RUSSELL ON ARBITRATION

Twenty-Third Edition

AUSTRALIA
Lawbook Co.
Sydney

CANADA and USA
Carswell
Toronto

HONG KONG
Sweet & Maxwell Asia

NEW ZEALAND
Brookers
Wellington

SINGAPORE and MALAYSIA
Sweet & Maxwell Asia
Singapore and Kuala Lumpur

Russell on Arbitration
Twenty-Third Edition

by

David St. John Sutton
BA, FCI Arb

Judith Gill
MA (Oxon), Dip Int Arb, FCI Arb

Matthew Gearing
BA (Oxon), MCI Arb

LONDON
SWEET & MAXWELL
2007

Published in 2007 by
Sweet & Maxwell Limited of 100 Avenue Road,
Swiss Cottage, London, NW3 3PF
http://www.sweetandmaxwell.co.uk
Typeset by Interactive Sciences Ltd,
Gloucester
Printed and bound in Great Britain by
TJ International, Padstow, Cornwall

No natural forests were destroyed to make this product;
only farmed timber was used and re-planted

British Library Cataloguing in Publication Data

A CIP catalogue record for this book
is available from the British Library
ISBN 978 0 421 96680 2

©
Sweet & Maxwell
2007

FOREWORD

Russell on Arbitration is one of the classic legal reference works. It has stood the passage of time and established, and in recent editions reinvented, its own distinct persona and importance in legal literature. Few other texts have become institutions due to acceptance and reliance on by the legal fraternity, including the courts, practitioners and all those involved with arbitration in England and under English law. For many foreign lawyers representing parties in arbitrations in England *Russell* is a reference tool for them too.

Anecdotal evidence suggests there are an ever increasing number of arbitrations in England. Whilst difficult to substantiate, this may be the result of the momentum of the alternative dispute resolution movement which has resulted in decreasing numbers of cases being taken to the courts. Yet hard facts on the number of arbitrations are not available and perhaps impossible to obtain. This is due in large part to the very many different kinds of arbitration, resorted to by parties from different industries, involving arbitrators from different backgrounds and professional experience, and many involving factual issues rather than legal principles. These arbitrations are domestic (i.e. where both parties are from England and the subject matter is in England), international (involving some non-UK element), commercial (involving some business element), investment (arising out of bilateral investment treaties or investments by a party into another country), ad hoc and institutional (such as ICC, LCIA or Stockholm Institute), commodities (food and grain) and industry specific (shipping, insurance, construction).

The only evidence that exists is the annual number of known decisions arising out of, concerning or affecting arbitration in the English courts. A rough estimate suggests that in almost five years since the 22nd edition of *Russell*, there have been 70–80 such decisions a year over this period. However what is important is not the numbers but how the English courts use their power to support and give effect to the agreement of the parties to submit their differences to arbitration. The Arbitration Act 1996 greatly narrowed the opportunities for the English courts to review and interfere with the arbitration process. Happily that approach has been supported and followed in the main by the English courts.

With the passage of 10 years since its enactment, the Arbitration Act 1996 continues to be interpreted and applied with its intended purpose, i.e. giving primary place to the will of the parties and then upholding the authority of the arbitrators to conduct proceedings appropriately in the circumstances of the case. It is also noteworthy that the English courts are looking at factors and influences from outside the United Kingdom, especially the UNCITRAL Model Law of International Commercial Arbitration, the New York Convention and the decisions of other national and international courts on related commercial arbitration issues.

There are four main areas where reported decisions of the English courts have covered important areas of the 1996 Arbitration Act.

1. The courts have sought to give effect to party autonomy and to oblige parties to adhere to their commitment to arbitrate. This has meant the staying of proceedings commenced in the courts despite the existence of a valid arbitration agreement and recognising the differences that exist in the conduct of arbitrations generally. The effect may be to preclude a party from seeking to challenge an award in a country other than the place of arbitration and even, perhaps in due course, ordering a party to participate in an arbitration based on a valid arbitration agreement. A breach of the arbitration agreement could also give an entitlement to monetary damages.

2. Injunctive relief, by way of anti-suit or anti-arbitration injunctions, is a widely sought remedy in the face of an arbitration agreement and gives rise to many concerns of excessive jurisdiction being exercised by the courts. These cases have provided the opportunity for the English courts to consider the interaction between the duty of the court to recognise the autonomy of the arbitration and therefore the importance of not interfering in the process, and the need to exercise jurisdiction and make orders which give effect to the decision of the parties to submit their differences to arbitration. In practise the court's powers have been used sparingly, and only to enforce arbitration agreements and support arbitral practice. They generally are not used to interfere with arbitrations taking place in another country and under some other law.

3. The doctrine of separability, resisted for some time in England, is now well accepted in English law and given effect to in the Act. The English courts have recognised that, with few exceptions, it is for arbitrators to determine the extent of their own jurisdiction, and that the arbitration and the arbitration agreement may be subject to a different national law to that governing the underlying contract. Most significantly, the House of Lords decision in *Premium Nafta Products Ltd & Others v Fili Shipping Co Ltd & Others* (the *Fiona Trust* case) recognised that an arbitral tribunal will not be deprived of jurisdiction where the underlying contract is alleged to have been induced by bribery, or for that matter even if this allegation is upheld.

4. An area where the courts have had some involvement is with respect to the duties of arbitrators. These are stated in section 33 of the Arbitration Act 1996 in language which, whilst original and perhaps revolutionary, expresses the general expectation and understanding of the duty of arbitrators in unique terms. These obligations are to "act fairly and impartially as between the parties", "giving each party a reasonable opportunity of putting his case" and adopting procedures which "avoid unnecessary delay or expense". The meaning and application of these basic standards have still to be thoroughly considered in the English courts. They have however been tested in the English courts largely in the context of applications to challenge awards for serious irregularity under section 68. The English courts have also had the opportunity to consider the IBA Guidelines on

Conflict of Interest in International Arbitration in reviewing standards for impartiality and independence of arbitrators.

This 23rd edition of *Russell on Arbitration*, more than 150 years after the first edition, reflects the law on these and other issues up to date in 2007. It will continue to be an indispensible aid to lawyers and non-lawyers involved with arbitration or wishing to understand the principles of the law applicable to arbitration in England. The authors, distinguished and experienced practitioners in all forms of international and domestic arbitration, are to be commended for continually raising the bar in respect of this ever more valuable book.

Julian D M Lew Q.C.
October 2007

PREFACE

This book deals with the English law of arbitration as at June 30, 2007, although wherever possible an attempt has been made to incorporate subsequent developments up to the date of finalising the proofs for publication in early October 2007. For example, reference has been included to the potentially important first instance decisions in *Albon v Naza Motor Trading Sdn Bhd (No.4)*, where the court exceptionally granted an injunction to restrain a foreign arbitration, and to *Tamil Nadu Electricity Board v ST-CMS Electric Co Private Ltd*, which deals with the interplay between the law of the matrix contract and the law of the agreement to arbitrate. Both of these cases were decided in July 2007.

Even more recently, in the final days of reviewing the proofs of the book, the House of Lords handed down the important decision in *Premium Nafta Products Ltd v Fili Shipping Co Ltd*. We had given extensive treatment to the decision of the Court of Appeal in this case (there entitled *Fiona Trust & Holding Corp v Yuri Privalov*). The House of Lords decision further bolsters the principle of separability of the agreement to arbitrate contained in section 7 of the Act and lays down sensible and modern guidance on the construction of the wording of agreements to arbitrate and we have therefore sought to incorporate reference to it in so far as possible in the time available.

More than ever, the development of arbitration law is moving at a fast pace and the temptation, which we have resisted, was to postpone publication of this 23rd edition until certain important developments had crystallised, not least because in the five years since the 22nd edition almost every area of arbitration law has received judicial attention and time is now ripe for a fresh statement of the law. One evolving issue worthy of particular note is the continued ability of the courts to grant anti-suit injunctions to restrain proceedings brought in other Brussels Convention countries commenced in breach of an agreement to arbitrate is in doubt following the reference of this question to the European Court of Justice by the House of Lords in *West Tankers Inc v Ras Riuione Adriatica di Sicurata*. The ECJ is not expected to consider the reference until 2009 at the earliest. In Chapter 7, we summarise the current position pending this decision and the arguments for and against the use of anti-suit injunctions.

Finally, we should thank our colleagues at Allen & Overy LLP and elsewhere who have given us great assistance in the process of preparing this addition, in particular, Hannah Ambrose, Chris Mainwaring-Taylor and Conan Lauterpacht, colleagues in the arbitration group at Allen & Overy. We also wish to express our thanks for the tireless secretarial support provided by Maria Iannella, and for the invaluable support and guidance given by our publishers at Sweet & Maxwell.

David St John Sutton, Judith Gill, Matthew Gearing
October 2007

CONTENTS

ABBREVIATIONS

Act

The Arbitration Act 1996.

Brussels Regulation

Council Regulation (EC) No.44/2001 of December 22, 2000 on jurisdiction and the recognition and enforcement of judgments in civil and commercial matters, including, if applicable, its application to Denmark as from July 1, 2007 by virtue of an agreement made on October 19, 2005 between the European Community and the Kingdom of Denmark on jurisdiction and the recognition and enforcement of judgments in civil and commercial matters.

Brussels Convention

EC Convention on Jurisdiction and the Enforcement of Judgments in Civil and Commercial Matters, Brussels 1968. The Brussels Convention has been largely replaced by the Brussels Regulation. With respect to legal proceedings instituted and to documents formally drawn up or registered as authentic instruments before July 1, 2007, the Brussels Regulation is not applicable to Denmark. Nor does it apply to certain overseas territories which fall within the geographical scope of the Brussels Convention. The Brussels Convention therefore continues to have a residual application.

ADR

Alternative dispute resolution.

Arbitration PD

The *Practice Direction—Arbitration* which supplements CPR Pt 62.

Chitty

Beale and others, *Chitty on Contracts* (29th edn, Sweet & Maxwell, 2006).

CIArb

Chartered Institute of Arbitrators.

Commercial Court

The part of the Queen's Bench Division of the English High Court of Justice devoted to commercial cases, including all arbitration applications and appeals.

Convention award

An arbitration award made in a country which is party to the New York Convention. The use of the expression "Convention award" derives from a statutory definition in the Arbitration Act 1975, s.7: that Act has been repealed. The Arbitration Act 1996, s.100(1) uses the expression "New York Convention award" for awards made outside the United Kingdom under the New York Convention; there are of course other conventions for the enforcement of awards made outside the United Kingdom. However, the expression "Convention award" in the narrower sense is likely to continue to be used.

CPR
The Civil Procedure Rules in force as at September 2007.

DAC
Departmental Advisory Committee on Arbitration Law set up by the United Kingdom's Department of Trade and Industry.

DAC Report
The DAC (see above) produced a number of reports. Where none is specified, the reference is to their report on the Arbitration Bill of February 1996. If the reference number is to another of the committee's reports, the title of that report is given in full.

Dicey & Morris
Dicey, Morris & Collins, *Conflict of Laws* (Lawrence Collins and other eds, 14th edn, Sweet & Maxwell, 2006).

Kendall
J Kendall, *Expert Determination* (3rd edn, Sweet & Maxwell, 2001).

FIDIC
Federation Internationale des Ingenieurs-Conseils.

FOSFA
Federation of Oils and Seeds and Fats Association.

GAFTA
Grain and Feed Trade Association.

Geneva Convention
Convention on the Execution of Foreign Arbitral Awards signed at Geneva on behalf of His Majesty on September 26, 1927

Handbook
Bernstein's *Handbook of Arbitration Practice* (4th edn, Sweet & Maxwell, 2003).

IBA Guidelines
IBA Guidelines on Conflicts of Interest in International Arbitration.

IBA Rules
IBA Rules on the Taking of Evidence in International Commercial Arbitration.

ICC
International Chamber of Commerce.

ICCA
International Council for Commercial Arbitration.

ICC Rules
Rules of Arbitration of the ICC.

ICE
Institution of Civil Engineers.

ICSID
International Centre for the Settlement of Investment Disputes.

ICSID Convention
The Convention on the Settlement of Investment Disputes between States and Nationals of Other States, 1965.

JCT
Joint Contracts Tribunal.

LCIA
London Court of International Arbitration.

LCIA Rules
LCIA Arbitration Rules.

LMAA
London Maritime Arbitration Association.

Lugano Convention
Convention of September 16, 1988 on jurisdiction and the enforcement of judgments in civil and commercial matters. Its effects are materially the same as the Brussels Convention and it governs issues of jurisdiction and enforcement between the European Union member states and the European Free Trade Association countries other than Liechtenstein (namely Iceland, Switzerland and Norway).

Merkin
Robert Merkin, *Arbitration Law* (LLP, 1991).

Model Law

The UNCITRAL Model Law on International Commercial Arbitration.

Mustill and Boyd

Michael Mustill and Stewart Boyd, *Commercial Arbitration* (2nd edn, 1992), as supplemented by a *2001 Companion* (Butterworths, 2001).

NEMA guidelines

Guidelines, laid down by the House of Lords in *BTP Tioxide Ltd v Pioneer Shipping Ltd, "The Nema"* [1982] A.C. 724, for appeals from arbitration awards to the courts.

New York Convention

The New York Convention on the Recognition and Enforcement of Foreign Arbitral Awards of 1958.

Redfern & Hunter

Alan Redfern, Martin Hunter, Nigel Blackaby and Constantine Partasides, *Law and Practice of International Commercial Arbitration* (4th edn, Sweet & Maxwell, 2004).

RIBA

Royal Association of British Architects.

RICS

Royal Institution of Chartered Surveyors.

RSC

Rules of the Supreme Court of England and Wales now largely replaced by the CPR.

UNCITRAL

United Nations Commission on International Trade Law.

UNCITRAL Rules

Arbitration Rules of the United Nations Commission on International Trade Law, 1976.

WHITEBOOK

The CPR and Practice Directions, with Commentary, contained in two volumes.

TABLE OF CASES

TABLE OF STATUTES

*References in **bold** indicate where legislation is reproduced in full*

TABLE OF STATUTORY INSTRUMENTS

*References in **bold** indicate where legislation is reproduced in full*

TABLE OF CIVIL PROCEDURE RULES

References in **bold** *indicate where legislation is reproduced in full*

CHAPTER 1

INTRODUCTION

1. ARBITRATION LAW

Modern law. A comprehensive review of the law and practice of arbitration[1]   1–001
culminated in the Arbitration Act 1996 and new rules[2] made under that Act.
Although not a complete code of arbitration law,[3] the Arbitration Act 1996 does
contain a coherent and modern framework. Except for ss.85–87,[4] the Act has been
in force since January 31, 1997.[5] Since that date, much has been done to fill out

---

[1] This review was undertaken by a committee set up by the Department of Industry, and under the
chairmanship of successive distinguished judges that committee produced a succession of reports
(the DAC reports) which explain the background and reasoning for modernising the English law of
arbitration: see para.1–053.

[2] The rules consist of Pt 62 of the Civil Procedural Rules 2002 ("CPR"), referred to in this book as
"CPR 62" as developed by a Practice Direction: see paras 7–009 and 8–181 *et seq.*

[3] The last attempt to enact a code of arbitration failed before the Common Law Procedure Act, 1854.
A general arbitration act was urged by Francis Russell, the first author of Russell on Arbitration in
his letter to the then Lord Chancellor, Lord Brougham and Vaux dated October 20, 1853 published
in (1997) 13 Arbitration Int. 3 at 253.

[4] It has been decided not to bring these sections into force, see para.2–005.

[5] See Arbitration Act 1996 (Commencement No.1) Order (SI 1996/3146) dated December 16,
1996.

the framework. That work, which is discussed in this book, includes hundreds of decisions by the courts.

1–002 Content of Arbitration Act 1996. Part 1 of the Act contains the principal provisions relating to arbitration pursuant to a written arbitration agreement.[6] The provisions of Pt II which are in force[7] are those relating to consumer arbitration agreements,[8–9] statutory arbitrations,[10] and the provision for the exceptional appointment of a judge as arbitrator.[11] Part III contains provisions for the recognition and enforcement of certain foreign awards,[12] and Pt IV contains some general provisions.[13]

1–003 Scope of the Arbitration Act 1996. The scope of the application of the provisions of Pt 1 of the Act is stated in s.2(1) to apply where the seat of the arbitration is in England and Wales[14] or Northern Ireland.[15] Conversely, except as stated below, the provisions of Pt 1 of the Act do not apply if the seat of the arbitration is elsewhere.

The expression "the seat of the arbitration" is defined in s.3 of the Act to mean the juridical seat of the arbitration designated

- by the parties to the arbitration agreement, or

- by any arbitral or other institution or person vested by the parties with powers in that regard, or

- by the arbitral tribunal if so authorised by the parties.

or determined in the absence of any such designation, having regard to the parties' agreement and all the relevant circumstances.[16]

When the seat of the arbitration is in England,[17] Pt 1 of the Act will apply irrespective of the proper law,[18] and even if the arbitration is conducted abroad.[19] Even if the seat of the arbitration is abroad or no seat has been designated or

---

[6] As defined in s.6 of the Arbitration Act 1996. The requirement for writing is contained in s.5(1) of the Arbitration Act 1996.

[7] As mentioned, ss.85–87 of the Arbitration Act 1996 relating to domestic arbitration has not been brought into force.

[8–9] Sections 89–91 of the Arbitration Act, 1996—see para.2–084.

[10] Sections 94–98 of the Arbitration Act, 1996—see Appendix 3.

[11] Section 93 of the Arbitration Act, 1996—see para.4–019.

[12] Sections 99–104 of the Arbitration Act, 1996—see Ch.8.

[13] Sections 105–110 of the Arbitration Act, 1996—s.105 defines the court—see para.7–008.

[14] England and Wales constitute a single legal system. Scotland has a different arbitration law.

[15] Section 108(2) provides that ss.92 and 93 of the Act do not apply to Northern Ireland.

[16] Section 3 of the Arbitration Act 1996—see also Ch.2 for a discussion about the seat of the arbitration.

[17] To avoid frequent repetition of the phrase "England and Wales or Northern Ireland", the authors have taken the liberty of using the abbreviation "England".

[18] The subject of proper law as applied both to the merits of the dispute and to the arbitration agreement is discussed in Ch.2.

[19] See para.2–107 for a discussion about the difference between the seat of the arbitration and the place where the arbitration is conducted.

determined,[20] the provisions of the Act relating to the stay of legal proceedings[21] and the enforcement of arbitral awards[22] will apply[23] as will certain other powers of the court in support of the arbitration.[24] Those powers are referred to in a later section of this chapter.[25]

Mandatory provisions. The terms of an arbitration agreement may be overridden in whole or in part by mandatory provisions of English law. The Arbitration Act 1996 contains a list of such provisions[26] within Pt I of that Act.[27] For example, the court may on the application of a party to an arbitration agreement extend the time agreed for beginning proceedings in respect of certain claims and this power cannot be excluded by the terms of an arbitration agreement.[28]

1–004

2. ARBITRATION AND ITS FEATURES

Features. Three features arising out of the Act deserve particular mention:

1–005

- party autonomy is recognised as paramount[29] and court intervention is expressly excluded except as specified in the Act[30];

- a general duty is imposed on the arbitral tribunal to act fairly and impartially and to adopt procedures that avoid unnecessary delay or expense[31]; and

- English arbitration law is uniform, the same law applying to all arbitrations, whether domestic or international, provided that they are governed by English law.[32]

---

[20] Section 2 of the Act foresees that situation when, despite the broad definition of "the seat of the arbitration" in s.3, the seat of the arbitration is not designated or determined—see para.2–102.

[21] Section 9 of the Arbitration Act 1996, but also ss.10 and 11—see paras 7–010 *et seq.*

[22] Section 66 of the Arbitration Act 1996—see para.8–003.

[23] Section 2(3) of the Arbitration Act 1996. See *Weissfisch v Julius* [2006] EWCA 218 where a stay of the court action was requested on this basis.

[24] Section 44 of the Arbitration Act 1996—see paras 7–180 *et seq.*

[25] See s.4 of this chapter entitled "The role of the English Court" at para.1–019.

[26] Schedule 1 to the Arbitration Act 1996. The mandatory duty imposed on the arbitral tribunal by s.33 of that Act is mentioned: in para.1–004.

[27] Part I of the Arbitration Act 1996 applies to most arbitrations, but its provisions are modified in respect of the arbitrations specified in Pt II of the Act and do not apply to Pt III of the Act.

[28] Arbitration Act 1996, s.12: see paras 7–067 *et seq.*

[29] Section 1 of the Arbitration Act 1996 states as a general principle that "the parties should be free to agree how their disputes are resolved, subject only to such safeguards as are necessary in the public interest".

[30] Section 1 of the Arbitration Act 1996 states as another general principle, that in matters governed by Pt 1 of the Act "the court should not intervene except as provided by this Part".

[31] This general duty is specified in s.33 of the Arbitration Act 1996: see para.4–104 and para.5–032.

[32] The uniform treatment of domestic and international arbitration governed by English law results from the decision not to bring into force ss.85–87 of the Act which make provisions for a "domestic arbitration agreement". For details of that decision, see para.2–005 and footnote.

1–006 **General principles.** The general principles of arbitration, which are complementary to party autonomy and the tribunal's general duty, are expressed in the first section of the Act, and are said to be founded on the following principles and to be construed accordingly[33]:

- the object of arbitration is to obtain the fair resolution of disputes by an impartial tribunal without unnecessary delay or expense;

- the parties should be free to agree how their disputes are resolved subject only to such safeguards as are necessary in the public interest[34]; and

- intervention by the courts should be restricted.[35]

1–007 **Public interest.** The first statement recognises that unnecessary expense and delay can and should be avoided without compromising the fair resolution of disputes. The need for an impartial tribunal is of course imperative and is discussed later in this book.[36] Equally significant is the emphasis on party autonomy,[37] which is "subject only to such safeguards as are necessary in the public interest".[38] There is no definition of the words quoted in the previous sentence,[39] so they must be considered in the light of the mandatory provisions of the Arbitration Act 1996, including in particular s.33 of the Act[40]:

> "It seems to us that the public interest dictates that [section] 33 must be mandatory, i.e. that the parties cannot effectively agree to dispense with the duty laid on arbitrators under that section."[41]

Although court intervention is limited by the mandatory provisions of the Arbitration Act 1996,[42] within that constraint there is scope for ensuring that party autonomy does not override matters that affect the public interest.[43]

---

[33] The general principles on which Pt 1 of the Arbitration Act 1996 is "founded" and is to be "construed accordingly" are set out in s.1 of the Arbitration Act 1996.

[34] The qualification of "public interest" on party autonomy is mentioned in para.1–039 and footnote to that paragraph.

[35] The general principles are stated to apply to the provisions of Pt I of the Arbitration Act 1996. The third principle has been paraphrased. See Appendix 1 for the full text of the 1996 Act.

[36] See paras 4–023 *et seq.*

[37] The emphasis on party autonomy became more apparent after the UK acceded to the New York Convention in 1975. See paras 1–048 *et seq.*

[38] Arbitration Act 1996, s.1(b).

[39] The consequences of public interest are however discussed in the DAC report at para.19. See Appendix 2.

[40] See paras 5–032 *et seq.* for a discussion of this duty.

[41] DAC report para.155. The whole of the paragraph, which is reproduced in Appendix 2, and the following paragraphs in that report are worth reading on this subject—see also para.5–053.

[42] Arbitration Act 1996, s.1(c) and para.1–019. There is no inherent common law jurisdiction that permits the court to supervise arbitrations, although certain common law rights are saved by s.81(1) of the Arbitration Act 1996: see para.7–003.

[43] The role of the court in arbitration is discussed in Chs 7 and 8. See para.1–040 for public policy and pubic interest.

Definition of arbitration. As a means of resolving disputes, arbitration has   1–008
been employed in England and elsewhere for centuries.[44] The need for a definition
has always been subsidiary to its purpose although attempts have from time to
time been made at a definition.

> "An arbitration is a reference to the decision of one or more persons, either with or
> without an umpire, of some matter or matters in difference between the parties".[45]

The Arbitration Act 1996 does not contain a definition[46] of arbitration (as
opposed to the arbitration agreement).[47] Perhaps the absence of an accepted
definition of arbitration, which encompasses its many facets but precludes other
forms of dispute resolution, simply demonstrates the diverse scope of the subject.
In any event, courts and practitioners have managed to resolve questions about
what is and is not arbitration when these have arisen based on well-recognised
features of the process.[48]

It is difficult to identify the exact combination of features[49] which sets arbitration apart from other methods of dispute resolution, but certain features are
usually found in arbitration. They are the need for a provision referring the
dispute to arbitration, the privacy of the proceedings, a determination of the
dispute and the finality of the decision.

Arbitration agreement. Compare a court action, which is another means   1–009
of dispute resolution. Like arbitration, it involves adjudication leading to a final
decision, sometimes after appeal, but it does not require the agreement of the
parties or some other provision referring the dispute for decision by the tribunal.
By contrast, an arbitration agreement (whether contained in a submission agreement[50] or in a clause in a commercial contract) identifies the parties to the
dispute[51] and defines the dispute or types of dispute referred to arbitration. It
contains the tribunal's mandate.[52] It may also specify how the tribunal is to be
appointed and, expressly or by implication, the procedure to be adopted in the

---

[44] References to arbitrament, as arbitration used to be called, appear in the Year Books. For an early
example, see Anon (1468) Y.B., 8 Edw. IV., fo.1, p.1.
[45] Definition of arbitration provided by Romilly M.R. in *Collins v Collins* (1858) 26 Beav. 306 at 312
reported in English cases at 916–919. The definition could apply to other forms of dispute
resolution. The problems of defining arbitration are discussed in *Mustill and Boyd*, pp.38–50.
[46] The omission was deliberate. See DAC report, para.18 and the April 1995 Interim Report of DAC,
reproduced in Appendix 2.
[47] Section 6 of the Arbitration Act 1996 defines an "arbitration agreement". See Ch.2 for a full
discussion.
[48] In *O'Callaghan v Coral Racing Ltd*, *The Times*, November 26, 1998, CA the court decided that a
procedure for resolving disputes over a gaming transaction could not be an arbitration process.
[49] The features mentioned here refer to arbitration generally rather than to the English law of
arbitration, which has already been mentioned in para.1–005.
[50] See para.2–003 for a definition of "submission agreement".
[51] In the case of an arbitration clause, the parties are usually identified in the main agreement that
contains the clause, although not all parties to an arbitration agreement in a contract need to be
parties to the particular dispute.
[52] The tribunal's mandate is also governed by the scope of the reference to it of the particular
arbitration.

proceedings. It is this agreement which gives rise to the consensual and predominantly bilateral nature of arbitration to the exclusion of third parties.[53] The nature and content of the arbitration agreement is addressed in Ch.2 and the parties to that agreement are discussed in Ch.3. Arbitration pursuant to an investment treaty is referred to briefly at the end of s.7 of this chapter[54] and arbitration pursuant to statute is referred to in Appendix 3.

1–010 **Privacy and confidentiality.** An arbitration is heard in private, whereas at least some part of a court action may be heard in public at the trial or hearing. The tribunal, the parties and their representatives are the only persons allowed to participate in the proceedings unless the parties and the tribunal agree otherwise. A witness may be required to give evidence to the tribunal but that testimony is only heard by those persons allowed to be present. The public has no right to attend a hearing before an arbitral tribunal. Privacy, and the related subject of confidentiality, are discussed in greater detail in a later chapter.[55] They are subject to numerous qualifications, which is why no specific provision was made for them in the Arbitration Act 1996,[56] but they are said to be implicit in the parties' choice to arbitrate in England.[57]

1–011 **Determination.** Privacy and agreement of the parties are not peculiar to arbitration. Alternative dispute resolution ("ADR") procedures, including conciliation and mediation, are also held in private and depend on an agreement between the parties, but ADR differs from arbitration[58] in that a conclusion can be reached only if all the parties agree. ADR gives the parties the opportunity to meet and negotiate with each other often with the assistance of a neutral third party adviser. Agreement to ADR does not however guarantee that there will be a final and binding decision.[59] By contrast, once an arbitral tribunal has been appointed, it must proceed with the reference by determining the issues and making an award[60] unless the tribunal is released from that obligation.[61] One party cannot avoid the

---

[53] Multi-party arbitrations are an exception, although even they are based on agreement see paras 3–040 *et seq.*

[54] Paragraph 1–041.

[55] See para.5–182.

[56] The omission is justified in the DAC report (paras 11–17). For a commentary on that decision see Patrick Neill Q.C. "Confidentiality in Arbitration" [1996] 12(3) Arbitration Int. 287, and observations made in *Associated Electric & Gas Insurance Service Ltd v European Reinsurance Co of Zurich* [2003] UKPC 11.

[57] *Moscow City Council v Bankers Trust Co* [2004] EWCA Civ 314.

[58] Sometimes arbitration is subsumed within the definition ADR, because it is an alternative to litigation, but in this book arbitration is treated separately from other ADR techniques: see paras 2–024 *et seq.*

[59] For a thorough review of ADR procedures see J Tackaberry and A Marriott, *Bernstein's Handbook of Arbitration and Dispute Resolution Practice.*

[60] See Ch.6 for a full discussion on the Award.

[61] This may occur in several ways (e.g. by agreement of the parties, death of a sole arbitrator, revocation of the appointment or removal of the tribunal). See paras 4–159 *et seq.* An arbitrator may be relieved of liability for breach of this obligation if the court is satisfied that it was reasonable for him to resign: see the Arbitration Act 1996, s.25(4) and para.7–133.

decision of an arbitral tribunal by refusing to go on with the proceedings.[62] Although the parties must have committed to arbitrate in the first place,[63] once a binding commitment to arbitrate is made, sometimes years before the dispute arises, an enforceable arbitration award may result despite the objection of one of the parties.

Expert determination. It is difficult to distinguish arbitration from expert determination. One distinction may be found in the type of procedure the parties intend to use to resolve their difference rather than in the nature of the difference itself. For example, parties appoint a valuer to determine a fair price of something. His expert opinion is required rather than an award based on submissions from the parties, although expert determination has expanded into the area of general dispute resolution.[64] His decision cannot be challenged in the same way as the award of an arbitral tribunal.[65] A valuer may however be sued if he provides a negligent valuation.[66] On the other hand, an arbitral tribunal can be appointed only where there is express reference to arbitration of a matter which it must decide after taking account of any evidence and argument of the parties to that dispute. Further, the Arbitration Act 1996 does not apply at all to expert determination.

1–012

Variety of procedures. As for the procedures used in arbitration, there are those akin to High Court practice, where it is assumed that the parties will exchange full written submissions, make voluntary disclosure of documents and call witnesses to give evidence orally and be cross-examined. There are others, which though formal and often conducted under the auspices of an arbitral institution,[67] reflect more closely procedures used abroad, permitting little, if any, document disclosure or cross-examination. Increasingly common in international arbitration is a form of hybrid procedure, taking elements of both common and civil law systems.[68] Then, there are the more informal procedures, which apply in many consumer cases. In some of those informal procedures there is a hearing, where the parties are often not represented by lawyers; in others the tribunal

1–013

---

[62] See para.5–228 for termination by mutual consent.

[63] The Commitment is frequently made by an arbitration agreement, (see Ch.2) but it may also be contained in a statute (see Appendix 3) or in a treaty (see para.1–041).

[64] For a full treatment of this subject, see J Kendall, *Expert Determination*. See also paras 2–028 *et seq.*

[65] See *Halifax Life Ltd v The Equitable Life Association Co* [2007] EWHC 503 where the challenge of such a decision was decided by Cressell J., who reviewed previous authorities. Challenges to arbitral awards are discussed in paras 8–051 *et seq.*

[66] The Arbitration Act 1996, s.29 gives the arbitral tribunal an immunity unless its acts or omissions are shown to have been in bad faith. This provision has removed the doubt about an arbitrator's immunity from suit that followed the decisions of *Sutcliffe v Thackrah* [1974] A.C. 727 and *Arenson v Arenson* [1975] All E.R. 901. See paras 4–200 *et seq.*

[67] See paras 3–052 *et seq.* for the role of an "arbitral institution".

[68] This approach is reflected in the IBA Rules on the Taking of Evidence in International Commercial Arbitration.

decides the dispute on the basis of documents submitted by the parties, and without a hearing.[69]

1–014 **Domestic and international.** Many of the disputes referred to arbitration are of a wholly domestic kind and are conducted under consumer schemes that provide a tribunal with the relevant expertise (not necessarily legal) and a simplified procedure. Other disputes are truly international, the only connection with England being the choice of London as a neutral seat for the arbitration. In between, many disputes would be considered international because one or more of the parties was from a different jurisdiction.

1–015 **Finality.** An arbitral tribunal may make one or more awards,[70] each of which is final as to the matters decided. The finality of the award and its consequences are treated fully in Ch.6. For the purpose of this introduction it will suffice to say that recourse against an award is limited. Permission to appeal may only be obtained in special circumstances,[71] and the grounds for otherwise challenging an award are restricted.[72] An application to enforce an award may be made immediately after the award has been published to the parties. Such applications are very often granted summarily,[73] because of the limited scope for opposition.[74]

3. THE ARBITRAL TRIBUNAL

1–016 **The decision-maker.** Once the parties have agreed to arbitrate, they will need to provide for a decision-maker to resolve their disputes or differences. That is the arbitral tribunal, which may consist of one or more persons.[75] An arbitration agreement will often provide for each party to appoint an arbitrator and for a third person, either a third arbitrator or an umpire, to be appointed immediately after or some time later in order to make up the tribunal.[76] In this book reference is usually made to "the arbitral tribunal" or simply "the tribunal" because that is the

---

[69] See paras 5–089 *et seq.* for a discussion on the different procedures available.

[70] Arbitration Act 1996, s.47, see paras 6–009 *et seq.*

[71] See paras 8–119 *et seq.* and the Arbitration Act 1996, s.69 which restates the previous law contained in the Arbitration Act 1979, s.1(4) as applied in *Pioneer Shipping BTP Tioxide Ltd (The "Nema")* [1981] 3 W.L.R. 292 and *The "Antaios"* [1985] A.C. 191. See also *Bisichi Mining v Bass Holdings* [2002] EWHC 375 (Ch), Jacob J. and *Losinjska v Valfracht Maritime (The "Lipa")* [2001] 2 Lloyd's Rep. 17.

[72] See paras 8–051 *et seq.* and the Arbitration Act 1996, s.67 (challenge as to substantive jurisdiction) and s.68 (challenge for serious irregularity).

[73] See paras 8–002 *et seq.* and the Arbitration Act 1996, s.66.

[74] Although the scope for opposition is limited, it varies according to the type of award (e.g. an award made in England or one made abroad, such as a New York Convention Award) (see paras 8–010 *et seq.*)

[75] In maritime and commodity disputes it is common for each party to appoint an arbitrator and for the two arbitrators to determine the dispute. If they cannot agree an umpire enters upon the reference. See para.4–007

[76] The significance of the different tribunals is discussed in paras 4–062 *et seq.*

term used in the Arbitration Act 1996[77] and because it more accurately reflects the fact that awards can be made by a sole arbitrator, two or more arbitrators or an umpire.[78] The word arbitrator[79] in the singular is used from time to time, which will serve as a reminder that a large number of arbitrations that take place in England are conducted by a single or sole arbitrator. Also, the tribunal does not always act as one, and an application to remove an arbitrator[80] need not extend to the whole tribunal.[81]

Appointment by the parties. Whatever their number, one, two, three or more, the arbitral tribunal must be impartial[82] and act judicially in determining the parties' disputes in accordance with their agreement and the law.[83] An arbitrator differs from a judge, however, in that he is appointed not by the State but by the parties or by an individual or institution chosen by the parties.[84] He therefore owes duties to the parties themselves, (as explained in Ch.4), and is not accountable to Parliament or to the public at large.   1–017

Variety of expertise. The arbitrator may differ from a judge in another important respect. He can be chosen by the parties because of his expertise in the subject matter of the dispute. A judge is trained in the law in order to decide legal issues. Very often the arbitrator is an experienced lawyer, but there are occasions when an arbitrator trained in another discipline is more appropriate to decide upon technical issues outside the law.[85]   1–018

---

[77] Sections 15 to 29 of the Arbitration Act 1996 are concerned with the arbitral tribunal.

[78] See s.21 of the Arbitration Act 1996 for a definition of "umpire". An umpire will only decide the matter if there is a reference to two arbitrators and an umpire and the two arbitrators cannot agree on a decision—see para.4–007.

[79] The word "arbitrator" is defined in the Arbitration Act 1996, s.82(1), and includes an umpire.

[80] Arbitration Act 1996, s.24 provides a mechanism for the court to remove an arbitrator (see paras 7–110 *et seq.*) but arbitration rules often provide for an arbitral institution to remove an arbitrator in certain circumstances.

[81] If the whole tribunal is affected or tainted by the bias of one, they may all have to be removed. See *ASM Shipping v Harris* [2007] EWHC 1513 (Comm) at para.4–115.

[82] A partial arbitrator may be removed by the court (Arbitration Act 1996, s.24(1)(a)). For a discussion of the arbitrator's duty to act fairly and impartially see paras 4–106 *et seq.* The rules of the LCIA ("LCIA Rules") provide that the tribunal "shall be and remain at all times impartial and independent" (Art.5.2). The ICC Rules of Arbitration provide that the tribunal shall be independent (Art.7.1). The two requirements overlap: see DAC report, para.101.

[83] As the arbitrator usually derives his mandate from an agreement of the parties, it is axiomatic that he must have regard to that agreement in reaching his conclusion. Apart from the general duty specified in s.33 of the Arbitration Act 1996, the arbitral tribunal must also apply the law unless the parties agree otherwise. (Arbitration Act 1996, s.46, see also *President of India v La Pintada* [1985] 1 All E.R. 104, *per* Lord Brandon at 119.) These matters are discussed in more detail later in this work: see para.4–141.

[84] The parties have no say in the appointment of a judge as he is appointed by the State. (The judge-arbitrator is an anomaly: see paras 4–019 *et seq.*) Parties often leave the selection of the arbitral tribunal to an individual office-holder (e.g. the President of the Law Society) or to an independent appointing authority like the International Court of Arbitration of the International Chamber of Commerce (ICC) or the LCIA, although the tribunal may be appointed by the court if all else fails: see paras 4–026 and 4–027.

[85] The composition of tribunals is developed in paras 4–035 *et seq.*

4. THE ROLE OF THE ENGLISH COURT

1–019 **Non-intervention.** English arbitration law recognises and gives effect to party autonomy, and, in matters governed by Pt I of the Act, the court is directed not to intervene except as provided by that part of the Act.[86] This direction, which is stated as a general principle in the first section of the Act, has been observed[87] and emphasised by the courts at the highest level.[88] Nevertheless, the Act recognises that court intervention may occasionally be necessary to support the arbitral proceedings.[89] Chapters 7 and 8 of this book discuss the powers available to the English courts and how they have been exercised since the Act came into force.

1–020 **Powers of the court.** All the powers specified in Pt 1 of the Act as exercisable by the court apply when the seat of the arbitration is in England.[90] Some of those powers may, however, apply even when the seat of arbitration is outside England[91] or when no seat has been designated or determined.[92] Mention has already been made of the court's powers to stay legal proceedings in breach of an arbitration agreement,[93] and to enforce an arbitration award made abroad.[94] Another important power, which the court may exercise even though the seat of the arbitration is outside England or no seat has been designated or determined, is the court's power to grant interim measures.[95] This is not a term used in the Act, but it aptly describes the matters listed in s.44(2).[96] The court's power to grant urgent relief is particularly useful before the arbitral tribunal is appointed. Once appointed, the tribunal has power to grant interim measures,[97] although occasionally the court's assistance is still required during the reference.[98]

Section 2(3) of the Act contains specific reference to the court's powers conferred by s.43 (securing the attendance of witnesses),[99] and s.44 (powers exercisable in support of arbitral proceedings),[100] although in those cases the Act

---

[86] Section 1(c) of the Arbitration Act 1996.
[87] For a discussion of the limited intervention of the courts, see lecture dated March 14, 2006 of Coleman J. "Arbitrators and Judges—How much interference should we tolerate?"
[88] *Lesotho Highlands Development Authority v Impregilo SpA* [2005] UKHL 43.
[89] The exception to s.1(c) of the Act reflects this recognition, which is expressed in later sections of the Act. Section 1(c) copies the words of Art.5 of the Model Law—see Appendix 4.
[90] Section 2(1) of the Arbitration Act 1996, which refers to "England and Wales or Northern Ireland".
[91] Section 2(2) to (7) of the Arbitration Act 1996. "Outside England" is used in this chapter as a shorthand for the words "outside England and Wales or Northern Ireland".
[92] Reference to this last phrase in s.2 of the Act has already been mentioned in an earlier footnote.
[93] Section 2(2)(a) of the Arbitration Act 1996, which refers expressly to s.7 of the Act—see paras 7–010 *et seq.*
[94] Section 2(2)(b) of the Arbitration Act 1996, which refers expressly to s.66 of the Act—see para.8–003.
[95] Section 2(3)(b) of the Arbitration Act 1996, which refers to s.44 of the Act.
[96] It is a term used in the Model Law, Art.9, which was acknowledged by the DAC to correspond to s.44—see para.214 of DAC report in Appendix 2.
[97] See paras 5–074 *et seq.*
[98] See Ch.7 for a full discussion about the court's power.
[99] See paras 7–202 *et seq.*
[100] See paras 7–180 *et seq.*

provides that the court may refuse to exercise its power if, in the opinion of the court, the fact that the seat is abroad or, when determined, is likely to be abroad makes it inappropriate to do so.[101]

Seat abroad or not determined. The powers of the court to intervene 1–021
when the seat of an arbitration is abroad or not determined are not limited, however, to the sections specifically mentioned,[102] because s.2(4) of the Act provides that the court may exercise a power conferred by any provision of Pt 1 of the Act not already mentioned for the purpose of supporting the arbitral process where:

- No seat of the arbitration has been designated or determined, and
- by reason of a connection with England and Wales or Northern Ireland the court is satisfied that it is appropriate to do so.

Further, where the law applicable to the arbitration agreement[103] is English law,[104] s.7 (separability of arbitration agreement),[105] and s.8 (death of a party)[106] apply even if the seat of the arbitration is abroad or not determined.[107]

5. THE ADVANTAGES OF ARBITRATION

The choice of arbitration. With all the other means of resolving disputes 1–022
available, why should anyone choose to arbitrate? After all, the parties, or one of them, must pay the fees of the arbitral tribunal and the expenses of the venue, whereas a judge and the use of the courts largely come free. There are several reasons why parties agree to arbitration.

Privacy and choice in the tribunal. Mention has already been made of 1–023
the privacy and confidentiality of arbitration proceedings. Some parties prefer to know in advance that their disputes will be determined out of the public gaze. The right to choose or to have a say in the choice of one or more members of the arbitral tribunal is also regarded as an advantage. Even if the degree of influence is minimal because the choice is left to an appointing authority, there has nevertheless been some involvement in the selection process by agreeing to that appointing authority, and the parties may take comfort from the institution's previous experience of appointing and working with particular arbitrators. Parties

---

[101] Section 2(3) of the Arbitration Act 1996.
[102] Sections 9–11, 66, 43 and 44 of the Act.
[103] That law may be different to the law governing the merits of the dispute—see para.2–094.
[104] The words used in s.2(5) of the Act are "the law of England and Wales or Northern Ireland".
[105] See para.2–007.
[106] See para.3–026.
[107] Section 2(5) of the Arbitration Act 1996.

find it reassuring not to be dependent on the luck of the draw from a court list.[108] Further, some disputes involve highly technical issues and it can be useful to have at least one member of the tribunal who is familiar with the technical issues or applicable law by virtue of his training and so does not have to be educated by the parties in order to understand them.

1–024 **Flexibility.** Arbitration can be much more flexible both in time and procedure. If the dispute needs urgent resolution, the parties can choose a tribunal who will act promptly rather than wait their turn in the queue.[109] As arbitration is consensual, the parties can choose the most suitable procedure. Neither they nor the tribunal are tied to formal rules of court. Written submissions in letter form may be appropriate for a dispute over the interpretation of a written agreement, whereas examination of witnesses may be required for the determination of disputed facts. The parties can also be represented by anyone of their choice because they are not bound by rules limiting appearance to persons with particular legal qualifications.[110]

1–025 **Neutrality and equality.** Where the parties come from different countries, arbitration may be preferable to litigation because quite often neither party is willing to submit to the jurisdiction of the national court of the other. Arbitration offers them neutrality in the choice of law, venue, procedure and tribunal. The parties may agree upon the law and procedure of a third country or leave the choice to the tribunal. They can appoint an arbitrator from another country or request an international arbitral institution to make the appointment either of the sole arbitrator or one or more members of the tribunal.[111] In so doing the parties may be more confident that there will be equality of treatment.

1–026 **Enforceability of award.** A further important advantage of arbitration is the extensive enforceability of the award. Having incurred the cost of proceedings, a successful claimant wants to be in a position to enforce the award, if necessary.

---

[108] The listing procedure of the English courts is based largely upon the availability of the judges and there are provisions for transfer of business to another court.

[109] In an urgent case a decision may be required in a matter of days or hours. Although the court will respond to urgent applications (e.g. for interim measures like an injunction), an arbitral tribunal has more flexibility to adapt its procedure, for example, to give a final decision immediately after oral and/or written submissions from the parties.

[110] Unless the litigant appears in person, only barristers and solicitors with advocacy certificates have a right of audience before the higher courts in England. There is no such restriction in arbitrations (Arbitration Act 1996, s.36). The parties may be represented by any person of their choice (e.g. a foreign lawyer or someone experienced in the issue in dispute).

[111] The ICC Rules of Arbitration provide expressly that where the circumstances so demand the sole arbitrator or chairman of the arbitral tribunal shall be of a different nationality to that of the parties (Art.9.5). Compare Art.6.1 of the LCIA Rules.

As a result of various conventions, arbitral awards are recognised and enforceable in many more countries than English court judgments.[112]

Summary of advantages. To summarise, parties choose arbitration 1–027 because of the flexibility and privacy of the proceedings, their ability to choose (directly or indirectly) the tribunal and the enforceability of the award. Perhaps most importantly though, in the modern world of cross-border transactions and collaborations, arbitration can provide elements of neutrality as regards location, governing law and constitution of the tribunal, which make it a very attractive proposition in international commerce.[112a]

6. THE DISADVANTAGES OF ARBITRATION

What are the snags? In order to get a full picture it is necessary to mention 1–028 the cons as well as the pros of arbitration. Expense and delay immediately spring to mind, but they are features of litigation as well. Certainly, there is an extra cost in respect of the fees of the arbitral tribunal,[113] but in many cases the tribunal can more than pay its way by taking control of the proceedings from the outset and conducting them in an efficient manner. Its general duty[114] combined with the exhortation in the first section of the Arbitration Act 1996[115] requires an arbitral tribunal to avoid unnecessary delay or expense.

Expense and delay. Some delays are peculiar to arbitration. For example, 1–029 there are those that can occur at the beginning of the proceedings as a result of the procedures for appointing the tribunal, particularly if challenges are made to the arbitration agreement or to an arbitrator.[116] As against that the limited scope for recourse against the award may save time in the end by avoiding the possibility of one or more appeals. It is often said that the limited coercive powers of the

---

[112] The principal convention which provides for recognition and enforceability of awards made in England and elsewhere is the New York Convention, which was adopted by the UK in 1975: see paras 8–020 *et seq.* on this subject. Although there are certain treaties under which court judgments are enforceable, these are more limited in application than the New York Convention. For example, there is no treaty between the UK and the USA for the enforcement of judgments but both countries have acceded to the New York Convention.

[112a] *Premium Nafta Products Ltd & others v Fili Shipping Co Ltd & others* [2007] UKHL 40, *per* Lord Hoffmann at [6].

[113] The fees will increase if there is more than one member of the tribunal and/or if an arbitral institution is involved. In addition to the arbitration fees, there may be the expenses of the place (offices or hotel) where hearings take place.

[114] The general duty of the tribunal specified in s.33 of the Arbitration Act 1996 includes the avoidance of "unnecessary delay or expense": s.33(1)(b) see paras 4–131 and 5–032.

[115] The Arbitration Act 1996 states as the object of arbitration the fair resolution of disputes by an impartial tribunal "without unnecessary delay or expense": s.1(a).

[116] Challenges of both kinds do occur, particularly in international cases.

tribunal[117] make arbitration vulnerable to delay. There is some truth in this statement, but once appointed an experienced tribunal will take control of the proceedings, and proceed, despite an obstructive party, in order to maintain a reasonable timetable.[118]

1–030 **No summary procedures.** The summary and third party procedures used in the English courts are not available in arbitration.[119] An arbitral tribunal must give each party a reasonable opportunity of putting his case and dealing with that of his opponent,[120] which does not allow a summary decision in favour of the claimant on the ground that the respondent has no real prospect of successfully defending its claim.[121]

1–031 **No joinder or consolidation.** Because of the consensual nature of arbitration, an arbitral tribunal will usually lack the power to add or substitute a party to the proceeding without the consent of all the existing parties.[122] For the same reason an arbitral tribunal has no power to consolidate its arbitration with another in order to bring before one tribunal related claims for determination. Even if there is express power for the claims to be consolidated,[123] consolidation may not be possible once arbitration proceedings have commenced.

1–032 **Quality of decision making.** Criticism is sometimes made because decisions or reasoning of a tribunal are not up to the standard expected by one or other party to the arbitration. When a party has a choice in the nomination or appointment of the tribunal care should be taken so as to ensure that members of the tribunal are well qualified to decide the particular dispute.[124]

7. MATTERS REFERRED AND REFERABLE TO ARBITRATION

1–033 **What can be referred to arbitration?** The question of whether particular disputes can be referred to arbitration (arbitrability) should not be confused

---

[117] The tribunal can dismiss for want of prosecution and can proceed even if a party chooses not to participate but peremptory orders may need to be enforced by an application to the court—see ss.41 and 42 of the Arbitration Act 1996 and paras 5–202, 5–224 and 7–198.

[118] "The calibre, experience and industry of the tribunal, and the nature and quality of the procedure employed in individual cases, are of paramount importance": statement attributed to the late Sir Michael Kerr. For powers of the tribunal in case of default, see paras 5–192 *et seq.*

[119] CPR Pts 19 and 24.

[120] This is part of the general rule in the Arbitration Act 1996, s.33. Contrast the power to strike out a claim for delay: s.41(3). See para.4–089.

[121] Contrast court's powers under CPR Pt 24.2.

[122] See para.3–044

[123] For example, claims by an employer against a contractor and related claims by the contractors against sub-contractors

[124] See para.4–014.

with the question of what disputes fall within the terms of a particular arbitration agreement (the scope of the arbitration agreement). The latter is a matter of interpretation of the particular arbitration clause and is dealt with in Ch.2. The subject of arbitrability has not received much attention from the English courts,[125] although it has been considered by some other common law courts, including the Supreme Court of the United States of America.[126] Paradoxically, the reason may lie in the huge range of different disputes that are referred to arbitration in England and the procedures adopted to determine them, which inhibit any attempt to limit arbitrability at least in the commercial field. In order to get an idea of what can be referred to arbitration in England one need go no further than the City of London which has witnessed a large variety of commercial and financial disputes. To those cases concerning maritime, insurance and commodity contracts, can be added disputes arising out of building and civil engineering projects, energy and utilities, information and technology, intellectual property, rent review clauses in commercial leases, partnership agreements, manufacturing, imports and exports and general trading.[127] Another approach is to observe the differently constituted arbitral tribunals[128] and the variety of procedures adopted in arbitrations conducted under the rules of institutions as well as in "ad hoc" arbitrations.[129]

Arbitrability.[130] The issue of arbitrability can arise at three stages in an   **1–034** arbitration: first, on an application to stay the arbitration, when the opposing party claims that the tribunal lacks the authority to determine a dispute because it is not arbitrable; second, in the course of the arbitral proceedings on the hearing of an objection that the tribunal lacks substantive jurisdiction[131]; and third, on an application to challenge the award[132] or to oppose its enforcement. The New York

---

[125] The English courts have frequently considered the scope of specific arbitration clauses (e.g. *Ashville Investments Ltd v Elmer Contractors Ltd* [1988] 2 All E.R. 577 and *Fiona Trust & Holding Corp & ors v Privalov & ors* [2002] EWCA Civ 20 *(affirmed) Premium Nafta Products Ltd & others v Fili Shipping Co Ltd & others* [2007] UKHL 40) but the subject of arbitrability has received little attention. The subject was raised, but rejected summarily, in *Re Vocam Europe Ltd* [1998] B.C.C. 396 at 398 and has since been considered in respect of anti-trust issues (see para.1–036). Indeed, in considering the Model Law, the DAC report of 1989 gave short shrift to the subject as follows: "Such matters as are not arbitrable in England (e.g. civil status, liability for criminal offences, etc.) lie almost wholly outside the commercial field" Appendix 1. For a different view see Eric A Schwartz "The Domain of Arbitration and Issues of Arbitrability: The View from the ICC", Vol.9, Foreign Investment Law Journal No.1, 17.

[126] See for example *First Options of Chicago Inc v Kaplan* (1995) 514 U.S. 938.

[127] The first three cases were treated as special categories in the Arbitration Act 1979, s.4 but are not given that treatment in the Arbitration Act 1996.

[128] The composition of arbitral tribunals is referred to in para.1–016 and developed in paras 4–035 *et seq.*

[129] See paras 2–006 and 3–051.

[130] Some observations on arbitrability and the problems of terminology are made in the *2001 Companion to Mustill & Boyd, Commercial Arbitration*, pp.70–76.

[131] The objection may be made to the tribunal or, subject to conditions, to the court: see ss.31 and 32 of the Arbitration Act 1996.

[132] The challenge would be to the tribunal's substantive jurisdiction under s.67 of the Arbitration Act 1996: see paras 8–054 *et seq.*

Convention, for example, refers to non-arbitrability as a ground for a court refusing to recognise and enforce an award.[133]

1-035 **Crime.** An obvious area where disputes are not arbitrable is criminal responsibility. Only judges and magistrates can punish criminals and there will be few occasions where an arbitral tribunal must consider whether a crime has been committed, but a defence might be raised to a commercial claim which, if proved, could mean that one or both of the parties had committed a crime.[134] The procurement of a contract by bribery of a public officer is an example.[135] In order to decide whether the defence is well founded the tribunal must investigate the allegation. If the defence is established the claim may be dismissed, but, whatever its decision, an arbitral tribunal cannot under English law impose criminal sanctions.

1-036 **Anti-trust.** Issues relating to competition or anti-trust arising from alleged breaches of securities legislation are arbitrable.[136] Thus, an arbitrator can, and may have to,[137] apply the competition law of the European Union which has direct effect in Member States. Insofar as that law affects the validity of the main contract, the arbitration agreement will be severable as a result of s.7 of the Arbitration Act 1996 and may survive such invalidity.[138] Failure by an arbitrator to apply EU competition law where relevant may lead to an appeal against his decision.[139] Even if an appeal has been excluded it has been suggested that the court may intervene in order to fulfil its own duty under EU law.[140]

1-037 **Limits of jurisdiction.** In *Et Plus SA v Welter*,[141] the court stayed court proceedings and said that it would be for the arbitral tribunal to decide finally on the merits of claims under Arts 81 and 82 of the EC Treaty. The scope and

---

[133] Article V(2)(a) permits enforcement to be refused if the court finds that the subject of the difference is "not capable of settlement by arbitration under the law of that country": see para.8–043.

[134] The Supreme Court of the USA has held that claims under the Racketeer Influences and Corrupt Organisations (RICO) Act are arbitrable by a tribunal appointed under the Federal Arbitration Act. See *Shearson and American Express Inc v McMahon* [1987] 482 U.S. 220.

[135] An agreement to split the proceeds of a crime was another example given by the Court of Appeal in *Soleimany v Soleimany* [1998] 3 W.L.R. 911 at 821. On the subject of illegality, see para. 8–031.

[136] *ET Plus SA v Welter* [2005] EWHC 2115; [2006] 1 Lloyd's Rep. 251 in respect of claims of breaches of Arts 81 and 82 of the EC Treaty.

[137] *Mustill and Boyd, Companion*, p.80, suggests that it follows from the decision in the *Municipality of Almelo v Energiebedriff-Jellemij* [1994] E.C.R. 1–1477 that the duty to apply European law exists even where the arbitrator is empowered, pursuant to s.46(1)(b) of the 1996 Act, to decide according to "other considerations" than an applicable law.

[138] See para.2–007 for the doctrine of separability.

[139] It would be a matter of English law for the purpose of s.69 of the Act: see para.8–119.

[140] *Mustill and Boyd, Companion*, p.82 suggests that the common law power under s.81(1) of the Arbitration Act 1996 gives scope for intervention by the court on public policy grounds, but this is doubtful.

[141] [2005] EWHC 2115 at [51] and [2006] 1 Lloyd's Rep. 251 at 264. The arbitration was seated in Paris.

application of the duty of an arbitral tribunal to apply competition law is uncertain. In successive decisions, the Supreme Court of the United States of America has held on an application for a stay that an arbitral tribunal can decide issues relating to anti-trust and securities legislation.[142] In a rider to the *Mitsubishi* judgment, however, the Supreme Court said that on an application for enforcement the court would consider "the effect of an arbitral tribunal's failure to take cognisance of the statutory cause of action".[143] The implication of this rider is that if an arbitral tribunal decides that there has been a breach of anti-trust legislation but does not award the punitive damages prescribed by the legislation (because the tribunal regards it as penal or possibly because another law is applied), the enforcing court may review the award. This result may not be surprising in domestic cases, that is, those involving two parties normally resident within the jurisdiction of the court, but it does raise an important issue in non-domestic or international cases.[144]

Human rights. The European Convention on Human Rights ("ECHR") has been incorporated into English domestic law by the Human Rights Act 1996 ("HRA") and is relevant to an arbitration whose seat is in England.[145] Section 3(1) of the HRA requires that primary legislation, which includes the Arbitration Act 1996 and subordinate legislation "must be read and given effect in a way which is compatible with Convention rights". Subordinate legislation includes the rules made under the Arbitration Act 1996. Thus, in considering any application or appeal concerning an arbitration, the court will have regard to the ECHR[146] because arbitration is directed at determining the civil rights and obligations of the parties.[147]   1–038

Fair hearing. Article 6(1) of the ECHR provides: 1–039

"In the determination of his civil rights and obligations ... everyone is entitled to a fair and public hearing within a reasonable time by an independent and impartial tribunal established by law ... ".

---

[142] *Mitsubishi Motors Corp v Soler Chrysler Plymouth Inc* [1985] 473 U.S. 614 (anti-trust claims) and *Shearson and American Express Inc v McMahon* [1987] 482 U.S. 220 (securities and RICO claims). A similar subject was considered in *Att-Gen of New Zealand v Mobil Oil N2 Ltd* [1989] 2 N.Z.L.R. 649 where the High Court in New Zealand refused to stay an arbitration in respect of anti-trust claims. In *IBM Australia Ltd v National Distribution Services Ltd* [1991] 100 A.L.R. 361 the Supreme Court of New South Wales approved the New Zealand decision in upholding an agreement to refer to arbitration the decision and relief to be granted under consumer protection provisions.

[143] *Mitsubishi*, above at 636–637.

[144] In the *Mitsubishi* case the parties chose Swiss law to govern their contract, but there is some more recent authority in the USA that the "second look doctrine" will not excuse enforcement of Convention awards (*Brandeis Intsel Ltd v Calabrain Chemicals Co* 656 F. Supp. 160).

[145] Part 1 of the Arbitration Act 1996 applies to an arbitration whose seat is in England or Wales or Northern Ireland. However, what is said about an arbitrator's duty in para.1–039 has wider application and extends in principle to arbitration conducted in other States that have acceded to the ECHR.

[146] See the decision of the European Court of Human Rights in *Suovaniemi v Finland* (February 23, 1999).

[147] Article 6(1) of the ECHR. See *Stretford v Football Association* [2007] EWCA Civ 238 at [34].

Although an arbitral tribunal is not a "tribunal" within the meaning of Art.6 of ECHR,[148] an arbitrator is required to observe duties that are broadly compatible with Convention rights. Duties imposed on an arbitral tribunal by s.33 of the Arbitration Act 1996 require an arbitrator to "act fairly and impartially as between the parties, giving each party a reasonable opportunity of putting his case and dealing with that of his opponent . . . "[149] A party who voluntarily[150] agrees to arbitration is treated as having waived his right to a public hearing in the arbitration,[150a] but the waiver does not extend to the other rights guaranteed by Art.6(1) of the ECHR, including the right to a fair hearing within a reasonable time by a tribunal that is impartial and independent.[151] Thus, although the Arbitration Act 1996 is compatible with the ECHR,[152] it is important that the tribunal bears in mind the ECHR and its jurisprudence[153] as well as the Arbitration Act. Failure to do so will make the tribunal's decision susceptible to challenge.[154] The court has already considered the effect of the ECHR on its former practice of not giving full reasons for a refusal to grant permission for leave to appeal against an arbitration award, and concluded that some reasons should be given.[155]

1–040   **Public policy.** Under the Arbitration Act 1996, the parties are free to submit all arbitrable issues, including those involving fraud, to the tribunal for determination.[156] The court does, however, retain limited powers in respect of matters that affect public policy or the public interest.[157] Section 1 of the Arbitration Act 1996

---

[148] For a further discussion on this subject see Jonathan Haydn-Williams, "Arbitration and the Human Rights Act 1998" (Journal of Chartered Institute of Arbitrators) Vol.67, p.289. For primary sources see *www.echr.co.int*.

[149] See also s.1 of the Arbitration Act 1996 for a statement of the objective of an arbitration and *Stretford, ibid.*, paras 35–38. See para.5–032.

[150] The waiver to a public hearing only applies where the parties have voluntarily (or freely) entered into an agreement to arbitrate. See *Streford, ibid.*, para.45. This waiver does not extend to arbitrations imposed on a party by statute.

[150a] See *Premium Nafta Products Ltd & others v Fili Shipping Co Ltd & others*, in which it was confirmed that "[t]he European Convention was not intended to destroy arbitration" and that as arbitration is based on agreement, parties can by agreement waive the right to have their disputes determined by a court (*per* Lord Hoffmann, at [20]).

[151] See *Stretford, ibid.*, para.65, *Sumukan Ltd v Commonwealth Secretariat* [2007] EWCA Civ 243 at [59] and *Kazakhstan v Istil Group Inc* [2007] EWCA Civ 471 at [19], which reviewed the Strasbourg jurisprudence.

[152] Although compatible, there are differences. The obvious difference is that Art.6(1) of the ECHR requires a tribunal to be independent as well as impartial: see para.4–128.

[153] The ECHR is said to be a "living instrument", which means that the principles stated in it will be developed by the Commission and the European Court of Human Rights.

[154] A challenge to the tribunal's jurisdiction was made unsuccessfully in *Istil, ibid.*

[155] See *North Range Shipping v Seatrans Shipping Corp* [2002] EWCA Civ 405, which overturned the decision in *Mousaka Inc v Golden Seagull Maritime* [2002] W.L.R. 395, and *BLCT Ltd v J Sainbury Plc* [2003] EWCA Civ 884 at [44]–[48]. See para.8–152.

[156] When however an award is obtained by fraud or the award or the way in which it was procured is contrary to public policy, that constitutes a "serious irregularity" which would enable a party to apply to the court to challenge the award. Section 68(2)(g) of the Arbitration Act 1996: see para.8–076.

[157] Public policy and public interest are not the same thing but they may overlap. Public interest has been explained in the DAC report in terms of the mandatory duty imposed on a tribunal by s.33 of the Arbitration Act 1996. Public policy is described in para.8–044.

qualifies the autonomy of the parties by "such safeguards as are necessary in the public interest".[158] Further, enforcement of an award may be opposed on the ground that it is contrary to public policy,[159] and an application may be made to set aside an award because of a serious irregularity causing substantial injustice to the applicant where the award was "obtained by fraud or the award or the way in which it was procured [was] contrary to public policy."[160] The court has even granted an injunction restraining enforcement and publication of an award obtained by fraud.[161]

Investment disputes. Though disputes arising out of bilateral and multi-lateral investment treaties have increased in recent years, they raise legal considerations that are beyond the scope of this book.[162]   1–041

8. THE SOURCES OF ARBITRATION LAW

Where arbitration law is to be found. There is no single source of English arbitration law. Prior to the Arbitration Act 1996, there was not even a partial statutory code for the conduct of arbitrations. The Arbitration Acts 1950–1979 were more concerned with filling the gaps in an incomplete arbitration agreement[163] and specifying the powers of the High Court.[164] The greatest source of arbitration law was to be found elsewhere, as the following quotation indicated: 1–042

> "A user of the process and his foreign or non-specialist adviser cannot quickly hope to ascertain, simply by reading the Arbitration Acts and other statutes which contain individual provisions concerning arbitration, how arbitration in England works in practice, and still less how to confront the kind of problem which is likely to arise if the conduct of the reference goes wrong. The law on these topics lies almost entirely in the reported cases, beyond the reach of lay users of arbitration, and indeed of non-specialist foreign and English lawyers."[165]

---

[158] Arbitration Act 1996, s.1(b). For a discussion on the effect of s.33 of the Act in the context of this provision, see paras 155 *et seq.* of the DAC report—see also para.5–065.

[159] See Arbitration Act 1996, s.103(3) which provides that recognition or enforcement of a New York Convention Award may be refused "if it would be contrary to public policy to recognise or enforce the award"—see also para.8–044.

[160] Arbitration Act 1996, s.68(2)(g) and see para.8–076.

[161] *Arab National Bank v El Abdali* [2004] EWHC 2381.

[162] The reader is referred to specialist texts such as *Foreign Investment Disputes* by Bishop, Crawford and Reisman (Kluwer, 2005).

[163] Arbitration Act 1950, s.6, for example.

[164] Arbitration Act 1950, s.12(6) and Arbitration Act 1979, s.1(2), for example.

[165] Extract from para.103 of the DAC report on the UNCITRAL Model Law dated June, 1989. The report recommended that the Arbitration Acts 1950–1979 should be replaced by a new Act, which became the Arbitration Act 1996. See Appendix 2.

The Arbitration Act 1996 restated the former arbitration legislation[166] with some changes and it also codified principles established by previous case law. Further, the Civil Procedure Rules ("CPR") Pt 62 and the Arbitration Practice Direction made under those rules specify the procedure applicable to arbitration applications made to the English courts.[167] Nevertheless, the decisions of judges on arbitration matters that come before them continue to play an important role in the development of the English law of arbitration.[168] Further, much of the practice of arbitration is contained in awards of tribunals which are generally not published. It is in this area that textbooks such as this come into their own because they identify and comment upon the law and practice of arbitration. The court has recognised that, in relation to cases arising in an international commercial context regard may be had to comparative law and the approach taken to relevant matters in other jurisdictions.[168a]

9. DEVELOPMENTS IN ARBITRATION LAW

1-043 **Arbitration Act 1996.** This is the principal English arbitration statute.[169] It replaced the Arbitration Acts 1950–1979 as amended following a comprehensive review of the English law and practice of arbitration[170] as well as the UNCITRAL Model Law on International Commercial Arbitration.[171]

> "One of the major purposes of the Arbitration Act 1996 was to set out most of the important principles of the law of arbitration in England and Wales in a logical order and expressed in a language sufficiently clear and free from technicalities to be readily comprehensible to the layman. It was to be 'in user-friendly language'.[172]
>
> It is also not merely a consolidating Act. I would accept that the Act was intended to make the law of arbitration clear and more straightforward. Furthermore, the Act makes the law less technical than it has been hitherto. If it is appropriate for me to say so, the underlying spirit of the Arbitration Act is very much in accord with the underlying spirit of the new procedural rules applicable to the civil courts in this jurisdiction . . . it sets out in readily understandable terms for parties to an arbitration what is required of them."[173]

---

[166] The former arbitration legislation is to be found principally in the Arbitration Acts 1950–1979. The Arbitration Act 1996 appears in Appendix 1 of this book. Only Part II of the Arbitration Act 1950 remains in force in respect of the enforcement of certain foreign awards: see para.8–020.

[167] For the procedure under CPR Pt 62 and the Arbitration Practice Direction see paras 8–178 *et seq.*

[168] The decision of the House of Lords in *Porter v Magill* [2001] UKHL 67 is a case in point. That decision finally decided the test for impartiality. See para.1–051.

[168a] *Premium Nafta Products Ltd & ors v Fili Shipping Co Ltd & ors* [2007] UKHL 40, *per* Lord Hope at [29]–[32]. The court further recognised that the UK, as a centre for international commercial arbitration cannot risk being isolated internationally by virtue of its approach to questions of interpretation of clauses (*per* Lord Hope at [293]).

[169] Appendix 1 contains the full text of the Arbitration Act 1996.

[170] This is the review mentioned in para.1–001.

[171] The text of the Model Law with a commentary on its Articles appears in Appendix 4.

[172] *Seabridge Shipping v Orssleff* [1999] 2 Lloyd's Rep. 685 at 690.

[173] *Patel v Patel* [1999] 3 W.L.R. 322, *per* Lord Woolf M.R. at 325. Lord Woolf played a leading role in the reform of the procedural rules applicable to the civil courts in England and Wales, referred to as the Woolf Reform.

Although it restates the previous legislation on arbitration with some changes, the Arbitration Act 1996 also takes account of developments that have occurred in English arbitration law.[174] Some of those developments occurred as a result of work undertaken by the United Nations,[175] and two landmarks in that work and their sequel deserve to be mentioned as well as the former arbitration legislation. This will be done in chronological order, followed by a reference to the influence of case law and the preparatory work that preceded the Arbitration Act 1996.

A report has since been made following a survey into how the Act has worked in practice.[175a]

Arbitration Act 1950. For many years this was the principal arbitration Act. 1–044
With the exception of Pt II of that Act,[176] which relates only to the enforcement of a certain limited number of foreign awards,[177] the Arbitration Act 1950 has been repealed.[178] Many of its provisions, with modifications, were re-enacted by the Arbitration Act 1996.

The New York Convention. The Convention for the Recognition and 1–045
Enforcement of Foreign Arbitral Awards, which was made in June 1958 in New York,[179] had a profound effect on English arbitration law.[180] Although the United Kingdom did not accede to the New York Convention until 1975, its enactment by the Arbitration Act 1975 was to bring about fundamental changes to the law and practice of arbitration. The effect on domestic arbitration occurred gradually as a result of the introduction into English law of a temporary distinction between a "domestic arbitration agreement"[181] and a non-domestic or international arbitration agreement. The changes and their consequences are mentioned in the following paragraphs.

Arbitration Act 1975. This Act, which implemented the New York Conven- 1–046
tion into English law, limited the discretion of the High Court to stay any action

---

[174] For example the decision of the Court of Appeal in *Harbour Assurance Co (UK) Ltd v Kansa General International Insurance Co Ltd* [1993] 1 Lloyd's Rep. 455 concerning severability of the arbitration agreement: see para.2–007.
[175] The work had been done in the main by successive working parties established by the Trade Commission of the United Nations (UNCITRAL). The New York Convention and Model Law provoked changes and a thorough review of English arbitration law.
[175a] Report on the Arbitration Act 1996, Arbitration Int. vol.23, no.3, p.437.
[176] Section 99 of the Arbitration Act 1996 preserves Pt II of the Arbitration Act 1950 for this purpose, see para.8–020.
[177] The awards concerned are enforceable under the Geneva Convention.
[178] Section 107(2) of the Arbitration Act 1996. There were some transitional provisions.
[179] See para.8–021.
[180] The New York Convention is described in the DAC report as "the cornerstone of international disputes resolution"—para.347.
[181] The distinction was introduced by the Arbitration Act 1975, s.1(4). It is restated in the Arbitration Act 1996, s.85(2), although it has been decided not to bring that section into force. Thus, the distinction has not been preserved: see para.2–005.

brought in breach of an arbitration agreement which was not a domestic arbitration agreement. A stay was mandatory, if one of the parties to a non-domestic arbitration agreement requested it, unless the court was satisfied that the agreement was null and void, inoperative or incapable of being performed or there was not in fact any dispute between the parties with regard to the matters agreed to be referred.[182] The Arbitration Act 1996 restates this provision except that it follows the text of the New York Convention and omits the last clause concerning the absence of a dispute.[183] Under the 1975 Act, the High Court maintained a discretion in respect of domestic arbitration agreements[184] but that changed with the Arbitration Act 1996. There is no longer a discretion and a stay is mandatory.[185]

The Arbitration Act 1975 also introduced a new category of arbitration award, namely, the Convention award, which was to extend the special status given to a "foreign award" some 45 years earlier.[186] The court was required to recognise and enforce a Convention award except where there was opposition on specific and limited grounds.[187] The amendments made by the Arbitration Act 1975 as described in this paragraph revealed a modest change in policy towards party autonomy in arbitration proceedings and away from court intervention. The following paragraphs indicate how that policy continued to develop.

1–047   **Commercial Court Committee.** The subject of judicial review of arbitration awards was examined by this Committee in 1978. In particular, the Committee considered the powers of the High Court both to set aside an award if it appeared from the award itself or from documents incorporated into the award that the arbitral tribunal had reached some erroneous conclusions of fact or law, and the power to require the tribunal to state an award or part of it in the form of a special case for the opinion of the court.[188] The former was known as "error on the face of the award" and the latter as "the stated case procedure". Review for an error on the face of the award had led to tribunals declining to give reasons for their awards, and the stated case procedure had resulted in delays while the opinion of the High Court on the award was awaited. The Committee recommended that these two forms of review be replaced by a new right of appeal confined to questions of law, leaving decisions on questions of fact to the arbitral tribunal.

---

[182] Arbitration Act 1975, s.1(1).
[183] Arbitration Act 1996, s.9(4): see paras 7–046 and 7–047.
[184] Arbitration Act 1975, s.1(2).
[185] Although the Arbitration Act 1996, s.86(2) re-enacted with amendments s.4 of the 1950 Act, it has been decided not to bring s.86 into force: see para.2–005 and footnote.
[186] A "foreign award" is defined in the Arbitration Act 1950, s.35 and includes an arbitral award made in a State that has acceded to the Convention on the Execution of Foreign Arbitral Awards signed in Geneva in September 1927, which was enacted by the Arbitration (Foreign Awards) Act 1930 and re-enacted by the Arbitration Act 1950, Pt II, which remains in force: see s.99 of the Arbitration Act 1996.
[187] The grounds were set out in the Arbitration Act 1975, s.5 and are restated in Arbitration Act 1996, s.103(2): see paras 8–022 *et seq.*
[188] Commercial Court Committee report on Arbitration, July 1978, Cmnd. 7284.

Arbitration Act 1979. This Act implemented the recommendations of the   1–048
Commercial Court Committee and gave the High Court a new jurisdiction limited
to determining a question of law arising in the course of the reference[189] and to
hearing an appeal on a question of law arising out of an award provided that certain
conditions were fulfilled.[190] Further, with the exception of three special categories
of cases,[191] which no longer apply,[192] this new jurisdiction of the court could be
excluded at any time in respect of a non-domestic arbitration agreement if the
parties entered into an agreement in writing to that effect.[193] Now the parties can
at any time and in respect of any arbitration agreement[194] exclude either or both
an application to determine a preliminary point of law and an appeal from any
arbitration award.[195]

UNCITRAL Model Law. This is the other[196] outstanding contribution   1–049
made by the United Nations to international arbitration which has influenced the
development of English law.[197] The full text of the Model Law on International
Commercial Arbitration[198] which was adopted by the United Nations Commission
on International Trade Law (UNCITRAL) on June 21, 1985 and has since been
amended appears in Appendix 4 to this book with some comments on how
provisions of the Model Law have been incorporated into the Arbitration Act
1996. The DAC reports[199] contain a comprehensive review of the UNCITRAL
Model Law, and the following chapters of this book cross refer by way of footnote
the sections of the Arbitration Act 1996 with various Articles of the Model
Law.

Case law. The changes introduced by the Arbitration Acts 1975 and 1979 were   1–050
duly implemented by the courts. The Judicial Committee of the House of Lords
led the way in a series of judgments that affected various stages of the arbitration
proceedings. A clause containing an arbitration agreement was enforced and court
proceedings stayed even though the words of s.1 of the Arbitration Act 1975, then

---

[189] Arbitration Act 1979, s.2(1) restated in the Arbitration Act 1996, s.45: see paras 7–165 *et seq.*
[190] Arbitration Act 1979, s.1 restated in the Arbitration Act 1996, s.69, paras 8–119 *et seq.*
[191] Arbitration Act 1979, s.4(1) The special category of cases concerned a question or claim falling
within the Admiralty jurisdiction of the High Court (maritime disputes) and disputes arising out
of a contract of insurance or a commodity contract, as defined in subs.4(2) of the 1979 Act.
[192] The special category cases were not retained in the Arbitration Act 1996, so the exception no longer
applies.
[193] Arbitration Act 1979, s.3(1). Even in domestic cases the jurisdiction could be excluded by
agreement after the dispute had arisen.
[194] See s.6 of the Arbitration Act 1996 for the definition of arbitration agreements under the Act.
[195] The distinction between domestic and non-domestic arbitration agreements is no longer in force
(see para.2–005).
[196] The New York Convention referred to above was the first major contribution which has been made
by the United Nations to international arbitration.
[197] The structure and content of the Arbitration Act 1996 owes much to the Model Law: see the DAC
report, para.4 reproduced in Appendix 2.
[198] The UNCITRAL Model Law should not be confused with the UNCITRAL Rules of Arbitration.
Both are products of the United Nations Commission on International Trade Law.
[199] See para.1–053.

in force, did not literally require a stay.[200] The proposition that the High Court had an inherent jurisdiction to supervise the conduct of an arbitration beyond the powers then contained in the Arbitration Acts 1950–1979 was rejected by the House of Lords with a statement that the tribunal was the master of the procedure to be followed in the arbitration.[201]

Strict guidelines were established for the High Court to follow in deciding whether to grant leave to appeal against a question of law arising out of an award made in England.[202] Further, in respect of New York Convention awards, the courts demonstrated a willingness to recognise and enforce an award as such even though the State where the arbitration took place was not a party to the New York Convention when the award was made[203] and despite evidence that the award was not made in the place intended by the parties to the arbitration agreement.[204]

1-051 **Some leading decisions.** Case law continues to play an important role in the development of arbitral law. The courts have approved a broad approach to the construction of an arbitration clause and have endorsed the separability of that clause from the rest of the contract.[204a] The test for apparent bias has been restated by the House of Lords,[205] and a distinction made between excess of powers and a mistaken exercise of an arbitrator's power.[206] The use of an anti-suit injunction to restrain a party to an arbitration agreement from commencing or prosecuting court proceedings in another Member State has been referred by the House of Lords to the European Court of Justice for a ruling.[207] The subject of illegality has twice been considered by the Court of Appeal in the context of enforcing an arbitration award[208] and the subject of joinder has been considered by the Privy Council.[209] The courts have also been required to give effect to changes introduced by the Arbitration Act 1996[210] and other legislation.[211]

1-052 **Pre-1996 decisions.** Caution has been expressed by the court about the use of cases that pre-date the Arbitration Act 1996.

> "Reference to such cases should only generally be necessary in cases where the Act does not cover the point—as, for example, in relation to confidentiality or where for some

---

[200] *Channel Tunnel Group Ltd v Balfour Beatty Construction Ltd* [1993] 1 All E.R. 664.
[201] *Bremer Vulcan Schiffbau und Maschinenfabrik v South India Shipping Corp* [1981] 1 All E.R. 289.
[202] *Pioneer Shipping BTP Tioxide Ltd (The "Nema")* [1981] 3 W.L.R. 292 and *The "Antaios"* [1985] A.C. 191. These guidelines have been codified by the Arbitration Act 1996, s.69(3).
[203] *Kuwait Minister of Public Work v Sir Frederick Snow & Partners* [1984] 1 All E.R. 733.
[204] *Hiscox v Outhwaite (No.1)* [1991] 3 All E.R. 641.
[204a] *Premium Nafta Products Ltd & ors v Fili Shipping Co Ltd & ors* [2007] UKHL 40.
[205] *Porter v Magill* [2001] UKHL 67—see paras 4–110 *et seq.*
[206] *Lesotho Highlands Development Authority v Impregilo SpA* [2005] UKHL 43.
[207] *West Tankers Inc v RAS Riunione (The "Front Comor")* [2007] UKHL 4.
[208] *Soleimany v Soleimany* [1998] 3 W.L.R. 811 and *Westacre Investment Inc v Jugoimport—SPDR Ltd* [1999] 2 Lloyd's Rep. 65. See para.8–032 and para.8–033.
[209] *The Bay Hotel and Resort v Cavalier Construction Co Ltd* [2001] UKPC 34.
[210] Decisions on s.68 (challenging the award for serious irregularity) are a good example—see paras 8–072 *et seq.*
[211] For example, the Human Rights Act 1998—see para.1–038.

other reason it is necessary to refer to the earlier cases—a court should, in general, comply with the guidance given by the Court of Appeal and rely on the language of the Act."[212]

This book does refer to a few cases that were based on the old law. They are not strictly limited to cases where the Act does not cover the point. They are occasionally used to illustrate situations, particularly where those points have not been considered by the court since the 1996 Act came into force. In other areas, such as challenges to awards, reference to the pre-1996 case law, which applied a different regime, is no longer appropriate.

The DAC reports. In 1987 an Advisory Committee of the Department of   1–053
Industry ("the DAC") was established to consider the UNCITRAL Model Law and to examine the operation of the Arbitration Acts 1950–1979 in the light of that Model Law.[213] In 1989, the DAC recommended that England and Wales should not adopt the Model Law but should have a new and up-to-date Arbitration Act which in general applied to domestic and international arbitrations alike.[214] In 1994, a consultation paper was published together with a draft arbitration bill. Following a period of consultation[215] a new draft arbitration bill was circulated for public comment in July 1995. The Arbitration Act 1996 is based on that bill.

A further report of the DAC was published in February 1996[216] which commented clause by clause on the Arbitration Bill. A supplemental report followed in January 1997.[217] These two reports have been referred to with approval by the court,[218] and are of considerable assistance with regard to the interpretation of the Arbitration Act 1996.[219]

Party autonomy—the perception. The public policy summarised in   1–054
the comment: "There must be no Alsatia in England where the King's writ does not run,"[220] no longer applies to English arbitration law. Not only has party autonomy been formally enshrined in the Arbitration Act 1996,[221] but it is also

---

[212] *Seabridge Shipping v Orssleff* [1996] 2 Lloyd's Rep. 685 at 690. See also *Lesotho Highlands v Impreglio SpA* [2005] UKHL 43.

[213] Departmental Advisory Committee on Arbitration law, A Report on the UNCITRAL Model Law on International Commercial Arbitration 1989 (the "DAC Committee Report" 1989), Terms of Reference, p.1. The text of the Model Law with a commentary on its Articles appears in Appendix 3.

[214] The DAC report (1989) at 34.

[215] Consultation Paper dated February 1994.

[216] The DAC report on the Arbitration Bill of February 1996, referred to in this book as the DAC report, Appendix 2.

[217] The DAC supplementary report on the Arbitration Act 1996 dated January 1997 is also at Appendix 2.

[218] The reported decisions that have quoted the DAC reports are too many to enumerate, but many of them are referred to in *Cetelem SA v Roust Holding Ltd* [2005] EWCA Civ 618.

[219] The DAC report and supplementary report are also reproduced in Appendix 2. CPR Pt 62, the Arbitration Practice Direction and the allocation and commencement orders are at Appendix 1.

[220] *Czarnikow v Roth Schmidt and Co* [1922] 2 K.B. 478, *per* Scrutton L.J.

[221] Section 1(b) of the Arbitration Act 1996 is in effect a statement of the principle of party autonomy. It is reinforced by the following subs.1(c) which restricts court intervention.

applied in practice. In most cases, the agreement to arbitrate is recognised and indirectly enforced by means of a stay, the tribunal is left alone to conduct the reference and to determine the dispute, the award is not reviewed and it is summarily enforced. The powers of intervention of the Court have been curtailed and are identified in the Arbitration Act 1996.[222] The DAC reports[223] indicate how the courts should apply the Arbitration Act 1996. There continue to be applications to the court, particularly while there is a need to clarify some provisions of the Act,[224] but the decisions made after the Act reveal[225] that the spirit of the legislation as expressed by the DAC is being adhered to, and the scope for interference with the arbitral process is very limited.

10. Summary of Following Chapters

1–055   **The rest of the book.** This introduction is intended to whet the appetite for the subject of arbitration. What follows is an explanation of the modern law and practice of arbitration in England. The chapters have been arranged so as to lead the reader from the beginning to the end of an arbitration and to enable him to pick out particular aspects of interest.

1–056   **Chapter 2** examines all aspects of the arbitration agreement (often referred to simply as the arbitration clause) and contains a checklist for the draftsman. What formalities are needed? How important are the terms of the arbitration agreement or arbitration clause? When and how can they be varied? How does the choice of the place or "seat"[226] affect the law of the arbitration?

1–057   **Chapter 3** is devoted to the parties and institutions. Who can and cannot enter into an arbitration agreement? How should one verify the capacity of a proposed party for the purposes both of entering into an arbitration agreement and of executing on assets? What changes (e.g. bankruptcy) might occur before and during the arbitration proceedings and what can be done about them?

---

[222] Section 1(c) of the Arbitration Act 1996 provides that the court should not intervene in matters governed by Pt I of the Act except as provided by that Part of the Act, although the court does retain a limited inherent jurisdiction. See paras 7–003 *et seq.*

[223] The DAC report, as supplemented, expresses clear views on how the courts should approach the Arbitration Act 1996.

[224] As in, e.g. *McLean Homes SE Ltd v Blackdale*, unreported, November 2, 2001 QBD (TCC), H. Lloyd Q.C. and *North Range Shipping Ltd v Seatrans Shipping* [2002] EWCA Civ 405.

[225] Permission to appeal may have been given too readily on occasion, but information given by Colman J. in his lecture "Arbitrators and Judges—How much interference should we tolerate?" (March 14, 2006) suggests that judges have followed the dictate of the House of Lords in *Lesotho Highlands, ibid.*, [2005] UKHL 43 that the purposes of the Arbitration Act is to reduce dramatically court intervention.

[226] See Arbitration Act 1996, s.3 for a definition of the "seat" of an arbitration and paras 2–102 *et seq.*

Chapter 4 addresses the subject of the arbitral tribunal. How is a tribunal 1–058
appointed, and when is an appointing authority needed? When are particular
qualifications required? What of the tribunal's powers, duties and liabilities? How
and when does the authority of the tribunal come to an end? How are fees
determined?

Chapter 5 considers the ways in which arbitration proceedings are conducted. 1–059
When and how are these proceedings (the reference) commenced? What matters
need to be considered and at what stage of the reference? What procedure should
be adopted in the reference? Is there to be a hearing? If so, how is it to be
conducted? How is the reference terminated?

Chapter 6 concentrates on the award. What are the formal and substantive 1–060
requirements for a valid award? What relief and remedies may a tribunal award?
How are the costs of the reference and the award assessed? What is the effect, if
any, of an award on the parties to the reference and on third parties?

Chapter 7 focuses on the role of the English court before and during the 1–061
arbitration. Will the court stay legal proceedings brought in breach of an arbitration agreement? How and when may the court intervene in an arbitration during
the reference and for what purpose? What interim measures are available? How are
disputes about recoverable costs to be resolved?

Chapter 8 concludes with the role of the court after the award has been made. 1–062
How can that award be enforced? How can it be challenged? Is there a right of
appeal? What are the grounds?

In the last section of Ch.8, there is a description of the procedure for arbitration
applications with cross-references to the relevant rules.

Appendices. There are several Appendices, consisting of (1) the Arbitration 1–063
Act 1996 and CPR Pt 62 and the Arbitration Practice Direction with court forms,
(2) the DAC report, February 1996 and the DAC supplementary report of January
1997, (3) a description of Statutory Arbitration, (4) an annotated version of the
UNCITRAL Model Law, and (5) a list of appointing authorities.

At the front of the book there is also a glossary which includes the abbreviations
that are used throughout the book and particularly in the footnotes.

CHAPTER 2

THE ARBITRATION AGREEMENT

1. INTRODUCTION

2–001   **Contents of the chapter.** This chapter is concerned with the arbitration agreement. It begins by considering what constitutes an arbitration agreement. This involves examining the statutory definition, the nature of an arbitration agreement and different types of arbitration agreements. It also considers how an arbitration agreement is distinguished from other types of dispute resolution clause. The next two sections examine respectively the form and content of an arbitration agreement. There is clearly an overlap between the two, but the meaning of an agreement in writing for the purposes of the Arbitration Act 1996 and incorporation of arbitration agreements by reference to other documents are dealt with in the former section. The section dealing with the content of the arbitration agreement provides a checklist of the matters to be included as well as considering the scope of the arbitration agreement and different wordings commonly used in arbitration agreements. The laws to be applied to the arbitration are then examined. Finally, the chapter looks at how the arbitration agreement may be terminated.

2. WHAT IS AN ARBITRATION AGREEMENT?

(a) Statutory definition of arbitration agreement

Definition in the 1996 Act. Section 6 of the Arbitration Act 1996 contains a definition of an arbitration agreement.[1] It provides[2] that an arbitration agreement is "an agreement to submit to arbitration present or future disputes (whether they are contractual or not)". An arbitration agreement is therefore a contractual undertaking by two or more parties to resolve disputes by the process of arbitration,[3] even if the disputes themselves are not based on contractual obligations.[4] The term "disputes" includes "any difference".[5] It is important to note also: **2–002**

(1) The Arbitration Act 1996 will only apply to an arbitration agreement if it is in writing or evidenced in writing.[6]

(2) Reference to a written form of arbitration clause or to a document containing an arbitration clause constitutes an arbitration agreement if the reference is such as to make that clause part of the agreement.[7]

Agreement to submit present or future disputes. It is clear from the definition set out above that the term "arbitration agreement" covers both (i) an arbitration clause in a contract (or matrix agreement) by which the parties agree   **2–003**

---

[1] The definition applies to Pt I of the Arbitration Act 1996. It does not therefore apply to arbitration agreements that fall outside the Arbitration Act 1996, e.g. because they are not made in writing, or to statutory arbitration, which is dealt with in Appendix 3.

[2] Section 6(1) of the Arbitration Act 1996.

[3] An arbitration agreement is not contrary to Art.6 of the European Convention on Human Rights: *Stretford v Football Association* [2007] EWCA Civ 238 at [34]. See further para.1–039 above.

[4] e.g. disputes involving tort claims: see para.2–004 below.

[5] Section 82(1)of the Arbitration Act 1996. The DAC report explained that there was some authority for the proposition that "difference" is wider than "dispute": see para.41 of the DAC report. See also dicta in *Amec Civil Engineering Ltd v Secretary of State for Transport* [2005] 1 W.L.R. 2339 suggesting the words "dispute or difference" might mean something more than "dispute" alone.

[6] Section 5(1) of the Arbitration Act 1996: see paras 2–038 *et seq.* below.

[7] Section 6(2) of the Arbitration Act 1996: see paras 2–044 *et seq.* below.

that disputes between them in the future arising out of that contract will be referred to arbitration and (ii) a separate agreement not forming part of another contract to refer an existing dispute to arbitration. This separate agreement,[8] sometimes known as a "submission agreement"[9] or an ad hoc agreement,[10] deals only with the setting up of machinery to resolve the particular dispute which has arisen between the parties.

2–004 **Non-contractual claims.** The statutory definition of an arbitration agreement[11] makes clear that disputes may be referred to arbitration whether they arise in contract or otherwise. Accordingly, claims based on a cause of action arising in tort, restitution, breach of a statutory duty or some other non-contractual cause of action may fall within an arbitration agreement. Provided the terms of the arbitration agreement are broad enough to encompass such claims they can in principle be the subject of an arbitration. Whether they do so in any particular case requires an examination of the arbitration agreement but the courts have generally given a broad interpretation to the scope of arbitration agreements in this regard.[12] In this context it may be possible to conclude that the non-contractual claims are so intimately connected with a contract that even an arbitration clause designed primarily for contractual claims will extend to connected non-contractual claims.[13] In *Asghar v Legal Services Commission* claims for conspiracy, misfeasance in public office and inducement to commit breach of conduct were all found to be within the arbitration agreement because "the resolution of the contractual claims cannot sensibly or practically be divorced from the resolution of the non-contractual claims."[14] Many such cases relate to claims in tort[15] based on breach of a duty of care which arises under a contract and an arbitration agreement which covers disputes "arising out of" a contract will be wide enough to include such tort claims.[16]

The Court of Appeal in *Fiona Trust v Primalov* has stated that it is time for "a line of some sort to be drawn and a fresh start made" in relation to the fine and sometimes inconsistent distinctions previously made on the basis of particular

---

[8] The importance of ensuring that clear agreement has been reached was underlined in *LG Caltex Gas Co Ltd v China National Petroleum Corp* [2001] 1 W.L.R. 1892 where the Court of Appeal held that no separate agreement had in fact been entered into.

[9] See also Art.7.1 of the Model Law at Appendix 4.

[10] See para.2–006 below.

[11] Section 6(1) of the Arbitration Act 1996; the words " . . . disputes (whether they are contractual or not)" were not in the statutory predecessor, s.32 of the Arbitration Act 1950.

[12] See para.2–075 below.

[13] *Woolf v Collis Removal Service* [1948] 1 K.B. 11. For arbitration of the tort of conspiracy, see *Lonrho Ltd v Shell Petroleum Co Ltd*, *The Times*, February 1, 1978, Ch D, Brightman J.

[14] [2004] EWHC 1803 at [18].

[15] See further para.2–075 below.

[16] The *"Playa Larga"* [1983] 2 Lloyd's Rep. 171; The *"Ermopoulis"* [1990] 1 Lloyd's Rep. 160; The *"Angelic Grace"* [1995] 1 Lloyd's Rep. 87; *Abdullah M Fahem & Co v Mareb Yemen Insurance Co and Tomen (UK) Ltd* [1997] 2 Lloyd's Rep. 738. See further para.2–078 below. Similarly claims for breach of duty as a bailee would be covered.

wordings used in arbitration agreements.[17] Consistent with that general instruction, although some analysis of the nature of the non-contractual claims being made and the terms of the particular arbitration agreement will be necessary it seems likely that the sort of distinctions previously encountered[18] will be replaced by a broader approach to construing arbitration agreements as widely as their terms reasonably permit. Whatever the wording of the arbitration agreement, non-contractual claims may of course become part of the reference if they are included in a pleading and no point is taken by the other party, even if there had originally been no contractual relationship between the parties.[19]

Domestic arbitration agreements. There were restrictions imposed under the previous law in relation to domestic arbitration agreements. These restrictions affected the right to obtain a stay of legal proceedings brought in breach of an arbitration agreement and meant that parties were permitted to exclude the right to a determination by the court of a preliminary point of law or the right to appeal only after the arbitration had begun.[20] This is no longer the case. The distinction between domestic and international arbitration agreements which applied under previous legislation is no longer effective.[21]   2–005

Meaning of "ad hoc". Although it is not referred to specifically in the legislation, the expressions "ad hoc arbitration" or "ad hoc submission" are sometimes used to describe an agreement to refer an existing dispute to arbitration, as contrasted with an arbitration agreement providing for future disputes to be so referred.[22] This should not be confused with the quite different sense in which the phrase "ad hoc arbitration" is also used, namely to signify an arbitration conducted without an arbitration institution administering the proceedings or supplying the procedural rules for the arbitration. This second sense is more common in international arbitrations.   2–006

---

[17] *Fiona Trust & Holding Corp & ors v Yuri Privalov & ors* [2007] EWCA Civ 20 at [17]. Affirmed in *Premium Nafta Products Ltd v Fili Shipping Co Ltd* [2007] UKHL 40 at [12] where Lord Hoffmann, applauding the Court of Appeal's decision said that the linguistic distinctions drawn in earlier cases "reflect no credit upon English commercial" law.

[18] See para.2–076 below.

[19] *Almare Società di Navigazione SpA v Derby & Co Ltd (The "Almaea Prima")* [1989] 2 Lloyd's Rep. 376. The right to object would be lost under s.73 of the Arbitration Act 1996.

[20] Under s.1 of the Arbitration Act 1975.

[21] Sections 85, 86 and 87 of the Arbitration Act 1996 have not been brought into force: The Arbitration Act 1996 (Commencement No.1) Order 1996 (SI 1996/3146). A decision has been taken that they will not be brought into force. The press release issued by the Department of Trade and Industry on January 30, 1997 quoted the Corporate and Consumer Affairs Minister, John Taylor, as saying: " . . . I have also decided that all arbitrations, whether domestic or international, should be treated in the same way . . . This means the court will no longer have discretion to order legal proceedings to be stayed or halted if there is a valid arbitration agreement. Also, parties are now free to enter into an agreement at any time that they will not involve the courts on point [sic] of law."
See also DAC supplementary report on the Arbitration Act 1996, January 1997, para.47–50 at Appendix 2.

[22] See, e.g. *LG Caltex Gas Co Ltd v China National Petroleum Corp* [2001] 1 W.L.R. 1892, although in that case the Court of Appeal held that no ad hoc agreement had in fact been entered into.

(b) Separability of the arbitration agreement

2–007 **The doctrine of separability.** An arbitration agreement specifies the means whereby some or all disputes under the matrix contract in which it is contained are to be resolved. It is however separate from the matrix contract: "An arbitration clause in a commercial contract . . . is an agreement inside an agreement. The parties make their commercial bargain . . . but in addition agree on a private tribunal to resolve any issues that may arise between them."[23] This is known as the doctrine of separability and s.7 of the Arbitration Act 1996 provides a statutory codification of the previous case law on this subject.[24] As the House of Lords noted in *Lesotho Highlands v Impreglio SpA*, "it is part of the very alphabet of arbitration law as explained in *Harbour Assurance Co (UK) Ltd v Kansa General International Insurance Co Ltd* . . . and spelled out in section 7 of the Act, the arbitration agreement is a distinct and separable agreement from the underlying or principal contract".[25]

2–008 **Statutory provision for separability.** Section 7 provides that "unless otherwise agreed by the parties, an arbitration agreement which forms or was intended to form part of another agreement (whether or not in writing) shall not be regarded as invalid, non-existent or ineffective because that other agreement is invalid, or did not come into existence or has become ineffective, and it shall for that purpose be treated as a distinct agreement."[26] This provision confirms by statute the separability doctrine which had evolved in the earlier case law.[27] In particular the use of the words "or was intended to form part of another agreement" make clear that even if the matrix contract never came into existence,

---

[23] *per* Saville J. in *Union of India v McDonnell Douglas Corp* [1993] 2 Lloyd's Rep. 48.
[24] See in particular *Heyman v Darwins Ltd* [1942] A.C. 356 and *Harbour Assurance Co (UK) Ltd v Kansa General Insurance Co Ltd* [1993] 1 Lloyd's Rep. 455. See also Model Law, Art.16(1) (see Appendix 4). See para.2–008 below.
[25] [2006] 1 A.C. 221 at [21].
[26] Section 7 of the Arbitration Act 1996: cf. Model Law, Art.16(1), see Appendix 4.
[27] The House of Lords rejected the theory that an arbitration clause is terminated by breach of the contract of which it forms part in *Heyman v Darwins Ltd* [1942] A.C. 356. They held that neither repudiation nor accepted repudiation entails the termination of the obligation to refer disputes to arbitration. On the contrary, the injured party can insist on having the consequences of the repudiation assessed by arbitration. The reasoning behind the doctrine of separability was that the arbitration clause constitutes a self-contained contract collateral or ancillary to the underlying or matrix contract: *Bremer Vulkan Schiffbau und Maschinenfabrik v South India Shipping Corp Ltd* [1981] 1 Lloyd's Rep. 253 at 259. It had long been held that an arbitration agreement can continue to be implied as one of the terms of the relationship between parties after the formal expiry of an agreement between them containing an arbitration clause. Typically, this is the case with leases and partnership deeds: see *Morgan v William Harrison Ltd* [1907] 2 Ch. 137; *Cope v Cope* (1885) 52 L.T. 607; and *Gisborne Harbour Board v Spencer* [1961] N.Z.L.R. 204 at 211. Case law went on to confirm that an arbitration clause could also survive invalidity of the underlying contract: *Harbour Assurance Co (UK) Ltd v Kansa General Insurance Co Ltd* [1993] 1 Lloyd's Rep. 455. The Court of Appeal have recently confirmed the position in *Fiona Trust & Holding Corp & ors v Yuri Privalov & ors* [2007] EWCA Civ 20 affirmed by the House of Lords in *Premium Nafta Products Ltd v Fili Shipping Co Ltd* [2007] UKHL 40. See also Peter Gross Q.C., "Separability Comes of Age in England: *Harbour v Kansa* and Clause 3 of the Draft Bill" (1995) 11 Arbitration Int. 85.

the arbitration agreement may still be binding.[28] Similarly, the fact that the matrix contract subsequently fails or is found to be invalid or never to have come into existence will not of itself mean that the arbitration agreement is necessarily undermined also.[29] Section 7 of the Arbitration Act 1996 applies where the law applicable to the arbitration agreement is the law of England and Wales or Northern Ireland even if the seat of the arbitration is outside England and Wales or Northern Ireland or has not been designated or determined.[30]

Consequences of separability. The doctrine of separability underlines the potential width of an arbitration agreement because it establishes that an arbitration agreement has a separate life from the matrix contract for which it provides the means of resolving disputes. This enables the arbitration agreement to survive breach or termination of the matrix contract of which it forms part. The consequence of this separate existence is that even if the matrix contract has been brought to an end, for example by accepted repudiation or frustration, the arbitration agreement continues in being in order to deal with any disputes in respect of liabilities under the matrix contract arising before or after termination.[31]   2–009

Invalidity of matrix contract. Section 7 of the Arbitration Act 1996 enables the arbitration agreement to survive not just termination or breach of the matrix contract but also more serious defects. Unless otherwise agreed by the parties, the arbitration agreement may survive as a distinct agreement even if the contract in which it is contained is regarded as invalid, non-existent or ineffective.[32] The validity of the matrix contract may therefore be determined by arbitration in accordance with the arbitration agreement, and the resulting award will be enforceable, even if the tribunal determines that the matrix contract is invalid.   2–010

Void contracts. Similarly, even where the matrix contract is held to be void, the arbitration agreement which forms part of it may still be upheld as a valid and   2–011

---

[28] In *Glaxosmithkline Ltd v Department of Health* [2007] EWHC 1470 it was alleged that the parties had entered into a purely non-binding and voluntary agreement such that there was no intention to create legal relations. Accordingly it was said that, notwithstanding the doctrine of separability, the arbitration agreement was no more binding than the larger whole of which it formed part, such that there was no "award" for the purposes of an appeal under s.69 of the Arbitration Act 1996. The court found that there was no agreement between the parties that the award should not be final and binding so as to displace ss.58 and 66 of the Arbitration Act 1996, the effect of which was that an award is binding and enforceable.

[29] See paras 2–051 *et seq.* below.

[30] Section 2(5) of the Arbitration Act 1996.

[31] Such as claims for sums accrued due prior to termination or claims in respect of post-termination obligations. See generally *DDT Trucks of North America Ltd v DDT Holdings Ltd* [2007] EWHC 1542. See also *Kruse v Questier & Co Ltd* [1953] 1 Lloyd's Rep. 310; *Heyman v Darwins* [1942] A.C. 356; *Government of Gibraltar v Kenney and Another* [1956] 2 Q.B. 410.

[32] See also *Fiona Trust & Holding Corp & ors v Yuri Privalov & ors* [2007] EWCA Civ 20 affirmed in *Premium Nafta Products Ltd v Fili Shipping Co Ltd* [2007] UKHL 40.

independent agreement, so that any disputes must be referred to arbitration.[33] As Colman J. put it in *Vee Networks Ltd v Econet Wireless International Ltd*: "If, in accordance with s.7 [of the Arbitration Act 1996], an arbitrator determines that the matrix contract is, for example, void ab initio by reason of illegality and it is not in issue whether the arbitration agreement is also illegal and void, the tribunal can continue to exercise such jurisdiction under the arbitration agreement as its scope permits. For example, if there were an alternative claim in tort or for restitution which was within the scope of the clause, the tribunal would continue to have jurisdiction conclusively to determine that claim."[34]

2–012 **Invalidity of arbitration agreement.** The position differs however where the arbitration agreement itself is impeached[35] or the existence of an arbitration agreement is disputed.[36] In these circumstances, if the matter comes before the court,[37] the question of jurisdiction may never reach the arbitrators because it will be determined the court.[38] In this regard the court draws a distinction between disputes as to the existence of the arbitration agreement, which are likely to be for the court, and disputes as to its validity, which wherever possible should be left to the tribunal.[39] However if the argument that there is no jurisdiction because the arbitration agreement itself is invalid or non-existent, the tribunal may decide that question[40] but its decision will not be conclusive and can be reviewed by the court.[41] It is only in exceptional circumstances however that the arbitration agreement itself will be impugned and, as stated above, attacks on the matrix contract will not generally suffice to prevent the arbitration agreement being upheld as conferring jurisdiction on the tribunal to determine the parties' disputes.[42] For example, in *Fiona Trust v Privalov*[43] allegations of bribery were raised in general terms but not so as to specifically impugn the arbitration agreement. The court upheld the application of the arbitration agreement by declining to decide the question of jurisdiction itself and referring the matter instead to the arbitrators:

---

[33] *Vee Networks Ltd v Econet Wireless International Ltd* [2004] EWHC 2909; [2005] 1 Lloyd's Rep. 192.

[34] [2004] EWHC 2909; [2005] 1 Lloyd's Rep. 192 at [21].

[35] *Harbour Assurance Co (UK) Ltd v Kansa General Insurance Co Ltd* [1993] 1 Lloyd's Rep. 455; *Vee Networks Ltd v Econet Wireless International Ltd* [2004] EWHC 2909.

[36] See, e.g. *Cigna Life v Intercaser SA* [2002] 1 All E.R. (Comm) 235 where it was held that a contract of re-insurance did not incorporate an arbitration agreement in respect of two of the parties to proceedings. See also *Phoenix Finance v FIA* [2002] EWHC 1028; *Anglia Oils Ltd v Owners and/or Demise Charterers of the Marine Champion* [2002] EWHC 2407; *Albon v Naza Motor Trading Sdn Bhd (No.3)* [2007] EWHC 327.

[37] For example on an application to stay under s.9 of the Arbitration Act 1996, see para.7–024 below.

[38] As in *Albon v Naza Motor Trading Sdn Bhd (No.3)* [2007] EWHC 327.

[39] See paras 7–028 *et seq.* below.

[40] Under s.30 of the Arbitration Act 1996.

[41] Under s.67 of the Arbitration Act 1996 which is a mandatory provision pursuant to s.4(1) and Sch.1 of the Arbitration Act 1996; see for example *LG Caltex Gas Co Ltd v China National Petroleum Corp* [2001] EWCA Civ 788. See generally paras 8–054 *et seq.*

[42] See paras 2–010 above and 7–030 below.

[43] [2007] EWCA Civ 20, affirmed in *Premium Nafta Products Ltd v Fili Shipping Co Ltd* [2007] UKHL 40.

"If the arbitrators can decide whether a contract is void for initial illegality, there is no reason why they should not decide whether a contract has been procured by bribery, just as much as they can decide whether a contract has been procured by misrepresentation or non-disclosure. Illegality is a stronger case than bribery which is not the same as non est factum or the sort of mistake which goes to the question of whether there was any agreement ever reached. It is not enough to say that the bribery impeaches the whole contract unless there is some special reason for saying that the bribery impeaches the arbitration clause in particular."[44]

By contrast, where it was alleged that the signature of one of the parties to the matrix contract had been forged, and hence no matrix contract or agreement to arbitrate had been reached, then this was a question going to whether there was any agreement ever reached and would be decided by the court.[45]

Illegality affecting the contract. This question of invalidity of the arbitration agreement has arisen in a number of cases concerning contracts alleged to be void by virtue of illegality,[46] and the courts examine whether the particular form of illegality renders not just the matrix contract but also the arbitration agreement void. This involves a consideration of the purpose and policy of the rule of illegality and whether this would be defeated by allowing the issue to be determined by arbitration.[47] In *Soleimany v Soleimany*[48] Waller L.J. noted[49] that: "There may be illegal or immoral dealings which are, from an English law perspective, incapable of being arbitrated because an agreement to arbitrate them would itself be illegal or contrary to public policy under English law." However, in that case the Court of Appeal found the arbitration agreement to be valid notwithstanding that the resulting award upholding the contract was unenforceable due to illegality.[50] In contrast, in *O'Callaghan v Coral Racing Ltd*,[51] the same court was faced with a clause in a gaming contract under which disputes were to be referred for arbitration to the editor of *The Sporting Life*. The court held that the illegality of the contract meant that any claim was bound to fail owing to the transaction being null and void under s.18 of the Gaming Act 1845, and the "arbitration clause" could not survive independently. 2–013

Application of terms of matrix contract. The doctrine of separability does not prevent the application to the arbitration agreement of provisions 2–014

---

[44] *Fiona Trust & Holding Corp & ors v Yuri Privalov & ors* [2007] EWCA Civ 20 at [29], affirmed in *Premium Nafta Products Ltd v Fili Shipping Co Ltd* [2007] UKHL 40.

[45] As in *Albon v Naza Motor Trading Sdn Bhd (No.3)* [2007] EWHC 327.

[46] Several have been concerned with the enforcement of arbitration awards made pursuant to contracts alleged to be illegal: see paras 8–031 *et seq.*

[47] *per* Hoffmann L.J. in *Harbour Assurance Co (UK) Ltd v Kansa General Insurance Co Ltd* [1993] 1 Lloyd's Rep. 455 at 469.

[48] [1999] Q.B. 785.

[49] At 797.

[50] The contract was found to be contrary to the revenue laws and export controls of the country of performance.

[51] *The Times*, November 26, 1998. For further background on the wider circumstances of the case, not relevant to the separability of the agreement to arbitrate, see *Locabail (UK) Ltd & Others v Bayfield Properties and Others* [2000] Q.B. 451, [98] *et seq.*

in the matrix contract which are stated to apply to all clauses of the matrix contract.[52] So for example if variations of any clause in the matrix contract are required to be in writing, that will apply equally to the arbitration clause as to other provisions of the matrix contract.[53]

(c) Arbitration agreements falling outside the 1996 Act

2–015 **Oral arbitration agreements.** An oral agreement to arbitrate, sometimes known as a parol submission, is valid as a matter of English law[54] but are not subject to the provisions of the of the Arbitration Act 1996.[55] Oral agreements were outside the scope of previous legislation because of the definition of an arbitration agreement.[56] The Arbitration Act 1996[57] contains a much broader definition of writing and some agreements which would previously have been oral agreements are now treated as "in writing" for the purposes of the Act.[58] The statute also makes it difficult to participate in arbitration proceedings arising out of an arbitration agreement which is alleged to be oral without it being construed as an agreement in writing.[59] An oral agreement to arbitrate is unusual in most modern commercial contexts.[60] Where the whole of the contract, including the agreement to arbitrate, is oral, the existence and validity of the entire contract may also be in doubt.[61] Clearly therefore oral agreements to arbitrate should be avoided by reducing them to writing so that they will fall within the terms of the 1996 Act.

2–016 **Implied agreement to refer existing disputes to arbitration.** An agreement to refer existing disputes to arbitration can in some cases be implied by the conduct of the parties. Where a party denies that it has entered into an agreement to arbitrate, the court will consider whether a reasonable person, knowing the relevant background and observing matters in the place of the party asserting the existence of the arbitration agreement, would have concluded from the other party's conduct that it was agreeing to participate in the proposed arbitration.[62]

---

[52] *JSC Zestafoni G Nikoladze Ferroalloy Plant v Ronly Holdings Ltd* [2004] EWHC 245.
[53] *JSC Zestafoni G Nikoladze Ferroalloy Plant v Ronly Holdings Ltd* [2004] EWHC 245.
[54] At common law. Oral agreements to arbitrate are acknowledged in s.81(1)(b) of the Arbitration Act 1996.
[55] Section 5(1) of the Arbitration Act 1996.
[56] Section 32 of the Arbitration Act 1950.
[57] Section 5 of the Arbitration Act 1996.
[58] See paras 2–039 *et seq.* below.
[59] Section 5(5) of the Arbitration Act 1996.
[60] Save in the context of salvage contracts: see further *Brice on Maritime Law of Salvage* (4th edn) Sweet & Maxwell 2002. See though for example *RJT Consulting v DM Engineering (Northern Ireland) Ltd* [2002] EWCA Civ 270.
[61] As, for example, in *E Turner & Sons Ltd v Maltind Ltd* (1985) 5 Const. L.J. 273, where the court found that there was no offer and acceptance.
[62] *Athletic Union of Constantinople v National Basketball Association* [2002] 1 All E.R. (Comm) 70. The court found in that case that a reasonable person would have so concluded.

However, since the introduction of the Arbitration Act 1996, there will rarely be any need to rely on an implied arbitration agreement. This is because the very broad definition of writing under the Arbitration Act 1996[63] means that in many cases there will be a written arbitration agreement for the purposes of the statute rather than an implied arbitration agreement. For example, if a tribunal has no jurisdiction to hear a dispute pursuant to the arbitration agreement, but the parties proceed with the reference and exchange written submissions alleging an arbitration agreement which is not denied, the written submissions will be sufficient to constitute an arbitration agreement in writing.[64] Even if there is no specific allegation of an arbitration agreement, if the parties proceed with a reference without objecting to the lack of jurisdiction they will lose the right to object and the tribunal will be entitled to proceed to determine the matters referred.[65]

There may however be situations in which one party alleges that there is an implied agreement to arbitrate based on the parties' conduct notwithstanding the absence of an arbitration agreement for the purposes of the Arbitration Act 1996. In these circumstances, if one of the parties makes a timely objection to jurisdiction, the tribunal will have to consider the existence of an implied agreement. The conduct from which the implication may be drawn can arise in the context of an arbitration concerned with other disputes or in connection with proceedings whose status as a proper reference of the disputes in question is itself the subject of controversy.[66] In the former case it will not be the existence of an arbitration agreement that is in dispute, but rather its scope, i.e. whether the particular claim being made is within the arbitration agreement. One effect of an implied arbitration agreement can be to overcome objections to the enlargement of the scope of the reference beyond the tribunal's existing jurisdiction.[67] As stated above, it would be extremely rare for there to be an implied agreement to arbitrate in these circumstances which did not fall within the statutory definition of arbitration agreement. In principle, however, the parties can enter into an implied agreement to arbitrate which would not constitute a written arbitration agreement for the purposes of s.5 of the Arbitration Act 1996.[68] It would then take effect as an oral arbitration agreement to which the Arbitration Act 1996 will not apply.[69]

---

[63] Section 5 of the Arbitration Act 1996: see para.2–039 below.

[64] Section 5(5) of the Arbitration Act 1996. In *Athletic Union of Constantinople v National Basketball Association* [2002] 1 All E.R. (Comm) 70 the parties were agreed that if there was an agreement to arbitrate the merits of the dispute it fell within s.5 of the Arbitration Act 1996 as an agreement in writing and was subject to the provisions of the 1996 Act.

[65] Section 73 of the Arbitration Act 1996: see para.5–065 below. See also *Athletic Union of Constantinople v National Basketball Association* [2002] 1 All E.R. (Comm) 70.

[66] *Westminster Chemicals & Produce Ltd v Eicholz & Loeser* [1954] 1 Lloyd's Rep. 99; *Aktiebolaget Legis v V Berg & Sons Ltd* [1964] 1 Lloyd's Rep. 203; *Luanda Exportadora SARL v Wahbe Tamari & Sons Ltd* [1964] 2 Lloyd's Rep. 535; *The "Tuyuti"* [1984] Q.B. 838; *Higgs & Hill Building Ltd v Campbell Denis Ltd* [1982] 28 B.L.R. 47; *Cia Maritima Zorroza SA v Sesostris SAE (The "Marques de Bolarque")* [1984] 1 Lloyd's Rep. 652; *Almare Società di Navigazione SpA v Derby & Co Ltd (The "Almaea Prima")* [1989] 2 Lloyd's Rep. 376; *Furness Withy (Australia) Pty Ltd v Metal Distributors (UK) Ltd (The "Amazonis")* [1990] 1 Lloyd's Rep. 236; *Allied Vision Ltd v VPS Film Entertainment GmbH* [1991] 1 Lloyd's Rep. 99.

[67] See paras 5–060 *et seq.* For agreements to which the Arbitration Act 1996 applies, continuing with the reference may lead to a loss of the right to object pursuant to s.73: see para.5–065.

[68] See paras 2–039 *et seq.* below.

[69] See para.2–015 above.

(d) Mutuality

2–017 **Mutuality not required.** Until 1986 English law required an arbitration agreement to be "mutual" in that it had to give both parties the same right to refer disputes to arbitration.[70] In *Pittalis v Sherefettin*,[71] a rent review case, the Court of Appeal redefined this requirement, seeing no lack of mutuality in an agreement between two persons which conferred on one of them alone the right to refer the dispute to arbitration.[72] As Fox L.J. said:

> "There is a fully bilateral agreement which constitutes a contract to refer. The fact that the option is exercisable by one of the parties only seems to me to be irrelevant. The arrangement suits both parties . . . the landlord is protected, if there is no arbitration, by his own assessment of the rent as stated in his notice: and the tenant is protected, if he is dissatisfied with the landlord's assessment of the rent, by his right to refer the matter to arbitration. Both sides have, therefore, accepted the arrangement and there is no lack of mutuality."[73]

Since then it has become well established that there is no requirement under English law for an arbitration agreement to confer on the parties a mutual right to initiate a reference[74] and an arbitration agreement providing an option for one party alone to refer disputes to arbitration is valid.[75] A party who is not empowered to initiate a reference to arbitration will be entitled to pursue litigation in respect of a dispute in the absence of agreement on some other mechanism such as expert determination,[76] although if the option is validly invoked[77] a stay of those proceedings will be granted.[78] Further, once the option is validly invoked by a party it cannot subsequently change its mind and unilaterally opt for litigation.[79] In practice an increasing number of clauses give only one party the right to refer disputes to arbitration, particularly in international derivatives transactions with counterparties in jurisdictions where English court judgments would not be enforced. In these cases it is typical for there to be a clause conferring jurisdiction on the courts of one or more jurisdictions with an option exercisable at the instance of only one party to insist that any dispute be referred to arbitration. Obviously it is important if adopting this approach to ensure that the precise

[70] *Baron v Sunderland Corp* [1966] 2 Q.B. 56 at 64 A/B, a case about statutory arbitration. This was followed in *Tote Bookmakers v Development & Property Holding Co Ltd* [1985] Ch. 261. The dictum in *Baron v Sunderland* was subsequently held (in *Pittalis v Sherefettin* discussed below) to be wider than necessary because it had been a case where there was no arbitration clause at all, not just an agreement lacking mutuality.

[71] [1986] 1 Q.B. 868.

[72] For the position where such right is conferred on both parties see para.2–067 below.

[73] *Pittalis v Sherefettin* [1986] 1 Q.B. 868 at 875, following *Woolf v Collis Removal Service* [1948] 1 K.B. 11.

[74] See for example *Nine Gladys Road Ltd v Kersh* [2004] EWHC 1080; *NB Three Shipping Ltd v Harebell Shipping Ltd* [2005] 1 Lloyd's Rep. 509.

[75] *NB Three Shipping Ltd v Harebell Shipping Ltd* [2005] 1 Lloyd's Rep. 509.

[76] See para.2–028.

[77] The option could not be invoked after a party had taken a step in the action or otherwise led the other party to believe on reasonable grounds that the option to arbitrate would not be exercised: *NB Three Shipping Ltd v Harebell Shipping Ltd* [2005] 1 Lloyd's Rep. 509.

[78] *NB Three Shipping Ltd v Harebell Shipping Ltd* [2005] 1 Lloyd's Rep. 509.

[79] *Whiting v Halverson* [2003] EWCA Civ 403.

circumstances in which the option may be exercised are clearly set out. Provided this is done, the clause will be valid under English law, although if the seat of the arbitration is in another country the relevant local law will have to be examined. Should enforcement of the resulting award be required in some other jurisdiction it would also be prudent to check that the law of the place of enforcement considers such clauses to be valid.[80]

Unilateral option to litigate. Similarly it is also now established that a 2–018
disputes provision which contains an arbitration agreement between the parties but also provides one party with an option to litigate will be upheld provided it is clear and unequivocal.[81] The effect of such a provision will be that one party has a choice of litigating or arbitrating any dispute, whereas the other party can be forced to arbitrate.[82] Again a party cannot "blow hot and cold" and if it starts, or participates in, an arbitration it will have waived the right to opt for litigation instead.[83] However, provided the party exercising its option to litigate has not participated in the arbitration, it will not be precluded from exercising its option by virtue of the fact that the other party has already commenced arbitration.[84]

(e) Variations

Disputes where contract varied. Disputes may arise about whether a 2–019
contract which has been varied includes or excludes the original arbitration agreement. For example in *Faghirzadeh v Rudolf Woolf SA (Pty) Ltd* a variation of a contract for the sale of steel bars was found to be unintelligible except by reference back to the original contract and its arbitration clause.[85] Further, questions may arise as to whether time-bars in the original arbitration agreement still apply.[86]

---

[80] See para.2–107 below.
[81] *Law Debenture Trust Corp Plc v Elektrim Finance BV* [2005] EWHC 1412.
[82] The question arises whether, if a party exercises its option to litigate, the other party can pursue any counterclaims in those proceedings or would be compelled to arbitrate them. In *Law Debenture Trust Corp Plc v Elektrim Finance BV* [2005] EWHC 1412 it was accepted (at [42]) that counterclaims would be entertained in the litigation, but in that case the disputes provision specifically contemplated such counterclaims. Absent such provision it is likely that a party could insist on the counterclaims being brought in separate arbitration proceedings, however inconvenient that may be.
[83] *Law Debenture Trust Corp Plc v Elektrim Finance BV* [2005] EWHC 1412 at [42].
[84] It was suggested in *Law Debenture Trust Corp Plc v Elektrim Finance BV* [2005] EWHC 1412 (by Mann J. at [45]) that if the situation were otherwise then whether the dispute were to be arbitrated or litigated would depend on "potential accidents of timing or conceivably an unseemly scramble".
[85] [1977] 1 Lloyd's Rep. 630.
[86] In *EB Aaby's Rederi A/S v Union of India* [1974] 2 Lloyd's Rep. 57 a charterparty containing a CENTROCON arbitration clause stated that any claim had to be made within 12 months of final discharge, or the claim would be barred. An undertaking was given to pay after the general average statement was drawn up, a process which apparently took "many years" and when the claim was finally presented, the defendants pleaded the time-bar. The House of Lords held that neither the arbitration clause nor the time bar had survived the variation.

2–020 **Effect of variation.** The effect of the variation may be to terminate the arbitration agreement altogether, although this will be a matter of construction of the varied contract. In most cases a variation of the terms of the matrix contract will not impugn the parties' agreement to arbitrate disputes under the contract as varied absent express provision doing so.

(f) Conditions precedent

2–021 **Conditions precedent.** Conditions precedent to the operation of an arbitration agreement must be fulfilled before a tribunal will have jurisdiction to determine disputes under it. So for example an arbitration agreement which provides for disputes to be submitted to arbitration "at the request of any party" will not make arbitration of any dispute compulsory unless and until a party requests it.[87] Similarly where a building contract contained an arbitration clause which provided that the "reference shall not be opened until after completion of the works", the court decided, with regret, that the arbitrator had no jurisdiction to determine whether the works had been completed, that in fact they had not been completed and therefore an award by the arbitrator was invalid.[88] Where the disputes provision is a multi-tiered clause, the steps to be taken prior to commencing arbitration may constitute conditions precedent in which case they must be complied with.[89]

2–022 *Scott v Avery* **clauses.** The parties to a contract may agree that no action shall be brought upon it until an arbitration award has been made, or (what amounts to the same thing) may agree that the only obligation arising out of a particular term of the contract shall be to pay whatever sum a tribunal may award.[90] This is known as a *Scott v Avery* clause. It does not prevent litigation being initiated on a contract containing a clause of this type, but the condition precedent is a defence to the action.[91] A *Scott v Avery* clause does not preclude injunctive proceedings brought for the purpose of enforcing the arbitration agreement itself.[92]

2–023 **No effect if stay granted.** The court used to have power to discharge *Scott v Avery* agreements, which has been repealed.[93] In order to avoid the combination

---

[87] *Secretary of State of the Environment, Transport and the Regions, Ex p. The Channel Group Ltd and France Manche SA* [2001] EWCA Civ 1185.

[88] *Smith v Martin* [1925] 1 K.B. 745, citing *Pethick Brothers v Metropolitan Water Board*, CA from *Hudson Building Contracts* (6th edn), Vol.2, p.456. See also *May v Mills* (1914) 30 T.L.R. 287.

[89] See para.2–036 below.

[90] *Scott v Avery* (1856) 25 L.J. Ex. 308. For a recent example see *Jagger v Decca Music Group Ltd* [2004] EWHC 2542.

[91] *Viney v Bignold* (1887) 20 Q.B.D. 172.

[92] *Toepfer International GmbH v Société Cargill France* [1998] 1 Lloyd's Rep. 379 where the application was to restrain proceedings brought in a foreign jurisdiction in breach of the arbitration agreement.

[93] Section 109 of the Arbitration Act 1996 has repealed Pt 1 of the Arbitration Act 1950, including this provision at s.25(4).

of an unworkable arbitration clause and no right to bring legal proceedings,[94] it is now enacted that if the court refuses to stay legal proceedings in favour of arbitration, any provision that an award is a condition precedent to the bringing of legal proceedings in respect of any matter is of no effect in relation to those proceedings.[95] The *Scott v Avery* condition precedent is also disregarded for limitation purposes.[96]

(g) Other types of clauses distinguished

Types of dispute resolution clauses. One reason why arbitration 2–024
agreements are sometimes ineffective is because of a failure properly to distinguish between the different forms of dispute resolution available and the extent to which, if at all, they can be combined.[97] In particular, consideration needs to be given to whether a contract should provide for dispute resolution by the court, or by arbitration or by expert determination, all of which can lead to a binding decision. These procedures may be combined with adjudication or ADR processes. Each of these is considered below.

Jurisdiction clauses. A jurisdiction clause provides expressly for the courts 2–025
of a particular country to have jurisdiction to deal with disputes arising under a contract.[98-99] It may provide that the courts of a particular country have exclusive jurisdiction, in which case no other court can usually take jurisdiction. Or it may provide that the courts of a particular country have non-exclusive jurisdiction, in which case the chosen court has jurisdiction but both parties also have the right to commence proceedings in any other court of competent jurisdiction in certain circumstances. The third alternative is to provide that the courts of a particular country have non-exclusive jurisdiction for the benefit of one party only, in which case the party benefiting from the provision (generally the one with the stronger negotiating position) can sue in any court of competent jurisdiction whereas the other party is confined to bringing an action in the courts of the named country only.

Even if the parties have agreed on the courts of a particular country in their jurisdiction clause, it may be overridden by provisions in relevant Regulations and Conventions[100] which provide for certain courts to have exclusive jurisdiction to deal with particular types of disputes regardless of the domicile of the parties, e.g.

---

[94] DAC report, para.57.

[95] Section 9(5) of the Arbitration Act 1996.

[96] Section 13(3) of the Arbitration Act 1996: see paras 5–014 and 8–177.

[97] In *David Wilson Homes Ltd v Survey Services Ltd (in liquidation)* [2001] 1 All E.R. (Comm) 449 a clause provided simply for disputes to be "referred to a Queen's Counsel of the English Bar to be mutually agreed [between the parties]". At first instance the judge held that the clause was not an arbitration clause but was a clause providing either for expert determination or for a non-binding opinion. The Court of Appeal disagreed and held it was an arbitration clause because the parties intended there to be a procedure in the nature of a judicial inquiry.

[98-99] The law relating to exclusive and non-exclusive jurisdiction clauses is outside the scope of this work. See further, *Civil Jurisdiction and Judgments*, Briggs, Rees (4th edn, 2005).

[100] Notably the Brussels Regulation; the Brussels Convention and the Lugano Convention.

those involving immovable property and proceedings concerning registration or validity of intellectual property rights. There are also special rules concerning insurance, consumer contracts and employment contracts.

2–026 **Incompatibility of jurisdiction clauses and arbitration agreements.** Save where the disputes provisions are of a hybrid nature,[101] a jurisdiction clause is an alternative to an arbitration agreement and they should not be combined in the same contract.[101a] This is because a valid reference to arbitration is a contractual obligation to pursue any disputes before an arbitration tribunal to the exclusion of the courts.[102] There have been a number of cases where the court has had to consider clauses providing for resolution of disputes by both arbitration and the courts and it then has to endeavour to ascertain the parties' intentions. That is not always a straightforward task. However, where the circumstances warrant, it seems the court will strive to give effect to apparently conflicting provisions by construing the references to the jurisdiction of the court as relating to its supportive and supervisory jurisdiction over the tribunal.[103]

2–027 **The court's approach.** The courts take a pragmatic approach to the difficulties that can arise when parties agree both a jurisdiction clause and an arbitration agreement in the same contract. So, for example, where printed conditions provided for the jurisdiction of the courts of Lima, Peru but a typed clause provided for "arbitration according to the conditions and laws of London", this was held to be an express choice of arbitration in London. Kerr L.J. asked the rhetorical question: "How would the judge in Lima like to conduct a case according to English procedural law?"[104] In another case a clause in an international commercial contract provided for ICC arbitration, whilst another clause in the same contract provided for English law and that the courts of England should have exclusive jurisdiction. Steyn J. rejected the argument that there was a hopeless inconsistency between the clauses, and held, on the proper construction of the clauses, that the second clause provided the law governing the arbitration and the reference to the jurisdiction of the courts referred to their supervisory powers.[105] Similarly a contract on GAFTA Form 100 provided that "the Court of England or arbitrators appointed in England, as the case may be, shall, except for

---

[101] See para.2–037.
[101a] See though paras 2–017 *et seq.* in relation to options to arbitrate or litigate which may necessitate provision for both forms of dispute resolution in the parties' contract.
[102] Save insofar as the court may be asked to use its supervisory or supportive powers in relation to an arbitration: see Chs 7 and 8 below.
[103] See, e.g. *Paul Smith v H&S International Holding Inc* [1991] 2 Lloyd's Rep. 127 discussed in the following paragraph.
[104] *Naviera Amazonica Peruana SA v Compania Internacional de Seguros del Peru* [1988] 1 Lloyds Rep. 116.
[105] *Paul Smith v H&S International Holding Inc* [1991] 2 Lloyd's Rep. 127; followed in *Axa Re v Ace Global Markets Ltd* [2006] EWHC 216. See also *Daval Aciers D'Usinor et de Sacilor v Armare Srl (The Nerarno)* [1996] 1 Lloyd's Rep. 1. In *Shell International Petroleum Co Ltd v Coral Oil Co Ltd* [1999] 1 Lloyd's Rep. 72 the reference to the English courts was held to be confined to disputes about the proper law of the contract. Cf. *Indian Oil Corp v Vanol Inc* [1991] 2 Lloyd's Rep. 634.

the purpose of enforcing any award made in pursuance of the arbitration clause hereof, have exclusive jurisdiction over all disputes which may arise under this contract". This was followed by an arbitration clause covering any dispute arising out of or under the contract. Colman J. found that those disputes which were within the ambit of the arbitration agreement fell within the exclusive jurisdiction of the arbitrators and all others were within the jurisdiction of the court.[106] The Court of Appeal disagreed and concluded that the exclusive jurisdiction clause was intended to apply both where the contract provides for arbitration and where it does not, so that if provision for arbitration is included, as it was here, the exclusive jurisdiction of the English court does not take effect.[107]

Expert determination (or valuation).[108] Like arbitration, expert   2–028
determination provides for the final resolution of disputes by a private individual or individuals to whom issues are referred for a binding decision. Traditionally a distinction has been drawn between the two on the basis that a tribunal must act judicially by applying the law whereas an expert, unless the parties agree some other basis for his decision, decides according to his own expert opinion.[109] This has become a less clear distinction now that, if agreed by the parties, a tribunal is entitled to base its decision on "other considerations",[110] although if the require-ment to act judicially can be established it will resolve the issue.[111] Experts are often appointed more to get the benefit of their professional (non-legal) expertise in deciding technical issues, but arbitrators appointed for their technical expertise have long been a feature of English arbitration.[112] Experts have traditionally been involved in determinations prior to the existence of a dispute, whereas an arbitra-tion tribunal deals with disputes after they have arisen. A more recent develop-ment is the use of experts, notably lawyers, to decide all aspects of a dispute, rather than particular technical issues. As a result of these factors the distinction between experts and arbitrators has in some cases become somewhat blurred although there are significant practical differences since expert determination is not governed by the Arbitration Act 1996.[113]

Construction of contractual provision. Whether a contract's chosen   2–029
form of dispute resolution is expert determination or arbitration is a matter of construction of the contract, which involves an objective inquiry into the inten-tions of the parties. The express words used may give a strong indication of the parties' intentions and the phrase "as an expert and not as an arbitrator" is frequently used to signify that the process is intended to be one of expert

---

[106] *Toepfer International GmbH v Société Cargill France* [1997] 2 Lloyd's Rep. 98.
[107] *Toepfer International GmbH v Société Cargill France* [1998] 1 Lloyd's Rep. 379 at 386.
[108] See generally, Kendall J., *Expert Determination* (3rd edn, 2001).
[109] *Re Carus-Wilson v Green* (1886) 18 Q.B. 7; *David Wilson Homes Ltd v Survey Services Ltd (in liquidation)* [2001] 1 All E.R. (Comm) 449.
[110] Section 46 of the Arbitration Act 1996. See further para.2–091.
[111] *David Wilson Homes Ltd v Survey Services Ltd (in liquidation)* [2001] 1 All E.R. (Comm) 449.
[112] See paras 6–075 *et seq.* below.
[113] See for example *In Re British Aviation Insurance Co* [2005] EWHC 1621 at [130]–[132].

determination. The terminology used is likely to be persuasive,[114] although not always conclusive.[115] Where the express wording is ambiguous, the court looks first at the other provisions of the contract to try to resolve the ambiguity.[116] If that does not resolve the matter the court will refer to certain guidelines which may serve to distinguish which process the parties intended to adopt.[117] Of these, the most important used to be whether there was an "issue" between the parties, such as the value of an asset, on which they had not taken defined positions, in which case the procedure was held to be expert determination. If there was a "formulated dispute" between the parties where defined positions had been taken, the procedure was held to be arbitration.[118] This concept is in many cases somewhat artificial as the parties will often be in dispute about a matter before it is referred to an expert, but in appropriate cases this guideline is still relied on.[119] A further guideline, as noted above, is the judicial function of a tribunal as opposed to the application of his professional expertise by the expert.[120] A tribunal arrives at its decision on the evidence and submissions of the parties and must apply the law or, if the parties agree, other considerations.[121] An expert, unless it is agreed otherwise, makes his own inquiries, applies his own expertise and decides on the basis of his own expert opinion.[122] This distinction does not apply in the case of "look-sniff arbitrations",[123] although these are rare.[124] A further distinction, that the parties agree to accept an expert's decision as final, whereas a tribunal's award can be appealed, has become less important because of the restrictions on appeals from arbitration awards.[125] It is also the case that regardless of the agreement between the parties, the courts will review a decision of an expert in certain limited circumstances.[126]

2–030 **Procedural differences distinguishing expert determination.** One of the main differences between expert determination and arbitration has

[114] *Palacath Ltd v Flanagan* [1985] 2 All E.R. 161.
[115] *Taylor v Yielding* (1912) 56 S.J. 253. See also *Re Hammond and Waterton* (1890) 62 L.T. 808. Inconsistent headings cannot prevail over the express wording of the clause if that is clear: *Cott UK Ltd v FE Barber Ltd* [1997] 3 All E.R. 540.
[116] *Langham House Developments Ltd v Brompton Securities Ltd* (1980) 256 E.G. 719.
[117] Or "indicia", established by Lord Wheatley in *Arenson v Casson Beckman Rutley & Co* [1975] 3 W.L.R. 815.
[118] *Collins v Collins* (1856) 26 Beav. 306 at 312; *Tharsis Sulphur & Copper Co Ltd v Loftus* (1872) L.R. 8 CP 1; *Chambers v Goldthorpe* [1901] 1 Q.B. 624; *Sutcliffe v Thackrah* [1974] 1 A.C. 727 at 762; *C and D Leigh v English Property Corp Ltd* [1976] 2 Lloyd's Rep. 298; *North Eastern Cooperative Society Ltd v Newcastle upon Tyne City Council* [1987] 1 E.G.L.R. 142 at 146A; *Capricorn Inks Pty Ltd v Lawter International (Australia) Pty Ltd* [1989] 1 Q.B. 8 at 15; *Ipswich Borough Council v Fisons Plc* [1990] 1 W.L.R. 108.
[119] *Ipswich Borough Council v Fisons Plc* [1990] 1 W.L.R. 108 at 115D.
[120] *David Wilson Homes Ltd v Survey Services Ltd (in liquidation)* [2001] 1 All E.R. (Comm) 449.
[121] Section 46 of the Arbitration Act 1996.
[122] *Palacath v Flanagan* [1985] 2 All E.R. 161 at 166.
[123] *Finnegan v Allen* [1943] 1 K.B. 425; *Mediterranean and Eastern Export Co Ltd v Fortress Fabrics (Manchester) Ltd* [1948] 2 All E.R. 186. See para.5–110.
[124] Perhaps because the procedure contemplated is more suited to expert determination.
[125] Section 69 of the Arbitration Act 1996. See paras 8–119 *et seq.*
[126] See for example *Veba Oil Supply & Trading GmbH v Petrotrade Inc* [2001] EWCA Civ 1832; [2002] 1 All E.R. 703. An expert's decision can be reviewed for material manifest error or a material failure to follow instructions.

traditionally been the procedure adopted to reach the decision.[127] There is usually a greater degree of formality in arbitration which arises from the judicial nature of the decision (in most cases) and the court's role in supervising the conduct of arbitration pursuant to its statutory powers.[128] However, under the 1996 Act, subject to any contrary agreement between the parties, a tribunal is given a great deal of flexibility in determining the procedure to be adopted.[129] The Arbitration Act 1996 makes clear that the tribunal may take the initiative in ascertaining the facts and the law,[130] and it can direct that there should be no oral evidence or oral submissions.[131] A tribunal has to comply with its statutory duty of fairness,[132] and machinery exists to permit its removal for failure to do so,[133] but otherwise it has considerable scope for determining the procedure most suited to the needs of the case, subject to any agreement of the parties. There is also authority that an expert is subject to an implied duty to act fairly when conducting an expert determination.[134]

Expert determination treated differently from arbitration. 2–031
The following features demonstrate how expert determination is treated differently from arbitration in a number of important respects.

- An expert determination is constrained by the terms of the clause referring the matter to expert determination, whereas much is incorporated into an arbitration agreement by statute and by judicial precedent. For example, the court generally has no power to appoint an expert, whereas statute provides the court with the power to appoint an arbitrator.[135] Similarly there is no obligation of confidentiality in relation to expert determination unless one has been contractually agreed.

- An arbitration award can be challenged on grounds of "serious irregularity" in the conduct of the arbitration,[136] but this is a statutory remedy for which there is no common law analogue in expert determination.[137]

- An expert's decision can only be enforced as a matter of contract and not pursuant to the statutory machinery available in respect of an arbitration award.[138]

---

[127] So for example in *Town & City Properties v Wiltshier Southern Ltd and Gilbert Powell* [1988] 44 B.L.R. 109 an arbitrator who said that the hearing should take the form of meetings between himself and the technical representatives of the parties, and not a trial-type hearing with oral evidence, cross-examination and speeches, was said by the court to have adopted a process which was "really that of a valuation, rather than an arbitration" (at 119).
[128] See generally Chs 7 and 8.
[129] Pursuant to s.34(1) of the Arbitration Act 1996.
[130] Section 34(2)(g) of the Arbitration Act 1996.
[131] Section 34(2)(h) of the Arbitration Act 1996.
[132] See paras 4–106 and 5–032 *et seq.*
[133] See paras 7–116 *et seq.*
[134] *Worrall v Topp* [2007] EWHC 1809.
[135] Section 18 of the Arbitration Act 1996.
[136] See paras 8–072 *et seq.*
[137] See though *Worrall v Topp* [2007] EWHC 1809 where it was held that there existed an implied obligation on the expert to act fairly.
[138] See paras 8 002 *et seq.*

- An expert can be sued for negligence,[139] while an arbitrator has immunity.[140]

- There can be no appeal on a point of law from an expert determination, unless the wrong law has been applied to the issue for determination,[141] in which case there is not, strictly speaking, an appeal, but rather the decision can be challenged.[142] The parties to an arbitration can appeal against a tribunal's award on a point of law in certain limited circumstances.[143]

2–032 **Adjudication.** The word adjudication suggests a judicial decision-making process, but it is also used to refer to a system of interim dispute resolution used specifically in connection with construction contracts. Adjudication was for many years found only in some of the standard forms of construction contracts and was reserved for certain kinds of disputes. It is now mandatory for all disputes under many types of construction contracts.[144] Dyson J. (as he then was) in *Macob Civil Engineering Ltd v Morrison Construction Ltd*,[144a] explained that: "The intention of Parliament in enacting the Act was plain. It was to introduce a speedy mechanism for settling disputes in construction contracts on a provisional interim basis, and requiring the decisions of adjudicators to be enforced pending the final determination of disputes by adjudication, litigation or agreement."

2–033 **Relationship of adjudication to arbitration.** The relationship of adjudication to arbitration was described in *London & Amsterdam Properties Ltd v Waterman Partnership Ltd*[145] as follows: "Arbitration and adjudication are dispute resolution procedures which have many similarities, they are privately conducted and confidentiality may attach to information received in relation to both. Arbitration gives rise to a final determination which is capable of registration for enforcement. Adjudication gives rise to a provisional determination which is only binding until the dispute is arbitrated, litigated or agreed. Adjudication further is subject to very restrictive time limits, and no matter how complex the dispute "one size fits all". Arbitration has no such limits imposed by Parliament." It will be observed that, although adjudication produces interim rather than final decisions, those decisions are binding pending agreement of the parties altering their effect or the reference of disputes about them to arbitration or litigation.[146] It is

---

[139] *Arenson v Casson Beckman Rutley & Co* [1975] 3 W.L.R. 815.
[140] See paras 4–152 *et seq.*
[141] *Nikko Hotels (UK) Ltd v MEPC Plc* [1991] 28 E.G. 86.
[142] As was sought, unsuccessfully, in *Nikko.*
[143] Section 69 of the Arbitration Act 1996. See paras 8–119 *et seq.*
[144] Section 108 of the Housing Grants, Construction and Regeneration Act 1996. For the wide definition of construction contracts, see s.104. For the operations excepted from the statutory provisions, see s.105(2). See generally *Keating on Building Contracts* (8th edn, 2006) at para.16–100.
[144a] [1999] B.L.R. 93 at [24].
[145] [2003] EWHC 3059; [2004] B.L.R. 179 at [136].
[146] Housing Grants, Construction and Regeneration Act 1996, s.108(3). See also *Carillion Construction Ltd v Devonport Royal Dockyard Ltd* [2005] EWCA Civ 1358 at [85]–[87].

therefore perfectly consistent to make provision for adjudication followed by the possibility of challenge to the adjudicator's decision by arbitration.[147] Indeed this is employed in many construction contracts.

Enforcement of adjudicator's decision. The court has held that an 2–034 adjudication decision cannot be enforced as an arbitration award[148] but should be enforced by the court's summary judgment procedure under CPR Pt 24.[149] The existence of an arbitration agreement pursuant to which the dispute will be finally resolved does not prevent enforcement by the court of the adjudicator's decision on a temporary basis.[150] Nor will an application to stay court proceedings under s.9 of the Arbitration Act 1996[151] be effective to prevent enforcement of the adjudicator's decision.[152]

ADR. Alternative dispute resolution (ADR) is regarded by English practitioners 2–035 as any system of dispute resolution which is non-binding. By "non-binding" is meant that the parties are under no obligation to comply with any decision or determination resulting from the process, if indeed there is one.[153] Nor are the parties obliged to participate in or continue with the process in the absence of express contractual provision to that effect. Where the parties do agree to adopt an ADR process they may be obliged to refer their dispute to a third party who is to act in some facilitative[154] or evaluative[155] capacity. The third party is not empowered to impose a decision on the parties, and, unless the parties agree on a settlement, the ADR process will not reach any binding agreement resolving the dispute. Thus ADR does not guarantee a binding result, although it can lead to one, and this is a key distinction between ADR and arbitration. Accordingly the parties should ensure that they have a binding system of dispute resolution to fall back on if they cannot agree a settlement following ADR. If no system is mentioned, the parties always have the right to litigate the dispute in court after failure to settle. ADR procedures include negotiation, mediation and conciliation,[156] mini-trial or executive tribunal, structured settlement conference, "med-

---

[147] Any contractual requirements of the arbitration agreement will still need to be complied with: *JT Mackley & Co Ltd v Gosport Marina Ltd* [2002] EWHC 1315. As to the scope of what is referred to arbitration see *Amec Civil Engineering Ltd v Secretary of State for Transport* [2005] 1 W.L.R. 2339.

[148] *Cameron (A) Ltd v Mowlem (John) & Co Plc* [1990] 52 B.L.R. 24.

[149] *Outwing Construction Ltd v H Randall and Son Ltd* [1999] B.L.R. 158

[150] *Absolute Rentals Ltd v Gencor Enterprises Ltd* (2001) 17 Const. L.J. 322, *The Construction Group Centre v Highland Council* [2002] B.L.R. 476, [2002] C.I.L.L. 1906 and *Macob Civil Engineering Ltd v Morrison Construction Ltd* [1999] B.L.R. 93.

[151] See para.7–024.

[152] See *Comsite Projects Ltd v Andritz AG* [2003] EWHC 958; (2004) 20 Const. L.J. 24 at [21].

[153] Which is unlikely unless the form of ADR chosen calls for some form of "early neutral determination".

[154] Assisting the negotiation without giving an opinion on the issues.

[155] Giving an opinion on the issues.

[156] The expressions "mediation" and "conciliation" are often used interchangeably, and the processes are difficult to distinguish in practice. The term "mediation" has become more popular in recent years.

arb" and expert evaluation or non-binding appraisal.[157] They place a premium on party involvement. Like arbitration and expert determination, they are private and confidential, but they are also without prejudice, in the sense that oral and written exchanges cannot be disclosed in any subsequent legal proceedings.[157a] The use of mediation in particular has greatly increased in the last decade, particularly following court-led initiatives to impose it upon litigating parties in an effort to resolve disputes without the need for a full trial.[158]

2–036 **Multi-tier clauses.** Many contracts containing arbitration clauses also provide for the parties first to try to settle the matter by negotiation or discussion between senior executives and, if that fails, the dispute must be referred to mediation or some other ADR process. Only when these steps have failed is the matter to be referred to arbitration. This type of clause, which contemplates at least two different levels of dispute resolution procedure, is known as a multi-tier or multi-level clause.[159] Depending on the form of words used, these clauses may or may not give rise to a binding obligation to submit to the different forms of dispute resolution before starting an arbitration, but an obligation simply to negotiate is not binding.[160] Where such preliminary steps are expressed in mandatory terms so as to constitute a condition precedent to the right to arbitrate they must be complied with.[161] In many cases however they will not be mandatory and it is then possible for the claimant to commence arbitration even without complying with them.[162] When drafting a multi-tier clause it is important to set out time limits within which each stage of the process is to be completed, so that the parties can be certain about when they can proceed to the next level. In some cases the decisions made during the initial steps are binding on the parties, at least until a court or tribunal rules on the point.[163] An application can be made for a stay of court proceedings brought in breach of an agreement to arbitrate[164] even where the matter is to be referred to arbitration only after the exhaustion of other dispute

---

[157] See generally Brown & Marriott, *ADR Principles and Practice* (2nd edn, Sweet & Maxwell, 1999). "Med-arb" is different because if a mediation fails the mediator is then to act as an arbitrator. Apparently popular in the United States, "med-arb" is regarded with suspicion in some countries, including England, because of the difficulties arising from the private disclosures made to the mediator who then becomes an arbitrator.

[157a] See, for example, *Aird v Prime Meridian Ltd* [2006] EWCA Civ 1866 at [5].

[158] CPR Pt 26, r.4.

[159] See for example *National Boat Shows Ltd v Tameside Marine* [2001] W.L. 1560826.

[160] See *Courtney & Fairbairn Ltd v Tolaini Brothers (Hotels) Ltd* [1975] 1 W.L.R. 297, where an agreement to negotiate price was held to be unenforceable; *Itex Shipping Pte Ltd v China Ocean Shipping Co (The "Jing Hong Hai")* [1989] 2 Lloyd's Rep. 522.

[161] See *JT Mackley & Co Ltd v Gosport Marina Ltd* [2002] EWHC 1315 where, amongst other things, failure to comply with a condition precedent rendered the arbitration notice invalid.

[162] Although not an arbitration case, see *Halifax Financial Services Ltd v Intuitive Systems Ltd* [1999] 1 All E.R. (Comm) 303.

[163] *Channel Tunnel Group Ltd v Balfour Beatty Construction Ltd* [1993] A.C. 334. See also the system of adjudication in building contracts at para.2–032 above.

[164] See generally paras 7–024 *et seq.*

resolution procedures, which includes both binding and non-binding systems.[165]

Hybrid clauses. Some contracts provide that particular disputes will be   2–037
resolved by one form of dispute resolution and other types of dispute by some
other method. For example, it is common in an agreement for the sale and
purchase of a business for disputes concerning the calculation of deferred consideration to be referred to expert determination whilst all other disputes under
the agreement are to be resolved by arbitration or by the courts. Some questions
of default, such as the failure to pay an instalment due, might be settled more
effectively by litigation, whose summary procedures[166] have no direct counterpart
in arbitration, whilst valuation and/or technical questions in the same contract
might be settled more simply by expert determination. Some clauses distinguish
between resolving disputes as to liability, which fall within the arbitration agreement, and those as to damages, which do not. The key issue when dealing with
such provisions is to ensure that it is clear precisely which types of disputes fall
to be resolved by each mechanism.[167] It may assist to provide expressly how this
is to be determined in the event of disagreement between the parties. So, for
example, the expert might be empowered to determine whether particular disputes
fall within his jurisdiction and the parties agree to be bound by that decision.
Alternatively, the clause might provide that unless both parties agree that the
dispute falls to be considered by the expert then it shall be dealt with by
arbitration, but this effectively gives each party a right of veto.

3. FORM OF AN ARBITRATION AGREEMENT

(a) "A written agreement"

Requirement of writing. To constitute an arbitration agreement to which   2–038
the Arbitration Act 1996 applies, the agreement must be in writing.[168] The same
requirement applies to other agreements between the parties.[169] However, the

---

[165] Section 9(2) of the of the Arbitration Act 1996, following the decision in *Channel Tunnel Group Ltd v Balfour Beatty Construction Ltd* [1993] 1 Lloyd's Rep. 291, HL.

[166] Under CPR Pt 24.

[167] See, for example, *May & Hassell Ltd v Vsesojuznoje Objedinenije Exportles* (1940) 66 Lloyd's Rep. 103 and *May & Hassell Ltd v Vsesojuznoje Objedinenije Exportles (No.2)* (1941) 69 Lloyd's Rep. 102.

[168] Section 5 of the Arbitration Act 1996 states that an agreement has to be in writing to bring it within Pt I of the Act. If an arbitration agreement is not in writing it is not completely ineffective: s.81(1)(b) of the Arbitration Act 1996, and see para.2–015 above. See also the definition of international arbitration agreements in Art.II.2 of the New York Convention which specifically includes exchange of letters and telegrams; Model Law, Art.7.2 (see Appendix 4).

[169] "Other agreements" are those on the powers of the tribunal and the procedure to be followed in the arbitration and any matter on which the parties may agree pursuant to the Arbitration Act 1996: see para.2–060.

agreement need not be signed by the parties[170] and the agreement can be found in an exchange of communications,[171] which need not be signed.

2–039 **What constitutes writing?** The requirement of writing can also be satisfied by[172]:

    (i) the arbitration agreement being "evidenced in writing",[173] which includes the arbitration agreement being recorded by one of the parties, or by a third party, with the authority of the parties to the agreement[174] or

    (ii) the arbitration agreement being made in some medium other than writing which refers to terms which are in writing[175] or

    (iii) an exchange of written submissions (in arbitration or court proceedings) in which the existence of an arbitration agreement in some medium other than writing is alleged and not denied.[176]

"Writing" includes being recorded by any means.[177]

This very wide meaning given to the words "in writing" in the 1996 Act was considered justified on the basis of English law as it then stood.[178] It was also intended to reflect that in these times of rapidly evolving technology "writing" should include recording by any means.[179]

2–040 **Meaning of "evidenced in writing".** The meaning of "evidenced in writing" has been considered by the Court of Appeal in the context of s.107 of the Housing Grants, Construction and Regeneration Act 1996, which so far as is material is in the same terms as s.5 of the Arbitration Act 1996.[180] The court concluded that for an agreement to be in writing the whole contract has to be

---

[170] Section 5(2)(a) of the Arbitration Act 1996; see para.2–043 below.

[171] Section 5(2)(b) of the Arbitration Act 1996.

[172] For an exhaustive if now slightly out-of-date study of international practice in this area, see Landau, *The Requirement for a Written Form of Arbitration Agreement: when Written means Oral.* ICCA Congress Series, no.11 (2003), pp.19–81.

[173] Section 5(2)(c) of the Arbitration Act 1996; see para.2–040 below. See also, for example, *National Boat Shows Ltd v Tameside Marine* [2001] W.L. 1560826, where the acceptance of an offer in a prospectus by submission of an application form was held to include an agreement to be bound by the terms of the prospectus and thereby to constitute an agreement in writing.

[174] Section 5(4) of the Arbitration Act 1996.

[175] Section 5(3) of the Arbitration Act 1996.

[176] Section 5(5) of the Arbitration Act 1996. It seems from the wording of the section that it is specifically the existence of an arbitration agreement which has to be alleged and not denied. If the parties simply proceed with the arbitration without specifically alleging an arbitration agreement, they may nevertheless be taken to have impliedly agreed to arbitrate: see para.2–016.

[177] Section 5(6) of the Arbitration Act 1996.

[178] *Zambia Steel & Building Supplies Ltd v Clark & Eaton Ltd* [1986] 2 Lloyd's Rep. 225.

[179] DAC report, para.34.

[180] *RJT Consulting v DM Engineering (Northern Ireland) Ltd* [2002] EWCA Civ 270.

evidenced in writing.[181] It is not sufficient merely to show that there are documents which indicate the existence of the agreement.[182]

Reference to a written agreement. Where contracts for the salvage of 2–041
ships are agreed orally by reference to a Lloyd's standard form of salvage agreement containing an arbitration clause, the exigencies of the disaster may remove the opportunity to sign the necessary documents.[183] Occasions when this arises have been said to be frequent and important.[184] To deal with this difficulty, it is now enacted that when parties agree otherwise than in writing by reference to terms which are in writing, they make an agreement in writing.[185] Outside the context of salvage contracts there may be little scope for the application of this provision. In principle however the parties could agree orally essential terms such as price and performance and also agree that the contract will be on certain standard terms and conditions which are in writing and include an arbitration agreement.[186]

Formality and incorporation. It is not necessary that an arbitration 2–042
agreement be a formal agreement, or that all the terms should be contained in one document. Issues as to whether an arbitration agreement has been established can arise however when it is purportedly incorporated from another document[187] or where further steps are required to make it effective.[188] If an arbitration agreement is not in writing, even in the broad sense used in the Act, it will not be governed by the Arbitration Act 1996. It may nevertheless be a valid oral agreement, in which case it will be governed by the common law.[189]

Signature unnecessary. Signature of a written agreement by the parties is 2–043
not required for an arbitration agreement to be valid under the UNCITRAL

---

[181] The majority considered that all the terms must be in writing, but Auld L.J. considered it sufficient if the material in issue in the reference are evidenced in writing.
[182] Applied in *Carillion Construction Ltd v Devonport Royal Dockyard Ltd* [2003] B.L.R. 79, another case under s.107 of the Housing Grants, Construction and Regeneration Act 1996.
[183] For an example of an appeal from an arbitration award from a Lloyd's salvage contract, see *The Owners of the Motor Vessel Tojo Maru v NV Bureau Wijsmuller (The "Tojo Maru")* [1972] A.C. 242.
[184] DAC report, para.36.
[185] Section 5(3) of the Arbitration Act 1996.
[186] The limitations of a provision in identical terms in the Housing Grants, Construction and Regeneration Act 1996 in the context of construction contracts were observed in *Carillion Construction Ltd v Devonport Royal Dockyard Ltd* [2003] B.L.R. 79.
[187] See paras 2–044 *et seq.*
[188] For example in *Oceanografia SA de CV v DSND Subsea AS (The "Botnica")* [2006] EWHC 1360, a charter-party containing a London arbitration clause was agreed "subject to the signing of mutually agreeable contract terms and conditions" which in fact were signed by one party only. Following a challenge to the tribunal's jurisdiction the court held that, having proceeded with the charter-party, the parties were bound by its terms, including the arbitration clause, on the basis of both waiver and estoppel by convention, and the tribunal accordingly had jurisdiction.
[189] See para.2–015.

Model Law[190] nor is signature obviously a mandatory requirement of the New York Convention.[191] Signature is also not required under English law[192] but problems may arise if an award which is based on an unsigned arbitration agreement is sought to be enforced in another jurisdiction under the New York Convention. These problems can be overcome by having all parties sign terms of reference.[193]

(b) Incorporation by reference

2–044   **Reference to another document.** The terms of a contract may have to be ascertained by reference to more than one document. Ascertaining which documents constitute the contractual documents and in what, if any, order of priority they should be read is a problem encountered in many commercial transactions, particularly those involving shipping and construction. This issue has to be determined by applying the usual principles of construction and attempting to infer the parties' intentions by means of an objective assessment of the evidence. This may make questions of incorporation irrelevant[194] if for example it is clear that the contractual documents in question are entirely separate and no intention to incorporate the terms of one in the other can be established. However, the contractual document defining and imposing the performance obligations may be found to incorporate another document which contains an arbitration agreement. If there is a dispute about the performance obligations, that dispute may need to be decided according to the arbitration provisions of that other document. This very commonly occurs when the principal contractual document refers to standard form terms containing an arbitration agreement.[195] However the standard form wording may not be apt for the contract in which the parties seek to incorporate it, or the reference may be to another contract between parties at least one of whom is different. In these circumstances it may be possible to argue that the purported incorporation of the arbitration agreement is ineffective.[196] The draftsmen of the Arbitration Act 1996 were asked to provide specific

---

[190] Article 7, see Appendix 4. The 2006 amendments to the Model Law contain a long and short form option which deals with the writing requirement. Neither expressly require signature. Option 1, see Art.7(3), is in expressly very broad terms and provides that an agreement is in writing if its content is recorded in any form, even if the agreement has been concluded orally.

[191] Article II(2). See also generally, Landau, *The Requirement for a Written Form of Arbitration Agreement: when Written means Oral.* ICCA Congress Series, no.11 (2003), pp.19–81.

[192] Section 5(2) of the Arbitration Act 1996.

[193] e.g. pursuant to Art.18 of the ICC Rules.

[194] As in *The President of India v Metcalfe Shipping Co Ltd* [1969] 2 Q.B. 123.

[195] See para.2–048 below. In *Stretford v Football Association Ltd* [2006] EWHC 479, which was affirmed at [2007] EWCA Civ 238 though this point was not the subject of appeal, a licence was issued which required compliance with Rules of Association which contained an arbitration clause. The obligation to observe the Rules was held to be a term of the licence and the arbitration agreement was incorporated into it. See also *Whiting v Halverson* [2003] EWCA Civ 403 where a Rotary Club member was held bound by an arbitration agreement contained in a club's constitution.

[196] See paras 2–046 *et seq.* below.

guidance on the issue, but they preferred to leave it to the court to decide whether there had been a valid incorporation by reference.[197]

Statutory guidance. The key question is whether the reference in an 2–045 agreement to a written form of arbitration clause or to a document containing an arbitration clause constitutes an arbitration agreement. Section 6(2) of the Arbitration Act 1996 provides: "The reference in an agreement to a written form of arbitration clause or to a document containing an arbitration clause constitutes an arbitration agreement if the reference is such as to make that clause part of the agreement." The provision begs the question *when* is the reference such as to make the clause part of the agreement. The courts struggled to find a consistent answer before the passing of the 1996 Act,[198] although a more consistent approach has now developed.

A matter of construction. The basic juridical exercise involved in all these 2–046 cases is the proper construction of general words of incorporation in one contract referring to the terms of another contract or document.[199] "The imputed mutual intention of the parties has to be arrived at by general principles of construction applicable to any other contractual term."[200] In practice however specific rules of construction have been applied in this context and differing views have been advanced as to the proper approach to be adopted. This is perhaps best illustrated by the decision in *Aughton Ltd v MF Kent Services Ltd*[201] where a sub-contractor's order provided for a sub-sub-contract to be "on GC/Works/1" (a standard form contract used by the British government as employer). The sub-sub-contractors claimed that this was a reference to the contract between the main contractor and the sub-contractor, which included an arbitration clause. The Court of Appeal disagreed[202] for two distinct reasons:

(i) *per* Ralph Gibson L.J.: The reference "on GC/Works/1" was not a reference to the contract between the sub-contractor and the main contractor, because the conditions of that contract could not be applied to the sub-sub-contract without significant modification. It was therefore not a written agreement[203]: it was a "direction in writing to a place where the terms of the arbitration agreement [were] to be found".[204]

---

[197] See DAC report, para.42.
[198] In *Trygg Hansa Insurance Co Ltd v Equitas Ltd* [1998] 2 Lloyd's Rep. 439 it was held that the pre-1996 Act authorities were to be applied to determine whether the clause was indeed made part of the agreement in the absence of any indication in s.6(2) as to how this was otherwise to be determined. This was apparently also the intention of the drafters of the legislation: see DAC report, para.42. The Arbitration Act 1950 was silent on incorporation by reference.
[199] *Excess Insurance Co Ltd v Mander* [1997] 2 Lloyd's Rep. 119.
[200] *per* Colman J. at 124.
[201] [1991] 57 B.L.R. 1.
[202] *Aughton Ltd v MF Kent Services Ltd* [1991] 57 B.L.R. 1.
[203] Within what is now s.5 of the Arbitration Act 1996.
[204] Gibson L.J. in *Aughton* at [29].

(ii) *per* Sir John Megaw: There are three factors peculiar to arbitration agreements to be considered. First, an arbitration agreement may preclude the parties from bringing a dispute before a court. Second an arbitration agreement has to be a written agreement,[205] and third an arbitration agreement is of a different nature from other types of clauses and constitutes a self-contained collateral contract. These factors apply equally to engineering contracts as they do to arbitration clauses in charterparties which it is sought to incorporate into bills of lading, with the result that, as in the charterparty cases,[206] there must be distinct and specific words expressing the parties' intention to make the incorporation.[207]

Sir John Megaw therefore concluded that specific words were necessary to incorporate an arbitration clause and that the reference in a sub-contract to another contract's terms and conditions would not suffice to incorporate the arbitration clause into the sub-contract.[208] His reasoning for imposing the requirement of specific words of incorporation was based on three important factors peculiar to arbitration agreements outlined above. However, in the same case, Ralph Gibson L.J. reached the conclusion that express words of incorporation were not always necessary and in some circumstances general words would be sufficient to effect incorporation depending on the terms of the arbitration agreement. His preferred approach was to look at the precise words of the contract alleged to permit incorporation and to the precise terms of the arbitration agreement. If the terms of the arbitration clause are such that they only apply to the contract in which they appear, Ralph Gibson L.J.'s view was that general words of incorporation would be insufficient, but if they apply to both then general words of incorporation are sufficient.

2–047 **Development of the case law.** Sir John Megaw's view in *Aughton* followed the approach previously adopted in *Thomas & Co v Portsea SS Co Ltd*,[209] and a number of cases both before and after the 1996 Act have adopted the same approach. In *Barrett & Son (Brickwork) Ltd v Henry Boot Management Ltd*[210] Lloyd J. relied on both Sir John Megaw's approach in *Aughton* and the dicta of Lord Diplock in *Bremer Vulcan v South India Shipping*[211] to support the conclusion that if a contract is to be incorporated into another contract there must be

---

[205] The case was decided under the previous legislation but the requirement for writing is now contained in s.5 of the Arbitration Act 1996: see para.2–038.
[206] *Thomas & Co v Portsea SS Co Ltd* [1912] A.C. 1: see also para.2–056 below.
[207] Sir John Megaw in *Aughton* at [31] *et seq.*
[208] At [31].
[209] [1912] A.C. 1. Although as Bowsher J. pointed out in *Secretary of State for Foreign and Commonwealth Affaris v Percy Thomas Partnership & Kier International* (1998) 65 Con. L.R. 11, the *Bremer Vulkan* case was not dealing with incorporation. See also *Federal Bulk Carriers Inc v Itoh & Co Ltd* [1989] 1 Lloyd's Rep. 103.
[210] (1995) C.I.L.L. 1026. See though *Roche Products v Freeman Process Systems Ltd* [1996] 80 B.L.R. 102; and *Secretary of State for Foreign and Commonwealth Affairs v Percy Thomas Partnership* (1998) 65 Con. L.R. 11.
[211] [1981] A.C. 909.

express reference to it in that other contract.[212] Hicks J. on the other hand concluded in *Roche Products Ltd v Freeman Process Systems Ltd*[213] that he should give effect to the intentions of the contracting parties even if that was expressed as a general reference to a document to be incorporated. He saw no justification for a rule which artificially restricts the intention of the parties by requiring them to use particular forms of words to achieve incorporation.

Subject to drawing a distinction between incorporation of an arbitration agreement contained in a document setting out standard form terms and one contained in some other contract between different parties,[214] judicial thinking seems to have favoured the approach of Sir John Megaw in *Aughton*, namely that general words of incorporation are not sufficient. Rather, particular reference to the arbitration clause needs to be made to comply with s.6 of the Arbitration Act 1996, unless special circumstances exist. This was the view taken by Judge Raymond Jack Q.C. following a review of the relevant authorities in *Trygg Hansa Insurance Co Ltd v Equitas Ltd*[215] and it was supported and confirmed by Evans L.J. in *Anonymous Greek Co of General Insurances, (The "Ethniki") v AIG Europe (UK)*.[216]

Reference to standard form terms. If the document sought to be incorporated is a standard form set of terms and conditions the courts are more likely to accept that general words of incorporation will suffice.[217] This is because the parties can be expected to be more familiar with those standard terms, including their arbitration clause.[218] In *Sea Trade Maritime Corp v Hellenic Mutual War Risks Association (Bermuda) Ltd, (The "Athena") No.2*[219] the court drew a distinction between what it described as a "two-contract case", that is where the arbitration clause is contained in a secondary document which is a contract to which at least one party is different from the parties to the contract in question, and "a single contract case" where the arbitration clause is in standard terms to be found in another document.[220] Relying on dictum of Bingham L.J. in *Federal*

2–048

---

[212] See also *Cooperative Wholesale Society v Sanders & Taylor* (1995) 11 Constr. Law Jo. 118; *Trygg Hansa Insurance Co Ltd v Equitas Ltd* [1998] 2 Lloyd's Rep. 439; *Excess Insurance Co Ltd v CJ Mander* [1997] 2 Lloyd's Rep. 119. In *Alfred McAlpine Construction Ltd v RMG Electrical* [1998] A.D.R.L.J. 33 it was held that reference to terms applying to a sub-contract "as if fully set out hereunder and . . . fully incorporated herein" and the sub-contractor acknowledging that he fully appreciates and understands them was sufficient to meet Sir John Megaw's requirement of express words of incorporation.

[213] [1996] 80 B.L.R. 102.

[214] See para.2–048 below.

[215] [1998] 2 Lloyd's Rep. 439. Applied in *Cigna Life Insurance Co of Europe SA-NV v Intercaser SA de Seguros y Reaseguros* [2002] 1 All E.R. (Comm) 235; *American International Specialty Lines Insurance Co v Abbott Laboratories* [2002] EWHC 2714.

[216] [2000] 2 All E.R. 566 at 575.

[217] The same will apply to standard rules and regulations which are incorporated into a contract: *Stretford v Football Association Ltd* [2006] EWHC 479; *Whiting v Halverson* [2003] EWCA Civ 403.

[218] See *Modern Building Wales v Limmer and Trinidad Co* [1975] 2 Lloyd's Rep. 318; *Extrudakerb (Maltby Engineering) Ltd v Whitemountain Quarries Ltd* [1996] N.I. 567; *Hackwood Ltd v Areen Design Services Ltd* (2006) 22 Const. L.J. 68. See also Andrew Tweeddale, "Incorporation of Arbitration Clauses", Arbitration (2002), Vol.68, No.1 at 48.

[219] [2006] EWHC 2530.

[220] At [62].

Bulk Carriers Inc v C Itoh & Co Ltd (The "Federal Bulker"),[221] Langley J. said that: "In principle, English law accepts incorporation of standard terms by the use of general words and, I would add, particularly so when the terms are readily available and the question arises in the context of dealings between established players in a well-known market. The principle, as the dictum makes clear, does not distinguish between a term which is an arbitration clause and one which addresses other issues. In contrast, and for the very reason that it concerns other parties, a 'stricter rule' is applied in charterparty/bills of lading cases. The reason given is that the other party may have no knowledge nor ready means of knowledge of the relevant terms. Further, as the authorities illustrate, the terms of an arbitration clause may require adjustment if they are to be made to apply to the parties to a different contract." The court therefore reinforced the distinction between incorporation by reference of standard form terms and of the terms of a different contract, and concluded that in a single contract case general words of incorporation are sufficient, whereas by its nature a two-contract case may require specific reference to the other contract.

2–049 **When specific reference required.** In *Trade Maritime Corp v Hellenic Mutual War Risks Association (Bermuda) Ltd, (The "Athena") No.2*[222] the court referred in particular to the stricter approach which requires specific reference to the arbitration agreement as being applicable in charterparty/bills of lading cases. It has also been applied in other areas, notably reinsurance contracts and construction contracts.[223] In principle however the rationale for requiring specific words of incorporation, notably the absence of knowledge of the terms of another contract between different parties and the need for adjustment of the terms as written, is not limited to those situations. It is suggested therefore that the same approach would apply generally in two contract cases even outside those particular fields.

2–050 **Contrast with the Model Law.** The current position therefore seems to be that if the arbitration agreement is incorporated from a standard form a general reference to those terms is sufficient, but at least in the case of reference to a non-standard form contract in the context of construction and reinsurance contracts and bills of lading a specific reference to the arbitration agreement is necessary. As for reference to an arbitration agreement in non-standard form terms outside those particular fields the position is less clear, but it seems that generally a specific reference is needed.[224] This leads to the rather odd result that the English courts have in a number of cases applied the wording of s.6(2) of the Arbitration Act 1996 to support a restrictive approach, whilst courts in other jurisdictions interpreting

---

[221] [1989] 1 Lloyd's Rep. 103 at 105.
[222] [2006] EWHC 2530.
[223] The submissions in *Sea Trade Maritime Corp v Hellenic Mutual War Risks Association (Bermuda) Ltd (The "Athena") No.2* [2006] EWHC 2530 at [62] referred specifically to reinsurance contracts and construction contracts. For incorporation by reference in reinsurance contracts see para.2–055, in construction contracts see para.2–053 and in bills of lading see para.2–056 below.
[224] See para.2–047 above.

the very similar wording of the pre-2006 version of Art.7(2) of the Model Law[225] have taken a more liberal approach. This is tempered somewhat by the distinction drawn in *Trade Maritime Corp v Hellenic Mutual War Risks Association (Bermuda) Ltd, (The "Athena") No.2*[226] but in any event the different approaches were justified in *Trygg Hansa* on the basis that the DAC report did not simply intend to apply Art.7(2) of the Model Law and the more liberal approach because it specifically suggested that existing case law should be applied.[227] This guidance has led the English courts, in some cases at least, to apply the more restrictive approach that appeared in the pre-1996 cases.

Company articles of association. A company's articles of association 2–051 may incorporate an arbitration agreement. The question has arisen whether the arbitration agreement applies to:

• disputes between members, and, if so, whether only to disputes which relate to the affairs of the company or

• disputes between the company and its members and, if so, whether only to disputes with members in their capacity as members and not some other capacity.[228]

It is a matter of construction of the individual article, but provisions of this type are likely to be construed restrictively and, as a general rule, they apply only to disputes between the company and one of its members in his capacity as a member.[229] Disputes have also arisen between members of a trading association where the trading association has been a company and its articles include an arbitration clause. The courts have rejected claims that the trading association's articles of association oblige the parties to submit their dispute to arbitration, and held that the dispute is not caught by the arbitration clause.[230]

Leases and other assignments of real property. Obligations 2–052 between landlord and tenant may last for a considerable time. As a result of the length of the relationship documents other than the original lease, including sub-leases, assignments, deeds and correspondence, come into existence. One or more of the documents may contain an arbitration clause, and others may not. The court has to decide as a matter of construction whether to read the documents together and give effect to the arbitration clause. In *Wade-Gery v Morrison*, for

---

[225] See Appendix 4.
[226] [2006] EWHC 2530.
[227] Paragraph 42 of the DAC report.
[228] *Hickman v Kent and Romney Marsh Sheep Breeders' Association* [1915] 1 Ch. 881; *Beattie v Beattie Ltd* [1938] Ch. 708; *London Sack & Bag Co Ltd v Dixon and Lugton Ltd* [1943] 2 All E.R. 763.
[229] Note however that certain matters such as a winding up petition or a petition by a shareholder for relief from unfairly prejudicial conduct under s.459 of the Companies Act 1985 cannot be referred to arbitration in any event: see para.7–039.
[230] *London Sack & Bag Co Ltd v Lugton Ltd* [1943] 2 All E.R. 763.

example, a supplemental deed varied the covenants in a lease, but the court held that it did not vary the provision for arbitration.[231]

2–053 **Construction contracts and sub-contracts.** Construction projects usually involve sub-contractors and a common problem is whether the terms of the main contract, including its arbitration clause, have been incorporated into a sub-contract. As noted above[232] the courts have not always been consistent about whether these arbitration clauses are validly incorporated. For example in *Modern Buildings Wales Ltd v Limmer and Trinidad Co Ltd* an order placed on sub-contractors specified that it should be in the "appropriate form for nominated subcontractors (RIBA 1965 edition)". There was no such form but the court held that the parties meant to refer to the "green form"[233] commonly used for sub-contracts. Like the RIBA forms, the green form contained an arbitration clause, which was held to be binding on the parties.[234] In *Aughton*[235] however, which was also a construction case,[236] the court declined to incorporate the arbitration agreement into a sub-sub-contract. While the decisions are not always consistent,[237] the court will in each case examine the language of the contracts in question to see whether, applying general principles of construction, it provides a clear indication of an intention to incorporate the arbitration provisions of the main contract.[238] Construction contracts are a field where the use of standard forms are commonplace and accordingly the approach taken in *Trade Maritime Corp v Hellenic Mutual War Risks Association (Bermuda) Ltd (The "Athena") No.2*[239] may be particularly appropriate. Indeed even when dealing with a two-contract case, if the secondary document is stated to be based on standard form terms containing an arbitration agreement then presumably specific reference to the arbitration clause would not be needed.[240]

---

[231] (1878) 37 L.T. 270.

[232] See para.2–047.

[233] Published by the construction industry associations NFBTE and FASS.

[234] *Modern Buildings Wales Ltd v Limmer and Trinidad Co Ltd* [1975] 1 W.L.R. 1281. The Court of Appeal reached a similar conclusion, where the reference was again to an RIBA form, in *Brightside Kilpatrick Engineering Services v Mitchell Construction (1973) Ltd* [1975] 2 Lloyd's Rep. 493.

[235] Paragraph 2–046.

[236] See also *Giffen (Electrical Contractors) Ltd v Drake & Scull Engineering Ltd, Femwork Ventilation Ltd v Same* (1993) 37 Con. L.R. 84 and *Astel-Reiniger Joint Venture v Argos Engineering and Heavy Industries Co Ltd* (1995) A.D.L.R.J. 41, where general rules of construction were applied. Contrast *Lexair Ltd (in administrative receivership) v Edgar W Taylor Ltd* [1993] 65 B.L.R. 87, where *Thomas v Portsea* (cited above) was applied. Bingham M.R. in *Giffen* suggested that the difference between the two approaches might not be so large as it might seem but he preferred that of Gibson L.J. *Portsea* has subsequently been applied in *Co-operative Wholesale Society Ltd v Saunders & Taylor Ltd* (1994) 39 Con. L.R. 77 and in *Barrett & Son (Brickwork) Ltd v Henry Boot Management Ltd* (1995) C.I.L.L. 1026. See also Roche *Products Ltd and Celletech Therapeutics Ltd v Freeman Process Systems Ltd and Haden Maclellan Holdings Plc and Black Country Development Corp v Kier Construction Ltd* [1996] 80 B.L.R. 102.

[237] See also *Barrett & Son (Brickwork) Ltd v Henry Boot Management Ltd* (1995) C.I.L.L. 1026; *Roche Products v Freeman Process Systems Ltd* [1996] 80 B.L.R. 102; and *Secretary of State for Foreign and Commonwealth Affairs v Percy Thomas Partnership* (1998) 65 Con. L.R. 11.

[238] See para.2–047.

[239] [2006] EWHC 2530: see para.2–048 above.

[240] See para.2–046.

Unsigned construction contracts. It is, and has been, common com-   2–054
mercial practice in the construction industry for the employer to delay signing
contract documents even though the contractor starts work. The practice can lead
to disputes about whether an arbitration agreement has been entered into at all.[241]
These disputes are resolved by reference to the same principles of construction as
apply to determine whether a contract has come into existence,[242] namely by a
careful examination of whether all the terms have been agreed, despite the absence
of formality.

Re-insurance contracts. Re-insurance contracts often contain a provision   2–055
that, save as expressly provided, they follow the same form as the primary
insurance.[243] This is not normally sufficient to incorporate the arbitration clause
in the primary policy, which is regarded as ancillary to the main subject matter.[244]
A specific reference to the arbitration clause is usually required, even applying the
approach *Sea Trade Maritime Corp v Hellenic Mutual War Risks Association
(Bermuda) Ltd, (The "Athena") No.2.*[245]

Bills of lading and charterparties. The question frequently arises in   2–056
shipping cases as to whether arbitration clauses in charterparties have been
incorporated into bills of lading.[246] A bill of lading is a negotiable instrument and
a document of title, and this has been thought to affect the approach to be taken
to construction of its terms.[247] It is clear however that specific reference is
necessary to incorporate in a bill of lading an arbitration agreement in a charterparty. This is so whether the requirement for specific reference which Sir John

---

[241] See, e.g. *Birse Construction Ltd v St David Ltd* [1999] B.L.R. 194.
[242] See *Coltman Precast Concrete Ltd v W&J Simons (Contractors) Ltd* 35 Con. L.R. 127 and *Smith and Gordon Ltd v John Lewis Building Ltd* (1993) 44 Con. L.R. 11. In *Smith and Gordon* the Court of Appeal was told that this practice was common in the building industry: Mann L.J. said he had little sympathy, and that it was for parties to ensure they had a contract, and that they could not expect the courts to find one for them.
[243] Various formulations are used, such as "same terms, exclusions, conditions, definitions and settlements" or "same terms, clauses, conditions and warranties".
[244] *Trygg Hansa Insurance Co Ltd v Equitas Ltd* [1998] 2 Lloyd's Rep. 439; *Excess Insurance Co Ltd v CJ Mander* [1997] 2 Lloyd's Rep. 119; *Pine Top Insurance Co Ltd v Unione Italiana Anglo Saxon Reinsurance Ltd* [1987] 1 Lloyd's Rep. 476; *Cigna Life Insurance Co of Europe SA NV v Intercaser SA de Seguros y Reaseguros* [2002] 1 All E.R. (Comm) 235.
[245] [2006] EWHC 2530. See para.2–048 above.
[246] See, e.g. *N.V. Reederij Amsterdam v President of India (The "Amstelmolen")* [1960] 2 Lloyd's Rep. 82; *The "Elizabeth H"* [1962] 1 Lloyd's Rep. 172; *Merak, The (Owners of Cargo on Board) v The Merak (Owners) (The "Merak")* [1965] P. 223; *The "Phonizien"* [1966] 1 Lloyd's Rep. 150; *Tradax SA v Volkswagenwerk AG* [1969] 2 Q.B. 599, affirmed [1970] 1 Q.B. 537; *Federal Bulk Carriers Inc v C Itoh & Co Ltd (The "Federal Bulker")* [1989] 1 Lloyd's Rep. 103; *Daval Aciers D'Usinor et de Sacilor v Armare Srl (The "Nerarno")* [1996] 1 Lloyd's Rep. 1.
[247] In particular, subsequent endorsees might never have seen the charterparty and in the absence of specific words of incorporation might not appreciate that they had become bound by provisions in another contract which precluded them enforcing their rights in the courts: *Excess Insurance Co Ltd v CJ Mander* [1997] 2 Lloyd's Rep. 119. See also the comments of Bingham L.J. in *Federal Bulk Carriers Inc v C Itoh & Co Ltd (The "Federal Bulker")* [1989] 1 Lloyd's Rep. 103 at 105 endorsed in *Trade Maritime Corp v Hellenic Mutual War Risks Association (Bermuda) Ltd, (The "Athena") No.2* [2006] EWHC 2530.

Megaw advanced in *Aughton*[248] as applicable to incorporation of arbitration agreements in contracts generally, or just to certain two-contract cases as discussed in *Trade Maritime Corp v Hellenic Mutual War Risks Association (Bermuda) Ltd, (The "Athena") No.2*.[249] General words of incorporation in a bill of lading will not be construed as incorporating the terms of an arbitration agreement in a charterparty.[250] It is only where the charterparty or the bill of lading make specific provision to that effect that the incorporation will be effected.[251]

In addition to the fact that a bill of lading is a negotiable instrument, the reasoning put forward for this approach in the bill of lading context is that general, as distinct from specific, words of incorporation must be taken to cover only those contractual provisions that are in substance germane or directly relevant to the subject matter of the contract into which they are to be incorporated. They must also be capable of operating in conjunction with that contract if so incorporated.[252] An arbitration agreement between a ship owner and charterer is not considered germane to the contractual rights and obligations that arise under the bill of lading.[253]

2–057   **Applicability of the arbitration agreement.** The courts are reluctant to give effect to arbitration clauses which on their face are inapplicable to the contract into which it is sought to incorporate them.[254] Some flexibility will be permitted, however, depending on the degree to which the clause can be said to be inapplicable.[255] Thus in *The "Rena K"*[256] a charterparty provided "any disputes which may arise under this charter to be settled by arbitration in London". The bills of lading provided that: "All terms, clauses, conditions and exceptions including the arbitration clause . . . are hereby incorporated." It was held that the use of these specific words meant that the parties to the bill of lading intended the arbitration clause to apply to disputes arising under the bill of lading, even though, (i) prima facie the words were apt to cover disputes arising only under the

---

[248] See para.2–046 above.
[249] [2006] EWHC 2530. See para.2–048 above.
[250] *The Delos, Owners of Cargo v Delos Shipping Ltd* [2001] 1 All E.R. (Comm) 763; *Federal Bulk Carriers Inc v Itoh & Co Ltd (The "Federal Bulker")* [1989] 1 Lloyd's Rep. 103; *Skips A/s Nordheim and Others v Syrian Petroleum Co Ltd and Petrofina SA (The "Varenna")* [1983] 2 Lloyd's Rep. 592; *Siboti K/S v BP France SA* [2003] EWHC 1278.
[251] *Thomas & Co Ltd v Portsea SS Co Ltd* [1912] A.C. 1; *Merak, The (Owners of Cargo on Board) v The Merak (Owners) (The "Merak")* [1965] P. 223; *"Michael S" Evryalos Maritime Ltd v China Pacific Insurance Co Ltd (The "MV Michael S")*, (December 20, 2001); *Daval Aciers D'Usinor et de Sacilor v Armare Srl (The "Nerarno")* [1996] 1 Lloyd's Rep. 1; *The Delos, Owners of Cargo v Delos Shipping Ltd* [2001] 1 All E.R. (Comm) 763; *Welex AG v Rosa Maritime Ltd* [2002] EWHC 762; [2002] 1 All E.R. (Comm) 939 affirmed at [2003] EWCA Civ 938.
[252] *The "Annefield"* [1971] 1 All E.R. 394.
[253] *Thomas & Co Ltd v Portsea SS Co Ltd* [1912] A.C. 1; *The "Annefield"* [1971] P. 168.
[254] *The "Annefield"* [1971] P. 168, affirmed by the Court of Appeal at [1971] 1 Lloyd's Rep. 1. As Brandon J. noted in that case at 173 "when the arbitration agreement is, by its terms, applicable only to disputes under the charterparty, general words will not incorporate it into the bill of lading so as to make it applicable to disputes under the [bill of lading]".
[255] Or, as was said in *Siboti K/S v BP France SA* [2003] EWHC 1278, if "undue manipulation" is required.
[256] [1978] 1 Lloyd's Rep. 545.

charterparty and (ii) it was necessary to manipulate or adapt part of the wording of the clause to give effect to the parties' intention.[257]

4. CONTENT OF AN ARBITRATION AGREEMENT

(a) Drafting the arbitration agreement

Level of detail. One of the briefest arbitration agreements to be reported merely stated: "arbitration to be settled in London".[258] Although that agreement was enforced, it required a court action to achieve that result.[259] Greater detail is desirable to achieve clarity and thereby certainty as to the parties' intentions, and to avoid unnecessary and expensive disputes prior to consideration of the substantive issues. Ultimately, if an agreement contains jurisdictional references which are completely contradictory, the jurisdictional agreement may be void for uncertainty.[260]   2–058

Further, whilst it is possible that parties might reach agreement on some issues concerning the conduct of the arbitration after a dispute has arisen, that is often more difficult than securing agreement at the time of negotiating the arbitration agreement. Accordingly it is usually preferable to consider such matters at the contract drafting stage.

Checklist of matters to be considered. When drafting an arbitration agreement care needs to be taken to ensure that it is appropriate for the particular circumstances of the case. The following is a checklist of the matters which need to be considered when drafting an arbitration agreement, together with references to where they are addressed in this book. It may not be necessary to include provision for all of them, but thought should be given as to whether they need to be addressed in the particular circumstances of the case: 2–059

1. Have the parties been properly identified?—para.3–003.

2. Is there a clear reference to arbitration?—para.2–065.

3. What disputes are to be referred to arbitration?—para.2–072

4. Where is the seat of the arbitration to be?—paras 2–100 and 5–071 *et seq.*

5. How is the substance of the dispute to be determined?—paras 2–090 *et seq.*

---

[257] See also *Daval Aciers D'Usinor et de Sacilor v Armare Srl (The "Nerarno")* [1996] 1 Lloyd's Rep. 1; *Film Finance Inc v The Royal Bank of Scotland* [2007] EWHC 195.
[258] *Tritonia Shipping Inc v South Nelson Forest Products Corp* [1966] 1 Lloyd's Rep. 114.
[259] See generally the approach of the courts at para.2–068.
[260] See e.g. *EJR Lovelock v Exportles* [1968] 1 Lloyd's Rep. 163 and see generally paras 2–026 *et seq.*

The Arbitration Agreement

6. What is the law of the arbitration to be?—paras 2–095 *et seq.*

7. Is there a choice of the procedural law?—paras 2–101 *et seq.*

8. How will the tribunal be appointed?—paras 4–024 *et seq.*

9. Is there an appointing authority?—para.2–062.

10. Is the tribunal required to have any particular attributes or qualifications? —paras 4–017 *et seq.*

11. How many members of the tribunal will there be?—para.4–016.

12. Are procedural and/or evidential rules or the rules of an institution to be adopted, and, if so, which ones?—paras 2–061 and 5–089 *et seq.*

13. What will be the language of the arbitration?—paras 5–167 *et seq.*

14. Should the tribunal be given power to make provisional awards under s.39 of the Arbitration Act 1996?—para.5–085.

15. Is specific provision for confidentiality required?—paras 5–182 *et seq.*

16. Should applications and appeals to the court be excluded?—para.2–063.

17. Is a waiver of sovereign immunity required?—para.3–036.

18. Are provisions for multi-party arbitration, consolidation or concurrent hearings required?—paras 3–040 *et seq.*

2–060 **Amending the statutory regime.** In addition to the matters set out above, consideration should also be given more generally to whether the parties wish to amend the statutory regime which will otherwise apply by virtue of the Arbitration Act 1996.[261] The parties are specifically given the right to make agreements in writing[262] about a wide range of matters subject only to "such safeguards as are necessary in the public interest".[263] They may do so by adopting a foreign procedural law.[264] In many instances the statute sets out the provisions that apply in the absence of agreement otherwise between the parties. Some provisions apply only if the parties agree that they should.[265] In other respects the fallback position is that it is for the tribunal to decide matters where the parties have not agreed them.[266]

---

[261] Section 4(2) of the Arbitration Act 1996 makes clear that the parties are allowed to make their own arrangements by agreement in respect of the non-mandatory provisions of the 1996 Act.

[262] The requirement for any agreement to be "in writing" stems from s.5(1) of the Arbitration Act 1996 although the section gives the expression a broad meaning.

[263] This gives effect to the principle of party autonomy set out in s.1(b) of the Arbitration Act 1996.

[264] Section 4(5) of the Arbitration Act 1996 and see para.2–103 below. The choice of a foreign law to govern the substance of the dispute, for example as the proper law of the contract in question, will not constitute an agreement as to the non-mandatory provisions of the of the Arbitration Act 1996: see *Lesotho Highlands Development Authority v Impreglio SpA* [2005] UKHL 43 at [37]; *C v D* [2007] EWHC 1541 at [38]; *XL Insurance Ltd v Owens Corning* [2000] 2 Lloyd's Rep. 500 at 508.

[265] Such as the power to order consolidation of proceedings or concurrent hearings under s.35 or the power to make a provisional award under s.39 of the Arbitration Act 1996.

[266] Section 34(1) of the Arbitration Act 1996.

The matters on which the parties may make agreements under the Arbitration Act 1996, with references to the relevant section numbers in the statute, are as follows.

The seat of the arbitration—s.3

Application of institutional rules—s.4(3)

Separability of arbitration agreement—s.7

Commencement of arbitral proceedings—s.14

The tribunal: number of arbitrators—s.15

The tribunal: whether third arbitrator to act as chairman—s.15

Procedure for appointment of arbitrators, including choice of an appointing authority—s.16

Power in case of default to appoint sole arbitrator—s.17

Failure of appointment procedure—s.18

Chairman—s.20

Umpire—s.21

Decision-making where no chairman or umpire—s.22

Revocation of arbitrator's authority—s.23

Procedure for challenge to arbitrators—s.24(2)

Resignation of arbitrator—s.25

Death of person by whom arbitrator appointed—s.26(2)

Filling of vacancy—s.27

Competence of tribunal to rule on its own jurisdiction—s.30

Procedural and evidential matters—s.34

Consolidation of proceedings and concurrent hearings—s.35

Legal or other representation—s.36

Power to appoint experts, legal advisors or assessors—s.37

General powers exercisable by the tribunal—s.38

Power to make provisional awards—s.39

Powers of tribunal in case of party's default—s.41

Enforcement of peremptory orders of tribunal—s.42

Court powers exercisable in support of arbitral proceedings—s.44

Determination of preliminary point of law—s.45

Rules applicable to substance of dispute—s.46

Awards on different issues—s.47

Remedies—s.48

Interest—s.49

Extension of time for making award—s.50

Settlement—s.51

Form of award—s.52

Place where award treated as made—s.53

Date of award—s.54

Notification of award—s.55

Correction of award or additional award—s.57

Effect of award—s.58

Award of costs—s.61

Effect of agreement or award about costs—s.62

The recoverable costs of the arbitration—s.63

Recoverable fees and expenses of arbitrators—s.64

Power to limit recoverable costs—s.65

Appeal on point of law—s.69

Service of notices—s.76

Powers of court in relation to service of documents—s.77

Reckoning periods of time—s.78

Power of court to extend time limits relating to arbitral proceedings—s.79

2–061   **Application of institutional rules.** The 1996 Act specifically contemplates that the parties may amend the statutory regime which will otherwise
apply by adoption of institutional arbitration rules.[267] Some of the institutions who
promulgate rules also offer their services in the administration of arbitrations. The
United Nations does not administer arbitrations, but its UNCITRAL Rules are
useful for ad hoc arbitrations, particularly because they offer a means of ensuring
the appointment of the tribunal.[268] The relevant UNCITRAL working group is
currently considering a proposal to amend the UNCITRAL Rules, which were

---

[267] Section 4(3) of the Arbitration Act 1996. On institutions and their rules see further paras 3–051 *et
seq.* and 5–090 *et seq.* and in particular paras 5–101 to 5–103.
[268] When using the UNCITRAL Rules it is recommended that an appointing authority be expressly
provided for, as the mechanism in the rules for appointing one is cumbersome.

published in 1976.[269] The rules of a particular institution are not necessarily incorporated into an arbitration agreement merely because a particular institution has been made the appointing authority, and many institutions offer this as a separate service. It is important therefore to provide for the arbitration to be conducted in accordance with the institution's rules and not just that it shall appoint the tribunal. The incorporation of institutional rules in an arbitration agreement is not essential, but it may well be useful and may save time and money by providing a framework for the conduct of the arbitration.[270] The institutional rules will also circumscribe the tribunal's powers and jurisdiction, subject to the terms of the arbitration agreement.[271] Individual provisions within sets of institutional rules should be considered to see if they give the parties what they want. For example, do they want to give the tribunal all the powers conferred by Art.22 of the LCIA Rules, which include a power to join third parties against the wishes of one of the existing parties? Do they want the tribunal to have a very broad power to grant interim and conservatory measures as provided by Art.23 of the ICC Rules? Are there other matters not dealt with that the parties need addressed in the arbitration agreement?[272] If appropriate the parties can amend the institutional rules by express provision in the arbitration agreement, though it is then sensible to make clear that the rules are adopted save as varied by the arbitration agreement.

Appointing authority. An arbitration agreement should state how the   2–062
tribunal is to be appointed, in default of agreement between the parties. The use of an institution to appoint the tribunal, where they take on the role of "appointing authority", may be considerably more effective, cheaper and quicker than applying to the court. As mentioned in the previous paragraph, acting as an appointing authority is offered by many institutions as a separate service from the administration of arbitrations so it is important to clarify in the arbitration agreement which role is to be performed. Adoption of an institution's rules will usually make the institution responsible for appointment of the tribunal.[273] In England the court may also appoint arbitrators.[274]

Exclusion agreements. The parties to an arbitration agreement may   2–063
exclude the right to seek (i) leave to appeal to the court on points of law[275] and (ii) determinations of preliminary points of law by the court.[276] An agreement to dispense with reasons for the tribunal's award constitutes an agreement to exclude

---

[269] See *Revision of the UNCITRAL RULES*, Paulsson and Petrochilos, discussed at the 45th Seession of Working Group II, *www.uncitral.org*
[270] See paras 5–101 *et seq.*
[271] *The Bay Hotel and Resort Ltd v Cavalier Construction Co Ltd* [2001] UKPC 34.
[272] In particular the matters specified at para.2–059.
[273] But note that the UNCITRAL Rules provide for ad hoc rather than institutional arbitration so a separate provision for an appointing authority should be included, although there is a default procedure.
[274] See paras 7–095 *et seq.*
[275] Section 69(1) of the Arbitration Act 1996.
[276] Section 45(1) of the Arbitration Act 1996.

the court's jurisdiction in these respects.[277] The exclusion agreement may be incorporated into the arbitration agreement by reference to another document in which it is contained.[278] In domestic cases parties used to be permitted to exclude the right to appeal only after the arbitration had begun, but this is no longer the case.[279] There used also to be a statutory limitation on this right in maritime, commodity and insurance cases[280] unless the exclusion agreement was entered into after the commencement of the arbitration or the contract was governed by a law other than the law of England and Wales.[281] Again this has been abolished[282] so the law is now the same in all cases: appeals and determinations of preliminary points of law can be excluded at the time of making the arbitration agreement. The ICC Rules[283] and the LCIA Rules[284] contain a valid exclusion agreement.[285] Appeals are excluded to the extent permitted by law if these rules are adopted. The wording of an exclusion agreement can be relatively straightforward: "The parties hereby exclude all rights under sections 45 and 69 of the Arbitration Act 1996 to seek a determination of a preliminary point of law by the High Court, or to appeal from any arbitration award."

2–064   **Standard form arbitration clauses.** A reliable method of ensuring that the more important features of an arbitration agreement are included is to use one of the standard forms.[286] Using these standard forms provides a good measure of comfort that an effective arbitration agreement has been entered into, and these arbitration clauses, in conjunction with the rules which they incorporate, will include many of the matters referred to in the checklist at para.2–059. However, consideration should also be given to whether the particular features of the transaction suggest further provisions are necessary. The particular rules chosen should be examined to establish whether there are matters they omit to cater for but which, in the particular circumstances of the case, need to be addressed. For example, if the agreement containing the arbitration agreement is one of several related contracts or there are several parties to the agreement all of whom are likely to be involved in any dispute, then additional provision for multi-party arbitration should be considered.[287] Many standard form clauses do not address this, and nor

---

[277] Section 69(1) of the Arbitration Act 1996.
[278] *Sukuman Ltd v The Commonwealth Secretariat* [2006] EWHC 304.
[279] Section 87 of the Arbitration Act 1996, see para.2–005.
[280] The so-called "special categories".
[281] Section 4(1) of the Arbitration Act 1979.
[282] Section 109(2) of the Arbitration Act 1996.
[283] Article 28.6.
[284] Article 26.9.
[285] *Arab African Energy Corp Ltd v Olieprodukten Nederland BV* [1983] 2 Lloyd's Rep. 419; *Marine Contractors Inc v Shell Petroleum Development Co of Nigeria Ltd* [1984] 2 Lloyd's Rep. 77; *Sanghi Polyesters Ltd v The International Investor* [2000] 1 Lloyd's Rep. 480.
[286] For example the recommended clauses from the LCIA and ICC. Various other arbitration institutions, including trade or professional associations, have their own suggested clauses, and reference should be made to the institutions concerned.
[287] See paras 3–040 *et seq.*

do the rules which they incorporate.[288] Similarly confidentiality is a matter for which specific provision may be desirable.[289]

Terms must be clear and certain. To be valid and enforceable, the   2–065
terms of an arbitration agreement must be clear and certain.[290] It is obviously
desirable for there to be a clear reference to arbitration,[291] and the procedure
envisaged by the clause, to the extent that it is articulated, must be consistent with
a provision for arbitration.[292] Whether the arbitration agreement meets the
requirement for clarity and certainty is assessed in the same way as it would be for
any other contract. In the absence of a clear reference to arbitration the court may
be forced to conclude that there is no arbitration agreement at all.[293] Even if there
is an arbitration agreement, disputes about its terms, whether it has been incorporated into the relevant contract and so forth can be costly and may delay or derail
altogether the arbitration. It is of fundamental importance that the parties'
agreement clearly and unequivocally reflects their wish to make arbitration the
means for final and binding resolution of disputes between them.[294]

Multiple Agreements. Where a transaction comprises a series of agree-   2–066
ments between the same parties, it is important to consider the dispute resolution
provisions in relation to each of them. Failure to do so may result in disputes
under the different agreements being resolved in different fora, which carries the
risk of additional expense and inconsistent decisions.[295] Depending on the scope
of the arbitration agreement it may be possible to bring disputes under different,
related agreements in one proceeding, but to avoid issues arising in relation to the
tribunal's jurisdiction to do so it is advisable to provide specifically for arbitration
in the same terms in each agreement, or to cross refer to the applicable arbitration

---

[288] The ICC Rules, for example, provide at Art.10 for what is to happen as regards formation of the tribunal where there are multiple parties to an arbitration, but they do not empower the tribunal to consolidate arbitrations or to join third parties or to hold concurrent hearings.

[289] See paras 5–182 *et seq.* below.

[290] *Lobb Partnership Ltd v Aintree Racecourse Co Ltd* [2000] B.L.R. 65.

[291] Failure to do so may not necessarily be fatal—see *Plant v Plant* [2002] EWHC 2283, a case where there was no express reference to arbitration. The clause in question provided that disputes were "to be determined by the decision of a Chancery or Commercial Queen's Counsel appointed by the parties . . . and such decision shall be final and binding". The court proceeded to consider the proper construction of the clause in the context of an application to stay court proceedings in favour of arbitration. See also *David Wilson Homes Ltd v Survey Services Ltd (in liquidation)* [2001] 1 All E.R. (Comm) 449.

[292] See e.g. *AIG Europe SA v QBE International Insurance Ltd* [2001] Lloyd's Rep. 268 where the clause in question was held to be "at best a procedure for conciliation which might or might not result in a compromise of the dispute" despite express reference to the appointment of "an arbitrator".

[293] As for example in *Al Midani v Al Midani* [1999] 1 Lloyd's Rep. 923. See also *Flight Training International Inc v International Fire Training Equipment Ltd* [2004] EWHC 721.

[294] In *Finnegan v Sheffield City Council* [1988] 43 B.L.R. 124 a construction contract contained a clause to the effect that the question whether disputes under the contract were to be referred to arbitration was to be a matter for further negotiation. This was held not to be an arbitration clause. See also *AIG Europe SA v QBE International Insurance Ltd* [2001] Lloyd's Rep. 268.

[295] See, for example, *Sawyer v Atari Interactive Inc* [2006] I.L. Pr. 8.

agreement. Such provisions are often known as consolidation and joinder provisions and require considerable care when drafting to ensure that all relevant factors are covered.[295a]

2–067   **Option to arbitrate.**[296] A disputes clause providing for the jurisdiction of the courts subject to an option for either of the parties to refer the dispute to arbitration is valid.[297]

2–068   **The approach of the court.** The court seeks to give effect to the parties' intention to refer disputes to arbitration, and to allow the tribunal full jurisdiction except in cases of hopeless confusion. So for example in *Mangistaumunaigaz Oil Production Association v United World Trade Inc*[298] an oil contract provided for "Arbitration, if any, by ICC rules in London". The respondents argued that the words "if any" were inconsistent with an unconditional contractual undertaking to arbitrate future disputes but the court found that the words were either surplusage or an abbreviation for "if any dispute arises". On the other hand an agreement referring "any dispute and/or claim" to arbitration in England followed by a clause referring "any other dispute" to arbitration in Russia was held to be void for ambiguity, and was neither effective nor enforceable.[299]

If the circumstances allow, the court will lean in favour of upholding the arbitration agreement[300] in order to give effect to the parties' intentions.[301] Where the wording used shows reasonably clearly that the parties intended to submit their disputes to arbitration, then the court will uphold the arbitration agreement even in the absence of mandatory language requiring disputes to be submitted to arbitration.[302] Further, following the approach laid down in *Investors Compensation Scheme v West Bromwich Building Society*,[303] the court may conclude that something has gone wrong with the language used and may correct that error.[304]

2–069   **No presumption in favour of arbitration.** There is no presumption either in favour of or against arbitration and the construction of disputes clauses will not be influenced by some general notion of favouring or disapproving of the

---

[295a] See paras 3–044 *et seq.*
[296] Unilateral options to arbitrate or litigate are dealt with at paras 2–017 to 2–018 above.
[297] *Westfal-Larsen and Co A/S v Ikerigi Compania Naviera SA (The "Messiniaki Bergen")* [1983] 1 Lloyd's Rep. 424; *Navigazione Alta Italia SpA v Concordia Maritime Chartering AB (The "Stena Pacifica")* [1990] 2 Lloyd's Rep. 234.
[298] [1995] 1 Lloyd's Rep. 617.
[299] *Lovelock Ltd v Exportles* [1968] 1 Lloyd's Rep. 163.
[300] *Astro Vendeor Compania Naviera SA v Mabanaft GmbH* [1970] 2 Lloyd's Rep. 267, Mocatta J.
[301] In *Paul Smith Ltd v H&S International Holdings Inc* [1991] 2 Lloyd's Rep. 127, the court found a way of reconciling two apparently conflicting clauses. See also *Shell International Petroleum Co Ltd v Coral Oil Co Ltd* [1999] 1 Lloyd's Rep. 72 and other cases referred to at para.2–027.
[302] *Lobb Partnership Ltd v Aintree Racecourse Co Ltd* [2000] B.L.R. 65.
[303] [1998] 1 All E.R. 98.
[304] *Nine Gladys Road Ltd v Kersh* [2004] EWHC 1080.

process.[305] Rather in each case it is a matter of the proper cons
parties' agreement. The Court of Appeal has however said that an
arbitration clause in an international commercial contract sh(
construed.[306]

The presumption of "one-stop adjudication". The legislative pur-   2–070
pose behind the 1996 Act was the promotion of one-stop adjudication.[307] Accordingly, in considering the scope of an arbitration clause the court will apply the
presumption that the parties have agreed to one forum for dispute resolution.[308]
Where the parties have agreed an arbitration clause they are presumed to have
intended to resolve their disputes through arbitration, and not by means of several
different forms of dispute resolution including both arbitration and the courts.[309]
This presumption has been given forceful judicial expression, most recently in
Fiona Trust & Holding Corp v Yuri Privalov[310] where it was described as a
"powerful" reason for a liberal interpretation of arbitration clauses,[311] and *Premium Nafta Products Ltd v Fili Shipping Co Ltd*.[311a] The Court of Appeal considered that no commercial man would knowingly create a system that required
that the court should first decide whether the contract should be rectified or
avoided or rescinded, before the arbitrator could go on to resolve the dispute that
had arisen. Often cited also is the reluctance expressed by Bingham L.J. "to
attribute to reasonable parties an intention that there should in any foreseeable
eventuality be two sets of proceedings".[312] Citing that dictum, Hoffmann L.J.
stated that the presumption "merely reassures one that the natural meaning of the
words [of the arbitration agreement] produce a sensible and business-like
result".[313] The judiciary also showed their awareness of the adverse effects of the

---

[305] *Overseas Union Insurance Ltd v AA Mutual International Insurance Co Ltd* [1988] 2 Lloyd's Rep. 63.
The courts will however strive to give effect to the arbitration process where at all possible and to
uphold arbitration awards where at all possible. See for example *London Underground Ltd v Citylink
Telecommunications Ltd* [2007] EWHC 1749 (TCC).
[306] *Fiona Trust & Holding Corp v Yuri Privalov* [2007] EWCA Civ 20. See further paras 2–074—2–075,
affirmed in *Premium Nafta Products Ltd v Fili Shipping Co Ltd* [2007] UKHL 40.
[307] See *Lesotho Highlands Development Authority v Impreglio SpA* [2005] UKHL 43 at [34]. In *Capital
Trust Investments Ltd v Radio Design TJ AB* [2002] 2 All E.R. 159.
[308] See, for example, *Asghar v The Legal Services Commission* [2004] EWHC 1803; *Et Plus SA v Welter*
[2006] 1 Lloyd's Rep. 251.
[309] See for example *Capital Trust Investments Ltd v Radio Design TJ AB* [2002] 2 All E.R. 159 where
the court emphasised that the parties would have wanted one tribunal to determine all claims which
could fairly be said to arise out of an application for shares, including claims for fraudulent or
negligent misrepresentation.
[310] [2007] EWCA Civ 20.
[311] See also *Benford Ltd v Lopecan SL* [2004] EWHC 1897; [2004] 2 Lloyd's Rep. 618 where the court
applied the presumption to construe a proviso to an arbitration agreement as covering both claims
and cross claims amounting to a transactional set-off such that the court was entitled to retain
jurisdiction over both.
[311a] [2007] UKHL 40 at [13].
[312] *Ashville Investments v Elmer Contractors Ltd* [1989] 1 Q.B. 488 at 517, similarly, Balcombe L.J. at
503.
[313] *Harbour Assurance Co (UK) Ltd v Kansa General International Insurance Co Ltd* [1993] 1 Lloyd's
Rep. 455 at 470. See also Rix J. in *Aggeliki Charis Compania Maritima SA v Pagnan SpA* [1994] 1
Lloyd's Rep. 168 at 172: Leggatt L.J. in the same case on appeal at [1995] 1 Lloyd's Rep. 87 at
91.

contrary view on London's continuing pre-eminence as a centre for international arbitration,[314] which fortified the presumption for "one-stop adjudication".

(b) Scope of the arbitration agreement

2–071 **Submitting disputes to arbitration.** In order to determine whether a particular dispute has been validly referred to arbitration a number of aspects need to be considered. First, is the dispute capable of being referred to arbitration at all? For example, disputes about a person's civil status or criminal liability are not amenable to arbitration. This issue of arbitrability is dealt with in Ch.1.[315] Secondly, is the type of dispute that has arisen within the scope of the particular arbitration agreement? This will be the focus of the following paragraphs. Thirdly, even if disputes of the type in question are within the terms of the arbitration agreement, does the dispute fall within the scope of what was actually referred by the parties in the particular reference? This aspect is addressed in Ch.5.[316]

2–072 **What matters are within the scope of the arbitration agreement?** The question over what matters does the arbitration agreement confer jurisdiction on the tribunal turns on the particular form of words used. The trend is against drawing fine distinctions on the basis of the form of words used[317] or, as Evans J. put it in *Overseas Union Insurers Ltd v AA Mutual International Insurance Co Ltd*[318]: "[having] the lawyers engage in minute semantic analysis in the guise of ascertaining what the parties' intentions were." Hirst J. expressed little relish for "an intricate and often regrettably hair-splitting exercise in weighing and contrasting the effect of [the] . . . prepositions encountered in arbitration agreements",[319] while Mustill L.J. has referred to the tendency to avoid nice distinctions and give the language of the arbitration agreement its natural meaning.[320] Nevertheless a party is entitled to object to a tribunal assuming jurisdiction over a dispute which falls outside what the parties have agreed in their arbitration agreement to refer,[321] and it is therefore important to consider the scope of the arbitration agreement and whether the dispute which has arisen falls within its terms on a true construction of that agreement.[322] Whilst it is very common for arbitration agreements to refer all disputes[323] arising under a particular contract to

---

[314] Leggatt L.J. in *Harbour Assurance Co (UK) Ltd v Kansa General International Insurance Co Ltd* [1993] 1 Lloyd's Rep. 455 at 466.

[315] At paras 1–033 *et seq.*

[316] See para.5–026 below.

[317] *Fiona Trust & Holding Corp v Yuri Privalov* [2007] EWCA Civ 20, affirmed in *Premium Nafta Products Ltd v Fili Shipping Co Ltd* [2007] UKHL 40. See further paras 2–074 *et seq.* below.

[318] [1988] 2 Lloyd's Rep. 63 at 67.

[319] *Ethiopian Oilseeds & Pulses Export Corp v Rio Del Mar Foods Inc* [1990] 1 Lloyd's Rep. 86.

[320] *Société Commerciale de Reassurance v ERAS (Internationale) Ltd (formerly ERAS (UK))* [1992] 1 Lloyd's Rep. 570.

[321] See generally paras 5–060 *et seq.*

[322] *Metal Distributors (UK) Ltd v ZCCM Investment Holdings Plc* [2005] EWHC 156. For the position on cross claims, set-off and counterclaims see para.6–016.

[323] As regards use of the terms "differences" or "disputes" in an arbitration agreement see para.5–003 below.

arbitration, the parties may deliberately have chosen to refer some but not all types of dispute under their contract to arbitration.[324] This occurs for example where the parties wish some disputes, such as those relating to technical or valuation issues, to be submitted to expert determination.[325] Alternatively if the arbitration agreement forms part of a settlement agreement rather than a transactional agreement it may well limit the scope of the matters which may be submitted to arbitration.[326] Accordingly a close examination of the scope of what has been referred will be necessary as the tribunal will only have jurisdiction to hear disputes that fall within the arbitration agreement.

When does the issue arise? Issues concerning the scope of the arbitration   2–073
agreement and therefore the tribunal's jurisdiction can arise at several stages:

- at the outset of the reference, the question arises whether a particular issue is or is not one that should be referred to arbitration under the terms of the arbitration agreement;

- during arbitration proceedings, issues may be raised concerning whether a reference as constituted is wide enough to resolve a particular dispute or aspect of a dispute; and

- at the enforcement stage, the enforcing court may need to decide whether the scope of the award is wider than permitted by the agreement to arbitrate and/or the terms of the reference.

The discussion which follows should be read in the light of the statutory restrictions on the right to make tardy objections to jurisdiction[327] and the courts' desire to give effect to the wishes of parties and their choice of dispute resolution mechanisms in particular. Even if arguments can be deployed to defeat the tribunal's jurisdiction on the basis of the original arbitration agreement, it may be possible to argue that there has been an "ad hoc" submission agreement[328] and/or that the other party is estopped from challenging jurisdiction as a result of an implied agreement to arbitrate.[329]

---

[324] See also para.2–004 above in relation to non-contractual causes of action.

[325] See para.2–037 above in relation to hybrid clauses.

[326] See, for example, *Plant v Plant* [2002] EWHC 2283 where it was held that the relevant clause was only applicable to disputes arising under specific provisions of a settlement agreement and did not apply to disputes generally under the agreement. See also *T&N Ltd v Royal & Sun Alliance Plc* [2004] Lloyd's Rep. 102.

[327] Section 73 of the Arbitration Act 1996, cf. Model Law, Art.4 (see Appendix 4) and see paras 5–065 and 8–065.

[328] See para.2–006.

[329] As in *Jones Engineering Services Ltd v Balfour Beatty Building Ltd* (1992) A.D.L.R.J. 133. This was also argued, without success in *Cia Maritima Zorrosa SA v Sesostris SAE, (The "Marques de Bolarque")* [1984] 1 Lloyd's Rep. 652 and *Allied Vision Ltd v VPS Film Entertainment GmbH* [1991] 1 Lloyd's Rep. 392. In both these cases there were reservations of the right to object to an arbitrator's jurisdiction which were not overridden by subsequent ad hoc submissions. See also *Almare Società di Navigazione SpA v Derby and Co Ltd (The "Almaea Prima")* [1989] 2 Lloyd's Rep. 376; *Jones v Balfour Beatty* (1992) A.D.L.R.J. 133 was distinguished in *MJ Gleeson Group Plc v Wyatt of Snetterton Ltd* (1994) 42 Con. L.R. 14. See also *Lesser Design & Build Ltd v University of Surrey* [1991] 56 B.L.R. 57. For implied agreements to arbitrate see para.2–016.

(c) Specific wordings

2-074   **Current position.** In *Fiona Trust & Holding Corp v Yuri Privalov*[330] the Court of Appeal reviewed the authorities on the meanings to be given to different formulations of arbitration agreement wordings. Longmore L.J., accepting that *"not all these authorities are readily reconcilable"*, went on to say[331]:

> "Hearings and judgments get longer as new authorities have to be considered. For our part we consider that the time has now come for a line of some sort to be drawn and a fresh start made at any rate for cases arising in an international commercial context. Ordinary business men would be surprised at the nice distinctions drawn in the cases and the time taken up by argument in debating whether a particular case falls within one set of words or another very similar set of words. If business men go to the trouble of agreeing that their disputes be heard in the courts of a particular country or by a tribunal of their choice they do not expect (at any rate when they are making the contract in the first place) that time and expense will be taken in lengthy argument about the nature of particular causes of action and whether any particular cause of action comes within the meaning of a particular phrase they have chosen in their arbitration clause."

The approach advocated by the Court of Appeal was that any jurisdiction or arbitration clause in an international commercial contract should be liberally construed. The words "arising out of" should cover every dispute except a dispute as to whether there was ever a contract at all. Although previously the words "arising under the contract" had sometimes been given a narrower meaning, that should no longer be so. The words "out of" and "under" should be widely construed.[331a] This approach was whole heartedly endorsed by the House of Lords in *Premium Nafta Products Ltd v Fili Shipping Co Ltd*.[331b]

2-075   **Broad interpretation favoured.** *Fiona Trust*[332] provided a welcome statement of principle from the Court of Appeal[332a] which has now been endorsed by the House of Lords in *Premium Nafta Products Ltd v Fili Shipping Co Ltd*.[333] It reflects what has tended to be a broad approach to the construction of arbitration clauses which has been prevalent since the coming into force of the Arbitration Act 1996. A recurring question is the extent to which tort claims fall within arbitration agreements contained in a contract.[334] Clearly they can do so, but there

---

[330] [2007] EWCA Civ 20.
[331] At [17].
[331a] At [18].
[331b] [2007] UKHL 40 at [12].
[332] [2007] EWCA Civ 20 at [17].
[332a] Subsequent decisions indicate the approach is well received: *Film Finance Inc v The Royal Bank of Scotland* [2007] EWHC 195; *Mabey and Johnson Ltd v Danos and others* [2007] EWHC 1094.
[333] [2007] UKHL 40.
[334] See for example *Empresa Exportadora de Azucar v Industria Azucarera Nacional SA (The "Playa Larga" and The "Marble Islands")* [1983] 2 Lloyd's Rep. 171; *The "Angelic Grace"* [1994] 1 Lloyd's Rep. 168; *Astro Vencedor Compania Naviera SA v Mabanaft GmbH* [1970] 2 Lloyd's Rep. 267; *Ulysses v Huntingdon* [1990] 1 Lloyd's Rep. 160.

was some authority that particular wording may not be sufficient to achieve that.[335] The tendency now is very much to treat claims based on other causes of action as within the tribunal's jurisdiction, particularly if they relate to the same facts as other contractual claims falling within the arbitration agreement. So, for example, in *Et Plus SA v Welter*[336] a clause submitting to arbitration "any potential disputes regarding the performance or the interpretation of this contract" was held to extend to tort claims, provided they were sufficiently connected to the performance or non-performance of the contract. Similarly in *Asghar v Legal Services Commission*[337] the relevant provision covered "disputes . . . concerning alleged breaches of this contract". Lightman J. held that the tort claims that were raised had "the closest possible connection with the contract and the rights and duties of the parties thereunder and at the very least critical issues in respect of each of those causes of action would be the subject of arbitration. The resolution of the contractual claims could not sensibly or practically be divorced for the resolution of the non-contractual claims."[338]

Standard wordings and court rulings. In light of the clear and   2–076
authoritative statements in *Fiona Trust & Holding Corp v Yuri Privalov*[339] and *Premium Nafta Products Ltd v Fili Shipping Co Ltd*[339a] it seems likely that the case law, and in particular some of the fine if not inconsistent distinctions,[340] that evolved as to the scope of what particular words or phrases refer to arbitration are now very likely to fall into disuse.[341] In any event it should be borne in mind that previous rulings are of limited assistance and should be treated with caution given the need to construe the particular arbitration agreement in question. As Evans J. said in *Overseas Union Insurers Ltd v AA Mutual International Insurance Co Ltd*[342]: "reported decisions in earlier cases, even of high authority, cannot necessarily be

---

[335] *Ashville Investments Ltd v Elmer Contractors Ltd* [1989] Q.B. 488 at 508; *Fillite (Runcorn) Ltd v Aqua-Lift (a firm)* [1989] 45 B.L.R. 27.
[336] [2006] 1 Lloyd's Rep. 251; [2005] EWHC 2115.
[337] [2004] EWHC 180.
[338] See generally para.2–004 above in relation to non-contractual claims.
[339] [2007] EWCA Civ 20.
[339a] [2007] UKHL 40.
[340] For example, in *Ashville Investments Ltd v Elmer Contractors Ltd* [1989] Q.B. 488 claims for mistake and misrepresentation were held to be covered by an arbitration agreement which referred "any matter or thing of whatsoever nature arising thereunder or in connection therewith" to arbitration. However, in *Fillite (Runcorn) Ltd v Aqua-Lift (a firm)* [1989] 45 B.L.R. 27, claims for misrepresentation and negligent misstatement were found not to be covered by an arbitration agreement which referred "any dispute or difference arising under these heads of agreement" to arbitration. There is no substantive difference in effect between a clause "thereunder" and "under" and so it was the expression "in connection therewith" as used in *Ashville v Elmer* which widened its scope. See also *Chimimport Plc v G D'Alesio SAS (The "Paola d'Alesio")* [1994] 2 Lloyd's Rep. 366 at 372.
[341] The Court of Appeal referred specifically to the international commercial context, but it is suggested that the same should apply in the domestic context. It must be doubtful whether businessmen in England would respond any differently from the their counterparts in the international context. Whilst there may be a greater awareness of the historical limitations of particular forms of wording the area has always been subject to some uncertainty and of course if particular claims are sought to be excluded from the scope of the arbitration agreement that can be achieved by express provision to that effect.
[342] [1988] 2 Lloyd's Rep. 63 at 66.

binding in later cases, unless exceptionally the relevant words and all the relevant circumstances are the same in both cases. Even then, the binding nature of the earlier decision would only become relevant if the Court in the later case, if unaided by authority, would reach a contrary conclusion as to the natural and proper meaning of the words in question." That said, it is perhaps premature to abandon entirely the guidance given, so the following paragraphs will address particular wordings albeit that the authorities referred to have now to be treated with considerable circumspection given the recent authorities referred to above.

2–077 **"All" or "any" differences, disputes or claims.** The most comprehensive forms of wording are those which refer to the decision of the tribunal each and every dispute between the parties by use of the words "all" or "any". This may be expressed by reference to the terms differences, disputes or claims.[343] An arbitration agreement referring "any dispute or difference" to arbitration was found wide enough to cover the effects of exceptional dislocation and delay notwithstanding that the disputes clause provided that they were to be assessed by mutual agreement. Once the parties had clearly agreed to differ about those issues they fell within the arbitration clause.[344]

2–078 **Disputes "arising out of" or "arising under" the contract.** As mentioned above,[345] the phrases "disputes arising under the contract" and "disputes arising out of the contract" were specifically considered by the Court of Appeal in *Fiona Trust*[346] who concluded that they should cover every dispute except a dispute as to whether there was ever a contract at all.[347] Although previously the words "arising under the contract" had sometimes been thought to have a narrower meaning, that should no longer be so.[348] The words "out of" and "under" should be widely construed.[349] Accordingly the earlier case law suggesting that a provision referring "disputes arising out of the contract" would not include claims for a contribution under the Civil Liability (Contribution) Act

---

[343] *Government of Gibraltar v Kenney* [1956] 2 Q.B. 410; *Re an arbitration between Hohenzollern Actien Gesellschaft fur Locomotivban and the City of London Contract Corp* (1886) 54 L.T. 596; *Ashville Investments Ltd v Elmer Contractors Ltd* [1989] Q.B. 488 at 508. See paras 5–003 *et seq.* for the significance of the terminology used.

[344] *Vosper Thorneycroft v Ministry of Defence* [1976] 1 Lloyd's Rep. 58.

[345] See para.2–074.

[346] [2007] EWCA Civ 20. See also *Premium Nafta Products Ltd v Fili Shipping Co Ltd* [2007] UKHL 40 which affirmed the Court of Appeal's decision.

[347] See *Mustill & Boyd* at 120 referred to in *Fiona Trust* and also in *Ethiopian Oilseeds & Pulses Export Corp v Rio Del Mar Foods Inc* [1990] 1 Lloyd's Rep. 86. See also *Fillite (Runcorn) Ltd v Aqua-Life (a firm)* [1989] 45 B.L.R. 27 where Nourse L.J. said at 44 that the preposition "under" presupposes that the noun which it governs has some existence, and therefore an arbitration clause with that wording cannot be used to question the contract's existence.

[348] In *Heyman v Darwins Ltd* [1942] A.C. 356 both Lord Wright (at 385) and Lord Porter (at 399) indicated that "arising out of" had a wider meaning than "arising under"; see also *Government of Gibraltar v Kenney* [1956] 2 Q.B. 410 at 421; *Chimimport v D'Alesio* [1994] 1 Lloyd's Rep. 366. Cf. *Union of India v EB Aaby's Rederi A/S (The "Evje")* [1975] A.C. 797 at 814 and 817; *Ulysses Compania Naviera SA v Huntingdon Petroleum Services Ltd (The "Ermoupolis")* [1990] 1 Lloyd's Rep. 160.

[349] See also *Mabey and Johnson Ltd v Danos and others* [2007] EWHC 1094.

1978[350] or that "disputes arising under the contract" would not cover rectification claims[351] would no longer seem to apply. The words "disputes arising out of" have generally been held to have a wide meaning[352] but the Court of Appeal's approach represents a shift towards a broader interpretation of the words "arising under of the contract".[353]

Disputes "in connection with", "in relation to", or "regard- 2–079
ing" a contract. These words, which are frequently encountered and are to be given the same meaning,[354] were at one time given a restricted interpretation,[355] but are now well established as having a broad meaning.[356] They have been held[357] to include claims for rectification of a contract,[358] as well as mistake and misrepresentation.[359] They may also be sufficient to catch disputes arising under another contract related to the contract containing the arbitration clause.[360]

Disputes "concerning alleged breaches of the contract". This 2–080
phrase was held not to be confined to causes of action for breach of contract but to include all disputes which have at their heart the issue of breach of contract including claims for conspiracy, misfeasance in public office and inducement to commit breach of contract.[361]

Disputes "with respect to the construction of". Where the arbitra- 2–081
tion agreement applies to disputes concerning "the construction" of a document

---

[350] *X Ltd v Y Ltd* [2005] B.L.R. 341. See para.6–111 for the tribunal's power to award a contribution.
[351] *Heyman v Darwins* [1942] A.C. 356; *Government of Gibraltar v Kenney* [1956] 2 Q.B. 410; *Crane v Hegeman-Harris Co Inc* [1939] 1 All E.R. 622; and *Ashville Investments Ltd v Elmer Contractors Ltd* [1989] Q.B. 488. The significance of these authorities was in any event doubtful given the statutory power, absent agreement otherwise, for tribunals to order rectification under s.48(5)(c) of the Arbitration Act 1996: see para.6–132 below.
[352] *Heyman v Darwins Ltd* [1942] A.C. 356; *Government of Gibraltar v Kenney* [1956] 2 Q.B. 410; *Kruse v Questier & Co Ltd* [1953] 1 Q.B. 669; *Mantovani v Carapelli SpA* [1978] 2 Lloyd's Rep. 63; *Empresa Exportadora de Azucar v Industria Azucarera Nacional SA (The "Playa Larga" and The "Marble Islands")* [1983] 2 Lloyd's Rep. 171; *Ethiopian Oilseeds & Pulses Export Corp v Rio Del Mar Foods Inc* [1990] 1 Lloyd's Rep. 86. For a recent example see *Capital Trust Investments Ltd v Radio Design TJ AB* [2002] 2 All E.R. 159.
[353] With regard to claims in tort see para.2–004 and para.2–075 above.
[354] *Et Plus SA v Welter* [2006] 1 Lloyd's Rep. 251.
[355] As in *Lawson v The Wallassey Local Board* (1882) 11 Q.B.D. 229, where "any difference . . . concerning anything in connection with this contract" was held not to cover a dispute about an implied term that certain other work on the site should not be delayed.
[356] *Woolf v Collis Removal Service* [1948] 1 K.B. 11; *A&B v C&D* [1982] 1 Lloyd's Rep. 166; *Jagger v Decca Music Group Ltd* [2004] EWHC 2542; *el Nasharty v J Sainsbury Plc* [2003] EWHC 2195; *Faghirzadeh v Rudolf Wolff* [1977] 1 Lloyd's Rep. 630 at 641.
[357] *Ashville Investments Ltd v Elmer Contractors Ltd* [1989] Q.B. 488.
[358] This remedy is now available in any event under s.48(5)(c) of the Arbitration Act 1996: see para.6–114.
[359] See the cases referred to at para.2–076.
[360] *A&B v C&D* [1989] 1 Q.B. 488.
[361] *Asghar v The Legal Services Commission* [2004] EWHC 1803 at [21].

this refers to the meaning or interpretation of the document.[362] That would not cover claims for rectification.[363] However in *Macepark (Whittlebury) Ltd v Sargeant (No.1)* case[364] it was held that the addition of the words "or effect" to "the construction" of a document did encompass a jurisdiction to deal with a claim for rectification. The court reasoned that the words "or effect" suggested something more was intended that just the meaning of the document and would include what it is the parties must do or not do under the document as a matter of substance, which would include rectification.

2–082   **Preference for wording in wide terms.** The preceding paragraphs demonstrate that in most cases the preferred course is to draft an arbitration agreement covering future disputes in the widest possible terms. Such a broad formula was used in *Government of Gibraltar v Kenney*[365]: "any dispute or difference which arises or occurs between the parties in relation to any thing or matter arising out of or under this agreement". The ICC recommended wording is "All disputes arising out of or in connection with the present contract shall be finally settled under the Rules of Arbitration . . . " The LCIA form is more explicit: "Any dispute arising out of or in connection with this contract, including any question regarding its existence, validity or termination, shall be referred to and finally resolved by arbitration . . . "

(d) Particular types of dispute

2–083   **Fraud.** Fraud claims can be within the scope of an arbitration agreement. Under previous legislation,[366] the court could revoke the authority of a tribunal to deal with claims involving issues of fraud and determine those claims itself. This provision has been repealed.[367]

2–084   **Consumers contracts.** Under earlier legislation[368] consumers were not always bound by their arbitration agreements. The provisions were unsatisfactory[369] and were found by the Court of Appeal to be contrary to Arts 6 and 59 of the Treaty of Rome because they discriminated against non-English parties by preventing them from having the same right that English parties had to treat the arbitration provisions as optional.[370] Consumer arbitration agreements are now dealt with in ss.89 to 91 of the Arbitration Act 1996 which give effect to the Unfair

---

[362] *Ashville Investments Ltd v Elmer Contractors Ltd* [1989] Q.B. 488 at 508; *Macepark (Whittlebury) Ltd v Sargeant (No.1)* [2002] W.L. 1876043, Ch D.
[363] *Macepark (Whittlebury) Ltd v Sargeant (No.1)* [2002] W.L. 1876043, Ch D.
[364] *Macepark (Whittlebury) Ltd v Sargeant (No.1)* [2002] W.L. 1876043, Ch D.
[365] [1956] 2 Q.B. 410.
[366] Section 24(2) of the Arbitration Act 1950.
[367] Section 107(2) of the Arbitration Act 1996.
[368] Consumer Arbitration Agreements Act 1988.
[369] See DAC report, paras 332 *et seq.*
[370] *Philip Alexander Securities and Futures Ltd v Bamberger: Same v Gilhaus* [1996] C.L.C. 1757.

Terms in Consumer Contracts Regulations 1999.[371] Under these provisions an arbitration agreement[372] where one of the parties is a consumer is unfair insofar as it relates to a claim for an amount which does not exceed a figure specified by statutory instrument, currently £5,000.[373] A consumer is a natural or legal person[374] who, in making a contract, is acting for purposes which are outside his trade, business or profession.[375] The effect of the arbitration agreement being unfair is that it cannot be enforced against the consumer. The rest of the contract continues to bind the parties, with litigation available for dispute resolution.[376] Sections 89 to 91 of the Arbitration Act 1996 apply whatever the law applicable to the arbitration agreement.[377]

Building and engineering disputes. Previous case law[378] suggested that arbitration agreements in building and engineering contracts gave arbitral tribunals wider jurisdiction in some respects than that of the court. This was said to arise from the drafting of arbitration clauses in standard form construction contracts which give the arbitrator power to "open up, review, and revise any certificate, opinion, decision, requisition or notice . . . and to determine all matters in dispute", a power that the court was said not to possess.[379] The House of Lords subsequently rejected this suggestion and a provision conferring this power upon the arbitrator is not to be construed as removing them from the court.[380]   2–085

Prior reference to engineer. In many standard form construction contracts, disputes are first decided upon by the engineer. Following that decision the dispute will in many cases then be referred to adjudication,[381] and thereafter to arbitration or litigation. The parties are not limited in the arguments they can put to the tribunal by not having raised the same points with the engineer.[382] However there is often a time limit within which the engineer's decision must be challenged, failing which it becomes binding, and if that time limit is not complied with the right to refer the matter to arbitration may be lost.[383]   2–086

---

[371] Section 89 refers to the Unfair Terms in Consumer Contracts Regulations 1994 including any regulations amending or replacing those regulations. The 1994 Regulations were indeed repealed and replaced by the 1999 Regulations.

[372] Consumer arbitration agreements are defined in s.89 of the Arbitration Act 1996 using slightly different wording from the definition in s.6(1) of the Arbitration Act 1996.

[373] Section 91 of the Arbitration Act 1996. SI 1999/2167 establishes the figure at £5,000.

[374] Section 90 of the Arbitration Act 1996.

[375] Regulation 3 of the Unfair Terms in Consumer Contracts Regulations (SI 1999/2083).

[376] Regulation 8(2) of the Unfair Terms in Consumer Contracts Regulations (SI 1999/2083).

[377] Section 89(3) of the Arbitration Act 1996.

[378] *Northern Regional Health Authority v Crouch (Derek) Construction Co Ltd* [1984] 1 Q.B. 644.

[379] *Northern Regional Health Authority v Crouch (Derek) Construction Co Ltd* [1984] 1 Q.B. 644.

[380] *Beaufort Developments (N.I.) Ltd v Gilbert-Ash (N.I.) Ltd* [1999] 1 A.C. 266.

[381] See para.2–032 above.

[382] *Mid Glamorgan County Council v Land Authority for Wales* [1990] 49 B.L.R. 61.

[383] *JT Mackley & Co Ltd v Gosport Marina Ltd* [2002] EWHC 1315 (TCC).

5. LAWS TO BE APPLIED TO AN ARBITRATION

(a) Introduction

2–087 **General.** In arbitrations between parties in England and Wales the issue of the choice of law to be applied does not usually arise. Unless there is some other provision,[384] the arbitration will be subject in all respects to English law. However the issue does arise in every international arbitration and can be of fundamental importance, because:

- the parties are free to choose the applicable laws, whether they make an express choice or provide how the laws are to be chosen;

- different laws can operate simultaneously on different aspects of the arbitration;

- if the parties fail to make express choices and/or fail to make clear how the laws are to be chosen the matter will usually have to be investigated in the course of the arbitration, and

- the result of that determination can have a radical effect on the outcome of the dispute.

2–088 **Different laws applicable.** It is possible for several different laws to apply to a dispute referred to arbitration. First, there is the law governing the substance of the dispute. Where the dispute concerns the performance of obligations under a matrix contract, this will usually be the "governing law" or the "proper law of the contract".[385] Secondly, there is the law of the arbitration agreement which governs the obligation to submit disputes to arbitration and to honour any award.[386] Thirdly, there is the procedural law which is the law governing the conduct of the arbitration, also known as the curial law or *lex arbitri*.[387] These three are perhaps the most commonly encountered laws applicable in the context of an arbitration, but there are others that may be relevant including the law of the particular reference to arbitration,[388] the law applicable to the capacity of the

---

[384] For example where the parties have chosen to have their dispute determined under a different law or in accordance with some other considerations than English law pursuant to s.46(1) of the Arbitration Act 1996.

[385] See paras 2–092 *et seq.* below.

[386] *Union of India v McDonnell Douglas Corp* [1993] 2 Lloyd's Rep. 48.

[387] This book will refer to the law governing the conduct of the reference as the procedural law, as this perhaps conveys most clearly the nature of what is being discussed. Strictly speaking however the concept of curial law is more accurate because, as explained in *Dubai Islamic Bank PJSC v Paymentech Merchant Services Inc* [2001] 1 Lloyd's Rep. 65 at 71 the 1996 Act uses the concept of seat rather than procedural law to determine when the provisions of Pt 1 apply.

[388] See para.2–099 below. In practice this is almost always the same as the law governing the arbitration agreement, or, possibly, where it differs from the law of the arbitration agreement, the curial law.

parties to enter into the reference,[389] the law of any place other than the seat where hearings in the arbitration are to take place,[390] the law of the place or places where recognition and enforcement will be sought[391] and the law applicable to any compromise of the dispute.[392]

Interplay of the different laws. The substantive rights and obligations of   2–089
the parties have to be determined according to the rules[393] governing the substance
of the dispute. Where the dispute is contractual this will usually be the proper law
of the contract. If the claim is based on some other cause of action then the
applicable law may need to be ascertained on a different basis.[394] The arbitration
agreement often forms part of a matrix contract and will often, but not always,[395]
be governed by the same law.[396] This may be significant if, for example, the
arbitration agreement is valid according to the law which is alleged to govern it but
not under the proper law of the contract.[397] The arbitration proceedings themselves are regulated by the procedural law, which governs matters of procedure in
the conduct of the reference and may for example deny one of the parties a remedy
which would have been available under the proper law of the matrix contract. The
procedural law will usually be that of the seat of arbitration unless for example the
parties have expressly chosen a different law.[398]

(b) The rules governing the substance of the dispute

Statutory Provision. The substance of the dispute is to be determined in   2–090
accordance with the law chosen by the parties as applicable to the substance of the

---

[389] Questions of capacity to enter into an arbitration agreement will usually be determined, in the case of an individual, by the law of his domicile or, in the context of an international contract, the proper law of the contract. In the case of a corporate entity they will usually be governed by the law of the place of incorporation, although again the proper law of the contract may be relevant in the international context: see *Redfern & Hunter*, paras 3–025 to 3–029. See also para.3–003 below.

[390] See para.2–107 below.

[391] See para.2–109 below.

[392] *Halpern v Halpern* [2006] EWHC 603, which confirmed at [64] that the Rome Convention will apply in determining the law applicable to any compromise of the dispute.

[393] The term "rules" is used as the parties may adopt rules which are not the laws of a country: see para.2–091 below.

[394] The reader is referred generally to *Dicey & Morris* and in particular to Ch.34 in relation to claims in restitution and Ch.35 in relation to tort claims.

[395] See for example *C v D* [2007] EWHC 1541, where the matrix contract was governed by New York law but the arbitration agreement by English law, and *Tamil Nadu Electricity Board v ST-CMS Electric Co Private Ltd* [2007] EWHC 1713, where the matrix contract was governed by Indian law but the arbitration agreement by English law.

[396] *Sonatrach Petroleum Corp v Ferrell International Ltd* [2002] 1 All E.R. (Comm) 627.

[397] See for example *XL Insurance Ltd v Owens Corning* [2000] 2 Lloyd's Rep. 500.

[398] Whilst it is possible to do so, this course adds a layer of complication as regards the interplay of those laws as interpreted by the courts of each jurisdiction and is therefore to be avoided.

dispute[399] or, if they so agree, in accordance with such other considerations as are agreed by them or determined by the tribunal.[400] Absent such choice or agreement, the tribunal has to apply the law determined by the conflict of laws rules it considers applicable.[401]

2–091 **Other considerations.** The 1996 Act brought English law into line with the approach in many other jurisdictions by permitting the parties to choose to have their dispute resolved by considerations other than the rules of a particular national law.[402] It is now clear that if the parties choose to have the tribunal decide the dispute *"ex aequo et bono"* or as an *"amiable compositeur"* or on the basis of non-national law principles or indeed on the basis of any other considerations, that choice will be binding so long as it is ascertainable.

2–092 **Absence of choice or agreement on rules governing the substance of the dispute.** As mentioned above, where the parties have neither chosen a law nor agreed other considerations to govern the substance of their dispute, the tribunal has to apply the law determined by the conflict of laws rules it considers applicable.[403] That will usually involve determining the law using the conflict of law rules of the seat of arbitration,[404] but the 1996 Act does not inhibit the tribunal's choice in this regard. If the arbitration is being conducted under a set of institutional or other rules they may indicate how the tribunal is to determine the applicable law.[404a] Under English law, the rules applicable to the determination of the proper law of a contract are those set out in the Rome Convention on the Law Applicable to Contractual Obligations.[405] The Rome Convention was given effect in England by the Contracts (Applicable Law) Act 1990.[406] While the Rome Convention rules do not apply to arbitration agreements,[407] they do apply to the determination of the proper law of the matrix contract.[408] The rules of the Rome Convention apply whenever there is a choice to be made between the laws of different countries, even if the parties and the laws

---

[399] Excluding the conflict of laws provisions: see s.46(2) of the Arbitration Act 1996.
[400] Section 46(1) of the Arbitration Act 1996.
[401] Section 46(3) of the Arbitration Act 1996.
[402] Section 46(1) of the Arbitration Act 1996; *Halpern v Halpern* [2007] EWCA Civ 291 at [37]–[38].
[403] Section 46(3) of the Arbitration Act 1996.
[404] *CGU International Insurance Plc v Astrazeneca Insurance Co Ltd* [2006] C.L.C. 162.
[404a] See, for example, Art.17 of the ICC Rules.
[405] The Rome Convention was opened for signature in Rome on June 19, 1980 and signed by the United Kingdom on December 7, 1981. There are some exceptions to its application: see Contracts (Applicable Law) Act 1990, Sch.1: Rome Convention, Art.1.2.
[406] For contracts made after April 1, 1991. The statute gives effect not just to the Rome Convention but also to the Luxembourg Convention, the Brussels Protocol and the Funchal Convention. Amendments are pending which will add also the 1996 Accession Convention.
[407] Contracts (Applicable Law) Act 1990, Sch.1: Rome Convention, Art.1.2(d).
[408] See *Dicey & Morris*, para.32–036.

concerned are those of countries which are not signatories to the Rome Convention.[409] Essentially the Rome Convention provides that where the parties have not chosen an applicable law a contract is governed by the law of the country with which it is most closely connected.[410]

Effect of seat on choice of proper law of contract. Under the 2–093 Contracts (Applicable Law) Act 1990, the selection of a seat of arbitration may be regarded as an implied choice of a proper law for the substantive contract in appropriate circumstances. The requirement in Art.3(1) of the Rome Convention is that the choice of law by the parties must be "express or demonstrated with reasonable certainty".[411] Previously the choice of a seat was given considerable weight as an indication of the proper law of the contract.[412] Now the test is whether it is sufficient to demonstrate the choice with reasonable certainty. It has been held that a standard form contract which stipulated London as the seat if, as was the case, the parties failed to agree on a seat, demonstrated the choice of English law with reasonable certainty.[413] Provisions stipulating for arbitration by a local arbitral tribunal or institution, or, for example, for the appointment of an arbitrator by the English High Court, may strengthen the inference. However, the inference to be drawn from the choice of seat may be weaker where arbitration is to be under the auspices of an international arbitral institution such as the ICC, because the appointment of a tribunal is effected by the institution and is therefore less connected with the seat.[414] Where the parties make an ad hoc submission to arbitration with no express choice of proper law applicable to the substance of the dispute, following an arbitration agreement with an express choice, the fact of the original choice will not be conclusive as to the proper law to be applied in the later submission.[415]

---

[409] Article 1(1) of the Rome Convention.
[410] Contracts (Applicable Law) Act 1990, Sch.1: Rome Convention, Art.4.1.
[411] Contracts (Applicable Law) Act 1990, Sch.1: Rome Convention, Art.3.1. See also *Dicey & Morris*, para.32–094.
[412] *Compagnie d'Armement Maritime SA v Cie Tunisienne de Navigation SA* [1971] A.C. 572; *Bangladesh Chemical Industries Corp v Henry Stephens Shipping Co Ltd and Tex-Dilan Shipping Co Ltd (The "SLS Everest")* [1981] 2 Lloyd's Rep. 389; *Compania Naviera Micro SA v Shipley International Inc (The "Parouth")* [1982] 2 Lloyd's Rep. 351, CA; *Astro Venturoso Compania Naviera v Hellenic Shipyards SA (The "Marianina")* [1983] 1 Lloyd's Rep. 12, CA; *Steel Authority of India Ltd v Hind Metals Inc* [1984] 1 Lloyd's Rep. 405; *Ilyssia Compania Naviera SA v Ahmed-Qawi Bamodah (The "Elli 2")* [1985] 1 Lloyd's Rep. 107, CA; cf. *Atlantic Underwriting Agencies Ltd v Compagnia di Assicuranzione di Milano* [1979] 2 Lloyd's Rep. 240; *James Miller & Partners Ltd v Whitworth Street Estates (Manchester) Ltd* [1970] A.C. 583; *Mitsubishi Corp v Castletown Navigation Ltd (The "Castle Alpha")* [1989] 2 Lloyd's Rep. 383. See also D. Rhidian Thomas, "Commercial Arbitration Agreements as a Signpost of the Proper Law", (1984) L.M.C.L.Q. 141.
[413] *Egon Oldendorff v Libera Corp No.2* [1996] 1 Lloyd's Rep. 380.
[414] See *Dicey & Morris*, para.32–096. No inference as to the proper law to be applied can be drawn where the place of arbitration is to be selected by a third party such as the ICC Court of Arbitration or where the arbitration clause contemplates alternative places of arbitration: see *Star Shipping AS v China National Foreign Trade Transportation Corp (The "Star Texas")* [1993] 2 Lloyd's Rep. 445.
[415] A particularly confused situation discussed in *Furness Withy (Australia) Pty Ltd v Metal Distributors (UK) Ltd (The "Amazonia")* [1990] 1 Lloyd's Rep. 236.

(c) The law of the arbitration agreement

2–094   **Choice of law rules applicable to the arbitration agreement.**
The Arbitration Act 1996 gives guidance on both the rules applicable to the
substance of the dispute and on ascertaining the seat of arbitration,[416] but it does
not address the determination of the law applicable to the arbitration agreement.
It is not therefore entirely clear what choice of law rules should be applied.[417] The
Rome Convention provides choice of law rules for contracts generally, but it does
not apply to arbitration agreements.[418] It has been suggested[419] that the New York
Convention gives an indication of the applicable choice of law rules by providing
that recognition or enforcement of an award may be refused if "the arbitration
agreement was not valid under the law to which the parties subjected it or, failing
any indication thereon, under the law of the country where the award was
made".[420]

2–095   **The law of the arbitration agreement.** As a matter of English law
however the arbitration agreement will be governed by the law chosen by the
parties.[421] Where the arbitration agreement is contained in a matrix contract, the
law of the arbitration agreement will often follow the proper law of that matrix
contract.[422] However an arbitration agreement is separable[423] from the matrix
contract between the parties, and an arbitration agreement may be subject to a
different law from that of the matrix contract in which it is contained.[424] Not only
may the parties choose different laws for the matrix agreement and the arbitration
agreement, other factors may indicate that different laws should apply.[425] Within
the arbitration agreement itself it is also open to the parties to specify a procedural
law for the arbitration which is different from the law governing the arbitration
agreement and, again, other factors may indicate that different laws should

---

[416] Sections 46 and 3 of the Arbitration Act 1996 respectively.
[417] In *Halpern v Halpern* [2006] EWHC 603 it was suggested at [52] that common law principles
    applied. The case went to the Court of Appeal at [2007] EWCA Civ 291 but they dealt with the case
    as one requiring determination of the applicable law of the compromise agreement in question to
    which the Rome Convention applied.
[418] Contracts (Applicable Law) Act 1990, Sch.1: Rome Convention, Art.1.2(d).
[419] *Dicey & Morris*, para.16–014.
[420] This provision appears as s.103(2)(b) of the Arbitration Act 1996.
[421] *Naviera Amazonica Peruana SA v Compania Internacional de Seguros del Peru* [1988] 1 Lloyd's Rep.
    116; *Tamil Nadu Electricity Board v ST-CMS Electric Co Private Ltd* [2007] EWHC 1713.
[422] *ABB Lummus Global Ltd v Keppel Fels Ltd* [1999] 2 Lloyd's Rep. 24; *Sonatrach Petroleum Corp v
    Ferrell International Ltd* [2002] 1 All E.R. (Comm) 627; *Tonicstar Ltd (t/a Lloyd's Syndicate 1861)
    v American Home Assurance Co* [2005] Lloyd's Rep. 32; *Svenska Petroleum Exploration AB v
    Lithuania (No.2)* [2006] 1 Lloyd's Rep. 181. For the law applicable to an arbitration agreement
    formed pursuant to the provisions of an investment treaty see *Republic of Ecuador v Occidental
    Exploration and Production Co* [2006] 2 W.L.R. 70.
[423] Unless otherwise agreed by the parties, s.7 of the Arbitration Act 1996: see para.2–007 above.
[424] *Black-Clawson International Ltd v Papierwerke Waldhof-Aschaffenburg AG* [1981] 2 Lloyd's Rep. 446
    at 453; *Naviera Amazonica Peruana SA v Cia Internacional de Seguros del Peru* [1988] 1 Lloyd's Rep.
    116 at 119; *Sumitomo Heavy Industries Ltd v Oil and Natural Gas Commission* [1994] 1 Lloyd's Rep.
    45 at 57; *Channel Tunnel Group Ltd v Balfour Beatty Construction Ltd* [1993] A.C. 334 at 357;
    Sonatrach Petroleum Corp v Ferrell International Ltd [2002] 1 All E.R. (Comm) 627; *XL Insurance
    Ltd v Owens Corning* [2000] 2 Lloyd's Rep. 500; *C v D* [2007] EWHC 1541; *Tamil Nadu Electricity
    Board v ST-CMS Electric Co Private Ltd* [2007] EWHC 1713.
[425] *XL Insurance Ltd v Owens Corning* [2000] 2 Lloyd's Rep. 500; *C v D* [2007] EWHC 1541.

apply.[426] In particular, ad hoc submission agreements drawn up after disputes have arisen do not form part of any matrix contract, and there may be less reason to imply that the same law is applicable to the arbitration agreement as to the underlying contract in respect of which disputes have arisen. Where the parties have made no specific choice of law for the arbitration agreement, the applicable law may be the law of the country where enforcement is sought under the New York Convention.[427]

Effect of seat on the law of the arbitration agreement. Where   2–096
there is no express choice of a proper law of the matrix contract nor of the arbitration agreement, but the seat of the arbitration is specified, the law of that place may govern both the matrix contract[428] and the arbitration agreement.[429] Indeed express reference to the law of the seat may determine the law of the arbitration agreement even if there is a different proper law of the contract.[430]

Matters covered by the law of the arbitration agreement. The   2–097
law of the arbitration agreement regulates substantive matters relating to that agreement,[431] including in particular the interpretation, validity, effect and discharge of the agreement to arbitrate.[432] It also governs the identification of the parties to the arbitration agreement.[433] The law of the arbitration agreement also governs similar issues relating to the reference and enforcement of the award.[434] An issue as to whether a particular dispute falls within the scope of an arbitration agreement will therefore be governed by the law of the arbitration agreement.[435]

---

[426] *Black-Clawson International Ltd v Papierwerke Waldhof-Aschaffenburg AG* [1981] 2 Lloyd's Rep. 446; *Naviera Amazonica Peruana SA v Cia Internacional de Seguros del Peru* [1988] 1 Lloyd's Rep. 116 at 119, CA; *Deutsche Schachtbau-und Tiefbohr-Gesellschaft GmbH v Shell International Petroleum Co Ltd (Trading as Shell International Trading Co)* [1990] 1 A.C. 295 at 309–310, CA, reversed on other grounds at 329; *Channel Tunnel Group Ltd v Balfour Beatty Construction Ltd* [1993] A.C. 334 at 357.

[427] Section 5(2)(b) of the Arbitration Act 1975, now re-enacted as s.100 of the Arbitration Act 1996, explained by Steyn L.J. (as he then was) in *Star Shipping AS v China National Foreign Trade Transportation Corp (The "Star Texas")* [1993] 2 Lloyd's Rep. 445 at 450.

[428] See para.2–093 above.

[429] Particularly where the law of the arbitration agreement follows that of the matrix contract: see *Sonatrach Petroleum Corp v Ferrell International Ltd* [2002] 1 All E.R. (Comm) 627.

[430] *XL Insurance Ltd v Owens Corning* [2000] 2 Lloyd's Rep. 500; *C v D* [2007] EWHC 1541.

[431] See *Heavy Industries Ltd v Oil and Natural Gas Commission* [1994] 1 Lloyd's Rep. 45, in which Potter J. stated (at 57) that the proper law of the arbitration agreement covered, inter alia, "questions as to the validity of the arbitration agreement, the validity of the notice of arbitration, the constitution of the tribunal and the question whether an award lies within the jurisdiction of the arbitrator".

[432] *Dalmia Dairy Industries Ltd v National Bank of Pakistan* [1978] 2 Lloyd's Rep. 223; *Black-Clawson International Ltd v Papierwerke Waldhof-Aschaffenburg AG* [1981] 2 Lloyd's Rep. 446; *XL Insurance Ltd v Owens Corning* [2000] 2 Lloyd's Rep. 500; *Svenska Petroleum Exploration AB v Lithuania (No.2)* [2006] 1 Lloyd's Rep. 181; *Weissfisch v Julius* [2006] EWCA Civ 218.

[433] *Petersen Farms Inc v C&M Farming Ltd* [2004] EWHC 121; [2004] 1 Lloyd's Rep. 603.

[434] It is an implied term of the arbitration agreement that the parties will perform the award: see para.6–163 below. See also *C v D* [2007] EWHC 1541; *Tamil Nadu Electricity Board v ST-CMS Electric Co Private Ltd* 2007 EWHC 1713.

[435] *Nova (Jersey) Knit Ltd v Kammgarn Spinnerei* [1977] 1 W.L.R. 713, HL; *Dalmia Dairy Industries Ltd v National Bank of Pakistan* [1978] 1 Lloyd's Rep. 223, CA; *The "Marques de Bolarque"* [1984] 1 Lloyd's Rep. 652 at 660; *Et Plus SA v Welter* [2006] 1 Lloyd's Rep. 251; *Abu Dhabi Investment Co v H Clarkson & Co Ltd* [2007] EWHC 1267.

2–098   **Distinguishing law of the arbitration agreement and procedural law.** A distinction has to be drawn between, on the one hand, substantive matters relating to the arbitration agreement which are governed by the law of the arbitration agreement and, on the other hand, procedural matters relating to a reference under that agreement which are governed by the procedural law of the arbitration. In the past the court has been driven to conclude that matters which would generally be considered procedural, such as the granting of an extension of time for the bringing of an arbitration, were subject to the law governing the arbitration agreement.[436] The position is now considerably clearer under Pt I of the Arbitration Act 1996 which provides guidance as to the matters governed by the procedural law.[437]

2–099   **The law of the reference.** Mention is sometimes made of a "proper law of the reference".[438] This is based on there being a separate agreement to arbitrate the particular dispute. The reference therefore arises from an agreement subsidiary to but separate from the arbitration agreement itself, and the agreement comes into effect by the reference of a particular dispute or disputes to arbitration. At this stage a new set of mutual obligations arises in relation to the conduct of the reference.[439] The proper law of the reference is said to govern the question of whether the parties have been discharged from the obligation to continue with the particular reference (while leaving intact the arbitration agreement to refer future disputes). The proper law of the reference will almost always be the same as the proper law of the arbitration agreement.[440]

(d) The "seat" of the arbitration and the procedural law

2–100   **The "seat" or place of arbitration.**[441] In England it is essential for an arbitration to have a "seat",[442] which is the geographical location to which the arbitration is ultimately tied. English law does not recognise the concept of

---

[436] *International Tank and Pipe SAK v Kuwait Aviation Fuelling Co KSC* [1975] Q.B. 224. See also *CM van Stillevoldt BV v El Carriers Inc, The Times,* July 8, 1982; *Mitsubishi Corp v Castletown Navigation Ltd (The "Castle Alpha")* [1989] 2 Lloyd's Rep. 383.

[437] See para.2–106 below.

[438] See, e.g. *Sumitomo Heavy Industries Ltd v Oil and Natural Gas Commission* [1994] 1 Lloyd's Rep. 45 at 57; and *C v D* [2007] EWHC 1541 where it was referred to as the agreement to refer.

[439] *Sumitomo Heavy Industries Ltd v Oil and Natural Gas Commission* [1994] 1 Lloyd's Rep. 45 at 57; *Bremer Vulcan Schiffbau und Maschinenfabrik v South India Shipping Corp* [1981] 1 Lloyd's Rep. 253 at 263; *Black-Clawson International Ltd v Papierwerk Waldhof-Aschaffenburg AG* [1981] 2 Lloyd's Rep. 446.

[440] *Sumitomo Heavy Industries Ltd v Oil and Natural Gas Commission* [1994] 1 Lloyd's Rep. 45 at 57.

[441] See para.5–071.

[442] *Naviera Amazonica Peruana v Cia Internacional de Seguros del Peru* [1988] 1 Lloyd's Rep. 116; *Dubai Islamic Bank PJSC v Paymentech Merchant Services Inc* [2001] 1 Lloyd's Rep. 65.

"delocalised" arbitral procedures which are "floating in the transnational firmament", unconnected with any national system of law.[443] Section 3 of the Arbitration Act 1996 defines the seat of an arbitration as its "juridical seat", which is the place to which it is legally attached. As the seat is the legal, rather than the physical, place of arbitration proceedings,[444] hearings can be held in other jurisdictions.[445] The seat of the arbitration is often specified in the arbitration agreement by the selection of a particular place or country in which the arbitration is to be held. In the absence of a clear indication to the contrary, there is a strong presumption that the place where the arbitration is to take place will constitute its seat.[446] The expression "seat" is often used to refer to the particular city chosen, rather than the country (for example, "arbitration in London") and while the parties' agreement is on a city, the crucial choice is of the jurisdiction in which the city is located.[447]

Choice of seat. The parties are free to choose a seat.[448] Under English law the   2–101
procedural law of an arbitration is generally the law of the country in which the arbitration has its seat (and vice versa).[449] So in the absence of agreement otherwise,[450] the choice of seat prescribes the procedural law of the arbitration and the choice of a procedural law will determine the seat. The parties' choice of a seat is therefore extremely important,[451] not simply in relation to the proper law of the contract,[452] but also because the law of the seat may contain provisions which have important consequences for the conduct of the proceedings.[453] Indeed, most provisions of the Arbitration Act 1996 will only apply to arbitrations whose seat is in England and Wales or Northern Ireland.[454]

Ascertaining the seat. If the seat has not been agreed on by the parties,   2–102
either expressly or by the choice of a procedural law, the matter may fall to be

---

[443] *Bank Mellat v Helliniki Techniki SA* [1984] 1 Q.B. 291 at 301; *Arab National Bank v El-Abdali* [2004] EWHC 2381. See also Sir Michael Mustill, "Transnational Arbitration and English Law", Current Legal Problems (Stevens, 1984), pp.133–152. The exception is arbitrations conducted pursuant to the ICSID arbitration rules. Awards of such arbitrations are enforceable in England under the ICSID Convention.

[444] *Union of India v McDonnell Douglas Corp* [1993] 2 Lloyd's Rep. 48.

[445] See para.2–107.

[446] *Channel Tunnel Group Ltd v Balfour Beatty Construction Ltd* [1993] A.C. 334; *Halpern v Halpern* [2006] EWHC 603.

[447] *Tongyuan (USA) International Trading Group v Uni-clan Ltd* [2001] W.L. 98036.

[448] Section 3(a) of the Arbitration Act 1996.

[449] *Naviera Amazonica Peruana SA v Compania Internacional de Seguros del Peru* [1988] 1 Lloyd's Rep. 116; *ABB Lummus Global Ltd v Keppel Fels Ltd* [1999] 2 Lloyd's Rep. 24; *Arab National Bank v El-Abdali* [2004] EWHC 2381; *C v D* [2007] EWHC 1541.

[450] Even if the parties agree on a different procedural law, the mandatory provisions of the law of the seat will apply: see para.2–103 below.

[451] See further para.5–072 below.

[452] See paras 2–093 *et seq.*

[453] e.g. provisions prescribing the degree of intervention by the court in the arbitral process. See further para.2–106 below.

[454] Section 2(1) of the Arbitration Act 1996 applies Pt I of the statute to arbitrations in England and Wales or Northern Ireland. The remaining subsections set out particular provisions that apply, or may apply, even if the seat is outside those countries or has not been designated.

resolved by an arbitration institution or some other person the parties have agreed should have the power to designate the seat,[455] or by the tribunal if authorised to do so.[456] If the parties have agreed that a set of arbitration rules are to apply they may contain a means of establishing the seat of arbitration in the absence of express agreement by the parties.[457] In all other cases it is necessary to look at the parties' agreement and all the relevant circumstances.[458] Provision in an arbitration agreement stipulating for arbitration by a local tribunal or institution may indicate the appropriate place of arbitration.[459] If the arbitration agreement is silent as to the seat of the arbitration and the applicable procedural law, but does specify a governing law, that law may apply as the procedural law and serve to determine the seat of the arbitration.[460]

2–103 **Procedural law different from law of seat?** The procedural law of the arbitration may be, and often is, different from the proper law of the matrix contract and the proper law of the arbitration agreement.[461] Though undesirable it is also possible for the parties to choose to hold an arbitration in one country but make it subject to the procedural laws of another country.[462] The Arbitration Act 1996 specifically recognises that the parties may choose a different procedural law where the seat of the arbitration is in England.[463] Where they do so, that law will apply as an agreement made by the parties in respect of the non-mandatory provisions of the 1996 Act.[464] The mandatory provisions of the of the Arbitration Act 1996 will still apply however, regardless of what the chosen procedural law says, as they cannot be excluded in respect of arbitrations whose seat is in England.[465] This gives rise to the unattractive prospect of a reference being

---

[455] Section 3(b) of the Arbitration Act 1996 acknowledges the possibility of the seat being designated by an arbitral or other institution or person.

[456] Section 3(c) of the Arbitration Act 1996; see also *Dubai Islamic Bank PJSC v Paymentech Merchant Services Inc* [2001] 1 Lloyd's Rep. 65. In *Arab National Bank v El-Abdali* [2004] EWHC 2381 it was held that s.3(c) of the Arbitration Act 1996 applies even where a party takes issue with the tribunal's authority to act in the arbitration.

[457] See, e.g. ICC Rules, Art.14.1, LCIA Rules, Art.16, UNCITRAL Rules, Art.16.

[458] Section 3 of the Arbitration Act 1996. See *Arab National Bank v El-Abdali* [2004] EWHC 2381 for an example of the court determining the seat on the basis of all the relevant circumstances.

[459] *Whitworth Street Estates (Manchester) Ltd v James Miller & Partners Ltd* [1970] A.C. 583 at 607, 612, 616; *Bank Mellat v Helliniki Techniki SA* [1984] Q.B. 291 at 301; *Naviera Amazonica Peruana SA v Cia Internacional de Seguros del Peru* [1988] 1 Lloyd's Rep. 116 at 119; *Sumitomo Heavy Industries Ltd v Oil and Natural Gas* [1994] 1 Lloyd's Rep. 45 at 56–59.

[460] *Egon Oldendorff v Libera Corp* [1995] 2 Lloyd's Rep. 64; *The Bay Hotel and Resort Ltd v Cavalier Construction Co Ltd* [2001] UKPC 34.

[461] *Union of India v McDonnell Douglas Corp* [1993] 2 Lloyd's Rep. 48 at 50, and s.3(a) of the Arbitration Act 1996. See also s.34(2)(a) of the Arbitration Act 1996 and para.5–072.

[462] *Black-Clawson International Ltd v Papierwerke Waldhof-Aschaffenburg AG* [1981] 2 Lloyd's Rep. 446 at 453; *Naviera Amazonica Peruana SA v Compania Internacional de Seguros del Peru* [1988] 1 Lloyd's Rep. 116 at 120; *Union of India v McDonnell Douglas* [1993] 1 Lloyd's Rep. 48 at 50–51; *ABB Lummus Global Ltd v Keppel Fels Ltd* [1999] 2 Lloyd's Rep. 24.

[463] Section 4(5) of the Arbitration Act 1996. The choice of a law applicable to the substance of the dispute will not be sufficient for the purposes of s.4(5): *Lesotho Highlands Development Authority v Impreglio SpA* [2005] UKHL 43 at [37]; *C v D* [2007] EWHC 1541 at [38]; *XL Insurance Ltd v Owens Corning* [2000] 2 Lloyd's Rep. 500 at 508.

[464] Section 4(2) and (5) of the Arbitration Act 1996.

[465] Mandatory provisions apply: see ss.2(1), 4(1) of and Sch.1 to the Arbitration Act 1996.

governed by two procedural laws: that of the seat of the arbitration in so far as its provisions are mandatory (England) and that of the parties' express choice.[466]

Floating seat/procedural law possible. The procedural law of the   2–104
arbitration may be determined only after the reference has been initiated.[467] So whilst a "floating" proper law of a contract is not permissible as a matter of English law,[468] a "floating" seat is allowed, even if they are contained in the same provision.[469]

Brussels Regulation and Brussels and Lugano Conventions   2–105
do not apply. When considering procedural remedies under English law, it should be borne in mind that arbitration is excluded from the scope of the Brussels Regulation and the Brussels and Lugano Conventions on jurisdiction and enforcement of judgments in civil and commercial matters.[470] The Conventions also do not generally apply to court proceedings ancillary to arbitration proceedings[471] although they can apply to the jurisdiction of the court to order provisional measures in support of arbitration proceedings.[472] The precise scope of the exclusion has however been a matter of some uncertainty[473] but the test seems to be whether the, or perhaps a, principal focus of the proceedings is arbitration.[474]

---

[466] *Union of India v McDonnell Douglas Corp* [1993] 2 Lloyd's Rep. 48 at 51.

[467] *Star Shipping AS v China National Foreign Trade Transportation Corp (The "Star Texas")* [1993] 2 Lloyd's Rep. 445, CA. See also, *EJR Lovelock Ltd v Exportles* [1968] 1 Lloyd's Rep. 163.

[468] *Armar Shipping Co Ltd v Caisse Algerienne* [1981] 1 All E.R. 498; *The "Iran Vojdan"* [1984] 2 Lloyd's Rep. 380; *Sonatrach Petroleum Corp v Ferrell International Ltd* [2002] 1 All E.R. (Comm) 627.

[469] *Sonatrach Petroleum Corp v Ferrell International Ltd* [2002] 1 All E.R. (Comm) 627; cf. *The "Iran Vojdan"* [1984] 2 Lloyd's Rep. 380.

[470] Article 1 of each convention. The conventions were given effect in English law by the Civil Jurisdiction and Judgments Acts 1982 and 1991—see generally Ch.11 of *Dicey & Morris*.

[471] e.g. proceedings to set aside or enforce arbitration awards, or to appoint or dismiss arbitrators, and even where proceedings involve the question of the existence or validity of an arbitration agreement: *Marc Rich & Co AG v Societa Italiana Impianti PA (The "Atlantic Emperor")* [1992] 1 Lloyd's Rep. 342, ECJ; *Allied Vision Ltd v VPS Entertainment GmbH* [1991] 1 Lloyd's Rep. 392; *Marc Rich & Co AG v Societa Italiana Impianti PA (No.2) (The "Atlantic Emperor")* [1992] 1 Lloyd's Rep. 624, CA. See also Audit (1993) 9 Arbitration Int. 1; Kaye (1993) 9 Arbitration Int. 27; Volkovittsch (1993) 2 American Review of International Arbitration 501.

[472] *Van Uden Maritime BV v Deco-Line* [1999] 2 W.L.R. 1181. In relation to anti-suit injunctions see *Navigation Maritime Bulgaria v Rustal Trading (The "Ivan Zagubanski")* [2002] 1 Lloyd's Rep. 106; cf. *West Tankers Inc v RAS Riunione Adriatica di Sicurta SpA and Others* [2007] UKHL 4 and see further paras 7–012 *et seq.* and 7–184.

[473] *The "Heidberg"* [1994] 2 Lloyd's Rep. 287; *The "Angelic Grace"* [1994] 1 Lloyd's Rep. 168; *The "Xing Su Hai"* [1995] 2 Lloyd's Rep. 15; *Toepfer International GmbH v Molino Boschi Srl* [1996] 1 Lloyd's Rep. 510; *Lexmar Corp and Steamship Mutual Underwriting Association (Bermuda) Ltd v Nordisk Skibsrederforening and Northern Tankers (Cyprus) Ltd* [1997] 1 Lloyd's Rep. 289; *Toepfer International GmbH v Société Cargill France* [1998] 1 Lloyd's Rep. 379; *Through Transport Mutual v New India Assurance Co Ltd* [2004] EWCA Civ 1598; *West Tankers Inc v RAS Riunione Adriatica di Sicurta SpA and Others* [2007] UKHL 4. See generally *Dicey & Morris*, paras 11–035 *et seq.*

[474] *Navigation Maritime Bulgaria v Rustal Trading (The "Ivan Zagubanski")* [2002] 1 Lloyd's Rep. 106; *Through Transport Mutual v New India Assurance Co Ltd* [2004] EWCA Civ 1598; *A v B* [2006] EWHC 2006.

2–106   **Matters covered by the procedural law.** An exhaustive list of the matters covered by the procedural law of an arbitration in each jurisdiction is not possible. Their nature and scope are determined by the particular law concerned. Conflicts may arise between the procedural law, the proper law of the contract and the law of the arbitration agreement or the law of the place of enforcement, particularly in relation to questions of arbitrability and validity of the contract, appointment of a tribunal, time limits and the form and validity of the award.[475] In England, the procedural law of arbitration is principally set out in Pt I of the Arbitration Act 1996[476] and by section 2 it applies whenever the seat of the arbitration is in England, Wales or Northern Ireland. So under English law, the choice of an English seat[477] will, subject to agreement otherwise,[478] incorporate the various matters addressed in the Act, including questions relating to the appointment and revocation of the authority of the arbitration tribunal, the powers and duties of the tribunal and remedies for breach of duty, and any challenges to the award.[479] Foreign procedural law may also be relevant to enforcement of a foreign award in England.[480]

2–107   **Hearings in different locations.** In international arbitrations, meetings or hearings may take place in several countries, without changing the seat.[481] In these cases it is important not to confuse the seat with what is simply the appropriate or convenient geographical location for particular hearings.[482] It will be necessary to ensure compliance with any mandatory local law requirements of the place where the meeting or hearing takes place.

2–108   **Procedural rules distinguished.** The procedural law applicable to the reference must be distinguished from procedural rules which the parties might

---

[475] See for example *C v D* [2007] EWHC 1541 where an award made in England was not susceptible to challenge under the Arbitration Act 1996 but was alleged to be subject to be subject to review in the United States based on the nationality of the parties and the proper law of the contract.

[476] Although the common law is expressly preserved in so far as it is consistent with the Arbitration Act 1996: s.81(1).

[477] It is in fact the choice of England as the seat of the arbitration, rather than the choice of English procedural law which is the determinative factor, though in most cases the choice of seat and the choice of procedural law will be the same: see para.2–101 above.

[478] e.g. by selection of a different procedural law in relation to the non-mandatory provisions of the 1996 Act: see para.2–103.

[479] The supervisory jurisdiction of the courts of the seat has been emphasised recently by the Court of Appeal in *Weissfisch v Julius* [2006] EWCA Civ 218; see also *A v B* [2006] EWHC 2006; *C v D* [2007] EWHC 1541. Invoking the jurisdiction of the courts elsewhere is a breach of the agreement vesting supervisory jurisdiction in the courts of the seat and is remediable in damages or, in appropriate circumstances, an order for costs on an indemnity basis: see *A v B (No.2)* [2007] EWHC 54; *C v D* [2007] EWHC 1541. Declaratory or injunctive relief may also be available: see *Noble Assurance Co v Gerling-Konzern General Insurance Co* [2007] EWHC 253.

[480] *Dalmia Dairy Industries Ltd v National Bank of Pakistan* [1978] 2 Lloyd's Rep. 223.

[481] This is because the "seat" is the legal, rather than the physical place of arbitration, see para.2–100. The rules of various arbitration institutions specifically contemplate hearings in different locations: see, e.g. LCIA Rules, Art.16. 2, ICC Rules, Art.14.2 and UNCITRAL Rules, Art.16(2). The ICC Rules expressly provide that the tribunal may conduct its deliberations at any location: see Art.14.3 of the ICC Rules.

[482] *Naviera Amazonica Peruana v Cia Internacional de Seguros del Peru* [1988] 1 Lloyd's Rep. 116 at 117, 121.

choose to apply to the reference, such as those of the ICC or LCIA.[483] The latter are rules for the conduct of the arbitration which have effect only because they have been agreed to by the parties. In contrast, the applicable procedural law as the law of the seat[484] will apply regardless of the parties' wishes; but the parties may agree amendments to details of the procedure in so far as this is permitted by the relevant national law.[485]

Law of the place of enforcement. As mentioned above[486] regard must 2–109
also be had to the law of the place or places where recognition and enforcement of the award will be sought. Any mandatory requirements of the law of the place of enforcement should be complied with, although in some cases the parties may not know in precisely which jurisdictions they will, if successful, seek to enforce the award. In any event consideration should be given to enforcement at an early stage so that any mandatory requirements of the relevant law can be ascertained. In addition to mandatory requirements, there may be a particular feature of the procedure or the arbitration agreement which is contrary to the law of the place of enforcement, for example a lack of mutuality.[487] Again this is something that the parties would want to identify at an early stage so that they can attempt to address it, for example by seeking to enforce elsewhere or altering the relevant procedure or agreeing an ad hoc submission to arbitration which addresses the issue.

6. TERMINATION OF THE ARBITRATION AGREEMENT

(a) Termination by agreement

Termination of the arbitration agreement. The parties can by 2–110
agreement bring the agreement to arbitrate to an end. Arbitration is consensual and there is no reason why the parties cannot agree to vary their arbitration agreement so as to bring about its termination.[488] The parties might for example jointly agree that all future disputes should be dealt with by the court rather than pursuant to the arbitration agreement contained in their contract. There is no statutory requirement for the termination of the arbitration agreement to be in writing[489] although the matrix contract may provide that any variation of its provisions are to be in writing and this can apply equally to the arbitration agreement.[490] In any event a written record is desirable for evidential purposes.

---

[483] See, e.g. *Paul Smith Ltd v H&S International Holding Inc* [1991] 2 Lloyd's Rep. 127.
[484] See though para.2–103 above as to the possibility of choosing a different procedural law from that of the seat.
[485] See para.2–060 above as to the scope for agreeing procedural matters under English law.
[486] See para.2–088 above.
[487] See para.2–017 above.
[488] Termination by agreement is expressly contemplated by s.23(4) of the Arbitration Act 1996.
[489] Section 23(4) of the Arbitration Act 1996; see also DAC report, para.40.
[490] *JSC Zestafoni G Nikoladze Ferroalloy Plant v Ronly Holdings Ltd* [2004] EWHC 245.

Otherwise the nature of an arbitration agreement means that, even if parties decide to adopt a different dispute resolution mechanism for a particular dispute that arises under the arbitration agreement, that will not of itself bring about the termination of the arbitration agreement. Any subsequent dispute that arises within the ambit of the arbitration agreement will fall to be determined in accordance with its provisions.

Referring a dispute to mediation or some other non-binding process will not of itself rescind a prior agreement to refer the dispute to arbitration.[491]

(b) Repudiation of the right to arbitrate

2–111   **Express or implied repudiation.** A party may repudiate the arbitration agreement and if the other party accepts that repudiation the arbitration agreement will come to an end. The repudiation may be express or may be inferred from the conduct of a party who acts in a way that is inconsistent with the continued operation of the arbitration clause and evinces an intention not to be bound by it.[492] However a failure to comply with the general duty to do all things necessary for the proper and expeditious conduct of the arbitral proceedings is not a repudiation of the arbitration agreement.[493] The repudiation may be by anticipatory breach of the arbitration agreement.[494] Acceptance of the repudiation may be demonstrated by the commencement of proceedings in court.[495]

2–112   **Repudiation by commencing proceedings.** A party may repudiate the arbitration agreement by commencement of proceedings in court in breach of its terms, but such breach will only be repudiatory if done in circumstances that show the party in question no longer intends to be bound by the agreement to arbitrate.[496] Such an intention can only be inferred from conduct which is clear and unequivocal.[497] If there was some reason for the breach, such as confusion as to the correct course, the court will not infer that the party bringing the proceedings intended to renounce its obligation to arbitrate.[498]

---

[491] *Frota Oceanica Brasiliera SA v Steamship Mutual Underwriting Association (Bermuda) Ltd (The "Frotanorte")* [1996] Lloyd's Rep. 461, *per* Longmore J. The point was not addressed when the case came before the Court of Appeal.

[492] *Traube v Perelman* [2001] W.L. 1251816.

[493] *Elektrim SA v Vivendi Universal SA* [2007] EWHC 11 at [124]. The court reasoned that s.40 imposes statutory obligations, the remedy for breach of which is set out in the Act. It does not create duties by way of implied terms of the arbitration agreement of which there can be a repudiatory breach. It is of course possible for a party to commit a breach of an arbitration agreement which is not repudiatory and which does not therefore allow the other party to bring the agreement to arbitrate to an end.

[494] *Downing v Al Tameer Establishment* [2002] EWCA Civ 721.

[495] *Traube v Perelman* [2001] W.L. 1251816; *Downing v Al Tameer Establishment* [2002] EWCA Civ 721.

[496] *BEA Hotels NV v Bellway LLC* [2007] EWHC 1363.

[497] *BEA Hotels NV v Bellway LLC* [2007] EWHC 1363.

[498] *Rederi Kommanditselskaabet Merc-Scandia IV v Couniniotis SA (The "Mercanaut")* [1980] 2 Lloyd's Rep. 183. See also *World Pride Shipping Ltd v Daiichi Chuo Kisen Kaisha (The "Golden Anne")* [1984] 2 Lloyd's Rep. 489.

Tribunal to determine dispute as to repudiation. If there is a   2–113
dispute about whether the arbitration agreement has been repudiated, that is a
question going to the jurisdiction of the tribunal and is therefore to be determined
by the tribunal under s.30(1)(a) of the Arbitration Act 1996 rather than the court
(unless the requirements of s.32 of the Arbitration Act 1996 are met.[499]

(c) Abandonment of the arbitration agreement

Similarly a party may abandon its right to arbitrate, for example by delay or   2–114
inaction,[500] or by commencing court proceedings in breach of an arbitration
agreement.[501] However the courts are slow to find such abandonment without very
clear evidence of an intention to abandon the right to arbitrate together with
reliance by the other party to its detriment.[502] Even if the right to arbitrate a
particular dispute has been abandoned, that does not necessarily mean that the
arbitration agreement itself has been abandoned.[503]

---

[499] See paras 5–060 *et seq.*
[500] *Wakefield (Tower Hill Trinity Square) Trust v Janson Green Properties Ltd* [1998] E.G.C.S. 95. See
though *Indescon Ltd v Ogden* [2005] 1 Lloyd's Rep. 31.
[501] See para.2–112, as commencing proceedings in breach of an agreement to arbitrate does not
automatically entitle the other party to treat the agreement to arbitrate as being at an end. *World
Pride Shipping Ltd v Daiichi Chuo Kisen Kaisha (The "Golden Anne")* [1984] 2 Lloyd's Rep. 489.
[502] *Shell International Petroleum Co Ltd v Coral Oil Co Ltd* [1999] 1 Lloyd's Rep. 72.
[503] See para.5–229 concerning the abandonment of a particular reference.

CHAPTER 3

PARTIES AND INSTITUTIONS

1. INTRODUCTION

3–001 **Contents of the chapter.** This chapter concerns the persons, corporations, states and other entities which can be parties to an arbitration. This involves largely contractual and constitutional issues, with some specific rules affecting particular situations. Then follows a consideration of the position where there are disputes between three or more parties rather than the usual bilateral arrangement. The chapter concludes with a consideration of the status of arbitral institutions.

2. PARTIES

3–002 **The general rule.** Contract law governs the capacity of a party to enter into an arbitration agreement.[1] Subject to the qualifications set out in the following paragraphs, in principle any individual or corporate body (or indeed any other entity, e.g. a partnership, which the law recognises as having the necessary

---

[1] See generally *Chitty* (29th edn) Chs 8–11. For statutory arbitrations, see Appendix 3.

capacity) can be party to an arbitration agreement. Nevertheless, it is important to give consideration to the capacity of the parties to an arbitration agreement in order to establish whether they are capable of creating a legally enforceable obligation to arbitrate. This is particularly so when dealing with foreign entities[2] whose legal status is governed by the law of their home jurisdiction.[3]

Capacity and identity. It is perhaps self-evident that care needs to be taken   3–003
to ensure that the right person or entity is identified as a party to the arbitration agreement and in any arbitration proceedings.[4] Whether an error in this regard will be fatal depends on the circumstances and the courts have drawn a distinction between a mistake as to identity, which will generally invalidate the proceedings, and a mere misnomer, which will not.[5]

It may also be necessary to verify the capacity of a party to enter into an arbitration agreement[6] or to bring or defend arbitration proceedings.[7] How this is done depends on the circumstances. It may, for instance, be sufficient, in the case of an English company, to carry out a search of the official register of UK companies maintained by Companies House,[8] but more sophisticated enquiries to obtain the relevant constitutional documents may be necessary for partnerships, unincorporated associations and companies incorporated outside England. Questions of the capacity of parties and verification of their identity may also have to be considered by the arbitral institution and/or the tribunal to which a dispute has

---

[2] See, e.g. *Hussman (Europe) Ltd v Al Ameen Development & Trade Co* [2000] 2 Lloyd's Rep. 83 where a distributorship was entered into with a Saudi "Establishment" which under Saudi law had no legal personality separate or distinct from its owner.
[3] In *Continental Enterprises Limited v Shandong Zhucheng Foreign Trade Group Co* [2005] EWHC 92 at para.72 Steel J. found, applying Chinese law, that a lack of capacity to enter into a contract also invalidated the arbitration agreement.
[4] See also para.5–024.
[5] See for example *Unisys International Services Ltd v Eastern Counties Newspapers Ltd* [1991] 1 Lloyd's Rep. 538 where arbitration was commenced in the name of the contracting party but that party had since changed its name and the original name had been given to its subsidiary company. The Court of Appeal upheld the contracting party as a party to the arbitration as a matter of construction of the notice commencing the arbitration. In contrast, in *Internaut Shipping GmbH v Fercometal Sarl, The Elikon* [2003] EWCA Civ 812 the conduct of an arbitration commenced in the name of "Owners" but pursued in the name of a party found not in fact to be the Owners under a charterparty, was held to be a nullity (though the original reference to arbitration was still valid and potentially capable of being pursued by the true "Owners"). See also *Kenya Railways v Antares Co Pte Ltd (The "Antares") (Nos 1 and 2)* [1987] 1 Lloyd's Rep. 424; *Hussman (Europe) Ltd v Al Ameen Development & Trade Co* [2000] 2 Lloyd's Rep. 83 and *Hussmann (Europe) Ltd v Pharaon* [2003] EWCA Civ 266; [2003] 1 All E.R. (Comm) 879.
[6] See, e.g. the decision of Longmore J. in *Frota Oceanica Brasiliera SA v Steamship Mutual Underwriting Association (Bermuda) Ltd (The "Frotanorte")* [1995] 2 Lloyd's Rep. 254 where it was held that a claim being pursued by reinsurers by virtue of subrogation rights would have to be brought in the name of the insured, and consequently any agreement to arbitrate must therefore be with the insured. The Court of Appeal took a different approach, holding that the parties had not in fact concluded a binding arbitration agreement at all because they were not of the same mind as to who the parties to the agreement were: [1996] Lloyd's Rep. 461.
[7] Such issues will often arise for example in the context of substituted parties, as to which see para.3–016 below.
[8] See the official website at *www.companieshouse.gov.uk*.

been referred. They should in the first instance address these questions to the parties by the institution/tribunal. Once an issue has come to light concerning the capacity of one or more parties this should be addressed at the earliest opportunity so that, if it is capable of being resolved, steps are taken to do so and in any event unnecessary costs[9] are avoided.

3. INDIVIDUALS UNDER DISABILITY

3–004   **General.** Under English law most individuals have the capacity to enter into an arbitration agreement in the same way as they do contracts generally. The exceptions are minors[10] and patients suffering from mental disorder.[11] As far as arbitration agreements are concerned, the position of minors and patients follows the general law of contract.

3–005   **Minors.** A contract for "necessaries"[12] sold and delivered to a minor[13] or a contract of service, education, apprenticeship or instruction which is of benefit to a minor is binding on him.[14] It therefore follows that a minor will be bound by an arbitration agreement contained in such a contract.[15] All other contracts where one party is a minor are voidable at the option of the minor but binding on the other party, and arbitration agreements follow this rule.[16]

3–006   **Patients.** A patient is generally bound by any contract he enters into, including an arbitration agreement, but mental incapacity may in some circumstances render the arbitration agreement voidable. A party seeking to avoid an arbitration agreement based upon mental incapacity at the time of entering into the arbitration agreement will need to demonstrate that owing to his mental incapacity he did not know what he was doing and that the other party was aware of his incapacity.[17] A patient's affairs are also subject to the wide discretionary powers of the court.[18]

---

[9] For example the costs of proceeding with an arbitration against a party lacking capacity and against whom any award will be unenforceable.

[10] Individuals under 18 years of age, see s.1 of the Family Law Reform Act 1969.

[11] Section 1 of the Mental Health Act 1983. The capacity of patients will be governed by the Mental Capacity Act 2005 if and when the relevant provisions of that statute are brought into force.

[12] Defined in s.3(3) of the Sale of Goods Act 1979 as "goods suitable to the condition in life of the minor or other person concerned and to his actual requirements at the time of the sale and delivery".

[13] Section 3 of the Sale of Goods Act 1979. The minor is required to pay a reasonable price rather than the contractually stipulated sum.

[14] *Clements v London and North Western Railway Company* [1894] 2 Q.B. 482 at 491.

[15] *Slade v Metrodent LD* [1953] 2 Q.B. 112.

[16] See generally *Chitty*, Ch.8.

[17] *Imperial Loan Co Ltd v Stone* [1892] 1 Q.B. 599. For a more recent example where such a claim failed see *Irvani v Irvani* [2000] 1 Lloyd's Rep. 412.

[18] Part VII of the Mental Health Act 1983. These provisions will be replaced by the Mental Capacity Act 2005 if and when it is brought into force.

Bankrupts. This subject is considered under the general heading of "Insolvent   3–007
Individuals and Companies".[19]

4. CORPORATE BODIES

Companies incorporated under the Companies Acts. Com-   3–008
panies can bind themselves to arbitration agreements under English law. Their
capacity to do so cannot be called into question on the ground of lack of capacity
by reason of anything in the company's constitution.[20] When a company ceases to
exist, an arbitration to which it is a party also comes to an end,[21] but an arbitration
would not necessarily come to an end simply because the company is in liquidation, administration or receivership.[22] Where a company has been restructured,
privatised or nationalised, it is important to ensure that the entity which originally
entered into the arbitration agreement continues to exist and is the appropriate
participant in the arbitration proceedings.

Limited Liability Partnerships. Despite the designation as a "partner-   3–009
ship", a limited liability partnership is a corporate entity with legal personality
separate from that of its members.[23] It has capacity to enter into an arbitration
agreement.[24]

Statutory corporations.[25] Where a corporation has been established by   3–010
statute, an express provision in its constitution may affect its capacity to enter into
an arbitration agreement, but in the absence of any special provision, a statutory
corporation has full capacity to enter into an arbitration agreement.

Insolvent companies. This subject is considered under the general heading   3–011
of "Insolvent Individuals and Companies".[26]

[19] See paras 3–027 *et seq.*
[20] Section 35(1) of the Companies Act 1985, as amended by s.108(1) of the Companies Act 1989, and
s.65(1) and Sch.6, para.20 of the Charities Act 1993. This will be replaced by s.39(1) of the
Companies Act 2006 which is due to come into force on October 1, 2008.
[21] *Morris v Harris* [1927] A.C. 252; *Baytur SA v Finagro Holdings SA* [1991] 4 All E.R. 129. This
assumes of course that there has been no assignment or novation of the rights and obligations to a
third party: see para.3–016 below.
[22] See further paras 3–030 *et seq.*
[23] Section 1(2) of the Limited Liability Partnerships Act 2000. The law of partnership does not apply:
s.1(5) of the Limited Liability Partnerships Act 2000.
[24] Section 1(3) of the Limited Liability Partnerships Act 2000.
[25] See para.3–033 on state entities and public authorities, and para.3–039 on international organisations. For the position with ecclesiastical corporations such as bishops see *Halsbury's Laws*
(4th edn), Vol.14, paras 1253–1256.
[26] See paras 3–027 *et seq.*

5. PARTNERSHIPS AND UNINCORPORATED ASSOCIATIONS

3–012 **Partnerships.** Partners who enter into ordinary commercial contracts containing arbitration clauses bind the partnership and all the partners to the agreement to arbitrate.[27] There is old authority that the power to refer disputes to arbitration outside the ordinary course of business of the partnership, such as a reference following a dissolution to get in the partnership debts,[28] cannot be exercised by one partner without special authority.[29] The remaining partners may however adopt an unauthorised reference and their conduct may make it binding upon them.[30]

3–013 **Unincorporated associations.** An unincorporated association is not a legal entity and does not therefore have capacity to enter into a contract such as an arbitration agreement.[31] A contract purportedly made by or with an unincorporated association does not bind all the members for the time being of that association[32] but it may bind those persons who actually entered into it as well as those members for whom they had express or implied authority to contract as agents.[33] The rules of an unincorporated association may constitute a contract between the members and an arbitration agreement in those rules would then be binding in relation to disputes between the members.[34]

6. THIRD PARTIES[35]

3–014 **Statutory rights of third parties.** Under s.1 of the Contracts (Rights of Third Parties) Act 1999, a person who is not a party to a contract may nevertheless enforce a term of that contract if the contract expressly provides that he may do so or if it purports to confer a benefit on him. Where the contract in question contains an arbitration agreement whose scope is wide enough to cover the dispute, then pursuant to s.8(1) of the Contracts (Rights of Third Parties) Act 1999 the third party is treated as being a party to the arbitration agreement as regards the enforcement of his right pursuant to the contract,[36] such that he is not just entitled but can be required to arbitrate any dispute.[37] Section 8(1) of the 1999

---

[27] Partnership Act 1890, ss.5 and 6.
[28] As in *Hatton v Royle* (1858) 3 H. & N. 500.
[29] Lindley & Banks on Partnership (18th edn), para.12–44.
[30] *Thomas v Atherton* (1878) 10 Ch. D. 185.
[31] See generally *Chitty*, Ch.9. There are exceptions based on statutory provision.
[32] *Walker v Sur* [1914] 2 K.B. 930.
[33] *Chitty*, para.9–068.
[34] See for example *Whiting v Halverson* [2003] EWCA Civ 403.
[35] See also Substituted Parties at para.3–016 and Multiparty Disputes at para.3–040.
[36] See for example *Mulchrone Swiss Life (UK) Plc* [2005] EWHC 1808, although in that case the 1999 Act did not apply as the relevant contract pre-dated its coming into force.
[37] *Nisshin Shipping Co Ltd v Cleaves & Co Ltd* [2003] EWHC 2602.

Act does not apply to non-contractual disputes such as claims arising in tort. These may be covered by s.8(2) which allows a third party to enforce a term providing for disputes between the third party and the contracting party to be submitted to arbitration even where the third party does not fall within s.8(1).[38]

Guarantors, sureties and indemnifiers. A third party such as a guarantor, surety or indemnifier may enter into obligations relating to the performance of one of the parties to a contract incorporating an arbitration agreement in circumstances where the statutory provision does not apply.[39] If it is intended that an award against the principal debtor will bind the guarantor (or similar third party) then the guarantee (or surety agreement or indemnity) should contain express provision to that effect. Failure to include that provision may make the award unenforceable against that third party.[40] Agreements containing guarantees or similar obligations often provide that the creditor can proceed against the guarantor, surety or indemnifier without first having to obtain an arbitration award (or a judgment, as the case may be) against the debtor. This type of provision leaves open the possibility of simultaneous proceedings, with unnecessary duplication and the risk of inconsistent results. The court cannot impose solutions to the problem.[41] The right course is, at the drafting stage, to include provisions in the various contracts which specifically deal with the issue, either by limiting the parties' rights to proceed under both contracts simultaneously or by providing that all disputes under both contracts are to be referred either to the court or to arbitration. If they are to be referred to arbitration, provision should be made for them to be consolidated,[42] so that all the issues and relevant parties are brought before one tribunal.

3–015

7. Substituted Parties

When substitution of parties occurs. If a party is claiming under or through a party to the arbitration agreement, then the provisions of the Arbitration Act 1996 will apply to him.[43] The assignment of a contract is perhaps the

3–016

---

[38] Section 8(2) is obscurely drafted. See generally "The Third Man: The 1999 Act Sets Back Separability?" by Anthony Diamond Q.C. in (2001) 17 Arbitration Int. 211. See also *Nisshin Shipping Co Ltd v Cleaves & Co Ltd* [2003] EWHC 2602; [2004] 1 Lloyd's Rep. 38 at [36] which quotes the Lord Chancellor's Department Explanatory Notes in relation to s.8.

[39] For example because they have entered into a separate contract of guarantee which would form the basis of any claim rather than a party seeking to enforce a term of the principal contract.

[40] *In Re Kitchin Ex p. Young* (1881) 17 Ch. D. 668; *Bruns v Colocotroonis (The "Vasso")* [1979] 2 Lloyd's Rep. 412.

[41] See the unsuccessful attempts in *Alfred McAlpine Construction Ltd v Unex Corporation Ltd* [1994] 70 B.L.R. 26 and *Roche Products Ltd and Celltech Therapeutics Ltd v Freeman Process Systems Ltd and Haden Maclellan Holdings Plc: Black Country Development Corp v Kier Construction Ltd* [1996] 80 B.L.R. 102. These cases were decided prior to the Arbitration Act 1996 but the principle still holds good. Indeed the court no longer has a discretion whether or not to enforce an arbitration agreement: Arbitration Act 1996, s.9 and para.2–023.

[42] As contemplated by s.35(1) of the Arbitration Act 1996. See further paras 3–044 *et seq.*

[43] Section 82(2) of the Arbitration Act 1996.

most common situation when this arises and the assignee may be substituted for the assignor in the arbitration agreement or in any arbitration proceedings. However substitution may also occur due to legal or corporate reconstruction of an entity or group of entities, for example by way of merger, which may or may not take effect by way of assignment.[44] Investigation will need to be made in each case as to the nature and effect of what has occurred as regards the legal status and obligations of the entities involved under the laws applicable to them. For example, under many foreign laws a merger may take effect by way of universal succession such that the rights and obligations of one entity transfer to the other as a matter of law and no notice is required to give effect to this as regards third parties.[45] The transferring entity may or may not then cease to exist. In any event, if the substituting party wishes to pursue a claim under a contract he will be bound by any arbitration agreement contained in it.[46]

3–017   **Notice required under English law.** As a matter of English law, notice to the other parties and the tribunal is required for a substituted party to proceed with arbitration proceedings and for any award to take effect.[47] The notice must be given within a reasonable time and failure to do so may bring the arbitration to an end.[48] Many of the reported cases involving substituted parties concern corporate reorganisations which are not reflected in ongoing arbitration proceedings or they concern proceedings being commenced in the name of a party that either no longer has an interest in the proceedings or has ceased to exist. In such cases it is necessary to consider whether the error in naming the party is essentially a misnomer, in that the proper party was in fact joined to the proceedings, or subsequently ratified them, or submitted to the jurisdiction of the tribunal even if not formally named as a party.[49] However where the proceedings have been started on behalf of a party that does not exist, as opposed to there being an error in naming the proper party, the proceedings will be a nullity.[50]

---

[44] In *Through Transport Mutual Insurance Association (Eurasia) Ltd v New India Assurance Co Ltd (The "Hari Bhum") (No.2)* [2005] EWHC 455 the claimant was described as a "statutory transferee", its right to pursue a claim under a contract between two other parties arising not by way of assignment but under a Finnish statute. It was nevertheless claiming "under or through a party to the agreement" for the purposes of s.82(2) of the Arbitration Act 1996.

[45] As under German law, for example: *Eurosteel Ltd v Stinnes AG* [2000] C.L.C. 470.

[46] *Through Transport Mutual Insurance Association (Eurasia) Ltd v New India Assurance Co Ltd (The "Hari Bhum") (No.2)* [2005] EWHC 455.

[47] *The Republic of Kazakhstan v Istil Group Inc* [2006] EWHC 448; *Baytur SA v Finagro Holding SA* [1991] 4 All E.R. 129; *Eurosteel Ltd v Stinnes AG* [2000] C.L.C. 470.

[48] *NBP Developments Ltd and Others v Buildko and Sons Ltd (formerly William Thomson and Sons Ltd) (in liquidation)* (1992) 8 Const. L.J. 377.

[49] *SEB Trygg Holding AB v Manches* [2005] 2 EWHC 35 affirmed at [2005] EWCA Civ 1237; *Harper Versicherungs AG v Indemnity Marine Assurance Co Ltd* [2006] EWHC 1500; *Unisys International Services Ltd v Eastern Counties Newspapers Ltd* [1991] 1 Lloyd's Rep. 538.

[50] *SEB Trygg Holding AB v Manches* [2005] EWHC 35 affirmed at [2005] EWCA Civ 1237. See also *Internaut Shipping GmbH and Another v Fercometal Sarl (The "Elikon")* [2003] EWCA Civ 812. See also para.5–024 below.

Rights of assignees.[51] Where there is a valid assignment of a contract   3–018
containing an arbitration agreement the assignee will be bound by the arbitration
agreement.[52] He may invoke the arbitration agreement to pursue a claim but will
also be subject to the arbitration agreement in the event of a claim by the other
party.[53] The assignee is not limited to commencing arbitration proceedings following the assignment, but may also join existing proceedings.[54] References under Pt
I of the Arbitration Act 1996 to a party to an arbitration agreement include any
person, such as an assignee, claiming through or under a party to the agreement.[55]

Legal assignees. A legal assignee obtains rights pursuant to statute.[56] To be   3–019
effective as a legal assignment the transfer has to be absolute and not by way of
charge only; it must be in writing and express notice must have been given to the
other party. By following that procedure an assignee can succeed to an assignor's
rights in an arbitration provided that notice is given to both the other party and
to the tribunal.[57] A legal assignee can bring or defend arbitration proceedings in
its own name.

Equitable assignees. The position of an equitable assignee in the context of   3–020
arbitration was considered by the Court of Appeal in *Baytur SA v Finagro Holding
SA*.[58] In that case an award had been made after the claimant had ceased to exist
and the respondent sought to avoid liability. (The claimant was a French company
whose assets and liabilities had been transferred to two other companies: under
French law, as soon as the transfers were completed, the transferor company was
dissolved.) The court held that an equitable assignee must first give notice of the
assignment to the other party[59] and then submit to the jurisdiction of the
arbitrator. If that is not done and the assignor ceases to exist in the meantime, the
arbitration and any award made in it may lapse.[60] Concerns have been expressed

---

[51] For assignment generally see *Chitty*, Ch.20.
[52] *Schiffahrtsgesellschaft Detleu Von Appen GmbH v Voest Alpine Intertrading GmbH* [1997] 2 Lloyd's
Rep. 279; *Starlight Shipping Co v Tai Ping Insurance Co Ltd* [2007] EWHC 1893; *Aspel v Seymour*
[1929] W.N. 152; *Shayler v Woolf* [1946] 1 Ch. 320. See also *The "Padre Island" (No.1)* [1984] 2
Lloyd's Rep. 408 and *(No.2)* [1990] 2 Lloyd's Rep. 191 where the transferee of an insolvent
assured's rights against his insurer under the Third Parties (Rights against Insurers) Act 1930 was
held to be bound by an arbitration clause.
[53] *Schiffahrtsgesellschaft Detleu Von Appen GmbH v Voest Alpine Intertrading GmbH* [1997] 2 Lloyd's
Rep. 279.
[54] As was the case in both *Baytur SA v Finagro Holding SA* [1991] 4 All E.R. 129 and *Montedipe SpA
v JTP-RO Jugotanker, The "Jordan Nicolov"* [1990] 2 Lloyd's Rep. 11. See also *Charles M. Willie
and Co (Shipping) Ltd v Ocean Laser Shipping Ltd (The "Smaro")* 1999 1 Lloyd's Rep. 225.
[55] Arbitration Act 1996, s.82(2).
[56] Law of Property Act 1925, s.136.
[57] Hobhouse J. in *Montedipe SpA v JTP-RO Jugotanker, The "Jordan Nicolov"* [1990] 2 Lloyd's Rep.
11. The judge drew attention to the analogous procedure used in litigation under the old RSC,
Ord.15, r.7(2)—see now CPR Pt 19, r.4.
[58] [1992] 1 Lloyd's Rep. 134.
[59] On the analogy of the procedure in litigation under the old RSC, Ord.15, r.7.
[60] That was the conclusion reached in *Baytur SA v Finagro Holding SA*, but *Eurosteel Ltd v Stinnes
AG* [2000] C.L.C. 470 is authority that it does not apply in cases of universal succession.

that this could lead to a situation where liability might be avoided by entities merging and choosing not to give the requisite notice.[61]

An equitable assignee must join the assignor as a party to any arbitration.

3–021   **Novation.** Novation occurs when the parties to a contract agree that a third party should replace one of them as regards relations with the other. The third party must also of course agree to do so. Novation involves the creation of a new agreement between the party to the existing contract and the third party. In the arbitration context it means bringing one or more substitute parties to an arbitration agreement who can enforce the agreement in place of the original party. As a result of there being a new agreement the remedies sought by the new or substitute party are not necessarily limited to those that would have been available under the agreement to the original party.[62] Novation can arise either by act of the parties[63] or by statute, as for instance under the Third Parties (Rights against Insurers) Act 1930.[64]

Where a novation occurs, the new party may be able to join in arbitration proceedings between the original parties, at least where his claim is based on identical facts.[65]

3–022   **Group of companies doctrine.** Under English law the scope of an arbitration agreement is limited to the parties who entered into it and those claiming under or through them.[66] However in the international context there has developed what has become known as the "group of companies doctrine" whereby an arbitration agreement entered into by a company within a group of companies can bind its non-signatory affiliates if the circumstances demonstrate that the mutual intention of all the parties was to bind the both the signatories and the non-signatory affiliates.[67] This theory has been applied in a number of arbitrations so as to justify a tribunal taking jurisdiction over a party who is not a signatory to the contract containing the arbitration agreement.[68] However the English courts have firmly rejected the group of companies doctrine.[69] Though there was earlier

---

[61] *per* Longmore J. in *Eurosteel Ltd v Stinnes AG* [2000] C.L.C. 470, following *Industrie Chimiche Italia Centrale v Alexander G Tsavlinis & Sons Maritime Co (The "Choko Star")* [1996] 1 W.L.R. 774.

[62] See *Charles M. Willie and Co (Shipping) Ltd v Ocean Laser Shipping Ltd (The "Smaro")* [1999] 1 Lloyd's Rep. 225.

[63] Such as the respondent turning from a partnership into a company, as in *Oakland Metal Company Ltd v D Benaim & Co Ltd* [1953] 2 Q.B. 261.

[64] *Firma C-Trade SA v Newcastle Protection and Indemnity Association* and *Socony Mobil Oil and others v West of England Shipowners Mutual Insurance Association (London) Ltd No.2 The "Padre Island"* [1991] 2 A.C. 1.

[65] This was the opinion given by Rix J. in *Charles M Willie and Co (Shipping) Ltd v Ocean Laser Shipping Ltd (The "Smaro")* [1999] 1 Lloyd's Rep. 225.

[66] Section 82(2) of the Arbitration Act 1996.

[67] The doctrine originated in an ICC case involving the Dow Chemical group of companies: *Dow Chemical v Isover Saint Gobain* ICC Interim Award of September 23 of 1982 in Case No.4131.

[68] See generally Craig, Park & Paulsson, *International Chamber of Commerce Arbitration* (3rd edn, 2000), pp.75–78 and *French Arbitration Law and Practice* by Delvolvé, Rouche and Pointon, paras 216–241.

[69] *Petersen Farms Inc v C&M Farming Ltd* [2004] EWHC 121; [2004] 1 Lloyd's Rep. 603.

authority[70] that a company which was not a party to the arbitration agreement was claiming "through or under"[71] its parent company and the contract signatory, that approach is unlikely now to be followed.[72]

8. AGENTS AND LAWYERS

Agents generally.[73] An agent may enter into an arbitration agreement on 3–023 behalf of his principal.[74] If however his authority to act is successfully challenged[75] the arbitration agreement will not be binding on the principal and the agent may incur personal liability for any losses suffered by the other party.[76] To avoid this the agent should ensure that he has full authority from his principal to conclude the contract including the arbitration agreement. Further, the agent should either (i) enter into the contract expressly on behalf of his named principal or, if that is not possible, (ii) consider obtaining a comprehensive secured indemnity from the principal for any liability arising out of his having entered into the contract on behalf of the principal.

No claim by agent. An agent entering into a contract for an undisclosed 3–024 principal will not himself be entitled to claim substantive relief under the contract, nor will he be able to participate in an arbitration as he is not a party to the arbitration agreement.[77]

Lawyers. Lawyers, in practice usually solicitors in England, need authorisation 3–025 to act as agent to bind their client to arbitration. The other party can rely on the ostensible authority of the lawyer acting as agent on behalf of his client and if the solicitor lacks authority he may be liable for breach of warranty of authority, which would make him liable for wasted costs.[78]

---

[70] *Roussel-Uclaf v GD Searle & Co Ltd* [1978] 1 Lloyd's Rep. 225.
[71] This case was decided under the old law but the concept has been preserved by s.82(2) of the Arbitration Act 1996.
[72] It was the subject of criticism in *Grupo Torras v Al-Sabah* [1995] 1 Lloyd's Rep. 374.
[73] See generally *Bowstead & Reynolds on Agency* (18th edn).
[74] Usually it will be in the agent's best interests to have the principal enter into the contract containing the arbitration agreement in his own name, but that is not always feasible and this section assumes that the agent is entering into the contract on the principal's behalf.
[75] As, for example, in *The "City of Calcutta"* (1898) 79 L.T. 517, where the master of a ship was held not to have the authority to bind the shipowners to arbitration.
[76] Losses in relation to the arbitration agreement would generally be limited to costs incurred, e.g. in pursuing abortive arbitration proceedings against the alleged principal.
[77] *Electrosteel Castings Ltd v Scan-Trans Shipping & Chartering Sdn Bhd* [2002] EWHC 1993.
[78] Cordery On Solicitors, Division F, Section 1.A.14.

9. EXECUTORS, ADMINISTRATORS AND TRUSTEES

3–026   **Effect of death of a party.** Section 8(1) of the Arbitration Act 1996 provides that unless otherwise agreed by the parties an arbitration agreement is not discharged by the death of a party to the agreement, and it may be enforced by or against the personal representatives of that party.[79] By s.8(2) of the Arbitration Act 1996 this is subject to any rule of law by which a person's death extinguishes that person's cause of action.[80] These provisions apply where the law applicable to the arbitration agreement is the law of England and Wales or Northern Ireland even if the seat of the arbitration is elsewhere or has not been designated or determined.[81] A personal representative or trustee may submit to arbitration any matter relating to an estate or trust and may enter into agreements for these purposes without being personally liable, provided he exercises such care and skill as is reasonable in the circumstances.[82] Trustees' powers may be expressly set out in the trust instrument, which will supersede the general rule and should be examined. Trustees who submit to arbitration should clarify that they are acting in their capacity as trustees in the arbitration agreement and provide expressly that they are liable only to the extent of the trust property in their hands.

10. INSOLVENT INDIVIDUALS AND COMPANIES

3–027   **Bankrupt can submit to arbitration.** A bankrupt is not deprived of his right to contract, but his estate passes to his trustee in bankruptcy and is subject to the insolvency legislation.[83] A bankrupt can therefore submit to arbitration personally,[84] without binding his estate in bankruptcy, although he cannot by so doing improve his position at the expense of his creditors, nor can the other party improve his position as regards other creditors.

3–028   **Position of the trustee in bankruptcy.** Where the bankrupt is party to a contract containing an arbitration clause the trustee in bankruptcy may choose whether or not to adopt the contract. If he does so then the arbitration agreement is enforceable both by and against him.[85] Should the trustee in bankruptcy choose

---

[79] Section 8(1) of the Arbitration Act 1996. For a discussion of the practical consequences of this, see David M. Richards, "The Death of a Party in Arbitration Proceedings", (1995) 61 Arbitration Int. 1 at 43. See also para.4–161.

[80] Section 8(2) of the Arbitration Act 1996. The best-known instance of a cause of action "abating" is in defamation, see *Gatley on Libel and Slander* (9th edn), para.8.12.

[81] Section 2(5) of the Arbitration Act 1996.

[82] Section 15 of the Trustee Act 1925 which applies the duty of care set out in s.1(1) of the Trustee Act 2000.

[83] Parts VIII–XI of the Insolvency Act 1986.

[84] *Re Milnes and Robertson* (1854) 15 C.B. 451.

[85] Section 349A(2) of the Insolvency Act 1986 inserted by s.107(1) and Sch.3 to the Arbitration Act 1996.

not to adopt the contract and a dispute arises under the contract which needs to be resolved for the purposes of the bankruptcy then either the trustee in bankruptcy, with the permission of the creditors' committee, or any other party to the contract may apply to the court for a determination as to whether the matter should be referred to arbitration.[86] If the court orders that the matter should be referred to arbitration then the trustee in bankruptcy will be bound by the arbitration agreement for the purposes of that reference. A trustee in bankruptcy also has power to refer to arbitration any dispute concerning debts, claims or liabilities between the bankrupt and any person who may have incurred liability to the bankrupt.[87]

Existing proceedings. Where the bankrupt is a party to existing arbitration proceedings, the fact of his bankruptcy does not of itself effect a stay of the arbitration, but at any time when bankruptcy proceedings are pending or after the making of a bankruptcy order the court may order a stay of any arbitration proceedings.[88] After the making of a bankruptcy order, no creditor who is a party to an arbitration agreement with the bankrupt but who could prove in the bankruptcy may commence arbitration proceedings without permission of the court.[89]   3–029

Administration and administrative receiverships. An administrator or administrative receiver (subject to the provisions of the debenture under which he is appointed) has the power to refer to arbitration any question affecting the company.[90] When an administration order has been made, no arbitration proceedings may be brought against the company or its property without consent of the administrator or permission of the court.[91]   3–030

Voluntary winding-up. Companies can be wound up voluntarily in what are known as creditors' or members' voluntary winding-up.[92] In such cases the liquidator may start or defend an arbitration in the name of and on behalf of the company without seeking permission from the court,[93] save that in a creditors' voluntary winding up permission of the court is required during the period before the holding of a creditors' meeting pursuant to s.98 of the Insolvency Act 1986. Permission of the court is not needed to continue arbitration proceedings against   3–031

---

[86] Section 349A(3) of the Insolvency Act 1986, inserted by s.107(1) and Sch.3 to the Arbitration Act 1996.
[87] Section 314 and para.6 of Sch.5 to the Insolvency Act 1986.
[88] Section 285(1) of the Insolvency Act 1986.
[89] Section 285(3)(b) of the Insolvency Act 1986.
[90] Paragraph 5 of Sch.1 to the Insolvency Act 1986.
[91] Para.43(6) of Sch.B1 to the Insolvency Act 1986 inserted by the Enterprise Act 2002.
[92] Under Pt IV, Chs II, III, IV and V of the Insolvency Act 1986.
[93] Insolvency Act 1986, s.165(3) and Sch.4, Pt II(4).

a company which is being voluntarily wound up. Once the winding-up is completed the company ceases to exist and any arbitration agreement previously entered into by it will become a nullity.[94]

3–032 **Compulsory winding-up.** Alternatively a company may be wound up by the court in a compulsory winding-up.[95] Where a company is being wound up by the court, the liquidator may, with permission of the court or the liquidation committee, bring or defend arbitration proceedings in the name of and on behalf of the company.[96] If a vesting order has been made[97] the liquidator can bring an arbitration in his own name.[98] There is no automatic stay of arbitration proceedings against a company upon the presentation of a winding-up petition, but the court may order a stay at any time after presentation of the petition and before a winding-up order is made.[99] Once a winding-up order has been made or a provisional liquidator appointed, arbitration proceedings may not be brought or continued against the company or its property without permission of the court.[100] As in the case of a voluntary winding-up, once the winding-up is completed the company ceases to exist and any arbitration agreement previously entered into will become a nullity.[101]

11. STATES, STATE ENTITIES AND PUBLIC AUTHORITIES

3–033 **States, state entities and public authorities.** The importance of arbitration involving states and state entities has increased dramatically in recent years, due in part to the proliferation of investment treaties. Many states, including the United Kingdom, have entered into bilateral or multilateral[102] investment treaties which confer upon investors certain rights aimed at protecting their investments which are directly enforceable against the host state. "Investment" is usually defined very broadly so as to encompass a wide range of commercial transactions and interests. Typically these treaties provide a remedy for investors against the host state which may be pursued by arbitration or in the local courts at the investor's option. Where arbitration is selected as the means for resolving

---

[94] *Morris v Harris* [1927] A.C. 252; *Foster Yates & Thom Ltd v HW Edgehill Equipment Ltd* (1978) 122 S.J. 860; *Baytur SA v Finagro Holding SA* [1992] 1 Lloyd's Rep. 134.
[95] Under Pt IV, Ch.VI of the Insolvency Act 1986. The circumstances in which a company may be wound up by the court in a compulsory winding-up are set out in s.122 of the Insolvency Act 1986 and include that the company is unable to pay its debts.
[96] Section 167(1)(a) and Sch.4, Pt II(4) of the Insolvency Act 1986. The provision refers to "any action or other legal proceeding" and this would include arbitration proceedings: *Bristol Airport Plc v Powdrill, Re Paramount Airways Ltd* [1990] B.C.C. 130.
[97] Pursuant to s.145(1) of the Insolvency Act 1986.
[98] Section 145(2) of the Insolvency Act 1986.
[99] Section 126 of the Insolvency Act 1986.
[100] Section 130(2) of the Insolvency Act 1986.
[101] See para.3–031 above.
[102] For example the Energy Charter Treaty signed in December 1994 which deals with cross-border energy co-operation and includes arbitration procedures for disputes arising between contracting states and investors of other contracting states: see further *www.encharter.org*.

disputes between the state and the investor, often there is a choice between arbitration proceedings before ICSID, the ICC or ad hoc proceedings pursuant to the UNCITRAL Rules.

Involvement of the English court. As recent cases before the English 3–034 court have shown, where the seat of arbitration is in England these investment arbitrations may be subject to the Arbitration Act 1996[103] and accordingly subject to the English court's supervisory jurisdiction, notwithstanding that they involve interpretation of international treaties between foreign states.[104] Similarly, even if the arbitration has its seat elsewhere, the English court may be asked to enforce a resulting award. The increase in arbitrations involving states and state entities, both under investment treaties and otherwise, has also brought greater focus on issues such as the juridical distinctions to be drawn between states and different state entities, both as regards their submission to arbitration[105] and the enforcement of awards.[106] A detailed analysis of investment and other arbitrations involving states is beyond the scope of this book,[107] but in any dealings with or on behalf of states or state-owned entities it is important to consider the extent to which any treaties or laws[108] give rise to a cause of action which may be submitted to arbitration.[109]

Capacity of a state or state entity to enter into arbitration 3–035 agreements. Under English law, the Crown has the capacity to be a party to an arbitration agreement.[110] However some states may not have the power to enter into arbitration agreements or may only enter into arbitration agreements on specific terms.[111] The capacity of foreign states to enter into an arbitration agreement depends on their constitution. No general rule of English law limits the

---

[103] *Republic of Ecuador v Occidental Exploration and Production Co* [2005] EWHC 774, affirmed by the Court of Appeal at [2005] EWCA Civ 1116.

[104] An exception is arbitrations conducted under ICSID rules: s.3(2) of the Arbitration (International Investment Disputes) Act 1966.

[105] See, for example, *The Republic of Kazakhstan v Istil Group Inc* [2006] EWHC 448; *Svenska Petroleum Exploration AB v Lithuania (No.2)* [2005] EWHC 2437 affirmed by the Court of Appeal at [2006] EWCA Civ 1529.

[106] See para.3–038 below.

[107] See further R Doak Bishop, James Crawford, W Michael Reisman (eds), *Foreign Investment Disputes: Cases, Materials and Commentary* (The Hague: Kluwer Law International, 2005) especially chs 2, 4, 12 and 13.

[108] In addition to treaties, many countries have national legislation which itself may confer similar rights upon investors.

[109] This needs to be done at the outset, as some of the treaties have what is known as a "fork in the road" provision which in effect means that the choice of a particular form of dispute resolution mechanism under the treaty precludes an investor from subsequently adopting an alternative route, even if it was one originally available under the treaty.

[110] Section 106 of the Arbitration Act 1996 provides that the Crown is bound by Pt I of that Act.

[111] For example, state entities in some jurisdictions only have capacity to enter into agreements providing for arbitration seated in their home jurisdiction. See further Jeremy Winter, "International Arbitration under Public Works Contracts" in *International and ICC Arbitration*, Centre of Construction Law and Management, King's College (London, 1990), pp.175–183.

capacity of state entities and public authorities to enter into arbitration agreements, unlike the position in certain civil law jurisdictions.[112]

3–036 **Sovereign immunity.** When dealing with a foreign state, state entity or public authority[113] it is important for both parties to consider whether they may be able to claim sovereign immunity.[114] The laws of many jurisdictions provide that if the state becomes involved in commercial activities then its ability to claim immunity is restricted, but some degree of immunity is given in respect of the state's activities.[115] In the arbitration context the types of immunity which are most likely to be of relevance are those relating to jurisdiction, enforcement and prejudgement proceedings such as an application for a freezing injunction. Each of these may be irrevocably waived by express contractual provision.

3–037 **Statutory provision.** The State Immunity Act 1978 provides[116] that a foreign state is not able to claim immunity in respect of proceedings in the courts of the United Kingdom which relate to arbitration.[117] However this does not override contrary provisions in the arbitration agreement and does not apply to arbitrations between states.[118]

3–038 **Relationship between states and state entities.** Subject to questions of sovereign immunity an arbitration award may be enforced against a state or a state entity.[119] More complicated is the relationship between the two and the question whether each can be held responsible for awards made against the other. This issue should be addressed at the outset of arbitration proceedings as enquiry may need to be made whether the state entity is to be treated as legally distinct from the state.[120] That will often require an investigation not only of the relevant

---

[112] See essay by Jeremy Winter cited above. A special statute was required for the Ile-de-France to have capacity to enter into an arbitration agreement for the EuroDisney project: Matthieu de Boisseson "Interrogations et doutes sur une évolution legislative: l'article 19 de la loi du 19 août 1986" [1987] Revue de l'arbitrage, 3–21.

[113] Or indeed an international organisation—see para.3–039 below.

[114] Consideration should be given to whether, even if immunity from jurisdiction has been waived, a claim might still be made to immunity from enforcement of any resulting award or from execution against the state's assets. See *Svenska Petroleum Exploration AB v Lithuania (No.2)* [2005] EWHC 2437 affirmed by the Court of Appeal at [2006] EWCA Civ 1529.

[115] The position under English law is set out in the State Immunity Act 1978.

[116] Section 9 of the State Immunity Act 1978.

[117] This includes proceedings to enforce a foreign arbitration award: *Svenska Petroleum Exploration AB v Lithuania (No.2)* [2005] EWHC 2437 affirmed by the Court of Appeal at [2006] EWCA Civ 1529.

[118] Section 9(2) of the State Immunity Act 1978.

[119] *Svenska Petroleum Exploration AB v Lithuania (No.2)* [2005] EWHC 2437 affirmed by the Court of Appeal at [2006] EWCA Civ 1529.

[120] An order requiring the Republic of the Ukraine to comply with an arbitrator's award was set aside because it was made against two separate and distinct parties, The State Property Fund of Ukraine and The Republic of Ukraine, whereas the award was against a single entity, namely The Republic of the Ukraine through the State Property Fund of Ukraine: *Norsk Hydro ASA v The State Property Fund of Ukraine* [2002] EWHC 2120.

constitutional documents but also of the manner in which they operate in order to determine whether the state entity in question is in fact an organ of the State.[121]

12. INTERNATIONAL ORGANISATIONS

Organisations created by treaty. A number of international organisa- 3–039 tions have been created by treaty. Care should be taken to examine the terms of the relevant treaty and constitution of the organisation when entering into any arbitration agreement with it, as the organisation may not be a legal person in English law and may therefore lack the capacity to take part in legal proceedings.[122] Even if the international organisation does have the capacity to enter into an arbitration agreement, it may seek to claim sovereign immunity.[123]

13. MULTI-PARTY DISPUTES

Introduction. Arbitration is generally a bilateral affair because the arbitration 3–040 agreement is typically made between two parties to a contract containing an arbitration clause. However contracts may be made between several parties, or there may be several related contracts comprised in a transaction and these may involve different parties. Claims may also arise against non-parties in relation to the same or a similar subject matter as that of an agreement with an arbitration clause. The situations described are quite distinct, but all give rise to potential difficulties as regards combining the different claims and parties in arbitration proceedings. At the heart of these difficulties is the common theme that arbitration is a consensual process and this will usually prevent the introduction into the proceedings of claims or parties which were not within the scope of what the contracting parties agreed to.[124] This section will examine the extent to which the further claims or parties can be dealt with in the same arbitration proceedings and how that result may be achieved.[125]

---

[121] See *Walker International Holdings Ltd* v *République Populaire du Congo and others* [2005] EWHC 2813 (Comm). In that case it was sought to enforce against the assets of a state entity although the award was against the state. The reverse of that situation occurred in *The Republic of Kazakhstan v Istil Group Inc* [2006] EWHC 448.

[122] See, for instance, *Arab Monetary Fund v Hashim and others (No.3)* [1991] 1 All E.R. 890. In *JH Rayner (Mincing Lane) Ltd v Department of Trade and Industry* [1990] 2 A.C. 418 an unsuccessful attempt was made to impose liability on the members of an international organisation in respect of an arbitration award obtained against the international organisation itself.

[123] See para.3–036.

[124] This sentence in an earlier edition of this book was cited with approval in *Metal Distributors (UK) Ltd v ZCCM Investment Holdings Plc* [2005] EWHC 156. For name-borrowing arbitrations, see para.6–182. See also paras 6–016 *et seq.* in relation to claims for deduction or set-off.

[125] For substituted parties, see para.3–016.

3–041 Reasons for objecting. Of course a party may have legitimate reasons for objecting to the introduction of further claims or parties. To do so could significantly add to the costs of the proceedings and the time necessary for his claims to be resolved. On the other hand, it may be more efficient overall for the claims or parties or both to be joined and this would avoid the risk of inconsistent decisions from different tribunals.

3–042 Parties to the same arbitration agreement. Perhaps the simplest situation is where there are more than two parties in dispute who are all parties to the same arbitration agreement, usually because it is contained in a contract to which they are all parties. In this situation there is little difficulty in conducting multi-party arbitration proceedings in relation to the particular dispute, provided that the mechanism for appointment of the tribunal can be properly established.[126] Various institutional rules now deal specifically with this aspect to ensure that the tribunal may be validly constituted.[127]

3–043 Disputes arising at different times. Problems may however occur if more than one dispute arises between the parties to the agreement at different times. Absent express provision for doing so it will not usually be possible to require consolidation of these disputes in the same arbitration proceedings. This is because the jurisdiction of the arbitrators in relation to the first dispute will already have been determined and the scope of the reference, which determines the tribunal's jurisdiction, cannot subsequently be enlarged to encompass the second dispute. Of course this is always subject to the parties and the tribunal expressly agreeing that the scope of the reference should be enlarged to encompass the later disputes.

3–044 Related claims, consolidation of arbitrations and concurrent hearings. Disputes may arise which, although connected, are the subject of two or more separate arbitration agreements. This would be the case where for example a party has entered into two separate agreements with different parties relating to the same subject matter. A good example is a construction project, where the main contractor enters into separate contracts with the employer and the sub-contractors. Each of the parties may agree in their arbitration clauses to have all related disputes[128] arising between any of them heard together in one arbitration. Alternatively the parties' arbitration agreements may contemplate having the disputes dealt with in separate arbitration proceedings but allowing those proceedings to be consolidated or for there to be concurrent hearings.[129]

---

[126] In particular the arbitration agreement should make clear which party or parties are to appoint members of the tribunal. It should be borne in mind that in some jurisdictions (e.g. France) the award will be vulnerable to challenge if all parties have not had an equal right to participate in the appointment of the tribunal.

[127] See, e.g. LCIA Rules, Art.8 and ICC Rules, Art.10.

[128] The question of who is to decide what disputes are related is addressed in para.3–045 below.

[129] As contemplated by s.35(1) of the Arbitration Act 1996.

There need be no agreement to which they are all party, provided the agreement into which each has entered demonstrates their consent to the chosen mechanism for dealing with disputes. So, in the above example, there will usually be no arbitration agreement entered into between the employer and the sub-contractor, but they may nevertheless both be bound to have their disputes heard in the same tripartite arbitration proceeding with the main contractor.[130] The court however has no power to consolidate arbitration proceedings or to order concurrent hearings.[131]

Drafting considerations. Careful drafting is needed in relation to these   3–045
agreements to ensure not just that the relevant provisions in the different agreements are clear and consistent but also that the mechanism proposed is workable. In particular, if the joining of disputes or proceedings is limited to those involving "related disputes", it will need to be clear what is meant by this[132] and who is to determine whether one dispute is related to another.[133] Often the parties will confer the power to make this determination on the tribunal already appointed which will be in a position to make an impartial assessment of the degree of overlap. Alternatively it may be left to one of the parties to decide, and in making the decision he may have regard solely to his own commercial interests.[134] Another approach is to provide that both parties have to agree that the disputes are related in order for the provision to operate and failing agreement they will be dealt with in separate arbitrations.[135]

Further matters to be considered. Timing can also be an important   3–046
factor. If an arbitration proceeding is at an advanced stage it may be inconvenient, inefficient and expensive to seek to join further claims, even if this is contemplated by the parties' agreement.[136] In order to address this it may be sensible to give the tribunal discretion as to whether additional claims, consolidation or concurrent hearings should be allowed. Alternatively the arbitration agreement may expressly

---

[130] *Trafalgar House Construction (Regions) Ltd v Railtrack Plc* [1995] 75 B.L.R. 55.

[131] *Elektrim SA v VivendiUniversal SA (No.2)* [2007] EWHC 571 at [72].

[132] In *City & General (Holborn) Ltd v AYH Plc* [2005] EWHC 2494 the arbitration agreement referred to "issues which are substantially the same as or are connected with issues raised in related disputes". The court held that this was to be construed having regard to the commercial purpose of avoiding multiplicity of proceedings and it was sufficient that a material portion of the issues were the same as or connected with the issues in dispute.

[133] Absent agreement or a provision as to who should make this determination it may be necessary to apply to the court for the appointment of an arbitrator under s.18(3) of the Arbitration Act 1996 and the court can then decide the issue: *City & General (Holborn) Ltd v AYH Plc* [2005] EWHC 2494.

[134] *Lafarge Redland Aggregates Ltd v Shephard Hill Civil Engineering Ltd* [2000] 1 W.L.R. 1621, *per* Lord Hobhouse at 1642. The Court of Appeal had expressed the view that the decision had to be made in good faith, and even contemplated that the party concerned had an obligation to act reasonably: [1999] C.I.L.L. 1457.

[135] Of course this effectively provides both parties with a right of veto.

[136] Article 19 of the ICC Rules allows new claims which fall outside the terms of reference to be added only where authorised by the tribunal which shall consider the nature of the new claims, the stage of the arbitration and other relevant circumstances.

limit the power to do so to cases where the further claims are brought within a certain time or before particular steps have been taken.[137]

3–047 Joining third parties to arbitration proceedings. The position of third parties who have not entered into any binding agreement to refer their disputes to arbitration is rather different. In the ordinary course they would not be permitted to join in the arbitration proceedings unless the parties and, if already appointed, the tribunal agree. The parties may however make provision in their arbitration agreement for third parties to be allowed to join the proceedings. For example,[138] Art.22.1(h) of the LCIA Rules expressly empowers the tribunal to allow a third party to join the proceedings if the third party and one of the existing parties agree.[139] Again careful drafting would be necessary to ensure clarity as to the precise circumstances in which participation of the third party is permitted and what the nature of his role is to be.

3–048 Absence of express agreement. A tribunal has no power to order consolidation of proceedings or concurrent hearings without the agreement of all the parties.[140] Problems can arise where a contract provides for any disputes arising under it to be determined in the same arbitration as disputes arising under another contract, but that other contract contains no corresponding provision. In these circumstances neither the courts nor the tribunal can insist upon a tripartite arbitration. However, the court will strive to allow the claims to proceed in separate arbitrations.[141]

---

[137] For example it may need to be done before an arbitrator has been agreed or appointed to determine the later dispute: *Trafalgar House Construction (Regions) Ltd v Railtrack Plc* [1995] 75 B.L.R. 55. There was authority prior to the 1996 Act that if a party pursues an arbitration and, some time later, commences a further arbitration against another party, the court may decline to enforce an agreement to consolidate because it could unfairly delay the conclusion of the first arbitration to the detriment of the other party: see *Higgs and Hill Building Ltd v Campbell Denis Ltd* [1982] 28 B.L.R. 47, and *Hyundai Engineering Construction Co Ltd v Active Building and Civil Construction Pte Ltd* [1989] 45 B.L.R. 62. It is unlikely these decisions would now be followed given the emphasis on party autonomy in s.1(b) of the Arbitration Act 1996 and the terms of s.35(1) of the Arbitration Act 1996.

[138] The UNCITRAL Working Group currently considering revisions to the UNCITRAL Arbitration Rules is also considering introducing a similar provision to those rules: see paras 121 *et seq.* of the Report of the 46th Session in New York, February 2007, at *www.uncitral.org.*

[139] This rule has rarely been invoked and doubts have been expressed about the enforceability of any resulting award in favour of the third party. However by adopting the LCIA Rules the parties are agreeing to third parties being joined on these terms. The resulting award ought therefore to be enforceable, even against a party who opposed the third party joining the proceedings. See also *The Bay Hotel and Resort Ltd v Cavalier Construction Co Ltd* [2001] UKPC 34.

[140] Arbitration Act 1996, s.35(2).

[141] *Lafarge Redland Aggregates Ltd v Shephard Hill Civil Engineering Ltd* [2000] 1 W.L.R. 1621. That case involved a sub-contract under the FCEC Blue Form which provided for disputes to be dealt with jointly with disputes under the main contract. The disputes clause in the main contract contained no reciprocal provision obliging the employer to participate in a tripartite arbitration, and arbitration under the main contract was delayed pending negotiations between the employer and the main contractor. A majority of the House of Lords decided that the sub-contractor could proceed with a separate arbitration if the employer declined to co-operate with a tripartite arbitration or if the contractor failed to initiate the arbitration under the main contract within a reasonable time.

Statutory provision. Judges have noted the benefits that could result from   3–049
the abolition of the restriction preventing the joining of third parties and consolidation of arbitrations,[142] but the draftsmen of the Arbitration Act 1996 decided
this would be too great an interference with the principle of party autonomy.[143]
Section 35 of the Act, which deals with the subject, has no teeth. After confirming
that parties are free to agree on consolidation and concurrent hearings, s.35 goes
on to state that an arbitral tribunal has no power to order consolidation or
concurrent hearings without the agreement of the parties.

Court powers. Nothing is said in the Arbitration Act 1996 about any power   3–050
of the court to order consolidation of arbitrations or concurrent hearings, with the
result that the court does not have these powers.[144] The court may however be
called upon to assist in the appointment of the tribunal in the absence of
agreement between the parties on the tribunal or on an appointing authority. In
these circumstances the court can appoint the same tribunal to hear a number of
different disputes in consecutive hearings.[145] The court cannot require the parties
to agree to that tribunal hearing the different cases concurrently.

14. ARBITRAL INSTITUTIONS

General. Arbitral institutions exist to provide arbitration services, either as   3–051
their sole or principal purpose, or as ancillary to other functions of a trade or
professional association.[146] For instance, the principal purpose of the LCIA and
the Chartered Institute of Arbitrators is to provide arbitration (and ADR) services.[147] The ICC is a world trade organisation, one of whose divisions provides
arbitration and conciliation services. The Royal Institution of Chartered Surveyors
is a professional association of English surveyors which provides arbitration
services as one part of its activities. ICSID is an autonomous arbitral institution
affiliated to the World Bank.[148]

---

[142] Goff J. (as he then was) in *Interbulk Ltd v Aiden Shipping Co Ltd, The "Vimeira"* [1984] 2 Lloyd's
Rep. 4664 at 467, Lloyd J. (as he then was) in *World Pride Shipping Ltd v Daiachi Chuo Kisen Kaisha,
The "Golden Anne"* [1984] 2 Lloyd's Rep. 489 at 491, Steyn J. (as he then was) in *Property
Investments Holdings Ltd v Byfield Building Services* (1985) 31 B.L.R. 47 at 56, Staughton L.J. in
Furness Withy (Australia) Pty Ltd v Metal Distributors (UK) Ltd (The "Amazonia") [1990] 1
Lloyd's Rep. 236 at 240.
[143] DAC report, paras 177 *et seq.*
[144] Arbitration Act 1996, s.1(c).
[145] *Abu Dhabi Gas Liquefaction Co Ltd v Eastern Bechtel Corp and Chiyoda Chemical Engineering &
Construction Co Ltd* [1982] 2 Lloyd's Rep. 425.
[146] Care should be taken to ensure selection of an appropriate institution: see *Flight Training International Inc v International Fire Training Equipment Ltd* [2004] EWHC 721 where an agreement
provided for the submission of disputes to ACAS which in fact dealt only with employment
disputes and not commercial disputes.
[147] Although both also have an important educational role in relation to arbitration.
[148] See *www.worldbank.org/icsid*.

3–052 **Role of institutions in arbitration agreements.**[149] Arbitration institutions can play an important role in arbitration agreements. They and their rules are often specified in the arbitration agreement, although the parties may agree to take advantage of the services offered by an institution after a dispute has arisen. An arbitral institution may adopt a number of different roles in relation to the arbitration proceedings depending upon what the parties have agreed their role should be. In particular the institution may:

(a) provide arbitration rules pursuant to which the arbitration will be conducted;

(b) act as the appointing authority which, in the absence of agreement between the parties, appoints the tribunal to hear the dispute and may also deal with any challenges to or replacement of arbitrators[150];

(c) act as an account holder for fees and deposits and administer the funds necessary to pay for the tribunal's fees and expenses[151];

(d) supervise the conduct of the arbitration by acting as an administrator for the proceedings.

These functions are not mutually exclusive and an institution will frequently act in a combination of some or all of these roles.[152]

3–053 **Administration by institution.** Administration services and a degree of supervision of the arbitration is offered by certain institutions, including the ICC and the LCIA. For example, the services provided by the ICC include:

● ensuring that all parties and the tribunal receive written submissions;

● approving the terms of reference[152a];

● assisting the parties and the arbitrators to deal with administrative issues;

● encouraging the tribunal to make an award without delay; and

● checking the award for clerical and similar errors.[152b]

The LCIA starts proceedings with all communications being sent through its Registrar, but once the tribunal is formed it usually directs that communications between it and the parties take place directly. The LCIA's Registrar still receives copies of correspondence and submissions between the tribunal and the parties and continues to administer the arbitration, depending upon the needs of the

---

[149] See further para.2–061.
[150] The institution may also provide a list of suitably qualified arbitrators to assist a party in selecting an arbitrator.
[151] The LCIA in particular regularly provides this service.
[152] See paras 2–061 *et seq.* and 4–075.
[152a] Terms of reference are dealt with in Art.18 of the ICC Rules.
[152b] Awards are scrutinised by the ICC Court: see Art.27 of the ICC Rules.

parties and the tribunal. The LCIA supervision of administered arbitrations is less extensive than that provided by the ICC, and in particular there are no terms of reference and no formal "scrutiny" of the award. Administration by an arbitral institution naturally involves some cost to the parties,[152c] but this may be out-weighed by the value of the services offered. Proper administration can make a real contribution to the effectiveness of an arbitration by helping to keep the proceedings moving along. The pace of an arbitration can be significantly slowed down by one or (both) of the parties failing to co-operate in the conduct of the proceedings; an institution may be able to communicate with and influence an uncooperative party or a tardy tribunal.

Immunity. Arbitration institutions[153] are not liable for anything done or 3–054
omitted in the discharge or purported discharge of the function of appointing or nominating arbitrators unless the act or omission is shown to have been in bad faith.[154] Nor can liability attach to the appointing institution as a consequence of the act of appointment or nomination, for the acts and omissions of the arbitrator (or his employees or agents) in the discharge or purported discharge of the functions of an arbitrator.[155] Employees or agents of arbitral or other institutions are also protected.[156] The DAC report gave two reasons for this statutory immunity. First, there is a risk that attempts would be made to hold institutions or individuals responsible for the consequences of their appointments in terms of what the arbitrators do or fail to do, which would reopen matters referred to arbitration. Second, arbitral institutions do not have "deep pockets" and might not be able to afford the cost of insurance; vulnerability to lawsuits might drive them out of existence.[157] It would not be easy to show bad faith, particularly in the case of an appointing authority, so the institution will be kept in line by the desire to maintain its reputation rather than by the desire to avoid law suits. The immunity does not extend to actions or omissions other than in connection with the appointment of arbitrators, and therefore does not provide a defence to the negligent administration of arbitrations or dealings with funds deposited by the parties.

[152c] Most arbitration institutions, including the ICC and the LCIA, levy a fixed, non-returnable registration fee from the claimant. From then on institutions diverge between charging scale fees and time-related rates. the ICC Court of Arbitration fixes its administrative costs and arbitrators' fees on the basis of a percentage of the amount in dispute. The LCIA charges administration fees and arbitrators' fees at hourly rates, split between the parties.
[153] And individuals acting as appointing authorities.
[154] Section 74(1) of the Arbitration Act 1996.
[155] Section 74(2) of the Arbitration Act 1996.
[156] Section 74(3) of the Arbitration Act 1996.
[157] DAC report, paras 299–301.

CHAPTER 4

THE TRIBUNAL

1. INTRODUCTION

Contents of chapter. This chapter is devoted to the tribunal which consists   4–001
of the person or persons appointed to decide a dispute submitted to arbitration.
It begins by defining who is and who is not an arbitrator and by distinguishing the
different types of arbitral tribunal. It then discusses the qualifications needed for
an arbitrator before turning to the way the tribunal is appointed and remunerated.
Discussion follows on the powers of the tribunal. Then, the general and specific
duties of the tribunal are identified with detailed attention being given to the
important subjects of impartiality and independence.[1] The chapter concludes with
a short discussion on the liabilities of an arbitral tribunal and how its authority
may be terminated.

2. DEFINITIONS

(a) The arbitrator

Role of an arbitrator. An arbitrator's task is to determine disputes referred   4–002
to him, either alone if he is appointed as the sole member of an arbitral tribunal
or jointly with other members of a tribunal, on the basis of the evidence and
submissions, according to the law chosen by the parties or other considerations
agreed by them or determined by the tribunal,[1a] and within the general obligation
of a fair resolution by an impartial tribunal without unnecessary delay or expense.[2]
Despite the apparent similarities with the role of a judge, an arbitrator is not a
judge in the sense of an appointee of the state who presides over lawsuits. The
authority of an arbitral tribunal arises entirely from the agreement between the
parties.[3] However, as will be seen below,[4] a judge very occasionally may be
appointed an arbitrator. Another feature which distinguishes an arbitrator from a

---

[1] See paras 4–106 *et seq.*
[1a] For example, if a choice of "internationally accepted principles of law governing international
 relations" does not count as substantive law it could be treated as a choice of "such other
 considerations as are agreed by the parties"—s.46(1)(b) of the Arbitration Act 1996. See *Deutsche
 Schachtbau-und Tiefbohrgesellschaft GmbH v R'As Al Khaimah National Oil Co* [1987] 3 W.L.R.
 1023.
[2] Section 1(1) of the Arbitration Act 1996.
[3] This is usually the case, although authority may be derived from statute or treaty—see Appendix
 3 for statutory arbitrations.
[4] See paras 4–019 *et seq.*

judge is that an arbitrator almost always performs his task in private. This arises from the wishes of the parties, sometimes expressed and, where not expressed, always implied, that the arbitration is to be private.[5]

4–003   **Experts and valuers.** There is a traditional distinction between the role of arbitrators and experts, including valuers, appointed to determine issues "as an expert and not as an arbitrator". The role of an expert fulfils many of the requirements set out in the previous paragraph, particularly those concerning the private, contractual aspects. But there are a number of differences. The most significant is that an expert need not act judicially.[6] This has two consequences: an expert can apply his own expertise to deciding the question referred and an expert is not bound to give each party an opportunity to put its case and to deal with that of the other party.[7]

4–004   **Quasi-arbitrators.** The term "quasi-arbitrator" is obsolete except for one limited sense, having lost its former meaning of a valuer/expert possessing arbitral immunity.[8] The term is now properly applied only to the exceptional case of an arbitrator acting at common law and not under the Arbitration Act where the submission to arbitration is oral.[9]

(b) Different types of tribunal

4–005   **A range of roles.** The word "arbitrator" is used to embrace a number of roles arising from the different types of arbitral tribunal that can be established:

- a tribunal consisting of a sole arbitrator appointed by joint agreement of the parties or otherwise;

- a member of a tribunal of two arbitrators;

- an arbitrator/advocate[10];

- an umpire;

- a party-appointed arbitrator, sitting as a member of a tribunal of three or more arbitrators; or

- a third arbitrator, or "president" or "chairman".

---

[5] See para.1–010.
[6] See para.2–028.
[7] Sections 33(1)(a) and 34(2)(g) of the Arbitration Act 1996.
[8] See J Kendall, *Expert Determination* (3rd edn). The effect of s.5 of the Arbitration Act 1996 is to reduce the number of potential members of this species to close to zero.
[9] See para.2–015 and Lord Simon in *Arenson v Casson Beckman Rutley & Co* [1975] 3 W.L.R. 815 at 824.
[10] See para.4–008 for this unusual hybrid.

In this book, as elsewhere, the word "arbitrator" is used to cover all these functions, but where a distinction has to be drawn between them the text makes this clear. The Arbitration Act 1996 makes frequent use of the expressions "tribunal" and "arbitral tribunal", and it is appropriate to use these expressions in preference to the word "arbitrator" where, as is usually the case, the position of a tribunal is in issue, not that of any individual member. The reason for the historical English preference for the term "arbitrator" rather than tribunal arises from the fact that, as can be seen from the case reports, many arbitral tribunals in England have traditionally consisted of only one arbitrator.[11]

Sole arbitrator. A sole (or single) arbitrator is a complete tribunal. He may be   **4–006**
appointed by agreement of the parties, an appointing authority or the court. Unless a contrary intention is expressed, every arbitration agreement is deemed to include a provision that the reference shall be to a single arbitrator.[12] The intention may be expressed in rules of arbitration referred to in the arbitration agreement, but rules of arbitration differ where the agreement itself is silent about the number of arbitrators to be appointed.[13] Therefore, it is preferable to state in the arbitration agreement if a sole arbitrator is to be appointed.

A member of a tribunal of two arbitrators. English law allows a   **4–007**
tribunal of two arbitrators, and it presumes, in the absence of other evidence, that the parties intended to appoint a tribunal of two arbitrators where they had agreed on decision by "arbitrators", on the basis that the irreducible minimum is two not three.[14] This could lead to deadlock between the two arbitrators, but for the statutory provision that, unless otherwise agreed by the parties, an agreement that the number of arbitrators shall be two[15] shall be understood as requiring the appointment of an additional arbitrator as chairman of the tribunal[16]: there has to be specific agreement if the third arbitrator is to act as an umpire.[17] In practice the tribunals which are subject to the parties' specific agreement for an umpire are usually found in trade and commodity arbitrations conducted in the City of London.[18]

An arbitrator/advocate. The role of arbitrator and that of advocate are   **4–008**
usually completely separate, because an arbitrator is expected to be impartial

---

[11] See para.1–016.

[12] Section 15(3) of the Arbitration Act 1996. Under the Model Law, Art.10(2) (see Appendix 4), the number of arbitrators is three unless the parties determine otherwise.

[13] Compare, for example, LCIA Rules, Art.5.4 with ICC Rules of Arbitration, Art.8.2.

[14] *Fletamentos Maritimos SA v Effjohn International BV* [1995] 1 Lloyd's Rep. 311.

[15] Or any other even number.

[16] Section 15(2) of the Arbitration Act 1996.

[17] Sections 15(2) and 21 of the Arbitration Act 1996. Under the previous legislation umpires were the "default" for all two-member tribunals who disagreed (see the Arbitration Act 1950, s.8).

[18] The ICC declined jurisdiction in an arbitration of this sort, *Sumitomo Heavy Industries v Oil and Natural Gas Commission* [1994] 1 Lloyd's Rep. 45. The two-arbitrator tribunal does not easily fit into the scheme of the ICC's Rules, and parties are encouraged to agree to a tribunal of three arbitrators.

however appointed.[19] Where, however, there is a tribunal of two arbitrators and the third member is not the chairman but is to act as an umpire, the arbitrators may, in certain arbitrations, once they have been replaced as the tribunal by the umpire, become advocates for the parties who appointed them and argue the dispute before the umpire.[20]

4–009 **An umpire.** If parties agree that the third arbitrator is to act as an umpire,[21] the umpire is appointed by the party-appointed arbitrators at any time and forthwith if they disagree about the dispute referred to them.[22] The umpire system is a "peculiarly English concept": those responsible for drafting the Arbitration Act 1996 considered, but eventually decided against, recommending its abolition.[23] Parties are free to agree on whether the umpire attends proceedings immediately after his appointment and when he replaces the other arbitrators: if there is no agreement, there is a statutory code.[24]

4–010 **A party-appointed arbitrator sitting as a member of a tribunal.** Each party may be entitled to appoint its own arbitrator, but a party-appointed arbitrator has no special role to play other than as a member of the tribunal.[25] A party-appointed arbitrator does not change his status on the completion of the tribunal by its third member. This should be contrasted with the position described above[26] where a tribunal originally consisted of two arbitrators who were unable to reach agreement and were replaced as the tribunal by the umpire. A tribunal of three or more does not always allow for the appointment or even nomination by each party of an arbitrator. The arbitration agreement may provide that all the arbitrators are to be appointed by an independent appointing authority. In certain cases, arbitration rules provide for appointment of the whole tribunal by an appointing authority.[27]

4–011 **A third arbitrator (or "president" or "chairman").** Where parties agree that there will be a tribunal of three arbitrators, the third acts as the chairman unless the parties agree he should act as an umpire.[28] Arbitration rules and provisions made in ad hoc arbitrations may make a distinction between the chairman and the other members of the tribunal. For instance, the chairman may be given the power to make procedural rulings, and to give the casting vote where

---

[19] See para.4–106 for a discussion of this duty.
[20] This was a practice in some shipping arbitrations, for example, before the Arbitration Act 1996: see for instance *Rahcassi Shipping Co SA v Blue Star Line Ltd* [1969] 1 Q.B. 173. Perhaps specific agreement is now needed on this pursuant to s.15 of the Arbitration Act 1996.
[21] Otherwise, the third arbitrator acts as chairman: s.15(2) of the Arbitration Act 1996.
[22] Section 16(6)(b) of the Arbitration Act 1996: cf. Arbitration Act 1950, s.8(2).
[23] DAC report, para.94. See para.4–150.
[24] Section 21 of the Arbitration Act 1996, see para.4–165 below.
[25] See paras 4–145 *et seq.* The exception of the arbitrator/advocate has already been mentioned.
[26] See para.4–009.
[27] The ICC Rules, Art.10 contain such a provision in the case of multi-party arbitrations.
[28] Section 15(1) and (2) of the Arbitration Act 1996.

otherwise there would be no majority decision.[29] In the absence of agreement, there is a statutory code providing that decisions, orders and awards shall be made by all or a majority of the arbitrators (including the chairman) and the view of the chairman shall prevail in relation to a decision, order or award in respect of which there is neither unanimity nor a majority.[30] The chairman's fees may be fixed at a higher rate than those of the party-appointed arbitrators to reflect that the chairman will usually bear a greater burden when it comes to writing the award.

A member of a larger tribunal. Some tribunals have a membership of a higher odd number than three. An appeal board composed of five persons hears appeals from two-arbitrator panels in certain commodity arbitrations.[31] The number of arbitrators for the Iran-United States Claims Tribunal has been nine.[32]   4–012

3. QUALIFICATIONS OF AN ARBITRATOR

(a) General considerations

Who may be appointed as an arbitrator? The law does not impose general restrictions on who may be appointed an arbitrator. It is not a recognised profession like that of solicitor or barrister although it is becoming increasingly common for some individuals to practice solely as arbitrators. It is a feature of English arbitration practice that non-lawyers may become arbitrators in specialist fields such as rent reviews, engineering, shipping and construction. The Chartered Institute of Arbitrators runs courses and examinations and awards recognition to those it regards as suitably qualified to act as an arbitrator. Other professional bodies in England which act as appointing authorities for arbitrators also take steps to ensure that professional standards are maintained by running courses, by providing continuing education and by periodically reviewing the membership lists and removing certain names.[33] However, arbitration does not form part of the compulsory training of either solicitors or barristers, although arbitration is now being taught in postgraduate courses attended by lawyers in the fields of commercial and construction law.[34] There are in fact no minimum requirements at all,   4–013

---

[29] ICC Rules, Art.25.1.

[30] Section 20 of the Arbitration Act 1996. See para.4–147.

[31] For example, those run by FOSFA and GAFTA, see Derek Kirby Johnson, "Commodity Trade Arbitration", in Bernstein's Handbook of Arbitration and Dispute Resolution Practice (4th edn, Sweet & Maxwell, 2003), p.46.2.

[32] Or any agreed larger multiple of three, Claims Settlement Declaration of January 19, 1981, Art.III.1, quoted in (1982) VII Yearbook Commercial Arbitration, at 258.

[33] As was done by the Royal Institution of Chartered Surveyors in 1993: Estates Gazette 28, February 12, 1994.

[34] For example, the Master of Laws (LLM) Programme of the University of London entitled International and Comparative Commercial Arbitration.

because the authority of the arbitral tribunal arises from the parties' contract, and the law allows contracting parties complete freedom to choose their tribunal.

4–014 **Unsuitable appointees.** Common sense usually, but not always, prevents the appointment of completely unsuitable people[35] and an appointing authority may reserve the right not to confirm the nomination of an arbitrator who is considered unsuitable.[36] But parties and their advisers wish to appoint the most suitable candidate(s), and not simply avoid those that are unsuitable. Advice should be taken and references obtained where the proposed candidates are not known. Even after that stage, it may be difficult to secure the appointment of the preferred candidate where the other party's agreement is required because the other party may reject the proposal. In those circumstances the appointing authority will make the selection.[37] From a practical point of view, one of the most important qualifications for any arbitrator is that he should remain alive and well for the duration of the proceedings. Parties who are concerned about the serious consequences of having to replace tribunal members who die or become infirm take out insurance on the arbitrators' life and health. This will at least help to cover the costs of fresh hearings should an original appointee become too ill to continue or die in the course of the reference.

4–015 **Personal nature of arbitral function.** An arbitration agreement does not have to refer disputes to a tribunal of immediately identified individuals. The parties may refer disputes to a fluctuating body of persons whose individual members vary from time to time, provided that body fulfils the requirement to appoint arbitral tribunal members when the particular dispute comes for decision.[38]

What, then, is the effect of an arbitration agreement referring a dispute to a partnership or a corporation? By analogy with *Keighley Maxsted*[39] the arbitration agreement must be construed as requiring that the firm or corporation would select suitable arbitrators from its own members. There is authority that a partnership can be appointed to act as an arbitral tribunal.[40]

Once, however, an arbitrator is appointed there is no doubt that it is a personal function and an arbitrator's authority ceases on his death.[41]

---

[35] Most rules of arbitration provide a challenge procedure, which safeguards against the choice of a partial arbitrator. See paras 4–051 *et seq*.

[36] The LCIA Rules, Art.7.1, for example, contains such a provision.

[37] See para.4–049.

[38] *Keighley Maxsted & Co v Bryan Durant & Co* [1893] 1 Q.B. 405, where the court upheld an award made by a panel of five chosen by a committee of the London Corn Trade Association.

[39] Cited above in fn.38. Presumably a similar selection is carried out by the British Boxing Board of Control but the point is not discussed in the judgment in *Watson v Prager and another* [1991] 3 All E.R. 487.

[40] For an example of a finding that an agreement to refer a valuation to a partnership was a reference to that partnership to act as arbitrators, see *Leigh v English Property Corp Ltd* [1976] 2 Lloyd's Rep. 298.

[41] Section 26(1) of the Arbitration Act 1996.

Tribunals of specific number of members. Where an arbitration   4–016
agreement provides for a tribunal of a specific number of members, a tribunal
composed of a different number of members does not have jurisdiction[42] unless
the parties to the arbitration agree to vary or waive the requirement, or a party is
in default of appointment[43] or loses the right to object.[44]

If a vacancy occurs because one member of the tribunal dies, resigns or is
removed, the parties may agree not to replace him in which case the remaining
members of the tribunal (a truncated tribunal) may proceed with the arbitration
and make an award.[45]

(b) Special qualifications

Special qualifications and jurisdiction. The arbitration agreement   4–017
may provide that the member(s) of the tribunal must have some special qualification. It is then a ground of objection to the jurisdiction of a tribunal that one or
more of its members does not have that qualification.[46] The sort of qualification
required may be:

- membership of a particular trade association[47] or;

- being "commercial men"[48] or;

- being a Queen's Counsel.

Special qualifications that tribunal members must have may be imposed:

- either expressly by the words of the arbitration agreement or;

- indirectly by the rules incorporated into an arbitration agreement.

The requirement that members of a tribunal hold a particular qualification does
not extend to the umpire appointed in the same reference unless the arbitration
agreement, or the rules it incorporates, require the umpire to have that same
qualification.[49] The courts strive to uphold the jurisdiction of a tribunal if the
deviation from the qualification is not clearly established.[50]

---

[42] *Mallozzi v Carapelli SpA* [1976] 1 Lloyd's Rep. 407.
[43] Section 17 of the Arbitration Act 1996.
[44] Section 73(1)(d) of the Arbitration Act 1996, see para.7–127.
[45] Section 27(1)(a) of the Arbitration Act 1996 contemplates this possibility as do some arbitration
rules, e.g. ICC Rules, Art.12.5.
[46] See para.7–114 for discussion of this challenge as a ground for applying to the court for removing
the arbitrator.
[47] *Oakland Metal Co v Benaim (D) & Co* [1953] 2 Q.B. 261; *Jungheim, Hopkins & Co v Foukelmann*
[1909] 2 K.B. 948.
[48] See para.4–018.
[49] *Macleod Ross & Co v Craddock Manners Ltd* [1954] 1 Lloyd's Rep. 258—contrast *Rahcassi Shipping
Co SA v Blue Star Line* [1969] 1 Q.B. 173.
[50] *Pan Atlantic Group Inc and others v Hassneh Insurance Co of Israel Ltd* [1992] 2 Lloyd's Rep. 120,
where the Court of Appeal dismissed a challenge to an arbitrator who had resigned from a position
that met the requirements.

The effect of a successful challenge to an arbitrator on the ground that he does not have a special qualification required by the arbitration agreement is that the appointment, and all proceedings which follow, including the award, are void, because the arbitrator lacks jurisdiction.[51] Further, a mistake as to his qualification may vitiate a party's consent to the appointment,[52] but the right to object can be lost if it is not exercised in a timely fashion.[53]

4-018 **"Commercial Men".** Arbitration clauses sometimes specify that tribunals are to be composed of "commercial men". The courts are reluctant to lay down general principles as to the meaning of this expression, preferring to construe the expression in its context. For example, someone who had formerly been a solicitor, but was for many years a full-time maritime arbitrator, was held to be within the class of persons to whom the parties to a charterparty were referring when using the expression "commercial men". What mattered was the "arbitrator's practical commercial experience".[54]

(c) Judges[55]

4-019 **Judges may sit as arbitrators.** In special circumstances, a judge of the Commercial Court or the Technology and Construction Court (a TCC judge) may accept appointment as a sole arbitrator or as an umpire,[56] although such appointments are rare. The award of a judge who sits as an arbitrator or umpire is subject to appeal in the same way as an award made by an arbitrator who is not a judge, except that appeals from the decision of a judge-arbitrator are to the Court of Appeal.[57] Such an appeal against the decision of a judge—arbitrator was made in *Henry Boot Ltd v Alstom Combined Cycles.*[58] The Court of Appeal in that case also found that the appeal raised a question of general importance, but it was not sufficient to justify giving leave to appeal to the House of Lords.[59] An application that a judge at the trial of an action sit in the dual capacity of judge and arbitrator

---

[51] *Rahcassi Shipping Co SA v Blue Star Line Ltd* cited above in fn.20, *Pando Compania Naviera SA v Filmo SAS* [1975] 1 Q.B. 742.
[52] In *Continental Grain Co v China Petroleum Technology & Development Corp*, Mance J., December 4, 1998, the court reviewed different kinds of mistake and found on the evidence that the mistake by one party (unilateral mistake) was not sufficiently fundamental to vitiate consent to the appointment of the arbitrator concerned.
[53] Section 73(1)(a) of the Arbitration Act 1996, see para.7-127 and footnote.
[54] *Pando Compania Naviera SA v Filmo SAS* cited above in fn.51.
[55] See DAC report, para.340-3.
[56] Section 93(1) of the Arbitration Act 1996. A judge may not, therefore, accept appointment as a party-appointed arbitrator or as a chairman of a tribunal.
[57] Section 93(6) of the Arbitration Act 1996 and Sch.2, para.2(1).
[58] [2005] EWCA Civ 814.
[59] *Henry Boot* cited above in fn.58, paras 82-86.

was refused on the basis that no one person can fulfil both functions at the same time.[60] Where a judge is appointed as arbitrator, his fees are paid to the court.[61]

Judges of the Commercial Court. The Commercial Court is frequently   4–020
concerned with disputes over contracts of the type which contain arbitration clauses, classically, commodity and shipping contracts. The commercial court also supervises arbitrations arising from commercial contracts of that type and is the court which generally deals with points of law arising from any arbitration.[62] Judges of the Commercial Court are therefore suited to be chosen as arbitrators in commercial cases.[63] However, a judge of the Commercial Court is not permitted to accept an appointment unless the Lord Chief Justice has informed him that, having regard to the state of business in the High Court and the Crown Court, he can be made available.[64] In practice, appointments of commercial judges as arbitrators are very rare although the judiciary has made a recent attempt to change this practice.[65]

TCC judges. Previously known as Official Referees, the judges of the Technol-   4–021
ogy and Construction Court decide a broad scope of claims that are not limited to technology and building disputes.[66] A TCC judge may, if in all the circumstances he thinks fit, accept an appointment as sole arbitrator, or as umpire under an arbitration agreement. He will not, however, be permitted to accept an appointment unless the Lord Chief Justice has informed him, that, having regard to the state of the court's business, he can be made available.[67]

County court judges. There is no similar statutory provision permitting   4–022
County Court judges to be appointed by parties as arbitrators, but they do act as statutory arbitrators in county court claims.[68]

---

[60] *Wilson v Keen*, unreported, Court of Appeal, June 25, 1991.
[61] Section 93(4) of the Arbitration Act 1996, cf. Administration of Justice Act 1970, s.4.
[62] CPR Pt 62(12).
[63] A commercial claim means "any claim arising out of the transaction of trade and commerce", including the specific claims listed in CPR Pt 58.
[64] Section 93(2) of the Arbitration Act 1996.
[65] On May 7, 2007, Mr Justice David Steel, the judge in charge of the Commercial Court, wrote to all heads of chambers and law firms in London to make sure that sets were "aware" that judges "may accept appointments as a sole arbitrator". Reported at *www.thelawyer.com*.
[66] CPR Pt 60. The Practice Direction made under this Part gives examples of the TCC claims—see White Book, 2E–10.
[67] Section 93(3) of the Arbitration Act 1996, cf. Arbitration Act 1950, s.11, as amended by Court and Legal Services Act 1990, s.99.
[68] Section 92 of the Arbitration Act 1996, see Appendix 3.

(d) Impartiality and disinterest

4-023   **General.** The general proposition that arbitrators should be impartial and disinterested is uncontroversial. It is more difficult to provide an adequate definition of partiality and interest, but the law has been clarified. Section 33 of the Act imposes on the tribunal a duty to act fairly and impartially as between the parties,[69] but as will be seen from the discussion in the section, Duties of the Arbitral Tribunal,[70] the tribunal may, because of arbitration rules incorporated into the arbitration agreement,[71] have an additional duty to be independent of the parties. The subjects of impartiality and independence, as well as the related subject of neutrality, are discussed in that later section of this chapter.[72]

4. APPOINTMENT OF AN ARBITRAL TRIBUNAL

(a) Introduction

4-024   **Appointment by agreement of the parties.** Arbitration agreements usually give the parties an opportunity to agree on the appointment of the arbitral tribunal. The most satisfactory result is where the parties agree on the tribunal. This is because, if parties do not agree on who to appoint, they lose control over the composition of the tribunal. The control then passes to an appointing authority, or to the court. Parties are free to agree on the procedure for appointing the tribunal, including the procedure for appointing a chairman.[73] Whatever procedure they adopt, parties should look at each other's nominations objectively and try to rationalise any suspicion they feel about a particular nomination. Unless a procedure for appointment has already been agreed and implemented,[74] simultaneous exchange of lists may help to avoid such suspicion. Each party puts forward a list of names[75] proposed for appointment as arbitrator. Parties exchange and compare each other's lists to see if any of the names appear on both lists. The same nominee(s) appearing on both lists may or (if that is the parties' agreement) will be selected. Even if there are no common names, there may be one or more candidates on the lists which are acceptable to both parties. If necessary, lists can continue to be exchanged until there are sufficient matches to constitute a tribunal.

---

[69] Section 33(1)(a) of the Arbitration Act 1996.
[70] Paragraphs 4–104 *et seq.*
[71] For example, LCIA Rules, Art.5.2 and ICC Rules, Art.7.1. See further paras 4–112 to 4–113.
[72] See paras 4–107 *et seq.*
[73] Section 16(1) of the Arbitration Act 1996.
[74] The exchange of lists is best suited for appointment of a sole arbitrator or chairman of a tribunal. When a claimant has already nominated an arbitrator pursuant to an agreed procedure, the opportunity for exchanging lists will only arise for the appointment of a chairman.
[75] In one Canadian case, unreported but known to the authors, the lists were of as many as 10 nominations for each member of a three-arbitrator tribunal.

Statutory appointment procedure. If there is no agreement on the   4–025
procedure for appointment, the Act provides the following[76]:

  (i) Tribunal of one arbitrator: parties jointly appoint the arbitrator not later
      than 28 days after service of a request in writing by either party to do
      so.[77]

 (ii) Tribunal of two arbitrators: each party appoints one arbitrator not later
      than 14 days after the service of a request in writing by either party to do
      so.[78]

(iii) Tribunal of three arbitrators: each party appoints one arbitrator not later
      than 14 days after service of a request in writing by either party to do so,
      and the two so appointed forthwith appoint a third arbitrator as the
      chairman of the tribunal.[79]

 (iv) Tribunal of two arbitrators and an umpire: each party appoints one
      arbitrator not later than 14 days after service of a request in writing by
      either party to do so. The two so appointed may appoint an umpire at any
      time after they themselves are appointed and shall do so before any
      substantive hearing or forthwith if they cannot agree on any matter relating
      to the arbitration.[80]

  (v) Upon the failure of any of the above, and in any other case: parties should
      apply to the court.[81]

Appointment by an appointing authority.[82] If the parties fail to   4–026
agree on the appointment of the tribunal, the arbitration agreement usually
provides that those powers of appointment are exercisable by a third party known
as an appointing authority. In international arbitrations whose seat[83] is outside
England, specifying an appointing authority in the arbitration agreement is crucial
to the effectiveness of the parties' chosen dispute resolution procedure if the court
in the country where the seat is located will not appoint a tribunal. The jurisdiction of the English court as an appointing authority does not extend to arbitrations

[76] Section 16(2)–(7) of the Arbitration Act 1996, cf. Model Law, Art.11(2) and (3): (see Appendix
   4).
[77] Section 16(3) of the Arbitration Act 1996. If there is no agreement as to the number of arbitrators,
   the Arbitration Act 1996 provides that the tribunal shall consist of a sole arbitrator. See s.15(3),
   Arbitration Act 1996 and para.4–006.
[78] Section 16(4) of the Arbitration Act 1996. See also s.15(2) of the Arbitration Act 1996 and
   para.4–007 for the meaning given to an agreement to appoint two arbitrators.
[79] Section 16(5) of the Arbitration Act 1996, cf. Model Law, Art.11(3)(a): (see Appendix 4).
[80] Section 16(6) of the Arbitration Act 1996.
[81] Sections 16(7) and 18(2) of the Arbitration Act 1996, see paras 7–097 *et seq.*
[82] See para.4–049.
[83] See paras 2–100 *et seq.*

where the seat is not in England, unless no seat has been designated or determined[84] and because of some connection with England, the court is satisfied that it is appropriate to exercise that power.[85]

4–027 **Appointment by the court and settling the type of tribunal.**
The failure by the parties to agree on an appointment procedure in circumstances for which the Act does not provide a procedure[86] or the breakdown of any appointment procedure can be resolved by an application to the court[87] as long as the seat of arbitration is in England.[88] There must however be a failure in the procedure for appointment and the statutory requirements of s.18 of the Act must be fulfilled.[89] The court has regard to any agreement of the parties as to the qualifications of the arbitrators.[90] The court also has to deal with arbitration agreements which fail to be specific about the tribunal. For example:

- Disputes arising under a contract were to be settled "by arbitration in the usual way", which the court interpreted to mean the way in which disputes arising out of the particular commodity or class of commodity were settled in London, namely, by two arbitrators, and by an umpire if they disagreed.[91]

- A charterparty provided "arbitration, if any, is to be settled in London according to British law in the customary manner". This was held to require the decision of two arbitrators and an umpire if they disagreed. The court found it was not customary to refer disputes of this kind to a single arbitrator.[92]

Despite the vagueness of the wording, specific choices were held to have been made by the parties in these two examples. Had the court not made those findings, a single arbitrator would have been appointed. English law presumes that every arbitration agreement contains a provision that the reference shall be to a single arbitrator,[93] unless a contrary intention is shown.[94] Internationally, tribunals of three arbitrators are much more common.[95]

---

[84] An appointing authority can determine a seat of arbitration when the parties have not chosen one (see e.g. Art.14.1 of the ICC Rules of Arbitration).

[85] Section 2(4) of the Arbitration Act 1996.

[86] Categories (i) to (iv) in para.4–025 specify the statutory procedure. They do not provide for the unusual agreement for the appointment of more than three arbitrators.

[87] Section 18 of the Arbitration Act 1996. See paras 7–097 *et seq.*

[88] Even if England is not the seat of arbitration, the court may help in the circumstances described above in para.4–026 (s.2(4) of the Arbitration Act 1996).

[89] See decision of Eddy J. in *Glidepath v Thompson* [2004] EWHC 2234 (Q.B.) at [49].

[90] Section 19 of the Arbitration Act 1996. See para.7–105.

[91] *Scrimaglio v Thornett & Fehr* [1924] 131 L.T. 174 on appeal; (1924) 18 Ll. L. Rep. 148.

[92] *Laertis Shipping Corp v Exportadora Espanola de Cementos Portland SA, The "Laertis"* [1982] 1 Lloyd's Rep. 613.

[93] Section 15(3) of the Arbitration Act 1996. See *"The Lapad"* [2004] EWHC 1273 (Comm) for such a case and see para.4–006.

[94] Although the two examples referred to above were decided on the basis of the previous legislation, we consider that the court would come to the same conclusion under the present law.

[95] See UNCITRAL Rules, Art.5, Model Law, Art.10(2) (see Appendix 4). The ICC and the LCIA have a discretion respectively under ICC Rules, Art.2.3, and LCIA Rules, Art.3.2.

(b) Appointment by the parties

Time for appointment. In arbitration agreements for future disputes it is **4–028** not usual to appoint named individuals as tribunal members before the dispute has arisen. Time is likely to pass between the making of the original contract and the dispute arising. By then the individual(s) named in the arbitration agreement may have died, retired, become ill, have conflicts of interest or be otherwise unavailable. Parties generally agree to appoint a tribunal after the dispute has arisen. The usual forms of arbitration clause prevent them from doing so in advance of a dispute. When the dispute has arisen it will be a matter of concern to the party or parties who wish to make progress in the arbitration to appoint a tribunal without delay, because, until a tribunal is appointed, little progress can be made in an arbitration.

The arbitration agreement often specifies a time within which an arbitrator must be appointed, failing which a party may lose the right to nominate[96] or appoint an arbitrator, which may even result in the other party's nominee being appointed as the sole arbitrator.[97] In the absence of agreement the time limit is provided by statute.[98]

In submission agreements[99] the identification of members of the arbitral tribunal is one of the matters for agreement between the parties. The tribunal is commonly agreed to in the submission agreement; or at the very least, the arbitration agreement will set out the mechanism by which the arbitrator(s) are to be appointed.[100]

Formalities. The general law has no formal requirements for the appointment **4–029** of arbitral tribunals.[101] Appointment is often effected on the parties' behalf by agents, such as their solicitors or brokers. Where the tribunal is to consist of a single arbitrator, and the parties agree on the name, a letter from each of the parties or their representatives to the proposed arbitrator, and his acceptance, are sufficient to achieve his appointment. Where there is to be a two-member tribunal with one arbitrator appointed by each party, a letter nominating one member of that tribunal will be sufficient to appoint, because the other party's agreement is not necessary: in that case the letter should go to both that arbitrator and the opposing party and, if known, the other arbitrator. Special formalities (such as appointment by deed) may be prescribed by the arbitration agreement, but are

---

[96] Under many rules of arbitration each party has a right to nominate an arbitrator, but the appointment is made or confirmed by the appointing authority.
[97] This situation occurred in *Minermet SpA v Luckyfield Shipping Corp* [2004] EWHC 729.
[98] Arbitration Act 1996 s.16(3), (4), (5) and (6).
[99] Arbitration agreements to refer existing disputes, see para.2–003.
[100] For example, by an appointing authority, see para.4–049.
[101] The practice of appointing by deed has become rare. Documents executed as deeds may be subject to stamp duty.

now rarely encountered. When they are, they should be followed, although the court may be able to correct a defective appointment.[102]

4–030 **Completing a valid appointment.** There are three requirements for the completion of a valid appointment[103]:

    (1) informing the other party;

    (2) informing the nominee; and

    (3) securing the nominee's agreement to act.

4–031 **Informing the other party.** The importance of informing the other party should be obvious, and it is now a statutory requirement.[104] In giving this information care should be taken to specify the correct name and address of the person nominated as arbitrator and the party making the nomination.[105]

4–032 **Informing the person nominated as arbitrator.** It is important to inform the person nominated as arbitrator because he may need to take some time to consider whether to accept the appointment, for instance by establishing whether he has a conflict of interest. Also, he may have to start acting immediately he accepts the appointment.[106] As long as he accepts it does not matter whether the nominee is told (and accepts) before or after notification to the other party, but it is preferable that he be informed beforehand in case he cannot accept.

4–033 **Securing agreement to act.** The appointment cannot be complete without the person nominated as arbitrator having indicated his agreement to act.[107] Unless the arbitration agreement provides otherwise, no particular form of acceptance is required, but an acceptance in writing or confirmed in writing is advisable.

4–034 **All appointments must be valid and co-extensive.** Where the reference is to a tribunal of more than one arbitrator, all must be properly appointed, and all must be appointed to decide the same dispute. Otherwise the

---

[102] *Finzel Berry & Co v Eastcheap Dried Fruit Co* [1962] 1 Lloyd's Rep. 370 when the court found that the failure to follow the mechanical route of communication did not invalidate the appointment.

[103] *per* Lord Denning M.R. in *Tradax Export SA v Volkswagenwerk AG* [1970] 1 Lloyd's Rep. 62 at 64.

[104] Section 17(2) of the Arbitration Act 1996, and DAC report, para.83. Previously it could arise under contract: *Tew v Harris* (1848) 11 Q.B. 7.

[105] See para.5–024 for discussion about getting the notice of arbitration right.

[106] *Bunge SA v Kruse* [1979] 1 Lloyd's Rep. 279.

[107] *Tradax Export SA v Volkswagenwerk AG, "La Loma"* [1970] Q.B. 537.

award may be challenged.[108] A party may lose the right to object by not objecting to an appointment forthwith or within such time as is allowed by the arbitration agreement.[109]

(c) Sole arbitrator

The simplest system. Some arbitration agreements specify a reference to   4–035
a sole arbitrator. Where no choice is made, the law implies a reference to a tribunal consisting of a sole arbitrator.[110] If no procedure for appointment has been agreed, parties should appoint jointly not later than 28 days after service of a request in writing by either party to do so.[111] The parties may agree on the identity of the proposed arbitrator, in which case they can complete the appointment provided the nominee accepts the appointment. If the parties do not agree on who to appoint, the appointment will fall to be made by the appointing authority specified in the arbitration agreement, or by an appointing authority agreed on by the parties specifically for the purpose, or by the court[112]: the court can give directions as to the making of an appointment, direct how the tribunal is to be constituted, revoke an appointment as well as making the necessary appointment itself.[113] The court can also provide similar assistance where an appointed single arbitrator ceases to hold office.[114]

(d) Tribunal of two arbitrators

City of London. Tribunals of two arbitrators have been and continue to be   4–036
found in trade, insurance, shipping and commodity arbitrations in the City of London. English law presumes the parties' choice of a tribunal of two arbitrators where the arbitration agreement uses the simple word "arbitrators" on the basis that two is the irreducible minimum.[115] Any reference to two arbitrators implies the appointment of an additional arbitrator as chairman,[116] so there has to be specific agreement if the third arbitrator is to act as an umpire, or for there to be

---

[108] For challenges of an award or a tribunal to its substantive jurisdiction, see Arbitration Act 1996 s.67(1) and para.8–054. *Davies and another v Price* (1862) 6 L.T. 713, where one arbitrator's authority was expressly limited to construction of a lease.

[109] Section 73 of the Arbitration Act 1996, see para.7–127. Before this was enacted, questions of acquiescence and estoppel arose. For instance in *Oakland Metal Co Ltd v D Benaim & Co Ltd* [1953] 2 Q.B. 261 a party was estopped from objecting, after the award, that the arbitrator he had nominated was not properly qualified.

[110] Section 15(3) of the Arbitration Act 1996.

[111] Section 16(3) of the Arbitration Act 1996.

[112] The court granted the claimant's application to appoint a sole arbitrator in *Atlanska Plovidba v Asturianos (The "Lapad")* [2004] EWHC 1273 (Comm).

[113] Section 18 of the Arbitration Act 1996, cf. Model Law, Art.11(4): see Appendix 4.

[114] Section 27 of the Arbitration Act 1996.

[115] See para.4–007.

[116] Section 15(2) of the Arbitration Act 1996.

two arbitrators and no chairman.[117] An agreed award by a tribunal of two is completely valid.[118]

4-037 **Sole arbitrator appointed in default.** The Act provides that, unless the parties agree otherwise,[119] where each of the two parties is to appoint an arbitrator and one party refuses[120] to do so (known as the party in default), or fails to do so within the time specified,[121] the other party, having duly appointed his arbitrator, may give notice to the party in default that he proposes to appoint his arbitrator as sole arbitrator.[122] If the party in default does not within seven clear days of that notice make the required appointment and notify the other party that he has done so, the other party may appoint his arbitrator as sole arbitrator whose award shall be binding on both parties as if he had been so appointed by agreement.[123] Those responsible for drafting the Arbitration Act 1996 found that the procedure was in common use and preferable to having to make an application to the court.[124] The safeguard against abuse is that the party in default may apply to the court for an extension of time to appoint a second arbitrator and to set aside the appointment of the sole arbitrator,[125] which the court is likely to do provided that the application is made promptly,[126] and that the partiers have not otherwise agreed.[127]

4-038 **Strings of contracts.** Special arbitration rules[128] have been evolved to deal with disputes about "strings" of contracts where the same goods have been sold on several times, to avoid the necessity for a party in the middle of the string to appoint an arbitrator.[129] Under the GAFTA No.125 Arbitration Rules, the party initiating the claim secures the acceptance of his arbitrator, and gives notice of his intention to proceed to arbitration and of the appointment of his arbitrator to the next person in the string. Provided that person passes on notice of the appointment without undue delay, up or down the string as the case may be, that is

---

[117] Sections 15 and 21 of the Arbitration Act 1996.
[118] *Tarmarea SrL v Rederiaktiebolaget Sally (The "Dalny")* [1979] 2 Lloyd's Rep. 439, and s.22 of the Arbitration Act 1996.
[119] This exception is important, because the arbitration agreement or rules incorporated into that agreement often provide for appointment in default by an appointing authority (see para.4–049).
[120] In the case of a refusal there is no need to wait for the expiry of the relevant time period, DAC report, para.86.
[121] See *"The Lapad"* [2004] EWHC 1273 (Comm) where this occurred.
[122] Section 17(1) of the Arbitration Act 1996, cf. Arbitration Act 1950, s.7.
[123] Section 17(2) of the Arbitration Act 1996, cf. Arbitration Act 1950, s.7. This was done in *Minermet SpA Milan v Luckyfield Shipping Corp SA* [2004] EWHC 729.
[124] DAC report, para.84.
[125] Section 17(3) of the Arbitration Act 1996 and para.7–099.
[126] The grounds are specified in the Act, as the DAC recommended that they were best left to the courts to develop in the light of the overall philosophy of the Act (DAC report, para.876).
[127] In *Minermet SpA Milan v Luckyfield Shipping Corp SA* [2004] EWHC 729, the parties had agreed otherwise by an express term of their contract and the court was unable to extend the time to appoint pursuant to s.17 of the Act.
[128] Refined Sugar Association, r.4, GAFTA 125, r.5.
[129] There were 40 parties in the string reported in *EDM JM Mertens & Co PVBA v Veevoeder Import Export Vimex BV* [1979] 2 Lloyd's Rep. 372, based on a previous wording of GAFTA 125.

sufficient and there is no need for an intermediate party to appoint his own arbitrator. Under the Refined Sugar Association Arbitration Rules, it is a matter within the absolute discretion of the Association's council whether this procedure can be invoked. It is difficult to see how the procedure could work except for quality disputes.[130]

Where there is a vacancy. Ideally, each party appoints an arbitrator and those arbitrators complete the reference. If a vacancy arises, the parties are free to agree on how to fill it, whether and if so to what extent the previous proceedings should stand and what effect (if any) the arbitrator's ceasing to hold office has on any appointment made by him, whether alone or jointly.[131] If they cannot agree,[132] the parties are to follow the statutory procedure.[133] This requires the party whose appointed arbitrator has ceased to hold office to make a fresh appointment not later than 14 days after service of a request in writing by the other party to do so.[134] If that fails, the default procedure can be invoked, unless the parties otherwise agree.[135]   4–039

"Ceases to hold office". The Act provides how a vacancy should be filled when an arbitrator ceases to hold office.[136] This will arise when an arbitrator has died,[137] or his authority has been revoked by the court[138] or he has been removed by the court.[139] Resignation is now given statutory recognition and it is clear from the wording of the section that resignation necessarily implies ceasing to hold office.[140] If an arbitrator fails or neglects to act, but does not resign, steps will have to be taken to remove him before there can be a vacancy.[141]   4–040

"Having duly appointed his arbitrator". A party giving notice to the other to nominate an arbitrator must have nominated, or must simultaneously nominate, an arbitrator otherwise his notice is invalid.[142]   4–041

Action by recipient of notice. The party who receives notice to appoint an arbitrator must not only make the appointment, but also give notice of that   4–042

---

[130] Derek Kirby Johnson, "Commodity Trade Arbitration" in *Bernstein's Handbook of Arbitration and Dispute Resolution Practice* (4th edn, Sweet & Maxwell, 2003) at para.44.8.
[131] Section 27(1) of the Arbitration Act 1996, cf. Model Law, Art.15, see Appendix 4.
[132] Section 27(2) of the Arbitration Act 1996.
[133] Section 27(3) of the Arbitration Act 1996 brings in the provisions of s.16 and s.18.
[134] Section 16(4) of the Arbitration Act 1996. We suggest this is the right interpretation. It would be odd if the party whose arbitrator had not ceased to hold office could be obliged to make a second appointment.
[135] Section 17 of the Arbitration Act 1996.
[136] Section 27(1) of the Arbitration Act 1996.
[137] Section 26(1) of the Arbitration Act 1996.
[138] Section 18(3)(c) of the Arbitration Act 1996.
[139] Section 24 of the Arbitration Act 1996: see paras 7–111 *et seq.*
[140] Section 25 of the Arbitration Act 1996.
[141] Section 24(1)(d) of the Arbitration Act 1996.
[142] Section 17(1) of the Arbitration Act 1996, and see *Vulcaan NV v Mowinckels Rederi* [1938] 2 All E.R. 152 on the earlier wording in the Arbitration Act 1950, s.7(b).

appointment to the other party within seven clear days[143] in order to avoid appointment by default. This may involve appointment by an agreed appointing authority, or in the absence of agreement appointment by the other party of his arbitrator as sole arbitrator in the reference.[144]

4–043 **Appointment to act as sole arbitrator.** There must be an actual appointment to act as sole arbitrator.[145] Giving the other party more time to appoint will not of itself invalidate the appointment.[146]

(e) Appointment of third arbitrator or umpire

4–044 **Status and role of third arbitrator.** Formerly in England when two party-appointed arbitrators appointed a third arbitrator, he became an umpire. This ran counter to international practice, in which umpires are unknown. Since 1979 any method of appointing a three-person tribunal, unless a contrary intention is expressed, results in a panel of three arbitrators, not two arbitrators plus one umpire.[147] This has the important consequence that, unless otherwise agreed by the parties,[148] the award of any two of the arbitrators is binding.[149] That third arbitrator is the chairman, unless the parties agree otherwise.[150] Parties are free to agree on what the functions of the chairman are to be in relation to the making of decisions, orders and awards.[151] If or to the extent there is no agreement, the statutory provisions provide that decisions, orders and awards are to be made by all or a majority of the arbitrators (including the chairman), and the view of the chairman prevails only in relation to a decision, order or award in respect of which there is neither unanimity nor a majority.[152]

4–045 **Status and role of umpire.** Where the parties have agreed that there is to be an umpire, they are free to agree what the functions of the umpire are to be, and in particular whether he is to attend the proceedings and when he is to replace the other arbitrators as the tribunal with power to make decisions, orders, and awards.[153] If or to the extent there is no agreement, statutory provisions apply as

---

[143] Section 17(2) of the Arbitration Act 1996.
[144] The appointment as sole arbitrator of the person appointed by the other party is discussed earlier in this section of the chapter—see para.4–037.
[145] *Drummond v Hamer* [1942] 1 K.B. 352, where the court set aside an award made by a sole arbitrator, because the landlord's notice had not been an appointment of the sole arbitrator and, even if it constituted an appointment, it was made before the expiration of the agreed time limit.
[146] *Kiril Mischeff Ltd v British Doughnut Co Ltd* [1954] 1 Lloyd's Rep. 237, CA.
[147] Section 15(2) of the Arbitration Act 1996. The law before 1979 was contained in s.9 of the Arbitration Act 1950, which was amended by s.6(2) of the Arbitration Act 1979.
[148] Section 22(1) of the Arbitration Act 1996.
[149] Section 22(2) of the Arbitration Act 1996.
[150] Section 15(2) of the Arbitration Act 1996.
[151] Section 20(1) of the Arbitration Act 1996.
[152] Section 20(2)–(4) of the Arbitration Act 1996.
[153] Section 21(1) of the Arbitration Act 1996.

follows. The umpire attends the proceedings and is supplied with the same documents and other materials as are supplied to the other arbitrators. Decisions, orders, and awards are made by the other arbitrators unless and until they cannot agree on any matter relating to the arbitration, in which event they forthwith give notice to the parties and the umpire, and the umpire replaces them as the tribunal with power to make decisions, orders and awards as if he were sole arbitrator. There is provision for application to the court to resolve difficulties.[154]

Form of appointment. No particular form of appointment of a third   4-046
arbitrator or umpire is necessary, but it should be in writing and state clearly whether an umpire or a third arbitrator is being appointed, and whether, if he is not to be an umpire, he is to act as chairman. It should also comply with any special requirements set out in the arbitration agreement.

The arbitration agreement often states that the third arbitrator or umpire is to be appointed by the existing members of the tribunal. Arbitrators with this power are under no obligation to obtain the parties' approval of their selection, and the fact that the parties are dissatisfied with the choice does not for that reason alone affect the validity of the appointment.[155] However in practice it is common for the parties to be consulted on the identity of the third arbitrator or umpire and then for the two arbitrators formally to make the appointment.[156]

Consultation should be limited to the identity of the third arbitrator to justify departure from the rule against unilateral communication between one party and an arbitrator.

Third arbitrator declining appointment. The attempted appoint-   4-047
ment of a third arbitrator or umpire who declines to accept the appointment is of no effect. The person(s) who attempted to appoint him may appoint another in his place.[157]

The court has power to appoint where a replacement third arbitrator or umpire[158] "ceases to hold office".[159]

Third arbitrator failing to act. An appointment of a third arbitrator or   4-048
umpire which has been made by the two party-appointed arbitrators exhausts the power of appointment, and appointors have no power to revoke the appointment made or to make a fresh appointment.[160] If the person appointed will not then act

---

[154] Section 21(2)–(6), see ss.4–172 of the Arbitration Act 1996.
[155] *Oliver v Collings* (1880) 11 East. 367.
[156] The practice of consultation does not remove the choice from the two arbitrators, but it helps to avoid problems of conflicts, and enables the parties to comment on the suitability of the persons proposed.
[157] *Trippet v Eyre* (1684) 3 Lev. 263, see also *Reynolds v Gray* (1698) 1 L.D. Raym. 223, where an appointment is conditional on the proposed umpire's acceptance of office, the arbitrators can reappoint if the post is refused.
[158] Section 27 of the Arbitration Act 1996.
[159] See para.4–050.
[160] *Oliver v Collings* (1880) 11 East. 367.

in the arbitration, and unless the parties agree to make some other arrangement,[161] application to the court is the only recourse.

(f) Appointment by an appointing authority

4–049   **Where the parties do not agree.** Arbitration agreements often provide for an appointing authority[162] to appoint an arbitrator if the parties cannot agree. This mechanism is most commonly applied in cases of the appointment of a sole or third arbitrator, but it can also apply where one party has the right to appoint an arbitrator but fails to appoint him. It is a useful arrangement which provides a cheaper and quicker route to an appointment than application to the English court or to another institution in default.[163] As is apparent from their names, some of the appointing authorities are specialist professional institutions or trade associations and should be nominated only in arbitration agreements providing for the resolution of disputes within their particular expertise. Others are specialist arbitration bodies.

The means by which the parties apply to an appointing authority for the appointment of arbitrators is likely to be specifically laid down by each appointing authority. A fee is almost invariably charged. Reference to an appointing authority usually follows attempts by the parties to agree on an appointment in which one or more names may have been considered. An appointing authority may be unwilling to appoint a person who has been put forward by one party and rejected by the other party. This sometimes leads to the curious tactic of not putting one's preferred candidate forward for agreement by the other party, nor mentioning that candidate in the application to the appointing authority, in the hope that this increases the chances of the preferred candidate actually being appointed. The risks inherent in this tactic are obvious. We favour the direct method of making the identity of one's preferred candidate clear from the outset and, if necessary, the parties can agree that if the appointment falls to be made subsequently by an appointing authority, the names of prior suggested candidates will not be disclosed. Parties often make representations to an appointing authority about the identity, qualifications and characteristics of appointees. An appointing authority is not bound to follow representations which do not track any requirements for arbitrators contained in the arbitration agreement, unless, possibly, both parties agree on them and they do not conflict with the arbitration agreement. Once an appointing authority starts dealing with the appointment, parties are not able to influence the procedure. There are no legal safeguards as appointing authorities are immune from suit unless the act or omission complained of is shown to have been in bad faith.[164] So it may be only in their reputation that appointing authorities can be affected by the consequences of a misguided appointment.

---

[161] Section 27(1) of the Arbitration Act 1996.
[162] For list of appointing authorities, see Appendix 5.
[163] Parties who choose the UNCITRAL Rules, for example, should name an appointing authority in their arbitration agreement rather than leave it in default to be designated on request by the Secretary General of the Permanent Court of Arbitration at The Hague (Art.6.2).
[164] Section 74. See para.3–047 of the Arbitration Act 1996.

(g) Appointment by the court

Where the court has power to appoint. The court's power to appoint   4–050
arbitrators and umpires has been touched on in the preceding sections and is
discussed fully in Ch.7.[165]

(h) Challenges to appointment

Challenge procedures. Before accepting an appointment, an arbitrator   4–051
should consider whether he is suited to the particular case. Does he have the
required qualifications? Is he impartial and disinterested?[166] If not, he may be
challenged. A party who wishes to challenge an arbitrator should examine the
provisions of any arbitration rules which apply to the arbitration.[167] If no arbitration rules apply, application will have to be made to the court.[168] But where
arbitration rules provide machinery for challenge, the terms of those rules are
likely to make it essential to use that machinery rather than apply to the court, at
least in the first instance.[169] In any event, this is required by the Act, which
provides that if there is an arbitral institution or person vested by the parties with
power to remove an arbitrator, the court shall not exercise its power of removal
unless satisfied that the applicant has first exhausted any available recourse to that
institution or person.[170] The machinery for challenge, as set out in the various
arbitration rules, often requires challenges to be made by a party within a short
period of becoming aware of the ground for challenge, with the supervising
authority deciding the question if it is contested.[171] Otherwise, there is no time
limit for applying to the court under s.24 of the Act for the removal of an
arbitrator, although by delaying a party can lose his right to relief.[172] A successful
challenge would result in an order for removal.

5. REMUNERATION OF AN ARBITRAL TRIBUNAL

(a) The right to remuneration

Express or implied. In most cases the tribunal enters into an express   4–052
agreement with the parties about the level of fees and the right to be paid certain

---

[165] See paras 7–095 *et seq.*
[166] See paras 4–023 *et seq.* above.
[167] For example, there are challenge procedures in the LCIA Rules, Art.10, and the ICC Rules,
   Art.11.
[168] See paras 7–110 *et seq.*
[169] In the *AT&T* case [2002] 2 All E.R. (Comm) 625, the first challenge was made to the ICC Court
   of Arbitration.
[170] Section 24(2) of the Arbitration Act 1996.
[171] ICC Rules, Art.2.8–11, ICSID Rules, Art.9, LCIA Rules, Art.3.7–8, Model Law, Art.13 (see
   Appendix 4). Where the challenge is decided by the tribunal, as in the case of ICSID and the Model
   Law, there are procedures for appeal.
[172] See para.7–086.

expenses. It is in the interests of the parties as well as the tribunal for this to be done no later than the time of the tribunal's appointment. Where there is no express agreement about fees and expenses, the right to remuneration has been understood to depend on an undertaking, to be implied from the appointment of an arbitrator, to pay reasonable remuneration for his services and those of the third arbitrator or umpire[173]: statute now makes this a joint and several liability of the parties, which they cannot agree to exclude,[174] and qualifies the obligation to pay such reasonable fees and expenses by adding the words "(if any) as are appropriate in the circumstances".[175] This qualification protects the parties in respect of attempts by an arbitrator to charge fees or expenses that are excessive.[176] An arbitrator's expenses are usually limited to travel and hotel bills but in certain cases they may extend to the cost of a secretary[177] or the fees of a legal adviser or expert.[178] A wise arbitrator ensures that, so far as possible, the parties contract directly with suppliers for the other expenses, such as the hiring of suitable accommodation for the hearing.[179]

4–053   **Invalid appointments.** Where an appointment is invalid, depending on the circumstances, the party who appointed the arbitrator is generally liable for his fees. However, where an arbitrator to his own knowledge has no jurisdiction, for instance because he lacks the necessary qualification,[180] and his appointor was not aware of the lack of the qualification, the arbitrator ought not to be entitled to recover fees.[181]

4–054   **Where no award made.** The implied undertaking to pay reasonable expenses to an arbitrator used not to apply unless the arbitrator had delivered an award.[182] The statutory provision has no such limitation.[183] In many cases no award is delivered, either because the parties settle the dispute, or because the claimant gives up. The law now entitles an arbitrator to reasonable fees for work done until the time when activity ceased, plus his reasonable expenses. It is however much more satisfactory for there to be an express agreement between the parties and the arbitrator entitling the arbitrator to payments in these circumstances.

---

[173] *Brown v Llandovery Terra Cotta and Co Ltd* (1909) 25 T.L.R. 625; *John Anthony Tackaberry v Phaidon Navegacion SA* [1992] A.D.L.R.J. 112.
[174] Section 28(1) of the Arbitration Act 1996, s.4 and Sch.1.
[175] Section 28(1) and (5) of the Arbitration Act 1996, DAC report, para.123.
[176] A charge for typing services on top of a reasonable hourly rate of fees may be excessive: *Hussman (Europe) LLT v Al Ameen Development* [2000] 2 Lloyd's Rep. 83—see para.4–059.
[177] See para.5–173.
[178] See para.5–160.
[179] But see para.4–082 on the cost of tribunal experts.
[180] See paras 4–017 *et seq.*
[181] We do not know any precedent to support either of the propositions of law set out in this paragraph, but submit they are right on general contract principles.
[182] See *Brown v Llandovery Terra Cotta and Co Ltd* (1909) 25 T.L.R. 625.
[183] Section 28(1) of the Arbitration Act 1996.

Where arbitrator is removed or resigns. Where the court removes an 4–055
arbitrator or an application is made consequent upon his resignation, the court
may make orders with respect to his entitlement to fees or expenses, or the
repayment of any fees and expenses already paid.[184] Presumably the level of fees
which the arbitrator might properly charge should be determined by the extent of
his fault in the circumstances leading to his removal: in the case of a resignation,
the court will have regard to whether it was reasonable in all the circumstances for
the arbitrator to resign.[185] The court's power to order an arbitrator to make
repayment of his fees on removal or resignation is a means by which the court may
sanction an arbitrator for breach of his duties. Apart from a possible reduction of
fees, an arbitrator who resigns may incur liability for costs that arise as a result of
that resignation,[186] and the statutory immunity does not affect any liability
incurred by an arbitrator by reason of his resigning.[187]

(b) Fixing the level of fees

Bases of fee levels. The level of fees may be agreed directly with each 4–056
arbitrator as normally occurs in an "ad hoc" arbitration or be fixed by the
institution supervising the arbitration in accordance with the terms of appointment that are usually specified in the relevant arbitration rules. In the latter case
the chosen institution will invariably charge a fee for services rendered,[188] which
is in addition to fees and expenses paid to the tribunal. For instance, the ICC
charges arbitrators' fees based in part on a percentage scale of the amount in
dispute. The ICC has regard to the time spent, the complexity of the dispute and
other relevant circumstances, and then brings the fee within the wide percentage
specified in Appendix 3 to the ICC Rules. The LCIA charges according to the
time spent but the hourly rates are on a scale. These are the two usual methods
by which fees are fixed. Another method is to agree a lump sum for the whole
arbitration, but this is rarely done, for if a case does not proceed to an award,
disputes could arise over the arbitrator's right to payment: or, if the case goes on
much longer than expected, the arbitrator's rate of remuneration can decline
considerably.[189]

The parties and the tribunal should agree beforehand on the basis of charge
where there is no award because the dispute is settled first. Where there is no
established arrangement,[190] the level of fees is generally negotiated between the
tribunal and the parties, either on the basis of a proportion of the amount in

---

[184] Sections 24(4) and 25(3) of the Arbitration Act 1996, and see paras 7–133 *et seq.*
[185] Section 25(4) of the Arbitration Act 1996, see para.7–135.
[186] See para.4–158 for circumstances in which such liability may occur.
[187] Arbitration Act, s.29(3). For the relief that may be granted by the court, see s.25(3)(a) of the Act
and para.7–133.
[188] The charge may be limited to an appointment fee if the institution is only required to appoint the
tribunal or may be based on a small percentage of the claim or time spent where the institution is
expected to provide some supervision of the arbitration.
[189] This can also be the effect with the ICC's basis of charges.
[190] See para.4–062 for cancellation fees.

dispute or the time spent by the tribunal. When there is no agreement, the fees must be reasonable.[191]

4–057   **Adjustment by the court.** Any party may apply to the court[192] for an order that the amount of the arbitrator's fees and expenses shall be considered and adjusted. Repayment can be ordered, but only if it appears reasonable to do so.[193]

4–058   **No implied right to increases.** The level of fees and provision for increases in fees if the case continues over a long period should be fixed at the start of the arbitration, and not just before a hearing.[194] The rules of contract law, which arguably apply to this issue, do not permit a tribunal to impose an increase in its fees during a case. Attempts to increase fees have led to allegations of bias and of what used to be called misconduct,[195] and could, if pursued unreasonably, lead to an application to remove the arbitrator[196] and even to a challenge of any award made by him[197] because of breach of the duty to avoid unnecessary expense.[198]

4–059   **Excessive fees.** If the fees of the tribunal are agreed by the parties, there is no basis for reducing those fees even if they are excessive.[199] If the fees that are alleged to be excessive have been fixed by an appointing authority agreed by the parties, it is doubtful whether the parties have a remedy.[200] If the fees have not been agreed by the parties or fixed by an appointing authority, they must be reasonable.[201] On the application of a party, the court may order the amount of an arbitrator's fees and expenses to be adjusted, or repaid if they have already been paid.[202] Such an application may be made by a party who does not wish to be liable for excessive

[191] See para.4–054.
[192] On notice to the other parties and the arbitrators. Section 28(2) of the Arbitration Act 1996.
[193] This is implied from the preceding subsection, which talks of "reasonable fees and expenses": cf. s.28(3) of the Act.
[194] Avoiding the embarrassment of *Guardian Royal Assurance Group v Phillips and Another*, unreported, July 30, (1993) Q.B.D. Commercial Court, Waller J., where a barrister's clerk's "strong negotiating letter" was misunderstood and resulted in the resignation of the barrister from his appointment as arbitrator.
[195] See *Town Centre Securities Plc v Leeds City Council* [1992] A.D.L.R.J. 54; *Sea Containers v ICT Pty Ltd* [2002] N.S.W.C.A. 84.
[196] Such an attempted increase was mentioned in *Andrews & Bredshaw* [2000] B.L.R. 6 at 16 but was not directly in issue.
[197] Section 68 of the Arbitration Act 1996.
[198] Section 33(1)(b) of the Arbitration Act 1996.
[199] Section 28(5) of the Arbitration Act 1996. The arbitrator has a contractual right to his fees. Usually the tribunal will not release the award until the fees have been paid, so the practical option of withholding payment of the fees is not available if the award is wanted by one or more of the parties.
[200] The question was raised but not decided in *Hussman (Europe) Ltd v Al Ameen Development and Trade Corp* [2002] 2 Lloyd's Rep. 83.
[201] *Agrimex Ltd v Tradigrain SA* [2003] EWHC 1656. See paras 7–212 *et seq.*
[202] The application can be made at any time, and in principle should be made as soon as it is known that the fees are or will be excessive—*Hussman* cited above at fn.201, where an application was made at the end of the arbitration. For challenging the arbitrator's lien, see para.4–064.

fees of an arbitrator appointed by the other party,[203] but the application should be made promptly otherwise the right to recovery of the excess may be lost.[204]

(c) Deposits, commitment fees and interim fees

Advance payments. It is common practice for arbitration institutions and arbitral tribunals to take steps to secure their fees in advance. This may take the form of seeking deposits and/or commitment fees to cover the loss of business likely to result if the arbitration hearings, sometimes booked to run for a period of several weeks, are postponed because the parties are not ready or cancelled at short notice because the parties settle the dispute. Arbitrations such as those run by the ICC commonly require that the parties make deposits with the arbitral institution on account of arbitrators' fees and the administrative expenses of the arbitration. Some arbitration rules give the arbitral tribunal the power to make orders securing its fees.[205] As the powers are part of the arbitration agreement, the orders are enforceable. The right to a commitment fee is not an implied term of an arbitrator's appointment, and the matter should therefore be dealt with by express agreement at the time of his appointment. Before the Arbitration Act 1996, it could be misconduct to insist on a commitment fee as a condition of continuing as arbitrator after the initial appointment had been accepted without reservation.[206] Under the Act, an application can be made to the court to remove an arbitrator who persists with such a demand on the ground that he had refused or failed properly to conduct the proceedings or to use all reasonable dispatch in conducting the proceedings or making an award.[207]   **4-060**

Interim payments. Commitment fees should be distinguished from interim payments. A right to require the payment of interim fees may arise when the arbitration agreement or rules provide for such payment or even when an arbitration becomes more extensive than originally expected and reasonable notice of the required payment is given.[208]   **4-061**

---

[203] See *United Tyre Co Ltd v Born* [2004] EWCA 1236. If the application to the court is successful, however, as it was in this case the applicant would be relieved of the liability for the excess which might have to be borne in full by the appointing party: s.28(3) of the Arbitration Act 1996 and DAC report, paras 1, 2, 3. See para.7–212.

[204] There was delay in the *United Tyre* case, cited above at fn.203, but by a narrow margin the judge decided to grant the application.

[205] For example, ICE Arbitration Procedure (1997), r.7.5(6).

[206] *KS Norjarl A/S v Hyundai Heavy Industries Co Ltd* [1991] 1 Lloyd's Rep. 524: considered in *Turner v Stevenage Borough Council* [1998] C.L. 28. See also *Sea Containers v ICT Pty Ltd* [2002] N.S.W.C.A. 84.

[207] Section 24(1)(d) of the Arbitration Act 1996. Proof of substantial injustice would have to be proved, which would be difficult unless a complete impasse had been arrived at.

[208] *Turner v Stevenage Borough Council* [1998] C.L. 28 at 36 *et seq.*, CA where an application to remove the arbitrator for retaining part of an interim payment was approved. Although based on the previous legislation, it is still good law.

4–062 **Cancellation fees.** As mentioned in the preceding paragraph, a commitment, often secured by a deposit or advance payment, is frequently demanded by an arbitral tribunal in case the arbitration is "abandoned, suspended or concluded by agreement or otherwise, before the final award is made".[209] Absent agreement of the parties there is no right to a commitment fee and to continue to insist upon a commitment fee in circumstances where the parties do not agree to provide them can provide grounds for removal.[210] In an "ad hoc" arbitration, an arbitrator will often ask as one of the terms of his appointment for staged payment of his fees, so that if the arbitration settles he will receive an agreed amount according to the stage reached. Under this arrangement the arbitrator agrees to devote a specific time to reading the written submissions and documents and to hearing oral testimony and submissions. In return, the parties (or any party appointing him) will agree to pay him anything from a third to the whole of his fees, depending on how close the arbitration settles to the reading period or hearing.

(d) Award not delivered until fees paid

4–063 **Lien.** The traditional method by which arbitral tribunals have secured payment has been to withhold the award from the party or parties seeking to take it up until any outstanding fees have been paid, effectively to exercise a lien over the award. This is now sanctioned by the Act in a provision that the parties cannot exclude.[211] When the award is ready for delivery, the tribunal notifies the parties that it is available on payment of its fees. Either party or both may then take up the award, on payment of the fees. It does not concern the tribunal which party pays the fees. Where the party who takes up the award is not, under its terms, liable to pay the fees, he may recover from his opponent all the costs the award imposes, including the tribunal's fees.[212] If neither party takes up the award, the tribunal may have no sanction but to forego its fees or to sue for them.

4–064 **Challenging an arbitral tribunal's lien.**[213] Where the parties have agreed the level of fees with the tribunal, the agreement cannot be reviewed by the court,[214] because the tribunal has a contractual right to payment. The court's adjustment procedures assist a party who has not agreed the level of fees with the tribunal,[215] is unable to obtain delivery of the award without paying those fees in full because the tribunal is exercising its lien, and claims that the tribunal's demands are excessive. The court (or any arbitral or other institution with powers

[209] The words quoted are taken from the LCIA Rules, Art.28.5.
[210] *K/S Norjarl A/S v Hyundai Heavy Industries Ltd* [1992] 1 Q.B. 863; *Sea Containers v ICT Pty Ltd* [2002] N.S.W.C.A. 84.
[211] Section 56(1) of the Arbitration Act 1996.
[212] *Hicks v Richardson* (1797) 1 Bos. & Pul. 93; *Smith and Another v Troup* (1849) 7 C.B. 757.
[213] See para.6–068.
[214] Section 28(5) of the Arbitration Act 1996.
[215] Including an arbitrator who has ceased to act and an umpire who has not replaced the other arbitrators: s.56(5) of the Arbitration Act 1996.

in relation to the delivery of the tribunal's award)[216] may order that the tribunal is to deliver the award on payment into court by the applicant of the fees and expenses demanded, or such lesser amount as the court may specify. Another possible order is that the amount of fees and expenses properly payable is to be determined by such means and upon such terms as the court may direct. Finally, the court can order that, out of the money paid into court, there shall be paid out such fees and expenses as may be found properly payable and the balance if any is to be paid to the applicant.[217] The amount properly payable is any amount ascertained under the process now known as adjustment[218] at which the tribunal is entitled to be heard.[219] No application to the court may be made where there is another available process provided, for example, by an arbitral institution, for appeal or review of the amount of the fees or expenses demanded.[220] There is authority that a party who has paid an excessive sum to obtain delivery of an award may recover the excess beyond what is reasonable in an action against the tribunal in restitution.[221] Except when the Act does not apply,[222] parties are better advised to seek an adjustment from the court under its statutory powers,[223] as an action in restitution is a costly and uncertain means of attacking an exorbitant level of fees.

(e) Costs awards

Arbitrators' fees included in costs awards. For the impact of costs   4–065
awards on arbitrators' fees, see Ch.6.[224]

6. POWERS OF AN ARBITRAL TRIBUNAL

(a) Introduction and sources

Preface. This section considers the powers of arbitral tribunals. The next   4–066
section will discuss their duties. A list of powers follows the introduction. Arguably, some items in the list fall into the category of both powers and duties. For
instance it is both a power and a duty to issue an award. In order to keep the

---

[216] Section 56(6) of the Arbitration Act 1996, cf. ICC Rules, Art.23.1.

[217] Section 56(2) of the Arbitration Act 1996, see para.6–071.

[218] Section 28(2) of the Arbitration Act 1996, see para.4–057.

[219] This follows from s.28(2) of the Arbitration Act 1996 which requires notice to be given to the arbitrators.

[220] Section 56(4) of the Arbitration Act 1996. The DAC have taken care to avoid the use of the word "taxation" which appeared in the earlier legislation. The word "taxation" is used to describe similar procedures for the adjustment of costs incurred in court cases, CPR Pt 62.

[221] In the matter of an arbitration between *JM Coombs and JW Freshfield* (1850) 4 Ex. 839 and *Barnes v Braithwaite and Nixon* (1857) 2 H. & N. 569.

[222] Such an action may apply if the seat of arbitration was abroad, but the arbitrator was ordinarily resident in England and the arbitration agreement was governed by English law.

[223] Section 28 of the Arbitration Act 1996.

[224] See paras 6–130 *et seq.*

distinction between powers and duties, we have not listed the same function in both categories: but a tribunal often discharges one of its duties by exercising one of its powers. Those powers and duties which relate to the conduct of the reference are dealt with in detail in Ch.5, those which relate to the award in Ch.6, and those which relate to the court and to enforcement in Chs 7 and 8.

4–067 **The arbitration agreement and arbitration rules.** The first source of a tribunal's powers is the arbitration agreement between the parties under which the tribunal has been appointed. There is considerable flexibility as to the powers the parties can agree to give to the tribunal.[225] Before accepting appointment, each prospective member of a tribunal should review the arbitration agreement and any other agreements the parties have made about procedure, whether incorporated from the rules of an arbitration institution or trade association or contained in an express agreement, to ensure that those agreements can be complied with. The courts have upheld the parties' agreement unless the agreed form for the conduct of the arbitration is so contrary to fundamental principles that it is held to be unenforceable as contrary to public policy,[226] and continues to do so under the Act.[227]

4–068 **Statute.** The Act[228] gives tribunals a wide discretion in procedural matters,[229] subject to the parties' agreement in many cases. The exercise of that discretion is subject to the tribunal discharging its duty to act impartially as between the parties, giving each party a reasonable opportunity of putting its case and dealing with that of its opponent. In so doing the tribunal also has the duty to adopt procedures suitable to the circumstances of the particular case, avoiding unnecessary delay or expense, so as to provide a fair means for the resolution of the matters falling to be determined.[230] The tribunal discharges that duty by the exercise of its powers under numerous provisions of the Act, notably ss.34, 37, 38, 39, 41 and 65. In the positive language of the Act, "parties should be free to agree how their disputes are resolved, subject only to such safeguards as are necessary in the public interest".[231] The Act empowers a tribunal, subject to the right of the parties to agree any matter,[232] to decide whether and to what extent the tribunal should itself take the initiative in ascertaining the facts and the law,[233] and to decide whether there should be a hearing.[234] If a tribunal is to take the initiative in ascertaining the facts and the law, in an "inquisitorial" as opposed to an "adversarial" procedure,

---

[225] See paras 2–058 *et seq.*
[226] *Naumann v Edward Nathan & Co Ltd* (1930) 36 Ll. L. Rep. 268 on appeal; 37 Ll. L. Rep. 249, Scrutton L.J.
[227] Section 1 of the Arbitration Act 1996, and see paras 5–039 *et seq.*
[228] Section 34 of the Arbitration Act 1996.
[229] See paras 4–072 *et seq.*
[230] Section 33(1) of the Arbitration Act 1996. See paras 4–112 *et seq.* and paras 5–032 *et seq.*
[231] Section 1(b) of the Arbitration Act 1996.
[232] Section 34(1) of the Arbitration Act 1996.
[233] Section 34(2)(g) of the Arbitration Act 1996.
[234] Section 34(2)(h) of the Arbitration Act 1996.

each party must have the same opportunity to present its case and to rebut the material.[235] All these matters are discussed in more detail in Ch.5.[236]

(b) Powers of tribunals

Powers generally. An arbitral tribunal, in discharging its duty to determine 4–069
the dispute has certain powers, which are listed below. A summary of the powers
follows which in turn refers to the more detailed discussion in other chapters.
Each of the following powers is subject to the right of the parties to agree that the
power shall not be exercised or that it is to be exercised in a different way[237]:

- to rule on jurisdiction[238];

- to decide all procedural and evidential matters,[239] including;

- location and timing of proceedings[240];

- language and the need for translations[241];

- the form, timing and possible amendment of any statement of claim or
  defence[242];

- disclosure of documents[243];

- parties' questions to each other[244];

- rules, weight, time, manner and form of evidence[245];

- whether the tribunal should take the initiative in ascertaining facts and
  law[246];

- whether there should be oral or written evidence or submissions[247];

---

[235] *Town and City Properties (Development) Ltd v Wiltshier Southern Ltd and Gilbert Powell* [1988] 44
B.L.R. 109, commenting on an arbitration held under the JCT Arbitration Rules, where the
arbitrator was said to have carried out a "process really that of a valuation, not an arbitration". See
para.5–099 on inquisitorial procedure.
[236] See paras 5–032 *et seq.* and paras 5–089 *et seq.*
[237] The right of the parties to make agreements to this effect is expressed within each of the relevant
sections of the Arbitration Act 1996. There are only a few powers of a tribunal which the parties
cannot exclude or vary, and they are better described as rights. They are:
    (1) the liability of the parties for arbitrators' fees and expenses: s.28;
    (2) arbitrators' immunity: s.29; and
    (3) arbitrators' lien over the award: s.56.
    See also s.4(1) of the Arbitration Act 1996 and Sch.1.
[238] Section 30 of the Arbitration Act 1996.
[239] Section 34 of the Arbitration Act 1996.
[240] Section 34(2)(a) of the Arbitration Act 1996.
[241] Section 34(2)(b) of the Arbitration Act 1996.
[242] Section 34(2)(c) of the Arbitration Act 1996.
[243] Section 34(2)(d) of the Arbitration Act 1996.
[244] Section 34(2)(e) of the Arbitration Act 1996.
[245] Section 43(2)(f) of the Arbitration Act 1996.
[246] Section 34(2)(g) of the Arbitration Act 1996.
[247] Section 34(2)(h) of the Arbitration Act 1996.

- to appoint experts, legal advisers and assessors[248];

- to order security for costs[249];

- to give directions about property the subject of proceedings[250];

- to direct that a witness be examined on oath or affirmation[251];

- to make provisional orders[252];

- to act in case of a party's default[253];

- to apply to the court for a peremptory order[254];

- to make awards on different issues at different times on different aspects[255];

- to make a declaration[256];

- to order payment of a sum of money in any currency[257];

- to order a party to refrain from doing something[258];

- to order specific performance of a contract other than land[259];

- to order rectification, setting aside or cancellation of a deed or other document[260];

- to award interest[261];

- to terminate arbitral proceedings if the dispute is settled by the parties[262];

- to decide the date of the award[263];

- to correct an award[264];

- to make an additional award on matters in issue but not covered by the award[265];

- to allocate costs between the parties[266];

---

[248] Section 37 of the Arbitration Act 1996.
[249] Section 38(3) of the Arbitration Act 1996.
[250] Section 38(4) of the Arbitration Act 1996.
[251] Section 38(5) of the Arbitration Act 1996.
[252] Section 39 of the Arbitration Act 1996.
[253] Section 41 of the Arbitration Act 1996.
[254] Section 42(2) of the Arbitration Act 1996.
[255] Section 47 of the Arbitration Act 1996.
[256] Section 48(3) of the Arbitration Act 1996.
[257] Section 48(4) of the Arbitration Act 1996.
[258] Section 48(5)(a) of the Arbitration Act 1996.
[259] Section 48(5)(b) of the Arbitration Act 1996.
[260] Section 48(5)(c) of the Arbitration Act 1996.
[261] Section 49 of the Arbitration Act 1996.
[262] Section 51(2) of the Arbitration Act 1996.
[263] Section 54 of the Arbitration Act 1996.
[264] Section 57(3)(a) of the Arbitration Act 1996.
[265] Section 57(3)(b of the Arbitration Act 1996).
[266] Section 61(1) of the Arbitration Act 1996.

- to determine the costs recoverable[267];

- to limit recoverable costs to a specific amount.[268]

(c) Powers and jurisdiction

Powers distinct from jurisdiction. The powers and the jurisdiction of   4–070
an arbitral tribunal are sometimes confused but they are quite distinct. If the
tribunal lacks jurisdiction (competence) it cannot determine the dispute at all. If
the tribunal has jurisdiction, it has the necessary competence to conduct the
reference, but should consider the extent of its powers when determining how it
should do so.[269]

Ruling on jurisdiction. Unless otherwise agreed by the parties, an arbitral   4–071
tribunal is expressly given the power to rule on its own substantive jurisdiction, as
to (i) whether there is a valid arbitration agreement, (ii) whether the tribunal is
properly constituted, and (iii) what matters have been submitted to arbitration in
accordance with the arbitration agreement.[270] Case law used to encourage arbitral
tribunals to make the first ruling on their own jurisdiction[271]: the statutory
provision defines the power precisely and its limits. Any ruling can be challenged
by any available arbitral process of appeal or review or by the court,[272] although the
court will be slow to reverse a well-founded decision by the arbitral tribunal.[273]

(d) Procedural and evidential powers

General. An arbitral tribunal has the power to decide all procedural and   4–072
evidential matters, subject to the right of the parties to agree any matter.[274] This
is a very general provision, drawn so as to have the potential to include matters not
covered by the list of matters specified in s.34(2) of the Act. Although the general
power conferred by this statutory provision is extensive, it is subject to modification by the parties to the arbitration. Frequently, rules of arbitration incorporated
into the arbitration agreement do to a limited extent modify the powers listed in
s.34 of the Act.[275]

---

[267] Section 63(3) of the Arbitration Act 1996.
[268] Section 65 of the Arbitration Act 1996.
[269] See paras 4–135 *et seq.* and paras 5–060 *et seq.*
[270] Section 30(1) of the Arbitration Act 1996. In the Model Law, Art.16 (see Appendix 4), this power
   is not subject to the parties' agreement, it is given to the tribunal in all cases.
[271] *Brown (Christopher) Ltd v Genossenschaft Oesterreicher Waldbesitzer R GmbH* [1954] 1 Q.B. 8.
[272] Section 67 of the Arbitration Act 1996 and paras 8–054 *et seq.*
[273] The court dismissed an appeal against the award of an arbitrator and upheld his finding that he had
   no jurisdiction: *Stanstead Shipping Co v Shenzen Nantian Oil Mills* (August 21, 2000) Thomas J.
[274] Section 34(1) of the Arbitration Act 1996, cf. Arbitration Act 1950, s.12(1)–(3) and Model Law, Arts
   19, 20, 22, 23 and 24: see Appendix 4.
[275] For example, the ICC rules give the International Court of Arbitration rather than the arbitrators
   power to fix the place of arbitration in the absence of agreement by the parties Art.14.1.

4–073 **Time and place for proceedings.**[276] The tribunal may decide when and where any part of the proceedings is to be held.[277] This provision does not override the designated seat of arbitration.[278]

4–074 **Language and translations.**[279] The tribunal may decide the language or languages to be used in the proceedings and whether translations of any relevant documents are to be supplied.[280]

4–075 **Statement of claim and defence.**[281] The tribunal may decide whether and if so what form of written statements of claim and defence are to be used, when these should be supplied and the extent to which such statements can be later amended.[282]

4–076 **Disclosure of documents.**[283] The tribunal may decide whether and if so which documents or classes of documents should be disclosed and at what stage.[284–285]

4–077 **Questions to the parties.**[286] The tribunal may decide whether and if so what questions should be put to and answered by the respective parties and when and in what form such material should be exchanged and presented.[287] In civil litigation, such questions take the form of "requests for information", and can be about the case put forward and/or the evidence to support it. In arbitration, the

---

[276] See paras 5–073 *et seq.* and 5–197.

[277] Section 34(2)(a) of the Arbitration Act 1996: derived from Model Law, Art.20 (see Appendix 4), which is fuller. The Model Law adds that the tribunal should have regard to the convenience of the parties: arguably this is part of the tribunal's general obligation under s.33 of the Arbitration Act 1996: DAC report, para.169. See Appendix 2.

[278] Section 3 of the Arbitration Act 1996: see para.5–071.

[279] See paras 5–167 *et seq.*

[280] Section 34(2)(b) of the Arbitration Act 1996 derived from Model Law, Art.22: see Appendix 4.

[281] See paras 5–120 *et seq.*

[282] Section 34(2)(c) of the Arbitration Act 1996. This is derived from Model Law, Art.23: see Appendix 4. Under the old law the power was held to exist from the vague wording of the Arbitration Act 1950, s.12(1): " . . . [to] do all other things the arbitrator . . . may require", interpreted in *T Sloan & Sons (Builders) Ltd and Another v Brothers of Christian Instruction* [1974] 3 All E.R. 715. See para.5–127.

[283] See paras 5–133 *et seq.*

[284–285] Section 34(2)(d) of the Arbitration Act 1996. The words disclosed "between parties and produced by the parties" also appear in the subsection but have not been repeated above because they suggest a two-stage process of lists of documents followed by inspection, which is rare nowadays.

[286] See para.5–141.

[287] Section 34(2)(e) of the Arbitration Act 1996. Under the old law the arbitrator was held to have this power, see *Kursell v Timber Operators and Contractors Ltd* [1923] 2 K.B. 202. Breach was formerly remediable by court order, but this was abolished by the Courts and Legal Services Act 1990, s.103, itself now repealed by s.107(2) of the Arbitration Act 1996.

scope and form of such questions are left to the discretion of the tribunal but are not common.

Rules about evidence.[288] The tribunal may decide whether to apply strict   4–078
rules of evidence (or any other rules) as to the admissibility, relevance or weight of any material (oral, written or other) sought to be tendered on any matters of fact or opinion, and the time, manner and form in which such material should be exchanged and presented.[289] Before the Act was passed, there was concern about the application of strict rules of evidence to arbitration. It was reflected in Professor Goode's trenchant criticism of the rule: "the only rule about evidence should be that the arbitrator acts fairly and in conformity with the rules of natural justice".[290] Difficult doctrines like the parol evidence or hearsay rules need not now concern an arbitral tribunal unless, exceptionally, it is decided to apply strict rules of evidence in the arbitration.

Ascertaining the facts and the law.[291] The tribunal may decide   4–079
whether and to what extent it should itself take the initiative in ascertaining the facts and the law.[292] This provision was introduced by the Act. It was designed to counter the tendency of common law tribunals not to take the initiative and simply to decide on the representations of the parties. The provision allows the tribunal to be more interventionist and "inquisitorial", which is said to be more in line with civil law practice. If the tribunal does take the initiative in obtaining evidence, it must give all parties a reasonable opportunity of commenting on it.[293]

Presentation of evidence and submissions.[294] The tribunal may   4–080
decide whether and to what extent there should be oral[295] or written evidence or submissions.[296] This provision allows the tribunal to decide whether there is to be a hearing, unless both parties agree on the issue.[297] Previously one of the parties could insist on a hearing, even if neither the tribunal nor the other party wanted a hearing to take place[298]: the same is true of the Model Law.[299]

---

[288] See para.5–130.

[289] Section 34(2)(f) of the Arbitration Act 1996.

[290] "The adaptation of English law to International Commercial Arbitration", 8 Arbitration Int. 1 at 6.

[291] See paras 5–094 *et seq.*

[292] Section 34(2)(g) of the Arbitration Act 1996.

[293] Section 33(1)(a), DAC report, para.172 of the Arbitration Act 1996.

[294] See paras 5–130 *et seq.*

[295] In *Brandeis & Black* [2001] 2 All E.R. (Comm) 980, the court found no objection in the arbitrators permitting one party to call and cross-examine witnesses of the other party.

[296] Section 34(2)(h) of the Arbitration Act 1996, derived from Model Law, Art.24(1) (see Appendix 4).

[297] This provision is subject to the parties agreeing otherwise. Some rules of arbitration incorporated into the arbitration agreement give each party the right to insist upon a hearing (e.g. ICC Rules, Art.20.2).

[298] *Henry Sotheran Ltd v Norwich Union Life Insurance Society* [1992] 31 E.G. 70.

[299] Article 24(1), second sentence.

4–081 **Time for compliance.**[300] The tribunal is given the power to fix the time within which any directions given by it are to be complied with, and the power to extend the time so fixed (whether or not is has expired).[301]

(e) Experts

4–082 **Experts, legal advisers and assessors.**[302] A tribunal may appoint experts or legal advisers[303] to report to it and the parties or appoint assessors to assist it on technical matters and may allow any such expert, legal adviser or assessor to attend the proceedings.[304] Parties must have a reasonable opportunity to comment on any information, opinion or advice proffered by any expert, legal adviser or assessor.[305] Their fees count as expenses of the arbitrators, a provision the parties are not free to vary or depart from by agreement.[306]

(f) Securing claim, costs and evidence[307]

4–083 **Agreed powers.** Parties are free to agree on the powers exercisable by the arbitral tribunal for securing a claim or an award, or costs or evidence.[308] For example, arbitration rules may empower the tribunal to order a respondent to a claim or a counterclaim to provide security for all or part of the amount in dispute.[309] Unless otherwise agreed by the parties the tribunal has the powers set out as follows.[310]

4–084 **Security for costs.**[311] An arbitral tribunal has the power to order a claimant (or counterclaiming respondent) in an arbitration to give security for the costs of the arbitration in such form as the tribunal determines.[312] The tribunal must not,

---

[300] See para.5–138.
[301] Section 34(3) of the Arbitration Act 1996.
[302] See para.5–159.
[303] The right to seek legal advice was mentioned in *National Boat Shows v Thameside Marine* (August 1, 2001), QBD (Comm).
[304] Section 37(1)(a) of the Arbitration Act 1996.
[305] Section 37(1)(b) of the Arbitration Act 1996.
[306] Section 37(2) of the Arbitration Act 1996, a mandatory provision, because an agreement between the parties to a different effect would prevent the tribunal from recovering, from those parties, expenses properly incurred, DAC report, para.188. For arbitrators' expenses, see the s.28(1) of the Arbitration Act 1996, which makes the parties jointly and severally liable for such reasonable fees and expenses (if any) as are appropriate in the circumstances. Thus the appropriateness of the cost of a tribunal expert could be an issue, which presumably could cover whether the expert should have been instructed at all as well as the amount of the expense.
[307] See paras 5–074 *et seq.*
[308] Section 38(1) of the Arbitration Act 1996.
[309] See for example LCIA Rules, Art.25–1(a) and para.5–084—compare limited power of the court, see para.7–207.
[310] Section 38(2) of the Arbitration Act 1996.
[311] See para.5–079.
[312] Section 38(3) of the Arbitration Act 1996. This power, which was formerly exercised by the High Court, is now exclusively the province of the arbitral tribunal. The court's powers are specified in s.44 of the Act and do not include power to order security for costs: see para.7–207.

however, exercise its power on the ground that the claimant is an individual ordinarily resident outside the United Kingdom or that it is a corporation or association formed or seated abroad.[313]

Directions about property.[314] The tribunal may give directions in relation   4–085
to any property which is the subject of the proceedings or as to which any question arises in the proceedings, and which is owned by or is in the possession of a party to the proceedings.[315]

Oaths and affirmations.[316] The tribunal may direct that a party or witness   4–086
shall be examined on oath or affirmation, and may for that purpose administer any necessary oath or take any necessary affirmation.[317]

Preservation of evidence.[318] An arbitral tribunal may give directions to a   4–087
party for the preservation for the purpose of the proceedings of any evidence in his custody or control.[319] For example, a tribunal could order a party to keep documentary records which had been created some time earlier, say at the beginning of a project, and which might otherwise be destroyed.

(g) Default

Default.[320] Parties have an obligation to do all things necessary for the proper   4–088
and expeditious conduct of the arbitral proceedings.[321] This includes complying without delay with any determination of the tribunal as to procedural or evidential matters, or with any order or directions of the tribunal.[322] Parties are free to agree on the powers of the tribunal in case of a party's failure to do something necessary for the proper and expeditious conduct of the arbitration.[323] Unless otherwise agreed by the parties, the following provisions apply.[324]

Delay.[325] If the claimant has been guilty of "inordinate and inexcusable delay"   4–089
in pursuing his claim in arbitration and the delay gives rise to, or is likely to give

---

[313] This prohibition is expressed in s.38(3) of the Arbitration Act 1996. See also DAC report, para.366.
[314] See paras 5–081 and 5–082.
[315] Section 38(4) of the Arbitration Act 1996. This provision expands considerably on Art.17 of the Model Law (see Appendix 4), from which it is derived.
[316] See paras 5–157 and 5–164.
[317] Section 38(5) of the Arbitration Act 1996.
[318] See para.5–083.
[319] Section 38(6) of the Arbitration Act 1996.
[320] See paras 5–191 *et seq.*
[321] Section 40(1) of the Arbitration Act 1996.
[322] Section 40(2)(a) of the Arbitration Act 1996.
[323] Section 41(1) of the Arbitration Act 1996. Cf. Model Law, Art.25: see Appendix 4.
[324] Section 41(2) of the Arbitration Act 1996.
[325] See paras 5–224 *et seq.*

rise to a substantial risk that it is not possible to have a fair resolution of the issues in that claim, or the delay has caused, or is likely to cause serious prejudice to the respondent, the tribunal may make an award dismissing the claim.[326] Inordinate and inexcusable delay is a long period of time, years not months, for which no satisfactory explanation is given.[327]

4–090   **Non-attendance and non-compliance.**[328] If a party fails to attend or be represented at a hearing or, where matters are to be dealt with in writing, fails to submit written evidence or make written submissions, the tribunal may proceed in the absence of that party, or without any written evidence or submissions on his behalf, and make an award on the basis of the evidence before it.[329] The tribunal must have given the party an opportunity to put his case and answer that of his opponent.[330]

4–091   **Peremptory orders.**[331] If without showing sufficient cause a party fails to comply with an order, the tribunal may make a peremptory order.[332] If a claimant fails to comply with a peremptory order of the tribunal to provide security for costs, the tribunal may make an award dismissing his claim.[333] If a party fails to comply with any other kind of peremptory order the tribunal may direct that the party in default shall not be entitled to rely on any allegation or material which is the subject-matter of the order and/or draw adverse inferences from the act of non-compliance and/or make an award on the basis of the materials provided and/or make an order as to the payment of costs.[334] The tribunal may instead apply to the court for an order requiring a party to comply with a peremptory order made by the tribunal.[335]

(h) Orders and Awards[336]

4–092   **Awards on different issues at different times on different aspects.**[337] Unless empowered by the parties to grant relief on a provisional basis,[338] the tribunal must make a final award on the issues that were put to it and

---

[326] Section 41(3) of the Arbitration Act 1996. If the arbitration has not been commenced, the court may treat the arbitration agreement as having been frustrated: *The "Hannah Blumenthal"* [1982] 1 Lloyd's Rep. 582, CA.
[327] For a discussion of this standard, see the notes at CPR Pt 25, r.1(6).
[328] See paras 5–202 *et seq.*
[329] Section 41(4) of the Arbitration Act 1996.
[330] Section 33(1)(a) of the Arbitration Act 1996, DAC report, para.208.
[331] See further paras 5–191 *et seq.*
[332] Section 41(5) of the Arbitration Act 1996.
[333] Section 41(6) of the Arbitration Act 1996.
[334] Section 41(7) of the Arbitration Act 1996.
[335] Section 42 of the Arbitration Act 1996.
[336] See paras 6–002 *et seq.*
[337] See paras 6–009 *et seq.*
[338] See para.4–093.

the failure to do so is an irregularity.[339] However, unless otherwise agreed by the parties, the tribunal may make more than one award at different times on different aspects of the matters to be determined.[340] In particular, the tribunal may make an award relating (a) to an issue affecting the whole claim, or (b) to a part only of the cross-claims submitted to it for decision.[341] If a tribunal does so, it shall specify in its award the issue,[342] or the claim or part of a claim, which is the subject-matter of the award.[343] The purpose of this provision is to allow tribunals to decide disputes in a way that avoids one very long hearing and encourages a managerial approach, with the selection of issues for early determination to encourage settlement of the rest of the dispute.[344] A partial or interim award creates an estoppel as respects the issue determined by that award. Neither party can at any subsequent hearing in the arbitration advance arguments or adduce evidence on that issue directed to disputing the correctness of the determination previously made.[345]

Provisional order.[346] There is also power, exercisable only by agreement of the parties, to make "provisional orders",[347] by which is meant any orders on a provisional basis of relief that the tribunal would have the power to grant in a final award. This includes, for instance, an order for the payment of money or the transfer of property between the parties, or an order for an interim payment on account of costs.[348] Any provisional order is subject to subsequent final adjudication by the tribunal, whether on the merits or costs.[349] Without the parties' agreement to confer this power on the tribunal, the tribunal has no such power.[350]   **4–093**

Remedies.[351] The parties are free to agree on the powers exercisable by the tribunal as regards remedies.[352] Unless otherwise agreed by the parties, the remedies are as follows.[353] The tribunal may make a declaration as to any matter to be determined in the proceedings.[354] The tribunal may order the payment of a sum of money, in any currency.[355] The tribunal has the same powers as the court: **4–094**

---

[339] *Ronly Holdings Ltd v JSC Zestafoni G Nikoladze Ferroalloy Plant* [2004] EWHC 1354.
[340] Section 47(1) of the Arbitration Act 1996.
[341] Section 47(2) of the Arbitration Act 1996.
[342] This issue may, for example, be the tribunal's jurisdiction to decide some or all of the dispute.
[343] Section 47(3) of the Arbitration Act 1996.
[344] DAC report, paras 226–233.
[345] *Westland Helicopters v Al-Hejailan* [2004] EWHC 1625.
[346] See further paras 5–085 *et seq.* and 6–020 *et seq.* on this, and on the terminology.
[347] Section 39(1) of the Arbitration Act 1996.
[348] Section 39(2) of the Arbitration Act 1996.
[349] Section 39(3) of the Arbitration Act 1996.
[350] Section 39(4) of the Arbitration Act 1996.
[351] See paras 6–096 *et seq.*
[352] Section 48(1) of the Arbitration Act 1996.
[353] Section 48(2) of the Arbitration Act 1996.
[354] Section 48(3) of the Arbitration Act 1996 and see paras 6–109 *et seq.*
[355] Section 48(4) of the Arbitration Act 1996, see paras 6–098 *et seq.*

(a) to order a party to do or to refrain from doing anything,[356] (b) to order specific performance of a contract (other than a contract relating to land),[357] and (c) to order the rectification, setting aside or cancellation of a deed or other document.[358]

4–095 **Interest.**[359] The parties are free to agree on the powers of the tribunal as regards the award of interest,[360] but only an agreement in writing as defined in the Act can qualify as an agreement to the contrary under s.49 of the Act.[361] Unless otherwise agreed, the following applies.[362] The tribunal may award simple or compound interest from such dates, at such rates and with such rests as it considers meets the justice of the case: (a) on the whole or part of any amount awarded by the tribunal, in respect of any period up to the date of the award, (b) on the whole or part of any amount claimed in the arbitration and outstanding at the commencement of the arbitral proceedings but paid before the award was made, in respect of any period up to the date of payment.[363] The tribunal may award simple or compound interest from the date of the award (or any later date) at such rates and with such rests as it considers meets the justice of the case, on the outstanding amount of any award (including any award of interest under s.49(3) and any award as to costs).[364] Previously, a tribunal could award only simple interest.[365] The power to award compound interest should be used on a compensatory basis, and not a punitive basis.[366]

4–096 **Terminating proceedings in case of a settlement.**[367] If during arbitral proceedings the parties settle the dispute, unless the parties otherwise agree, the tribunal shall terminate the substantive proceedings and, if so requested by the parties and not objected to by the tribunal, shall record the settlement in the form of an agreed (or "consent") award.[368]

4–097 **Reasons.**[369] A tribunal now has the power (and the duty) to give reasons as part of an award, unless the parties agree to opt out of this provision.[370]

---

[356] See paras 6–107 *et seq.*
[357] See paras 6–108 *et seq.*
[358] Section 48(5) of the Arbitration Act 1996, see paras 6–114 *et seq.*
[359] See paras 6–115 *et seq.*
[360] Section 49(1) of the Arbitration Act 1996.
[361] *Lesotho Highlands Development Authority v Impregilo* [2005] UKHL 43. For statutory arbitrations see *Durham CC v Darlinghom BC* [2003] EWHC 2598.
[362] Section 49(2) of the Arbitration Act 1996 in addition to any other powers the tribunal may have to award interest, s.49(6) of the Arbitration Act 1996.
[363] Section 49(3) of the Arbitration Act 1996.
[364] Section 49(4) of the Arbitration Act 1996.
[365] Section 39(2) of the Arbitration Act 1996.
[366] DAC report, para.237.
[367] See paras 6–024 *et seq.*
[368] Section 51(1) and (2) of the Arbitration Act 1996.
[369] See further paras 6–028 *et seq.* and 6–051.
[370] Section 52(4) of the Arbitration Act 1996, Model Law, Art.31 (see Appendix 4).

Deciding the date of an award.[371] Unless otherwise agreed by the 4–098
parties, the tribunal may decide what is to be taken as the date on which the award
was made.[372]

Notifying the parties of an award. Unless otherwise agreed by the 4–099
parties, the tribunal has the power (and the duty) to notify the award by service of
copies on the parties without delay after the award is made.[373]

Correcting an award and issuing an additional award.[374] The 4–100
parties are free to agree on the powers of the tribunal to correct an award or make
an additional award.[375] If there is no agreement, the tribunal has powers to correct
an existing award so as to remove any clerical mistake or error arising from an
accidental slip or omission or to clarify or remove an ambiguity. The tribunal may
also make an additional award in respect of any claim (including a claim for
interest or costs) which was presented to the tribunal but was not dealt with in the
award.[376]

Summary award.[377] Unless arbitration rules allow it,[378] the jurisdiction to 4–101
make an award whose effect is like that of a summary judgment is regarded as
exceptional[379] and no provision has been made for it in the Act.

The very different power to make a provisional order, with consent of the
parties, is mentioned above.[380]

(i) Costs[381]

Awarding costs. Subject to the parties' right to agree what costs of the 4–102
arbitration are recoverable,[382] the tribunal has the power to determine by award the
recoverable costs of the arbitration on such basis as it thinks fit. If it does so and
does not limit those costs to a specific sum,[383] the tribunal must specify the basis
on which it has acted and the item of recoverable costs and the amount referable

---

[371] See para.6–053.
[372] Section 54(1) of the Arbitration Act 1996.
[373] Section 55(1) and (2) of the Arbitration Act 1996.
[374] See paras 6–036 and 6–167 *et seq.*
[375] Section 57(1) of the Arbitration Act 1996. Model Law, Art.33 (see Appendix 4).
[376] Section 57(2) and (3) of the Arbitration Act 1996.
[377] See para.1–029.
[378] See for instance, ICE Arbitration Procedure (1997) r.15.
[379] *Modern Trading Co Ltd v Swale Building and Construction Ltd* (1990) 24 Con. L.R. 59.
[380] See para.4–093.
[381] See paras 6–129 *et seq.*
[382] Section 63(1) of the Arbitration Act 1996.
[383] See para.4–103.

to each.[384] If the tribunal does not determine the recoverable costs of the arbitration, the court may do so on the application of a party to the arbitration.[385]

4–103 Limiting recoverable costs. Unless otherwise agreed by the parties, the tribunal may direct that the recoverable costs of the arbitration, or any part of the arbitral proceedings, shall be limited to a specified amount.[386] Exercising this power is part of the general duty of the tribunal to avoid unnecessary expense.[387]

7. DUTIES OF AN ARBITRAL TRIBUNAL

(a) Introduction

4–104 General duty. The Act imposes on the tribunal a general duty in conducting the arbitration proceedings, in its decisions on matters of procedure and evidence and in the exercise of all other powers conferred on it.[388] As is described more fully in the following paragraphs, this wide-ranging duty consists in acting fairly and impartially and adopting procedures suitable for the arbitration, and expresses in positive form what was implicit at common law. This general duty of the tribunal finds its complement in s.40 of the Act, which imposes a general duty on the parties.[389] The fact that both duties now have a statutory basis and are mandatory emphasises their importance to the arbitral process.

Breach by an arbitrator of his general duty can have serious consequences. Depending on the breach, it may, for example, form the basis of an application to remove him[390]; it is also a ground for challenging his award[391]; and if bad faith is established on his part it may even lead to a claim for damages against him.[392]

4–105 Specific duties. The specific duties of an arbitral tribunal may be listed as follows[393]:

- to act fairly and impartially between the parties[394];

[384] Section 63(3) of the Arbitration Act 1996. See paras 6–141 *et seq.*
[385] Section 63(4) of the Arbitration Act 1996.
[386] Section 65(1) of the Arbitration Act 1996. See further paras 6–147 and 6–148.
[387] Section 33(1)(b) of the Arbitration Act 1996, DAC report, para.272.
[388] Section 33 of the Arbitration Act 1996, greatly expanded from Model Law, Art.18 (see Appendix 4).
[389] See para.5–191.
[390] Section 24 of the Arbitration Act 1996. See paras 7–112 *et seq.*
[391] Section 68 of the Arbitration Act 1996. See paras 8–072 *et seq.*
[392] This possibility is discussed at paras 4–154 *et seq.*
[393] A tribunal's powers in relation to awards tend to overlap with its duties in relation to awards, see the examples in paras 4–097 and 4–099, which are not listed again in this section, exercising its power to issue awards.
[394] Section 24(1)(a) and s.33(1)(a) of the Arbitration Act 1996.

- to possess the qualifications required by the arbitration agreement[395];

- to be physically and mentally capable of conducting the proceedings[396];

- to conduct the proceedings properly[397];

- to use all reasonable despatch in conducting the proceedings or making an award[398];

- to give each party a reasonable opportunity of putting his case and dealing with that of his opponent[399];

- to adopt procedures suitable to the circumstances of the particular case[400];

- to avoid unnecessary delay or expense[401];

- to provide a fair means for the resolution of the matters falling to be determined[402];

- to attend hearings and participate in deliberations of the tribunal[403];

- not to exceed its substantive jurisdiction[404];

- not to exceed its powers[405];

- to conduct the proceedings in accordance with the procedure agreed by the parties[406];

- to deal with all the issues put[407];

- to ensure that any award is neither uncertain nor ambiguous[408];

- to ensure that any award is not obtained by fraud or procured in a way contrary to public policy[409];

- to ensure that any award complies with requirements as to its form[410];

- to act judicially[411];

---

[395] Section 24(1)(b) of the Arbitration Act 1996.
[396] Section 24(1)(c) of the Arbitration Act 1996.
[397] Section 24(1)(d)(i) of the Arbitration Act 1996.
[398] Section 24(1)(d)(ii) of the Arbitration Act 1996.
[399] Section 33(1)(a) of the Arbitration Act 1996.
[400] Section 33(1)(b) of the Arbitration Act 1996.
[401] Section 33(1)(b) of the Arbitration Act 1996.
[402] Section 33(1)(b) of the Arbitration Act 1996.
[403] Implicit in the above.
[404] Section 67 of the Arbitration Act 1996.
[405] Section 68(2)(b) of the Arbitration Act 1996.
[406] Section 68(2)(c) of the Arbitration Act 1996.
[407] Section 68(2)(d) of the Arbitration Act 1996.
[408] Section 68(2)(f) of the Arbitration Act 1996.
[409] Section 68(2)(g) of the Arbitration Act 1996.
[410] Section 68(2)(h) of the Arbitration Act 1996.
[411] *Re Hopper* (1867) L.R. 2 Q.B. 367, explained by Lord Salmon in *Sutcliffe v Thackrah* [1974] A.C. 727 at 763D, *Fisher v PG Wellfair Ltd (In Liquidation); Fox v PG Wellfair Ltd (in liquidation)* [1981] 2 Lloyd's Rep. 514.

- to keep the subject-matter of the arbitration confidential[412];

- to make its own decision[413];

- to decide according to the law or, if agreed, according to other considerations.[414]

Breach of these duties:

- can lead to an arbitrator's removal and repayment of fees[415];

- can justify intervention by the court during a reference[416];

- can lead to an award being remitted or set aside or declared to be of no effect[417] and;

- could result in a claim for damages in the event of bad faith.[418]

(b) The duty to act fairly and impartially

4–106 **Duty of fairness.**[419] As part of the tribunal's general duty, it must act fairly as well as impartially as between the parties, in conducting the arbitral proceedings, in its decisions on matters of procedure and evidence and in the exercise of other powers conferred on it. The subject of impartiality is discussed fully in the following paragraphs, but it is important not to overlook the additional duty of fairness, which affects every aspect of the arbitration. Section 33 of the Act also gives specific instances of what is meant by fair treatment, namely:

- each party should be given a "reasonable" opportunity of putting his case and dealing with that of his opponent, and

- suitable procedures should be adopted by the tribunal that avoid unnecessary delay and expense, so as to provide a "fair" means for resolving the particular dispute.[420]

In fulfilling its duty of fairness, the tribunal may have to balance conflicting demands of the parties. It is not always easy to find the right balance, but the

---

[412] See para.5–182.
[413] See para.6–056.
[414] Section 46 of the Arbitration Act 1996.
[415] Sections 24, 25 and 68 of the Arbitration Act 1996.
[416] See paras 7–111 *et seq.*
[417] See paras 8–072 *et seq.*
[418] See paras 4–154 *et seq.*
[419] See paras 5–032 *et seq.*
[420] A restatement of s.33 of the Arbitration Act 1996.

tribunal must do its best to ensure that each party has a reasonable opportunity of putting his case and dealing with that of his opponent.[421]

Duty of impartiality. An obligation to act impartially[422] as between the parties is also required as part of the general duty imposed on the tribunal by s.33 of the Act. Failure to observe this fundamental requirement may lead to the removal of the arbitrator on the grounds of actual or apparent bias.[423] 4–107

Actual and apparent bias. A distinction is often made between actual bias and apparent bias, although both give grounds for removal. Actual bias is rarely alleged and even more rarely established.[424] More often there is a suspicion of bias which has been variously described as apparent or unconscious or imputed bias. In such majority of cases, it is often emphasised that the challenger does not go so far as to suggest the arbitrator is actually biased, rather that some form of objective apprehension of bias exists. 4–108

Same test for judges and arbitrators. Since *R. v Gough*[425] it has been clear that the same test for removal of an arbitral tribunal for bias ("actual" or "apparent") will apply to judges, and other judicial decision takers. In *AT&T*,[426] Lord Woolf M.R. did suggest that if different standards were to apply to judges and arbitrators, a higher standard should apply to arbitrators, but the court upheld the application of the same standard. For all practical purposes, there is no significant distinction between the "real possibility" test and the "justifiable doubts" test referred to in s.24(1)(a) of the Act. 4–109

As discussed below, the IBA Guidelines on Conflicts of Interest in International Arbitration do provide some guidance on particular circumstances which may give risc to a real possibility of bias.[427]

The real possibility test: the fair minded and informed observer. In weighing the evidence the court will consider whether the circumstances bearing on the allegation of the partiality "would lead a fair-minded and 4–110

---

[421] In *Badwith Shipping Corp v Intaari (the "Magdalena Oldenouff")* [2006] EWHC 2532, an award was challenged, albeit unsuccessfully, on the ground that the arbitral tribunal had failed to give the applicant a reasonable opportunity to deal with the case of the respondent. See paras 5–042 *et seq.* below for a discussion on the parties' procedural rights.

[422] See paras 4–023 *et seq.*

[423] Section 24(1)(a) of the Arbitration Act 1996; see also Model Law, Art.12(1) (see Appendix 4).

[424] In an arbitration in which one party was Portuguese, the arbitrator was overheard saying that Portuguese people were liars. The arbitrator was removed for failing to act fairly and without partiality between the parties. *Re The Owners of the Steamship "Catalina" and Others* and *The Owners of the Motor Vessel "Norma"* (1938) 61 Ll. L. Rep. 360. For a less obvious example, see *Turner (East Asia) Pte Ltd v Builders Federal (Hong Kong) Ltd and Josef Gartner & Co* [1988] 42 B.L.R. 122.

[425] [1993] A.C. 646. See further the comments of Rix J. in *Laker Airways v FLS Aerospace* [2000] 1 W.L.R. 113 at 117E–H.

[426] *AT&T Corp v Saudi Cable Co* [2000] 2 All E.R. (Comm) 625 at 638 B–D.

[427] Approved on May 22, 2004 by the Council of the International Bar Association. See *www.ibanet.org/legalpractice/arbitration.cfm*.

informed observer to conclude that there was a real possibility... that the
[arbitrator] was biased", replacing the previous 'real danger' of basis test set out
in *R. v Gough*.[428] The emphasis is very much on the hypothetical third party
observer[428a]; it has been variously observed that assertions by an arbitrator who is
the subject of a challenge that he had an open mind or was otherwise not biased
are often unlikely to be helpful and should be accorded little or no evidential
weight.[429] The court (or institution, as the case may be) will usually try and put
itself in the position of the reasonable man. The fair-minded observer is imputed
with knowledge of all relevant facts and takes account of the professional standing
of the impugned arbitrator, so that a highly experienced arbitrator with impeccable
credentials is assumed to have a lower propensity to bias than someone less
experienced.[430] The standard also appears to vary depending on the type of
arbitration. Technical arbitrators chosen by the parties for their skill and knowledge in a particular area might not necessarily adopt "*the kind of management
regime that would be imposed by a Queen's Counsel fulfilling the same function.*"[431] In
similar vein, it has been suggested that, in the context of trade or commodity
arbitration, the court should take a "*fairly robust view of commercial dealings between
a particular arbitrator and one of the parties, or for that matter between an individual
arbitrator and the market generally.*"[432] Less clear is the extent to which the
hypothetical third party observer is attributed with a trans-national identity or
whether the fact that a challenger may be a foreign party and therefore unfamiliar
with certain features of the English legal system can strengthen a challenge,
although the likely position now is that, "*The interpolation of the observer does, I
think, make it unnecessary to give special regard to foreigners.*"[433]

4–111   **Substantial injustice.** In deciding whether to remove an arbitrator on the
ground of apparent bias the court should apply the same test as for a finding of
serious irregularity under s.68 of the Act, which also requires the court to consider
whether the irregularity of the arbitrator has caused or will cause substantial

---

[428] The current test was formulated in *Re Medicaments & Related Classes of Goods* [2001] 1 W.L.R. 700
and was modified by the House of Lords in *Porter v Magill* [2001] UKHL 67. This alteration to the
test brought English law into line with the European Convention on Human Rights jurisprudence,
according to which a judge must be both subjectively (actually) impartial but also objectively
impartial: he must be seen to be impartial. Neither case involved an arbitral tribunal but the courts
reviewed all the previous authorities including those relating to arbitrators.

[428a] Other common law jurisdictions adopt the same or very similar test. For example, the "fair-minded
and informed fictitious observer" test is applied in Hong Kong. See *Pacific China Holdings Ltd v
Grand Pacific Holdings Ltd* HCCT 5/2007.

[429] *Re Medicaments & Related Classes of Goods (No.2)* [2001] 1 W.L.R. 700, *per* Lord Hope at 495.

[430] *Sumukan Ltd v Commonwealth Secretariat* [2007] EWHC 188 (Comm) at [71], where the court said
that a fair minded observer would look beyond narrow questions relating to the rules relating to the
arbitrator's appointment.

[431] *Norbrook Laboratories v Tank* [2006] EWHC 1055, *per* Colman J., at [153].

[432] *Argonaud Insurance Co and others v Republic Insurance Co* [2003] EWHC 547, David Steel J, who
cited with approval the reasons given by Moore-Bick J. in *Rustal Trading Ltd v Gill & Duffus SA*
[2000] 1 Lloyd's Rep. 14 at 18.

[433] *ASM Shipping Ltd of India v TTMI Ltd of England* [2005] EWHC 2238 (Comm) (considering
Rustal Trading Ltd v Gill & Duffus SA) [2000] 1 Lloyd's Rep. 14 at [39].

injustice to the applicant. Substantial injustice will normally follow as a matter of course in cases of actual or apparent bias.[434–435]

Role of institutions. For arbitrations governed by institutional rules, it is usual for those rules to provide that the challenge must first be decided by the institution. Section 24(2) provides that if an arbitral institution is vested with the power to remove an arbitrator then the court shall not intervene unless the applicant has first exhausted any available recourse to that institution. In practice, institutions deciding challenges under English law are likely to have regard to the same principles and authorities as the court, although as mentioned in the next paragraph, the grounds for the challenge may not be identical. For example, arbitration rules often require an arbitrator to be independent[436] as well as "impartial". Section 24(1) is mandatory, so even if an institution's rules refer to its decision being final then an application will still be capable of being made to the court, assuming that the seat of arbitration is England.[437]   4–112

The ICC,[438] the LCIA[439] and ICSID[440] have taken steps to prevent the suspicion that arbitrators they appoint lack independence, but not without controversy. For example, the ICC Rules of Arbitration oblige a prospective arbitrator to disclose in writing to the Secretary-General of the ICC Court any facts or circumstances which might be of such a nature as to call into question the arbitrator's independence in the eyes of the parties. The form the prospective arbitrator must complete states that the arbitrator has to take into account "whether there exists any past or present relationship, direct or indirect, with any of the parties or their counsel, whether financial, professional, or of another kind, and whether the nature of such relationship is such that disclosure is called for". The LCIA and ICSID have similar procedures. Swiss commentators have been concerned that disclosure could jeopardise client confidentiality, and that the result could be that inexperienced arbitrators are appointed. One commentator has suggested an amendment to the ICC Rules excluding the need to disclose mere prior acquaintance between an arbitrator and the lawyer for one of the parties.[441] These sorts of procedures are followed as a matter of course only in arbitrations administered by the major institutions. In ad hoc arbitrations where no institutional supervision is provided the only sure way to obtain the relevant information is to carry out one's own investigations and ask pertinent questions of proposed arbitrators.   4–113

[434–435] *Rustal Trading v Gill & Duffus SA* and *ASM Shipping Ltd v TTMI Ltd* [2005] EWHC 2238 (Comm). See para.7–123.

[436] For a discussion about the duty of independence, see para.4–128.

[437] Section 2(1) of the Arbitration Act 1996. In *AT&T Corp v Saudi Cable* [2000] 2 All E.R. (Comm) 625, a challenge under s.24 of the Act to an ICC arbitrator was made to the English court following a rejection of the challenge by the ICC Court, notwithstanding Art.7(4) of the ICC Rules which provides that decisions of the ICC Court as to a challenge to an arbitrator shall be final.

[438] Article 11, ICC Rules of Arbitration.

[439] LCIA, r.10.3.

[440] ICSID, r.6(2).

[441] See 1990/3 Swiss Arbitration Association Bulletin, 226–234, and 1991/2, 85–89.

4–114 **Strategic considerations.** Allegations of conflict of interest have received heightened attention in recent years, and there is a concern within the arbitral community that many challenges are brought as tactical devices simply to disrupt or derail proceedings. For this reason, any prospective challenger should not only consider carefully whether the proposed challenge really is justified on the facts but also try to avoid as much collateral damage to the progress of the proceedings as possible. In many cases, this will involve bringing the challenge at the earliest opportunity, rather than waiting to see how proceedings develop first[442] and in other cases constructive suggestions can be made to demonstrate the good faith of the challenger. In *ASM Shipping Ltd of India v TTMI Ltd of England*,[443] where an objection to an arbitrator/umpire was raised at a hearing, the court noted: "*The objection to X QC was not an attempt to disrupt the arbitration, as the owners had indicated their wish to continue with the two appointed arbitrators and without an umpire and, unless they disagreed, a replacement umpire was not needed.*"[444] The Court of Appeal has made it clear that the stage of the proceedings at which a challenge is brought does not of itself matter, subject of course to there having been no waiver of rights pursuant to s.73.[445] These views of the Court of Appeal were expressed in response to some judicial reluctance to sustain challenges brought at an advanced stage of proceedings where a large amount of work has been undertaken and where hearings may have to be repeated.[446]

4–115 **Infection of bias.** In certain circumstances, it is possible that co-arbitrators may become tainted by the apparent bias of an arbitrator who is removed but only, it is submitted, where the co-arbitrators strongly and inappropriately associate themselves with the removed arbitrator's position. There is no rule that if follows as a matter of law that the remaining arbitrators are tainted by the apparent bias of the removed arbitrator.[447]

4–116 **Pecuniary interest.** There is an automatic disqualification for an arbitrator who has a direct pecuniary interest in one of the parties.[448] The question of removal is to be considered in the light of all relevant circumstances.

---

[442] Of course, a delayed challenge may be barred under s.73.

[443] [2005] EWHC 2238 (Comm).

[444] Paragraph 41. For an unsuccessful attempt to circumvent the first instance judge's refusal to grant leave to appeal his decision see the decision of the Court of Appeal under the same name, [2006] EWCA 1341.

[445] *Morrison v AWG Group Ltd* [2006] EWCA Civ 6 at [29]–[30].

[446] In *Re Medicaments & Related Classes of Goods (No.2)* [2001] 1 W.L.R. 700, the entire tribunal was removed even though the trial was in progress and had already lasted some five weeks. The IBA Guidelines state, "no distinction should be made regarding the stage of the arbitral procedure", Pt 1, Explanation to General Standard 3, at para.3(d).

[447] *ASM Shipping Ltd v Bruce Harris & Others* [2007] EWHC 1513, at [42]–[46]. Contrast *Re Medicaments & Related Classes of Goods* [2001] W.L.R. 700, in which it was held that a lay member of the Restrictive Practices Court was tainted by apparent bias, leading to the disqualification of the other two members of the court.

[448] *AT&T Corp v Saudi Cable* [2000] 2 All E.R. (Comm) 625. The challenged arbitrator held 300 common shares in one of the parties, a listed entity, and was not challenged on this basis.

In *AT&T*, the chairman of an arbitral tribunal was a non-executive director and shareholder in a competitor company that was an unsuccessful bidder for the agreement in relation to which disputes subsequently arose between the parties. The Court of Appeal (upholding the decision reached at first instance) dismissed the challenge because, among other things, the arbitrator did not have a direct pecuniary interest in either of the parties. His shareholding in a competitor of one of the parties was sufficiently small to be of no consequence.[449] Further, the court found that he was not part of the management of the competitor company and that his directorship was incidental rather than a vital part of his professional life. The arbitrator did not attach any real importance to his directorship, as illustrated by his readiness to resign it when he was challenged.

Past or present positions held by arbitrator. In exceptional cases, the past or present positions held or roles performed by the arbitrator outside of the particular case before him can give rise to a real possibility of bias. In *Locabail v Bayfield Properties*[450] the Court of Appeal sought to give guidance on factors that could not ordinarily provide a basis for an allegation of bias. These include the judge's gender, religion, background, family,[451] friendships,[452] memberships of clubs or associations, previous decisions, extra-curricular utterances, previous receipt of instructions to act for or against any one engaged in a case now before him and membership of the same chambers. However, this list is of a general nature only and does not preclude any of the listed matters from giving rise to a successful challenge in particular circumstances. 4–117

Role of IBA Guidelines on Conflicts of Interest. The IBA Guidelines on Conflicts of Interest in International Arbitration, although clearly not representative of English law, also contain helpful guidance on specific situations relating to past or present positions.[452a] The Guidelines contain certain general principles and also attach lists of particular circumstances which have arisen in practice and which are classified as red, orange or green depending upon the degree or of objection, if any, to the particular circumstance. For example, the fact that the arbitrator is a director, otherwise controls or has a significant financial interest in one of the parties appears on the Non-Waivable Red List, which means that the arbitrator should not act in any circumstances. The situation where an arbitrator is a lawyer in the same firm as counsel to one of the parties is on the 4–118

---

[449] *AT&T Corp v Saudi Cable* [2000] 2 All E.R. (Comm) 625, at [16].
[450] [2000] Q.B. 451 at 480.
[451] In *Tembec v United States*, an investment treaty case under the North American Free Trade Agreement, ICSID refused to remove an arbitrator on the grounds of (1) the arbitrator's marriage to a first cousin of the US President, and (2) the arbitrator's position some 20 years previously as US State Department Legal Advisor. Investment Treaty News, June 15, 2006, *www.iisd.org/investment/itn*.
[452] See *Morrison v AWG Group Ltd* [2006] EWCA Civ 6.
[452a] The earlier IBA Rules of Ethics for International Arbitrators, available at *www.ibanet.org*, also contain some helpful guidance.

Waivable Red List, which means that the arbitrator may act with consent of the other party.[453] Far less clear cut are situations appearing on the Orange List which, the Guidelines suggest, should be disclosed as each situation may "in the eyes of the parties give rise to justifiable doubts as to the arbitrator's impartiality or independence". Green List circumstances do not need to be disclosed and do not give rise to objection. Certain examples of these situations will be discussed below. The application of the IBA Guidelines were considered in *ASM Shipping Ltd of India v TTMI Ltd of England*. The facts of that case could not be made to fit into any of the examples given in the Guidelines, leading the court to conclude that they "*say . . . nothing about the true answer to the questions in this case*".[454] In appropriate circumstances, however, it is suggested that the court could derive assistance from the Guidelines when considering challenges.

4–119   Unequal involvement in appointment process. The court has rejected an application to set aside an award based on apparent bias where the tribunal was appointed by the head of a body which would always be a party to any case before the tribunal, the body provided administrative services to the tribunal and met certain expenses and had power to amend its statute.[455] Rejecting the complaint, the court noted that steps had been taken to ensure the high professional standing of the tribunal members. In the same case, the court also rejected a related complaint relating to the ad hoc process by which one of the arbitrators had been appointed, saying that a "*properly informed, independent observer*" would not have concluded that there was a real possibility of bias. The decision appears to have been influenced by the fact that the body in question was the Commonwealth Secretariat, an international organisation designed to organise and promote the interests of the Commonwealth of Nations, and not a commercial institution, where it seems likely that the direct ability to appoint all three members of the tribunal would not be tolerated.

4–120   Arbitrator previously acted for/against a party. In *ASM Shipping Ltd of India v TTMI Ltd of England* apparent bias was made out where a Queen's Counsel had appeared seven months previously for a third party (instructed on a disclosure application by one of the solicitors in the case before him) against one of the parties to the case in which he now sat as arbitrator. At issue in the arbitration was an allegedly dishonest approach to disclosure by the challenging party, and a similar issue had arisen in the context of the separate disclosure application made by the Queen's Counsel against the party in the earlier case. "*The nature of the allegations, the pattern of them, the involvement of the same*

---

[453] Paragraphs 1.1, 2.3.3.
[454] [2005] EWHC 2238 (Comm).
[455] *Sukuman Ltd v Commonwealth Secretariat* [2007] EWHC 188.

solicitors, X QC's involvement in the disclosure process a short time before sitting as an arbitrator in judgment on the alleged dishonest party persuades me, for the reasons I have given, that X QC should have recused himself."[456] If the arbitrator had not been involved in making allegations of dishonesty against one of the parties then it is suggested that apparent bias may not have been made out. An arbitrator was also removed where he had previously acted as a consultant expert and advised on the defence of non-parties (in the arbitration) to an insurance fraud case. His involvement was limited to a two week period, some three and a half years before the arbitration commenced but nonetheless related to a fraud which was said to constitute the "central fact" in the arbitration. In these circumstances, the court removed the arbitrator because of the real risk that the arbitrator may have formed certain views as to the issues and relevant individuals from his previous engagement which he could not now disclose to the court, as his previous advice was privileged, but which may give rise to an appearance of bias.[457]

Arbitrator's law firm associated with a party. An arbitrator was removed where the firm in which he was salaried partner carried out a large amount of separate legal work for an associated company of one of the parties.[458] A similar argument was rejected by the Court of Appeal in the *Locabail v Bayfield Properties*,[459] one of five applications relating to judicial bias heard together. The court found that the link between the firm of solicitors in which the judge was a senior partner and one of the parties was too remote to allow disqualification on the basis of a direct pecuniary bias or apparent bias.   4–121

Repeated appointments. Other forms of past contact between a party and an arbitrator may also constitute grounds for removal; each case turns on its particular facts. For example, a pattern of significant and repeated appointments from one party in favour of a particular arbitrator may be sufficient, especially if it can be shown that the arbitrator is dependent upon a particular party for a significant portion of his or her business. The Orange List of the IBA Guidelines suggests that more than three previous appointments by an arbitrator by the same   4–122

---

[456] [2005] EWHC 2238 (Comm). This was a challenge under s.68 of the Act. The award was not set aside because the applicant delayed until the award was delivered and accordingly had fallen foul of s.73 of the Act. However, the court felt that the arbitrator "should not continue to act in this matter" (at 390), even though no application was apparently made under s.24, because the court felt that his continued involvement in the case was unacceptable as apparent bias had been made out. For comment on this case see, Friel, "Apparent Bias" and "Serious Irregularity" in English Arbitration, Int. A.L.R. 2006, 9(1), N1–3. For an unsuccessful attempt to circumvent the first instance judge's refusal to grant leave to appeal his decision see the decision of the Court of Appeal under the same name, [2006] EWCA 1341. See also *ASM Shipping Ltd v Harris* [2007] EWHC 1513 for an unsuccessful attempt to remove the two remaining arbitrators.
[457] *Sphere Drake Insurance v American Reliable Insurance Co* [2004] EWHC 796.
[458] *Save & Prosper Pensions Ltd v Homebase Ltd* [2001] L. & T. Rev. 11.
[459] [2000] 1 All E.R. 65.

counsel or law firm in three years, and more than one previous appointment by the same party or its affiliates should be disclosed.[460]

4-123 **Arbitrator/counsel links.** In principle, the mere fact that an arbitrator is being addressed in a case by counsel with whom he sits as co-arbitrator in a separate, unrelated case is unlikely to constitute sufficient grounds for removal of the arbitrator.[461] A close personal friendship between an arbitrator and counsel or someone else involved in the case, such as a witness, may also give rise to a real possibility of bias.[462] The existence of significant animosity between an arbitrator and counsel or someone else involved in the case may also give rise to a real possibility of bias.[462a]

4-124 **Previous views expressed by arbitrator.** In certain circumstances, previously expressed views of an arbitrator, which suggest a certain pre-disposition to a particular course of action, outcome or in favour of a party, can constitute grounds for removal. One of the *Locabail v Bayfield* applications[463] against a judge was successful on this basis. The judge had written four strongly worded articles which led the court to conclude that an objective apprehension of bias may arise on the part of one of the parties. However, a challenge against a sole arbitrator in a trade arbitration which alleged apparent bias because the arbitrator had previously been involved in a dispute with one of the parties failed. The judge found this on the facts to be no more than "an ordinary incident of commercial life" occurring in the relatively small field of trade arbitrations where it was thought the parties and arbitrators were quite likely to have had prior dealing with each other.[464] Similarly, the fact that an insurance arbitrator had previously given a statement in another arbitration (and may have been called to give evidence subsequently) about the meaning of a standard form clause which might have had a tentative bearing on the present arbitration would not give grounds for removal.[465] There is foreign authority to suggest that apparent bias might be made out in circumstances where an arbitrator also appears simultaneously as counsel in a case raising very similar issues and in his capacity as counsel takes a position

---

[460] Orange list, paras 3.1.3, 3.3.7. No objection was taken to 10 sets of previous instructions over 11 years to the arbitrator (to act as counsel) by one of the solicitors in the arbitration in *ASM Shipping Ltd of India v TTMI Ltd of England* [2005] EWHC 2238 (Comm). This was seen in the context of the arbitrator's overall number of 400 instructions in the same period: [15].

[461] This approach has been confirmed by the Swiss Supreme Court in a series of cases involving the Court of Arbitration for Sport. *X v Y*, August 4, 2006, Swiss Supreme Court, 1st Civil Chamber, reported at *www.kluwerarbitration.com*.

[462] In *Sir Alexander Morrison & Another v AWG Group Ltd & Another* [2006] EWCA 6, a case of apparent judicial bias, the Court of Appeal removed a judge who declined to recuse himself when he realised, on the eve of the trial, that he had known a major proposed witness for over 30 years.

[462a] *Howell & Others v Millais Rothers* [2007] EWCA 720, a case of apparent judicial bias, where a judge who had unsuccessfully applied for a job with a firm of solicitors later showed animosity to that firm when it represented a party before him. The judge was removed.

[463] *Timmins v Gormley* [2000] 1 All E.R. 65 at 92–93.

[464] *Rustal Trading Ltd v Gill and Duffas SA* [2000] 1 Lloyd's Rep. 14.

[465] *Argonaut Insurance Co v Republic Insurance Co* [2003] EWHC 547.

which is adverse to a party in the case in which he sits as arbitrator.[466] Whether the English court would follow this approach would, it is suggested, depend very much on the circumstances as an unduly strict application of such a principle could lead to parties seeking removal of an arbitrator when the confluence of the issues was really quite remote.[467]

Barristers from the same chambers. In international arbitrations 4–125 parties unfamiliar with the organisation and traditions of English barristers have questioned the participation in an arbitration of barristers from the same chambers in different capacities: for instance, one appearing as an arbitrator, and another appearing as advocate. The English courts have to date maintained that this practice is not sufficient evidence of apparent bias[468] but if chambers develop stronger corporate identities one can expect further questions to be raised.[469] Where a party was represented by a barrister from the same chambers as one of the arbitrators, the court declined to remove the arbitrator on an application under s.24(1)(a) of the Act. The court found that, to succeed with such an application, the applicant must show that either (i) the organisation of chambers gives rise to the necessary justifiable doubts because of the danger of accidental or improper dissemination of confidential information, or (ii) the arbitrator may not observe the rule against holding conversations with one party outside the presence of all parties to the arbitration.[470]

Same chambers and conditional fee arrangements. To these two 4–126 possibilities, one can also conceivably add the situation where an arbitrator may have to bear a greater share of chambers' running expenses if other members of chambers earn less, in other words where expenses are paid in proportion to earnings. If counsel is conducting an arbitration on a conditional fee arrangement then in theory a situation may arise where, if the arbitrator who is a member of the same chambers and becomes aware of the conditional fee arrangement and would under the rules of chambers, have to pay more towards expenses if counsel earns

[466] *Ghana v Telekom Malaysia Berhad*, October 18, 2004; November 5, 2004; District Court of The Hague, reported at *www.kluwerarbitration.com*. The case involved two investment treaty cases. The Dutch court admitted Ghana's challenge to the arbitrator unless the arbitrator resigned as counsel, which he did, and then rejected a second challenge based on the fact that the arbitrator had already been involved in a number of decisions of the tribunal.
[467] In non-investment treaty confidential arbitrations, a prospective challenger would not usually be aware of the position being taken by the arbitrator as counsel, or indeed as arbitrator, in other confidential cases.
[468] *Laker Airways v FLS Aerospace* [2000] 1 W.L.R. 113; see also *PPG Industries Inc v Pilkington Plc* (1989) unreported decision of Saville J., Commercial Court, November 1, see also *Nye Saunders and Partners (a firm) v Alan E Bristow* [1987] 37 B.L.R. 92. French law has recognised the same principle as part of English law. See further Kendall, "Barristers, Independence and Disclosure" in (1992) 8 Arbitration Int. 287.
[469] This situation appears on the Orange List of the IBA Guidelines, at para.3.3.2, which suggests that the principle that a successful challenge cannot be founded on this basis is not inviolate. See also a commentary on this issue in Background Information issued by the IBA Working Group.
[470] *Laker Airways v FLS Aerospace* [2000] 1 W.L.R. 113. Considered in *ASM Shipping Ltd of India v TTMI Ltd of England* [2005] EWHC 2238 (Comm) and cited with approval in *Smith v Kvaerner Cementation* [2006] EWCA 242, at [17].

less, the fair minded observer may conclude that the arbitrator might be inclined to favour the case being advanced by the fellow member of his chambers or at least that his exercise of discretion in relation to the award of costs may be open to question.[471]

4–127 **Early disclosure advised.** When an arbitrator has a prior interest that might raise doubts about his impartiality, he should disclose that interest at the earliest opportunity. This enables the issue to be debated before much time and money have been spent on the arbitration proceedings. If it is not disclosed by the arbitrator at an early stage, but discovered by one of the parties at a later stage, there is much more likelihood of suspicion arising from the apparent concealment. In those circumstances it is at least likely that there will be objections to the continued involvement of the arbitrator and much more risk that substantial costs will have been wasted if he has to be replaced. The statement "Early disclosure advised" should not be taken to extremes however; unnecessary disclosure can also raise an incorrect implication in the minds of the parties that the disclosed circumstances constitute an open invitation to object to or remove that arbitrator. Excessive disclosure can therefore undermine the process, with unfounded objections being taken by the parties on the basis of over-broad disclosure at the early stages of proceedings.

In certain circumstances, it is arguable that failure to disclose of itself may give rise to the necessary justifiable doubts,[472] especially if the failure to disclose is shown to be culpable, for example in relation to an obviously relevant matter.

(c) The duty to be independent

4–128 **Independence.** If an arbitrator accepts an appointment, and his independence is questioned by one or more of the parties, he cannot be challenged under the Act solely on that ground unless the lack of independence gives rise to justifiable doubts as to his impartiality.[473] Possible distinctions between independence and impartiality have been the subject of much comment.[474] The DAC decided to leave out a specific requirement of independence, as lack of independence would often raise justifiable doubts about impartiality and therefore independence was thought to be often included within the concept of impartiality.[475] It is arguable that the requirement in Art.6 of the European Convention on Human Rights, incorporated

---

[471] Some support for this view can be found in the *obiter* comments of the Court of Appeal in *Smith v Kvaerner Cementation* [2006] EWCA 242 at [17].

[472] Such an argument was made before the Court of Appeal in *AT&T Corp v Saudi Cable* [2000] 2 All E.R. (Comm) 625, although on the facts the argument was rejected because the initial failure to disclose the directorship was "due to secretarial error and was innocent" (at 630B). Whilst advising early and prudent disclosure, the IBA Guidelines do not suggest that non-disclosure of itself should make an arbitrator partial. See Pt II, para.5.

[473] Section 24(1)(a) of the Arbitration Act 1996 and para.4–023. DAC report, paras 100–102.

[474] See Eastwood, "A Real Danger of Confusion? The English Law Relating to Bias in Arbitrators" in *Arbitration Int.*, Vol.17, No.3, and the further references at fn.24 of the article.

[475] DAC report, paras 101–102.

into domestic law by the Human Rights Act 1998, which includes the right to be heard by "an independent and impartial tribunal" has introduced the concept of independence into English arbitration law in any event.[476] In *ASM Shipping Ltd of India v TTMI Ltd of England*, Morison J. commented that there was a "difference without distinction" between the two concepts.[477]

Neutrality. Neutrality is not the same concept as independence: it is much   4-129
broader. It has been said[478] that an international arbitrator, particularly when appointed chairman of a tribunal, must be neutral not only as between the countries of the parties and their political systems, but also as between their legal systems and use of legal concepts. The ICC's practice is to appoint as chairman a national of a different country from the countries of both the parties and the party-appointed arbitrators.[479] Some would go further, and insist that the chairman does not come from the same kind of country as well. This might, we suppose, produce the following result: in an arbitration between, for instance, an African party and a US party, the chairman of the tribunal could not be a national of any African country or of the United States: on the basis of this doctrine the United Kingdom, (and even perhaps other common law jurisdictions) and possibly other countries, might also be excluded. The resulting choice might be a national of a European, South American or Pacific Rim country.[480] A balance has to be struck between the need to find a tribunal experienced enough to discharge its mandate effectively, but in whom the parties can objectively have confidence. English law does not however draw any distinction between the standards of impartiality required from a chairman as opposed to party-appointed arbitrators.[481]

(d) Duty to adopt suitable procedure and to avoid expense and delay

Suitable procedures.[482] A tribunal has an obligation to adopt procedures   4-130
suitable to the circumstances of the particular case.[483] Thus, where an arbitration turns on a single issue of law it would not be appropriate to arrange a full trial with

---

[476] See Sandy, Independence, Impartiality and the Human Rights Act in England, Arbitration Int., Vol.20, No.2, 2004; Gearing "A Judge in his own Cause?, Actual or Unconscious Bias of Arbitrators", (2000) Int. A.L.R. 246 and Eastwood, above, "The English Law Relating to Bias in Arbitrators". See also para.1–038.

[477] Paragraph 14.

[478] Professor Pierre Lalive "On the neutrality of the arbitrator and of the place of arbitration" (1984) Essays on International Arbitration at paras 23 *et seq.* and Rosabel Goodman-Everard, "Cultural Diversity in International Arbitration—A Challenge for Decision-Makers and Decision-Making" (1991) 2 Arbitration Int. 155.

[479] See also LCIA Rules, Art.3.3.

[480] In the dispute involving the former firm of Arthur Andersen, the choice of tribunal was severely limited because of the number of partners practising in different parts of the world.

[481] Save that if it is accepted that a party-appointed arbitrator can have unilateral discussions with the party who appointed him over the identity of the chairman, where it falls to the party-appointed arbitrators to appoint the chairman.

[482] See paras 5–089 *et seq.*, where the range of possible procedures is discussed.

[483] Section 33(1)(b) of the Arbitration Act 1996.

cross-examination of witnesses: a suitable procedure may be the submission of
written arguments with no hearing.

4–131 **The duty to avoid unnecessary delay or expense.**[484] A tribunal has
the duty, in adopting suitable procedures, to avoid unnecessary delay or expense.[485]
The first part of this obligation is similar to the duty to "use all reasonable
dispatch" under the former legislation and its breach is a ground for removal
under the Arbitration Act 1996.[486] There is no precedent, however, for the
obligation to avoid unnecessary expense. The duty might for example be discharged in part by using the power to limit recoverable costs.[487] It is clearly very
closely connected to the duty to adopt suitable procedures. In the example given
above[488] the written procedure may be more cost effective than one involving a
hearing.[489]

(e) Conduct of proceedings

4–132 **Mental and physical capacity.** An arbitrator must be mentally and
physically capable of conducting proceedings. If he is not or there are justifiable
doubts as to his capacity, he may be removed.[490]

4–133 **Proper conduct of proceedings.** The tribunal's duties in respect of the
proper conduct of the proceedings are discussed in Ch.5.[491] These include
conducting the arbitration with reasonable despatch,[492] attending hearings and
participating in deliberations,[493] following the agreed procedure[494] and dealing
with all the issues.[495]

4–134 **Requirements of an award.** An award should be certain and unambiguous,[496] it must not be obtained by fraud or be contrary to public policy[497] and it
must comply with requirements as to form.[498] The tribunal's duties relating to an
award are dealt with in Chs 6 and 8.[499]

[484] See paras 5–032 *et seq.*
[485] Section 33(1)(b) of the Arbitration Act 1996.
[486] Section 24(1)(d)(ii) of the Arbitration Act 1996, cf. Arbitration Act 1950, s.13(3).
[487] Under s.65 of the Arbitration Act 1996, see para.4–103.
[488] In para.4–130.
[489] See para.5–108.
[490] Section 24(1)(c) of the Arbitration Act 1996, see para.7–115.
[491] See paras 5–032 *et seq.*
[492] Section 24(1)(d)(ii) of the Arbitration Act 1996.
[493] Implicit in the general duty under s.33(1)(a) of the Arbitration Act 1996.
[494] Section 68(2)(c) of the Arbitration Act 1996.
[495] Section 68(2)(d) of the Arbitration Act 1996.
[496] Section 68(2)(f) of the Arbitration Act 1996.
[497] Section 68(2)(g) of the Arbitration Act 1996.
[498] Section 68(2)(h) of the Arbitration Act 1996.
[499] See paras 6–044 *et seq.* and paras 8–072 *et seq.*

(f) Duty not to exceed jurisdiction or powers

Not to exceed jurisdiction.[500] An arbitral tribunal should not exceed its   4–135
jurisdiction; if it does so, the award may be unenforceable, either in whole or in
part.[501] The corollary to this negative duty is that every tribunal should aim to
make an award that can be enforced if necessary. This aim is stated as an express
objective in some rules of arbitration.[502]

Not to exceed powers.[503] An arbitral tribunal should not exceed its powers   4–136
in conducting an arbitration, or any resulting award may be challenged for serious
irregularity.[504] A distinction is made, however, between an excess of powers and
the incorrect exercise of powers. In the latter case, a decision may not be
successfully challenged.[505]

(g) Qualifications

Duty to possess the required qualifications. An arbitrator must   4–137
possess the qualifications required by the arbitration agreement,[506] otherwise he
can be removed and/or his award may be set aside.[507]

(h) Other duties

To respect confidentiality. One of the reasons for choosing arbitration is   4–138
that it is thought to keep disputes confidential.[508] An arbitral tribunal is subject to
a duty to keep the subject-matter of the arbitration confidential except when
required by law to disclose it.[509]

To act judicially.[510] This duty is best expressed in the general duty imposed   4–139
on an arbitral tribunal by s.33 of the Arbitration Act, 1996.[511] That duty is
mandatory. Though it is sometimes said that an arbitrator must act judicially, the
duties of judge and an arbitrator differ. For example, the parties may agree that an

---

[500] Section 67(1) of the Arbitration Act 1996.
[501] See further paras 5–060 *et seq.*
[502] For example, see ICC Rules, Art.35.
[503] Section 68(2)(b) of the Arbitration Act 1996.
[504] See paras 8–041 *et seq.*
[505] *Lesotho Highlands Development Authority v Impregilo* [2005] UKHL 43.
[506] Section 24(1)(b) of the Arbitration Act 1996.
[507] See Chs 7 and 8.
[508] The confidentiality attaching to arbitration is qualified—see paras 5–184 *et seq.*
[509] See paras 5–182 *et seq.*
[510] *Re Hopper* (1867) L.R. 2 Q.B. 367, explained by Lord Salmon in *Sutcliffe v Thackrah* [1974] A.C.
    727 at 763D, *Fisher v PG Wellfair Ltd (in liquidation)*; *Fox v PG Wellfair Ltd (in liquidation)* [1981]
    2 Lloyd's Rep. 514. See paras 5–032 *et seq.*
[511] See paras 5–062 and 6–078.

arbitrator may apply "considerations" other than the law.[512] The nature of an arbitral tribunal's judicial role has been qualified somewhat by the provision enabling a tribunal to take the initiative in ascertaining the facts and the law.[513] However, in taking the initiative, the tribunal would have to operate openly and would have to give the parties an opportunity to deal with any new material it intended to rely on.

The duties of the tribunal in the conduct of the conference are discussed in Ch.5.[514] The substantive requirements of an award are discussed in Ch.6.[515] Challenges to decisions made by arbitrators are discussed in Ch.8.[516]

4–140   To make one's own decision. The tribunal has a duty to reach a decision on the issues submitted for determination. A tribunal cannot delegate its function to decide between the parties.[517] Further, each member of the tribunal is expected to participate in the decision-making process even if the result is not unanimous.[518]

4–141   To decide according to the law. It used frequently to be said to be an arbitrator's duty was to decide disputes according to the law,[519] and that this duty was an implied term.[520] The position is now clearly stated in the Act. The tribunal must decide a dispute: (a) in accordance with the law chosen by the parties as applicable to the substance of the dispute, or (b), if the parties so agree, in accordance with "such other considerations" as are agreed by them or determined by the tribunal.[521] A reference to the substantive law of a country is not a reference to its conflict of laws rules.[522] If or to the extent that there is no such choice or agreement, the tribunal applies the law determined by conflict of laws rules it considers applicable.[523] "Such other considerations" are discussed in the following paragraphs.[524]

4–142   "Equity" clauses. The tribunal has a duty to decide a dispute in accordance with the legal rights of the parties, rather than in what the tribunal considers a fair and reasonable way,[525] unless there is specific agreement between the parties to the contrary. The tribunal may, however, be specifically instructed by the arbitration

---

[512] Section 46(1) of the Arbitration Act 1996.
[513] Section 34(2)(g) of the Arbitration Act 1996. See also paras 151–163.
[514] See paras 5–032 *et seq.*
[515] See paras 6–072 *et seq.*
[516] See paras 8–051 *et seq.*
[517] See paras 6–057 and 6–076 *et seq.*
[518] See *European Grain v Johnston* [1982] 2 Lloyd's Rep. 550 at 554.
[519] *Orion Compania Espanola de Seguros v Belfort Maatshappij Voor Algemene Verzekgringen* [1962] 2 Lloyd's Rep. 257.
[520] For instance, *NV Vulcaan v Mowinvkels Rederi* [1938] 2 All E.R. 152.
[521] Section 46(1) of the Arbitration Act 1996. Cf. Model Law, Art.28: (see Appendix 4).
[522] Section 46(2) of the Arbitration Act 1996.
[523] Section 46(3) of the Arbitration Act 1996.
[524] See also para.2–091
[525] *David Taylor & Son Ltd v Barnet Trading Co* [1953] 1 W.L.R. 563 at 568.

agreement to decide the dispute on some basis other than the law. An agreement to this effect has generally become known as an "equity clause". For example, the parties may agree that the tribunal is to decide the dispute in accordance with concepts variously known as "honourable engagement", "amiable composition", "equity", "*ex aequo et bono*", the "general principles of law recognised by civilised nations" or the "*lex mercatoria*".[526] The expression "*lex mercatoria*" is not usually found in arbitration clauses, and some commentators have doubted whether it has any meaning. Those who do assign it a meaning differ as to whether it is a separate body of international commercial law or equivalent to freedom from strict legal constraint.[527] Various wordings are encountered in arbitration agreements, and each has to be carefully interpreted.

Court's attitude to "equity" clauses. It is expected that the courts will interpret the statutory provision allowing a tribunal to decide a dispute in accordance with such other considerations as are agreed or determined[528] as obliging them to uphold equity clauses.[529] In agreeing that a dispute shall be resolved this way, the parties are in effect excluding any right of appeal to the court, there being no question of law to appeal.[530]   4–143

Facilitating a settlement. From time to time an arbitral tribunal is asked to facilitate a settlement between the parties.[531] An arbitrator must proceed very carefully with this task and not compromise his role as an arbitrator with that of a mediator even if both parties agree. In *Weissfisch v Julius*,[532] the Respondent had attempted, but failed, to mediate disputes between the parties and then proceeded to fulfil his role as arbitrator. An application was made to the court by one of the parties to restrain him from continuing to act as an arbitrator in circumstances where he had performed a role, described by the Court of Appeal, as coming close to an amalgam of arbitrator and mediator. The application failed, but litigation ensued.[533]   4–144

(i) Party-appointed arbitrators

Duty to act judicially, fairly and impartially. Party-appointed arbitrators[534] have the same duty to act judicially, fairly and impartially as any   4–145

---

[526] Model Law, Art.28(3) (see Appendix 4) refers to "*ex aequo et bono*" and "*amiable compositeur*".
[527] David Rivkin, "The enforceability of arbitral awards based on *lex mercatoria*", (1993), 9 Arbitration Int., 1 at 67.
[528] Section 46(1)(b) of the Arbitration Act 1996.
[529] See DAC report, paras 222 *et seq.*
[530] DAC report, para.223.
[531] This is often done in other jurisdictions, e.g. in Germany.
[532] [2006] EWCA Civ 218.
[533] The parties had in that case expressly waived any conflict arising from the arbitrator's prior involvement with the parties. The litigation continued under the title *A v B* [2007] 1 Lloyd's Rep. 237, 358.
[534] See Murray Smith, "The Impartiality of the party-appointed arbitrator", 6 Arbitration Int. 4 at 320.

other member of the tribunal (e.g. the chairman), although they have been appointed by one of the parties, rather than by both parties, or by an appointing authority or by the court.[535] As Russell wrote in the first edition of this book:

> "The arbitrators so selected [i.e. one by each side] are not to consider themselves the agents or advocates of the party who appoints them. When once nominated, they are to perform the duty of deciding impartially between the parties, and they will be looked on as acting corruptly if they act as agents or take instructions from either side".[536]

The consequence is that unless consulting about the appointment of a third arbitrator, a party-appointed arbitrator must not confer unilaterally with the party who appointed him, or with any of that party's legal or other representatives, unless the other party, or its representatives, are present. An exception to this rule allows a party-appointed arbitrator to discuss the identity of the chairman with the party who appointed him.[537] Normally, the tribunal, as a whole, should communicate with the parties unless the chairman is authorised to do so alone.[538] If the arbitrator appointed by one party becomes sole arbitrator, in default of appointment by the other, he is in the same position as a single arbitrator,[539] and must of course act judicially.

4–146 Party-appointed arbitrators appointing and then sitting with an umpire. Party-appointed arbitrators have a duty to act judicially when appointing an umpire.[540] After the appointment the position may become somewhat different when sitting with the umpire, because party-appointed arbitrators have as a matter of practice in certain arbitrations acted as advocates following their replacement by the umpire as the decision-maker. Arbitrators in this role should approach their task as follows:

> "The arbitrators are appointed to perform a judicial function unless and until they disagree and the umpire enters upon the reference. Thereafter they can and do act as advocates for the party who appointed them. Until that point is reached, and it is only in a minority of cases that it is reached, neither arbitrator has any special relationship with the party which appointed him and each arbitrator is under the same duty of fairness, openness and impartiality to both parties."[541]

4–147 Each arbitrator must act, but majority awards are allowed. Unless the contrary intention is expressed in the arbitration agreement, in any case

---

[535] The only exception is a tribunal originally composed of two arbitrators where there has been disagreement and an umpire is appointed, see para.4–150.

[536] At pp.206–207, in a section on the disadvantages of tribunals of more than one arbitrator published in 1849.

[537] See IBA Rules of Ethics for International Arbitrators, Art.5.2; *Pacific China Holdings Ltd v Grand Pacific Holdings Ltd* HCCT 5/2007, a decision of the Hong Kong High Court.

[538] *Veritas Shipping* cited above at fn.537, at 77.

[539] *Cooper v Shuttleworth* (1856) 25 L.J. Ex. 114 at 115.

[540] *Prescod v Prescod* (1887) 58 L.T. 76.

[541] *The Owners of the MV Myron v Tradax Export SA* [1970] 1 Q.B. 527, Lord Donaldson M.R. at 533B.

where there is a reference to three arbitrators, the decision, order or award of two of the arbitrators is binding: but where one of the three is to act as chairman the view of the chairman prevails in cases where there is neither unanimity nor a majority.[542] Where the reference is to two arbitrators, there must be unanimity in order to make a valid award,[543] but together they have power to make decisions, orders and awards until they cannot agree on a substantive matter in the arbitration.[544] If and when they disagree, an umpire will usually take over the conduct of the arbitration, and his power is the same as if he were sole arbitrator.[545]

All arbitrators must have the same jurisdiction. All arbitrators **4–148** must be given jurisdiction over all the questions they are to decide: for an award cannot be made about a matter over which one arbitrator has no jurisdiction.[546]

(j) Third arbitrators, chairmen and umpires

Different types of third arbitrator. In most jurisdictions the third **4–149** arbitrator, or chairman (or president) of the tribunal holds a position no different from that of the other arbitrators, except that he chairs or presides over meetings of the tribunal.[547] English law accords one type of third arbitrator, the umpire, a different status. He is, effectively, a sole arbitrator.[548] He is appointed by the existing two arbitrators[549] to take over the reference from arbitrators who are unable to agree amongst themselves. In general he is in the same position as a sole arbitrator, and must possess the same qualifications or absence of disqualifications.[550] The powers and duties of an umpire, when he is called upon to act, are in general the same as those of a sole arbitrator.

Role of umpire. The parties may agree on what the functions of their umpire **4–150** are to be, and in particular whether he is to attend the first stage of the proceedings which take place before the two party-appointed arbitrators, and when he is to replace those arbitrators as the tribunal with the power to make decisions, orders,

---

[542] Section 20 of the Arbitration Act 1996. This is similar to ICC Rules, Art.19, and UNCITRAL Rules, Art.31(2) for procedural matters. There is no analogue for it in the Model Law (see Appendix 4) or the former English legislation.

[543] This obvious statement seems to be supported by the terms of s.22(2) of the Arbitration Act 1996 which uses the word "all" when there is no possibility of a majority of arbitrators.

[544] Section 21(4) of the Arbitration Act 1996.

[545] Section 21 of the Arbitration Act 1996.

[546] *Davies and Another v Price* (1864) 11 L.T. (N.S.) 203. The jurisdiction is established by the terms of the arbitration agreement, the appointments and any other similar documents arising between the parties and/or the arbitrators.

[547] See para.4–011.

[548] Section 21(5) of the Arbitration Act 1996.

[549] Section 16(6)(b) of the Arbitration Act 1996.

[550] For instance, the absence of undisclosed interest, *Blanchard v Sun Fire Office* (1890) 6 L.T.R. 365: cf. paras 4–023 *et seq.*

and awards.[551] If or to the extent there is no such agreement, the following provisions apply.[552] The umpire's authority begins after notice of disagreement has been given by the two party-appointed arbitrators either to him or the parties.[553] There is no definite rule as to what constitutes disagreement, but it has been widely construed: "non-agreement is disagreement".[554] The court may order the umpire to replace the other arbitrators as the tribunal with power to make decisions, orders and awards "as if he were sole arbitrator" at any time after his appointment, on the application of either party.[555] If the umpire fails to start acting within a reasonable time he may be removed by the court on application of either party.[556] What the parties usually want is for the arbitrators to sit with the umpire and to assist him in understanding the evidence and arguments presented to them. For this reason the practice is found of the two arbitrators expressing their disagreement early to save the costs of dealing with the same matters twice. An umpire may sit with the arbitrators and hear the evidence, which is no ground for objection to the validity of an award subsequently made by the umpire after the arbitrators failed to agree provided the umpire does not participate in the arbitrators' deliberations.[557] An arbitration agreement providing for decision by "arbitrators" was held to contemplate the appointment of the umpire before he entered on the reference, and consequently to enable the arbitrators to request the attendance of the umpire at the hearing even though one of the parties to the reference did not consent.[558]

4–151 **Umpire's jurisdiction and duty with regard to evidence and the hearing.** Where the umpire enters upon the reference and replaces the arbitrators[559] he needs to review the evidence and submissions only on those matters about which the arbitrators have disagreed.[560] The umpire has a duty to hear the evidence of the parties and their witnesses, if application is made to him by either party, even if the same evidence has already been adduced before the arbitrators (but not the umpire).[561] The umpire may not take any part of the evidence from the notes of the arbitrators, unless the parties both agree.[562] The umpire must conduct the hearing impartially.[563]

---

[551] Section 21(1) of the Arbitration Act 1996.
[552] Section 21(2) of the Arbitration Act 1996.
[553] Section 21(4) of the Arbitration Act 1996.
[554] *Winteringham v Robertson* (1858) 27 L.J. Exch. 301.
[555] Section 21(5) of the Arbitration Act 1996.
[556] Section 24(1)(d)(ii) of the Arbitration Act 1996.
[557] *Flag Lane Chapel v Sunderland Corp* (1859) 5 Jurist. N.S. 894.
[558] *Fletamentos Maritimos SA v Effjohn International BV* [1995] 1 Lloyd's Rep. 311.
[559] Under s.21(5) of the Arbitration Act 1996.
[560] *Orion Compania Espanola de Seguros v Belfort Maatschappij Voor Algemen Verzeigringeen* [1962] 2 Lloyd's Rep. 257.
[561] *Re Salkeld and Slater* (1840) A. & E. 768.
[562] *Fletamentos Maritimos SA v Effjohn International BV (No.2)* [1997] 2 Lloyd's Rep. 302 at 305–306; *Re Jenkins and Leggo* (1841) L.J. Q.B. 71; and *Re Firth and Howlett* (1850) 19 L.J. Q.B. 169.
[563] *Re Hawley and North Staffordshire Railway* (1848) 12 Jur. 389.

8. LIABILITIES OF ARBITRATORS

(a) Introduction

Immunity and claims. Arbitrators enjoy statutory immunity for their acts **4–152** and omissions[564] except where bad faith is shown. This gives arbitrators a defence to many types of claim. This section considers this immunity and the "bad faith" exception, and reviews the types of claims that have been made in the light of this provision. Arbitral institutions have a similar immunity in respect of appointments.[565]

Statutory immunity. Under s.29 of the Arbitration Act 1996, an arbitrator **4–153** is not liable for anything done or omitted to be done in the purported discharge of his functions as arbitrator unless the act or omission is shown to have been in bad faith.[566] This is a very broad statement, covering all types of claims. The immunity extends to an employee or agent of an arbitrator.[567] Previous attempts to achieve immunity, such as a statutory instrument under the Supply of Goods and Services Act 1982 and various contractual exclusions found in arbitration rules are very much a secondary consideration.[568]

Bad faith. It is not possible to succeed with an action against an arbitrator **4–154** unless one can prove bad faith. "Bad faith" is not defined in the Arbitration Act, but the expression is used from time to time, and has been used in the case of both judges[569] and regulatory authorities.[570] It was used in the case of judges to set limits to their immunity at common law, but without definition. In the case of regulatory authorities subject to a very similarly drafted statutory provision[571] it has been said to mean: "(a) malice in the sense of personal spite or desire to injure for improper reasons, or (b) knowledge of absence of power to make the decision in question".[572] In any action against an arbitrator the burden of proof is on the

[564] Section 29 of the Arbitration Act 1996.
[565] Section 74. See para.3–047 of the Arbitration Act 1996.
[566] Section 29(1) of the Arbitration Act 1996. This immunity does not affect liability caused by resigning: see para.4–158.
[567] Section 29(2) of the Arbitration Act 1996.
[568] Supply of Goods and Services Regulations (SI 1985/1), and exclusions such as those found in the LCIA and CI Arb Rules.
[569] In *Sirros v Moore and others* [1975] 1 Q.B. 118.
[570] Financial Services Act 1986, s.186 and *Melton Medes Ltd and another v Securities and Investments Board* [1995] 3 All E.R. 880.
[571] Financial Services Act 1986, s.187(3).
[572] *Melton Medes* cited above in fn.580, at 889/890. The judge (Lightman J.) cited Wade, *Administrative Law* (6th edn) p.782, itself citing *Bourgoin SA v Ministry of Agriculture, Fisheries and Food* [1985] Q.B. 716. In administrative law "bad faith" is shown if the power to decide or act has been exercised for purposes other than those for which the power was conferred or without regard to the relevant, or only the relevant, considerations. The judge applied the restrictive meaning set out in the text to misfeasance in public office—sometimes called "deliberate misuse of power".

party asserting bad faith, and there would have to be cogent evidence to justify the allegation.

(b) Types of claims

4–155 **Professional negligence.** "Professional negligence" is a generic term covering claims for damages against professionals, usually for breach of contract[573] or, more rarely in recent years, for breach of a duty giving rise to liability in the tort of negligence.[574] There is no case law on the professional negligence of arbitrators. Where an arbitrator is extravagant or dilatory,[575] the remedy is limited to his removal as an arbitrator and forfeiture of the right to fees, and does not of itself give rise to a cause of action for damages for losses arising from the arbitrator's incompetence, such as the extra costs of rehearing the case before a fresh tribunal. Other manifestations of incompetence may give rise to charges of serious irregularity justifying the arbitrator's removal, but similarly do not carry an express right to damages. Professional negligence on its own is unlikely to surmount the requirement to show bad faith if the arbitrator is to be held liable for damages; it will have to be coupled with personal malice or deliberate excess of powers.

4–156 **Serious irregularity.** The arbitrator has a number of duties arising from the manner in which the proceedings are conducted, breach of which can lead to his removal and the setting aside of the award on the grounds of serious irregularity.[576] The remedies for serious irregularity are limited to those provided by the Act.[577] If an action were to be brought for damages based on serious irregularity committed by the arbitrator, statutory immunity[578] will provide a complete defence, in the absence of some element of personal or deliberate misbehaviour as evidence of bad faith.

4–157 **Deliberate and serious misbehaviour.** The following are recorded instances[579] of serious and deliberate breaches of an arbitrator's duties:

- deliberately obstructing the proceedings by, for instance, failing to appear at hearings without a reasonable excuse;
- refusing to participate in the tribunal's deliberations; and

---

[573] *Bolam v Friern Hospital Management Committee* [1957] 1 W.L.R. 582; Supply of Goods and Services Act 1982, s.13.
[574] *Hedley Byrne & Co Ltd v Heller & Partners Ltd* [1964] A.C. 465, and numerous authorities, including *Henderson v Merrett Syndicates Ltd* [1995] 2 A.C. 145.
[575] Section 24(1)(d)(ii) of the Arbitration Act 1996, see also ss.33 and 68(2) of the Arbitration Act 1996.
[576] See paras 8–072 *et seq.*
[577] See paras 8–113 *et seq.*
[578] SI 1985/1, noted at para.4–153.
[579] Collected by VV Veeder in ICCA Congress Series No.5, Kluwer 1991.

- "leaking" details of the tribunal's deliberations before the publication of the award.

It may be possible to show bad faith in each of these examples. Further, if the rules governing the arbitration do not provide a remedy for such conduct, an application could be made to the court to remove the arbitrator on the basis that he has refused or failed properly to conduct the proceedings.[580]

Resigning. Resignation, previously a difficult subject, is now governed by statute.[581] Parties are free to agree with an arbitrator the consequences of his resignation as regards his entitlement (if any) to fees or expenses, and any liability incurred for resigning.[582] If or to the extent they do not agree, the following will apply. An arbitrator who resigns his appointment may, on notice to the parties, apply to the court for relief from any liability incurred by the resignation, and for an order about his entitlement to fees or expenses.[583] The court can grant relief from liability on whatever terms it thinks fit, if satisfied it was reasonable in all the circumstances for the arbitrator to resign.[584] This provides a structure for settling disputes about resignation, but offers no guidance on how it would be operated. What would be reasonable? Would it, for instance, be reasonable for a tribunal to resign when in disagreement with both the parties about the procedure?[585] Or would it be reasonable for an arbitrator to resign on having ceased to be a self-employed lawyer and accepted full-time employment as, say, a judge or an ambassador?[585a] In this latter case, should the arbitrator have discussed the risk that he might have to resign before accepting an appointment? Whatever the circumstances, both the parties will be caused expense and delay in reconstituting a tribunal and appraising that new tribunal of all the issues, and where part only of a tribunal resigns the other members will also be put to inconvenience. Parties do not expect to incur this extra expense which may exceed any amount paid to the resigning arbitrator. Thus, the court may be asked not to limit its order to the repayment of any fees and expenses already paid to the resigning arbitrator. The use of the word "liability" in s.25 of the Act suggests that his responsibility for resignation without reasonable cause[586] may go beyond repayment of any fees and expenses, and s.29 of the Act (immunity) does not affect this liability.[587]

4–158

---

[580] Section 24(1)(d)(i) of the Arbitration Act 1996. See para.7–121.
[581] Section 25 of the Arbitration Act 1996, see para.7–133.
[582] Section 25(1) of the Arbitration Act 1996.
[583] Section 25(3) of the Arbitration Act 1996.
[584] Section 25(4) of the Arbitration Act 1996.
[585] See para.5–056.
[585a] VV Veeder in ICCA Congress Series No.5, Kluwer 1991, topic 8, refers to a case where a sole arbitrator faced action after resigning to take up an appointment to a public office.
[586] As is the position under Austrian law, see Werner Melis, *The Immunity of Arbitrators* (ed. Lew, Lloyd's of London Press Ltd, 1990).
[587] Section 29(3) of the Arbitration Act 1996.

9. CHALLENGE AND TERMINATION OF AUTHORITY OF ARBITRATORS

(a) Termination generally

4–159   **Tribunal's authority continues until terminated.** Once a tribunal has been appointed, it continues in place with full authority until that authority is terminated. Termination comes about by operation of law, by act of the parties, by act of an appointing authority, or by a court order.

(b) Termination by operation of law

4–160   **Death of arbitrator.** The authority of an arbitrator is personal and ceases on his death.[588] There are statutory provisions for replacement in the absence of an agreed appointment procedure.[589]

4–161   **Death of party appointing an arbitrator.** Unless otherwise agreed by the parties, the death of the person by whom an arbitrator was appointed does not revoke the authority of an arbitrator.[590]

4–162   **Insolvency.** The insolvency of an arbitrator is unlikely to affect his formal capacity to continue to act.[591]

4–163   **Discharge of duty.** When an arbitrator has made his final award on all the issues submitted to him for decision, he has no further function, and his authority over the parties has come to an end.[592]

(c) Termination by act or omission of the arbitrator

4–164   **Resigning.** An arbitrator's authority terminates on his resignation,[593] whether the parties accept it or not.

---

[588] Section 26(1) of the Arbitration Act 1996. See para.4–015.
[589] Section 27 of the Arbitration Act 1996. See paras 4–040 and 7–130.
[590] Section 26(2) of the Arbitration Act 1996. See para.3–026 generally on the effect of the death of a party.
[591] There is no authority in support of this statement, but as a matter of principle it seems correct. For the effect on arbitrations of the insolvency of one of the parties, see paras 3–027 *et seq.*
[592] See paras 5–218 *et seq.* and 6–166 *et seq.*
[593] This is the necessary implication of s.25 of the Arbitration Act 1996. See also DAC report, paras 111 *et seq.* The theory used to be that an arbitrator could not resign without the consent of the parties: see para.4–158.

Umpire's entry into reference. Where the parties have agreed that there   4–165
is to be an umpire, the arbitrators will be replaced by the umpire usually upon
notice that the arbitrators cannot agree on a matter relating to the arbitration.[594]
Whenever replacement occurs, the arbitrators' authority will then be terminated.

(d) Termination by act of the parties

Parties may agree to terminate tribunal's authority. Parties   4–166
acting together can remove the arbitral tribunal in whole or in part, or agree to
revoke the reference itself.[595] A party cannot unilaterally terminate the authority
of a arbitrator by withdrawing the claim.[596] A party who wishes to remove an
arbitrator must challenge the appointment under any procedure in the arbitration
agreement or rules, or in the absence of such a procedure, apply to the court for
revocation of the arbitrator's authority.[597]

Settlement. The parties may also terminate the tribunal's authority by settling   4–167
the dispute. The terms of the settlement must be examined to assess their effect
on the arbitration proceedings. In particular, the tribunal will want to be satisfied
that all claims in the arbitration have been disposed of in the settlement. Unless
otherwise agreed by the parties, it is still for the tribunal to terminate the
"substantive" proceedings.[598] The tribunal will record the terms of settlement in
the form of an agreed award, if the parties so request and the tribunal does not
object.[599]

(e) Termination by appointing authority

Termination in accordance with rules. An appointing authority can   4–168
remove an arbitrator, if the removal is in accordance with its rules. For instance,
under the ICC Rules,[600] challenges can be made, "for an alleged lack of independence or otherwise", to the ICC International Court of Arbitration,[601] and if the
challenge is accepted, that same body may replace the arbitrator.[602]

---

[594] Section 21 of the Arbitration Act 1996 provides that the parties are free to agree on, among other
things, when the umpire is to replace the other arbitrators on the tribunal (s.21(1)(b)) but failing
agreement the replacement occurs when the arbitrators give notice of their disagreement
(s.21(4)).
[595] Section 23 of the Arbitration Act 1996, see para.5–228.
[596] See observations made by the Court of Appeal in *John Roberts Architects Ltd v Parkcase Homes
(No.2) Ltd* [2006] EWCA Civ 64 at [18].
[597] See paras 4–051 and 7–074.
[598] Section 51 of the Arbitration Act 1996, cf. Model Law, Art.30: (see Appendix 4).
[599] Section 51(2) of the Arbitration Act 1996, DAC report, para.24, see para.6–025.
[600] Article 11.1.
[601] See para.4–051.
[602] ICC Rules, Art.12.1.

(f) Termination by court order

4–169   **Removal and revocation of authority.** These remedies are discussed in
Ch.7.[603]

---

[603] See paras 7–110 *et seq.*

CHAPTER 5

THE CONDUCT OF THE REFERENCE

1. INTRODUCTION

(a) Contents of the chapter

This chapter deals with the conduct of a reference to arbitration. It begins by **5–001** looking at when and how to commence arbitral proceedings, including a consideration of the relevant statutory requirements and time limits. It then addresses the general duties of the tribunal in conducting the reference and in particular those imposed by s.33 of the Arbitration Act 1996. The following section sets out some preliminary matters which may need to be considered by the tribunal at the outset of the reference, including the important matter of jurisdiction, and then looks at how the tribunal should ascertain the procedure to follow in the arbitration. The hearing itself is also considered, and in particular what form the procedure at the hearing might take. Finally, this chapter looks at termination of the reference.

(b) Application of statutory provisions

5–002   This chapter focuses on the practical aspects of conducting an arbitration and considers the many statutory provisions in the Arbitration Act 1996 which are relevant in this regard. It is worth emphasising, however, that these statutory provisions relating to the tribunal's conduct of the arbitration only apply where the seat of arbitration is in England, Wales and Northern Ireland.[1] They do not generally apply to the conduct of an arbitration by a tribunal in any other jurisdiction, even if English law is the substantive law applied to the merits of the dispute. The two exceptions to this are the provisions relating to the separability of the arbitration agreement and the death of a party.[2] The court may, however, exercise certain of its powers even where no seat has been designated or determined.[3]

2. COMMENCING THE ARBITRATION

(a) When to commence proceedings

5–003   **Existence of a dispute.** Normally, it will only be appropriate to commence arbitral proceedings once a dispute has arisen between the parties.[4] This is reflected in the fact that most arbitration agreements refer specifically to "disputes" or "differences" being submitted to arbitration,[5] and in such cases a

---

[1] Section 2(1) of the Arbitration Act 1996. See further paras 2–100 *et seq.* above in relation to designation of the seat of arbitration.

[2] Section 2(5) of the Arbitration Act 1996. Separability is dealt with in s.7 of the Act and death of a party in s.8.

[3] Section 2(2)–(4) of the Arbitration Act 1996.

[4] Common sense also suggests that it will usually be precipitate to set in motion arbitral proceedings where the proposed respondent has not yet had an opportunity to accept liability or comply with whatever is being demanded of him, unless the claimant is facing an approaching time bar and needs to start arbitration proceedings to protect his position.

[5] See para.2–077 above. Under the Arbitration Act 1996 "dispute" includes any difference, see s.82(1) of the Arbitration Act 1996. See though dicta in *Amec Civil Engineering Ltd v Secretary of State for Transport* [2005] 1 W.L.R. 2339 suggesting the words "dispute or difference" might mean something more than "dispute" alone.

tribunal will not have jurisdiction to deal with the matter until a dispute or difference has arisen which has been referred to them for determination. The question whether there exists a dispute has been considered in a number of recent cases. It has arisen in particular in the context of applications to stay court proceedings due to the existence of an arbitration agreement,[6] the argument being that no stay is necessary if there is no dispute between the parties to be referred to arbitration because the claim is unanswerable.[7] This argument has been firmly rejected and a claim that has not been admitted gives rise to a dispute however unanswerable that claim is said to be.[8] The court adopts an inclusive rather than a restrictive interpretation of what constitutes a dispute.[9] Indeed so long as it can reasonably be inferred that the claim is not admitted that will suffice to constitute a dispute.[10] Even where the claim is admitted but a party seeks to defer the time for payment that will constitute a dispute if the revised payment terms are not accepted.[11]

Dispute or claim? The question whether there is a dispute or merely a claim 5–004 may also arise where a party wishes to include a claim within the terms of an existing reference covering other, clearly disputed, issues. The courts tend to take a fairly broad view of what constitutes a dispute in this context also. In *Lesser Design & Build Ltd v University of Surrey*[12] claims made under a JCT building contract were held to be "in dispute" simply because they were not agreed: the claims had not actually been rejected and the time for payment had not yet arrived. By contrast, however, the court felt unable in the same case to extend the reference

---

[6] See, for example, *Ellerine Brothers (Pty) Ltd v Klinger* [1982] 1 W.L.R. 1375; *Halki Shipping Corp v Sopex Oils Ltd (The "Halki")* [1998] 1 Lloyd's Rep. 465. The existence of a dispute is also sometimes an issue in the context of references to an engineer, or to an adjudicator under s.108(1) of the Housing Grants, Construction and Regeneration Act 1996: see for example *London & Amsterdam Properties Ltd v Waterman Partnership Ltd* [2003] EWHC 3059; [2004] B.L.R. 179; *Amec Civil Engineering Ltd v Secretary of State for Transport* [2005] EWCA Civ 291; [2005] 1 W.L.R. 2339; *Beck Peppiatt Ltd v Norwest Holst Construction Ltd* [2003] EWHC 822; [2003] B.L.R. 316.

[7] As Rix L.J. pointed out in *Amec Civil Engineering Ltd v Secretary of State for Transport* [2005] EWCA Civ 291; [2005] 1 W.L.R. 2339 at 2358 if arbitration is sought and it turns out there is no dispute because the claim is admitted then matters are unlikely to proceed. On the other hand if the claim is disputed the courts are unlikely to be receptive to an argument that the arbitration was not justified because there was no dispute at the time it was started.

[8] *Halki Shipping Corp v Sopex Oils Ltd (The "Halki")* [1998] 1 Lloyd's Rep. 465. See also the various decisions in relation to what constitutes a dispute in the context of adjudication: *Sindall Ltd v Solland* (2001) 80 Con.L.R. 152; *Beck Peppiatt Ltd v Norwest Holst Construction Ltd* [2003] EWHC 822; [2003] B.L.R. 316; *CIB Properties Ltd v Birse Construction Ltd* [2004] EWHC 2365; [2005] 1 W.L.R. 2252; *London & Amsterdam Properties Ltd v Waterman Partnership Ltd* [2003] EWHC 3059; [2004] B.L.R. 179.

[9] *Amec Civil Engineering Ltd v Secretary of State for Transport* [2005] EWCA Civ 291. See also the propositions advanced by Jackson J. at first instance in that case at [2004] EWHC 2339.

[10] *Collins (Contractors) Ltd v Baltic Quay Management (1994) Ltd* [2004] EWCA 1757 at [63]; *Amec Civil Engineering Ltd v Secretary of State for Transport* [2005] EWCA Civ 291; *Wealands v CLC Contractors Ltd* [1999] 2 Lloyd's Rep. 739; *Halki Shipping Corp v Sopex Oils Ltd (The "Halki")* [1998] 1 Lloyd's Rep. 465.

[11] *Exfin Shipping (India) Ltd v Tolani Shipping Co Ltd* [2006] EWHC 1090.

[12] 56 B.L.R. 57.

to matters which had not even been claimed at the time the arbitration was commenced.[13]

(b) Time limits for commencing proceedings

5–005   The procedures for commencing an arbitration and constituting the tribunal will depend upon what the parties have agreed (or not agreed) as the first step or steps to be taken.[14] The parties are also free to agree when the arbitration is to be regarded as having commenced, both for the purposes of the Arbitration Act 1996 and for limitation purposes,[15] failing which statutory provisions apply.[16] The parties are also free to agree on the method to be adopted for reckoning periods of time, but again if there is no agreement then statutory provisions apply.[17] Identification of the date of commencement may be of critical importance to the parties in view of contractual or statutory time limits for commencement of the arbitration.[18] Once arbitration is commenced time stops running and there can be no question of the time limit subsequently expiring as regards causes of action included in the reference.[19]

5–006   **Contractual time limits.** A contractual time limit, whether contained in an arbitration agreement or some other provision of the contract, or indeed in arbitration rules referred to in the arbitration agreement, may (1) impose a time limit for commencing arbitration proceedings, and/or (2) provide that a claim shall be barred or extinguished if arbitration is not commenced within the time limit.[20] These provisions are not necessarily found together. The parties' agreement may limit the time for commencing arbitration without barring or extinguishing the claim, so that a party who is out of time loses his right to arbitrate and will be confined to whatever remedy, if any, is available in the courts.[21]

---

[13] See also *A/S Det Dansk-Franske Dampskibsselskab v Compagnie Financière 'd'Investissements Transatlantiques SA (Compafina) (The "Himmerland")* [1965] 2 Lloyd's Rep. 353 at 360; *Cruden Construction Ltd v Commission for the New Towns* (1995) C.I.L.L. 1035; *Ellerine Brothers (Pty) Ltd v Klinger* [1982] 1 W.L.R. 1375 and *Carillion Construction Ltd v Devonport Royal Dockyard Ltd* [2003] B.L.R. 79 as to what constitutes a "dispute". The wording of the notice of arbitration may however encompass claims arising subsequently to the commencement of the arbitration: see *Harper Versicherungs AG v Indemnity Marine Assurance Co Ltd* [2006] EWHC 1500 at [53] and para.5–026 below.

[14] *Emson Contractors Ltd v Protea Estates Ltd* [1987] 39 B.L.R. 126.

[15] Section 14(1) of the Arbitration Act 1996.

[16] Section 14(2)–(5) of the Arbitration Act 1996: see para.5–021 below.

[17] Section 78 of the Arbitration Act 1996.

[18] See for example *Lafarge (Aggregates) Ltd v Newham LBC* [2005] EWHC 1337 (Comm).

[19] See *Leif Hoegh & Co A/S v Petrolsea Inc (The "World Era")* [1992] 1 Lloyd's Rep. 45; *Triad Shipping Co v Stellar Chartering & Brokerage Inc (The "Island Archon")* [1993] 2 Lloyd's Rep. 388.

[20] In construction contracts it is common to find provisions for the initial determination of disputes (for example by an adjudicator under the contract) which become final and binding if their decision is not referred to arbitration within a specific period of time. Such provisions are strictly construed: *Lafarge (Aggregates) Ltd v Newham LBC* [2005] EWHC 137 (Comm).

[21] Such clauses are now exceptional, *per* Hobhouse J. in *Leif Hoegh & Co A/S v Petrolsea Inc (The "World Era")* [1992] 1 Lloyd's Rep. 45 at 50.

Alternatively, and much more commonly, the parties' agreement may make compliance with a time limit a condition of any claim, without limiting the operation of the agreement to arbitrate, so that a claimant who is out of time may still have a right to arbitrate,[22] but the respondent may raise a time bar by way of defence to the claim.[23] If the contract does not make clear which of the above is intended but simply requires notice of a claim to be given or arbitration to be commenced within a certain period of time, then if the notice is not given or the arbitration is not commenced the claim will be barred.[24] It is possible for a respondent to waive any objection to arbitration, while still relying on a limitation clause as barring or extinguishing the claim.[25]

Impossibility of compliance. Even where a claim could not have been brought forward within the contractual time limit, for example because the cause of action giving rise to the claim had not arisen or come to the knowledge of the claimant until too late to enable him to comply, the claim may still be barred.[26] However time bar clauses will be construed strictly against the party relying upon them.[27] A time bar clause can be unilateral.[28]   5–007

Tribunal's power to extend time. Certain arbitration rules give the tribunal or an institution a discretion to extend the time for commencing arbitration proceedings or for the appointment of an arbitrator.[29] If there is a power for   5–008

---

[22] See though *JT Mackley & Co Ltd v Gosport Marina Ltd* [2002] EWHC 1315 where a declaration of invalidity of a notice of arbitration was sought because, amongst other things, it did not comply with the parties' contractually agreed time limit. The declaration was granted and the court endorsed the need to comply with the requirements of the arbitration agreement, although the decision was based upon failure to comply with a condition precedent to commencing the arbitration rather than failing to comply with the time limit.

[23] See also, for example, the JCT Standard Form of Building Contract 1998 edition (now replaced by 2005 edition) which provides by cl.30.9.3 that the final certificate is conclusive evidence as to the adjustments to be made to the contract sum unless arbitration is commenced within 28 days of its receipt. An attempt to re-open the certificate thereafter would be met by a defence based on further evidence being barred by virtue of the conclusive evidence provision: *McLaughlin & Harvey Plc v P&O Developments Ltd* [1991] 55 B.L.R. 101.

[24] *Metalfer Corp v Pan Ocean Shipping Co Ltd* [1998] 2 Lloyd's Rep. 632; *Smeaton Hanscomb & Co Ltd v Sassoon I Setty, Son & Co* [1953] 2 Lloyd's Rep. 580; *Metalimex Foreign Trade Corp v Eugenie Maritime Ltd* [1962] 1 Lloyd's Rep. 378.

[25] See generally *Aktiebolaget Legis v V Berg & Sons Ltd* [1964] 1 Lloyd's Rep. 203 at 212–213 where Roskill J. (as he then was) approved the position summarised in an earlier edition of this book; *Smeaton Hanscomb & Co Ltd v Sassoon I Setty, Son & Co (No.1)* [1953] 2 Lloyd's Rep. 580.

[26] *A/S Det Dansk-Franske Dampskibsselskab v Compagnie Financière d'Investissements Transatlantiques SA (Compafina) (The "Himmerland")* [1965] 2 Lloyd's Rep. 353. The court noted that cases of undue hardship could be dealt with by what is now s.12 of the Arbitration Act 1996. See paras 5–009 and 7–071 *et seq.* below. See also *Smeaton Hanscomb & Co Ltd v Sassoon I. Setty, Son & Co (No.1)* [1953].

[27] *Minister of Materials v Steel Brothers & Co Ltd* [1952] 1 T.L.R. 499.

[28] *WJ Alan and Co Ltd v El Nasr Export and Import Co* [1971] 1 Lloyd's Rep. 401. Such a clause may give rise to public policy objections under the New York Convention in certain jurisdictions.

[29] See, e.g. GAFTA 125, r.21 and *Ets Soules & Cie v International Trade and Development Co Ltd* [1979] 2 Lloyd's Rep. 122.

the tribunal or an institution to grant an extension of time, this must be pursued prior to any application to court under s.12 of the Arbitration Act 1996.[30]

5–009 **Court's power to extend time.** Section 12 of the Arbitration Act 1996[31] empowers the court to extend contractual (but not statutory) time limits for the commencement of arbitration proceedings. It may do so only where it is satisfied that (a) the circumstances are such as were outside the reasonable contemplation of the parties when they agreed the provision in question, and that it would be just to extend the time, or (b) that the conduct of one party makes it unjust to hold the other party to the strict terms of the provision in question.[32] Any available arbitral process[33] for extending time must first be exhausted. The court can extend time even if an extension was refused following the arbitral process, but it will be a rare case indeed where it will do so.[34]

5–010 **Statutory time limits.** Statutory time limits, whether imposed by the Limitation Act 1980 or any other limitation enactment, apply to arbitrations as they do to legal proceedings.[35] The effect of a statutory time limit is to provide a procedural bar to the remedy which has to be raised by way of defence to the claim. It does not go to the jurisdiction of the tribunal, but it does provide a defence to the claim.[36]

5–011 **Contractual claims and statutory time limits.** Where the claim being submitted to arbitration lies in contract[37] and a statutory time limit is raised, it is for the claimant to show prima facie evidence of (a) the date upon which the arbitration commenced and (b) a breach of contract, causally connected with the damage sought to be recovered, and accruing within the six years immediately preceding commencement. It is then for the respondent to show, if he can, either that (a) though apparently flowing from the breach complained of, the damage in

---

[30] Section 12(2) of the Arbitration Act 1996.
[31] Replacing and substantially amending s.27 of the Arbitration Act 1950: see paras 7–067 *et seq.* below.
[32] See paras 7–067 *et seq.* below.
[33] Such as an application to the tribunal or to an administering institution with power to grant the extension sought.
[34] See further para.74(ii) of the DAC report.
[35] Section 13(1) of the Arbitration Act 1996. A detailed analysis of limitation periods is beyond the scope of this book and the reader is referred to *Limitation Periods* (5th edn) by Andrew McGee (2006).
[36] *Leif Hoegh & Co A/S v Petrolsea Inc (The "World Era")* [1992] 1 Lloyd's Rep. 45. As explained in that case, the existence of a time bar does not deprive the arbitrator of jurisdiction, but in the context of a party seeking to expand his existing claim in the arbitration after the time limit has elapsed, there may well also be want of jurisdiction because the relevant cause of action was not included in the original reference.
[37] Different considerations may apply to certain claims in tort which are actionable only on proof of damage, for example negligence.

reality flowed from some earlier breach outside the limitation period, or (b) that the arbitration was in fact commenced on some later date.[38]

No extension of statutory time limits. The court's power to extend time under s.12 of the Arbitration Act 1996 does not extend to statutory time limits.[39]   5–012

Award set aside. Where an award is, in whole or in part, set aside or declared to be of no effect,[40] the court may further order that the period between the commencement of the arbitration and the date of the court's order shall be excluded in computing the limitation period for that dispute.[41]   5–013

Scott v Avery **clauses.** A term in an arbitration agreement to the effect that no cause of action shall accrue until an award is made will not be effective to extend the limitation period in respect of the matter to be referred to arbitration. For limitation purposes, the cause of action is deemed to have accrued at the time when it would ordinarily have done so but for that term in the agreement.[42]   5–014

(c) Manner of commencing proceedings

Contractual provisions. There may be specific provision in the arbitration agreement as to the manner of commencement of the arbitration and it is important that this is followed.[43] The particular step which is to be performed in order to commence the proceedings may, for example, be the making of a claim,[44] the appointment of an arbitrator,[45] the notification of such appointment to the other party, the sending of a notice to the other party requiring him to agree to the appointment of an arbitrator, or the serving of a request for arbitration.[46] The precise formulation may reflect the type of arbitration or the constitution of the tribunal.[47] Where, for example, the arbitration is to be conducted in accordance with specific arbitration rules, there may well be particular steps to be taken to   5–015

---

[38] *NV Stoomv Maats "De Maas" v Nippon Yusen Kaisha (The "Pendrecht")* [1980] 2 Lloyd's Rep. 56.
[39] Section 12(5) of the Arbitration Act 1996.
[40] See below paras 8–153 *et seq.*
[41] Section 13(2) of the Arbitration Act 1996.
[42] Section 13(3) of the Arbitration Act 1996. For *Scott v Avery* clauses generally see para.2–022.
[43] See para.5–019 below for the consequences of failure to comply with contractual provisions.
[44] No particular form of words is required for making a claim provided it is clear that a claim is being made: *Cathiship SA v Allanasons Ltd (The "Catherine Helen")* [1998] 3 All E.R. 714.
[45] See generally paras 4–024 *et seq.* above.
[46] A "request for arbitration" is required where, for example, the ICC Rules have been incorporated into the arbitration agreement, ICC Rules Art.4(1). It then substitutes for a "notice of arbitration": see paras 5–022 and 5–023 below.
[47] i.e. whether each of the parties is to appoint an arbitrator, or both parties are to concur in the appointment of a sole arbitrator.

commence proceedings under those rules.[48] The claimant may have validly commenced arbitration proceedings under the 1996 Act even if the specific steps required by those arbitration rules are not strictly complied with.[49]

5–016 Preliminary steps to be taken. The arbitration agreement may also provide that certain steps have to be taken prior to commencing arbitration proceedings. For example, the disputes clause may provide for a tiered process of dispute resolution. This typically requires the dispute to be submitted to particular officers within the corporate structure of the parties and, failing agreement between them, to mediation before resort is had to arbitration. When drafting such provisions it is vital to ensure that there are clear time limits for each step of the process so as to be certain when the dispute can be escalated to the next stage.[50]

Where such preliminary steps are expressed in mandatory terms so as to constitute a condition precedent to the right to arbitrate they must be complied with.[51] In many cases however they will not be mandatory and it is then possible for the claimant to commence arbitration even without complying with them.[52]

5–017 Service of claim not a condition precedent. There is no implied term of an arbitration agreement that service of a claim on the proposed respondent is a precondition to a valid request for arbitration.[53] It may, of course, be an express term.

5–018 Absence of contractual provision. In many cases the arbitration agreement will be silent as to the steps to be taken. In these circumstances the statutory provisions of s.14 of the Arbitration Act 1996 apply and the arbitration must be commenced by the service of a notice of arbitration on the other party.[54] The notice must be in writing[55] and should follow as closely as possible the terms of s.14 of the Arbitration Act 1996.

5–019 Consequence of failure to comply with contractual provisions. The consequence of failure to comply with a contractual requirement for commencing the arbitration is that the arbitration will not have been validly

---

[48] Under the ICC Rules, for example, a party must submit a Request for Arbitration, containing information specified in the rules, to the Secretariat of the ICC Court.

[49] See para.5–021 below.

[50] See para.2–036 above.

[51] See para.2–021 above. See also *JT Mackley & Co Ltd v Gosport Marina Ltd* [2002] EWHC 1315 where, amongst other things, failure to comply with a condition precedent rendered the arbitration notice invalid.

[52] Although not an arbitration case, see *Halifax Financial Services Ltd v Intuitive Systems Ltd* [1999] 1 All E.R. (Comm) 303.

[53] *Paul Smith Ltd v H&S International Holding Inc* [1991] 2 Lloyd's Rep. 127.

[54] See para.5–021 below.

[55] Section 14(3) to (5) of the Arbitration Act 1996.

commenced. This may be of crucial importance if a limitation period has subsequently expired, because the claimant will not be able to remedy the position by having a second go at commencing the proceedings.[56]

Remedying default. Assuming that there is no limitation point to be taken, in the event that the arbitration has not been validly commenced the safest course is to serve a further notice complying with the contractual requirements. Alternatively the claimant may be able to remedy any default so that the proceedings can go forward as from the date on which the contractual requirements were met. For example, if the arbitration clause requires service of a notice of arbitration and the appointment of an arbitrator, and the claimant served the notice but failed to appoint, he may subsequently make the appointment and the arbitration will proceed as from the date the contractual requirements are fulfilled.[57] The proposed respondent may of course waive any objection to the failure to comply with the contractual requirements,[58] and the arbitration will then proceed as from the original date. The respondent may also lose the right to object if he takes part in the reference without making his objection known.[59]

5–020

Commencement for limitation purposes. The parties are free to agree when an arbitration is to be regarded as commencing both under the Arbitration Act 1996 and for limitation purposes.[60] In the absence of agreement the provisions of s.14 of the Arbitration Act 1996 apply. Under that section an arbitration is treated as being commenced when a notice in writing is served[61] on the other party requiring him to agree to the appointment of an arbitrator or, if the parties are each to make an appointment, requiring him to appoint an arbitrator.[62] The party giving the notice does not have to already have appointed his own arbitrator.[63] Where, however, the arbitration agreement specifies the person to be appointed as arbitrator, the arbitration is treated as being commenced when a notice in writing is served on the other party requiring him to submit the dispute to that person.[64] Finally, if the arbitrator is to be appointed by someone other than a party to the arbitral proceedings, such as an arbitral institution, the arbitration is treated as being commenced when notice in writing is given to that other person

5–021

---

[56] Unless there is some arbitral process available for doing so or he can persuade the court to extend time under s.12 of the Arbitration Act 1996: see paras 7–067 *et seq.* below.

[57] Assuming that the arbitration clause did not stipulate that the appointment must be stated in the notice.

[58] For example by proceeding to agree the appointment of the tribunal.

[59] Section 73 of the Arbitration Act 1996.

[60] Section 14(1) of the Arbitration Act 1996.

[61] As to service, see s.76 of the Arbitration Act 1996: see para.5–028 below.

[62] Section 14(4) of the Arbitration Act 1996, replacing s.34(3)(a) of the Limitation Act 1980. An error as to the number of arbitrators to be appointed will not necessarily invalidate the notice of arbitration: see *Swiss Bank Corp v Novorissiysk Shipping Co (The "Petr Shmidt")* [1995] 1 Lloyd's Rep. 202.

[63] *Petredec Ltd v Tokomaru Kaiun Co Ltd* [1994] 1 Lloyd's Rep. 162. There may, however, be a contractual requirement to do so, e.g. the Centrocon arbitration clause bars the claim in default of appointment of a claimant's arbitrator within a stipulated time.

[64] Section 14(3) of the Arbitration Act 1996, replacing s.34(3)(b) of the Limitation Act 1980.

requesting him to make the appointment.[65] It is prudent to send to the respondent a copy of the notice addressed to the person requested to make the appointment as this may avoid arguments about when the notice was given.

5–022   **Notice of arbitration pursuant to s.14.** The "notice" referred to in s.14(3) to (5) of the Arbitration Act 1996 must be in writing and its contents must comply with the requirements for commencing arbitration set out in the subsections. The requirements of s.14 will be interpreted broadly and flexibly.[66] Prior to the Arbitration Act 1996 there were a number of cases which addressed the form of notice to be given in order to commence arbitration for the purposes of s.34(3) of the Limitation Act.[67] This line of authority has been superseded by s.14.[68]

5–023   **The form of the notice.**[69] Subject to complying with the requirements of s.14 of the Arbitration Act 1996,[70] there are otherwise no specific requirements as to the form of the notice.[71] It must be in writing[72] and is often simply in the form of a letter[73] from the proposed claimant to the proposed respondent. Provided the notice is objectively clear about who is being asked to do what, the giving of a notice addressed to a proposed arbitrator and merely copied to the other party to the arbitration would be sufficient.[74] It is not unusual to impose a time limit for compliance, failing which, if appropriate, an application can be made to court to have the arbitrator appointed.[75]

5–024   **The parties to the notice.** The notice of arbitration must identify the party or parties to whom it is addressed. Failing correctly to do so, or naming parties not

---

[65] Section 14(5) of the Arbitration Act 1996.

[66] *Seabridge Shipping AB v AC Orssleff's Eftf's A/S* [1999] 2 Lloyd's Rep. 685. Thomas J. indicated that s.14 of the Act will be construed broadly enough to include an implied request to appoint an arbitrator. See also *Atlanska Plovidba v Consignaciones Astrurianas SA (The "Lapad")* [2004] EWHC 1273.

[67] *Nea Agrex SA v Baltic Shipping Co Ltd* [1976] 1 Q.B. 933; *Surrendra Overseas Ltd v Government of Sri Lanka* [1977] 1 Lloyd's Rep. 653; *Peter Cremer GmbH & Co v Sugat Food Industries Ltd (The "Rimon")* [1981] 2 Lloyd's Rep. 640; *Petredec Ltd v Tokumaru Kaiun Co Ltd (The "Sargasso")* [1994] 1 Lloyd's Rep. 162; *Allianz Versicherungs AG v Fortuna Co Inc* [1999] 2 All E.R. 625; *Charles M Willie and Co (Shipping) Ltd v Ocean Laser Shipping Ltd (The "Smaro")* [1999] 1 Lloyd's Rep. 225; cf. *Vosnoc Ltd v Transglobal Projects Ltd* [1998] 1 W.L.R. 101.

[68] *per* Thomas J. in *Seabridge Shipping AB v AC Orssleff's Eftf's A/S* [1999] 2 Lloyd's Rep. 685. Reference to the pre-Act cases would, he said, be "a retrograde step".

[69] See also para.5–015 with regard to any contractual requirements.

[70] Thomas J. in *Seabridge Shipping AB v AC Orssleff's Eftf's A/S* [1999] 2 Lloyd's Rep. 685 considered but left open the question whether methods for commencing arbitration other than those set out in s.14 were permitted.

[71] *Blackpool Borough Council v F Parkinson Ltd*, 58 B.L.R. 85.

[72] Sub-sections 14(3) to (5) of the Arbitration Act 1996 specifically contemplate notice in writing but any agreement pursuant to s.14(1) of the Arbitration Act 1996 would also need to be "in writing" pursuant to s.5(1) of the Arbitration Act 1996. Section 5 gives the expression "in writing" a broad meaning.

[73] It can also be in the form of an email: *Bernuth Lines Ltd v High Seas Shipping Ltd* [2005] EWHC 3020.

[74] *Seabridge Shipping AB v AC Orssleff's Eftf's A/S* [1999] 2 Lloyd's Rep. 685.

[75] See paras 3–050? above and 7–095 *et seq.* below.

all of whom are party to the arbitration agreement, can have potentially serious consequences as regards the jurisdiction of the tribunal.[76] If proceedings are started on behalf of the wrong party or a party that does not exist they will be a nullity. If on the other hand there is simply an error in naming the party concerned, that error may be treated as "a mere misnomer" capable of correction.[77] In *JT Mackley & Co Ltd v Gosport Marina Ltd*[78] it was held that an attempt to commence tripartite arbitration when one of the parties was not party to the arbitration agreement rendered the notice of arbitration invalid. The better view however is that the notice of arbitration will only be valid as against the other party to the arbitration agreement and not the third party.

Specifying matters in dispute. Whilst it is not a requirement of the   5–025
statute, the notice of arbitration will often specify the matters in dispute and indeed there may be a contractual requirement to do so. Care should be taken to specify all the matters in dispute which are to be determined in the arbitration.[79] This is because the tribunal will have jurisdiction to decide only those matters actually referred,[80] and if there is doubt about whether a particular matter has been included the tribunal's jurisdiction to deal with it will be open to challenge.[81] Consequently it is advisable to include in the notice of arbitration some general wording which embraces all the outstanding matters in dispute between the parties, as well as specific wording identifying clear and discrete issues to be decided which can be described in the notice.[82]

Scope of the reference. Whether a particular matter is within the reference   5–026
will be determined as a matter of construction of the notice of arbitration,[83] giving the words used their natural meaning in the context in which they were used and applying an objective test.[84] The factual background to the giving of the notice and

---

[76] See for example *Internaut Shipping GmbH v Fercometal Sarl (The "Elikon")* [2003] EWCA Civ 812; [2003] 2 Lloyd's Rep. 430; *Hussman (Europe) Ltd v Al Ameen Development & Trade Co* [2000] 2 Lloyd's Rep. 83 and *Hussmann (Europe) Ltd v Pharaon* [2003] EWCA Civ 266; [2003] 1 All E.R. (Comm) 879; *SEB Trygg Holding AB v Manches* [2005] EWHC 35 affirmed at [2006] EWCA Civ 1237.

[77] *SEB Trygg Holding AB v Manches* [2005] EWHC 35 affirmed at [2006] EWCA Civ 1237; *Harper Versicherungs AG v Indemnity Marine Assurance Co Ltd* [2006] EWHC 1500; *Unisys International Services Ltd v Eastern Counties Newspapers Ltd* [1991] 1 Lloyd's Rep. 538. See further paras 3–003 et seq.

[78] [2002] EWHC 1315.

[79] In *Atlanska Plovidba v Consignaciones Astrurianas SA (The "Lapad")* [2004] EWHC 1273 a notice of arbitration which accurately described the dispute but referred to it arising under the wrong contractual document was found to be effective.

[80] Although the parties, with the agreement of the arbitrator, may enter into an ad hoc agreement to arbitrate disputes not originally included in the reference: see paras 2–003 and 2–006 above.

[81] See *Triad Shipping Co v Stellar Chartering & Brokerage Inc (The "Island Archon")* [1993] 2 Lloyd's Rep. 388; *London Borough of Lewisham v Shephard Hill Civil Engineering Ltd* unreported, July 30, 2001 QBD (T&CC).

[82] See further *Cruden Construction Ltd v Commission for the New Towns* (1995) C.I.L.L. 1035.

[83] Although the scope of the reference may subsequently be expanded or reduced by agreement of the parties: see *Westland Helicopters Ltd v Al-Hejailan* [2004] EWHC 1625.

[84] *Lesser Design & Build Ltd v University of Surrey*, 56 B.L.R. 57.

any previous communications between the parties concerning the issues between them will also be relevant in construing the scope of the reference to arbitration.[85] If, by the time the notice of arbitration is given, the parties' previous communications indicate that it would be natural to expect the reference to arbitration to include all the outstanding disputes, that fact may be taken into consideration. The reference may also include claims arising subsequent to the commencement of the arbitration if appropriately drafted.[86]

5–027   **Disputes about notice of arbitration.** Any disputes about the validity of a notice of arbitration should in the first instance be determined by the tribunal on the basis of its power to rule on its own jurisdiction pursuant to s.30 of the Arbitration Act 1996.[87] Alternatively, in exceptional circumstances,[88] and where the conditions of s.32 are met, application may be made to the court. There is some authority that even where s.32 is inapplicable, the court retains a general jurisdiction to grant declaratory relief, but this would appear contrary to the principle laid down in s.1(c) of the Arbitration Act 1996 which provides that in matters governed by the Act the court should not intervene except as provided in the statute. It was recognised in *Vale do Rio doce Navegacao SA v Shanghai Bao Steel Ocean Shipping Co Ltd*[89] that use of the word "should" rather than "shall" in the subsection "shows that an absolute prohibition on intervention by the court in circumstances other than those specified in Part 1 was not intended . . . However it is clear that the general intention was that the courts should usually not intervene outside the general circumstances specified in Part 1 of the 1996 Act".[89a] In *JT Mackley & Co Ltd v Gosport Marina Ltd.*[90] a question was raised as to whether there was a lacuna in the tribunal's powers under s.30 to decide whether there has been a valid reference at all. That would seem to be an unduly narrow reading of s.30.[91] Without deciding the point, the court proceeded to find that as the questions raised as to the validity of the notice of arbitration were "significant generally" it would proceed under its general jurisdiction and granted the declaration of invalidity sought. This decision appears to be an isolated case and is unlikely to be followed save perhaps where there is good reason why the matter cannot be resolved by the tribunal.

---

[85] *Lesser Design & Build Ltd v University of Surrey*, 56 B.L.R. 57.

[86] *Harper Versicherungs AG v Indemnity Marine Assurance Co Ltd* [2006] EWHC 1500 at [53].

[87] *JT Mackley & Co Ltd v Gosport Marina Ltd* [2002] EWHC 1315 (TCC); *Vale do Rio doce Navegacao SA v Shanghai Bao Steel Ocean Shipping Co Ltd* [2000] 2 All E.R. (Comm) 70. For the tribunal's power under s.30 of the Arbitration Act 1996, see para.5–062 below.

[88] *Vale do Rio doce Navegacao SA v Shanghai Bao Steel Ocean Shipping Co Ltd* [2000] 2 All E.R. (Comm) 70.

[89] *Vale do Rio doce Navegacao SA v Shanghai Bao Steel Ocean Shipping Co Ltd* [2000] 2 All E.R. (Comm) 70.

[89a] At [52].

[90] [2002] EWHC 1315.

[91] The relevant provision is a power to determine "what matters have been submitted to arbitration in accordance with the arbitration agreement" and the suggestion in *JT Mackley & Co Ltd v Gosport Marina Ltd* was that this might be confined to deciding the scope of a valid reference as opposed to whether there had been a valid reference at all.

Service of the notice of arbitration. The parties are free to agree how   5–028
the notice of arbitration is to be served.[92] Commercial contracts often contain
specific provisions setting out how service is to be effected, for example by
requiring service by registered post at a particular address and marked for the
attention of a named individual. Service of a notice of arbitration will be valid if
effected in accordance with such contractual provisions.

Effective means of service. In the absence of agreement on how the notice   5–029
of arbitration is to be served, it may be served on a person by any effective means.[93]
In other words, if the process leads to the notice being delivered to the person[94]
on whom it is to be served that will suffice and the method of service adopted does
not matter. Any recognised means of communication effective to deliver the
document will suffice,[95] but the burden of showing that it has been duly received
lies on the server.[96] The notice of arbitration may, for example, be validly served
by telex,[97] facsimile[98] or electronic mail.[99] In the case of an English registered
company a telex[100] is served when it is received at the registered office whether or
not this is in normal business hours or at a time when for some other reason the
registered office is closed.[101] In the case of a foreign company, no such specific rule
can be applied, and the approach must be to apply the principles (a) that a claimant
should have his full six years,[102] and (b) that the notice need not come to the
attention of any officer of the company immediately, to the facts of each case.[103]
Time of receipt of the telex must, however, be local time at the place of receipt.[104]
Presumably the same would apply to other methods of giving notice, e.g. by
facsimile or electronic mail.

The "fail-safe method". If there is some doubt as to whether a particular   5–030
method will be effective, a "fail-safe" method[105] of service is provided in s.76(4)

---

[92] Section 76(1) of the Arbitration Act 1996.
[93] Section 76(3) of the Arbitration Act 1996.
[94] Service on the relevant party will suffice and it is not necessary that the notice come to the attention of particular managerial or legal staff: *Bernuth Lines Ltd v High Seas Shipping Ltd* [2005] EWHC 3020.
[95] *Bernuth Lines Ltd v High Seas Shipping Ltd* [2005] EWHC 3020.
[96] *Schumacher t/a Vita Konzern v Laurel Island Ltd (The "Santa Cruz Tres")* [1995] 1 Lloyd's Rep. 208; *Bernuth Lines Ltd v High Seas Shipping Ltd* [2005] EWHC 3020.
[97] *NV Stoomv Maats "De Maas" v Nippon Yusen Kaisha (The "Pendrecht")* [1980] 2 Lloyd's Rep. 56.
[98] *Petredec Ltd v Tokumaru Kaiun Co Ltd (The "Sargasso")* [1994] 1 Lloyd's Rep. 162; *Swiss Bank Corp v Novorissiysk Shipping Co (The "Petr Shmidt")* [1995] 1 Lloyd's Rep. 202.
[99] *Bernuth Lines Ltd v High Seas Shipping Ltd* [2005] EWHC 3020.
[100] Telex is now seldom used as a means of communication but the same principles would presumably apply in relation to service by other means such as fax and email.
[101] *NV Stoomv Maats "De Maas" v Nippon Yusen Kaisha (The "Pendrecht")* [1980] 2 Lloyd's Rep. 56.
[102] Assuming the usual limitation period for contract claims applies and that no shorter contractual time limit has been agreed.
[103] *NV Stoomv Maats "De Maas" v Nippon Yusen Kaisha (The "Pendrecht")* [1980] 2 Lloyd's Rep. 56.
[104] *NV Stoomv Maats "De Maas" v Nippon Yusen Kaisha (The "Pendrecht")* [1980] 2 Lloyd's Rep. 56.
[105] See the comments at para.304(iii) of the DAC report.

of the Arbitration Act 1996. This provides that the notice will be treated as effectively served if it is addressed, pre-paid and delivered[106] by post:

(a) to the addressee's last known principal residence or, if he is or has been carrying on a trade, profession or business, his last known principal business address; or

(b) where the addressee is a body corporate, to the body's registered or principal office.

If that is done the notice will be treated as effectively served.[107]

5–031 **Court assistance with service.** Where service of a notice of arbitration in accordance with the parties' agreement or under the provisions of s.76 of the Arbitration Act 1996 set out above is not reasonably practicable, the court may intervene to assist.[108] This power is subject to contrary agreement between the parties and any available arbitral processes must first be exhausted.[109] The court may order service in a particular manner or may dispense with service altogether.[110] The provisions for service contained in s.76 of the Arbitration Act 1996 do not apply in relation to court proceedings.[111]

3. DUTIES OF THE TRIBUNAL IN RELATION TO THE CONDUCT OF THE REFERENCE

(a) Duty under s.33 of the Arbitration Act 1996[112]

5–032 **Statutory obligations.** Section 33 of the Arbitration Act 1996 imposes a mandatory duty on the tribunal with regard to the way in which it conducts the reference.[113] This duty reflects the general principle set out in s.1(a) of the Arbitration Act 1996 that the object of arbitration is to obtain the fair resolution of disputes by an impartial tribunal without unnecessary delay or expense. Section 33 provides:

---

[106] The requirement that it be delivered indicates that service is effective only once actual delivery of the notice has occurred and not when the notice is sent.

[107] Section 76(4) of the Arbitration Act 1996.

[108] Section 77 of the Arbitration Act 1996. This may be, for example, where the respondent is evading service.

[109] Section 77(3) of the Arbitration Act 1996.

[110] Section 77(2) of the Arbitration Act 1996.

[111] Section 76(5) of the Arbitration Act 1996.

[112] See also paras 4–104 *et seq*.

[113] The section cannot be excluded by agreement of the parties: see s.4 and Sch.1 to the Arbitration Act 1996.

"(l) The tribunal shall—

(a) act fairly and impartially as between the parties, giving each party a reasonable opportunity of putting his case and dealing with that of his opponent, and

(b) adopt procedures suitable to the circumstances of the particular case, avoiding unnecessary delay or expense, so as to provide a fair means for the resolution of the matters falling to be determined.

(2) The tribunal shall comply with that general duty in conducting the arbitral proceedings, in its decisions on matters of procedure and evidence and in the exercise of all other powers conferred on it."

Section 33(1) has two limbs. The first, subs.33(1)(a), effectively requires the tribunal to act in accordance with natural justice and broadly reflects Art.18 of the Model Law.[114] This is dealt with at paras 5–038 *et seq.* below. Secondly, subs.33(1)(b) imposes a positive duty on the tribunal to adopt suitable procedures for the fair resolution of the dispute and avoid unnecessary delay and expense. Section 33(2) confirms the overriding nature of the duty imposed by s.33(1).

Complying with the obligations. The section makes clear that the procedures to be adopted will depend upon the circumstances of the particular case. There is no prescribed procedure that will be suitable in all cases and the tribunal will be expected to adopt a flexible approach as the needs of the case dictate. Simply adopting in every case procedures based on the CPR will no longer do and a party who argues for full pleadings, disclosure of documents, expert evidence and hearings with live testimony should be required to justify why this is necessary for the fair resolution of the dispute. Despite the flexibility available, the tribunal has a positive duty under s.33 to ensure that suitable procedures are adopted and it will be in breach of its obligation if, for example, it fails to ensure that the issues in the reference are properly defined.[115]   5–033

Guidance from the Act. The tribunal is given some guidance in the 1996 Act itself as to how it should approach the duty imposed by s.33. In particular, s.34(2) may be treated as a non-exhaustive checklist of issues for the tribunal to consider in establishing the procedure for the reference.[116] s.34(1) provides that these are matters for the tribunal to decide, subject to any agreement on them between the parties.[117]   5–034

---

[114] Article 18 refers to each party being given a "full" opportunity to present its case whereas s.33(1)(a) refers to a "reasonable" opportunity. This reflects that it may not always be necessary, efficient or fair to allow a party the opportunity to present his case as fully as he may wish and it is considered sufficient for him to be allowed a reasonable opportunity to do so: see para.5–043 below.

[115] *RC Pillar & Sons v Edwards* [2002] C.I.L.L. 1799.

[116] For a fuller checklist and discussion of the procedural issues see paras 5–118 *et seq.* below.

[117] It was apparently a matter of much debate whether the final word on procedural and evidential matters should be with the tribunal or with the parties. Section 34(1) is an interesting compromise. It gives an overriding right to the parties to agree the procedure, but is drafted in such a way as to give apparent prominence to the tribunal's right to decide such matters.

5–035　**Exercise of the tribunal's powers.** Section 33(2) makes clear that the tribunal must have regard to the general duty set out in s.33(1) when exercising its various powers in the course of the reference. It must therefore consider whether it would assist the fair, speedy and most efficient resolution of the dispute for it to exercise the powers available including, for example, the power to limit recoverable costs under s.65 of the Act.[118]

5–036　**Remedies for failure to comply.** Where a party considers that the tribunal has failed to comply with the duty under s.33(1) he has two basic remedies. First, he may apply under s.24 of the Arbitration Act 1996 for the tribunal to be removed. Secondly, he may seek to challenge any resulting award under s.68 of the 1996 Act. An application for removal under s.24 might be appropriate if a party learned of the failure to comply with the duty under s.33(1) during the course of the hearing. He would in any event have to raise his objection forthwith[119] or within such time as the arbitration agreement specifies because otherwise the right to object will be lost.[120] Having made his objection a party may nevertheless choose to continue to take part in the proceedings. If he does so, or if the failure to comply with the duty under s.33(1) only becomes apparent on publication of the award, the second alternative of challenging the award would be appropriate. It will often be combined with an application for removal under s.24 so that, if the challenge is successful, the award will not be remitted to the same tribunal.[121]

5–037　**Challenge to the award.** A party who considers that the tribunal has failed to comply with its duty under s.33(1) can also seek to challenge any resulting award on grounds of serious irregularity under s.68(2)(a) of the Arbitration Act 1996.[122] Additionally the applicant must show "substantial injustice" has been or will be caused. Challenges under s.68 of the Arbitration Act 1996 are dealt with in Ch.8.[123] Whilst it is possible to describe the sort of behaviour on the part of a tribunal which may give grounds for objection on the basis of a breach of the duty under s.33(1), the question whether in any given case a remedy will be available has to be considered in the specific context of s.68 and whether in the particular circumstances it gave rise to substantial injustice. In this context, the Court of Appeal has indicated that "pursuit of the overall objective of arbitral proceedings as set out in s.1(a) of the 1996 Act ('the fair resolution of disputes by an impartial tribunal without unnecessary delay or expense') requires that . . . the courts

---

[118] See paras 6–147 *et seq.*

[119] This has been held to mean "as soon as reasonably possible": see *Margulead Ltd v Exide Technologies* [2004] EWHC 1019; [2005] 1 Lloyd's Rep. 324.

[120] Section 73 of the Arbitration Act 1996. See for example *Sinclair v Woods of Winchester Ltd* [2005] EWHC 1631; 102 Con. L.R. 127.

[121] Removal of an arbitrator is dealt with in paras 7–111 *et seq.* below.

[122] As His Honour Judge Lloyd Q.C. pointed out in *Weldon Plant Ltd v The Commission for the New Towns* [2000] EWHC Technology 76; [2000] B.L.R. 496 at [30], although a failure to comply with s.33 is placed first in s.68(2) "it is in reality more in the nature of a general provision of which section 68(2) contains further examples".

[123] See paras 8–072 *et seq.*

should accord a reasonably generous margin of appreciation to arbitrators in the discharge of their functions."[124] More specifically, His Honour Judge Lloyd Q.C. in *Weldon Plant Ltd v The Commission for the New Towns*[125] held that the mere fact that there was an error in the award which was unfair to a party did not mean that there must have been a failure to comply with s.33 of the Act and therefore a serious irregularity for the purposes of s.68(2)(a).[126] Accordingly, whilst there is clearly a link between the duty under s.33 and the ability to challenge an award for serious irregularity under s.68, breach of the duty will not necessarily give rise to a remedy under the latter section.

(b) *Natural justice and fairness*

Statutory provision. English law requires the tribunal to comply with rules   5–038
of natural justice in the conduct of the reference and an award may be challenged or enforcement resisted if it is made in breach of them.[127] The minimum requirements are set out in the first limb of the tribunal's duties under s.33 of the Arbitration Act 1996. That section provides that the tribunal shall "act fairly and impartially as between the parties, giving each party a reasonable opportunity of putting his case and dealing with that of his opponent". This reflects the two traditional limbs of natural justice, namely the requirement that the tribunal hearing a case must be unbiased and disinterested, and the requirement that each party must be given a fair opportunity to be heard.[128]

Agreement otherwise? Section 33(1) is one of the mandatory provisions in   5–039
the 1996 Act,[129] so the parties cannot agree that the tribunal may act in breach of the duty imposed. The parties may, however, agree to what would otherwise constitute a breach of natural justice under common law.[130] For example, the parties may agree to waive any objection to the appointment of an arbitrator who has an interest which he discloses.[131] Or they may agree to the incorporation of a

---

[124] *per* Parker L.J. in *Warborough Investments Ltd v S Robinson & Sons (Holdings) Ltd* [2003] EWCA Civ 751 at [60].

[125] [2000] EWHC Technology 76; [2000] B.L.R. 496 at [30].

[126] See also *Sinclair v Woods of Winchester Ltd* [2005] 102 Con. L.R. 127 at [20] and *Newfield Construction Ltd v Tomlinson* [2004] EWHC 3051.

[127] See paras 8–077, 8–010 and 8–028.

[128] See paras 5–042 *et seq.*

[129] See s.4 and Sch.1 to the Arbitration Act 1996. As regards enforcement of the duty see para.5–036 above.

[130] *London Export Corp Ltd v Jubilee Coffee Roasting Co Ltd* [1958] 1 W.L.R. 271: see though *W Naumann v Edward Nathan & Co Ltd* [1931] 37 Lloyd's Rep. 249. The common law is maintained insofar as it is not inconsistent with the statute: see s.81 of the Arbitration Act 1996.

[131] In *Weissfisch v Julius* [2006] EWCA Civ 218 the parties agreed to appoint a solicitor as arbitrator who was authorised to continue to represent them outside the arbitration, for reward. They also expressly waived any rights to challenge his appointment on any ground including his having been engaged in the mediation of their disputes and his having been legal adviser to them. The Court of Appeal noted these "extraordinary features" but declined to allow an appeal against the refusal of an injunction restraining the arbitrator from proceeding with a hearing to determine his jurisdiction. This was however a case where the arbitration agreement was governed by Swiss law rather than English law.

custom or trade practice that might otherwise be considered unreasonable and in breach of natural justice. Express agreement will be required[132] but if it is forthcoming then the tribunal cannot be said to have conducted the proceedings improperly. This is subject to what has been agreed not requiring the tribunal to act in breach of its duty under s.33(1).

5–040 **Impartial.** Section 33(1) of the Arbitration Act 1996 states that the tribunal must act "impartially".[133] An arbitrator must also appear impartial[134] and if there are justifiable doubts as to his impartiality this will provide a ground for his removal by the court under s.24(1)(a) of the Arbitration Act 1996[135] or may mean that the award can be challenged.[136]

5–041 **Unilateral communication with a party.** Whilst there is no absolute rule against the arbitrator having unilateral discussions with one party only, an arbitrator should avoid doing so as it can lead to removal for failure to conduct the proceedings properly[137] or for a reasonable apprehension of bias,[138] especially if discussions are intentional or frequent, go beyond administrative matters or are not promptly disclosed to the other party.[139] In practice unilateral communications frequently occur between an arbitrator and the legal representatives of his appointing party in the context of both his own appointment and consideration of potential candidates for appointment as the third arbitrator.[139a] This practice is unobjectionable provided the discussion does not stray into the substance of the dispute and both parties are made aware that the discussions are taking place.[140]

5–042 **A reasonable opportunity of putting case.** Each party must be given a reasonable opportunity to present his own case.[141] This means he must be given an opportunity to explain his arguments to the tribunal and to adduce evidence in

---

[132] *London Export Corp Ltd v Jubilee Coffee Roasting Co Ltd* [1958] 1 W.L.R. 271.

[133] See generally para.5–032 and para.4–107 above.

[134] *K/S Norjarl A/S v Hyundai Heavy Industries Co Ltd* [1991] 1 Lloyd's Rep. 524.

[135] This subject is dealt with more fully in paras 4–107 *et seq.*

[136] Under s.68(2)(g) of the 1996 Act and subject, of course, to the loss of the right to object under s.73(1); see para.8–065.

[137] Under s.24(1)(d)(i) of the Arbitration Act 1996: see paras 7–116 *et seq.*

[138] Under s.24(1)(a) of the Arbitration Act 1996: see paras 4–107 *et seq.*

[139] *Norbrook Laboratories Ltd v Tank* [2006] EWHC 1055.

[139a] See *Pacific China Holdings Ltd v Grand Pacific Holdings Ltd* HCCT 5/2007, a first instance decision from Hong Kong, where an application to remove an arbitrator as a result of such communication was rejected. See also r.5.2 of the IBA's Rules of Ethics for Arbitrators at *www.ibanet.org*.

[140] The Chartered Institute of Arbitrators has published a "Guideline on the Interviewing of Prospective Arbitrators" which sets out a suggested procedure for pre-appointment interviews with arbitrators. The Guideline has received a mixed reception from practitioners, in part because it is seen as proposing an unduly formal and burdensome regime.

[141] Section 33(1)(a) of the Arbitration Act 1996 and see *Montrose Canned Foods Ltd v Eric Wells (Merchants) Ltd* [1965] 1 Lloyd's Rep. 597.

support of his case[142] and a sufficient period of time should be allowed for this.[143] If an arbitrator bifurcates the proceedings so as to determine certain issues in advance of others and holds a hearing on that basis, he cannot subsequently make an award on the postponed issues without giving an opportunity to address those also.[144] Failure to afford a party a reasonable opportunity of putting his case may render the award subject to challenge under s.68[145] of the Arbitration Act 1996,[146] but only if it is such as results in substantial injustice.[147] It could also lead to the arbitrator's removal under s.24(1)(d) of the Arbitration Act 1996.[148] A party's inability to present his case is also a ground for refusing enforcement of the resulting award under the New York Convention.[149]

Qualification of the right. The need to allow a party a reasonable opportunity to present his case can give rise to difficulties. To what extent can the tribunal intervene where, for example, a party's submissions or evidence is needlessly long, repetitive, focuses on irrelevant issues or is sought to be made over an extended period of time? What if a party ignores procedural deadlines imposed by the tribunal but maintains he still has points to put before it in support of his case? Inevitably each situation has to be dealt with in its own context but the following general considerations should be taken into account.   5–043

No unfettered right. The right to present his case does not mean that a party has an unfettered right to make submissions or present evidence as and when he wishes. It is noteworthy that s.33(1)(a) of the Arbitration Act 1996 refers to a reasonable opportunity whereas Art.18 of the Model Law on which it is based refers to a full opportunity. This reflects the DAC's intention that the right to   5–044

---

[142] Prior to the Arbitration Act 1996 a party had to be permitted an oral hearing if he requested one, unless there was some agreement to the contrary: see *Henry Sotheran Ltd v Norwich Union Life Insurance Society* [1992] 31 E.G. 70. However, absent agreement between the parties, this is now a matter to be decided by the tribunal under s.34(2)(h) of the Arbitration Act 1996. English law therefore differs from the UNCITRAL Model Law on this, Art.24(1) of which allows either party to insist on a hearing, see Appendix 4.

[143] *Norbrook Laboratories Ltd v Tank* [2006] EWHC 1055.

[144] *Benaim (UK) Ltd v Davies Middleton & Davies Ltd* [2005] EWHC 1370.

[145] In *Icon Navigation Corp v Sinochem International Petroleum (Bahamas) Co Ltd* [2002] EWHC 2812 a tribunal found in favour of a party on an issue which that party alleged it had not had an opportunity properly to address. The other party appealed against the award under s.69 of the Arbitration Act 1996, thereby raising the prospect of a successful appeal on the issue in question. The court determined that in this situation the appropriate course is to oppose the application for leave to appeal on the grounds that it is not just and proper in all the circumstances for the court to determine the question of law in respect of which leave to appeal is sought. An oral hearing of the application for leave to appeal may be appropriate in these circumstances.

[146] See paras 8–077 *et seq.* See also *Henry Sotheran Ltd v Norwich Union Life Insurance Society* [1992] 31 E.G. 70 and *Lovell Partnerships (Northern) Ltd v AW Construction Plc* [1996] 81 B.L.R. 83, both cases under the old law but demonstrating the type of conduct which is likely to give rise to serious irregularity under s.68 in this context. See also *Williams v Wallis* [1914] 2 K.B. 478.

[147] *Warborough Investments Ltd v S Robinson & Sons (Holdings) Ltd* [2002] EWHC 2502, affirmed by the Court of Appeal at [2003] EWCA Civ 751. See also paras 8–104 *et seq.* below.

[148] *Benaim (UK) Ltd v Davies Middleton & Davies Ltd* [2005] EWHC 1370. See para.7–116 *et seq.*

[149] See the Arbitration Act 1996, s.103(2)(c) implementing Art.V(1)(b) of the Convention, dealt with at para.8–034.

present the case should not be without limit. The tribunal's duty under s.33 of the Arbitration Act 1996 has to be considered in light of s.34 of the same Act which, in the absence of agreement between the parties, requires the tribunal to determine all procedural and evidential matters.[150] The combination of these provisions means the tribunal must actively manage the proceedings in order to comply with its duty under s.33.

5–045   **Limits.** A party is required to comply with procedural orders and directions from the tribunal,[151] including those imposing limits as to time and content of submissions and evidence.[152] On the other hand, if the tribunal's directions in this regard can be said to be unfair or to operate unfairly against one of the parties, that party may have a genuine ground of complaint.[153] In practice the tribunal will usually allow some latitude to a party who has further relevant submissions or evidence to put forward, but will need to draw the line at some point.[154] Provided it has made clear to the parties exactly where that line will be drawn, for example by giving advance warning of a cut-off date for evidence and submissions, and provided of course it is not unreasonable to draw the line in that way, the tribunal should not fall foul of the requirement to give the parties a reasonable opportunity to present their case.[155]

5–046   **Managing the proceedings.** Similarly, a tribunal cannot be expected to sit through extended oral hearings listening to long-winded submissions on irrelevant matters. The tribunal is entitled, and under s.33 is obliged and encouraged, to avoid the unnecessary delay and expense that would be caused by such an approach. The tribunal should take a grip on the proceedings from the outset and indicate to the parties those areas on which it particularly wishes to be addressed and those which it does not consider relevant to the real issues in dispute. If a party fails to heed such guidance, the tribunal might seek to focus the proceedings by fixing times for written submissions and allocating the remaining hearing time between the parties. This the tribunal is entitled to do, provided it will allow a reasonable time for both parties to put forward their argument and evidence.[156]

5–047   **Late raising of issues.** The question whether new issues can be raised at a late stage of the proceedings will depend upon the circumstances of the particular

[150] See para.5–034 above.
[151] See generally paras 5–191 *et seq.* below.
[152] There can be no doubt in view of the general principles set out in s.1 of the Arbitration Act 1996 and the duties imposed on the tribunal under s.33(1)(b) of the Arbitration Act 1996 that the tribunal has the power and indeed the duty to impose such limits where it is appropriate in the circumstances of the case. See also *Overseas Fortune Shipping Pte Ltd v Great Eastern Shipping Co Ltd (The "Singapore Fortune")* [1987] 1 Lloyd's Rep. 270 on the imposition of time limits.
[153] *Damond Lock Grabowski v Laing Investments (Bracknell) Ltd*, 60 B.L.R. 112. This was a case under the old law but the point could be made even more strongly in view of the principle of fairness required under ss.1 and 33(1)(a) of the 1996 Act.
[154] *Shuttari v Solicitors' Indemnity Fund* [2004] EWHC 1537 (Ch).
[155] *Overseas Fortune Shipping Pte Ltd v Great Eastern Shipping Co Ltd (The "Singapore Fortune")* [1987] 1 Lloyd's Rep. 270.
[156] See para.5–042 above.

case and whether it will cause injustice. The ability of the other party to be given a reasonable opportunity to address those new issues will be crucial. As Moore-Bick J. said in *Icon Navigation Corp v Sinochem International Petroleum (Bahamas) Co Ltd*[157]: "No tribunal likes to shut out genuine issues if it can avoid doing so, but it is necessary to ensure that the other party has a fair opportunity to deal with any new point that is put forward. Provided the arbitrators are satisfied that there will be no prejudice to the opposing party they are entitled to allow new points to be raised at any stage of the proceedings, even in closing submissions."[158]

Assisting a party to put his case. Another issue which arises in this context is the extent to which, if at all, a tribunal is obliged to assist a party in putting his case. There was some authority under the old law that if a tribunal has in mind certain findings of fact arising out of the evidence given which would establish a defence to a claim, and it requires that defence to be formulated in the pleadings, it should spell this out to the party concerned and failure to do so could render the award susceptible to challenge for "procedural mishap".[159] The scope for any such challenge based on the failure by one of the parties properly to put his case has been removed by the Arbitration Act 1996.[160] The position now appears to be that, although a tribunal should make sure that a party properly understands the case being put to him,[161] there is no positive obligation for a tribunal to make a party's case for him, even where that party is not legally represented. Of course, the other party must prove his case to succeed in any event. 5–048

A reasonable opportunity to deal with the case of the other party. Section 33(1)(a) of the Arbitration Act 1996 also requires the tribunal to allow each party a reasonable opportunity to deal with the other side's case. This means that each party is entitled to know,[162] and should have an opportunity to address,[163] all evidence and submissions made by the other party.[164] Failure by a party to insist on being given information will not absolve the arbitrator from his 5–049

---

[157] [2003] 1 All E.R. (Comm) 405.
[158] As the judge noted, there may however be costs consequences of raising issues late in the proceedings.
[159] *Indian Oil Corp Ltd v Coastal (Bermuda) Ltd* [1990] 2 Lloyd's Rep. 407. However, see the comments of Lord Donaldson in *King v Thomas McKenna Ltd* [1991] 1 All E.R. 653, CA at 655–656.
[160] See the grounds for challenge for serious irregularity listed in s.68(2) of the Arbitration Act 1996 and dealt with in paras 8–076 *et seq.*
[161] Both as a matter of good practice and arguably to comply with the duty under s.33(1) of the Arbitration Act 1996.
[162] *Ajay Kanoria and others v Tony Francis Guinness* [2006] EWCA Civ 222. That case concerned enforcement of a New York Convention award being resisted on the basis of a party's inability to present its case under s.103(2)(c) of the Arbitration Act 1996 but the reasoning is equally applicable in the present context.
[163] *Norbrook Laboratories Ltd v Tank* [2006] EWHC 1055.
[164] See, for example, *Montrose Canned Foods Ltd v Eric Wells (Merchants) Ltd* [1965] 1 Lloyd's Rep. 597 and *Ceval Alimentos SA v Agrimpex Trading Co Ltd* [1995] 2 Lloyd's Rep. 380, cases under the old law but underlining the right now embodied in s.33(1)(a) of the Arbitration Act 1996.

overriding duty in this regard.[165] Accordingly, where there are material communications between the tribunal and a party, the tribunal should ensure that they take place in the presence of both parties.[166] If this is for some reason not possible, the tribunal should be careful to inform the other party of the content of such communications, providing copies of any which are in writing. A tribunal wishing to avoid criticism would be well advised to take a broad view of what is "material" and to err on the side of caution. As Megaw L.J. noted in *Government of Ceylon v Chandris*: "It is, I apprehend, a basic principle, in arbitrations as much as in litigation in the Courts (other, of course, than ex parte proceedings), that no one with judicial responsibility may receive evidence, documentary or otherwise, from one party without the other party knowing that the evidence is being tendered and being offered an opportunity to consider it, object to it, or make submissions on it. No custom or practice may over-ride that basic principle."[167]

5–050   **The right to deal with any issue which will be relied on by the tribunal.**[168] To comply with its duty under s.33(1) of the Arbitration Act 1996 to act fairly, the tribunal should give the parties an opportunity to deal with any issue which will be relied on by it as the basis for its findings.[169] The parties are entitled to assume that the tribunal will base its decision solely on the evidence and argument presented by them[170] prior to the making of the award,[171] and if the tribunal is minded to decide the dispute on some other point, the tribunal must give notice of it to the parties to enable them to address the point.[172] That said, a tribunal does not have to refer back to the parties its analysis or findings based

---

[165] *Mohan Lal Mirpuri v Amarjit Singh Jass* [1997] 56 Con. L.R. 31. In that case an arbitrator in a "documents-only" arbitration proceeded to make an award when he knew that one of the parties had not received documents which he had received from the other party. The solicitor for the party who had not received the documents knew of the omission but did not take positive steps to obtain the documents. This inaction was held not to override the arbitrator's duty to ensure each party knew the case which was put against them and the award was remitted.

[166] Unilateral communications may lead to the removal of an arbitrator: see para.7–118 below.

[167] [1963] 1 Lloyd's Rep. 214.

[168] See *Pacol Ltd v Joint Stock Co Rossakhar* [2000] 1 Lloyd's Rep. 109 which referred to this and the following paragraph as they appeared in the 21st edition of this book.

[169] *Gbangbola v Smith & Sherriff Ltd* [1998] 3 All E.R. 730; *Pacol Ltd v Joint Stock Co Rossakhar* [2000] 1 Lloyd's Rep. 109; *Bulfracht (Cyprus) Ltd v Boneset Shipping Co Ltd (The "Pamphilos")* [2002] 2 Lloyd's Rep. 681; *Omnibridge Consulting Ltd v Clearsprings (Management) Ltd* [2004] EWHC 2276; *Vee Networks Ltd v Econet Wireless International Ltd* [2004] EWHC 2909; [2005] 1 Lloyd's Rep. 192.

[170] Unless an inquisitorial approach is adopted, see para.5–099 below, but even then the parties should be given a reasonable opportunity to deal with any issue the tribunal will rely on.

[171] This will usually be limited to the evidence and argument presented by the time the hearing is concluded but may extend to post-hearing submissions made prior to the making of the award.

[172] *Gbangbola v Smith & Sherriff Ltd* [1998] 3 All E.R. 730; *Pacol Ltd v Joint Stock Co Rossakhar* [1999] 2 All E.R. 778; *Guardcliffe Properties Ltd v City & St James* [2003] 25 E.G. 143; *Cameroon Airlines v Transnet Ltd* [2004] EWHC 1829; *St George's Investment Co v Gemini Consulting Ltd* [2004] EWHC 2353; [2005] 01 E.G. 96; *Vee Networks Ltd v Econet Wireless International Ltd* [2004] EWHC 2909; [2005] 1 Lloyd's Rep. 192. This follows the position prior to the Arbitration Act 1996: *Top Shop Estates Ltd v C Danino* [1985] 1 E.G.L.R. 9; *Zermalt Holdings SA v Nu-Life Upholstery Repairs Ltd* [1985] 2 E.G.L.R. 14; *Handley v Nationwide Anglia Building Society* [1992] 29 E.G. 123; *Unit Four Cinemas Ltd v Tosara Investments Ltd* [1993] 44 E.G. 121; *Henry Boot Construction Ltd v Mooney* (1996) 12 Constr. L.J. 37. See also para.8–081.

on the evidence or argument before it.[173] Indeed, the tribunal is entitled to derive an alternative case from the parties' submissions as the basis for its award, so long as an opportunity is given to address the essential issues which led the tribunal to those conclusions.[174] If an issue is raised but not pursued by one party, and the other party chooses not to address the point, it may still be open to the tribunal to rely upon that issue so long as it has been "put into the arena".[175] In most cases of course the tribunal would want to solicit submissions on the point rather than leave it unaddressed by one party but the right conveyed by s.33(1) is to be given an opportunity to deal with the issue and it is ultimately for a party to decide whether to avail itself of that opportunity.[176]

The tribunal's view of the facts. Similarly, if a tribunal forms a view of   5–051
the facts which is different from that given in the evidence adduced by the parties,[177] and it might produce a contrary result to that which emerges from the evidence, then the tribunal should bring its view to the attention of the parties and give them an opportunity to address it.[178] However not every observation or inference of fact need be referred back to the parties for them to make submissions if such observation or inference is not material or significant and is simply an ordinary incident of the arbitral process based on the arbitrator's power to make findings of fact.[179]

Tribunal's expert knowledge. A tribunal may be entitled to rely on its   5–052
own expert knowledge in deciding the case.[180] Unless it is clear that members of the tribunal will be relying on their experience of the trade,[181] and indeed they

---

[173] *ABB AG v Hochtief Airport GmbH* [2006] 1 All E.R. 529 (Comm); *Bulfracht (Cyprus) Ltd v Boneset Shipping Co Ltd (The "Pamphilos")* [2002] EWHC 2292; [2002] 2 Lloyd's Rep. 681; *Bandwith Shipping Corp v Intaari* [2006] EWHC 2532.
[174] *ABB AG v Hochtief Airport GmbH* [2006] 1 All E.R. 529 (Comm); *The Trustees of Edmond Stern Settlement v Simon Levy* [2007] EWHC 1187; *JD Wetherspoon Plc v Jay Mar Estates* [2007] EWHC 856.
[175] *Warborough Investments Ltd v S Robinson & Sons (Holdings) Ltd* [2002] EWHC 2502, affirmed by the Court of Appeal at [2003] EWCA Civ 751; *Bandwith Shipping Corp v Intaari* [2006] EWHC 2532; *JD Wetherspoon Plc v Jay Mar Estates* [2007] EWHC 856. See further para.8–080.
[176] In *JD Wetherspoon Plc v Jay Mar Estates* [2007] EWHC 856, the arbitrator conducting a rent review arbitration offered the parties the opportunity to accompany him on his inspection of comparable properties, which they declined. The court held that no criticism could be made of the arbitrator that he proceeded with the inspection in their absence.
[177] Or the parties' agreed view of the facts: *Omnibridge Consulting Ltd v Clearsprings (Management) Ltd* [2004] EWHC 2276; *Walsall Metropolitan Borough Council v Beechdale Community Housing Association Ltd* [2005] EWHC 2715.
[178] *Société Franco-Tunisienne d'Armement-Tunis v Government of Ceylon* [1959] 2 Lloyd's Rep. 1; [1959] 1 W.L.R. 787; *R. v Paddington and St Marylebone Rent Tribunal* [1949] 1 K.B. 666; *Aiden Shipping Ltd v Interbulk Ltd (The "Vimeira")* [1986] A.C. 965. See para.8–081 below.
[179] *Bulfracht (Cyprus) Ltd v Boneset Shipping Co Ltd (The "Pamphilos")* [2002] EWHC 2292. See also *Tame Shipping Ltd v Easy Navigation Ltd (The "Easy Rider")* [2004] EWHC 1862.
[180] See paras 4–139 above and 6–075 et seq. below.
[181] See for example *Hawk Shipping Ltd v Cron Navigation Ltd* [2003] EWHC 1828 where Toulson J. observed at [19] that: "When the parties choose the LMAA small claim procedure they do so in the expectation that the Arbitrator will bring his own specialist knowledge to bear in determining the claim".

have been appointed for that purpose, (as happens, for example, in disputes about the quality of commodities), they should disclose the matters within their own knowledge on which they intend to rely to avoid any subsequent argument that the parties should have been given an opportunity to address them. That said, the courts in recent years have taken a more robust approach to tribunals relying on their own experience and knowledge.[182] So, for example, there can be no objection to arbitrators using their experience and technical knowledge when applying the law or evaluating the evidence before them and making findings of fact.[183] In *Checkpoint Ltd. v Strathclyde Pension Fund*[184] the court drew a distinction between the arbitrator supplying new evidence by using his own knowledge and him using that knowledge to evaluate and adjudicate upon the evidence before him. The arbitrator is fully entitled to make use of his own experience and knowledge in evaluating the evidence before him and in reaching his conclusions, provided that it is of a kind and in the range of knowledge that one would reasonably expect the arbitrator to have, and provided he uses it to evaluate the evidence called and not to introduce new and different evidence.[185] Accordingly the tribunal can draw an inference from the evidence even if that inference has not specifically been raised by either party.

5–053 **Scope of the statutory duty.** The scope of the duty to "act fairly" under s.33(1) of the Act is not precisely defined. One of the problems in discussing this area is that the concepts involved are general and vague. As the DAC acknowledged,[186] this vagueness, and the consequent wide scope of s.33(1), flow from one of the main objectives of the Act, namely the provision of a flexible system of arbitration. On the face of it the scope of s.33(1) appears to facilitate challenges for serious irregularity under s.68(2)(a). However a successful applicant under s.68 needs to show "substantial injustice", which creates a high threshold. The DAC indicated[187] that having chosen arbitration, parties cannot validly complain of substantial injustice "unless what has happened simply cannot on any view be defended as an acceptable consequence of that choice". It emphasised that s.68 was designed as a long stop, only available in extreme cases where the tribunal has gone so wrong in its conduct of the arbitration that justice calls out for it to be corrected. The DAC also expressed a hope that the court would take a dim view of those who tried to attack awards because of alleged breaches of s.33 which have

---

[182] In *Checkpoint Ltd v Strathclyde Pension Fund* [2004] EWCA Civ 84 the Court of Appeal suggested that an acceptable test for whether the arbitrator had wrongly used his personal experience of the market is whether or not the information relied upon by the arbitrator is information of the kind and within the range of knowledge which he would reasonably be expected to have. The arbitration agreement in that case specifically contemplated an arbitrator with "relevant local knowledge".

[183] *Bulfracht (Cyprus) Ltd v Boneset Shipping Co Ltd (The "Pamphilos")* [2002] EWHC 2292; *Benaim (UK) Ltd v Davies Middleton & Davies Ltd* [2005] EWHC 1370; *Hawk Shipping Ltd v Cron Navigation Ltd* [2003] EWHC 1828.

[184] [2003] EWCA 84. See also *JD Wetherspoon Plc v Jay Mar Estates* [2007] EWHC 856.

[185] *Checkpoint Ltd v Strathclyde Pension Fund* [2003] EWCA Civ 84; *JD Wetherspoon Plc v Jay Mar Estates* [2007] EWHC 856 at [10].

[186] Paragraph 150 of the DAC report.

[187] Paragraph 280 of the DAC report.

no real substance.[188] In practice, the courts have not been inundated with spurious claims based upon alleged breaches of s.33, despite the apparent width and vagueness of the duty. This is no doubt in part due to the robust approach the courts have taken towards the requirement for an applicant to demonstrate substantial injustice.[189]

Intervention by the court. In its approach to s.33 and the requirement of fairness the court has to take account of the non-interventionist principle.[190] This principle is expressed in s.1(c) of the 1996 Act and by s.34 of the Act which makes it clear that procedural and evidential matters are for the tribunal to determine in the absence of agreement between the parties. These provisions lend support to the approach advocated by the DAC outlined in para.5–053 above. Additionally, whilst there were a number of authorities under the old law showing the court's willingness to intervene where it was felt the tribunal had erred in relation to evidential and procedural matters,[191] those decisions are not applicable to the statutory regime embodied in the Arbitration Act 1996.[192]   5–054

(c) Relationship between duties, principles and party autonomy

Duties, principles and party autonomy. The Arbitration Act 1996 sets out in s.1 the general principles on the basis of which it is to be construed.[193] It makes clear that the parties are free to agree how their arbitration is to be conducted, subject to such safeguards as are necessary in the public interest.[194] These safeguards are reflected in the fact that various provisions in the Act are mandatory.[195] Section 33(1) of the Arbitration Act 1996 imposes specific duties on the arbitrators.[196] These duties are mandatory and cannot be excluded by agreement. However the parties are free to agree all procedural and evidential matters under s.34(1) of the Arbitration Act 1996. The question arises as to what is the relationship between these provisions and whether there is a tension between them?[197]   5–055

---

[188] Paragraph 151 of the DAC report.
[189] See paras 8–072 *et seq.* for a detailed discussion of the court's approach.
[190] The principle of non-intervention was stated clearly by the House of Lords in *Lesotho Highlands v Impreglio SpA* [2005] UKHL 43.
[191] For example as to evidential weight, relevance and admissibility which are now dealt with in s.34(2)(f) of the Arbitration Act 1996.
[192] This reflects the position generally in relation to the 1996 Act. In *Seabridge Shipping AB v AC Orssleff's Eftf's A/S* [1999] 2 Lloyd's Rep. 685 at 690 Thomas J. (as he then was) observed that "it would in my view be a retrograde step if when a point arose reference had to be made to pre-Act cases" and he referred to the guidance given by the Court of Appeal in *Patel v Patel* [2000] Q.B. 551 that reliance should be had on the wording of the Arbitration Act 1996. These statements were endorsed by the House of Lords in *Lesotho Highlands v Impreglio SpA* [2005] UKHL 43.
[193] See paras 1–004 and 1–005 above.
[194] Section 1(b) of the Arbitration Act 1996.
[195] Set out in Sch.1 of the Arbitration Act 1996.
[196] See paras 5–032 *et seq.* above.
[197] See generally paras 154 to 163 of the DAC report.

5–056   **Differing views of the parties and the tribunal.** In particular, what happens if the parties purport to agree something which the tribunal considers is contrary to the principles and duties laid down in ss.1 and 33 of the Arbitration Act 1996? s.33(1) cannot be excluded by agreement but on the other hand the tribunal cannot override the agreement of the parties, nor should they proceed against the wishes of the parties. In these circumstances the tribunal would want to explore the predicament with the parties and ask them to modify their agreement. If the parties were unwilling to do so the tribunal may have to resign.[198] The only alternative to resignation, assuming the parties are unwilling to modify their agreement as to how they wish the tribunal to proceed, is for the tribunal to follow the parties' wishes notwithstanding their own reservations about the proposed course. The tribunal would have to satisfy itself that this course can be reconciled with its mandatory obligation under s.33, but having brought about this situation the parties could not justifiably complain if the tribunal did so, nor would they be able to show substantial injustice in order to challenge the resulting award.

4. PRELIMINARY CONSIDERATIONS

(a) Rules applicable to substance of the dispute

5–057   **Determining the applicable rules.** An issue which frequently arises for determination by the tribunal at a preliminary stage is the question of the law or rules to be applied to the merits of the dispute.[199] This is however just one aspect of a broader issue and the following three categories of applicable law or rules may need to be considered[200]:

(1) The law of a particular country or some other considerations agreed between the parties may govern the rights and obligations arising out of the parties' substantive agreement.[201] If a national law is selected this is referred to as the governing or proper law of the contract.

(2) A different law may apply to the rights and obligations arising out of the agreement to arbitrate. This is known as the law of the arbitration agreement.[202]

---

[198] This was the view of the DAC—see paras 154 to 163 of the DAC report.

[199] For a fuller discussion of this subject see paras 2–090 *et seq.* above. See also s.46 of the Arbitration Act 1996. Section 46(1)(b) makes clear that the parties may choose either a "law" to apply to the dispute or "other considerations". This opens the door to "equity clauses" and the like: See paras 4–141 and 4–142 above.

[200] There may be other applicable laws, such as the law governing the particular reference to arbitration. See para.2–094 above.

[201] Section 46(1) of the Arbitration Act 1996. See paras 2–090 *et seq.* above. See also *Compagnie d'Armement Maritime SA v Compagnie Tunisienne de Navigation SA* [1971] A.C. 572 at 604 and *Bank Mellat v Helliniki Techniki SA* [1984] Q.B. 291 at 301.

[202] See for example *C v D* [2007] EWHC 1541. See paras 2–094 *et seq.* above.

(3) A law other than the law of the arbitration agreement may govern the procedures to be adopted in an arbitration.[203] This is known as the procedural law or the curial law of the arbitration.

Law of place of enforcement.[204] It is also necessary to have regard to the laws of the place or places where recognition and enforcement will be sought in order to ensure that the resulting award complies with any mandatory requirements they might impose.   5–058

For a fuller discussion of the applicable law (or rules) in their different contexts, and how they are to be determined by the tribunal, see paras 2–087 *et seq.* above. The court's power to determine preliminary points of law is dealt with at paras 7–165 *et seq.* below.   5–059

(b) Jurisdiction[205]

Tribunal to consider jurisdiction. A tribunal should consider the existence and scope of its jurisdiction. Usually, if there are concerns about the tribunal's jurisdiction then one of the parties will raise them. Indeed, if the parties fail to raise objections to jurisdiction in a timely fashion they may lose their right to do so at a later stage.[206] Even if neither of the parties raises any objection to jurisdiction, the tribunal may still wish to consider the position. It will want to be satisfied, for example, that it is a bona fide reference. If there are specific concerns, for example about whether the particular dispute falls within the scope of the arbitration clause, the tribunal may want to satisfy itself that it has jurisdiction to proceed. Depending on the circumstances, however, it may consider it more appropriate to continue with the reference unless and until a timely objection is raised by one of the parties.[207]   5–060

Tribunal investigating its jurisdiction. Often the tribunal will have accepted its appointment before being in a position to ascertain its jurisdiction, but once it is able to do so the tribunal may decide to assess for itself whether it has jurisdiction to hear the dispute. The tribunal does so by obtaining from the parties and examining the arbitration agreement, the notice of arbitration and any other documents which are relevant to the jurisdiction issue. If the tribunal   5–061

---

[203] *James Miller & Partners v Whitworth Street Estates (Manchester) Ltd*, [1970] A.C. 583; *Union of India v McDonnell Douglas Corp* [1993] 2 Lloyd's Rep. 48 at 50. See paras 2–100 *et seq.* above.

[204] See para.2–109 above.

[205] For a fuller discussion of the tribunal's jurisdiction, arising from the scope of the arbitration agreement, see paras 2–071 *et seq.* above.

[206] See para.5–065.

[207] Given that the parties may lose their right to object, the tribunal may feel there is no harm in proceeding because jurisdiction will be conferred by the parties having proceeded with the reference: see para.2–016.

decides to investigate its jurisdiction it should inform the parties accordingly. The parties can then seek to satisfy the tribunal that it has jurisdiction to hear the dispute on the basis of the existing agreement to arbitrate. Provided the tribunal is so satisfied it should proceed with the reference. It will then be for a party who objects to the tribunal's jurisdiction to decide what steps to take and it may be that a ruling from the tribunal or the court will follow,[208] provided the objection is made in a timely fashion.[209] If on the other hand the tribunal has concerns that it in fact has no jurisdiction to determine the dispute, it can raise them with the parties so that they can be properly explored and, if necessary, the parties can agree an ad hoc submission to put the matter beyond doubt. Alternatively, if the tribunal is not satisfied that it has jurisdiction and the parties do not agree to enter into an ad hoc submission, the tribunal can rule on the issue.

5–062 **Determination by the tribunal.** The principle that the tribunal should determine its own jurisdiction is firmly enshrined in s.30 of the Act which provides that, unless the parties have agreed otherwise in writing,[210] the tribunal may rule on its own jurisdiction,[211] that is:

"(a) whether there is a valid arbitration agreement;

(b) whether the tribunal is properly constituted[212]; and

(c) what matters have been submitted to arbitration in accordance with the arbitration agreement."[213]

Accordingly, if the tribunal is not satisfied that it has jurisdiction, the parties should be informed of this and that the tribunal proposes ruling on the issue. The tribunal will usually give the parties an opportunity to make submissions on the jurisdiction issue prior to making any ruling[214] and will then proceed to make its decision on jurisdiction. This should be done in the form of an award.[215] If the tribunal declines to act on the basis of lack of jurisdiction, either the claimant can seek to pursue his case in court or he can apply to the court to challenge the

---

[208] See paras 5–064 and 7–143 *et seq.* below.

[209] See para.5–066.

[210] The requirement for any agreement between the parties to be "in writing" stems from s.5(1) of the Arbitration Act 1996, although the section gives the expression a broad meaning.

[211] On occasions the court will nonetheless effectively determine the tribunal's jurisdiction when considering an application for a stay of court proceedings pursuant to s.9 of the Arbitration Act 1996. The Court of Appeal in *Fiona Trust and Others v Yuri Privalov & Others* [2007] EWCA 20 (affirmed in *Premium Nafta Products Ltd v Fili Shipping Co Ltd* [2007] UKHL 40) has confirmed however that the presumption is that the tribunal should be left to determine its own jurisdiction first if at all possible. See further para.7–029 below.

[212] Challenges to arbitrators are dealt with at paras 4–159 *et seq.* above.

[213] The quotation is taken from s.30(1) of the Arbitration Act 1996.

[214] It may be appropriate for the parties to be heard in order to comply with the tribunal's general duty to act fairly under s.33(1) of the Arbitration Act 1996, but this will depend upon the circumstances of the particular case and the lack of jurisdiction may be so obvious that no purpose would be served by receiving submissions from the parties.

[215] So that a party who wishes to have the tribunal's decision reviewed by the court may do so under s.67 of the Arbitration Act 1996: see paras 8–054 *et seq.*

tribunal's award as to jurisdiction under s.67 of the Arbitration Act 1996.[216] It has been suggested that there may be a lacuna in the tribunal's jurisdiction in that sub-paragraph (c) quoted above might not entitle it to determine that there has been no valid reference of any matters to arbitration.[217] That would appear to be an unnecessarily restrictive interpretation of the provision and one which is unlikely to be followed.

Objection to the tribunal's jurisdiction by a party. The previous paragraphs dealt with the situation where the tribunal has concerns about jurisdiction. However, a party may dispute that the tribunal has jurisdiction over him, even if the tribunal itself considers that it does have jurisdiction and that the reference may proceed. For example, a party may maintain that he never entered into the arbitration agreement, or that he is not bound by it because it is invalid, or he may dispute that the issues which the other party is attempting to refer to arbitration fall within the scope of the arbitration agreement. Where one party claims that the arbitration agreement (as opposed to the matrix agreement) has been terminated by acceptance of a repudiatory breach of that agreement, this again requires the tribunal to address whether there is a valid subsisting arbitration agreement and is a matter of jurisdiction for the tribunal to determine.[218]   **5–063**

Courses of action available. The party contesting jurisdiction has various courses of action open to him as follows[219]:   **5–064**

- he can refuse to participate at all in the arbitration and can then, if necessary, exercise his right to challenge the award after it has been made,[220] or can resist its enforcement.[221] It is also possible for the party contesting jurisdiction to commence court proceedings to pursue a substantive cause of action and resist any application for a stay of those proceedings.[222] If the other party has commenced arbitral proceedings and applies to the court for the appointment of an arbitrator under s.18 of the Arbitration Act 1996, the party contesting jurisdiction may oppose that application.[223] Alternatively he may

---

[216] See also paras 8–054 *et seq.* for challenges under s.67 of the Arbitration Act 1996.

[217] *JT Mackley & Co Ltd v Gosport Marina Ltd* [2002] EWHC 1315 (TCC).

[218] Pursuant to Arbitration Act 1996, s.30(1)(a); see *ABB Lummus Global Ltd v Keppel Fels Ltd* [1999] 2 Lloyd's Rep. 24.

[219] *Azov Shipping Co v Baltic Shipping Co* [1999] 1 All E.R. 476.

[220] Under s.67 of the Arbitration Act 1996. The award can be challenged whether or not it deals expressly with jurisdiction: see *Vee Networks Ltd v Econet Wireless International Ltd* [2004] EWHC 2909; [2005] 1 Lloyd's Rep. 192; *LG Caltex Gas Co Ltd v China National Petroleum Corp* [2001] 1 W.L.R. 1892.

[221] For example under s.66(3) of the Arbitration Act 1996. See, for example, *Allied Vision Ltd v VPS Film Entertainment GmbH* [1991] 1 Lloyd's Rep. 392 where the defendant resisted enforcement under s.26 of the Arbitration Act 1950 which preceded s.66 of the Arbitration Act 1996.

[222] Under s.9 of the Arbitration Act 1996 or under the court's inherent jurisdiction: see paras 7–024 *et seq.*

[223] See paras 7–095 and 7–096 below.

apply to court for a declaration or injunction in relation to the tribunal's jurisdiction[224];

- he may object to the tribunal's jurisdiction under s.31 of the Arbitration Act 1996 and seek a ruling from the tribunal on the question of jurisdiction under s.30 of the Arbitration Act 1996. The tribunal's ruling may be given by way of an award on jurisdiction or as part of the tribunal's award on the merits. Assuming the tribunal decides against him, he must exhaust any arbitral process available for resolving the issue and, if that is unsuccessful, he may seek to challenge the tribunal's award on jurisdiction or seek a declaration from the court that an award on the merits is of no effect, in whole or in part, for lack of jurisdiction[225]; or

- he may seek an immediate determination from the court on the preliminary question of the tribunal's jurisdiction under s.32 of the Arbitration Act 1996.[226] He may take this course where, for example, the parties have agreed that the tribunal should not have power to rule on jurisdiction, or where the tribunal has declined to make an award on jurisdiction, but he will need either the tribunal's permission or agreement of all the parties and there are various other criteria to be met as set out in paras 7–143 *et seq.* below.

5–065 Loss of right to object. What a party contesting jurisdiction cannot do is to participate in the reference without making clear his objection to the tribunal's jurisdiction. If he does, the right to object will be lost and he cannot then seek to challenge the tribunal's jurisdiction after the award has been made, either by challenging it under s.67 of the Arbitration Act 1996[227] or by resisting its enforcement.[228]

5–066 Time for raising objections. A party who takes part in the arbitration proceedings and who objects to the tribunal's jurisdiction must raise his objection promptly. If the objection arises at the outset then it must be made not later than the point at which that party takes his first step in the proceedings[229] to contest the merits on a matter in relation to which he disputes jurisdiction.[230] Appointing or participating in the appointment of an arbitrator will not however preclude a party from objecting to jurisdiction.[231] If the basis for objection arises during the course

---

[224] Section 72 of the Arbitration Act 1996; see para.7–146. The scope of s.72 is limited and is to be read in light of the Court of Appeal's decision in *Fiona Trust and Others v Yuri Privalov & Others* [2007] EWCA 20.

[225] Under s.67 of the Arbitration Act 1996.

[226] See for example *Esso Exploration & Production UK Ltd v Electricity Supply Board* [2004] EWHC 723.

[227] See paras 8–054 *et seq.*

[228] He will have lost the right to object: s.73(1) and (2) of the Arbitration Act 1996.

[229] Seeking an extension of time within which to make submissions may amount to such a first step: *Itex Shipping Pte Ltd v China Ocean Shipping Co (The "Jing Hong Hai")* [1989] 2 Lloyd's Rep. 522.

[230] Section 31(1) of the Arbitration Act 1996.

[231] Section 31(1) of the Arbitration Act 1996.

of the proceedings, it must be raised as soon as possible thereafter.[232] In either case the tribunal may allow a late objection if it considers the delay justified.[233] Failure to make a timely objection may lead to the loss of the right to object under s.73 of the Arbitration Act 1996.[234]

Refusing to participate in the arbitration. It is always open to a 5–067
party who denies that the tribunal has jurisdiction to ignore the arbitration proceedings altogether and, if necessary,[235] either to challenge[236] or to resist enforcement of any award.[237] Section 72(2)(a) of the Arbitration Act 1996 specifically confers on a party who takes no part in the proceedings the same right to challenge an award for lack of jurisdiction as is given to a party to the reference. This is a high risk strategy, however, and there are usually very good reasons for wanting an early ruling on jurisdiction from the tribunal or the court. In particular, there is a risk that a party may be held to have taken part in the proceedings and consequently to have lost the right to object.[238] Even if this does not apply, at the enforcement stage the only question will be whether the tribunal had jurisdiction and there will be no re-opening of the merits of the case. By taking this course therefore a party will have lost the opportunity to contest the dispute on its merits. Alternatively, a party who takes no part in the reference may apply to the court for a declaration or injunction in relation to the tribunal's jurisdiction.[239] This avoids many of the problems referred to. Section 72(1) of the Arbitration Act 1996 imposes no specific time limit within which the application must be made, but it will usually make sense for all parties to have the application dealt with at an early stage.

Obtaining an award on jurisdiction. Rather than refusing to partici- 5–068
pate in the arbitration, a party may raise with the tribunal his challenge to the jurisdiction to proceed with the reference. He may ask the tribunal to receive submissions on the point and then to make an award dealing with the issue of jurisdiction.[240] He cannot compel the tribunal to give an award on jurisdiction alone,[241] but if it does so the only recourse for a party who disagrees with the ruling is to challenge the tribunal's decision under s.67 of the Arbitration Act 1996[242]; there can be no challenge of the tribunal's decision to rule on its

---

[232] Section 31(2) of the Arbitration Act 1996.
[233] Section 31(3) of the Arbitration Act 1996.
[234] See para.8–065 below.
[235] i.e. because an award has been made against him.
[236] Under s.67 of the Arbitration Act 1996. See paras 8–054 *et seq.* below.
[237] Section 66(3) of the Arbitration Act 1996. See para.8–004 below.
[238] Under s.73 of the Arbitration Act 1996. See para.8–065 below.
[239] Section 72(1) of the Arbitration Act 1996. See paras 7–146 *et seq.* below.
[240] See s.31(4)(a) of the Arbitration Act and para.6–013 below.
[241] *Exmar BV v National Iranian Tanker Co (The "Trade Fortitude")*, [1992] 1 Lloyd's Rep. 169.
[242] See generally paras 8–054 *et seq.* There can be no challenge under s.67 to a tribunal's decision to decline jurisdiction: see *LG Caltex Gas Co Ltd v China National Petroleum Corpn* [2001] EWCA Civ 788.

jurisdiction.[243] It is common for the tribunal to agree to issue an award on jurisdiction alone where so requested because, if its decision is to be challenged in the courts, that process can be commenced without delay. The tribunal will be aware of the potential delay and expense if it refuses to deal with an objection to its jurisdiction until the issue of its final award, by which time the merits of the substantive issues in the reference will have been considered in full, and its decision is that it in fact had no jurisdiction to deal with the matters in dispute. On the other hand the nature of the objection may be such that the tribunal could not properly form a view on jurisdiction until it had heard evidence on the merits of the case. In these circumstances the tribunal can exercise its power to deal with the objection to jurisdiction in its award on the merits.[244] If the tribunal adopts this course then, provided the objection to jurisdiction has been raised,[245] the objecting party will have 28 days from the date of the award on the merits to challenge the jurisdictional determination under s.67 of the Arbitration Act 1996.[246]

5–069   **Status of tribunal's determination.** Although the tribunal can and should inquire into the merits of any objection to jurisdiction, its determination on the matter is subject to challenge, whether it has been made in an award on jurisdiction or in an award on the merits.[247] The party who is challenging the tribunal's jurisdiction must therefore accept the tribunal's decision or apply promptly to the court. The court will then look at the issue afresh[248] and may confirm the award, vary it or set it aside in whole or part.[249]

5–070   **Applying to the court.**[250] Instead of seeking an award from the tribunal, a party may apply immediately to the court for a preliminary ruling on the tribunal's jurisdiction under s.32 of the Arbitration Act 1996. However, this is only available if all the parties agree or the tribunal gives its permission. If the application is made with the permission of the tribunal but not all the parties agree to the application, the applicant will have to persuade the court that there is good reason why it (rather than the tribunal) should make the determination and set out the grounds on which it is based. The applicant will also in these circumstances have

---

[243] *Kalmneft JSC v Glencore International AG* [2002] 1 All E.R. 76. That case involved an attempt to challenge the underlying decision to rule on jurisdiction under s.67 of the Arbitration Act 1996, but it is difficult to see how any other form of challenge to a decision to rule on jurisdiction would succeed either.

[244] Section 31(4)(b) of the Arbitration Act 1996.

[245] To satisfy the requirements of s.73(1) of the Arbitration Act 1996: see para.8–065 below.

[246] Under s.70(3) of the Arbitration Act 1996. See para.8–063 below. See for example *People's Insurance Co of China (Hebei Branch) v Vysanthi Shipping Co Ltd (The "Joanna V")* [2003] EWHC 1655; [2003] 2 Lloyd's Rep. 617.

[247] Under s.67 of the Arbitration Act 1996. See paras 8–054 *et seq.* below.

[248] The same applies in the context of resisting enforcement of an award on the basis of a challenge to the tribunal's jurisdiction: *Allied Vision Ltd v VPS Film Entertainment GmbH* [1991] 1 Lloyd's Rep. 392.

[249] Section 67(3) of the Arbitration Act 1996.

[250] Applications to the court to resolve questions of jurisdiction during the arbitration are dealt with more fully in paras 7–143 *et seq.* below.

to show that it is likely to produce substantial savings in costs and that the application was made without delay. An application to court may be appropriate where, for example, the parties have exercised their right to agree that the tribunal shall not have power to deal with an objection to jurisdiction.[251]

(c) Seat of the arbitration[252]

Establishing the seat of the arbitration. The tribunal will also need   5–071
to give consideration to the seat of the arbitration. Under English law an arbitration always has to have a seat,[253] even though it may not be determined until the arbitration is commenced.[254] Section 3 of the Arbitration Act 1996 provides that the seat of the arbitration means the "juridical seat" designated by the parties to the arbitration agreement or by any institution[255] or person vested with that power or by the tribunal if it is so authorised by the parties.[256] Once the seat is established, it can only be moved in accordance with the provisions of s.3.[257]

Importance of the seat. Determining the "seat" of an arbitration is   5–072
extremely important, for a number of reasons. First, it will usually (but not necessarily[258]) be where meetings or hearings will take place. What happens if the tribunal holds hearings elsewhere contrary to the express agreement of the parties? To hold the hearings in another country would render any award subject to challenge for serious irregularity, provided substantial injustice could be demonstrated.[259] To hold the arbitration in a location different from, but within the same country as, that expressly agreed between the parties will not necessarily do so.[260] In many cases, however, the parties will either be willing to vary their agreement so as to allow the hearing to be held elsewhere or, if the arbitration is subject to institutional rules, they may empower the tribunal to do so.[261]

Second, the seat of an arbitration is important because it establishes the curial law of the arbitration and may determine each of the procedural law applicable to the arbitration,[262] the law of the arbitration agreement[263] and the proper law of the

---

[251] Under s.30(1) of the Arbitration Act 1996.
[252] The seat of arbitration is dealt with more fully at paras 2–100 *et seq.* above.
[253] *Dubai Islamic Bank PJSC v Paymentech Merchant Services Inc* [2001] 1 Lloyd's Rep. 65.
[254] See para.2–102.
[255] The ICC Rules provide (Art.14.1) that in the absence of agreement between the parties the place of arbitration is fixed by the ICC Court.
[256] Many institutional rules authorise the tribunal to determine the seat in the absence of agreement between the parties: see e.g. Art.16.1 of the UNCITRAL Arbitration Rules.
[257] *Dubai Islamic Bank PJSC v Paymentech Merchant Services Inc* [2001] 1 Lloyd's Rep. 65.
[258] See para.5–073.
[259] See paras 8–072 *et seq.* below. Substantial injustice may indeed be caused if the proceedings are subject to a different procedural law as a result.
[260] *Tongyuan (USA) International Trading Group v Uni-clan Ltd*, unreported [2001] QBD (Comm).
[261] See, e.g. Art.16.2 of the LCIA Rules. This provision is not expressed to be subject to agreement otherwise by the parties.
[262] See para.2–100.
[263] See para.2–096.

substantive contract.[264] It will also determine which provisions of the Arbitration Act 1996 apply[265] and in particular what powers exist to support the arbitral process and whether the English court has jurisdiction to review any award.[266] Agreement as to the seat of an arbitration is akin to agreement to an exclusive jurisdiction clause in that it confers on the courts of the seat the exclusive right to exercise a limited supervisory jurisdiction over the arbitration.[267] Accordingly, any challenge to any interim or final award is to be made only in the courts of the place designated as the seat of the arbitration.[268]

The seat of the arbitration is also important in the context of the recognition and enforcement of any award and it is relevant in determining whether it is a "New York Convention award" to which Pt III of the Arbitration Act 1996 applies.[269] The grounds for challenging or resisting enforcement of a New York Convention award are limited and the seat of the arbitration is specifically relevant to certain of those grounds.[270] Finally, the seat must be determined because s.52(5) of the Arbitration Act 1996 requires the award to state the seat of the arbitration and s.53 confirms that, where the seat of the arbitration is in England, Wales or Northern Ireland, an award is treated as having been made there unless otherwise agreed in writing[271] by the parties.

5–073   **Place of hearings.** Although the seat is important for the reasons set out above, the tribunal may select some other place or places for the arbitration hearing or part of it to take place. They may do so for reasons of convenience, for example in connection with the taking of evidence from particular witnesses who are located somewhere other than the seat of arbitration. Subject to the general duty imposed by s.33(1) of the Arbitration Act 1996, the tribunal has a wide discretion to decide upon when and where any part of the proceedings shall take place, subject to agreement in writing between the parties.[272] The fact that hearings may take place in other locations does not of itself alter the seat of arbitration.[273]

---

[264] See paras 2–093 *et seq.*
[265] The scope of application of the 1996 Act and the way in which the seat is to be determined are dealt with in ss.2 and 3 of the Act.
[266] *Weissfisch v Julius* [2006] EWCA 218; *A v B* [2006] EWHC 2006; *C v D* [2007] EWHC 1541; *Dubai Islamic Bank PJSC v Paymentech Merchant Services Inc* [2001] 1 Lloyd's Rep. 65.
[267] *A v B* [2006] EWHC 2006.
[268] *C v D* [2007] EWHC 1541; *A v B* [2006] EWHC 2006.
[269] As defined in s.100(1) of the Arbitration Act 1996, or indeed whether it is a Washington Convention award under the Arbitration (International Investment Disputes) Act 1966 or a "foreign award" under Pt II of the Arbitration Act 1950. See further paras 8–020 *et seq.*
[270] Arbitration Act 1996, s.103(2)(b)—validity under the law of the place where it was made, s.103(2)(e)—composition of tribunal or arbitral procedure not in accordance with law of country where it took place, and s.103(2)(f)—setting aside or suspension by a competent authority of the country in which made: see paras 8–031, 8–038 and 8–040.
[271] The requirement for any agreement between the parties to be "in writing" stems from s.5(1) of the Arbitration Act 1996, although the section gives the expression a broad meaning.
[272] Section 34(2)(a) of the Arbitration Act 1996.
[273] *Dubai Islamic Bank PJSC v Paymentech Merchant Services Inc.* [2001] 1 Lloyd's Rep. 65.

(d) Interim measures

Types and purpose of interim measures. Consideration should also 5–074 be given at an early stage to whether interim measures should be ordered. The term "interim measures" is not used in the 1996 Act, but is adopted here to refer to orders or directions on such matters as security for costs, interim preservation orders and injunctions. These orders are often designed to protect the position of the parties and/or preserve the status quo pending the outcome of the arbitration.[274] However, they may also be preservation orders where the tribunal exercises its procedural powers in relation to evidential matters.[275]

From whom to seek interim measures.[276] The parties are free to 5–075 agree what powers the tribunal is to have with regard to interim measures,[277] but unless the parties have agreed otherwise in writing then the tribunal has the powers set out in s.38(3), (4) and (6) of the Arbitration Act 1996.[278] Interim measures may also be sought from the court,[279] but in the ordinary course the parties would be expected to apply to the tribunal in those cases where the tribunal has the power to make them.[280] For the court's powers in this regard see paras 7–180 *et seq.* This section deals with the position of the tribunal in relation to which the following matters should be considered[281]:

1. Availability or effectiveness of the tribunal—If the tribunal is not yet constituted,[282] or cannot act effectively, or is not immediately available to act, or the relief sought relates to third parties over whom the tribunal has no jurisdiction, then an application should be made to the court. Certain institutions offer the facility to constitute the tribunal on an expedited basis in cases of exceptional urgency[283] or provide other ways in which expedited relief can be sought.[284] If this facility is available, the applicant is then faced with a choice as to whether to seek the formation of an

---

[274] In the context of the court granting orders in support of arbitration, see Lord Mustill's categorisation into three groups described in para.7–006 below.

[275] See in particular s.38(4) and (6) of the Arbitration Act 1996.

[276] For the position in relation to interim injunctions see para.5–077 below.

[277] Section 38(1) of the Arbitration Act 1996.

[278] See paras 5–076 *et seq.*

[279] Under s.44 of the Arbitration Act 1996. See generally paras 7–179 *et seq.* below. The power to order security for costs is however reserved exclusively to the tribunal: see para.5–079 below.

[280] See s.44(5) of the Arbitration Act 1996 and para.189 of the DAC report. This ties in with the general principle of non-intervention set out in s.1(c) of the Arbitration Act 1996. See further though para.5–077 below.

[281] For enforcement of the tribunal's procedural orders see paras 5–191 *et seq.* below.

[282] See for example *Cetelem SA v Roust Holdings Ltd* [2005] EWHC 300.

[283] See Art.9 of the LCIA Rules. The application to the LCIA Court must set out "*specific grounds for exceptional urgency*". If the application is granted by the LCIA Court, even a three member tribunal can be constituted in a matter of a few days.

[284] The ICDR, affiliated to the AAA, has introduced a procedure in its International Arbitration Rules effective from May 1, 2006 whereby an application can be made to an interim, emergency arbitrator, who is appointed urgently by the ICDR solely for the purpose of considering an application for interim relief.

expedited tribunal from whom to seek the interim measure or to make an application to the court under s.44(3) of the Arbitration Act 1996, although any order made under s.44 will normally only inure until the tribunal is able to consider the matter itself.[285]

2. Breadth of relief available—Subject to the considerations set out in the previous paragraph, the applicant should consider the scope of the relief available from the court and the tribunal respectively when deciding from whom to seek the desired interim measures. The court retains a relatively broad discretion to grant interim measures.[286] The powers available to the tribunal under the Act cover security for costs, orders relating to property which is the subject matter of the proceedings and preservation of evidence.[287] These powers apply unless agreed otherwise. In addition the parties may agree to confer on the tribunal a power to make provisional awards under s.39 of the Arbitration Act 1996, including orders as to payment of money or the disposition of property.[288] If however the arbitration is being conducted pursuant to institutional or other arbitration rules,[289] the scope of relief available is likely to be governed by those rules and not by the default provisions of the Act. Institutional rules vary in the extent to which they allow tribunals to grant interim relief[290] and this may mean an application to court is needed to secure the relief sought.

3. Third parties—A tribunal does not have jurisdiction over a third party, even though that third party may hold the money, goods or property in dispute. So if an order which binds third parties is required an application should be made to the court.

4. Need for a without notice order—In some cases, a without notice order will be more effective because it is feared that the respondent will take action to frustrate the order if he is given advance notice of it, such as by paying funds out of a targeted bank account. The willingness of the court to grant without notice injunctions presents a considerable advantage to the applicant when compared with applying to the tribunal for relief;

---

[285] See *Econet Wireless Ltd v Vee Networks Ltd and Others* [2006] EWHC 1568 at [13]–[14]. In that case, an interim ex parte injunction granted under s.44 was discharged because, among other reasons, the applicant had taken no steps subsequent to the interim order to commence LCIA arbitration proceedings or otherwise to avail itself of the ability to seek expedited formation of an LCIA tribunal under Art.9(1) of the LCIA Rules in cases of exceptional urgency.

[286] See paras 7–179 *et seq.* below.

[287] Section 38 of the Arbitration Act 1996.

[288] See paras 5–085 and 6–021 below.

[289] See para.5–101 below.

[290] Contrast Art.23(1) of the ICC Rules: the tribunal may "order any interim or conservatory measure it deems appropriate", with Art.25.1(b) and (c) of the LCIA Rules which allow the tribunal to order the preservation of property which is the subject matter of the dispute and to order on a provisional basis any relief which the tribunal would have the power to grant in its award.

tribunals cannot at present grant without notice applications.[291] Even before the court however very good reason is needed to justify a hearing without notice and an interim injunction obtained without notice will be discharged if it is subsequently determined that the order should not have been given on a without notice basis.[292]

5. Effectiveness—It is sometimes the case that the interim measure is not complied with and has to be enforced. The applicant will need to weigh up the relative effectiveness of obtaining an order from the court or the tribunal if enforcement is likely to be necessary. A striking example of the potential ineffectiveness of the tribunal's orders occurred in *Kastner v Jason*[293] where the parties agreed to arbitration under Jewish law and the Beth Din ordered by consent that the respondent could not sell the property in dispute. The property was nevertheless sold in breach of the order. The claimant subsequently obtained a monetary award against the respondent but was unable to enforce against the property, notwithstanding the registration of a caution by the claimant of which the third party purchaser had constructive notice, because the Beth Din's orders gave no proprietary right against the property.[294]

Scope of tribunal's powers. As mentioned above[295] the parties may agree 5–076 on what powers the tribunal should have to grant interim measures. However, the Arbitration Act 1996 provides a default provision so that unless the parties have agreed otherwise in writing, the tribunal has the powers set out in s.38(3), (4) and (6) of the Act relating to security for costs, preservation of property and preservation of evidence. These powers are addressed in paras 5–079 *et seq.* below. Before doing so, the tribunal's power to grant interim injunctions will be considered.

Interim injunctions. Parties often seek interim measures in the form of an 5–077 interim injunction directed at the other party to the reference requiring them to do or refrain from doing something in relation to the dispute. The interim injunction continues according to its terms during the course of the reference until the award is made, when it may or may not be replaced by a final injunction.[296] On

---

[291] Following much debate revised articles of the Model Law have now been published which contemplate the tribunal making a preliminary order directing a party not to frustrate the purpose of an interim measure: see Appendix 4. At the time of publication, revision of the UNCITRAL Arbitration Rules was under discussion. Previous suggestions that the rules be amended to include a power to grant ex parte or without notice interim measures have been rejected. For details of the ongoing process see Notes of the UNCITRAL Working Group II (Arbitration), in particular draft amendments to the rules considered at the Group's 45th session, dated December 6, 2006 (*www.uncitral.org*).

[292] *Econet Wireless Ltd v Vee Networks Ltd and Others* [2006] EWHC 1568 at [12].

[293] [2004] EWCA Civ 1599; [2005] 1 Lloyd's Rep. 397 affirming decision at [2004] EWHC 592; [2004] 2 Lloyd's Rep. 233.

[294] The Model Law has been revised in an attempt to enhance the enforceability of interim measures: see Appendix 4.

[295] Paragraph 5–075.

[296] See para.6–107.

the face of it, the power to grant interim injunctions is within the wording of s.48(5)(a) of the Arbitration Act 1996 which confers on the tribunal the same powers as the court to order a party to do or refrain from doing anything. However that provision appears in the Act under the sub-heading "Award"[297] and it is doubtful that the tribunal could issue an interim injunction in the form of an award, because an award must finally dispose of the issues with which it deals[298] and many interim injunctions are not sought on the basis that they constitute a final determination of the issues in question. Rather they are intended to preserve the status quo pending the outcome of the arbitration. Accordingly, s.48(5)(a) of the Arbitration Act 1996 would not seem to confer a power to grant an interim injunction in the form of an award. The parties may however have agreed pursuant to s.39 of the Arbitration Act 1996 that the tribunal should have power to make provisional awards,[299] in which case the tribunal may issue an interim injunction in the form of a provisional award under that section.[300] Absent such agreement the question then arises whether a tribunal may instead issue a procedural order or direction rather than an award requiring a party to do or refrain from doing something. The answer would seem to be yes, provided the order or direction is within the powers conferred by s.38 of the Arbitration Act 1996 in that it relates to property which is the subject matter of the proceedings or the preservation of evidence or is a power that the parties have agreed the tribunal should have.[301]

5–078   **Practical limitations.** The limitations on the tribunal's powers described in the previous paragraphs as regards availability, third parties, without notice orders and effectiveness[302] are particularly relevant in the context of interim injunctions, because they are often required urgently at the outset of the proceedings in order to preserve the status quo. Putting those matters on one side, how useful will an interim injunction from the tribunal be in practice? Even if the tribunal has been established and exercises its power to order an injunction, the tribunal does not have the coercive powers[303] of the court to deal with any breach. A tribunal may take a very dim view of one of the parties to the reference ignoring an injunction it has granted, but there is little the tribunal can do in practice to require compliance within the urgent time frame on the basis of which most interim

---

[297] It covers ss.46 to 58 of the Arbitration Act 1996.

[298] See paras 6–078 *et seq.* above.

[299] See paras 5–085 and 6–020 *et seq.* The power to make provisional awards is often expressly set out in institutional rules: see e.g. Art.25 of the LCIA Rules and Art.23 of the ICC Rules.

[300] Assuming the tribunal has power to order a final injunction under s.48(5)(a). In *Vertex Data Science Ltd v Powergen Retail Ltd* [2006] EWHC 1340 the parties excluded the power to grant injunctions under s.48 and though they conferred power to make a provisional award under s.39 that is only available in respect of any relief the tribunal would have power to grant in a final award. Accordingly the tribunal had no power to grant injunctive relief in relation to performance of the contract.

[301] For example by the adoption of arbitration rules containing a broad power to grant interim measures such as that contained in Art.23 of the ICC Rules.

[302] See para.5–075 above.

[303] e.g. the imposition of a fine or even a term of imprisonment for contempt of court when orders are breached.

injunctions are sought.[304] It may be that ultimately a peremptory order could be made by the tribunal and enforced by the court pursuant to s.42 of the Arbitration Act 1996 but this is likely to take some time. If the interim injunction is in the form of an order,[305] it is not possible to make use of the court's coercive powers by enforcing it as an award through the courts.[306] Even if the injunction is in the form of an award, enforcement takes time. These considerations suggest that where there is no urgency, no third parties are involved and the tribunal has power to grant the required injunctive relief, a party should apply to the tribunal rather than the court. Otherwise, and particularly where a party is seeking urgent measures to preserve assets or evidence,[307] these may need to be sought from the court under s.44(2)(e) of the Arbitration Act 1996.[308]

Security for costs. Section 38(3) of the Arbitration Act 1996 enables the tribunal to order a claimant to provide security for the costs of the arbitration.[309] This was a major change from the position prior to the 1996 Act when application had to be made to court in the absence of agreement by the parties to confer this power on the tribunal. Also, the House of Lords had decided that the court had power to order security for costs even in the context of an international arbitration under institutional rules where the only connection of the parties or the dispute to England was that they had agreed, directly or indirectly, to arbitrate here.[310] That decision was widely criticised and s.38(3) reinforces that this is a matter for the tribunal, not the court. Section 38(3) also provides that the power shall not be exercised on the ground that the claimant is:

5–079

(a) an individual ordinarily resident outside the United Kingdom; or

(b) a corporation or association incorporated or formed under the law of a country outside the United Kingdom, or whose central management and control is exercised outside the United Kingdom.

---

[304] The tribunal's powers under s.41 of the Arbitration Act 1996 are cumbersome and directed to the "proper and expeditious" conduct of the reference, rather than to the sort of matters for which interim injunctive relief might be sought: see paras 5–192 *et seq.* above.

[305] Which is likely unless it has been granted as a provisional award pursuant to a power conferred under s.39 of the Arbitration Act 1996: see para.5–077 above.

[306] See para.6–003. On the other hand, the powers under ss.41 and 42 of the Arbitration Act 1996 would not apply to an award granting an interim injunction which would have to be dealt with by the normal mechanism for enforcement of an award by the court: see paras 8–002 *et seq.* For the court's powers to grant interim injunctions under s.44 of the Arbitration Act 1996, see paras 6–107 and 7–195 below.

[307] i.e. a freezing injunction or search order.

[308] See comments in the DAC report, para.201 that these powers were intentionally left to be applied by the courts. See also para.6–021 for a discussion of the availability of such relief by way of provisional award.

[309] See generally paras 190 to 198 of the DAC report. The power extends to counter-claimants by virtue of s.82(1) of the 1996 Act.

[310] *Coppee-Lavalin SA/NV v Ken-Ren Chemicals and Fertilizers Ltd (In Liquidation)* [1994] 2 All E.R. 449, HL.

Certain institutional rules also provide expressly that the tribunal has power to order security for costs.[311]

5–080 Basis of order for security. Save as mentioned the 1996 Act does not specify the basis on which security for costs should, or should not, be granted and the tribunal therefore has a broad discretion.[312] It seems likely though that in practice the tribunal will have regard to similar considerations as those applied by the court in dealing with applications under CPR Pt 25.[313] Security may be given in various forms including typically by way of bank guarantee, although it is important to ensure that the guarantee will remain in place pending the final determination of costs payable, even if that is to be done by the court pursuant to s.63(4) of the Arbitration Act 1996.[314]

5–081 Preservation of property. Section 38(4) of the Arbitration Act 1996 provides that the tribunal may give directions in relation to property[315] subject to two provisos. First, the property must be the subject-matter of the reference or property as to which a question arises in the proceedings. Secondly, the property must be owned by or be in the possession of a party to the proceedings. This reflects the tribunal's inability to enforce its orders against third parties.[316] Relief may be sought from the court if the provisos are not met or for some other reason the tribunal is unable to act or to act effectively.[317]

5–082 Types of order relating to property. Section 38(4) specifies that the tribunal may order:

(a) the inspection, photographing, preservation, custody or detention of the property by the tribunal, an expert or a party; or

(b) that samples be taken from, or any observation be made of or experiment conducted upon, the property.

5–083 Preservation of evidence. Section 38(6) of the Arbitration Act 1996 empowers the tribunal to give directions for the preservation of any evidence.

---

[311] See for example Art.25.2 of the LCIA Rules.
[312] In *Rotary Watches Ltd v Rotary Watches (USA) Inc*, [2004] W.L. 3200214 at para.6, security for costs was said to have been granted both on the basis that the respondent was impecunious and because it was outside the jurisdiction.
[313] See though the discussion at paras 364 to 369 of the DAC report.
[314] In *Rotary Watches Ltd v Rotary Watches (USA) Inc*, [2004] W.L. 3200214 the bank guarantees were due to expire before the court could conclude a detailed assessment of costs but in the circumstances the court issued a certificate for interim costs on a summary assessment.
[315] Replacing the power previously derived from s.12(1) of the Arbitration Act 1950: see *The "Vasso"* [1983] 3 All E.R. 211.
[316] See para.5–075 above.
[317] Under s.44(2) of the Arbitration Act 1996. See para.7–193 below.

Again the order can only be directed at a party to the proceedings and applies to evidence in his custody or control. There may however be relief available from the court if third parties are involved or for some other reason the tribunal is unable to act or to act effectively.[318] Any directions from the tribunal for the preservation of evidence must be made for the purposes of the particular reference to arbitration and not to preserve evidence for some other proceeding, actual or contemplated.[319]

Security for the award. In the absence of agreement between the parties **5–084** specifically conferring the power to do so, a tribunal cannot order security for the award. Some institutional rules permit the tribunal to order security for the award.[320]

It appears that even if the parties agree to confer on the tribunal power to order provisional relief under s.39 of the Arbitration Act 1996,[321] that would not be sufficient to allow the tribunal to order security for the award. This is because such an order is not "relief which [the tribunal] would have power to grant in a final award" as required by the statutory provision.

(e) Provisional relief[322]

Power to grant provisional relief. If the parties have conferred on the **5–085** tribunal the power under s.39 of the Arbitration Act 1996 to order provisional relief, consideration should be given as to whether it is appropriate to exercise that power. The power, if conferred, enables the tribunal to order on a provisional basis any relief which it can order in a final award.[323] The power is exercised by the making of a provisional award and is therefore an exception to the principle that an award must finally determine the issues with which it deals.[324] It must be emphasised, however, that the power to grant provisional relief only arises if the parties have agreed in writing[325] that the tribunal is to have it.

Types of provisional relief. Some guidance is given in s.39(2) of the **5–086** Arbitration Act 1996 as to the types of provisional relief envisaged.[326] In particular it provides that the power includes:

---

[318] Under s.44(2) of the Arbitration Act 1996. See para.7–192 below.

[319] Although there may of course be some other means of doing so, e.g. by an application to court.

[320] See, e.g. Art.25.1(a) of the LCIA Rules.

[321] See para.5–085 below.

[322] This is dealt with more fully in paras 6–020 *et seq.* below.

[323] For the relief and remedies which a tribunal can award see paras 6–096 *et seq.* below.

[324] See para.6–020 below.

[325] The requirement for any agreement between the parties to be "in writing" stems from s.5(1) of the Arbitration Act 1996, although the section gives the expression a broad meaning.

[326] Though not specifically mentioned, relief by way of interim injunction may presumably also be granted pursuant to this section: see para.6–021 below.

"(a) a provisional order for the payment of money or the disposition of property as between the parties; or

(b) an order to make an interim payment on account of the costs of the arbitration."

Section 39 would not empower an arbitrator to order a freezing injunction or search order.[327]

5–087 **When provisional relief appropriate.** The power to grant provisional relief may be very useful for example in trades and industries where cash flow is of particular importance.[328] The construction industry is one example, although the mandatory reference of disputes to adjudication under most construction contracts renders applications for provisional relief from the tribunal less frequent. Nevertheless it is still included in the standard form rules used in that industry.[329] Similarly in the shipping field it may be useful to give the tribunal power to grant interim payment of freight or to order the sale of cargo, prior to the final determination of the dispute. Provisional relief may also be appropriate where the contractual scheme agreed between the parties envisages that payment will be made in the circumstances which have transpired.[330]

5–088 **Provisional decision subject to final award.** It is clear from s.39(3) of the Arbitration Act 1996 that any provisional relief is subject to the final decision of the tribunal on the case. It must therefore be taken into account and finally determined in a subsequent award or awards of the tribunal dealing with the merits of the dispute and/or costs. Section 39 also specifically makes clear that it does not affect the power under s.47 of the 1996 Act to make more than one award.

5. ASCERTAINING THE PROCEDURE

(a) General considerations

5–089 **Freedom of the parties to choose the procedure.** Section 1(b) of the Arbitration Act 1996 sets out the general principle that party autonomy prevails subject only to "such safeguards as are necessary in the public interest". This principle reflects the fact that arbitration is consensual and, subject to certain restrictions, the parties are free to determine the procedure which is to be followed

---

[327] See para.6–021.
[328] See para.203 of the DAC report.
[329] See, e.g. r.10 of the Construction Industry Model Arbitration Rules.
[330] *BMBF (No.12) Ltd v Harland and Wolff Shipbuilding and Heavy Industries Ltd* [2001] EWCA Civ 862.

in the reference.[331] Where the law governing the procedure is English law their freedom is restricted by the mandatory provisions of the Arbitration Act 1996[332] and the public interest,[333] including principles of natural justice and fairness.[334] In the international context unfairness or other failures to comply with provisions of international conventions as to procedure may lead to the setting aside of an award or problems with recognition or enforcement.[335] Apart from such considerations, the principle of party autonomy governs the procedures to be followed.[336]

Options available to the parties. The parties may specify their own   5–090 procedure, or they may adopt a set of procedures by specifying arbitration under particular institutional or other rules.[337] They may give the tribunal a specific power to regulate the procedure as it thinks fit,[338] or they may not consider the position at all. Where the arbitration agreement is contained in a clause by which the parties agree to submit future disputes to arbitration, without specifying that any institutional rules are to apply, there will often be few, if any, specific procedural provisions set out in the arbitration agreement. The parties may nevertheless seek to agree the procedural and evidential rules to be adopted, although this will often prove more difficult after the dispute has arisen. If they are unable to do so the tribunal will control the procedure and form of the arbitration and make decisions on evidence.[339] Under English law, the parties' agreed procedure will prevail over the tribunal's wishes and it cannot waive or dispense with matters agreed between them.[340] A material departure by the tribunal from such agreed procedure may constitute a serious irregularity under s.68(2)(c) of the Arbitration Act 1996, and may result in the award being remitted, set aside or

---

[331] Section 34(1) gives an overriding right to the parties to agree the procedure, but is drafted in such a way as to give apparent prominence to the tribunal's right to decide such matters: see further para.5–034 above.

[332] Section 4(1) and Sch.1 to the Arbitration Act 1996.

[333] Section 1(b) of the Arbitration Act 1996.

[334] These are of course in any event now required in accordance with the general duty on the tribunal under s.33(1) of the Arbitration Act 1996, which is consistent with the ECHR: see para.1–038. See also paras 5–038 *et seq.* above.

[335] See Redfern & Hunter, (4th edn, 2004), para.6–01.

[336] Sections 34(1) and 38(1) of the Arbitration Act 1996. See also the comments of Lord Mustill in *Coppee-Lavalin SA/NV v Ken-Ren Chemicals and Fertilizers Ltd (In Liquidation)* [1994] 2 All E.R. 449 at 458, HL. This principle is also enshrined in the Model Law, Art.19(1) of which states: "Subject to the provisions of this Law, the parties are free to agree on the procedure to be followed by the tribunal in conducting the proceedings." In *Sinclair v Woods of Winchester Ltd* [2005] EWHC 1631; 102 Con. L.R. 127, the court rejected as "plainly wrong and almost grotesquely unfair to the arbitrator" the submission that he should have disregarded the agreement reached between counsel that a particular report should not be referred to by him.

[337] See para.5–101 below.

[338] *Amalgamated Metal Corp Ltd v Khoon Seng Co* [1977] 2 Lloyd's Rep. 310 at 317.

[339] Section 34(1) of the Arbitration Act 1996.

[340] Section 34(1) of the Arbitration Act 1996. See also *Amalgamated Metal Corp Ltd v Khoon Seng Co* [1977] 2 Lloyd's Rep. 310. The position is less clear with regard to a procedure agreed by the parties after the arbitrator has been appointed and to which he has some fundamental objection. Presumably the arbitrator can resign if for good reason he objects to what the parties have agreed subsequent to his appointment. See the discussion at para.5–067 above.

declared to be of no effect.[341] If however the digression from the parties' agreed procedure was insignificant it would not be a serious irregularity because it would not cause substantial injustice.[342]

5-091 **Institutional rules.** Where the arbitration agreement specifies that the arbitration is to be conducted in accordance with particular institutional rules, the tribunal's power to regulate the procedure will be limited by those rules. So, for example, Art.15 of the ICC Rules provides:

> "The proceedings before the Arbitral Tribunal shall be governed by these Rules, and, where these Rules are silent, by any rules which the parties or, failing them, the Arbitral Tribunal may settle on . . . "

5-092 **Limiting scope for agreement.** Similarly, having chosen to conduct the arbitration in accordance with institutional rules, the parties may to some extent limit their ability thereafter to regulate the procedure by agreement. For example, under r.6 of the 2006 ICE Arbitration Procedure the tribunal may require the parties to submit short statements on the disputes or differences and may summon the parties for a preliminary meeting for the purpose of giving directions.[343] No doubt the tribunal would pay heed to any agreement between the parties on these matters, but it is not bound to adopt the parties' views as to the need for a preliminary meeting or for such statements on the disputes or differences, even if the parties are agreed as between themselves. On the other hand it is common for many provisions of institutional rules to allow the parties to agree the point in question, or to be expressly subject to the parties agreeing otherwise.[344]

5-093 **Which version of rules to apply.** Institutional rules are modified from time to time and the question of which set of rules is applicable to the arbitration may then arise. The institution's rules may themselves deal with the question of which version is to apply.[345] Further, parties sometimes provide expressly in their contract either for the institution's rules in force at the time of making the contract to apply to any subsequent dispute or for the rules in force at the time the arbitration is commenced to apply. The former approach should be treated with caution because later versions of the rules are generally introduced to make

---

[341] See also *London Export Corp Ltd v Jubilee Coffee Roasting Co Ltd* [1958] 1 W.L.R. 271; *Amalgamated Metal Corp Ltd v Khoon Seng Co* [1977] 2 Lloyd's Rep. 310, HL. For a fuller discussion of serious irregularity see paras 8–072 *et seq.* below.

[342] See para.8–072.

[343] The latest (2006) version of the ICE Arbitration Procedure includes at r.6.3 a provision that the parties may agree the directions to be given and submit them to the tribunal for approval, which approval must not be unreasonably withheld.

[344] See, for example, the ICC Rules and the LCIA Rules, both of which contain many provisions which are subject to the parties' agreement otherwise.

[345] The introduction to the LCIA Rules for example makes clear the parties agree that the arbitration shall be conducted in accordance with the following rules "or such amended rules as the LCIA may have adopted hereafter to take effect before the commencement of the arbitration."

improvements or reflect changes in relevant laws. It may be that arbitration under the earlier rules is not appropriate or feasible in light of such developments. In the absence of express provision, the courts will interpret a reference to institutional rules as a reference to the rules in force at the time of commencement of the arbitration.[346]

The arbitrator as master of his own procedure. The above   5–094
comments with regard to party autonomy contemplate that the parties are in agreement as to the procedure to be adopted. However all too often they are not, particularly after a dispute has arisen. In these circumstances, the tribunal will decide on the procedure to be adopted, subject to the general duty set out in s.33(1) of the Arbitration Act 1996.[347] An arbitrator must act judicially,[348] but is "master of his own procedure"[349] and the court will not interfere with the exercise of his discretionary powers for dealing with procedural and evidentiary matters during the course of the reference unless his conduct is so extreme as to warrant his removal.[350]

The range of procedures available.[351] One of the advantages of   5–095
arbitration is its flexibility with regard to the procedures that may be adopted. Whereas courts tend to be bound by relatively rigid procedures, arbitrations are capable of being tailored to the needs of the parties and the particular dispute. That said, it does in practice usually require both a firm tribunal and a degree of co-operation from both sides for the real benefits of arbitration's flexibility (i.e. savings in time and costs) to materialise. A tribunal will rightly tend to err on the side of being fair rather than on the side of being robust in its conduct of the arbitration. This is in part because it will be concerned to comply with its duty under s.33 of the Arbitration Act 1996[352] and also because it will want to do all it can to ensure that the resulting award is enforceable.

The extremes. The parties may prefer a quick and cheap resolution of their   5–096
dispute to a slow, expensive solution, and may be prepared, up to a point, to bear any consequent cutting-down of the opportunities to put their case across. At one

---

[346] *China Agribusiness Development Corp v Balli Trading* [1998] 2 Lloyd's Rep. 76.
[347] See also *Anangel Peace Compania Naviera SA v Bacchus International Commerce Corp ("The Anangel Peace")* [1981] 1 Lloyd's Rep. 452.
[348] *Henry Sotheran Ltd v Norwich Union Life Insurance Society* [1992] 31 E.G. 70.
[349] See *Bremer Vulkan Schiffbau und Maschinenfabrik v South India Shipping Corp* [1981] A.C. 909. See also, by way of example, *Carlisle Place Investments v Wimpey Construction UK Ltd* [1980] 15 B.L.R. 1109 and *Three Valleys Water Committee v Binnie & Partners* 52 Build. L.R. 42.
[350] Pursuant to s.24(1)(d) of the Arbitration Act 1996: see further paras 7–111 *et seq.* See also *Bremer Vulkan Schiffbau und Maschinenfabrik v South India Shipping Corp* [1981] 1 All E.R. 289; [1981] A.C. 909; *K/S A/S Bill Biakh v Hyundai Corp* [1988] 1 Lloyd's Rep. 187; *Three Valleys Water Committee v Binnie & Partners* 52 B.L.R. 42. There may of course be a remedy in relation to the resulting award if the tribunal has behaved in a way that constitutes serious irregularity under s.68 of the Arbitration Act 1996: see paras 8–072 *et seq.* below.
[351] See also para.1–022 above.
[352] See para.5–032 above.

extreme the procedure in an arbitration may be very similar to that applicable to proceedings in court, with full oral hearings, strict adherence to rules of evidence, pleadings, extensive disclosure of documents, and factual and expert witnesses. At the other extreme, it may be agreed that the tribunal should decide the dispute on the basis of a limited range of documents, with no hearings,[353] pleadings or submissions (oral or written). Between these extremes procedures may be modified or mixed as desired and of course the tribunal must always bear in mind its overriding duty under s.33(1) of the Arbitration Act 1996.[354]

5–097　**Procedure tailored for the case.** In practice, unless the parties make their particular wishes clear, there has in the past been a tendency for the procedures adopted to be those with which the tribunal and the parties' representatives are most familiar, or a combination of such procedures. This can lead to arbitrations being conducted in such a way as to effectively mirror court proceedings. Such a tendency is perhaps less common in light of the duty imposed by s.33(1) of the Arbitration Act 1996 which requires the tribunal to consider in each case how the procedure can be tailored to ensure a fair resolution of the case without unnecessary delay or expense. There does seem to have been a shift to more streamlined procedures in many cases, particularly with regard to the disclosure of documents and the length of hearings. One way to approach this is for the tribunal to consider in turn each of the matters set out in s.34(2) of the 1996 Act, together with any other relevant issues about which procedural directions might be sought.[355] This will assist in forming a view as to what provisions are really necessary in the context of the particular reference and how they can most effectively be implemented.

5–098　**Adversarial procedure.** In English courts an adversarial procedure is adopted whereby each party puts forward its case and the judge's role is essentially to determine which party's case he considers should succeed. A similar adversarial procedure has traditionally been adopted in English arbitrations, although the tribunal may be more disposed to intervene in the course of the hearing, for example to put questions to witnesses, and of course it must be careful to ensure that it gives the parties an opportunity to deal with any issue upon which it intends to base its findings.[356]

5–099　**Inquisitorial procedure.** The inquisitorial approach is generally adopted in the courts of civil law countries. The judge's role is to investigate the merits of the case and reach a conclusion, the parties and their representatives assisting him in this process. Under this approach the judge is more inclined to initiate and pursue with the parties his own ideas and theories about the case, rather than relying on

[353] See para.5–196 below.
[354] See para.5–032 above.
[355] See para.5–117 below.
[356] See para.5–050 above.

the parties to put forward their own. Arbitrations in England are rarely conducted under the inquisitorial approach in its true sense, save to an extent in the context of quality arbitrations.[357] However this is now one of the matters for the tribunal to consider under s.34(2) of the Arbitration Act 1996. Subsection (g) specifically refers to "whether and to what extent the tribunal should itself take the initiative in ascertaining the facts and the law". It may be appropriate to adopt this procedure where, for example, the tribunal or one or more of the parties is from a civil law background or where the arbitrator has been appointed because of his expert knowledge and the parties wish him to investigate the dispute himself.[358] In any event it is always subject to the overriding duty in s.33(1) of the Arbitration Act 1996.[359]

Nature of the dispute. The degree of formality adopted in the arbitration   5–100
will also be influenced by the nature of the dispute. Thus there is no requirement for formal pleadings, extensive disclosure of documents and so on, in an arbitration conducted by a tribunal which is experienced in the trade in question but which has chosen to proceed with a high degree of informality.[360] Nevertheless there is a requirement for natural justice and fairness taking into account all the circumstances, including the informality of the proceedings.[361] Again, however, the guiding principle is the duty laid down in s.33(1) of the Arbitration Act 1996.[362]

Institutional arbitration and arbitration rules. Various institutions   5–101
promulgate rules for use in arbitrations which set out, in varying degrees of detail, the procedure to be adopted in an arbitration conducted under those rules. These institutions include both commercial associations (such as GAFTA and FOSFA) and institutions whose very existence is designed to facilitate arbitration (such as the Chartered Institute of Arbitrators and, in the international context, the ICC and LCIA).[363] A reference in the arbitration clause to such rules of arbitration constitutes an agreement in writing for the purposes of s.5 of the Arbitration Act

---

[357] See para.5–110 below.
[358] In *Checkpoint Ltd v Strathclyde Pension Fund* [2003] L. & T.R. 22 the agreed procedure contemplated that the arbitrator might use inquisitorial powers but he would inform the parties of his findings and ask them to comment on them. The court found that the arbitrator in that case had not in fact used inquisitorial powers but had simply applied his own knowledge.
[359] In *Norbrook Laboratories Ltd v Tank* [2006] EWHC 1055 it was held to be a breach of s.33 for the arbitrator to contact potential witnesses in the absence of both parties and without producing any record of the witnesses' remarks. As to s.33 see generally para.5–032 above.
[360] *Krohn & Co (Import-Export GmbH & Co KG) v PT Tulung Agung Indah* [1992] 1 Lloyd's Rep. 377.
[361] *Krohn & Co (Import-Export GmbH & Co KG) v PT Tulung Agung Indah* [1992] 1 Lloyd's Rep. 377.
[362] See para.5–032 above.
[363] See paras 3–051 *et seq* and 5–171 *et seq*.

1996 and may therefore be an agreement between the parties for the purposes of the non-mandatory provisions of the 1996 Act.[364]

5–102 **Advantages of institutional arbitration.** The institution concerned may perform a number of different roles in connection with arbitration proceedings.[365] However, its principal function will usually be to deal with the administration of the reference in accordance with its rules.[366] The main advantages of having the arbitration administered by an institution in this way are that:

- it provides a procedural framework for the case;

- it may be able to provide specialist services or arbitrators with particular expertise;

- it may serve to relieve the parties and the tribunal of some of the administrative burden of conducting the reference;

- the institution can deal with challenges to and replacement of arbitrators without the need to involve the courts.

5–103 **Disadvantages of institutional arbitration.** The main disadvantage of institutional arbitration is that it may add to the expense of arbitration, because the institution concerned will have to be paid for its efforts. It may also delay the proceedings.[367]

5–104 **Arbitration rules where no institution.** Not all arbitration rules involve administration of the reference by an institution. The UNCITRAL Arbitration Rules, for example, are specifically designed for use in "ad hoc" arbitrations and, despite the name, arbitrations under the LMAA Terms are also "ad hoc".[368]

5–105 **Rules providing procedural framework.** Whether administered or not, arbitration under the different rules is intended to provide a procedural

---

[364] See s.4(3) of the Arbitration Act 1996. The phrases "unless otherwise agreed by the parties" and "the parties are free to agree" are the two formulae adopted in numerous sections of the Act to signify that either the parties may opt for certain provisions to apply or that the parties' agreement prevails over the default provisions in the statute. The question arises as to how specific the provisions in the institutional rules must be in order to constitute an agreement between the parties for these purposes. If the rules make express provision there is no problem but if, for example, the tribunal is conferred with a general power to decide or order something and that general power could encompass an alternative approach from that in the 1996 Act, will it be an "agreement otherwise"? It seems unlikely unless there is some indication that the alternative approach was specifically envisaged.

[365] See paras 2–061 and 3–052 above for the various roles played by institutions in arbitration.

[366] See para.5–171 below.

[367] See, for example, the comments of Lord Mustill in *Coppee-Lavalin SA/NV v Ken-Ren Chemicals and Fertilizers Ltd (In Liquidation)* [1994] 2 All E.R. 449 at 459, HL.

[368] See para.2–006 above for the meaning of "ad hoc".

framework for the conduct of the reference. The rules do not provide an exhaustive code designed to cover all points that might arise in the course of the arbitration, but rather set out the powers, duties and obligations of the tribunal and the parties so that they know what can and cannot be done, and by whom, in determining the procedure to be adopted in the particular reference. Similar guidance is given by the Arbitration Act 1996, but the arbitration rules will normally provide a more complete code than the framework provided by the Act, for example by specifying time limits for the service of written submissions and appointment of the tribunal. They will often also constitute an agreement between the parties for the purposes of many of the non-mandatory provisions of the 1996 Act.[369]

Terms of reference. A tribunal will sometimes draw up terms of reference 5–106
for the arbitration. In the context of arbitration under institutional rules these are relatively commonplace[370] and are for example required by the ICC Rules which set out those matters to be included.[371] Even in the absence of a requirement for terms of reference the Tribunal may choose to draw up a document which sets out the terms of its appointment, the scope of its jurisdiction, the agreed remuneration of the tribunal and similar matters, and seek the parties' agreement to it. Terms of reference agreed between the tribunal and the parties may amend or supplement the terms of the parties' arbitration agreement and may be a specific source of the tribunal's powers.[372] The terms of reference will normally be a separate document from the tribunal's procedural order or directions setting out specific steps to be taken by the parties in the conduct of the hearing.[373]

Speedy arbitration. Certain arbitration institutions have introduced proce- 5–107
dures which the parties may elect to follow and which are designed to improve the speed, cost and efficiency of the arbitration process.

The ICC has introduced a "Pre-Arbitral Referee" procedure under which an independent referee may order provisional or conservatory measures before the tribunal embarks on the reference. This Pre-Arbitral Referee procedure was introduced in 1990 but is still rarely encountered in practice. The conclusion to be drawn from this is not necessarily that the parties do not want such a procedure, but perhaps rather that it is not very well known and is not therefore being addressed at the contract drafting stage. Once a dispute has arisen it may be difficult to secure agreement of the parties to it. Any decision rendered by the Pre-Arbitral Referee is not an award capable of enforcement and this may also in part explain the apparent reluctance to adopt the procedure.

---

[369] See para.5–101 above.
[370] The ICC Rules are perhaps the best known international arbitration rules that provide for terms of reference, but so do others such as the rules of the Belgian arbitration institution CEPANI. Other sets of rules, such as those of the LCIA, have no such requirement.
[371] Article 18 of the ICC Rules.
[372] *Lesotho Highlands Development Authority v Impreglio SpA* [2005] UKHL 43; [2006] 1 A.C. 221, *per* Lord Steyn at [21].
[373] See para.5–111 below.

The LMAA has a Small Claims Procedure suggested for claims up to US$ 50,000.[374] It is designed for relatively straightforward disputes, but a problem has been parties submitting complex matters for which the procedure is not really suitable.[375] Similarly, GAFTA has a Simple Dispute Arbitration Rule No.126 for dealing with small and straightforward claims.

The parties may also make provision in their arbitration agreement for a speedy arbitration, for example by imposing specific time limits for particular steps or for the making of the tribunal's award.[376]

5–108   **Documents only arbitrations.** It is customary in some fields of arbitration for disputes to be determined on the basis of documents submitted to the tribunal but without any oral hearing or cross examination of witnesses.[377] Whether to adopt this type of procedure is a matter to be considered by the tribunal under s.34(2)(h) of the Arbitration Act 1996.[378] In such "documents only" or "paper" arbitrations, as they are sometimes called, there would normally be written submissions and documentary evidence produced by each party on the basis of which the tribunal would reach its decision, but no oral evidence or oral submissions. The written submissions may simply take the form of a letter to the tribunal from the party or his representative, or may be a more formal document produced by lawyers.

5–109   **Need for vigilance.** It is particularly important in documents only arbitrations for the tribunal to be alive to the danger of introducing into its award matters which are not actually in issue between the parties on the basis of their written submissions.[379] Without the benefit of an oral hearing to clarify what exactly is in dispute, the tribunal may be more at risk of referring to matters in its award which the parties have not had an opportunity to address, giving rise to the risk of serious irregularity under s.68(2)(a).[380] If the tribunal is in any doubt it should seek written clarification from the parties as to the issues between them prior to making the award.

5–110   **Quality or look-sniff arbitrations.** A particular type of arbitration procedure which has traditionally stood alone is that adopted in quality or "look-

---

[374] This is the total amount claimed in the arbitration by either party excluding interest and costs. A claim may therefore be commenced under the Small Claims Procedure but become no longer applicable in the event of a counterclaim which exceeds that sum: *Bernuth Lines Ltd v High Seas Shipping Ltd* [2006] 1 All E.R. (Comm) 359.

[375] See the commentary on the LMAA Small Claims Procedure (2006) at *www.lmaa.org.uk*.

[376] Care needs to be taken that the procedure is workable, but for example it is relatively common to find a provision in the arbitration agreement that the tribunal will make its final award within a certain period of time following its appointment.

[377] Dispensing with an oral hearing is common, for example, in shipping cases.

[378] For guidance on when an oral hearing would be appropriate, see the comments, *obiter*, of Tomlinson J. in *Boulos Gad Tourism & Hotels Ltd v Uniground Shipping Co Ltd* [2001] W.L. 1676909. Many arbitration rules give the parties a right to insist upon an oral hearing on the merits of the case: see for example Art.19.1 of the LCIA Rules.

[379] *Pacol Ltd v Joint Stock Co Rossakhar* [1999] 2 All E.R. 778.

[380] See paras 5–049 *et seq.* and para.8–080.

sniff" arbitrations. These generally concern disputes relating to commodity sales where the issue to be resolved is the quality of the commodity in question. The established practice in such cases is for an expert arbitrator in the field to examine the commodity concerned (or samples of it) and to give the parties his decision on its quality based on that inspection. There are no formal hearings or submissions by the parties. Such a procedure can be very useful in this type of case as it provides a quick and straightforward solution to a particular kind of problem that commonly arises. However, even in the commodity field the number of cases decided in this way is very small indeed[381] and the procedure is perhaps more appropriately conducted by way of expert determination rather than arbitration.[382]

(b) Directions from the tribunal in the course of the reference

Directions generally. During the course of a reference the tribunal will often wish to communicate to the parties that certain procedural steps are to be taken and to set out the timetable for doing so. These are often recorded in a formal document known as an "Order for Directions" or "Procedural Order". Whatever the document is called its purpose will be to provide a record for both the parties and the tribunal of the procedural steps which it has ordered or directed shall be taken. Such an order may record the tribunal's jurisdiction to deal with the dispute, but it will not itself confer substantive jurisdiction upon the tribunal.[383] In most arbitrations directions will be given on several occasions as the case progresses, and the later directions may amend those previously given. 5–111

Who should give directions. Generally the full tribunal will give procedural directions in the course of the reference. In the absence of agreement otherwise by the parties, decisions and orders have to be made by all the members of the tribunal or (if unanimity cannot be reached) a majority of them.[384] However, it is common in practice, particularly in international arbitrations where the arbitrators may be located in different countries, for procedural decisions to be delegated to one or more members of the tribunal, usually the chairman.[385] This has the advantage of facilitating speedy decisions and avoiding the cost and inconvenience of consulting all members of the tribunal. 5–112

Fixing time and method for compliance. The tribunal may, and usually will, fix the time for compliance with its procedural directions. This may 5–113

---

[381] Even GAFTA nowadays has virtually no arbitrations conducted in this way.
[382] For the distinction between arbitration and expert determination see para.2–028 above.
[383] *Persaud v Beynon* [2005] EWHC 3073. Where however the procedural order sets out the tribunal's jurisdiction and the arbitration proceeds without objection being taken to the scope of the jurisdiction so described, the right to object may be lost under s.73 of the Arbitration Act 1996.
[384] Sections 20(3), 21(4) and 22(2) of the Arbitration Act 1996.
[385] See for example Art.14.3 of the LCIA Rules.

specify not just the date but also the time by which despatch or receipt is required. The tribunal may also extend a time limit, whether or not it has expired.[386] It is also common for directions to specify how steps are to be taken, for example permitting service of submissions and evidence by email with hard copies to follow by post or courier.

5–114 **The preliminary meeting.** There will often be a preliminary meeting held between the tribunal and the parties at a relatively early stage of the reference.[387] There is no legal requirement for a preliminary meeting,[388] but it is often useful in giving the participants an opportunity to meet and obtain directions from the tribunal for the future conduct of the reference. The need for a meeting will depend upon the extent to which the procedure and any directions to be sought from the tribunal can be agreed between the parties. The costs involved may also be an important consideration, particularly if the arbitration involves parties and their representatives from different jurisdictions. It is becoming relatively commonplace in these circumstances for the preliminary meeting to take the form of a video-conference or a telephone conference call rather than a meeting in person.

5–115 **Timing of preliminary meeting.** In practice the tribunal, and indeed the parties, will want to understand at least in broad terms the likely issues in the case before anything more than procedural directions for the provision of initial submissions by the parties are made. The tribunal may also wish to consider certain substantive issues at the preliminary meeting, such as questions of jurisdiction or applicable law, and it will need an understanding of the case in order to do so. The preliminary meeting therefore often takes place only after each party has served a written document setting out its case which the tribunal has had an opportunity to consider.[389]

5–116 **Agreeing directions in advance.** The parties should try to identify in advance of the preliminary meeting the matters needing to be dealt with and, if possible, to agree on the procedure and any directions to be sought from the tribunal. Section 34(1) of the Arbitration Act 1996 specifically recognises the right of the parties to agree any procedural or evidential matter. If agreement can be reached this will save time and costs at the preliminary meeting itself and may even render a meeting unnecessary. Endeavouring to agree matters will also, particularly in the international context, help to identify any differing expectations

---

[386] Section 34(3) of the Arbitration Act 1996. For the reckoning of periods of time see s.78 of the Arbitration Act 1996.

[387] An exception is shipping cases, where such meetings are generally unknown: see "Procedural reform in maritime arbitration" by Bruce Harris [1995] A.D.R.L.J. 18.

[388] Certain institutional rules contemplate a preliminary directions hearing: see, e.g. Art.18 of the ICC Rules which contemplates terms of reference being drawn up "on the basis of documents or in the presence of the parties".

[389] See para.5–120 below.

between the parties of the way in which the reference should be conducted from a procedural point of view. The parties may of course have reached agreement on some matters by incorporating procedural rules into the arbitration agreement[390] which cover the position. Any agreement reached between the parties should then be put before the tribunal so that it has an opportunity to express its views on the feasibility and appropriateness of the agreed approach.

Matters about which directions may be required. Section 34(2) of 5–117
the Arbitration Act 1996 may be treated as a non-exhaustive list of procedural and evidential matters for the tribunal to consider, subject to their having been agreed by the parties. However, the range of matters which might need to be addressed is very wide indeed. Consideration should be given to whether the matters set out in para.5–118 below should be dealt with at the preliminary meeting (or, if no preliminary meeting is to be held, whether they are in any event matters on which an award or procedural directions[391] should be sought from the tribunal).[392] It will be a rare case indeed when all the issues will need to be considered and the tribunal should hesitate before dealing with matters upon which no direction is really necessary as this may add to the scope for dispute between the parties and cause delay. Further, even if there has been a preliminary meeting at which certain matters were not dealt with, it is open to the tribunal to give directions at some later stage during the course of the reference.

A checklist. By way of a checklist, the following matters may require con- 5–118
sideration:

- Any terms in the arbitration agreement as to how and by whom the reference is to be conducted;

- The law or rules to be applied to the merits of the dispute and, if a foreign law is to apply, how it is to be presented[393];

- Any mandatory laws of the seat of the arbitration or other place where hearings or meetings are to be held, insofar as they might affect the conduct of the reference or the award;

- Any mandatory laws of the place where enforcement of an award will be sought, insofar as they might affect the conduct of the reference or the award;

- The tribunal's jurisdiction;

---

[390] For example the rules of an arbitration institution: see para.5–101 above.
[391] See para.6–002 below for the distinction between an award and procedural directions.
[392] See the UNCITRAL Notes on Organising Arbitral Proceedings whose stated purpose is "to assist arbitration practitioners by listing and briefly describing questions on which appropriately timed decisions on organising arbitral proceedings may be useful".
[393] This second aspect is dealt with at para.5–209.

- The procedural or evidential rules incorporated into the arbitration agreement or which the parties or the tribunal otherwise wish to adopt;

- Whether (and if so what) interim measures are appropriate;

- Whether provisional relief can and should be granted;

- How the issues are to be defined;

- Whether there should be a determination of particular issues before others;

- What documents (if any) to be provided;

- Whether (and if so how) the evidence of witnesses of fact is to be adduced;

- Whether (and if so how) expert evidence is to be adduced by the parties;

- Whether the tribunal wishes to appoint any expert(s), legal adviser or assessor;

- Administration of the reference;

- Arrangements for the hearing(s);

- The place or places at which hearings are to be conducted;

- Language(s) to be used in the reference;

- Fees and deposits;

- Any other issues arising, e.g. confidentiality restrictions, arrangements specific to multiparty or consolidated arbitrations, etc.

A number of these topics have been dealt with above.[394] The remaining topics are addressed in the following paragraphs.

(c) Terms of the arbitration agreement

5–119   **Consideration of special terms.** The arbitration agreement may contain specific requirements as to qualifications that the members of the tribunal are required to possess[395] or as to how the reference is to be conducted. For example, it might provide that the tribunal is to act as "amiable compositeur".[396] The tribunal should consider any such terms at an early stage, and preferably prior to accepting appointment, to establish whether it can comply with them. If it cannot

---

[394] Namely the law or rules to be applied to the merits of the dispute (paras 5–057 and 2–090 *et seq.*), mandatory laws of the seat (paras 2–100 *et seq.* and 5–071) or place of enforcement (paras 2–109 and 5–058), the tribunal's jurisdiction (paras 5–060 *et seq.* and 2–071 *et seq.*), the place at which hearings or meetings are to be conducted and any mandatory laws applicable there (paras 2–107 and 5–073), the adoption of procedural rules (paras 5–101 *et seq.*), interim measures (paras 5–074 *et seq.*), provisional relief (paras 5–085 *et seq.*) and fees and deposits (paras 4–052 *et seq.*).

[395] See para.4–017

[396] See paras 4–141 and 4–142 above.

or is unwilling to do so, it may seek some form of variation of the arbitration agreement or waiver from the parties or otherwise decline the appointment.[397]

(d) Defining the issues

How the issues are to be defined. The issues in a reference are the matters in dispute between the parties, which are often described only in the most general terms in the notice of arbitration. The nature, scope and number of the issues in a particular reference may have a considerable influence upon the procedure to be adopted and the choice of a suitable tribunal to determine the dispute, and it is obviously desirable for the tribunal and the parties to have a clear idea of the issues at an early stage.[398] The tribunal will need to know the precise matters which it is required to determine, and possibly in what order, so that its award is directed only at those issues,[399] and determines all of them.[400] Early definition of the issues avoids wasting time and costs on matters which are not in dispute, and focusing on the real issues between the parties may also encourage settlement.[401] Failure by the tribunal to ensure that the issues are properly defined may be a breach of its duty under s.33 of the Arbitration Act 1996.[402]

5–120

Choice of methods. Under s.34(2)(c) of the Arbitration Act 1996 the tribunal should consider[403] "whether any and if so what form of written statements of claim and defence are to be used [and] when these should be supplied". The tribunal's choice will depend upon factors such as the type and complexity of the dispute and the qualifications and experience of the tribunal. If there are complex issues of law it may assist to have the issues defined by methods similar to pleadings in court proceedings. If the dispute is a technical matter before a tribunal with technical expertise and there is effectively only one factual issue (for example a quality assessment of a particular commodity), there may be no need for any written statements of claim or defence at all. There are no hard and fast rules as to the form or nomenclature to be adopted, but the following paragraphs

5–121

---

[397] Resignation would be a last resort—see para.5–056.

[398] See for example *Newfield Construction Ltd v Tomlinson* [2004] EWHC 3051; 97 Con. L.R. 148 where the tribunal made an award of costs on the basis of a misunderstanding of the dispute between the parties as set out in the pleadings.

[399] If the award purports to determine matters not in dispute between the parties it may be vulnerable to challenge: *Pacol Ltd v Joint Stock Co Rossakhar* [1999] 2 All E.R. 778.

[400] A tribunal will not be criticised for failing to determine an issue which was never part of the reference: see *Vee Networks Ltd v Econet Wireless International Ltd* [2004] EWHC 2909; [2005] 1 Lloyd's Rep. 192 where it was held that an objection to substantive jurisdiction could not be made under s.67 of the Arbitration Act 1996 in circumstances where the issue in question had never been raised before the tribunal.

[401] The ICC Rules require preparation of terms of reference which include both a summary of the parties' respective claims and relief sought and, unless the tribunal considers it inappropriate, a list of the issues to be determined: Art.18 of the ICC Rules and para.5–106 above.

[402] As in *RC Pillar & Sons v Edwards* [2002] C.I.L.L. 1799. The facts in that case were described as "extreme" in *Sinclair v Woods of Winchester Ltd* [2005] EWHC 1631; 102 Con. L.R. 127 at [21].

[403] Unless there is agreement of the parties on the matter.

address the use of court style pleadings and also the less formal statement of case procedure.

Whichever method is adopted, the parties' written submissions may assist in defining the issues in the case but will not usually determine the scope of the reference, which is contained in the notice of arbitration.[404] However, where particular issues are addressed in both parties' written submissions without either side (or the tribunal) taking exception to them, that would normally be sufficient to confer jurisdiction to deal with them, albeit that the scope of the reference may thereby be enlarged.[405]

5–122   **Pleadings.** Pleadings are formal documents in which the parties set out their respective cases.[406] The claimant usually serves Points of Claim setting out the facts and matters upon which he relies. The respondent then responds by serving Points of Defence addressing the allegations made in the Points of Claim. Points of Reply may be served by the claimant, and there may occasionally be further pleadings in response.[407] If allegations in the pleadings of either party are inadequately set out, further details may be sought. The use of pleadings will enable each party to see the nature of the case made against them and to identify the material facts upon which that case is based. Matters of evidence and legal argument do not usually appear in English pleadings, but in practice it is not uncommon in arbitrations to encounter them in documents purporting to be formal pleadings.

5–123   **Statement of case procedure.** Alternatively the arbitration may proceed by service of a statement of case, followed by a statement of defence or some other document setting out the response. These documents are generally less formal than traditional pleadings and, at least in international cases, are becoming the norm. Typically they will set out the relevant facts, refer to evidence (relevant documents are often annexed) and develop arguments, including arguments on the law.[408] Statements of case are often less structured than formal pleadings, and

---

[404] *London Borough of Lewisham v Shephard Hill Civil Engineering Ltd*, 2001, unreported, July 30, 2001, QBD (TCC), [2001] W.L. 825511. See para.5–025 above.

[405] *Ward Bros Plant Hire Ltd v Banlaw (Europe) Ltd*, unreported, November 19, 1999, QBD (TCC). This would also follow from the fact that any right to object to the enlarged jurisdiction is lost if no objection is taken under s.73 of the Arbitration Act 1996.

[406] The term "pleadings" is often used to describe any form of document which sets out a party's case, but in order to draw out the distinctions between different types of documents it is used here in the sense of formal pleadings similar to those found in court litigation.

[407] Although it is not specifically addressed in s.34(2) of the Arbitration Act 1996, the position is presumably the same as under the old law where the question of whether to allow service of a Reply and further pleadings was a matter for the discretion of the tribunal, as was the question whether their service should be allowed out of time: *Three Valleys Water Committee v Binnie & Partners* 52 B.L.R. 42.

[408] Statements of case will sometimes be accompanied by a full set of the documents relied upon and that party's factual and expert witness evidence. In such circumstances they will be akin to memorials: see para.5–125 below. The advantage of this approach is that it can save considerable time by requiring service of evidence simultaneously rather than fixing a series of dates for the different evidential stages. It does however raise logistical issues with regard to coordinating the submission of evidence which may be inter-dependent. Alternatively the tribunal may order the exchange of documents and witness evidence in sequential steps.

consequently they may be less clear and concise. A pleading in response to another pleading generally deals with each allegation in turn, setting out the case made in response on each particular point. However if in response to the claimant's statement of case the respondent produces a document directed more towards "telling the story" than addressing the matters raised by the other party's case, the precise issues in dispute may be more difficult to ascertain, and it may not be very easy to sort out the relevant from the irrelevant. Accordingly, some care is required when adopting the statement of case procedure, in order to structure the analysis and define the issues with clarity. If necessary the tribunal can require the parties to seek to distil a list of issues in a separate document from the statements of the parties' cases. In view of the duties imposed on the tribunal under s.33 of the Arbitration Act 1996,[409] there are strong arguments in favour of the statement of case procedure, for example where the issues are straightforward or where the tribunal is experienced and less formal submissions provide all the "help" it needs.[410] Where one or more of the parties are represented by lawyers who are unfamiliar with formal English pleadings, the statement of case procedure will usually be adopted.

Form of statement of case procedure. At its most informal a state- 5–124
ment of case may consist simply of short letters from each of the parties. More usually it will consist of written submissions, prepared either by the parties or their legal advisers. At its most formal it may be similar to enlarged pleadings, or to the "briefs" used in litigation in the United States of America.

Memorials. The document that sets out a party's case is sometimes referred 5–125
to as a "memorial".[411] A memorial is a form of statement of case. It will usually be accompanied by all the evidence relied on by the serving party, including relevant documents, factual witness statements and expert reports. Like a statement of case, a memorial will often contain submissions on the evidence and the law.

Other informal methods. The issues may be defined orally, or may be 5–126
ascertained from documents, without the need for written clarification or definition. This might be appropriate if the issues are very clear and straightforward, or are well known to the particular tribunal concerned. Whichever method is used, the tribunal must be able to identify and isolate the matters which are in dispute and which it is required to determine.

Amendments. Under s.34(2)(c) of the Arbitration Act 1996 the tribunal is to 5–127
consider[412] the extent to which amendments may be made to the parties' written

---

[409] See para.5–032 above.
[410] See Bruce Harris, "Procedural Reform in Maritime Arbitration" [1995] A.D.R.L.J. 18.
[411] See for example r.31 of the ICSID Arbitration Rules.
[412] Subject to any agreement of the parties on the matter.

submissions.[413] The parties may apply to amend their written submissions at any time in the course of the reference. Amendment of submissions is more restricted in the arbitration context than in court proceedings, however, in that it is subject to the further constraint that the proposed amendment cannot, without agreement from both parties[414] and the tribunal, extend the issues beyond the scope of what has been submitted to arbitration in that reference.[415] In other words, the tribunal's jurisdiction is defined by the issues that have been referred to arbitration, and that jurisdiction cannot be enlarged by subsequent amendment of the parties' written submissions without the agreement[416] of both parties, and the tribunal. Conversely, the scope of the issues that fall within the reference to arbitration is not narrowed by the parties' written submissions so as to preclude subsequent amendments which fall within the reference to arbitration.[417] An amendment may be refused because the claim sought to be introduced is subject to a limitation period which is different from that which applies to the original claim.[418]

5–128 Agreed statement of facts. It may also help to define the issues and to save time and costs if the parties produce an agreed statement of facts. The tribunal can then proceed with the reference on the basis of those agreed facts without requiring the parties to prove them. The tribunal cannot, without notice to the parties, simply choose to ignore them for the purposes of its award.[419] It is, however, open to the tribunal, in its discretion, to release the parties from their agreement if, for example, the statement of facts proves ambiguous or unworkable or gives rise to unforeseen consequences. This is provided of course that the tribunal gives the parties an opportunity to be heard on the point and, if they decide not to follow the agreed statement of facts, they give the parties an opportunity to present their cases fully.[420]

5–129 Determination of preliminary issues.[421] One or both of the parties may suggest, or it may be apparent from the parties' written submissions, that

---

[413] Again this highlights the point that the submissions themselves do not usually determine the scope of the reference. See *Excomm Ltd v Guan Shipping (Pte) Ltd (The "Golden Bear")* [1987] 1 Lloyd's Rep. 330 where the respondents alleged that the claimants had abandoned a claim by not including it in the Points of Claim. The court noted that the tribunal had a discretion to allow the claim to be restored by amendment. See also paras 5–025 and 5–121 above.

[414] Their agreement may arise from the adoption of institutional arbitration rules: see for example Art.19 of the ICC rules.

[415] *Leif Hoegh & Co A/S v Petrolsea Inc (The "World Era")* [1992] 1 Lloyd's Rep. 45.

[416] Which need not be in writing.

[417] *Ulysses Compania Naviera SA v Huntingdon Petroleum Services Ltd and others (The "Ermoupolis")* [1990] 1 Lloyd's Rep. 160, *Persaud v Beynon* [2005] EWHC 3073; see though *Three Valleys Water Committee v Binnie & Partners* 52 B.L.R. 42, where the pleading was the submission to arbitration.

[418] *Mosvolds Rederi AS v Food Corp of India, The "Arras"* [1989] 1 Lloyd's Rep. 131.

[419] *Techno Ltd v Allied Dunbar Assurance Plc* [1993] 22 E.G. 109.

[420] *Techno Ltd v Allied Dunbar Assurance Plc* [1993] 22 E.G. 109.

[421] See generally paras 6–009 *et seq.* below.

determination of a particular issue or issues at an early stage would be appropriate.[422] This might arise where the determination will save time or costs or both in relation to the future conduct of the reference, or where the determination is likely to be decisive of the whole or a significant part of the dispute. Thus it may be expedient to make an award on jurisdiction at an early stage, or to deal with issues of liability before those relating to quantum, or to deal with a number of principal issues or claims which the parties believe will assist them in resolving the remaining matters in dispute between them.

(e) Evidence

Application of the rules of evidence.[423] There was some doubt under the old law as to whether the tribunal was, or indeed should be, under a duty to apply the rules of evidence.[424] Section 34(2)(f) of the Arbitration Act 1996 now makes clear that one of the matters for the tribunal to consider[425] is "whether to apply strict rules of evidence (or any other rules) as to the admissibility, relevance or weight of any material (oral, written or other) sought to be tendered on any matters of fact or opinion, and the time, manner and form in which such material should be exchanged and presented".[426]   5–130

Disclosure of documents in court proceedings. Disclosure is the process by which a party to civil proceedings in court obtains documents from another party in advance of the hearing.[427] In English court proceedings there is generally "standard disclosure" by the parties to the action which requires them to produce the documents on which they rely, documents which adversely affect their own case or another party's case, documents which support another party's case and any documents required to be disclosed by a relevant Practice Direction.[428] A party may also apply to the court at any time for an order for specific disclosure or specific inspection of particular documents or classes of documents.[429] Disclosure is given by listing the documents.[430] Each party is also entitled to look at the documents in the other party's list and this part of the disclosure process is known as "inspection". Certain classes of document can be   5–131

---

[422] The tribunal has power to make awards on different issues under s.47 of the Arbitration Act 1996: see para.6–009 below.

[423] See also para.1–012 above.

[424] See, for example, Mustill & Boyd *Commercial Arbitration* (2nd edn, 1989) at p.352, cf. Lord Steyn (1994) 10 Arbitration Int. 1.

[425] Subject to any agreement of the parties on the matter. In particular, the parties may have agreed to adopt a set of evidential rules, such as the IBA Rules on the Taking of Evidence in International Commercial Arbitration available at *www.ibanet.org*.

[426] This is discussed in more detail in para.4–078 above.

[427] See generally Hollander, *Documentary Evidence* (9th edn, 2006); CPR Pt 31. See also Steyn J. in *Sunderland Steamship P and I Association v Gatoil International Inc (The "Lorenzo Halcoussi")* [1988] 1 Lloyd's Rep. 180 at 184.

[428] CPR Pt 31, r.6. See CPR Pt 31 generally for the rules on disclosure of documents in court litigation.

[429] CPR Pt 31, r.12.

[430] CPR Pt 31, r.10.

withheld from inspection.[431] Such documents nonetheless have to be listed, and described in terms which enable a challenge to be made in respect of any claim for withholding the document from inspection.

5–132 **Failings of the disclosure process.** The disclosure process has been criticised as being expensive and time-consuming.[432] There are also very real doubts as to how effective it is in eliciting evidence of real probative value. In any event it is a widely held view that the sometimes huge expense of dealing with the disclosure process in court litigation is out of all proportion to the benefit gained in terms of useful and important evidence. The trend, even in court proceedings, is now very much towards seeking to control the scope of disclosure in order to implement proper case management in accordance with the CPR.[433]

5–133 **Disclosure of documents in arbitration.** Under s.34(2)(c) of the Arbitration Act 1996 the tribunal is to consider[434] "whether any and if so which documents or classes of documents should be disclosed between and produced by the parties and at what stage".[435] The use of the word "any" makes it clear that there does not in fact have to be any disclosure at all. The tribunal's discretion can, however, be restricted or excluded by agreement between the parties,[436] and in an appropriate case the tribunal may encourage the parties to adopt a more international disclosure standard.[437]

5–134 **Scope of document disclosure.** In certain cases the scope of disclosure may be similar to that given in court litigation but in many, if not most, cases it will be both more limited and more focussed. Indeed it may be open to the tribunal to dispense with disclosure of documents altogether, provided that is not inconsistent with the duties imposed on the tribunal under s.33 of the Arbitration Act 1996. Although the tribunal can order disclosure of any documents within the possession or power of the parties, it can only do so if this is necessary for the purpose of

---

[431] CPR Pt 31, r.19.
[432] Although the current regime is an improvement on the previous procedure under RSC Ord.24 which has been replaced by CPR Pt 31.
[433] CPR Pt 31.
[434] Subject to any agreement of the parties on the matter.
[435] Disclosure of documents is a matter for the tribunal, not the court: *NB Three Shipping Ltd v Harebell Shipping Ltd* [2004] EWHC 2001. However if the application is urgent the court may exercise its power to preserve evidence or assets under s.44 of the Arbitration Act 1996: see *National Insurance & Guarantee Corp Ltd v M Young Legal Services Ltd* [2004] EWHC 2972. See also para.7–192 below.
[436] Section 34(1) of the Arbitration Act 1996 and para.5–136.
[437] See for example the IBA Rules on the Taking of Evidence in International Commercial Arbitration available at *www.ibanet.org*.

determining the dispute before it in the particular reference.[438] It will rarely be appropriate to adopt wholesale CPR disclosure.

Questions of privilege. Under the Arbitration Act 1950 the obligation to produce documents was "subject to any legal objection",[439] so that, for example, parties could object to the production of documents over which privilege could be asserted.[440] There is no similar provision in the Arbitration Act 1996.[441] However questions of privilege frequently arise in arbitration and fall to be determined by the tribunal, subject to agreement of the parties, pursuant to s.34(2)(d). Interesting conceptual issues arise in cases involving parties from different jurisdictions where the approach to questions of privilege may be radically different. What law should a tribunal apply in these circumstances? Should it be the law of the seat of the arbitration? Or that of the jurisdiction where the document was created? In practice a combination of wishing to preserve the privilege of a party who under the rules of his own jurisdiction had a legitimate expectation of it, and not wishing to treat the parties differently, means that in most cases both parties will be able to claim privilege in accordance with whichever applicable rules are most restrictive about the requirement to disclose.

5–135

Arbitration practice. Although the tribunal has power to order wide-ranging disclosure, it should consider restricting disclosure to those documents which are "relevant and material"[442] to the issues. Frequently the parties will agree to produce voluntarily the documents upon which they each wish to rely and the tribunal is then only asked to determine what further documents they should be compelled to disclose. Arbitrators are generally more amenable than the court to limiting the scope of disclosure and are reluctant to entertain extensive disclosure requests for documents of peripheral relevance. The provisions of the 1996 Act encourage this trend. The tribunal will usually dispense with a costly and time-consuming listing exercise and the production of large numbers of documents which are of no real interest or value but which would be required if standard

5–136

---

[438] *Kirkawa Corp v Gatoil Overseas Ltd (The "Peter Kirk")* [1990] 1 Lloyd's Rep. 154. This was a case under the old law but a tribunal that sought to order disclosure of wholly irrelevant documents would be in breach of its obligations under s.33(1)(b) of the Arbitration Act 1996: see para.5–032.

[439] Section 12(1) of the Arbitration Act 1950.

[440] i.e. documents which fall within one of the recognised categories of documents protected from production under the relevant applicable law. As a matter of English law these categories include confidential communications with a lawyer for the purpose of giving or receiving legal advice and communications generally which come into existence for the sole or dominant purpose of advice or evidence in pending or prospective litigation. Documents may also be privileged if they incriminate the party concerned. See generally Hollander, *Documentary Evidence* (9th edn, 2006) and in relation to without prejudice documents para.5–140 below.

[441] Where the IBA Rules on the Taking of Evidence in International Commercial Arbitration have been adopted r.9(2)(b) will apply which specifically recognises "legal impediment or privilege under the legal or ethical rules determined by the Tribunal to be applicable" as a reason for excluding documents.

[442] This is the test used in the IBA Rules on the Taking of Evidence in International Commercial Arbitration. It provides a good yardstick for tribunals generally.

disclosure along the lines of that available in court proceedings were to be given. In shipping cases, for example, a party may seek voluntary disclosure of certain documents or may seek an order from the tribunal for their production, but formal disclosure procedures involving lists of documents and inspection are unusual. On the other hand, limited document disclosure has not historically been a prominent feature of construction arbitrations although this has begun to change, presumably as a result of the duties imposed on arbitrators under s.33 of the Arbitration Act.[443] If the listing of documents is dispensed with, the parties may simply make the documents available for inspection or deliver copies of the documents to each other. Another useful mechanism is adoption of what is known as a Redfern Schedule.[444] Again there are no hard and fast rules, and both the appropriate level of disclosure and the approach to be adopted will depend on the particular circumstances of the case.

5-137 **Disclosure from third parties.** A tribunal has no power to require disclosure from a third party. If documents held by a third party are required it will be necessary to make an application to court, either pursuant to s.43 or s.44 of the Arbitration Act 1996.[445]

5-138 **Timing.** Section 34(2)(c) of the Arbitration Act 1996 makes clear that it is for the tribunal to determine[446] at what stage disclosure of documents is to be given. This means that the tribunal may order disclosure of documents or classes of documents at any stage in the course of the reference and whether or not it has made a previous order for disclosure.

5-139 **Use of documents obtained in an arbitration.** There is an implied obligation on a party obtaining documents in an arbitration not to disclose or use them for any purpose other than the dispute in which they were obtained.[447] This duty of confidence extends to "any documents prepared for and used in the arbitration, or disclosed or produced in the course of the arbitration, or transcripts or notes of the evidence in the arbitration or the award".[448] It is qualified, however,

---

[443] See para.5–032 above.
[444] Named after Alan Redfern, author of "Law and Practice of International Commercial Arbitration" by Redfern, Hunter and Blackaby (4th edn, Sweet & Maxwell, 2004), it is a schedule containing four columns, the first of which describes the documents of which disclosure is sought, the second sets out the disclosing party's objections to producing them, the third gives the responses of the party seeking disclosure to the objections raised and the fourth column is for the tribunal's ruling. Each column is completed as the request for disclosure proceeds. The advantage of this type of schedule is that it collates the information in relation to each document or category of document into a convenient summary for both the parties and the tribunal.
[445] See paras 7–192 and 7–204.
[446] Subject to any agreement of the parties on the matter.
[447] *Dolling-Baker v Merrett and Others* [1991] 2 All E.R. 891 at 899, CA; *Hassneh Insurance Co of Israel and Others v Stuart J Mew* [1993] 2 Lloyd's Rep. 243. A similar but express obligation applies to documents disclosed in court litigation subject to certain exceptions including where the document has been read to or by the court: CPR Pt 31, r.22.
[448] *per* Parker L.J. in *Dolling-Baker v Merrett and Others* [1991] 2 All E.R. 891, CA.

in relation to the award itself (and perhaps other documents) and may be displaced by consent or by order or permission of the court.[449]

"Without prejudice" communications. Communications between the   5–140
parties or their representatives which are made for the purpose of reaching a settlement of the dispute and on a "without prejudice" basis cannot be admitted in evidence in litigation.[450] In the arbitration context similar considerations apply as in relation to privileged documents generally.[451] Arbitrators tend to apply to all parties whichever of the potentially applicable laws confers most protection on such communications, so as not to frustrate legitimate expectations of the author of the document that it will not need to be produced.

Questions. Section 34(2)(e) of the Arbitration Act 1996 provides for the   5–141
tribunal to decide[452] "whether any and if so what questions should be put to and answered by the respective parties and when and in what form this should be done". This gives the tribunal scope, amongst other things, to order a party to answer written questions on oath in a similar way to the procedure of seeking further information in court.[453]

Evidence of witnesses of fact. The parties to an arbitration will often   5–142
wish to rely on the evidence of witnesses of fact.[454] If they do, it is usual for such evidence to be given in the form of written witness statements which are exchanged[455] prior to the hearing of the arbitration.[456] If the evidence is disputed the witnesses then appear at the hearing for cross-examination, although it is clear from s.34(2)(e) of the Arbitration Act 1996[457] that it is for the tribunal to decide[458] if, when and how questions are to be put to the witnesses. Indeed this provision gives the tribunal considerable scope as to how the evidence of witnesses of fact is to be given and this may for example include witness conferencing.[459] Hearsay evidence may be given even if strict rules of evidence apply.[460]

---

[449] See further paras 5–184 *et seq.* below.
[450] For the policy behind this rule see *Rush and Tompkins Ltd v Greater London Council* [1989] A.C. 1280.
[451] See para.5–135 above.
[452] Subject to any agreement of the parties on the matter.
[453] Pursuant to CPR Pt 18. In court proceedings a party is required to endorse the answers with a statement of truth: CPR Pt 22, r.1.
[454] See paras 7–202 *et seq.* below for the powers of the court to secure the attendance of witnesses in arbitration proceedings.
[455] It is of course possible for the tribunal to order sequential service of witness statements but mutual exchange between the parties is more common.
[456] The court has followed this practice: see CPR Pt 32, r.4.
[457] See para.5–141 above.
[458] Subject to any agreement of the parties on the matter.
[459] See para.5–212 below.
[460] Civil Evidence Act 1995, ss.1 and 11. Notice must be given to the other parties of the intention to rely on hearsay evidence: see s.2 of the 1995 Act. As to strict rules of evidence applying, see para.5–130 above.

5–143   Advantages of written witness statements. The main advantages of written witness statements are as follows. First, they save time and costs at the hearing by largely replacing the witnesses' evidence in chief.[461] Second, written witness statements should reduce the likelihood of fresh issues emerging during the giving of evidence at the hearing which require further investigation and, possibly, an adjournment. Where there has been a direction from the tribunal for exchange of written statements, a party should not normally be allowed to raise entirely new points with the witness by way of examination in chief at the hearing, unless there is some compelling reason why they could not have been dealt with in the written exchange. Third, by requiring the parties to set out their factual witness evidence in advance of the hearing it forces them to focus on the strengths and weaknesses of their case, as well as that of the other side, which may in turn promote a settlement of the dispute.

5–144   Disadvantages of written witness statements. There are, however, disadvantages to having written witness statements. In particular there is a danger that the witness statements will have been prepared by lawyers and may not fully reflect the evidence of the witness, or at least might not reflect the way that witness would himself express his evidence.[462] There may also be concerns that a tribunal will tend to concentrate on what occurs during the hearing and, if it has not properly read and digested the witness statements beforehand, it might not get a balanced picture when the case is begun by launching into cross-examination of the claimants' witnesses.

5–145   Direction to be obtained. If the evidence is to be given in written witness statements then a direction should be obtained from the tribunal providing for the exchange of the statements. The exchange should be fixed for a specific date or for a date which is capable of being precisely determined by reference to other events in the arbitration, for example a certain number of days after disclosure or before the hearing. The directions may also provide for the exchange of witness statements in reply prior to the hearing.

5–146   Number of factual witnesses. It would be unusual specifically to limit the number of factual (as opposed to expert) witnesses, although this may be appropriate in certain circumstances, for example to minimise costs and to avoid repetition of evidence by several witnesses. Again the overriding duties imposed on the tribunal under s.33 of the Arbitration Act 1996 come into play.[463] The

---

[461] See para.5–210 below. Evidence in chief is referred to as "direct examination" in some jurisdictions.

[462] This may become apparent in the course of the hearing when the witness is cross-examined or responds to questions from the tribunal.

[463] See para.5–032 above.

tribunal would have to balance any such restriction against the parties' right to be given a reasonable opportunity to present their respective cases.[464]

Examination on oath. The tribunal has a discretion as to whether any party 5–147 or witness is to be examined on oath or affirmation and has power to administer the oath or affirmation itself.[465] This is subject to agreement otherwise by the parties.[466] It happens less and less that witnesses in arbitrations in England are sworn, save for example where allegations of dishonesty arise.[467] Instead the tribunal will often require the witness to confirm the truth of the testimony to be given. Arbitration rules sometimes contain provision as to the confirmation to be given by a witness.[468]

Compelling attendance of witnesses. A tribunal does not have the 5–148 power to require the attendance of a witness who refuses to attend and give evidence, although if that witness is within the control of one of the parties, the tribunal may in appropriate circumstances be justified in drawing an adverse inference from his failure to do so. A party may, however, use the available court procedures, such as the issuing of witness summonses, to require the attendance of witnesses before the tribunal or to secure that their evidence is available for use at the arbitration hearing.[469] There are, however, limits on the court's ability to compel attendance, notably that agreement of the tribunal or the other parties is required, and the witness summons procedure can only be used in relation to witnesses within the United Kingdom.[470]

Expert evidence called by the parties.[471] The parties may wish to 5–149 adduce expert opinion evidence to support their respective cases in the arbitration and, if so, they should obtain an appropriate direction from the tribunal. The direction should cover the form in which the experts' evidence is to be given, and in many cases it will also specify the maximum number of experts on whose evidence the parties may rely and, in broad terms at least, the nature of the evidence to be given. So, for example, it may provide that each party may adduce evidence from one expert in relation to the particular technical issues raised by the case and from one expert in relation to the computation of the alleged loss. Specifying these matters in the direction will avoid a multiplicity of experts from

---

[464] See further paras 5–042 *et seq.* above.
[465] Section 38(5) of the Arbitration Act 1996.
[466] Section 38(2) of the Arbitration Act 1996.
[467] See para.5–164 below in relation to the giving of false evidence.
[468] See for example ICSID r.35.
[469] Section 43 of the Arbitration Act 1996 and Arbitration Practice Direction, para.7.1; see also paras 7–202 *et seq.* and 7–191 below.
[470] Section 43(2) and (3) of the Arbitration Act 1996. See para.7–203 below. The court also has power to assist in the taking of evidence from witnesses outside the jurisdiction but this is rarely invoked: see para.7–191.
[471] Matters of foreign law, which are occasionally dealt with by way of expert evidence, are addressed in para.5–209.

a party on the same issue. It will also help prevent a situation where each party adduces expert evidence on different aspects of the case and there are delays whilst they then seek to address the case put forward by the other.

5–150　**Tribunal-appointed expert(s).** The tribunal has power under s.37 of the Arbitration Act 1996 to appoint experts, legal advisers[472] or technical assessors and may allow them to attend the hearing.[473] Their fees and expenses fall to be included as expenses of the arbitrators and can therefore form part of the tribunal's award on costs.[474] The parties need not be consulted on the instructions to the tribunal-appointed expert[475] but it will usually be useful to do so in order to ensure all areas where the expert's views need to be sought are covered. The legal advice sought by the tribunal may relate to procedural as well as to substantive matters to be determined.[476] The expert or legal adviser is to report to the tribunal and to the parties whereas an assessor simply assists the tribunal on technical matters[477] but in each case the parties must be given an opportunity to comment on "any information, opinion or advice offered by any such person".[478] The tribunal should not meet the expert to discuss his evidence without the parties being present unless they consent to this.[479] The tribunal must also of course reach its own decision and cannot delegate this to the expert, legal adviser or technical assessor.[480]

5–151　**Provision of reports.** Expert evidence is almost invariably given in the form of a written report which is produced[481] prior to the hearing and the author of the report is required to attend the hearing so that he may be questioned on it by the parties and the tribunal. As with factual witnesses, the direction should specify a date on which the reports are to be produced or the date should be capable of being precisely determined by reference to other events in the arbitration.

5–152　**Meetings of experts.** It is not uncommon for a direction to be given that the parties' experts are to meet following exchange of their reports so as to discuss the issues and identify those on which they can agree, thereby narrowing those to be

---

[472] Including those who can advise on foreign law, as in *Hussman (Europe) Ltd v Al Ameen Development & Trade Co* [2000] 2 Lloyd's Rep. 83.
[473] Unless otherwise agreed by the parties: see s.37(1) of the Arbitration Act 1996.
[474] Section 37(2) of the Arbitration Act 1996 and see paras 6–158 and 6–159 below.
[475] *Hussman (Europe) Ltd v Al Ameen Development & Trade Co.* [2000] 2 Lloyd's Rep. 83.
[476] See for example *Home of Homes Ltd v Hammersmith and Fulham LBC* [2003] EWHC 807; 92 Const. L.R. 48 at [41] where the tribunal took leading counsel's opinion in relation to both jurisdictional issues and the exercise of its power to limit recoverable costs under s.65 of the Arbitration Act 1996.
[477] This follows from the wording of s.37(1)(a)(i) as contrasted with s.37(1)(a)(ii).
[478] Section 37(1) of the Arbitration Act 1996.
[479] *Hussman (Europe) Ltd v Al Ameen Development & Trade Co* [2000] 2 Lloyd's Rep. 83
[480] See para.6–074 below.
[481] The parties usually simultaneously exchange the reports of their respective experts.

pursued at the hearing.[482] The experts may be required to produce a minute of the meeting or a schedule of agreed points, or there may be provision for supplemental reports following the initial exchange and/or meeting.

Tribunal meeting with experts. Tribunals have occasionally sought to preside over meetings of the experts in the absence of the parties and their legal representatives.[483] This should be avoided as it may give rise to doubts about the fairness of the procedure.[484]

5–153

Giving false evidence. Where it becomes apparent that a witness is not telling the truth, his evidence will be discredited. The tribunal will take the fact of his having given false evidence into account when considering the weight, if any, that can be attributed to his testimony as a whole. On a more formal level, it is perjury for a person lawfully sworn as a witness or interpreter in an arbitration to make a statement, material in the proceedings, which he knows to be false or does not believe to be true.[485] The requirement that he be lawfully sworn means that unless the witness is examined on oath or affirmation he cannot subsequently be prosecuted for perjury. As modern practice is not generally for witnesses to be examined on oath in arbitration[486] such prosecutions are very rare indeed.

5–154

Criminal liability. It is a criminal offence to interfere with the course of justice by manufacturing false evidence intended to deceive and mislead a tribunal, even if the evidence is never actually used.[487]

5–155

Directions in relation to property and evidence. The tribunal may also need to consider at the preliminary meeting (if it has not already done so) the exercise of any powers it may have under ss.38(4) and (6) of the Arbitration Act 1996 to give directions in relation to property and evidence. These may include directions for the inspection, photographing, preservation, custody or detention of property or for the taking of samples. This is dealt with in the section on interim measures at paras 5–074 *et seq.* above.[488]

5–156

---

[482] In practice such meetings may not produce much of substance because, despite their independence, all too often the parties' respective experts are briefed to concede as little as possible at this preliminary stage. A "without prejudice" meeting between the experts to discuss the issues followed by an open document recording matters of agreement may be more productive.

[483] See, e.g. *How Engineering Services Ltd v Lindner Ceilings Floors Partitions Plc* [1999] 2 All E.R. 374.

[484] Which could lead to a challenge for serious irregularity under s.68(2)(a) for failure to comply with the duty imposed by s.33(1)(b) of the Arbitration Act 1996: see paras 5–032 and 8–072. In *How Engineering Services Ltd v Lindner Ceilings Floors Partitions Plc* [1999] 2 All E.R. 374 a meeting between the tribunal and the expert in the absence of the parties and their legal advisers was held not to be unfair, but the case highlights the potential difficulties.

[485] Section 1(1) and (2) of the Perjury Act 1911.

[486] See para.5–157.

[487] *R. v Vreones* [1891] 1 Q.B. 360.

[488] See, in particular paras 5–081 and 5–083.

(f) Language(s) of the reference

5–157 Selection of language(s) to be used. The language or languages to be used in the proceedings and whether translations of any relevant documents are to be supplied is one of the matters for the tribunal to consider under s.34(2)(b) of the Arbitration Act 1996. This is subject to the right of the parties to agree on the language to be used. The language used in the reference will not necessarily be the language of the place of arbitration or that of the underlying substantive contract.

5–158 Importance of choosing the language(s). The choice of language may be an important consideration both from a practical point of view and in the context of ensuring procedural fairness and equality. The tribunal may, for example, be faced with parties of different nationalities, perhaps with agreements expressed in both their languages, and may be reluctant to favour one party's language over that of another. In some international arbitrations the parties and the individual members of the tribunal may not have the same mother tongue, yet it is important that the tribunal can communicate effectively in the language of the arbitration. In such cases an early decision on the language or languages to be used in the arbitration is vital if it has not already been agreed between the parties. Provision may need to be made for translations of documents or for translators to assist in the giving of witness evidence. Translation issues may influence the choice of language to be used[489] and should also be considered at an early stage.

5–159 Agreement of the parties. As stated above, the parties are free to agree the language(s) to be used, and an agreed language is specifically included in many arbitration agreements. Indeed if the choice of language is likely to be troublesome in the event of a dispute arising, it is usually better to deal with it at the stage of contract negotiation. Most institutional arbitration rules are to the same effect as English law, namely that if the parties do not agree upon the language to be used it will fall to the tribunal to decide.[490]

5–160 Determination by the tribunal. If the choice of a language falls to the tribunal to decide, it may be a difficult issue to determine.[491] It must of course

---

[489] For example because the majority of the documents to be used as evidence in the reference are in a particular language.

[490] Section 34(1) and (2)(b) of the Arbitration Act 1996 and see Art.17.3 of the LCIA Rules, Art.16 of the ICC Rules and Art.17.1 of the UNCITRAL Rules. This is also the position under the Model Law, Art.22(1) which provides that "The parties are free to agree on the language or languages to be used in the arbitral proceedings. Failing such agreement, the arbitral tribunal shall determine the language or languages to be used in the proceedings . . . "

[491] In ICC arbitrations the tribunal is given some guidance by Art.16 of the ICC Rules, which provides that the tribunal shall determine the language or languages of the arbitration "due regard being given to all relevant circumstances, including the language of the contract."

comply with the overriding duty imposed by s.33 of the Arbitration Act 1996.[492] The tribunal will also have to ensure that it is capable of dealing properly with the arbitration in the chosen language (if necessary with the assistance of translators), and that it calls for proper translations of documents which it does not properly understand.[493] In practice the tribunal is likely to resolve the issue by looking to the language of the parties' contract and any subsequent communications to determine the language(s) of the arbitration, and if necessary providing for oral testimony to be given in the mother tongue of the witness, subject to the provision of a proper translation of that evidence.

(g) Administrative matters

Administration during the reference. If the arbitration is being conducted under the auspices of an arbitral institution, it is common for that institution to be involved in the administration of the reference.[494] For example, it will commonly arrange service on the other party and the tribunal of the notice of arbitration and any written submissions, and may act as a conduit for communications between the tribunal and the parties. This latter approach can, however, be very inefficient, for example in the context of trying to fix dates and venue for a preliminary meeting or corresponding on procedural issues, and it is in practice often replaced by direct communications, with the institution simply being kept informed of what has been agreed.   **5–161**

Tribunal or parties to carry out administration. In an ad hoc arbitration,[495] the tribunal as a whole or the chairman may carry out the necessary administration during the reference, but often it is left to the parties or their advisers to co-ordinate this. It would not be appropriate to leave the administration to one party or their adviser unless the other party agrees, but agreement may be forthcoming where for example greater resources are available to one of the parties to achieve an orderly administration of the reference, or where it is very much easier for one party to deal with administration because of physical location.   **5–162**

Secretary to the tribunal. The tribunal may appoint a secretary to assist with administration of the reference, particularly in very large cases. Prior agreement of the parties to the appointment should be obtained, particularly if it is intended that the parties should meet the cost of the secretary's services. There has been some controversy over the role of the secretary and whether it is   **5–163**

---

[492] See para.5–032 above.
[493] *E Rotheray & Sons Ltd v Carlo Bedarida & Co* [1961] 1 Lloyd's Rep. 220. See also Art.17.4 of the LCIA Rules and Art.17.2 of the UNCITRAL Rules. The position under English law is also reflected in Art.22(2) of the Model Law which states that the tribunal "may order that any documentary evidence shall be accompanied by a translation into the language or languages agreed upon by the parties or determined by the arbitral tribunal".
[494] See para.2–061.
[495] See para.2–006.

acceptable for this to extend to assisting the tribunal by producing a draft of the award or some sections of it.[496] If either party has any concerns in this regard it should raise them when the proposal to appoint a secretary is first aired by the tribunal so that the precise role can be clarified and agreed.

5–164 **Fixing the date of the hearing.** If an oral hearing is to take place[497] the time and venue should be arranged far enough in advance to allow the parties adequate time for preparation. Although it may be possible to fix a date at the stage of appointment of the tribunal, it is frequently more appropriate to wait until the issues have been defined by the exchange of written submissions[498] and a clearer assessment is possible of the issues in dispute, the likely length of the hearing and also the length of time required for preparation.[499] Accordingly the main oral hearing date will often be set at the preliminary hearing, if there is one, or otherwise at the stage when directions are given by the tribunal setting out the procedural timetable for the conduct of the reference.

5–165 **Tribunal's obligation to be available.** In the absence of express agreement to do so, the tribunal is under no obligation to make particular dates available for hearings; the obligation is to sit on such dates as may reasonably be required having regard to all the circumstances, including the arbitrators' own commitments.[500] Having said that, if an arbitrator is unable to sit for the required number of days within a reasonable period it may be preferable for him to offer to resign, depending of course on the circumstances, including the stage to which the case has progressed.[500a]

5–166 **Proper planning needed.** If the procedural stages and any hearings are well-planned this will help ensure the parties and their advisers are properly prepared and can also reduce costs. The tribunal, the parties and their representatives will be able to set aside the necessary time for each stage in their diaries. Subject of course to the tribunal's duty to ensure that the reference is conducted without unnecessary delay,[501] the procedural timetable laid down should be achievable and flexible, and the length of time set aside for the hearing itself ought as far as possible to be a realistic assessment of what is required, otherwise further hearings may be necessary. Adjournments will result in delay and additional costs,

---

[496] Assisting with the drafting of an award is not of itself objectionable, though most arbitrators would be expected to be able and willing to do it themselves: see para.6–056 below.

[497] There is no entitlement to an oral hearing see para.5–196 below.

[498] Assuming there are to be any, see paras 5–120 *et seq.* above.

[499] Where interim measures are sought however it may be necessary for the tribunal to convene a hearing as a matter of urgency immediately following its constitution.

[500] *K/S Norjarl A/S v Hyundai Heavy Industries Co Ltd* [1991] 1 Lloyd's Rep. 524, CA.

[500a] Though under a different statutory regime, see *Enterra Pty v ADI Ltd* [2002] N.S.W.S.C. 700, an Australian case in which the New South Wales Supreme Court held that an arbitrator could not be removed on grounds of his being "unsuitable" merely because of undue delay in fixing a hearing date.

[501] Section 33 of the Arbitration Act 1996: see para.5–032 above.

and the evidence and issues discussed at the first hearing will inevitably be less immediate and fresh in the minds of all concerned when the hearing is reconvened.

Pre-trial hearing or conference. The arrangements for the substantive   5–167
hearing may include a pre-trial hearing or conference at which the parties and/or their advisors are required to attend before the tribunal[502] on a date some time before the substantive hearing. This is particularly useful where there are specific issues which the parties wish to have dealt with before the start of the substantive hearing, but in most cases some form of preparatory hearing or conference will be of assistance. The purpose is usually to ensure that the case will be ready for the substantive hearing, to ensure that the parties and their representatives understand the arrangements that have been made and know what to expect when the hearing begins, and to address any outstanding procedural steps. It may also provide an opportunity for seeking to narrow the issues in dispute between the parties.

Venue for the hearing. Whoever is administering the reference[503] will need   5–168
to arrange a suitable venue for the hearing. Obviously a room will be required for the hearing itself, but it may also be useful to have retiring rooms for each of the parties and for the tribunal, so that they can discuss the case and work on documents in private. The venue will usually be a neutral location, such as a conference room in a hotel or rooms available for the purpose from a local institution or chamber of commerce. Various arbitration institutions have rooms available for arbitrations and there are some commercial enterprises with suitable facilities for hire. Occasionally, the parties may for reasons of cost or convenience agree to hold the arbitration hearing in one of their own offices or those of their advisers or indeed in the offices of a member of the tribunal.

Room hire charges. A deposit will usually be required in advance for the   5–169
cost of the room hire and this is usually borne equally between the parties or by the claimant alone. The cost of the venue hire forms part of the costs of the arbitration and can therefore be reimbursed if appropriate following a decision on costs by the tribunal in its award.[504]

Other administrative arrangements. The parties should also consider   5–170
what other administrative arrangements need to be made for the hearing. For example, they may want a transcript of the proceedings and, if so, a firm of shorthand writers (or court reporter) should be retained or recording equipment installed. It is common in larger cases for simultaneous transcription to be

---

[502] Physical attendance at a pre-trial conference is not always required and it may, for example, be possible to arrange video-conferencing or a telephone conference call.
[503] See paras 5–171 *et seq.* above.
[504] See paras 6–132 and 6–133 below.

available on laptop computers and other computer based technologies are also sometimes used for the presentation of documents or submissions. Appropriate arrangements need to be made well in advance of the hearing to ensure set-up and operation of these systems runs smoothly. If any of the witnesses are to give their evidence in a language other than English it may be necessary to arrange for the attendance of a translator.[505] If the evidence is to be given on oath or affirmation, a bible or other relevant text needs to be on hand. On a more mundane level, refreshments should be arranged, both for the parties and for the tribunal.

5–171 **Arrangements in multiparty arbitrations.** Save for possible complications concerning the constitution of the tribunal,[506] there are no special procedural requirements of multiparty or consolidated arbitrations. However, the involvement of several parties may make the proceedings more complex to manage from an administrative viewpoint and the need for procedural directions from the tribunal even greater.[507]

(h) Privacy and the obligation of confidentiality

5–172 **Privacy and confidentiality.** It has long been assumed that arbitrations in England are private and confidential. By this it is meant that the proceedings, including any hearing,[508] are a private matter between the parties and the tribunal, from which strangers are generally excluded. The proceedings are also confidential, so that neither party is entitled to publish details of the case to third parties.[509] These general principles derive from the arbitration agreement rather than from any privilege attaching to information used in or relating to the arbitration. They are subject to exceptions as discussed below,[510] but the privacy and confidentiality of the process has often been cited as one of the key virtues of arbitration when compared with litigation. As Leggatt J. stated: the concept of privacy in arbitration "derives simply from the fact that the parties have agreed to submit to arbitration particular disputes arising between them and only between

---

[505] See further para.5–168 above.
[506] See paras 3–040 *et seq.* on multi-party arbitrations generally, and para.3–042 concerning appointment of the tribunal.
[507] See the UNCITRAL Notes on Organising Arbitral Proceedings, s.18, paras 86 to 88, which set out some of the areas that may be more complex in a multi-party case.
[508] *Oxford Shipping Co Ltd v Nippon Yusen Kaisha (The "Eastern Saga")* [1984] 3 All E.R. 835 at 379; *Hassneh Insurance Co of Israel v Stuart J Mew* [1993] 2 Lloyd's Rep. 243.
[509] The mere fact that parties to whom disclosure is contemplated are in the same beneficial ownership and management as the party to whom the obligation of confidentiality is owed is not sufficient to displace it: *Ali Shipping Corp v Shipyard Trogir* [1998] 2 All E.R. 136. However even an express confidentiality provision will not prevent a party relying on an arbitration award as conferring rights upon him in other proceedings between the same two parties: *Associated Electric & Gas Insurance Services Ltd v European Reinsurance Co of Zurich* [2003] 1 W.L.R. 1041.
[510] See paras 5–086 *et seq.*

them".[511] The obligation of confidentiality is implied into the arbitration agreement as a matter of law and arises as an essential corollary of the privacy of arbitration proceedings.[512]

Absence of statutory provision. Despite the widespread acceptance of 5–173 privacy and confidentiality as characteristics of arbitration, there is no statutory provision in the Arbitration Act 1996 or elsewhere dealing with privacy and confidentiality in the arbitration context.[513] The reason for this is that "grave difficulties arose over the myriad exceptions" and the formulation of any statutory principles was ultimately rejected on the basis that it would impede the current practice in English arbitrations as regards privacy and confidentiality and give rise to more litigation.[514] As a result both the principles and the exceptions to them[515] have to be gleaned from the case law and cannot be said yet to be fully explained. As Potter L.J. noted in *Ali Shipping Corp v Shipyard Trogir*[516]:

"While . . . the boundaries of the obligation of confidence . . . have yet to be delineated . . . , the manner in which that may best be achieved is by formulating exceptions of broad application to be applied in individual cases, rather than by seeking to reconsider, and if necessary adapt, the general rule on each occasion in the light of the particular circumstances and presumed intentions of the parties at the time of their original agreement."

Reservations have been expressed by the Privy Council about the desirability or merit of characterising a duty of confidentiality as an implied term subject to exceptions, because it fails to recognise the different types of confidentiality attaching to different types of documents.[517] The Privy Council did not however advance an alternative approach but indicated that, at least so far as the award itself is concerned, it may have to be referred to for a number of different purposes including the enforcement of the rights it confers.

Scope of the obligation of confidentiality. The fact that an obligation 5–174 of confidentiality exists does not prevent any mention whatsoever of the arbitration. In *Department of Economic Policy and Development of the City of Moscow v Bankers Trust Co*[518] Cooke J. noted that: "There can in my judgment be no breach

---

[511] In *Oxford Shipping Co Ltd v Nippon Yusen Kaisha (The "Eastern Saga")* [1984] 3 All E.R. 835 at 842.

[512] *Ali Shipping Corp v Shipyard Trogir* [1998] 2 All E.R. 136, overruling Colman J. in *Hassneh Insurance Co v Mew* [1993] 2 Lloyd's Rep. 243 on this point.

[513] By contrast, s.14 of the New Zealand Arbitration Act 1996 contains a specific obligation.

[514] See further paras 11 to 17 of the DAC report and the commentary on that decision by Sir Patrick Neill Q.C., "Confidentiality in Arbitration" (1996) 12 Arbitration Int. 287.

[515] The exceptions established in case law to date are addressed in paras 5–186 to 5–189 below.

[516] [1998] 2 All E.R. 136 at 147.

[517] *Associated Electric & Gas Insurance Services Ltd v European Reinsurance Co of Zurich* [2003] 1 W.L.R. 1041.

[518] [2003] EWHC 1377; [2003] 1 W.L.R. 2885 at [51]. The case was reversed in part on appeal at [2004] EWCA Civ 314; [2004] 2 Lloyd's Rep. 179, but the Court of Appeal did not take issue with the proposition quoted.

of duty in disclosing the fact of commencement of arbitration, the existence of an arbitration or the result of that arbitration where there is any legitimate reason to do so. Equally, the existence of any challenge to an award, the existence of litigation relating to it and the result of that litigation would for similar reasons not amount to a breach if disclosed." These comments were *obiter* and perhaps reflect a more liberal approach than some would consider warranted. They do however highlight the difficulty which results from the relatively undefined scope of the obligation of confidentiality imposed at common law. The judge was clearly influenced by the need for disclosure of such matters where there is a commercial necessity or legitimate commercial interest, but it is not clear whether disclosure is limited to such circumstances. Disclosure will obviously be permitted where legally required.[519] Beyond this it is not clear what commercial necessity or legitimate commercial interest really means for these purposes. Would disclosure of the existence of an arbitration be a breach of the obligation of confidentiality absent some commercial necessity or legitimate commercial interest? The answers to questions of this sort are not readily to hand in the case law and if parties are concerned about such matters the best course is to deal with them expressly in their arbitration agreement.[520]

5–175 **Contractual provision for confidentiality.** Whilst it is clear that under English law the general principles of confidentiality and privacy apply to arbitration, there is no reason to be complacent, or to regard the current position as beyond question, particularly in the light of decisions such as *Esso/BHP v Plowman*.[521] In that case the High Court of Australia reviewed the English authorities on the subject in detail with substantial input from leading English lawyers, yet concluded that under Australian law there was no implied obligation of confidentiality. Certainly if privacy and confidentiality are of great importance to any or all of the parties, for example because the subject matter of the arbitration includes technical or commercial secrets, the safest course is to make specific provision in the arbitration agreement that can if necessary be backed up by an order of the tribunal or the court.

5–176 **Exceptions to the duty of confidentiality.** As stated above, there are a number of exceptions to the duty of confidentiality. In practice problems most frequently arise where one party wants to use documents obtained in an arbitration for some other purpose.[522] The private nature of arbitration gives rise to an implied obligation on a party obtaining documents in an arbitration not to disclose or use them for any purpose other than the dispute in which they were obtained.[523]

---

[519] For example by a company under the rules of a Stock Exchange on which its shares are listed.
[520] See para.5–185 below.
[521] (1995) 11 Arbitration Int. 234.
[522] Similar considerations will apply where a non-party seeks disclosure in relation to an arbitration or in relation to court proceedings concerning a dispute in relation to which there is a binding arbitration agreement: see *Glidepath BV v Thompson* [2005] 2 Lloyd's Rep. 549.
[523] *Dolling–Baker v Merrett and Others* [1991] 2 All E.R. 890 at 899, CA; *Hassneh Insurance Co of Israel and Others v Stuart J Mew* [1993] 2 Lloyd's Rep. 243.

This duty of confidence extends to "any documents prepared for and used in the arbitration, or disclosed or produced in the course of the arbitration, or transcripts or notes of the evidence in the arbitration or the award".[524] There are exceptions to this duty of non-disclosure where the disclosure takes place with the consent of the other party or by order or permission of the court, where it is reasonably necessary or where it is in the interests of justice. These exceptions are examined in the following paragraphs.

Disclosure of documents following consent, order or permission of the court. The obligation not to disclose or use documents arises from the implied obligation in the arbitration agreement to maintain confidentiality, rather than any confidentiality or privilege being conferred on the document itself by virtue of its use in the arbitration. The obligation may accordingly be displaced by consent of the other party to the arbitration. It will also be displaced where disclosure is pursuant to an order or permission of the court.[525] Where a third party seeks disclosure of documents on the court file prior to proceedings being stayed in favour of arbitration, the court will only grant its permission where the parties to the arbitration consent or there are overriding interests of justice requiring disclosure.[526] This also applies to applications for ancillary relief and related evidence.

5–177

Disclosure reasonably necessary. The duty of confidence is qualified in relation to the award when disclosure is reasonably necessary to establish or protect a party's legal rights as against a third party[527] by founding a cause of action or a defence to a claim.[528] In these circumstances disclosure of the award, including any reasons given, will not be a breach of the duty of confidentiality.[529] This also applies to pleadings, written submissions, proofs of witnesses, transcripts and notes of the evidence, provided of course such disclosure is reasonably necessary to establish or protect a party's legal rights as against a third party.[530]

5–178

---

[524] *per* Parker L.J. in *Dolling-Baker v Merrett and Others* [1991] 2 All E.R. 891 at 899, CA.

[525] *Dolling-Baker v Merrett and Others* [1991] 2 All E.R. 890, CA; *London & Leeds Estates Ltd v Paribas Ltd (No.2)* [1995] 2 E.G. 134; *Ali Shipping Corp v Shipyard Trogir* [1998] 2 All E.R. 136.

[526] *Glidepath BV v Thompson* [2005] EWHC 818 and para.5–189 below. See though *Department of Economic Policy and Development of the City of Moscow v Bankers Trust Co* [2004] EWCA Civ 314; [2004] 2 Lloyd's Rep. 179 where it was held that the parties' election for confidential arbitration does not dictate the position in respect of arbitration claims brought before the court, but the court can take into account the parties' expectations in this regard.

[527] The position is even stronger where a party seeks disclosure in the context of subsequent proceedings between the same two parties: *Associated Electric & Gas Insurance Services Ltd v European Reinsurance Co of Zurich* [2003] UKPC 11.

[528] For example where the disclosure is necessary in order for a party to pursue a subsequent claim against his insurers in respect of the same loss.

[529] *Hassneh Insurance Co of Israel and Others v Stuart J Mew* [1993] 2 Lloyd's Rep. 243; *Ali Shipping Corp v Shipyard Trogir* [1998] 2 All E.R. 136.

[530] *Ali Shipping Corp v Shipyard Trogir* [1998] 2 All E.R. 136, *per* Potter L.J. at 147. It was previously thought that this principle applied only to an award and not to materials such as pleadings, witness statements, disclosure, etc., used in the arbitration process leading up to the award. Indeed, in *Hassneh* Colman J. justified the distinction between the award and other materials on the grounds that, unlike other documents used in an arbitration, an award determines the parties' rights and obligations, and it is also potentially a public document in the context of supervision or enforcement

Reasonably necessary in this context means more than simply evidentially relevant to the legal rights in question. It must be shown that the information will play an essential part in establishing the right or defence in question, such that serious prejudice will be caused if access is denied.[531] However a degree of flexibility will be applied taking account of such matters as the issues to which the information is directed and the practicality and expense of obtaining it elsewhere.[532]

There is also an exception to the duty of confidentiality to the effect that a party may put the award and any reasons before a court if there is an application seeking to invoke the court's supervisory powers in relation to the arbitration, or if the court's assistance is sought with regard to enforcement of the award.[533]

5-179　**Disclosure in the interests of justice.** A further limited exception to the obligation of confidentiality arises where disclosure is required in the interests of justice. This exception was referred to by Mance J. in *London & Leeds Estates Ltd v Paribas Ltd (No.2)*[534] as arising where disclosure is required in the public interest. In that case disclosure was sought to demonstrate prior inconsistent views expressed by an expert in arbitration proceedings. The "interests of justice" and the "public interest" might appear to be open-ended concepts, but as Potter L.J. explained in *Ali Shipping Corp v Shipyard Trogir*[535] the exception is based on the interests of justice in ensuring that the judicial decision in the particular case was based on accurate evidence rather than any public interest in the broader sense.

5-180　**Enforcement of confidentiality obligations.** The usual remedy in the event of threatened breach of the confidentiality obligation is injunctive relief, either from the tribunal if it has power to do so[536] or from the court.[537] It is not necessary to show that prejudice will be caused by the disclosure.[538]

(i) Enforcement of procedural orders

5-181　**Duty to comply with the tribunal's procedural orders.** Section 40(1) of the Arbitration Act 1996 imposes a mandatory general duty on the parties to do all things necessary for the proper and expeditious conduct of the reference.

---

by the court. See also *Insurance Co v Lloyd's Syndicate* [1995] 1 Lloyd's Rep. 272 as to the scope of the qualification.
[531] *Glidepath BV v Thompson* [2005] 2 Lloyd's Rep. 549.
[532] *per* Potter L.J. in *Ali Shipping Corp v Shipyard Trogir* [1998] 2 All E.R. 136.
[533] *Hassneh Insurance Co of Israel and Others v Stuart J Mew* [1993] 2 Lloyd's Rep. 243.
[534] [1995] 2 E.G. 134.
[535] [1998] 2 All E.R. 136 at 148.
[536] See para.6–107.
[537] See para.7–195.
[538] *Ali Shipping Corp v Shipyard Trogir* [1998] 2 All E.R. 136.

By s.40(2)(a) this specifically includes complying without delay with any order or direction of the tribunal on evidential or procedural matters.[539]

Powers of the tribunal in case of default. Section 41 of the Arbitration Act 1996 sets out the tribunal's powers in cases of default, unless the parties have agreed otherwise.[540] These powers fall into three categories. First, there is a power to dismiss the claim for want of prosecution and this is dealt with in paras 5–224 to 5–227 below. Second, the tribunal is empowered to continue the proceedings even if a party fails to attend the hearing or submit evidence. This is dealt with in para.5–202 below. Third, there are powers exercisable by the tribunal where there has been a failure to comply with an order it has made. In addition to these powers of the tribunal, the court may make an order requiring a party to comply with a peremptory order of the tribunal.[541] The court can then apply its coercive powers in the event of a failure to comply.

5–182

Failure to comply with an order of the tribunal. If a party fails to comply with an order of the tribunal, without showing sufficient cause (i.e. satisfying the tribunal that there were justifiable reasons for the failure) then the tribunal may make a peremptory order.[542] The peremptory order must stipulate the time for compliance and must be to the same effect as the order which has been disobeyed. The tribunal cannot therefore seek to penalise non-compliance with its order by making a peremptory order on some other matter unconnected with the default. Nor can the peremptory order be more onerous than the order which has been disobeyed,[543] save of course in relation to the time limit imposed for compliance which is within the discretion of the tribunal.

5–183

Failure to comply with a peremptory order for security for costs. The consequences of a party failing to comply with a peremptory order will depend upon whether it relates to security for costs or to some other matter. If the order relates to security for costs, failure to comply entitles the tribunal to make an award dismissing the claim.[544]

5–184

Failure to comply with any other kind of peremptory order. In the event of failure to comply with any other kind of peremptory order the tribunal

5–185

---

[539] As to the remedies for failure to comply with the duty, see para.205 of the DAC report. They include the ability of the tribunal to exercise its powers under s.41 of the Arbitration Act 1996—see para.5–192.

[540] Section 41(1) and (2) of the Arbitration Act 1996. Subsection (1) emphasises the parties' freedom to agree the powers they wish to confer on the tribunal to deal with a party's default. Subsection (2) makes clear that unless the parties have agreed otherwise, the default provisions set out in subss.(3) to (7) of s.41 apply.

[541] Section 42 of the Arbitration Act 1996 dealt with in paras 7–198 *et seq.* below.

[542] Section 41(5) of the Arbitration Act 1996.

[543] This results from the words "to the same effect" in s.41(5) of the Arbitration Act 1996.

[544] Section 41(6) of the Arbitration Act 1996. Security for costs orders are distinguished to avoid the prospect of the reference being stayed indefinitely. It also follows the practice of the court, see para.210 of the DAC report.

has a discretion under s.41(7) of the Arbitration Act 1996 to do any of the following:

(a) direct that the party in default shall not be entitled to rely upon any allegation or material which was the subject matter of the order;

(b) draw such adverse inferences from the act of non-compliance as the circumstances justify;

(c) proceed to an award on the basis of such materials as have been properly provided to it;

(d) make such order as it thinks fit as to the payment of costs of the arbitration incurred in consequence of the non-compliance.

These remedies do not include the power to proceed immediately to a summary award against the defaulting party as this was considered too draconian,[545] but nevertheless they provide the tribunal with powers to impose sanctions as appropriate.

6. THE HEARING

(a) Attendance and representation

5–186 **No entitlement to oral hearing.** Prior to the Arbitration Act 1996 the parties or either of them were entitled to require an oral hearing before the tribunal.[546] That is no longer the case. Unless all parties agree that there shall be an oral hearing, it is for the tribunal to decide whether there should be oral evidence or submissions.[547] Many arbitration rules reverse this position by allowing a party the right to insist on an oral hearing on the merits.[548]

5–187 **When and where to hold hearings.** If there is to be an oral hearing the tribunal decides when and where the hearing or indeed any part of the proceedings shall be held.[549] This is subject to the right of the parties to agree these matters.[550] It might, for example, be convenient to hold part of the proceedings in a particular location in order to accommodate several witnesses or an important witness who is unable to travel to the seat of the arbitration.[551] It should always be made clear

---

[545] See para.211 of the DAC report. Such a remedy might also lead to difficulties in the enforcement of the award in other jurisdictions.

[546] *Henry Sotheran Ltd v Norwich Union Life Insurance Society* [1992] 31 E.G. 70. This was subject to agreement otherwise by the parties.

[547] Section 34(2)(h) of the Arbitration Act 1996.

[548] See for example Art.19.1 of the LCIA Rules.

[549] Section 34(2)(a) and (h) of the Arbitration Act 1996. See further para.2–107 above.

[550] Section 34(1) of the Arbitration Act 1996.

[551] It is also becoming increasingly common for less important witnesses to give their evidence by video conferencing if for some reason they are unable to attend the hearing: see para.5–210 below.

by the tribunal where the seat[552] of the arbitration is, particularly if hearings are being held in other locations.

Who may attend. The categories of persons who may attend an arbitration hearing are not clearly defined, but will include the parties themselves and persons attending on behalf of the parties, for example their legal representatives. Third parties (other than witnesses) are excluded from the hearing,[553] unless of course both parties and the tribunal agree otherwise.[554] Any expert, legal advisor or technical assessor appointed by the tribunal may be allowed to attend the hearing.[555]

5–188

Representation at the hearing. Parties may wish to be represented at the hearing by an advocate. Unless the parties have agreed otherwise, this may be a lawyer or "other person".[556] The refusal of a party's request for representation by an advocate chosen by him, or seeking to limit the level of representation,[557] may give grounds for challenging the award, particularly in complex cases.[558] However, a party cannot insist upon a particular individual if, for example, that person is unsuitable[559] or unavailable.[560] In these circumstances some other individual would have to be chosen. Legal representation may be excluded by the parties' arbitration agreement.[561] It is excluded by the rules of certain trade associations,[562] but is expressly permitted by other institutional rules.[563] Many sets of rules are

5–189

---

[552] For the seat of arbitration generally see paras 2–099 *et seq.* and 5–071 *et seq.*

[553] *Oxford Shipping Co Ltd v Nippon Yusen Kaisha (The "Eastern Saga")* [1984] 2 Lloyd's Rep. 373 at 379; *Hassneh Insurance Co of Israel and Others v Stuart J Mew* [1993] 2 Lloyd's Rep. 243. In practice, the need to exclude the public will rarely arise, precisely because the proceedings are private and the venue privately arranged between the parties and the tribunal.

[554] The Court of Appeal have confirmed that by agreeing to arbitrate the parties waive their right to a public hearing and this does not infringe Art.6 of the European Convention on Human Rights: see *Stretford v Football Association Ltd* [2007] EWCA 238. See also para.1–039 and *Premium Nafta Products Ltd v Fili Shipping Co Ltd* [2007] UKHL 40 at [20].

[555] Section 37(1) of the Arbitration Act 1996.

[556] Section 36 of the Arbitration Act 1996. See also *Piper Double Glazing Ltd v DC Contracts* 31 Con. L.R. 149 and *Hookway & Co Ltd v Alfred Isaacs & Sons* [1954] 1 Lloyd's Rep. 491.

[557] *Norbrook Laboratories Ltd v Tank* [2006] EWHC 1055. If the level of representation is inappropriate that may affect the recovery of the cost of such representation.

[558] For failure to comply with the duty under s.33 of the Arbitration Act 1996. See also *Hookway & Co Ltd v Alfred Isaacs & Sons* [1954] 1 Lloyd's Rep. 491 and *How Engineering Services Ltd v Lindner Ceilings Floors Partitions Plc* [1999] 2 All E.R. 374, both cases under the old law.

[559] e.g. because he is a close personal friend or business partner of a member of the tribunal. There is little authority on what criteria should be applied in determining unsuitability, and a tribunal should be hesitant about excluding a chosen representative on the grounds of unsuitability unless it has real concerns that the progress of the hearing would be undermined or that the resulting award would be rendered vulnerable to challenge.

[560] See para.184 of the DAC report.

[561] See for example *Virdee v Virdi* [2003] EWCA Civ 41. This will not preclude the appointment of a legal advisor to the tribunal pursuant to s.37 of the Arbitration Act 1996.

[562] e.g. Art.16.2 of the GAFTA Arbitration Rules, No.125 excludes legal representation at oral hearings at the first instance stage unless the parties agree otherwise.

[563] e.g. UNCITRAL Rules, Art.4; LCIA Rules, Art.18.1.

silent on the point, and the practical effect of this is that the parties may be legally represented if they so wish.

5–190 **Exclusion of a party's representative.** The parties are entitled to have persons attending to assist them in presenting their case,[564] and if such persons are excluded without good reason when their presence is desired by a party, the award may be subject to challenge.[565]

5–191 **Exclusion of a party.** Although there will be some types of behaviour which would justify the exclusion of a party (or a person whom a party wishes to be present to assist with the presentation of his case), the importance of the parties' right to be present at the hearing means that such exclusion will be justified only in very extreme and exceptional circumstances. Because of the serious risk that the award will be challenged if a party or his chosen representative is excluded,[566] such action should be viewed by the tribunal as the very last resort.

5–192 **Hearings in the absence of one of the parties.** The tribunal has power to proceed in the absence of a party, and a hearing may take place even if one of the parties is not present and the case proceeds in the absence of submissions, evidence or indeed any case at all from one of the parties.[567] Obviously it is desirable that all of the parties should present their respective cases. However, if the tribunal were not able to proceed in the absence of a party, it would be possible for that party to circumvent the arbitration agreement by simply refusing or failing to participate in the reference. Where one party does not participate the tribunal should record in detail in its award the opportunities to participate that the absent party was given.

5–193 **Due notice of hearing required.** Before proceeding, a tribunal should ensure that a non-attending party has been given due notice of the hearing[568] and indeed of the reference generally.[569] In order to comply with its duty under s.33

---

[564] See para.5–199 above.
[565] In the words of Turner L.J. in *Re Haigh, Haigh v Haigh* (1861) 31 L.J. (Ch), 420 at 424: "I certainly do not mean to lay it down that an arbitrator is bound to submit to insults from those who attend him but I think that before he excludes anyone from attending on behalf of any of the parties interested, they are bound to ascertain that there is good reason for the exclusion, and to take the best care he can that the party who is affected by the exclusion is not prejudiced by it." That was a case under the old law but it would presumably now be challenged as a serious irregularity under s.68 of the Arbitration Act 1996 on the basis of a failure to allow the party concerned a reasonable opportunity to put his case and/or to act fairly in accordance with the duty imposed by s.33 of the Arbitration Act 1996. It would be necessary to show substantial injustice: see paras 8–072 *et seq*.
[566] i.e. for failing to give that party a fair opportunity to be heard.
[567] Section 41(4) of the Arbitration Act 1996.
[568] This is required by s.41(4)(a) of the Arbitration Act 1996.
[569] *Schumacher t/a Vita Konzern v Laurel Island Ltd (The "Santa Cruz Tres")* [1995] 1 Lloyd's Rep. 208.

of the Arbitration Act 1996,[570] if the tribunal has any doubts about whether a party's absence is inadvertent it should adjourn the hearing and make inquiries.[571] If it proposes to proceed in the absence of a party, the tribunal should make absolutely clear to the party in default that the arbitration will go ahead anyway.[572]

Conduct of hearing with a party absent. The fact that a claim is   5–194
undefended does not mean that the tribunal is obliged to accept it without question. Nor is it under an obligation to protect the party who is absent. Rather, the tribunal's function is "to hold the scales as evenly as [it can] and to act fairly and judicially in the conduct of the hearing".[573] In practice this means that where an arbitration hearing proceeds in the absence of one of the parties, the tribunal should consider the evidence and submissions before it in order to determine whether they are sufficient to establish the claim. They are not bound to accept the evidence of the party attending and may find,[574] even if it is uncontroverted, that it falls short of establishing the case to be proved.[575]

Submissions and evidence of the absent party. The tribunal should   5–195
consider any evidence or submissions which have been tendered at any time by the absent party, so that it takes into account the absent party's case to the extent this is possible on the materials before it.

Role of the tribunal. If only one party is represented, it frequently happens   5–196
that the tribunal becomes more interventionist, so as to ensure both sides of the case are fairly developed. In such circumstances there is a fine line between being alert to ensure procedural fairness, which the tribunal must ensure happens, and acting as an advocate for the unrepresented party, which the tribunal must not do. Of course the tribunal may adopt an inquisitorial role in this situation.[576] In any event the need to be fair to both parties should be borne in mind at all times.[577]

(b) The course and structure of the hearing

Structure of the hearing. Subject to the overriding principles and duties   5–197
set out in ss.1 and 33(1) of the Arbitration Act 1996, there are no mandatory

---

[570] See para.5–032 above.
[571] *Montrose Canned Foods Ltd v Eric Wells (Merchants) Ltd* [1965] 1 Lloyd's Rep. 597 at 602.
[572] *The "Myron" (Owners) v Tradax Export SA* [1969] 1 Lloyd's Rep. 411 at 417. This was a case under the old law but it seems likely that the requirement would still be imposed as part of the duty under s.33 of the Arbitration Act 1996.
[573] *per* Dunn, L.J. in *Annie Fox and Others v PG Wellfair Ltd* [1981] 2 Lloyd's Rep. 514 at 528, CA.
[574] *The "Myron" (Owners) v Tradax Export SA* [1969] 1 Lloyd's Rep. 411 at 416–417.
[575] *Lewis Emanuel & Son Ltd v Sammut* [1959] 2 Lloyd's Rep. 629 at 634.
[576] See para.5–099 above.
[577] *Town & City Properties v Witshier* 44 B.L.R. 109. This was a case under the old law but the requirement still applies as part of the duty to act fairly under s.33 of the Arbitration Act 1996.

requirements concerning the structure of the hearing.[578] The following paragraphs describe a frequently followed structure, similar to that adopted in court proceedings, which begins with opening statements, followed by the evidence of witnesses for the claimant and the respondent respectively and ends with closing submissions. Whilst each of these may be undertaken it is not uncommon for some or all to be omitted or curtailed, or for oral procedures to take a different course (such as witness conferencing[579]) or to be replaced by written submissions.

5–198 **Opening statements.** Opening statements are intended to introduce the tribunal to the parties' respective cases, although the tribunal will usually be expected to have read the parties' written submissions and evidence in advance of the hearing. The written submissions will often include a summary of its case from each party[580] which each will then develop orally at the hearing. Opening statements may also address specifically the key documents relied upon, and set out the party's arguments and the case it will seek to establish in the course of the hearing. However, lengthy opening statements reading aloud large numbers of documents are not usually tolerated in arbitration proceedings and should very much be discouraged.[581] Indeed it is becoming relatively common, particularly where the parties have served written pre-hearing submissions or skeleton arguments summarising their respective cases, for tribunals to allow only very short opening submissions before moving on to witness testimony.

5–199 **Dealing with foreign law.** Where the applicable substantive law is a law other than English law, the tribunal will have to determine whether it will be addressed by way of expert evidence or by way of submissions. English courts treat foreign law as a question of fact to be proved by expert evidence and tribunals have occasionally in the past adopted the same approach. Indeed, the tribunal may instruct its own expert on foreign law issues.[582] Nowadays, however, foreign law is almost always dealt with in arbitration by way of submissions from the parties' advocates who may or may not be from the jurisdiction concerned.

In the absence of either party or the tribunal itself raising an issue under the applicable foreign law that is different from English law, the tribunal is free to decide the case on the presumption that the applicable foreign law is the same as English law.[583]

---

[578] There is no requirement to follow procedures as would apply under English court procedure: *Margulead Ltd v Exide Technologies* [2004] EWHC 1019.

[579] See para.5–212 below.

[580] Or, in some cases, a fully argued submission including references to the evidence and legal authorities relied upon.

[581] See, e.g. the comments of Lord Justice Saville that this was "the antithesis of fairness" in Construction & Engineering Law, June/August 1996.

[582] Under s.37 of the Arbitration Act 1996; see para.5–160. This happened for example in the case of *Hussman (Europe) Ltd v Al Ameen Development & Trade Co* [2000] 2 Lloyd's Rep. 83.

[583] *Hussman (Europe) Ltd v Al Ameen Development & Trade Co* [2000] 2 Lloyd's Rep. 83.

Witness evidence.[584] Where the witness evidence is in the form of written   **5–200**
witness statements and experts' reports which are exchanged prior to the hearing
of the arbitration, these largely replace the witnesses' evidence in chief. At the
hearing the witness will at the outset normally only be asked a few questions by
the party calling him, so as to establish his identity and to address any corrections
to his written statement. Exceptionally, the witness may also be permitted to
address additional matters not covered in his statement but usually this will be
limited to elaborating on matters dealt with rather than raising new ones. Following the initial questioning of the witness by the party calling him, the witness will
be tendered for cross-examination by the other parties.[585] If considered appropriate, the witness will then be re-examined.[586] The evidence may be given on oath
but this is done less and less.[587] On the other hand, the giving of evidence by video
conference where witnesses are abroad is becoming increasingly common, particularly where the evidence of the witness is not central to the case, credibility is not
in issue and the expense and inconvenience of travelling to the hearing are not
warranted.

Questioning by the tribunal. The tribunal may ask questions of the   **5–201**
witnesses during the course of the evidence or after the parties have completed
their questioning. If however the tribunal is adopting an inquisitorial approach it
will take the lead in conducting the questioning.[588]

Witness conferencing or "hot-tubbing". In recent years tribunals in   **5–202**
some cases have adopted a method of hearing witness evidence which involves a
number of witnesses giving evidence simoultaneously.[589] This method is generally
only adopted with the parties' agreement[590] and is often used for some but not all
witnesses in a case. It has been applied to both factual and expert witnesses,
though it is not usual to mix the two when adopting such a procedure. The precise
methodology varies but typically the tribunal will take the lead in questioning the
witnesses, each of whom are asked the same questions. The witnesses are each
given an opportunity to respond, both to the tribunal's question and to the
comments of the other witness or witnesses.[591] The parties are sometimes consulted in advance and invited to suggest questions that might be put to the

---

[584] See paras 5–142 *et seq.* above.
[585] This is the traditional approach to witness evidence in England. See however para.5–212 for the
practice of witness conferencing.
[586] Re-examination is limited to matters arising out of the cross-examination.
[587] See para.5–157 above.
[588] See para.5–099 above.
[589] See further Wolfgang Peter "Witness Conferencing" in (2002) 18 Arbitration Int. 47.
[590] Given that, absent agreement of the parties, the tribunal can decide pursuant to s.34(2)(g) whether
and to what extent it should itself take the initiative in ascertaining the facts and the law, it could
arguably impose the approach against the wishes of one of the parties but this is not generally
done.
[591] Witness conferencing can be undertaken with any number of witnesses. In one LCIA case, 10
factual witnesses gave contemporaneous evidence using this technique. In most cases however, the
witness conferencing will be limited to the one witness dealing with a particular area (such as a
specific expert discipline) called by each party.

witnesses, though the tribunal will not be limited to these and may also ask their own questions. In any event the parties should be given an opportunity, at the end of the tribunal's questioning, to ask any further supplemental questions they wish to put to the witnesses, although in practice the scope of examination at this stage is usually very limited and falls well short of a typical cross-examination.[592] Experiences of this technique, which tends to be favoured particularly by arbitrators from civil law jurisdictions, are varied. It can undoubtedly save time and costs, but the parties' representatives are unable to utilise cross-examination techniques which they may consider a disadvantage.

5-203 **Closing submissions.** The parties or their representatives often make oral closing submissions at the end of the hearing, summarising their case and the evidence in support, and addressing the case put forward by the other party. It is usual for the respondent to make its closing submissions prior to those of the claimant, so that the claimant "gets the last word". Whoever makes its closing submissions first, there is no right of reply.[593] Alternatively, it is increasingly common in arbitrations for there to be mutual exchange of written post-hearing submissions and, where this procedure is adopted, they may replace oral closing submissions altogether. If there are to be written post-hearing submissions, it is important for the tribunal to set a date by which they are to be produced in order to bring finality to the proceedings.[594]

5-204 **Closure of the proceedings.** Some arbitration agreements and arbitration rules[595] make specific provision for the tribunal to declare the proceedings closed at a certain point and that thereafter no further submissions may be made or evidence produced unless requested by the tribunal or unless specific permission is given by the tribunal. Even absent a specific provision the tribunal will often want to draw a line under the proceedings and may indicate that permission will be required for any further evidence or submissions.

5-205 **Stay of arbitration proceedings.** Subject to the agreement of the parties, it is for the tribunal to decide when and where any part of the proceedings is to be held.[596] In principle therefore, and subject of course to its general duty to avoid unnecessary delay,[597] it is for the tribunal to decide whether there should be an

---

[592] Failure to afford this opportunity would potentially give rise to a challenge under s.68(2)(a) of the Arbitration Act 1996 for failure to comply with the duty under s.33 of the Arbitration Act 1996 which includes giving each party a reasonable opportunity of putting his case and dealing with that of his opponent.

[593] *Margulead Ltd v Exide Technologies* [2005] 1 Lloyd's Rep. 324.

[594] Article 22.1 of the ICC Rules specifically requires the tribunal to declare the proceedings closed once the parties have had a reasonable opportunity to present their cases. Thereafter no further submission or argument may be made or evidence produced unless requested or authorised by the tribunal.

[595] See for example Art.22 of the ICC Rules.

[596] Section 34(2)(a) of the Arbitration Act 1996.

[597] Section 33(1)(b) of the Arbitration Act 1996.

adjournment or stay of the arbitration proceedings.[598] Whether it is appropriate to do so will depend on the particular circumstances of the case, but a tribunal will want very cogent and persuasive grounds that granting a stay will be consistent with its duties under s.33 of the Act.[599]

(c) Notes of proceedings

Arbitrators' notes. As a general practice, the tribunal should themselves carefully take notes of everything material stated by witnesses, and of material points made in oral submissions. This will enable it properly to sift the evidence and arguments, for example by comparing the oral performance of witnesses with their statements and the documents, and also with the evidence of other witnesses. Where a transcript is available the tribunal's reliance on its own notes is obviously diminished, but an arbitrator will usually want to keep a note in any event as a precautionary measure.

5–206

Transcripts. The tribunal's task may be made much easier if they are provided with a transcript of the proceedings taken by a firm of shorthand writers or produced from a recording of the proceedings. Whilst this is commonly done, it can be expensive and the parties may be unwilling to incur the additional expense. The tribunal may wish to explore with the parties the different options available and what is suitable for the particular case.[600] This may vary from the luxury of a simultaneous computerised transcript to a transcript of a mechanical recording received some time later.

5–207

7. TERMINATION OF THE REFERENCE

(a) Termination following a final award

Functus officio. The proceedings will close after the oral hearings have finished and any post-hearing submissions have been made. Thereafter the tribunal makes its award.[601] Once a final award is made,[602] the tribunal becomes *functus officio.* This means that its authority to act ceases, the reference terminates and the award cannot thereafter be amended.

5–208

---

[598] See *Elektrim SA v VivendiUniversal SA (No.2)* [2007] EWHC 571 at [71].

[599] See para.5–040 above. In *Elektrim SA v VivendiUniversal SA (No.2)* [2007] EWHC 571, the tribunal refused to stay the proceedings on three occasions.

[600] See para.5–180 above.

[601] For the position where the parties settle the dispute during the reference see para.5–223 below.

[602] In the case of an award which determines all the outstanding issues in the arbitration, i.e. all those not previously dealt with in earlier awards. See para.6–005 below.

5-209 **Amendment to or additional award.** There are, though, exceptions under the Arbitration Act 1996 to the rule that the tribunal becomes functus officio. First, the tribunal has power under s.57 of the Arbitration Act 1996 to correct clerical mistakes or errors or to clarify or remove any ambiguity in the award.[603] Second, it can make an additional award in respect of any claim presented to the tribunal which was not dealt with in the award.[604] Third, the court has power to remit matters to the tribunal under ss.68(3)(a) and 69(7)(c) of the Arbitration Act 1996.[605]

5-210 **Providing reasons.** Under s.70(4) of the Arbitration Act 1996[606] the court may also order the tribunal to state the reasons for its award in sufficient detail to enable the court properly to consider a challenge to or appeal against the award.[607] The order only arises where a challenge to or appeal against the award has actually been made.

5-211 **Fresh evidence prior to the final award.** The tribunal has a discretion whether to hear further evidence after the proceedings have closed but prior to making its award. The key issues will be whether the evidence is material and whether it could have been produced earlier.[608] If it is not material, or if it could have been produced earlier, the tribunal is unlikely to exercise its discretion in favour of allowing it to be given. If for some reason it could not have been given earlier, the tribunal is likely to be more sympathetic to the application for it to be taken into account. A tribunal should not receive and act on fresh evidence obtained after the proceedings have closed without giving the parties an opportunity to be heard on it.[609]

5-212 **Fresh evidence after the final award.** If fresh evidence comes to light subsequent to the making of the award, the tribunal cannot deal with it of its own volition. Prior to the 1996 Act the court could remit the award to the tribunal for the fresh evidence to be considered,[610] but it is very doubtful whether this would now fall within the meaning of serious irregularity for the purposes of challenging the award under s.68 of the 1996 Act.[611]

---

[603] See paras 6–166 *et seq.* below.
[604] See paras 6–036 *et seq.* below
[605] See para.8–163 below.
[606] See paras 6–031 and 8–095 below.
[607] See paras 8–162 *et seq.*
[608] See *JH Rayner & Co v Fred Drughorn Ltd* [1924] 18 Lloyd's Rep. 269.
[609] *Sociedad Iberica de Molturacion SA v Nidera Handelscompagnie BV* [1990] 2 Lloyd's Rep. 240. This would fall within the duty imposed by s.33(1) of the Arbitration Act: see paras 5–032 above and 8–167 below.
[610] But again would only do so if it was material and could not have been obtained earlier: see *Albany Marine Inc v South Loyal Shipping Inc and Another (The "Ville De Titana")* [1994] 1 Lloyd's Rep. 541.
[611] *Profilati Italia SRL v Paine Webber Inc* [2001] 1 All E.R. (Comm) 1065. See also para.8–099.

Settlement. Where the parties settle their dispute, and whether or not the tribunal issues an agreed award,[612] the tribunal is required to terminate the substantive proceedings.[613] This is subject to agreement in writing[614] otherwise by the parties.[615]

5–213

(b) Dismissal for want of prosecution

Statutory power. The tribunal has power to make an award dismissing a claim for want of prosecution,[616] subject to agreement otherwise by the parties and also subject to the following conditions.[617] First, there must have been inordinate and inexcusable delay on the part of the claimant in pursuing the claim and, secondly, the delay must give rise or be likely to give rise to a substantial risk that it is not possible to have a fair resolution of the issues in the claim or the delay must have caused, or be likely to cause, serious prejudice to the respondent.

5–214

Retrospective application. The statutory power to dismiss for want of prosecution under the old law applied retrospectively, both in relation to arbitration agreements made and references commenced before it came into force and in respect of delay occurring before that time.[618] The same would apply to s.41(3) of the Arbitration Act 1996.

5–215

Contractual power. In addition to the statutory power, there may also be a contractual power to dismiss for want of prosecution contained in the arbitration agreement or in the arbitration rules incorporated by reference.[619]

5–216

Position where no tribunal appointed. The position is more complicated where arbitration has been commenced by service of a notice of arbitration which stops the limitation period running, but no tribunal has ever been appointed. In those circumstances, absent factual evidence of abandonment, or

5–217

---

[612] See paras 6–025 *et seq.*

[613] Section 51(2) of the Arbitration Act 1996.

[614] The requirement for any agreement to be "in writing" stems from s.5(1) of the Arbitration Act 1996 although the section gives the expression a broad meaning.

[615] Section 51(1) of the Arbitration Act 1996.

[616] Section 41(3) of the Arbitration Act 1996, replacing s.13A of the Arbitration Act 1950 (inserted by the Courts and Legal Services Act 1990, s.102). Prior to this enactment there had been various attempts to assert a power to terminate stale arbitration proceedings, which were largely rejected by the courts: see *Bremer Vulkan Schiffbau Und Maschinenfabrik v South India Shipping Corp (The "Bremer Vulkan")* [1981] 1 All E.R. 289; [1981] A.C. 909; *Paal Wilson & Co A/S v Partenreederei Hannah Blumenthal (The "Hannah Blumenthal")* [1983] 1 All E.R. 34; *Food Corp of India v Antclizo Shipping Corp (The "Antclizo")* [1988] 2 All E.R. 513.

[617] Section 41(3) of the Arbitration Act 1996.

[618] *L'Office Cherifien Des Phosphates and Unitramp SA v Yamashita-Shinnihon Steamship Co Ltd (The "Boucraa")* [1994] 1 Lloyd's Rep. 251.

[619] See, e.g. Art.22 of the GAFTA Arbitration Rules, No.125.

some express or implied provision to proceed without delay, the reference continues and the right to appoint an arbitrator subsists.[620]

(c) Termination by mutual consent

5-218   Termination by agreement. The parties may agree to terminate the reference and if they do so this operates as a consensual withdrawal of the tribunal's jurisdiction,[621] i.e. the parties are agreeing to revoke the authority of the tribunal.[622] The parties may also agree to terminate the arbitration agreement[623] and whether this will also terminate the particular reference will depend upon the circumstances of the case. The revocation must be in writing unless the arbitration agreement is also terminated.[624]

5-219   Abandonment by conduct of the parties. The conduct of the parties in failing to proceed with an arbitration may be sufficient to justify the inference that they have mutually agreed[625] to abandon the contract to arbitrate.[626] Ordinary contractual principles apply in determining whether the parties have agreed on the abandonment.[627] However, the circumstances in which silence and inactivity can lead to an inference of abandonment by mutual consent are very limited.[628] Indeed, unless the period of silence is so long that all possibilities other than an inferred agreement to abandon can be plainly excluded, or at least that an

---

[620] *Indescon Ltd v Ogden* [2005] 1 Lloyd's Rep. 31.

[621] *Chimimport Plc v G D'Alesio SAS (The "Paola D'Alesio")* [1994] 2 Lloyd's Rep. 366.

[622] See s.23(3) of the Arbitration Act 1996. Revocation of the tribunal's authority would not necessarily operate as an agreement to terminate the reference, however.

[623] See para.2–110.

[624] Section 23(4) of the Arbitration Act 1996. For the meaning of "writing" see s.5 of the Arbitration Act 1996. It was considered impracticable to require agreement in writing to terminate the arbitration agreement, see para.99 of the DAC report.

[625] Neither party can treat inactivity by the other party as a repudiatory breach of the arbitration agreement and bring the arbitration to an end by accepting it, since both parties would be in breach of the mutual obligation to proceed with the arbitration and neither could therefore rely on the other's breach: *Bremer Vulkan Schiffbau Und Maschinenfabrik v South India Shipping Corp (The "Bremer Vulkan")* [1981] 1 All E.R. 289. Nor can an arbitration agreement be frustrated by delay: *The "Hannah Blumenthal"* [1983] 1 All E.R. 34.

[626] *The "Splendid Sun"* [1981] 2 Lloyd's Rep. 29; [1981] Q.B. 694; *The "Multitank Holsatia"* [1988] 2 Lloyd's Rep. 486; *Thai-Europe Tapioca Service Ltd v Seine Navigation Co Inc (The "Maritime Winner")* [1989] 2 Lloyd's Rep. 506. The first of these cases was expressly approved by the House of Lords in *The "Hannah Blumenthal"* [1983] 1 All E.R. 34.

[627] *The "Hannah Blumenthal"* [1983] 1 All E.R. 34.

[628] See *Francaise D'Importation et de Distribution SA v Deutsche Continental Handelsgesellschaft* [1985] 2 Lloyd's Rep. 592 at 598–599; *The "Leonidas D"* [1985] 2 Lloyd's Rep. 18 at 24–25; *Food Corp of India v Antclizo Shipping Corp (The "Antclizo")* [1988] 2 All E.R. 513; *The "Multitank Holsatia"* [1988] 2 Lloyd's Rep. 486 at 491; *Thai-Europe Tapioca Service Ltd v Seine Navigation Co Inc (The "Maritime Winner")* [1989] 2 Lloyd's Rep. 506 at 513–515; *The "Golden Bear"* [1987] 1 Lloyd's Rep. 331; *Unisys International Services Ltd v Eastern Counties Newspapers Ltd* [1991] 1 Lloyd's Rep. 538, CA. See also *Indescon Ltd v Ogden* [2004] EWHC 2326.

agreement to abandon was the most probable inference, mere silence can never amount to such an agreement.[629]

Limited scope of application. The case law on abandonment by conduct 5–220
pre-dates the coming into force of s.41(3) of the Arbitration Act 1996[630] which gave the tribunal power to make an award dismissing a claim where there has been inordinate and inexcusable delay in pursuing it. The circumstances in which a case based on abandonment at common law would nowadays be brought must be very limited. It is not inconceivable, however, that the reference could be abandoned by mutual consent even though s.41(3) would not apply, for example because the respondent is unable to demonstrate the requisite prejudice[631] or because the parties have excluded the power under s.41(3).

---

[629] *Unisys International Services Ltd v Eastern Counties Newspapers Ltd* [1991] 1 Lloyd's Rep. 538, CA.
[630] See further para.5–224.
[631] See, e.g. the comments of Potter J. in *Thai-Europe Tapioca Service Ltd v Seine Navigation Co Inc (The "Maritime Winner")* [1989] 2 Lloyd's Rep. 506 at 517 where he drew a distinction between estoppel, for which prejudice is required, and contractual abandonment.

CHAPTER 6

THE AWARD

1. INTRODUCTION

(a) Contents of the chapter

This chapter deals with the award. It begins by considering what an award is 6–001
and describing the different types of award. It then looks at the formal and
substantive requirements of a valid award and also at the relief and remedies which
a tribunal may give in an award, including the award of interest. This is followed
by a consideration of costs and how these should be dealt with in the award.
Finally the chapter deals with the effect of an award including its effect on the
reference, on the parties and on third parties.

(b) What is an award?

No statutory definition. There is no statutory definition of an award in 6–002
English arbitration law despite the important consequences which flow from an
award being made. In principle an award is a final determination of a particular
issue or claim in the arbitration. It may be contrasted with orders and directions
which address the procedural mechanisms to be adopted in the reference.[1] Such
procedural orders and directions are not necessarily final in that the tribunal may
choose to vary or rescind them altogether.[2] Thus, questions concerning the
jurisdiction of the tribunal or the choice of the applicable substantive law are
suitable for determination by the issue of an award. Questions concerning the
timetable for the reference or the extent of disclosure of documents are procedural
in nature and are determined by the issue of an order or direction and not by an
award. The distinction is important because an award can be the subject of a
challenge or an appeal to the court,[3] whereas an order or direction in itself cannot
be so challenged.[4] A preliminary decision, for example of the engineer or adjudicator under a construction contract, which is itself subject to review by an arbitration tribunal, is not an award.[5]

---

[1] Section 34(3) of the Arbitration Act 1996 refers to "directions" given by the tribunal in relation to
procedural and evidential matters. Sections 20 and 22 refer to "decisions, orders and awards" of the
tribunal. See generally para.5–111 above.
[2] See for example *Home of Homes Ltd v Hammersmith and Fulham LBC* [2003] EWHC 807; 92 Const.
L.R. 48 where an arbitrator rescinded his earlier orders limiting recoverable costs pursuant to s.65
of the Arbitration Act 1996. See also *Charles M Willie and Co (Shipping) Ltd v Ocean Laser Shipping
Ltd ("The Smaro")* [1999] 1 Lloyd's Rep. 225.
[3] Under ss.67, 68 or 69 of the Arbitration Act 1996: see paras 8–054, 8–072 and 8–119 *et seq.*
below.
[4] This is because ss.67, 68 and 69 of the Arbitration Act 1996, which deal with challenges and appeals,
all specifically refer to awards: see paras 8–054, 8–072 and 8–119 *et seq.* below. In *Charles M Willie
and Co (Shipping) Ltd v Ocean Laser Shipping Ltd ("The Smaro")* [1999] 1 Lloyd's Rep. 225 Rix
J. suggested that arbitrators may have a discretion to render a procedural or evidential decision in
the form of an award if it raises a question of such principle or importance that subjecting it to the
mechanism for leave to appeal would be appropriate.
[5] *Cameron (A) Ltd v John Mowlem & Co Plc* [1990] 52 Build. L.R. 24, CA. Relief is, however,
available from the court to give effect to such a decision, see for example *Drake & Scull Engineering
Ltd v McLaughlin & Harvey Plc* 60 B.L.R. 102; *Macob Civil Engineering Ltd v Morrison Construction Ltd* [1999] B.L.R. 93 at [24].

6–003 **Procedural orders and directions.** The distinction referred to above between an award and procedural orders may in some circumstances become blurred.[6] The tribunal may issue a document which purports to be an award but which in fact deals only with procedural issues. In *Exmar BV v National Iranian Tanker Co (The "Trade Fortitude")*[7] Judge Diamond Q.C. had to consider a document described by the tribunal as an "Interim Final Award" which contained the decision that it would not issue an interim award[8] in the claimants' favour pending the determination of the respondents' counterclaims. The document also gave detailed reasons for this decision. The judge found it impossible to say that the document, being a decision in respect of matters referred to the tribunal for decision, was incapable by reason of its procedural nature of constituting an award. He therefore concluded, albeit somewhat reluctantly, that he had jurisdiction to review the tribunal's decision.[9] A stricter approach towards attempts to challenge an "award" dealing with procedural matters is now likely to be taken in accordance with the general non-interventionist philosophy of the Arbitration Act 1996, and tribunals should in any event take care to distinguish their procedural orders and directions from awards on substantive issues.

(c) A final award

6–004 **Meaning of "final award".** There are three senses in which an award may be said to be "final". First, an award may be final in that it determines all the issues in the arbitration, or determines all the issues which remain outstanding following earlier awards dealing with only some of the issues in the arbitration.[10] Second, an award must be final in the sense of being a complete decision on the particular issues considered without leaving aspects of those issues to be dealt with subsequently or by a third party.[11] Third, an award is final under s.58(1) of the

---

[6] See, e.g., *Leif Hoegh & Co A/S v Petrolsea Inc (The "World Era") (No.2)* [1993] 1 Lloyd's Rep. 363 and *Urban Small Space Ltd v Burford Investment Co Ltd* [1990] 2 E.G.L.R. 120. In both of these cases the tribunal made an award dealing with disclosure of documents. In the latter case leave to appeal against the award was refused on the ground that the appeal would not substantially affect a party's rights, but no objection to the application seems to have been taken on the grounds that it was in fact a procedural direction rather than a final determination of an issue or issues in the arbitration. Cf. *Three Valleys Water Committee v Binnie & Partners* 52 B.L.R. 42 where the court refused to order an arbitrator to state reasons under s.1(5) of the Arbitration Act 1979, (now s.70(4) of the Arbitration Act 1996—see para.6–031 below) for his decision on the service of a pleading because it was not an award but simply a ruling. See also *The "Sennar" (No.2)* [1985] 1 W.L.R. 490.

[7] [1992] 1 Lloyd's Rep. 169.

[8] Under s.14 of the Arbitration Act 1950. The term "interim award" was deliberately not used in s.47 of the Arbitration Act 1996 which replaced s.14 of the 1950 Act. See further paras 6–009 *et seq.* below.

[9] See also *Cargill SpA v P Kadinopoulos SA* [1992] 1 Lloyd's Rep. 1, HL.

[10] The phrase has been very commonly used in this sense and this has continued notwithstanding that the previous distinction between final and interim awards is no longer appropriate: see para.6–009 below.

[11] See paras 6–007 and 6–078 below.

Arbitration Act 1996 in that it is final and binding on the parties.[12] These three senses are discussed further in the following paragraphs.

Final award determining all outstanding issues in the arbitration. 6–005

A "final" award in this sense is descriptive of the kind of award rather than its effect. It describes an award which determines all the outstanding issues in the arbitration, i.e. all those not previously dealt with in earlier awards. A tribunal can make only one final award in this sense of the term in the absence of some specific authority to make more than one.[13] Subject to the matters discussed in para.6–005 below, once its final award is made the tribunal is "*functus officio*". This means that its jurisdiction over the matters referred to arbitration comes to an end.[14]

Exceptions. 6–006

There are three exceptions under the Arbitration Act 1996 to the general rule that once the tribunal has made its final award, it becomes "*functus officio*" and cannot subsequently amend the award. First, the court has power to remit matters to the tribunal under ss.68(3)(a) and 69(7)(c) of the Arbitration Act 1996.[15] Secondly, the tribunal has power under s.57(3)(a) of the Arbitration Act 1996 to correct clerical mistakes or errors or to clarify or remove any ambiguity in the award.[16] Thirdly, under s.57(3)(b) of the Arbitration Act 1996, the tribunal can make an additional award in respect of any claim presented to the tribunal which was not dealt with in the award.[17]

Complete decision. 6–007

The second sense in which an award must be final is the requirement for it to be a complete decision on the matters dealt with. A tribunal may not, for example, leave matters open for the decision of a third party.[18]

Final and binding. 6–008

The concept of a final award described above should not be confused with the sense in which an award is "final" under s.58(1) of the Arbitration Act 1996.[19] Section 58(1) provides:

---

[12] See paras 6–008 and 6–162 below. Section 39 of the Arbitration Act 1996 refers to a final award, apparently giving it this meaning.

[13] Such authority might arise under statute, e.g. under the provisions of the Arbitration Act 1996 discussed in para.6–006. Alternatively, it might arise from the terms of the arbitration agreement: see, e.g. the power to make additional awards under the LCIA Rules, Art.27.3.

[14] See para.5–218 above.

[15] See paras 8–113 and 8–153 below.

[16] See paras 6–167 *et seq.* below.

[17] See paras 6–171 below.

[18] See para.6–078 below.

[19] In *Pirtek (UK) Ltd v Deanswood Ltd* [2005] EWHC 2301; [2005] 2 Lloyd's Rep. 728 it was held that a tribunal had no power to make an award of interest because an earlier award dealing with quantum was final and binding on the parties. However it was because the earlier award was final in the sense of having finally determined all the outstanding issues in the arbitration that the making of a further award was precluded, rather than because it was final and binding under s.58(1) of the Arbitration Act 1996.

"Unless otherwise agreed by the parties, an award made by the tribunal pursuant to an arbitration agreement is final and binding both on the parties and on any persons claiming through or under them."

"Final" in this context means that, as between the parties to the reference and persons described in s.58(1),[20] the award is conclusive as to the issues with which it deals, unless and until there is a successful challenge to the award.[21] The award can therefore be enforced, even if there are other issues outstanding in the reference.[22] In this sense all awards are final and binding under s.58(1) as to the particular issues with which they deal,[23] even if they are not the final award made in the reference.[24] This provision is subject to the parties agreeing otherwise but selection of a foreign governing law will not suffice as agreement otherwise for these purposes.[25]

(d) Awards on different issues

6–009   **Power to make more than one award.** An award may dispose of only some of the issues in the arbitration, leaving others to be determined in a subsequent award or awards. In some jurisdictions and certain sets of arbitration rules these awards are referred to as "partial awards".[26] Section 47 of the Arbitration Act 1996 provides that the tribunal may make more than one award at different times on different aspects of the matters to be determined. This is a general power to determine the issues in more than one award and the section

---

[20] Persons claiming through or under a party would include, for example, assignees: see para.3–018.

[21] In *Equatorial Traders Ltd v Louis Dreyfus Trading Ltd* [2002] EWHC 2023 (QBD (Comm)) an arbitration award was subject to appeal under the arbitration rules of a trade association but became final and binding if a statement of case in the appeal was not served within a given time limit or any extension granted. The deadline having been missed, the court found that the arbitration award could not be the subject of a second appeal as it had become final and binding by operation of the rules.

[22] *Marine Contractors Inc v Shell Petroleum Company of Nigeria Limited* [1984] 2 Lloyd's Rep. 77; *Overseas Fortune Shipping Pte Limited v Great Eastern Shipping Co Ltd (The "Singapore Fortune")* [1987] 1 Lloyd's Rep. 270.

[23] See however *The Republic of Kazakhstan v Istil Group Inc* [2006] EWHC 448 where a partial award on jurisdiction was subsequently held by the tribunal to be a nullity when it transpired that a party had ceased to exist at the time of the partial award. The court ruled that any challenge to the tribunal's approach on the basis that it constituted an irregularity should have been, but was not, made within the time limits set out for serious irregularity challenges under s.68 of the Arbitration Act 1996. Nevertheless it offered the provisional view that the partial award was not a nullity.

[24] In *Glaxosmithkline Ltd v Department of Health* [2007] EWHC 1470 it was alleged that the parties had entered into a purely non-binding and voluntary agreement with no intention to create legal relations and that the arbitration agreement was not therefore binding and there was no "award" for the purposes of an appeal under s.69 of the Arbitration Act 1996. This was rejected by the court and Cooke J. noted at [27] that: "When regard is then had to the terms of the Arbitration Act, attention is directed to sections 58 and 66. These show that, absent contrary agreement, an Award is binding and may, with the leave of the court, be enforced. I find no agreement between the parties that the Award should not be final and binding."

[25] *C v D* [2007] EWHC 1541.

[26] See, e.g. ICC Rules, Art.2(iii).

imposes no time limit as to when any further award is to be made.[27] The power is subject to agreement otherwise by the parties.[28] The section specifically avoids using the term "interim award"[29] on the basis that it was thought to be confusing[30] but it is still used from time to time. The section also makes clear that the tribunal may, in particular, make an award relating—

(a) to an issue affecting the whole claim, or

(b) to a part only of the claims or cross-claims submitted to it for decision.[31]

Scope and content of awards on different issues. An award dealing only with certain issues or claims must clearly state that it is an award relating to those issues or claims only and specify the issue or claim or part of a claim with which it deals,[32] otherwise the award may be subject to challenge.[33] An award must also comprise a determination of an issue or claim which is in dispute. It cannot therefore be used to provide a "payment on account" of sums claimed, without actually deciding that those sums are due and owing.[34]   6–010

When awards on different issues appropriate. Section 47 was drafted not so as to alter the existing powers of the tribunal to make several awards,[35] but rather to emphasise how those powers should be exercised in appropriate cases.[36] Whether to make more than one award is a matter over which the tribunal has a complete discretion,[37] subject to complying with the duty under s.33(1) of the Arbitration Act 1996.[38] However, some guidance is given in paras 226–233 of the DAC report.[39] In particular, it is intended that they should be used in large, complex cases where issues may be selected for early decision which will be commercially, even if not legally, determinative of the case. As is pointed out in   6–011

---

[27] *Sea Trade Maritime Corp v Hellenic Mutual War Risks Association (Bermuda) Ltd* [2006] EWHC 578.
[28] Section 47(1) of the Arbitration Act 1996.
[29] This was the term used in earlier legislation: s.14 of the Arbitration Act 1950.
[30] Because it suggests a temporary decision: see para.233 of the DAC report.
[31] Section 47(2) of the Arbitration Act 1996.
[32] Section 47(3) of the Arbitration Act 1996 confirming *SL Sethia Liners Ltd v Naviagro Maritime Corp (The "Kostas Melas")* [1981] 1 Lloyd's Rep. 18.
[33] Under s.68(2)(f) and/or (h) of the Arbitration Act 1996: see (under the previous law) *Leach (SH) v Haringey London Borough Council, The Times*, March 23, 1977.
[34] See para.231 of the DAC report approving the reasoning in *The "Kostas Melas"* [1981] Lloyd's Rep. 18. There is power under s.39 of the Arbitration Act 1996 to make temporary financial adjustments between the parties pending resolution of the dispute: see paras 6–020 *et seq.* below.
[35] Under s.14 of the Arbitration Act 1950. Where the reference to arbitration is of a composite dispute, the tribunal may not isolate an individual point and decide it as a separate issue: *Minerals and Metals Trading Corp of India Ltd v Encounter Bay Shipping Co Ltd (The "Samos Glory") (No.2)* [1988] 1 Lloyd's Rep. 51.
[36] Paragraph 232 of the DAC report.
[37] *Exmar BV v National Iranian Tanker Co (The "Trade Fortitude")* [1992] 1 Lloyd's Rep. 169.
[38] See para.230 of the DAC report.
[39] See Appendix 2.

the DAC Report, this is consistent with the approach adopted in both the Commercial Court and the Official Referees' Court[40] in England.

6–012 **Examples.** By way of example, the making of awards on different issues may be appropriate:

(1) Where the determination of a particular issue or issues at an early stage will save time or costs or both in relation to the future conduct of the reference. This may be the case, for example, where there are objections to the jurisdiction of the tribunal[41] or where there is a dispute as to the law applicable to the substantive issues in the case.[42]

(2) Where the determination of a particular issue or issues is likely to be decisive of the whole or a significant part of the dispute. Thus it may be expedient to deal with issues of liability before those relating to quantum or to deal with a number of principal issues or claims which the parties believe will from a commercial viewpoint assist them in resolving the remaining matters in dispute between them.

(3) Where an ascertainable minimum sum is clearly due from one party to the other, notwithstanding that there may be further sums in dispute or further claims or cross-claims which may give rise to liability.[43] Thus, an award may be sought from the tribunal[44] where a party maintains that there is no defence to some part of the claim,[45] or where there is an ongoing loss or cause of action. In the latter case, the tribunal may issue an award for losses incurred to the date of its award and leave open the option of a further award or awards for future losses.

(4) Where the proceedings are of a size and complexity that the only practical course is to deal with the issues or groups of issues in stages.

6–013 **Award on jurisdiction.** The tribunal can issue an award on jurisdiction under s.31(4)(a) of the Arbitration Act 1996.[46] The power is frequently exercised

---

[40] Now called the Technology and Construction Court.

[41] See paras 6–013 below and 5–060 *et seq.*

[42] Although depending upon the circumstances it may be better to deal with these matters at the same time as the other substantive issues in the case: see para.5–067.

[43] Section 47(2)(b) of the Arbitration Act 1996 specifically contemplates the tribunal making an award on part only of the claims or cross-claims referred. See for example *SL Sethia Liners Ltd v Naviagro Maritime Corp (The "Kostas Melas")* [1981] 1 Lloyd's Rep. 18. See also para.6–016 below for the position where deduction or set-off is claimed.

[44] The tribunal may also have power to make provisional awards in these circumstances under s.39 of the Arbitration Act 1996, as to which see paras 6–020 *et seq.* below.

[45] This is different from the court's power to grant summary judgment under CPR Pt 24 where it considers that there is no prospect of success on a claim or issue because, unlike a court, a tribunal would need to conduct an investigation of any disputed law or facts to satisfy itself that there is no defence to the claim before issuing its award.

[46] Assuming it has power to rule on its own jurisdiction under s.30 of the Arbitration Act 1996: see para.5–062 above.

where either the tribunal itself has concerns about its jurisdiction or where one of the parties raises a challenge to the tribunal's jurisdiction to proceed with the reference.[47] The tribunal cannot be compelled to give an award on jurisdiction prior to its final award,[48] but it is common in these circumstances for the tribunal to agree to do so, because if its decision is to be challenged in the courts that process can be commenced without delay.[49]

Dangers of multiple awards. In an appropriate case the issue of more than one award may be extremely useful. A multiplicity of awards can, however, be detrimental, and tribunals should be wary of adopting such an approach. By dealing with the case in the piecemeal fashion that several awards necessarily entails, there may be a danger that resolution of the dispute as a whole will be delayed and the parties will be put to additional expense. The decision to make an award on a particular issue or issues will also often be made at an early stage of the proceedings. There is a danger that it may subsequently prove to be less determinative, legally or commercially, than originally envisaged. For example, as the case unfolds, it may become clear that it is more complex than originally thought. The tribunal should therefore consider whether there is any real advantage to any of the parties in proceeding with the partial award at all, or whether it will simply add to the costs of the reference and cause unnecessary delay.[50] The tribunal should focus on what it is intended to achieve by the issue of the award, whether that is the most appropriate and efficient way of dealing with the reference and the likelihood of the award achieving that object. In considering these matters the tribunal should of course keep in mind its duties under s.33 of the Arbitration Act 1996.[51]

6–014

Imposition of conditions. Where a tribunal is minded to exercise its discretion to issue an award dealing with particular issues or claims only, it may impose conditions on its doing so. For example, a tribunal may refuse to make the award unless the claimant provides reasonable security for the respondent's cross-claims.[52] The tribunal cannot, however, make an order for disclosure of documents in the arbitration conditional upon the honouring of an earlier partial award by the party seeking disclosure.[53]

6–015

Claim for deduction or set-off. The question arises whether a tribunal has jurisdiction to consider a set-off said to constitute a defence to a claim before

6–016

---

[47] See paras 5–060 *et seq.*
[48] *Exmar BV v National Iranian Tanker Co (The "Trade Fortitude")* [1992] 1 Lloyd's Rep. 169.
[49] See generally paras 5–060 *et seq.* above and in particular para.5–068.
[50] See further *Exmar BV v National Iranian Tanker Co (The "Trade Fortitude")* [1992] 1 Lloyd's Rep. 169 as to the circumstances in which an award on particular issues or claims is appropriate.
[51] See paras 5–032 *et seq.*
[52] *Japan Line Ltd v Aggeliki Charis Compania Maritima SA (The "Angelic Grace")* [1980] 1 Lloyd's Rep. 288; *Exmar BV v National Iranian Tanker Co (The "Trade Fortitude")* [1992] 1 Lloyd's Rep. 169 and see also *Glafki Shipping Co SA v Pinios Shipping Co (No.1) (The "Maira")* [1982] 1 Lloyd's Rep. 257, CA.
[53] *Kirkawa Corp v Gatoil Overseas Ltd (The "Peter Kirk")* [1990] 1 Lloyd's Rep. 154.

the tribunal, when such set-off arises under some separate agreement.[54] The tribunal will need to be satisfied that it has jurisdiction over the claimed set-off on the true construction of the arbitration agreement.[55] A distinction may also need to be drawn between transaction set-off, which relates to matters arising under the same or a closely related contract, and independent set-off, which concerns an unrelated contract.[56] A tribunal will be more readily willing to accept jurisdiction in a case of transaction set-off than where what is claimed is an independent set-off but again it will depend upon the tribunal having jurisdiction on the true construction of the arbitration agreement in question.[57]

The difficulty lies in determining in each case whether there is jurisdiction to deal with set-off claims in circumstances where no clear indication is given in the arbitration agreement.[58] In principle it is perhaps preferable for a tribunal to be able to determine a claim for set-off, at least where the respective agreements are part of the same transaction or series of transactions, on the basis that it can then determine whether a defence is properly available in respect of claims which the tribunal is required to determine.[59] This reasoning applies to a set-off as a defence to a claim but not perhaps to the bringing of a counterclaim. The jurisdiction of a tribunal to deal with a cross claim or set off by way of counterclaim (as opposed to a defence to a claim) will only be available if they fall clearly within the arbitration agreement.[60]

---

[54] For contractual rights of set-off see para.6–017 below.

[55] *Econet Satellite Services Ltd v Vee Networks Ltd* [2006] EWHC 1664; [2006] 2 Lloyd's Rep. 423. In that case the arbitration agreement covered disputes "arising under, out of or by virtue of this Agreement" and was subject to the UNCITRAL Arbitration Rules, Art.19.3 of which provides that "In his statement of defence . . . the respondent may make a counter-claim arising out of the same contract or rely on a claim arising out of the same contract for the purpose of a set-off". Field J. held that the effect of these provisions was that the respondent could raise a set-off only if it was founded on a claim arising out of the same contract as that on which the claimant's claim was based. Cf. the provisional view expressed by Gross J. in *Ronly Holdings Ltd v JSC Zestafoni G Nikoladze Ferroalloy Plant* [2004] EWHC 1354; [2004] B.L.R. 323 that a tribunal does or should have a general jurisdiction to allow a transaction set-off.

[56] *Aectra Refining & Manufacturing Inc v Exmar NV (The New Vanguard and The Pacifica)* [1994] 1 W.L.R. 1634.

[57] *Metal Distributors (UK) Ltd v ZCCM Investment Holdings Plc* [2005] EWHC 156; [2005] 2 Lloyd's Rep. 37

[58] Where the arbitration agreement incorporates arbitration rules which deal expressly with the question of a claim for set-off, as in *Econet Satellite Services Ltd v Vee Networks Ltd* [2006] EWHC 1664; [2006] 2 Lloyd's Rep. 423, the position is relatively straightforward, but many arbitration agreements will be silent on the point.

[59] This was the view expressed on a provisional basis by Gross J. in *Ronly Holdings Ltd v JSC Zestafoni G Nikoladze Ferroalloy Plant* [2004] EWHC 1354; [2004] B.L.R. 323 at [33]. The objection to it is that the tribunal would thereby be effectively assuming jurisdiction in respect of the separate agreement over which it has no jurisdiction. Difficulties arise however where the tribunal determines a set-off defence arising under a separate agreement and that agreement is or may be the subject of separate proceedings. Even if it could be said that in fact no determination under the separate agreement was being made but rather simply an assessment of the validity of the defence being advanced, it is quite possible that the determination would give rise to an issue estoppel: see para.6–019 below. That said, the alternative is that the tribunal are unable to consider what would otherwise be a valid defence to the claim due to the limits of their jurisdiction, which is also undesirable as those issues would have to be determined in separate proceedings.

[60] *Metal Distributors (UK) Ltd v ZCCM Investment Holdings Plc* [2005] EWHC 156; [2005] 2 Lloyd's Rep. 37.

Contractual deduction or set-off. The position is more straightforward 6–017 where the claim for deduction or set-off is based on an express provision in the parties' contract. There is authority that where a party is entitled to, and does, claim a contractual right of deduction or equitable set-off against sums due, a tribunal may only in "exceptional circumstances" make an award in respect of those sums without a full hearing of the matters alleged to give rise to the deduction or set-off.[61] For these purposes "exceptional circumstances" arise where the party claiming deduction or set-off does not satisfy the tribunal that he does so in good faith and on reasonable grounds, or where the sum awarded is undoubtedly due even on the figures presented by the party claiming deduction or set-off.[62] Otherwise, if a tribunal makes an award for a sum to be immediately payable without properly considering a claimed right of set-off, the award may be subject to challenge.[63]

The effect of an award on particular issues or claims. An award 6–018 dealing only with particular issues or claims is an "award" for the purposes of the Arbitration Act 1996.[64] Accordingly it is final and binding as between the parties to the arbitration (and those claiming through or under them[65]) in relation to the issues disposed of by it, unless and until there is a successful appeal or challenge to the award.[66] The statutory provisions relating to the challenge and enforcement of awards, which are discussed in Ch.8 below,[67] also apply.

Issue estoppel. An award dealing with particular issues creates an "issue 6–019 estoppel" between the parties in relation to the matters with which it deals.[68] The tribunal does not have power either to reopen its award at some later stage of the reference, or to make a subsequent determination of issues previously disposed of in an interim award. Once it makes an award, the tribunal becomes *"functus officio"*[69] in relation to that part of its mandate which comprised the issues disposed of and the tribunal thereby redefines its mandate for the future. Any

---

[61] *The Modern Trading Co Ltd v Swale Building and Construction Ltd* [1992] A.D.R.L.J. 174; 24 Con. L.R. 59.

[62] *The Modern Trading Co Ltd v Swale Building and Construction Ltd* [1992] A.D.R.L.J. 174 24 Con. L.R. 59; *SL Sethia Liners Ltd v Naviagro Maritime Corp (The "Kostas Melas")* [1981] 1 Lloyd's Rep. 18. See also *Industriebeteiligungs & Handelsgesellschaft v Malaysian International Shipping Corp Berhad (The "Bunga Melawis")* [1991] 2 Lloyd's Rep. 271.

[63] Under s.68(2)(a) and/or (d) of the Arbitration Act 1996. See paras 8–077 and 8–093 *et seq.*

[64] Section 47 of the Arbitration Act 1996.

[65] Persons claiming through or under a party would include, for example, assignees: see para.3–018.

[66] Section 58(1) of the Arbitration Act 1996. Unlike s.14 of the Arbitration Act 1950 this is not expressly stated in the Arbitration Act 1996, but it is implicit in the treatment of awards under the statute and the commentary at para.232 of the DAC report which makes clear that there was no intention to change the previous powers in relation to interim awards. This was also confirmed in *Gbangbola v Smith & Sherriff Ltd* [1998] 3 All E.R. 730.

[67] See paras 8–051 *et seq.* and 8–002 *et seq.* below.

[68] See paras 6–176 *et seq.* below.

[69] See para.5–218 below.

determination in a later award on an issue already disposed of in an earlier award is therefore outside the tribunal's jurisdiction and void.[70]

(e) Provisional award[71]

6–020 **Power to make a provisional award.** Section 39 of the Arbitration Act 1996 introduced a new provision enabling the parties to empower the tribunal to make provisional awards. It must be emphasised that this is an "opt in" provision which only applies where the parties have agreed that it should[72]; however, a number of institutional rules include it.[73] The power, if conferred, enables the tribunal to order on a provisional basis any relief which it can order in a final award.[74] The parties could also, if they wished, confer more limited powers in relation to provisional awards.[75]

6–021 **Types of provisional award.** Some guidance is given in s.39(2) of the Arbitration Act 1996 as to the types of provisional award envisaged. In particular it provides that the power includes, for instance:

"(a) a provisional order for the payment of money or the disposition of property as between the parties or

(b) an order to make an interim payment on account of the costs of the tribunal."

The power does not, however, allow arbitrators to grant freezing injunctions or search orders on the application of one party alone.[76] This rather begs the question of whether such relief could be granted against a party following a hearing at which he was present. This was raised but not resolved in *Kastner v*

---

[70] What is said in this paragraph does not however apply to provisional awards under s.39 of the Arbitration Act 1996: see para.6–020 *et seq.* below. It is also subject, of course, to the exceptions discussed at para.6–006.

[71] Section 39 of the Arbitration Act 1996 contemplates the making of provisional "orders", but the heading of the section refers to "provisional awards" and the cases dealing with or referring to the section contemplate a power to make an award rather than simply an order: see *BMBF (No.12) Ltd v Harland and Wolff Shipbuilding and Heavy Industries Ltd* [2001] EWCA Civ 862, where provisional relief under s.39 of the Arbitration Act 1996 was given in the form of an award and subsequently reviewed by the court without any objection being taken. In *Ronly Holdings Ltd v JSC Zestafoni G Nikoladze Ferroalloy Plant* [2004] EWHC 1354 Gross J. referred to relief granted pursuant to s.39 of the Arbitration Act 1996 as an exception to the principle that an award must be final as to all issues decided.

[72] Section 39(1) of the Arbitration Act 1996. The parties may do so however by adopting a law or procedure which confers such a power: see *Kastner v Jason* [2004] EWCA Civ 1599.

[73] See for example LCIA Rules, Art.25.1(c) and r.10 of the Construction Industry Model Arbitration Rules.

[74] For the relief and remedies which a tribunal can award see paras 6–096 *et seq.* below.

[75] In accordance with the general principle of party autonomy set out in s.1(b) of the Arbitration Act 1996. The wording of s.39(1) of the Arbitration Act 1996 would accommodate this.

[76] See para.201 of the DAC report.

Jason.[77] It seems the tribunal would not ordinarily have power to make such an order under s.39 because it is not relief which the tribunal would have power to grant in a final award. However at first instance in *Kastner v Jason* Lightman J. considered s.48(1) of the Arbitration Act 1996 sufficiently wide to enable the parties to confer on arbitrators the power by the final award to make freezing directions pending satisfaction or securing the final award.[78] If this were done, then there is no reason why a provisional award to like effect could not be made under s.39. Alternatively the power to make these types of orders may in principle be conferred on the tribunal by agreement of the parties pursuant to s.38(1) of the Arbitration Act 1996. If the order is confined to dealing with property which is the subject of the arbitration proceedings, then s.38(4) of the Arbitration Act 1996 might apply. Generally, though, as the DAC report notes,[78a] these draconian powers are best left to be applied by the court.

When provisional award appropriate. The power to make a provi-   6–022
sional award may be very useful, for example in trades and industries where cash flow is of particular importance.[79] Such clauses have proved popular in the construction industry, and indeed several of the standard form contracts and arbitration rules used in that industry have such provisions.[80] Similarly, in the shipping field it may be useful to give the tribunal power to grant interim payments of freight or to order the sale of cargo prior to the final determination of the dispute.

Provisional decision subject to final award. It is clear from s.39(3)   6–023
of the Arbitration Act 1996 that any provisional award is subject to the final decision of the tribunal in the case. It must therefore be taken into account and finally determined in a subsequent award or awards of the tribunal dealing with the merits of the dispute and/or costs.[81] Section 39 also specifically makes clear that it does not affect the power under s.47 of the Arbitration Act 1996 to make more than one award.

(f) Agreed award

Power to make an agreed award. Many cases settle before reaching the   6–024
stage of a final award. Where the parties settle their dispute in the course of the arbitration, s.51 of the Arbitration Act 1996 enables the tribunal to issue an award

---

[77] [2004] EWHC 592 and, on appeal, at [2004] EWCA Civ 1599.
[78] [2004] EWHC 592 at [27].
[78a] At para.201 of the DAC report.
[79] See para.203 of the DAC report.
[80] See for example r.10 of the Construction Industry Model Arbitration Rules.
[81] See the comments of Gross J. referred to above in *Ronly Holdings Ltd v JSC Zestafoni G Nikoladze Ferroalloy Plant* [2004] EWHC 1354 that relief granted pursuant to s.39 of the Arbitration Act 1996 is an exception to the principle that an award must be final as to all issues decided.

recording the terms agreed.[82] Section 51 is an "opt out" provision so it applies unless the parties have agreed that it should not.[83] The section apparently does not apply where the parties settle part only of their dispute.[84] The tribunal may nevertheless at common law make an award dealing both with the issues requiring determination and recording the terms agreed in relation to issues settled by agreement between the parties.[85] Various arbitration rules also expressly provide for any settlement to be recorded in an award. The ICC Rules, for example, specifically provide that the tribunal may issue a consent award.[86]

6–025   **Obligation of the tribunal.** Where s.51 does apply and the case settles, the tribunal is required to terminate the reference.[87] If requested by the parties, and provided the tribunal does not object to doing so, it must issue an agreed award recording the terms of the settlement.[88] If the tribunal does object, the parties cannot compel the issue of an agreed award. This proviso is important as a control mechanism to ensure the agreed award procedure is not misused by parties seeking an award in terms which would or might mislead third parties or is designed for example to permit the laundering of funds.[89] If the tribunal suspects an ulterior motive of this sort, it may refuse to issue an agreed award.

6–026   **Status and form of an agreed award.** An agreed award has the same status and effect as any other award on the merits.[90] Accordingly, an agreed award is enforceable even though the tribunal has not actually made a decision but simply recorded agreed terms. This is reinforced by the fact that an agreed award must state that it is an award of the tribunal, but need not state that it is an agreed award.[91] Some institutional rules do, however, require that the award state that it

---

[82] This reflects Art.30 of the Model Law.

[83] Section 51(1) of the Arbitration Act 1996.

[84] The wording of s.51 of the Arbitration Act 1996 seems to contemplate any settlement of "the dispute" as a whole. The tribunal would not, for example, "terminate the substantive proceedings" under s.51(2) since this appears to mean the proceedings as a whole. The parties might by agreement seek from the tribunal a consent award dealing with the settlement of part of the dispute but this would not be pursuant to s.51(2) to (5) of the Arbitration Act 1996.

[85] The common law is preserved so far as it is consistent with the Arbitration Act 1996: see s.81(1) of the Arbitration Act 1996.

[86] ICC Rules, Art.26. See also LCIA Rules, Art.26.8.

[87] Section 52(2) of the Arbitration Act 1996. The section refers to terminating "the substantive proceedings", but it is in practice terminating the reference subject possibly to the need to deal with costs: see para.6–026 below.

[88] Section 51(2) says that in these circumstances the tribunal "shall" record the settlement in an agreed award.

[89] See the discussion at paras 241–242 of the DAC report.

[90] Section 51(3) of the Arbitration Act 1996.

[91] This proposition derives from s.51(3) of the Arbitration Act 1996 which requires only that an agreed award shall state that it is an award of the tribunal. Paragraph 244 of the DAC report makes clear that it was deliberately decided not to make any statement that the award is an agreed award a mandatory requirement, although the tribunal are at liberty to record that it is if they consider it appropriate to do so, unless the parties agree otherwise. Paragraph 378 of the DAC report suggested that on an application for enforcement the court should be informed that the award is an agreed award if that is not apparent from the award itself. That suggestion was not adopted in s.66 of the Arbitration Act 1996.

is made by consent.[92] The provisions in the Arbitration Act 1996 relating to awards[93] apply equally to an agreed award[94] and in particular it must comply with the requirements as to form set out in s.52 of the Arbitration Act 1996.[95] The requirement in s.52(4) for an award to contain reasons does not however apply to an agreed award. As regards costs, the terms agreed between the parties may deal with these but, if they do not, ss.59 to 65 of the Arbitration Act 1996 concerning costs of the arbitration apply.[96]

Why seek an agreed award? The advantage of a settlement being incorpo-   6–027
rated in an agreed award is that enforcement of an award is likely to be more straightforward than bringing proceedings to enforce the terms of the settlement itself. If the award is to be enforced abroad, it may be recognised and enforced as a New York Convention award.[97] An agreed award is not strictly necessary, however, unless enforcement of the award is required. The parties would usually want some form of writing recording what has been agreed but this may take the form of an exchange of correspondence or a written settlement agreement rather than an award. The parties will often have informed the tribunal that they are seeking to negotiate a settlement. Whether or not this has been done, once terms are agreed the parties can simply inform the tribunal that a settlement has been reached disposing of the issues referred to arbitration. Subject to payment of any outstanding fees and expenses of the tribunal, the arbitration is brought to an end. In most cases, however, it will be in the parties' interests to have an agreed award under s.51 of the Arbitration Act 1996 for reasons of clarity about what has been agreed and, above all, to facilitate enforcement if that proves necessary.[98]

(g) Reasoned award

Meaning of "reasoned award". A reasoned award is one in which the   6–028
tribunal sets out the reasons for its decision and these reasons form part of the award itself. A reasoned award is also sometimes referred to as a "speaking award" or a "motivated award".

Reasons must be given. Under s.52(4) of the Arbitration Act 1996 an   6–029
award must contain the reasons for the determinations made by the tribunal unless

---

[92] See, e.g. LCIA Rules, Art.26.8.
[93] Sections 52 to 58 of the Arbitration Act 1996.
[94] Section 51(4) of the Arbitration Act 1996.
[95] See paras 6–044 *et seq.* below.
[96] Section 51(5) of the Arbitration Act 1996. These provisions are dealt with at paras 6–129 *et seq.* below.
[97] See paras 8–021 *et seq.* below.
[98] See, e.g. *Chimimport Plc v G D'Alesio SAS (The "Paola D'Alesio")* [1994] 2 Lloyd's Rep. 366 where it was decided that a subsequent challenge to a settlement agreement could not be determined by the arbitrator.

either it is an agreed award or the parties have agreed to dispense with reasons.[99] Parties to an arbitration, and particularly the losing party, are entitled to know the reasons for the tribunal's decision by which they are bound, unless they have specifically agreed in writing[100] to dispense with reasons.[101] Further, reasons are effectively a prerequisite for any appeal against the tribunal's decision, because in practice it will only be possible to argue that there has been an error of law if the tribunal has explained the basis of its findings by giving reasons.[102] It is sufficient for the purposes of a reasoned award under s.52(4) of the Arbitration Act 1996 that the tribunal complies with the parties' requirements for reasons even if they fall short of what would usually be required under English law.[103]

The only reasons that *have* to be given are those "for" the award, i.e. those in favour, and not those of a dissenting arbitrator.[104] It is, however, common practice for the reasons of any dissenters to be given also, and though these are sometimes included within the award document, they do not form part of the award itself.[105]

6–030 **Specifying the matters in dispute.** It is not strictly necessary that the award should specify the matters in dispute,[106] although the requirement to give reasons for the decision[107] will usually encompass an indication, expressly or implicitly, of the disputed issues.[108] In *Checkpoint Ltd v Strathclyde Pension Fund*[109] a distinction was drawn between a point of dispute, which did not have to be specifically dealt with, and an issue for the purposes of s.68(2) of the Arbitration Act 1996, which did. It is however desirable for the award to indicate the matters in dispute so that the parties can see that the tribunal has addressed them, and the award can be relied upon in resisting any subsequent challenge on the grounds

---

[99] The court has power to require the tribunal to state the reasons for its award if it has failed to do so under s.70(4) of the Arbitration Act 1996: see para.6–031. In an extreme case of failure to do so the award may be susceptible to challenge, see para.8–095 below. A failure to give reasons for the decision on costs is an irregularity as to form within the terms of s.68(2)(h) of the Arbitration Act 1996 and can lead to an application that the court should exercise its powers to order reasons to be given under s.70(4): See *Norbrook Laboratories Ltd v Tank* [2006] EWHC 1055 at [127].

[100] The requirement for any agreement between the parties to be "in writing" stems from s.5(1) of the Arbitration Act 1996, although the section gives the expression a broad meaning.

[101] See para.247 of the DAC report.

[102] The court may take into account post-award communications from the tribunal which set out the reasons for the award: *Newfield Construction Ltd v Tomlinson* [2004] EWHC 3051; 97 Con. L.R. 148 at [21].

[103] *The Bay Hotel and Resort Ltd v Cavalier Construction Co Ltd* [2001] UKPC 34. In that case the Privy Council decided that an award which would not have constituted a reasoned award under English law nevertheless fulfilled the requirement of "a written explanation of the award" under the Construction Industry Arbitration Rules of the American Arbitration Association which the parties had incorporated into their arbitration agreement.

[104] *Cargill International SA v Sociedad Iberica de Molturacion SA* [1998] 1 Lloyd's Rep. 489.

[105] *Stinnes Interoil GmbH v Halcoussis & Co* [1982] 2 Lloyd's Rep. 445. See further para.6–058 below.

[106] *Smith v Hartley* (1851) 20 L.J.C.P. 169.

[107] Unless it is an agreed award or the parties have agreed to dispense with reasons: See para.6–029 above.

[108] For the form of a reasoned award see para.6–032 below.

[109] [2003] EWCA Civ 84.

either that the tribunal has failed to deal with all the issues that were put to it[110] or, alternatively, that it has exceeded its substantive jurisdiction by determining matters that were not referred to it.[111]

Reasons ordered by the court. Under s.70(4) of the Arbitration Act   **6–031** 1996[112] the court may order the tribunal to state the reasons for its award in sufficient detail to enable the court properly to consider a challenge to or appeal against the award.[113] The jurisdiction will be sparingly exercised[114] and the court when making such an order can also deal with how the additional costs incurred as a result of its order are to be met.[115] A distinction must be drawn between a failure to give reasons and a failure to deal with an issue in the award.[116] In the latter case the position cannot simply be remedied by requiring the tribunal to state its reasons. Equally, if the complaint is a deficiency of reasons the initial application should be made under s.70(4) and not on the basis of serious irregularity under s.68.[117]

Form of a reasoned award.[118] No particular form is required for a   **6–032** reasoned award although "the giving of clearly expressed reasons responsive to the issues as they were debated before the arbitrators will reduce the scope for the making of unmeritorious challenges".[119] When giving a reasoned award the tribunal need only set out what, on its view of the evidence, did or did not happen, and explain succinctly why, in the light of what happened, the tribunal has reached its decision, and state what that decision is.[120] In order to avoid being vulnerable to challenge the tribunal's reasons must deal with all the issues that were put to

---

[110] Section 68(2)(d) of the Arbitration Act 1996: See para.8–093 below.

[111] Section 67 of the Arbitration Act 1996: See paras 8–054 *et seq.* below.

[112] Replacing s.1(5) of the Arbitration Act 1979. There are two key changes from the previous provision. First, the court may initiate the order whereas previously the statute required an application by a party to the reference. Second, and following from the first, the order only arises where a challenge to or appeal against the award has actually been made, whereas previously an order for reasons could be sought in anticipation of such an application.

[113] See paras 8–070, 8–093 and 8–130.

[114] *per* Kerr L.J. in *Universal Petroleum Co Ltd v Handels und Transport GmbH* [1987] 1 Lloyd's Rep. 517, CA at 528. This was a decision under the 1979 Act but it seems likely that a similar approach will be taken under the Arbitration Act 1996.

[115] Section 70(5) of the Arbitration Act 1996.

[116] *Hussman (Europe) Ltd v Al Ameen Development & Trade Co* [2000] 2 Lloyd's Rep. 83; *Fidelity Management SA v Myriad International Holdings BV* [2005] EWHC 1193.

[117] *Margulead Ltd v Exide Technologies* [2004] EWHC 1019; *World Trade Corp Ltd v C Czarnikow Sugar Ltd* [2004] EWHC 2332; *Norbrook Laboratories Ltd v Tank* [2006] EWHC 1055.

[118] See also paras 8–093 *et seq.* below concerning challenges based on a failure to deal with all the issues and the relationship between that and a failure to give sufficient reasons.

[119] *per* Tomlinson J. in *ABB AG v Hochtief Airport GmbH* [2006] EWHC 388. He added that: "Reasons which were a little less compressed at the essential points might have been more transparent as to their meaning and might even have dissuaded the unsuccessful party from challenging the award or, at any rate, from mounting so wide-ranging a challenge."

[120] *per* Donaldson L.J. in *Bremer Handelsgesellschaft GmbH v Westzucker GmbH (No.2)* [1981] 2 Lloyd's Rep. 130 at 132–3. The parties may agree that something less is required: *The Bay Hotel and Resort Ltd v Cavalier Construction Co Ltd* [2001] UKPC 34 and see para.6–029 above.

it.[121] It should set out its findings of fact[122] and its reasoning so as to enable the parties to understand them and state why particular points were decisive. It should also indicate the tribunal's findings and reasoning on issues argued before it but not considered decisive, so as to enable the parties and the court to consider the position with respect to appeal on all the issues before the tribunal.[123] When dealing with controversial matters, it is helpful for the tribunal to set out not only its view of what occurred, but also to make it clear that it has considered any alternative version and has rejected it. Even if several reasons lead to the same result, the tribunal should still set them out.[124] That said, so long as the relevant issues are addressed there is no duty to deal with every possible argument[125] or to explain why the tribunal attached more weight to some evidence than to other evidence.[126] The tribunal is not expected to recite at great length communications exchanged or submissions made by the parties.[127] Nor is it required to set out each step by which it reached its conclusion or to deal with each and every point made by the parties.[128] It is sufficient that the tribunal should explain what its findings are and the evidential route by which it reached its conclusions.[129]

Where objection has been taken to the tribunal's substantive jurisdiction this issue should be addressed in the award. However if the tribunal fails to do so but goes on to determine the merits of the case, thereby determining the objection to jurisdiction, that may be taken as an implied award on substantive jurisdiction notwithstanding that it is not expressly dealt with.[130]

6–033   **Reasons not forming part of the award.** In the past tribunals have sometimes adopted a practice of providing the parties with reasons whilst stating expressly that they do not form part of the award itself and imposing restrictions

---

[121] Section 68(2)(d). See para.8–093 below.

[122] A failure to make relevant, clear or sufficient findings of fact may render an award susceptible to appeal under s.69 of the Arbitration Act 1996: see *Skanska Construction (Regions) Ltd v Anglo-Amsterdam Corp Ltd* [2002] 84 Con. L.R. 100. However the court will look at substance rather than form, particularly when interpreting the findings of a tribunal not comprised of lawyers: *Bottiglieri di Navidgazione SpA v Cosco Qingdao Ocean Shipping Co (The "Bunga Saga Lima")* [2005] EWHC 244; [2005] 2 Lloyd's Rep. 1 at [22]. See also *Action Navigation Inc v Bottiglieri Navigation SpA* [2005] EWHC 177; [2005] 1 Lloyd's Rep. 432.

[123] See the comments of Mance J. in *Transcatalana de Commercio SA v Incobrasa Industrial Commercial Brazileira SA* [1995] 1 Lloyd's Rep. 215 at 217.

[124] *Universal Petroleum Co Ltd v Handels und Transport GmbH* [1987] 1 Lloyd's Rep. 517, CA.

[125] *Ascot Commodities NV v Olam International Ltd* [2002] 2 Lloyd's Rep. 277. See also *Checkpoint Ltd v Strathclyde Pension Fund* [2003] EWCA 84 where a distinction was drawn between a point of dispute, which did not have to be specifically dealt with, and an issue for the purposes of s.68(2) of the Arbitration Act 1996, which did.

[126] *World Trade Corp Ltd v C Czarnikow Sugar Ltd* [2004] EWHC 2332; *Protech Projects Construction (Pty) Ltd v Al-Kharafi & Sons* [2005] EWHC 2165.

[127] *Transcatalana de Commercio SA v Incobrasa Industrial e Commercial Brazileira SA* [1995] 1 Lloyd's Rep. 215.

[128] *Petroships PTE Ltd v Petec Trading and Investment Corp. (The "Petro Ranger")* [2001] 2 Lloyd's Rep. 348; *Hawk Shipping Ltd v Cron Navigation Ltd* [2003] EWHC 1828.

[129] *per* Donaldson L.J. in *Bremer Handelsgesellschaft GmbH v Westzucker GmbH (No.2)* [1981] 2 Lloyd's Rep. 130 at 132–133. See also *Torch Offshore LLC v Cable Shipping Inc* [2004] 2 Lloyd's Rep. 446; *World Trade Corp Ltd v C Czarnikow Sugar Ltd* [2005] 1 Lloyd's Rep. 422 and para.6–083 below.

[130] *Vee Networks Ltd v Econet Wireless International Ltd* [2004] EWHC 2909; [2005] 1 Lloyd's Rep. 192; *LG Caltex Gas Co Ltd v China National Petroleum Corp* [2001] EWCA Civ 788.

on their use, e.g. that they may not be used in connection with the award or without the tribunal's consent.[131] This was particularly common, for example, in arbitrations conducted under the LMAA Terms. Reasons must now be given under s.52(4) of the Arbitration Act 1996 unless the parties agree otherwise in writing.[132] It seems they rarely do so[133] and the practice of giving reasons not forming part of the award seems unlikely to continue to any great extent.[134]

Use of reasons not forming part of the award. There were a 6–034 number of authorities under the old law on the question whether reasons not forming part of the award could be used in connection with an appeal against an award.[135] Under the 1996 Act, if the parties agree that the reasons should not form part of the award then it seems likely that will constitute an agreement to dispense with reasons for the purposes of s.52(4) of the Arbitration Act 1996. In such circumstances there can be no appeal against the award.[136] However the court will look at reasons not forming part of the award where a party is resisting enforcement or seeking to challenge the award even if the parties have agreed that they are not to be referred to in proceedings relating to the award.[137] Where the tribunal gives reasons stated not to form part of the award, but the parties have not agreed that the reasons should be restricted in this way, it seems likely that the court would look at those reasons despite their being expressed not to form part of the award.[138]

[131] This practice stemmed from the possibility, prior to the Arbitration Act 1979, of setting aside an award on the grounds that it disclosed an error of fact or law on its face. By providing reasons in a way which meant they did not become a part of the award itself and therefore not apparent on its face, the tribunal could satisfy the parties' wish to know why the particular result has obtained and yet prevented any error contained in its reasons being relied upon for the purpose of setting aside the award. Setting aside an award on these grounds was abolished by the Arbitration Act 1979.

[132] The requirement for any agreement between the parties to be "in writing" stems from s.5(1) of the Arbitration Act 1996, although the section gives the expression a broad meaning. This will help avoid disputes about whether the reasons are or are not intended to form part of the award, see *The General Valdes* [1982] 1 Lloyd's Rep. 17; *BP Chemicals Ltd v Kingdom Engineering (Fife) Ltd* [1994] 2 Lloyd's Rep. 373.

[133] *Tame Shipping Ltd v Easy Navigation Ltd (The Easy Rider)* [2004] EWHC 1862 proceeded on the assumption that there had been an agreement between parties that the reasons would not be referred to in any proceedings relating to the award by virtue of their adopting the LMAA Small Claims Procedure, though in fact it had been amended in 2002.

[134] The principal advantage of having reasons not forming part of the award was that it hindered any appeal against the award, see *Mutual Shipping Corp v Bayshore Shipping Co Ltd (The "Montan")* [1985] 1 Lloyd's Rep. 189; [1985] 1 W.L.R. 625. A more effective means of excluding an appeal was to enter into an exclusion agreement under s.3 of the Arbitration Act 1979. However the right to enter into an exclusion agreement was limited in the three "special categories" of cases under s.4(1) of the 1979 Act and as a result the practice of providing reasons not forming part of the award served a purpose in such cases. As the "special categories" have not survived into the Arbitration Act 1996, there is no longer good reason for this practice to be followed.

[135] See in particular *Mutual Shipping Corp v Bayshore Shipping Co Ltd (The "Montan")* [1985] 1 Lloyd's Rep. 189.

[136] Section 69(1) of the Arbitration Act 1996.

[137] *Tame Shipping Ltd v Easy Navigation Ltd (The Easy Rider)* [2004] EWHC 1862.

[138] Alternatively the court could order the tribunal to state its reasons under s.70(4) of the Arbitration Act 1996 but there are a number of reasons why it might not wish to do so. First, it is a cumbersome step given that the tribunal's reasons are already to hand. Second, as the parties have not agreed that use of the reasons should be restricted, it is not obvious why the court should treat them as such simply because the tribunal has sought to impose this. Third, there is of course a risk of

(h) Majority award

6–035   **When majority award appropriate.** Unless the parties have agreed otherwise in writing,[139] if the reference is to three or more arbitrators, their decisions, orders and awards can be made by a majority of them. This applies whether or not a chairman has been appointed.[140] Majority awards and the position when there is no majority are dealt with at para.6–057 below.

(i) Additional award

6–036   **Power to make an additional award.** A tribunal has power under s.57(3)(b) of the Arbitration Act 1996 to make an additional award in respect of any matter, including interest or costs, which was presented to it in the course of the reference but which the tribunal did not deal with in its award. Additional awards are dealt with at paras 6–171 *et seq.* below.

(j) Convention awards

6–037   **New York Convention award.** Part III of the Arbitration Act 1996 (replacing the Arbitration Act 1975) gives effect to the New York Convention on the Recognition and Enforcement of Foreign Arbitral Awards[141] by incorporating into English law provision for the enforcement of awards covered by the New York Convention. Section 100(1) of the Arbitration Act 1996 defines a "New York Convention award" as:

> "an award made, in pursuance of an arbitration agreement, in the territory of a state (other than the United Kingdom) which is a party to the New York Convention."

6–038   **The ICSID Convention.** The Convention on the Settlement of Investment Disputes between States and Nationals of other States (the "ICSID Convention")[142] was implemented in English law by the Arbitration (International Invest-

---

inconsistencies between the restricted reasons originally given and those provided pursuant to s.70(4).

[139] The requirement for any agreement between the parties to be "in writing" stems from s.5(1) of the Arbitration Act 1996, although the section gives the expression a broad meaning.

[140] Sections 20(3) and 22(2) of the Arbitration Act 1996.

[141] The Convention on the Recognition and Enforcement of Foreign Arbitral Awards adopted by the United Nations Conference on International Commercial Arbitration on June 10, 1958. See further paras 8–021 *et seq.* below for enforcement of New York Convention awards.

[142] The ICSID Convention was opened for signature in Washington on March 18, 1965 and is sometimes referred to as "the Washington Convention".

ment Disputes) Act 1966.[143] That Act continues in force with only minor consequential amendments as a result of the Arbitration Act 1996.[144]

Meaning of "Convention award". Section 7(1) of the Arbitration Act 1975 referred to a New York Convention award as a "Convention award". Although the Arbitration Act 1996 is more specific, a reference to a "Convention award" is generally taken to mean a New York Convention award rather than to an award made under another international convention on arbitration, such as the Geneva Convention[145] or the ICSID Convention. For obvious reasons it is preferable to avoid referring simply to a "Convention award".   6–039

Enforcement of awards. Whether an award is a New York Convention award under s.100(1) of the Arbitration Act 1996 or an award pursuant to some other convention on arbitration will determine the scope of the court's jurisdiction in relation to it, particularly in relation to enforcement.[146]   6–040

(k) Foreign awards

Meaning of "foreign award". Part II of the Arbitration Act 1950 concerns the enforcement of certain foreign awards. That part of the 1950 Act continues to apply, notwithstanding that the remainder of it has been repealed by the Arbitration Act 1996.[147] Section 35(1) refers to a "foreign award" as one   6–041

(1) pursuant to an arbitration agreement to which the 1923 Protocol on Arbitration Clauses[148] applies and

(2) between parties subject to the jurisdiction of Contracting States to the Geneva Convention[149] and

(3) made in the territory of a Contracting State to the Geneva Convention.

Whether or not an award is a foreign award will determine the scope of the court's jurisdiction in relation to enforcement of it under Pt II of the Arbitration Act 1950.[150]   6–042

[143] See para.1–041 in relation to investment arbitrations, many of which are conducted under the auspices of ICSID, which was set up pursuant to the ICSID Convention.
[144] See further paras 8–048 *et seq.* for enforcement of ICSID Convention awards.
[145] See para.8–047 below for enforcement of Geneva Convention awards.
[146] See paras 8–020 *et seq.* below.
[147] Section 99 of the Arbitration Act 1996.
[148] Protocol on Arbitration Clauses signed on behalf of His Majesty at a Meeting of the Assembly of the League of Nations held on the September 24, 1923.
[149] Convention on the Execution of Foreign Arbitral Awards signed at Geneva on behalf of His Majesty on September 26, 1927.
[150] See para.8–047 below.

6–043   In this book, the term foreign award is also used more generally to designate an award made outside England.

2. FORMAL REQUIREMENTS OF AWARD

(a) Form of the award

6–044   **Statutory requirements.** Section 52 of the Arbitration Act 1996 provides:

> "52. (1) The parties are free to agree on the form of an award.
>
> (2) If or to the extent that there is no such agreement, the following provisions apply.
>
> (3) The award shall be in writing signed by all the arbitrators or all those assenting to the award.
>
> (4) The award shall contain the reasons for the award unless it is an agreed award or the parties have agreed to dispense with reasons.
>
> (5) The award shall state the seat of the arbitration and the date when the award is made."

The starting point therefore is that the award must comply with any requirements as to form agreed between the parties and in the absence of agreement the statutory provisions in ss.52(3) to (5) apply. This section is very similar to Art.31 of the Model Law.[151]

6–045   **Failure to comply with agreed or statutory requirements.** Failure to comply with any requirements as to form agreed between the parties or derived from the Arbitration Act 1996 will render the award susceptible to challenge.[152] What if the requirements are of an immaterial character? Under the Arbitration Act 1996 failure to comply with the requirements as to form is of itself a "serious irregularity",[153] but a party wishing to challenge the award under that section must also show that the irregularity has or will result in "substantial injustice" to him. This seems extremely unlikely if the requirement is immaterial.[154] In any event, if there were a successful application the court would usually seek to remit the award to the tribunal so that it can remedy the defect.

---

[151] See Appendix 4.
[152] Under s.68(2)(h) of the Arbitration Act 1996.
[153] Section 68(2)(h) of the Arbitration Act 1996. See further para.8–098 below.
[154] This is addressed in para.234 of the DAC report in the context of the requirement under s.52(5) of the Arbitration Act 1996 that the award state the seat of the arbitration. The Report points out that the seat is only of importance in international arbitrations and in the domestic context this requirement is likely to be immaterial: see also *Tongyuan (USA) International Trading Group v Uni-Clan Ltd* [2001] W.L. 98036 where the arbitration agreement provided for arbitration in Shenzhen or Shanghai but in fact the hearing was held in Beijing.

Effect on time limits. It may be that a failure to comply with agreed or   6–046
statutory requirements can be remedied. For example, even if the tribunal fails to
sign or date the award when it is notified to the parties, they may do so at a later
date. The award will then take effect from the date upon which the requirements
have been met so that any time limits for challenge or appeal against the award will
run from that date.[155]

Award to be in writing. Section 52(3) of the Arbitration Act 1996 requires   6–047
the award to be made in writing.[156] Having the tribunal's decision in written form
facilitates both the enforcement of the award and any challenge to it. Various sets
of arbitration rules similarly provide for awards made under them to be in
writing.[157]

Parol awards. The parties may agree that a parol award, i.e. one made orally,   6–048
may be given,[158] although it will be a very rare case indeed where the parties will
be content with such an award. To constitute a valid parol award the tribunal must
make an express determination: "In the absence of a declaration, what evidence
would there be of a sole arbitrator having made up his mind? The test of the
making of an award is, can the arbitrator change his mind? So long as it remains
in his power to do so, he has not made an award."[159]

Award to be signed. Section 52(3) of the Arbitration Act 1996 also requires   6–049
the award to be signed by all the arbitrators or all those who assent to it. A
dissenting arbitrator need not sign.[160] The signature may be attested by a witness,
though there is no legal requirement for this and it is merely done to provide
evidence of the signature.

Place of signing. There is old authority that where an award is made by more   6–050
than one arbitrator then, for it to be valid, all the arbitrators should sign it in each

---

[155] *Weldon Plant Ltd v The Commission for the New Towns* [2000] B.L.R. 496. Lloyd J. left open the
possibility in that case of circumstances in which an inference could be drawn that the award was
in fact signed and dated. The court might look to draw such an inference where, e.g. the evidence
shows that the failure to sign is an oversight but the contractually agreed time limit for making the
award has expired. Where the requirement is capable of being remedied, as it was in *Weldon*, it is
preferable for this to be done.
[156] As to parol awards see para.6–048 below.
[157] For example LCIA Rules, Art.26.1. The Model Law, Art.31 also requires the award to be in writing
and signed by the tribunal.
[158] Prior to the Arbitration Act 1996 a parol award was valid unless the reference to arbitration required
the award to be made in writing, see *Cocks v Macclesfield* (1562) 2 Dyer 218 b Benloe 97; *Rawling
v Wood* (1735) Barnes 54. The Arbitration Act 1996 has reversed this so that a parol award will now
only be valid if the parties have agreed that the award may be made orally and in the absence of
agreement a parol award will not suffice.
[159] *Thompson v Miller* (1867) 15 W.R. 353.
[160] Unless required to do so by the relevant arbitration rules: see, e.g. Arbitration Rules No.125 of
GAFTA, r.7.1 and *Cargill International SA v Sociedad Iberica de Molturacion SA* [1998] 1 Lloyd's
Rep. 489.

other's presence.[161] That is inappropriate in the context of modern communications and the courts have indicated that it is unlikely to be followed.[162] Certainly there is no such requirement laid down in the Arbitration Act 1996 and as the court should not intervene in matters governed by the Act save as provided for in the Act[162a] there would seem to be no basis for a challenge on these grounds. In practice the award is often signed separately by the arbitrators, particularly where they are located in different parts of the world and the inconvenience and expense of bringing them together for the signing of the award would be considerable. Section 53 of the Arbitration Act 1996 confirms that unless the parties have agreed otherwise in writing,[163] any award is treated as having been made at the seat of arbitration, even if it has been signed elsewhere.[164]

6–051 **Reasons.** Under s.52(4) of the Arbitration Act 1996 the tribunal is required to give a reasoned award unless either it is an agreed award[165] or the parties have agreed that the tribunal's reasons for its decision need not be given. This reversed the position under the previous law when there was only an obligation to give reasons where this had been stipulated by the parties. For a fuller discussion of reasoned awards see paras 6–028 *et seq.* above.

6–052 **Seat to be specified.** Section 52(5) of the Arbitration Act 1996 requires the award to state the seat of the arbitration[166] and s.53 confirms that where the seat of the arbitration is in England, Wales or Northern Ireland, an award is treated as having been made there unless otherwise agreed in writing[167] by the parties. Requiring the seat to be stated in the award will assist in determining which provisions of the Arbitration Act 1996 apply[168] and in particular what powers exist

---

[161] *Wade v Dowling* (1854) 4 E. & B. 44.

[162] *European Grain & Shipping Ltd v Johnston* [1982] 3 All E.R. 989 *Bank Mellat v GAA Development Construction Co* [1988] 2 Lloyd's Rep. 44. Article 22 of the LMAA Terms specifically provides that the members of the tribunal need not meet together for the purpose of signing their award.

[162a] Section 1(c) of the Arbitration Act 1996. The requirement for signature is governed by s.52(3) of the Act, albeit that no reference is made in the subsection to whether or not the arbitrators must sign in each other's presence.

[163] The requirement for any agreement between the parties to be "in writing" stems from s.5(1) of the Arbitration Act 1996, although the section gives the expression a broad meaning.

[164] This addresses a particular problem that arose under the previous statutory regime in relation to the court's supervisory jurisdiction over an award made in a country other than the place of arbitration: *Hiscox v Outhwaite* [1992] 1 A.C. 562; [1991] 3 All E.R. 641; [1991] 3 W.L.R. 297; [1991] 2 Lloyd's Rep. 435.

[165] See paras 6–024 *et seq.* above.

[166] Article 31 of the Model Law refers to the "place of arbitration" but the meaning is the same and the reference to the seat is consistent with the terminology used in ss.2 and 3 of the Arbitration Act 1996: see further para.250 of the DAC report.

[167] The requirement for any agreement between the parties to be "in writing" stems from s.5(1) of the Arbitration Act 1996, although the section gives the expression a broad meaning.

[168] The scope of application of the Arbitration Act 1996 and the way in which the seat is to be determined are dealt with in ss.2 and 3 of the Act. See paras 2–100 *et seq.*

to support the arbitral process and whether the English court has jurisdiction to review any award.[169] This may be of considerable importance given that the scope of review available will differ from country to country.[170] The seat of the arbitration is also important in the context of the recognition and enforcement of any award and it may be necessary to determine whether it is a "New York Convention award" to which Pt III of the Arbitration Act 1996 applies.[171] The grounds for challenging or resisting enforcement of a New York Convention award are limited and the seat of the arbitration is specifically relevant to certain of those grounds.[172]

Dating of the award. Section 52(5) of the Arbitration Act 1996 provides 6–053
that the award must state the date on which it is made. This will be of assistance in calculating interest due on the award and in determining whether a contractual time limit for the making of the award has been complied with. The time limit for any challenge or appeal also runs from the date of the award.[173] Under s.54 of the Arbitration Act 1996 the tribunal may decide when an award is to be taken as made, subject to agreement in writing[174] otherwise by the parties. If the tribunal does not fix the date of the award, it may be taken as being the date on which it is signed by the sole arbitrator or by the final member of the tribunal to sign.[175] Alternatively of course the award may be challenged[176] and remitted to the tribunal for clarification of the date on which it was made.[177]

---

[169] *Weissfisch v Julius* [2006] EWCA 218; *A v B* [2006] EWHC 2006; *C v D* [2007] EWHC 1541; *Dubai Islamic Bank PJSC v Paymentech Merchant Services Inc* [2001] 1 Lloyd's Rep. 65. See para.5–072 on the importance of the seat.

[170] For the powers of the English court see paras 8–054, 8–072 and 8–119 *et seq.* below. They are, for example, more extensive than those of the French courts.

[171] As defined in s.100(1) of the Arbitration Act 1996 (replacing s.7(1) of the Arbitration Act 1975), or indeed whether it is an ICSID Convention award under the Arbitration (International Investment Disputes) Act 1966 or a "foreign award" under Pt II of the Arbitration Act 1950: see further paras 6–037 *et seq.* above and 8–020 *et seq.* below.

[172] Arbitration Act 1996, s.103(2)(b)—validity under the law of the place where it was made, s.103(2) (e)—composition of tribunal or arbitral procedure not in accordance with law of country where it took place, and s.103(2)(f)—setting aside or suspension by a competent authority of the country in which made: see generally paras 8–028 *et seq.* and in particular paras 8–031, 8–038 and 8–040 below. By s.53 of the Arbitration Act 1996, where the seat of the arbitration is in England, Wales or Northern Ireland, an award is treated as made there unless otherwise agreed by the parties.

[173] Section 70(3) of the Arbitration Act 1996.

[174] The requirement for any agreement between the parties to be "in writing" stems from s.5(1) of the Arbitration Act 1996, although the section gives the expression a broad meaning.

[175] Section 54(2) of the Arbitration Act 1996. This reflects the court's approach in *Hiscox v Outhwaite* [1992] 1 A.C. 562; [1991] 3 All E.R. 641; [1991] 3 W.L.R. 297; [1991] 2 Lloyd's Rep. 435. That case concerned where an award was "made" for the purposes of determining whether it was a Convention award under the Arbitration Act 1975, s.7(1), but the court's comments in relation to *Brooke v Mitchell* (1840) 6 M. & W. 473 9 L.J. Ex. 269 suggest that it was intended to be of wider application. Presumably if the parties have agreed that an unsigned award will suffice, the award will be made when it is published, i.e. when the tribunal gives notice to the parties that the award is ready. (See also *Thompson v Miller* (1867) 15 W.R. 353.)

[176] See para.6–045 above.

[177] Although this course may not be appropriate if the time limit for a proposed further challenge to or appeal against the award will have expired by the time the date is clarified.

6–054 **Recitals.** Formal recitals are used much less often in awards now than they were when there was a "special case" procedure.[178] It is still useful for an award to set out the information which recitals traditionally contained but this is now usually done in the body of the award rather than in recitals. If they are to be adopted the tribunal can use recitals to set out the circumstances leading to the award, so that for example they will record the contractual relationship between the parties, the matters giving rise to the dispute, the appointment of the tribunal and its authority to decide the dispute (i.e. the arbitration agreement), and, if applicable, the hearings which have taken place. Recitals are not necessary though, and their absence will not render the award invalid. Similarly an award cannot be challenged on the grounds of an error in the recitals,[179] nor would such an error constitute a question of law arising out of the award for the purposes of an appeal under s.69 of the Arbitration Act 1996.

6–055 **Effect of recitals on tribunal's authority.** Though recitals are not essential, they can be used to show on the face of the award that the tribunal had authority to determine the dispute as it did, but a tribunal cannot by a false recital give itself an authority beyond that given to it by the parties' submission to arbitration.[180]

6–056 **Delegating the drafting of the award.** A tribunal may obtain legal advice on the drawing up of its award to ensure that it is in a proper form and may even delegate the drafting of the award.[181] It may also consult an expert on some issue required to be dealt with in the award.[182] However the tribunal may not delegate the making of its decision to another[183] and when employing a draftsman, it remains the function of the tribunal itself to decide on findings of fact, to evaluate and analyse the submissions of law and to arrive at their own reasons for their decision. The tribunal must exercise its own judgment in deciding the issues.[184]

---

[178] i.e. prior to the introduction of the present appeal system in the Arbitration Act 1979, now replaced by s.69 of the Arbitration Act 1996.

[179] See, e.g. *Harlow v Read* (1845) 14 L.J. C.P. 239, where the award recited that the tribunal had "considered the decision of the umpire" when there had in fact been no consultation with the umpire. An error in the recitals would not meet the requirements for a challenge under s.68 of the Arbitration Act 1996.

[180] *Price v Popkin* (1839) 8 L.J. Q.B. 198. The same would apply where the statement of authority to determine the dispute is contained in the body of the award.

[181] As in *Agrimex Limited v Tradigrain SA* [2003] EWHC 1656; [2003] 2 Lloyd's Rep. 537. It was noted in that case however at [32] that: "For some time and certainly since the enactment of the Arbitration Act 1996 it has been part of the skill ordinarily to be expected of a competent arbitrator that he should produce his own reasoned award".

[182] e.g. taking Counsel's opinion on points of law, as in *Gladesmore Investments Ltd v Caradon Heating Ltd* [1994] E.G. 159. The tribunal is given a specific power to appoint experts, legal advisers or assessors by s.37(3) of the Arbitration Act 1996, subject to agreement of the parties otherwise: see para.5–160 above.

[183] *National Boat Shows Ltd v Tameside Marine* [2001] W.L. 1560826. See further para.6–074 below.

[184] *Agrimex Ltd v Tradigrain SA* [2003] EWHC 1656; [2003] 2 Lloyd's Rep. 537 at [33].

(b) Awards by more than one arbitrator or by an umpire

Chairmen and majority awards. The parties may agree to appoint a chairman of the tribunal and to decide what his functions will be in relation to the making of decisions, awards and orders.[185] If they do appoint a chairman then unless otherwise agreed in writing[186] any decisions, orders and awards are to be made by all the arbitrators or, if the reference is to three or more arbitrators, by a majority of them. If no majority can be achieved, the chairman decides.[187] If, however, there is no chairman then decisions, orders and awards must be made by all or a majority of the tribunal.[188]   6–057

Dissenting opinions. Any member of the tribunal who does not assent to an award need not sign it[189] and may set out his own views of the case in a "dissenting opinion", although he should not do so unless there is a good reason for expressing his dissent, because a dissenting opinion may encourage a challenge to the award.[190] This is for the parties' information only and does not form part of the award,[191] but it may add weight to the arguments of a party wishing to appeal against the award.   6–058

Award of the umpire. Where there is an umpire, either he replaces the other arbitrators as the tribunal,[192] in which case the award is his alone, or he does not replace them, in which case he takes no part in the making of the award.[193] The fact that the arbitrators (or one of them) purport, after their authority has expired, to join with the umpire in his award, will not invalidate it. The award will stand as the award of the umpire alone.[194]   6–059

Award by a stranger. Similarly, an award will not be susceptible to challenge because a stranger to the reference purports to assent to it, provided that the award   6–060

---

[185] Section 20(1) of the Arbitration Act 1996.
[186] The requirement for any agreement between the parties to be "in writing" stems from s.5(1) of the Arbitration Act 1996, although the section gives the expression a broad meaning.
[187] Section 20(4) of the Arbitration Act 1996, which replaced and expanded s.9 of the Arbitration Act 1950 (as amended by s.6(2) of the Arbitration Act 1979). Various of the arbitration rules also provide for majority decisions and, in the absence of a majority, for the chairman of the tribunal to decide: see, for example, ICC Rules, Art.25.1 and LCIA Rules, Art.26.3.
[188] Section 22(2) of the Arbitration Act 1996.
[189] Section 52(3) of the Arbitration Act 1996.
[190] See further the 2003 Freshfields Lecture "Dissenting Opinions in International Commercial Arbitration—The Good, the Bad and the Ugly" by Alan Redfern in 20 Arbitration Int. (2004), 223–242.
[191] See para.6–029 above.
[192] Section 21(4) of the Arbitration Act 1996: see para.4–045 above.
[193] Even though he will often have attended the proceedings and been given copies of all the documents, s.21(3) of the Arbitration Act 1996.
[194] *Beck v Sargent* (1812) 4 Taunt. 232.

is issued by the tribunal properly appointed and the stranger does not play any part in the decision-making process.[195]

(c) Time for making award

6–061 **Statutory time limits.** Generally, subject to the matters discussed in para.6–062 below, the tribunal may make its award or awards at any time, unless otherwise agreed in writing by the parties.[196] However, the Arbitration Act 1996 imposes specific time limits for making an award in three situations. First, where an award is remitted by the court,[197] the tribunal shall, unless the court directs otherwise, make its award within three months from the date of the order for remission.[198] Second, any correction of the award[199] must be made within 28 days from when the application was received by the tribunal or, if the correction is made at the initiative of the tribunal itself, within 28 days of the award.[200] Third, if the tribunal is to make an additional award[201] it must do so within 56 days of the original award.[202] The time limits for corrections and additional awards are capable of being extended by agreement of the parties.[203]

6–062 **Award to be produced promptly.** The tribunal must, however, produce its award promptly after the conclusion of the hearing.

"At the end of the hearing [the tribunal] will be in a position to give a decision and the reasons for that decision. They should do so at the earliest possible

---

[195] In *Itex Shipping Pte Ltd v China Ocean Shipping Co (The "Jing Hong Hai")* [1989] 2 Lloyd's Rep. 522 an arbitration clause in a charterparty provided for each party to appoint an arbitrator and the two so appointed to appoint a third. Disputes arose and each party appointed its arbitrator. Before a third arbitrator was appointed the parties entered into a settlement agreement which itself referred any disputes to the tribunal already appointed. The charterers failed to make payments under the settlement agreement and the owners sought an award for the sums due. The two arbitrators appointed a third arbitrator and an award was issued by all three of them. The court held that it was to be implied that the same mechanism was to apply for appointment of the tribunal as in the original arbitration clause, but that even if there was an irregularity it was sufficient that the two arbitrators had issued the award. In these circumstances, an argument that there has been a serious irregularity entitling a party to challenge the award under s.68 of the Arbitration Act 1996 would almost certainly fail on the ground that it has caused no substantial injustice. Enforcement abroad may be difficult however because the composition of the arbitral tribunal not being in accordance with the agreement of the parties provides grounds for refusing recognition and enforcement of an award under Art.VI(d) of the New York Convention.

[196] Section 47(1) of the Arbitration Act 1996. The agreement otherwise may, for example, be set out in the arbitration agreement—see para.6–063 below. For removal of a dilatory arbitrator who refuses or fails to use all reasonable dispatch in making an award see s.24(1)(d)(ii) of the Arbitration Act 1996 and paras 7–122 *et seq.* below. The requirement for any agreement between the parties to be "in writing" stems from s.5(1) of the Arbitration Act 1996, although the section gives the expression a broad meaning.

[197] Under ss.68 or 69 of the Arbitration Act 1996: see paras 8–113 and 8–153 below.

[198] Section 71(3) of the Arbitration Act 1996.

[199] Under s.57(3)(a) of the Arbitration Act 1996: see para.6–167 below.

[200] Section 57(5) of the Arbitration Act 1996.

[201] Under s.57(3)(b) of the Arbitration Act 1996: see para.6–171 below.

[202] Section 57(6) of the Arbitration Act 1996.

[203] Sections 57(5) and (6) of the Arbitration Act 1996.

moment. The parties will have made their submissions as to what actually happened and what is the result in terms of their respective rights and liabilities. All this will be fresh in the arbitrators' minds . . . above all [the award] is something which can and should be produced promptly and quickly at the conclusion of the hearing. That is the time when it is easiest to produce an award with all the issues in mind."[204]

This is now reflected within the general principles and duties set out in the Arbitration Act 1996. In particular, s.1(a) sets out the general principle that the object of arbitration is the fair resolution of disputes by an impartial tribunal without unnecessary delay or expense, and s.33 requires the tribunal to comply with a general duty to adopt suitable procedures avoiding unnecessary delay or expense.[205] An arbitrator can also be removed if he fails to use all reasonable despatch in making an award.[206]

Contractual time limits. Time limits for the making of the tribunal's final award are frequently imposed in the arbitration agreement entered into by the parties. For example it may be specified that the award must be made within 90 days after the conclusion of the oral hearing.[207] The tribunal should endeavour to comply with the time limit, but should this not be possible it should seek the parties' written agreement to an extension of time. Alternatively, if the parties do not agree to the extension the tribunal or one of the parties can apply to the court, which has power to extend any time limit imposed for the making of the award where a substantial injustice would otherwise be done and whether or not that time limit has expired.[208]   6–063

(d) Taking up the award

Notification of the award. The Arbitration Act 1996 focuses on the concept of "notification" rather than "publication" of the award.[209] Unless the parties agree otherwise in writing[210] the award is notified to the parties by service of copies[211] of it on them.[212] It must be notified without delay, subject to the   6–064

---

[204] *per* Donaldson L.J. in *Bremer Handelsgesellschaft GmbH v Westzucker GmbH (No.2)* [1981] 2 Lloyd's Rep. 130 at 132–3.

[205] See generally paras 5–032 *et seq.*.

[206] Section 24(1)(d)(ii) of the Arbitration Act 1996. See paras 7–122 *et seq.*.

[207] Various sets of arbitration rules also impose time limits for the making of the award. See, for example, Art.24.1 of the ICC Rules, which requires the award to be made within six months of the signing of Terms of Reference, although this period can be, and in practice often is, extended.

[208] Section 50 of the Arbitration Act 1996: see paras 7–081 *et seq.* below.

[209] Section 55 of the Arbitration Act 1996 refers to notification and s.56 to "delivery" of the award: see para.6–067 below.

[210] The requirement for any agreement between the parties to be "in writing" stems from s.5(1) of the Arbitration Act 1996, although the section gives the expression a broad meaning.

[211] The Act refers to service of "copies" but it is more usual for each party to receive an original document.

[212] Section 55(2) of the Arbitration Act 1996. Accordingly notification for the purposes of s.55 is not simply telling the parties that the award is ready but also transmitting copies of it to them and therefore incorporates delivery of the award, subject to s.56 of the Arbitration Act 1996.

tribunal's right to withhold the award in case of non-payment of its fees and expenses.[213] Notification must be given to all parties to the reference.[214] It is particularly important that no delay occurs in notification of the parties, since any appeal or application to challenge the award must be brought within 28 days of the date of the award, regardless of whether notification has been given,[215] although time may be extended by the court.[216]

6–065 **Making and publishing the award.** Some arbitration agreements refer to the tribunal "making and publishing" its award. Subject to agreement in writing[217] otherwise by the parties, if the tribunal does not fix the date of the award, it is taken as being made on the date when it is signed by the sole arbitrator or by the final member of the tribunal to sign.[218] There is no specific reference in the Arbitration Act 1996 concerning when an award is published to the parties, but case law lays down that an award is published when the tribunal gives notice to the parties that the award is ready.[219] It is not dependent upon the parties taking up the award.[220] Consequently, a requirement that the award be "made and published" will be satisfied when it has been signed and the parties have been given notice that it is ready. This does not require service on the parties of a copy of the award as contemplated by s.55(2) of the Arbitration Act 1996.

6–066 As stated in para.6–064, the relevant time limits for appeals and challenges to the award under ss.67, 68 and 69 of the Arbitration Act 1996 are determined by reference to the date of the award.[221] However, where the parties have agreed that the tribunal shall "make and publish" its award this must be complied with and it is arguably not a valid award capable of challenge until it is. In practice any requirement that the award be published may be complied with by the tribunal contacting the parties to tell them that the award is ready and available on payment of its fees.[222] Where the reference to arbitration provides for "publication to the parties", it would appear that publication to all the parties is a condition precedent to a valid award.[223]

---

[213] Sections 55(3) and 56 of the Arbitration Act 1996: see also paras 4–063 above and 6–069 below.
[214] See para.255 of the DAC report.
[215] Section 70(3) of the Arbitration Act 1996.
[216] CPR Pt 62 r.9(1): see para.8–212.
[217] The requirement for any agreement between the parties to be "in writing" stems from s.5(1) of the Arbitration Act 1996, although the section gives the expression a broad meaning.
[218] Section 54(2) of the Arbitration Act 1996, see para.6–053 above.
[219] *Brooke v Mitchell* (1840) 6 M. & W. 473 9 L.J. Ex. 269; see also *Bulk Transport Corp v Sissy Steamship Co Ltd (The "Archipelagos" and "Delfi")* [1979] 2 Lloyd's Rep. 289; *Hiscox v Outhwaite* [1992] 1 A.C. 562; [1991] 3 All E.R. 641; [1991] 3 W.L.R. 297; [1991] 2 Lloyd's Rep. 435.
[220] *International Petroleum Refining & Supply SDAD Ltd v Elpis Finance SA (The "Faith")* [1993] 2 Lloyd's Rep. 408; *Handley v Nationwide Anglia Building Society* [1992] 29 E.G. 123; *Bulk Transport Corp v Sissy Steamship Co Ltd (The "Archipelagos" and "Delfi")* [1979] 2 Lloyd's Rep. 289.
[221] Section 70(3) of the Arbitration Act 1996.
[222] See paras 4–063 above and 6–069 below.
[223] This seems to have been assumed in both *Brooke v Mitchell* (1840) 9 L.J. Ex. 269 6 M. & W. 473 and *Bulk Transport Corpn v Sissy Steamship Co Ltd (The "Archipelagos" and "Delfi")* [1979] 2 Lloyd's Rep. 289.

Delivery of award. It may be stipulated in the arbitration agreement that the 6–067
award must be delivered or be "ready to be delivered" by a specified date.[224]
Under the previous law delivery of the award occurred when one of the parties
took up the award, i.e. collected it from the tribunal, all parties having been
informed that it was available.[225] However, given the requirement in s.55(2) of the
Arbitration Act 1996 for the award to be notified by service of copies on "the
parties", which means all of them,[226] delivery now involves copies of the award
being served on both parties, in the absence of agreement otherwise in writing.[227]
Delivery now therefore equates to notification under s.55(2) and a requirement
that the award be delivered will be satisfied when it has been notified to the parties
by service of a copy on each one of them.[228]

Ready to be delivered. An award is "ready to be delivered" as soon as it has 6–068
been made.[229] Provided the award is ready for delivery (and the parties so
informed) by the date specified, the fact that it is not actually delivered by that date
will not affect its validity,[230] although it will additionally have to be notified to
them to fulfil the statutory requirement under s.55(2) of the Arbitration Act
1996.[231]

Retention of award pending payment of outstanding fees.[232] It 6–069
is usual for the tribunal to retain the award until its outstanding fees and expenses
have been paid or secured.[233] The tribunal will normally inform the parties that
the award is ready and at the same time provide details of any sums outstanding
in respect of its fees.[234] At this stage the parties would usually be expected to meet
the outstanding fees in equal shares, reflecting their joint and several liability for
them,[235] following which the award will be notified to them by service of copies on
them pursuant to s.55(2) of the Arbitration Act 1996. If one party fails to do so

---

[224] See for example *Riley Gowler Ltd v National Heart Hospital Board of Governors* [1969] 3 All E.R.
1401, CA. That case concerned an arbitration under the London Building Acts (Amendment) Act
1939, s.55(n) of which provided for an appeal "within 14 days after the delivery of an award made
under this section . . . "
[225] *Riley Gowler Ltd v National Heart Hospital Board of Governors* [1969] 3 All E.R. 1401, CA.
[226] See para.255 of the DAC report.
[227] The requirement for any agreement between the parties to be "in writing" stems from s.5(1) of the
Arbitration Act 1996, although the section gives the expression a broad meaning.
[228] Delivery of the award to the parties may be withheld until full payment of the tribunal's fees and
expenses has been made: see s.56(1) of the Arbitration Act 1996: see para.6–069.
[229] See para.6–065 above.
[230] *Brown v Vawser* (1804) 4 East 584.
[231] Agreeing that an award be ready to be delivered by a certain date does not of itself involve
notification of the award to the parties and would not therefore be an agreement on the requirements for notification of the award pursuant to s.55(1).
[232] See para.4–063.
[233] They are expressly entitled to do so under s.56(1) of the Arbitration Act 1996.
[234] Where an arbitral institution is administering the arbitration it will normally take responsibility
both for ensuring the deposits held on account of the tribunal's fees and expenses are sufficient and
for notifying the award: see for example Art.28.1 of the ICC Rules.
[235] Under s.28 of the Arbitration Act 1996: see further para.4–052 above.

the other party may make payment in full in order to obtain the award from the tribunal. The party who has made payment can subsequently look to the other party for the sums paid in respect of fees which the tribunal or the court directs are recoverable costs which the other party should pay.[236] By paying the tribunal's outstanding fees and expenses to secure the release of the award a party does not lose his right to challenge the award,[237] nor his right under s.28 of the Arbitration Act 1996 to challenge the amount of the tribunal's fees and expenses.[238]

6–070 **Importance of taking up the award.** A delay in taking up the award may have serious consequences in the context of applications to court challenging or appealing against the award. A 28-day time limit for any challenge to the award or appeal is laid down in s.70(3) of the Arbitration Act 1996, although it may be extended upon application to the court.[239] Time runs from the date of the award, whether or not it has been notified or delivered to the parties.[240] The tribunal has an obligation to notify the parties of the award without delay[241] but may refuse to deliver it pending payment of its fees and expenses.[242] A party who is delaying taking delivery of the award, perhaps in the hope that the other party will, at least initially, bear the burden of any outstanding fees and expenses, should keep in mind the 28-day time limit if he is likely to want to mount a challenge or appeal against the award.[243] The better course will usually be to pay the outstanding fees and expenses[244] in order to secure delivery of the award and be able to determine whether an appeal or challenge is appropriate. If necessary, those fees and expenses can subsequently be challenged under s.28 of the Arbitration Act 1996.[245]

---

[236] *International Petroleum Refining & Supply SDAD Ltd v Elpis Finance SA (The "Faith")* [1993] 2 Lloyd's Rep. 408. However, if the amount to be paid is not fixed by the award then it may be determined, or the means for it to be determined specified, by the court under s.63(4) of the Arbitration Act 1996. This applies notwithstanding that one party has already paid to the tribunal the full sum demanded: *Llandrindod Wells Water Co v Hawksley* (1904) 20 T.L.R. 241; *Re Prebble and Robinson* [1892] 2 Q.B. 602. An alternative is to use the procedure in s.56(2) of the Arbitration Act 1996 (replacing s.19 of the Arbitration Act 1950): see para.6–071 below.

[237] *Rokopoulas v Esperia SpA* (1978) 122 S.J. 127.

[238] Section 56(8) of the Arbitration Act 1996.

[239] See para.8–212 below.

[240] See para.6–067 above. A party seeking to challenge or appeal against an award must first exhaust any process of appeal or review available under the arbitration agreement and if such process exists the 28-day time limit runs from the date when that party was notified of the result of it: s.70(3) of the Arbitration Act 1996.

[241] Section 55(2) of the Arbitration Act 1996.

[242] Section 56 of the Arbitration Act 1996; see also para.6–069 above.

[243] See *International Petroleum Refining & Supply SDAD Ltd v Elpis Finance SA (The "Faith")* [1993] 2 Lloyd's Rep. 408. The court may, however, exercise its discretion to extend time under CPR Pt 62 r.9(1); see para.7–092 below. See also s.80(5) of the Arbitration Act 1996. Paragraph 294 of the DAC report suggests that time may be extended under s.79 of the Act, but in fact on its wording that section would not apply: see also para.382 of the DAC report. See also *Handley v Nationwide Anglia Building Society* [1992] 29 E.G. 123; *Zermalt Holdings SA v Nu-Life Upholstery Repairs Ltd* [1985] 2 E.G.L.R. 14; *Nature Conservancy Council for England v Deller* [1992] 43 E.G. 137.

[244] Either to the tribunal or into court: see para.6–071 below.

[245] See paras 4–059 and 7–212 *et seq.*

Payment into court of tribunal's fees and expenses. Alternatively, 6–071
where the tribunal refuses to deliver its award unless its outstanding fees are paid,
the court can order that it do so on payment into court of the fees demanded or
some lesser amount specified by the court. The court then directs how the fees and
expenses properly payable are to be determined and these are met from the funds
in court, the balance (if any) being paid out to the applicant.[246] This provides a
remedy for a party who wants to take up the award but considers the tribunal's fees
are excessive and wants them reviewed.[247] The application to court may be made
by any party to the reference,[248] but the procedure is not available if the arbitration
agreement itself provides any process for appeal or review of the tribunal's fees and
expenses.[249]

3. SUBSTANTIVE REQUIREMENTS OF AWARD

Requirements of a valid award. To be valid, an award must comprise a 6–072
decision by the tribunal on the matters referred with which it deals. An award
must also be final, in the sense of being a complete decision without leaving
matters to be dealt with subsequently or by a third party, and it must be certain.[250]
An award may be susceptible to challenge[251] if the tribunal exceeds its powers,[252]
or if the award is obtained by fraud or is contrary to public policy,[253] or if the
requirements as to form are not complied with.[254] The converse of these grounds
for challenge should be considered as requirements for a valid award.[255] The
courts are inclined to uphold the validity of an award and there is a presumption
in favour of it being a final and sufficiently certain decision on the matters in
dispute.[256]

---

[246] Section 56(2) of the Arbitration Act 1996 (replacing s.19(1) of the Arbitration Act 1950). See paras 7–213 *et seq.* below.

[247] It would not however assist a party who considers the fees to be excessive where the other party has already paid the tribunal's fees.

[248] The proviso to s.19(2) of the Arbitration Act 1950, that the application could not be made by a party if the fees demanded had been fixed by written agreement between that party and the arbitrator, no longer applies. However, the same result is achieved by s.56(3) of the Arbitration Act 1996 which provides that the fees and expenses properly payable are those for which the applicant is liable under s.28 of the Arbitration Act 1996 (dealt with at para.4–052 above) or under any agreement in relation to payment of the tribunal.

[249] Section 56(4) of the Arbitration Act 1996.

[250] *Tongyuan (USA) International Trading Group v Uni-Clan Ltd* [2001] W.L. 98036.

[251] See generally paras 8–072 *et seq.* below.

[252] See paras 8–089 *et seq.* below.

[253] As in *Arab National Bank v The Registrar of Companies* [2005] EWHC 3047. See paras 8–099 *et seq.* below.

[254] See paras 8–098 *et seq.*

[255] Even though a party would have to show that the other requirements of s.68 have been satisfied in order to mount a successful challenge.

[256] *Wood v Griffith* (1818) 1 Swanst. 43; *Harrison v Creswick* (1852) 13 C.B. 399 21 L.J.C.P. 113; *Cargey v Aitcheson* (1823) 2 B. & C. 170 1 L.J. (O.S.) K.B. 252; *Bland v Russian Bank for Foreign Trade* (1906) 11 Com. Cas. 71.

(a) Award must comprise a decision by the tribunal[257]

6–073   **Form of decision.** Any form of words amounting to a decision on the matters referred will be sufficient. No technical expressions are necessary[258] but it is clearly desirable that the award should be in clear and unambiguous terms. The words "I am of opinion that A is entitled to claim of B £134 for non-performance of his contract" were held a sufficient award.[259] However, where the arbitrator wrote a letter saying, "To meet the circumstances of the case in a liberal manner I propose that B should pay A £10", this was held not to be an award because it did not express a decision that A was entitled to the £10, but only recommended that that sum should be paid to him.[260]

6–074   **Decision may not be delegated.** The tribunal may consult an expert on some issue required to be dealt with in the award.[261] However the tribunal may not delegate the making of its decision to another[262] and must exercise its own judgment in deciding the issues.[263] An award seeking to delegate the decision to a third party will not be valid.[264]

6–075   **Decision based on own expert knowledge.** An arbitrator who is appointed because of his knowledge and experience of a particular trade, is entitled to decide the dispute on the basis of that expert knowledge and experience.[265] This applies in particular where the issues in dispute relate to questions of quality, compliance of bulk with sample and the like and also to questions of valuation.[266] Further, by appointing an arbitrator with expert knowledge the parties are taken

---

[257] See also for comparison the authorities in the context of expert determination, e.g. *Shorrock v Meggitt* [1991] B.C.C. 471.

[258] *Eardley v Steer* (1835) 4 Dowl. 423 4 L.J. Ex. 293.

[259] *Matson v Trower* (1824) Ry. & Moo. 17. See also *Smith v Hartley* (1851) 20 L.J.C.P. 169 where a "request" was held to be equivalent to a direction to pay.

[260] *Lock v Vulliamy* (1833) 5 B. & Ad. 600.

[261] e.g. taking Counsel's opinion on points of law, as in *Gladesmore Investments Ltd v Caradon Heating Ltd* [1994] E.G. 159. The tribunal is given a specific power to appoint experts, legal advisers or assessors by s.37(3) of the Arbitration Act 1996, subject to agreement of the parties otherwise: see para.5–160 above.

[262] *National Boat Shows Ltd v Tameside Marine* [2001] W.L. 1560826. See further para.6–078 below.

[263] *Agrimex Ltd v Tradigrain SA* [2003] EWHC 1656; [2003] 2 Lloyd's Rep. 537 at [33].

[264] In *Johnson v Latham* (1850) 19 L.J.Q.B. 329 disputes arose between the owners of two mills on a river. An arbitrator, appointed to define the water rights and depths of the defendant's weir and authorised to order any erections to be put up about the weir, awarded that the defendant was entitled to maintain his weir at a depth of 14 inches and no more, and for the purpose of marking the depth ordered such durable marks and erections to be placed about the weir as B might direct. The court held that the direction as to the depth of the weir was sufficient, but that the award was to be remitted as a result of the arbitrator delegating to B the fixing of the marks. See though para.6–078 below.

[265] See generally paras 5–050—5–052 above.

[266] Many of the recent decisions on this subject concern rent review arbitrations: see for example *JD Wetherspoon Plc v Jay Mar Estates* [2007] EWHC 856; *Warborough Investments Ltd v S. Robinson & Sons (Holdings) Ltd* [2002] EWHC 2502; *Checkpoint Ltd v Strathclyde Pension Fund* [2003] EWCA Civ 84.

to have assented to him using that general knowledge of the trade in reaching his decision.

General and specific knowledge. A distinction must be drawn, however, between such general knowledge of the trade and knowledge of special facts relating to a particular case. In the latter case the arbitrator is only entitled to rely on such knowledge provided he indicates the matters on which he intends to rely and gives the parties an opportunity to make submissions to him on those matters.[267] More recently the distinction has been described in terms that the arbitrator is fully entitled to make use of his own experience in reaching his conclusions, provided that it is of a kind and in the range of knowledge that one would reasonably expect the arbitrator to have, and providing that he uses it to evaluate the evidence called and not to introduce new and different evidence.[268] In other words, an arbitrator cannot supply new evidence by using his own knowledge but he can use that knowledge to evaluate and adjudicate upon the evidence before him. So, for example, in assessing rents, an expert arbitrator can rely on his general knowledge of comparable rents in the district, but if he knows of a particular comparable case, then he should disclose details of it before relying on it for his award.[269]

6–076

Disclosure of matters to be relied upon. As a matter of caution, a tribunal should always disclose the matters within its own knowledge on which it intends to rely to avoid subsequent argument about whether they were, or were not, simply its general knowledge of the trade or matters which the parties should have been given an opportunity to address.[270]

6–077

(b) Award must be a complete decision

A complete decision. An award must be final in the sense that, in relation to the issues or claims with which it deals, it is a complete decision on the matters requiring determination.[271] A tribunal cannot reserve to itself, or delegate to

6–078

---

[267] *Mediterranean and Eastern Export Co Ltd v Fortress Fabrics (Manchester) Ltd* (1948) 81 Ll. L. Rep. 401; [1948] 2 All E.R. 186; *Annie Fox and Others v PG Wellfair Ltd* [1981] 2 Lloyd's Rep. 514; *Anangel Peace Compania Naviera SA v Bacchus International Commerce Corp ("The Anangel Peace")* [1981] 1 Lloyd's Rep. 452; *Top Shop Estates Ltd v C Danino* [1985] 1 E.G.L.R. 9; *Zermalt Holdings SA v Nu-Life Upholstery Repairs Ltd* [1985] 2 E.G.L.R. 14; *Unit Four Cinemas Ltd v Tosara Investments Ltd* [1993] 44 E.G. 121; *Mount Charlotte Investments Plc v Prudential Assurance* [1995] 10 E.G. 129; see also paras 5–050 *et seq.* above.

[268] *Checkpoint Ltd v Strathclyde Pension Fund* [2003] EWCA Civ 84 which approved the dicta in *Annie Fox and Others v PG Wellfair Ltd* [1981] 2 Lloyd's Rep. 514; *JD Wetherspoon Plc v Jay Mar Estates* [2007] EWHC 856.

[269] This was one of the examples given by Dunn L.J. in *Annie Fox and Others v PG Wellfair Ltd* [1981] 2 Lloyd's Rep. 514, CA at 529.

[270] See paras 5–050—5–052 above.

[271] *Ronly Holdings Ltd v JSC Zestafoni G. Nikoladze Ferroalloy Plant* [2004] B.L.R. 323. This has long been the position: see *Whitworth v Hulse* (1866) L.R. 1 Ex. 251; *Randall v Randall* (1805) 7 East 81; *Samuel v Cooper* (1835) 2 A. & E. 752. See *Re Wright and Cromford Canal Co* (1841) 1 Q.B. 98.

another, the power of performing in the future any act of a judicial nature in relation to matters dealt with in the award. The tribunal's duty is to make a complete and final decision by its award, and it is a breach of that duty to leave any part of the decision to be determined subsequently or by another.[272] The tribunal may, however, reserve to itself or delegate to another purely ministerial acts, even after the time limited for making the award has expired,[273] though care should be taken to ensure that the act is not in fact the collation of further evidence.[274]

6–079 **Failure to deal with all issues submitted.** If the award fails to deal with an issue which the submission requires the tribunal to determine, it will be susceptible to challenge under s.68(2)(d) of the Arbitration Act 1996.[275] However any challenge will only succeed if the issue said to have been omitted is an important or fundamental one, as it is only then that the necessary substantial injustice could be caused.[276] The award does not have to deal with issues which it becomes unnecessary to resolve given the tribunal's determination on other issues.[277]

6–080 **Withdrawal of claims.** Where a party withdraws some or all of his claims or chooses not to pursue them, the tribunal should nevertheless deal with the claims in its award by recording that they were submitted and then withdrawn. This would enable the other party to rely on the award as showing that the claims were included within the scope of the reference to arbitration and that they have been disposed of by the tribunal. Accordingly, it would be possible to raise a plea of res judicata or issue estoppel[278] if it was sought to resurrect the claims in subsequent proceedings.[279]

6–081 **Matters on which no decision required.** No objection based on want of finality can be made if the matter not dealt with was one upon which there was

---

[272] *Ronly Holdings Ltd v JSC Zestafoni G. Nikoladze Ferroalloy Plant* [2004] B.L.R. 323. See also *Re O'Connor and Whitlaw* (1919) 88 L.J.K.B. 1242; *Johnson v Latham* (1850) 19 L.J.Q.B. 329 and see *Cogstad v Newsum* [1921] A.C. 528.

[273] In *Thorp v Cole* (1835) 2 C.M. & R. 367 the tribunal was entitled to award a specified rate to be charged per acre for land valuation, though the number of acres was to be ascertained by measurement, because measuring is a ministerial act. See though *Tandy and Tandy* (1841) 9 Dowl 1044 where the award was held invalid because it reserved to the tribunal a power to appoint a counsel or solicitor to settle the proper deeds required to give effect to the transfer of premises in accordance with the award.

[274] See *Sociedad Iberica de Molturacion SA v Nidera Handelscompagnie BV* [1990] 2 Lloyd's Rep. 240.

[275] For a detailed discussion of this requirement see paras 8–093 *et seq.* below.

[276] *Fidelity Management SA v Myriad International Holdings BV* [2005] EWHC 1193; *World Trade Corp Ltd v C Czarnikow Sugar Ltd* [2004] EWHC 2332; *Checkpoint Ltd v Strathclyde Pension Fund* [2003] EWCA Civ 84.

[277] *HBC Hamburg Bulk Carriers GmbH & Co KG v Tangshan Haixing Shipping Co Ltd* [2006] EWHC 3250.

[278] See para.6–176 below.

[279] Those parts of an award dealing with such claims would presumably be considered as being by consent. The Arbitration Act 1996 deals with "agreed awards" in s.51 but refers to "the dispute" being settled rather than just some part of it. Agreed awards are dealt with at paras 6–024 *et seq.* above.

no dispute between the parties and therefore no decision was required. Nor can objection be made if the award deals with all matters brought to the tribunal's attention, though there are other matters within the scope of the submission which are not put to it. In order to invalidate the award, the point which it is alleged the award fails to deal with must have been specifically raised.[280]

Award to be based on evidence and argument presented. The **6–082** award must be based solely on the evidence and argument presented by the parties,[281] and if the tribunal is minded to decide the dispute on some point which has not been dealt with, it must give notice of it to the parties to enable them to address it.[282] That said, it will not amount to a serious irregularity if the tribunal decides the case on the basis of a point that was *"in play or, to use a different expression, 'in the arena' in the proceedings"* even if not strictly argued or pleaded by a party. [283]

No need to deal with all arguments raised. Though it must deal **6–083** with all matters required to be determined, the award need not expressly address each and every argument raised.[284] A distinction is to be drawn between consideration of the arguments advanced, which need not be specifically addressed in the award, and reasons for a decision on the claims and issues in dispute, which must be set out in the award.[285]

Decision on matters actually submitted. On the other hand, the **6–084** tribunal must decide the matters actually submitted. The tribunal is not entitled to direct what it considers to be some suitable arrangement without deciding the matters submitted.[286] Nor can an arbitrator adjust the sums due under his award

---

[280] This is reflected in s.68(2)(d) of the Arbitration Act 1996: see paras 8–093 *et seq.* below. It is worth noting also that under s.69(3)(b) of the Arbitration Act 1996, leave to appeal against an award will only be given if the tribunal was asked to determine the question of law concerned.

[281] Unless an inquisitorial approach is adopted: see para.5–099 above.

[282] *Ascot Commodities NV v Olam International Ltd* [2002] C.L.C. 277; *Cosemar SA v Marimarna Shipping Co Ltd (The "Mathew")*, [1990] 2 Lloyd's Rep. 323; *Annie Fox and Others v PG Wellfair Ltd* [1981] 2 Lloyd's Rep. 514; *Fairclough Building Ltd v Vale of Belvoir Superstore Ltd* [1990] 56 B.L.R. 74. See also paras 5–061 *et seq.* above and also para.8–080 below on the possibility of challenge where the tribunal bases its award on a point which the parties have not been given an opportunity to argue before it.

[283] *ABB AG v Hochtief Airport GmbH* 2006 EWHC 388, following *Bulfracht (Cyprus) Ltd v Boneset Shipping Co Ltd (The "Pamphilos")* [2002] EWHC 2292; *Warborough Investments Ltd v S Robinson & Sons (Holdings) Ltd* [2003] EWCA Civ 751; *Bandwith Shipping Corp v Intaari* [2006] EWHC 2532. See further para.8–080 below.

[284] *World Trade Corp Ltd v C Czarnikow Sugar Ltd* [2004] EWHC 2332. See also paras 8–093 *et seq.* below.

[285] In *Checkpoint Ltd v Strathclyde Pension Fund* [2003] EWCA Civ 84 a distinction was drawn between a point of dispute, which did not have to be specifically dealt with, and an issue for the purposes of s.68(2) of the Arbitration Act 1996, which did. See also *Benaim (UK) Ltd v Davies Middleton & Davies Ltd* 102 Con L.R. 1 and paras 6–028 *et seq.* above and in particular para.6–031.

[286] In *Ross v Boards* (1838) 8 A. & E. 290 L.J. Q.B. 209, on a reference of all questions relating to an agreement for the sale of land, the sufficiency of the vendor's title was disputed. An award that the purchaser should take a conveyance of the title with all its faults, receiving an indemnity, was held invalid as not finally settling the question of title.

to take account of matters in dispute which are beyond the scope of his jurisdiction.[287] Nor, if the tribunal disagrees with the formulation of the submission, is it entitled to determine the issues which it thinks should have been put before it, though in fact they were not.[288]

6–085 **Where several claims made.** Where several claims are made between the parties, the tribunal must decide upon each of them in the award in order to comply with the duty to express conclusions on all claims and counterclaims submitted and to avoid the need for the award to be remitted. Thus, unless there is clear evidence of express or implied abandonment of certain points, the tribunal must deal with all the issues raised in the parties' written statements of claim and defence, even if they are not subsequently argued and elaborated upon at the hearing or in written submissions.[289]

6–086 **Failure to mention particular claim.** The failure to deal explicitly with a particular claim or a pleaded issue does not necessarily mean that the award will be susceptible to challenge if it is to be inferred from the circumstances that the tribunal did not in fact overlook that claim or issue when making its award.[290] Thus, it is not necessary for the award formally to express that it is an award on all the matters submitted if that is clear from its face,[291] but it may be advisable to do so.

6–087 **Counterclaims.** In the absence of special circumstances requiring that matters should be dealt with separately, where there is a counterclaim which is sought to be used as a set-off or excess,[292] the award need not deal separately with the two

---

[287] *Ronly Holdings Ltd v JSC Zestafoni G Nikoladze Ferroalloy Plant* [2004] EWHC 1354 although as noted in that case if a defence of set-off is raised the tribunal may be required to investigate it: see para.6–016 above. See also *Metal Distributors (UK) Ltd v ZCCM Investment Holdings Plc* [2005] EWHC 156; [2005] 2 Lloyd's Rep. 37 at [18.6].

[288] In *Jager v Tolme* [1961] 1 K.B. 939 a contract contained a clause to the effect that in the event of war rendering performance impracticable, either party might "appeal to the Council" (of a trade association) "for a decision". It was held that the Council must decide the parties' rights according to law and an award substituting a new contract for the old one was invalid. The Arbitration Act 1996 does however provide some scope for the tribunal to base its decision on considerations other than a particular law if the parties so agree: see para.2–091 and paras 4–141 *et seq.* above.

[289] *Cobelfret NV v Cyclades Shipping Co Ltd (The "Linardos")* [1994] 1 Lloyd's Rep. 28. Even if claims have been withdrawn or abandoned it may be helpful for the tribunal to include them in the award: see para.6–080 above.

[290] In these circumstances it is unlikely that substantial injustice will have occurred: see para.8–104 below. See also *Sig Bergesen DY A/S and Another v Mobil Shipping and Transportation Co (The "Berge Sund")* [1992] 1 Lloyd's Rep. 460; *Gray v Gwennap* (1822) 1 B. & A. 106; *Craven v Craven* (1817) 7 Taunt. 644; *Dunn v Warlters* (1842) 9 M. & W. 792 11 L.J. Ex. 188; *Perry v Mitchell* (1844) 12 M. & W. 792 14 L.J. Ex. 88; *Jewell v Christie* (1866) L.R. 2 C.P. 296 36 L.J.C.P. 168.

[291] *Re Brown and Croydon Canal Co* (1839) 9 A. & E. 522 8 L.J.Q.B. 92.

[292] See para.6–016 above.

issues of claim and counterclaim, but it must explain how the result is arrived at.[293]

Composite award as to quantum. As to quantum, a tribunal may make   6–088
a composite award in respect of amounts which arise as a result of various
interacting events, the consequences of which cannot be separated so as to
attribute a part to each claim.[294]

(c) Award must be certain

Need for certainty. An award must be certain in the sense that the tribunal's   6–089
decision on the matters dealt with must be clear from its face, as must the nature
and extent of the duties it imposes on the parties. If the effect of the award is
uncertain or ambiguous, it will be susceptible to challenge.[295]

Clarity as to what is required. The need for certainty with regard to the   6–090
effect of the award means that it must be clear exactly what is required to be done
and by whom. Where the award directs the payment of money, it must be clear
what amount is to be paid,[296] by whom and to whom.[297] Where a tribunal ordered
payment of a sum of money sufficient to secure the release of securities, the award
was held to be invalid because it did not ascertain the actual amount which was
required to be paid.[298]

Failure to deal with quantum. Where the award in effect comprises a   6–091
decision on liability but fails to decide the amount due or to make provision for
payment,[299] it may be remitted to the tribunal for it to deal with these further

---

[293] *Compagnie Financière pour le Commerce Extérieur SA v Oy Vehna A.B.* [1963] 2 Lloyd's Rep. 178.
[294] *J. Crosby & Sons Ltd v Portland UDC* [1967] 5 B.L.R. 121; *London Borough of Merton v Stanley Hugh Leach Ltd* [1985] 32 B.L.R. 51.
[295] Under s.68(2)(f) of the Arbitration Act 1996. See para.8–098 below.
[296] *Margulies Bros Ltd v Dafnis Thomaides & Co (UK) Ltd* [1958] 1 Lloyd's Rep. 250 [1958] 1 W.L.R. 398; *River Plate Products Netherlands BV v Establissement Coargrain* [1982] 1 Lloyd's Rep. 628. See also *Oricon Waren-Handels GmbH v Intergraan N.V.* [1967] 2 Lloyd's Rep. 82 at 98–9 and *Montrose Canned Foods Ltd v Eric Wells (Merchants) Ltd* [1965] 1 Lloyd's Rep. 597.
[297] In *Re Tidswell* (1863) 33 Beav 213 an arbitrator was required to award and apportion a trust estate among the persons entitled. He found that a certain sum was due from a party and directed him to pay or account for it to the trust estate. The award was held uncertain, on the grounds that it ought to have specified to whom and in what proportions the money ought to be paid. See also *Bulk Trading SA v Moeller* [2006] EWCA Civ 1294 where it was unsuccessfully argued that an award was unclear as to which of two parties, one of whom was the agent of the other, it was made against.
[298] *Hewitt v Hewitt* [1841] 1 Q.B. 110.
[299] In *Montrose Canned Foods Ltd v Eric Wells (Merchants) Ltd* [1965] 1 Lloyd's Rep. 597 an award provided that "the Buyers pay the Sellers for all the losses arising from the non-payment of documents on presentation. We also award the Arbitration fees and expenses for account of buyers". The court held that the award was defective and should be remitted because it merely decided the question of liability without either deciding the amount to be paid or making provision for payment.

points.[300] Alternatively the tribunal may be able to make an additional award dealing with quantum.[301]

6–092 **Who must do what?** The award must not only make clear exactly what is required to be done but also which of the parties is required to do it.[302] The person who is to receive payment or otherwise to receive benefit from performance, or towards whom performance of the award is to be directed, must also be sufficiently identified, even if not named.[303]

6–093 **Method of calculation sufficient.** It is, however, sufficiently certain if the award sets out the method of calculation of the amount due to be paid, so that all that is required to determine the actual amount is "mere arithmetic".[304]

6–094 **Time limit not required.** An award will be sufficiently certain even if it imposes no time limit for compliance. It must be performed within a reasonable time, or, if the requirement for performance is conditional upon a request to do so, within a reasonable time of the request. A demand for compliance with the award will normally be given before a party seeks to enforce an award, particularly if no time limit for performance is specified in the award.

6–095 **Award in the alternative.** An award may be sufficiently certain and final though it is in the alternative. Where an award directs that one of two things be done, and one of them is uncertain or impossible, the award is nevertheless sufficiently certain and final if the other alternative is certain and possible and it will be incumbent on the party concerned to perform the award.[305]

---

[300] Under s.68 of the Arbitration Act 1996; see paras 8–093 and 8–113 below. If the tribunal is not in a position to make an award on quantum it will usually be open to it to make an award dealing with liability and defer issues of quantum until a subsequent or final award: see paras 6–009 *et seq.* above. See also *Cremer v Samanta and Samanta* [1968] 1 Lloyd's Rep. 156.

[301] See para.6–171 below.

[302] *Lawrence v Hodgson* (1826) 1 Y. & J. 16; *Re Smith and Wilson* (1848) 2 Ex. 327; *Rainforth v Hamer* (1855) 25 L.T.(O.S.) 247.

[303] *Hare v Fleay* (1851) 11 C.B. 472 20 L.J.C.P. 249. See also the comments of Roskill J. concerning the importance of properly identifying the parties in the award in *SG Embiricos Ltd v Tradax Internacional SA (The "Azuero")* [1967] 1 Lloyd's Rep. 464.

[304] *Higgins v Willes* (1828) 3 M. & R. 382; *Hopcraft v Hickman* (1824) 2 S. & S. 130 3 L.J. (O.S.) Ch. 43; *Wohlenberg v Lageman* (1815) 6 Taunt. 251; *Plummer v Lee* (1837) 2 M. & W. 495 6 L.J. Ex. 141.

[305] Where an award directed that the respondent should cause satisfaction to be entered on the judgment-roll in a certain action, or pay a sum of money, and there was in fact no such action, the award was held good to compel the respondent to pay the money: *Wharton v King* (1832) 2 B. & Ad. 528 9 L.J. (O.S.) K.B. 271. See also *Simmons v Swaine* (1809) 1 Taunt. 549.

4. Relief and Remedies Available to the Tribunal

Relief and remedies available. The Arbitration Act 1996 sets out the 6–096
range of relief and remedies which the tribunal may grant. Section 48 provides:

"48. (1) The parties are free to agree on the powers exercisable by the arbitral
        tribunal as regards remedies.
    (2) Unless otherwise agreed by the parties, the tribunal has the following
        powers.
    (3) The tribunal may make a declaration as to any matter to be determined
        in the proceedings.
    (4) The tribunal may order the payment of a sum of money, in any cur-
        rency.
    (5) The tribunal has the same powers as the court—

        (a) to order a party to do or refrain from doing anything;
        (b) to order specific performance of a contract (other than a contract
            relating to land);
        (c) to order the rectification, setting aside or cancellation of a deed or
            other document."

Party autonomy. As with so many provisions of the Arbitration Act 1996, 6–097
s.48 makes clear that party autonomy prevails and preserves the parties' right to
extend or restrict the tribunal's powers as regards remedies by agreement in
writing.[306] Indeed the parties may agree to confer on the tribunal powers which
would not be available to the court.[307] In the absence of contrary agreement
between the parties the tribunal has the powers set out in s.48(3) to (5), although
these are not necessarily the only powers it will have.[308]

(a) Directing payment of money

Directing payment. The most common form of relief granted in an award 6–098
is a direction for the payment of money. [309] This may be either as a debt due or
by way of damages or as a payment due in satisfaction of a claim for restitution.[310]
Section 48(4) confirms the tribunal's power to order the payment of a sum of

---

[306] The requirement for any agreement between the parties to be "in writing" stems from s.5(1) of the
Arbitration Act 1996, although the section gives the expression a broad meaning.
[307] This was clearly the intention: see para.234 of the DAC report. See also the discussion in relation
to exemplary damages at paras 6–103 *et seq.* below.
[308] See, e.g. para.6–113 below concerning the tribunal's power to order an indemnity. Also the parties
may agree to confer powers under s.48(1) in addition to those under s.48(3) to (5).
[309] See also paras 6–115 *et seq.* below on interest payable on monies awarded.
[310] As in *Cameroon Airlines v Transnet Ltd* [2004] EWHC 1829.

money, provided the parties have not agreed otherwise in writing[311] in the arbitration agreement.

6–099 **To whom payment should be made.** Where an award directs the payment of money, it will usually be payment by one party to the reference to the other party and the award should set out clearly who is to make payment to whom.[311a] There is old authority that an award directing payment of a sum of money to a third party is void unless the payment is for the benefit of one of the parties to the reference, and the onus of showing that benefit is on the party seeking to enforce the award.[312]

6–100 **Terms of payment.** A tribunal may fix the time at which payment is to be made[313] and it may direct that payment be made in instalments, with the whole becoming payable if one instalment remains unpaid.[314] There is old authority that a tribunal may order the payment of additional sums for delay in carrying out its award and that this will be regarded as in the nature of liquidated damages rather than as a penalty.[315] It seems unlikely that such a course would now be adopted in the light of the statutory provision for the tribunal to award interest.[316]

6–101 **Currency of payment.** Section 48(4) of the Arbitration Act 1996 provides that an award may order payment to be made in any currency. The proper construction of this section was considered by the House of Lords *Lesotho Highlands Development Authority v Impreglio SpA* where Lord Phillips explained that there are two possible ways of interpreting the provision.[317] The first is to treat it as simply conferring a procedural power to make an award in any currency, not thereby affecting the existing substantive law concerning awards in a foreign currency. This was the view favoured by the majority in *Lesotho Highlands Development Authority v Impreglio SpA*. The alternative approach, favoured by Lord Steyn, was that s.48(4) represented a change in the substantive law, by introducing an unconstrained power to make an award in any currency. This was rejected by the majority on the basis that if those who drafted the Act had intended to give such a broad discretion they would have done so more clearly, but the matter cannot be considered entirely free from doubt.[318]

---

[311] The requirement for any agreement between the parties to be "in writing" stems from s.5(1) of the Arbitration Act 1996, although the section gives the expression a broad meaning.

[311a] See para.6–092 above.

[312] *Wood v Adcock* (1852) 7 Ex. 468 21 L.J. Ex. 204.

[313] *Armitage v Walker* (1855) 2 Kay & J. 211.

[314] *Royston v Rydal* (1605) Rolle Ab. Arb. H 8 Com. Dig. Arb. E. 15; *Kockill v Witherell* (1672) 2 Keb. 838.

[315] *Parfitt v Chambre* (1872) L.R. 15 Eq. 36.

[316] Section 49 of the Arbitration Act 1996 and see further para.6–115 below.

[317] [2005] UKHL 43; [2006] 1 A.C. 221 at [49].

[318] Although the remaining four Law Lords questioned Lord Steyn's interpretation, Lord Hoffmann preferred to express no opinion on the point.

Assuming that the existing principles of English law do apply to the exercise of discretion under s.48(4)[319] then the tribunal should make the award in the proper currency of the contract under which the dispute arose unless the parties have expressly or impliedly agreed otherwise in writing.[320] The proper currency of the contract is the currency with which payments under the contract have the closest and most real connection or, if there is none, the currency which most truly expresses the claimant's loss.[321] An award in a foreign currency may be enforced in England without the need to convert it to sterling.[322]

Certificates as a condition precedent. Certain building and engineer- 6–102
ing contracts make the issue of an architect's or engineer's certificate a condition precedent to a contractor's right to payment for the work done. Where there has been no certificate and the contractor claims payment, the tribunal may still be able to decide the rights and obligations of the parties, including what sum should be paid to the contractor.[323] Assuming that the tribunal does have such jurisdiction, its award may itself take the place of the certificate, depending upon whether this power has been conferred on the tribunal.

Exemplary damages. English law permits the award of exemplary or, as 6–103
they are known in some jurisdictions, punitive damages in actions in tort in three cases.[324] In the arbitration context, there are two issues to be considered in relation to exemplary damages. The first is whether the tribunal has power to make an award providing for the payment of exemplary damages. The second is whether, assuming the tribunal does make such an award, it is enforceable. The present discussion of the topic will be limited to addressing these two issues in the context of English law on the subject.

Power to award exemplary damages. The first issue is whether a 6–104
tribunal sitting in England and applying English substantive law would only be entitled to award exemplary damages in cases in which an English court applying English law would be able to do so, i.e. in the three cases set out in the footnote

---

[319] In *Lesotho Highlands Development Authority v Impreglio SpA* [2005] UKHL 43; [2006] 1 A.C. 221 Lord Phillips specifically referred to the following statement of the position set out in the 22nd edition of this book.

[320] The requirement for any agreement between the parties to be "in writing" stems from s.5(1) of the Arbitration Act 1996, although the section gives the expression a broad meaning.

[321] *Jugoslavenska Oceanska Providba v Castle Investment Co Inc* [1974] Q.B. 292; *Services Europe Atlantique Sud (Seas) of Paris v Stockholms Rederiaktiebolag Svea of Stockholm ("The Folias")* [1979] A.C. 685.

[322] *Miliangos v George Frank (Textiles) Ltd* [1976] 1 Lloyd's Rep. 201.

[323] See further *Keating on Building Contracts* (8th edn), para.5–015.

[324] These are, first, oppressive, arbitrary or unconstitutional actions by servants of the government; second, where the defendant's conduct has been calculated by him to make a profit for himself which may well exceed the compensation payable to the plaintiff; and, third, where there is express authorisation by statute: *Rookes v Barnard* [1964] A.C. 1129, HL. A detailed discussion of the subject is beyond the scope of this book but the reader is referred to *McGregor on Damages* (17th edn) Ch.11.

to the previous paragraph. Prior to the Arbitration Act 1996 the answer was probably yes,[325] although there was no direct authority on the point. Given that most arbitrations are concerned with contractual rather than tortious claims, this lack of any decided cases on the point was perhaps unsurprising. Different considerations would have applied, however, to a tribunal sitting in England and applying a foreign substantive law. The scope of the tribunal's power to award exemplary or punitive damages would in such cases have been determined, first, by the scope of the arbitration agreement, (i.e. whether it was sufficiently widely drafted so as to permit, or at least not to exclude, such an award) and, secondly, by the extent to which, if at all, the foreign substantive law permits such an award.

6–105 **Has the Arbitration Act 1996 changed the position?** Arguably the position has changed with the passing of the 1996 Act, at least where the parties have agreed that the tribunal shall have power to award exemplary damages. Section 48 of the Arbitration Act 1996 makes clear that the parties are free to agree in writing[326] on what powers the tribunal should have as regards remedies and they are not restricted to those that would be available to the court.[327] Presumably, therefore, the parties could by agreement give the tribunal an unfettered right to award exemplary damages if it considered this appropriate.[328]

6–106 **Enforcement of award of exemplary damages.** There is no decided case on the question whether an English court would enforce an award of exemplary damages made in an arbitration with its seat in England and, if so, in what circumstances. In the light of s.48 of the Arbitration Act 1996 it seems likely that it would do so if the parties had expressly agreed to give the tribunal power to award exemplary damages or had chosen an applicable substantive law that permits the award of exemplary damages in the circumstances of the particular case. The court would, however, look very closely at the agreement and would seek to construe it narrowly. If a tribunal purported to award exemplary damages in the absence of express agreement between the parties that it should do so, and in circumstances where under English law there is no entitlement to them, the award would be vulnerable to challenge for both serious irregularity under s.68 and for error of law pursuant to s.69 of the Arbitration Act 1996.

Difficulties may arise in the context of international arbitrations where, for example, an award has been made at a seat of arbitration and under an applicable

---

[325] On the basis that the availability of exemplary damages concerns heads of damage rather than quantification and is therefore to be determined by the substantive law.

[326] The requirement for any agreement between the parties to be "in writing" stems from s.5(1) of the Arbitration Act 1996, although the section gives the expression a broad meaning.

[327] See para.6–097 above.

[328] There are at least two possible arguments against this. First, it would involve the tribunal deciding the case other than in accordance with English law. The tribunal is entitled to do so if empowered by the parties under s.46 of the Arbitration Act 1996. Secondly, it is arguably contrary to public policy and the exclusion of exemplary damages would be considered a "safeguard . . . necessary in the public interest" under s.1(b) of the Arbitration Act 1996. This is considered further in the context of enforcement of an award of exemplary damages: see para.6–106 below.

substantive law both of which permit the award of exemplary damages, and enforcement is sought in another jurisdiction which does not permit such awards, or at least not in those circumstances. If enforcement is being sought of a New York Convention award[329] an English court would be likely to enforce the award notwithstanding that it provides for exemplary damages in circumstances where they would not be available under English law. The most obvious ground for not doing so would be to assert that the award is contrary to public policy but it is difficult to see what concerns of this nature would arise given that exemplary damages are available as a matter of English law, albeit in limited circumstances.

(b) Injunctive relief

Power to grant injunctions. The Arbitration Act 1996 has clarified the power of the tribunal to grant injunctive relief. Unless the parties have agreed otherwise in writing,[330] under s.48(5)(a) it has the same power as the court to order a party to do or refrain from doing anything. A tribunal can therefore include in its award permanent injunctive relief.[331] The position in relation to interim injunctions is dealt with at paras 5–077 above.

6–107

(c) Specific performance

Power to order specific performance. Section 48(5)(b) of the Arbitration Act 1996 provides that the tribunal has the same power as the court to order specific performance of a contract other than a contract relating to land.[332] A contract relating to land is one which creates or transfers an interest in land.[333] In the event of a failure to comply with the tribunal's award, the coercive powers of the court may be available once steps have been taken to enforce the award.[334]

6–108

(d) Declaratory relief

Power to make declarations. A tribunal has power under s.48(3) of the Arbitration Act 1996 to make declarations in an award as to any matter to be

6–109

---

[329] See further paras 8–021 *et seq.* below for enforcement of New York Convention awards.

[330] The requirement for any agreement between the parties to be "in writing" stems from s.5(1) of the Arbitration Act 1996, although the section gives the expression a broad meaning. See for example *Vertex Data Science Ltd v Powergen Retail Ltd* [2006] EWHC 1340 where the parties excluded the power to grant injunctions under s.48.

[331] In contrast, the court's power under s.44 of the Arbitration Act 1996 is limited to interim injunctive relief: see paras 7–180 *et seq.* below.

[332] Formerly s.15 of the Arbitration Act 1950. The proviso in s.15 referred to contracts relating to land or any interest in land, but there was no intention to change the law in this regard: see para.234 of the DAC report.

[333] *Telia Sonera AB v Hilcourt (Docklands) Ltd* [2003] EWHC 3540. That case also clarified that it is the relevant contractual obligation of which specific performance is sought that must not relate to land, not the contract as a whole.

[334] The English court may be unable to lend its coercive powers if the respondent and/or the subject matter of the award is abroad, but a foreign court may enforce the award. As to enforcement, see paras 8–002 *et seq.* below.

determined in the proceedings, provided the parties have not agreed otherwise in writing[335] in the arbitration agreement.[336] A declaration may be made with or without a decision on a related money claim and will be appropriate, for example, where the parties simply want a decision on their rights, or to determine the existence or meaning of a contract. Declarations are often sought together with orders for specific performance. The reference in the statute to "any matter to be determined" suggests that the power is to be construed widely.

6–110　**When declaratory relief appropriate.** A tribunal should take a similar approach to the court in deciding when to grant declaratory relief.[337] In particular, it should avoid making declarations on academic or hypothetical questions or in respect of claims which have not actually been made. As Lord Diplock said in *Gouriet v Union of Post Office Workers*, "it is when an infringement of the plaintiff's rights in the future is threatened or when, unaccompanied by threats, there is a dispute between parties as to what their respective rights will be if something happens in the future, that the jurisdiction to make declarations of right can be most usefully invoked. But the jurisdiction of the court is not to declare the law generally or to give advisory opinions; it is confined to declaring contested legal rights, subsisting or future, of the parties represented in the litigation before it and not those of anyone else."[338] It may also be appropriate to seek a declaration of a subsisting right, such as an entitlement to indemnification under a policy of insurance, although this will usually be accompanied by a request for an order for payment of monies due under the policy.

(e) Contribution

6–111　**Power to order a contribution.** A tribunal may have power to order a contribution under s.1 of the Civil Liability (Contribution) Act 1978. The position was considered by the Court of Appeal in *Société Commerciale de Reassurance v Eras (International) Limited and Others*[339] but, at least in relation to a tribunal sitting in England, no firm conclusion was reached. However in *Wealands v CLC Contractors Ltd*[340] the same court expressed the view that the tribunal did have such power. This decision was followed in *X Ltd v Y Ltd*[341] where the court made clear that if the arbitration clause is drafted in appropriate terms, it may encom-

---

[335] The requirement for any agreement between the parties to be "in writing" stems from s.5(1) of the Arbitration Act 1996, although the section gives the expression a broad meaning.
[336] As to enforcement of declaratory awards see para.8–012.
[337] The court's power is set out in CPR, r.40.20.
[338] [1978] A.C. 435 at 501. CPR r.40.20, introduced since that case was decided, does not expressly limit the power to declarations "of rights". See generally Woolf, *The Declaratory Judgment* (3rd edn).
[339] [1992] 1 Lloyd's Rep. 570.
[340] [1999] 2 Lloyd's Rep. 739.
[341] [2005] B.L.R. 341.

pass a claim for contribution under the Civil Liability (Contribution) Act 1978, notwithstanding that such claims are not specifically addressed in s.48 of the Arbitration Act 1996.

The current position. It is clear that if the arbitration agreement specifically 6–112 confers jurisdiction to order a contribution under the 1978 Act then this will be upheld, given the parties' right to agree on the remedies available[342–343] The position is more uncertain in the absence of a clear provision in the arbitration agreement conferring jurisdiction to order a contribution. In *Wealands v CLC Contractors Ltd*,[344] where a party sought to resist a stay of court proceedings, the court decided that even if an arbitrator would lack power to determine a right of contribution under the 1978 Act that would not be a good reason for refusing a stay, because, by agreeing to arbitration, the parties would be deemed to have agreed to forego any right to that remedy. The court went on to consider, *obiter* dicta, the existence of the jurisdiction and, relying on the argument that tribunals in England have implied powers to exercise "every right and discretionary remedy given to a Court of law",[345] the court concluded, somewhat tentatively, that an arbitrator was empowered to order a contribution. In *X Ltd v Y Ltd*,[346] although it was accepted in principle that an arbitration agreement may be drafted in sufficiently wide terms so as to encompass a claim for contribution under the Civil Liability (Contribution) Act 1978, a provision in that case that "all disputes, differences or questions between the parties to the Contract with respect to any matter or thing arising out of or relating to the Contract . . . shall be referred to the arbitration" was held not to achieve that result. The safest approach if it is contemplated that a claim for a contribution is to fall within the tribunal's jurisdiction is to provide for this expressly in the arbitration agreement.

(f) Indemnity

Power to order indemnity. Whether there is power to order an indemnity 6–113 is not specifically addressed in s.48 of the Arbitration Act 1996, perhaps because it is subsumed within the power to order the payment of a sum of money and/or to make a declaration of the right to be indemnified. If the amount of the indemnity cannot be ascertained, for example because it will depend upon the

---

[342–343] Pursuant to s.48(1) of the Arbitration Act 1996.

[344] [1999] 2 Lloyd's Rep. 739.

[345] The argument (which was set out by Mustill L.J. in the *Eras* case) is that it is to be implied that the tribunal has the same powers as would have been available in a court of law having jurisdiction to decide the same subject matter. This argument is based on the quoted text from Tucker L.J. in *Chandris v Isbrandtsen-Moller* [1951] 1 K.B. 240; [1950] 2 All E.R. 618 relying on *Edwards v Great Western Railway* (1851) 11 C.B. 588. In the latter case the award was the result of a reference by consent order in a trial at Nisi Prius and accordingly it would have been natural to assume that the tribunal's powers concerning interest were the same as those of the jury whom it replaced. It is questionable how much weight can be placed on this argument given the number of implied terms specifically mentioned in the Arbitration Act 1996 and the terms of the 1978 Act itself, but it nevertheless formed the basis of the court's tentative decision in the *Wealands* case.

[346] [2005] B.L.R. 341.

amount, if any, payable to a third party, then the tribunal may grant a declaration of the right to be indemnified and/or may refrain from issuing its final award until the amount payable can be fixed.

(g) Rectification, setting aside or cancellation of a deed or other document

6–114 **Power to make order.** Section 48(5)(c) of the Arbitration Act 1996 provides that the tribunal has the same power as the court to order the rectification, setting aside or cancellation of a deed or other document. This statutory provision has clarified an area of the law which previously turned on construction of the arbitration agreement and whether it was in sufficiently broad terms to confer this power.[347]

(h) Interest

6–115 **Statutory power to award interest.** The tribunal has a power to award interest under s.49 of the Arbitration Act 1996.

6–116 **Party autonomy.** As with so many provisions of the Arbitration Act 1996, s.49 makes clear that party autonomy prevails and preserves the parties' right to agree what powers, if any,[348] the tribunal shall have as regards the award of interest. Again the parties may agree to confer on the tribunal powers which would not be available to the court.[349] In the absence of agreement between the parties[350] the tribunal has the powers set out in s.49(3) to (5), although these are not necessarily the only powers it will have as s.49(6) of the Arbitration Act 1996 preserves any other power of the tribunal to award interest.[351]

---

[347] The trend was generally towards construing arbitration clauses so as to permit the tribunal to order rectification: *Ethiopian Oilseeds & Pulses Export Corp v Rio Del Mar Foods Inc* [1990] 1 Lloyd's Rep. 86; *Ashville Investments Ltd v Elmer Contractors Ltd* [1988] 2 Lloyd's Rep. 73, CA; [1988] 3 W.L.R. 867. Cf. *Crane v Hegeman-Harris Co Inc* [1939] 4 All E.R. 68, CA; *Printing Machinery Co Ltd v The Linotype & Machinery Ltd* [1912] 1 Ch. 566; *Fillite (Runcorn) Ltd v Aqua-Lift* 26 Con. L.R. 66 45 B.L.R. 27.

[348] See *Socony Mobil Oil Co Inc v West of England Ship Owners Mutual Insurance Association Ltd (The "Padre Island") (No.2)* [1989] 1 Lloyd's Rep. 239, CA. The intention to exclude interest need not be contained in the arbitration clause itself, provided it can be construed as part of the arbitration agreement.

[349] The DAC report does not spell this out as it does at para.234 in relation to remedies under s.48 of the Arbitration Act 1996, but the freedom given to the parties to agree these powers is on the face of it the same subject perhaps to public policy considerations.

[350] Selection of a particular governing law will not constitute agreement between the parties for the purposes of s.49 because it does not constitute an agreement in writing in accordance with s.5(1) of the Arbitration Act 1996: see *Lesotho Highlands Development Authority v Impreglio SpA* [2005] UKHL 43; [2006] 1 A.C. 221 at [37].

[351] See also para.6–127 below.

Pre- and post-award interest. The section draws a distinction between   6–117
interest payable up to the date of the award, and interest payable thereafter on the
sums awarded. The former is dealt with in s.49(3) and the latter in s.49(4). The
provisions are the same save for the period over which interest may be awarded and
on what. Pre-award interest may be given on any amount awarded by the tribunal
or any sum which is claimed in the arbitration[352] and post-award interest may be
given on the outstanding amount of any award. Prior to the 1996 Act post-award
interest accrued automatically.[353] It no longer does so and, unless there is provision
for post-award interest in the arbitration agreement or any applicable rules,[354] it
should be the subject of a specific claim in the arbitration.[355]

Interest on sums which are claimed in the arbitration. It is clear   6–118
from s.49(3)(b) that the tribunal has power to award interest on sums paid even
though it has not reached the stage of making an award in respect of them,
provided that those sums were claimed in the arbitration. Correspondingly, the
tribunal has no power under the section to award interest on sums paid prior to
the arbitration being commenced because they are not claimed in the arbitration.

Amounts payable following declaratory award. Interest may also   6–119
be awarded where a sum is payable in consequence of a declaratory award made by
the tribunal under s.49(5) of the Arbitration Act 1996. The provision was considered in *Durham CC v Darlington BC*[356] and the court concluded that it had to
be construed consistently with the remainder of the section, such that a tribunal
was only empowered to award interest in circumstances where, had it made a
monetary award, interest could have been awarded under s.49(3).[357]

Simple or compound interest. Unlike its predecessor,[358] which referred   6–120
only to simple interest, ss.49(3) and (4) of the Arbitration Act 1996 give the
tribunal power to award simple or compound interest.[359] This reflects the position
under the rules of various arbitration institutions which empower the tribunal to

---

[352] Assuming that the sum claimed became payable prior to the making of the award: see *Durham CC
v Darlington BC* [2003] EWHC 2598.

[353] Pursuant to s.20 of the Arbitration Act 1950.

[354] *Pirtek (UK) Ltd v Deanswood Ltd* [2005] EWHC 2301; [2005] 2 Lloyd's Rep. 728. See for example
art.26.6 of the LCIA Rules.

[355] *Walker v Rowe* [2000] 1 Lloyd's Rep. 116. The respondent is named in the official transcript as
Rome, rather than Rowe.

[356] [2003] EWHC 2598.

[357] Although there was a declaratory award in that case, nothing fell due until service of a notice and
the sum was not therefore payable consequent upon the declaratory award.

[358] Section 19A of the Arbitration Act 1950.

[359] See further para.237 of the DAC report which addresses the concerns which had been expressed
about conferring a power to award compound interest.

award compound interest.[360] Compound interest is to be awarded on a compensatory basis and the power should not be used in order to punish the payer.[361] In most cases however compound interest will reflect more accurately than simple interest the loss caused to a party by not having the sum awarded at his disposal.[362]

6–121 **Rate of interest.** The tribunal has a discretion as to the rate of interest to be applied, but it should keep in mind that the purpose of interest is to compensate the successful party for not having had at his disposal the amount awarded for a period of time. This is underlined by the reference in ss.49(3) and (4) to interest being awarded as the tribunal considers meets the justice of the case. The contract may itself specify an interest rate for unpaid sums. Alternatively, the tribunal may adopt a rate at or above the bank borrowing rate(s) for the period in question.[363] As regards post-award interest it is usual to award a similar rate to the prevailing "judgment rate".[364]

6–122 **Period of pre-award interest.** Section 49(3) also gives the tribunal a discretion as to the dates from which interest is to be paid and with what rests. Interest may be awarded under this subsection up to the date of payment of any sum which is claimed in the arbitration or on any amount awarded up to the date of the award, whichever is the earlier. Interest will usually be awarded from the date when the sum paid or awarded originally fell due and the cause of action in respect of that sum arose.[365]

6–123 **Period of post-award interest.** Subsection 49(4) gives the tribunal a discretion to award interest from the date of its award, or any later date, until payment on the outstanding amount of any award. It may also award rests in

---

[360] See, e.g. the LCIA Rules, Art.26.6.

[361] See para.237 of the DAC report.

[362] See the discussion in *Sempra Metals Ltd (formerly Metallgesellschaft Ltd) v Inland Revenue Commissioners* [2007] UKHL 34.

[363] As to the rate of interest to be applied generally, see *Tate & Lyle Food and Distribution Ltd v Greater London Council* [1981] 3 All E.R. 716.

[364] 8% per annum as at July 2007. Section 49(4) has introduced a substantive change by giving the tribunal considerably more discretion with regard to post-award interest. Its predecessor, s.20 of the Arbitration Act 1950, specifically provided for an award to carry interest at the same rate as a judgment debt unless the award directed otherwise. Thus there was an entitlement to post-award interest where the award itself was silent on the issue. The tribunal could direct that no post-award interest was payable, but it did not have power to give post-award interest at any rate other than that applicable to a judgment debt: see *Timber Shipping Co SA v London and Overseas Freighters Ltd* [1972] A.C. 1 at [21]. There is apparently no such restriction as to the rate to be applied under s.49(4).

[365] *BP Chemicals Ltd v Kingdom Engineering (Fife) Ltd* [1994] 2 Lloyd's Rep. 373.

interest during this period. The subsection makes clear that the power extends to awarding interest on awards in respect of interest and/or costs.[366]

Power should normally be exercised. The tribunal should normally   6–124
exercise its power to award interest in the absence of a good reason not to.[367] As Lord Denning M.R. stated in *Panchaud v Pagnan:* "In a commercial transaction if the plaintiff has been out of his money for a period, the usual order is that the defendant should pay interest for the time for which the sum has been outstanding. No exception should be made except for good reason."[368]

Effect of delay. Delay in bringing a claim is not of itself a good reason for   6–125
refusing interest unless the delay is exceptional and inexcusable.[369–370]

Award silent on interest. If a party has sought interest on sums payable or   6–126
found to be due but the award is silent on the subject, it may be susceptible to challenge on the grounds of serious irregularity under s.68(2)(d) of the Arbitration Act 1996 for failing to deal with an issue put to the tribunal.[371] Where the omission is due to a clerical mistake or error arising from an accidental slip or omission, it may be corrected by the tribunal under s.57(3)(a) of the Arbitration Act 1996.[372] However, it will usually be more appropriate to exercise the power under s.57(3)(b) to make an additional award in relation to interest.[373]

Other power to award interest. Section 49(6) specifically preserves any   6–127
power of the tribunal to award interest other than under the statute. This is a saving provision, such that the other power to award interest will not be ousted by the statutory regime, but nor does the existence of the other power preclude the

---

[366] The liability to pay interest under s.49 is a liability in debt and can be enforced as such, with interest accruing on the unpaid debt: *Coastal States Trading (UK) Ltd v Mebro Mineraloelhandelsgesellschaft GmbH* [1986] 1 Lloyd's Rep. 465. Further, s.49 has removed a possible anomaly under the earlier statute whereby, as the entitlement to post-award interest arose by statute rather than under the award, it may not have been recoverable when seeking to enforce the award in another jurisdiction under the New York Convention.

[367] *Wildhandel N.V. v Tucker and Cross* [1976] 1 Lloyd's Rep. 341.

[368] [1974] 1 Lloyd's Rep. 394 at 411.

[369–370] *Panchaud v Pagnan* [1974] 1 Lloyd's Rep. 394. In *Antclizo Shipping Corporation v Food Corporation of India (The "Antclizo") (No.2)* [1991] 2 Lloyd's Rep. 485 arbitrators were appointed in 1975 to hear disputes under a charterparty. There followed a prolonged delay and both arbitrators died. Two fresh arbitrators and an umpire were appointed in July 1989. The umpire found that the failure to pursue the arbitration for eight years from 1975 to 1983 was due in part to the pendency of other arbitrations between the same parties raising similar issues. However, there was no agreement to "freeze" the arbitration. He found that the delay was an inordinate and unreasonable failure to prosecute the claim and declined to award interest for those eight years. The court would not interfere, holding that he was entitled to take an overall view of the position in exercising his discretion.

[371] See paras 8–093 *et seq.*. below.

[372] See *Pancommerce SA v Veecheema BV* [1983] 2 Lloyd's Rep. 304 and see para.6–167 below.

[373] See para.6–171 below.

exercise of the powers under the remaining provisions of s.49.[374] In practice such "other" power will most commonly arise where there is an express or implied contractual right to interest.[375] Various sets of arbitration rules contain such a power.[376]

6–128 **Overriding contractual right to interest.** Subject to what the parties may have agreed shall be the tribunal's powers as to interest, under s.49 the tribunal has a discretion whether to exercise its power to award interest, although as set out in para.6–124 the power should normally be exercised. If, however, there is a contractual right to interest then it must be awarded. The contractual right may be to receive compound interest and, if so, this must be awarded.[377]

5. COSTS

(a) Description of costs

6–129 **Terminology used.** A distinction has traditionally been drawn between "costs of the reference" and "costs of the award", the former being in broad terms the costs incurred by the parties in putting their respective cases in the arbitration and the latter being the administration costs of the reference, including the tribunal's fees and expenses.[378] These two types of costs were referred to in the previous legislation[379] and the distinction was often relevant in practice because tribunals would commonly award a party the costs of the reference to be agreed or "taxed"[380] whereas the costs of the award would be awarded as a lump sum.[381] This terminology has been replaced in s.59 of the Arbitration Act 1996 which refers only to the "costs of the arbitration", which comprise both costs of the reference and of the award. All these terms will nevertheless be considered below as both the parties and tribunals may still find it convenient to distinguish between them in the context of how recoverable costs are to be dealt with.

---

[374] *Lesotho Highlands Development Authority v Impreglio SpA* [2005] UKHL 43; [2006] 1 A.C. 221 at [38].

[375] Mustill & Boyd p.393 identify a number of other circumstances which could give rise to some "other power" to award interest. These are (1) interest as special damages for the late payment of money, (2) the equitable right to interest in relation to profits arising from a breach of fiduciary duty, and (3) where the claim is one which falls within the Admiralty jurisdiction of the High Court but is referred to arbitration.

[376] See for example LCIA Rules, Art.26.6.

[377] *National Bank of Greece SA v Pinios Shipping Co (No.1) and George Dionysios Tsitsilianis (The "Maira") (No.3)* [1990] 1 Lloyd's Rep. 225.

[378] Many of the administrative costs such as room hire and shorthand writer fees will have been paid in advance by the parties jointly or by one of them but are then recoverable following the tribunal's award on costs.

[379] Section 18(1) of the Arbitration Act 1950 referred to "costs of the reference and award" and s.18(4) of the Arbitration Act 1950 to "costs of the reference".

[380] i.e. assessed by the tribunal or by a Taxing Master at court, now known as a "costs judge": CPR Pt 43.2.

[381] *Government of Ceylon v Chandris* [1963] 2 Q.B. 327 at 333.

Costs of the arbitration. These are defined in s.59(1) of the Arbitration   6–130
Act 1996 as:

(a) the arbitrators' fees and expenses,

(b) the fees and expenses of any arbitral institution concerned, and

(c) the legal or other costs of the parties.[382]

It will be seen that broadly speaking (a) and (b) fall within what have previously
been termed the costs of the award and (c) comprise the costs of the reference.
Section 59(2) makes clear that the costs of the arbitration also include the costs of
or incidental to any proceedings to determine the amount of the recoverable costs
of the arbitration, such as the costs of any application to court under s.63(4) to
determine the recoverable costs.[383] Presumably they would also include the costs
of negotiating and settling the terms of any submission to arbitration.[384]

Costs of the reference. These comprise all costs properly and reasonably   6–131
incurred by either party[385] in preparing and presenting their case in the arbitration, including of course costs incurred in rebutting the case put forward by the
other party. They include the costs of legal or lay[386] representation,[387] expenses of
fact witnesses and fees of expert witnesses or advisers retained to assist one or
other party with the preparation of their case.[388] They presumably also include the
costs of negotiating and settling the terms of the submission to arbitration.[389]
Conditional fee agreements may be entered into in relation to arbitration proceedings,[390] and subject to meeting the requirement of reasonableness pursuant to

---

[382] This includes costs of a lay representative in arbitration proceedings: *Piper Double Glazing Ltd v D
C Contracts* 31 Con. L.R. 149.

[383] But not the costs of other arbitration applications unrelated to the determination of recoverable
costs.

[384] Which are costs of the reference: *Re Autothreptic Steam Boiler Co and Townsend, Hook & Co* (1888)
21 Q.B.D. 182.

[385] *Re Autothreptic Steam Boiler Co and Townsend, Hook & Co* (1888) 21 Q.B.D. 182.

[386] The costs of lay representatives are recoverable: see *Piper Double Glazing Ltd v DC Contracts* 31
Con. L.R. 149.

[387] The costs of in-house counsel and a party's management staff are not usually recoverable on the
basis that their salaries would be incurred in any event and are not therefore an additional cost
attributable to the arbitration. The position may be different where a party can show that they have
recruited additional resources specifically to deal with the arbitration.

[388] Experts will usually charge professional fees for their services as an expert witness together with out
of pocket expenses. Fact witnesses are not usually remunerated for time spent giving evidence
although if they are not in the employment of the party calling them it may be appropriate to pay
for lost earnings as a result of their preparation and attendance at the hearing. Any such payments
should be limited to reasonable compensation for losses actually incurred, so that they cannot be
characterized as "buying" the evidence to be given which might undermine its credibility. There
is no objection to paying the reasonably incurred out of pocket expenses of fact witnesses.

[389] See para.6–130.

[390] *Protech Projects Construction (Pty) Ltd v Al-Kharafi & Sons* [2005] EWHC 2165; *Bevan Ashford v
Geoff Yeandle (Contractors) Ltd (in liquidation)* [1998] 3 All E.R. 238. In the latter case Sir Richard
Scott V.C. decided that although a conditional fee agreement relating to arbitration proceedings
does not fall within s.58 of the Courts and Legal Services Act 1990 (inserted by s.27(1) of the Access
to Justice Act 1999) and the regulations made under it, nevertheless if such an agreement complies
with those provisions then it would not be contrary to public policy and would be enforceable.

s.63(5) of the Arbitration Act 1996 or falling within the parties' agreement as to recoverable costs pursuant to s.63(1), the appropriate uplift may also form part of the costs of the reference.[391]

The term "costs of the reference" is sometimes used to mean the costs discussed above together with the costs of the award, in other words all costs incurred in connection with the arbitration.[392] However, even under the previous legislation a distinction was drawn between the two types of costs, and this broader meaning of the term "costs of the reference" should no longer be used, particularly in the light of the statutory definition of "costs of the arbitration" in s.59 of the Arbitration Act 1996.

6–132 **Costs of the award.** During the course of an arbitration, costs will arise which relate to the setting up and administration of the arbitration. These are termed the "costs of the award" and include, for example, the tribunal's fees and expenses,[393] the fees and expenses of any arbitral institution concerned, the cost of hiring rooms for hearings, shorthand writers' fees[394] and translators' fees. The cost of photocopying documents for use by the tribunal at the hearing is also a cost of the award as are any special expenses incurred in connection with the arbitration by the tribunal with the consent of the parties, such as the fees and expenses of a secretarial service retained by the tribunal to assist it with the case.[395] The fees and expenses of an expert or legal adviser or assessor appointed under s.37 of the Arbitration Act 1996 are treated as expenses of the arbitrators and are therefore also costs of the award.

(b) Jurisdiction and manner of awarding costs

6–133 **Power to award costs.** Section 61(1) of the Arbitration Act 1996 provides that: "The tribunal may make an award allocating the costs of the arbitration as between the parties, subject to any agreement of the parties." Accordingly, the tribunal has a discretion to award the costs of the arbitration as between the parties, although this power is subject to anything that the parties have agreed and is also subject to the general principle set out in s.61(2) that costs follow the event.[396]

---

[391] *Protech Projects Construction (Pty) Ltd v Al-Kharafi & Sons* [2005] EWHC 2165. It would seem therefore that foreign counsel could recover on the basis of fee arrangements that would not be permitted under English law, provided they are considered reasonable or fall within what the parties have agreed should be recoverable costs.

[392] *Re Walker & Brown* (1882) 9 Q.B.D. 434.

[393] *Government of Ceylon v Chandris* [1963] 2 Q.B. 327 at 333.

[394] The parties should seek to agree in advance whether transcripts of the hearing will be required. The tribunal may also have views on this. These costs should be treated as costs of the award (rather than costs of the reference) even where only one of the parties has arranged to receive transcripts, particularly if the tribunal has also received them.

[395] See para.5–173 above.

[396] See para.6–138 below.

Agreement between the parties as to costs. The parties are in 6–134
general at liberty to agree who shall pay the costs and on what principles costs shall
be awarded.[397] The parties do not however have a completely unfettered right to
agree how the costs of the arbitration shall be allocated between them. Section 60
of the Arbitration Act 1996 provides that: "An agreement which has the effect that
a party is to pay the whole or part of the costs of the arbitration in any event is only
valid if made after the dispute in question has arisen." So a provision in an
agreement to refer future disputes to arbitration to the effect that the parties will
each bear their own costs, or that one party will bear his own costs in any event,
or that one party will bear all the costs of the arbitration, is void. Such a provision
can only be valid in an agreement to submit an existing dispute to arbitration or
if it is confirmed or validated after the dispute has arisen. However an agreement
that the losing party will pay the costs of the arbitration would not be void, as it
is not an agreement that a particular party will pay the costs in any event.

Further, unless otherwise agreed, the parties' obligations to each other as 6–135
regards costs relate only to "recoverable costs" in the arbitration.[398] Section 62 of
the Arbitration Act 1996 provides that: "Unless the parties otherwise agree, any
obligation under an agreement between them as to how the costs of the arbitration
are to be borne, or under an award allocating the costs of the arbitration, extends
only to such costs as are recoverable."

Exercise of the discretion. The court will not interfere with the tribunal's 6–136
exercise of its discretion to award costs merely because the court would itself have
exercised that discretion differently.[399] The tribunal must exercise its discretion,
however, and must not disable itself from doing so by adopting an invariable rule
in relation to certain costs.[400]

Exercise of discretion. Prior to the Arbitration Act 1996 the courts had 6–137
held that in exercising its discretion the tribunal must act judicially, which means
in the same manner as would be adopted by a judge in a court of law.[401]

There is, however, now clear guidance in the Arbitration Act 1996 as to the
tribunal's powers with regard to the award of costs.[402] It has been said that as a
result it is no longer helpful to ask whether an arbitrator has acted judicially.[403]
The focus of inquiry will be on compliance with the statutory provisions and any
additional powers that the parties agree the tribunal shall have with regard to the
award of costs. Where the Crown is a party to the arbitration, the discretion as to

---

[397] Section 61 of the Arbitration Act 1996. Arbitration rules often also make provision for the approach
to costs: see for example Art.40 of the UNCITRAL Rules and Art.28.2 of the LCIA Rules.
[398] See para.6–141 below.
[399] *Channel Island Ferries Ltd v Cenargo Navigation Ltd ("The Rozel")* [1994] 2 Lloyd's Rep. 161.
[400] *James Allen (Liverpool) Ltd v London Export Corp Ltd* [1982] 2 Lloyd's Rep. 632.
[401] *Everglade Maritime Inc v Schiffahrtsgesellschaft Detlef Von Appen GmbH (The "Maria")* [1992] 2
Lloyd's Rep. 167; [1993] 1 W.L.R. 33; [1992] 3 All E.R. 851 (Judge Diamond Q.C.); [1993] 3
W.L.R. 176 (Court of Appeal); *President of India v Jadranska Solbodna Plovidba* [1992] 2 Lloyd's
Rep. 274; *Metro-Cammell Hong Kong Ltd v FKI Engineering Ltd* 77 B.L.R. 84.
[402] Section 61(2) of the Arbitration Act 1996; see para.6–138 below.
[403] *Fence Gate Limited v NEL Construction Limited* [2002] C.I.L.L. 1817.

costs is in general to be exercised in the same way as in proceedings between subjects.[404]

6–138 **Costs follow the event.** Section 61(2) of the Arbitration Act 1996 provides that:

> "Unless the parties otherwise agree, the tribunal shall award costs on the general principle that costs should follow the event except where it appears to the tribunal that in the circumstances this is not appropriate in relation to the whole or part of the costs."

Usually, therefore, costs will "follow the event" so that the successful party will be awarded his costs.[405] If the tribunal is going to depart from this it should set out clearly its reasons for doing so,[406] and its decision must be justified as the exercise of a discretion in accordance with the 1996 Act.[407] If the tribunal fails to appreciate the result of its award, such that it purports to award costs on the principle that they follow the event but in fact awards them to the loser, the decision will be vulnerable to challenge.[408]

6–139 **What constitutes the event?** Where one of the parties is the clear winner on all issues it will be a straightforward task to award costs in a way that follows the event. In many cases however parties will succeed on some claims but not on others, and win on some of the contested issues and arguments but lose on others. How then is a tribunal to go about determining the relevant event for these purposes? The answer is that in most cases the tribunal will look at the overall result to determine which party can be said to have won the arbitration. That does not involve an issue by issue analysis, but rather requires the tribunal to decide which party overall can be said to have succeeded in the reference. Of course it

---

[404] Section 7 of the Administration of Justice (Miscellaneous Provisions) Act 1933. The section contains savings for special cases, including cases where the Crown is "required" to be made a party.

[405] For cases under the old law see *Semco Salvage & Marine Pte Ltd v Lancer Navigation Co Ltd (The "Nagasaki Spirit")* [1996] 1 Lloyd's Rep. 449; *Channel Island Ferries Ltd v Cenargo Navigation Ltd ("The Rozel")* [1994] 2 Lloyd's Rep. 161; *The "Erich Schroeder"* [1974] 1 Lloyd's Rep. 192; *Smeaton Hanscomb & Co Ltd v Sassoon/Setty, Son & Co (No.2)* [1953] 1 W.L.R. 1481; *Blue Horizon Shipping Co SA v ED & F Man Ltd (The "Aghios Nicolaos")* [1980] 1 Lloyd's Rep. 17; *Heaven & Kesterton Ltd v Etablissements Francois Albiac et Cie* [1956] 2 Lloyd's Rep. 316.

[406] *Lewis v Haverfordwest Rural District Council* [1953] 1 W.L.R. 1486; *Smeaton Hanscomb & Co Ltd v Sassoon/Setty, Son & Co (No.2)* [1953] 1 W.L.R. 1481. In the absence of agreement to dispense with them, the tribunal is under an obligation to provide reasons in any event, see para.6–029 above. See also para.6–144 for the type of situation where departure from the normal approach may be appropriate.

[407] *Gbangbola v Smith & Sherriff Ltd* [1998] 3 All E.R. 730. In that case the arbitrator took into account matters which he ought to have given the parties an opportunity to address before making his award as to costs but failed to do so and thereby breached his duty under s.33(1)(a): see further para.5–050.

[408] *Newfield Construction Ltd v Tomlinson* [2004] EWHC 3051; 97 Con. L.R. 148 at [21]. The challenge was upheld under s.68 of the Arbitration Act 1996 but the award was also successfully appealed on a point of law under s.69 of the Arbitration Act 1996.

may be that neither party can be said to have "won", in which case it may be appropriate to order that each party shall bear its own costs. Often when considering "the event" a tribunal will consider, at least in broad terms, on which of its claims a party has succeeded and will adjust the proportion of recoverable costs awarded to reflect the fact that the other party has defeated certain claims or indeed won on other claims it has brought.[409] This is not an exact science but in broad terms a tribunal should start from the premise that the successful party should recover its costs and then make appropriate adjustments to reflect what the tribunal considers a fair allocation of costs in light of the overall result and state the reasons for making them.

Review by the court. As stated above,[410] where the tribunal has exercised its   6–140
discretion as to costs, the court will not seek to replace that decision with its own, even if the court would have exercised the discretion in a different way. The court will, however, review whether the discretion has been exercised properly in accordance with the principles set out in the Arbitration Act 1996 in so far as they apply.

The court's review of an order as to costs will usually be founded on an error of law[411] following an application brought under s.69 of the Arbitration Act 1996.[412] Alternatively, and depending on the particular circumstances, it may be possible to challenge the costs order on the grounds of serious irregularity, provided the matters for complaint fall within the categories set out in s.68 of the Arbitration Act 1996.[413] The "central principles" to be applied were summarised in *Newfield Construction Ltd v Tomlinson*[414] as follows:

- For the complaint about a costs award to arise in the form of an appeal (under s.69 of the Act), it must be one that can be expressed in the form of a clear question of law.

- If the complaint is that the decision the tribunal arrived at was wrong because of an error in its appreciation or understanding of the material used as the basis of the award, it may amount to a serious irregularity (under s.68 of the Act). However, it does not give rise to a question of law.

---

[409] See for example *Rotary Watches Ltd v Rotary Watches (USA) Inc* [2004] W.L. 3200214.
[410] At para.6–136 above.
[411] *Donald Campbell & Co Ltd v Pollak* [1927] A.C. 732; *President of India v Jadranska Slobodna Plovidba* [1992] 2 Lloyd's Rep. 274; *Fence Gate Ltd v NEL Construction Ltd* [2002] C.I.L.L. 1817.
[412] If the parties have agreed to dispense with reasons, there can be no appeal: s.69(1) of the Arbitration Act 1996. Nor can the tribunal's exercise of its discretion to award costs be challenged in proceedings by the tribunal to recover its costs: see *Cohen v Baram* [1994] 2 Lloyd's Rep. 138.
[413] See *Gbangbola v Smith & Sherriff Ltd* [1998] 3 All E.R. 730; *Fence Gate Ltd v NEL Construction Ltd* (2001) Con. L.R. 41; *Newfield Construction Ltd v Tomlinson* [2004] EWHC 3051; 97 Con. L.R. 148. See also para.8–098 below.
[414] [2004] EWHC 3051; 97 Con. L.R. 148 at [27]. The principles were drawn from the decision of His Honour Judge Thornton Q.C. in *Fence Gate Ltd v NEL Construction Ltd* (2001) Con. L.R. 41 at [37]–[40].

- The tribunal must not take into account matters which the law or the powers given to it by the parties or the general law preclude it from acting on and, conversely, it must not fail to take account of, and give effect to matters that the law requires it to take account of. Moreover, since the tribunal must observe and give effect to the law, the overall discretionary exercise must not be perverse nor one that a reasonable tribunal properly directing itself could not have reached.

- A question of law can arise, if it is contended that the tribunal misdirected itself by taking into account factors which it should not have done or by failing to take into account factors it should have done.

(c) Recoverable costs

6–141 **Determining the recoverable costs.** In contrast to s.61, which is concerned with the allocation of recoverable costs, ss.63 and 64 of the Arbitration Act 1996 deal respectively with the recoverable costs of the arbitration and the recoverable fees and expenses of the tribunal. Section 63 provides that the parties are free to agree what costs of the arbitration are recoverable, but in the absence of agreement certain default provisions apply. These default provisions are that the tribunal may determine the recoverable costs of the arbitration on such basis as it thinks fit and, if it does so, the tribunal must specify the basis on which it has acted, the items of recoverable costs and the amount referable to each.[415] If the tribunal does not determine the recoverable costs, either party may apply to the court which will either determine them on such basis as it thinks fit, or order that they shall be determined by such means and upon such terms as it may specify.[416]

6–142 **The recoverable fees and expenses of the tribunal.** Section 64 of the Arbitration Act 1996 provides that unless otherwise agreed in writing[417] by the parties, the recoverable costs of the arbitration include only such reasonable fees and expenses of the tribunal as are appropriate in the circumstances.[418] If there is any dispute about this, and the matter is not already before the court on an application under s.63(4),[419] either party may apply to the court for it to determine the matter or order that it be determined by such means and upon such terms as the court may specify.[420] Although this establishes a means of determining what

---

[415] Section 63(3) of the Arbitration Act 1996; see also para.6–150 below.
[416] Section 63(4) of the Arbitration Act 1996; see also para.6–153 below.
[417] The requirement for any agreement between the parties to be "in writing" stems from s.5(1) of the Arbitration Act 1996, although the section gives the expression a broad meaning.
[418] Section 64(1) of the Arbitration Act 1996. This is, of course, subject to any order of the court under ss.24(4) or 25(3)(b) as to entitlement to fees or expenses of an arbitrator in case of removal or resignation: see s.64(3) of the Arbitration Act 1996.
[419] See para.6–141 above.
[420] Section 64(2) of the Arbitration Act 1996; see also para.6–153 below.

fees and expenses of the tribunal are recoverable as between the parties, it does not affect any right of the tribunal to payment of its fees and expenses.[421]

How much is recoverable? Section 63(5)(a) of the Arbitration Act 1996 **6–143** sets out the basis for assessing what costs are recoverable, namely that "there shall be allowed a reasonable amount in respect of all costs reasonably incurred". This reflects the test applied under CPR Pt 44 r.4 for the standard basis of assessment of costs.[422] Section 63(5)(b) confirms that any doubt as to whether costs were reasonable or reasonably incurred is to be resolved in favour of the paying party. This is subject to the tribunal determining that some other basis should be adopted, so that in a suitable case the test might be amended to reflect the indemnity basis of assessment of costs under CPR Pt 44 r.4, i.e. to resolve any doubt about whether the costs were reasonable or reasonably incurred in favour of the receiving party. The practice however in many international arbitrations where the seat is London is rather more flexible. It is not uncommon for the successful party to be awarded more than would be recoverable under the standard basis of costs and tribunals often reach this conclusion without distinguishing between the standard and indemnity bases of awarding costs but rather focussing on what is considered reasonable in all the circumstances.

Determining recoverable costs on some other basis. As stated **6–144** above, the basis set out above under s.63(5) of the Arbitration Act 1996 is subject to the tribunal or court "determining otherwise". This they might do where, for example, the successful party has grossly exaggerated his claim, or where substantial time has been spent on unnecessary evidence or on discrete issues of fact on which that party was unsuccessful. This is especially so if the successful party's conduct has been unreasonable. Similarly, the tribunal or court may decline to award a party the costs of a procedural hearing or step in the reference prior to the substantive hearing on the grounds that the party's conduct in relation to that aspect of the case was unreasonable, even though he may ultimately succeed in the arbitration. However, it is not appropriate to refuse a successful party the entirety of his costs solely on the ground that he has recovered significantly less than claimed.[423]

The right to payment of fees, etc. Section 63(7) of the Arbitration Act **6–145** 1996 makes clear that the right to payment of fees and expenses of arbitrators, experts, institutions and the like is not affected by whether those fees and expenses are recoverable as between the parties as costs of the arbitration. Similarly, the

---

[421] Section 64(4) of the Arbitration Act 1996; see also para.6–145.

[422] Although CPR Pt 44 r.4 imposes an additional requirement that the costs are proportionate to the matters in issue.

[423] *Channel Island Ferries Ltd v Cenargo Navigation Ltd ("The Rozel")* [1994] 2 Lloyd's Rep. 161; *Lewis Emanuel and Son Ltd v Sammut* [1959] 2 Lloyd's Rep. 629. See also *Rosen & Co v Dowley and Selby* [1943] 2 All E.R. 172.

court's powers to determine whether the tribunal's fees and expenses are recoverable does not affect their right to payment.[424]

6–146 Payment of costs by a third party. The court may in some circumstances order that the costs of an action be paid by a person who is not a party to that action.[425] A tribunal has no jurisdiction to do so.[426]

6–147 Power to limit recoverable costs. One of the more innovative provisions of the Arbitration Act 1996 is s.65, which provides that, unless otherwise agreed by the parties, the tribunal may direct that the recoverable costs of the arbitration, or of any part of the arbitral proceedings, shall be limited to a specified amount.[427] Any direction under this section may be made or varied at any stage, but this must be done sufficiently in advance of the incurring of costs to which it relates, or the taking of any steps in the proceedings which may be affected by it, for the limit to be taken into account.[428]

This provision was introduced by the Arbitration Act 1996[429] and gives the tribunal power to limit the amount of recoverable costs in advance. The intention was that this power would enable tribunals to dissuade the parties from incurring unnecessary costs by making clear beforehand that above the stated limit they will not be recoverable from the other side, even if a party is successful in relation to the matters to which the costs relate.[430] It does not of course prevent parties incurring those costs anyway if they so choose, but they will do so at their own expense. The tribunal will usually wish to give the parties an opportunity to make representations in relation to such a proposed order, but it is not necessary for the tribunal to give reasons explaining their decision to impose a cap on recoverable costs under the section.[431] Any order may be varied pursuant to s.65(2) of the Arbitration Act 1996 and that includes the power to remove altogether any previously imposed cap.[432]

6–148 Requirement for a specified amount. Under s.65(1) the recoverable costs may be limited to a "specified amount". The tribunal is not therefore entitled to order a cap limited to "reasonable costs" or to "those costs reasonably incurred".

[424] Section 64(4) of the Arbitration Act 1996. The tribunal's fees and expenses may, however, be challenged under s.28 of the Arbitration Act 1996: see paras 4–059 and 7–212 *et seq.* above.
[425] *Aiden Shipping Ltd v Interbulk Ltd (The "Vimeira")* [1986] A.C. 965 [1986] 2 All E.R. 409, HL; CPR Pt 48 r.2.
[426] *Maritime Transport Overseas GmbH v Unitramp (The "Antaios")* [1981] 2 Lloyd's Rep. 284; *The "Takamine"* [1980] 2 Lloyd's Rep. 205. Thus s.61(1) of the Arbitration Act 1996 empowers the tribunal to award costs of the arbitration "as between the parties".
[427] Section 65(1) of the Arbitration Act 1996.
[428] Section 65(2) of the Arbitration Act 1996.
[429] There is no equivalent provision in the earlier statutes or in the Model Law.
[430] See further para.272 of the DAC report.
[431] *Home of Homes Ltd v Hammersmith and Fulham LBC* [2003] EWHC 807; 92 Const. L.R. 48.
[432] *Home of Homes Ltd v Hammersmith and Fulham LBC* [2003] EWHC 807; 92 Const. L.R. 48.

Is it being used? The aim of s.65 is undoubtedly worthwhile. It presents the   **6–149**
tribunal with a real opportunity to control the costs of an arbitration because a
party will in many cases be reluctant to incur costs that will not be recoverable
even if that party wins. There is of course usually an element of irrecoverable costs
in arbitrations, but the exercise by the tribunal of its power under s.65 may focus
the minds of the parties on this. There have been few reported decisions on the
exercise of the power under s.65 but when given the opportunity the court has
been supportive of its use.[433] This may reflect the potential controversy of an order
being made, but there is no doubt that there are cases where the power can be used
to good effect, for example where future costs are likely to become as significant
as, or outweigh, the sums at stake and this is not considered by the tribunal to be
justified in all the circumstances. In due course there may well develop a body of
case law on issues such as the circumstances in which an order should be made and
how long is "sufficiently in advance . . . for the limit to be taken into account".[434]
For the time being it remains an under-used but potentially very useful addition
to the tribunal's powers, particularly in helping it to comply with the duty to avoid
unnecessary expense under s.33(1)(b) of the Arbitration Act 1996.[435]

(d) Determination of costs by the tribunal

Power to determine recoverable costs. As stated above,[436] under   **6–150**
s.63(3) of the Arbitration Act 1996 the tribunal may determine the recoverable
costs of the arbitration on such basis as it thinks fit. When doing so it must specify
the basis adopted, the items of recoverable cost and the amount recoverable for
each, and must assess the amount which is to be paid and for what. In the absence
of specific agreement there is no obligation on the tribunal to determine the
recoverable costs and if it declines to do so[437] the parties will need either to agree
the amount of costs or to pursue an application to the court.[438] In these circumstances the tribunal's award may still deal with who is to pay the costs and for
what, but not the amount that is to be paid. If the tribunal does determine the
recoverable costs of the arbitration, its assessment of the amount to be paid forms

---

[433] *Home of Homes Ltd v Hammersmith and Fulham LBC* [2003] EWHC 807; 92 Const. L.R. 48. The
judge commended the arbitrator's attempts to impose a limit on recoverable costs pursuant to s.65
of the Arbitration Act 1996 several times in the course of his judgment.

[434] In *Home of Homes Ltd v Hammersmith and Fulham LBC* [2003] EWHC 807; 92 Const. L.R. 48 an
order under s.65(1) of the Arbitration Act 1996 was made 10 working days before the commencement of the substantive hearing and purportedly covered not just the hearing itself but also costs
incurred during a period prior to the making of the order. The arbitrator subsequently rescinded
the order on the basis of legal advice that this was too late a stage at which to make such an
order.

[435] See para.5–032 above.

[436] At para.6–141 above.

[437] Unless there is good reason not to the tribunal should deal with costs rather than leaving it to the
court: see para.6–156 below.

[438] See para.6–153 below.

part of the award and is binding on the parties unless and until the award is set aside.[439]

6–151 Independent judgment. Where the tribunal determines the recoverable costs of the arbitration, it must apply its own independent mind and judgment to the amounts claimed in order to be satisfied that they are of a reasonable amount and were reasonably incurred.[440]

6–152 Tribunal's own fees and expenses. The tribunal's power under s.63(3) of the Arbitration Act 1996 to determine the recoverable costs of the arbitration, includes the power to determine the extent to which its own fees and expenses are recoverable, and to include these as part of the award.[441] This is subject to any agreement between the parties pursuant to s.63(1) of the Arbitration Act 1996 on the matter. However, it would obviously be inappropriate for the tribunal to have the last word on whether their fees and expenses are reasonable and therefore recoverable. Unless the fees and expenses of the tribunal have been agreed in advance,[442] any party may therefore apply to the court to determine what fees and expenses are recoverable as costs of the arbitration.[443] The court may determine the matter itself[444] or may decide the means and terms on which they are to be determined.[445]

(e) Determination of costs by the court

6–153 Application to court. If the tribunal does not determine the recoverable costs of the arbitration the court has jurisdiction to do so or to order the means and terms upon which they shall be determined.[446] This is of course subject to the parties having already agreed the recoverable costs under s.63(1) of the Arbitration Act 1996. If they are to be determined by the court this will be carried out by a particular type of judge known as a "costs judge" who deals with the assessment of allowable costs.[447]

---

[439] *Re Gilbert and Wright* (1904) 20 T.L.R. 164. This case was decided under a statutory provision which gave the tribunal power to "tax or settle" costs, but the same reasoning would apply under the Arbitration Act 1996.

[440] *Government of Ceylon v Chandris* [1963] 1 Lloyd's Rep. 214. This case was decided under the old law but the reasoning still applies.

[441] The tribunal's contractual right to be paid is not affected: s.64(4) of the Arbitration Act 1996.

[442] See para.4–052 above.

[443] Section 64(2) of the Arbitration Act 1996: see para.6–142 above. The tribunal's fees and expenses may also be challenged under s.28 of the Arbitration Act 1996: see paras 4–059 above and 7–212 below.

[444] s.64(2)(a).

[445] s.64(2)(b).

[446] Under s.63(4) of the Arbitration Act 1996: see para.7–210 below. Where the arbitration agreement requires the tribunal to fix the costs, it must do so rather than leaving it to the court: *Morgan v Smith* (1842) 9 M. & W. 427.

[447] For the court's powers generally see CPR Pts 43–48 and related Practice Direction.

Scale of costs and basis of determining them. Under the previous   6–154
legislation an arbitrator could direct that costs should be assessed or "taxed" in the
High Court, and this carried an implication that they should be assessed on the
High Court scale and not on the County Court scale, even if the amount of the
award was a small one.[448] The test under the Arbitration Act 1996 is somewhat
different; it is a question of determining whether the costs are of a reasonable
amount and were reasonably incurred, any doubt being resolved in favour of the
paying party.[449] This is subject to the court (or the tribunal) determining that
some other basis should be adopted, so that in a suitable case the test might be
amended to reflect indemnity costs under CPR Pt 44 r.4, i.e. to resolve any doubt
about whether the costs were reasonable or reasonably incurred in favour of the
receiving party.[450]

(f) Approach to costs

Costs to be "determined if not agreed". Perhaps the most frequently   6–155
made order for costs under the previous statutory regime was that they should be
"taxed if not agreed". This meant that the tribunal was inviting the parties to
reach agreement as to the amount of costs and, failing agreement either to revert
to the tribunal for them to assess the costs[451] or to apply to the court for them to
be "taxed". This terminology is no longer appropriate,[452] but the equivalent order
would be for costs to be "determined if not agreed". A tribunal may still decline
to determine recoverable costs itself, leaving the parties to agree them or apply to
court for their assessment.[453]

Tribunal determines recoverable costs. The tribunal has power to   6–156
determine the amount of recoverable costs under s.63(3) of the Arbitration Act
1996[454] and include in the award details of the amounts allowed by it in respect of
costs, and giving a total figure. The tribunal should follow this course unless there
are good reasons not to do so. When there is a dispute over the amount of
recoverable costs, it is an issue in the arbitration which the tribunal should
determine unless there is a particular reason for leaving it to the court.[455]

Lump sum. It was not uncommon under the previous statutory regime for the   6–157
tribunal to award a lump sum in respect of costs of the reference and/or of the
award. So far as the costs of the reference were concerned, the lump sum was

---

[448] *Perkins (HG) v Brent-Shaw* [1973] 1 W.L.R. 975.
[449] Section 63(5) of the Arbitration Act 1996: see para.6–143 above.
[450] See para.6–144 above.
[451] Under s.18(1) of the Arbitration Act 1950: *M/S Alghanim Industries Inc v Skandia International Insurance Corp* [2001] All E.R. (Comm.) 30.
[452] See para.6–155 above.
[453] Under s.63(4) of the Arbitration Act 1996.
[454] See para.6–150 above.
[455] See para.6–153 for determination by the court.

normally based on (but less than) the actual costs incurred by the party in whose favour the award of costs is made, details of these having been obtained by the tribunal in advance of making its award. The award of a lump sum was allowed even if that sum was clearly less than would have been allowed on a taxation.[456] However, in view of the requirement in s.63(3)(b) of the Arbitration Act 1996 that the tribunal specifies the items of recoverable costs and the amount referable to each, the award of a single lump sum would not now be acceptable.

(g) Sealed offers

6–158　**What is a sealed offer?** A sealed offer has been described as the arbitral equivalent of making a payment into court.[457] It will usually be in the form of a letter[458] which is expressed to be "without prejudice save as to costs" and will offer terms for settlement of the arbitration which are open for acceptance for a stated period.[459] If the offer is accepted that constitutes a settlement of the arbitration. If it is not accepted it may have an effect on the way in which costs are dealt with in the award or by the court. The principal difference between a payment into court and a sealed offer is that a sealed offer does not involve an actual payment being made unless and until it is accepted.

6–159　**Who may make a sealed offer?** Following the introduction of the CPR, a Pt 36 offer is not limited to an offer to settle by a defendant but also covers an offer to settle by a claimant. If the claimant does better than what he proposed in his offer then the court may order interest at a high level to be paid by the defendant on sums found to be due and may order costs to be assessed on an indemnity basis and to carry interest at a high level.[460] Given the tribunal's discretion to award interest and costs under the Arbitration Act 1996[461] there seems no reason in principle why a tribunal could not adopt a similar approach when faced with a settlement offer from a claimant that the respondent fails to beat.

6–160　**Effect of sealed offer.** In deciding the effect of a sealed offer, the question for a tribunal is whether the successful party has achieved more by rejecting the offer and going on with the arbitration than he would have achieved if he had accepted the offer.[462] In considering this question the tribunal is limited to a

---

[456] *Bradshaw v Air Council* [1926] Ch. 329; cf. *The "Maria"* [1992] 2 Lloyd's Rep. 167.
[457] *Tramountana Armadora SA v Atlantic Shipping Co SA* [1978] 1 Lloyd's Rep. 391; [1978] 2 All E.R. 870 at 876, *per* Donaldson J.
[458] This type of letter is also known as a *Calderbank* letter after the case of that name: [1975] 3 W.L.R. 586.
[459] Usually 21 days, by analogy with CPR Pt 36 r.2.
[460] See CPR Pt 36 r.14(3).
[461] See paras 6–115 *et seq.* and 6–133 *et seq.*
[462] *Tramountana Armadora SA v Atlantic Shipping Co SA* [1978] 1 Lloyd's Rep. 391; [1978] 2 All E.R. 870 at 877, *per* Donaldson J. If the sealed offer was made by the claimant, the test would be whether he achieved more than the offer made.

comparison of what he has achieved in respect of the principal sum claimed and interest. It is not entitled to take into account how costs are to be awarded.[463] If the successful party has failed to achieve more by rejecting the offer, the tribunal should order it to pay both parties' costs of the arbitration from the date specified for acceptance of the sealed offer.[464]

When to inform tribunal of sealed offer. A sealed offer may be given 6–161 to the tribunal for it to open and consider only after it has decided upon the substantive award. This may avoid the expense of reconvening for a further hearing to deal with costs, but it does of course mean that the tribunal will know that some offer has been made, even though it does not know the amount. Rightly or wrongly, parties are sometimes concerned that this knowledge might colour the tribunal's thinking in reaching its decision.[465] The alternative, therefore, is to invite the tribunal to make an award dealing with the substantive issues and to postpone determining the question of costs pending further submissions and/or a further hearing. The extent to which such a request will itself suggest the existence of a sealed offer will depend upon the circumstances of the case and whether, for example, potentially complex costs issues may not need to be addressed at all if the tribunal's decision goes a particular way.

6. EFFECT OF AN AWARD

(a) Effect generally

Effect under statute of an award. Under s.58(1) of the Arbitration Act 6–162 1996[466] an award made by the tribunal pursuant to an arbitration agreement is final and binding both on the parties and on any persons claiming through or under them, unless otherwise agreed in writing[467] by the parties. This means that, as between the parties to the reference and persons claiming through or under them, the award is conclusive as to the issues with which it deals, unless and until there is a successful challenge or appeal against the award.[468] Thus the award itself creates new rights between the parties, in most cases superseding their previous

---

[463] *Everglade Maritime Inc v Schiffahrtsgesellschaft Detlef Von Appen GmbH (The "Maria")* [1992] 2 Lloyd's Rep. 167 [1993] 1 W.L.R. 33; [1992] 3 All E.R. 851; [1993] 3 W.L.R. 176, CA.

[464] Or, if no date was specified, then from a reasonable time after the offer was made. The equivalent period under CPR Pt 36 is 21 days.

[465] The DAC have expressed the view, albeit in a slightly different context, that a tribunal, properly performing its duty under s.33, should not be influenced by such matters: see para.196 of the DAC report.

[466] Replacing s.16 of the Arbitration Act 1950.

[467] The requirement for any agreement between the parties to be "in writing" stems from s.5(1) of the Arbitration Act 1996, although the section gives the expression a broad meaning.

[468] Section 58(2) makes clear that the fact the award is final and binding does not affect the right of appeal or challenge.

rights in relation to the matters referred.[469] It is also immediately enforceable and many awards are implemented without the need for further enforcement proceedings. If, however, a party refuses to comply with the award, enforcement proceedings may be commenced to secure compliance.[470]

6–163   **Obligation to perform.** Not only is the award final and binding upon the parties but they are also obliged to perform in accordance with its terms. As stated by Lord Hobhouse in *Associated Electric and Gas Insurance Services Ltd v European Reinsurance Co of Zurich*, "it is an implied term of an arbitration agreement that the parties agree to perform the award".[471] An obligation to similar effect also appears in many sets of arbitration rules.[472]

6–164   **When award takes effect.** An award takes effect from the date upon which it is made[473] and the time limits for challenges and appeals against an award relate to the date of the award rather than its notification.[474] An award does not have to be performed in order to take effect.

6–165   **Award does not transfer property.** An award cannot operate as a transfer of property, whether realty[475], or personalty;[476] it can only declare rights to the property and (where there is power to order specific performance[477]) direct that the parties execute appropriate conveyances or otherwise transfer the property concerned.[478]

(b) Effect on the reference

6–166   **Tribunal "functus officio".** Subject to the exceptions set out below, once a final award is made, the tribunal becomes "functus officio".[479] This means that

---

[469] *per* Fletcher-Moulton L.J. in *Doleman v Ossett* [1912] 3 K.B. 257 at 267; *Bremer Oeltransport GmbH v Drewry* (1933) 45 Ll. L. Rep. 133; [1933] K.B. 753; *F.J. Bloemen Pty Ltd v Council of the City of Gold Coast* [1973] A.C. 127, PC; *Stargas SpA v Petredec Ltd (The "Sargasso")* [1994] 1 Lloyd's Rep. 412. See though para.6–180 below and quaere whether it applies to all awards, including those where, for example, only declaratory relief is given.

[470] See paras 8–002 *et seq.* below.

[471] [2003] UKPC 11 at [9]. See also *Purslow v Baily* (1704) 2 Ld Raym. 1039; *Bremer Oeltransport GmbH v Drewry* [1933] 1 K.B. 753 at 760, 764; *Bloemen v Gold Coast City Council* [1973] A.C. 115. .

[472] See, for example, art.26.9 of the LCIA Rules and art.28.6 of the ICC Rules.

[473] See para.6–065 above.

[474] Section 70(3) of the Arbitration Act 1996.

[475] *Henry v Kirwan* (1859) 9 Ir. C.L. Rep. 459.

[476] *Hunter v Rice* (1812) 15 East 100.

[477] See above para.6–122.

[478] *Johnson v Wilson* (1741) Willes 248. In *Thorpe v Eyre* (1834) 1 A. & E. 926 the terms on which a party was holding certain land was referred to arbitration, and the award found that the holding was as tenant. The court subsequently held that the award did not have the effect of transferring the property in the land or in the growing crops which would pass with the land.

[479] *International Petroleum Refining & Supply SDAD Ltd v Elpis Finance SA (The "Faith")* [1993] 2 Lloyd's Rep. 408; *Fidelitas Shipping Co Ltd v V/o Exportchleb* [1966] 1 Q.B. 630.

its authority to act ceases and the reference terminates. The tribunal cannot reopen the case even if fresh evidence comes to light that would have been material to the decision reached.[480] However, the tribunal[481] has power under s.57(3)(a) of the Arbitration Act 1996 to correct clerical mistakes or errors arising from an accidental slip or omission or to clarify or remove any ambiguity in the award, and also power under s.57(3)(b) to make an additional award.[482] Save for these situations, the tribunal has no power to amend or recall an award once it has been made and notified to the parties unless it is remitted by the court.[483]

Correction of clerical mistakes, etc. The tribunal has power to correct 6–167 its award in respect of any clerical mistake or error arising from any accidental slip or omission or to clarify or remove any ambiguity in the award, unless the parties have agreed in writing[484] otherwise.[485] Any correction then forms part of the award.[486] The power covers three distinct situations. The first is a clerical mistake, a slip of the pen or something of that kind, and the second is an error arising from an accidental slip or omission, i.e. something is wrongly put in or left out by accident.[487] The third situation was introduced in the Arbitration Act 1996 and enables the tribunal to clarify or remove any ambiguity in the award.

Meaning of "accidental slip". In *The "Trade Fortitude"*[488] Lloyd L.J. 6–168 explained further what was meant by an "accidental slip". He said:

"In one sense, of course, all errors are accidental. You do not make a mistake on purpose. But here the words take their colour from their context. I do not

---

[480] Under the previous legislation, the court would remit an award to the tribunal in these circumstances but there is no equivalent provision in the 1996 Act: *Elektrim SA v Vivendi Universal SA* [2007] EWHC 11 at [76]. It may however be possible to obtain relief from the court under s.68 of the Arbitration Act 1996 in these circumstances including remission of the award to the tribunal under s.68(3)(a): see Waller L.J. in *Westacre Investments Inc v Jugoimport-S.P.D.R. Holding Co Ltd* [2000] Q.B. 288 at 307; *Thyssen Canada Ltd v Mariana Maritime SA* [2005] EWHC 219; [2005] 1 Lloyd's Rep. 640; and paras 8–100 and 8–113 below.

[481] The power rests with the tribunal, not the court: *Ronly Holdings Ltd v JSC Zestafoni G. Nikoladze Ferroalloy Plant* [2004] EWHC 1354.

[482] There have been occasions when parties have sought to rely on s.57(3) to invite the tribunal to revisit or to correct the substance of its decision on the merits on the basis that the party concerned believes the decision to be wrong: see for example *Hawk Shipping Ltd v Cron Navigation Ltd* [2003] EWHC 1828; *C v D* [2007] EWHC 1541 at [12]. Such a request is beyond the proper scope of s.57(3) of the Arbitration Act 1996.

[483] *Re Calvert & Co and Wyler* (1899) 106 L.T.J. 288; *Re Stringer and Riley Bros* [1901] 1 Q.B. 105; *Inland Revenue Commissioners v Hunter* [1914] 3 K.B. 423. Where an award is set aside or is declared of no effect by the court, the tribunal's jurisdiction is not exhausted and it may proceed to make an award: *Hussman (Europe) Ltd v Pharaon* [2003] EWCA Civ 266.

[484] The requirement for any agreement between the parties to be "in writing" stems from s.5(1) of the Arbitration Act 1996, although the section gives the expression a broad meaning.

[485] Section 57(3)(a) of the Arbitration Act 1996. This is to the same effect as the court's power under CPR Pt 40 r.12. Both are often referred to as the "slip rule".

[486] Section 57(7) of the Arbitration Act 1996.

[487] *Sutherland & Co v Hannevig Brothers Ltd* [1921] 1 K.B. 336. See also *Mutual Shipping Corp v Bayshore Shipping Co Ltd (The "Montan")* [1985] 1 Lloyd's Rep. 189; [1985] 1 W.L.R. 625.

[488] *Food Corp of India v Marastro Cia Naviera SA (The "Trade Fortitude")* [1986] 2 Lloyd's Rep. 209.

suggest that [the section] is limited to clerical mistakes. But, in general, the error must, in the words of Rowlatt J. in *Sutherland & Co v Hannevig Brothers Ltd*, [1921] 1 K.B. 336 at 341, be an error affecting the expression of the tribunal's thought, not an error in the thought process itself . . . The fact that the error . . . was an elementary error is not sufficient to make it accidental".

He did not consider an error in subtracting steaming time from time on demurrage instead of adding it to laytime to be an error arising from "an accidental slip or omission" within the meaning of s.17 of the Arbitration Act 1950 (replaced by s.57(3)(a) of the Arbitration Act 1996).[489]

6–169   Use of the slip rule. Thus, if the tribunal assesses the evidence wrongly or misconstrues or fails to appreciate the law, it cannot correct the resulting errors in its award under the slip rule.[490] Nor can it use the slip rule to reconsider a decision once made.[491] Where, however, the tribunal has transposed the parties, or has incorrectly calculated the amount payable under the award as a result of accepting the evidence of a particular witness but attributing that witness to the wrong party, it may correct the award under the slip rule.[492] If the correction under the slip rule reveals other errors, for example in relation to costs, they may also be considered as "arising from" the slip and therefore within the tribunal's power to correct the award.[493]

6–170   Ambiguity in the award. Section 57(3)(a) of the Arbitration Act 1996 also provides the tribunal with an ability to correct an award to clarify or remove any ambiguity in it. This would cover a situation where the tribunal's reasoning or decision is not sufficiently clear and clarification or correction is therefore warranted. The courts have drawn a distinction between seeking to effect a change in the tribunal's decision and referring a matter to the tribunal for clarification of what it has decided.[494] An award which contains inadequate rationale or incomplete reasons for a decision is likely to be ambiguous and need clarification.[495] The

---

[489] See, though, *Gannet Shipping Ltd v Eastrade Commodities Inc* [2002] 1 Lloyd's Rep. 713 where an error in failing to incorporate an agreed figure for demurrage was held to be an accidental slip. *Per* Langley J. at 717: "It was a slip because it was wrong. It was accidental because he did not mean to use the wrong figure and he misread some manuscript amendments . . . "

[490] *Mutual Shipping Corp v Bayshore Shipping Co Ltd (The "Montan")* [1985] 1 Lloyd's Rep. 189; [1985] 1 W.L.R. 625. If the tribunal admits to the mistake, however, this would provide a party with grounds for an application to the court under s.68(2)(i), although whether such an application would succeed would depend, amongst other things, on the nature and importance of the mistake and whether "substantial injustice" has been caused by it: see further para.8–103 below.

[491] See by analogy *R. v Cripps Ex p. Muldoon* [1984] 1 Q.B. 686, a case on RSC Ord.20, r.11 (now replaced by CPR Pt 40 r.12).

[492] *Mutual Shipping Corp v Bayshore Shipping Co Ltd (The "Montan")* [1985] 1 Lloyd's Rep. 189; [1985] 1 W.L.R. 625. Sir Roger Ormrod referred at 198 to the accidental slip being "the mental lapse which caused the arbitrator to transpose in his mind the parties".

[493] *Gannet Shipping Ltd v Eastrade Commodities Inc* [2002] 1 Lloyd's Rep. 713.

[494] *Al Hadha Trading Co v Tradigrain SA* [2002] 2 Lloyd's Rep. 512, approved in *Torch Offshore LLC v Cable Shipping Inc* [2004] EWHC 787.

[495] *Al Hadha Trading Co v Tradigrain SA* [2002] 2 Lloyd's Rep. 512

sub-section may therefore provide a means to request further reasons from the tribunal or to request reasons where none have previously been given in relation to a particular issue[496] but only where there is genuine ambiguity.[497]

Power to make an additional award. The tribunal also has power   6–171
under s.57(3)(b) of the Arbitration Act 1996 to make an additional award in respect of any claim, including a claim for interest or costs.[498] The power is limited to claims which were presented to the tribunal but omitted from the award.[499] It cannot therefore provide a means of raising new claims after the award has been made which were not presented during the course of the reference.[500] Nor can it be used to deal with an issue which arises under a claim that has been decided by an award, even if that issue remains undetermined.[501]

Time limit for application. The powers under s.57(3) of the Arbitration   6–172
Act 1996 are exercisable by the tribunal on its own initiative or on the application of either party. Any application must be made within 28 days of the date of the award or such longer period as the parties may agree. This could work harshly in that the parties may not receive the award until some time after its date[502] and securing agreement to extend the period during which an application to the tribunal may be made may not be easy. The court may however extend time under s.79 of the Arbitration Act 1996 where substantial injustice would otherwise result.[503] Where an application has been made within the time limit for a correction to the award, the tribunal should consider all possible accidental slips, omissions or ambiguities in the award even if some are not drawn to its attention until after the time limit has expired.[504]

Time limit for exercise of powers. Subject to the parties agreeing   6–173
otherwise[505] in writing,[506] any correction of the award must be made within 28

---

[496] *Al Hadha Trading Co v Tradigrain SA* [2002] 2 Lloyd's Rep. 512; *Torch Offshore LLC v Cable Shipping Inc* [2004] EWHC 787. See also *Groundshire v VHE Construction* [2001] B.L.R. 395.

[497] *Benaim (UK) Ltd v Davies Middleton & Davies Ltd* 102 Con. L.R. 1.

[498] This addition to the previous "slip rule" reflects Art.33 of the Model Law which gives the tribunal both the "slip rule" power and the power to make an additional award.

[499] Reserving a decision on costs to a future award is not failing to deal with a claim: *Sea Trade Maritime Corp v Hellenic Mutual War Risks Association (Bermuda) Ltd* [2006] EWHC 578.

[500] *Pirtek (UK) Ltd v Deanswood Ltd* [2005] EWHC 2301; [2005] 2 Lloyd's Rep. 728.

[501] *Torch Offshore LLC v Cable Shipping Inc* [2004] EWHC 787; *World Trade Corp Ltd v C Czarnikow Sugar Ltd* [2004] EWHC 2332. This approach to s.57(3)(b) is consistent with the wording used in the sub-section and prevents any attempt to reopen a decided claim by raising an issue relevant to that claim. It may however be appropriate in such circumstances to make an application under s.57(3)(a).

[502] By s.54(1) of the Arbitration Act 1996 this is the date on which the award is signed by the arbitrator or the last of them if there are more than one: see para.6–053 above.

[503] *Gold Coast Ltd v Naval Gijon SA* [2006] EWHC 1044. See para.7–089 below.

[504] *R.C. Pillar & Sons v Edwards* [2002] C.I.L.L. 1799.

[505] For example in *Home of Homes Ltd v Hammersmith and Fulham L.B.C.* [2003] EWHC 807; 92 Const. L.R. 48 the parties agreed that a s.57 application in relation to a partial award should be dealt with in due course when the tribunal made a further, subsequent award.

[506] The requirement for any agreement between the parties to be "in writing" stems from s.5(1) of the Arbitration Act 1996, although the section gives the expression a broad meaning.

days of the date the application was received by the tribunal or, where the correction is made by the tribunal on its own initiative, within 28 days of the date of the award.[507] The date upon which the correction is made, or the date upon which the tribunal determines not to make any correction following an application under s.57(3) of the Arbitration Act 1996, then becomes the date of the award for the purposes of s.54(2) of the Arbitration Act 1996.[508] Any additional award must be made within 56 days of the date of the original award, again subject to the parties agreeing in writing[509] otherwise.[510] Whether a request for an additional award will defer the date of the award for the purposes of s.54(2) of the Arbitration Act 1996 will depend upon whether the dispositive parts of the award are affected by the proposed additional award.[511]

6–174   **Notice to the parties.** Where the tribunal is minded to exercise its power to correct the award or to make an additional award, it must give the parties notice of its intention to do so and give them a reasonable opportunity to make representations if they wish to do so.[512] If the tribunal declines to exercise the power under s.57, a party might in limited circumstances apply to the court to have the award remitted for the tribunal to reconsider the point.[513]

6–175   **Exhaustion of section 57 remedies.** No application or appeal can be made to the court in relation to an award[514] unless any available recourse under s.57 of the Arbitration Act 1996 for the correction of the award or for the making of an additional award has been exhausted.[515] Does this mean that that a party must go back to the tribunal and ask for the award to be corrected even if they believe it to be unsalvageable or "so bad that it [is] not susceptible of any clarification or further expansion"? This question was answered in the affirmative in *Sinclair v Woods of Winchester Ltd.*[516] This is particularly pertinent where an award or its effect is ambiguous, as both ss.57(3)(a) and 68(2)(f) expressly use that

---

[507] Section 57(5) of the Arbitration Act 1996.

[508] *McLean Homes South East Ltd v Blackdale Ltd* [2001] W.L. 1560746. Thus, the time limit of 28 days pursuant to s.70(3) of the Arbitration Act 1996 for any appeal or challenge to the award will run from the date of the correction or decision not to correct.

[509] The requirement for any agreement between the parties to be "in writing" stems from s.5(1) of the Arbitration Act 1996, although the section gives the expression a broad meaning.

[510] Section 57(6) of the Arbitration Act 1996.

[511] *McLean Homes South East Ltd v Blackdale Ltd* [2001] W.L. 1560746.

[512] Section 57(3) of the Arbitration Act 1996.

[513] Where, for example, there is a clerical error which the tribunal declines to correct but which creates "uncertainty or ambiguity as to the effect of the award" under s.68(2)(f) of the Arbitration Act 1996 and the other requirements of s.68 are met: see paras 8–098 *et seq.* below. If the tribunal declines to make an additional award there is apparently no remedy unless it has failed to "deal with all the issues that were put to it" under s.68(2)(d) of the Arbitration Act 1996: see para.8–093 below.

[514] i.e. under ss.67, 68 or 69 of the Arbitration Act 1996.

[515] Section 70(2) of the Arbitration Act 1996 and see para.8–109 below. See also *Torch Offshore LLC v Cable Shipping Inc* [2004] 2 Lloyd's Rep. 446; *Omnibridge Consulting Ltd v Clearsprings (Management) Ltd* [2004] EWHC 2276.

[516] [2005] EWHC 1631 at [38]. The judge in that case discerned a deliberate ploy not to seek correction of the award as a decision to challenge the award was said to have already been made.

term. If the matters complained of are within the scope of s.57 then unless an application is made to the tribunal within the time limit for exercise of its powers under s.57 the right to challenge for serious irregularity will be lost.[517] However, the fact that particular aspects of the award should have been taken up with the arbitrator pursuant to s.57 will not preclude an application or appeal in respect of other aspects of the award.[518] Further, if the tribunal refuses the request for recourse under s.57 or is unable to correct the irregularity the application to the court can proceed.[519]

(c) Effect on other proceedings between the same parties

Valid award a bar to fresh proceedings. A valid award[520] will create an estoppel with regard to the matters with which it deals, preventing either party from pursuing those matters in a later stage of the arbitration[521] or in subsequent proceedings.[522] To the extent that a cause of action has been decided by the award, a party will be prevented from asserting or denying, as against the other party, its existence or non-existence in subsequent proceedings.[523] Any attempt to do so may be met by a plea of *res judicata*. Where one or more issues have previously been determined,[524] albeit that the cause of action is different, a party will again be prevented from seeking to contradict the earlier findings on those issues, on the basis of "issue estoppel".[525] In an appropriate case, the court can issue an anti-suit injunction to restrain a party from pursuing proceedings which amount to a collateral attack on a binding award.[526] It may even be possible to prevent issues being raised in subsequent proceedings which could and should have been raised in the earlier proceedings, i.e. those issues which properly belong to the subject of

6–176

---

[517] *Omnibridge Consulting Ltd v Clearsprings (Management) Ltd* [2004] EWHC 2276.

[518] *Gbangbola v Smith & Sherriff Ltd* [1998] 3 All E.R. 730.

[519] *Sinclair v Woods of Winchester Ltd* [2005] EWHC 1631 at [36]–[39].

[520] The award must also be final, conclusive and not susceptible to challenge or appeal: *Svenska Petroleum Exploration AB v Lithuania (No.2)* [2006] 1 Lloyd's Rep. 181. See though the comments of the Court of Appeal at [2006] EWCA Civ 1529 at [91].

[521] *Westland Helicopters Ltd v Al-Hejailan* [2004] 2 Lloyd's Rep. 523.

[522] *Fidelitas Shipping Co Ltd v V/o Exportchleb* [1965] 1 Lloyd's Rep. 223, CA; *Siporex Trade SA v Comdel Commodities Ltd* [1986] 2 Lloyd's Rep. 428; *Noble Assurance Co v Gerling-Konzern General Insurance Co* [2007] EWHC 253. This would include proceedings to enforce the award: *Svenska Petroleum Exploration AB v Lithuania (No.2)* [2006] 1 Lloyd's Rep. 181 affirmed by the Court of Appeal at [2006] EWCA Civ 1529.

[523] This applies only to a decision on the merits and not to matters of procedure: *Charles M. Willie and Co (Shipping) Ltd v Ocean Laser Shipping Ltd ("The Smaro")* 1999 1 Lloyd's Rep. 225.

[524] The determination must be a necessary part of the ealier decision, not simply collateral to it: see *Sun Life Assurance Co of Canada v Lincoln National Life Insurance Co* [2004] EWCA Civ 1660.

[525] *Associated Electric & Gas Insurance Services Ltd v European Reinsurance Co of Zurich* [2003] 1 W.L.R. 1041; See generally Spencer Bower, Turner and Handley, *The Doctrine of Res Judicata* (3rd edn, 1996) and *Johnson v Gore Wood* [2002] 2 A.C. 1.

[526] *C v D* [2007] EWHC 1541; *Noble Assurance Co v Gerling-Konzern General Insurance Co* [2007] EWHC 253 although in that case the court considered that justice was sufficiently served by the grant of declaratory relief as to the interpretation, scope and validity of the award.

the earlier proceedings.[527] This principle has been specifically applied to arbitrations.[528]

6–177	**Bar limited to questions referred.** Subject to the previous paragraph, only the claims actually referred are concluded by an award.[529] Whether a particular claim was within the reference and will be a question of fact in each case. Fresh proceedings might properly be brought on a demand which, though it existed as a claim at the time of the reference, was not then a matter in dispute and was not referred to the tribunal.[530] Similarly, where the award declares an entitlement to payment of a sum of money without directing payment, fresh proceedings may be brought to enforce payment. The award will be conclusive evidence both of the obligation to pay and of the amount due.[531] Depending on the circumstances, an alternative would be to seek an additional award under s.57(3)(b) of the Arbitration Act 1996 or possibly remission of the award to the tribunal under s.68 for it to include a direction as to payment.[532]

6–178	**Scope of bar to fresh proceedings.** The bar to fresh proceedings applies to claims coming within the reference whether or not the claims were actually brought before the tribunal.[533]

---

[527] See *Henderson v Henderson* (1843) 3 Hare 100; *Yat Tung Investment Co v Dao Heng Bank Ltd* [1975] A.C. 581; *Johnson v Gore Wood & Co* [2001] 2 W.L.R. 72.
[528] *Fidelitas Shipping Co Ltd v V/o Exportchleb* [1965] 1 Lloyd's Rep. 223, CA; *Arnold v National Westminster Bank* [1991] 3 All E.R. 41.
[529] *Crane v Hegermann-Harris Co* [1939] 4 All E.R. 68; *Steers v Lashley* (1794) 6 T.R. 61; *H.E. Daniels Ltd v Carmel Exporters & Importers Ltd* [1953] 2 Q.B. 242. In *Compagnie Granière SA v Fritz Kopp A.G.* [1980] 1 Lloyd's Rep. 463 buyers referred to arbitration a dispute relating to non-delivery of goods in terms which limited the reference to the issue of liability. The tribunal found in favour of the buyers who then submitted a debit note to the sellers. The sellers refused to pay and the buyers referred the claim for damages to arbitration. The sellers claimed the buyers were estopped, as they should have advanced all their claims in the first arbitration and had failed to do so. The court held that, as in the first arbitration the issue of damages was never raised at all, the buyers were not estopped. The rule in litigation that there could be no serial claims for damages based upon the same cause of action applied to arbitration, but the buyers here had not put forward two claims for damages.
[530] *Ravee v Farmer* (1791) 4 T.R. 146; *Golightly v Jellicoe* (1769) 4 T.R. 147n.; *Upton v Upton* (1832) 1 Dowl. 400. Cf. *Lesser Design & Build Ltd v University of Surrey* [1991] 56 B.L.R. 57 and para.5–004 above.
[531] *Whitehead v Tattersall* (1834) 1 Ad & El 491. See also *FJ Bloemen Pty Ltd v Council of the City of Gold Coast* [1973] A.C. 115, PC.
[532] See para.6–091 above.
[533] In *Willday v Taylor* (1977) 241 E.G. 835 the claimants entered into two contracts, the second supplemental to the first, both relating to the building of the same house and both containing an arbitration clause. In an arbitration under the second contract the claimants obtained a small award in respect of dampness. They then brought legal proceedings under the first contract, also in respect of dampness. The court held that the contracts were so related that an award under the second effectively disposed of a claim under the first in respect of the same defects, the claimants having expressly agreed that the award in the arbitration should be in complete satisfaction of their claim. See also *Dunn v Murray* (1829) 9 B. & C. 780 7 L.J. (O.S.) K.B. 390; *Dicas v Jay* (1830) 6 Bing. 519 8 L.J. (O.S.) C.P. 210; *Collins v Powell* (1788) 2 T.R. 756; *Clegg v Dearden* (1848) 12 Q.B. 576 17 L.J.Q.B. 223; *Smith v Johnson* (1812) 15 East 213.

Unsatisfied award. There can be no fresh proceedings simply because the   6–179
award remains unsatisfied, enforcement of the award being the appropriate
course.[534] Nor can there be fresh proceedings to recover additional losses arising
from a cause of action already determined.[535] If it is thought likely that there will
be further losses coming to light, the tribunal may be asked not to make a final
award, thus leaving open the possibility of a further award or awards in respect of
later losses. This would be better than relying on the tribunal's discretion to make
an additional award if, indeed, it has power in the circumstances to do so.[536]

Rights in rem. An award does not bar a claimant from proceeding in rem on   6–180
the same cause of action unless of course the cause of action has been satisfied by
performance of the award. Where, however, a foreign award is the subject of an
action on the award in England, the claimant cannot proceed in rem because the
claim arises out of the arbitration agreement rather than in relation to the use or
hire of a ship.[537]

Valid award conclusive evidence of law and facts found. As   6–181
between the parties, a valid award is conclusive evidence of the law and facts found
by it.[538] So long as it has not been set aside, evidence to contradict the award or
any of the individual issues of law or fact with which it deals will be inadmissible.[539] An award is not however admissible as evidence of the facts found by
it in criminal proceedings.[540]

Name-borrowing arbitrations. Some contracts, particularly in the con-   6–182
struction field, provide for "name-borrowing" so that a party (e.g. the sub-
contractor) can bring arbitration proceedings against a third party (e.g. the

---

[534] *Purslow v Baily* (1705) 2 Ld. Raym. 1039. Given that it is an implied term of the arbitration
agreement to comply with the award as set out in para.6–163 above, breach of this obligation could
give rise to an action in damages. However enforcement of the award will usually be the most
efficient way of seeking redress.

[535] "The rule in *Conquer v Boot*", see Mustill and Boyd p.411. See also *Compagnie Graniere SA v Fritz
Kopp AG* [1980] 1 Lloyd's Rep. 463.

[536] See para.6–171 above.

[537] *The "Bumbesti"* [1999] 2 Lloyd's Rep. 481. In *The "Sylph"* (1867) L.R. 2 A. & E. 24 a claim made
by a diver for injuries received from the respondent's steamer was referred to arbitration, with a
clause in the submission agreement that if the award was not performed by the respondent then all
the claimant's rights were reserved. The respondent failed to pay the sum awarded. The court held
that the claimant was entitled to proceed in rem against the steamer. It seems that the decision
would have been the same had there been no reservation of the claimant's rights. See also *The "Rena
K"* [1978] 1 Lloyd's Rep. 545 at 560.

[538] *Whitehead v Tattersall* (1834) 1 Ad. & El. 491 see also *Leicester Waterworks Co v Cropstone Overseers*
(1875) 44 L.J. M.C. 92; *Hill v Ball* (1828) 2 Bli. N.S. 1; *Sybray v White* (1836) 1 M. & W. 435. An
award may in particular be conclusive evidence between the parties as to the title to land: see *Doe
d Morris v Rosser* (1802) 3 East 15.

[539] *Gueret v Audouy* (1893) 62 L.J. Q.B. 633.

[540] *R. v Fontaine Moreau* (1848) 11 Q.B. 1028 at 1035.

employer) in the name of another (e.g. the main contractor).[541] This is a device that was used to avoid problems in relation to privity of contract,[542] although it is no longer necessary to adopt this mechanism if the third party has itself acquired rights under the contract.[543] Name-borrowing arbitrations can give rise to a number of procedural and logistical problems because the sub-contractor conducting the proceedings is not actually a party to them. It will often be preferable to provide for a tripartite arbitration instead.[544] The party whose name is borrowed will be bound by the terms of any award which is made in an arbitration conducted in accordance with the name-borrowing provisions (which will be strictly construed) or otherwise authorised by him.[545]

(d) Effect on third parties

6–183   **Award not generally binding on third parties.** Save where a third party agrees to be bound by it,[546] an award is generally only effective as regards the parties to it and persons claiming through or under them.[547] It cannot generally be relied on in proceedings involving a third party as evidence either of the facts found or of reputation.[548] The principle was applied in *Sacor Maritima SA v Repsol Petroleo SA*[549] where Mance J. confirmed that a finding in an arbitration between disponent owners and head charterers as to the cause of damage to cargo was not binding in a subsequent arbitration between the head charterers and sub-charterers.

6–184   **Exceptions.** There are exceptions to this general rule. In particular, the contractual context may give rise to third party rights.[550] There have also been cases where this general rule appears to have been departed from on grounds of

---

[541] For a recent example, see *Belgravia Property Company Ltd v S & R (London) Limited* [2001] B.L.R. 424.

[542] *Northern Regional Health Authority v Derek Crouch Construction Co* [1984] 2 All E.R. 175 [1984] Q.B. 644; *Lorne Stewart v William Sindall Plc* (1986) 11 Con. L.R. 99; *Gordon Durham & Co Ltd v Haden Young Ltd*, 27 Con. L.R. 109.

[543] See para.3–014.

[544] *Belgravia Property Co Ltd v S & R (London) Limited* [2001] B.L.R. 424.

[545] *Gordon Durham & Co Ltd v Haden Young Ltd*, 27 Con. L.R. 109 at 135.

[546] *Jackson v Henderson, Craig & Co* (1916) 115 L.T. 36.

[547] *Tunbridge Wells Local Board v Ackroyd* (1880) 5 Ex. D. 199; *Martin v Boulanger* (1883) 8 App. Cas. 296. Persons claiming through or under the parties are clearly bound: s.58(1) of the Arbitration Act 1996.

[548] *Sun Life Assurance Co of Canada v Lincoln National Life Insurance Co* [2004] EWCA Civ 1660; *Re Kitchin Ex p. Young* (1881) 17 Ch. D. 668.

[549] [1998] 1 Lloyd's Rep. 518.

[550] In *Co-operative Wholesale Society Ltd v Birse Construction Ltd* [1997] T.L.R. 454, CA an arbitrator's award in a building dispute between an employer and a contractor awarded sums in respect of sub-contract works. The employer failed to make payment owing to insolvency. Both the main contract and the sub-contract were on the standard JCT forms of contract. The Court of Appeal decided on the basis of those contracts that the sub-contractor was entitled to recover from the contractor sums found in the award to be due in respect of the sub-contract works. Cf. Lord Cooke in *Lafarge Redland Aggregates Ltd v Shephard Hill Civil Engineering Ltd* [2000] 1 W.L.R. 1621 at 1638.

acquiescence and ratification.[551] An award may also in some circumstances be relied upon in a claim against a third party for an indemnity or as quantifying the loss suffered (subject to showing a failure to mitigate or that the award was perverse or unreasonable).[552] The Court of Appeal have now rejected the suggestion advanced by Saville J. in *George Moundreas & Co. Ltd v Navimpex Centrala Navala*[553] that where an award determines the rights or obligations of parties to a contract, it may be possible for a third party to treat that award as in effect part of the contract between the original parties and rely upon the award as having determined the contractual position as between the original parties.[554]

Disclosure of award to third parties. In the absence of an express   6–185
agreement about confidentiality there is an implied obligation on a party obtaining documents in an arbitration not to disclose or use them for any purpose other than the dispute in which they were obtained.[555] It is qualified, however, when disclosure is reasonably necessary to establish or protect a party's legal rights as against a third party by founding a cause of action or a defence to a claim. In these circumstances disclosure of the award, including any reasons given, will not be a breach of the duty of confidentiality.[556] It is also an exception to the duty of confidentiality that a party may put the award and any reasons before the court if there is an application seeking to invoke the court's supervisory powers in relation to the arbitration or the award, or if the court's assistance is sought with regard to enforcement of the award.[557]

[551] See *Govett v Richmond* (1834) 7 Sim. 1; *Thomas v Atherton* (1877) 10 Ch. D. 185.
[552] *Stargas SpA v Petredec Ltd ("The Sargasso")* [1994] 1 Lloyd's Rep. 412; *Sun Life Assurance Co of Canada v Lincoln National Life Insurance Co* [2004] EWCA Civ 1660. Cf. *Alfred McAlpine Construction Ltd v Unex Corp Ltd* [1994] 70 B.L.R. 26.
[553] [1985] 2 Lloyd's Rep. 515 at 520.
[554] *Sun Life Assurance Co of Canada v Lincoln National Life Insurance Co* [2004] EWCA Civ 1660.
[555] *Dolling-Baker v Merrett and Others* [1991] 2 All E.R. 891 at 899, CA; *Hassneh Insurance Co of Israel and Others v Steuart J. Mew* [1993] 2 Lloyd's Rep. 243. A similar obligation applies to documents disclosed in High Court litigation: *Distillers Co (Biochemicals) Ltd v Times Newspapers Ltd* [1975] Q.B. 613; *Riddick v Thames Board Mills* [1977] Q.B. 881; CPR Pt 31 r.22.
[556] See para.5–188 above.
[557] *Hassneh Insurance Co of Israel and Others v Steuart J Mew* [1993] 2 Lloyd's Rep. 243.

CHAPTER 7

THE ROLE OF THE COURT BEFORE AND DURING THE ARBITRATION

1. INTRODUCTION

7–001 **Role of the court generally.** This chapter and Ch.8 examine the direct role of the English court in arbitration. The general principle is stated in Pt.1 of the Arbitration Act 1996 as follows:

> "In matters governed by this Part [of the Act] the court should not intervene except as provided by this Part."[1]

---

[1] Arbitration Act 1996, s.1(c). Compare Art.5 of the UNCITRAL Model Law on International Commercial Arbitration, reproduced in Appendix 4, which uses "shall" instead of the 1996 Act's use of "should" which is arguably less prescriptive.

This statement of principle in the very first section of the Arbitration Act 1996 is clear recognition of the policy of party autonomy underlying the Act and the desire to limit and define the court's role in arbitration so as to give effect to that policy. What led to the statement is discussed in Ch.1.[2] The extent of the court's powers before and during the arbitration is the subject of this chapter, whereas the court's role after the award is dealt with in Ch.8.

The statement of principle indicates two possibilities as to when the court can intervene in an arbitration. Under the first, the paradigm case, the court should only intervene where there is a provision in Pt 1 of the Arbitration Act 1996 that permits court intervention. The principle of non-intervention was stated clearly by the House of Lords in *Lesotho Highlands v Impreglio SpA*[3] where Lord Steyn quoted with approval statements made by Lord Wilberforce during the second reading of the Arbitration Bill before the House of Lords: "It has given to the court only those essential powers which I believe the court should have". In the same vein, the Court of Appeal in *Cetelem v Roust*[4] stated that, "a central and important purpose of the 1996 Act was to emphasise the importance of party autonomy and to restrict the role of the courts in the arbitral process. In particular the Act was intended to ensure that the powers of the court should be limited to assisting the arbitral process and should not usurp or interfere with it". **7–002**

In the second (and exceptional) case, however, the court may also intervene to prevent a substantial injustice even if there is no relevant provision in Pt 1 of the Act. The powers of the court in the latter case will only be exercised in "very exceptional circumstances".[5]

Inherent jurisdiction? Section 1(c) of the Act makes it clear that the general position is that there is no inherent common law jurisdiction of the court to supervise arbitration outside the framework of the Arbitration Act 1996. Section 1(c) is arguably subject to two limitations. First, it does not regulate intervention in the arbitral process in matters not governed by Pt 1, and, secondly, the use of the word "should" as opposed to the word "shall" shows that an absolute prohibition on court intervention was not intended.[6] The usual position taken by the courts is to restrict court intervention to the minimum necessary under the Act, but this is not always the case. For example, in *Virdee v Virdi*,[7] the judge at first instance had made various directions following appointment of a tribunal as to whether legal representation should be allowed and as to whether costs should be recovered. One party took issue with the terms of these directions, although apparently not the court's discretion to make them, and appealed. The Court of Appeal noted, " . . . The parties were not invoking the express jurisdiction of the court on any of the sections of the Arbitration Act 1996 when asking for the **7–003**

---

[2] See paras 1–043 *et seq.*
[3] [2006] 1 A.C. 221 at [18].
[4] [2005] 1 W.L.R 3555 at 3571.
[5] *Faruqi v Commonwealth Secretarial* [2002] W.L. 498805 where the court refused to intervene because the circumstances were not exceptional. See also *Fletamentos Maritimos v Effjohn International* [1997] 2 Lloyd's Rep. 302 and *The "Smaro"* [1999] 1 Lloyd's Rep. 225.
[6] For the pre-1996 position, see *Bremer Vulkan Schifbau v South India Shipping* [1981] A.C. 909.
[7] [2003] EWCA Civ 41.

judge's help in this respect . . . On the face of it, therefore, if it is right that the Arbitration Act itself does not have a provision barring access to this court in relation to the kind of relief which was being sought . . . then the ordinary rules as to access to this court should apply."[8] This decision in *Virdee* should be treated with caution. The parties were not legally represented before the Court of Appeal, which itself said "this case should not be regarded as binding precedent".[9] For this reason, *Virdee* should not be viewed as endorsing a general supervisory jurisdiction over arbitrations

7–004　　　Far less controversially, the inherent jurisdiction has been used in a supportive way to mitigate an unduly narrow application of certain terms of the Act. A clear example of a supportive use of the inherent jurisdiction can be found in *A v B*[10] where Colman J. endorsed the use of the inherent jurisdiction to stay English proceedings in favour of arbitration in a case where the court could not be certain of the existence of an arbitration agreement as required under s.9 of the Act.

7–005　　　A residual inherent jurisdiction also extends to the granting of leave to appeal. Despite the apparently unequivocal words of the Act which in many cases appear to require leave to appeal from the decision of the court at first instance,[11] the Court of Appeal also retains a residual jurisdiction to set aside the judge's decision in the case of unfairness relating to the process of the decision. Where, "the judge's refusal of leave to appeal was arbitrary or unfair: or was the product of a failure of intellectual engagement with the arguments put before him; or amounted actually or metaphorically to the absence of a decision on the issue" the Court of Appeal can of its own motion consider appeals even where leave of the first instance judge has not been given although these are "exceptionally rare cases."[12]

7–006　　　In *Coppée-Lavalin SA/NV v Ken-Ren Chemicals and Fertilisers Ltd*,[13] which was decided before the Arbitration Act 1996 was enacted, a distinction was drawn between three groups of measures that involve the court in arbitration, the first being purely procedural steps which an arbitral tribunal cannot order or cannot enforce (e.g. issuing a witness summons to a third party), the second being

---

[8] Paragraph 18. The court was apparently proceeding on the basis that as no express provision of the Arbitration Act was being relied upon (other than in relation to s.18, a separate point which is considered below) then the court, both at first instance and on appeal, had inherent jurisdiction to intervene. It is presumed that this analysis is based on s.1(3), "*In matters governed by this Part the court should not intervene except as provided by this Part*". However, ss.63 to 65 do at least provide extensive provision as to costs, and these provisions appear not to have been considered by the Court of Appeal.

[9] Paragraph 4. See also *JT Mackley & Co Ltd v Gosport Marina Ltd* [2002] EWHC 1315 where the existence of a general, albeit very limited, supervisory jurisdiction outside of the Arbitration Act 1996 was recognised. At [52] the court noted "*It is clear that the general intention was the courts should not usually intervene outside the general circumstances specified in Pt 1 of the 1996 Act*".

[10] [2006] EWHC 2006.

[11] See for example s.44(7).

[12] *CGU International Insurance Plc and Others v Astra Zeneca Insurance Co Ltd* [2006] EWCA 1340, *per* Rix L.J. at [100]. Following *Cetelem SA v Roust Holdings Ltd* [2005] EWCA Civ 618 the Court of Appeal can also bypass the requirement of leave from the first instance judge where the judge did not have jurisdiction to make the impugned order. See the discussion of *Cetelem* in *Kazakhstan v Istil Group Inc* [2007] EWCA 471.

[13] [1994] 2 All E.R. 449, where by a majority the House of Lords ordered a party to an arbitration to provide security for costs. The court (as opposed to an arbitrator) no longer has this power. See para.4–128.

designed to maintain the status quo (e.g. the granting of an interim injunction under s.44) and the third being designed to ensure the award has its intended practical effect by providing a means of enforcement if the award is not voluntarily complied with. It was pointed out that the three groups entail differing degrees of encroachment on the arbitral tribunal's task of deciding the merits of the dispute and that the extent of such intrusion should "condition to an important extent" the court's approach.[14] Despite the changes made by the Arbitration Act 1996, the distinction remains valid.

Contents. This chapter examines the court's role at all stages up to the publication of the final award, including the costs of the arbitration. Chapter 8 deals with the court's role in matters concerning the award, other than costs. Chapter 8 also specifies the procedure for applications to the court.   7–007

This chapter begins with applications to stay court proceedings which have been brought in breach of an arbitration agreement.[15] The court has no power to compel arbitration, save indirectly by refusing the claimant a remedy through the courts, so that if he wants to pursue his claim he can only do so by arbitration.[16] The court may also help where arbitration proceedings are wrongly brought and this is also addressed.[17]

The chapter proceeds to examine how the court may intervene while arbitration proceedings are pending and its powers to do so. They include power to extend time limits for commencing the arbitral proceedings[18] and for making the award,[19] power to appoint an arbitrator,[20] to decide disputes about the arbitrator's jurisdiction[21] and to determine points of law.[22] The court also has power to remove an arbitrator[23] and to appoint a replacement.[24] Other orders may also be made by the court during the reference, and these too are examined.[25]

Finally, this chapter deals with the court's power to determine the recoverable costs of the arbitration, including the fees and expenses of the arbitrator, when they are disputed.[26]

The court. The Commercial Court has primary responsibility for the administration and monitoring of the court's supervisory jurisdiction over arbitration and   7–008

---

[14] *per* Lord Mustill in *Ken-Ren* op. cit. at 469–470.
[15] See paras 7–010 *et seq*. below.
[16] The court usually achieves this by granting a stay of the legal proceedings, but in exceptional cases an anti-suit injunction may be obtained. See para.7–011.
[17] Paragraphs 7–057 *et seq*.
[18] Paragraphs 7–068 *et seq*.
[19] Paragraphs 7–081 *et seq*.
[20] Paragraphs 7–095 *et seq*.
[21] Paragraphs 7–143 *et seq*.
[22] Paragraphs 7–164 *et seq*.
[23] Paragraphs 7–111 *et seq*.
[24] Paragraphs 7–140 *et seq*.
[25] Paragraphs 7–179 *et seq*.
[26] Paragraphs 7–210 *et seq*.

awards under the Arbitration Act 1996.[27] Arbitration applications can also be made to certain other courts.[28–29]

7–009   Procedure. The Civil Procedural Rules 1998, as amended ("CPR") contain the procedural code that applies to all proceedings brought before the civil courts of England and Wales. Pt 62 of the CPR specifies the rules that apply generally to arbitration applications to the court[30] and will be referred to in this book as CPR Pt 62 or more simply r.62, followed by the rule number.[31] There is also a Practice Direction that supplements CPR Pt 62,[32] which will be referred to in this book as the Arbitration Practice Direction or as PD 62 followed by the relevant paragraph number.[33]

Depending on the court in which an arbitration claim is made, rules in other parts of the CPR and other practice directions may need to be consulted.[34]

Part I of CPR Pt 62 is concerned with applications to which the Arbitration Act 1996 applies. Part II is concerned with matters to which the pre-Act arbitration law applies. Part III applies to all enforcement proceedings other than by action or claim on the award. This book will consider Pt I in this chapter and Pt III in Ch.8, except that the general procedure for all arbitration applications will be specified in Ch.8.[35]

With limited exceptions, which will be mentioned in the relevant parts of Chs 7 and 8, the general rule is that "proceedings under this Act"[36] are to be commenced or taken in the High Court.[37]

2. STAYING COURT PROCEEDINGS

7–010   Introduction. An arbitration agreement is a contractual undertaking by which the parties agree to settle certain disputes by way of arbitration rather than by proceedings in court.[38] When a dispute arises however one of the parties may

---

[27] Whitebook, note 2E–45 to CPR PD 62.
[28–29] For a complete list of the courts in which an arbitration claim form may be issued, see para.8–178.
[30] CPR Pt 62 and CPR PD 62 (Arbitrations) were brought into force by the Civil Procedure (Amendment No.5) Rules 2001 (SI 2001/4015).
[31] CPR r.62.1, for example, indicates the first rule in CPR Pt 62.
[32] CPR PD 62 (Arbitrations).
[33] PD 62, para.1.1, for example, indicates the first subsection in the Arbitration Practice Direction.
[34] CPR Pts 58, 59 and 60 together with practice directions and guides apply to claims in the Commercial Court, Mercantile Courts and TCC respectively. See para.8–182.
[35] Paragraphs 8–178 *et seq.* Specific provisions of procedure will be mentioned with the relevant subject (e.g. an application for a stay of court proceedings).
[36] This expression appears in the Arbitration Act 1996, s.105(2) and (3).
[37] High Court and County Courts (Allocation of Arbitration Proceedings) Order 1996 (SI 1996/3215)—see Appendix 1.
[38] See Arbitration Act 1996, s.6(1) for definition of "arbitration agreement" for the purposes of the Act: see also para.2–002.

nevertheless commence court proceedings[39] either because he challenges the existence or validity of the arbitration agreement or because he means to breach it. A party may also wait until an unfavourable award is received and then start proceedings in an inappropriate jurisdiction to attack, set aside or otherwise impugn the award.[40]

In the first case the action may be entirely justified because arbitral proceedings must be founded on a valid arbitration agreement.[41] Therefore, rather than wait for arbitral proceedings, which he would then have to challenge as being wrongly brought,[42] the claimant may take the initiative by commencing a court action and then opposing an application to stay it.[43]

Where the court action is commenced in breach of an arbitration agreement the other party may apply to stay the court action, unless he is content to forego his right to have the dispute referred to arbitration and to defend the action before the court.[44]

Where the other party wishes to have the dispute referred to arbitration he must apply without delay to the court for a stay of the proceedings brought in breach of the agreement to arbitrate.[45] If granted, the stay will confront the other party with a choice between arbitrating the claim or not pursuing it at all, for if a stay is granted there is no third option of having it dealt with by the court.

Anti-suit injunctions. One option open to a party who faces court proceed-   7–011
ings brought in breach of an agreement to arbitrate is to apply for an anti-suit injunction. The jurisdiction to grant an anti-suit injunction is most usually directed at proceedings commenced in the early stages of an arbitration but can also be used where proceedings to challenge an award are commenced abroad.[46] Such an injunction is directed at the respondent, not to a foreign court (although there is much debate about the true effect of such an injunction) and directs the party to take no further steps in the proceedings brought in breach of the agreement to arbitrate. However, the use of an anti-suit injunction is a secondary remedy to be deployed in situations where a stay under s.9 of the Arbitration Act will not be or is unlikely to be effective. This will particularly be the case in respect

---

[39] The court will not decline to accept jurisdiction in an action simply because of the existence of the arbitration clause, see, for example, *McKellar and Westerman Ltd v Rosemary Dawn Eversfield* [1994] A.D.R.L.J. 140. It is for one of the parties to the arbitration agreement to take objection to the matter proceeding in court by applying for a stay.

[40] *Noble Assurance Co and Others v Gerling-Konzen General Insurance Co—UK Branch* [2007] EWHC 253; *C v D* [2007] EWHC 1541.

[41] There may also be a statutory reference (see Appendix 3).

[42] See para.7–057.

[43] The court action need not be commenced before the arbitral proceedings; it could be commenced after arbitral proceedings have been begun and the two may run in parallel unless and until one or other is stopped.

[44] The pros and cons of arbitration are discussed in paras 1–022 *et seq.*

[45] An injunction to restrain the breach of an agreement to arbitrate might instead be appropriate where the court proceedings are brought abroad, and the grant of a stay by the English court is not appropriate. See para.7–011.

[46] *Noble Assurance Co and Others v Gerling-Konzen General Insurance Co—UK Branch* [2007] EWHC 253 at [87]; *C v D* [2007] EWHC 1541.

of proceedings brought abroad in breach of an agreement to arbitrate, in which case s.9 proceedings clearly cannot be maintained in "the court in which the proceedings have been brought", at least not under s.9. In this situation, the party seeking to rely on an arbitration agreement will usually apply to the relevant foreign court for a stay, especially where the foreign court is situated in a country that has acceded to a Convention[47] that recognises and enforces arbitration agreements. However, where the party is unsure of the reception it will receive in that foreign court, and where England is the seat of the arbitration, an anti-suit injunction may be sought. In theory, it may be possible to seek an anti-suit injunction where England is not the seat of the arbitration but where the respondent is otherwise amenable to the jurisdiction of the English courts, for example where the court exercises in personam jurisdiction over the respondent.[48] However, particularly in the light of recent authority asserting the importance of the exclusive supervisory jurisdiction of the court's of the seat,[49] it is submitted that the English court is most unlikely to act in such situations.[50]

7–012 **Availability in the EU.** The grant by the English courts of anti-suit injunctions is becoming increasingly controversial. They are no longer available in matters covered by the Brussels Regulation regime,[51] where it is now firmly established that the question of jurisdiction is, pursuant to Art.27 of the Brussels Convention on Jurisdiction (previously Art.21 of the Convention) a matter for the court first seised of the dispute. In *Turner v Grovit*[52] the ECJ held that an anti-suit injunction ordered by the English court to restrain a defendant from taking proceedings in another Contracting State of the Brussels Regulation regime is inconsistent with that regime even where it could be shown that the foreign proceedings are vexatious or oppressive. The same conclusion was reached by the ECJ in *Eric Gasser GmbH v Misat Srl*[53] in respect of an exclusive jurisdiction

---

[47] e.g. The New York Convention, 1958.
[48] *IPOC International Growth Fund Ltd v OAO "CT-Mobile" and Another*, Court of Appeal of Bermuda, Nos 22, 23 of 2006, March 23, 2007. The Court of Appeal of Bermuda upheld the grant of an anti-suit injunction against a respondent incorporated in Bermuda where the seat of the arbitrations in question was Switzerland and Sweden. The court considered extensive English authority, although not it seems the Court of Appeal decision in *Weissfisch v Julius and Others* [2006] EWCA 218.
[49] *Weissfisch v Julius and Others* [2006] EWCA 218; *A v B* [2006] EWHC 2006.
[50] See however *Albon (t/a NA Carriage Co) v Naza Motor Trading Sdn Bhd & Anor (No.4)* [2007] EWHC 1879 (Ch), where an anti suit injunction was granted to restrain court and arbitration proceedings in Malaysia. The effect of the decision is probably confined to situations where the court has decided that it must decide an issue as to the existence of an arbitration agreement upon a s.9 stay application having been made and the court is anxious not to allow the arbitrators to decide the same issue pending the court's decision.
[51] The Brussels Regulation regime refers to the Brussels Convention on Jurisdiction 1965 as subsequently amended. The relevant rules are no contained in Council Regulation (EC) Regulation 44/2001. The Regulation has direct effect which is recognised in the Civil Jurisdiction and Judgments Order 2001 (SI 2001/3929) and is reflected in CPR r.6.19.
[52] [2004] 2 Lloyd's Rep. 169.
[53] [2005] 1 All E.R. (Comm) 538.

clause.[54] In the arbitration context, as is described below, anti-suit injunctions are currently available in support of arbitration wherever the respondent is domiciled. This is because proceedings seeking anti-suit injunctions in support of an arbitration agreement are outside the scope of the Brussels Regulation jurisdictional regime. There is a question however as to whether this state of affairs will continue. Recognising the need for the issue to be resolved by the ECJ, the House of Lords has now referred the following question to the ECJ: "Is it consistent with EC Regulation 44/2001 for a court of a Member State to make an order to restrain a person from commencing or continuing proceedings in another Member State on the ground that such proceedings are in breach of an arbitration agreement?"[55] The House of Lords expressed the firm view that the maintenance of arbitration (and in particular London seated arbitration) as an attractive alternative to litigation, free in the main from the competing requirements of domestic jurisdictions, requires that anti-suit injunctions continue to be available, " . . . in cases concerning arbitration, falling outside the Regulation, it is in my opinion equally necessary that Member States should trust the arbitrators (under the doctrine of Kompetenz-Kompetenz) or the court exercising supervisory jurisdiction to decide whether the arbitration clause is binding and then to enforce that decision by orders which require the parties to arbitrate and not litigate".[56]

Current position. Anti-suit injunctions in respect of proceedings not brought in the courts of EU Member States will be unaffected by the ECJ's decision.[57] Pending an answer from the ECJ the position in its Member States is as follows: 7–013

Notwithstanding the effect of the decisions in *Turner v Grovit* and *Eric Gasser*, the Court of Appeal has held that anti-suit injunctions can still be granted in the context of breaches of agreements to arbitrate, indeed in any situation relating to

---

[54] Anti-suit injunctions are still available in respect of court proceedings where the parties are not domiciled in countries party to the Brussels Regulation regime. Completing the trilogy of cases, see also *Owusu v Jackson (t/a Bal Inn Villas)* [2005] Q.B. 801, where the claimant was injured in a swimming accident in Jamaica and sued one English and several Jamaican defendants for damages for personal injuries. The ECJ held, applying Art.2 of the Convention, that there was no scope for an application of forum non conveniens where a defendant was domiciled in a Member State. It made no difference that the dispute centered on a non-member state and involved acts and omissions of other defendants who were domiciled in that state. The Brussels Convention regime as applied in *Turner* and *Eric Gasser* has been subject to heavy academic criticism in England as being inflexible. See Mance L.Q.R. 2004, 120 (Jul), 357–365; Briggs L.Q.R. 2004, 120 (Oct), 529–533.

[55] *West Tankers Inc v RAS Riunione Adriatica di Sicurta SpA and Others* [2007] UKHL 4, a "leapfrog" appeal from [2005] EWHC 454 in the light of the Court of Appeal's decision in *Through Transport Mutual Insurance (Eurasia) Ltd v New India Assurance Co Ltd* [2004] EWCA Civ 1598.

[56] *per* Lord Hoffmann, at [20]. Similar sentiments are expressed in the very short opinion of Lord Mance, at [26]–[30].

[57] See for example *Noble Assurance Co and Others v Gerling-Konzen General Insurance Co—UK Branch* [2007] EWHC 253, at [84]–[98], a post West Tankers case where the court considered it had power to grant an anti-suit injunction in respect of Vermont proceedings. See also *C v D* [2007] EWHC 1541; *Elektrim SA v (1) Vivendi Universal SA (2) Vivendi Telecommunication International SA (3) Elektrim Telekomunikacja SP Zoo (4) Carcom Warszawa SP Zoo* (2007) 2 Lloyd's Rep. 8 and *Starlight Shipping and Others v Tai Ping Insurance and Others* [2007] EWHC 1893.

arbitration or litigation not covered by the Brussels Regulation regime.[58] Arbitration currently falls outside the scope of the Brussels Regulation[59]; and hence proceedings in relation to arbitration usually fall within the arbitration exception in Art.1(2)9(d) of the Regulation.[60] The breadth of this exclusion has been the subject of some debate. The approach of the English court, as enunciated by the Court of Appeal in *Through Transport Mutual Insurance (Eurasia) Ltd v New India Assurance Co Ltd*, where the Court of Appeal found that the proceedings fell within the arbitration exception, is to assess whether the "principal focus" of the proceedings is arbitration.[61] This, the court said, embraces proceedings concerning the validity or existence of an arbitration agreement, the appointment of arbitrators, injunctions and other ancillary assistance in the context of arbitration proceedings and the recognition and enforcement of awards. It also extends to proceedings the aim of which is to set aside, disrupt or stop the arbitration.[62] The ECJ has however held that the exception does not however extend to pure provisional measure applications.[63] A simple starting point is to ask: does the essential subject matter of the claim concern arbitration?[64] If the answer to this question is yes, then the arbitration exception should apply. The question is one of substance and not form, so if the aim of proceedings is to circumvent or render nugatory an arbitration clause the English court will conclude that the proceedings

[58] The principles governing the grant of an anti-suit injunction after the *Eric Gasser* line of decisions are summarised by the Court of Appeal in *OT Africa Line Ltd v Magic Sportswear Corp* [2005] EWCA Civ 710. See in particular the comments of Rix L.J. at [51]. Sir Anthony Clarke M.R., speaking extra-judicially, has recognized "that there is scope for argument as to whether that [the English court's approach to the grant of anti-suit injunctions] is correct or not" in "*The differing approach to commercial litigation in the European Court of Justice and the courts of England and Wales*", Institute of Advanced Legal Studies, London, February 23, 2006, available at *www.dca.gov.uk/judicial/speeches/2006*.

[59] *Through Transport Mutual Insurance (Eurasia) Ltd v New India Assurance Co Ltd* [2004] EWCA Civ 1598, applied in *West Tankers Inc v Ras Riunione Adriatica di Sicurta SpA* [2005] All E.R. (D) 350 (see the House of Lords' reference to the ECJ [2007] UKHL 4). The Brussels Regulation (Council Regulation (EC) No.44/200)1 took effect on March 1, 2002 and replaced the previous Brussels Convention concerning issues of jurisdiction between all EU Member States except Denmark. The same issue applies under the Lugano Convention which governs jurisdictional issues between EU Member States and Iceland, Norway and Switzerland. See also, Jolly K., *Anti-Suit Injunction and the Arbitration Exception in the Brussels Regulation: New India Assurance v Through Transport Mutual Insurance* (2005) 71 Arbitration 3.

[60] See further para.7–184.

[61] [2004] EWCA Civ 1598. An anti-suit injunction was not granted in this case where a third party was pursuing a statutory right under Finnish law in the Finnish courts against an insurer. See a discussion of the effect of the *Turner v Grovit* line of cases and *Through Transport* by Sir Anthony Clarke M.R. speaking extra-judicially, "The differing approach to commercial litigation in the European Court of Justice and the courts of England and Wales", Institute of Advanced Legal Studies, London, February 23, 2006, available at *www.dca.gov.uk/judicial/speeches/2006*.

[62] The principal focus/principal objective test was applied in *A v B* [2006] EWHC 2006 at [87]–[97].

[63] *Van Uden Maritime BV v Kommarditgesellschatt* in *Firma Deco-Line* [2002] E.C.R. 1–7091. The distinction between pure provisional measure applications, which may fall outside the exception, and essentially all other types of arbitration-related exceptions which fall within the exception is unclear along the dividing line.

[64] *Through Transport*, above, *per* Clarke L.J., at paras 44–47; adopting the analysis of Advocate General Darmon in *Marc Rich & Co AG v Societa Italiana PA (The "Atlantic Emperor")* [1992] 1 Lloyd's Rep. 342.

in question have arbitration as their principal focus and hence fall within the arbitration exception.[65]

Test to be applied. In these situations (i.e. where the proceedings come within the scope of the arbitration exception), the English court has generally maintained the line that there should be no hesitation in granting an anti-suit injunction against a party who are in clear breach of an agreement to arbitrate.[66] Furthermore, the likely attitude of the foreign court is irrelevant as the target of the anti-suit injunction is the party in breach of the agreement to arbitrate, not the court.[67] Certain considerations, such as of comity, may however persuade the court to grant appropriate declaratory relief rather than an anti-suit injunction in certain situations.[68] Upon proof by the applicant of a valid arbitration agreement and an actual or threatened breach of its terms, an injunction will normally be granted unless it can be shown that the applicant has submitted to the jurisdiction of the foreign court or has otherwise unduly delayed in making the application for an anti-suit injunction.

7–014

Availability generally. Subject to the above threshold issue concerning availability of the remedy in respect of proceedings before EU Member States and other considerations mentioned, an application may be made to the court for an injunction to restrain a defendant from pursuing proceedings abroad in breach of an arbitration agreement,[69] provided the application is made

7–015

---

[65] *A v B* [2006] EWHC 2006. If the ECJ adopts this approach in the *West Tankers* reference then it is likely that the court will answer the question referred in the affirmative.

[66] *Through Transport*, paras 85–92. A classic exposition of the principles relevant to the grant of an anti-suit injunction can be found in *Aggeliki Charis Compania Maritima SA v Pagnan SpA (The "Angelic Grace'")* [1995] 1 Lloyd's Rep. 87, *per* Millett L.J. at 96, although in the light of more recent development this might be regarded as representing the "high water mark" of the jurisdiction. Nonetheless, the *"Angelic Grace"* test has been cited with approval after *West Tankers*. See *C v D* [2007] EWHC 1541, at [55]. *Starlight Shipping and Others v Tai Ping Insurance and Others* [2007] EWHC 1893 at [12]–[15]. In addition to the statement of approach in *The Angelic Grace* see also *Donohue v Armco* [2002] 1 Lloyd's Rep. 425 at 432 *et seq.*; *HL and Akai Pty Ltd v People's Insurance Co Ltd* [1998] 1 Lloyd's Rep. 90. See more recently *Goshawk Dedicated Ltd v ROP Inc* [2006] EWHC 1730, where an anti-suit injunction was granted to restrain the respondent from pursuing proceedings in the United States in breach of an English arbitration agreement. Contrast however the comments of Morision J in *Markel v Craft* [2006] EWHC 3150 at [30] concerning the need for the remedy to be used only sparingly.

[67] *Through Transport*, above. But contrast the comments of Morision J. in *Markel v Craft* [2006] EWHC 3150 to the effect that although the traditional justification for an anti-suit injunction is that it is directed at the party and not the foreign court, there is a growing realisation that even in arbitration cases an anti-suit injunction can be seen as interference with another court's jurisdiction. For this reason, Morison J. suggested that it is a remedy which should be used only sparingly.

[68] See *Noble Assurance Co and Others v Gerling-Konzen General Insurance Co—UK Branch* [2007] EWHC 253, where the court adopted this route.

[69] The *"Angelic Grace"* was the first in a series of cases that granted an anti-suit injunction. It followed the decision of the Court of Appeal on exclusive jurisdiction clauses in *Continental Bank v Acakas Compania Naviera* [1994] 1 Lloyd's Rep. 505. Other decisions where an anti-suit injunction has been made outside Europe include *Shell v Coral Oil* [1999] 1 Lloyd's Rep. 72; *Bankers Trust v Jakarta Intl* [1999] 1 Lloyd's Rep. 910; and *Sea Premium v Sea Consortium DBD* (Adm Ct) Steel J. (April 11, 2001). The exclusion by the Court of Appeal in the *Through Transport* case, of the application of *Turner v Grovit* principles to anti-suit injunctions relating to agreements to arbitrate makes it clear that the approach outlined in the *Angelic Grace* still prevails.

promptly.[70] The construction of an arbitration clause is governed by the proper law of the arbitration agreement rather than the law of the seat or the law of governing law of the matrix contract, and it is the proper law of the arbitration agreement which the court will apply in determining whether there is an actual or threatened breach of the agreement to arbitrate. The law of the arbitration agreement may be different from the procedural law of the arbitration and the governing law of the matrix contract.[71]

As to delay, this is fact specific: it has been suggested in one case that a delay of more than a year between the commencement of the foreign proceedings and the application for an anti-suit injunction would constitute sufficient grounds for declining the injunction on grounds of delay.[72] Where the foreign proceedings which were the subject of the anti-suit injunction had been on foot for over six months, the court declined to grant an anti-suit injunction as "*it may have the appearance of interference in the affairs of the other court, especially where the other court has already devoted considerable time to considering issues in the action*".[73] The court will also take account of any other special factors in the particular case militating against the grant of an anti-suit injunction.[74] The court may make an interim or a permanent injunction.[75] The jurisdiction also extends to the grant of so-called "anti-anti-suit injunctions" which require the respondent to refrain from pursuing their own anti-arbitral relief in the foreign court.[76]

7–016 **Third party statutory rights.** A related issue is whether an anti-suit injunction will be granted against a third party pursuing a statutory right derived from a contract in foreign proceedings, such as a third party bringing a claim directly against an insurer, where the underlying contract (such as between insurer and insured) refers disputes to English arbitration. Depending on the nature of the particular statutory right, the issue will turn on whether it can be said that the third party's reliance on the statutory right is a breach of the arbitration clause, rather than the applicant being only entitled to a declaration that the third party should pursue all of its claims against the applicant including the statutory claim in arbitration.[77]

---

[70] The need for prompt action was emphasised in *Bankers Trust v Jakarta Intl* [1999] 1 Lloyd's Rep. 910.

[71] See *C v D* [2007] EWHC 1541; *Tamil Nadu Electricity Board v St-CMS Electric Company Private Ltd* [2007] EWHC 1713 at [35]. See also *OT Africa Line Ltd v Magic Sportswear Corp* [2005] EWCA Civ 710.

[72] *Markel v Craft* [2006] EWHC 3150 at [32]. The injunction was refused on other grounds.

[73] *Noble Assurance Co and Others v Gerling-Konzen General Insurance Co—UK Branch* [2007] EWHC 253 (Comm); [2007] 1 C.L.C. 85, *per* Toulson L.J. at [100].

[74] For example, to avoid inconsistent decisions in multi-party disputes. See *Donohue v Armco op. cit.* See also *Navigation Maritime Bulgaria v Rustal Trading (The "Ivan Zagubanski")* [2002] 1 Lloyd's Rep. 106.

[75] Both injunctions were made in *The "Ivan Zagubanski"* at different stages of the proceedings. For the procedure relating to injunctions and their service see para.7–196.

[76] For an example of a case where such relief was granted in conjunction with an anti-suit injunction see *Goshawk Dedicated Ltd v ROP Inc* [2006] EWHC 1730.

[77] *Through Transport Mutual Insurance (Eurasia) Ltd v New India Assurance Co Ltd* [2005] 1 Lloyd's Rep. 67, followed in *Markel v Craft* [2006] EWHC 3150.

Recognition by foreign court. A further issue to consider is that even in 7–017
circumstances where an anti-suit injunction is granted in support of an agreement to arbitrate such an injunction may not be recognised by the court in the
foreign jurisdiction. This is especially so where the practice of that legal system
does not recognise the concept of anti-suit injunctions,[78] although the likely
reaction of the foreign court will not deter the English court from granting the
order.[79] The Court of Appeal has suggested that considerations of comity are
to some extent built into the basic requirements for the principled exercise of
the jurisdiction to grant an anti-suit injunction.[80] Even if the court is that its
injunction will be ignored by the foreign court, it may still proceed to issue the
injunction on the basis that a respectable foreign party is not likely to disregard
its order.[80a]

Jurisdictional basis. It had previously been the case that anti-suit injunc- 7–018
tions were made under the court's inherent jurisdiction conferred by s.37 of
the Supreme Court Act 1981 and not under s.44 of the Act.[81] The Court of
Appeal in *Cetelem v* Roust[82] noted the apparent tension between s.37 of the
Supreme Court Act 1981 and s.44 of the Arbitration Act 1996. Although the
tension has not been resolved, there remains an acceptance that orders under
s.37 can be made in the context of arbitration. Notwithstanding the comments
in *Cetelem v Roust*, the House of Lords in *West Tankers* made it clear that anti-
suit injunctions are (at least usually) granted under s.37 of the Supreme Court
Act 1981.[83] In a subsequent decision, the application was brought on the two
alternative basis. The court did not indicate on which basis it granted the
injunction.[84] In *Elektrim SA v Vivendi Universal SA and Others*[85] the court
assumed that s.37 could be used to grant arbitral relief in the context of arbitration. Where the court proceeds under s.37 of the Supreme Court Act, it
should have regard to the same factors as arise under s.44 of the Arbitration
Act.[85a] It is suggested that the court could also attempt to use the language of
s.44(2)(e) to grant anti-suit injunctions, although an anti-suit injunction made
under this sub-section could not be a final injunction.[86]

[78] For example, the Greek Court of Appeal has refused to recognise an anti-suit injunction ordered by
the English court in relation to a London arbitration, finding that orders restraining a party from
accessing the courts is contrary to the Greek Constitution: [2004] Piraiki Nomologia 92 (available
at *www.kluwerarbitration.com*).
[79] *West Tankers Inc v Ras Riunione Adriatica di Sicurta SpA* [2005] All E.R. (D) 350, *per* Colman J.,
at [51]–[52]. But see the House of Lords' reference to the ECJ in [2007] UKHL 4.
[80] See *OT Africa Line Ltd v Magic Sportswear Corp* [2005] 2 Lloyd's Rep. 170 at [62]–[69].
[80a] *Starlight Shipping and Others v Tai Ping Insurance and Others* [2007] EWHC 1893 at [43].
[81] *Welex AG v Rosa Maritime* [2003] 2 Lloyd's Rep. 509 at [36], [40]. Anti-suits injunctions have
hitherto probably been granted under s.37 of the Supreme Court Act 1981 because they are usually
final injunctions.
[82] *Cetelem SA v Roust Holdings Ltd* [2005] EWCA Civ 618.
[83] *West Tankers Inc v RAS Riunione Adriatica di Sicurta SpA and Others* [2007] UKHL 4 at [8].
[84] *C v D* [2007] EWHC 1541.
[85] [2007] 2 Lloyd's Rep. 8.
[85a] *Starlight Shipping and Others v Tai Ping Insurance and Others* [2007] EWHC 1893, [19].
[86] See *Starlight Shipping and Others v Tai Ping Insurance and Others* [2007] EWHC 1893, [20]–[28].
The argument runs that the anti-suit injunction is necessary to preserve the contractual rights of
the applicant to arbitrate. It has been accepted in *Cetelem SA v Roust Holdings Ltd* [2005] 1 W.L.R.

7–019 Damages for breach of the agreement to arbitrate. In certain circumstances it is not possible to obtain an effective stay to restrain proceedings brought in breach of an agreement to arbitrate. In particular, this may be the case where proceedings in breach of an agreement to arbitrate are brought in a foreign jurisdiction and where the courts of that jurisdiction neither stay the proceedings, nor recognise an order of either the arbitral tribunal or the court at the seat of the arbitration which attempts to restrain the party concerned from bringing proceedings in breach of an arbitration agreement. However, there is no reason in principle why an unsuccessful attempt to restrain the proceedings brought in breach should be a condition precedent to an action for damages in this context. In such situations, a party should consider the availability of an action for damages for breach of the agreement to arbitrate. In *Donohue v Armco*[87] the House of Lords accepted in principle that damages were available in cases of breach of a jurisdiction clause. The damages recoverable in such an action may extend to any additional liability incurred in the foreign jurisdiction (such as punitive damages, for example) as well as the costs of defending the foreign proceedings. In *Union Discount v Zoller*[88] it was decided by the Court of Appeal that where a party had incurred costs in successfully applying in New York to strike out proceedings against it brought in breach of an English jurisdiction clause but, due to local costs rules, it could not obtain an order for costs in New York, it could recover damages in English proceedings against the respondent including all costs reasonably expended on the New York application. The English court has also accepted that costs of defending the foreign proceedings may be recovered in England even where those costs could in theory be obtained in the foreign proceedings.[89] An action for damages may be maintained both for breach of the arbitration agreement itself and for breach of the jurisdiction agreement vesting supervisory jurisdiction in the courts at the seat.[90]

7–020 Overlap between remedies. Situations will also arise where a party may obtain an anti-suit injunction restraining the proceedings in breach of an arbitration agreement and may also bring an action for damages in respect of losses to date caused to it as a result of the proceedings brought in breach. However, the scope of an anti-suit injunction and an action for damages for breach of an agreement to arbitrate is not co-extensive. There will be situations where an anti-suit injunction may be obtained in circumstances where an action for damages for breach of the agreement to arbitrate has not yet accrued, for example against a subrogated insurer who pursues court proceedings inconsistent with an agreement

---

3555 that contractual rights are assets within the terms of s.44(3). An anti-suit injunction to restrain breach of an agreement to arbitrate was granted in *Goshawk Dedicated Ltd v ROP Inc* [2006] EWHC 1730 but the judgment does not contain any discussion of the basis of the court's jurisdiction to grant the relief. See further para.7–196.

[87] [2001] 1 Lloyd's Rep. 425.

[88] [2001] EWCA 1755.

[89] *A/S D/S Svendborg af 1912 A/S Bodies Corporate trading in partnership as "Maersk Sealand" v Akar* [2003] EWHC 797 (Comm.).

[90] *A v B (Costs)* [2007] EWHC 54 at [16].

to arbitrate binding on its assured.[91] There will also be situations where, although the applicant may be entitled to a declaration that the other party should refer all claims to arbitration, the action of the third party in maintaining foreign proceedings will not constitute a breach of the agreement to arbitrate (such as where a third party brings foreign court proceedings against an insurer relying on a foreign statutory right) and hence no anti-suit injunction will be granted.[92]

English Proceedings. It is also possible of course to bring an action for 7–021
damages where the proceedings in breach of an arbitration agreement are brought in England and Wales but in practice it is unlikely that any substantial loss will have been suffered other than the costs of applying to the court for a stay, unless perhaps concurrent arbitration proceedings have been commenced. In principle if costs of the English court proceedings are awarded on a standard basis then the shortfall between the standard basis and actual costs could be recovered in an action for damages although this is a "formalistic and cumbersome procedure which would in itself involve more costs and judicial time" and so should be avoided if possible.[93]

Costs on an indemnity basis. Where proceedings have been brought in 7–022
breach of an agreement to arbitrate, the usual approach is that costs of the relevant English proceedings will be awarded against the party acting in breach of the agreement to arbitrate on an indemnity basis.[94]

Domestic and non-domestic. Although the Arbitration Act 1996 makes 7–023
a distinction between domestic and non-domestic arbitration agreements,[95] those provisions in the Act relating to domestic arbitration agreements will not be brought into force.[96] Accordingly, no further mention of those provisions will be found in this chapter.

---

[91] *West Tankers Inc v Ras Riunione Adriatica di Sicurta SpA* [2005] All E.R. (D) 350, *per* Colman J. at [67]–[68]. But see the House of Lords' reference to the ECJ [2007] UKHL 4.

[92] As in *Through Transport Mutual Insurance (Eurasia) Ltd v New India Assurance Co Ltd* [2005] 1 Lloyd's Rep. 67.

[93] *A v B (Costs)* [2007] EWHC 54 at [10].

[94] *A v B (Costs)* [2007] EWHC 54 at [10]–[11]; *Kyrgyz Mobil Tel and Others v Fellowes International Holdings and Another* [2005] EWHC 1329, at [42].

[95] The distinction, which was introduced by the Arbitration Act 1975, is apparent from ss.85–87 inclusive of the Arbitration Act 1996. The definition of "domestic arbitration agreement" appears in s.85(2) of the Arbitration Act 1996.

[96] The decision appears in the statement made on January 30, 1997 by the Parliamentary Under Secretary of State for Corporate and Consumer Affairs, Department of Trade and Industry. It followed the Arbitration Act 1996 (Commencement No.1) Order 1996 which excepted ss.85–87 from coming into force with the rest of the Act on January 31, 1997, see para.2–005.

7-024 The court's powers to grant a stay of legal proceedings.[97] An application for a stay of legal proceedings will usually be made under s.9 of the Arbitration Act 1996, whose provisions are mandatory.[98] Section 9 will apply even if the seat of the arbitration is abroad or no seat has been designated or determined but clearly the legal proceedings to which the stay relates must be proceedings before the court which is asked to consider the application.[99] To give an example of the court's approach, where the seat of an arbitration was in Abu Dhabi, and the scope of the arbitration agreement was governed by Abu Dhabi law, the court heard expert evidence as to Abu Dhabi law in order to determine the scope of the arbitration clause.[100] Under s.9 a stay must be granted unless the court is satisfied that the arbitration agreement is "null and void, inoperative, or incapable of being performed".[101]

The Brussels Regulation regime,[102] where it is now firmly established that the question of jurisdiction is, pursuant to Art.27 of the Brussels Convention (previously Art.21 of the Convention), a matter for the court first seised of the dispute, does not alter the effect of s.9 (or the court's exercise of its inherent jurisdiction to grant a stay) provided that, as will usually be the case, the principal focus of the proceedings is arbitration. If this is the case the arbitration exception in Arts 1(2), 9(d) of the Regulation will be triggered.[103]

7-025 Courses of action open to the court. As to determining whether the matter is within s.9 of the Act, a number of courses are in principle open to the court. They include[104]

- To determine on the available evidence that there is, or is not, an applicable arbitration agreement and accordingly to grant or dismiss the application for a stay; or

- to stay the legal proceedings pending a determination by the arbitral tribunal of its own jurisdiction under s.30 of the Arbitration Act[105]; or

---

[97] "Legal proceedings" is used in the Arbitration Act 1996 to mean "civil proceedings in the High Court or a County Court": see s.82(1) of the Act.

[98] See s.4 of the Arbitration Act 1996 and Sch.1 to the Act for the mandatory provisions.

[99] Arbitration Act 1996, s.2(2).

[100] *Abu Dhabi Investment Co and Others v H Clarkson & Co Ltd* [2006] EWHC 1252. In that case the dispute did not fall within the scope of the arbitration agreement and a stay was refused.

[101] Arbitration Act 1996, s.9(4). See para.7–046 for a commentary on this phrase.

[102] The Brussels' regime refers to the Brussels Convention on Jurisdiction 1965 as subsequently amended. The relevant rules are now contained in Council Regulation (EC) Regulation 44/2001. The Regulation has direct effect which is recognised in Civil Jurisdiction and Judgments Order 2001 (SI 2001/3929) and is reflected in CPR r.6.19.

[103] *A v B* [2006] EWHC 2006 at [87]–[97]. See also discussion of the scope of the arbitration exception at para.7–013.

[104] *Birse Construction v St David* [1999] B.L.R. 194. Cited with approval in *Al-Naimi v Islamic Press Agency, Inc* [2000] 1 Lloyd's Rep. 522 at 524; *Anglia Oits Ltd v Owners of Marine Champion (The "Marine Champion")* [2002] EWHC 2407 and by the Court of Appeal in *Fiona Trust and Others v Yuri Privalov & Others* [2007] EWCA 20 at [37].

[105] In *Albon v Naza Motor Trading SDN BHD (No.3)* [2007] EWHC 665, Lightman J. at [16], expressed the view that this course could only be followed under the court's inherent jurisdiction.

- not to decide the question immediately but to give directions for an issue to be tried; or

- To decide that there is no arbitration agreement and to dismiss the application for a stay.[106]

Whilst the principle that the tribunal should determine its own jurisdiction is firmly enshrined in s.30 of the Act, on occasions the court will nonetheless effectively determine the tribunal's jurisdiction when considering an application for a stay. The Court of Appeal in *Fiona Trust and Others v Yuri Privalov & Others*[107] said that the presumption is that the tribunal should be left to determine its own jurisdiction first if at all possible, " . . . it is contemplated by the Act that it will, in general, be right for the arbitrators to be the first tribunal to consider whether they have jurisdiction to determine the dispute".[108] These comments were echoed by the Court of Appeal in *Kazakstan v Istil Group Inc*, "A party which wishes to challenge the jurisdiction of the arbitrators must take the point before the arbitrators, and will lose the right to challenge it before the court unless it has taken the point before the arbitrators".[109] Jurisprudence on this issue is not uniform however and it is clear that the courts will decide issues of jurisdiction, especially where it is alleged that no agreement was concluded.[110] The court also has an inherent jurisdiction (in addition to its jurisdiction under s.9) to grant a stay of legal proceedings in certain circumstances,[111] and will usually exercise this jurisdiction when it is virtually certain that there is an arbitration agreement or there is only a dispute about its scope but that the formal requirements of a s.9 stay cannot be met.[112]

Conditions applied. When acting under its statutory jurisdiction under s.9   7–026
there are certain conditions applied by the court to an application for a stay. Those conditions are considered in the following paragraphs.

There must be an arbitration agreement to which the section   7–027
applies. The existence of an arbitration agreement must be shown, although as explained below it is not necessary for its validity to be unchallenged.[113] For these

---

[106] The fourth ground is in reality a sub-set of the first ground.
[107] [2007] EWCA 20.
[108] *Fiona Trust and Others v Yuri Privalov & Others* [2007] EWCA 20 at [34]. Affirmed *Premium Nafta Products Ltd & Others v Fili Shipping Co Ltd & Others* [2007] UKHL 40. The Court of Appeal's decision in *Fiona Trust* has the rare distinction among arbitration cases of being reported in the Financial Times. "*Courts reinforce respect for arbitration process*", *The Financial Times*, January 29, 2007.
[109] [2007] W.L. 1425725, *per* Toulson L.J. at para.35.
[110] See *Albon v Naza Motor Trading SDN BHD (No.3)* [2007] EWHC 665, *per* Lightman J. at [20].
[111] See para.7–055.
[112] *A v B* [2006] EWHC 2006; *Al-Naimi v Islamic Press Agency Inc* [2000] 1 Lloyd's Rep. 522 at 525, CA: see para.7–055, considered in *T & N Ltd v Royal & Sun Alliance Plc* [2004] Lloyd's Rep. I.R. 102.
[113] *Ahmed Al-Naimi v Islamic Press Agency* [2000] 1 Lloyd's Rep. 522 at 525, *per* Waller L.J.

purposes "arbitration agreement" is defined as an "agreement" to submit to arbitration present or future disputes, whether they are contractual or not.[114] The provisions of the Arbitration Act 1996 apply only where the arbitration agreement is in writing,[115] although the expression "agreement in writing" is defined broadly and includes an agreement contained in a written exchange of communication and an agreement evidenced in writing.[116] The agreement relied upon will usually be produced to the court on the application to stay. The House of Lords has suggested that an arbitration agreement can exist for these purposes if it is contained in a matrix agreement the terms of which remained to be agreed.[116a] If there is not an agreement to arbitrate but an agreement to submit disputes to other forms of alternative dispute resolution without containing the ultimate requirement to arbitrate, the court will not be bound to grant the mandatory stay contemplated by s.9 but will instead will adopt a discretionary approach equivalent to that which prevailed in respect of arbitration before the enactment of the Arbitration Act 1996.[117]

7–028   **Existence and validity of the arbitration agreement.** The existence[118] of an arbitration agreement between the parties to the dispute must be proved by the applicant[119] in order to secure a stay of the court proceedings.[120] As is explained below, the court now draws a distinction between existence of the arbitration agreement, which is likely to be a matter for the court, (unless a stay under the inherent jurisdiction is granted) and its validity, which wherever possible should be left to the arbitrators. See *Premium Nafta Products Ltd & Others v Fili Shipping Co Ltd & Others* [2007] UKHL 40, *per* Lord Hoffmann at [7], noting that it was very unlikely that rational businessman would intend that the question of whether the contract was repudiated should be decided by arbitrators but the question of whether it was induced by misrepresentation should be

---

[114] Arbitration Act 1996, s.6(1) contains the principal definition which is adopted elsewhere in the Act. See para.1–033 above on what is and what is not capable of settlement by arbitration.

[115] Arbitration Act 1996, s.5(1) and see paras 2–002 and 2–038 above.

[116] Arbitration Act 1996, s.5(2) and see para.2–039 above.

[116a] *Premium Nafta Products Ltd & Others v Fili Shipping Co Ltd & Others* [2007] UKHL 40.

[117] For an example of the doctrine of a discretionary stay being considered see *Thames Valley Power Ltd v Total Gas & Power Ltd* [2005] EWHC 2208, where the court declined to grant a discretionary stay in favour of expert determination because it formed the view that the position of one of the parties was untenable and a swift resolution of the dispute would be achieved if all claims were to be determined immediately by the court.

[118] The arbitration agreement must be in existence at the date of the commencement of the legal proceedings: *Traube v Perelman* (July 25, 2001), Ch D, Jacobs J.; *A v B* [2006] EWHC 2006.

[119] *Premium Nafta Products Ltd & Others v Fili Shipping Co Ltd & Others* [2007] UKHL 40. See also *Cigna Life v Intercaser SA* [2002] 1 All E.R. (Comm) 235 where it was held that a contract of re-insurance did not incorporate an arbitration agreement in respect of two of the parties to proceedings. See also *Pheonix Finance v FIA* [2002] E.W.H.E. 1028, and para.2–012.

[120] See *Unum Life Insurance Co v The Israel Pheonix Ass Co* (March 16, 2001), QBD (Comm.), Andrew Smith J. (upheld on appeal), where the applicant for a stay failed to prove the existence of an arbitration agreement that bound the claimant, and a stay was refused. For a similar case see *Sun Life Asurance Co of Canada v CX Reinsurance Co Ltd* [2003] EWCA Civ 283 where the Court of Appeal held that as the agreement for reinsurance containing the arbitration clause had never been signed the parties had never intended to be bound by an agreement to arbitrate, and a stay under s.9 was accordingly refused.

decided by a court.[120a] The doctrine of separability, as discussed in Ch.2,[121] enables the arbitration agreement to survive the termination by breach of any contract of which it forms part . As the House of Lords noted in *Lesotho Highlands v Impreglio SpA*, "it is part of the very alphabet of arbitration law as explained in *Harbour Assurance Co (UK) Ltd v Kansa General International Insurance Co Ltd* . . . and spelled out in section 7 of the Act, the arbitration agreement is a distinct and separable agreement from the underlying or principal contract".[122]

Court or tribunal to decide? As noted above[123], the court has in essence four courses open to it when faced with an application to stay court proceedings. The options boil down to leaving the jurisdictional issue to be determined by the tribunal itself or the court stepping in and deciding the jurisdictional issue, either on witness statement evidence or after a trial of the issue. Even if the underlying contract is alleged to be void or voidable, the parties are presumed to have wanted their disputes resolved by an arbitral tribunal. In the light of the presumption of "one-stop adjudication", the court will usually strive to give effect to the arbitration agreement by granting a stay of court proceedings and allowing the tribunal to investigate whether the contract is valid, but it will not do so in every case.[124] In *Fiona Trust and Others v Yuri Privalov and Others*[125] the allegation of bribery was in general terms and did not specifically impugn the arbitration agreement. The court declined to decide the jurisdiction issue itself, referring the matter instead to the arbitrators: 7–029

> "If the arbitrators can decide whether a contract is void for initial illegality, there is no reason why they should not decide whether a contract has been procured by bribery, just as much as they can decide whether a contract has been procured by misrepresentation or non-disclosure. Illegality is a stronger case than bribery which is not the same as non est factum or the sort of mistake which goes to the question of whether there was any agreement ever reached. It is not enough to say that the bribery impeaches the whole contract unless there is some special reason for saying that the bribery impeaches the arbitration clause in particular."[126]

When the court will decide the jurisdictional issue. The court's approach will depend upon whether it is the matrix agreement that is challenged, or whether the objection is specifically directed at the arbitration agreement itself. If the existence of the arbitration agreement is challenged then as noted the court will decide the issue itself. The court will decide the issue if it is alleged that the 7–030

[120a] *Premium Nafta Products Ltd & Others v Fili Shipping Co Ltd & Others* [2007] UKHL 40 at [17]. See also Lord Hope at [32]–[35].

[121] See paras 2–007 *et seq.* and s.7 of the Arbitration Act 1996.

[122] [2006] 1 A.C. 221 at [21].

[123] At para.7–025.

[124] This was the law even before the Arbitration Act 1996 came into effect: see *Harbour Assurance Co (UK) Ltd v Kansa General Insurance Co Ltd* [1993] 3 All E.R. 897. It is reinforced by ss.7 and 30 of the Arbitration Act 1996.

[125] [2007] EWCA 20.

[126] *Fiona Trust* at [29].

matrix agreement containing the arbitration agreement has been forged.[127] This approach is justified on the basis that s.9(1) requires there to be an arbitration agreement to be in existence for a stay to be granted.[128] A challenge to the existence of the main agreement does not necessarily impugn the existence of the arbitration agreement provided the court can be satisfied that the arbitration clause has been agreed.[128a]

The court will also usually decide the jurisdictional issue itself if a specific allegation has been made which directly impugns the agreement to arbitrate, rather than the matrix agreement. This approach is justified on the basis that s.9(4) requires a stay to be granted unless the arbitration agreement itself is null, void, inoperative or incapable of being performed. Whilst the issue of whether there has ever been a concluded arbitration agreement binding on the party against whom a stay of English proceedings is the threshold point which is normally decided by the courts, the circumstances may sometimes justify a stay under the inherent jurisdiction of the court so as to enable the arbitrator to decide this issue.[129]

However, if the arbitration agreement itself is not challenged the court will have to ascertain only that an arbitration clause exists before granting a stay of the legal proceedings; it should not usually determine questions relating to the validity of the arbitration agreement before referring the matter to the arbitrators. As noted, this applies even in situations where there is a claim to set aside the matrix agreement on the grounds of fraud or bribery.[130]

7–031 **Need for further evidence?** If it is appropriate for the court to decide jurisdiction itself, such as where there is a claim of non *est factum*, forgery in relation to the matrix contract,[130a] denial that there was a concluded agreement[131] or a specific allegation of fraud or misrepresentation going to the arbitration agreement itself, the court may be able to do so on the evidence before it.[132] On the majority of occasions however it will have to give directions for service of evidence for that purpose, if necessary staying the proceedings pending determination of the issue. However, if the court's preliminary view is that a detailed enquiry is likely to find that a valid arbitration agreement does exist, the court

---

[127] See *Premium Nafta Products Ltd & Others v Fili Shipping Co Ltd & Others* [2007] UKHL 40, *per* Lord Hope at [34]. *Albon v Naza Motor Trading SDN BHD (No.3)* [2007] EWHC 665.

[128] *A v B* [2006] EWHC 2006 at [107].

[128a] *Premium Nafta Products Ltd & Others v Fili Shipping Co Ltd & Others* [2007] UKHL 40 at [18].

[129] *A v B* [2006] EWHC 2006 at [109]; *Etri Fans Ltd v NMB (UK) Ltd* [1987] 1 W.L.R. 1110; *Al Naimi v Islamic Press Agency* [2000] 1 Lloyd's Rep. 522.

[130] *Fiona Trust and Others v Yuri Privalov and Others* [2007] EWCA 20 at [23]. Affirmed *Premium Nafta Products Ltd & Others v Fili Shipping Co Ltd & Others* [2007] UKHL 40.

[130a] *Albon v Naza Motor Trading SDN BHD (No.3)* [2007] EWHC 665.

[131] As in *Sun Life Assurance Co of Canada v CX Reinsurance Co Ltd* [2003] EWCA Civ 283, and *Glidepath Holding BV v Thompson* [2005] 1 All E.R. (Comm) 434.

[132] *Stretford v Football Association Ltd* [2006] EWHC 479, where the court concluded that the respondent was bound by an agreement to arbitrate.

should not determine that issue itself but stay the court proceedings and leave the matter to the arbitrator.[133]

Trial of the issue. If the court feels it has no option but to decide the matter   7–032
of jurisdiction itself, it may direct a trial of the issue rather than decide the matter on the basis of witness statements [134] Indeed, it has been suggested that it will be a "rare case" in which it is appropriate for the court to resolve issues of fact on written evidence alone, unless the parties agree.[135] Consideration of whether to order a trial of the issue will depend in many cases on whether its resolution will involve findings of fact which impact upon substantive rights and obligations of the parties which are already in issue, and on whether the trial is likely to encompass a broad area of investigation. If either of these questions is answerable in the affirmative then the appropriate course will likely be for the tribunal to resolve the issue.[136] However, the court may take the view that if the issue turns on a pure question of construction, which does not involve a wide ranging factual enquiry, then it would be both unfair and inefficient to require the applicant to go before the tribunal with his objections. In light of the more recent decisions in *Fiona Trust* and *A v B* the question of construction would have to go specifically to initial invalidity of the arbitration agreement.[137] As noted the presumption should be (and indeed usually is) that the tribunal should be left to determine its own jurisdiction if at all possible subject to the noted qualifications concerning the existence of the agreement to arbitrate and that the issue is within the scope of the arbitration agreement.[138]

Effect of potential section 67 challenge. The possibility of a sub-   7–033
sequent s.67 challenge to an award on jurisdiction should not militate in favour of the court deciding the jurisdictional issues upon a s.9 application being made. If the evidence relevant to the jurisdictional issue is likely to be difficult to contain and is likely to impinge upon matters relevant to the substance of the dispute, the possibility of a subsequent s.67 application is a "risk worth taking", especially as the tribunal will then be in a strong position to resolve the substantive issues

---

[133] See the comments of Waller L.J. in *Ahmed Al-Naimi v Islamic Press Agency* [2000] 1 Lloyd's Rep. 522 at 525, made in the context of the court's inherent jurisdiction but nonetheless providing useful guidance. See also CPR r.62.8(3).
[134] This course was adopted in *Albon v Naza Motor Trading SDN BHD* [2007] EWHC 665, Lightman J.
[135] See the comments of Chadwick L.J. in *Ahmed Al-Naimi v Islamic Press Agency* [2000] 1 Lloyd's Rep. 522.
[136] *Al Naimi v Islamic Press Agency* [2000] 1 Lloyd's Rep. 522, CA.
[137] See for example *Law Debenture Trust Corp Plc v Elektrim Finance BV* [2005] 2 Lloyd's Rep. 755 at 765–766.
[138] The suggestion that arbitrators should not decide jurisdiction in the face of "*root and branch objections to their jurisdiction*", *per* Mann J. in *Law Debenture Trust* is not, we suggest, a valid consideration nor one which finds any support in the Act. The comments of Mann J. on the jurisdictional approach of the court must now be read in the light of the decisions in *Fiona Trust* (including the House of Lords in *Premium Nafta Products*) and *A v B*.

quickly.[139] To some extent there will almost always be the risk on any s.9 application of a subsequent challenge under s.67 of the Act, so if the court paid undue attention to this consideration it would invariably err on the side of deciding jurisdictional issues itself, which as the Court of Appeal and the House of Lords made clear in *Fiona Trust v Yuri Privalov Premium Nafta Products* is the exception and not the rule under the Act.

7–034 **The applicant must be a party to the arbitration agreement.**[140] Before the Arbitration Act 1996 was passed, it was unclear whether a party to the legal proceedings could obtain a stay notwithstanding that he was not a party to the arbitration agreement or a person claiming through or under a party to the arbitration agreement.[141] The terms of s.9 of the Act remove any doubt and make clear that the application to stay must be made by a party to the arbitration agreement.

Where there are several defendants any one of them who is a party to an arbitration agreement with the plaintiff can make the application to have the action stayed. It is not necessary that all the defendants should join in the application. The action will only be stayed under s.9 as against those defendants who are a party to the arbitration agreement, although the other defendants may seek a stay of the action on case management grounds alone.

7–035 **Scope of arbitration clause.** The dispute which arises or has arisen between the parties must fall with the scope of the arbitration clause.[142] Otherwise a stay of the legal proceedings will not be granted under s.9 of the Act, even though a valid arbitration agreement exists between the parties.[143] although a stay may be granted pursuant to the court's inherent jurisdiction.[144] Usually, arbitration agreements are drafted in wide terms but if they are in narrow terms the court will not stay proceedings which appear to be outside the agreement to arbitrate. So where claims for fraudulent misrepresentation were found by the court to be outside the proper scope of an agreement to arbitrate disputes in Abu Dhabi no stay would be granted.[145] When faced with issues relating to the separability of the

---

[139] See for example the comments of Waller L.J. in *Al-Naimi v Islamic Press Agency* [2000] 1 Lloyd's Rep. 522, CA at p.6 of the judgment. For the contrasting and apparently now out-dated view see the comments of Mann J. in *Law Debenture Trust Corp Plc v Elektrim Finance BV* [2005] 2 Lloyd's Rep. 755 at 766.

[140] See paras 3–016 *et seq.* on substituted parties.

[141] In *Roussel-Uclaf v GD Searle & Co Ltd* [1978] 1 Lloyd's Rep. 225, the court got around this difficulty by holding that the first defendant, which was not a party to the arbitration agreement, was claiming "through or under" its parent company to whom a stay was also granted, but that decision is not free from criticism—see *Grupo Torras v Al-Sabah* [1995] 1 Lloyd's Rep. 374.

[142] This proposition was accepted in *Re Vocam Europe Ltd* [1998] B.C.C. 396 at 398, although it failed on the facts of that case. However, it succeeded in *Sonatrach Petroleum Corp v Ferrell International* [2002] 1 All E.R. (Comm) 627.

[143] *T&N Ltd v Royal & Sun Alliance Plc* [2004] Lloyd's Rep. 102, although in this case there was also an issue as to whether one of the defendants was a party to the arbitration agreement (see para.19 of the decision).

[144] This possibility was considered in the *T&N* case, but not pursued. See para.7–055.

[145] *Abu Dhabi Investment Co and Others v H Clarkson & Co Ltd* [2006] EWHC 1252.

arbitration agreement the court will usually first consider the scope of the arbitration agreement before proceeding to consider issues of separability.[146]

Approach of the court. The court has provided guidelines on its approach   7–036
as to what is covered by the arbitration agreement. Old authorities seeking to draw nice distinctions between differently worded clauses, such as "arising out of", "arising under", "arising in connection with" are no longer relevant in the light of the guidelines set out by the Court of Appeal in *Fiona Trust v Yuri Privalov*, where the court said "the time has now come for a line of some sort to be drawn and a fresh start made at any rate for cases arising in an international commercial context". This approach was fully endorsed by the House of Lords, affirming the Court of Appeal's decision.[147]

In *Ashgar and Others v The Legal Services Commission and Another*[148] proceedings were commenced for a variety of causes of action including breach of contract, trespass and conspiracy. The agreement to arbitrate covered "all disputes . . . concerning alleged breaches of the Contract". The court found that resolution of the contractual claims could not sensibly be divorced from resolution of the non-contractual claims and determined that all the causes of action maintained by the claimant should be covered by the stay. The highly unattractive alternative would have been to allow the closely related non-contractual claims to be determined by the court whilst the contractual claims were referred to arbitration. Separate proceedings under regulatory legislation allowing a regulatory body to seek disclosure of documents would also be stayed where there was a pending arbitration during the course of which documents would be disclosed.[149]

Claims against the tribunal. Section 9(1) does not apply however in the   7–037
unusual situation where one of the parties to the arbitration agreement brings claims against the tribunal for a declaration or injunction against the tribunal on the grounds of invalidity of the arbitration agreement or of its appointment. The issue of the appropriateness of a stay in these circumstances will fall to be considered under the court's inherent jurisdiction.[150]

Stays regarding optional clauses. It is now clear that a stay will be   7–038
ordered to protect a unilateral option to arbitrate even where the contract in question also submits disputes to the English Courts, subject to one party's option to arbitrate.[151] A stay will not be ordered in the converse situation, namely where

---

[146] *Fiona Trust v Yuri Privalov and Others* [2007] EWCA 20 at [18]–[19]; affirmed, *Premium Nafta Products Ltd & Others v Fili Shipping Co Ltd & Others* [2007] UKHL 40.
[147] See para.2–074. *Fiona Trust v Yuri Privalov and Others* [2007] EWCA 20 at [17]. Affirmed, *Premium Nafta Products Ltd & Others v Fili Shipping Co Ltd & Others* [2007] UKHL 40. *Birse Construction Ltd v St Davids Ltd* [1999] B.L.R. 194, approved in *Al-Naimi v Islamic Press Agency* [2000] 1 Lloyd's Rep. 522, CA.
[148] [2004] EWHC 1803. See also *Legal Services Commission v Aaronson* [2006] EWHC 1162 at [28].
[149] *Legal Services Commission v Aaronson* [2006] EWHC 1162.
[150] *A v B* [2006] EWHC 2006 at [74].
[151] N.B. *Three Shipping v Harebell Shipping Ltd* [2005] 1 Lloyd's Rep. 509.

there is a broad agreement to arbitrate subject to one party's right to bring proceedings before the English courts and that party wishes to assert its right to litigate. In both of these situations involving optional rights, provided a party wishing to exercise his option has not waived his right to do so, such as by participating in the other proceedings, then the optional rights will be given effect to.[152] Accidents of timing or attempts by one party to jump the gun by starting its preferred set of proceedings first will not dictate the court's approach, so it does not matter for example if a party who wishes to stay court proceedings in favour of arbitration pursuant to an effective option in these terms fails to start arbitration proceedings before the court proceedings.[153]

7–039 **Legal proceedings must have been brought against the applicant in respect of a matter to be referred.** There must be legal proceedings, which is defined in the Act to mean "civil proceedings in the High Court or a County Court in England and Wales and Northern Ireland".[154] Service of a demand for payment of a debt under the Insolvency Act, known as a statutory demand, has been held not to be legal proceedings for the purpose of seeking a stay under s.9 of the Act.[155] By contrast, a winding up petition is a species of legal proceeding but is not brought by way of claim or counterclaim, required by the bracketed words in s.9(1), and hence outwith the scope of the section.[156] Furthermore, a petition by shareholders for relief from unfairly prejudicial conduct under s.459 of the Companies Act 1985 would not be stayed under s.9 because statutory rights of shareholders to petition the courts for relief are inalienable and cannot be diminished or removed by contract.[157] Employment tribunal proceedings are also not caught by s.9, because Pt I of the Arbitration Act 1996 does not apply to proceedings before an employment tribunal.[158]

---

[152] *Law Debenture Trust Corp Plc v Elektrim Finance BV* [2005] 2 Lloyd's Rep. 755.

[153] See the discussion of timing of proceedings in *Law Debenture Trust Corp Plc v Elektrim Finance BV* [2005] 2 Lloyd's Rep. 755, *per* Mann J. at [43]–[47]. The court was keen to avoid endorsing "an unseemly scramble" to be the first to start proceedings ([45]). See also the earlier decision *Whiting v Halverston* [2003] EWCA Civ 403 where the court decided that a party who had exercised his option to arbitrate could not oppose a stay of court proceedings by resiling from his election.

[154] The term is defined in s.82(1) of the Arbitration Act 1996. See also s.2(1) of the Arbitration Act 1996.

[155] *Shalson v DF Keane Ltd* [2003] EWHC 599. The court rejected a submission in this case to the effect that as the statutory demand would lead to bankruptcy proceedings which were legal proceedings within the terms of s.82 of the Arbitration Act 1996 and that a stay could then be granted, the "doomed process" should be "nipped in the bud" by the granting of a stay at the statutory demand stage, *per* Blackburne J. at [18]–[21].

[156] *Best Beat Ltd v Rossall* [2006] EWHC 1494 at [15]. The judge's findings on this point are *obiter*.

[157] *Exeter City AFC Ltd v Football Conference Ltd* [2004] 1 W.L.R. 2910.

[158] Section 6(2) of the Employment Tribunal Act 1996 and Arbitration Act 1996, Sch.3, para.62. Section 8 of the Employment Rights (Dispute Resolution) Act 1998 limits the circumstances in which a pre-existing agreement to arbitrate is effective to prevent the bringing of a claim under certain employment legislation (such as the Sex Discrimination Act, Race Relations Act, Disability Discrimination Act or the Employment Act). It applies in relation to arbitration agreements entered into after August 1, 1998.

Stay of part only of legal proceedings. An application may be made   7–040
to stay some part of legal proceedings, even where other parts are not subject to
an agreement to arbitrate. The legal proceedings will continue in respect of those
other parts. This may occur, for example, where the claims are made in contract
and in tort and the scope of the arbitration agreement is confined to contractual
claims. The applicant for a stay will have to show that the legal proceedings have
been brought against him (as opposed to any other party) and that they deal with
a dispute which falls within the terms of the arbitration agreement. If they do not,
because, for example, the dispute arises not out of the contract containing the
arbitration clause, but out of another contract which has no such clause,[159] the
court will have no jurisdiction to grant a stay under s.9 of the Act.

Arbitration need not have started. There is no requirement that the   7–041
reference to arbitration must have been started. This is clear from the words in
s.9(1), "a matter which under the agreement is to be referred to arbitration".[160]
Despite this, on occasion the courts apparently have placed some weight on the
fact that arbitration has not been and indeed might never be started.[161] Indeed,
the fact that the dispute cannot immediately be referred to arbitration, because the
exhaustion of other dispute resolution procedures is first required,[162] will not
prevent the court from ordering a stay.[163] For example, in a situation where a
disputes procedure required a process of internal review, followed by mediation
which in turn was followed by arbitration if necessary, it did not matter that the
initial processes of review had not been undertaken at the time proceedings were
commenced such that there was no arbitration underway at the time the legal
proceedings were commenced nor at the time of the application for a stay. There
was a clear agreement within the terms of s.6 of the Act to submit future disputes
to arbitration and hence a stay would be granted to protect the ultimate agreement
to arbitrate.[164]

There must have been an acknowledgement of service in the   7–042
legal proceedings. Section 9 of the Act refers to the procedure for acknowledgement of service of the claim form or other process which initiated the
proceedings in court. The application for a stay cannot be made until service of the

---

[159] This possibility was considered in *Al-Naimi v Islamic Press Agency, ibid.*, although in that case the
court proceedings were stayed because the court found that the dispute fell within the scope of the
arbitration clause.
[160] *Enco Civil Engineering Ltd v Zeus International Development Ltd* [1991] 56 B.L.R. 43 approved by
the Court of Appeal in *Channel Tunnel Group Ltd v Balfour Beatty Construction Ltd* [1992] Q.B 656
and subsequently affirmed by the House of Lords [1993] A.C. 334.
[161] *Shalson v DF Keane Ltd* [2003] EWHC 599 at [18]–[19].
[162] As is common, for example, in construction contracts where there is a reference in the first instance
to adjudication and only after that decision, or the failure to make a decision within a specified time
period, is the dispute referred to arbitration.
[163] Arbitration Act 1996, s.9(2) which followed the decision in *Channel Tunnel Group Ltd and Others v
Balfour Beatty Construction Ltd and Others* [1993] 1 Lloyd's Rep. 291, HL.
[164] *Ashgar and Others v The Legal Services Commission and Another* [2004] EWHC 1803.

originating process has been acknowledged by the applicant.[165] Where the court is asked to grant leave to serve proceedings out of the jurisdiction, and evidence is submitted that the dispute in question is governed by an agreement to arbitrate and the parties to be served would be likely to apply for a s.9 stay, no leave to serve out should be granted. To do otherwise would be an exercise in futility.[166]

7-043 **The party making the application must not have taken any step in the proceedings to answer the substantive claim.**[167] By serving a defence or taking other steps in the proceedings that answer the substantive claim[168] a party submits to the jurisdiction of the court in respect of the claim and will not thereafter be able to obtain a stay requiring the other party to pursue his claim, if at all, by arbitration. In other words, by accepting the court's jurisdiction to hear the substantive case he is treated as electing to have the matter dealt with by the court rather than insisting on his contractual right to arbitrate. The same applies to a counterclaim, and a party seeking to stay a counterclaim must not have taken any step in connection with the proceedings by way of counterclaim.[169] When an amendment is introduced into existing proceedings and a stay is then sought, the defendant not having objected to the original proceedings, the question for the court is whether the matters introduced by the amendment were part and parcel of the dispute of which the court was already seised, or whether they were discrete matters in respect of which s.9 entitles the defendant to insist that they are arbitrated.[170]

The requirement is not to take "any step" in the proceedings. It is a lower test than that for proceedings under s.72 which is only available to a party "who takes no part in the proceedings".[171] A step in the proceedings must, however, be one which "impliedly affirms the correctness of the legal proceedings and the willingness of the defendant to go along with a determination by the courts instead of arbitration".[172] First, the conduct of the applicant (and defendant to the legal proceedings) must be such as to demonstrate an election to abandon his right to a stay in favour of allowing the action to proceed. Second, the act in question must have the effect of invoking the jurisdiction of the court.[173] Further, an act which would otherwise be regarded as a step in the proceedings will not be treated as

---

[165] Arbitration Act 1996, s.9(3). For acknowledgment of service, see CPR Pt 10.
[166] *A&B v C&D* [1982] 1 Lloyd's Rep. 166, at 171, 172, a decision under s.1 of the Arbitration Act 1975.
[167] Arbitration Act 1996, s.9(3).
[168] Certain assertions in an answer to American proceedings were not considered to be a step in the proceedings: *Thyssen v Calypso* [2000] 2 Lloyd's Rep. 243 at 247. Similar considerations may apply where there is no provision in a foreign court's procedure for doing anything other than filing a defence.
[169] *Chappell v North* [1891] 2 Q.B. 252; *Radio Publicity (Universal) Ltd v Cie Luxembourgeoise de Radiodifusion* [1936] 2 All E.R. 721.
[170] *Ahad and Another v Uddin* [2005] EWCA 883.
[171] See para.8–053. See also *Law Debenture Trust v Elektrim Finance BV* [2005] EWHC 1412.
[172] *Eagle Star v Yuval* [1978] 1 Lloyd's Rep. 357, *per* Denning M.R. at 361, which was followed in *Kuwait Airways v Iraq Airways* [1994] 1 Lloyd's Rep. 276.
[173] These two propositions of Mustill & Boyd were adopted with approval in *Patel v Patel* [1999] 1 All E.R. (Comm.) 923 at 925.

such if the applicant has specifically stated that he intends to seek a stay.[174] Thus, a party who applied for leave to defend as well as asking for a default judgment to be set aside did not take a step in the proceedings,[175] nor did someone who applied for summary judgment "in the event that its application for a stay was unsuccessful".[176] An action taken to resist an interim injunction would also not be a step in the proceedings,[177] nor would the making of an application for interim relief to the court (provided the purpose of the application related to the arbitral proceedings[178]), whereas applying for disclosure[179] of documents or asking for an order for particulars of the substantive claim will constitute a step in the proceeding. Unsurprisingly, an application for a stay is not itself a submission to the jurisdiction of the court.[180]

Making the application to stay. In order to apply to stay legal proceedings commenced in breach of an arbitration agreement, the defendant must first acknowledge service of the claim form.[181] Then, without taking a further step in the proceedings to answer the substantive claim, the defendant should promptly make an application to stay those proceedings.[182]   **7–044**

Service of application to stay legal proceedings. An application under s.9 of the Arbitration Act 1996 must be served on the party bringing the relevant legal proceedings and on any other party to those proceedings.[183] Provision is also made in the rules for service on a party who has not given an address for service.[184]   **7–045**

Null and void, inoperative, or incapable of being performed. Where the conditions mentioned in the preceding paragraphs are satisfied the court must make an order under s.9 of the Act staying the proceedings unless either: **7–046**

- The court is satisfied, on the standard of proof set out later in this section, that the arbitration agreement is null and void. This will be the case where the arbitration agreement (as opposed to the matrix agreement) was never

---

[174] *Patel v Patel* [1999] 1 All E.R. (Comm) 923.
[175] *Patel v Patel* [1998] 3 W.L.R. 322, CA.
[176] *Capital Trust v Radio Design* [2002] 2 All E.R. 159, CA.
[177] *Roussel-Uclaf v GD Searle & Co Ltd* [1978] 1 Lloyd's Rep. 225.
[178] *Glidepath BV v Thompson* [2005] 2 Lloyd's Rep. 549.
[179] *Parker, Gaines & Co Ltd v Turpin* [1918] 1 K.B. 358.
[180] *Finnish Marine Insurance Co Ltd v Protective National Insurance Co* [1989] 2 Lloyd's Rep. 99.
[181] See para.7–042 above.
[182] The application is in Form 8 and is made to the court in which the legal proceedings are pending (see Appendix 1). The procedure for arbitration applications generally is described in paras 7–009 *et seq.*
[183] CPR r.62.8(1): see para.8–189.
[184] CPR r.68.2(2). See para.8–189.

entered into[185] or where it was entered into but has subsequently been found to have been void *ab initio*. In *Stretford v Football Association*[186] the Court of Appeal rejected an argument that the agreement to arbitrate was null and void by reason of art.6 of the Convention for the Protection of Human Rights and Fundamental Freedoms.[187] The Court of Appeal found that the right to a public hearing by a tribunal established by law was capable of being waived provided the arbitration agreement was entered into without constraint.

- The court is satisfied, on the standard of proof set out later in this section, that the arbitration agreement is inoperative or incapable of being performed. It will be inoperative where, for example, the arbitration agreement has been repudiated or abandoned[188] or it contains such an inherent contradiction that it cannot be given effect.[189] An arbitration agreement will be incapable of performance where, even if the parties were both ready, willing and able to do so, it could not be performed by them.[190] Poverty of the proposed claimant will not render the arbitration agreement incapable of being performed,[191] nor will inability of the party seeking the stay to satisfy any subsequent award.[192]

The phrase "null and void, inoperative, or incapable of being performed" which appears in s.9(4) of the Act is taken directly from Art.II.3 of the New York Convention.[193] The burden of proving that any of the grounds in s.9(4) of the Act has been made out lies upon the claimant (in the proceedings, i.e. the respondent to the stay application), and, if the defendant/applicant can raise an arguable case in favour of validity, a stay of the proceedings should be granted and the matter left to the arbitrators.[194]

A stay will not be refused on the grounds that a particular right or remedy which might have been granted by the court will not be available in arbitration proceedings.[195]

If a defendant in court proceedings (i.e. the applicant in the stay application) asserts as a defence of set-off a cross-claim under a separate agreement which

---

[185] In *Sunlife Assurance Co of Canada v CX Reinsurance Co Ltd* [2004] Lloyd's Rep. I.R. 58, the Court of Appeal found on the evidence that an arbitration agreement had not been concluded and upheld a dismissal of an application to stay court proceedings.

[186] [2007] Bus. L.R. 1052.

[187] Incorporated into domestic legislation by the Human Rights Act 1998, Sch. 1, Pt 1, art.6.

[188] See para.2–118. and *Elektrim v Vivendi Universal* [2007] EWHC 11 at [123]–[132]. In *Downing v Al Tameer* [2002] EWCA Civ 721 the defendant denied the existence of any contractual relationship, following which the claimant started court proceedings. The Court of Appeal found on the facts that the defendant had repudiated the arbitration agreement and refused the defendant's application to stay the court proceedings. See also *Traube v Perelman* [2001] W.L. 1251816.

[189] See the pathological arbitration clauses referred to in para.2–003.

[190] *Janos Paczy v Haendler & Natermann GmbH* [1981] 1 Lloyd's Rep. 302, CA.

[191] *ibid.*

[192] An argument to the contrary was rejected by Sheen J. and not pursued in the Court of Appeal in *The "Tuyuti"* [1984] Q.B. 838 at 842–843.

[193] For the New York Convention and its ratification by the UK see paras 8–021 *et seq.*

[194] *Hume v AA Mutual International Insurance* [1996] L.R.C.R. 19; *Downing v Al Tameer* [2002] EWCA Civ 721; *Albon v Naza Motor Trading SDN BHD (No.3)* [2007] EWHC 665 at [23].

[195] *Société Commerciale de Réassurance v Eras (International) Ltd and Others* [1992] 1 Lloyd's Rep. 570, CA.

refers disputes to arbitration, then the defendant's application for a stay of the court proceedings can only be resisted if the claim which is to be arbitrated operates in total or partial extinction or defeasance of the claim being advanced by the claimant. If it does not, then a stay will be granted.[196]

Existence of a dispute.[197] Before the Arbitration Act 1996 was enacted a   7–047
stay of legal proceedings, even in the case of a non-domestic arbitration agreement, would not be granted if the court was satisfied that there was in fact no substantive dispute between the parties with regard to the matter agreed to be referred. This situation arose out of a controversial provision in a previous Arbitration Act,[198] which has been repealed and gave rise to a body of cases in which the alleged absence of a defence to a claim was said to mean there was in fact no dispute between the parties. As a result of the repeal the court may no longer refuse to grant a stay where, for example, there is no arguable defence to the claim. The previous case law on the subject can be disregarded. Once the court is satisfied that there is a dispute, it is obliged under s.9 of the Arbitration Act 1996 to grant the defendant a stay of the legal proceedings unless the arbitration agreement is null and void, inoperative or incapable of being performed. For the purposes of s.9, the word "dispute" is to be given its ordinary meaning and includes any claim which the other party refused to admit or did not pay, whether or not there is any answer to the claim in fact or in law.

Third parties involved. There is no longer any scope for the court refusing   7–048
a stay of proceedings on the ground that third parties are involved and that it would be preferable for the dispute to be dealt with in one forum to avoid the possibility of inconsistent decisions.[199] In *Abu Dhabi Investment Co v H Clarkson*[200] legal proceedings would have continued against other defendants not party to the agreement to arbitrate even if the court had granted a stay of proceedings in relation to certain defendants. This factor could not be taken into account by the court when deciding whether or not a stay should be granted. Further, the court will uphold the right to a stay notwithstanding the fact that a claim against a third party is not within the reference to arbitration.[201]

On the other hand, the court does have an inherent jurisdiction to stay court proceedings brought in England against a third party by a claimant involved in arbitration proceedings with another party, even if the arbitration proceedings are

---

[196] *Prekons Insaat Sanyi As v Rowlands Castle Contracting Group* [2007] 1 Lloyd's Rep. 98.
[197] See further para.5–003, existence of a dispute.
[198] Arbitration Act 1975, s.1(1), replaced by the Arbitration Act 1996, s.9(4).
[199] See *Bulk Oil (Zug) AG v Trans Asiatic Oil Ltd* [1973] 1 Lloyd's Rep. 129 and the authorities reviewed in that decision, including *Taunton Collins v Cromie* [1964] I W.L.R. 633. See also *Coltman Precase Concrete Ltd v W & J Simons (Contractors) Ltd* (1993) 35 Con. L.R. 127; *John Rew and Others v Malcolm John Cox and Others, The Times*, November 29, 1995 and also *Berkshire Senior Citizens Housing Association v McCarthy E Fitt and National Westminster* 15 B.L.R. 27.
[200] [2006] EWHC 1252 at [28]. On the facts of that case no stay was granted and so the prospect of further fragmentation of proceedings did not arise.
[201] *Wealands v CLC Contractors* [1999] 2 Lloyd's Rep. 739, CA, when it was argued that the arbitrator could not award the contribution claimed—see para.6–125.

being conducted abroad.[202] Such a stay will only be granted in exceptional and compelling circumstances and will not be allowed to stifle the claim indefinitely.

7–049 **Poverty of defendant.** Poverty is not itself a ground for refusing to grant a stay,[203] although, if the poverty is caused by a breach of the contract on the part of the defendant, that may alter the position.[204] When deciding whether to grant a stay, the court may not take into account the fact that the claimant would be unable to receive legal aid for arbitration proceedings.[205]

7–050 **The imposition of conditions.** In *John Mowlem & Co Plc v Carlton Gate Development Co Ltd*,[206] the judge indicated that he would exercise his discretion to grant a stay only subject to the condition that the arbitrator should be legally qualified and have knowledge of the building industry. As the court does not have a discretion under s.9 of the Arbitration Act 1996, this approach would not now be followed unless perhaps the stay is being granted pursuant to the court's inherent jurisdiction.[207]

7–051 **Adjudicator's decision.** An application to stay court proceedings pursuant to s.9 of the Act will not prevent the court enforcing a decision of an adjudicator,[208] even though arbitration is the contractually agreed method of dispute resolution. "Ultimately, a dispute may be determined by arbitration, but that does not prevent enforcement of the temporary decision of an adjudicator".[209]

7–052 **Refusal to stay.** Where the court refuses to stay legal proceedings the dispute will be determined in those proceedings and not by arbitration. Any term in the arbitration agreement making an award a condition precedent to the bringing of legal proceedings[210] will have no effect in respect of those proceedings.[211]

---

[202] *Reichold Norway v Goldman Sachs Intl* [2000] 1 W.L.R. 173. In this case, it was argued that the primary claim lay against the defendant to the arbitration and that there was no sensible reason for the claimant to pursue the English action against the third party. Distinguished in *Mabey & Johnson Ltd v Laszlo Danos and Others* [2007] EWHC 1094. See also para.7–055 below.

[203] *Edwin Jones v Thyssen (GB) Ltd* [1991] 57 B.L.R. 116; *Smith v Pearl Assurance* [1939] 1 All E.R. 95.

[204] *Fakes v Taylor Woodrow Construction Ltd* [1973] Q.B. 436; *Chrisphine Othieno v Cooper and Cooper* [1991] 57 B.L.R. 128; *Goodman v Winchester & Alton Railway Plc* [1985] 1 W.L.R. 141; *Andrews (Trustees) v Brock Builders Ltd* [1997] 3 W.L.R. 124. These decisions were made before the Arbitration Act 1996 and it is doubtful if they would be followed.

[205] *Edwin Jones v Thyssen (GB) Ltd* [1991] 57 B.L.R. 116, followed in *Al-Naimi v Islamic Press Agency* [2000] 1 Lloyd's Rep. 522, overruling *Fakes v Taylor Woodrow Construction Ltd* [1973] Q.B. 436 on this point.

[206] [1979] 51 B.L.R. 104, CA.

[207] Paragraph 7–055 below.

[208] Adjudication is dealt with at paras 2–032 *et seq.*

[209] *Comsite Projets Ltd v Andritz AG* [2003] EWHC 958.

[210] This condition precedent in an arbitration agreement is known as a *Scott v Avery* clause: see para.2–016.

[211] Arbitration Act 1996, s.9(5).

Appeal. An appeal to the Court of Appeal lies against the court's grant or   7–053
refusal of a stay of legal proceedings.[212] As the judge's decision is interlocutory,
leave to appeal to the Court of Appeal is required.[213]

Interpleader proceedings. Where someone does not dispute a claim but   7–054
does not know who to pay because of competing claims, he may seek relief from
the court by way of interpleader.[214] If the court grants that relief and the issue
between the claimants falls within the scope of an arbitration agreement to which
they are parties, the court will refer the issue to arbitration and stay the legal
proceedings unless the circumstances are such that legal proceedings brought by
the claimants would not be stayed.[215] If the court does not grant a stay, any
condition precedent about obtaining an award before bringing legal proceedings
will not affect the determination of the issue by the court.[216]

It is apparent from the terms of s.10(1) of the Arbitration Act 1996 that in
determining an application for a stay under this section the court will apply the
relevant conditions discussed above[217] in respect of s.9 of the Arbitration Act
1996.[218]

Both ss.9 and 10 apply even if the seat of the arbitration is abroad or no seat has
been designated or determined.[219]

Stay under the court's inherent jurisdiction. The court also has an   7–055
inherent jurisdiction to stay proceedings brought in breach of an agreement to
decide disputes by arbitration.[220] It is rarely necessary to invoke this power in view
of the statutory jurisdiction. However, the tool is a useful one as it allows the court
to stay proceedings where the strict requirements of s.9 cannot be met.[221] The
inherent jurisdiction may be appropriate though where:

   1. The court cannot be certain that an arbitration agreement exists as is
      required for a stay under s.9 but there is an issue whether the parties

---

[212] *Inco Europe Ltd v First Choice Distribution* [2000] 1 W.L.R. 586, HL.

[213] *Inco, ibid.* at 588. See CPR Arbitration PD 20 for application for permission to appeal.

[214] See generally RSC Ord.17 in Sch.1 to CPR.

[215] Arbitration Act 1996, s.10(1).

[216] Arbitration Act 1996, s.10(2).

[217] Paragraphs 7–026 *et seq.*

[218] *Bakwin Eire International Trading Co Inc v Sothebys*, QBD, Master Rose, November 22, 2005.

[219] Arbitration Act 1996, s.2(2).

[220] *Channel Tunnel Group Ltd v Balfour Beatty Construction Ltd* [1993] 1 Lloyd's Rep. 291, HL;
Al-Naimi v Islamic Press [2000] 1 Lloyd's Rep. 522, *per* Waller L.J. at 525; *Legal Services Commission
v Aaronson* [2006] EWHC 1162 at [36]–[37].

[221] *A v B* [2006] EWHC 2006, which exemplifies a broader approach to the use of the jurisdiction.
Contrast the more restrictive comments of Lightman J. in *Albon v Naza Motor Trading SDN BHD*
[2007] EWHC 665. at [24], " . . . the court should only exercise its inherent jurisdiction to order
such a stay and decline to decide the issue of the conclusion of the arbitration agreement or of the
scope of the arbitration agreement in an exceptional case. The inherent jurisdiction should be
exercised with particular caution where the issue is as to the conclusion of the arbitration agreement".

entered into a binding agreement to arbitrate or whether the subject matter of the action is within the scope of the arbitration.[222] The court will however usually need to be virtually certain that there was an agreement to arbitrate before exercising its discretion under the inherent jurisdiction.[223]

2. It is alleged that the arbitration agreement itself (rather than the matrix agreement) was induced by a misrepresentation, whether fraudulent or otherwise.[224]

3. Related claims extending beyond the parties to an arbitration but involving parties closely connected to those parties are brought and it would be wasteful of costs and risk conflicting outcomes to allow the closely related legal proceedings to proceed in tandem with the arbitration.[225] It is not enough however that the claims involving third parties not party to the agreement to arbitrate raise similar issues to those being arbitrated separately.[226] It is possible that a stay on this basis may be granted in cases involving the alleged application of the so-called group of companies theory, where for example one company in the group has signed a contract containing an arbitration clause and another group company has performed the contract and legal proceedings are brought against the latter company. In light of the decision in *Peterson Farms*[227] the granting of a stay would be based on the desire to avoid conflicting outcomes and to save costs rather than to provide support for the group of companies theory.

4. For some other reason the application falls short of the requirements for a stay under the Arbitration Act 1996.[228]

A stay under the inherent jurisdiction would not be granted if doing so would result in claims being determined in two separate fora.[229] This is in contrast to the position under s.9 where the court has no discretion to take such factors into account.

[222] *A v B* [2006] EWHC 2006, [107]; *Etri Fans Ltd v NMB (UK) Ltd* [1987] 1 W.L.R. 1110 at 1114; *Al Naimi v Islamic Press Agency* [2000] 1 Lloyd's Rep. 522 at 525.

[223] *El Nasharty v J Sainsbury Plc* [2004] 1 Lloyd's Rep. 309 at [28]–[31], applying (albeit with some reservation) the test laid down by Waller L.J. in *Al-Naimi*. In *Albon v Naza Motor Trading SDN BHD* [2007] EWHC 665, Lightman J., at paras 24–26, the court was not certain that an agreement to arbitrate existed.

[224] *A v B* [2006] EWHC 2006 at [109], [123].

[225] *A v B* [2006] EWHC 2006 at [127]–[128] where claims against the arbitrator falling outside the reference were stayed pending determination of the substantive claims in the arbitration. *Et Plus SA v Welter* [2006] 1 Lloyd's Rep. 251 at [91].

[226] See *Abu Dhabi Investment Co v H Clarkson* [2006] EWHC 1252 at [28]. The possible exercise of a stay under the inherent jurisdiction did not arise in this case but it is clear that one would not have been granted in any event.

[227] *Peterson Farms v C & M Farming Ltd & Another* [2004] 1 Lloyd's Rep. 614.

[228] For example because it was an oral agreement to arbitrate: see paras 7–027 and 2–015.

[229] *Exeter City AFC Ltd v Football Conference Ltd* [2004] 1 W.L.R. 2910.

3. INJUNCTIONS TO RESTRAIN ARBITRATIONS

Introduction. Even before the Arbitration Act 1996, the English court had   7–056
already expressed a reluctance to interfere in the conduct of arbitration proceedings, which they accepted should be left as far as possible to the arbitral tribunal.[230] The court had no general supervisory power over the conduct of
arbitrations beyond those powers conferred by the Arbitration Acts then in
force.[231] Thus, the tribunal's decisions during the course of a reference were not
reviewable by the court,[232] unless the tribunal exceeded its jurisdiction or it could
be shown that what the tribunal was doing or had done was something manifestly
contrary to natural justice.[233] The appropriate remedy during the course of the
reference was for the court to remove the tribunal.[234] If the award had already been
made, the appropriate application would have been for an order to set it aside on
the grounds of misconduct.[235]

The Arbitration Act 1996 restricted the courts ability to interfere in the arbitral
process yet further. The principle of non-intervention is expressed in s.1(c) of the
Act[236] and that principle is reflected throughout the body of the Act. Thus,
although the court retains wide powers to support the arbitral process (e.g.
appointment of arbitrators where the procedure breaks down) the scope of intervention in other areas has been curtailed. For example, the broad ground for
removing the tribunal during the reference for "misconduct"[237] has been limited
to specific grounds for removal[238] and to a challenge of the award for serious
irregularity, although a great many applications are still brought under this section.[239]

Arbitral proceedings wrongly brought. Before commenting on the   7–057
court's powers exercisable during the arbitration, it is appropriate to mention what
can happen when arbitral proceedings are wrongly brought. This is the reverse of
the situation where a party brings court proceedings in breach of an agreement to

---

[230] See the different views expressed in *K/S A/S Bill Biakh v Hyundai Corp* [1988] 1 Lloyd's Rep. 187;
Three Valleys Water Committee v Binnie & Partners [1990] 52 B.L.R. 42 and *Fletamentos Maritimos
SA v Effjohn International* [1997] 2 Lloyd's Rep. 302.
[231] The Arbitration Acts 1950 to 1979 which have now been largely replaced by the Arbitration Act
1996 but on this point see Lord Diplock in *Bremer Vulkan Schiffbau und Maschinenfabrik v South
India Shipping Corp* [1981] A.C. 909 at 979; [1981] 1 All E.R. 289 at 296.
[232] *Ulysses Compania Naviera SA v Huntingdon Petroleum Services Ltd and Others (The "Ermoupolis")*
[1990] 1 Lloyd's Rep. 160.
[233] *French Government v "Tsurushima Maru"* (1921) 7 Lloyd's Rep. 244.
[234] *Kirkawa Corp v Gatoil Overseas Inc (The "Peter Kirk") (No.2)* [1990] 1 Lloyd's Rep. 158; *Damond
Lock Grabowski v Laing Investments (Bracknell) Ltd* [1992] 60 B.L.R. 112.
[235] *K/S A/S Bill Biakh v Hyundai Corp* [1988] 1 Lloyd's Rep. 187; *Kirkawa Corp v Gatoil Overseas
Inc. (The "Peter Kirk") (No.2)* [1990] 1 Lloyd's Rep. 158. In neither case had an award been made
but both decisions indicated that this was the appropriate remedy.
[236] See further paras 7–001 *et seq.*
[237] Arbitration Act 1950, s.23(2) contained provision for removing an arbitrator for misconduct. This
provision has been repealed by the Arbitration Act 1996, see para.7–126.
[238] Arbitration Act 1996, s.24.
[239] Arbitration Act 1996, s.68, see paras 8–072 *et seq.*

arbitrate.[240] It occurs where arbitral proceedings are commenced against a party who maintains that he is not bound by an arbitration agreement or that the issues referred do not fall within the scope of the arbitration agreement entered into by him, i.e. that the tribunal lacks jurisdiction and that the arbitral proceedings have been wrongly brought. The courses of action that are open to a party in these circumstances are discussed in the context of disputes as to the jurisdiction of the tribunal.[241]

Whatever action is taken, the party concerned should act promptly in order not to lose his right to object to the tribunal exercising jurisdiction over him.

7–058 **Injunctions to restrain arbitral proceedings.** Injunctions to restrain arbitrations are, at least in England, few and far between and becoming fewer still over time. This is principally because of the acceptance of the principle that the arbitrator should usually determine his own jurisdiction and so to restrain an arbitration by way of injunction would be inconsistent with the scheme of the Arbitration Act 1996.[242] However, there are exceptional circumstances where an injunction to restrain an arbitration may be obtained. Such an injunction is different in nature from an injunction granted in support of arbitral proceedings,[243] but it is convenient to mention this type of injunction at this stage. Subject to the extreme limitations on the exercise of the court's discretion set out below,[244–245] the possibility of obtaining an injunction to restrain the continuation of arbitral proceedings can arise in the following cases:

Case 1: where one party commences an action before the court and successfully opposes a stay (whether under s.9 or the court's inherent jurisdiction) on the ground that the arbitration agreement is invalid and the arbitral proceedings based on the invalid agreement continue in defiance of the court's findings. This case is also likely to cover situations where the court has decided that it, rather than the arbitrators, must decide an issue as to the jurisdiction of the arbitrators upon a s.9 stay application having been made and where there is a risk that the arbitrators might proceed to consider the same jurisdictional issue pending the court's decision[246];

---

[240] Paragraph 7–010.
[241] Paragraphs 5–060 *et seq.*, 7–143 *et seq.* and 8–054 *et seq.*
[242] *Elektrim SA v Vivendi Universal SA and Others* (2007) 2 Lloyd's Rep. 8.
[243] Injunctions in support of arbitral proceedings are discussed in paras 7–011 and 7–195.
[244–245] Paragraph 7–059 below.
[246] See however *Albon (t/a NA Carriage Co) v Naza Motor Trading SDN BHD & Anor (No.4)* [2007] EWHC 1879 (Ch), where an anti suit injunction was granted to restrain court and arbitration proceedings in Malaysia. Because of the special circumstances of that case, namely a jurisdictional issue pending before the court, it is suggested that the decision is not supportive of any wider application of an anti-arbitral injunction jurisdiction. The decision of the court not to allow the arbitrators to continue and consider other aspects of the dispute pending the court's decision on jurisdiction is, it is suggested, questionable. *Per* Lightman J. at [28], [29].

Case 2: where a party does not wish to take part in the arbitral proceedings but disputes the substantive jurisdiction[247] of the tribunal and wants to prevent that tribunal determining claims against him. It is virtually impossible to obtain an injunction on this basis absent truly exceptional circumstances; and

Case 3: where all parties to an arbitration agreement apply to the court under s.32 of the Arbitration Act 1996 and despite their request for a suspension of the arbitral proceedings the tribunal proceeds with a view to making an award.

As in the case of all applications for an injunction, delay is a powerful factor against granting the relief. If a party has taken part in an arbitration for some time before seeking an injunction to restrain the arbitration, the act of taking part will almost certainly be fatal to the grant of an injunction.[248]

Exercise of the court's discretion. The court does retain a general 7–059 statutory jurisdiction to grant an injunction under s.37 of the Supreme Court Act 1981, although the extent of the applicability of this jurisdiction to arbitration proceedings has been doubted and has been the subject of some judicial debate.[249] The court will exercise its discretion to grant an injunction restraining the further conduct of an arbitration only in rare cases. The statutory scheme for dealing with questions relating to arbitral jurisdiction is set out in ss.30–32, 67, 70(2), 72 and 73 of the Arbitration Act 1996. As noted, the primary forum in which disputes as to jurisdiction should be decided is before the arbitration tribunal. Court interventions should usually be limited to the statutory scheme; "It is impossible to say that the 1996 Act includes features which provide some kind of analogy for the granting of an anti-arbitration injunction or the arrest of arbitration proceedings in circumstances similar to those arising in this case."[250] Even where the court is prepared to consider the exercise of its discretion under s.37 of the Supreme Court Act 1981, it will exercise that discretion extremely sparingly. In *Elektrim SA v Vivendi Universal SA and Others*,[251] the court found that even if the applicant could establish that one of its legal or equitable rights had been infringed or that the continuation of the arbitration was vexatious, oppressive or unconscionable,

---

[247] "Substantive jurisdiction" is defined in s.30(1) of the Arbitration Act 1996 and extends to not only the validity of the arbitration agreement, but also whether the tribunal has been properly constituted and what matters have been submitted to arbitration in accordance with the arbitration agreement.

[248] *Elektrim SA v (1) Vivendi Universal SA and Others* [2007] 2 Lloyd's Rep. 8, [83]–[85]. See also *The "Oranie" and the "Tunisie"* [1966] 1 Lloyd's Rep. 477, CA.

[249] *Cetelem SA v Roust Holdings Ltd* [2005] 1 W.L.R. 3555, at [74]. *Elektrim SA v Vivendi Universal SA and Others* [2007] 2 Lloyd's Rep. 8, [83]–[85]. See also *The "Oranie" and the "Tunisie"* [1966] 1 Lloyd's Rep. 477, CA.

[250] *A v B* [2006] EWHC 2006, [124].

[251] [2007] 2 Lloyd's Rep. 8.

the court would still not grant an injunction to restrain the arbitration as to do so would be inconsistent with the scheme of the 1996 Act.[252]

7–060 **When injunction unavailable.** Restraining injunctions (against an actual or prospective party to an arbitration or an arbitrator) will not be granted at all where:

1. The arbitrator has (or, we suggest, is likely to have) jurisdiction. "If in a case where an arbitrator does have jurisdiction to decide a particular dispute, he is to be restrained from so doing and no stay of court proceedings is to be granted, there is likely to be a potential breach of the United Kingdom's international obligations in relation to commercial arbitrations under the New York Convention of 1957 as enshrined in the 1996 Act."[253]

2. A party has taken part in the arbitration without objecting to jurisdiction and then seeks an injunction restraining the further conduct of the arbitration. This would be incompatible with the statutory scheme contained in ss.70(2), 72 and 73 of the Act.[254] This includes situations where a party has unsuccessfully asked the tribunal to stay the arbitration and then seeks an injunction effectively by way of appeal to the arbitrators' decision.[255]

7–061 **Declaration usually sufficient.** An injunction might be granted in the extreme case where the court has made an order that there is no valid arbitration agreement, such as for example under s.72(1)(a) of the Arbitration Act 1996, and there was some indication that the other party or the tribunal was intending not to comply with the court's declaration. Failing such indications, a declaration alone should be sufficient.[256]

7–062 **Injunction where foreign seat.** The discretion to grant an injunction to restrain an arbitration should be exercised even more sparingly where the seat of

---

[252] For a recent application of this approach, see *J Jarvis & Sons v Blue Circle Dartford Estates* [2007] EWHC 1262, at [39], [40]. The advocates in that case were unable to find any case since the enactment of the Arbitration Act 1996 in which the court had granted an injunction to halt an arbitration. An injunction to restrain a party from pursuing arbitration and court proceedings in Malaysia was however granted in *Albon (t/a NA Carriage Co) v Naza Motor Trading SDN BHD & Anor (No.4)* [2007] EWHC 1879 (Ch).

[253] *Fiona Trust and Others v Yuri Privalov and Others* [2007] EWCA 20 at [31]. Affirmed *Premium Nafta Products Ltd & Others v Fili Shipping Co Ltd & Others* [2007] UKHL 40.

[254] *A v B* [2006] EWHC 2006, at [12].

[255] *Elektrim SA v (1) Vivendi Universal SA (2) Vivendi Telecommunication International SA (3) Elektrim Telekomunikacja SP Zoo (4) Carcom Warszawa SP Zoo* [2007] 2 Lloyd's Rep. 8, paras 83–85. See also *The "Oranie" and the "Tunisie"* [1966] 1 Lloyd's Rep. 477, CA.

[256] A hypothetical situation discussed in *Fiona Trust and Others v Yuri Privalov and Others* [2007] EWCA 20 at [36]. See further para.7–066 below on declaratory relief. See also *Noble Assurance Co and Others v Gerling-Konzen General Insurance Co—UK Branch* [2007] EWHC 253, an anti-suit injunction case where declaratory relief was granted in lieu of an injunction.

the arbitration is outside England and Wales. In *Weissfisch v Julius and Others*,[257] the Court of Appeal considered an application for an interim injunction to restrain an arbitrator from holding a hearing to consider his own jurisdiction. The seat of the arbitration was Switzerland (and the governing law Swiss). The Court of Appeal found that a natural consequence of the express choice of the Swiss seat, upon which the parties had agreed following legal advice, was that questions relating to the agreement to arbitrate would fall to be considered by the Swiss courts. This accords with the principles to be adopted under the New York Convention which in turn are recognised by the 1996 Act. For an English court to restrain an arbitrator under an agreement providing for a foreign seat would infringe those principles save, the court noted, in undefined "exceptional circumstances".[258] Any other conclusion would arguably place at risk the system of international commercial arbitration and would replicate the mistakes of courts in certain jurisdictions who have in the past sought to assume for themselves supervisory jurisdiction over arbitrations with a seat outside of their jurisdiction.[259–260]

Need for legal proceedings. An injunction restraining the further conduct of a reference will almost always be an interim injunction. It is a determination of the validity of the reference and, if the injunction is granted, it will dispose of the arbitral proceedings, leaving the claimant to pursue a remedy in the courts if he so chooses. The court will not usually grant an injunction unless court proceedings have been commenced or an undertaking is given to do so.   7–063

Restraining the making of an award. There is no precedent for an injunction restraining the making of an award when the arbitration has already taken place, but an injunction might issue in these circumstances in an exceptional case.[261] In practice, if the reference has already proceeded to the stage where all that remains to be done is the making of an award, there is likely to have been delay by the applicant, making it inappropriate to grant an injunction. On the other hand, the party concerned may not have been made aware that the reference was taking place and, on discovering this, chooses to seek an injunction rather than   7–064

---

[257] [2006] EWCA 218.
[258] *Weissfisch v Julius and Others* [2006] EWCA 218 at [33]. But see *Albun (t/a NA Carriage Co) v Naza Motor Trading SDN BHD & Another (No.4)* [2007] EWHC 1879.
[259–260] For a notorious example of intervention by the Indian courts in a London-seated arbitration, see *ONGC v Western Co of North America* (1987) All India Rep. S.C. 674. More recently, see *IPOC International Growth Fund Ltd v OAO "CT-Mobile" and Another,* Court of Appeal of Bermuda, Nos 22, 23 of 2006, March 23, 2007. The Court of Appeal of Bermuda upheld the grant of an anti-suit injunction against a respondent incorporated in Bermuda where the seat of the arbitrations in question was Switzerland and Sweden.
[261] *The "Oranie" and the "Tunisie"* [1966] 1 Lloyd's Rep. 477 (CA). An exceptional case might arise, for example, if the arbitration had proceeded in the absence of the applicant and the applicant had learned of it only after the arbitration hearings had been held but before the award was made.

waiting until the award is made and then challenging it[262] or resisting its enforcement.[263] Even in such a case the applicant will have to present cogent reasons why the matter is not one for the tribunal in the first instance.

7–065 **Effect of application on the arbitration.** It is usual for both the other party and the tribunal to be joined as defendants to proceedings seeking such an injunction and, if granted, the injunction will be directed to them both. Once the tribunal becomes aware that there is an application being made to court to restrain the future conduct of the reference, the tribunal should decide whether or not to continue with the arbitral proceedings pending the outcome of the application for the injunction.[264] In arriving at its decision, the tribunal should have regard to its general duty[265] as well as to practical considerations.[266] If they believe that the injunction has been wrongly granted, many arbitrators are likely to take the view that it is their general duty to continue proceedings where at all possible in defiance of an injunction. Paramount amongst the considerations as to whether or not an injunction has been wrongly granted are, it is submitted, whether the injunction is issued by the court at the seat of the arbitration or by a foreign court and whether the court is acting within the confines of modern arbitral legislation or purporting to exercise a more general inherent jurisdiction.

7–066 **Declaratory relief.** In addition or as an alternative to an injunction, the court may grant a declaration that a reference is outside the jurisdiction of the tribunal. However, the scope for granting a declaration has been almost entirely superseded by s.32(2) of the Act,[267] which requires the agreement of all parties or the permission of the tribunal to an application under that section. There is no longer a right to a declaration at common law, at least where the seat of arbitration is in England or Wales,[268] and the court will be extremely reluctant to issue a declaration as to jurisdiction in respect of a foreign arbitration.

4. EXTENSION OF TIME

7–067 **Introduction.** The court may extend time limits under four separate sections of the Arbitration Act 1996. The first relates to any agreed time limit within which

---

[262] The subject of challenging an award is dealt with in Ch.8, as is opposing enforcement of awards.

[263] A party who considers the arbitration proceedings to have been wrongly brought will almost always want to raise the objection at an early stage because if he waits until the enforcement stage and the objection is not upheld, he will have lost the opportunity to contest the dispute on its merits.

[264] Sections 32(4) and 67(2) of the Arbitration Act 1996 give the tribunal discretion to continue with the arbitral proceedings, unless the parties agree otherwise.

[265] The general duty of the tribunal is contained in s.33 of the Arbitration Act 1996 and includes the avoidance of "unnecessary delay".

[266] There may be little point in the arbitral tribunal seeking to compel the parties to incur time and expense in taking further steps in arbitration proceedings which, if the injunction application is successful, will not be pursued.

[267] *ABB v Keppel* [1999] 2 Lloyd's Rep. 24 at 30.

[268] The court's power is now governed by the Arbitration Act 1996, s.32.

an arbitration is to commence.[269] The second concerns any agreed time limit for making an award.[270] The third is a general power to extend and applies to any other time limit agreed by the parties in relation to a matter in the arbitral proceedings or specified in Pt 1 of the Arbitration Act 1996 having effect in default of their agreement.[271] The fourth relates to extending time for making an application or appeal to the court under the Act.[272] Each power will be examined in turn.

(a) Extending time for commencing arbitration proceedings (section 12)

Power to extend time for commencing arbitration proceedings.[273] Where there is an arbitration agreement to refer future disputes to arbitration which imposes a time limit on the commencement of arbitration or other related dispute resolution procedures, the court has power under s.12 of the Arbitration Act 1996[274] to extend that time limit. This provision is mandatory[275] and applies to any step that is required to be taken by the arbitration agreement failing which the claim will be barred after a specified period elapses. The power will only be exercised however if the court is satisfied either that the need for an extension arises out of circumstances outside the reasonable contemplation of the parties when the time limit was agreed, or that one party's conduct makes it unjust to hold the other to the time limit.[276] **7–068**

Circumstances outside the reasonable contemplation of the parties. In order to succeed under this head the applicant must satisfy the court that the need for an extension arises out of circumstances that were "outside the reasonable contemplation of the parties" when the time limit was agreed. He will also have to satisfy the court that it would be "just" to extend the time limit.[277] For this purpose it will not be sufficient to show that the respective bargaining positions of the parties were unequal. Section 12 is not designed to deal with unequal bargaining power or consumer protection.[278] Thus previous case law on "undue or unreasonable hardship" is no longer relevant.[279] The Arbitration Act 1996 is intended to give effect to party autonomy. The court is encouraged to respect the parties' bargain and to recognise the wish of "commercial concerns **7–069**

---

[269] Arbitration Act 1996, s.12, see paras 7–068 *et seq.*
[270] Arbitration Act 1996, s.50, see paras 7–081 *et seq.*
[271] Arbitration Act 1996, s.79, see paras 7–089 *et seq.*
[272] Arbitration Act 1996, s.80(5), see paras 7–092 *et seq.*
[273] See paras 5–003 *et seq.* in relation to the time for commencing arbitration generally.
[274] Section 12 of the Arbitration Act 1996 replaces s.27 of the Arbitration Act 1950.
[275] Section 4 of the Arbitration Act 1996 and Sch.1 to the Act.
[276] Section 12(3) of the Arbitration Act 1996.
[277] Arbitration Act 1996, s.12(3)(a).
[278] DAC report para.71. See by contrast s.91 of the Arbitration Act 1996.
[279] *Cottiship SA v Allanasons Ltd* [1998] 3 All E.R. 714 and *Thyssen v Calypso* [2000] 2 Lloyd's Rep. 248.

(and indeed others) to draw a line beneath transactions at a much earlier stage than ordinary limitation periods would allow."[280] The court will examine the relevant circumstances of each case,[281] but will not interfere with a contractual bargain "unless the circumstances are such that if they had been drawn to the attention of the parties when they agreed the provision, the parties would at the very least have contemplated that the time bar might not apply; it then being for the court finally to rule as to whether justice requires an extension of time to be given."[282] Even where the fact of the relevant circumstances is accepted by the court, such as in *Monella v Pizza Express*[283] where a change in law made time of the essence in certain situations in rent review cases, the change in law must be shown actually to cause the failure of the applicant to give notice of arbitration in time.[284]

7–070   **Ignorance of agreed time limit insufficient.** Ignorance by the applicant of a time limit contained in the arbitration agreement or rules incorporated into it will not suffice. He will need to establish that the provision concerned was not within the reasonable contemplation of the parties when the agreement was concluded. This could occur, for example, where the arbitration agreement incorporates rules of arbitration that were amended after the conclusion of the agreement and the applicant states in the witness statement supporting his application that he was unaware that the amendments had included a specific time limit for commencing the arbitration. Case law has drawn a narrow and fine distinction between a mistake of law as to what suffices to refer a matter to arbitration within the meaning of a clause requiring arbitration to be commenced within a particular time, which may fall with s.12(3)(a), and a mistake of law as to what requires to be referred to arbitration within such a time, which will not.[285] Therefore, where the market has acted for a significant period on a court decision as to the construction of a standard form charterparty which has important time bar implications and if a different construction were subsequently arrived at, such as on appeal, it is likely that the s.12(3)(a) ground might be triggered.[286]

7–071   **Conduct of the other party.** Where the conduct of another party to the arbitration agreement causes or contributes to the need for an extension, the court

---

[280] DAC report para.68, referred to with approval in *Cottiship, ibid.* at 727.

[281] *Cottiship SA v Allansons, ibid.* at 726 and *Vosnoc Ltd v Transglobal Projects* [1998] 1 W.L.R. 101.

[282] *Harbour and General Works v Environmental Agency* [2000] 1 Lloyd's Rep. 65 at 81, where the Court of Appeal refused to extend the time limit by eight days. Applied in *Monella v Pizza Express* [2004] 1 E.G.L.R. 43.

[283] [2004] 1 E.G.L.R. 43.

[284] In that case, the court refused to extend time for service of a notice of arbitration in a rent review case after the Court of Appeal overturned a previous decision which suggested that time was not of the essence in certain standard form clauses of a lease. The decision arguably turns on the fact the Court of Appeal's decision was known for a year before the relevant review date arose, so the applicant's solicitors could have factored it into account when considering the timing of the notice of arbitration: See the comments of Morritt V.C at para.36.

[285] *Vosnoc Ltd v Transglobal Projects* [1998] 1 W.L.R. 101 at 112 and *Grimaldi Co v Sekimyo Line (The "Seki Rolette")* [1998] 3 All E.R. 943. Considered in *Borgship Tankers Inc v Product Transport Corp Ltd (The "Casco")* [2005] 1 Lloyd's Rep. 565 at 572.

[286] *The "Casco", per* Cresswell J., at 572, *obiter.*

may grant relief to the applicant.[287] The court will however require evidence of the conduct complained of and its relevance to the issue (e.g. how the applicant was misled about the time limit).[288] The court will also need to be persuaded that it would be "unjust" to hold the applicant to the original time limit.[289] The word unjust replaced the phrase "undue hardship" that was used in the previous legislation[290] and the applicant has the burden of satisfying the court that there would not only be hardship but that he would suffer real injustice if the time limit were not extended.[291]

The relevant disputes. Section 12 only applies to an agreement to refer future disputes, not to an agreement to refer an existing dispute to arbitration.[292] It does apply however even if the right to arbitrate is unilateral,[293] or if the agreement to refer disputes is conditional or depends upon the exercise of an option to go to arbitration rather than litigate in court. Although the section applies only to an agreement to refer future disputes, the dispute must have arisen before the application can be made.[294]

7–072

The section is limited to time limits imposed by virtue of the parties' contract; it does not give the court jurisdiction to extend statutory limitation periods.[295]

The claims or rights affected. Section 12 applies where the arbitration agreement provides that a claim will be barred[296] or the claimant's right extinguished unless the claimant takes some step within a particular time. That may include a failure to appoint an arbitrator in time, or to give notice to appoint, or to take some other step to commence arbitration proceedings within the time limit specified. The court may extend time where the failure to take the required step within the time limit either bars the claim by extinguishing the right itself or where it bars the remedy i.e. the right to commence arbitration proceedings.[297] It

7–073

---

[287] Arbitration Act 1996, s.12(3)(b).

[288] This was described as the threshold question in *Thyssen v Calypso* [2000] 2 Lloyd's Rep. 243 at 248. See also *Harbour and General Works v Environment Agency* [2000] 1 Lloyd's Rep. 65.

[289] This is also a requirement of s.12(3)(b) of the Arbitration Act 1996: *Thyssen v Calypso, ibid.* at 249.

[290] Section 27 of the Arbitration Act 1950 which has been replaced by s.12 of the Arbitration Act 1996.

[291] Case law based on the phrase "undue hardship" in s.27 of the Arbitration Act 1950 should not be relied upon: see DAC report paras 62 *et seq.*

[292] Arbitration Act 1996, s.12(1). The point was raised on the previous legislation in *Navigazione Alta Italia SpA v Concordia Maritime Chartering AB (The "Stena Pacifica")* [1990] 2 Lloyd's Rep. 234.

[293] *Pittalis v Sherefettin* [1986] 2 All E.R. 227, CA.

[294] Arbitration Act 1996, s.12(2), see also *Richurst Ltd v Pimenta* [1993] 2 All E.R. 559.

[295] Arbitration Act 1996, s.12(5). Note also that s.12(1) of the Arbitration Act 1996 refers to a provision in the arbitration agreement. See also *Kenya Railways v Antares Co Pte Ltd (The "Antares") (Nos 1 and 2)* [1987] 1 Lloyd's Rep. 424, CA, which was based on s.27 of the Arbitration Act 1950, which s.12 of the Arbitration Act 1996 has replaced. The subject of statutory time limits is discussed in para.7–080.

[296] See para.2–022 for this type of arbitration clause.

[297] This is apparent from the terms of s.12(1) of the Arbitration Act 1996. See also *Vosnoc Ltd v Transglobal Projects* [1998] 2 All E.R. 990, as reviewed in *Harbour and General Works v Environment Agency* [2000] 1 Lloyd's Rep. 65, CA. See also para.5–021.

cannot however do so where the time limit goes to the substantive rights of the parties but has no connection with the commencement of arbitration proceedings.[298] In other words, where the time limit provides a defence to the claim without affecting the right to commence arbitration proceedings, relief under s.12 is not available.

7–074 **Taking steps to begin arbitration proceedings or other dispute resolution procedures.** The court will also consider whether or not the act concerned commences, or is part of the process required to commence, arbitration or other dispute resolution procedures or if the step is merely a condition precedent to proceedings. If it is the latter, s.12 will not apply to give the court jurisdiction to extend the time for it to be taken.[299]

After reviewing several earlier authorities on s.27 of the Arbitration Act 1950, which preceded s.12 of the Arbitration Act 1996, the court decided that a landlord's notice to increase rent as a result of which arbitration proceedings could be commenced was not "some other step to commence arbitration proceedings" within the meaning of the section.[300]

7–075 **Exhaustion of other means for obtaining an extension.** The court will not entertain an application if the applicant has not exhausted "any available arbitral process for obtaining an extension of time".[301] Rules of Arbitration sometimes provide for extensions of time,[302] and if those rules are incorporated into the arbitration agreement the applicant should seek an extension in accordance with those rules before applying to the court under s.12.

7–076 **Delay.** The claimant should issue his application under s.12 without delay. Failure to do so is a factor which the court may take into account in the exercise of its discretion whether or not to grant the application.[303]

---

[298] *Babanaft International Co SA v Avant Petroleum Inc (The "Oltenia")* [1982] 1 Lloyd's Rep. 448 (affirmed by the Court of Appeal); *Mariana Islands Steamship Corp v Marimpex Mineraloel-Handelsgesellschaft GmbH & Co KG (The "Medusa")* [1986] 2 Lloyd's Rep. 328. The contrary decision in *McLaughlin & Harvey Plc v P & O Developments Ltd* [1991] 55 B.L.R. 101 was disapproved in *Crown Estate Commissioners v John Mowlen & Co Ltd* [1994] 70 B.L.R., CA. These decisions were based on the previous legislation but the principle still applies.
[299] See *Babanaft International Co SA v Avant Petroleum Inc, (The "Oltenia")* [1982] 1 Lloyd's Rep. 448, affirmed by the Court of Appeal in [1982] 1 W.L.R. 871, a decision based on s.27 of the Arbitration Act 1950 but which is still relevant to s.12 of the Arbitration Act 1996.
[300] *Richurst Ltd v Pimenta* [1993] 2 All E.R. 559. A tenant's counter-notice, even if out of time, requiring the rent increase to be determined by arbitration did however fall within s.27 of the Arbitration Act 1950 which has been replaced by s.12 of the Arbitration Act 1996: see *Pittalis v Sherefettin* [1986] 2 All E.R. 227, CA.
[301] Arbitration Act 1996, s.12(2).
[302] See for example art.4.7 of the LCIA Rules.
[303] Delay was a factor in the decision of the court in *Thyssen v Calypso* [2000] 2 Lloyd's Rep. 243 at 249. See also *Comdel Commodities Ltd v Siporex Trade SA (No.2)* [1990] 2 Lloyd's Rep. 207, a decision based on s.27 of the Arbitration Act 1950.

Making the application. The application is usually for an order extending   7–077
the time for commencing arbitration proceedings,[304] but as an alternative, and if all
parties consent, an application can be made that such an order is not needed.[305]
The alternative application may be made where, for example, there is a dispute
over the claimant's contention that the arbitration proceedings are being or have
been commenced in good time, but the arbitral tribunal is better placed to
investigate facts necessary to determine the dispute and will have to do so if any
party objects to the court doing so.[306] Either application can only be made by a
"party to the arbitration agreement".[307]

Exercise of the court's discretion. Even if the grounds for an extension   7–078
are established, the court has a discretion whether to grant the extension. In the
case of circumstances outside the reasonable contemplation of the parties, the
court will have to be persuaded that it would be just to extend the time.[308] That
means taking account of the position of all the parties. The mere fact that the
applicant's claim may be barred would not necessarily determine the matter if that
would be unfair to another party, for example, because of new commitments
entered into after the time limit had elapsed. The position is different where the
conduct of that party has contributed to the applicant's dilemma.[309] In that event
the court will have to consider the extent to which that conduct misled the
applicant and to what extent the applicant was also at fault.[310]

The order and its terms. If the court exercises its discretion, an order may   7–079
be made extending the relevant time limit "for such period and on such terms"
as the court thinks fit.[311] It is apparent from the terms of s.12(4) of the Act that
the court can make an order even if the time limit has expired or has already been
extended by a previous order of the court.[312] The length of the extension is left to
the court's discretion and will depend on the circumstances of each case.[313] The

---

[304] The procedure for an arbitration application is described in paras 8–178 *et seq.*
[305] The alternative application is not stated specifically in CPR Pt 62, but it was so provided in previous
versions of the rule (e.g. PD 21.1 made under former CPR Pt 49).
[306] *Grimaldi Compagnie v Sekihyo Line* [1998] 3 All E.R. 943.
[307] Arbitration Act 1996, s.12(2).
[308] This is the result of the words used in s.12(3)(a) of the Arbitration Act 1996.
[309] This is apparent from the different wording used in s.12(3)(b) of the Arbitration Act 1996.
[310] *Thyssen v Calypso* [2000] 2 Lloyd's Rep. 248.
[311] Arbitration Act 1996, s.12(4).
[312] See s.12(4) of the Arbitration Act 1996 and *Nea Agrex SA v Baltic Shipping Co Ltd (The "Agios
Lazavos")* [1976] 2 Lloyd's Rep. 47; *Navigazione Alta Italia SpA v Concordia Maritime Chartering
AB (The "Stena Pacifica")* [1990] 2 Lloyd's Rep. 234. These decisions were based on s.27 of the
Arbitration Act 1950, which has been repealed, but they support the general proposition.
[313] In *Phoenix Shipping v General Foods* [1997] 2 Lloyd's Rep. 703 the Court of Appeal upheld an order
that extended a time bar by 23 months, although the judge's decision was described as at the borders
of the latitude to be afforded in cases of this kind (at 709). See also analysis of Court of Appeal in
Irish Agricultural Wholesale v Partnerneedserei (The "Euro Trader") [1987] 1 Lloyd's Rep. 418.

court may also impose terms on the granting of an extension, such as requiring the applicant to appoint an arbitrator within a limited number of days.[314]

7–080 **Limitation Acts.** The Limitation Act 1980 and the Foreign Limitation Periods Act 1984 as well as "any other enactment (whenever passed) relating to the limitation of actions"[315] apply to arbitration proceedings as they apply to other legal proceedings,[316] and an order made to extend the period for commencing an arbitration will not affect the operation of the Limitation Acts.[317]

The Arbitration Act 1996 provides that the parties are free to agree when arbitration proceedings are to be regarded as commenced for the purposes of the Limitation Acts,[318] and makes provision for what is to happen when there is no agreement.[319] Whether arbitration has been commenced within the agreed time can lead to a dispute,[320] and it is important to give timely notice in accordance with the agreement.[321] Where an award has been set aside or declared to be of no effect in whole or in part the court may by order exclude the period from the commencement of the arbitration to the date of the order for the purpose of computing the time prescribed by the Limitation Acts for starting proceedings, including arbitration proceedings.[322] The Arbitration Act 1996 also provides that in determining for the purpose of the Limitation Acts when a cause of action accrued, any provision that an award is a condition precedent to the bringing of legal proceedings in respect of a matter to which an arbitration agreement applies shall be disregarded.[323]

(b) Extending time for making an award (section 50)

7–081 **Power to extend time for making an award.** Subject to anything to the contrary in the arbitration agreement, the tribunal may make an award at any time.[324] However, time limits for the making of the award are sometimes imposed by the arbitration agreement.[325] In that event the court may by order extend the

---

[314] This is apparent from the words of s.12(4) of the Arbitration Act 1996. See also *Patel v Peel Investments (South) Ltd* [1992] 30 E.G. 88. This decision was also based on s.27 of the Arbitration Act 1950, which has been replaced by s.12 of the Arbitration Act 1996, but the judge's observations about conditions still have some relevance.

[315] The words quoted from the definition of "the Limitation Acts" in s.13(4) of the Arbitration Act 1996 are designed to catch any enactment concerning limitation of action made after the Arbitration Act 1996 was enacted.

[316] Arbitration Act 1996, s.13(1).

[317] Arbitration Act 1996, s.12(5). As already mentioned the "Limitation Acts" is a defined term.

[318] Arbitration Act 1996, s.14(1).

[319] Arbitration Act 1996, ss.14(2) to (5) inclusive, see para.5–018.

[320] *West of England v Hellenic* [1999] 1 Lloyd's Rep. 93, and authorities referred to at 107.

[321] Paragraphs 5–006 *et seq.*

[322] Arbitration Act 1996, s.13(2), see para.5–013.

[323] Arbitration Act 1996, s.13(3), see para.5–014 for such provisions, which are referred to as *Scott v Avery* clauses.

[324] Arbitration Act 1996, s.47.

[325] As to the time for the making of an award generally: see paras 6–061 *et seq.*

period, whether or not that time limit has already expired[326] and whether or not the award has already been made,[327] unless the parties agree otherwise.

Excluding court's powers. Unlike s.12, s.50 of the Act is not mandatory.[328]   7–082
The parties can by agreement[329] exclude the court's power to extend a time limit for making an award.

Exhaustion of other means of obtaining an extension. The court   7–083
will not entertain an application under s.50 unless and until any available arbitration process for obtaining an extension of time has been exhausted.[330] If there is an available arbitral process which has been exhausted, it would be "a rare case indeed where the court extended the time notwithstanding that it had not been done through" such an arbitral process.[331]

Substantial injustice. In order to obtain an extension of time for making an   7–084
award, the court must be satisfied that a "substantial injustice would otherwise be done."[332] There is no definition of substantial injustice in s.50 but the courts have sought to derive assistance from discussion of the concept of substantial injustice in s.68 of the Act, citing with approval para.58 of the DAC Report to the effect that substantial injustice only arises "where it can be said that what has happened is so far removed from what could reasonably be expected of the arbitral process that we would expect the court to take action".[333] The intention is that the court should respect the parties' choice of arbitration so it must be satisfied that the consequence of observing the agreed time limit cannot be defended as an "acceptable consequence of that choice".[334] The Court of Appeal has however allowed an extension when the refusal of the judge was "disproportionate" in the circumstances.[335]

---

[326] Arbitration Act 1996, s.50(4).

[327] *Oakland Metal Co Ltd v D Benaim & Co Ltd* [1953] 2 Q.B. 261 at 266, a decision based on s.13(2) of the Arbitration Act 1950, which has been replaced by s.50(4) of the Arbitration Act 1996.

[328] This is apparent from the words "unless otherwise agreed by the parties" in s.50(1) of the Arbitration Act 1996 and the omission of s.50 from Sch.1 to the Arbitration Act 1996.

[329] This exclusion agreement can appear in the arbitration agreement itself or in rules incorporated into the agreement.

[330] Arbitration Act 1996, s.50(2). "Any available arbitral process" has the same meaning in this section as in s.12, of the Act. Such a process may be provided for in arbitration rules incorporated into the arbitration agreement. See para.7–091.

[331] DAC report, para.239.

[332] Arbitration Act 1996, s.50(3).

[333] *Gold Coast v Naval Gijon SA* [2006] All E.R. (D.) 209 at [24]–[28], a case under ss.57 and 79 of the Act. See para.8–104.

[334] DAC report, para.280. The words were applied to s.68(2) of the Arbitration Act 1996 but they seem to be appropriate here too.

[335] *Keith Peters v Dylan Jones*, unreported, May 22, 2000, CA.

7–085   The applicant. Either the tribunal or any party to the arbitral proceedings may apply for the extension.[336] Whoever applies, the tribunal and all other parties must have notice of the application.

7–086   The court's discretion. Subject to what has been said in the previous paragraphs,[337] the court has a complete discretion to extend the time for such period and on such terms as it considers fit.[338] The court may do so whether or not the time previously fixed (by the arbitration agreement or by a previous order) has expired.[339]

7–087   Consequences of an order. If the court makes an order extending the time for making an award under s.50 of the Act, the award and all else done in the arbitration during the extended period is rendered valid and effective.

7–088   Judge-arbitrator. The court's power to extend time for making an award does not apply to a judge-arbitrator or a judge-umpire but they have a similar power to extend time themselves under Sch.2 of the Arbitration Act 1996.[340]

(c) Extending agreed time limits (section 79)

7–089   Power to extend time limits relating to arbitral proceedings. In addition to the powers to extend a time limit for commencing arbitration[341] and for making an award,[342] the court has power to extend other time limits agreed by the parties in respect of the arbitral proceedings or specified in Pt 1 of the Arbitration Act 1996 as having effect "in default of such agreement".[343] This general power for the court to extend time limits relating to arbitration is contained in s.79 of the Arbitration Act 1996. It empowers the court to extend any time limits agreed by the parties in respect of the conduct of the arbitration other than the commencement of arbitration, which is governed by s.12 of that Act. Section 79 also authorises the court to extend any time limits specified in the Arbitration Act 1996 "in default of agreement".[344] The provision does not seem

---

[336] This is apparent from Arbitration Act 1996, s.50(2). The procedure for an arbitration application is described in paras 8–178 *et seq.*

[337] See paras 7–082—7–084 inclusive.

[338] Arbitration Act 1996, s.50(4).

[339] Arbitration Act 1996, s.50(4). See similar provision in s.12, and para.7–079 above.

[340] Paragraph 5(1) of Sch.2: see s.93(6) of the Arbitration Act 1996.

[341] Arbitration Act 1996, s.12: see paras 7–068 *et seq.*

[342] See paras 7–081 *et seq.*

[343] Arbitration Act 1996, s.79. For example, an agreed time limit for submission of a statement of case: see *Equatorial Traders Ltd v Louis Dreyfus Trading Ltd* [2002] 2 Lloyd's Rep. 638 where the extension was refused.

[344] For example, the procedure contained in s.16 of the Arbitration Act 1996 for the appointment of members of the tribunal.

to apply to other time limits imposed by the 1996 Act,[345] and it would not apply to time limits imposed by another statute.

Rules of the court have however been made giving the court a discretion to extend the 28-day time limit for making an application to challenge or appeal against an award.[346]

Excluding court's powers. The provisions of s.79 are not mandatory. The parties can by agreement[347] exclude the court's powers to grant extensions under this section. 7–090

It would seem, however, that the parties may effectively agree that, unless the award is made within a certain time, it shall not be binding or have any effect, thus making time of the essence of the contract.[348]

Exercise of the court's discretion. The court has a wide discretion to extend time under s.79, which may be exercised whether or not the time has already expired, although the later an application is made the less likely it will be to succeed.[349] Further, any order by the court may be made on "such terms as the court thinks fit".[350] There are however restrictions on the exercise of the court's power which are identical to those mentioned in respect of s.50. Thus, the applicant should exhaust any available arbitral process for obtaining an extension of time before applying to the court[351] and he must satisfy the court that a substantial injustice would otherwise be done.[352] Where a party had failed to appoint its party-appointed arbitrator within the time allowed by the agreement to arbitrate resulting in the other party-appointed arbitrator becoming the sole arbitrator, no extension under s.79 for appointment of the second party-appointed arbitrator would be granted as the applicant could not show any substantial injustice likely to result from the appointment of a sole arbitrator.[353] In *Gold Coast v Naval Gijon*[354] the court extended retrospectively the time period under s.57 to allow correction of the award by the arbitrator for clerical mistakes and accidental slips or omissions. In this case, one application under s.57 had already been made 7–091

---

[345] DAC report, para.382 mentions that s.79 does not seem to apply to the 28-day time limit contained, for example, in s.70(3) of the Arbitration Act 1996 concerning an appeal or challenge to an award because it is not one stipulated as having effect in default of the agreement between the parties: see equivocation on this matter in DAC report, paras 294 and 382. This was confirmed in *Kalmneft v Glencore International* [2002] 1 All E.R. 76 at 87—see paras 7–092 and 8–106.

[346] CPR r.62.9 and PD 62, para.11.1 made pursuant to Arbitration Act 1996, s.80(5): see para.8–106.

[347] This is apparent from the words of s.79 and its omission from Sch.1 of the Arbitration Act 1996.

[348] *Randell v Thompson* (1876) 1 Q.B.D. 748 at 758, a decision on a submission agreement.

[349] Arbitration Act 1996, s.79(4). See *Equatorial Traders Ltd*, above.

[350] Arbitration Act 1996, s.79(5).

[351] Arbitration Act 1996, s.79(3)(a): see para.7–083.

[352] Arbitration Act 1996, s.79(3)(b): see para.7–084. See also DAC report, paras 308 and 309.

[353] *Minermet SpA Milan v Luckyfield Shipping Corp SA* [2004] 2 Lloyd's Rep. 348. The applicant had in fact made it clear that it "had no problem" with the identity of the sole arbitrator (para.11). Other submissions as to why a sole arbitrator would lead to a substantial injustice were rejected.

[354] [2006] 2 Lloyd's Rep. 400.

to the arbitrator within time and certain corrections were made. The arbitrator stated that his earlier award of interest had been incorrect and that he would have corrected it had he the power to do so, but the time limit under s.57 had already expired. The court found that there would be a substantial injustice to one of the parties if the arbitrator was not allowed to correct his award as to interest in these circumstances, especially where it was understandable why the error had not come to light earlier.[355] The applicant must explain why he had not taken action earlier, including where relevant why an earlier application under s.79 has not been made; "the section holds no scope for a 'wait and see' approach".[356] Indeed, delay in making an application under s.79 can be fatal to the success of such an application.[357]

(d) Extending statutory time limits (section 80(5))

7–092 **Power to extend time limit for applications and appeals.** Section 80(5) relates to time limits prescribed by Pt 1 of the 1996 Arbitration Act for making an application or appeal to the court and provides that the rules of court relating to the reckoning of periods, the extending or abridging of periods, and the consequences of not taking a step within the period prescribed by the rules apply. The effect of s.80(5) is therefore to introduce the broad discretionary approach as to extending time limits under the CPR[358] to applications or appeals to the court under the Arbitration Act 1996.[359] It has been pointed out that the court's approach to the exercise of its discretion under s.80(5) is different from that under s.79 since s.80(5) contains no threshold requirement of substantial injustice. In this respect, therefore, a lower unfairness threshold is presumed to have been intended in relation to applications under s.80(5).[360] Section 70(3) of the Arbitration Act 1996 imposes a 28-day time limit within which an application or appeal must be brought.[361] The time runs either from the date of the award or, if there has been an arbitral process of appeal or review, the date of notification of the outcome of such process.[362] An application may be made to the court under CPR r.62.9(1) to vary the time limit fixed by s.70(3).[363] The considerations that are likely to be material in such an application are identified in *Kalmneft v Glencore International*, and the procedure is discussed in Ch.8.[364]

---

[355] See also *RC Pillar v Edwards* [2001] W.L. 676628.
[356] *Equatorial Traders v Louis Dreyfus* [2002] Lloyd's Rep. 638 at 642.
[357] *Pirtek (UK) Ltd v Deanswood Ltd.* [2005] 2 Lloyd's Rep. 728. Although there was no s.79 application before the court in that case, the court indicated that it would not have granted one in any event, principally because of the applicant's inexplicable delay in raising the matter: *per* Aikens J. at [44]–[49].
[358] In particular CPR r.3.1.2 and CPR r.62.9.
[359] *Kalmneft v Glencore International* [2002] 1 Lloyd's Rep. 128 at [48].
[360] *Kalmneft v Glencore International* [2002] 1 Lloyd's Rep. 128, cited with approval in *Gold Coast* at [29].
[361] This subject is dealt with fully in Ch.8, but it is mentioned here for completeness.
[362] See, e.g. para.8–063.
[363] CPR r.62.9 was made pursuant to s.80(5) of the Arbitration Act 1996.
[364] See para.8–213.

The applicant. Either the tribunal or any party to the arbitral proceedings   7–093
may apply for the extension. Whoever applies, the tribunal and all other parties
must have notice of the application.[365]

Appeals. Permission of the court is required for any appeal from a decision of   7–094
the court to extend time under ss.12, 50 and 79 of the Act.[366] The court referred
to in the subsections is the court of first instance which decided the matter; so it
used to be the case that if permission of that court is not obtained there can be no
appeal. However, there are now at least two categories of cases where the Court of
Appeal will grant permission to appeal even though the judge at first instance has
refused permission. These are considered at para.7–201 which deals with wording
to the same effect under s.44(7).

In most cases, leave of the judge at first instance will still be required under
ss.12, 50 and 79 as the jurisdiction of the court to extend time is usually
uncontroversial.

5. APPOINTMENT OF AN ARBITRATOR OR UMPIRE[367]

Introduction. The arbitration agreement[368] should specify the number of   7–095
arbitrators (or arbitrators and an umpire) to be appointed and the manner in which
they are to be appointed. Subject to the terms of the arbitration agreement, the
parties should try to agree on the identity of the arbitral tribunal once a dispute
has arisen. If they cannot agree, then the parties or any one of them may request
that the appointment be made by the appointing authority,[369] if any, specified in
the arbitration agreement.[370] Failing this, an application may be made to the court
for the appointment of the arbitral tribunal.

The Arbitration Act 1996 provides not only that the parties are free to agree
upon a procedure to appoint the arbitral tribunal[371] and the consequences if that
procedure fails,[372] but also what is to happen if there is no agreed procedure,[373] or
the agreed procedure fails.[374]

---

[365] Arbitration Act 1996, s.79(2). The procedure for an arbitration application is described in paras
8–178 *et seq.*
[366] Arbitration Act 1996, ss.12(6), 50(5) and 79(6).
[367] See also paras 4–028 *et seq.* on the appointment of arbitrators by the parties.
[368] By "arbitration agreement" we mean to include any arbitration rules that are often incorporated
into the agreement by reference. Certain sets of arbitration rules leave the number of arbitrators to
be determined by the arbitration institution in question. So e.g. art.5.4 of the LCIA Rules provides
that a sole arbitrator will be appointed unless the parties have agreed otherwise, or unless the
Arbitration Court of the LCIA determines that in view of all the circumstances of the case a three-
member tribunal is appropriate. See also Art.8.2 of the ICC Rules.
[369] The term "appointing authority" means the individual or institution designated by the parties to
make the appointment. It may be a named individual or, more commonly, the present holder of a
particular office such as President of the Law Society. Alternatively it may be a particular body such
as the LCIA or a professional association.
[370] See para.4–049.
[371] Arbitration Act 1996, s.16(1).
[372] Arbitration Act 1996, s.18(1).
[373] Arbitration Act 1996, s.16(2)–(7) inclusive.
[374] Arbitration Act 1996, s.18.

To the extent that there is no agreed procedure, s.16 of the Act provides a default procedure for the appointment of a tribunal, depending on the number of arbitrators[375] to be appointed.[376] Nevertheless, the assistance of the court may be required where:

- an agreed procedure or, failing agreement, the statutory default procedure[377] does not result in the appointment of a complete tribunal; and

- the parties cannot agree on what is to happen in the event of a failure of the appointment procedure.[378]

Section 18 of the Act gives the court the necessary powers for this purpose. The powers are wide,[379] but they will not be used where the arbitration agreement provides for a method of appointment (such as appointment by an appointing authority) and that method has not been invoked.[380] Furthermore, the court will, as with many applications under the Arbitration Act 1996, examine on a prima facie basis whether or not an agreement to arbitrate exists. For example, where the agreement refers to a body which provides conciliation, mediation and arbitration services but the clause suggests the parties intended to mediate and not arbitrate, then no appointment will be made.[381]

Occasionally, the arbitration agreement will expressly empower the court to make an appointment[382] or the parties may specifically consent to the appointment being made by the court.[383]

7–096 **Exercise of the court's discretion to appoint a tribunal.** The court's jurisdiction depends on two conditions: First, a failure of the contractual procedure and, second, the absence of agreement between the parties on the steps to be taken as a result. There are "strong grounds for exercising the court's discretion in favour of constituting the tribunal except in the small number of cases in which it can be seen that the arbitral process cannot result in a fair resolution of the dispute".[384] This is important because often a failure to agree on

---

[375] The court may appoint an umpire in an appropriate case; s.18(3) uses the term "appointments", and the term "arbitrator" may include umpire—Arbitration Act 1996, s.82(1).

[376] If there is no agreement as to the number of arbitrators, the tribunal shall consist of a sole arbitrator: Arbitration Act 1996, s.15(3)—see para.4–035.

[377] Arbitration Act 1996, s.16(7) recognises that there may be instances where the statutory procedure will be inadequate to meet the situation (e.g. where there are more than two parties).

[378] Arbitration Act 1996, s.18(1) states that the parties are free to agree what is to happen in the event of a failure of the procedure for the appointment of the tribunal.

[379] See s.18(3) of the Arbitration Act 1996 and paras 7–098 *et seq.*

[380] This seems to be the effect of s.18(1) of the Arbitration Act 1996.

[381] *Flight Training International Inc v International Fire Training Equipment Ltd* [2004] 2 All E.R. (Comm) 568.

[382] *Medov Lines SpA v Traelandsfos A/S* [1969] 2 Lloyd's Rep. 225, Donaldson J. stated (at 227) that, in making the appointment, "the court is acting as an independent authority to whom resort is had by the parties consensually, rather than as a court acting by virtue of its inherent or statutory jurisdiction, but the appointments are nonetheless effective for that".

[383] *Tzortzis and Sykias v Monark Line A/B* [1968] 1 Lloyd's Rep. 337.

[384] *Atlanska Plovidba v Consignaciones Asturianas SA (The "Lapad")* [2004] 2 Lloyd's Rep. 109, *per* Moore-Bick J. at [24].

the identity of a tribunal, whether comprising one or three arbitrators, will arise not because of any concern over the attributes of individual arbitrators but because of more fundamental objections as to the existence or validity of an agreement to arbitrate. The court's discretion is broad and is not limited to a consideration of the factors that would provide grounds for refusing a stay under s.9 of the Arbitration Act 1996.[385] The court should be very slow to be influenced by submissions that arbitration would lead to unnecessary delay and expense or that the arbitration should not be allowed to proceed because proceedings raising the same issues have already been commenced abroad.[386] The concept of what constitutes failure of the contractual appointment procedure is not always entirely clear: an impasse over the appointment of an arbitrator may not satisfy the requirement, for example where it is clear that the parties have not reached an agreement to arbitrate at all and no arbitration proceedings have been commenced.[387] Usually, however, if one party proposes a particular arbitrator and the other party has declined to accept that suggestion (and no other suggestions are forthcoming) a failure within the terms of s.18 will have occurred.[388] The courts are likely to take a practical and non-formalistic approach to determining whether there has been agreement or not.[388a]

No agreement on appointment procedure. If the arbitration agreement does not contain a procedure for the appointment of the tribunal, s.16 of the Arbitration Act 1996 provides a default procedure. The statutory provisions vary according to the number and constitution of the tribunal.[389] The assistance of the court is not required unless the statutory procedure contained in s.16 fails or does not provide for the particular situation.[390] In that event the court can provide a remedy pursuant to s.18 of the Act, and in doing so the court has a discretion whether the dispute should be referred to a sole arbitrator or to a panel of three arbitrators.[391] 7–097

Failure to appoint a sole arbitrator. Where the arbitration agreement or the Arbitration Act 1996[392] provides for the appointment of a sole arbitrator and 7–098

---

[385] See paras 7–024 *et seq.* above.
[386] Atlanska, at [27]–[33], drawing a direct analogy between an agreement to arbitrate and an exclusive jurisdiction clause, the approach to which is laid down by the House of Lords in *Donohue v Armco* [2002] I Lloyd's Rep. 425.
[387] *Glidepath Holding BV v Thompson* [2005] 1 All E.R. (Comm) 434 at [46]–[50].
[388] *City & General (Holborn) Ltd v AYH Plc* [2006] B.L.R. 55, where an order to appoint an arbitrator was made under s.18, although one part of the dispute referred to arbitration was omitted from the reference as it fell outside of the agreement to arbitrate. *Through Transport Mutual Insurance Association (Eurasia) Ltd v New India Assurance Co Ltd (The "Hari Bhum") (No.2)* [2005] 2 Lloyd's Rep. 378.
[388a] See *Grid Corp of Ovissa v AES Corp & Others*, (2002) 7 Supreme Court Cases 736, a decision of the Indian Supreme Court concerning the form of agreement which is required when two arbitrators are required to agree upon a chairman.
[389] See paras 4–025 *et seq.* for a complete description of the provisions for appointment in s.16 of the Arbitration Act 1996.
[390] Arbitration Act 1996, s.16(7) provides that if there are more than two parties s.18 shall apply.
[391] *The "Villa"* [1998] 1 Lloyd's Rep. 195 at 197.
[392] Arbitration Act 1996, s.15(3).

the parties do not all concur in the appointment, the court may appoint an arbitrator pursuant to s.18 of the Act. Before making the application written notice to concur in the appointment should be given to the other party or parties to the dispute. That notice should include or be accompanied by the name of a suggested arbitrator and invite alternative suggestions from the other party, though this is not a statutory requirement. The notice does not need to be in a particular form and the court will be slow to invalidate it simply because the sender may have identified the wrong contractual document or otherwise made other non-material errors in the drafting of the notice.[393] If no agreement can be reached on the appointment within a reasonable time after service of the notice, application may be made to the court. Where the parties have agreed that related disputes shall be referred to the same arbitrator the court can use its power under s.18 to appoint the same arbitrator in all related disputes, provided there has been the requisite failure to appoint in each case.[394] The power to appoint an arbitrator will also be exercised where the failure to appoint results from disagreement not between the original parties to the agreement to arbitrate but between those claiming under or through an agreement to arbitrate.[395]

7–099 **Failure to appoint one of two party-appointed arbitrators.** Where each of two parties is to appoint an arbitrator, and one party makes an appointment but the other fails to do so, then by following the procedure in s.17 of the Arbitration Act 1996, the arbitrator who has been appointed can act as sole arbitrator.[396] If that procedure fails or the appointment is set aside, the court can give directions under s.18 of the Arbitration Act 1996. Section 17 applies even where the arbitration agreement contemplates the appointment of a third arbitrator by some other means such as agreement of the parties or their appointed arbitrators.[397]

An application to set aside an appointment made pursuant to s.17 of the Act may be made upon giving notice to the other party.[398] The application should be made without delay or the right to object may be lost,[399] and should set out the reason why the original appointment was not made. After hearing the application the court has power to set aside the appointment,[400] in which case the parties should then appoint arbitrators in accordance with the arbitration agreement. Whether the court will exercise its power to set aside an appointment will depend

---

[393] *Atlanska Plovidba v Consignaciones Asturianas SA (The "Lapad")* [2004] 2 Lloyd's Rep. 109, *per* Moore-Bick J. at [19].

[394] *City & General (Holborn) Ltd v AYH Plc* [2006] B.L.R. 55.

[395] *Through Transport*, above, involved an assignee of one of the original parties.

[396] The statutory procedure contained in s.17 of the Arbitration Act 1996 for appointing a party appointed arbitrator as the sole arbitrator is described in para.4–037.

[397] See, for example, *Minermet Spa Milan v Luckyfield Shipping Corp SA* [2004] EWHC 729 (Comm); [2004] 2 Lloyd's Rep. 348.

[398] Arbitration Act 1996, s17(3). The procedure for the application is described in paras 8–178 *et seq.*

[399] Arbitration Act 1996, s.73(1)(c).

[400] Arbitration Act 1996, s.17(3).

upon the specific circumstances of each case.[401] It is submitted that the court will be reluctant to remove an arbitrator under s.17(3) where the original failure to appoint is seen as part of an attempt to delay or disrupt the arbitral process. The court also has power to make an appointment where the s.17 procedure fails.[402]

Failure to appoint one of three arbitrators. Where the arbitration 7–100
agreement or the Arbitration Act 1996[403] provides for the appointment of three arbitrators, one to be appointed by each party and the third to be appointed by the two of them or in some other way, the court may appoint one or more of those arbitrators if the procedure for their appointment fails.[404] This situation can arise in one of two ways. First, a party refuses to appoint or fails to appoint in time or within a reasonable time the arbitrator to be appointed by him. In this situation, assuming he chooses not to adopt the procedure in s.17[405] of the Act, the other party should first give notice[406] to the defaulting party to appoint and then apply to the court to appoint the second arbitrator.

The second situation contemplated under this heading occurs when two arbitrators have been appointed (either by the parties or with the help of the court) but the third arbitrator is not appointed in due time. This situation is unusual but it may happen because the two arbitrators cannot agree who to appoint or because the third party nominated to appoint fails or refuses to do so. In that event the court can appoint, although before applying to the court notice should be given to the two arbitrators (and the appointing authority if appropriate) as well as to all other parties.

Failure to appoint an umpire. Umpires are rarely seen in English 7–101
arbitration following the 1996 Arbitration Act. However, the Act does still contain provision for the use of umpires, including their appointment by the court where necessary. An arbitration agreement which provides for the appointment of an umpire if the arbitrators appointed cannot agree should also provide how and when the umpire is to be appointed. For example, the arbitrators will notify the parties of their disagreement and invite the umpire to take over (or "enter upon") the reference and conduct the arbitration as if he were sole arbitrator. In the absence of an agreed mechanism s.21 of the Arbitration Act 1996 makes provision for how and when the umpire is to be appointed.[407]

If the arbitrators cannot agree on the appointment of the umpire but fail to give notice of the fact to the parties, or if any of them fails to join in the giving of notice,

---

[401] Section 17 does not specify the grounds on which the court should exercise its discretion to set aside an appointment. That was deliberate. See DAC report, para.85.

[402] Arbitration Act 1996, s.18.

[403] Arbitration Act 1996, s.15(2) provides that an agreement that the number of arbitrators shall be two is to be interpreted as requiring the appointment of an additional (third) arbitrator unless otherwise agreed by the parties. See para.4–036.

[404] Section 18 of the Arbitration Act 1996. This provision applies whether it is an agreed procedure that fails or in the absence of an agreed procedure s.16(5) applies but is not fully utilised.

[405] The provisions of s.17 of the Arbitration Act 1996 are discussed in para.4–037.

[406] Section 18(2) of the Arbitration Act 1996.

[407] See para.4–150.

any party to the arbitral proceedings may apply to the court to remedy the situation.[408] Notice of the application must be given to the other parties and to each member of the tribunal. Upon hearing the application, the court may "order that the umpire shall replace the other arbitrators as the tribunal with power to make decisions, orders and awards as if he were sole arbitrator".[409]

7–102 Default by an appointing authority. Under s.18 of the Arbitration Act 1996, the court also has power to appoint an arbitrator where the appointing authority specified in the arbitration agreement refuses or neglects to appoint or otherwise fails to do so. A party seeking to have the appointment made by the court should first serve on the authority concerned a written notice to appoint. If the appointment is not made within the time specified in the arbitration agreement or, if no time is specified, within a reasonable time after service of the notice,[410] then application may be made to the court. This is so whether the authority is to appoint in all cases or only if the parties fail to agree.[411]

7–103 To fill a vacancy. When an arbitrator ceases to hold office, s.27 of the Arbitration Act 1996 provides how the vacancy shall be filled (i.e. by the appointment of a replacement arbitrator if required). The vacancy may occur where an arbitrator (including a third arbitrator) or umpire who has been appointed refuses to act,[412] or is incapable of acting, or dies and the parties or the arbitrators do not fill the vacancy.[413] Unless the parties agree on how the vacancy is to be filled , the provisions of s.16 (procedure for appointment of arbitrators)[414] and s.18 (failure of appointment procedure) will apply in relation to the filling of the vacancy as in relation to an original appointment.[415] So if, for example, the vacancy is on a panel of three and arises in relation to an arbitrator appointed by one of the parties under the arbitration agreement, then unless the parties agree otherwise then the party who originally made the appointment will select a replacement pursuant to s.16 of

---

[408] Arbitration Act 1996, s.21(5). The procedure for an arbitration application is described in paras 8–178 *et seq.*

[409] Arbitration Act 1996, s.21(5).

[410] Normally seven clear days should suffice, and the appointing authority should then be notified of the application to the court. This period is not specified in s.18 but a similar length of notice appears in s.17.

[411] This was clear under s.10(2)(a) of the Arbitration Act 1950, and the words of s.18, which replace it are wide enough for that purpose.

[412] As to what constitutes a refusal or failure to act see paras 7–116 *et seq.*

[413] See, for example, *Rocco Guiseppe & Figli SpA v Tupinave (The "Graziela Ferraz")* [1992] 2 Lloyd's Rep. 452 where the court appointed a replacement for an arbitrator who had died after making an interim award but before the final award could be made. The court's order was made pursuant to s.10 of the Arbitration Act 1950 which has been replaced by s.18 of the Arbitration Act 1996.

[414] In *Federal Insurance v Transamerica* [1999] 2 Q.B. 286, the court indicated how s.27(I) of the Act should be construed with the s.16 procedure for the replacement of one member of the arbitral tribunal.

[415] Section 27(3) of the Arbitration Act 1996 replaced s.10(4) of the Arbitration Act 1950.

the Act. In the absence of an agreed procedure,[416] the parties should take care to observe the time limit in that section.[417]

When the parties cannot agree on how the vacancy is to be filled, either after it has arisen or beforehand (e.g. by the operation of a contractual appointment procedure),[418] and the statutory procedure[419] fails to fill the vacancy, any party to the arbitration agreement may apply for the court to exercise its powers under s.18 of the Act, which extend to appointing a replacement arbitrator or umpire.[420]

Practice. A party seeking to have the appointment made or set aside by the 7–104 court[421] should first serve written notice on the tribunal, if it has been fully or partially appointed, and on all the parties to the reference. The content of the notice will vary according to the application.[422] What is a reasonable length of time (e.g. 14 days or more) will depend upon the appointment.[423] If the appointment is not made within a reasonable time after service of the notice, then the court itself may make the appointment or give such directions as may be appropriate.[424]

What the court must consider in making appointments. When 7–105 considering how to exercise any of its powers under s.16 (procedure for appointment of arbitrators) or s.18 (failure of appointment procedure), the court must have due regard to any agreement of the parties as to the qualifications required of the arbitrators."[425] The court will begin by considering the arbitration agreement, including any rules referred to in it. If that agreement mentions that the arbitrator or umpire should have any particular qualifications s.19 requires the court to have regard to that requirement in making any appointment. Although not specified, it may appear to the court from the nature of the dispute that it would be desirable, for example, that a sole arbitrator should have legal training and some prior experience as an arbitrator. The court may also be asked to

---

[416] Arbitration Act, s.16(1) allows the parties to agree the appointment procedure, failing which ss.16(3) to (6) to apply.

[417] *Federal Insurance v Transamerica* [1999] 2 Q.B. 286, where the court found that the agreed time limit rather than the shorter time limit should apply.

[418] The ICC Rules, Art.12, contain a replacement procedure as do other arbitration rules (e.g. LCIA, Art.11.1).

[419] Arbitration Act 1996, s.16.

[420] Arbitration Act 1996, s.27(3) specifically provides that the provisions of s.18 shall apply "as in relation to the original appointment" (i.e. the court can appoint in the same way as it could have done when the tribunal was originally constituted).

[421] For the procedure relevant to the application to the court see paras 8–178 *et seq.*

[422] The court will not look at the precise wording of the written notice too finely: *In Re Eyre and the Corporation of Leicester* [1892] 1 Q.B. 136.

[423] Section 16 provides different time limits according to the size of the tribunal.

[424] The court has a discretion whether or not to appoint, but will usually do so unless there is substantial delay in making the application. Such an appointment would no longer be conditional upon the applicant giving security for costs as in *Re Bjornstad and The Ouse Shipping Co Ltd* [1924] 2 K.B. 673 in view of the provisions of s.38(3) of the Arbitration Act 1996. See also *Tritonia Shipping Inc v South Nelson Forest Products Corp* [1966] 1 Lloyd's Rep. 114.

[425] Section 19 of the Arbitration Act 1996 which derives from Art.11(5) of the Model Law.

consider imposing other necessary qualifications for members of the tribunal.[426]
The applicant should make clear to the court his own requirements for an
arbitrator. The parties may be required to submit lists of the arbitrators that they
would like appointed, but the court has a discretion whether and who to
appoint.

7–106   **Delay.** The court has a wide discretion whether to appoint an arbitrator under
s.18.[427] Nevertheless, the discretion must be exercised judicially and consistent
with the principles set out in s.1 of the Act. Thus, the court will not appoint an
arbitrator pursuant to s.18 when it is impossible to obtain a fair resolution of the
dispute by an impartial tribunal without unnecessary delay or expense. As noted
the circumstances in which it will decline to appoint an arbitrator are very
restricted, the presumption being that the court should give effect to the agreement to arbitrate and appoint an tribunal.[428]

7–107   **Ancillary powers.** As a corollary to the power to appoint an arbitrator or
umpire in the case of the failure or default of an appointment procedure, the court
has power to revoke an appointment already made under a defective appointment
procedure and to give directions as to how the tribunal should be constituted.[429]
In giving those directions the court will have regard to the intention of the parties
where it is reflected in the arbitration agreement or otherwise to the terms of s.15
of the Act. That section provides for a sole arbitrator if there is no agreement as
to the number of arbitrators and unless otherwise agreed for the appointment of
an additional arbitrator if the parties have provided for an even number of arbitrators.[430]

7–108   **Powers of arbitrator or umpire appointed by the court.** An
appointment made by the court will have the same effect as if made by or with the
agreement of the parties.[431] Thus, an arbitrator or umpire appointed by the court
has the same powers to act in the reference and to make an award as if he had been
appointed by consent or in accordance with the terms of the arbitration agreement. Where the case so requires, an arbitrator appointed by the court has the

---

[426] In *Virdee v Virdi* [2003] EWCA Civ 41, the judge at first instance decided that it was not essential
that members of the tribunal be members of the Sikh community. In *Federal Insurance v Transamerica* [1999] 2 Q.B. 286, the qualifications related to insurance experience.

[427] The *"Frotanorte"* [1996] 2 Lloyd's Rep. 461 at 468, CA, a decision based on the old arbitration law,
but referred to with approval in *Durthell & Sons v Secretary of State for Trade & Industry* [2001]
1 Lloyd's Rep. 275.

[428] See para.7–096 and *Atlanska*, above. Compare the decision in *Secretary of State v Percy Thomas
Partnership* [1998] 65 Con. L.R. 11 (where the application to appoint an arbitrator was refused) with
that in *Durthell, ibid.* at [60]–[65].

[429] Section 18(3) of the Arbitration Act 1996.

[430] See paras 4–006 *et seq.*

[431] Arbitration Act 1996, s.18(4).

same duty to appoint a third arbitrator as if he had been appointed under the arbitration agreement.[432]

Appeal. Permission of the "court"[433] is required for any appeal from a decision   7–109
of the court under ss.17, 18, or 21 of the Act.[434] It had been thought that court
meant the court which made the order and that in the absence of such leave the
Court of Appeal could not consider the matter. There are now at least two
categories of case where the Court of Appeal may give permission to appeal even
though the judge at first instance has not given permission. These cases are
discussed further at para.7–201 which deals with wording to the same effect under
s.44(7).

6. REMOVAL OF THE TRIBUNAL, RESIGNATION AND REVOCATION OF AUTHORITY

Introduction. A tribunal's authority runs from the time of its appointment   7–110
until a final award is made after which the tribunal has no further duties.[435] It is
possible, although rarely done, for the parties to agree in advance the circumstances in which the authority of an arbitrator may be revoked. If a settlement of
the dispute is reached, the parties may want to revoke the authority of the arbitral
tribunal rather than have an award which records the settlement. The Arbitration
Act 1996 empowers parties acting jointly by themselves or through an arbitral
institution to revoke the tribunal's authority[436] subject to the right of each member
of the tribunal to recover his reasonable fees and expenses.[437] When the authority
of the tribunal is revoked in the manner just described, there is no role for the
court to play.[438]

The court's power to revoke the appointment of an arbitrator or an umpire is
limited to the situation where the original appointment was made under s.18 of the
Act because of the failure of the appointment procedure.[439] The court no longer
has power to revoke the tribunal's authority on the ground that the dispute
involves a question of fraud.[440]

---

[432] This is implicit from s.18(4) of the Arbitration Act 1996.

[433] Section 105(1) of the Arbitration Act 1996, defining court as the court of first instance.

[434] Arbitration Act 1996, ss.17(4), 18(5) and 21(6). In *Virdee v Virdi* [2003] EWCA CIS 41, the judge
had refused leave to appeal against his decision on the appointment of an arbitrator and the Court
of Appeal concluded that it had no jurisdiction to entertain an appeal against his decision because
of the exclusion in s.18(5) of the Act.

[435] Hence the reference to arbitrators being "*functus officio*".

[436] Arbitration Act 1996, s.23(3).

[437] Arbitration Act 1996, s.28.

[438] Mention of this possibility appears in para.4–166.

[439] Section 23(5)(a) of the Arbitration Act 1996. See para.7–136.

[440] The provision was contained in the Arbitration Act 1950, s.24(2) but does not appear in the
Arbitration Act 1996. As to the meaning of "fraud" in this context, see *Watson v Prager* [1991] 3
All E.R. 487 at 510.

Even where an arbitrator resigns, the court's role is limited to granting him relief from any liability as a result of his resignation, and making an order in respect of his entitlement to any reasonable fees or expenses, if those matters cannot be agreed between him and the parties.[441]

In exceptional cases the court is empowered to remove an arbitrator[442] or an umpire[443] in the course of the reference upon the application of one or more of the parties to the arbitration.[444] The grounds for such an application are specified in s.24 of the Act and are considered below.

7–111 **Power to remove an arbitrator.**[445] Upon application of a party to the arbitral proceedings the court has power to remove an arbitrator under s.24 of the Arbitration Act 1996 on any of the four grounds specified in that section. Notice of the application must be given to the other parties, to the arbitrator[446] concerned and to any other arbitrator.[447] Each ground for removal will be examined in turn.

7–112 **First ground: partiality.** The Arbitration Act 1996 imposes a general duty on the tribunal "to act fairly and impartially as between the parties".[448] Of the four grounds for removal contained in s.24, this is the most significant and it is thought that most objections which are raised to an arbitrator are done so under this head, or under equivalent provisions contained in institutional rules. If there is actual bias on the part of an arbitrator not only will any award that he makes be subject to challenge for serious irregularity[449] but he may also be removed by the court on the application of one of the parties.[450] Even if there is no actual bias the arbitrator may be removed if the court is satisfied that there is apparent bias, namely that there are "justifiable doubts as to his impartiality" and the court will also consider setting aside any awards in these circumstances.[451] There is therefore a clear

---

[441] See para.7–136.
[442] Section 24 of the Arbitration Act 1996 provides for the removal of an "arbitrator", but it is possible for the court to remove more than one arbitrator (e.g. a tribunal of three) if a case for removal is made out against them all.
[443] Arbitration Act 1996, s.82(1) provides that "arbitrator", unless the context otherwise requires, includes an umpire.
[444] Arbitration Act 1996, s.24.
[445] The term "arbitrator" is used for convenience, but in this context it also includes an umpire if appropriate: Arbitration Act 1996, s.82(1).
[446] See *Miller Construction Ltd v James Moore Earthmoving* [2001] 2 All E.R. (Comm) 598 for the notice required to be given to the arbitrator concerned.
[447] Section 24(1) Arbitration Act 1996. For the procedure relevant to an application for removal see paras 8–178 *et seq.*
[448] See s.33(1)(a) of the Arbitration Act 1996 and paras 4–106 *et seq.* which contain a full discussion on this subject.
[449] Section 68(2)(a) of the Arbitration Act 1996 which deals with a failure to comply with the general duty to act "fairly and impartially" as between the parties. See para.8–077.
[450] Section 24(1)(a) of the Arbitration Act 1996.
[451] Section 24(1)(a) of the Arbitration Act 1996.

relationship between ss.24 and 68 of the Arbitration Act and challenges to awards on the basis of partiality are often brought under both grounds.[452]

Irregular conduct of the proceedings. Although relatively rare, the   7–113
arbitrator's conduct of proceedings can give rise to justifiable doubts as to his partiality, although there will be inevitable overlap with a failure properly to conduct proceedings under s.24(d)(i). The court will be slow to remove an arbitrator on this basis because of the understandable concern that objections are being raised by a party because he perceives that proceedings are going against him or because he has a general desire to disrupt or delay proceedings for fear of an unfavourable outcome. In this regard, the requirement imposed by s.73 to raise any "irregularity affecting the tribunal"[453] promptly is of central importance. However, on rare occasions where the arbitrator's conduct justifies it and when objection is raised promptly, an arbitrator will be removed as a result of his conduct of the proceedings. In *Norbrook Laboratories v Tank*,[454] a successful application was made to challenge an arbitrator after he had made an interim costs order against a party who had served notice under the applicable institutional rules that the short-form procedure should be terminated. The arbitrator had also contacted three potential witnesses unilaterally. Although he had not obtained witness statements from them, it was clear that he had spoken to them and he did not disclose the fact of his approaches or the content of his discussions to the parties. The arbitrator's exposure to these witnesses and to the disparaging remarks that they might be assumed to have made about one of the parties gave rise to a real possibility of bias. The unilateral contact with witnesses also gave rise to a failure properly to conduct proceedings under s.24(d)(i). Additionally, unilateral telephone contact with the parties is "generally to be deprecated" and falls to be considered as a failure properly to conduct the proceedings.[455] Other conduct by the arbitrator did not give rise to justifiable doubts as to partiality. This included:

1. a decision to award costs against the applicant upon his termination of the short form procedure, which the arbitrator clearly had the power to do under the relevant rules. The failure to give reasons for the decision on costs is an irregularity within the terms of s.68(1) and could have formed the basis of an application that the court should exercise its powers to order reasons to be given under s.70(4) but no such application was made.

2. an antagonistic relationship with the claimant's solicitors,[456] and

---

[452] The requirement of impartiality and the test to be applied by the fair minded and informed observer is discussed further at paras 4–106 *et seq.*

[453] Arbitration Act 1996, s.73(1)(d).

[454] [2006] EWHC 1055, where the arbitrator was removed and his partial award set aside.

[455] *Norbrook Laboratories v Tank*, at [132]. Arbitrators are well advised to ensure that their conduct cannot give rise to suspicion and so avoid private communications with either party even on trivial administrative matters. See para.7–118 below.

[456] For a decision where an antagonistic relationship between counsel and a judge gave rise to a reasonable apprehension of bias, see *R. v Lashley* [2005] EWCA Crim 2016. See also *Howell & Others v Millais & Others* [2007] EWCA 720.

3. expressions of views as to the value of in-house expert evidence as compared to independent expert evidence before hearing that evidence.

Ordinarily, the court will be slow to uphold a challenge on the basis that a particular decision of the tribunal shows a real possibility of lack of impartiality.[457] A challenge based on the alleged wrongful issue by the arbitrator of a peremptory order has been dismissed as "risible" and a challenge relating to the allegedly excessive time spent by the arbitrator in listening to and understanding counsel's submissions as "absurd", although in order to reach such a view the court did effectively review the arbitrator's behaviour in the context of the arbitration and reach its own view as to the arbitrator's conduct.[458]

7–114 **Second ground: absence of required qualifications.** In some cases the parties specify in the arbitration agreement that any arbitrator appointed must possess certain qualifications[459] and that requirement must be respected unless it is waived by all parties at the time of the appointment.[460] If an arbitrator is appointed by one party or by an arbitral institution and he does not possess the required qualifications another party to the arbitral proceedings may apply to the court to have him removed on that ground.[461]

7–115 **Third ground: incapacity.** The court may also remove the arbitrator on the basis that he is physically or mentally incapable of conducting the proceedings or that there are justifiable doubts as to his capacity to do so.[462] The court's power is not limited to an incapacity arising after the date of the appointment,[463] although in exercising its power to remove the court may take account of what the parties knew of the incapacity at the time of the appointment. In some cases the incapacity will be obvious[464] but in others it may be difficult to determine whether the incapacity justifies removal.[465] In the latter situation an applicant must satisfy the court on the evidence adduced that there are real doubts that the arbitrator concerned is capable of fulfilling his role as an arbitrator. The incapacity need not

---

[457] *ASM Shipping Ltd of India v TTMI Ltd of England* [2006] 1 Lloyd's Rep. 375 at [45], rejecting a ground for challenge based on the tribunal's failure to grant a requested adjournment. The judge's comment that the impugned decision of the arbitrators in this case was also the "right decision" arguably goes further than the courts should go when considering allegations relating to the conduct of an arbitration.

[458] See *Sinclair v Woods of Winchester Ltd* 102 Con. L.R. 127, at [41]–[46], [64]–[66].

[459] Qualification may include "Queen's Counsel", "Engineer" or "Commercial man" see para.4–017.

[460] The right to object may subsequently be lost, see s.73(d) of the Arbitration Act 1996 and para.7–127.

[461] Arbitration Act 1996, s.24(1)(b). The possibility of removal on this ground was discussed in *Continental Grain v China Petroleum* (December 4, 1998), Mance J., although the decision concerned an alleged mistake about qualifications of an arbitrator: see para.4–017. The subject of qualifications has also been mentioned in the context of s.19 of the Act: see para.7–105.

[462] Section 24(1)(c) of the Arbitration Act 1996.

[463] This view is based on the words of s.24(1) of the Arbitration Act 1996.

[464] A physical handicap that occurs after the arbitrator was appointed for example.

[465] The incapacity may manifest itself in failure to act, so that there will be overlap with the fourth ground specified in s.24(1).

be life-long, but it must be serious enough to put the arbitrator out of action altogether so far as the arbitration is concerned.[466] Where it is unclear whether deficiencies in the capability or performance of the arbitrator are due to incapacity or neglect the application for removal should be based on both the third and fourth grounds specified in s.24 of the Act.

Fourth ground: Refusal or failure properly to conduct pro- 7–116
ceedings. The fourth ground for removal is very broad and extends to many situations where an arbitrator breaches his general duty to the parties.[467] It is expressed in s.24(1) of the Act as follows:

"(d) that [the arbitrator] has refused or failed

  (i) properly to conduct the proceedings, or
  (ii) to use all reasonable despatch in conducting the proceedings or making an award,

and that substantial injustice has been or will be caused to the applicant."

Failure properly to conduct proceedings. As discussed above,[468] 7–117 allegations relating to the conduct of proceedings by arbitrators very rarely succeed. To the extent they do, the challenger will need to show that the arbitrator has failed to comply with the general duties under s.33 and s.68(2)(a), (b) and (c) of the Act. There will often be substantial overlap between allegations under this ground and the first ground above, where it is alleged that improper conduct of the proceedings manifests some objective lack of impartiality towards one of the parties.

In *Norbrook Labratories Ltd v Tank*,[469] the arbitrator's conduct[470] described above constituted a failure to conduct proceedings properly within the terms of s.24(d)(i). In particular each of:

1. unilateral telephone contact with the parties, not wholly confined to administrative matters, and

2. unilateral contact by the arbitrator with three fact witnesses compounded by a failure to make an exact record of what they said or to disclose such a record to the parties

---

[466] *Succula Ltd and Pomona Shipping Co Ltd v Harland and Wolff Ltd* [1980] 2 Lloyd's Rep. 381, a decision based on the previous legislation but whose comments at 388 are still relevant. Inability to comply with his duties to conduct the arbitration with reasonable despatch falls within s.24(1)(d)(ii) of the Arbitration Act 1996.
[467] See s.33 of the Arbitration Act 1996 and paras 5–040 *et seq.* for this duty.
[468] Paragraph 7–113.
[469] [2006] EWHC 1055.
[470] Paragraph 7–113.

did give rise to a failure properly to conduct the proceedings.[471] The court's decision to remove the arbitrator on the second of these complaints was also based on an appearance of lack of partiality.

7–118 Unilateral communications. Whilst there is no absolute rule against the arbitrator having unilateral discussions with one party only, the practice is, as noted in *Norbrook*, generally to be deprecated and can certainly lead to removal under this head or for a reasonable apprehension of bias, especially if discussions are intentional or frequent, go beyond administrative matters[472] or are not promptly disclosed to the other party.[473] Discussions concerning the appointment of the chairman fall within a generally recognised but not entirely clear exception to this rule.[473a] The Hong Kong Supreme Court refused to remove an arbitrator who refused to disclose the content of unilateral discussions with his appointing party over the identity of the chairman.[473b]

7–119 Other failures. The scope of a failure properly to conduct proceedings goes beyond unilateral contact with the parties. If an arbitrator has decided to deal with liability and quantum in two separate hearings, but then proceeds to make findings on quantum in the first hearing then a serious irregularity may result as well as possibly the removal of the arbitrator.[474]

7–120 Refusal to act. The fact that an arbitrator has refused either to conduct the proceedings or make an award as described in s.24 must be established by evidence. If in writing, the written refusal should be produced to the court. If the refusal was oral, the court should be informed of the words used by the arbitrator.

Whether an arbitrator has refused to act is a question for the court and not the arbitrator. From a practical point of view however the court will consider the arbitrator's view on the matter because if he was of the view that he had refused to act, and maintained his refusal, then the court would take into account that he could not be forced to continue with the arbitration against his will.[475]

---

[471] *per* Colman J. at [37].
[472] Minor administrative unilateral discussions, such as a telephone call to enquire about the whereabouts of papers or arrangements for a hearing, are it is suggested, not objectionable.
[473] For a case where an adjudicator held discussions with one party concerning issues of jurisdiction and accordingly gave rise to a reasonable apprehension of bias, see *Discain Project Services v Opecprime Development* [2000] B.L.R. 402.
[473a] Such discussions are permitted by the IBA Rules of Ethics for International Arbitrators, [5.2].
[473b] *Pacific China Holdings Ltd v Grand Pacific Holdings Ltd* HCCT 5/2007.
[474] *Benaim (UK) Ltd v Davies Middleton & Davies Ltd (No.2)* 102 Con. L.R. 1 at [31]. The allegation was not made out on the facts.
[475] *Succula Ltd and Pomona Shipping Co Ltd v Harland and Wolff Ltd* [1980] 2 Lloyd's Rep. 381.

If an arbitrator designated in an arbitration agreement seeks to delegate his duties by nominating someone else to act as arbitrator in his place, this may be treated as a refusal to act.[476]

Not every refusal to act will suffice. A refusal to make an award on an issue of jurisdiction may be justified provided that the tribunal is willing to proceed with the arbitration and to determine any issues of jurisdiction in their final award in due course.

Failure to act. It may be more difficult to show that an arbitrator has failed (as opposed to refused) to act in the manner specified in s.24(1)(d) of the Act. The failure must have a serious effect on the conduct or outcome of the arbitral proceedings as well as causing substantial injustice to the applicant. This occurred where an arbitration was conducted in such a manner that one party was denied the right to know the case to be met,[477] but mere lack of confidence in the tribunal is not a sufficient ground for removal.[478] Even a failure to comply with an order of the court may not suffice.[479] In order to support an application for removal, evidence should be adduced by the applicant of each failure relied upon.[480]   7–121

The dilatory arbitrator. The previous paragraphs mention cases where the tribunal has refused or failed properly to conduct the arbitral proceedings. There is however another kind of refusal or failure which can in exceptional circumstances lead to the tribunal's removal. That occurs where the proceedings are not conducted with reasonable despatch or an award is not made within a reasonable time. The tribunal is required to conduct the proceedings and adopt procedures that will avoid unnecessary delay.[481] A refusal or failure to conduct the proceedings or make an award with reasonable despatch can lead to the tribunal's removal, although the delay would have to be truly exceptional so as to cause substantial injustice to the applicant. What is reasonable despatch will depend on the circumstances. For instance, a decision in a "documents only" case[482] may be expected more quickly than in an arbitration where the testimony of many witnesses has to be considered. The subsection[483] is aimed at the type of delay which is serious and   7–122

---

[476] *Neale v Richardson* [1938] 1 All E.R. 753, *Succula Ltd and Pomona Shipping Co Ltd v Harland and Wolff Ltd* [1980] 2 Lloyd's Rep. 381.

[477] *Damond Lock Grabowski v Laing Investments (Bracknell) Ltd* [1992] 60 B.L.R. 112. Though based on the Arbitration Act 1950, the facts of this decision would justify removal under s.24 of the Arbitration Act 1996.

[478] *Groundshire v VHE Construction* [2001] B.L.R. 395 at 399. Parts of this decision have been doubted in subsequent cases: See *TTMI Ltd of England v ASM Shipping Ltd of India* [2006] 1 Lloyd's Rep. 401 at [34].

[479] *The Dredging and Construction Co Ltd v Delta Civil Engineering Co Ltd* (May 26, 2000), H.H. Judge Wilcox.

[480] This was done, for example, in *Home of Homes Ltd v Hammersmith and Fulham LBC* [2003] EWHC 807, although having considered the evidence adduced Forbes J. dismissed the application to remove the arbitrator.

[481] Arbitration Act 1996, s.33(1)(b).

[482] See para.5–108.

[483] Section 24(1)(d)(ii) of the Arbitration Act 1996.

inexcusable. Doing nothing will not justify complaint let alone removal if no one has asked the tribunal to do anything.[484]

7–123 **Substantial injustice.** In order to remove an arbitrator on any of the four grounds specified in s.24(1) of the Act, the applicant must persuade the court not only of the particular failure or refusal (as described in the preceding paragraphs) but also that he has suffered or will be caused substantial injustice if the arbitrator concerned is not removed.[485] As has already been mentioned[486] the expression "substantial injustice" is not defined in the Arbitration Act 1996. In the context of removing an arbitrator, guidance as to the intended meaning of the words can be obtained from para.106 of the DAC report in which it was said, "The provision is not intended to allow the court to substitute its own view as to how the arbitral proceedings should be conducted. Thus the choice by an arbitrator of a particular procedure, unless it breaches the duty laid on arbitrators by s.33, should on no view justify the removal of an arbitrator, even if the court would not itself have adopted that procedure."[487]

7–124 **Finding of bias imputes substantial injustice.** Once the court has found a real possibility of bias (i.e. it is satisfied as to the first ground of s.24) then substantial injustice will normally be imputed as a matter of course. In other words, in cases of actual or apparent bias there is no second hurdle to get over, or if there is it is a very low one. As Morison J. said in *ASM Shipping Ltd v TTMI Ltd*, "In my judgement there can be no more serious or substantial injustice than having a tribunal which was not, ex hypothesi, impartial, determine parties' rights."[488]

7–125 **The other three grounds.** In respect of the other three grounds of s.24, the second hurdle remains and if it cannot be surmounted the challenge will not be sustained. This was the case in *Norbrook Labratories Ltd v Tank*,[489] where unilateral telephone contact with the parties which amounted to a failure properly to conduct the proceedings did not lead to substantial injustice as it was in each case

---

[484] *Succula Ltd and Pomona Shipping Co Ltd v Harland and Wolff Ltd* [1980] 2 Lloyd's Rep. 381, a decision based on, among others, the former s.13 of the Arbitration Act 1950. See also *Enterra Pty Ltd v ADI Ltd*, September 1, 2002, Supreme Court of New South Wales, for an unsuccessful attempt to remove an arbitrator under s.44(c) of the Commercial Arbitration Act 1984 of New South Wales for failure to convene a hearing within a certain period of time.

[485] Section 24(1)(d) of the Arbitration Act 1996.

[486] See para.7–084.

[487] The words in square brackets have been inserted to apply them to the provisions in the Arbitration Act 1996. The words appearing in the report refer to the Arbitration Bill.

[488] [2006] 1 Lloyd's Rep. 375 at [39]. These comments were endorsed by Colman J. in *Norbrook Laboratories v Tank*, at [144]–[145] adding that substantial injustice would "normally" be inferred in bias cases and by Andrew Smith J. in *ASM Shipping Limited v Bruce Harris & Others* [2007] EWHC 1513, at [32]. The contrary finding in *Groundshire v VHE Construction* [2001] B.L.R. 395, at [33]–[34] can no longer be regarded as good law.

[489] [2006] EWHC 1055.

immediately disclosed to the other party.[490] Removal on this ground will only occur if the conduct of the arbitrator concerned is so unreasonable that justice demands that the arbitration should be temporarily halted or permanently brought to an end[491] and no other method of doing so is available to the court.[492]

Misconduct. This word does not appear in the Arbitration Act 1996 but under the previous law it covered a wide range of errors on the part of an arbitrator.[493] It ranged from a fundamental abuse of his position[494] to what was often referred to as "technical misconduct", i.e. where the arbitrator made errors but not in a culpable way or so as to impugn his integrity. Technical misconduct in that sense has no place in the law since the Arbitration Act 1996. Under the 1996 Act the grounds for removing an arbitrator are confined to the four grounds specified in s.24.[495]

7–126

Loss of right to object. A party who wants an arbitrator removed should apply to the court[496] as soon as he becomes aware that there are grounds for removal. He may lose his right to object if he delays. Section 73(1) of the Arbitration Act 1996 provides that the applicant may not raise an objection[497] before the court or tribunal[498] if he continued to take part in the arbitral proceedings without objecting "forthwith or within such time as is allowed by the arbitration agreement"[499] unless he shows that, at the time he took part in the proceedings, "he did not know and could not with reasonable diligence have discovered the grounds for the objection".[500] To be caught under this section the

7–127

---

[490] Paragraph 137. Meeting an expert witness without informing the parties beforehand has been found to be an irregularity under s.68 but may not be a serious one: *Hussman v Al Ameen* [2000] 2 Lloyd's Rep. 83 at 95. See also *Egmatra v Marco Trading Corp* [1999] 1 Lloyd's Rep. 862 and *Pacol v Rossakhar* [2000] 1 Lloyd's Rep. 109.

[491] Such a case was *Damond Lock Grabowski v Laing Investments* [1992] 60 B.L.R. 112. For a case at the opposite end of the spectrum, see *Dredging & Construction Co v Delta Civil Engineering* (May 26, 2000), H.H. Judge Wilcox.

[492] See *Wicketts & Sterndale v Brine Builders* [2002] C.I.L.L. 1805, where the arbitrator was removed under s.24(1)(d) because of inappropriate directions aimed at securing his fees.

[493] Atkin L.J. described "misconduct" in *Williams v Wallis & Cox* [1914] 2 K.B. 478: "That expression does not necessarily involve personal turpitude on the part of the arbitrator . . . The term does not really amount to much more than such a mishandling of the arbitration as is likely to amount to some substantial miscarriage of justice". See also *Annie Fox and Others v PG Wellfair Ltd* [1981] 2 Lloyd's Rep. 514.

[494] For example by accepting financial inducements to decide the case in favour of one of the parties.

[495] See paras 7–111 *et seq.*

[496] If there is a challenge procedure in the arbitration agreement itself or in any rules incorporated into that agreement (e.g. ICC Rules, Art.11), the applicant must, before applying to the court, exhaust that procedure—Arbitration Act 1996, s.24(2).

[497] The objection here means any objection on which the application for removal is based. There may, of course, be several objections (see the use of the words "that objection" in s.73(1) of the Arbitration Act 1996).

[498] Although s.73(1) refers to raising an objection "before the tribunal or the court" this phrase also embraces objections made under the relevant rules to arbitral institutions.

[499] The arbitration agreement itself or rules incorporated into it may contain a time limit within which any challenge must be made.

[500] Arbitration Act 1996, s.73(1).

applicant must have had knowledge of the essential facts constituting the irregularity or had grounds to believe that there was an irregularity.[501] The section does not therefore operate to catch a party who in a general sense had vague grounds to believe that some irregularity may have occurred, unless the circumstances were such as to put that party on a duty of further enquiry. A leading example of failing to act promptly can be found in *ASM Shipping Ltd of India v TTMI Ltd of England*.[502] Although apparent bias was made out the award was not set aside because the applicant delayed in making its challenge until the award was delivered and accordingly had fallen foul of s.73. What is striking about this case is that an objection to the arbitrator and an attempted reservation of rights was made as soon as the facts came to light at a hearing. However, once the arbitrator had declined to recuse himself the court found that a s.24 challenge should have been made promptly; it was not acceptable to continue the objection in correspondence and wait until the outcome of the award was known. "A 'heads we win, tails you lose' position is not permissible in law as s.73 makes clear".[503] In a related decision in the same litigation, the court reinforced this conclusion, noting that it was not sufficient to put down a marker, "An objection under s.73 must be stated in properly specific terms".[504] The *ASM Shipping* decisions serve as a salutary lesson to anyone who thinks that their position will be fully protected simply by sending a letter containing a reservation of rights. The loss of the right to object applies only to someone who takes part in the arbitral proceedings.[505] If he does not take part in those proceedings that section does not apply to him.

7–128   **Existence of non-waivable grounds for challenge.** A further issue in relation to the loss of the right to object is whether there are any non-waivable grounds for challenge in English law. The traditional and current prevailing view is that there are no non-waivable grounds in English law,[506] contrasting with the approach taken by the IBA Guidelines on Conflicts of Interest in International Arbitration[507] which includes a "non waivable" red-list. The traditional view was challenged in *Weissfisch v Julius and Others*[508] where a party disputed the effectiveness of the waiver it had given in circumstances where the arbitrator had acted for both parties to the arbitration and in fact had advised them on the dispute which was submitted to arbitration. The point was not decided as part of the injunction application then before the Court of Appeal.

---

[501] *Sumukan Ltd v Commonwealth Secretariat* [2007] EWHC 188.
[502] [2006] 1 Lloyd's Rep. 375. See para.7–113.
[503] Paragraphs 48–49. See also *Sinclair v Woods of Winchester Ltd* 102 Con. L.R. 127, at [33], where again conduct at the hearing could not be objected to as the challenger waited until after delivery of the award to make the challenge.
[504] *ASM Shipping Ltd v Bruce Harris & Others* [2007] EWHC 1513, at [53].
[505] *ASM Shipping Ltd of India v TTMI Ltd of England* [2006] 1 Lloyd's Rep. 375.
[506] See for example *Smith v Kvaerner Cementation* [2006] EWCA 242, a non-arbitration case where a recorder who acted for companies in the same group as one of the parties to a court action before him could decide the case if there was a sufficiently informed waiver to that effect.
[507] Available at *www.ibanet.org*.
[508] [2006] EWCA 218.

Orders the court can make. On an application for removal of an arbitrator   7–129
under s.24 of the Act the court can make one or more of the following
orders[509]:

- dismiss the application;

- remove the arbitrator against whom the application is made

- declare the entitlement (if any) to fees and expenses of the removed arbitrator; and

- direct any arbitrator removed to repay any fees or expenses already paid.

Filling of vacancy on removal. If the arbitrator is removed the vacancy   7–130
created by his ceasing to hold office will be filled in accordance with s.27 of the Act
which provides that in the absence of some other agreement by the parties the
same procedure as applied to the original appointment will apply,[510] to the extent
possible,[511] to fill the vacancy.[512]

Fees and expenses of removed arbitrator. The court may, as noted,   7–131
be asked to fix the fees and expenses of the arbitrator who is removed. If the
applicant wishes to recover any payment already made to the arbitrator an order
for repayment should be sought. As the DAC report noted, "We would expect this
power to be exercised where the behaviour of the arbitrator is inexcusable to the
extent that this should be marked by depriving him of all or some of his fees and
expenses."[513] The power to make orders (including a repayment order) in respect
of the fees and expenses of an arbitrator removed by the court[514] provides a means
of enforcing the general duty of the tribunal imposed by the Arbitration Act
1996.[515]

Rights of arbitral tribunal. A challenged arbitrator has the right to   7–132
appear and be heard on an application to remove him.[516] The arbitrator can also
provide written submissions or a witness statement to the court if he wishes
however it has been observed that assertions by an arbitrator who is the subject of
a challenge that he had an open mind or was otherwise not biased are often

---

[509] The court can also set aside any awards of the removed arbitrator under s.68 of the Arbitration Act
1996.
[510] Which, pursuant to s.16 of the Arbitration Act 1996, will be that agreed between the parties or, in
the absence of agreement, the default procedure set out in that section.
[511] Arbitration Act 1996, s.27(3) provides that s.18 of the Arbitration Act 1996 will apply where the
appointment procedure has failed.
[512] See para.7–103.
[513] DAC report, para.108.
[514] The court's power to make such orders is derived from s.24(4) of the Arbitration Act 1996.
[515] The general duty of the tribunal is set out in s.33 of the Arbitration Act 1996: see para.5–032.
[516] Section 24(5). The arbitrator exercised this right in *Norbrook Labratories Ltd v Tank* [2006] EWHC
1055. See *Miller Construction Ltd v James Moore Earthmoving* [2001] 2 All E.R. (Comm) 598 for the
arbitrator's right to notice and to take part in the application claim if he wishes to do so.

unlikely to be helpful and should be accorded little or no evidential weight.[517] The other members of the arbitral tribunal[518] will be concerned about such an application and are entitled to be notified of it.[519] The applicant also has an interest in keeping any other members of the tribunal informed because the arbitral proceedings may continue and an award may be made even though an application to the court for removal of an arbitrator is pending. If the applicant wants the tribunal to suspend the proceedings until the court has determined the matter he should ask for a suspension. The tribunal is not obliged to grant his request[520] and would be unlikely to do so where the proceedings could continue to run through various preparatory stages without prejudice to either party whilst the challenge is pending or where the challenge is seen as an attempt to derail arbitral proceedings.

7–133 **Relief for arbitrator who resigns.** An arbitrator or umpire who wishes to resign from his office before making his final award should seek the prior agreement of the parties. If he does not do so he may incur liability for the extra costs associated with replacing him and re-running part of the previous arbitral proceedings before his replacement.[521] He may be able to agree the extent of any liability with the parties consequent upon his resignation, in which case the agreement must be in writing,[522] but in default he may have to apply to the court to determine that liability as well as his entitlement, if any, to his own costs and expenses for what he did prior to his resignation.[523] It may be better for an arbitrator to take advantage of s.25(3) of the Arbitration Act 1996 rather than to wait until he is sued by the parties, particularly if fees and expenses are due to him.

7–134 **Limitations on relief from liability.** Although an arbitrator who resigns without the agreement of the parties may apply to the court for relief,[524] it is worth emphasising that such relief from liability will not be granted to an arbitrator unless he satisfies the court that his resignation was "reasonable in all the circumstances".[525] This requirement is consistent with the general duty that

---

[517] *Re Medicaments & Related Classes of Goods* [2001] 1 W.L.R. 700, *per* Lord Hope at 495.

[518] If the arbitrator concerned is the sole arbitrator he will be the tribunal, but there may be other members of the tribunal against whom no order is sought.

[519] Arbitration Act 1996, s.24(1). The procedure for an arbitration application is contained in paras 8–178 *et seq.*

[520] Arbitration Act 1996, s.24(3). The position is more difficult if a challenge is made just before a scheduled hearing is due to commence as the tribunal would be concerned that if the hearing goes ahead and the challenged arbitrator is subsequently removed that the hearing would have to be re-run.

[521] See para.4–158.

[522] Arbitration Act 1996, s.5(1) requires the agreement to be in writing. That section refers to "agreement between the parties" but as the resigning arbitrator will require both parties' agreement the requirement of writing would seem to apply.

[523] Arbitration Act 1996, s.25(3).

[524] The right to apply to the court is apparent from s.25(3) of the Arbitration Act 1996. For the procedure for an arbitration application see paras 8–178 *et seq.*

[525] Arbitration Act 1996, s.25(4).

arises when an arbitrator accepts his appointment,[526] it is an implied term of the arbitrator's retainer that he will complete the reference unless it is reasonable not do so. Failure to appreciate that the office would be onerous does not by itself justify resignation. The parties are likely to incur extra costs if an arbitrator has to be replaced particularly if some parts of the proceedings have to be re-heard, and this is a significant factor in determining the reasonableness of the arbitrator's resignation.

Relief granted on terms. The court's power to grant relief from liability may be made on terms.[527] Those terms may include an order that the arbitrator who resigns should bear all or at least some of any wasted costs. That can be achieved either by reducing any fees and expenses to which he would otherwise be entitled or by ordering him to repay any amounts already paid. The court has a complete discretion as to the terms of any order.   7–135

If the court decides not to grant the arbitrator relief from liability, he may have to settle the liability by making a payment out of his own personal funds.

Court's power to revoke arbitrator's appointment. In addition to the court's power to remove an arbitrator[528] the court may revoke an appointment under s.18 of the Arbitration Act 1996 when there has been a failure of a procedure for the appointment of an arbitral tribunal.   7–136

Effect of removal, revocation, death or resignation. When an arbitrator ceases to hold office, for whatever reason, a number of questions may arise, including: 7–137

- should he be replaced and if so how?

- to what extent will any previous proceedings in the arbitration stand?

- what effect, if any, will his ceasing to hold office have on any application made by him or a party?

- is he entitled to any fees or expenses?

The first three questions are suggested by s.27(1) of the Arbitration Act 1996 which provides that the parties are free to decide on the answers, but otherwise certain default provisions apply. As to how a vacancy should be filled, the procedure under s.16 for appointment of arbitrators applies[529] and an application may be made to the court for directions under s.18 of the Act if that procedure

---

[526] The general duty is specified in s.33 of the Arbitration Act 1996, see para.5–032. Although that position does not say that an arbitrator cannot resign without the parties' agreement it does require him to adopt procedures which would avoid unnecessary delay and expense.
[527] Arbitration Act 1996, s.25(4).
[528] The court's power to remove an arbitrator is discussed in the preceding paras 7–111 *et seq.*
[529] See para.7–097 for this procedure.

fails.[530] The question of fees has already been mentioned in connection with removal[531] and resignation.[532] The reconstituted tribunal then decides the extent to which the previous proceedings should stand.[533]

7–138 Provision in arbitration rules. If the arbitration is being conducted under one of the various sets of arbitration rules it is likely that those rules will themselves set out a procedure for removal of the arbitrator in certain circumstances, and for the appointment of a replacement. For example they may provide that the same procedure or mechanism by which the arbitrator so removed was appointed is to be adopted for the appointment of his replacement.[534] Whether this procedure or mechanism is to apply in the case of removal by the court (which jurisdiction cannot be excluded by agreement),[535] is a matter of construction of the rules in question.[536]

7–139 Effect of vacancy not being filled. If an arbitrator is removed but he is not replaced the remaining arbitrators, if any, will proceed with the reference. If there are no remaining arbitrators, the reference will cease.[537]

7–140 Replacement by the court. Where an arbitrator or an umpire resigns or dies or is removed by the court, or where his authority is revoked by the parties or by the court,[538] the court has power to fill the vacancy in the absence of agreement by appointing a replacement.[539]

7–141 The arbitration agreement ceasing to have effect. Under the Arbitration Act 1996 the court may fill a vacancy in the arbitral tribunal, but it is the parties who must agree to terminate their arbitration agreement.[540] The court has no power to terminate an otherwise valid arbitration.

---

[530] Section 27(3) of the Arbitration Act 1996.
[531] See para.7–131.
[532] See para.7–133.
[533] Section 27(4) of the Arbitration Act 1996.
[534] See for example ICC Rules, Art.12.4; LCIA Rules, Art.11; and UNCITRAL Rules, Art.12(2) which deal with replacement following the challenge procedures set out in the respective rules.
[535] Section 24 of the Arbitration Act 1996 is mandatory in accordance with s.4(1) and Sch.1 to the Arbitration Act 1996.
[536] The LCIA Rules in particular would seem to cover removal by the court.
[537] The possibility of the parties agreeing not to fill a vacancy is canvassed by s.27(1)(a) of the Arbitration Act 1996: "whether the vacancy is to be filled".
[538] The court's power to revoke is ancillary to its power to appoint under s.18 of the Arbitration Act 1996. See para.7–136.
[539] Section 27(3) of the Arbitration Act 1996 provides that s.18 will apply in relation to the filling of a vacancy as in relation to an original appointment: see paras 7–130 and 7–137.
[540] See the terms of s.23(4) of the Arbitration Act 1996.

Appeal. Permission of the "court"[541] is required for any appeal from a decision   **7–142**
of the court under ss.24 and 25 of the Act.[542] It had been thought that court meant
the court which made the order and that in the absence of such leave the Court
of Appeal could not consider the matter. There are now at least two categories of
case where the Court of Appeal may give permission to appeal even though the
judge at first instance has not given permission. These cases are discussed further
at para.7–201 which deals with wording to the same effect under s.44(7).

7. DETERMINING DISPUTES ABOUT THE TRIBUNAL'S JURISDICTION DURING THE ARBITRATION

Introduction. The jurisdiction of the arbitral tribunal is discussed in Ch.2.[543]   **7–143**
The courses of action open to a party who disputes the tribunal's jurisdiction are
set out in Ch.5.[544] These include:

- objecting in the arbitral proceedings that the tribunal lacks substantive
  jurisdiction under s.31 of the Arbitration Act 1996 and requesting a ruling by
  the tribunal under s.30 of the Act that it has no such jurisdiction;

- commencing an action in court and opposing a stay (under s.9 or the court's
  inherent jurisdiction) of that action;

- refusing to participate in the arbitration (and presumably resisting enforcement of an unfavourable award);

- opposing an application made to court for the appointment of an arbitrator[545];

- applying to the court for a declaration or injunction or other relief under s.72
  of the Act[546];

- applying to the court for a determination of the tribunal's jurisdiction under
  s.32 of the Act either with the written consent of all the parties or with the
  consent of the tribunal[547];

- applying to the court to challenge the tribunal's jurisdiction under s.67 when
  an award is made, whether or not it deals expressly with jurisdiction;

- applying to the court here or abroad for an anti-arbitral injunction,[548] and

---

[541] Section 105(1) of the Arbitration Act 1996, defining court as the court of first instance.
[542] Arbitration Act 1996, ss.24(6) and 25(5).
[543] See paras 2–072 *et seq.*
[544] See paras 5–063 *et seq.*
[545] See s.18(2) of the Arbitration Act 1996 and paras 7–095—7–096.
[546] See paras 7–146 *et seq.*
[547] An application can no longer be made at common law for a declaration that the tribunal lacks
jurisdiction: *ABB Lummus v Keppel* [1997] 2 Lloyd's Rep. 24 at 30.
[548] See paras 7–058 *et seq.*

- opposing enforcement of any award whenever it is made, for example, under s.66(3) of the Act.[549]

Not all of these courses of action are mutually exclusive.

7–144 Relevance for tribunal determination. The Arbitration Act 1996 states a clear preference for the tribunal to determine its own jurisdiction and for any challenge to be made to the court only after an award has been made on the subject.[550] This preference has been recognised on numerous occasions by the courts. The Court of Appeal in *Fiona Trust and Others v Yuri Privalov & Others* said that the presumption under the Arbitration Act 1996 is that the tribunal should be left to determine its own jurisdiction first if at all possible: " . . . it is contemplated by the Act that it will, in general, be right for the arbitrators to be the first tribunal to consider whether they have jurisdiction to determine the dispute".[551] In *Weissfisch v Julius and Others*, the Court of Appeal rejected an application for an interim injunction to restrain an arbitrator from holding a hearing to consider his own jurisdiction: "There is nothing untoward in Mr Julius considering a question of his own jurisdiction now that this has been put in issue.".[552]

7–145 Courses of action. The list of options open to the potential challenger to a tribunal's jurisdiction is relatively long. However, the scheme of the Act, combined with recent judicial pronouncements, epitomised by *Fiona Trust/Premium Nafta Products*[553] is that an application to a tribunal to determine its own jurisdiction is intended to be the usual step to take. Following one of the other courses may be problematic, the application for an anti-arbitral injunction being the most problematic of all.

7–146 Power of the court under s.72. On its face, s.72 empowers the court to determine a challenge to the jurisdiction of the arbitral tribunal by a person alleged to be a party to arbitral proceedings, provided that the person concerned has not taken part in the arbitration proceedings.[554] On the application of such a

---

[549] See, for example, *Allied Vision Ltd v VPS Film Entertainment GmbH* [1991] 1 Lloyd's Rep. 392 where the defendant resisted enforcement under s.26 of the Arbitration Act 1950 which preceded s.66 of the Arbitration Act 1996.

[550] See ss.30 and 32 of the Arbitration Act 1996 which are more in line with the UNCITRAL Model Law than with English law prior to the 1996 Act. See dicta of Tomlinson J. in *Zaporozkye Production Aluminium Plan Openshareholders Society v Ashly Ltd* [2002] EWHC 1410.

[551] *Fiona Trust and Others v Yuri Privalov & Others* [2007] EWCA 20 at [34]. This approach was fully endorsed by the House of Lords, *Premium Nafta Products Ltd & Others v Fili Shipping Co Ltd & Others* [2007] UKHL 40.

[552] [2006] EWCA 218 at [32].

[553] [2007] EWCA 20. Affirmed *Premium Nafta Products Ltd v Fili Shipping Co Ltd & Others* [2007] UKHL 40.

[554] Section 72 (1) of the Arbitration Act 1996. The right that such a person has to challenge an award under s.72 is referred to in paras 8–053 and 8–055.

person, the court may by declaration, injunction or other appropriate relief determine whether there is a valid arbitration agreement, whether the arbitral tribunal is properly constituted or what matters have been submitted to arbitration in accordance with the arbitration agreement.[555]

Where the court has to determine the tribunal's jurisdiction under this section, it will construe the scope agreement to arbitrate by reference to the governing law of the agreement to arbitrate. Considerations derived from the substantive law of the matrix agreement are not relevant to determining the issue of construction.[556]

Exercise of power. Although there is nothing on the face of s.72 to indicate any intended limitation upon the application of the court's power to grant relief under the section, the policy of the Act, namely that questions of jurisdiction should normally be decided by the arbitral tribunal,[557] requires that s.72 should play only a residual role in resolving jurisdictional disputes. The Court of Appeal in *Fiona Trust v Yuri Privalov* has remarked that "the courts should, in the light of section 1(1) of the Act, be very cautious about agreeing that its process [under s.72] should be so utilised."[558] Where the party who denies the existence of a valid arbitration agreement has started competing English proceedings the issue of the stay of those proceedings (under s.9 or the inherent jurisdiction)[559] should be decided first. A s.72 application does not "trump" a stay application but "s.72 might well be applicable if the party denying the existence of an arbitration agreement had not started English proceedings and did not wish to do so."[560]   7–147

Grounds for application. Subject to these limitations, an alleged party may bring a s.72 application on a number of grounds. It would cover a party who alleges that he is not a party to an agreement containing what is clearly an arbitration clause. It would also extend to a party who, whilst accepting that he is a party to an agreement to arbitrate, alleges that he is not a proper party to the proceedings, for example because the facts in dispute do not fall within the agreement to arbitrate. It would furthermore extend to a party who accepts that he is a party to an agreement to arbitrate but disputes for example the manner in which the tribunal has been constituted.[561]   7–148

---

[555] Section 72(1) of the Arbitration Act 1996.
[556] Subject to the possible application of the principle in *Ralli Bros v Compania Naviera SA* [1920] 2 KB 287. See *Tamil Nadu Electricity Board v ST–CMS Electric Co Private Ltd* [2007] EWHC 1713, where the arbitration agreement was governed by English law and the matrix agreement was governed by Indian law. The court construed the agreement to arbitrate without relevance to alleged Indian mandatory laws. *Per* Cooke J. at [35].
[557] See para.7–144.
[558] *Fiona Trust v Yuri Privalov and Others* [2007] EWCA 20 at [34]. Affirmed *Premium Nafta Products Ltd & Others v Fili Shipping Co Ltd & Others* [2007] UKHL 40.
[559] See paras 7–010 *et seq.*
[560] *Fiona Trust v Yuri Privalov and Others* [2007] EWCA 20 at [36]; affirmed *Premium Nafta Products Ltd & Others v Fili Shipping Co Ltd & Others* [2007] UKHL 40. *Tamil Nadu Electricity Board v ST-CMS Electric Co Private Ltd* [2007] EWHC 1713.
[561] *Law Debenture Trust Corp Plc v Elektrim* [2005] 2 Lloyd's Rep. 755 at [18].

Although s.72 is primarily intended to deal with the position at the interlocutory stages of an arbitration, where no award has yet been rendered, it can also be used to challenge an award once rendered.[562] It is probable however that the relief available under s.72(1) is narrower than that contemplated by s.72(2)(a) taken with s.67. Otherwise, if all the relief available under s.67 could be obtained by an alleged party by the "back door" under s.72(1), such an alleged party would have no reason ever to proceed under s.67. If an application is made under s.70(1) the effect of which is to challenge an award, such as by seeking a declaration that there is no valid agreement to arbitrate then the suggestion has been made that such an application should be subject to the same time-limit as a challenge under s.70(3), namely 28 days after the date of the award or the result of the outcome of any process of arbitral review.[563]

7–149 **Section 72 available where option to litigate.** In *Law Debenture Trust Corp Plc v Elektrim*,[564] a party to an agreement to arbitrate who also had an option to refer the dispute to the courts, could bring an application under s.72 as he was only an alleged party to the arbitration proceedings. It did not matter that, on a plain analysis, the respondent could show that there was an arbitration agreement to which the applicant was party. The Court of Appeal has subsequently sought to confine the application of this decision to clauses conferring an option to litigate,[565] noting that the court in *Law Debenture* did not need to consider the separability of the arbitration clause but only had to decide if the litigation option had been rightly exercised by the party seeking to litigate.[566]

7–150 **Relevance of seat.** Section 72 applies where the seat of arbitration is England.[567] However, the court will consider applications under this section where no seat has been expressly fixed but where it appears to the court that the seat is England by virtue of the operation of s.3 of the Act or if no seat has been fixed but there is an appropriate connection with England and Wales.[567a] In particular, if an arbitral award which is alleged to be the product of a fraud appears to assert that the seat of the fraudulently procured arbitration is England, then the court will treat that as the designation of a seat by the tribunal under s.3(c) of the Act, even where the tribunal's authority is at issue.[568] If the seat of the arbitration is clearly

---

[562] *Bernuth Lines Ltd v High Seas Shipping Ltd* [2006] 1 All E.R. (Comm) 359, *per* Christopher Clarke J. at [57]–[58].

[563] *Arab National Bank v El-Abdali* [2005] 1 Lloyd's Rep. 541, where s.72 was used to set aside an award which had been the produce of a fraud. See the discussion of the relationship between ss.67 and 72 at [57]–[58] of Christopher Clarke J.'s judgment.

[564] [2005] 2 Lloyd's Rep. 755.

[565] See para.2–018.

[566] *Law Debenture Trust Corp Plc v Elektrim* [2005] 2 Lloyd's Rep. 755 at [12]–[21]. See the comments of the Court of Appeal on this decision in *Fiona Trust v Yuri Privalov and Others* [2007] EWCA 20, and *Axa Re v Ace Global Markets Ltd* [2006] EWHC 216 where the applicant argued on a s.72 application that the arbitration clause had not been incorporated into the parties' agreement.

[567] Section 2(1) of the Arbitration Act 1996.

[567a] Section 2(3) of the Arbitration Act 1996.

[568] *Arab National Bank v El-Abdali* [2005] 1 Lloyd's Rep. 541 where s.72 was used to set aside an award which had been the product of a fraud.

not England, then the claimant who takes no part in the foreign arbitration may seek an injunction restraining the foreign arbitration, although this will only be granted in the most exceptional cases.[569]

"Takes no part". As to what constitutes taking no part for the purposes of 7–151 s.72(1), great caution needs to be exercised by a putative applicant. Corresponding with the arbitral institution for the purpose of trying to have the arbitration dismissed and indicating a conditional appointment of an arbitrator, subject to a clear reservation, did not constitute taking part for the purposes of s.72(1).[570] The words "who takes no part in the proceedings" do not extend to taking no part in the proceedings at any stage, whether before or after a s.72 challenge.[571] An unsuccessful applicant under s.72 will not therefore be debarred by the court from subsequent participation in the arbitration, which will be a matter for the tribunal. Therefore, it is possible that an applicant could try and defeat the arbitration under s.72 and, if he fails, engage in the proceedings for the purpose of arguing the merits of the case. It is likely however that an unsuccessful applicant cannot have "two bites of the cherry": he cannot make an unsuccessful application under s.72 and then seek to have the same jurisdiction issues decided again under ss.30 or 32.[572]

A further question arises as to whether a person who takes no part in the arbitration also enjoys the rights conferred on a "party to arbitral proceedings" under ss.67, 68 and 69 or is limited to only those rights specifically conferred upon him under s.72. A strict linguistic analysis would suggest that a non-party does not enjoy all of the rights to challenge an award conferred upon a party and that the Act has drawn a distinction between a party and a non-party or an alleged party for good reason. However, if this proposition is the right then a non-party would not be able to bring an appeal on a point of law under s.69 because this section is not incorporated by s.70(2).[573]

Need to act properly. A prospective applicant under s.72 should act 7–152 promptly. Declarations and injunctions are equitable remedies and will not be granted if there has been undue delay. It has also been suggested that where an application is made in respect of an award which has already been rendered, the 28-day time limit which applies to an application under s.67 by virtue of s.70(3) should apply.[574]

Overlap of powers. As noted, there is potential overlap between the court's 7–153 powers under ss.9, 18 and 72. A party commencing an arbitration cannot have

---

[569] See para.7–062.
[570] *Law Debenture Trust Corp Plc v Elektrim*, per Mann J. at [18].
[571] *Hackwood Ltd v Areen Design Services Ltd* (2006) Const. L.J. 68.
[572] *Hackwood Ltd v Areen Design Services Ltd*, per Field J. at [42].
[573] This point is discussed but not decided in *Bernuth Lines Ltd v High Seas Shipping Ltd (The "Eastern Navigator")* [2006] 1 Lloyd's Rep. 537, at [51].
[574] *Arab National Bank v El-Abdali* [2005] 1 Lloyd's Rep. 541 at [58].

recourse to s.72 and if faced with a recalcitrant respondent reluctant to join in formation of the tribunal may have to apply for appointment of the arbitrator under s.18 (or make an equivalent application to the relevant appointing authority). Because there is an issue as to the extent to which the court will examine the existence of an agreement to arbitrate upon a s.18 application,[575] the respondent in that situation may chose to make a cross-application under s.72(1) for a declaration that he is not party to the agreement to arbitrate.[576] The recalcitrant respondent may also chose to commence court proceedings, in which case the party commencing arbitration can seek a stay under s.9. As the Court of Appeal in *Fiona Trust* has made clear, in this situation the s.9 application should be heard before any s.72 application.[577] Another possible scenario is that when arbitration and court proceedings are started in competition with each other, the party who wishes to arbitrate may apply for an anti-suit injunction to restrain the court proceedings, whilst the party who wishes to litigate may apply under s.72 for a declaration that there is no valid agreement to arbitrate. In such a situation, the court is likely to hear both applications together.[578]

7–154 **Power of the court under section 32.** In certain limited circumstances it is possible to apply to the court under s.32 of the Arbitration Act 1996 to determine any question as to the substantive jurisdiction[579] of the tribunal[580] even if no ruling has yet been made by the tribunal on the subject.[581–582] The section is mandatory.[583] Notice of an application must be given to the other parties to the arbitral proceedings[584] unless they all agree in writing to the application. Notice to the tribunal is not required but it is desirable.[585] Precisely because of the restrictions on bringing a s.32 application, namely the need for consent of the parties or the tribunal, it is a relatively rarely used tool. Indeed, the scheme of the Act is to allow the arbitrators to decide their jurisdiction first and if the parties are dissatisfied with the decision they can challenge it under s.67.

---

[575] See paras 7–095 and 7–096.

[576] This course was adopted in *Sinochem v Fortune Oil Ltd* [2000] 1 Lloyd's Rep. 682.

[577] *Fiona Trust and Others v Yuri Privalov & Others* [2007] EWCA 20. Affirmed *Premium Nafta Products Ltd & Others v Fili Shipping Co Ltd & Others* [2007] UKHL 40.

[578] As happened in *Welex AG v Rosa Maritime Ltd (The "Epsilon Rosa") (No.2)* [2003] 2 Lloyd's Rep. 509. See in particular Tuckey L.J. at [37].

[579] For a definition of "substantive jurisdiction" see s.82(1) of the Arbitration Act 1996. See also paras 2–072 *et seq.* for matters within the tribunals jurisdiction.

[580] For the procedure for the application see paras 8–178 *et seq.*, but this application has special provisions in CPR Arbitration PD 19 which will be mentioned in the following paras 7–156 *et seq.*

[581–582] *Vale Do Rio v Shanghai Bao Steel* [2000] 2 Lloyd's Rep. 1. Where the tribunal has made a ruling on jurisdiction, that ruling can be challenged by applying to the court under s.67 of the Arbitration Act 1996, see paras 8–054 *et seq.*

[583] Section 4(1) and Sch.1 to the Arbitration Act 1996.

[584] Section 32(1) of the Arbitration Act 1996.

[585] Section 32(1) of the Arbitration Act 1996 requires notice "to the other parties" but if the applicant or the other parties do not want the tribunal to proceed with the arbitration until the question of jurisdiction is determined by the court notice of the application should be given to the tribunal.

Inherent jurisdiction of the court? Section 32 is arguably shadowed by   7–155
the court's inherent jurisdiction to determine a tribunal's jurisdiction at any time.
The effect of the policy of the 1996 Act, together with the express effect of s.1(c)
is that the court should not, save perhaps in exceptional cases, determine the
tribunal's jurisdiction under the court's inherent jurisdiction.[586]

Written agreement of all parties to the arbitral proceedings.   7–156
If all parties agree in writing, an application to the court under this section can be
made by any party to the arbitration proceedings.[587] In this event it does not
matter whether the tribunal agrees to the application or not, or that it has not been
invited to make a ruling on the matter.

Before the tribunal is appointed permission of all other parties to the dispute is
required for the purposes of an application under s.32 of the Act, and the court
"should not customarily be troubled with disputes as to the validity of the
reference to arbitration".[588] However, unlike applications made with the permission of the tribunal, where further conditions need to be satisfied before the court
will consider the matter,[589] when the parties consent to an application being made
there is no statutory basis at least on which the court can refuse to consider the
matter.[590] However, the court has expressed the view that it is not very satisfactory
for an application to be made under s.32 in respect of a partial objection to
jurisdiction only, where the arbitration was in any event going to proceed in
respect of the greater part of the dispute. In such case, the partial objection should
be reserved, to be dealt with by the arbitrators in the first instance and possibly by
the court on appeal under s.67 if needs be.[591]

Permission of the arbitral tribunal. If the applicant cannot secure the   7–157
agreement of all the parties to the arbitral proceedings he may still apply to the
court under s.32 if the tribunal agrees,[592] but in that event he must state in his
application the grounds on which he claims that the matter should be decided by
the court[593] rather than by the arbitral tribunal (e.g., the tribunal says that it

---

[586] *JT Mackley v Gossport Marina* [2002] B.L.R 367 where the court declined to exercise its inherent
jurisdiction to determine the tribunal's jurisdiction in the absence of the s.32 criteria having been
met.
[587] Section 32(2) of the Arbitration Act 1996. The subsection specifies that the agreement must be "in
writing". In *Elektrim v Vivendi Universal* [2007] EWHC 11, at [123] the court had not actually seen
any written agreement but was prepared to assume that one existed or would be prepared having
retrospective effect. The application need not be made by all the parties to the arbitration agreement
as long as they all agree in writing to the application.
[588] *JT Mackley's v Gosport Morris Ltd* [2002] EWHL 1315.
[589] Section 32(2)(b) of the Arbitration Act 1996.
[590] *Esso Exploration & Production Co UK Ltd v Electricity Supply Board* [2004] 1 All E.R. (Comm) 926,
where the court considered without question an application made by one party with the consent of
the other.
[591] *Peterson Farms v C&M Farming & Another* [2004] 1 Lloyd's Rep. 614 at [24].
[592] When there is more than one arbitrator and the parties have not agreed otherwise a majority
decision of the tribunal may suffice—see ss.20(3) and 22(2) of the Arbitration Act 1996—but the
fact that one arbitrator disagrees with the application will be a factor to be considered by the courts
in deciding whether to grant the application.
[593] Section 32(3) of the Arbitration Act 1996.

cannot decide the question of jurisdiction). He must also satisfy the court on the following conditions although if the tribunal has given its permission it is unlikely that the courts will scrutinise these pre-conditions very hard[594]:

- that the application was made without delay;

- that a determination by the court of the question of jurisdiction is likely to produce a substantial saving in costs; and

- that there is a good reason why the matter should be decided by the court at this stage of the proceedings and not by the tribunal.[595]

Each of these requirements must be met. The tribunal cannot apparently ask the court to determine its jurisdiction for it of its own motion. The circumstances in which the tribunal would encourage or consent to an application under s.32(b) of the Act are extremely limited. Exceptions might conceivably relate to a standard form agreement where the tribunal felt that the point was likely to arise repeatedly in other situations, but even then it is hard to envisage this would be enough to displace the presumption that the tribunal should determine its own jurisdiction.

7–158 **No delay.** The requirement that the application is made without delay is separate from the defence that may be raised by another party to the arbitral proceedings that the applicant has lost his right to object although in practice the two may overlap.[596]

7–159 **Substantial saving of costs.** The onus of satisfying the court on this condition also rests on the applicant. The use of the words "is likely to" in s.32[597] suggests that this requirement is not onerous, although the threshold is higher than "might produce substantial savings in costs" which appeared in another context in the former legislation.[598] There must be some evidence however that the saving of costs could be "substantial". This may, for example, include evidence that the court's determination would avoid the need to challenge a decision of the tribunal on the matter if an award were made although such reasoning may be too speculative to meet the "substantial savings" threshold.[599]

7–160 **Court decision is justified.** Not only must the applicant specify grounds why the court should decide the matter but he must also satisfy the court that

---

[594] See for example the brief approach taken to the satisfaction of the conditions in *Film Finance Inc v The Royal Bank of Scotland* [2007] EWHC 195 at [3].

[595] Section 32(2)(b) of the Arbitration Act 1996. In *Belgravia Property v S&R Ltd* [2001] B.L.R. 424, the court agreed that the matter was appropriate for decision by the court (at 434).

[596] Section 32(1) of the Arbitration Act 1996: see paras 7–162 *et seq.*

[597] See s.32(2)(b)(i) of the Arbitration Act 1996.

[598] See s.2(2)(a) of the Arbitration Act 1979, which has been replaced by s.45 of the Arbitration Act 1996.

[599] An identical provision appears in s.45(2)(b)(i) of the Arbitration Act 1996: see para.7–172.

there is a good reason for making an order in the course of the reference.[600] In the absence of the agreement in writing of all other parties to the arbitration proceedings, it is necessary but not sufficient that the tribunal consents to the application. In deciding whether or not to consider the application the court will take account of the witness statements filed by the parties setting out any evidence relied on in support of "their contention that the court should, or should not, consider the application".[601] The court will usually decide the matter without a hearing.[602] Section 32 is intended to deal only with exceptional cases.[603]

The application to court is for a declaration as to the arbitrator's jurisdiction which may be specified in terms of the proper construction of the arbitration agreement.

If the arbitrator has issued an award which contains a ruling on his jurisdiction, a party seeking to challenge his decision should apply to the court not under s.32 but under s.67.[604]

Effect of application on the arbitral proceedings. Unless the 7–161 parties agree otherwise, the tribunal may continue the arbitral proceedings and even make an award while an application to the court under s.32 is pending.[605] This is more likely to happen when the parties agree to apply jointly to the court than if the tribunal consents to the application to the court. In the first case the parties should notify the tribunal in writing of the proposed application and request it to suspend the arbitral proceedings if that is what is wanted. If the tribunal does not agree to suspend the parties should include in their application to the court a request for an injunction.[606]

Loss of right to object. Apart from the need to satisfy the court that the 7–162 application was made without delay[607] a party who wishes to take advantage of s.32 should apply to the court,[608] and give notice to the other parties, as soon as he becomes aware of any issue as to the substantive jurisdiction of the tribunal. He may lose his right to object if he delays.[609] The Arbitration Act 1996 provides that

---

[600] This is apparent from the terms of s.32(2)(b)(iii) and 32(3) of the Arbitration Act 1996.

[601] PD 62, para.9.2 requires the written evidence or witness statements to set out such evidence.

[602] PD 62, para.9.3.

[603] See DAC report, para.147 which states that this section is "not intended to detract from the basic rule as set out in [section] 30". (i.e. the competence of the tribunal to rule on its own jurisdiction).

[604] See paras 8–054 *et seq.*

[605] Section 32(4) of the Arbitration Act 1996.

[606] Section 32(4) of the Arbitration Act 1996 is subject to the qualification "unless otherwise agreed by the parties" which leaves open the possibility of applying for an injunction if the tribunal ignores the parties' agreement.

[607] Section 32(2)(b)(ii) of the Arbitration Act 1996: see para.7–158.

[608] There may be a challenge procedure in the arbitration agreement itself or in any rules incorporated into that agreement (e.g. ICC Rules of Arbitration, Art.11) but the applicant may apply to the court before exhausting that procedure although the intervention of the court would have to be justified.

[609] Section 32(1) of the Arbitration Act 1996 which refers to s.73 of the Arbitration Act 1996; see similar provisions referred to in paras 8–062 and 8–065.

the applicant may not raise an objection[610] before the court if he continued to take part in the arbitral proceedings without objecting "forthwith or within such time as is allowed by the arbitration agreement[611] unless he shows that, at the time he took part in the proceedings, he did not know and could not with reasonable diligence have discovered the grounds for the objection".[612]

7–163 **Appeal to Court of Appeal.** There are two possible appeals contemplated by s.32 of the Act. The first concerns the court's decision whether the conditions specified in subs.(2) have been met.[613] The second possible appeal concerns the decision of the court on the question of the jurisdiction of the tribunal, which is treated as a judgment of the court for the purpose of an appeal.[614] In both cases leave of the court making the decision is apparently required.

The court referred to in ss.32(5) and (6) is the court of first instance which decided the matter[615]; so it used to be the case that if permission of that court is not obtained there can be no appeal. However, there are now at least two categories of cases where the Court of Appeal will grant permission to appeal even though the judge at first instance has refused permission. These are considered at para.7–201 which deals with wording to the same effect under s.44(7).

8. DETERMINATION OF QUESTIONS OF LAW DURING THE ARBITRATION

7–164 **Introduction.** Normally the tribunal will decide all issues of fact and law that arise in the course of the reference. In a particular case however the tribunal and one or more of the parties may request the court to determine a question of law, although applications under s.45 are extremely rare. It may be appropriate to consider applying where it is apparent that the case will turn on the issue of law in question and that, whichever way it is decided by the tribunal, one or other of the parties will then seek to appeal against the award.[616] Given the need to seek leave of the court for any appeal against an award, it may be more convenient for all concerned to have the point determined by the court at the outset.[617] In these

---

[610] The objection here means any objection on which the application for removal is based. There may, of course, be several objections (see the use of the words "that objection" in s.73(1) of the Arbitration Act 1996).

[611] The arbitration agreement itself or rules incorporated into it may contain a time limit within which any challenge to jurisdiction must be made.

[612] Arbitration Act 1996, s.73(1).

[613] Section 32(5) of the Arbitration Act 1996—each one of the conditions have been described above in paras 7–158 *et seq.*

[614] Section 32(6) of the Arbitration Act 1996 first sentence.

[615] See definition of court in s.105(1) of the Arbitration Act 1996.

[616] Another example mentioned in the DAC report at para.218 is where an important point of law is of general interest and is potentially the subject of a large number of arbitrations. The subject of appeal against an award is dealt with in paras 8–119 *et seq.*

[617] There is though a requirement that the question of law, substantially affect the rights of one or more of the parties: see para.7–168 below.

circumstances it may save time and costs to have the point authoritatively determined by the court at an early stage and for the award to reflect that decision.

With the agreement of the other parties or the permission of the tribunal an application can be made to the court for the determination of a question of law during the arbitration. This procedure is not available however if neither the tribunal nor the other parties will agree to the determination of the question by the court. In that event it will fall to be determined by the tribunal in the course of the arbitration.[618–619]

Power of the court. In the circumstances mentioned in the following paragraphs, s.45 of the Arbitration Act 1996 empowers the court to decide any question of law arising in the course of an arbitration. The application may only be made by a party to the arbitral proceedings. It cannot be made by the tribunal alone. The other parties to the arbitral proceeding must be notified of any application under this section.[620]   7–165

Excluding court's power. The parties may agree not to apply to the court under s.45 and this is called an "exclusion agreement".[621] Alternatively, they may agree to dispense with reasons for any arbitral award, which will be construed as an exclusion agreement, and so prevent a determination by the court under that section.[622]   7–166

Question of law. The court's power under s.45(1) of the Arbitration Act 1996 is limited, as it is on an appeal,[623] to determining questions of law. The particular questions of law must be identified in the application.[624] The section cannot be used in relation to questions of fact, although the distinction is not always easy to make.   7–167

It is not practicable to produce an exhaustive list of the types of questions of law which may be referred for determination by the court, but the following warrant specific mention.

[618–619] If dissatisfied with the tribunal's award on a question of law an appeal may lie under s.69 of the Arbitration Act 1996 but permission of the court is required, unless all parties agree: see para.8–132.

[620] Section 45(1) of the Arbitration Act 1996. The procedure for a general arbitration application is contained in paras 8–178 *et seq.*, but special provisions apply to this application as is mentioned in para.7–174.

[621] The right to exclude the court's power is apparent from the opening words of s.45(1) of the Arbitration Act 1996. This right to exclude will also apply to a "domestic arbitration agreement" as s.87(1)(b) of the Arbitration Act 1996 has not been brought into force. It seems that exclusion agreements can still be made in general terms: See *Sumukan Ltd v Commonwealth Secretariat* [2006] 1 All E.R. (Comm) 621. Leave to appeal the decision was refused by the Court of Appeal, *Sumukan Ltd v Commonwealth Secretariat* [2007] EWCA 243; [2007] Bus. L.R. 1075.

[622] Arbitration Act 1996, s.45(1), second sentence.

[623] Section 69(1) of the Arbitration Act 1996. See para.8–119.

[624] Section 45(3) of the Arbitration Act 1996.

- Questions of construction: although often said to involve mixed questions of fact and law, questions of construction of an instrument may be considered by the court under s.45.[625]

- Questions of procedure: Questions may arise in the course of the reference whether the tribunal has the power or duty to make (or to refuse to make) a particular procedural order or direction. Determining these questions depends on matters such as the proper construction of the Arbitration Act 1996 and of the arbitration agreement. These are questions of law which are capable of being referred to the court for a preliminary determination under s.45, provided the other requirements of the section are fulfilled[626] and there is no exclusion agreement.[627] It is however necessary to distinguish questions concerning the exercise by the tribunal of a discretion to make (or refuse to make) an order or direction. These are not generally questions of law and cannot properly be the subject of an application under this section.[628]

- Question relating to appointment of arbitrators: these cannot be considered under s.45. They should be made under the appropriate appointment related section of the Arbitration Act, usually s.18.[629]

- Questions of jurisdiction: If the question which arises is whether the arbitrator has jurisdiction to determine a dispute, it will not be appropriate for this question to be resolved by an application to the court under s.45 because it is provided for expressly by ss.32 and 67 of the Act.[630]

- Questions of admissibility of evidence: Such questions in an arbitration cannot be the subject of an application under s.45, because they are to be decided by the tribunal. Section 34(2)(f) of the Act provides that the tribunal shall decide rules as to admissibility of evidence, subject to the right of the parties to agree some other rules.[631] An application under s.68 based in part on the tribunal's failure to grant disclosure was considered and rejected in *ABB AG v Hochtief Airport GmbH*.[632]

7–168 **Substantially affect the rights of one or more of the parties.**
Even if all parties or the tribunal agree to it, an application under s.45 of the Act

---

[625] *Beegas Nominees Ltd v Decco Ltd* [2003] 3 E.G.L.R 25.
[626] See paras 7–171 *et seq.* for these requirements.
[627] See, e.g. *Panchaud Freres SA v Etablissements General Grain Co* [1969] 2 Lloyd's Rep. 109; *Kursell v Timber Operators and Contractors Ltd* [1923] 2 K.B. 202.
[628] *Exmar BV v National Iranian Tanker Co (The "Trade Fortitude")* [1992] 1 Lloyd's Rep. 169; *Vasso (owners) v Vasso (cargo owners) (The "Vasso")* [1983] 3 All E.R. 211. Although decided before the Arbitration Act 1996, these decisions are relevant to this point.
[629] *City & General* (Holborn) Ltd, above, at paras 22–25.
[630] For a discussion of the ways in which jurisdiction may be challenged see paras 7–054 *et seq.* for a challenge under s.32, and paras 8–054 *et seq.* for a challenge under s.67 of the Arbitration Act 1996.
[631] See para.1–026 for a short discussion on the treatment of rules of evidence.
[632] [2006] 1 All E.R. (Comm) 529.

will not be granted unless the court is satisfied that the question of law substantially affects the rights of one or more of the parties.[633] This requirement reflects one of the conditions for leave to appeal against an award of the tribunal.[634] It may be satisfied if the sum involved is material[635] or if the determination of the question of law will resolve issues of title as to property which is the subject of the dispute.

Agreement of all parties. An application can be made under s.45 if all the parties to the arbitral proceedings agree[636] and the conditions mentioned in the preceding paragraphs[637] apply. The agreement can be given at the time when the dispute arises, or can be given in advance in the agreement to arbitrate.[638] In that event agreement of the tribunal is not required.   7–169

Permission of the arbitral tribunal. If the applicant cannot procure the agreement of all the parties to the arbitral proceedings to agree he may still apply to the court under s.45 if the tribunal agrees,[639] but in that event he must state in his application the grounds on which he claims that the matter should be decided by the court[640] rather than by the arbitral tribunal.[641] He must also satisfy the court on the following conditions: 7–170

- that the application was made without delay; and

- that a determination by the court of the question of jurisdiction is likely to produce a substantial saving in costs.

Each of these conditions must be met.[642]

---

[633] Section 45(1) of the Arbitration Act 1996. This requirement differs from the requirement contained in s.1(3)(b) of the Arbitration Act 1979, namely, that the question of law was one for which leave to appeal would be likely to be given. This change was deliberate because the previous requirement gave rise to great difficulty, both in theory and in practice, see DAC report, para.219.

[634] See s.69(3)(a) of the Arbitration Act 1996 and para.8–132.

[635] Decisions of the court based on s.1(4) of the Arbitration Act 1979, which has been re-enacted by s.69(3)(a) of the Arbitration Act 1996 and which contained a similar requirement are relevant to the meaning of this requirement: see for example, *The "Evimerie"* [1992] 1 Lloyd's Rep. 55.

[636] Although s.45(2)(a) of the Arbitration Act 1996 does not specify that the agreement of the other parties need be in writing (contrast s.32(2)(a) of the Act) an agreement is only effective for the purposes of Pt 1 of the Act "if in writing", see s.5(1) of the Arbitration Act 1996.

[637] See paras 7–167 and 7–168.

[638] As was the case in *Taylor Woodrow Holdings Ltd & Another v Barnes & Elliott Ltd* [2006] W.L. 2248800.

[639] When there is more than one arbitrator and the parties have not agreed otherwise a majority decision of the tribunal may suffice, see ss.20(3) and 22(2) of the Arbitration Act 1996. But the fact that one arbitrator disagrees with the application will be a factor to be considered by the court in deciding whether to grant the application.

[640] Section 45(3) of the Arbitration Act 1996.

[641] This may occur if the parties have agreed that the tribunal shall not have the power to decide the point of law.

[642] Section 45(2)(b) of the Arbitration Act 1996. See *ABB Lummus v Keppel* [1999] 2 Lloyd's Rep. 24 for a case where similar conditions were not met in respect of an application under s.32 of the Arbitration Act 1996.

7–171 **No delay.** If the application is to succeed it should be made as soon as the question of law can reasonably be identified and the permission of the tribunal obtained. Whether there has been delay in making the application is a matter of fact which will be determined by the court. The applicant must justify any apparent delay.[643]

7–172 **Substantial saving of costs.** The court must also be satisfied that the determination of the question is likely to produce substantial savings in costs to the parties.[644] The use of the words "is likely to" suggests that the hurdle in relation to saving costs is not very high. There must be some evidence however that the saving of costs could be substantial. It will usually be satisfied if a decision one way will determine the result altogether, or at least shorten the hearing. It does not matter that the decision may in fact go the other way.[645] Nevertheless, s.45 is aimed at the exceptional case.[646]

7–173 **Residual discretion.** Even where the threshold conditions are satisfied the court retains a discretion as to whether or not to decide the question of law.[647] In practice, the court is unlikely to refuse to decide the question if the conditions are satisfied.

7–174 **Procedure.** Where an application claim is made under s.45 of the Act with the agreement in writing of all the other parties to the arbitration proceedings, there is no need for evidence in support of their contention that the court should consider their claim,[648] although the parties should give reasons for their application. Where, however, the written consent of all the parties is not available but the tribunal has given its permission to the application claim under s.45, the written evidence or witness statements filed by the parties to the application must set out any evidence relied on in support of "their contention that the court should, or should not, consider the application".[649] Unless the court otherwise directs, it will decide without a hearing whether or not to consider the claim.[650] If the court

---

[643] Section 45(2)(b)(ii) of the Arbitration Act 1996.

[644] Section 45(2)(b)(i) of the Arbitration Act 1996—compare with the similar provision in s.32(2)(b)(i) in the Arbitration Act 1996 dealt with at para.7–159.

[645] *Vasso (owners) v Vasso (cargo owners) (The "Vasso")* [1983] 3 All E.R. 211. That case demonstrated the difficulty of complying with the terms of s.2(1) of the Arbitration Act 1979, which has been replaced by s.45 of the Arbitration Act 1996 in relation to a question whether the arbitrator had power to order the inspection of property. The difficulty was however ignored to the extent that the court proceeded to hear the application anyway.

[646] See para.7–178 and quotation from Court of Appeal in *Babanaft International SA v Avant Petroleum* [1982] 1 W.L.R. 871 at 882, a case about the court's non-interventionist policy.

[647] *Taylor Woodrow Holdings Ltd & Another v Barnes & Elliott Ltd* [2006] W.L. 2248800 at [55]–[62].

[648] This conclusion can be implied from PD 62 para.9.2. For procedure generally in respect of application claims, see paras 8–178 *et seq.*

[649] PD 62, para.9.2.

[650] PD 62, para.9.3.

decides to consider the claim, it will usually be determined in public,[651] although the court may order the claim to be heard in private.[652]

Effect of application on the arbitral proceedings. Unless the 7–175
parties agree otherwise, the tribunal may continue the arbitral proceedings and even make an award while an application to the court under s.45 is pending.[653] This is more likely to happen when the parties agree to apply jointly to the court than if the tribunal consents to the application to the court. In the first case the parties should notify the tribunal in writing of the proposed application and ask for the arbitral proceedings to be suspended if that is what is wanted. If the tribunal does not agree to suspend the parties should include in their application to the court a request for an injunction.[654]

Effect of the court's order. The court's decision on a question of law made 7–176
under s.45 is treated as a judgment of the court for the purposes of an appeal,[655] and can in principle be the subject of an appeal,[656] but an appeal will be allowed only in limited circumstances.[657] The court's decision whether or not to grant the application and decide the question of law is final unless permission to appeal is given.[658]

Costs of the application. It is important that the court should be asked to 7–177
deal with the costs of the application to the court as it is doubtful whether the tribunal would have jurisdiction to do so.[659] The court will apply the same principles as it usually does when considering who should bear the costs of an application.[660]

Appeal to Court of Appeal. There are two possible appeals contemplated 7–178
by s.45 of the Act. The first concerns the court's decision whether the conditions specified in subs.(2) have been met.[661] The second concerns the decision of the court on the question of law arising in the course of the arbitration, which is

---

[651] CPR r.62.10(3)(a).
[652] CPR r.62.10(1). The hearing may be in private where the evidence to be considered for or against the claim is particularly confidential.
[653] Section 45(4) of the Arbitration Act 1996.
[654] Section 45(4) of the Act is subject to the qualification "unless otherwise agreed by the parties" which leaves open the possibility of applying for an injunction if the tribunal ignores the parties' agreement.
[655] Section 45(6) of the Arbitration Act 1996.
[656] See s.45(6) of the Arbitration Act 1996 and the Supreme Courts Act 1981, s.16.
[657] The limited circumstances are described in para.7–178.
[658] This is the effect of s.45(6) of the Act. See para.7–178.
[659] Costs of an application to court under s.45 of the Act are arguably not recoverable costs of the arbitration under ss.63 and 64 of the Arbitration Act 1996: see paras 7–209 *et seq.*
[660] See CPR Pt 44.3 and commentary in the *White Book.*
[661] Section 45(5) of the Arbitration Act 1996. Each one of the conditions have been described above in paras 7–170 *et seq.*

treated as a judgment of the court for the purpose of an appeal.[662] In both cases leave of the court making the decision is apparently required. The court referred to in s.45(5) and (6) is the court of first instance which decided the matter[663]; so it used to be the case that if permission of that court is not obtained there can be no appeal. However, there are now at least two categories of cases where the Court of Appeal will grant permission to appeal even though the judge at first instance has refused permission. These are considered at para.7–201 which deals with wording to the same effect under s.44(7).

9. Court's Powers to Issue Injunctions and make Other Orders in Relation to Arbitral Proceedings

7–179   **Introduction.** In addition to extending time limits[664] appointing and removing arbitrators[665] and determining disputes as to jurisdiction[666] and questions of law,[667] the court has power to make a wide variety of orders in relation to arbitral proceedings. They include enforcing orders made by the arbitral tribunal,[668] securing the attendance of witnesses at the arbitration hearing[669] and making any orders relating to evidence or property, including the granting of injunctions, mentioned in s.44 of the Arbitration Act 1996. That section, which has attracted significant judicial attention culminating in the Court of Appeal's decision in *Cetelem v Roust*,[670] has been construed as being in broad terms and contemplates that an order may in an urgent case be made in advance of the commencement of an arbitration.[671] The following paragraphs will deal first with the powers under s.44[672] and will include in this discussion consideration of the existence of the court's inherent jurisdiction to grant injunctions.[673] It will then proceed to describe the court's powers under s.42[674] and appeals from orders under both these sections.[675] Various other powers of the court in relation to ongoing arbitrations are then dealt with,[676] concluding with a discussion of certain matters in relation to which the court no longer has power to make orders, namely disclosure

---

[662] Section 45(6) of the Arbitration Act 1996, first sentence.
[663] See definition of court in s.105(1) of the Arbitration Act 1996.
[664] See paras 7–067 *et seq.* above.
[665] See paras 7–095 *et seq.* above.
[666] See paras 7–143 *et seq.* above.
[667] See paras 7–164 *et seq.* above.
[668] Arbitration Act 1996, s.42.
[669] Arbitration Act 1996, s.43.
[670] *Cetelem SA v Roust Holdings Ltd* [2005] 1 W.L.R. 3555.
[671] *Tsakos Shipping v Orizon Tanker Co (The "Centaurus Mar")* [1998] C.L.C. 1.003. For urgent cases—see para.7–188.
[672] See paras 7–180—7–197 below.
[673] See para.7–196.
[674] See paras 7–198—7–200.
[675] See para.7–201.
[676] See paras 7–202—7–206.

of documents, answers to requests for information and security for costs in arbitrations.[677]

Power of the court to order interim injunctions and other orders during an arbitration. Section 44 of the Arbitration Act 1996 confers wide powers on the court in relation to the preservation of assets and evidence for an arbitration, including the important power to grant interim injunctions.[678] The court's powers under this section are the same as those exercisable in legal proceedings, save for urgent cases where it is now established that they are limited by the requirements of s.44(3).[679] The provisions of s.44 must be read in conjunction with the relevant rules of the court governing the exercise of those powers in relation to legal proceedings.[680]

7–180

Application to court or tribunal? When considering whether to seek an injunction or other interim order, the first decision to take is whether to apply for the relevant relief from the court or arbitral tribunal. The factors which should be taken into account when reaching this decision are dealt with in Ch.5.[681]

7–181

Should the court act? When an application is made to it, the court needs to consider the breadth of the its powers under s.44. There has been considerable recent debate over the extent of the powers available. For present purposes at least, the debate has been resolved by the Court of Appeal in *Cetelem v Roust Holdings*.[682] On the one hand, it is argued that the purpose of the 1996 Act is to make clear provision for the consensual resolution of disputes and to permit only a very limited role for the court. The Act made it clear that the court should not be given any powers that might be used to interfere with or usurp the arbitral process. Such an approach suggests that injunctive relief should be the preserve of the arbitral tribunal and should only be ordered by the court as a last resort, unless the court is acting at the request of the tribunal. On the other hand, it is argued that effective arbitrations are often secured by prompt, early injunctive relief of the sort that only the court can effectively give. This argument was largely accepted by the Court of Appeal who noted:

7–182

> "The whole purpose of giving the court power to make such orders is to assist the arbitral tribunal in cases of urgency or before there is an arbitration on foot. Otherwise it is all to easy for a party who is bent on a policy of non-cooperation to frustrate the arbitral process. Of course, in any case where the court is called upon to exercise the power, it

[677] These matters are dealt with at paras 7–207—7–208.
[678] The matters to which these powers relate are set out in s.44(2) of the Arbitration Act 1996 and are addressed in paras 7–191 *et seq.* below.
[679] Section 44(1) of the Arbitration Act 1996, "legal proceedings" means civil proceedings in the High Court or a County Court, s.82(1) of the Act.
[680] Principally the CPR.
[681] See paras 5–075 *et seq.*
[682] *Cetelem SA v Roust Holdings Ltd* [2005] 1 W.L.R. 3555.

must take great care not to usurp the arbitral process and to ensure, by exacting appropriate undertakings from the claimant, that the substantive questions are reserved for the arbitrator or arbitrators."[683]

7–183 **Foreign or no seat.** The powers contained in s.44 are available even if the seat of the arbitration is abroad or no seat has been designated or determined, but in that case the court may refuse to exercise the powers if it considers that it would be "inappropriate to do so".[684] Where the seat of arbitration is abroad the court will need a very good reason to exercise its jurisdiction under s.44: "As Mr Brindle QC submitted on behalf of the Respondents, 'The natural court for the granting of interim injunctive relief must be the court of the country of the seat of arbitration, especially where the curial law of the arbitration is that of the same country.' I agree.".[685]

7–184 **The Brussels regime.** Where the respondent is domiciled in another country that has acceded to the Brussels jurisdictional regime,[686] the question arises whether the arbitration exception embraces all types of provisional measures.[687] As noted,[688] the approach of the English court, as enunciated by the Court of Appeal in *Through Transport Mutual Insurance (Eurasia) Ltd v New India Assurance Co Ltd,* is to assess whether the "principal focus" of the proceedings is arbitration.[689] This was said to include proceedings involving ancillary assistance in the context of arbitration proceedings.[690] If the proceedings have arbitration as their principal focus then the arbitration exception is triggered. However, the ECJ has found that "provisional measures are not in principle ancillary to arbitration proceedings but are ordered in parallel to such proceedings and are intended as measures of support. They concern not arbitration as such but the protection of a wide variety of rights".[691] The ECJ found that a court-ordered provisional measure requiring the interim payment of sums claimed (in support of an

---

[683] *Cetelem SA v Roust Holdings Ltd* [2005] 1 W.L.R. 3555, *per* Clarke L.J. at [71].

[684] Section 2(3) of the Arbitration Act 1996. The words quoted indicate that the court has a complete discretion whether or not to exercise its powers in such a case. See *Commerce Insurance Co v Lloyd's Underwriters* [2002] 1 W.L.R. 132.

[685] *Econet Wireless Ltd v Vee Networks Ltd and Others* [2006] EWHC 1568 at [19]. See also *Weissfisch v Julius and Others* [2006] EWCA 218, not a decision under s.44, but relevant because the Court of Appeal refused to injunct a Swiss arbitration. See further the substantive decision in *A v B* [2006] EWHC 2006.

[686] See paras 7–012 *et seq.* above.

[687] See also the discussion of the arbitration exception in the context of anti-suit injunctions at para.7–013.

[688] At para.7–013.

[689] [2005] 1 Lloyd's Rep. 67 at [44], [47]–[49]. An anti-suit injunction was not granted in this case where a third party was pursuing a statutory right under Finnish law in the Finnish courts against an insurer. See a discussion of the effect of the *Turner v Grovit* line of cases and *Through Transport* by Sir Anthony Clarke M.R. speaking extra-judicially, "The differing approach to commercial litigation in the European Court of Justice and the courts of England and Wales", Institute of Advanced Legal Studies, London, February 23, 2006, available at *www.dca.gov.uk/judicial/speeches/2006*.

[690] See also *A v.B* [2006] EWHC 2006 and the cases cited at para.94 of Colman J.'s judgment.

[691] *Van Uden Maritime BV v KG Deco-Line* (Case C-391/95) [1999] 2 W.L.R. 1181 at 1256, ECJ.

underlying arbitration) was accordingly caught by the Brussels Convention on Jurisdiction. Accordingly, the court said that interim relief can only be granted by an English court where the measure is truly provisional and where there is a real connecting link between the subject matter of the measure sought and the territorial jurisdiction of the court. There is some conflict between the ECJ's construction of the arbitration exception and that taken by the English courts in *Through Transport* and subsequent cases. The position for now is that whilst it is clear that the Brussels jurisdictional regime does not embrace most arbitration-related proceedings there is a possibility that certain provisional measures will need to satisfy the *Van Uden* criteria where the respondent is domiciled in a member state. The scope of the arbitration exception is likely to be clarified by the ECJ in deciding the reference in *West Tankers*.[692]

Post award injunctions. Once an award has been issued and enforcement proceedings are on foot, it appears that the court's jurisdiction to grant injunctions is derived from its usual powers to issue injunctions to assist enforcement proceedings and not from s.44.[693] **7–185**

Excluding court's powers. Section 44 of the Act is not mandatory,[694] so an application cannot be made to the court if the parties have excluded the powers under this section.[695] **7–186**

Non-urgent cases. The section draws a distinction between urgent and non-urgent cases. Unless the case is one of urgency, the court can only act on the application of a party to the arbitral proceedings who has obtained the permission of the tribunal or the agreement in writing of all the other parties.[696] This requirement is consistent with the policy of the Arbitration Act 1996 to leave the **7–187**

---

[692] *West Tankers Inc v RAS Riunione Adriatica di Sicurta SpA and* others [2007] UKHL 4.
[693] *Celtic Resources Holdings Ltd v Arduina Holding BV* [2006] EWHC 2553 at [37]. When considering whether to continue a freezing order in aid of the execution of a judgment (which had been converted from an award), the court noted that it had an independent jurisdiction to consider whether a freezing order should be granted on usual principles. It appears that the arbitrator was functus officio in that case.
[694] This is apparent from the opening words of s.44(1) of the Arbitration Act 1996 and from its absence from Sch.1 of the Arbitration Act 1996.
[695] The terms of the exclusion clause must be clear—see *In Re Q's Estate* [1999] 1 Lloyd's Rep. 931. The arbitration clause or rules incorporated into it may contain an exclusion agreement in terms wide enough to prevent an application for some or all of the orders that can be made under s.44 of the Arbitration Act 1996. In *Sankofa v Football Association* [2007] EWHC 78, Simon J. at [16]–[18], expressed the preliminary view that the arbitration rules of the Football Association probably excluded the right to seek a court injunction under s.44. See also *Vertex Data Science v Powergen Retail* [2006] 2 Lloyd's Rep. 591, where the court found that an agreement to exclude the tribunal's power to grant injunctions under s.48(5) of the Arbitration Act 1996 did not necessarily mean that the parties also intended to exclude the court's powers under s.44.
[696] Section 44(4) of the Arbitration Act 1996. The evidence supporting the application should so state. For an example of one such application made with the permission of the tribunal, see *Assimina Maritime Ltd v Pakistan National Shipping Corp (The "Tasman Spirit")* [2005] I Lloyd's Rep 525, at [9].

conduct of the arbitration to the tribunal. Notice of any application must be given to the parties and the tribunal.[697] When these pre-conditions are met, the full range of the court's powers in subs.(2) are available. It is the application of the section to urgent cases which has aroused the greater controversy, probably because non-urgent applications, which effectively require consent, are relatively rare.

7–188   **Urgent cases.** Where there is urgency the courts may make an order in the absence of both the tribunal's permission and written consent of the other parties where it is necessary to do so "for the purposes of preserving evidence or assets".[698] The question considered in *Cetelem*[699] was whether the broad powers contained in subss.(1) and (2) were limited by subs.(3), so that in urgent cases those powers could only be exercised where the court thinks it is "necessary for the purpose of preserving evidence or assets".[700] The Court of Appeal agreed with this submission, overturning a previous line of authority which suggested that s.44 should not be construed in such a limited way, the power in subs.3 being merely permissive and not limiting the broad operation of the court's powers in subss.(1) and (2).[701–702] However, although at first sight the effect of the decision is to narrow the application of s.44 in urgent cases, in fact the practical difference between the position before and after *Cetelem*[703] is not great. Although the court confirmed that the order must be necessary for the purpose of preserving evidence or assets, assets are not to be limited to tangible assets but include choses in action, including contractual rights. In other words, a party may be able to justify an urgent application under s.44 to protect his contractual rights, even if no other more tangible assets can be identified.[703a] In that event the court may grant the application of a party (or even a proposed party) to the arbitral proceedings.

7–189   **Tribunal unable to act effectively.** Whether or not the case is urgent, the applicant will have to satisfy the court that the tribunal is "unable for the time being to act effectively".[704] This emphasises the fact that relief under s.44 will only be available from the court to the extent that it cannot be obtained from the arbitral process chosen by the parties. For this requirement to be satisfied, the tribunal must be unable to act effectively, either because it has not yet been constituted, which is the paradigm case,[705] or because, as the DAC report put it "in the nature of things it cannot act quickly or effectively enough".[706] Therefore,

---

[697] Section 44(4) of the Arbitration Act 1996. The subsection requires an agreement "in writing".
[698] Section 44(3) of the Arbitration Act 1996.
[699] *Cetelem SA v Roust Holdings Ltd* [2005] 1 W.L.R. 3555.
[700] Section 44(3) of the Arbitration Act 1996.
[701–702] *Cetelem SA v Roust Holdings Ltd* [2005] 1 W.L.R. 3555 overruled *Hiscox Underwriting v Dickson Manchester & Co Ltd* [2004] 2 Lloyd's Rep 438.
[703] *Cetelem SA v Roust Holdings Ltd* [2005] 1 W.L.R. 3555.
[703a] Applied *Starlight Shipping & Others v Tai Ping Insurance & Others* [2007] EWHC 1893 at [21]. Contractual rights include the right to have disputes referred to arbitration.
[704] Section 44(5) of the Arbitration Act 1996.
[705] This was the position in *Cetelem*.
[706] DAC report, para.215.

an application might be made to the court because a three member tribunal, even though already constituted, was not available to hear an urgent application quickly enough or because of the need to obtain an order binding upon third parties. If a fully constituted tribunal was available to act, the fact that their award might be ineffective in a particular jurisdiction would not, it has been suggested, make them unable to act effectively for the purposes of the sub-section.[706a] However, it has been suggested that the effect on a third party is a strong reason not to grant injunctive relief in support of an arbitration.[707] In the paradigm case, where an application is made to the court for an injunction, the applicant must undertake to refer the dispute to arbitration in due course.[708] It is also possible that the court may impose ancillary directions, such as a requirement that a party in whose favour an injunction has been granted undertakes to progress the arbitration proceedings as fast as possible.[709]

Practice in urgent cases. An application for an interim remedy under s.44 of the Act must be made in an arbitration claim form.[710] In an urgent case, however, the application may be made without prior notice to the respondent in which case the witness statement in support must contain reasons in addition to dealing with the matters that are required for all arbitration applications.[711] The additional reasons include:

7–190

- why the application is made without notice;

- why, if it is the case, it was not "practicable" to obtain permission of the tribunal or the agreement of all the other parties to the arbitral proceedings; and

- why the witness believes that the tribunal[712] has no power or is unable for the time being to act effectively.[713]

If the court does make an urgent order, it may direct that its order shall cease to have effect (in whole or in part) when the tribunal is properly constituted and

---

[706a] *Starlight Shipping and Others v Tai Ping Insurance and Others* [2007] EWHC 1893 at [27].

[707] *Sankofa v Football Association* [2007] EWHC 78, Simon J. at [22].

[708] *per* Staughton L.J. in *The Channel Tunnel Group Ltd and France Manche SA v Balfour Beatty Construction Ltd and Others* [1992] 2 Lloyd's Rep. 7 at 13, CA. Delay in commencing proceedings may lead to the discharge of the injunction: see *Siporex Trade SA v Comdel Commodities Ltd* [1986] 2 Lloyd's Rep. 428 at 435–436; *Weissfisch v Julius and Others* [2006] EWCA 218 at [9], and *Econet Wireless Ltd v Vee Networks Ltd and Others* [2006] EWHC 1568 at [14].

[709] *Engineered Medical Systems v Bregas AB* [2003] EWHC 3287, *per* Toulson J. at [25].

[710] PD 62 para.8.1.

[711] For the matters required for all arbitration applications see CPR r.62.4 and paras 8–087 *et seq.* Considerations which govern the grant of without notice injunctions generally will be applicable. In *Cetelem SA v Roust Holdings Ltd* [2005] 1 W.L.R. 3555, the initial injunction was granted on a without notice basis: [2005] 1 W.L.R. 3555 at [10].

[712] Section 44(5) of the Arbitration Act 1996 refers not only to the arbitral tribunal but also to "any arbitral of other institution or person vested by the parties with power to make the required order".

[713] There is a requirement in the Arbitration Act 1996 for the "condition in s.44(5) being satisfied". That condition has been addressed at para.7–189 above.

is in a position to make its own order.[714] This was described as a "novel provision" in the DAC report, said to follow from the philosophy that if a given power could possibly be exercised by the tribunal then it should be. In effect, therefore, the court hands over to the by now-effective tribunal the task of deciding whether or not the order should cease to have effect.[715] In *Econet Wireless Ltd. v Vee Networks*, the court went further and appeared to suggest that certain orders should be granted by the court only on terms that they inure until the matter can be considered by the tribunal, "the powers of the court under section 44 are plainly intended to cover over the crack between the moment of the application and the time when the arbitral tribunal can be formed and take its own decisions about preserving the status quo".[716] Despite these comments, it is not clear if or when a court must make an order only on terms that the matter be considered by the tribunal as soon as it is able. The words, "If the court so orders" in s.44(6) suggest the court has discretion as to the longevity of its orders. In certain matters, such as those which relate to third parties, the tribunal has no coercive jurisdiction over those third parties in any event and presumably at least in such cases the court may make an order that can last for the duration of the proceedings.[717]

7-191 **Taking the evidence of witnesses for use at the arbitration hearing.** In some situations it may not be possible to secure the attendance of a witness at the arbitration, because the conditions of s.43 of the Act cannot be met. For example, although the witness is in the United Kingdom the arbitration is being conducted abroad and the tribunal has no power to compel the witness to attend the hearing there. If all other requirements are met, an application may be made under s.44 (2)(a) of the Act.[718] In that event, the court may on the application of a party to the arbitration order that the witness attend for examination before an officer of the court appointed for that purpose,[719] although it may decline to make an order where it would be inappropriate to do so.[720] Although the court also has power to order evidence to be taken by witness statement or on affidavit,[721] the more likely request is to take evidence in a way that would enable the other party to cross-examine the witness because then greater weight can be attributed to it by the tribunal.

---

[714] Section 44(6) of the Arbitration Act 1996.

[715] Section 44(6) of the Arbitration Act 1996. DAC report, para.216.

[716] [2006] EWHC 1568 at [14].

[717] But see *Sankofa v Football Association* [2007] EWHC 78, Simon J., at [22], suggesting that effect on third parties is a reason not to grant an injunction under s.44 at all.

[718] Section 44 applies even if the seat is outside England, Wales or Northern Ireland. See Arbitration Act 1996, s.3(b).

[719] An application by a party under s.44 of the Act should be distinguished from a request by a foreign court under the Evidence (Proceedings in Other Jurisdictions) Act 1975 which enacted the 1970 Hague Convention on the Taking of Evidence Abroad in Civil or Commercial Cases.

[720] In *Commerce Insurance Co v Lloyd's Underwriters* [2002] 1 W.L.R. 1323, the court declined to make an order for the examination of witnesses for use in a New York arbitration because of the procedure adopted under the curial law.

[721] The court's powers as to ordering the giving of evidence by witness statements or affidavit are set out in CPR Pt 32. The powers of the High Court to order depositions to be taken are dealt with in CPR Pt 34.8 and its powers to enforce the attendance of witnesses for examination in CPR Pt 34.10.

The court also has power to order the issue to a foreign court of a commission or a request for the examination of a witness who is abroad for the purpose of an arbitration whose seat is in England, although this power is rarely invoked. The power may be exercised pursuant to an application under s.44 (2)(a) of the Act.

The fact that a witness is abroad may result in his evidence being admitted without his attending a hearing before the tribunal, although his absence and the inability to test his evidence by questioning him on it may affect the weight that will be attached to it. In substantial cases, overseas witnesses will usually travel to attend the hearing and give evidence in person.

Preservation of evidence. This is the second matter on which the court may make an order under s.44 of the Act if requested by a party to an arbitration or proposed arbitration.[722] The tribunal has a corresponding power,[723] so the court will only act where the tribunal is unable to act effectively.[724] It can extend to all types of evidence, whether physical or recorded in documentary, electronic, magnetic or photographic form. However, the sub-section cannot ordinarily be used to compel disclosure from a party to the arbitration as this is a matter for the tribunal[725] although in exceptional cases the court may order the production of limited documents if it felt they might otherwise be lost or unavailable to the tribunal. In a case involving a ship which had run aground in the port of Karachi, an order was made requiring a third party, a marine survey organisation, to produce the report which it had prepared for the port managers on the potential deepening of the harbour.[726] The power cannot be used as a means of obtaining ordinary disclosure of documents from a non-party. It is only where it can be shown that a question arises in relation to a particular document of a non-party that an order under this sub-section can be made. The documents of the non-party must therefore be capable of specific description, much as with a witness summons issued under s.43, which in practice overlaps with this sub-section.[727]

7–192

Orders relating to property. An application may also be made to the court under s.44 for orders relating to property.[728] The property concerned may either be the subject matter of the proceedings (e.g. when a party is claiming recovery of specific goods) or property as to which any question arises in the arbitral proceedings, (e.g. whether work was done on a particular building for which a claim is being made in the arbitration). In either case, the court can make a wide variety of orders as identified in s.44(2)(c)(i) and (ii), including the taking of samples, which are intended to have the effect of preventing the property being altered,

7–193

---

[722] For urgent cases where the arbitration has not yet been commenced see s.44(3) and para.7–188.
[723] For the tribunal's power to preserve evidence, see para.5–083.
[724] See s.44(5) of the Arbitration Act 1996. See para.7–189.
[725] NB: *Three Shipping Ltd v Harebell Shipping Ltd* [2005] 1 All E.R. (Comm) 200 at [14].
[726] *Assimina Maritime Ltd v Pakistan National Shipping Corp (The "Tasman Spirit")* [2005] 1 Lloyd's Rep 525.
[727] *Assimina Maritime Ltd v Pakistan National Shipping Corp (The "Tasman Spirit")* [2005] 1 Lloyd's Rep 525.
[728] See CPR Pt 25.1.

destroyed or disposed of before the evidence of its existing state can be secured for the purpose of the arbitration. For example, the physical evidence of a site at a particular time may be useful to reveal structural defects that might otherwise not be apparent.

Although it is more limited, the tribunal has a corresponding power to make orders in respect of property[729] so the court will only act where the tribunal is unable to do so effectively. For example, s.44 empowers the court to authorise any person to enter certain premises for "that purpose" (i.e. for the purpose of taking samples, making observations or otherwise preserving evidence). This means that the court may authorise the tribunal or another party to the proceedings or even a third party (e.g. an expert appointed by the tribunal or another party) to enter upon or into any land or building "in the possession or control" of any party to the arbitration in order to take samples, make observations or conduct experiments which may be necessary or expedient for the purpose of obtaining full information or evidence. To this extent the court's power goes beyond that of the tribunal. Thus, where the property in question is in the possession of a third party, it may well be necessary to invoke the court's jurisdiction to order its detention, preservation or inspection. Property in this regard can extend to documents held by third parties. There is therefore some overlap between the powers in ss.42(2)(b) and (c).[730] It is not clear whether property extends to intangible property, just as assets in s.44(3) extends to intangible assets by virtue of the Court of Appeal's decision in *Cetelem v Roust*.[731]

7–194   Orders for sale of goods. In addition to the detention, preservation or inspection of property (including goods) s.44 empowers the court to make orders for the sale of any goods which are the subject of the arbitral proceedings. If a sale is ordered, the court can then direct how the proceeds of sale are to be applied.[732] In *Cetelem v Roust*, the Court of Appeal gave the specific example of an order for the sale of a cargo of fish the value of which would otherwise be diminished or lost by putrefaction.[733] The powers under this sub-section are a specific example of the court's power to grant mandatory interim injunctions in certain limited cases.

7–195   Interim injunctions in support of arbitral proceedings. The court has power under s.44 (2)(e)[734] to grant interim injunctions in respect of arbitration proceedings.[735] A broad range of interim injunctions are available

---

[729] For the tribunal's power to give directions in relation to property see para.5–081.

[730] *Assimina Maritime Ltd v Pakistan National Shipping Corp (The "Tasman Spirit")* [2005] I Lloyd's Rep 525, where an order was made under s.42(b) and (c) in relation to specific documents held by a third party.

[731] *Cetelem SA v Roust Holdings Ltd* [2005] 1 W.L.R. 3555. The point may have limited practical effect given that inspection and detention of property must by definition in almost all cases be of tangible property.

[732] They may for example be paid into court pending the outcome of the arbitration.

[733] [2005] 1 W.L.R. 3555 at [65].

[734] This type of injunction should be distinguished from that which restrains arbitration proceedings, see para.7–058.

[735] The court's power to grant an interim injunction is specified in CPR Pt 25.1(1)(a).

under s.44 of the Act. The power certainly extends to the granting of a freezing injunction[736] with a view to preserving assets in appropriate cases.[737] The court also has power to grant a freezing order *quia timet* but the court will be astute to ensure that the order is used "properly and without abuse".[738] However, the Court of Appeal in *Cetelem* was not prepared to limit the power to grant interim mandatory injunctions to freezing injunctions or search orders (formerly Mareva and Anton Pillar injunctions), but accepted that a broader class of orders could fall with s.44(2)(e) including, in certain cases, an order for delivery up of documents required to satisfy a condition precedent in a share purchase transaction (the injunction sought in *Cetelem*) and an order for the vendor to deliver to the seller a share certificate in the case of imminent completion of a share purchase transaction.[739] The court will therefore on occasions extend the power to include the grant of an interim mandatory injunction, although this power must be exercised "very sparingly".[740] The power does not however extend to granting final injunctions[741] or to making a final determination of the rights of the parties, even if it may incidentally involve the initial determination of an issue which the parties have agreed to submit to arbitration. It seems likely that the court's power to grant anti-suit injunctions are more usually exercised under s.37 of the Supreme Court Act 1981 but, it is suggested, may also fall to be exercised under this sub-section.[741a]

The court has accepted that injunctions may be granted under s.44(2)(e) in the following circumstances:

- To restrain a law firm from appearing in arbitration proceedings where that law firm had previously acted for the applicant and possessed confidential information relevant to it.[742]

- To restrain ship owners on an interim basis from allowing two vessels to be employed inconsistently with the terms of two time charters pending the resolution of the arbitration. The Court of Appeal rejected an appeal on the

---

[736] A freezing injunction (formerly referred to as a "*Mareva*" injunction) is one which freezes assets of the party against whom it is granted and will be ordered where there is evidence that those assets would otherwise be "dissipated", i.e. removed from the jurisdiction of the court. This type of injunction is usually coupled with a requirement that the party against whom it is granted serves an affidavit giving details of his assets. It may also in limited circumstances be granted in a form which applies not just to assets within the jurisdiction of the English court but also to those held abroad. See *Dadourian Group Int Inc v Simms and Others* [2006] EWCA 399 for authoritative guidelines on when the court will enforce a worldwide freezing injunction. See generally CPR Pt 25 and PD 25.

[737] See, for example, *Aiglon Ltd and L'Aiglon SA v Gau Shan Co Ltd* [1993] 1 Lloyd's Rep. 164 and *Siporex Trade SA v Comdel Commodities Ltd* [1986] 2 Lloyd's Rep. 428.

[738] In *Re Q's Estate* [1999] 1 Lloyd's Rep. 931 at 938. Such an order is made before the cause of action arises.

[739] *Cetelem SA v Roust Holdings Ltd* [2005] 1 W.L.R. 3555 at [62]–[66].

[740] A "mandatory injunction" is one which requires the party against whom it is granted to take some positive step, as opposed to the usual form of injunction which requires the defendant to refrain from doing something. *Cetelem SA v Roust Holdings Ltd* [2005] 1 W.L.R. 3555 at [63]–[64].

[741] Although such power may exist under the court's inherent jurisdiction—see para.7–196 below.

[741a] See para.7–018.

[742] *Gus Consulting GmbH v Leboeuf Lamb Greene & Macrae* [2006] All E.R. (D.) 339. On the facts the injunction was refused.

basis that this was an impermissible form of mandatory injunction as it effectively compelled performance by the owners of the time charters.[743]

- To require on an interim basis for six months (not automatically for the whole period of the arbitration) that one party continue to supply a particular component part to the other.[744-745]

7–196   **Injunction under the court's inherent jurisdiction.** Until the decision in *Cetelem SA v Roust Holdings Ltd*[746] it was thought the court's power to grant an injunction in an exceptional case under the Supreme Court Act could be exercised notwithstanding the more specific power contained in s.44.[747] *Glidepath Holding BV v Thompson*[748] considered the relationship between s.44 of the Arbitration Act 1996 and the court's inherent powers to grant an injunction or other order under s.37 of the Supreme Court Act 1981. The court reached the view that the court's inherent powers are available in the context of arbitration and are broader than those existing under s.44 of the Arbitration Act 1996: "the inherent jurisdiction would not be so limited as that under the Arbitration Act".[749] However, this and earlier cases to the same effect need to be considered in the light of the Court of Appeal's comments in *Cetelem* which noted that there was a "tension" between the wide powers conferred on the court by s.37 of the Supreme Court Act and the much narrower powers conferred on the court by s.44.[750] A definitive decision on this point is awaited although the House of Lords in *West Tankers* supported the use of s.37 for the grant of anti-suit injunctions.[751] In *Elektrim SA v Vivendi Universal SA and Others*[752] the court also assumed that s.37 could be used to grant arbitral relief in the context of arbitration.[752a]

7–197   **Appointing a receiver.** The court is also empowered by s.44 (2)(e) of the Act to order the appointment of a receiver for the purpose of or in relation to arbitral proceedings.[753] The receiver so appointed is under a duty to collect in the

---

[743] *Lauritzen Cool AB v Lady Navigation Inc* [2005] 2 Lloyd's Rep. 63.
[744-745] *Engineered Medical Systems v Bregas AB* [2003] EWHC 3287.
[746] [2005] 1 W.L.R. 3555.
[747] These powers are contained in s.37 of the Supreme Court Act 1981. See also CPR Pt 25.1(1)(a).
[748] [2005] 1 All E.R. (Comm) 434.
[749] *per* Eady J. at [15]–[19]. There are a number of other recent cases where the court has accepted that an injunction may be granted under s.37 of the Supreme Court Act in the context of an arbitration. *National Insurance & Guarantee Corp Ltd v M Young Legal Services* [2005] 2 Lloyd's Rep. 46. See also the discussion of this case in *Cetelem SA v Roust Holdings Ltd* [2005] 1 W.L.R. 3555 at [42] and [43].
[750] *Cetelem SA v Roust Holdings Ltd* [2005] 1 W.L.R. 3555, at [74], *per* Clarke L.J., "The resolution of that tension must await another day".
[751] *West Tankers Inc v RAS Riunione Adriatica di Sicurta SpA and Others* [2007] UKHL 4 at [8] and see para.7–012 above.
[752] [2007] 2 Lloyd's Rep. 8.
[752a] An approach also supported in *Starlight Shipping and Others v Tai Ping Insurance and Others* [2007] EWHC 1893.
[753] The court's powers in respect of the appointment of receivers are set out in RSC Ord.30 in Sch.1 to CPR (sc 30).

property over which he is appointed, thereby ensuring its protection and preservation pending the arbitration in accordance with the directions of the court.[754]

Enforcement of peremptory order[755] of the tribunal. If a party 7–198 fails to comply with an order of the tribunal requiring him to do or stop doing something,[756] an application may be made to the court under s.12[757] of the Arbitration Act 1996 to enforce that order.[758] In most cases the tribunal's own powers to enforce its orders will suffice[759] but occasionally an application to the court to enforce a peremptory order of the tribunal may be necessary.[760] This section has been applied to enforce an order for payment made by an adjudicator under the Housing Grants, Construction and Regeneration Act 1996, even though the decision was referred to arbitration.[761] The circumstances in which such an application to the court can be made are described in the following paragraphs.

Excluding court's powers and exhausting other rights. Section 7–199 42 is not mandatory[762] so an application cannot be made to the court if the arbitration agreement[763] contains a provision to the effect that the court shall not make an order under that section. Further, if the arbitration agreement contains a procedure for what is to happen in the event of a failure to comply with an order of the tribunal that procedure must first be exhausted before an application can be made to the court.[764] Section 42 does not apply to foreign seated arbitrations, so for example it cannot be used to enforce an interim order made by a foreign tribunal against a party amenable to the jurisdiction of the English courts (unless no seat has been determined the court feels there is a sufficient appropriate connection for the purposes of s.2(4)(b)).

The applicant. Subject to what is stated in the preceding paragraph, an 7–200 application under s.42 can be made either by the tribunal or by a party to the

---

[754] See further *Kerr on Receivers* (17th edn), Ch.9.
[755] The expression "peremptory order" is defined in the Arbitration Act 1996, s.82(2).
[756] The tribunal may, for example, have ordered a party to produce evidence in his possession which is relevant to the issues to be decided.
[757] For construction contracts, a minor amendment has been made to s.42 by SI 1998/649.
[758] For the procedure on an application see paras 8–178 *et seq*.
[759] See s.41 of the Arbitration Act 1996 for powers of the tribunal in case of a party's default.
[760] The enforcement of the tribunal's order to preserve property is an example.
[761] *Macob Civil Engineering v Morrison Construction* [1999] C.L.C. 739. The court also decided in that case that a standard form of arbitration clause would not by itself exclude the application as is did not indicate that the parties were "otherwise agreed" for the purposes of the Arbitration Act 1996, s.42(1).
[762] This is apparent from the opening words of s.42(1) of the Arbitration Act 1996 and from its absence in Sch.1 to the Arbitration Act 1996.
[763] The arbitration clause or rules incorporated into it may contain an exclusion agreement in terms wide enough to prevent an application under s.42 of the Arbitration Act 1996.
[764] Section 42(3) of the Arbitration Act 1996.

arbitral proceedings.[765] Whoever makes the application must satisfy the court that the party concerned has failed to comply with an order within the time specified in the tribunal's order, or if no time is specified, within a reasonable time.[766]

Usually the tribunal will leave one of the parties to apply to the court, but if the tribunal does apply notice must be given to the parties.[767] One or more of the parties to the arbitration may apply for a court order under s.42 but unless the arbitration agreement provides that the court's powers under this section shall be available[768] the applicant must obtain the permission of the tribunal[769] and in any event notify the other parties. The fact that he has permission should be mentioned in the application.[770]

7–201   **Appeals.** Permission of the court is required to appeal from a decision of the court made under ss.42 and 44 of the Act.[771] It had been thought that reference to "the court" under both sections was to the court which made the order[772] and that in the absence of such an order from that court the Court of Appeal could not consider the matter. The former position was stated as follows, "Parliament has made it completely clear that in this respect the decision of the judge is to be final, unless the judge himself considers that there are matters which are fit to be considered by the Court of Appeal so as itself to grant leave".[773]

However, two separate lines of decisions of the Court of Appeal have weakened the proposition that the judicial decision taker at first instance is the only competent body to grant leave to appeal from his own decision. Following *Cetelem v Roust*,[774] which dealt with the provision in relation to appeals under s.44(7) of the Act, the distinction is now to be drawn between appeals to orders which the judge had jurisdiction to make, although it is alleged he erred in fact or in law in making the order, and orders which he had no jurisdiction to make. The Court of Appeal can give permission to appeal in respect of the latter type of orders, where the judge at first instance has no jurisdiction to make the order in question, even where the judge himself has refused leave to appeal. As the Court of Appeal noted in *Cetelem*:

"So long as the judge could make the order in the sense that it was within the jurisdiction specified in the relevant section, the buck stops with him. The order is made under the section. It is only where the judge makes an order which is outwith his jurisdiction, so

---

[765] Section 42(2) of the Arbitration Act 1996. For procedure on an application see paras 8–178 *et seq*.
[766] Section 42(4) of the Arbitration Act 1996.
[767] Section 42(2)(a) of the Arbitration Act 1996.
[768] Section 42(2)(c) of the Arbitration Act 1996.
[769] Where there is more than one arbitrator and the parties have not agreed otherwise a majority decision may suffice for this purpose, see ss.20(3) and 22(2) of the Arbitration Act 1996.
[770] The procedure for the application is mentioned in paras 8–178 *et seq*.
[771] Sections 42(5) and 44(7) of the Arbitration Act 1996.
[772] Because of the definition of court in s.105(1) of the Arbitration Act 1996.
[773] *Virdee v Virdi* [2003] EWCA Civ 41.
[774] *Cetelem SA v Roust Holdings Ltd* [2005] 1 W.L.R. 3555.

that he could not (as opposed to should not) make it, that s.44(7) and other similar provisions do not prevent an appeal to this court."[775]

Quite how easy this distinction is to operate in practice remains to be seen. In *Lesotho Highlands v Impreglio*,[776] the House of Lords when considering a challenge under s.68 of the Arbitration Act 1996 rejected an argument that an error as to the currency of an award constituted an excess of powers. However, this matter was argued strongly on both sides all the way up to the House of Lords and the concepts are elusive. The field of administrative law is full of examples of the difficulty in drawing a distinction between a simple error (within jurisdiction) and acting outside of jurisdiction.[777]

In a closely related decision, the Court of Appeal has held in respect of an appeal based on a preliminary point about whether a particular section (s.69) applies at all (because for example there is a question whether a valid exclusion agreement has been entered into) the Court of Appeal does have jurisdiction to grant leave in respect of such questions.[778] The Court of Appeal canvassed but did not decide the possibility that the opt out wording in s.44(1), "unless the parties otherwise agree" may also be a preliminary point as to whether that section applies at all.

The Court of Appeal also has a residual jurisdiction to set aside the judge's decision in the case of unfairness relating to the process of the judge's decision. The distinction is therefore to be drawn between appeals from the judge's refusal to give leave on the merits where, save for cases where there was no jurisdiction for the underlying decision, there is no appeal and cases where, "*the judge's refusal of leave to appeal was arbitrary or unfair: or was the product of a failure of intellectual engagement with the arguments put before him; or amounted actually or metaphorically to the absence of a decision on the issue*".[779] In such "exceptionally rare cases"[780] the Court of Appeal can of its own motion consider appeals even where leave of the first instance judge has not been given. The Court of Appeal has also rejected the argument that this residual discretion is contrary to Art.6 of the European Convention of Human Rights.[781]

---

[775] *Cetelem SA v Roust Holdings Ltd* [2005] 1 W.L.R. 3555, *per* Clarke L.J., at [25].

[776] [2006] 1 A.C. 221.

[777] *Pearlman v Keepers and Governors of Harrow School* [1978] 3 W.L.R 736 at 743: "The distinction between an error which entails absence of jurisdiction and an error made within jurisdiction is fine . . . it is rapidly being eroded".

[778] *Sukuman Ltd v Commonwealth Secretariat* [2007] EWCA 243; [2007] Bus. L.R. 1075 at [27]–[34].

[779] *CGU International Insurance Plc and Others v Astra Zeneca Insurance Co Ltd* [2006] EWCA 1340, *per* Rix L.J. at [98], approving *North Range Shipping Ltd v Seatrans Shipping Corp* [2002] 1 W.L.R. 2397. Approved in *Kazakhstan v Istil Group Inc*, [2007] W.L. 1425725, para.11. See also *ASM Shipping Ltd of India v TTMI Ltd* [2006] EWCA 1341, a decision under s.68(4), which is in the same terms as s.69(8).

[780] *CGU International Insurance Plc and Others v Astra Zeneca Insurance Co Ltd* [2006] EWCA 1340, *per* Rix L.J. at [100].

[781] *Kazakhstan v Istil Group Inc*, [2007] W.L. 1425725, following *CGU International Insurance Plc and Others v Astra Zeneca Insurance Co Ltd* [2006] EWCA 1340.

In all other cases, there is no right to appeal unless the judge at first instance gives leave to appeal. In that instance, "court" means the court which made the order.[782]

7–202   Securing the attendance of witnesses at the arbitration. Under s.43 of the Act, the same procedures may be used to secure the attendance before an arbitration tribunal of a witness as are available for court proceedings. Where a witness who is within the United Kingdom is unwilling to attend the hearing of an arbitration to give evidence on a voluntary basis, a party to arbitral proceedings who wants to compel the attendance of the witness before the tribunal[783] must apply for a witness summons in accordance with CPR Pt 34.[784]

7–203   Limitations on power to summon witness. The objective of a witness summons is to require a witness to attend an arbitration hearing in England[785] for the purpose of giving evidence and/or for the purpose of producing to the tribunal certain documents. Section 43 of the Arbitration Act 1996 is mandatory,[786] but a party can only issue a witness summons with the permission of the tribunal or the agreement of all the other parties.[787] Written evidence to that effect will be required before the summons is issued and can be served.[788] Further, this procedure can only be used if the witness concerned is in the United Kingdom and the arbitration hearing is being conducted in England.[789]

The requirement as to location of the hearing is only that "the arbitral proceedings are being conducted in England and Wales or, as the case may be, Northern Ireland." Subject to the limitations contained in subs.43(3) of the Act,[790] the powers contained in s.43 are available even if the seat of the arbitration is abroad or no seat has been designated or determined, but in that case the court may refuse to allow the powers to be exercised where the court considers that it would be "inappropriate to do so".[791] This raises the interesting possibility of a tribunal in a foreign seated arbitration agreeing to hold a hearing in England for the purpose of hearing a witness pursuant to a s.43 summons, thus triggering the

---

[782] *Cetelem SA v Roust Holdings Ltd* [2005] 1 W.L.R. 3555 at [25]. Considered *Kazakhstan v Istil Group Inc*, [2007] W.L. 1425725.

[783] This is authorised by s.43 of the Arbitration Act 1996 which envisages use of "the same court procedures as are available in relation to legal proceedings" to secure a witness's attendance.

[784] PD 62 para.7.1. A witness summons is a document issued by the court requiring a witness to (a) attend court to give evidence; or (b) produce documents to the court (CPR Pt 34, r.2).

[785] Or Northern Ireland.

[786] See s.4(1) of the Arbitration Act 1996 and Sch.1 of the Act.

[787] Section 43(2) of the Arbitration Act 1996. Contrast with the former s.12(4) of the Arbitration Act 1950 where no such limitation applied. See also Art.27 of the Model law and DAC report para.213.

[788] PD 62 para.7.3.

[789] Section 43(3) of the Arbitration Act 1996 refers to the proceedings as being conducted in "England, Wales, or as the case may be, Northern Ireland".

[790] These limitations are that the witness is in the United Kingdom and the arbitration proceedings are being conducted in England. For example, although the seat of arbitration is abroad, the parties and the tribunal may agree to conduct the proceedings in London.

[791] Section 2(3) of the Arbitration Act 1996. The words quoted give the courts a "wide discretion".

requirement of "conducting" the proceedings in England. The procedure and scope of a witness summons in court proceedings influences the court's approach to the granting of orders under s.43, in that only very narrow categories of documents can be sought from witnesses.[792] There is an overlap between the powers under s.43 and those available under s.44(2)(b).[793]

Limitation on production. In the case of a summons to produce docu- 7–204 ments, a witness cannot by virtue of s.43[794] be compelled to produce in the arbitration "any document or other material evidence" which he could not be compelled to produce in legal proceedings, i.e. if the matter were being heard in court. In this way the procedure is equivalent in substance to the procedure for a witness summons under the CPR. This provision is intended to protect the witness's rights in respect of evidence that is privileged from production.[795] Moreover, the witness summons process cannot be used as a means of obtaining disclosure of documents from a third party witness. Even though such a power is available in respect of court proceedings, it is not one endorsed by s.43. Indeed as the court's former power under s.12(6)(b) of the Arbitration Act 1950 has now been repealed, disclosure of any sort is primarily a matter for the tribunal. [796] For this reason, if a witness is ordered to produce documents those documents must be identified as a tightly defined group, by reference to individual documents or at the very least a compendious description.[797]

Practice. The application for a witness summons under s.43 of the Arbitration 7–205 Act 1996 may be made to the Admiralty and Commercial Registry of the High Court, or "if the attendance of the witness is required within the district of a district registry, at that registry at the option of the party".[798] A witness summons will not be issued until the applicant files written evidence which shows that the application is "made with the permission of the tribunal or the agreement of the other parties".[799] The summons will then be issued by the court office without the need for a specific court order. Normally, the court will serve the witness[800] and

---

[792] *Tajik Aluminium Plant v Hydro Aluminium AS* [2006] 1 Lloyd's Rep. 155, *per* Moore-Bick L.J. at [25].
[793] See para.7–193; *Assimina Maritime Ltd v Pakistan National Shipping Corp (The 'Tasman Spirit')* [2005] I Lloyd's Rep. 525.
[794] Section 43(4) of the Arbitration Act 1996. CPR Pt 34, r.2(5).
[795] For an account of what is "privileged" from production see commentary to CPR Pt 31 in *White Book*, paras 31.3–5 *et seq.*
[796] The leading case on s.43 is the decision of the Court of Appeal in *Tajik Aluminium Plant v Hydro Aluminium AS* [2006] 1 Lloyd's Rep. 155, applying principles enunciated in the earlier cases of *Assimina Maritime Ltd v Pakistan National Shipping Corp (The "Tasman Spirit")* [2005] I Lloyd's Rep 525 at [16]; *Tyneside Borough Council v Wickes Building Supplies Ltd* [2004] EWHC 2428; *BNP Paribas v Deloitte and Touche LLP* [2004] 1 Lloyd's Rep. 223. See also para.7–209 below.
[797] *Tajik Aluminium Plant v Hydro Aluminium AS* [2006] 1 Lloyd's Rep. 155 at [28]–[29].
[798] PD 62 para.7.2. The general procedure for an arbitration application is described in paras 8–178 *et seq.*
[799] PD 62 para.7.3.
[800] CPR Pt 34, r.6(1). See commentary to this paragraph in *White Book* and note time for service in CPR Pt 34.5.

"conduct money" must be tendered to the witness.[801] An application may be made to the court to set aside or vary a witness summons[802] but in the absence of such an application failure to comply with a witness summons validly served is punishable as a contempt of court.[803]

7–206   Security in respect of proceedings "in rem". A party to an arbitration may also pursuant to s.11 of the Arbitration Act 1996 invoke the "in rem" jurisdiction of the Admiralty Division of the High Court to arrest a vessel and to obtain security for his claim plus interest and costs.[804] The defendant will be entitled to apply for a stay of the proceedings pursuant to s.9 of the Act,[805] but even if the stay is granted the court may order the property arrested to be retained as security for the award in the arbitration or may order that the stay is conditional on the provision of equivalent security.[806] The same law and practice will apply in relation to property retained in pursuance of an order of the court made under s.11 of the Act as would apply if the property were held for the purposes of proceedings in the court making the order.[807] Further, s.11 applies even if the seat of the arbitration is abroad or no seat has been designated or determined.[808]

7–207   Security for costs. The court no longer has power to order security for costs in an arbitration. That power is expressly reserved to the arbitral tribunal.[809] The law was changed in the 1996 Act following the controversial decision of the House of Lords in *Coppee-Lavalin SA/NV v Ken-Ren Chemicals and Fertilizers Ltd (In Liquidation)* in which the majority held that the High Court had the power to order a claimant to provide security for costs in respect of an arbitration being conducted under the ICC Rules of Arbitration.[810] The court does have power, however, to order an applicant to provide security for costs of any arbitration application or appeal.[811] It may, but will not necessarily, make such an order where the applicant is a liquidator of an insolvent company.[812] The court's power will not

---

[801] Supreme Court Act 1981, s.36(4). CPR Pt 34.6(2).

[802] CPR Pt 34.3(4). For the grounds on which the court will set aside a subpoena see the commentary on this paragraph in the *White Book*. It may also be set aside if issued without the proper permission of the tribunal or agreement of all the other parties to the arbitration. See also *Sunderland Steamship P and I Association v Gatoil International Inc (The "Lorenzo Halcoussi")* [1988] 1 Lloyd's Rep. 180.

[803] See RSC Ord.52 re-enacted in Sch.1, CPR. The court will only punish a witness where there was no reasonable excuse for his absence.

[804] See, for example, *The "APJ Shalin"* [1991] 2 Lloyd's Rep. 62.

[805] See paras 7–010 *et seq.*

[806] Arbitration Act 1996, s.11. See *Greenmar Navigation Ltd v Owners of Ship ("Bazias 3") and ("Bazias 4") and Sally Line Ltd (The "Bazias 3" and "Bazias 4")* [1993] 1 Lloyd's Rep. 101.

[807] Section 11(2) of the Arbitration Act 1996.

[808] Section 2(2) of the Arbitration Act 1996.

[809] Section 38(3) of the Arbitration Act 1996. See para.5–098.

[810] [1994] 2 All E.R. 449, HL, a decision based on s.12 of the Arbitration Act 1950, which has now been repealed. For the arbitrator's power to grant security for costs see paras 5–079 *et seq.*

[811] Arbitration Act 1996, s.70(6).

[812] This conclusion is derived from the decision of H.H. Judge Dean Q.C. of January 19, 2000 in *Smith v UIC Insurance Co Ltd*, which was based on the old law.

be exercised on the ground that the appellant or applicant is an individual ordinarily resident outside the United Kingdom.[813]

Disclosure of documents and requests for information. The 7–208 court does not have the general power to order disclosure and answers to requests for information in an arbitration. An order that one party to an arbitration disclose documents to another should only be obtained from the tribunal,[814] although in principle an order requiring the production of very limited documents under s.44(2)(b) might be granted.[815] In certain circumstances the courts may also enforce a peremptory disclosure order made by the tribunal.[816]

10. DETERMINATION OF THE RECOVERABLE COSTS OF THE ARBITRATION

Introduction. The Arbitration Act 1996 gives the parties complete freedom to 7–209 agree what costs of the arbitration are recoverable,[817] and on what basis the costs are to be assessed.[818] In the absence of agreement by the parties the tribunal is empowered to determine by award the "recoverable costs of the arbitration" on such basis as it thinks fit,[819] failing which the court will determine the matter on the application of one of the parties.[820] The "recoverable costs of the arbitration" under s.63(3) does not incorporate by reference all the rules applicable to detailed assessment of costs in the courts, and ss.63(3) and (4) are to be read independently of each other.[821]

Court's power in respect of the recoverable costs of an arbi- 7–210 **tration.** Arbitral tribunals may make an order for costs (*e.g.* the respondent to

---

[813] Nor in the case of a corporation or association, that its place of incorporation or where its central management and control is exercised is outside the United Kingdom: s.70(6) of the Arbitration Act 1996.

[814] See paras 5–133 *et seq.* for the extent of the arbitrator's power. The court's power to order "discovery" and "interrogatories" (as disclosure and requests for information were formerly called) under s.12(6)(b) of the Arbitration Act 1950 was revoked by s.103 of the Courts and Legal Services Act 1990.

[815] See para.7–192 above.

[816] Section 42 of the Arbitration Act 1996, see para.7–198.

[817] Section 63(1) of the Arbitration Act 1996 which should be distinguished from s.60 of the Act. The latter section invalidates an agreement made before the dispute arises that one party should pay all or part of the costs of the arbitration. The recoverable costs referred to in s.63 include the legal costs incurred by the parties in the arbitration as well as the fees and expenses of the tribunal and any expert.

[818] Arbitration Act 1996, ss.63(1) and 64(1).

[819] Arbitration Act 1996, s.63(3). Such costs may include reasonable fees and expenses of the tribunal, s.64(1). See paras 6–141 *et seq.*

[820] Arbitration Act 1996, s.63(4).

[821] *Rotary Watches Ltd v Rotary Watches (USA) Inc,* Supreme Court Costs Office, December 17, 2004, unreported.

pay the claimant's costs on the usual basis) but leave the assessment of those costs, other than the fees and expenses of the tribunal, to be agreed by the parties or to be determined by the court.[822] If for whatever reason the tribunal does not determine the recoverable costs of the arbitration, the court may on the application of any party to the arbitral proceedings determine those costs on such basis as it thinks fit or order how they shall be determined.[823] Once the issue of costs is before the court under s.63, it can order summary of assessment of costs and payment on account of costs in the usual way.[824] The court may specify in the order the means by which and terms on which the recoverable costs shall be determined.[825] Notice of an application to the court under s.63 of the Act must be given to the other parties.[826]

7–211 **Basis on which costs of arbitration are assessed.** In the absence of any indication from the parties or the tribunal, the court has a complete discretion to determine the amount of costs recoverable from one or other of the parties or the basis on which those costs should be assessed. Unless however the court order specifies a particular sum or basis, the recoverable costs of the arbitration will be determined on the basis that there "shall be allowed a reasonable amount in respect of all costs reasonably incurred".[827] Section 63(5)(b) also states that any doubt as to whether costs were reasonably incurred or were reasonable in amount shall be resolved in favour of the paying party.

7–212 **Court's powers in respect of the tribunal's fees and expenses.** Normally the tribunal[828] or the appointing authority[829] will determine the tribunal's fees and expenses, which will be recovered in and be part of the award. Where however there is a question about what fees and expenses of the tribunal are reasonable and appropriate in the circumstances of a particular arbitration, the court has power to determine that question. The power will usually be exercised upon the application of one of the parties (upon notice to the other parties and to the tribunal) under s.28(2) of the Arbitration Act 1996 but the power may also be exercised in the course of an application under s.63(4), which has already been mentioned,[830] or upon the application of any party (upon notice to the other parties) under s.64(2) of the Act. The court also has power to make an order in

---

[822] See para.6–153.

[823] Arbitration Act 1996, s.63(4).

[824] *Rotary Watches Ltd v Rotary Watches (USA) Inc*, Supreme Court Costs Office, December 17, 2004, unreported.

[825] Section 63(4)(b) of the Arbitration Act 1996 (e.g. to be assessed by an expert, other than the courts taxing officer, on terms as to payment of the expert's fees).

[826] Section 63(4) of the Arbitration Act 1996.

[827] Section 63(5)(a) of the Arbitration Act 1996. For guidance on how the assessment is done see CPR Pt 44.7 and CPR Pt 47 and commentary on them in the *White Book*. See also para.6–143.

[828] Section 64(1) of the Arbitration Act 1996 provides that unless otherwise agreed by the parties the recoverable costs of the arbitration, which may be awarded, shall include reasonable fees and expenses of the tribunal as appropriate in the circumstances.

[829] See Arts 30 and 31 of the ICC Rules of Arbitration and Art.28 of LCIA Rules of Arbitration.

[830] See para.7–210. Section 63(7) makes clear that the provisions of s.63 do not affect the right of the arbitrators to payment of their fees and expenses. A similar provision appears in s.64(4).

respect of an arbitrator's entitlement to fees and expenses if he is removed by the court[831] or if he resigns.[832]

Section 28(3) provides that if the application under that section is made after any amount has been paid to an arbitrator by way of fees or expenses, the court may order the repayment of such amount (if any) as is shown to be excessive, but will not do so unless it is shown that it is reasonable in the circumstances to order repayment. The fact that an arbitrator makes an error is not ordinarily a ground for an adjustment to his fee for the time taken as a result of that error.[833] Where a party has agreed on an amount of fees and expenses to be payable to an arbitrator, s.28 will not affect his contractual liability for those fees and expenses.[834]

If the tribunal rather than the parties appoint an expert or legal adviser or assessor, his fees and expenses may be considered by the court as part of the tribunal's expenses.[835]

Court's power if the tribunal refuses to deliver an award without payment. The Arbitration Act 1996 recognises that the tribunal may refuse to deliver an award to the parties except upon full payment of all fees and expenses,[836] but in the event of a dispute about their amount, s.56(2) of the Act provides for resolution by the court in the absence of any available arbitral process for appeal or review of the amount of the fees or expenses demanded.[837] Notice of the application to the court must be given to the tribunal and to the parties.[838]   **7–213**

Various court orders in respect of arbitrators' fees and expenses. The Arbitration Act 1996 gives the court power to make various orders where there is a dispute about the fees and expenses of an arbitrator (whether or not he has ceased to act) or an umpire (even if he did not replace the arbitrators)[839] or even an arbitral institution.[840] Those orders include the following: **7–214**

- to review and if appropriate, to adjust the fees and expenses claimed by members of a tribunal[841];

- to order repayment of excessive sums paid by any party on account of fees and expenses[842];

---

[831] Section 24(4) of the Arbitration Act 1996.
[832] Section 25(3)(b) of the Arbitration Act 1996.
[833] *Hussman v Al Ameen* [2000] 2 Lloyd's Rep. 83 at 100.
[834] Arbitration Act 1996, s.28(5). A similar provision appears in s.56(8) of the Act: see para.7–214.
[835] The definition of "recoverable costs of the arbitration" in s.64(1) of the Arbitration Act 1996 includes the arbitrators' fees and "expenses".
[836] Section 56(1) of the Arbitration Act 1996.
[837] The application cannot be made to the court if there is an available arbitral process of the kind mentioned in s.56(4) of the Arbitration Act 1996.
[838] Section 56(2) of the Arbitration Act 1996. For procedure see para.8–195.
[839] Arbitration Act 1996, s.64(2).
[840] Arbitration Act 1996, s.56(6).
[841] Arbitration Act 1996, s.28(2).
[842] Arbitration Act 1996, s.28(3).

- to order delivery of an award on payment into court of the amount demanded for fees and expenses or a lesser sum[843];

- to direct how the amount of fees and expenses properly payable shall be determined and on what terms[844]; and

- to order payment out of court to an arbitrator of all or any part of the sum paid into court on account of his fees and expenses.[845]

The first two orders can be made at any time during the arbitration where there is a question as to the reasonableness of the tribunal's charges, and the court is empowered to "adjust fees and expenses even after they have been paid" to the tribunal.[846] The other orders may be made where the court is satisfied that the tribunal has demanded too much of the parties for the release of the award[847] although in that case "no application to the court may be made where there is any available arbitral process for appeal or review of the amount of the fees or expenses demanded".[848]

In determining the amount of fees and expenses properly payable to the tribunal the court will have regard to the terms of any agreement with the parties relating to payment of the tribunal. Where, for example, the parties have agreed a rate for each hour worked by the tribunal, that agreement will be enforced by the court[849] unless there are special grounds for setting the agreement aside.[850]

Section 56 also applies to an arbitral institution or other third party that has powers in relation to the delivery of the tribunal's award.[851]

7–215 **Appeal.** Permission of the court is required to appeal from a decision of the court under s.56 of the Act.[852] Although "court" is defined as the first instance court[853] making the decision, there are in fact two categories of cases where the Court of Appeal can grant leave to appeal notwithstanding the refusal of the first instance judge to grant leave. See the discussion at para.7–201 in respect of words to the same effect under s.44(7).

---

[843] Arbitration Act 1996, s.56(2)(a).
[844] Arbitration Act 1996, s.56(2)(b).
[845] Arbitration Act 1996, s.56(2)(c).
[846] See DAC report, paras 122–124.
[847] Section 56(3) of the Arbitration Act 1996 makes clear that the amount of fees and expenses properly payable "is the amount the applicant is liable to pay under s.28 on any agreement relating to the payment of the arbitrators".
[848] section 56(4) of the Arbitration Act 1996.
[849] Arbitration Act 1996, s.56(3)—see also para.4–052 on s.28 of the Arbitration Act 1996.
[850] Although this exception is not mentioned in s.56(3) of the Arbitration Act 1996, it should be implied where, for example, there has been a mutual mistake over the fees.
[851] Section 56(6) of the Arbitration Act 1996.
[852] Section 56(7) of the Arbitration Act 1996.
[853] Section 105(1) of the Arbitration Act 1996.

CHAPTER 8

THE ROLE OF THE COURT AFTER THE AWARD

1. INTRODUCTION

Contents of the chapter. This chapter examines the court's role after an   8–001
award has been issued to the parties.[1] It does not confine itself to considering the
court's role only after the arbitral proceedings have terminated as many arbitrations will involve multiple awards. As will be explained, it is possible to challenge
one award, for example as to jurisdiction, whilst the arbitration proceeds as regards
other issues to be determined. This chapter begins by explaining how an award
may be enforced either under the summary procedure provided for in s.66 of the

---

[1] The subject of "recoverable costs of the arbitration" is the only exception to this statement. For
convenience that subject is dealt with at the end of Ch.7. See paras 7–209 *et seq.* and 6–153.

Arbitration Act 1996[2] or by starting an action on the award.[3] It comments on the enforcement of certain foreign awards, including New York Convention Awards.[4] It then proceeds to examine the grounds for challenging[5] or appealing[6] against an award. The forms of recourse available, including the setting aside of the award and its remission to the arbitral tribunal,[7] are then examined.

This chapter also deals with the procedures to be adopted in relation to the various applications to the court.[8] They include provisions for service within and out of the jurisdiction.

2. Enforcement of Awards

8–002   **Introduction.** "Unless otherwise agreed by the parties, an award made by the tribunal pursuant to an arbitration agreement[9] is final[10] and binding both on the parties and on any persons claiming through or under them".[11] This means that, subject to any contrary agreement by the parties and to the right of challenge,[12] once the award[13] has been made it is immediately enforceable. Many awards are implemented without the need for further steps to be taken against the losing party, but if a party refuses to comply with the award, enforcement proceedings will be necessary.[14]

There are two principal methods of enforcement of an award available in England. The first method is to obtain permission or "leave"[15] of the court to enforce the award, "in the same manner as a judgment or order of the court to the same effect", under the summary procedure provided for by s.66 of the Arbitration Act 1996.[16] Judgment may also be entered in terms of the award[17] where that

---

[2] This section restates s.26 of the Arbitration Act 1950. See paras 8–003 *et seq.*

[3] Paragraphs 8–014 *et seq.*

[4] Paragraphs 8–020 *et seq.*

[5] Paragraphs 8–051 *et seq.*

[6] Paragraphs 8–119 *et seq.*

[7] Paragraphs 8–162 *et seq.*

[8] Paragraphs 8–178 *et seq.*

[9] "Arbitration Agreement" is defined in s.6(1) of the Arbitration Act 1996: see paras 2–002 *et seq.*

[10] See paras 6–004 *et seq.* for various meanings of "final".

[11] Arbitration Act 1996, s.58(1), replacing s.16 of the Arbitration Act 1950.

[12] This right is expressly reserved by s.58(2) of the Arbitration Act 1996. According to that subsection challenge may be done by "any available appeal or review or in accordance with the provisions of this Part" of the Arbitration Act 1996. The subject of challenge is dealt with in paras 8–051 *et seq.*

[13] What is sought to be enforced must be an arbitral award. See *Al Midani v Al Midani* [1999] 1 Lloyd's Rep. 923 and para.6–003.

[14] Enforcement proceedings should not be confused with proceedings for a declaration confirming the award in the country where it was made. Declaratory proceedings of that kind are common in some jurisdictions, for example, the USA, see *Rosseel NV v Oriental Commercial & Shipping Co (UK) Ltd* [1991] 2 Lloyd's Rep. 625, but not in England.

[15] The Arbitration Act 1996 uses the word "leave", but CPR Pt 62 and the Arbitration Practice Direction use the word "permission" which will generally be used in this book.

[16] Section 66(1) of the Arbitration Act 1996 has replaced s.26(1) of the Arbitration Act 1950. See paras 8–003 *et seq.*

[17] Section 66(2) of the Arbitration Act 1996. See para.8–007.

would make enforcement easier.[18] The second method of enforcement is to bring an action on the award and then to seek a judgment from the court for the same relief as is granted by the award.[19]

The procedure for enforcement and the grounds available for opposing enforcement depend to some extent on whether the award is made in England or abroad,[20] and in the latter case whether any Convention regulates its recognition and enforcement.[21]

Procedure to enforce awards summarily. The summary procedure available under s.66 of the Arbitration Act 1996[22] is normally used to enforce an arbitral award,[23] including an agreed award.[24] The section applies whether the seat of the arbitration is in England or abroad and even if no seat has been designated or determined.[25] Permission of the court is needed[26] but the procedure for obtaining it is straightforward. The application for the court's permission is usually made without notice to the other party[27] by an arbitration claim form[28] supported by a witness statement to which the arbitration agreement and the award or a copy of them (with an English translation if necessary) are exhibited.[29] Whilst comparisons are sometimes drawn between arbitration and adjudication, they are not valid in this area. Adjudication does not benefit from a corresponding provision to s.66, the absence of which means that an adjudicator's decision must be enforced by proceedings based on the contractual obligation to comply with the decision.[30]

8–003

---

[18] The pros and cons of entering judgment in the terms of the award as opposed to enforcing the award are discussed briefly in para.8–008.

[19] Section 66(4) of the Arbitration Act 1996 expressly provides that nothing in s.66 affects the recognition and enforcement of an award by "an action on the award".

[20] For a classification of awards see paras 6–002 *et seq.*

[21] See paras 8–020 *et seq.* for the principal conventions.

[22] The section is mandatory, and reflects s.35 of the Model Law.

[23] Not every award is enforceable under this section: see *Dalmia Cement Ltd v National Bank of Pakistan* [1974] 2 Lloyd's Rep. 98.

[24] An "agreed award" records a settlement reached by the parties to an arbitration and may be enforced in the same way as any other award on the merits of the case: see s.51 of the Arbitration Act 1996 and paras 6–024 *et seq.* above.

[25] Section 2(2) of the Arbitration Act 1996.

[26] Section 66(1) of the Arbitration Act 1996 requires "leave of the court" for enforcement of an award under that section.

[27] Orders were made on this basis and without a hearing in *Walker v Rowe* [2000] 1 Lloyd's Rep. 116 at 119 and *Socadec SA v Pan Afric Impex Co Ltd* [2003] EWHC 2086.

[28] The form of application and the procedure are described in para.8–178. Although the procedure for obtaining permission or "leave" of the court is usually without notice, the court may direct that notice should be given to another party—see CPR r.62.18(2). In any event, full and frank disclosure should be made in the witness statement of any matter that may affect the granting of leave, see *Curacao Trading Co BV v Harkisandas & Co* [1992] 2 Lloyd's Rep. 186, a decision based on s.26(1) of the Arbitration Act 1950, which has been re-enacted by s.66(1) of the Arbitration Act 1996.

[29] These exhibits are not mentioned in s.66 of the Arbitration Act 1996, although they are specified in s.102 of the Act in respect of New York Convention Awards. They are however required by CPR r.62.18(6). See *White Book*, 2E–33 and para.8–178 for details of the application.

[30] For a discussion of this distinction, see *VHE Construction Plc v RBSTB Trust Ltd* [2000] B.L.R. 187, *per* Judge Hicks at [55].

8–004   **Permission usually given.** Permission to enforce the award is usually
given, although the Arbitration Act 1996 directs the court not to grant "leave"
where, or to the extent that, the person against whom it is sought to be enforced
shows that "the tribunal lacked substantive jurisdiction to make the award".[31] In
practice, if there is no challenge to the award or if any applicable challenges to the
award under ss.67–69 have been determined against the applicant, then an order
for enforcement of the award under s.66(1) will usually follow.[32] A party who
wishes to oppose an application for permission to enforce an award, rather than
oppose an order made under s.66 of the Act,[33] must act promptly, because
permission may be granted without notice to him in the absence of his notifying
the court of his objection. The onus of showing that the arbitral tribunal "lacked
substantive jurisdiction"[34] and that he has not lost the right to object on this
ground[35] rests on the person opposing leave to enforce the award.

8–005   **Court discretion.** Even if the jurisdiction of the tribunal is not in issue, the
court has a discretion not to grant leave to enforce an award summarily.[36] s.66 is
a summary procedure; it is not suitable in cases involving complex objections to
enforcement requiring a full investigation of the facts.[37] The court may also not
give permission to enforce where the award is so defective in form[38] or substance[39]
that it is incapable of enforcement or its enforcement would be contrary to public
policy.[40] The court may also decline to enforce an award which purports to decide
matters that are not capable of resolution by arbitration[41] or grants relief which (if
enforced as a judgment or order of the court) would improperly affect the rights
of persons other than the parties to the arbitration agreement.[42]

These are exceptional cases. Wherever possible the court will give effect to the
award by granting permission to enforce it.

---

[31] Section 66(3) of the Arbitration Act 1996.

[32] *Persaud v Beynon* [2005] EWHC 3073 at [41].

[33] See paras 8–010 *et seq.* for opposing an order made under s.66 of the Arbitration Act 1996.

[34] See s.82(1) of the Arbitration Act 1996 for a definition of "substantive jurisdiction" and para.4–135,
as well as s.67 of the Act and para.8–054 for the right to challenge an award on this ground.

[35] Section 66(3) of the Arbitration Act 1996 makes clear that a right to object to "leave" on this ground
may be lost if the objection was not raised promptly (see also s.73 of the Act and para.8–065).

[36] The discretion is not finite: see DAC report, para.374.

[37] *Chaim Kohn v Sheva Wagschal & Others* [2006] W.L. 3854048, paras 13, 14; *ABCI v Banque Franco-
Tunisienne* [2002] 1 Lloyd's Rep. 511.

[38] Certain defects may be corrected under s.57 of the Arbitration Act 1996: see paras 6–186 *et seq.*
above. Under the ICC Rules of Arbitration, Art.27 a draft of the award is scrutinised for form
before it is approved by the ICC Court of Arbitration. The substance of the award is left to the
arbitral tribunal to decide.

[39] The defect in substance would have to be apparent on the face of the award, but see comments of
Lord Denning M.R. in *Middlemiss and Gould v Hartlepool Corp* [1972] 1 W.L.R. 1643 concerning
an award whose validity is doubtful.

[40] This is not stated in s.66 of the Arbitration Act 1996 but it was considered (see DAC report,
para.273) and it falls within the court's discretion. For "public policy" and illegality, see paras
8–031 and 8–044.

[41] For matters which are not arbitrable see paras 1–033 *et seq.*

[42] This was a formula suggested by the DAC report at para.374, but was not embodied in s.66 of the
Arbitration Act 1996. Nevertheless, the court retains a discretion.

Effect of permission to enforce given under section 66. Where 8–006
permission is given by the court, it is usually given on terms that the award may
be enforced in the same manner as a judgment or order of the court to the same
effect.[43] This means that all the methods of enforcing a judgment of the court[44]
are then available to enforce the award,[45] including an injunction.[46] Normally a
party who has obtained permission will proceed to enforce the award without
delay, but he is not obliged to do so.[47] Enforcement may be suspended pending the
determination of a challenge to the award.[48]

Judgment in terms of the award. Where permission to enforce is given, 8–007
judgment may also be entered in terms of the award.[49] That may be necessary in
order to comply with a contractual requirement[50] or to take advantage of some
convention for the enforcement of judgments abroad, but care should be taken
because if the award merges with the judgment, it may not be possible to take
advantage of the enforcement provisions of a particular arbitration convention.[51]

Which route to follow? The respective provisions of ss.66(1) and (2) of the 8–008
Arbitration Act 1996 are distinct, the former enables a party to use the court's
enforcement mechanisms for the purpose of enforcing an award, the latter enables
a party to obtain a judgment of the court in the terms of the award.[52] Both routes
provide effective means of enforcement, although one may be more appropriate
than the other if enforcement is sought in a jurisdiction where having either an
award or an English court judgment facilitates the process.

Stay of enforcement. Where the court grants permission to enforce an 8–009
award, it may also stay the execution of that order for a limited period. The effect
of the stay will be to suspend enforcement pending an application to challenge the
award. A party wanting to suspend enforcement should apply promptly to the
court for an order and combine that application with his challenge of the award
and opposition to its enforcement. The court will consider the prospects of
success of the challenge and whether enforcement might become more or less easy
if it is delayed.[53] An order for a stay that suspends enforcement of the award will
usually be subject to specific conditions. In one case, the court directed the

---

[43] Section 66(1) of the Arbitration Act 1996.
[44] This means the High Court or County Court: see s.105(1) of the Arbitration Act 1996.
[45] For the remedies available from the court see para.8–018.
[46] *Aiglon Ltd and L'Aiglon SA v Gau Shan Co Ltd* [1993] 1 Lloyd's Rep. 164, a case where worldwide
freezing injunctions were granted to enforce an award.
[47] *Curacao Trading Co BV v Harkisandas & Co* [1992] 2 Lloyd's Rep. 186.
[48] *Apis AS v Fantazia Kereskedelmi KFT* [2001] 1 All E.R. (Comm) 348.
[49] Section 66(2) of the Arbitration Act 1996.
[50] A requirement that judgment be entered in terms of the award is rare nowadays but it can be found
from time to time in arbitration agreements.
[51] See para.8–020.
[52] *ASM Shipping Ltd of India v TTMI of England* [2007] EWHC 927; [2007] 1 C.L.C 555 at [26].
[53] *Socadec SA v Pan Afric Impex Co Ltd* [2003] EWHC 2086.

respondent to pay a substantial sum into an escrow account.[54] In other cases, the court has ordered the applicant to make a payment into court as security.[55]

8–010   **Objections to summary enforcement of an award.** If permission is given to enforce an award under s.66 of the Act, the party (or parties) against whom the award is to be enforced may still challenge the award. There is a time after service of the order[56] during which an application may be made to set aside the order for permission to enforce the award.[57] The grounds for challenging an award[58] are not limited to the matter of jurisdiction mentioned in s.66(3) of the Act,[59] but they are certainly no wider than the rights available to challenge awards under the Arbitration Act 1996 more generally. The grounds for challenging some awards made abroad may be limited by a convention.[60] The subject of challenges and the grounds for opposing enforcement of awards are discussed in the following sections of this chapter.[61]

8–011   **Award must be pursuant to arbitration agreement.** Enforcement under s.66 is only available in respect of "an award pursuant to an arbitration agreement". It cannot therefore be used to enforce preliminary or interim decisions[62] which are themselves subject to review by an arbitral tribunal.[63] Nor can it be used to enforce procedural orders or directions, or any order of the tribunal granting relief on a provisional basis.[64]

---

[54] *Air India v Caribjet* [2002] 1 Lloyd's Rep. 314. An application to stay enforcement of a second award was refused because, if granted, it would be a long time before it was removed.

[55] *Apis AS v Fantazia Kereskedelmi KFT* [2001] 1 All E.R. (Comm) 348 where the court applied the same test for ordering security in respect of the suspension of an award made in England as is applied by the court when considering an application under s.103(5) of the Arbitration Act 1996. See para.8–046. *Socadec SA v Pan Afric Impex Co Ltd* [2003] EWHC 2086 where the court stayed enforcement for 28 days to allow security of US $4,000,000 to be put up. If this was done, the stay would continue.

[56] The time limit is 14 days after service of the order within the jurisdiction or such other period as the court fixes where the order is served outside the jurisdiction: see CPR r.62.18(9) and para.8–224.

[57] See para.8–224 for an application to set aside an award. If possible a party wishing to oppose enforcement should state his objections before permission is given: see para.8–004.

[58] The grounds are discussed in paras 8–051 *et seq.*

[59] Section 66(3) specifically mentions the case where it is shown that the tribunal "lacked substantive jurisdiction to make the award", but does not limit challenge to this ground. Some other grounds are discussed in connection with opposition to enforcement of New York Convention awards: see paras 8–028 *et seq.*

[60] The New York Convention, for example, see s.66(5) of the Arbitration Act 1996 and paras 8–021 *et seq.*

[61] See paras 8–051 *et seq.*

[62] Under some contractual provisions (e.g. cl.67 of the FIDIC Conditions of Contract) an engineer or adjudicator or other person may be required to make a decision before an arbitration commences.

[63] *Cameron (A) Ltd v John Mowlem & Co Plc* [1990] 52 B.L.R. 24, CA. Relief may however be available from the court to give effect to such a decision see *Drake & Scull Engineering Ltd v McLaughlin & Harvey Plc* 60 B.L.R. 102.

[64] The parties can empower a tribunal to make such an order which may be enforced as a "peremptory order" under s.42 of the Arbitration Act 1996 but not as an award because the tribunal's order is subject to final adjudication: see s.39(3) of the Act and para.5–088.

Form of award. Provided the terms of the award are sufficiently clear there 8–012
is now no reason why a declaratory award cannot be enforced under s.66. Indeed,
the courts do enforce declarations under s.66.[65] Previously expressed doubts about
whether an award which is couched in purely declaratory terms can be enforced
as a judgment under s.66 of the Act are, it is suggested, no longer applicable.[66] The
court will not however enforce an award which is in terms that are not clear nor
grant permission to enforce an award for the payment of money which does not
specify the sum due.[67] In order to be enforceable under this summary procedure
the award "must be framed in terms which would make sense if those were
translated straight into the body of a judgment".[68]

Security. The court has jurisdiction to order security for costs in respect of an 8–013
application under s.66.[69]

Action on the award. The provision in the Arbitration Act 1996 that "an 8–014
award made by the tribunal pursuant to an arbitration agreement is final and
binding"[70] supports an action on the award, although as stated above a party
wishing to enforce an award would normally adopt the summary procedure
provided by s.66 of the Act.[71] That procedure is only available however where
there is an "arbitration agreement" within the meaning of the Arbitration Act
1996.[72] When that procedure is not available for any reason[73] it may be possible to
commence an action on the award.[74]

Implied obligation to perform award. If the arbitration agreement 8–015
pursuant to which the award is made falls outside the broad statutory definition,[75]
the action will have to be based on the premise that the particular arbitration

---

[65] For one such example, see *Kohn v Wagschal* [2006] EWHC 3356 at [7].
[66] *Margulies Brothers, Ltd v Dafnis Thomaides & Co (UK), Ltd* [1958] 1 Lloyd's Rep. 250. See also
the observations of Moore Bick J. in *Tongyuan International v Uni-Clan Ltd* (January 19, 2001) QBD
(Comm) though in that case the judge found that the award was expressed in clear enough terms
to be capable of enforcement as a judgment pursuant to s.101 (2) of the Act. In any event, it would
apparently not apply to a New York Convention award made in declaratory form that is sought to
be enforced under s.101 of the Arbitration Act 1996: see s.66(4) of the Arbitration Act 1996.
[67] See *Margulies Brothers Ltd v Dafnis Thomaides & Co (UK) Ltd* [1958] 1 Lloyd's Rep. 250. The
correction of an award or an additional award may be required for this purpose: see s.57 of the
Arbitration Act 1996 and para.6–091.
[68] *Tongyuan International v Uni-Clan Ltd* (January 19, 2001) QBD (Comm), Moore Bick J.
[69] *Gater Assets Ltd v Nak Naftogaz Ukrainiy* [2007] 1 Lloyd's Rep. 522.
[70] Section 58(1) of the Arbitration Act 1996.
[71] See para.8–003.
[72] Section 6 of the Arbitration Act 1996 and para.2–002.
[73] The summary procedure under s.66 of the Act would not be available if, although an arbitration
agreement can be proved, it does not amount to an "arbitration agreement" within the meaning of
the Arbitration Act 1996, s.6.
[74] *Goldstein v Conley* [2002] 1 W.L.R. 281 at 294 where the award was not made "pursuant to an
arbitration agreement" within the meaning of the Arbitration Act 1996.
[75] A study of ss.5 and 6 of the Arbitration Agreement 1996 will reveal the breadth of the definition:
see para.2–002.

agreement contains an implied obligation to perform the resulting award[76] and failure to do so is a breach of that arbitration agreement. The successful party would be entitled to bring an action in respect of such breach and to obtain a judgment in the terms of the award.[77] The essential elements of the plaintiff's cause of action are that he must plead and prove:

- an arbitration agreement[78];

- that a dispute has arisen which falls within that arbitration agreement;

- the appointment of a tribunal in accordance with the arbitration agreement;

- the making of the award pursuant to the arbitration agreement; and

- failure to perform the award.[79]

8–016 **Defences to an action on the award.** With one exception, the same objections that can be raised to oppose the grant of permission to enforce an award under s.66 of the Act[80] can be raised by way of defence to an action on the award. They are not limited to the grounds specified in s.103(2) of the Act,[81] although those grounds give an indication of the defences available.[82]

A serious irregularity on the part of the tribunal cannot however be pleaded as a defence to an action on an award, and since an award cannot be set aside in an action commenced by a claim form, it cannot be set aside on a counterclaim.[83] A defendant to an action on an award cannot therefore seek by way of counterclaim an order that the award should be set aside or remitted to the tribunal for reconsideration. His proper course, if appropriate grounds exist, is to make a separate application[84] to have the award remitted or set aside and to refer to that

---

[76] *Purslow v Baily* (1704) 2 Ld. Raym. 1039; *Bremer Oeltransport GmbH v Drewry* [1933] 1 K.B. 753; *Bloemen v Gold Coast City Council* [1973] A.C. 103; see also *Lord Hobhouse in Associated Electric and Gas Insurance Services Ltd v European Reinsurance Co of Zurich* [2003] 1 W.L.R. 1041 at [9]. Section 8(1) of the Arbitration Act 1996 is consistent with the implied promise.
[77] This common law remedy is saved expressly by s.66(4) of the Arbitration Act 1996.
[78] Though not one that must comply with the definition in s.6 of the Arbitration Act 1996 because this enforcement mechanism is not confined to arbitration agreements under the Act.
[79] *Christopher Brown Ltd v Oesterreichischer Waldbesitzer, etc., R GmbH* [1954] 1 Q.B. 8 at 9 and *The "Saint Anna"* [1983] 1 Lloyd's Rep. 637.
[80] See para.8–010.
[81] See paras 8–028 *et seq.*
[82] Challenges to and appeals against an award are dealt with later in this chapter. See paras 8–051 *et seq.*
[83] *Birtley District Co-operative Society Ltd v Windy Nook & District Industrial Co-operative Society Ltd* [1959] 1 W.L.R. 142; [1959] 1 All E.R. 43; *Scrimaglio v Thornett and Fehr* (1924) 18 Ll. L. Rep. 148. In these decisions the former ground of misconduct was in issue, but the reasoning applies to serious irregularity.
[84] Part III of CPR Pt 62 does not apply to an action on the award, so the application to set aside would have to be made by originating motion.

application in his defence to the action on the award.[85] He should also consider applying to stay the action on the award pending the outcome of his own application.

Limitation Period. The limitation period for an action on the award will usually be six years,[86] although if the arbitration agreement is under seal it will be 12 years.[87] Time runs from the date of the breach of the arbitration agreement,[88] not from the date of the arbitration agreement or the date of the award.[89]   8–017

Remedies available from the court to enforce an award. The remedies available from the court to enforce an award reflect the scope of relief and remedies available to an arbitral tribunal.[90] In the case of an award of a sum of money, the court may give permission to enforce the award by any means of execution available for a judgment of the court or give judgment for that sum, including interest, as a debt.[91] The court may similarly enforce an award of damages.[92] The court may also enforce an award for specific performance.[93] It is also possible to sue for a declaration that the award is binding.[94]   8–018

The court may grant an injunction to assist in the enforcement of an arbitration award. The court also has power to charge property recovered in the arbitral proceedings with the payment of solicitors' costs.[95] This is an extension of the court's power to make declarations and orders in legal proceedings under s.73 of the Solicitors Act 1976.

The court may also grant an anti-suit injunction to prevent the award being challenged in a court other than the court of the seat of the arbitration.[96]

Enforcement of award after bankruptcy of party. The validity of an award is not affected by a party becoming bankrupt after the commencement   8–019

---

[85] This is the rule in *Thorburn v Barnes.* See also *Scrimaglio v Thornett and Fehr* (1924) 18 Ll. L. Rep. 148.

[86] Section 7 of the Limitation Act 1980.

[87] Section 8 of the Limitation Act 1980.

[88] The breach is an express or implied obligation to carry out the award.

[89] *Agromet Motoimport Ltd v Maulden Engineering Co* (Beds.) Ltd [1985] 1 W.L.R. 762.

[90] Section 48 of the Arbitration Act 1996 and see paras 6–103 *et seq.*

[91] *Coastal States Trading (UK) Ltd v Mebro Mineraloelhandelsgesellschaft GmbH* [1986] 1 Lloyd's Rep. 465. The tribunal's power to award interest appears in s.49 of the Arbitration Act 1996. See paras 6–115 *et seq.*

[92] *Bremer Oeltransport GmbH v Drewry* [1933] 1 K.B. 753. See also *Dalmia Dairy Industries Ltd v National Bank of Pakistan* [1978] 2 Lloyd's Rep. 223 at 274.

[93] See para.6–108.

[94] That would be unusual in view of the terms of s.58(1) of the Arbitration Act 1996 but the subsection is not mandatory, so there may be an issue as to the meaning of the parties' agreement. See *Birtley District Co-operative Society Ltd v Windy Nook & District Industrial Co-operative Society Ltd (No.2)* [1960] 2 Q.B. 1.

[95] Section 75 of the Arbitration Act 1996.

[96] *C v D* [2007] EWHC 1541.

of the reference but before enforcement of the resulting award,[97] and the award could form the basis of proof of a claim in the estate of the bankrupt. Further, a trustee in bankruptcy with permission of the court[98] may enforce an award or take action on it.[99]

3. RECOGNITION AND ENFORCEMENT OF CERTAIN FOREIGN AWARDS

8–020   **Introduction.** What has already been said about the enforcement of awards summarily or by an action on the award applies to awards made abroad as well as to awards made in England.[100] There are however several conventions which have been ratified by the United Kingdom concerning the recognition and enforcement of foreign arbitral awards.[101] Part III of the Arbitration Act 1996 deals with awards to which the New York Convention[102] applies, and it mentions that Pt II of the Arbitration Act 1950 continues to apply in relation to awards to which the Geneva Convention[103] applies which are not also New York Convention awards.[104] Awards made abroad may thus be enforceable in England under one or more conventions if the United Kingdom and the State where the award was made have ratified them. The terms of each convention should however be studied because they differ. The following paragraphs[105] will concentrate on enforcement of awards pursuant to the New York Convention because it is used most often as more countries have ratified it than any other convention,[106] but mention will also be made of the Geneva Convention and the Washington Convention.[107]

---

[97] *Ex p. Edwards* (1886) 3 Morrell's Bank. Rep. 179; s.3 of the Arbitration Act 1950 has been repealed, see para.3–027.

[98] Insolvency Act 1986, s.285(1). Permission to enforce the award would be necessary in any event under s.66 of the Arbitration Act 1996, but a trustee in bankruptcy should apply for permission under both Acts.

[99] For the position of a company which becomes subject to an administration or winding up order, see paras 3–030 *et seq.*

[100] An award made abroad which was not enforceable pursuant to a Convention (a "non-convention award") was enforced in *Dalmia Cement v National Bank of Pakistan* [1974] 2 Lloyd's Rep. 98.

[101] The New York Convention is the best known of these conventions, although it was preceded by the Geneva Convention which continues to apply to some awards. The UK has also ratified the Washington Convention which applies to certain investments disputes. Each of these conventions will be considered in turn.

[102] See s.100(4) of the Arbitration Act 1996 for a definition of the New York Convention.

[103] See the Schedules to the Arbitration Act 1950 for the text of the Geneva Protocol and Geneva Convention.

[104] See s.99 of the Arbitration Act 1996. See para.8–047 for awards to which the Geneva Convention applies.

[105] See paras 8–021 *et seq.*

[106] The New York Convention is described in the DAC report as "not only the cornerstone of international dispute resolution, it is an essential ingredient more generally of world trade" (para.347).

[107] See the Arbitration (International Investment Disputes) Act 1966 for provisions concerning the Washington Convention and para.8–048 for awards to which that Convention applies.

New York Convention Award. The Arbitration Act 1996[108] re-enacts   8–021
previous legislation which implemented the New York Convention[109] by incorporating into English law the provisions for the recognition and enforcement of
awards contained in the New York Convention. It defines a "New York Convention award" as an award made, in pursuance of an arbitration agreement,[110] in the
territory of a state (other than the United Kingdom) which is a party to the New
York Convention.[111] Note that there must be an agreement in writing to satisfy the
requirement of an arbitration agreement. Some instruments go so far as to provide
on their face that the writing requirement is satisfied.[112] The scope of the writing
requirements under the Convention and the Arbitration Act are not identical.[113]

Refusal of recognition and enforcement. The grounds on which   8–022
recognition of New York Convention awards will be refused under ss.101–103 of
the 1996 Act are very limited. Case law is replete with policy statements to this
effect: "There is an important policy interest, reflected in the country's treaty
obligations, in ensuring the effective and speedy enforcement of such international
arbitration awards".[114] Section 103 accordingly embodies a predisposition to
favour enforcement of New York Convention awards.[115] So unless the ground for
refusal falls within the terms of s.103, the court must recognise and enforce a New
York Convention award. The court also apparently has a very limited discretion to
enforce the award even where one or more of the grounds are made out.[116]

Scope of recognition and enforcement. Before turning to the detailed   8–023
terms of s.103, it is useful to set out the provisions of the preceding sections.
Section 101 of the Arbitration Act, 1996 reads:

> "101. (1) A New York Convention award shall be recognised as binding on the persons
> as between whom it was made, and may accordingly be relied on by those
> persons by way of defence, set-off or otherwise in any legal proceedings in
> England and Wales or Northern Ireland.

---

[108] Sections 100–103 of the Arbitration Act 1996.
[109] The Convention on the Recognition and Enforcement of Foreign Arbitral Awards adopted by the
United Nations Conference on International Commercial Arbitration on June 10, 1958; see
definition in s.101(1) of the Arbitration Act 1996.
[110] "Arbitration agreement" is defined as an agreement in writing (including an agreement contained
in an exchange of letters or telegrams) to submit to arbitration present or future differences capable
of settlement by arbitration: Arbitration Act 1996, s.6(1).
[111] Section 100(1) of the Arbitration Act 1996.
[112] For example, see Art.4(b) of the US/Ecuador bilateral investment treaty, referred to in *Ecuador v
Occidental Exploration & Production Co* [2006] 2 W.L.R. 70.
[113] Compare ss.100(2) and 5(2) of the Arbitration Act 1996.
[114] *Norsk Hydro ASA v State Property Fund of Ukraine* [2002] EWHC 2120 at [17].
[115] *IPCO (Nigeria) Ltd v Nigerian National Petroleum Corp* [2005] 2 Lloyds' Rep. 326, *per* Gross J. at
328.
[116] See para.8–028.

(2) A New York Convention award may, by leave of the Court, be enforced in the same manner as a judgment or order of the court to the same effect.
As to the meaning of "the court" see s.105.

(3) Where leave is so given, judgment may be entered in terms of the award."

The first part of s.101(1) is mandatory. A New York Convention Award is recognised under English law as binding on the persons as between whom it was made. The rest of the section specifies how a party may either enforce such an award[117] or rely upon it as a defence, set-off or otherwise in any legal proceedings in England.[118] In this way, the Convention extends beyond the paradigm situation where a claimant seeks recognition of an award so it can enforce a claim against the respondent. In *Svenska Petroleum Exploration AB v Lithuania (No.1)* the claimant persuaded the court to recognise a jurisdictional award of the tribunal under s.103(2) in response to an application by the respondent State to strike out the claimant's application to recognise the final award under ss.101–103 of the Arbitration Act 1996.[119] Enforcement can be sought directly under s.101(2) by applying for permission or "leave" of the court to enforce the award in the same manner as a judgment or order of the High Court or a county court.[120] Alternatively, where permission is obtained, judgment may be entered in terms of the award.[121] Where it was sought to enforce a single award against two separate and distinct parties, that order was a departure from the terms of the award and would not be an order "in terms of the award" under s.101(3).[122] These provisions reflect the terms of s.66, although because there is a special provision for the recognition and enforcement of a New York Convention award the Arbitration Act 1996 makes clear that nothing in that section affects the recognition or enforcement of an award under s.101 of the Act.[123]

Where a State has agreed in writing to submit a dispute to arbitration the effect of s.9(1) of the State Immunity Act 1978 is to extend the exemption from state

---

[117] Sections 101(2) and (3) which replaced s.3(2) of the Arbitration Act 1975, provide for enforcement of a New York Convention award.

[118] Section 101(1) which replaced s.3(2) of the Arbitration Act 1975, provides for using the award as a defence, set-off or otherwise. The word "otherwise" makes clear that the use to which a New York Convention award may be put is not limited.

[119] [2005] 1 Lloyd's Rep. 515. In this case, therefore, the claimant's initial application for recognition of the final award under the Convention led to it being able to rely on the tribunal's jurisdictional award under the Convention as a defence to the respondent's application to strike out its original application for recognition. The claimant also relied upon the principle of issue estoppel which was not made out at that stage, although it was subsequently on the hearing of the full application to register the award. See *Svenska Petroleum Exploration AB v Lithuania (No.2)* [2006] 1 Lloyd's Rep. 181 at [21], [22], [52]–[56], affirmed at [2006] EWCA 1529.

[120] Section 105(1) of the Arbitration Act 1996 defines "the court" as meaning the High Court or County Court.

[121] Section 101(3) of the Arbitration Act 1996.

[122] *Norsk Hydro ASA v State Property Fund of Ukraine* [2002] EWHC 2120 at [15]–[18].

[123] Arbitration Act 1996, s.66(4) replacing the Arbitration Act 1975, s.3(1)(a). This provision also extends to other enactments, including Pt II of the Arbitration Act 1950 (Geneva Convention awards) and to an action on the award. See also the corresponding provision in s.104 of the Arbitration Act 1996, which makes clear that a New York Convention award can also be enforced under s.66 of the Arbitration Act 1996 or by an action on the award.

immunity which that sub-section confers to an application under s.101 for leave to enforce the award as a judgment.[124]

Procedure for summary enforcement of a New York Conven-   8–024
tion award. The Arbitration Act 1996 s.102[125] specifies the procedure for recognising or enforcing a New York Convention award as follows:

"102.   (1)   A party seeking the recognition or enforcement of a New York Convention award must produce:

(a)   the duly authenticated original award or a duly certified copy of it, and

(b)   the original arbitration agreement or a duly certified copy of it.

(2)   If the award or agreement is in a foreign language, the party must also produce a translation of it certified by an official or sworn translator or by a diplomatic or consular agent."

Production of these documents suffices for the purpose of recognition of the award by the court.[126] The party seeking recognition does not have to show at that stage that the award was binding upon the party against whom recognition is sought. Any such question is for the latter to raise at the next stage under s.103 of the Act.[127]

Application without notice. The application is usually made without   8–025
notice to the other party[128] but the other party will be given a period of time within which to apply to the court to have the order set aside.

Enforcement of the award as made. Subject to the threshold require-   8–026
ment of production of documents referred to immediately above, and the exhaustive grounds on which enforcement of a New York Convention award may be refused,[129] the court is neither entitled nor bound to go behind the award in question, explore the reasoning of the arbitral tribunal or second guess its intention. Additionally, the court seeks to ensure that an award is carried out by making available its own domestic legal sanctions.[130] As a consequence, an order

---

[124] The Court of Appeal has confirmed that "proceedings which relate to the arbitration" under s.9(1) of the State Immunity Act 1978 cover proceedings in support of the arbitration, proceedings to challenge the award as well as proceedings to enforce the award. The exemption from immunity conferred by that sub-section does not extend however to enforcement by execution on property: *Svenska Petroleum Exploration AB v Lithuania* [2006] EWCA 1529 at [117] affirming the decision of Gloster J. in *Svenska Petroleum Exploration AB v Lithuania (No.2)* [2006] 1 Lloyd's Rep. 181.
[125] Section 102 of the Arbitration Act 1996 replaced s.4 of the Arbitration Act 1975.
[126] *Dardana Ltd v Yukos Oil Co (No.1)* EWCA Civ 543 at [10].
[127] *Svenska Petroleum v Lithuania (No.2)* 1 Lloyds' Rep. 515 at [18].
[128] *Svenska Petroleum and Exploration AB v Lithuania (No.2)* [2006] 1 Lloyds' Rep. 181 at 185. Affirmed by the Court of Appeal [2006] EWCA 1529.
[129] See para.8–028.
[130] *Norsk Hydro ASA v State Property Fund of Ukraine* [2002] EWHC 2120, *per* Gross J. at [17].

providing for enforcement of an award must follow the award. Minor slips and changes of name may be accommodated, but an award made against a single party cannot be enforced, for example, against two separate and distinct parties, because that would require the court "to stray into the arena of the substantive reasoning and intentions of the arbitral tribunal."[131]

8–027 **Service outside jurisdiction.** Permission may be sought to serve the arbitration claim form outside the jurisdiction of the court[132] and the presence of assets in the jurisdiction is not a pre-condition to the court exercising its discretion to grant permission.[133]

8–028 **Opposing enforcement of a New York Convention Award.** As stated above,[134] subject to production of the required documents the court has no discretion but to recognise and enforce a New York Convention award unless the party opposing enforcement proves one or more of the grounds specified in s.103 of the Arbitration Act 1996.[135] These grounds of refusal are exhaustive, and if none of the grounds is present the award will be enforced.[136] Much has been written about these grounds[137] and a detailed analysis is beyond the scope of this book but they will be treated summarily in this chapter.[138] The onus of proving the existence of a ground rests upon the party opposing enforcement, but that may not be the end of the matter. The court also has a discretion to refuse enforcement where one or more of the grounds are made out. This discretion is not to be exercised arbitrarily however because the word "may" in s.103(2) is intended to refer to the corresponding word in the New York Convention.[139] In any event the discretion is not open ended and should only be exercised where "despite the original existence of one or more of the listed circumstances, the right to rely on them had been lost by, for example, another agreement or estoppel", or where there are circumstances "which might on some recognisable legal principles affect the prima facie right to have an award set aside arising in cases listed in s.103(2)".[140] In *Svenska Petroleum Exploration AB v Lithuania (No.1)*, the claimant (responding to an application to strike out its application for recognition of an award) was able to satisfy the court that it should exercise this discretion. The

---

[131] *Norsk Hydro, supra* at [18], where an order and judgment enforcing an award were set aside.
[132] CPR r.62.18(4). This provision will apply whether the application is made to the High Court or to a County Court: see CCR, Ord.48C, CPR r.16 and para.8–191.
[133] *Rosseel NV v Oriental Commercial & Shipping Co (UK) Ltd* [1991] 2 Lloyd's Rep. 625.
[134] See para.8–024.
[135] Section 103 of the Arbitration Act 1996 replaced s.5 of the Arbitration Act 1975.
[136] Section 103(1) of the Arbitration Act 1996 replaced s.5(1) of the Arbitration Act 1975; *Rosseel NV v Oriental Commercial & Shipping Co (UK) Ltd* [1991] 2 Lloyd's Rep. 625.
[137] The reader is referred for example to Dr A J van den Berg, The New York Arbitration Convention of 1958 (Kluwer) and the updated commentary provided in the Arbitration Year Books.
[138] Challenges to and appeals against an award are however dealt with fully later at paras 8–051 *et seq.*
[139] *Ecuador v Occidental* [2006] 2 W.L.R. 70 at 101 following *Dardana v Yukos, ibid.* at 333.
[140] *Dardana Ltd v Yukos Oil Co (No.1)* [2003] 2 Lloyds' Rep 326, *per* Mance L.J. quoted with approval in *Svenska Petroleum Exploration AB v Lithuania (No.1)* [2005] 1 Lloyd's Rep. 515 at [19] and in *Kanoria v Guinness* [2006] EWCA Civ 222 at [25].

respondent state, which would otherwise have been able to prove that it was not a party to the agreement to arbitrate (and hence falling within s.103(2)(b)) had asked the tribunal to determine jurisdiction, had fought and lost that issue before the tribunal and then had participated in the merits stage of the arbitration without objecting or challenging the award on jurisdiction before the courts at the seat.[141] In this way, although s.73 of the 1996 Act[142] is not incorporated into ss.101–103, it is likely that the courts will approach the exercise of discretion under s.103(2) with the concept of the loss of a right to object firmly in mind.[143] However, as the Court of Appeal noted when affirming a subsequent decision in the same litigation, there can be no issue estoppel arising simply from the fact that the respondent failed to challenge the award before the court at the seat of arbitration.[144]

Nationality irrelevant. The New York Convention contains no nationality condition (unlike the Geneva Convention of 1927). So, whilst the New York Convention was primarily intended to facilitate the enforcement of awards against foreign parties, where an award is made abroad between parties of the same nationality, the New York Convention will also be available to a party seeking to enforce against assets of the other party in other convention countries. Therefore, a party's nationality would of itself be irrelevant to the consideration of any ground for refusing enforcement under s.103(2) or (3) of the Act.[145]   8–029

Incapacity. The court may refuse to enforce a New York Convention award upon proof by the party opposing enforcement that "a party to the arbitration agreement was (under the law applicable to him) under some incapacity".[146] That ground has been held to extend to someone who was so seriously ill that it was impossible for him to instruct a lawyer to present his defence.[147] Usually, it will be the incapacity of the party opposing the enforcement, but that will not always be the case.[148] The law of incorporation of a corporate party, which will often not be English law, may, for example prevent a party from entering into an arbitration agreement.[149]   8–030

---

[141] [2005] 1 Lloyd's Rep. 515, at [22], [27].

[142] See paras 8–065 and 8–110 below.

[143] *Svenska Petroleum Exploration AB v Lithuania (No.1)* [2005] 1 Lloyd's Rep. 515 at [26].

[144] *Svenska Petroleum Exploration AB v Lithuania* [2006] EWCA 1529 at [104], affirming the decision of Gloster J. in *Svenska Petroleum Exploration AB v Lithuania (No.2)* [2006] 1 Lloyd's Rep. 181.

[145] *IPCO (Nigeria) Ltd v Nigerian National Petroleum Corp* [2005] 2 Lloyd's Rep. 326, at [16]. See also *C v D* [2007] EWHC 1541.

[146] Section 103(2)(a) of the Arbitration Act 1996. See paras 3–004 *et seq.* for incapacity under English law.

[147] *Kanoria v Guinness* [2006] EWCA Civ 222 at [18] recording the decision of the judge at first instance. The party in question was suffering from a serious form of cancer.

[148] A claimant under some incapacity could conceivably obtain an award and seek to enforce it against a respondent who did not participate in the arbitration but pleaded the claimant's incapacity in opposition to enforcement proceedings.

[149] This occurred in *Continental Enterprises Ltd v Shandong* [2005] EWHC 92 (Comm) although the decision did not concern a New York Convention award. The incapacity of corporate entities bedevils international arbitration. See paras 3–003 *et seq.* on capacity of parties to an arbitration agreement under English law.

In order to oppose enforcement on this ground the party concerned must prove the incapacity to the satisfaction of the court. Expert evidence of any relevant foreign law may be required.

8–031 **Invalidity and illegality.** The validity of the arbitration agreement is fundamental to arbitration, and the enforcement of an award can be opposed if "the arbitration agreement was not valid under the law to which the parties subjected it[150] or, failing any indication thereon, under the law of the country where the award was made".[151] It is important to realise that this ground for opposing enforcement of the award relates to the validity of the arbitration agreement and not the validity of any underlying contract. The doctrine of separabilty which is enacted by the Arbitration Act 1996[152] will, unless the parties have agreed otherwise, treat the arbitration agreement as a distinct agreement from the rest of the contract for the purposes of determining its validity.[153] Nevertheless, illegality of the main contract can affect the enforceability of an arbitration award even under the New York Convention.[154]

8–032 **The *Westacre* Case.** *Westacre Investment Inc v Jugoimport–SPDR Ltd* proceeded on the basis that the arbitral tribunal had jurisdiction to decide whether the underlying contract was immoral and a nullity because of an alleged agreement to purchase personal influence and to pay bribes. The award, based on Swiss law and made in Geneva, concluded that the arbitration agreement and the underlying contract were valid, and an appeal to the Swiss Federal Tribunal on grounds of public policy was dismissed.

On hearing an application to set aside permission to enforce the award in England, the judge at first instance[155] summarised the effect of the English law authorities is as follows:

 (i) Where it is alleged that an underlying contract is illegal and void and that an arbitration award in respect of it is thereby unenforceable, the primary question is whether the determination of the particular illegality alleged fell within the jurisdiction of the arbitrators.

 (ii) There is no general rule that, where an underlying contract is illegal at common law or by reason of an English statute, an arbitration agreement, which is ancillary to that contract, is incapable of conferring jurisdiction on arbitrators to determine disputes arising within the scope of the agreement, including disputes as to whether illegality renders the contract unenforceable.

---

[150] The law chosen expressly or implicitly to govern the arbitration agreement and the underlying contract may be different. See paras 2–087 *et seq.*
[151] Arbitration Act 1996, s.103(2)(b).
[152] Section 7 of the Arbitration Act 1996: see para.2–008.
[153] See paras 2–011 *et seq.* for a discussion on this subject.
[154] *Westacre Investement Inc v Jugoimpor–SPDR Ltd* [1999] 2 Lloyd's Rep. 65, CA.
[155] *Westacre Investments v Jugoimport–SPDR* [1998] 3 W.L.R. 770 at 794.

(iii) Whether such an agreement to arbitrate is capable of conferring such jurisdiction depends on whether the nature of the illegality is such that, in the case of statutory illegality, the statute has the effect of impeaching that agreement as well as the underlying contract, and, in the case of illegality at common law, public policy requires that disputes about the underlying contract should not be referred to arbitration.

(iv) When, at the stage of enforcement of an award, it is necessary for the court to determine whether the arbitrators had jurisdiction in respect of disputes relating to the underlying contract, the court must consider the nature of the disputes in question. If the issue before the arbitrators was whether money was due under a contract which was indisputably illegal at common law, an award in favour of the claimant would not be enforced for it would be contrary to public policy for the court to enforce an award that ignored palpable and indisputable illegality.[156] If, however, there was an issue before the arbitrator whether the underlying contract was illegal and void, the court would first have to consider whether, having regard to the nature of the illegality alleged, it was consistent with the public policy which would, if illegality were established, impeach the validity of the underlying contract, that the determination of the issue of illegality should be left to arbitration. If it was not consistent, the arbitrators would be held to have no jurisdiction to determine that issue.

(v) If the court concluded that the arbitration agreement conferred jurisdiction to determine whether the underlying contract was illegal and by the award the arbitrators determined that it was not illegal, prima facie the court would enforce the resulting award.

(vi) If the party against whom the award was made then sought to challenge enforcement of the award on the grounds that[157] the contract was indeed illegal, the enforcing court would have to consider whether the public policy against the enforcement of illegal contracts outweighed the countervailing public policy in support of the finality of awards in general and of awards in respect of the same issue in particular.

By a majority the Court of Appeal upheld the decision of the court at first instance that refused to set aside permission to enforce the New York Convention award. The court also refused to set aside another New York Convention award, where the arbitrator had found that there was no bribery or corrupt practice, although public officers were lobbied in breach of a statutory provision.[158]

---

[156] This minor alteration in what Colman J. said in *Westacre* was suggested by the Court of Appeal in *Soleimany v Soleimany* [1998] 3 W.L.R. 811 at 826.

[157] In *Westacre*, Colman J. included the words "on the basis of facts not placed before the arbitrators", but these have been deleted from the passage quoted above because in *Soleimany v Soleimany, ibid.* the Court of Appeal said that in an appropriate case the court may inquire, as it did in *Soleimany*, into an issue of illegality even if the arbitrator found that there was no illegality (at 826).

[158] *OTV v Hilmarton* [1999] 2 Lloyd's Rep. 222.

8–033　**Application to awards wherever made.** The approach of the English court, as summarised above, to the enforcement of an award where there is an issue of illegality has been applied in relation to both awards made in England and abroad. In *Soleimany v Soleimany*,[159] the arbitrator found that money was due under a contract whose object involved smuggling items out of another country illegally. The award was made in England, and permission was granted to enforce the award summarily under the predecessor to s.66 of the Arbitration Act 1996. However, the Court of Appeal set aside the permission to enforce because the award referred on its face to an illegal object which the English court viewed as contrary to public policy.[160]

8–034　**Due process/Natural justice.** If the party opposing the award can prove that "he was not given proper notice of the appointment of the arbitrator or of the arbitration proceedings or was otherwise unable to present his case", that would be a ground for opposing a New York Convention award.[161] There is no definition in the Act of "proper notice"[162] which may vary depending, for example, on the applicable law, but in the exercise of its discretion the court will need to be persuaded that the complaint is not only a failure to comply with some notice requirement but that the party opposing enforcement really did not learn of the appointment of the arbitrator[163] or of the arbitration proceedings.[164]

8–035　**Inability to present case.** A party who received notice but who nevertheless claims that he was unable to present his case to the arbitral tribunal will have to state in his opposing witness statement exactly how he was prevented from presenting his case. This section will therefore normally cover the case where the procedure adopted has been operated in a manner contrary to natural justice.[165] This may include not only being prevented from putting his own case to the tribunal but also not having an opportunity to deal with that of his opponent. In *Irvani v Irvani*,[166] the Court of Appeal quashed a declaration that an award was valid and binding on the parties. On the face of the award, the Court of Appeal found that certain material findings were either unreasoned or suggested that the arbitrator had taken account of evidence that was not available to one of the parties. The court also found that the party concerned had not been invited to comment

---

[159] [1998] 3 W.L.R. 811.
[160] *Soleimany v Soleimany* [1998] 3 W.L.R. 811 at 828. See also para.8–044.
[161] Section 103(2)(c) of the Arbitration Act 1996. See also para.5–042. In *Kanoria v Guinness* [2006] EWCA Civ 222, the Court of Appeal declined to enforce the award on this ground.
[162] Section 80 of the Arbitration Act 1996 contains provisions and enabling legislation for notice requirements in respect of legal proceedings only.
[163] "The arbitrator" in this context would include one or more members of the arbitral tribunal and include an "umpire".
[164] By participating subsequently in the proceedings the party may waive the irregularity.
[165] This is consistent with the general duty of the tribunal stated in s.33(1)(a) of the Arbitration Act 1996, although that section applies to arbitrations whose seat is in England. *Minmetals Germany v Ferco Steel* [1999] C.L.C. 647 above, *per* Colman J. at [326], approved by the Court of Appeal in *Kanoria v Guinness* [2006] EWCA Civ 222.
[166] [2000] 1 Lloyd's Rep. 412 at 426.

on an investigation into the company in issue, nor was it clear from the award on what basis a claim was rejected. In the absence of an investigation by the judge into these matters, the Court of Appeal refused to enforce the award. In a similar and also exceptional case, *Kanoria v Guinness*,[167] the Court of Appeal refused to enforce an award where the party in question did not have notice of the allegation of fraud, which was the basis on which the arbitrator decided to make an award against him: "It seems to me quite clear on the natural wording of this clause that a party to an arbitration is unable to present his case if he is never informed of the case that he is called upon to meet."[168]

Denial of justice needed. It would not however be sufficient for a party to   8–036
say that his time for oral argument was limited if he was given an opportunity to supplement that argument with written submissions either before or after the hearing.[169] Nor would the refusal of a replacement arbitrator to allow a complete re-hearing where the parties had not required the taking of new evidence.[170] The tribunal's conduct would have to be a denial of justice for the court to refuse to enforce an award on this ground.[171]

Tribunal's jurisdiction. Enforcement of the award may also be opposed if   8–037
it "deals with a difference not contemplated by or not falling within the terms of the submission to arbitration or contains decisions on matters beyond the scope of the submission to arbitration",[172] although the court may distinguish between differences falling within and outside the ambit[173] of the arbitration agreement.

This ground for opposition is akin to challenging the award of the tribunal as to its substantive jurisdiction,[174] a subject which will be addressed later in this chapter,[175] and although dealt with in separate sections of the Act[176] the approach

---

[167] [2006] EWCA Civ 222.
[168] *per* Lord Phillips L.CJ., at [22].
[169] Some procedures do not contemplate long oral hearings. Further, questions to witnesses may have to be directed through the tribunal rather than via cross-examination. See *Minmetals Germany v Ferco Steel* [1999] C.L.C. 647 for difficulties encountered with an inquisitorial system, but where challenges to the award failed. See also para.5–045.
[170] *OTV v Hilmarton* [1999] 2 Lloyd's Rep. 222 at 226. The extent to which hearings need to be held anew following the replacement of an arbitrator are often set out in the applicable arbitral rules.
[171] It is doubtful whether every serious irregularity mentioned in s.68 of the Arbitration Act 1996 would suffice to justify refusal to enforce a New York Convention award (e.g. an uncertainty or ambiguity as to the effect of the award).
[172] Section 103(2)(d) of the Arbitration Act 1996.
[173] Section 103(4) of the Arbitration Act 1996.
[174] Section 67 of the Arbitration Act 1996. This ground of challenge is only available when the seat of arbitration is in England and Wales or Northern Ireland, which would not be the case if it were a New York Convention award. See *Metal Distributors (UK) Ltd v ZCCM Investment Holdings Plc* [2005] 2 Lloyd's Rep. 37, a challenge to an award under s.67, where the overlap with s.103(2)(d) appears to be recognised, at [18].
[175] See para.8–054.
[176] Section 67 (substantive jurisdiction challenge) and s.103(2)(d) of the Arbitration Act 1996.

of the court to the applications will be similar.[177] Both rest on the premise that the tribunal derives its competence or jurisdiction from the agreement by which the parties agreed to submit their disputes to arbitration and an award which exceeds the scope of that agreement will not be allowed to stand.[178]

8–038 **Procedure or composition of the tribunal is contrary to the agreement of the parties or the law of the place of arbitration.** The court may also refuse to enforce a New York Convention award upon proof "that the composition of the arbitral tribunal or the arbitral procedure was not in accordance with the agreement of the parties or, failing such agreement, with the law of the country in which the arbitration took place".[179] There are two parts to this ground for opposition. The first relates to the composition of the tribunal. Where, for example, the parties agreed that their disputes should be submitted to three arbitrators and a sole arbitrator appointed by one party proceeded to determine the dispute, the other party would have a ground to object to the enforcement of any award made by that arbitrator.[180] Opposition to enforcement on this ground would be likely to succeed if the party opposing enforcement did not take part in the arbitration. Where however he took part in the arbitration without objecting to the appointment of a sole arbitrator the court would be unlikely to exercise its discretion in his favour but would instead enforce the award.

8–039 **Adverse effect required.** The second ground for opposition rests on the departure from a procedure agreed by the parties, or failing their agreement, the procedural law of the place where the arbitration took place.[181] In order to persuade the court not to enforce the award on this ground, the procedure adopted by the tribunal would not only have to be materially different from that which had been agreed but would also have to affect adversely the objecting party's ability to present his case to the tribunal or address that of the other party. If he continued to take part in the proceedings, despite the different procedure, the court would need to be persuaded that he did not, or could not,[182] waive his right to object.[183]

---

[177] Although not bound to do so by s.103, the court is likely to consider, for example, whether the applicant should forfeit his right to object to the tribunal exceeding its jurisdiction.

[178] *Pirtek (UK) Ltd v Deanswood Wood Ltd* [2005] 2 Lloyds' Rep. 728, a decision based on s.67 of the Act. See paras 2–071 *et seq.* for a discussion as to the scope of the arbitration agreement.

[179] Section 103(2)(e) of the Arbitration Act 1996.

[180] Save where the appointment is pursuant to s.17 of the Arbitration Act 1996. See para.4–037.

[181] There may be some mandatory provisions concerning procedures for arbitrations conducted in a particular place.

[182] It is possible that under some law a particular procedural requirement is mandatory and cannot be waived.

[183] In *Minmetals Germany v Ferco Steel* [1999] C.L.C. 647 the court decided that the applicant had waived its right to object to the continuing omission of the arbitrators to disclose an award as required by the rules of arbitration. See para.8–110.

Not yet binding, set aside or suspended. Upon proof "that the award 8–040 has not yet become binding on the parties, or has been set aside or suspended by a competent authority of the country in which, or under the law of which, it was made",[184] the court may refuse to enforce a New York Convention award. If the arbitration agreement requires another step to be taken,[185] the award may not become binding on the parties until that step has been taken. Unless and until that event has occurred the court will not enforce the award.

Order of the competent authority. Where the relevant court has made 8–041 an order setting aside the award, the English court will usually, but not invariably, recognise that order and decline to enforce the award. The "competent authority" will almost invariably be the relevant court at the seat of the arbitration rather than the country under whose law it was made.[186] Where the competent authority suspends the binding effect of an award, the English court may dismiss the application for enforcement as premature or it may adjourn the application until the suspension is lifted.[187] For the purpose of this ground a suspension must have occurred as a result of a decision of a competent authority and not by operation of law.[188] The subsection is not triggered automatically by a challenge brought before the relevant court in that country, not least because s.103(5), which allows enforcement proceedings to be stayed whilst a challenge is pending elsewhere, would be "otiose, or at least curious".[189]

Application to set aside or suspend is pending. Section 103(5) 8–042 achieves a compromise between not allowing enforcement to be frustrated simply by making a challenge at the seat of the arbitration, and by not pre-empting pending challenge proceedings by the rapid enforcement of the award.[190] The court "may, if it considers it proper, adjourn the decision on the recognition or enforcement of the award".[191] In exercising its discretion the court will, without prejudging the matter, consider the strength of a number of factors pertaining to

---

[184] Section 103(2)(f) of the Arbitration Act 1996.

[185] For example, the arbitration agreement or the law which governs it, provides that an award shall not become binding unless and until it is confirmed by a judgment of the local court.

[186] See *C v D* [2007] EWHC 1541 on the inter-relationship between the curial and governing law with respect to review of awards. Where English law is the procedural law and it is the English court from which enforcement under the New York Convention is sought, under the Arbitration Act 1996, the court retains its supervisory jurisdiction over the arbitration. This is notwithstanding s.101(1) of the Arbitration Act 1996 which requires a New York Convention award to be recognised as binding: *Hiscox v Outhwaite* [1992] 1 A.C. 562.

[187] An adjournment will only be granted if the suspension is likely to be short-lived. Section 103(5) of the Arbitration Act 1996 permits an adjournment when an application to set aside an award or suspend its enforcement has been made to the competent authority.

[188] *White Knight ISA v Nu-Swift*: decision of Clarke J. on July 14, 1995. Suspension by operation of law may however fall under s.103(5) of the Arbitration Act 1996.

[189] *IPCO (Nigeria) Ltd v Nigerian National Petroleum Corp* [2005] 2 Lloyd's Rep. 326.

[190] *IPCO (Nigeria) Ltd v Nigerian National Petroleum Corp* [2005] 2 Lloyd's Rep. 326.

[191] Section 103(5) of the Arbitration Act 1996 which replaced s.5(3) of the Arbitration Act 1975.

the application to the competent authority and may adjourn only on terms that security is given by the party resisting enforcement of the award.[192]

8–043   **Non-arbitrable.** Enforcement of a New York Convention award may also be opposed if the award is "in respect of a matter which is not capable of settlement by arbitration", i.e. the subject of the dispute is non-arbitrable.[193] Although this ground has not yet come before the English courts for decision, it is apparent from the admissibility of competition or anti-trust issues to arbitration[194] that the courts will construe this ground narrowly. Nevertheless, English law does recognise that there are matters which cannot be decided by means of arbitration[195] and there have been decisions elsewhere that have recognised this ground.[196]

8–044   **Contrary to public policy.** A further ground for refusing to enforce an award is that "it would be contrary to public policy to recognise or enforce the award".[197] This ground, which is the source of much debate and potentially broad application in some jurisdictions is, as far as the English courts are concerned, confined to the public policy of England (as the country in which enforcement is sought) in maintaining the fair and orderly administration of justice.[198] Its application must be approached with "extreme caution"; it "was not intended to furnish an open-ended escape route for refusing enforcement of New York Convention awards".[199]

Although there are strong public policy considerations in favour of enforcing awards,[200] in *Soleimany v Soleimany*[201] the Court of Appeal refused on this ground (i.e. for reasons of public policy) to enforce an award made in England that referred on its face to the illegal object of the matrix contract. However, opposition to the enforcement of a New York Convention award on this ground failed in *Westacre v Jugoimport*[202] where the arbitral tribunal found that the underlying contract was valid.

---

[192] *Soleh Boneh International Ltd v The Government of the Republic of Uganda and Another* [1993] 2 Lloyd's Rep. 208. In *IPCO supra* Gross J. set out a list of considerations likely to be relevant to the court's consideration, at [15] and [16]. For the security that may be ordered see para.8–046 below.

[193] Section 103(3) of the Arbitration Act which replaces s.5(3) of the Arbitration Act 1975. See also paras 1–033 *et seq.* above.

[194] *ET Plus SA v Welter* [2006] 1 Lloyds' Rep 251, *per* Gross J. at 264 in respect of an application to stay court proceedings.

[195] Custody of children is one example.

[196] See para.1–036.

[197] Section 103(3) of the Arbitration Act 1996. See also s.68(2)(g) of the Act.

[198] *IPCO Nigeria Ltd v Nigerian National Petroleum Corp,* 2 Lloyds' Rep 326 at [24]. An application to set aside on these grounds was refused at [24].

[199] *IPCO Nigeria Ltd v Nigerian National Petroleum Corp,* 2 Lloyds' Rep 326 at [13]. See *Minmetals Germany v Ferco Steel* [1999] C.L.C. 647 at 661 where the court considered certain relevant considerations for determining whether such a ground is made out.

[200] *Tongyuan v Uni-clan* (January 19, 2001) Moore-Bick J.

[201] [1998] 3 W.L.R. 811.

[202] [1998] 3 W.L.R. 770, CA. See also *OTV v Hilmarton* [1999] 2 Lloyd's Rep. 222 and para.8–016.

Immunity[203]. Although not mentioned in the Arbitration Act 1996 or the   **8–045** New York Convention a party may be immune from enforcement proceedings. The defence of immunity is usually raised by sovereign States,[204] but it may also be available to other parties who do not participate in the arbitration proceedings.[205] Immunity may however be waived.[206]

Awards against States under investment treaty arbitrations are, subject to usual considerations of sovereign immunity, enforceable under the New York Convention. Indeed, some investment treaties specifically contemplate enforcement of non-ICSID awards under the New York Convention, although this is not a necessary pre-condition to enforcement of any award under the New York Convention.[207]

Security. The court may "on the application of the party claiming recognition   **8–046** or enforcement of the award order the other party to give suitable security".[208] On the question of security, both in terms of amount and whether it should be given at all, the court will consider both the strength of any argument that the award is invalid and the effect if enforcement is delayed by an adjournment.[209] In *Yukos Oil v Dardana Ltd*[210] the Court of Appeal decided that it was not an appropriate case to order security. The merits lent only modest support to such an application and no need was shown for any security during the adjournment of the enforcement proceedings. In *IPCO (Nigeria) Ltd v Nigerian National Petroleum Corp* the court ordered a stay of enforcement pending the resolution of challenge proceedings at the seat of the arbitration, Nigeria, upon payment of security and the sums indisputably due under the award.[211] In *Gater Assets Ltd v Nak Naftogaz Ukrainiy*,[212] Field J. ordered payment of security on the basis that a prima facie case of fraud in procuring the award had been made out. The Court of Appeal however, allowed the claimant's appeal by a majority. The court was prepared to assume (albeit not decide) that there is technical jurisdiction to order security for costs against an award creditor seeking to enforce an award but considered that the courts should be "reluctant" as a matter of principle, to order security for costs in such circumstances save in an exceptional case.[212a] The court found that the

---

[203] The doctrine of sovereign immunity is beyond the scope of this work and the reader is referred to *The Law of State Immunity* by Hazel Fox, 2002.

[204] See, for example, *Svenska Petroleum and Exploration AB v Lithuania (No.2)* [2006] 1 Lloyds' Rep. 181.

[205] See para.3–036. See also *AIG Capital Partners v The Republic of Kazakhstan and Another* [2005] EWHC 2239 for an unsuccessful attempt to execute under an ICSID award against funds beneficially owned by the State's Central bank.

[206] For example, as a result of the State Immunity Act 1978.

[207] *Ecuador v Occidental Exploration & Production Co* [2006] 2 W.L.R. 70.

[208] Section 103(5) of the Arbitration Act 1996 which replaced s.5(5) of the Arbitration Act 1975.

[209] *Soleh Boneh International Ltd and Another v Government of the Republic of Uganda and National Housing Corp* [1993] 2 Lloyd's Rep. 208, CA. Cited with approval in *IPCO*, at [15].

[210] [2003] 2 Lloyds' Rep. 326. The Court of Appeal reversed the decision of the judge at first instance who ordered security of US $2.5 million. See also *IPCO supra* at 335.

[211] [2005] 2 Lloyd's Rep. 326.

[212] [2007] 1 Lloyd's Rep. 522.

[212a] *Gater Assets Ltd v Nak Naffogaz Ukrainiy* [2007] EWHC 725, *per* Lord Justice Rix at [75].

ordering of security for costs was wrong in principle in this case as to do so would not be just.[212b]

8-047   **Enforcement of Geneva Convention awards.** Part II of the Arbitration Act 1950[213] contains provisions for the enforcement of certain awards[214] made pursuant to an agreement to arbitrate to which the Protocol set out in the first Schedule to that Act applies.[215] In order for those provisions to apply the place of arbitration and the parties to the arbitration[216] must be subject to a jurisdiction which has been recognised[217] as having reciprocal provisions pursuant to the Geneva Convention.[218] The Geneva Convention has been almost entirely overshadowed by the New York Convention.[219]

Awards covered by Pt II of the Arbitration Act 1950 are enforceable in England[220] either summarily[221] or by action on the award. They will be treated "as binding for all purposes on persons as between whom [the award] was made, and may accordingly be relied on by any of those persons by way of defence, set off or otherwise in any legal proceedings in England . . . ".[222] The conditions for obtaining enforcement of the award under these provisions[223] are specified in s.37 of the Arbitration Act 1950 and the evidence required is specified in the following section.[224]

8-048   **Enforcement by registration of ICSID Convention awards.** The Arbitration (International Investment Disputes) Act 1966 makes provision for the recognition and enforcement of awards rendered pursuant to the ICSID

[212b] To impose a security for costs order regime on an award creditor who sought enforcement under s.101 of the 1996 Act would be to impose substantially more onerous conditions than in the case of a domestic award under s.66 of the 1996 Act (where an award debtor would not be entitled to security for costs) and this would be in breach of Art.111 of the Convention. See *Gater Assets Ltd v Nak Naffogaz Ukrainiy* [2007] EWCA Civ 988, *per* Lord Justice Rix at [80] and [81].

[213] This part of the Arbitration Act 1950 is saved by the Arbitration Act 1996, s.99.

[214] These awards are described as "foreign awards" in Pt II of the Arbitration Act 1950.

[215] The Protocol on arbitration clauses signed on September 24, 1923 which is referred to in the Geneva Convention. See para.6–040.

[216] *Dalmia Cement Ltd v National Bank of Pakistan* [1974] Lloyd's Rep. 98.

[217] The recognition is made by Order in Council under s.35 of the Arbitration Act 1950.

[218] The Convention on the Execution of Foreign Arbitration Awards signed at Geneva on September 26, 1927.

[219] Many countries have acceded to both conventions (e.g. Austria, Belgium, German and Switzerland) and enforcement will usually be sought under the New York Convention because it contains fewer restrictions: see ss.100–103 of the Arbitration Act 1996 and paras 8–020 *et seq.* above.

[220] Section 36(1) of the Arbitration Act 1950. Similar words appear in s.101(1) of the Arbitration Act 1996 in respect of New York Convention awards.

[221] An application may be made under s.66 of the Arbitration Act 1996, which replaced s.26 of the Arbitration Act 1950 which is referred to in s.36(1) of the 1950 Act: see para.8–003.

[222] Section 36(1) of the Arbitration Act 1950.

[223] Enforcement of a "foreign award" pursuant to Pt II of the Arbitration Act 1950 is subject to the conditions specified in s.37 of that Act. Contrast the reversal of the burden of proof which appears in s.103 of the Arbitration Act 1996 in respect of New York Convention awards.

[224] Section 38 of the Arbitration Act 1950.

Convention.[225] That Convention provides for the settlement[226] by the International Centre for Settlement of Investments Disputes[227] of investment disputes[228] between Contracting States and nationals of other Contracting States.[229]

Application for registration and its effect. The Act of 1966 provides   8–049
that a person[230] seeking recognition or enforcement of an award made under the Washington Convention may register the award in the High Court "subject to proof of the prescribed matters[231] and to the other provisions of this Act".[232] An application to have such an award registered must be made in accordance with the CPR Pt 8 procedure[233] supported by a witness statement[234] which must state, among other things, whether enforcement of the award has been or might be stayed under the Convention.[235] The effect of registration in accordance with the Act of 1966 is to give the award "the same force and effect for the purposes of execution as if it had been a judgment of the High Court given when the award was rendered pursuant to the Convention and entered on the date of registration under this Act."[236] An application to stay execution of an award registered under the 1966 Act may be made and a stay of execution granted by the court if enforcement of the award is likely to be stayed pursuant to the Convention.[237] Apart from registration and an application to stay execution, no recourse to the

---

[225] The Convention on the Settlement of Investment Disputes between States and Nationals of Other States which was opened for signature in Washington on March 18, 1965. See para.6–038.

[226] The provisions of the Arbitration Act 1996 do not apply to "proceedings pursuant to the [ICSID] Convention", although an action in breach of an arbitration agreement to which the ICSID Convention applies may be stayed. The Lord Chancellor also has power to extend certain provision of the Arbitration Act 1996 to arbitration proceedings conducted under the ICSID Convention—see s.3 of the 1966 Act as amended by Sch.3 to the Arbitration Act 1996.

[227] This centre, referred to briefly in English as ICSID, was established under the auspices of the World Bank. Its headquarters are in Washington DC, USA.

[228] The jurisdiction of ICSID is specified in Art.25 of the Washington Convention.

[229] The UK is a Contracting State and has extended the application of the 1966 Act to several other territories—see SIs 1967/159 and 1967/249.

[230] "Person" here may mean a Contracting State that seeks to enforce an award against a national of the UK.

[231] CPR r.62.21(2) provides for the application of specified provisions of CPR r.74 with modifications suitable for an award in respect of the prescribed matters, which include a copy of the award certified pursuant to the Convention.

[232] Section 1(2) of the Arbitration (International Investment Disputes) Act 1966, as amended by the Arbitration Act 1996, Sch.3, para.24.

[233] CPR r.62.21(3).

[234] The witness statement must comply with CPR r.74, and exhibit a copy of the award certified pursuant to the Convention.

[235] CPR r.62.21(4).

[236] Section 2(1) of the Arbitration (International Investment Disputes) Act 1966. The subsection goes on to say that proceedings may be taken on the award so far as it relates to pecuniary obligations as if the award was a judgment of the High Court. In *AIG Capital Partners v The Republic of Kazakhstan and Another* [2005] EWHC 2239, proceedings relating to execution against certain assets of the State followed an order which was made under s.1 of the Act of 1966 to enforce an Award made under the 1992 USA-Kazakhstan bilateral investment treaty as a judgment of the court. The case concerns whether the judgment could be enforced against accounts in which the State's central bank held a beneficial interest.

[237] CPR r.62.21(5).

English court is possible under the Arbitration Act in respect of ICSID arbitration.[238] The so-called direct enforceability of ICSID awards is often cited as a reason why a disgruntled investor would chose to submit their disputes to arbitration under the ICSID Convention rather than to arbitration under another set of arbitral rules which would lead to an award enforceable under the New York Convention, the argument being that New York Convention awards are more open to challenge than ICSID awards.[239]

8–050 **Enforcement by registration of other awards made abroad.** The provisions for the registration and enforcement of the ICSID Convention also apply to an award made pursuant to the Multilateral Investment Guarantee Convention,[240] which was enacted by the Multilateral Investment Guarantee Agency Act 1988.

Other awards made abroad may be registered in England under Pt 1 of the Foreign Judgments (Reciprocal Enforcement) Act 1933, provided that they have become enforceable in the same manner as a judgment given by a court where the award was made.[241] This means of registering and enforcing the award is different from that where judgment is entered in terms of the award.[242] In the latter case the award merges into the judgment,[243] and it is the judgment that is enforced.

4. Challenge of Awards

8–051 **Introduction.** A party to an arbitration may apply to the court to challenge an award on the grounds of serious irregularity affecting the tribunal, the proceedings or the award,[244] or that the arbitral tribunal had no substantive jurisdiction[245] over the dispute in question.[246] It is also possible to appeal against an award on a question of law, but unlike the previous two grounds of challenge permission of the court is needed unless all parties to the proceedings agree.[247] The structure of this section of the chapter is as follows:

[238] Section 3(2) of the Arbitration (International Investments Dispute) Act 1966.
[239] Although beyond the scope of this work, it is generally thought to be the case that most ICSID awards have either been paid or settled. For examples of cases in foreign courts regarding enforcement of ICSID awards, see details of enforcement proceedings relating to awards of ICSID tribunals in the *Benvenuti & Bonfant v Congo*; *SOABI v Senegal* (French Courts) and *LETCO v Liberia* (US courts). Available at *www.kluwerarbitration.com*.
[240] The Convention was made in Korea on October 11, 1985 and provides for arbitration of disputes between the Agency and its members or former members arising out of that Convention.
[241] CPR r.62.20 which applies CPRs 74.1 to 74.7 and 74.9 to the award "as they apply in relation to a judgment", subject to the modifications in CPR r.62.20(2). This assumes that the law in force in the place where the award is made has a provision similar to that contained in ss.66 and 101 of the Arbitration Act 1996 for enforcing awards "in the same manner as a judgment" given by the court.
[242] The difference is apparent from the terms of s.66(1) and (2) of the Arbitration Act 1996.
[243] See para.8–007.
[244] Arbitration Act 1996, s.68. See paras 8–072 *et seq.*
[245] See definition of "substantive jurisdiction" in s.82(1) of the Arbitration Act 1996.
[246] Arbitration Act 1996, s.67.
[247] Arbitration Act 1996, s.69. See paras 8–119 *et seq.*

- Section 67—substantive jurisdiction challenge.[248]

- Section 68—serious irregularity challenge.[249]

- Section 69—appeal on a question of law.[250]

The grounds of challenge to an award under ss.67–69 of the 1996 Act are available if the seat of arbitration is England and Wales.[251] Because the effect of choice of the seat is to treat the courts of the seat as having exclusive supervisory jurisdiction,[252] when the seat is England and Wales, it will usually be inappropriate to commence proceedings abroad which have as their object or effect the setting aside or vacation of the English award. In *C v D*,[253] the court granted an anti-suit injunction to restrain threatened proceedings in New York to set aside an English award. The court rejected an argument that the choice of New York law as the substantive law of the contract provided grounds to commence challenge proceedings elsewhere. Highlighting the practical problems which any other approach wood give rise to, Cooke J commented:

> "No challenge has been made to the Partial Award in this country and it is to be regarded as binding therefore in this jurisdiction. If proceedings were brought in New York and the challenge was successful there, what would a third party country's courts do when faced with an application to enforce the award?"[254]

Challenges to awards made under investment treaties. Until   8–052
recently, most applications to challenge awards arose out of contractual arbitrations. However, it is now clear that applications to challenge awards can extend to cases brought under investment treaties (provided that the seat of arbitration is England). In *Ecuador v Occidental Exploration & Production Co*[255] the Court of Appeal confirmed that the court does have jurisdiction to hear challenges brought in respect of awards made under investment treaties rather than under contract. The treaty in question, the USA/Ecuador bilateral investment treaty, provided for arbitration under the UNCITRAL rules at a seat to be fixed by the tribunal. The fact of the tribunal having fixed London as the seat was sufficient to trigger the supervisory powers of the court over arbitral awards.[256] The Court of Appeal considered that investment treaties create *"direct rights in international law in favour of investors either from the outset or at least (and in this event retrospectively)*

---

[248] See para.8–054.
[249] See para.8–072.
[250] See paras 8–119 *et seq.*
[251] Section 2(1) of the Arbitration Act 1996.
[252] *A v B* [2007] 1 Lloyd's Rep. 237 at 255–256.
[253] [2007] EWHC 1541. See also *Noble Assurance Co and Others v Gerling-Konzern General Insurance Co UK Branch* [2007] EWHC 253.
[254] *C v D* [2007] EWHC 1541, *per* Cooke J. at [54].
[255] [2006] 2 W.L.R. 70.
[256] Similar proceedings reviewing awards made by tribunals in investment treaty cases have been heard by the courts in other jurisdictions, including Canada (see for example *Mexico v Metalclad Corp*, May 2, 2001) and Sweden, which reviewed issues of jurisdiction in the *Czech Republic v CME*. See *www.ita.law.uvic.ca*.

as and when they pursue claims in one of the ways provided."[257] As a result, the principle of non-justiciability of transactions between foreign states as enunciated in *Buttes Gas and Oil Co v Hammer*[258] would not be applied. Whilst agreements to arbitrate which allow investors to maintain claims directly against States are found in many investment treaties, the agreements to arbitrate themselves are not treaties but are, the Court of Appeal suggested, likely to be subject to international law and not to any domestic body of law.[259] The court may review decisions of tribunals in investment treaty cases under both ss.67 and 68. As to s.69, the English courts will (consistent with the approach in respect of contractual awards) only consider appeals on questions of English law which in most cases means that there would be no scope for a challenge based on an alleged error of international law.[260] The English court does not have jurisdiction to review awards of tribunals deciding cases under investment treaties sitting under the ICSID Convention. Section 3(2) of the Arbitration (International Investment Disputes) Act 1966 provides for the settlement of such disputes to the exclusion of domestic proceedings. Nor, it seems, does the English court have jurisdiction over state-to-state disputes which may also arise under investment treaties.[261–262]

8–053　**Challenge by a person taking no part in proceedings.** On its face, s.72 of the 1996 Act empowers the court to determine a challenge to the jurisdiction of the arbitral tribunal by a person alleged to be a party to arbitral proceedings, provided that the person concerned has not taken part in the arbitration proceedings. The operation of this section is considered at paras 7–146 *et seq.*

For obvious reasons that person need not exhaust any available recourse to the tribunal that made the award,[263] but he must make an application within 28 days of being notified of the award.[264]

5. Challenge of Substantive Jurisdiction[265]

8–054　**Substantive jurisdiction challenge.** A party to arbitral proceedings may (upon notice to the other parties and to the tribunal) apply to the court challenging any award of the arbitral tribunal as to its substantive jurisdiction,[266]

---

[257] *per* Mance L.J. at [18].
[258] *(No.3)* [1982] A.C. 888.
[259] The Court of Appeal did not decide this point however. See Mance L.J. at [33].
[260] A possible exception is a decision of a tribunal in an investment treaty case applying English law by virtue of a so-called "umbrella clause" contained in an investment treaty. See the brief comment on this issue in Mance L.J.'s judgment at [41].
[261–262] Mance L.J. at [39].
[263] Section 72(2) of the Arbitration Act 1996.
[264] *Bermuth Lines Ltd v High Seas Shipping Ltd* [2005] EWHC 3020 at [58] where Christopher Clarke J. confirmed that the time limit in s.70(3) applied to an application under s.72(2) of the Act.
[265] This is a defined term. See s.82(1) of the Arbitration Act 1996 and para.4–135.
[266] "Substantive jurisdiction" is defined in s.82(1) of the Arbitration Act 1996.

or for an order declaring an award made by the tribunal on the merits to be of no effect, in whole or in part, because the tribunal did not have substantive jurisdiction.[267] This type of challenge arises out of s.67 of the Arbitration Act 1996, and it should be distinguished from a party's objection during the arbitral proceedings that the tribunal lacks substantive jurisdiction to conduct the arbitration[268] and any determination made by the court under s.32 of the Arbitration Act 1996.[269] The right to challenge under s.67 of the Act is only available after an award dealing with jurisdiction has been made, but it is not subject to the same restrictions that apply to s.32.[270] Section 67 is mandatory.[271]

Timing of an application. The challenge may have been preceded by   8–055
other action. For example, one of the parties may have objected to the tribunal's jurisdiction which prompted the tribunal either to defer a decision on jurisdiction to the end of the arbitral proceedings, or to make an award early in those proceedings that the tribunal had jurisdiction to decide the disputes referred to it. The tribunal has a complete discretion in this respect[272] and a party cannot use s.67 of the Act to challenge its ruling as to what course to take.[273] However, once an award is published which expressly or implicitly[274] accepts that the tribunal has jurisdiction over the dispute, the party objecting to the tribunal's jurisdiction may, unless he has lost the right,[275] challenge the award by applying to the court under s.67 of the Arbitration Act 1996. That section also provides a means for challenging the jurisdiction of the tribunal by someone who took no part in the arbitral proceedings.[276]

Limited jurisdiction. An application under s.67 of the Act challenging any   8–056
award as to the arbitrator's jurisdiction confers on the court a strictly limited jurisdiction which is confined to determining whether an award as to jurisdiction should be confirmed, varied or set aside in whole or in part. If and to the extent that an award covers both jurisdiction and substantive issues as to the merits of the case the court has the power to declare the whole or part of that section of the

---

[267] Section 67(1) of the Arbitration Act 1996.
[268] See paras 5–060 and 7–143 *et seq.*
[269] See paras 7–154 *et seq.*
[270] Section 32(2) of the Arbitration Act 1996 requires the agreement of all the other parties or the permission of the tribunal: see paras 7–156 and 7–157.
[271] Section 4 of the Arbitration Act 1996 and Sch.1 to the Act.
[272] i.e. whether to decide his jurisdiction in an interim award or to deal with it when he makes a final award: Arbitration Act 1996 s.31(4). See para.6–013.
[273] *Kalmneft v Glencore* [2001] 2 All E.R. (Comm) 577.
[274] *Vee Networks Ltd v Econet Wireless* [2005] 1 Lloyds' Rep. 192 at [200].
[275] The right to object that the tribunal lacks substantive jurisdiction may be lost by taking part in the arbitration without making a timely objection: see s.73 of the Arbitration Act 1996 and para.8–065.
[276] Pursuant to s.72(2) of the Arbitration Act 1996; see para.8–053 above.

award which deals with the merits to be of no effect depending on the court's conclusion on jurisdiction.[277]

8–057 Relationship with sections 68 and 69. There is a conceptual difference between a challenge under s.67 and challenges under ss.68 and 69. Awards which are challenged under ss.68 and 69 have a presumptive validity unless or until they are set aside, whereas awards challenged under s.67 have no such presumptive validity: they were either made with jurisdiction or they were not.[278]

8–058 Party to proceedings. Sections 67 to 69 of the Act each refer to "a party to arbitral proceedings". This is not a defined term but must mean someone who has properly been made a party to the arbitration (i.e. somebody who is a party to the arbitration agreement or has agreed to become a party to the reference).[279]

8–059 Proper scope of the application. As with jurisdictional challenges made to the tribunal under s.30 and determination of points of jurisdiction by the court under s.32 of the 1996 Act, points raised under s.67 are likely to fall into essentially three categories.

- questions as to the existence and/or validity of the arbitration agreement,

- questions as to the proper constitution of the tribunal,[280] and

- questions as to the scope of the arbitration agreement, including questions as to the powers available to the tribunal.

8–060 Rehearing rather than a review. A section 67 hearing is a rehearing rather than a review: "*Appeals under that section are, after all, re-hearings not a completely fresh start as if there has been no previous challenge to the jurisdiction of the tribunal.*"[281] The court should not be put in a worse position than the arbitrator in determining the issue but, unlike under s.68 of the 1996 Act, the court's role is to confirm that the tribunal reached the right answer, not simply to decide that it was entitled to reach the decision it did.[282] If jurisdiction is to be challenged before the court, it will usually be the case that each ground of challenge must have been raised before the arbitrators first:

---

[277] *JSC Zestafoni v Ronly Holdings* [2004] 2 Lloyds' Rep 355. Section 30(1)(b) of the Arbitration Act 1996 which is also included in the definition of "substantive jurisdiction" by s.82(1) of the Act. Compare with s.103(2)(e) of the Act, which contains a similar ground for refusing to recognise or enforce a New York Convention award: see para.8–027.

[278] *Peterson Farms v C&M Farming Ltd & Another* [2004] 1 Lloyd's Rep. 614 at [26].

[279] *Vowles v Aston* [2005] EWHC 1459 at [21].

[280] *Lafarge v Newham LBC* [2005] 2 Lloyds' Rep. 577.

[281] *Primetrade AG v Ythan Ltd* [2006] 1 Lloyd's Rep. 457 at [62]. See also *Peterson Farms Inc v CM Farming Ltd* [2004] 1 Lloyd's Rep. 603 at [18].

[282] *Peterson Farms v C&M Farming Ltd & Another* [2004] 1 Lloyd's Rep. 603 at [17]–[18].

- Aikens J. in *Primetrade v Ythan* stipulated that "a *party objecting to jurisdiction, who has decided to take part in the arbitral proceedings should bring forward his objections in those proceedings before the arbitrators. He should not hold them in reserve for a challenge to jurisdiction in the court".*[283]

- As Colman J. put it in *JSC Zestafoni G Nikoladze Ferroalloy Plant v Ronly Holdings:* "*Were it otherwise, the policy of the sub-section could be frustrated by introducing at the last minute grounds of challenge not hitherto raised and thereby potential causes of delay and disruption of the application to the prejudice of the opposite party".*[284]

Raising new points. If a party wishes to raise a wholly new point it must 8–061
show good reason (such as that the point could not with reasonable diligence have
been discovered at the time) why the point was not raised before the arbitrator and
it will usually have to do this by adducing evidence.[285] The various references to
"objection" in s.73 have all been held to refer to the same objection and whilst the
court has resisted the temptation to lay down precise limits in the abstract, the
court will investigate whether the party is attempting to raise a new "objection".
The concept of objections does however appear to be construed relatively broadly;
objections do not have to be put in exactly the same way as they were put before
the arbitrators. Indeed, provided it falls within the same overall objection, a point
can be argued before the court which the arbitrators did not permit the objecting
party to take during the arbitration.[286]

If raised, the courts must investigate questions relating to the existence of the
agreement to arbitrate, such as whether or not it has been repudiated.[287]

Validity and scope of arbitration agreement. In relation to ques- 8–062
tions regarding the validity of the arbitration agreement, it will be necessary for
the court to determine, among other matters, disputes relating to whether or not
the arbitration clause has been incorporated by reference into the parties'
agreement.[288]

---

[283] *Primetrade AG v Ythan Ltd* [2006] 1 Lloyd's Rep. 457 at [59].
[284] [2004] 1 Lloyd's Rep 335 at [64].
[285] For a s.67 application where evidence was clearly not limited to that which was before the tribunal,
see *Kazakhstan v Istil Group Inc* [2006] 1 W.L.R. 596 at [23]. The judgment in the s.67 application
is [2006] EWHC 448. The Court of Appeal refused permission to appeal from the judge's decision,
see *Kazakhstan v Istil Group Inc* [2007] W.L. 1425725. The basis for Morison J.'s order as to new
evidence is not apparent from the judgments. See also *Aloot Kalmneft v Glencore International AG*
[2002] 1 Lloyd's Rep. 128; *Electrosteel Castings v Scan Trans Shipping & Chartering Sdn Bhd* [2003]
1 Lloyd's Rep. 190 for additional cases where new evidence has been admitted and new arguments
raised on s.67 applications. Note however that Gross J.'s classification of an arbitrator's decision on
jurisdiction as a "provisional determination" in *Electrosteel Castings* is doubted by Aikens J. in
Primetrade at [58].
[286] *Primetrade AG v Ythan Ltd* [2006] 1 Lloyd's Rep. 457 at [60]–[64].
[287] *BEA Hotels NV v Bellway LLC* [2007] W.L. 1623270. In relation to repudiatory breach of an
agreement to arbitrate, see further paras 2–111 *et seq.*
[288] See for example *Sea Trade Maritime Corp v Hellenic Mutual War Risks Association, The Athena*
[2006] EWHC 2530, where this question (whether the arbitration agreement had been incorporated
into the parties' agreement) was answered in the affirmative.

Set out below are certain examples of disputes relating to the scope of the agreement to arbitrate, including questions as to the powers available to the tribunal:

- The court will consider issues as to res judicata, so an award would be set aside in circumstances where it proceeded on the basis of an inconsistent finding on a matter which was res judicata.[289]

- The court will naturally consider the tribunal's jurisdiction to determine disputes arising out of claims of set-off or counterclaims made in the arbitration. The tribunal's jurisdiction over counterclaims depends on the true construction of the agreement to arbitrate and not on the rules of court in relation to counterclaims.[290]

- Where a tribunal's decision to award damages was, in part, based on the group of companies theory which formed no part of English law, the substantive law of the agreement, then the award would be set aside.[291]

- The court can set aside part only of the tribunal's award if it feels that the want of substantive jurisdiction extends to only part of the award.[292]

- Where a tribunal assumes jurisdiction based on a bilateral investment treaty, the court will as in all other cases examine whether the tribunal has decided matters outside the scope of the instrument by which jurisdiction was conferred on the tribunal. In such situations, the court will have to construe the scope of the relevant treaty, which is governed by public international law

---

[289] *Kazakhstan v Istil Group Inc* [2006] EWHC 448, at [75]–[83]; the French court had made findings that a party was not a proper party to the arbitration agreement and these findings were disregarded by the tribunal. Because of the earlier finding in relation to the loss of the right to object, this conclusion is *obiter*.

[290] *Metal Distributors (UK) Ltd v ZCCM Investment Holdings Plc* [2005] 2 Lloyd's Rep. 37. In *Vee Networks Ltd v Econet Wireless International Ltd* [2006] EWHC 1664 the court was asked to determine whether claims for set-off arising out of a different contract to that under which the primary claim as being made were within the agreement to arbitrate. The substantive law of the agreement was English law and the arbitration was conducted under the UNCITRAL rules, which provide that claims for set-off may be made (only) if arising out of the contract under which the claim was made. In these circumstances, the court would have regard to the provisions of the agreement to arbitrate in preference to the rules of English law, which advocates a broader approach to set-off. The court confirmed that the claims for set-off were outside of the scope of the agreement to arbitrate. See further para.6–016 above.

[291] *Peterson Farms v C&M Farming Ltd & Another* [2004] 1 Lloyd's Rep. 603. It did not matter that the same conclusion could conceivably have been reached by a different route, the doctrine of agency, as that was not the central basis relied upon by the tribunal, although the court did also consider and reject the suggestion that the award could be sustained on the basis of agency. See [51], [52], [63]–[66]. Note there are two *Peterson Farms* decisions, the first a decision of Tomlinson J. in respect of an application under s.70(7) to secure sums payable in respect of an ICC award subject to appeal under s.67 [2004] 1 Lloyd's Rep. 614 and the second a decision of Langley J. setting aside in part that award upon hearing the s.67 application [2004] 1 Lloyd's Rep. 603). The award was apparently doomed from the outset; although Tomlinson J. was charged only with the hearing of the s.70(7) application he was also clearly of the view that the award should be set aside, a view subsequently shared by Langley J.: " . . . on the face of it, the arbitrators have applied not the proper law of the agreement, not the curial law, not yet even some third system of law as being the system of law applicable to the arbitration, but rather have applied a doctrine which is not, at any rate on the face of the award, suggested to be grounded in any particular system of law", *per* Tomlinson J., at [31].

[292] *Peterson Farms v C&M Farming Ltd & Another* [2004] 1 Lloyd's Rep. 603.

and, as a treaty, its construction is governed by the rules on treaty interpretation contained in the Vienna Convention on the Law of Treaties 1969. In *Ecuador v Occidental Exploration & Production Co*[293] the Court of Appeal considered whether the tribunal's decision on matters of taxation fell outside the scope of the treaty in question and decided that it did not.[294] The court may not however consider a challenge to the jurisdiction of a tribunal if the arbitration was conducted under the ICSID rules.[295]

Timing of the application. In order to comply with s.70(3) of the Act, the application to the court must be brought within 28 days of the date of the award, unless there is an available arbitral process of appeal or review in which case the 28-day period will begin to run from the date when the applicant was notified of the result of any appeal or review on the question of the tribunal's substantive jurisdiction.[296] The court may however vary the period of 28 days fixed by the Act for challenging the award under s.67.[297] Further, although notice of the application must be given promptly, the application may be made without notice being served on any other party before the statutory period of 28 days expires.[298]   8–063

Exhaustion of other right.[298a] An application cannot be made under s.67 of the Arbitration Act 1996 if the applicant has not first exhausted any available recourse from the tribunal to correct the award or make an additional award[299] and any available process of appeal or review.[300]   8–064

Loss of right to object. A party who objects to the award on the ground that the tribunal lacks substantive jurisdiction should not only act promptly, but should also take care not to lose his right to object.[301] A party who takes part or continues to take part in the proceedings is in a different position from someone who takes no part in the proceedings. The latter cannot lose his right to object as long as he acts promptly to challenge the award once it is published.[302] The former must, however, state his objection to the tribunal's jurisdiction "either forthwith   8–065

---

[293] [2007] EWCA 656.
[294] See also the earlier decision, *Ecuador v Occidental Exploration & Production Co* [2006] 2 W.L.R. 70, where the Court of Appeal decided that the court does have jurisdiction to entertain applications under s.67 in respect of challenges to awards made under bilateral investment treaties.
[295] Section 3(2) Arbitration (International Investments Disputes) Act 1966. It would also be very unusual for the seat of an ICSID arbitration to be England.
[296] Section 70(3) of the Arbitration Act 1996.
[297] CPR r.62.9(1). This rule applies to applications made in respect of ss.67, 68 and 69 of the Act. See para.8–212.
[298] CPR r.62.9(2). For procedure generally see para.8–178.
[298a] See also the cases and principles cited at para.8–109.
[299] Section 70(2)(b) refers to s.57 which may possibly apply if it is unclear from the award made whether the tribunal has exceeded its jurisdiction.
[300] Section 70(2)(a) of the Arbitration Act 1996.
[301] Sections 67(1) and 73 of the Arbitration Act 1996.
[302] Section 72(2) of the Arbitration Act 1996 gives that person the same right of challenge as a party to the arbitral proceedings. See para.8–053 above.

or within such time as is allowed by the arbitration agreement or the tribunal".[303]

A further effect of s.73 is that usually only objections which have been taken before the tribunal can be raised before the court on a s.67 application.[304] If the applicable arbitral rules provide for two tiers of tribunals[305] then it will usually also be fatal to fail to object to the jurisdiction of the first instance tribunal if a party wishes to maintain a jurisdictional objection before the higher tribunal or the court.[306] The section also dictates in effect that if a tribunal proposes a particular course in respect of dealing with jurisdiction and the parties do not object, no objection whether on the basis of s.67 or otherwise can be maintained at a later stage. Where a tribunal concluded that an earlier partial award on jurisdiction was a nullity and no objection was taken to the tribunal's conduct in revisiting the issue then an objection on this basis could not be made once the final award incorporating the change to the partial award had been released to the parties.[307]

8–066   **The arbitral proceedings may continue pending an application.** The arbitral tribunal may continue the arbitral proceedings and even make "a further award" while an application to the court under s.67 of the Act is pending.[308] If the challenge is to a partial award on jurisdiction, and the proceedings on the merits are to continue, in most cases it would make case management sense to stay the arbitral proceedings pending the outcome of the court challenge. There may however be good reasons, relating to the likely strength of the challenge to jurisdiction, timing of the challenge or conduct of one of the parties, which would lead the tribunal to exercise their discretion to proceed with the arbitration.

8–067   **Procedure and variety of orders.** As noted, the challenge to an award under s.67 of the Arbitration Act 1996 will involve a re-hearing rather than simply a review.[309] Even if full argument on jurisdiction has been heard by the arbitral tribunal, the court may order a complete re-hearing with oral evidence where there are substantial issues of fact,[310] including foreign law.[311] On an application under s.67 of the Arbitration Act 1996, the court may confirm the award, vary it or set aside the award in whole or in part.[312] As noted, the question for the court is not

---

[303] Section 73(1) of the Arbitration Act 1996 which is incorporated by s.67(1) of the Act.
[304] This principle is discussed in detail above at para.8–061.
[305] Such as for example arbitration under the Rules of the Grain and Feed Trade Association.
[306] *Tradigrain SA v State Trading Corp of India* [2006] 1 Lloyd's Rep. 216 at [37]–[38].
[307] *Kazakhstan v Istil Group Inc* [2006] EWHC 448 at [41]–[42]. Permission to appeal was refused by the Court of Appeal, *Kazakhstan v Istil Group Inc* [2007] EWCA 471.
[308] Section 67(2) of the Arbitration Act 1996.
[309] See para.8–060.
[310] Such an order was made in *Azov Shipping v Baltic Shipping* [1999] 1 All E.R. 476, and having heard evidence the court set aside the arbitrator's order: [1999] 2 Lloyd's Rep. 159.
[311] *Astra Insurance v Sphere Drake* (May 17, 2000). Steel J. upheld the arbitrator's award that he had jurisdiction on the basis of findings of foreign law.
[312] Section 67(3) of the Arbitration Act 1996. *X Ltd v Y Ltd* [2005] EWHC 3769 at [36].

whether the tribunal was entitled to reach the decision to which it came, but whether they were right to do so.[313]

Further role of the tribunal. Where the court sets aside an award or decides that it, or part of it, is a nullity for jurisdictional reasons, the tribunal may make further award(s) within its jurisdiction, even where the award which has been set aside purported to be a final award.[314] Whilst the effect of an order to set aside an award clearly deprives that award of all legal effect, such an order does not mean that the entire arbitral process is thereby frustrated. No distinction is drawn between an order setting aside an award as to jurisdiction and an order setting aside a final award on the merits. In both cases, the arbitration may be able to carry on or revive as necessary unless of course the sustained jurisdictional objection relates to the identity or manner of appointment of the tribunal or validity of the agreement to arbitrate.[315] In this regard, it does not apparently matter that there is no express power to remit under s.67(3) as compared with s.68(3). 8–068

Security. The court may require the applicant to provide security for the costs of the application.[316] The court may also order that any money payable under the award shall be brought into court or otherwise secured pending the determination of the application.[317] The purpose of the power is to help avoid the risk that whilst an appeal is pending the ability of the losing party to honour the award is diminished whether "by design or otherwise".[318] This power is also available in respect of applications under ss.68 and 69 (the latter of which requires leave). Where however no leave is required, such as under ss.67 or 68, and the application is made as of right, the court will be very slow to exercise the power to order security.[319] It certainly cannot be used as a means of putting the winning party in the arbitration in a better position than he would otherwise have been in, for example, by requiring the losing party (or its backers) to put up funds which the winner can then take if the appeal fails but to which the winner would not otherwise have easy access. In any event, upon such an application the court will conduct a preliminary analysis of the strength of the appeal and will be less likely to grant the application if it believes that the challenge is well-founded.[320] 8–069

---

[313] *Electrosteel Castings Ltd v Scan Trans Shipping* [2002] EWHC 1993, Gross J. at [22] confirmed in *Peterson Farms v C&M Farming* [2004] EWHC 121 at [18].

[314] *Peterson Farms Inc v C&M Farming* [2004] EWHC 121 is an example of a decision to set aside an award only in part.

[315] *Hussmann (Europe) Ltd v Pharaon* [2003] 1 All E.R. (Comm) 879. The Court of Appeal also decided that there is no difference in principle between an order setting aside an award and a declaration of no effect. *Per* Rix L.J., at [81].

[316] Section 70(6) of the Arbitration Act 1996, which also provides that the application may be dismissed if an order for security is not complied with. See para.8–206 for discussion.

[317] Section 70(7) of the Arbitration Act 1996, which also provides that the court may direct that the application be dismissed if such an order is not complied with. See para.8–208 for discussion.

[318] DAC report, para.380.

[319] *Peterson Farms v C&M Farming Ltd & Another* [2004] 1 Lloyd's Rep. 614.

[320] *Peterson Farms v C&M Farming Ltd & Another* [2004] 1 Lloyd's Rep. 614.

8–070   **Insufficient reasons.** If necessary,[321] the court may also require the tribunal to state the reasons for its award in sufficient detail to enable the court properly to consider the application.[322]

8–071   **Appeals to Court of Appeal.** Appeals from decisions of the court under s.67 are dealt with at paras 8–115 *et seq.* in the context of applications under s.68 of the 1996 Act, as the wording of the relevant provisions is the same for both subsections.[323] Note however the comments of the Court of Appeal that, "The policy of the 1996 Act does not encourage such further appeals which in general delay the resolution of disputes by the contractual machinery of arbitration.".[324] This policy suggests that leave to appeal a decision rejecting a challenge under s.67 will very rarely be given.

6. CHALLENGE FOR SERIOUS IRREGULARITY CAUSING SUBSTANTIAL INJUSTICE

(a) Serious irregularity

8–072   **Challenge for Serious Irregularity.** An award may be challenged under s.68 of the Arbitration Act 1996 if there has been a serious irregularity of the kind described in s.68(2) of the Act. In these circumstances, "*a party to arbitral proceedings may (upon notice to the other parties and to the tribunal) apply to the court challenging an award in the proceedings on the ground of serious irregularity affecting the tribunal, the proceedings or the award*".[325] A person who is alleged to be a party to arbitral proceedings, but does not take part in the proceedings may also apply to the court in respect of a serious irregularity affecting him.[326] Section 68 of the Act is mandatory,[327] but the court will not grant the application unless it considers that the irregularity "has caused or will cause substantial injustice to the applicant",[328] except where the tribunal is shown to be biased, when substantial injustice will be assumed.[329] Section 68 involves what has been described as a two-

---

[321] Even if it would be helpful to have the tribunal's reasons, the court will not override any agreement by the parties that reasons need not be given.

[322] Section 70(4) of the Arbitration Act 1996. The court may make a further order of costs resulting from this order: see s.70(5) of the Act and para.6–031.

[323] Sections 67(4) and 68(4) of the Arbitration Act 1996.

[324] *Amec Civil Engineering Ltd v Secretary of State for Transport* [2005] 1 W.L.R. 2339, *per* May L.J. at [9].

[325] The procedure for an application to the court is contained in CPR Pt 62 and the Arbitration Practice Direction. See paras 8–178 *et seq.*, s.68(1) of the Arbitration Act 1996.

[326] Section 72(2)(b) of the Act, which makes clear that the serious irregularity must be within the meaning of s.68, although the duty to exhaust arbitral procedures does not apply to such a person. See para.8–053 above.

[327] Section 4 of the Arbitration Act 1996 and Sch.1 to that Act.

[328] Arbitration Act 1996, s.68(2). See para.8–104 for the meaning of this phrase.

[329] *ASM Shipping Ltd of India v TTMI* [2005] EWHC 2238 (Comm) at [39] and *Norbrook Laboratories Ltd v Tank* [2006] EWHC 1055 at [145].

stage investigation, viz, (1) has there been an irregularity of at least one of the nine kinds identified in the section[330] and (2) whether the incidence of such irregularity has caused or will cause substantial injustice.[331] If the court decides that there has not been an irregularity of that kind, there is no need to investigate the issue of substantial injustice.[332]

Overall approach of the courts. The starting point for any consideration   8–073 of the overall approach to s.68 is the decision of the House of Lords in *Lesotho Highlands*.[333] According to the House of Lords, s.68 is a *"high threshold"*. Their Lordships relied upon the purpose of the 1996 Act which was to *"reduce drastically the extent of intervention of courts in the arbitral process"*.[334] The Court cited with approval the DAC report, which described the section as a *"long stop, only available in extreme cases, where the tribunal has gone so wrong in its conduct of the arbitration in one of the respects listed in the section that justice calls out for it to be corrected"*.[335] The case law also contains numerous statements of the same type, relating to the need to limit court intervention in cases of asserted irregularity to only the extreme cases.[336]

Excess of powers. Implementing this firm policy, the House of Lords drew   8–074 a clear distinction between whether the tribunal purported to exercise a power which it did not have or whether it erroneously exercised a power that it did have. Only the former could give rise to a challenge under s.68. Provided that the tribunal is exercising a power which it does have, as opposed to one which it does not have, it does not matter how significant the error is: no relief will be afforded under s.68. The issue is not whether the tribunal has come to the right conclusion; the sole issue is whether it committed a serious irregularity resulting in a substantial injustice.

"It will be observed that the list of irregularities under s.68 may be divided into those which affect the arbitral procedure and those which affect the award. But

---

[330] Each of the irregularities are listed in para.8–076.

[331] *Bulfracht (Cyprus) Ltd v Boneset Shipping Co Ltd (the "Pamphilos")* [2002] 2 Lloyd's Rep. 681, *per* Colman J.

[332] *Warborough Investment Ltd v S Robinson and Sons (Holdings) Ltd* [2002] EWHC 2502.

[333] [2006] 1 A.C. 221. See also Park, "The Nature of Arbitral Authority: A Comment on Lesotho Highlands", in Arbitration Int., Vol.21, No.4.

[334] Paragraphs 26–28.

[335] DAC report para.280 quoted with approval in *Lesotho Highlands Development Authority v. Impreglio SpA* [2006] A.C. 221 and in many other decisions. See, for example, *Fidelity Management SA v Myriad International Holdings BV* [2005] 2 Lloyd's Rep. 508 at [5] but contrast the "note of caution" against treating this section of the DAC report, para.280, as if it were the statute itself. *Bandwith Shipping Corp v Intaari* [2006] EWHC 2532, at [60]–[61]. See also Macpherson and Mainwaring-Taylor, "Final and Binding? Challenges under the Arbitration Act 1996, s.68", in (2006) 72 Arbitration 2.

[336] For a useful summary of these pronouncements see the list of cases referred to in *ABB v Hochtief Airport GmbH* [2006] 1 All E.R. (Comm) 529 at [63].

nowhere is there any hint that a failure by the tribunal to arrive at the 'correct decision' could afford a ground for challenge under s.68".[337]

8–075   **Many challenges unmeritorious.** Because of the high threshold, the majority of challenges brought under this section have failed. Colman J., speaking extra-judicially, has remarked upon, "*the complete inability of a very large number of members of the legal profession in London to understand what the section means, judging by some of the applications which are run in the Commercial Court, particularly those which seek to establish that there has been a serious irregularity on the basis that the tribunal has not dealt on a blow-by-blow analysis with each submission in relation to the evidence.*"[338] Certain of the judgments under this section also contain comments which make it clear that many of the challenges which are made are weak and should never have been made. To cite just one example, "*In my view [this section 68 challenge] was a non-starter and had leave been required I have no doubt that leave would have been refused.*"[339] It is perhaps the absence of a leave requirement, together with other factors, which leads to so many weak challenges being brought under this section.

8–076   **Kinds of irregularity.** Serious irregularity for the purposes of s.68 of the Arbitration Act 1996 is an "irregularity of one or more of the following kinds,[340] which the court considers has caused or will cause substantial injustice to the applicant".[341] The requirements are substantial injustice,[342] and at least one of the irregularities listed in s.68(2) of the Act, namely:

  (a) failure by the tribunal to comply with its general duty of fairness under s.33 (general duty of tribunal);

  (b) the tribunal exceeding its powers (otherwise than by exceeding its substantive jurisdiction: see s.67);

  (c) failure by the tribunal to conduct the proceedings in accordance with the procedure agreed by the parties;

  (d) failure by the tribunal to deal with all the issues that were put to it;

  (e) any arbitral or other institution or person vested by the parties with powers in relation to the proceedings or the award exceeding its powers;

  (f) uncertainty or ambiguity as to the effect of the award;

---

[337] *Lesotho*, above *per* Lord Steyn at 236.
[338] Colman J., Arbitration and Judges—how much interference should we tolerate? Master's Lecture, London, March 14, 2006.
[339] *Fidelity Management SA v Myriad International Holdings BV* [2005] 2 Lloyd's Rep. 508, *per* Morison J. at [18]. See also *Sinclair v Woods of Winchester Ltd* 102 Con. L.R., *per* Judge Peter Coulson Q.C., at [71], "I consider it a great pity that these two allegations were ever made".
[340] An exhaustive list of irregularities appears in s.68(2) of the Arbitration Act 1996: see the following paragraphs of this chapter.
[341] Section 68(2) of the Arbitration Act 1996.
[342] "Substantial injustice" is described in para.8–104, which reveals it to be a considerable hurdle to a successful application under s.68.

(g) the award being obtained by fraud or the award or the way in which is was procured being contrary to public policy;

(h) failure to comply with the requirements as to the form of the award; or

(i) any irregularity in the conduct of the proceedings or in the award which is admitted by the tribunal or by any arbitral or other institution or person vested by the parties with powers in relation to the proceedings or the award.

Each irregularity will be discussed in the following paragraphs and, with two exceptions,[343] in the order that they appear in the subsection. The subject of substantial injustice will then be discussed.[344]

(i) Breach of general duty of fairness (ground a)

Overall approach. Section 33 of the Act imposes a general duty on the tribunal to: 8–077

- act fairly and impartially as between the parties, giving each party a reasonable opportunity of putting his case and dealing with that of his opponent, and

- adopt procedures suitable to the circumstances of the particular case, avoiding unnecessary delay or expense, so as to provide a fair means for the resolution of the matters falling to be determined.

The tribunal is required to comply with that general duty in conducting the arbitration proceedings, in its decisions on matters of procedure and evidence and in the exercise of the other powers conferred on the tribunal by the parties (expressly or implicitly).[345]

Permissible errors. Failure by the tribunal to comply with the duty will amount to an irregularity.[346] Whether it will be a serious enough irregularity to justify a challenge to an award will depend on the particular irregularity and the circumstances in which it occurred.[347] *"I do not accept the proposition that simply because the award contains an error which is unfair to a party there must have been a*   8–078

---

[343] Section 2(b) and (e) which concern excess of powers will be dealt with in two successive paras, 8–090 and 8–091, and 2(f) and (h) will be treated together in para.8–098.

[344] See para.8–104.

[345] See paras 5–032 *et seq.* for a discussion of this duty.

[346] Section 68(2)(a) of the Arbitration Act 1996.

[347] Bias on the part of the tribunal is an obvious example of a breach of the general duty. For a case at the opposite end of the spectrum see *Kalmneft v Glencore* [2002] 1 All E.R. 76. See also paras 4–107 *et seq.* and 5–041.

failure to comply with s.33 of the 1996 Act on the part of the tribunal and thus a serious irregularity for the purposes of s.68(2)(a) of the Act."[348]

8–079 **Overlap with section 67.** If it is alleged that proceedings were not validly commenced and therefore never came to the attention of the respondent, then this does not amount to a breach of the tribunal's duty to give each party a reasonable opportunity of presenting his case but would fall to be considered under s.67 as a complaint of lack of substantive jurisdiction.[349]

8–080 **Issue must be "in play".** It will not amount to a serious irregularity if the tribunal decides the case on the basis of a point not strictly argued or pleaded by a party; it will be enough that the issue was "*in play or, to use a different expression, 'in the arena' in the proceedings*".[350] However, if a point was not raised at all during the proceedings, depriving a party of the opportunity to address the arbitrator on it, and the arbitrator proceeds to base his decision on that point, ground (a) may be triggered.[351] The threshold is a relatively low one, and the tribunal does not need to spell out even a particularly crucial point for the parties before the end of the oral hearing.[352] It may be necessary for the court to examine the conduct of the proceedings in some detail to ascertain whether or not a particular point was actually "in play". In the same way, it has also been suggested, as regards issues of fact, that the tribunal has "an autonomous power to make findings of fact which may differ from the facts which either party contended for".[353]

---

[348] *Weldon Plant Ltd v The Commission for the New Towns* [2001] 1 All E.R. (Comm) 264 at [27]. See also *Sinclair v Woods of Winchester Ltd* [2005] 102 Con. L.R. 127 at [20] and *Newfield Construction Ltd v Tomlinson* [2004] EWHC 3051.

[349] *Bernuth Lines Ltd v High Seas Shipping Ltd (The Eastern Navigator)* [2006] 1 Lloyd's Rep. 537 at [53]–[54].

[350] *ABB AG v Hochtief Airport GmbH* [2006] 1 All E.R. (Comm) 529, [72], following *Bulfracht (Cyprus) Ltd v Boneset Shipping Co Ltd (The Pamphilos)* [2002] 2 Lloyd's Rep. 681 at 686; *Warborough Investments Ltd v S Robinson & Sons (Holdings) Ltd* [2003] 2 E.G.L.R. 149. *ABB AG v Hochtief Airport GmbH* and the other cases cited in this footnote were followed in *Bandwith Shipping Corp v Intaari* [2006] EWHC 2532, see [60]–[63].

[351] *Vee Networks Ltd v Econet Wireless International Ltd* [2005] 1 Lloyd's Rep. 192, where an arbitrator decided a point of construction by reference to certain amendments to the Bermudian Companies Act which were not addressed in the proceedings. This constituted a serious irregularity requiring the award to be remitted to the tribunal. See also *Cameroon Airlines v Transnet Ltd* [2004] EWHC 1829, where the tribunal decided an issue of quantum in a way other than that which was put by either party (although the issue was raised in the arbitration it was not raised in a way which afforded the challenger the opportunity to respond). See further *OAO Northern Shipping Company v Remol Cadores De Marin SL* [2007] EWHC 1821, where the tribunal had decided an award on the basis of a finding as to no representation on a particular point, when at least one of the parties had proceeded on the assumption that the point was in fact no longer an issue. These are three rare examples of successful challenges under s.68. Contrast these decisions with that of some months later in *ABB AG v Hochtief Airport GmbH. Vee* was cited in *ABB*, albeit not on this point: See [62].

[352] See *Bandwith Shipping Corp v Intaari* [2006] EWHC 2532 at [75]. The applicants complained unsuccessfully that the very narrow basis of the Tribunal's decision was not made sufficiently clear to them either in the pleadings or at the oral hearing but if it had been they would have had a good answer to it. Christopher Clarke J. rejected these submissions, finding that the point was "put into the arena" of the arbitration, at [60]–[63], [72].

[353] *London Underground Ltd v Citylink Telecommunications Ltd* [2007] EWHC 1749 at [37].

Treatment of new points. A direct refusal to hear evidence on a material   8–081
issue would be an irregularity,[354] but whether it is serious enough for the purposes
of s.68 will depend on the facts.[355] Unless an inquisitorial approach is adopted,[356]
the parties are entitled to assume that the tribunal will base its decision on the
evidence and argument presented by the parties.[357] If the tribunal is minded to
decide the dispute on a completely new point, the parties must be given notice of
it to enable them to address the point, but this does not mean that every nuance
or inference which the tribunal wishes to draw needs to be put to the parties if it
differs from that which has been precisely contended for in the arbitration.

> "It is of the very essence of a fair hearing that the parties should have an adequate
> opportunity of dealing with any substantial criticism of their claim or defence, whether
> the source of that criticism comes from the opposing party or the tribunal who makes the
> decision. It must, however, always be a question of fact and degree, whether or not such
> an opportunity has been denied."[358]

As noted, it is now enough if the point is "in play" or "in the arena" in the
proceedings, even if it is not precisely articulated.

Failure to consider evidence. An allegation that the arbitrators failed to   8–082
take into account a particular piece of evidence said to be relevant to an issue or
drew incorrect inferences from the evidence is not a failure to deal with an issue.[359]
The assertion that the arbitrator failed to take proper account of the evidence
could, in an exceptional case, give rise to a challenge if "an arbitrator genuinely
overlooked evidence that really mattered, or got the wrong end of the stick in
misunderstanding it. But there is all the difference in the world between such
cases and an arbitrator evaluating evidence but reaching factual conclusions on it
(as will happen in most arbitrations) which one party does not like".[360] A failure
to adjourn pending receipt of further evidence was not an irregularity.[361] However,
a departure in the award without warning from the way the case was presented
without giving the eventual losing party an opportunity to address the way the

---

[354] *Williams v Wallis & Cox* [1914] 2 K.B. 478, a decision based on "misconduct", but whose facts
could support a claim that the tribunal "failed to comply with s.33": see s.68(2)(a) of the Arbitration
Act 1996.

[355] In *Hussman (Europe) Ltd v Ahmed Pharaon* (April 16, 2002) Mr Brindle Q.C. found that there was
no serious irregularity when the tribunal declined to accept further evidence of a foreign law, even
though the reasons given by the tribunal were not good ones.

[356] Subject to the parties' agreement, the tribunal may itself "take initiative in ascertaining the facts and
the law" (s.34(2)(g)): see para.5–099.

[357] This will usually be limited to the evidence and argument presented by the time the hearing is
concluded but may extend to post-hearing submissions made prior to the making of the award.

[358] *Annie Fox and Others v PG Wellfair Ltd* [1981] 2 Lloyd's Rep. 514 at 520. Although that decision
was given before the Arbitration Act 1996, it has been cited with approval by the Court of Appeal
in *Checkpoint Ltd v Strathclyde Pension Fund* [2003] EWCA Civ 84 in the context of an application
under this section of the Act. See also The *"Vimeira"* [1984] 2 Lloyd's Rep. 66; *Fairclough Building
Ltd v Vale of Belvoir Superstore Ltd* [1990] 56 B.L.R. 74; and *Sanghi v TII* [2000] 1 Lloyd's Rep.
480 at 484. See para.5–061.

[359] *World Trade Corp Ltd v C Czarnikow Sugar Ltd* [2005] 1 Lloyd's Rep. 422, [45].

[360] *Arduina Holdings BV v Celtic Resources Holdings Plc* [2006] EWHC 3155, [46].

[361] *Shuttari v Solicitors' Indemnity Fund* [20004] EWHC 1537.

tribunal was now thinking was found to be a serious irregularity.[362] The court also set aside an award on this ground when the tribunal reverted to a previous case advanced by the claimant, without giving notice to the respondent, and missed a central point of the respondent's submission.[363]

8–083 **Procedural decisions.** Subject to agreements between the parties, the tribunal is the master of its own procedure. It is therefore rare, although not impossible, for a challenge to be sustained under this ground on the basis of the tribunal's choice of procedure, including for example relating to the decision of a tribunal to refuse a disclosure application. In *ABB AG v Hochtief Airport GmbH* the court rejected a challenge to the tribunal's decision to require only one party to the negotiations to disclose documents relevant to those negotiations, in respect of which there were allegations of lack of good faith. The decision was based on the IBA Rules on the Taking of Evidence which were adopted in that arbitration and which allow the tribunal to exclude any document from production on the ground of lack of sufficient relevance.[364] There is nothing in the decision to suggest that a decision to refuse a disclosure application could not in exceptional cases constitute a serious irregularity, although any such finding would need to be reconciled with the principle that under the 1996 Act disclosure is a matter for the discretion of the arbitrators.[365]

The court will, to a certain extent, be prepared to extrapolate reasoning from the award where that is necessary to make complete sense of the decision.[366]

8–084 **No need to adopt court procedures.** English court procedures do not have to be (and perhaps should not be) mimicked in arbitration. For example, failure to allow counsel for the claimant to reply orally to closing submissions will not be a serious irregularity. Where counsel were both allowed a single closing speech, contrary to English court procedure but in accordance with established international arbitral procedure, this was "well within the scope of what he [the arbitrator] was empowered to do".[367]

8–085 **Errors of fact.** An error of fact is not an irregularity, "The weight to be attached to each piece of evidence was entirely a matter for the arbitrator . . . It is not permissible to use ss.33 and 68 as a device to mount an appeal against the

---

[362] *Cameroon Airlines v Transnet* [2004] EWHC 1829 [108], although note at [109] the acceptance that "it cannot be said by Camair in this case that the point was never raised". See also *OAO Northern Shipping Co v Remol Cadores De Marin SL* [2007] EWHC 1821 and *Omnibridge Consulting Ltd v Clearsprings* [2004] EWHC 2276 at [43]–[48].

[363] *Ascot Commodities v Olam International* [2002] C.L.C. 277.

[364] [2006] 1 All E.R. (Comm) 529 at [84]–[85].

[365] See para.5–133.

[366] " . . . it is not necessary that the award should contain express findings of fact, provided that the necessary findings may be 'spelled out' ", *per* Gloster J. in *Bottiglieri di Navigazione SpA v Cosco Qingdao Ocean Shipping Co (The Bunga Saga Lima)* [2005] EWHC 244; [2005] 2 Lloyd's Rep. 1 at [22].

[367] *Margulead Ltd v Exide Technologies* [2004] EWHC 1019, [33].

decision of an arbitrator on a question of fact" [368] nor is s.68 "intended to provide a backdoor route to appeals on fact".[369] The fact that the tribunal's decision on the critical point of fact may, in the view of the court, be "debatable" does not provide the basis of a successful challenge under this head.[370] It would not be an irregularity if an arbitrator ignored a concession made by an expert witness as to a particular point and decided to reach a different conclusion on the point.[371]

Failure to manage the process. A failure to manage the arbitration with the result that there was no coherent identification of the issues and a significant increased cost was incurred was held to amount to a breach of the s.33 duty and therefore a serious irregularity.[372]   8–086

Emergence of new evidence. A challenge under this ground will not be made out if fresh evidence relied upon merely tends to throw doubt upon the veracity of a witness whose evidence was admitted by the tribunal. To succeed on this ground, a party will need to show that the award was procured by the fraud of the defendant or otherwise in way which was contrary to public policy (ground (g) below).[373]   8–087

Bias as a species of serious irregularity. As to a failure to observe principles of natural justice,[374] actual or apparent bias on the part of the tribunal would, if established, amount to a breach of the general duty and a serious irregularity under s.68(2)(a). There is considerable overlap between a challenge to an award on this ground as a result of actual or apparent bias and an application under s.24 to remove the arbitrator. In the right circumstances, the two applications may be brought together. However, the applicant may face the objection that he waived his right to object to the arbitrator under s.73 where he knew of the actual or apparent bias at an earlier stage in the proceedings and did not apply promptly to remove the arbitrator under s.24, but rather waited until the award   8–088

---

[368] *Claire & Co Ltd v Thames Water Utilities Ltd* [2005] B.L.R. 366, at [45]. Cited with approval in *Bandwith Shipping Corp v Intaari* [2006] EWHC 2532 at [77].

[369] *Arduina Holdings BV v Celtic Resources Holdings Plc* [2006] EWHC 3155, [45].

[370] *Bandwith Shipping Corp v Intaari* [2006] EWHC 2532, [77].

[371] *Claire & Co Ltd v Thames Water Utilities Ltd*, where it was acceptable for an arbitrator to ignore an alleged concession made by an expert as to the appropriate profit margin to be applied.

[372] *RC Pillar & Sons v Edwards* (January 11, 2001) H.H. Judge Thornton Q.C. Decisions based on the previous law are of very little value because of the higher threshold in s.68 of the Arbitration Act 1996. See comments of H.H. Judge Bowsher Q.C. in *Groundshire v VHE Construction* [2001] B.L.R. 395 at 400. See also paras 5–053 and 5–054.

[373] See the interesting discussion of this issue in *Thyssen Canada Ltd v Mariana Maritime SA* [2005] 1 Lloyd's Rep. 640 at [14]; see also the earlier decisions, *Scales v East London Waterworks* (1835) 1 Hodges 91 4 L.J.C.P. 195 and *Re Glasgow, etc., Ry. and London & North Western Ry.* (1888) 52 J.P. 215.

[374] What is stated in the first part of s.33 quoted above summarises the principles of natural justice. See paras 5–038 *et seq.* for a fuller discussion of this subject. In particular see paras 5–053 and 5–054.

had been issued before relying upon actual or apparent bias as a basis for challenging the award under s.68.[375]

(ii) Excess of powers of the arbitrator or institution (grounds b and e)

8–089	**Overall approach.** Ground b is described in s.68 of the Act[376] as *"the tribunal exceeding its powers, otherwise than by exceeding its substantive jurisdiction"*.[377] The excess of powers referred to in this section is of a different nature to the lack of substantive jurisdiction referred to in s.67 of the Act, although in practice there may be some overlap and an application may be made under both ss.67 and 68. For the purposes of s.68, excess of powers has to be distinguished from an incorrect exercise of powers. Thus, an alleged error of the arbitral tribunal in interpreting the underlying contract[378] cannot be an excess of powers so as to give the court power to intervene,[379] but is rather an error of law, which can only be challenged under s.69 of the Act if the right of appeal has not been excluded.[380] Jurisdiction goes to the tribunal's mandate whereas an excess of powers need not.[381] Where the gravaman of the complaint is that the tribunal lacked substantive jurisdiction, which includes whether the tribunal has been properly constituted and what matters have been submitted to arbitration in accordance with the arbitration agreement, the proper course is to apply under s.67 and not s.68.[382]

8–090	**Excess of powers.** The House of Lords in *Lesotho Highlands*[383] found that even if the tribunal had made an error of law in making its award in any currency under s.48(4) of the Act, such error did not amount to an excess of powers under s.68(2)(b). The distinction is to be drawn between *"whether the tribunal purported to exercise a power which it did not have or whether it erroneously exercised a power that it did have. If it is merely a case of erroneous exercise of power vesting in the tribunal no excess of power under s.68(2)(b) is involved."*[384] In other words, the mandatory provision of s.68(2)(b) cannot be used as a backdoor route for appealing errors of law, which appeals under s.69 are often excluded by clear the effect of institutional rules and in any event require leave of the court. Furthermore, by

---

[375] *ASM Shipping Ltd of India v TTMI Ltd of England* [2006] 1 Lloyd's Rep. 375; *Sumukan Ltd v Commonwealth Secretariat* [2007] EWHC 188. See paras 7–127 and 8–110.

[376] Section 68(2)(b) of the Arbitration Act 1996.

[377] Excess of substantive jurisdiction can be challenged under s.67 of the Arbitration Act 1996. See paras 8–054 *et seq.*

[378] An error in the interpretaion of provisions of the Arbitration Act, 1996, for example, would be treated similarly.

[379] The power is given by s.68 of the Arbitration Act 1996, for among others, the serious irregularity identified in s.68(2)(b).

[380] *Lesotho Highlands, ibid.*, HL. In that case, the right of appeal was excluded.

[381] See para.4–069 for a list of those powers.

[382] *National Bank v El-Abdali* [2005] 1 Lloyd's Rep. 541.

[383] [2006] 1 A.C. 221.

[384] *Lesotho Highlands, per* Lord Steyn at [24]. Lord Phillips dissented, taking a different view in particular on the scope of s.48(4) relating to the permissible currency of awards, finding that the arbitrators had purported to exercise a discretionary power which they did not in fact enjoy, amounting to an irregularity within ground (b).

analogy with Article V(1)(c) of the New York Convention which deals with "matters beyond the scope of the submission to arbitration" ground (b) should never lead to the re-examination of the merits of the award.[385]

To give an example of an error which may trigger ground (b) the tribunal may exceed its powers by appointing an expert to inspect the site of a property in dispute where such power is excluded in the arbitration agreement.[386]

Excess of powers by arbitral institution. As to excess of powers by an arbitral institution (ground e), an arbitration agreement will often provide for the appointment of the tribunal by a third party, usually an arbitral institution.[387] That institution would exceed its power of appointment, for example, by appointing a tribunal of three persons where the arbitration agreement specified a sole arbitrator. That excess of powers would be an irregularity.[388] There is a close affinity between grounds (b) and (e), the former relating to excess of powers by the tribunal, and the latter an excess of powers by the institution. The subsection is not limited to improper exercise of a power of appointment. It could extend, for example, to excessive scrutiny of an award.[389]

8–091

(iii) Breach of agreed procedures (ground c)

Approach of the court. The Arbitration Act 1996 gives the tribunal power to decide "*all procedural and evidential matters, subject to the right of the parties to agree any matter*".[390] The court will be reluctant to interfere with the tribunal's power to determine the proper procedure for a particular arbitration in the absence of a clear agreement to the contrary. The parties may all, for example, require a hearing.[391] It would then be an irregularity if an award were made without a hearing because the tribunal considered that the documents alone were sufficient for the purpose.[392]

8–092

---

[385] Paragraph 30, citing *Parsons & Whittemore Overseas Co Inc v Societe Generale de l'Industrie du Papier (RAKTA)* (1974) 508 F. 2d 969 (2nd Circuit).

[386] This example was given in *Lesotho* at [29]. The tribunal has power to appoint an expert for that purpose under s.37 of the Arbitration Act 1996 subject to the parties' agreement. When the arbitration agreement excludes that power, express agreement of the parties would be necessary.

[387] Section 68(2)(e) of the Act refers to "any arbitral or other institution or person vested by the parties with powers in relation to the proceedings or the award exceeding its powers". This covers both institutions like the ICC or LCIA and individual appointing authorities, such as the President of the Law Society.

[388] This example was given in *Lesotho* at [29]. Section 68(2)(e) of the Arbitration Act 1996.

[389] The ICC Rules of Arbitration authorise limited scrutiny of the tribunal's draft award by the ICC Court of Arbitration (Art.27). Interference with the substance of an award could be an irregularity within s.68(2)(e) of the Act.

[390] Section 34(1) of the Arbitration Act 1996.

[391] See para.5–196.

[392] Section 68(2)(c) of the Arbitration Act 1996 (failure by the tribunal to conduct the proceedings in accordance with the procedure agreed by the parties).

(iv) Failure to deal with all the issues put to it (ground d)

8-093   **Approach of the court.** There is substantial overlap between this ground
(d) and ground (a) and the commentary to both grounds should be read together.
Failure by the arbitral tribunal to deal with "all the issues that were put to it"
constitutes a procedural irregularity.[393] Construing the quoted words purposely
the Court of Appeal has said that they do not mean each and every point in
dispute. Rather they mean those issues which the tribunal has to resolve.[394]
However, the "issue" referred to in s.68(2)(d) must be an important or fundamental issue, for only a failure to deal with such could be capable of causing
substantial injustice. Further, the issue must have been put to the tribunal. There
is also a difference between a failure to deal with an issue and a failure to provide
sufficient reasons for a decision on that issue.[395] In the latter case the court may
upon application[396] require the tribunal to amplify the reasons for the award.[397]

8-094   **Need to decide essential issues.** The tribunal only has to decide matters
relevant to its ultimate decision. Ground (d) is therefore designed to cover those
issues the determination of which is essential to a decision on the claims or specific
defences raised. An irregularity will only result where the tribunal has not dealt at
all with a critical aspect of the case of a party. In other words, it *"is concerned with
a failure . . . where the tribunal has not dealt at all with the case of a party so that
substantial injustice has resulted . . . In the former instance the tribunal has not done
what it was asked to do, namely to give the parties a decision on all issues necessary to
resolve the dispute or disputes (which does not of course mean a decision on all the issues
that were ventilated but only those required for the award)"*.[398] The tribunal certainly
does not have to deal with every point which was raised in the proceedings. If an
award expresses no conclusion at all as to a specific claim or defence then that is
a clear failure to deal with the issue. The ground will also be triggered where the
decision cannot be justified as a key issue has not been decided which is crucial to
the result. It is certainly the case however that an award does not have to set out
each step by which a conclusion is reached. The courts shy away from conducting
a narrow textual analysis in an attempt to pick holes in the reasoning. Once a party
is reduced to alleging that particular sub-issues have not been properly explained
in the award then the challenge is very likely to fail.[399] If because of an incorrect
conclusion as to the applicable law an arbitrator fails to consider an issue which

---

[393] See s.68(2)(d) of the Arbitration Act 1996. See *Margulead v Exide* [2004] EWHC 1019.
[394] *Checkpoint Ltd v Strathclyde Pension Fund* [2003] EWCA Civ 84, *per* Ward L.J. at [48]–[49].
[395] *Fidelity Management SA v Myriad International Holdings BV* [2005] 2 Lloyd's Rep. 508 at 510.
[396] *World Trade Corp v Czarnikow Sugar* [2005] 1 Lloyd's Rep. 422 which was considered in *Fidelity* above at 510.
[397] *Petroships v Petec Trading (the "Petro Trader")* [2001] 2 Lloyd's Rep. 348.
[398] *Weldon Plant v Commission for the New Towns* [2001] 1 All E.R. (Comm) 264 at 279; *World Trade Corp Ltd v C Czarnikow Sugar Ltd*, at [16].
[399] *Fidelity Management SA v Myriad International Holdings BV* [2005] 2 Lloyd's Rep. 508; *Protech Projects Construction (Pty) Ltd v Al-Kharafi & Sons* [2005] 2 Lloyd's Rep. 779, at [34].

was put to him (because he felt that the issue was moot) then such a challenge is an error of law and should be brought, if at all, under s.69.[400]

Unclear reasoning. Ground (d) is also not triggered just because the   8–095
tribunal's reasoning is compressed, confusing or unsatisfactory. [401] If the court can deduce from the award and the other available materials before it, which may include extracts from evidence and the transcript of hearings, the thrust of the tribunal's reasoning then no irregularity will be found.[402] Equally, the court should bear in mind that when considering awards produced by non-lawyer arbitrators, the court should "*look at the substance of such findings, rather than their form, and that one should approach a reading of the award in a fair, and not in an unduly literal way.*"[403] On occasion the court has been prepared to embark on a detailed detective process, examining much of the evidence which was before the tribunal, in order to deduce the tribunals' reasoning and to uphold the award where at all possible to do so.[404] Whether this sort of wide ranging investigation was contemplated by the "long stop" language of the DAC report is doubtful.

Deficiency of reasons is also the subject of a specific remedy under s.70(4). As the Act is not presumed to have created two co-extensive remedies for deficiencies of reasons, one of which is a specific remedy for a specific problem (directing the tribunal to provide further reasons) and the other being a general remedy to set aside or remit awards which contain deficient reasons, this ground (d) is, as noted, reserved for only the extreme cases.[405]

Reasons separate from award. On occasion, particularly in maritime   8–096
arbitrations, the parties agree to receive reasons for the award separately from the award itself and may even agree not to make use of those reasons in any proceedings relating to the award. However, such an agreement has been found to be contrary to public policy in so far as it purports to restrict the court's access to the reasons. The court will look at restricted reasons for the purpose of considering a s.68 challenge; failure to look at the reasons would risk leaving a substantial injustice un-remedied.[406]

---

[400] *Protech Projects Construction (Pty) Ltd v Al-Kharafi & Sons* [2005] EWHC 2165; [2005] 2 Lloyd's Rep. 779, at [34].

[401] *ABB AG v Hochtief Airport GmbH* [2006] 1 All E.R. (Comm) 529, [79], [80], [87].

[402] For a contrary view, namely that s.68 does not justify "launching a detailed inquiry into the manner in which the tribunal considered the various issues" or an examination of the tribunal's evaluation of the evidence, see *Weldon Plant v The Commission for the New Towns* [2001] 1 All E.R. 264. Cited in *World Trade Corp Ltd v C Czarnikow Sugar Ltd*, at [16].

[403] *Bottiglieri di Navigazione SpA v Cosco Qingdao Ocean Shipping Co (The Bunga Saga Lima)* 2 Lloyd's Rep. 1, [22].

[404] *ABB AG v Hochtief Airport GmbH* [2006] 1 All E.R. (Comm) 529.

[405] *Fidelity Management SA v Myriad International Holdings BV* [2005] 2 Lloyd's Rep. 508, citing *World Trade Corp Ltd v C Czarnikow Sugar Ltd*.

[406] See for example the LMAA Small Claims Procedure. *Tame Shipping Ltd v Easy Navigation Ltd (The Easy Rider)* [2004] 2 Lloyd's Rep. 626.

8–097 **Reserving issues for future award.** It will also be sufficient for the tribunal to deal with an issue or a whole claim by reserving the matter for a further award. The tribunal has discretion to do this by virtue of s.47.[407]

(v) Uncertainty and ambiguity of award or formal deficiency (grounds f and h)

8–098 **Approach of the court.** An award may be challenged where it is ambiguous or its effect is uncertain, although in almost all cases of ambiguity the tribunal should first have been asked to correct the ambiguity under s.57(3)(a) or other agreed process of review.[408] The award may also be challenged if it does not comply with a particular requirement as to form.[409] The Arbitration Act 1996 provides that the parties are free to agree on the form of an award,[410] but that otherwise the award is to be in writing signed by all the arbitrators or by those assenting to the award, it must state the seat of the arbitration and the date when the award is made, and it must contain reasons unless it is an agreed award[411] or the parties have agreed to dispense with reasons.[412] A failure to give reasons for the decision on costs is an irregularity as to form within the terms of s.68(2)(h) and could form the basis of an application that the court should exercise its power to order reasons to be given under s.70(4).[413]

(vi) Fraud or contrary to public policy (ground g)

8–099 **Approach of the court.** This irregularity contemplates a situation where either the award was obtained by fraud[414] or the way it was procured was contrary to public policy.[415] Although the second part of the sub-section, "an award procured contrary to public policy" is wider on its face than the first part, "an award obtained by fraud" the courts have in fact interpreted the twin concepts

---

[407] *Sea Trade Maritime Corp v Hellenic Mutual War Risks Association (Bermuda) Ltd* [2006] EWHC 578.

[408] Section 68(2)(f) of the Arbitration Act 1996. See also s.70(2) and para.8–109 below.

[409] Section 68(2)(h) of the Arbitration Act 1996. See paras 6–044 *et seq.*

[410] The parties agreement about formal requirement will usually, but not always, be expressed in the arbitration agreement (e.g. the award will be written in a particular language). There may be specific, formal requirements for enforcement abroad.

[411] An agreed award may record a settlement reached by the parties: see s.51 of the Arbitration Act 1996 and para.6–024.

[412] Section 52 of the Arbitration Act 1996: see para.6–029.

[413] *Norbrook Labratories Ltd v Tank* [2006] EWHC 1055 at [127]. The applicant did not take the point.

[414] Fraud implies some act of deceit perpetrated on the tribunal (e.g. providing the tribunal with falsified certificates of ownership of property claimed), or on the other party (i.e. if the tribunal was party to the fraud). The latter case occurred in *Arab National Bank v El Abdali* [2005] 1 Lloyd's Rep. 541 and an injunction was granted.

[415] Section 68(2)(g) of the Arbitration Act 1996.

consistently.[416] The fact of fraud or procuration contrary to public policy must be established before there is any question of remission to the tribunal.[417] The award must be obtained by the fraud of a party to the arbitration or those privy to that party, not for example by the fraud of third party witnesses.[418] The term "public policy" is capable of covering a wide variety of matters, other than fraud. How illegality, for example, can affect the enforceability of an award has already been discussed.[419] Bribery or some other form of corruption would offend public policy,[420] and so may unconscionable conduct in certain circumstances.[421] The fact that witnesses can be shown to have lied when giving evidence does not of itself mean that any award subsequently produced by a tribunal will trigger this ground. It will need to be shown that the defendant can fairly be blamed for the adducing of the evidence and the deception of the tribunal[422] and that the evidence of deception, which could not have been produced at trial with reasonable diligence, could be expected to be decisive at a re-hearing.[423]

Evidence emerging after publication of award. It sometime happens that documents come to light after an award has been issued which cast doubt on the foundations on which the award has been based. Unlike the 1950 Arbitration Act which contained a power to remit an award in cases where new evidence had subsequently come to light after the award, the 1996 Act gives the court no such power. The court will thus now adopt a restrictive attitude in relation to fresh evidence that comes to light after an award has been made.[424] It does however amount to a fraud for the purpose of this sub-section if a party, through its directors, employees or lawyers, deliberately conceals a document which it knew should have been disclosed in the arbitration and the award will be "obtained by fraud" if the consequence of the deliberate concealment is an award in favour of the concealing party.[425] Even if a fraud or action contrary to public policy can be

8–100

---

[416] *Elektrim v Vivendi Universal and Others* [2007] EWHC 11, [87]. See also *Profilati Italia SrL v Paine Webber* [2001] 1 All E.R. (Comm) 1065 where an allegation of procuration contrary to public policy was found to require some form of reprehensible or unconscionable conduct by a party that has contributed in a substantial way to obtaining an award in his favour.

[417] *Thyssen Canada v Manon* [2005] 1 Lloyds' Rep 640 at 644.

[418] *Elektrim v Vivendi Universal and Others* [2007] EWHC 11, [80]; *Thyssen Canada Ltd v Mariana Maritime SA* [2005] EWHC 219, [2005] 1 Lloyd's Rep. 640 at 650 where there was perjured testimony of witnesses.

[419] See discussion at para.8–031.

[420] See *Westacre Investments v Jugoimport SPRD* [1999] 1 All E.R. (Comm) 865. Applied in *DDT Trucks of North America Ltd v DDT Holdings Ltd* [2007] EWHC 1542, [22].

[421] This last possibility was discussed in *Cuflet Chartering v Caroussel Shipping* [2001] 1 All E.R. (Comm) 398, although the misconduct in this case was found to be inadvertent.

[422] *Thyssen Canada Ltd v Mariana Maritime SA* [2005] 1 Lloyd's Rep. 640 at [14]. See also *Profilati Italia S.r.L. v Paine Webber* [2001] 1 Lloyd's Rep. 715 at 718 *per* Moore-Bick J.: "where the successful party is said to have procured the award in a way which is contrary to public policy, it will normally be necessary to satisfy the court that some form of reprehensible or unconscionable conduct on his part has contributed in a substantial way to obtaining an award in his favour".

[423] *DDT Trucks of North America Ltd v DDT Holdings Ltd* [2007] EWHC 1542.

[424] The tribunal cannot reopen the case in light of fresh evidence: see para.6–166 above.

[425] *Elektrim v Vivendi Universal and Others* [2007] EWHC 11, at [81]–[82], where an application based on alleged deliberate concealment of an important memorandum was dismissed. It could not be shown that the document had been deliberately concealed and even if that could have been shown it would not have made any difference to the terms of the award.

shown the applicant will then have to establish that it made a real difference to the outcome. An innocent or inadvertent failure to disclose material documents will not suffice especially if no substantial injustice results from the non-disclosure.[426] Inadvertently misleading the other party however carelessly[427] also does not fall within this ground.

8–101   **Illegality/public policy.** Further public policy will not be engaged merely because an arbitration agreement is illegal under the law of one party's domicile.[428]

The court may refuse to recognise or enforce a New York Convention award if to do so would be contrary to public policy.[429] The courts will apply similar concepts of public policy when enforcing awards and when considering s.68 challenges under this head.

8–102   **Trial of issues by court.** The court itself must establish the fraud or procuration contrary to public policy. This will entail the court holding a trial for this purpose in certain situations, although not apparently in all cases.[430] Even though the tribunal may be best placed to try these factual issues the court cannot remit the matter to the tribunal for this purpose, because it has no power to do so unless both serious irregularity and substantial injustice are properly made out.[431]

(vii) Admitted irregularity (ground i)

8–103   **Need for significant irregularity.** A party to the arbitral proceedings may also challenge an award where the tribunal or an arbitral institution[432] has admitted "any irregularity in the conduct of the proceedings or in the award".[433] The challenge can cite "any" irregularity; it need not be one of those mentioned in s.68 of the Act although as substantial injustice also has to be shown it must be a significant irregularity. An irregularity might be admitted, for example, where the tribunal subsequently recognises that it erred in an earlier partial award.[434]

---

[426] *Protech Projects Construction (Pty) Ltd v Al-Kharafi & Sons* [2005] 2 Lloyd's Rep. 779, [29]–[30]. This case is a good example of how the concepts of serious irregularity and substantial injustice are sometimes conflated, and if the court cannot see that the latter has resulted it will not find the former. See also *Profilati v Paine Webber* [2001] 1 All E.R. (Comm) 1065.

[427] *Cuflet Chartering v Caroussel Shipping* [2001] 1 All E.R. (Comm) 398.

[428] *JSC Zestafoni v Ronly Holdings* [2004] 2 Lloyds' Rep. 355 at [75].

[429] Section 103(3) of the Arbitration Act 1996, see para.8–044.

[430] In *Elektrim v Vivendi Universal and Others* [2007] EWHC 11 no oral evidence was adduced in support of the allegation of fraud. See [7].

[431] *Thyssen Canada Ltd v, Mariana Maritime SA* [2005] 1 Lloyd's Rep. 640, at [16].

[432] The words actually used are "any arbitral or other institution or person vested by the parties with powers in relation to the proceedings or the award", s.68(2)(i) of the Arbitration Act 1996.

[433] Section 68(2)(i) of the Arbitration Act 1996.

[434] As in *Kasakstan v Ishl Group Inc* [2006] EWHC 448 where the tribunal subsequently discovered that a party had ceased to exist at the time of its partial award.

(b) Substantial injustice

Meaning of substantial injustice. This term[435] is not defined in the Arbitration Act 1996, but a good idea of the meaning that it will be given by the court on an application made under s.68 of the Act can be gleaned from the DAC report in which it was said:

8–104

"The test of substantial injustice is intended to be applied by way of support for the arbitral process, not by way of interference with that process. Thus it is only in those cases where it can be said that what happened is so far removed from what could reasonably be expected of the arbitral process that we would expect the court to take action. The test is not what would have happened had the matter been litigated. To apply such a test would be to ignore the fact that the parties have agreed to arbitrate, not litigate. Having chosen arbitration, the parties cannot validly complain of substantial injustice unless what has happened simply cannot on any view be defended as an acceptable consequence of that choice. In short, [section] 68 is really designed as a long stop, only available in extreme cases when the tribunal has gone so wrong in its conduct of the arbitration that justice calls out for it to be corrected".[436]

The DAC report goes on to give as an example cases under the previous law when the court remitted awards to an arbitral tribunal because the lawyers acting for one party failed, or decided not to, put a particular point to the tribunal.[437] The clear inference from the report is that the court should not treat that kind of case as giving rise to substantial injustice and falling within the ambit of s.68 of the Act.

Burden on applicant. The burden is squarely on the applicant who invokes the "exceptional remedy" under s.68 to present findings of fact which establish substantial injustice. It cannot be simply assumed, other than in cases of actual or apparent bias.[438] Put simply, the question will be whether the applicant may have suffered unduly as a result if the irregularity. This can often be assessed by looking at the benefits, or windfalls, if any, which the other party receives as a result of the irregularity.[439]

8–105

Possibility of alternative outcome. The approach as laid down by Colman J. in *Vee Networks Ltd v Econet Wireless International Ltd*[440] namely, not to

8–106

---

[435] The same term is used in s.24(1)(d) of the Arbitration Act 1996, also without definition. See para.7–116.
[436] Paragraph 280 of the DAC report, quoted with approval on numerous occasions subsequently. See para.8–073.
[437] This happened in *India Oil Corp v Coastal (Bermuda) Ltd* [1990] 2 Lloyd's Rep. 407 and *King v Thomas McKenna* [1991] 1 All E.R. 653.
[438] *Lesotho Highlands* at [35]. See *ASM Shipping Ltd of India v TTMI Ltd of England* [2006] 1 Lloyd's Rep. 375 for the bias exception.
[439] See the discussion of this point in the dissenting judgment of Lord Phillips M.R. in *Lesotho Highlands*, at [52]–[53].
[440] [2005] 1 Lloyd's Rep. 192.

ascertain whether the arbitrator came to the wrong conclusion but to consider *"whether he was caused by inappropriate means to reach one conclusion whereas had he adopted appropriate means he might have reached another conclusion favourable to the applicant"*, is likely to be followed after the decision of the House of Lords in *Lesotho Highlands*.[441] In *Vee*, the court concluded that if an irregular procedure caused the arbitrator to decide a point against the applicant which, but for the irregularity, "he might well never have reached, provided always that the opposite conclusion is reasonably arguable" then substantial injustice will be made out.[442] The judge based this conclusion on the fact that it will not normally be appropriate for the court actually to try the issue of whether substantial injustice has been made out as that would be an entirely inappropriate inroad into the arbitral process. Whilst this sentiment of non-encroachment on the arbitral process is to be commended, the decision does appear to have lowered the intended threshold of substantial injustice somewhat by creating a presumption that injustice has arisen if the applicant can show that an irregularity deprived him of the opportunity of running other points even if they were not manifestly strong or, as it was put in *Vee*, the alternative argument was "not so weak that it had no realistic prospect of success".[443] This is in contrast with the approach taken in *Thyssen Canada Ltd*[444] where the court was prepared to embark on a full trial to determine whether fraud was made out as it did not feel that the award could be remitted to the tribunal unless or until a substantial injustice had been properly shown. In another case, in considering whether substantial injustice was caused by a tribunal's refusal to adjourn a hearing to receive further evidence, the court enquired whether the new evidence, if admitted, would have stood a realistic chance of reversing the award.[445] If therefore correcting or avoiding the serious irregularity would make no difference to the outcome, substantial injustice will not be shown.

8–107   **Order of issues.** In practice, therefore the usual approach of the courts is first to determine whether there has been any serious irregularity. If there has not been, then the question of substantial injustice cannot arise.[446] An alternative approach is to consider the substantial injustice issue first. If, for example, the court is convinced that the impugned decision is right, then no substantial injustice will have resulted even if the arbitrator reached the correct conclusion by adopting an unfair procedure.[447]

---

[441] *Lesotho Highlands Development Authority v. Impreglio SpA* [2006], A.C. 221.
[442] [2005] 1 Lloyd's Rep. 192 at [90]. See also *Conder Structures v Kvaener Constructions Ltd* [1999] A.D.R.L.J. 305, quoted with approval in *Hussman v Al Ameen, ibid.*
[443] Paragraph 91. Applied in *OAO Northern Shipping Co v Remol Coldores De Marin SL* [2007] EWHC 1821 at [25]–[30].
[444] Paragraph 16.
[445] *Shuttari v Solicitors Indemnity Fund* [2004] EWHC 1537 at [61].
[446] For a very clear exposition of this approach, see *Margulead Ltd v Exide Technologies* [2005] 1 Lloyd's Rep. 324, *per* Colman J. at [3].
[447] *Tame Shipping Ltd v Easy Navigation Ltd (The Easy Rider)* [2004] 2 Lloyd's Rep. 626 at [31].

(c) Application to court

Time limit for the application. A party to arbitration proceedings   8–108
wishing to apply to the court to challenge an award on the ground of *"serious
irregularity affecting the tribunal, the proceedings or the award"*[448] must give notice
to the other parties and the tribunal and bring the application *"within 28 days of
the date of the award or, if there has been any arbitral process of appeal or review, of
the date when the applicant . . . was notified of the result of that process"*.[449]

Exhaustion of other rights. Before making an application under s.68 the   8–109
party concerned must have first exhausted *"any available arbitral process of appeal
or review and any available recourse under section 57"* of the Act.[450] The reference
to recourse under s.57 means that before making his challenge the applicant must
have sought to remedy the irregularity by asking the tribunal to correct the award
to remove, among other things, any ambiguity, or to make an additional award in
respect of any claim which was presented to the tribunal but was not dealt with in
the award.[451] Only if the tribunal refuses that request or is unable to correct the
irregularity can the application to the court proceed.[452] Does this mean that that
a party must go back to the tribunal and ask for the award to be corrected even if
they believed it to be unsalvageable or "so bad that it was not susceptible of any
clarification or further expansion"? This question was answered in the affirmative
in *Sinclair v Woods of Winchester Ltd*.[453] There may however be cases where the
nature of the complaint is not caught by s.57(3), or its equivalent, and simply could
not be corrected by the tribunal even if asked, such as the omission to attach
sufficient weight to a piece of evidence. In those cases, there will be *"no available
recourse"* for the purpose of s.70(2)(b) and so the right to mount a challenge under
s.68 will not be lost if the matter is not raised with the tribunal in such circumstances.[453a]

Loss of right to object. A party who wishes to challenge an award for a   8–110
serious irregularity should not only act promptly in making his application to the
court but should also take care not to lose his right to object.[454] A party who takes
part or continues to take part in the proceedings must make his objection to the

---

[448] The words in quotes appear in s.68(1) of the Arbitration Act 1996.
[449] Section 68(1) of the Arbitration Act 1996, incorporating s.70(3) of that Act. The possibility of an
extension to this time limit is discussed at paras 8–212 *et seq.* See for example *Claire & Co Ltd v
Thames Water Utilities* [2005] EWHC 1022 where an extension was refused and *Tyssen Canada v
Manon* [2005] 1 Lloyd's Rep. 640.
[450] Sections 68(1) and 70(2) of the Arbitration Act 1996.
[451] Recourse under s.57 is not always available. That section is not mandatory and is subject to the
parties' agreement. See para.6–170.
[452] *Torch Offshore LLC & Amor v Cable Shipping Inc* [2004] EWHC 787; *Sinclair v Woods of Winchester
Ltd* [2005] EWHC 1631 at [36]–[39].
[453] Paragraphs 38. The judge in that case discerned a deliberate ploy not to seek correction of the award
as a decision to challenge the award was said to have already been made.
[453a] *World Trade Corp v C Czarnikow Sugar* [2004] EWHC 2332 at [8]–[15].
[454] Sections 68(1) and 73 of the Arbitration Act 1996. See para.7–127 for how the objection should be
made.

irregularity "*either forthwith or within such time as is allowed by the arbitration agreement or the tribunal*".[455] If that is not done, the party concerned may not be able to raise that objection before the court "unless he shows that, at the time he took part or continued to take part in the proceedings, he did not know or could not with reasonable diligence have discovered the grounds for the objection". Extreme caution is necessary however because it is unlikely to be enough to simply convey a reservation of rights. In *ASM Shipping Ltd of India v TTMI Ltd of England*,[456] a case brought under s.68 but also relevant to s.24, although apparent bias was made out the award was not set aside because the applicant delayed in making its challenge until the award was delivered and accordingly had fallen foul of s.73. What is striking about this case is that an objection to the arbitrator and an attempted reservation of rights was made almost as soon as the facts came to light at a hearing. However, once the arbitrator had declined to recuse himself the court found that a s.24 challenge should have been made promptly and certainly before taking up the award; it was not acceptable to continue the objection in correspondence and wait until the outcome of the award was known. "*A 'heads we win, tails you lose' position is not permissible in law as s.73 makes clear*".[457]

8–111   **Raising objection immediately.** Once the respondent can show that the applicant took part or continued to take part in the arbitration proceedings without objection, the burden shifts to the applicant to show that he did not know and could not with reasonable diligence have discovered the grounds for objection at the time. Taking part does not always require active participation: "*there might well be periods in the arbitration during which no formal step is required of one or other party but, during these periods, the parties will still be taking part in the proceedings.*"[458] In the case of an alleged procedural irregularity committed by an arbitrator during the conduct of proceedings, the point must therefore be raised immediately (unless there is no knowledge or means of knowledge, which will be a difficult hurdle to overcome). "*To wait until after the publication of the award or indeed after continuing to participate in the hearing . . . will be fatal to the right to mount a s.68 application*".[459] In *Thyssen Canada Ltd v Mariana Maritime SA*, a possible ground for objection (that the defendants had fraudulently concealed the true cause of a fire on board on a ship) was discovered shortly after the end of the hearing but several months before the publication of the award. The claimants did nothing to substantiate their knowledge (including by securing the witness statements which they subsequently obtained) and meanwhile continued to participate

---

[455] Section 73(1) of the Arbitration Act 1996, which is referred to in s.68(1). See also the authorities mentioned in footnote to para.8–065.

[456] [2006] 1 Lloyd's Rep. 375. See also *Arduina Holdings BV v Celtic Resources Holdings Plc* [2006] EWHC 3155, [36]–[38].

[457] Paragraphs 48–49. See also *Sinclair v Woods of Winchester Ltd* 102 Con. L.R. 127 at [33], where again conduct at the hearing could not be objected to as the challenger waited until after the delivery of the award to make the challenge.

[458] *Rustall Trading Ltd v Gill & Duffus SA* [2000] 1 Lloyd's Rep. 14 at 20, 21; cited with approval in *Thyssen Canada Ltd v Mariana Maritime SA* [2005] 1 Lloyd's Rep. 640 at [18]–[20].

[459] *Margulead Ltd v Exide Technologies*, per Colman J., at [34]. See also *ASM Shipping Ltd of India v TTMI Ltd of England* [2006] 1 Lloyd's Rep. 375 on the detailed operation of s.73.

in the proceedings including taking up the award. The s.68 application was therefore barred by s.73 of the 1996 Act.

Conduct of application. In most cases the court will decide the application 8–112 upon reviewing the available evidence and considering submissions. Evidence presented to the court can be substantial, perhaps overly so,[460] and there is an undecided issue as to how far the court should delve into the detailed conduct of proceedings and content of evidence presented to the tribunal. In certain cases, especially where it is alleged that the award has been procured by fraud, the court may need to give directions for a full trial including the cross examination of witnesses.[461]

Where an applicant wishes to put fresh evidence before the court, it is likely to have to satisfy the court that the fresh evidence was unavailable at the time of the arbitration, to explain why it was unavailable and that such evidence would have had an important influence on the result. The issue of fresh evidence will be particularly relevant where the applicant challenges the award under s.68(2)(g) where it alleges that the award was procured by fraud.[462]

Variety of orders. Upon an application under s.68 of the 1996 Act the court 8–113 can make an order in respect of the whole or part of the award by remitting it to the tribunal for reconsideration. When a fraud is established the court can grant an injunction restraining enforcement and publication of the fraudulent award[463] by setting it aside or by declaring the award to be of no effect. *"The court shall not exercise its power to set aside or declare an award to be of no effect, in whole or in part, unless it is satisfied that it would be inappropriate to remit the matters in question to the tribunal for reconsideration."*[464] The court may require the applicant to provide security for the costs of the application[465] or order that any money payable under the award shall be brought into court or otherwise secured pending the determination of the application.[466] If necessary,[467] the court may also require the tribunal to state the reasons for its award in sufficient detail to enable the court properly to consider the application.[468]

---

[460] See Colman J., Arbitration and Judges—how much interference should we tolerate? Master's Lecture, London, March 14, 2006; *ABB v Hochtief Airport GmbH* [2006] 1 All E.R. (Comm) 529, at [87], "Challenges such as this are immensely time-consuming and therefore costly".

[461] *Thyssen Canada Ltd v Mariana Maritime SA*, at [15].

[462] See the discussion of fresh evidence in the context of a s.68(2)(g) application in *Thyssen Canada Ltd v Mariana Maritime SA* [2005] 1 Lloyd's Rep. 640 at [58]–[66] and para.8–081 above.

[463] *Arab National Bank v El Abdali* [2005] 1 Lloyds' Rep. 541.

[464] Section 68(3) of the Arbitration Act 1996. As for what is inappropriate to be remitted, see para.8–163.

[465] Section 70(6) of the Arbitration Act 1996, which also provides that the application may be dismissed if an order for security is not complied with. See para.8–206 for discussion.

[466] Section 70(7) of the Arbitration Act 1996, which also provides that the court may direct that the application be dismissed if such an order is not complied with. See para.8–208 for discussion.

[467] Even if it would be helpful to have the tribunal's reasons, the court will not overrule any agreement by the parties that reasons need not be given.

[468] Section 70(4) of the Arbitration Act 1996. The court may make a further order of costs resulting from this order: see s.70(5) of the Act and para.6–029.

8-114   **Multiple applications.** Applications under s.68 of the Arbitration Act 1996 are often made together with an application for leave to appeal under s.69 of the Act. It is said that the logical approach to multiple applications of this kind is to set aside or remit for serious irregularity and to consider the question of permission to appeal once it is decided whether the award can stand.[469] Section 68 applications are also sometimes made together with an application to remove an arbitrator under s.24.[470] Indeed, on occasions the two applications will be interlinked, so that the practical effect of an application under one section will be linked to the success of an application under another section.[471]

(d) Appeals to the Court of Appeal

8-115   **Approach of the court.** This paragraph considers the leave requirements under both s.67(4) and s.68(4) as they are in the same form. Permission of the "court" is required for any appeal from a decision of the court under either ss.67 or 68.[472] It may be given "subject to conditions to the same or similar effect as an order" for security for costs or of the sum in dispute.[473] At first sight, this subsection appears to suggest that unless the judge at first instance gives leave to appeal there can be no appeal. Indeed, s.105(1) defines the "court" as the High Court or County Court. However, two separate lines of decisions of the Court of Appeal have weakened the proposition that the first instance judge alone is competent to grant leave to appeal from his own decision.

8-116   **Excess of jurisdiction.** Following *Cetelem v Roust*,[474] which dealt with the identical provision in relation to appeals under s.44(7) of the Act, the distinction is now to be drawn between appeals against orders which the judge had jurisdiction to make, although it is alleged he erred in fact or in law in making the order, and orders which he had no jurisdiction to make. The Court of Appeal can give permission to appeal in respect of the latter type of orders, where the judge at first instance has no jurisdiction to make the order in question, even where the judge himself has refused leave to appeal. As the Court of Appeal noted in *Cetelem*:

> "So long as the judge could make the order in the sense that it was within the jurisdiction specified in the relevant section, the buck stops with him. The order is made under the section. It is only where the judge makes an order which is outwith his jurisdiction, so that he could not (as opposed to should not) make it, that s.44(7) and other similar provisions do not prevent an appeal to this court."[475]

---

[469] *Bulfracht (Cyprus) Ltd v Boneset Shipping Co Ltd (the "Pamphilos")* [2002] 2 Lloyd's Rep. 681, *per* Colman J.
[470] *ASM Shipping Ltd of India v TTMI Ltd of England* [2006] 1 Lloyd's Rep. 375; *Sumukan Ltd v Commonwealth Secretariat* [2007] EWHC 188.
[471] *DDT Trucks of North America Ltd v DDT Holdings Ltd* [2007] EWHC 1542.
[472] Sections 67(4) and 68(4) of the Arbitration Act 1996.
[473] Section 70(8) of the Arbitration Act 1996.
[474] *Cetelem SA v Roust Holdings Ltd* [2005] 1 W.L.R. 3555.
[475] *Cetelem SA v Roust Holdings Ltd* [2005] 1 W.L.R. 3555, *per* Clarke L.J., at [25].

Quite how easy this distinction is to operate in practice remains to be seen. In *Lesotho Highlands v Impreglio*,[476] the House of Lords when considering a challenge under s.68 of the Arbitration Act 1996 rejected an argument that an error as to the currency of an award constituted an excess of powers. However, this matter was argued strongly on both sides all the way up to the House of Lords and the concepts are elusive. The field of administrative law is full of examples of the difficulty in drawing a distinction between a simple error (within jurisdiction) and acting outside of jurisdiction.[477]

Orders on preliminary points. In a closely related decision, the Court of Appeal has held in respect of an appeal based on a preliminary point about whether a particular section (s.69) applies at all (because for example there is a question whether a valid exclusion agreement has been entered into) that the Court of Appeal does have jurisdiction to grant leave in respect of such questions.[478] The Court of Appeal canvassed but did not decide the possibility that the opt out wording in s.44(1), "unless the parties otherwise agree" may also be a preliminary point as to whether that section applies at all. **8–117**

Residual jurisdiction regarding unfairness. The Court of Appeal also has a residual jurisdiction to set aside the judge's decision in the case of unfairness relating to the process of the judge's decision. The distinction is therefore to be drawn between appeals from the judge's refusal to give leave on the merits where, save for cases where there was no jurisdiction for the underlying decision, there is no appeal and cases where, "*the judge's refusal of leave to appeal was arbitrary or unfair: or was the product of a failure of intellectual engagement with the arguments put before him; or amounted actually or metaphorically to the absence of a decision on the issue*".[479] In such "exceptionally rare cases"[480] the Court of Appeal can of its own motion consider appeals even where leave of the first instance judge has not been given. The Court of Appeal has rejected the argument that this residual discretion is contrary to Art.6 of the European Convention of Human Rights.[481] **8–118**

---

[476] [2006] 1 A.C. 221.

[477] *Pearlman v Keepers and Governors of Harrow School* [1978] 3 W.L.R 736 at 743: "The distinction between an error which entails absence of jurisdiction and an error made within jurisdiction is fine . . . it is rapidly being eroded".

[478] *Sukuman Ltd v Commonwealth Secretariat* [2007] EWCA 243; [2007] Bus. L.R. 1075, at [27]–[34].

[479] *CGU International Insurance Plc and Others v Astra Zeneca Insurance Co Ltd* [2006] EWCA 1340, *per* Rix L.J. at [98], approving *North Range Shipping Ltd v Seatrans Shipping Corp* [2002] 1 W.L.R. 2397. Approved in *Kazakhstan v Istil Group Inc* [2007] W.L. 1425725, paras 11. See also *ASM Shipping Ltd of India v TTMI Ltd* [2006] EWCA 1341, a decision under s.68(4), which is in the same terms as s.69(8).

[480] *CGU International Insurance Plc and Others v Astra Zeneca Insurance Co Ltd* [2006] EWCA 1340, *per* Rix L.J. at [100].

[481] *Kazakhstan v Istil Group Inc* [2007] W.L. 1425725, following *CGU International Insurance Plc and Others v Astra Zeneca Insurance Co Ltd* [2006] EWCA 1340.

7. APPEAL ON QUESTION OF LAW

8–119   **Introduction.** Apart from applying to the court to challenge an award under s.67 (lack of substantive jurisdiction)[482] or s.68 (serious irregularity)[483] a party may be able to appeal to the court[484] on a question of law arising out of an arbitral award.[485] The right to appeal may be excluded by clear agreement and even if there is no exclusion agreement, which is often included by virtue of the parties choosing an institutional set of rules which contain a general exclusion of the right to appeal, there are a number of restrictions on the right to bring an appeal. Unless all the parties agree to the appeal, the appellant must obtain leave from the court, which will only be given if the court is satisfied on certain specific matters,[486] which will be discussed in the following paragraphs. A further restriction is that appeals can only be brought on questions of English law: this automatically rules out appeals on the great many international arbitrations seated in London pursuant to a foreign governing law. These restrictions mean that appeals on questions of law are often "dressed up" as challenges under s.68, which can be brought as of right.[487] Furthermore, few appeals under s.69 actually get over the leave requirement which has been designed to catch all but the most meritorious appeals.

8–120   **A necessary provision?** The very existence of s.69 has been criticised in some quarters as being an unwarranted encroachment on the powers of the tribunal to decide the case as they see fit. As Colman J. has said, it is the section "which gets most people hot under the collar."[488] However, in most quarters the provision is accepted as a necessary compromise between the desire to entrench arbitral authority on the one hand, and the desire on the other to continue the development of the body of English commercial law, with the link between the courts and tribunals remaining in place. There is no equivalent provision in the Model Law; this provision was derived very substantially from s.1 of the Arbitration Act 1975, which itself abolished the much criticised case stated procedure.

8–121   **Exclusion agreement.** Section 69 is not mandatory. The parties can agree to exclude an appeal to the court,[489] and this is generally known as an "exclusion

---

[482] See paras 8–054 *et seq.*

[483] See paras 8–072 *et seq.*

[484] Some arbitration rules provide for their own system of appeals, which may or may not be followed by a subsequent appeal to the court. See, e.g. the GAFTA Rules and the International General Produce Association Rules. See also the Rules of the International Centre for Settlement of Investment Disputes.

[485] Section 69 of the Arbitration Act 1996, replacing s.1 of the Arbitration Act 1979.

[486] The specific matters are contained in s.69(3) of the Arbitration Act 1996 and are listed in para.8–132.

[487] *Lesotho Highlands* is arguably one such case.

[488] Colman J., Arbitration and Judges—how much interference should we tolerate? Master's Lecture, London, March 14, 2006.

[489] This may be done before or after the commencement of the arbitration proceedings. Section 87(1)(b) of the Arbitration Act 1996 will not be brought into force: see para.2–005.

agreement".[490] Rules of arbitration often contain words wide enough to be treated as an exclusion agreement.[491] The nature of an exclusion agreement does not go to the substantive rights of the parties but relates to the ancillary arbitration agreement. It remains sufficient to include the exclusion agreement in general terms and to incorporate the exclusion agreement by reference. The previous case law has not been altered by the Human Rights Act and it is still the case that the exclusion agreement does not have to refer expressly to s.69 to be effective.[492] It is uncertain however whether an effective exclusion agreement is achieved by simply providing that a dispute shall be "finally settled . . . " by arbitration.[493] Further, if the parties agree to dispense with reasons for an award their agreement will be treated as an exclusion agreement.[494]

Exhaustion of other rights.[494a] An appeal may not be brought if the applicant "has not first exhausted any available arbitral process of appeal or review and any available recourse under s.57".[495] Section 57 of the Arbitration Act 1996 recognises that the parties are free to confer on the tribunal the power to correct an award or to make an additional award, and in the absence of such an agreement that section empowers the tribunal on its own initiative or on the application of a party to correct an award already made or to make an additional award in respect of a claim that was presented to the tribunal but not dealt with in the previous award.[496] Thus, if the point of law arises from an accidental slip or ambiguity that could be corrected or from the failure of the tribunal to deal with a claim in the award which was presented to it that could be the subject of an additional award, s.69 requires the applicant to request the tribunal to correct the matter (if necessary by an additional award) before appealing to the court. Only if the tribunal refuses that request or is unable to deal with the question can the appeal proceed.

8–122

Time limit. In order to comply with s.70(3) of the Arbitration Act, 1996, an appeal must be brought within 28 days of the date of the award or if there has been any arbitral process of appeal or review[497] (e.g. an additional award) from the date

8–123

---

[490] See para.2–063.

[491] e.g. Art.28.6 of the the ICC Rules of Arbitration (January 1, 1998) was found to exclude an appeal in *Lesotho*, at [3]. See also *Cameroon Airlines v Transnet* [2004] EWHC 1829.

[492] *Sukuman Ltd v Commonwealth Secretariat* [2006] 1 All E.R. (Comm). Upheld by the Court of Appeal, *Sukuman Ltd v Commonwealth Secretariat* [2007] EWCA 243; [2007] Bus. L.R. 1075.

[493] This point was raised but not decided in *Demco Investments & Commercial SA v SE Banken Forsakring Holding AB* [2005] 2 Lloyd's Rep. 650, at [6]. See also *Essex County Council v Premier Recycling Ltd* [2006] EWHC 3594 where a reference to "final and binding" was not sufficient to exclude the application of s.69.

[494] Section 69(1) of the Arbitration Act 1996.

[494a] The cases and principles cited at para.8–109 are of relevance to the application of s.57 to s.69 appeals.

[495] Section 69(2) incorporating s.70(2) of the Arbitration Act 1996. The use of the word "available" recognises that s.70 is not mandatory and that recourse to the tribunal may have been excluded by prior agreement.

[496] See paras 6–170 *et seq.*

[497] An additional award may result from a request to the tribunal or from an appeal board established under the rules governing the arbitration.

when the applicant was notified of the result of that process.[498] The possibility of an extension of this time limit is discussed earlier in this chapter.[499]

8–124 Question of law. The appeal to the court can only be made "on a question of law arising out of an award made in the proceedings"[500] and any application for permission to appeal must "identify the question of law to be determined and state the grounds on which it is alleged that leave to appeal should be granted".[501] A question of law is defined in s.82(1) of the Arbitration Act, 1996.[502] It does not include issues of foreign law,[503] even if the tribunal proceeds on the basis that for all practical purposes English law is the same as the foreign governing law.[504] The conditions on which the court must be satisfied before permission will be given are discussed later in this chapter.[505]

8–125 No appeal on facts. The tribunal's findings of fact are conclusive.[506] The appeal is only concerned with a question of law and must not encroach upon the facts. *"The arbitrators are the masters of the facts. On an appeal the Court must decide any question of law arising from an award on the basis of a full and unqualified acceptance of the findings of fact of the arbitrators. It is irrelevant whether the Court considers those findings of fact to be right or wrong. It also does not matter how obvious a mistake by the arbitrators on issues of fact might be, or what the scale of the financial consequences of the mistake of fact might be."*[507]

The court will not permit an appeal unless the tribunal's decision falls outside what has been described as the permissible range.

"The arbitrators plainly erred in their approach on this aspect. Yet it must be borne in mind that their decision was not one of pure law. It was a question of mixed law and fact. In such a situation their error in approach is not by itself decisive. It is still necessary to consider whether their actual decision in all the circumstances falls outside the permissible range of solutions open to arbitrators."[508]

---

[498] Section 69(2) incorporating s.70(3) of the Arbitration Act 1996.
[499] See para.8–063 and CPR r.62.9(1). See *Surefire Systems Ltd v Guardian ECL Ltd* [2005] EWHC 1860 for a comment on application for leave to appeal.
[500] Section 69(1) of the Arbitration Act 1996.
[501] Section 69(4) of the Arbitration Act 1996.
[502] For a court in England and Wales, it means a question of the law of England and Wales and for a court in Northern Ireland, it means a question of the law of Northern Ireland.
[503] *Egmatra AG v Marco Trading Corp* [1999] Lloyd's Rep. 862 at 865 and *Sanghi v TII* [2000] 1 Lloyd's Rep. 480 at 483.
[504] *Reliance Industries Ltd v Enron Oil and Gas India* [2002] 1 All E.R. (Comm) 59. The position would be different if the parties varied the agreement so that, for example, English law replaced the foreign law as the governing law.
[505] For example, the question of law must be one which the tribunal was asked to determine: see paras 8–129 *et seq.* below.
[506] See paras 8–085 *et seq. Boulos Gad Tourism v Uniground Shipping Co* (November 16, 2001) QBD (Comm), Tomlinson J.
[507] *Geogas SA v Trammo Gas Ltd (The "Baleares")* [1993] 1 Lloyd's Rep. 215 at 228, CA. Cited with approval in *Demco Investments & Commercial SA v SE Banken Forsakring*. Quoted in *Kershaw Mechanical Services Ltd v Kendrick Construction Ltd* [2006] EWHC 727, at [61].
[508] *Casimar SA v Marimarna Shipping Co Ltd* [1990] 2 Lloyd's Rep. 323, *per* Steyn J. at 326 cited with approval by HHJ. Peter Coulson Q.C. *Walsall MBC v Beachdale Community Housing Association* [2005] EWHC 2715 (TCC).

Even in matters concerning the construction of an agreement, which is ultimately a question of law (or mixed fact and law), the court will hesitate to vary the findings of a tribunal with commercial experience (but may still do so).[509]

Fact and law distinction. The distinction between questions of fact and law is a notoriously difficult one which arises generally in appellate practice.[510] Most cases take a restrictive view of what is a properly reviewable finding of law. Such a restrictive approach is illustrated by *Demco Investments & Commercial SA v SE Banken Forsakring*[511] where the court rejected a submission that a question of whether the tribunal was right to find a particular fact on the basis of the evidence before it was a question of law. The court remarked that the legislative intent of s.69(3) was to prevent parties seeking to dress up questions of fact as questions of law; any appeal on a question of law must take as its starting point the tribunal's findings of fact and then identify the question of law arising from the finding. In certain cases, a challenge under s.69 may succeed if the tribunal's findings of fact do not address a critical question which would need to be answered in order to substantiate the tribunal's conclusions.[512]

8–126

Construction of an instrument. However, a recent illustration of a broader approach can be found in a case where the court was prepared to intervene to overturn the arbitrator's decision that no binding agreement for the supply of a ship's engine had been concluded by an exchange of letters.[513] Relying upon the principle that the construction of a written instrument is a question of law[514] (or a mixed question of fact and law), the court reviewed the finding of the arbitrators and overturned it. This case is an extreme example of the application of s.69. The judgment conflates the identification of the relevant legal principles and their application to the facts. There is no suggestion in the judgment that the arbitrator's understanding of the law of offer and acceptance was incorrect: it is the application to the facts which the courts did not accept and hence the two stage approach outlined earlier in this paragraph appears not to have been followed. The decision in *Covington* is hard to reconcile with that in *Plymouth City Council v DR*

8–127

---

[509] *Covington Marine Corp v Xiamen Shipbuilding Industry Co Ltd* [2005] EWHC 2912 where Langley J. reviewed the relevant authorities [35]–[42]. Compare *Kershaw Mechanical Services Ltd v Kendrick Construction Ltd* [2006] EWHC 727 [51]–[57].

[510] See for example M Fordham, *Judicial Review Handbook* (4th edn, Hart), at 13.2.2, pp.281, 282.

[511] [2005] 2 Lloyd's Rep. 650. Applied in *Surefire Systems Ltd v Guardian ECL Ltd* [2005] B.L.R. 534. See also *Plymouth City Council v DR Jones (Yeovil) Ltd* [2005] EWHC 2356; *Kershaw Mechanical Services Ltd v Kendrick Construction Ltd* [2006] EWHC 727 and *London Underground v Citylink Telecommunications Ltd* [2007] EWHC 1749, [62]–[65].

[512] *Pentonville Shipping Ltd v Transfield Shipping Inc (The Jonny K)* [2006] 1 Lloyd's Rep. 666. The finding in question related to who was responsible for an order to sail given to a vessel during the course of loading. The tribunal's award had not clearly addressed this question and the award was remitted to them. The appeal was brought only under s.69 but could equally have been argued under s.68(2(d) (failure to deal with the issues), under which it fits more neatly. Alternatively, an order could have made under s.70(4)(b) requiring the tribunal to set out its reasoning in more detail.

[513] *Covington Marine Corp v Xiamen Shipbuilding Industry Co Ltd* [2005] EWHC 291 at [43]–[46].

[514] *The Trustees of Edmond Stern Settlement v Levy* [2007] W.L. 1623226, para.10, where the court held that the construction of the words in a contractual document was a question of law.

Jones (Yeovil) Ltd,[515] where the court expressed the view that questions as to (1) which documents were incorporated into a contract, and (2) what dates if any were incorporated into the contract were questions of fact and not law. [516]

On the basis that the court may review questions of construction as potential errors of law, the court should only intervene in the clearest of cases as questions of construction usually have to be answered against the background of relevant facts and the court will not have heard the evidence, unlike the arbitrator.[517]

8–128   **Qualifying errors of law.** The scope of an appeal under this section also includes a complaint that the tribunal has applied the wrong governing law and that the tribunal should have applied English law.[518] There can be no error of law if the arbitrator reached a decision within the permissible range of options open to him.[519] However, once the court has concluded that an error of law has been committed, the court will consider the issue of law in totality and is very likely to set out its view of the correct position.[520] If the award is then remitted to the tribunal under s.69(7) the tribunal must reconsider the issue on which it erred in the light of what the court has said.

If the tribunal wrongly records in an award that the parties were agreed on a point, this does not give rise to a question of law.[521] Rather, the parties should ask the tribunal to correct the award.[522]

8–129   **Arising out of the award.** The question of law, which is the subject of appeal, must arise out of an award made in the arbitral proceedings.[523] An issue may arise whether the "award" actually constitutes a decision which is capable of being the subject of an appeal.[524]

8–130   **Obtaining reasons from the tribunal.** The court is empowered to order the tribunal to state reasons for an award in sufficient detail for an appeal.[525] This may be necessary where the award does not contain any reasons or does not set out the tribunal's reasons in sufficient detail to enable the court properly to consider any question of law arising out of the award should an appeal be

[515] [2005] EWHC 2356.
[516] See paras 26, 33.
[517] *The Trustees of Edmond Stern Settlement v Levy* [2007] W.L. 1623226, para.13.
[518] *CGU International Insurance Plc v Astrazeneca Insurance Co Ltd* [2006] 1 C.L.C. 162.
[519] *Walsall MBC v Beechdale Community Housing Association Ltd* [2005] EWHC at [14], [26].
[520] For an example of this approach, see *Miranos International Trading Inc v VOC Steel Services BV* [2005] EWHC 1812.
[521] *Marc Rich & Co AG v Beogradska Plovidba (The "Avala")* L.M.L.N. 381, June 11, 1994.
[522] Unless the parties have excluded it, the tribunal has power to correct an award under s.57(3)(a) of the Arbitration Act 1996: see para.6–167.
[523] Section 69(1) of the Arbitration Act 1996.
[524] See paras 6–072 *et seq.* above.
[525] Section 70(4) of the Arbitration Act 1996 replacing s.1(5) of the Arbitration Act 1979. This would not apply where the parties had agreed that the tribunal should dispense with reasons for the award because that would amount to an exclusion agreement and no appeal would be possible: see para.8–121. It was done, however, in *Petroships v Petec Trading (The "Petro Ranger")* [2001] 2 Lloyd's Rep. 348 at 357.

pursued.[526] No application is required and the court may of its own motion order the tribunal to state the reasons for its award when the court has to consider an application or appeal.[527] The court may make an order in respect of any extra costs associated with its requests for reasons.[528]

Agreement to appeal. The parties may agree to an appeal to the court 8–131 against any award of the tribunal[529] and that agreement may be made before the dispute has arisen. Some standard forms of contract contain express consent to an appeal.[530] Such an agreement is expressly contemplated by s.69 of the Arbitration Act 1996.[531] In that event, a party wishing to exercise the right to appeal will not have to obtain permission from the court, but will have to fulfil the other conditions for an appeal.[532] In the absence of an agreed right of appeal, permission of the court will have to be obtained.

Requirements for permission to appeal. Even if there is no exclusion 8–132 agreement and the conditions mentioned above are met, the applicant will have to obtain permission of the court to proceed with the appeal unless all parties to the arbitral proceedings agree to the appeal.[533] Absent agreement, permission will only be granted if the court is satisfied:

"(a) that the determination of the question will substantially affect the rights of one or more of the parties;

(b) that the question is one which the tribunal was asked to determine;

(c) that on the basis of the findings of fact in the award (i) the decision of the tribunal on the question is obviously wrong, or (ii) the question is one of general public importance and the decision of the tribunal is at least open to serious doubt; and

(d) that, despite the agreement of the parties to resolve the matter by arbitration, it is just and proper in all the circumstances for the court to determine the question."[534]

---

[526] The power to demand reasons from the tribunal will be sparingly exercised: see para.6–031.

[527] It is apparent from the terms of s.70(4) of the Arbitration Act 1996 that no application is required.

[528] Section 70(5) of the Arbitration Act 1996.

[529] Agreement to an appeal was given in *Fence Gates Ltd v NEL Construction* (December 5, 2001) T&CC, H.H. Judge Thornton Q.C. See also *Robin Ellis Ltd v Vinexsa Internationa Ltd* [2003] B.L.R. 373.

[530] *Hallamshire Construction Plc v South Holland District Council* [2004] EWHC 8 (TCC), [2].

[531] Section 69(2)(a) of the Arbitration Act 1996. The word "agreement" in that subsection is not qualified, so it may include an agreement contained in an arbitration clause or in rules incorporated into that clause: see DAC report, para.292.

[532] Section 69(3) of the Arbitration Act 1996. See para.8–119. Further, the appellant must exhaust any other rights and comply with the time limit specified in s.70 of the Act.

[533] Section 69(2) of the Arbitration Act 1996.

[534] Section 69(3) of the Arbitration Act 1996, replacing s.1(4) of the Arbitration Act 1979. The second and third requirement were carefully considered by the Court of Appeal in *CMA CGM SA v Beteiligungs KG (The Northern Pioneer)* [2003] I Lloyd's Rep. 212.

The words appearing in s.69(3) of the Arbitration Act 1996 have been quoted above in full because of their importance to obtaining permission from the court. The requirements are cumulative and onus of satisfying the court on each of the matters quoted rests on the appellant. They will be examined in turn in the following paragraphs with illustrations, where appropriate, from decisions made by the courts.[535]

(a) Determination will substantially affect the rights of the parties

8-133   **Substantially affect rights of the parties.** The court will not grant permission to appeal unless it considers that, having regard to all the circumstances, the determination of the question of law concerned could substantially affect the rights of one or more of the parties to the arbitration agreement.[536] If there are a number of issues it is sufficient that taken together they have that effect.[537] This may be satisfied if a significant sum is involved but it is not necessarily the case that the sums have to be large.[538]

8-134   **Possibility of alternative outcome.** The requirement is a hurdle to overcome and will not be assumed: " . . . it is not good enough simply for a party to assert that the alleged issue in question must affect their rights simply because it goes to an aspect of the dispute in the arbitration."[539] In the *Northern Pioneer*,[540] the Court of Appeal held that the uncertain juridical basis of the right to withdraw a vessel for non-payment of hire within a reasonable time was enough to cast serious doubt on the arbitrator's decision, but not enough to pass the "substantially affect the rights of the parties" test. This was because the delay in purporting to cancel the chaterparty for over a month was inconsistent with an intention to terminate for non-payment. The Court of Appeal noted that it was "confident" that the arbitrators would have reached the same decision no matter what juridical basis they chose to base their decision on.[541] Equally, even where an arbitrator had made an error of law which satisfied the "obviously wrong" test, permission to appeal (or in the instant case, an extension of time to apply) would be refused where the rights of the parties would not be substantially affected as

---

[535] Pre-1996 decisions are still of some relevance to this subject. The previous law on requirements for "leave" to appeal was contained in s.1(4) of the Arbitration Act 1979, as interpreted by subsequent decisions of the courts. Section 69(3) of the Arbitration Act 1996 restates the previous law with some modifications (e.g. the express requirement that the question of law is one which the tribunal was asked to determine).

[536] Arbitration Act 1996, s.69(3)(a) which replaced the Arbitration Act 1979, s.1(4). See also the same requirement in s.45(1) of the 1996 Act.

[537] *Safeway Stores v Legal & General Insurance Soc Ltd* [2004] EWHC 415 at [7].

[538] *Miranos International Trading Inc v VOC Steel Services BV* [2005] EWHC 1812; *Secretary of State for the Environment v Reed International Plc* [1994] 06 E.G. 137. See also *Retla v Gryphon "The Evimeria"* [1982] 1 Lloyd's Rep. 55. See also para.7–168 for commentary on the similar provision contained in s.45(1) of the Arbitration Act 1996.

[539] *Walsall MBC v Beechdale Community Housing Association Ltd* [2005] EWHC at [15].

[540] *CMA CGM SA v Beteiligungs KG MS Northern Pioneer Schiffahrtsgesellschaft GmbH & Co* [2003] 1 W.L.R. 1015.

[541] Paragraphs 55, 56.

without success under related applications the claimant would still be left with a non-binding agreement.[542]

The rights affected must include rights which arise out of the award itself.[543]

Substantial sums involved. In the context of an intended challenge to an   8–135
award on costs, the applicant will have to show not only that the sum involved is sufficiently substantial but that, as with all appeals from awards, it depends upon the resolution of a question of law.[544]

Submitted to the tribunal. The second requirement on which the court   8–136
must be satisfied on an application for permission to appeal is that the question of law concerned is one that the tribunal was asked to determine.[545] Under the previous law[546] some applications for permission were made and granted on the basis that an examination of the reasons for the award revealed an error of law that had not been raised or debated in the arbitral proceedings.[547] The express provision in s.69(3)(b) of the Arbitration Act 1996 now prevents that happening.[548] If certain issues of law are not explored before the arbitrators but are then raised on an application for permission to appeal, the court should refuse permission.[549]

(b) Decision is obviously wrong

Approach of the court. An appellant needs to show that the decision is   8–137
obviously wrong or that it is one of general public importance and subject to serious doubt (a lower threshold than obviously wrong).[550] In successive decisions of the House of Lords made before the Arbitration Act 1996 a distinction was drawn between arbitration relating to a standard form of commercial contract and arbitration relating to a one-off contract of no general public importance. In the former case, leave to appeal was given if the decision of the tribunal on the question of law was open to serious doubt, or put another way, that there was a strong prima facie argument that the decision was wrong. In the latter case, leave would be given only if the judge was satisfied that the tribunal's decision on the question of law was "obviously wrong".[551] This distinction has been adopted by

---

[542] *DDT Trucks of North America Ltd v DDT Holdings Ltd* [2007] EWHC 1542 at [33], [34], [38].
[543] *President of India v Jadranska Solbodna Plovidba* [1992] 2 Lloyd's Rep. 274 which concerned the exercise by the tribunal of its discretion as to costs.
[544] *President of India v Jadranska Solbodna Plovidba* [1992] 2 Lloyd's Rep. 274. See para.6–140 above.
[545] Section 69(3)(b) of the Arbitration Act 1996.
[546] The previous law was contained in s.1(4) of the Arbitration Act 1979.
[547] See DAC report, para.286(ii).
[548] *Markland Ltd v Virgin Retail Ltd* [2003] EWHC 2428 at [32].
[549] *Northern Pioneer*, at [26]–[36].
[550] Section 69(3)(c) of the Arbitration Act 1996.
[551] *Pioneer Shipping Ltd v BTP Tioxide Ltd (The "Nema")* [1981] 2 All E.R. 1030; [1982] A.C. 724 and *Antaios Cia Naviera SA v Salen Rederierna AB (The "Antaios")* [1984] 3 All E.R. 229; [1985] A.C. 191.

the Arbitration Act 1996 which is intended to re-state the essence of those decisions.[552]

8–138 **Apparent error.** Colman J. has dispensed some helpful guidance on the meaning of the current term, when speaking extra-judicially *"What is obviously wrong? Is the obviousness something which one arrives at . . . on first reading over a good bottle of Chablis and some pleasant smoked salmon, or is 'obviously wrong' the conclusion one reaches at the twelfth reading of the clauses and with great difficulty where it is finely balanced. I think it is obviously not the latter."*[553]

8–139 **Need for a prima facie view.** Inevitably this exercise will entail the court coming to at least a prima facie view as to what it thinks the correct answer was.[554] To give two examples, an appeal was allowed from an award on a rent review provision where the decision was obviously wrong and the actual reasoning and language adopted by the arbitrator could not be defended.[555] An appeal was also allowed and the award was remitted to the arbitrator, where the court found after a hearing[556] that the arbitrator had taken the wrong legal approach in respect of the measure of damages.[557]

8–140 **Error apparent from award.** The obvious error must normally be demonstrable on the face of the award itself.[558] It is not normally appropriate to refer to transcripts, submissions and evidence in the arbitration, although the court will of course be able to examine any document referred to in the award.[559]

---

[552] Section 69(3)(c) of the Arbitration Act 1996: see DAC report, para.288. It was recognised that the guidelines set out in *The "Nema"* and *The "Antaios"* might require adaption in particular cases. See in this regard *CMA CGM SA v Beteiligungs KG MS Northern Pioneer Schiffahrtsgesellschaft mbH & Co* [2002] EWCA Civ 1878; [2003] 1 W.L.R. 1015, at [11]. The modification proposed by the Court of Appeal relates only to questions of public importance. If the question is not one of public importance and therefore needs to satisfy the "obviously wrong" test, the *Nema* guidelines will continue to prevail.

[553] Colman J., Arbitration and Judges—how much interference should we tolerate? Master's Lecture, London, March 14, 2006.

[554] See *Bottiglieri di Navigazione SpA v Cosco Qingdao Ocean Shipping Co (The "Bunga Saga Lima")* [2005] 2 Lloyd's Rep. 1 at [18]; *Stolt Tankers v Landmark Chemicals* [2002] 1 Lloyd's Rep. 786 at 796.

[555] *Bisichi Mining v Bass Holdings* [2002] EWHC 375, CL, Jacob. J.

[556] The judge who first considered the application for leave to appeal directed that it should be determined without a hearing, but the judge to whom it was referred for decision decided otherwise.

[557] *Horse Sport Ltd v Aintree Racecourse Co Ltd* [2003] B.L.R. 155, HH Judge Anthony Thornton Q.C. It is doubtful whether this decision observes the strictures of previous decisions on the test for "obviously wrong" particularly as the arbitrator's reasoning was scant (see para.47 of decision).

[558] *The Council of Plymouth v Jones* [2005] EWHC 2536 at [18] and TCC Guide (2nd Edn), para.10.2.4.

[559] *Kershaw Mechanical Services Ltd v Kendrick Construction Ltd* [2006] EWHC 727 at [44]–[45], modifying the test laid down in *Walsall MBC v Beechdale Community Housing Association Ltd* [2005] EWHC, [17], [21], [22]; *HOK Sport Ltd (formerly Lobb Partnership Ltd) v Aintree Racecourse Co Ltd* [2003] Lloyd's Rep. P.N. 148.

(c) Question of general public importance

An issue of general public importance. If it cannot be shown that the   8–141
decision is obviously wrong the appellant has the alternative of showing that the
issue is one of general public importance and that the decision on this point is
open to serious doubt.[560] For a question to be of general public importance "one
needs to have regard not only to the general significance of the point, but also to
the sort of situations in which it is likely to arise".[561] Even if the court finds that
there is a question of law of general public importance, it does not follow that
permission to appeal will be granted.[562] A question will not be of general public
importance if the circumstances in which the point arises are rare and unusual.

Open to serious doubt. What does "open to serious doubt" mean? In the   8–142
Northern Pioneer, the Court of Appeal said that these words impose a test which
is broader than Lord Diplock's test that permission should not be given "unless
the judge considered that a strong prima facie case has been made out that the
arbitrator had been wrong in his construction".[563] In that case, the uncertain
juridical basis of the right to withdraw a vessel from non-payment of hire within
a reasonable time was enough to cast serious doubt on the arbitrator's decision, but
not enough to pass the "substantially affect the rights of the parties" test.

Public importance. Standard forms of contracts which are regularly used in   8–143
a particular area of business are of general public importance.[564] The question of
law need not necessarily arise out of a standard form of contract, but the applicant

---

[560] Section 69(3)(c)(ii) of the Arbitration Act 1996.
[561] *Keydon Estates Ltd v Western Power* [2004] EWHC 996 at [21] for a brief consideration of this
requirement.
[562] *The Coal Authority v Trustees of Nostell Trust* [2005] EWHC 154.
[563] The Court of Appeal has stated that the *Nema* guidelines were "not intended to be all-embracing
or immutable, but subject to adaptation to match changes in practices when these occur or to
refinement to meet problems of kinds that were not foreseen, and are not covered by, what was said
by this House in *The Nema*". The Court of Appeal has concluded that "the statutory criteria are
strongly influenced by the Nema guidelines. They do not however follow these entirely. We have
concluded that they open the door a little more widely to the granting of permission to appeal than
the crack that was left by Lord Diplock." *CMA CGM SA v Beteiligungs KG MS Northern Pioneer
Schiffahrtsgesellschaft mbH & Co* [2002] EWCA Civ 1878 at [11]. As noted, the modification
proposed by the Court of Appeal relates only to questions of public importance.
[564] Lloyd's forms of insurance policies, various forms of building contracts and charterparties are
obvious examples. The applicant will have to satisfy the court that the particular contract in dispute
is used as a standard form. In *Losinjska v Valfracht Maritime (The "Lipa")* [2001] 2 Lloyd's Rep.
17, the court allowed an appeal on a point of construction on a charterparty on the Baltime form
where the decision of the tribunal was open to doubt. In *Miranos International Trading Inc v VOC
Steel Services BV* [2005] EWHC 1812, public importance was satisfied in respect of a point of
construction of a time charter. In *STX Pan Ocean Co Ltd v Ugland Bulk Transport AS, The Livanita*
[2007] EWHC 1317 public importance was satisfied in respect of a point of construction of a time-
charter party in modified NYPE form. In *Sea Trade Maritime Corp v Hellenic Mutual War Risks
Association, The Athena* [2006] EWHC 2530, at [107], the construction of a standard form contract
applicable to all members of the Hellenic War Risks Association was also one of public importance.

must satisfy the court that it is one of "general public importance".[565] If the issue at stake is one of public interest, that of itself will not elevate the issue to one of general public importance unless it can be shown that the clauses at issue "take a common form or that questions of construction which arise here will arise elsewhere."[566]

A point of general public importance can arise even if the dispute in question is of a relatively low value.[567]

8–144   **Faulty reasoning.** Provided the tribunal arrives at the right answer, permission to appeal will not be granted no matter how faulty the reasoning may have been.[568] This assumes that the tribunal gave sufficient reasons for the court to consider the question of law in issue. It should be contrasted with the situation where the tribunal gives no reasons or insufficient reasons to justify its conclusion. In the latter situation an application may be made to the court for permission to appeal coupled with a request for sufficient reasons.[569]

(d) Just and proper in all the circumstances

8–145   **Just and proper.** For the purposes of permission to appeal the court must also be satisfied that "despite the agreement of the parties to resolve the matter by arbitration, it is just and proper in all the circumstances for the court to determine the question of law".[570] The reason for this additional requirement has been explained as follows:

> " . . . we think it desirable that this factor should be specifically addressed by the Court when it is considering an application. It seems to us to be the basis on which the House of Lords acted as it did in *The Nema*. The Court should be satisfied that justice dictates that there should be an appeal and in considering what justice requires, the fact that the parties have agreed to arbitrate rather than litigate is an important and powerful factor".[571]

In order to oppose an application for permission to appeal on this ground, the proper procedure is to file evidence in support of the contention that it would not be "just and proper in the circumstances" to give permission to appeal and, if necessary, to ask for an oral hearing to develop this ground of opposition.[572]

---

[565] The expression is not defined in the Arbitration Act 1996. It may extend to the interpretation of a statutory provision.

[566] *Demco Investments & Commercial SA v SE Banken Forsakring Holding AB* [2005] 2 Lloyd's Rep. 650 at [52].

[567] *STX Pan Ocean Co Ltd v Ugland Bulk Transport AS, The Livanita* [2007] EWHC 1317.

[568] *Ipswich Borough Council v Fisons Plc* [1990] 1 All E.R. 730, CA.

[569] Section 70(4) of the Arbitration Act 1996: see para.8–113.

[570] Section 69(3)(d) of the Arbitration Act 1996. See *Keydon Estates v Western Power* [2004] EWHC 996 for a brief consideration of this requirement.

[571] Extract from the DAC report, para.290.

[572] *Icon Navigation Corp v Sinochem International Petroleum (Bahamas) Co* [2002] EWHC 2812, Moore Bick J.

Sweep-up discretion. The effect of this fourth condition for permission to   8–146
appeal is to give the court a final 'sweep-up' discretion which it can use to refuse
leave if the other three conditions are met. There is however precious little
guidance on the operation of the section. As a matter of practice, once the court
has wrestled with and overcome the "obviously wrong" or "serious doubt" test in
s.69(3)(c) then satisfaction of this condition is likely to follow as a matter of
course.[573]

(e) Application to court

Content of application. The application for permission to appeal against   8–147
the tribunal's decision on a question of law must in the arbitration claim form
"identify the question of law; and state the grounds on which the party alleges that
permission should be given".[574] This may not be easy where questions of fact and
law are mixed, but an attempt must be made. As the parties are not entitled to a
hearing,[575] it is particularly important that the grounds relied on for the application are carefully prepared. Depending on the particular case, such grounds
should include, for example, the fact that an identified point of law of public
importance is involved, with sufficient detail to enable the judge to make up his
mind without argument from the parties. Such other information should be
provided as will persuade the judge that it would be just and proper for the court
to determine the matter. However, "*Any written submission placed before the court in
support of an application for permission to appeal from findings in an arbitral award
should normally be capable of being read and digested by the judge within half an
hour . . . .*"[576]

Lengthy submissions which drew "fine lines" are at odds with both the spirit
of the legislation and the ethos of the Commercial Court.[577]

Extraneous evidence. The content of the written evidence in support of   8–148
and in opposition to the application are specified in the Arbitration Practice
Direction,[578] which must be followed strictly.[579] It is not normally appropriate to
refer to transcripts, submissions and evidence in the arbitration "but in addition
to the award the court should also receive a copy of any document referred to in

---

[573] The ground was not considered at all in *The Northern Pioneer CMA CGM SA v Beteiligungs KG* [2002] EWCA 1878.
[574] Practice Direction 62, para.12.1 which follows closely s.69(4) of the Arbitration Act 1996. The general procedure for applications to the court is described in paras 8–178 *et seq.* but an application for permission to appeal is subject to special provisions which are specified in PD 62, paras 12.2 and 12.3.
[575] Section 69(5) of the Arbitration Act 1996: see para.8–149.
[576] *The Northern Pioneer* (*CMA CGM SA v Beteiligungs KG* [2003] 1 Lloyd's Rep. 212) where the Court of Appeal criticised a lengthy submission.
[577] *The Northern Pioneer*, at [23].
[578] Practice Direction 62, paras 12.2 and 12.3.
[579] *Putrabali Ayamula v Epices and Another* [2003] 2 Lloyd's Rep. 700 where "exceptionally" the judge allowed argument of a ground that had not been identified in a response to the application for permission to appeal.

the award".[580] It should not include inadmissible evidence or argument about factual issues which the tribunal has decided.[581]

8–149 **Procedure on application for permission to appeal.** The court is required to determine the application for permission to appeal under s.69 on paper and without a hearing "unless it appears to the court that a hearing is required".[582] The parties are not entitled to demand a hearing. The Court of Appeal has said that it would be impossible to lay down guidelines for judges determining an application for an oral hearing under s.69(5) of the Act other than that they should seek to determine such applications "without unnecessary delay or expense."[583] This procedure differs from that of the previous legislation which permitted a brief argument.[584] The procedure may differ, however, where there are multiple applications.[585]

> "Although applications for leave to appeal under s. 69 are normally on paper without an oral hearing, the course adopted in the present case of hearing oral argument on the application for leave at the same hearing as for the s. 68 application is a sensible and a more . . . efficient approach, particularly [where] the underlying facts and legal submissions relevant to both applications are so related."[586]

8–150 **Multiple applications.** Nevertheless, attempts to get a hearing by raising in one application matters under s.69 as well as under ss.67 and/or s.68 have been criticised by the court.[587]

8–151 **Procedural issues.** Where the court decides that a hearing is required for the application for permission to appeal, one judge may hear that application and another will hear any appeal.[588] It is often more efficient however for the same judge to decide the appeal[589] particularly where there is some urgency, or where

---

[580] *Kershaw Mechanical Services Ltd v Kendrick Construction Ltd* [2006] EWHC 727 at [45]; *Walsall MBC v Beechdale Community Housing Association Ltd* [2005] EWHC, [17], [21], [22]; *Surefire Systems Ltd v Guardian ECL Ltd* [2005] B.L.R. 534, [22]; *HOK Sport Ltd (formerly Lobb Partnership Ltd) v Aintree Racecourse Co Ltd* [2003] Lloyd's Rep. P.N. 148.

[581] *Surefire Systems v Guardian ELC Ltd* [2005] EWHC 1860 for comments on an application for leave to appeal.

[582] Section 69(5) of the Arbitration Act 1996 and CPR r.69.10(4)(b). A hearing may take place when an application for permission to appeal is combined with an application to challenge the award under s.68 of the Act.

[583] *BLCT (13096) Ltd v J. Sainsbury Ltd* [2004] 2 P. & C.R. 3.

[584] *per* Lord Donaldson M.R. in *Ipswich Borough Council v Fisons Plc* [1990] 1 All E.R. 730 at 732, CA.

[585] See para.8–114.

[586] *Bulfracht (Cyprus) Ltd v Boneset Shipping Co Ltd (the "Pamphilos")* [2002] 2 Lloyd's Rep. 681, *per* Colman J.

[587] *Sinclair v Woods of Winchester* [2005] EWHC 1631; *Surefire v Guardian* [2005] EWHC 1850 (TCC) and *Plymouth v Jones* [2005] EWCH 2356 (TCC).

[588] This is a practice that developed in the Commercial Court before the Arbitration Act 1996: see *Hiscox v Outhwaite (No.2)* [1991] 3 All E.R. 143, CA.

[589] *The Agios Dimitrios* [2005] 1 Lloyd's Rep. 23, *per* Colman J. at [25] followed in *Miranos International v Voc Steel* [2005] EWHC 1812.

(despite the Lords' exhortations in *The "Nema"*) the matter has been argued in detail and the position is totally and unanswerably clear.[590]

Reasons for the grant or refusal of permission to appeal. If 8–152 permission to appeal is refused, the judge must give sufficient reasons to enable the losing party to understand why the judge has reached his decision. Such reasons can be very short.[591] At the very least an unsuccessful applicant for permission to appeal should be told which of the threshold tests in s.69(3) of the Act he failed. Usually it will not be necessary for the judge to go further and explain why the relevant test was not achieved.

Variety of orders. If permission is given and the court hears the appeal it 8–153 may by order confirm the award, which effectively means that the appeal is dismissed. On occasions the application for permission to appeal and the actual appeal, if permission is granted, will be heard together.[592] This would only happen if the court exercises its discretion to hold a hearing to consider the issue of permission. Even if a case is made out the court is not obliged to set aside the award, either in whole or in part, but may vary it[593] or may remit it to the tribunal in whole or in part for reconsideration in the light of the court's determination.[594] Indeed the court is directed not to "exercise its power to set aside an award, in whole or in part, unless it is satisfied that it would be inappropriate to remit the matters in question to the tribunal for reconsideration".[595] The court may require the appellant to provide security for the costs of any appeal[596] or order that any money payable under the award shall be brought into court or otherwise secured pending the determination of the appeal.[597]

Scope of discretion. It is apparent from what is said in the previous 8–154 paragraph that s.69(7) of the Act gives the court a measure of discretion when it

[590] *Brandeis (Brokers) v Black* [2001] 2 All E.R. (Comm) 980; *Hiscox v Outhwaite (No.2)* [1991] 3 All E.R. 143, CA; and *The "TFL Prosperity"* [1982] 1 Lloyd's Rep. 617. This situation will only occur where the court requires a hearing (see s.69(5) of the Arbitration Act 1996).

[591] Practice Direction, para.12.5. The change to previous practice of not giving reasons for refusal of permission to appeal was required by virtue of Art.6 of the Convention for the Protection of Human Rights and Fundamental Freedoms, as incorporated into English law by the Human Rights Act 1998. See *North Range Shipping Ltd v Seatrans Corp* [2002] 1 W.L.R. 2397; *Northern Pioneer* at [20].

[592] This procedure was adopted in *Miranos International Trading Inc v VOC Steel Services BV* [2005] EWHC 1812.

[593] In *Fence Gate Ltd v NEL Construction* (December 5, 2001) QBD (T&CC), H.H. Judge Thornton Q.C. varied an order for costs made by the arbitrator. A variation to the arbitrator's award was also made in *Galliford (UK) Ltd v Aldi Stores* (March 8, 2000) QBD (T&CC) H.H. Judge Bowsher Q.C.

[594] Section 69(7) of the Arbitration Act 1996. See, e.g. *Marc Rich Agricultural Trading SA v Agrimex Ltd* (April 6, 2000).

[595] Section 69(7) of the Arbitration Act 1996.

[596] Section 70(6) of the Arbitration Act 1996 which also provides that the appeal may be dismissed if an order for security is not complied with. See para.8–206 for discussion.

[597] Section 70(7) of the Arbitration Act 1996, which also provides that the court may direct that the appeal be dismissed if such an order is not complied with. See para.8–208 for discussion.

comes to deciding what order is most appropriate to give effect to its decision on an appeal against an arbitration award. That discretion does not, however, allow the court to take into account matters outside the scope of the appeal itself.[598] Where such matters do arise, the proper procedure suggested is to oppose the application for leave to appeal, file evidence in support of the matter and request an oral hearing. It is usually too late to raise the matter at the hearing of the appeal, although in order to avoid serious injustice, the court might be justified in reopening a decision giving permission to appeal.[599]

(f) Appeal to Court of Appeal

8–155	**Approach of the court.** Although the judge's decision on the application for permission to appeal against an arbitral award should usually be final, there are two possible means of appeal to the Court of Appeal. The first is against a grant or refusal of permission to appeal.[600] The second is against any decision of the court that hears an appeal on a question of law. In both cases permission of the court making the decision is ostensibly required (subject to the comments below in this paragraph), and in the second case the court must be of the view "that the question [of law concerned] is one of general importance or is one which for some other special reason[601] should be considered by the Court of Appeal".[602] Despite the clear language of s.69(8) the Court of Appeal can now override the judge's decision to refuse leave in certain cases.

8–156	**Meaning of "the court".** Permission of the court is required to appeal from a decision of the court made under s.69(8) of the Act.[603] It had been thought that reference to "the court" under both sections was to the court which made the order[604] and that in the absence of such an order from that court the Court of Appeal could not consider the matter. The former position was stated as follows, "Parliament has made it completely clear that in this respect the decision of the judge is to be final, unless the judge himself considers that there are matters which are fit to be considered by the Court of Appeal so as itself to grant leave".[605]

---

[598] *Ican Navigation Corp v Sinochem International Petroleum (Bahamas) Co* [2003] I All E.R. (Comm) 405, where the court refused to take account of the possibility of the tribunal having committed an irregularity if the court allowed the appeal.

[599] *Ican Navigation, supra, per* Moore Bick J.

[600] Section 69(6) of the Arbitration Act 1996. An appeal against the judge's refusal of leave was heard and dismissed in *CMA CGM SA v Beteiligungs KG and Another (The Northern Pioneer)* [2003] Lloyd's Rep. 212.

[601] It is doubtful whether the amount at stake would by itself constitute a special reason. Compare *British Gas Plc v Dollar Land Holdings Plc* [1992] 12 E.G. 141 with *Prudential Assurance Co Ltd v 99 Bishopsgate Ltd* [1992] 03 E.G. 120. The fact that the judge has differed from the views of an experienced arbitrator cannot be a special reason for these purposes: *The "Nicki R"* [1984] 2 Lloyd's Rep. 186. See also *The "Pera"* [1985] 2 Lloyd's Rep. 103.

[602] Section 69(8) of the Arbitration Act 1996, which replaced with some modifications s.1(7) of the Arbitration Act 1979.

[603] Sections 42(5) and 44(7) of the Arbitration Act 1996.

[604] Because of the definition of court in s.105(1) of the Arbitration Act 1996.

[605] *Virdee v Virdi* [2003] EWCA Civ 41.

Excess of jurisdiction. However, two separate lines of decisions of the   8–157
Court of Appeal have weakened the proposition that the judicial decision taker at
first instance is the only competent body to grant leave to appeal from his own
decision. Following *Cetelem v Roust*,[606] which dealt with the identical provision in
relation to appeals under s.44(7) of the Act, the distinction is now to be drawn
between appeals to orders which the judge had jurisdiction to make, although it is
alleged he erred in fact or in law in making the order, and orders which he had no
jurisdiction to make. The Court of Appeal can give permission to appeal in respect
of the latter type of orders, where the judge at first instance has no jurisdiction to
make the order in question, even where the judge himself has refused leave to
appeal. As the Court of Appeal noted in *Cetelem*:

> "So long as the judge could make the order in the sense that it was within the jurisdiction
> specified in the relevant section, the buck stops with him. The order is made under the
> section. It is only where the judge makes an order which is outwith his jurisdiction, so
> that he could not (as opposed to should not) make it, that s.44(7) and other similar
> provisions do not prevent an appeal to this court."[607]

Quite how easy this distinction is to operate in practice remains to be seen. In
Lesotho Highlands v Impreglio,[608] the House of Lords when considering a challenge
under s.68 of the Arbitration Act 1996 rejected an argument that an error as to the
currency of an award constituted an excess of powers. However, this matter was
argued strongly on both sides all the way up to the House of Lords and the
concepts are elusive. The field of administrative law is full of examples of the
difficulty in drawing a distinction between a simple error (within jurisdiction) and
acting outside of jurisdiction.[609]

Orders on preliminary points. In a closely related decision, the Court of   8–158
Appeal has held in respect of an appeal based on a preliminary point about
whether s.69 applies at all (because of a question whether a valid exclusion
agreement had been entered into) the Court of Appeal does have jurisdiction to
grant leave in respect of such questions.[610] The Court of Appeal canvassed but did
not decide the possibility that the opt out wording in s.44(1), "unless the parties
otherwise agree" may also be a preliminary point as to whether that section applies
at all.

Residual jurisdiction regarding unfairness. The Court of Appeal   8–159
also has a residual jurisdiction to set aside the judge's decision in the case of
unfairness relating to the process of the judge's decision. The distinction is

---

[606] *Cetelem SA v Roust Holdings Ltd* [2005] 1 W.L.R. 3555.
[607] *Cetelem SA v Roust Holdings Ltd* [2005] 1 W.L.R. 3555, *per* Clarke L.J., at [25].
[608] [2006] 1 A.C. 221.
[609] *Pearlman v Keepers and Governors of Harrow School* [1978] 3 W.L.R 736 at 743: "The distinction
between an error which entails absence of jurisdiction and an error made within jurisdiction is
fine . . . it is rapidly being eroded".
[610] *Sukuman Ltd v Commonwealth Secretariat* [2007] EWCA 243; [2007] Bus. L.R. 1075, [27]–[34].

therefore to be drawn between appeals from the judge's refusal to give leave on the merits where, save for cases where there was no jurisdiction for the underlying decision, there is no appeal and cases where, "*the judge's refusal of leave to appeal was arbitrary or unfair: or was the product of a failure of intellectual engagement with the arguments put before him; or amounted actually or metaphorically to the absence of a decision on the issue*".[611] In such "exceptionally rare cases"[612] the Court of Appeal can of its own motion consider appeals even where leave of the first instance judge has not been given. The Court of Appeal has also rejected the argument that this residual discretion is contrary to Article 6 of the European Convention of Human Rights.[613]

The sub-section also provides that a decision of the court on an appeal under this section shall be treated as a judgment of the court for the purposes of a further appeal, although it does not appear that these words in the first sentence of s.69(8) make any practical difference to the court's consideration of the question of the right to appeal.[614]

8–160　**Worthy of consideration by Court of Appeal.** *The "Nema"* guidelines as enacted by s.69(3) of the Act do not apply as such to applications for permission to appeal to the Court of Appeal.[615] Rather, the test for the judge deciding the matter is whether the question of law is worthy of consideration by the Court of Appeal. This can include situations where there are known to be different schools of thought on an issue and the Court of Appeal given its chance, might support one or the other of them.[616]

8–161　**Terms for appealing.** The court may impose such terms as it considers appropriate on the granting of permission[617] to appeal to the Court of Appeal. These terms may include security for costs or a requirement that any money payable under the award shall be brought into court.[618]

---

[611] *CGU International Insurance Plc and Others v Astra Zeneca Insurance Co Ltd* [2006] EWCA 1340, *per* Rix L.J. at [98], approving *North Range Shipping Ltd v Seatrans Shipping Corp* [2002] 1 W.L.R. 2397. Approved in *Kazakhstan v Istil Group Inc* [2007] W.L. 1425725, para.11. See also *ASM Shipping Ltd of India v TTMI Ltd* [2006] EWCA 1341, a decision under s.68(4), which is in similar terms as s.69(8).

[612] *CGU International Insurance Plc and Others v Astra Zeneca Insurance Co Ltd* [2006] EWCA 1340, *per* Rix L.J. at [100].

[613] *Kazakhstan v Istil Group Inc* [2007] W.L. 1425725, following *CGU International Insurance Plc and Others v Astra Zeneca Insurance Co Ltd* [2006] EWCA 1340.

[614] These words are also used as used in ss.32(6) and 45(6); the other two instances where the court is given jurisdiction to rule *de novo* on a substantive issue itself, rather than reviewing a decision of an arbitral tribunal. The wording is derived from s.2(3) of the Arbitration Act 1979 Act, which provided that a decision by the court on a preliminary point of law was "deemed to be a judgment of the court" within the meaning of s.27 of the Supreme Court of Judicature (Consolidation) Act 1925.

[615] *Geogas SA v Trammo Gas Ltd (The "Baleares")* [1991] 1 Lloyd's Rep. 349, CA, [1991] 2 W.L.R. 794. Cf. *The "Roachbank"* [1988] 2 Lloyd's Rep. 337.

[616] Paragraphs 58–60. Citing with approval Sir John Donaldson in *The Antaios* [1983] 1 W.L.R. 1362 at 1369–1370, but qualifying the test laid down in *The Nema*.

[617] Section 70(8) of the Arbitration Act 1996.

[618] Section 70(8) of the Arbitration Act 1996, replacing s.1(4) of the Arbitration Act 1979. See, e.g. *Nature Conservatory Council for England v Deller* [1992] 43 E.G. 137.

8. ORDERS IN RESPECT OF CHALLENGES AND APPEALS

Introduction. The Arbitration Act 1996 empowers the court to make orders   8–162
in connection with an application challenging an award[619] or an appeal against the
award.[620] If the court is inclined to grant such an application or permission to
appeal but considers that terms should be imposed it may order the applicant or
appellant to provide security for costs[621] or to bring into court any amount ordered
to be paid by an award.[622]

In the case of a successful challenge to substantive jurisdiction under s.67(3),
the court has no express power to remit the award but can only vary the award or
set it aside in whole or in part. However, the Court of Appeal has decided that in
such case the tribunal is not *functus officio* and the arbitration may in appropriate
cases carry on or revive as necessary, even if the tribunal had purported to issue
a final award on the merits.[623] In the other two cases (i.e. challenge for serious
irregularity or appeal on a question of law) the presumption is remission of the
award; the Arbitration Act states that the court shall not exercise its more
extensive powers (e.g. to set aside) unless it is satisfied that it would be inappropriate to remit the matters to the tribunal for reconsideration.[624] Whether it
would be inappropriate will depend on the particular irregularity, but some
guidance can be obtained from the decisions of the courts, as will be indicated in
the following paragraphs.[625] The prerogative orders applicable in judicial review
proceedings are not available against an arbitral tribunal.[626]

Remission of the award. The court has a discretion to remit an award to   8–163
the tribunal for reconsideration under the Arbitration Act 1996,[627] although the
exercise of that discretion is constrained by the need to preserve the finality of
arbitration awards.[628] Other factors may be taken into consideration including the

---

[619] Arbitration Act 1996, ss.67(3) and 68(3).
[620] Arbitration Act 1996, s.69(7).
[621] Section 70(6) of the Arbitration Act 1996.
[622] Section 70(7) of the Arbitration Act 1996.
[623] *Hussmann (Europe) Ltd v Pharaon* [2003] 1 All E.R. (Comm) 879.
[624] Arbitration Act 1996, ss.68(3) and 69(7).
[625] Some pre-1996 decisions are still useful in respect of remission and setting aside.
[626] *R v National Joint Council for the Craft of Dental Technicians (Disputes Committee), Ex p. Neate*
[1953] 1 Q.B. 704, CA. As explained in *Bremer Vulkan Schiffbau Und Maschinenfabrik v South India
Shipping Corp* [1981] 1 All E.R. 289 at 295–296, the jurisdiction of the court to supervise the
conduct of an arbitration is confined to exercising its powers under the arbitration legislation
(subject of course to the vexed issue of the exercise of inherent jurisdiction: see para.7–003
above).
[627] This was done in *Marc Rich Agriculture Trading SA v Agrimex Ltd* (April 6, 2000), Langley J. See
ss.68(3)(a) to 69(7)(c) of the Arbitration Act 1996 which replaced s.22 of the Arbitration Act 1950.
They apply respectively where there has been a serious irregularity or an error of law in the award.
This was also done in *Louis Dreyfus Trading Ltd v Reliance Trading Ltd* [2004] 2 Lloyd's Rep. 243
for the tribunal to reconsider quantum of damages.
[628] See, e.g. *Secretary of State for the Environment v Reed International Plc* [1994] 06 E.G. 137.

need to express clear findings in respect of the relevant issues.[629] Despite finding that two awards were made following serious irregularities[630] affecting both the proceedings and the awards, the court in *RC Pillar & Sons v Edwards*[631] decided to remit the awards to the tribunal in order to avoid serious injustice to at least one of the parties. An award will not be remitted, however, if doing so would serve no useful purpose, for example because it would be inevitable that the award would be varied as proposed by the court,[632] or there is no evidence on which the tribunal could reach any decision other than the one already made, in other words where the conclusion reached by the court is now the one which adopting the proper principles would have to be adopted by the tribunal.[633] Nor will an award be remitted unless there is something further for the tribunal to consider and upon which its judgment could be exercised afresh.[634]

Where the irregularity cannot be cured, the court may set the award aside. This may occur, for example, where the integrity of the tribunal is impugned.[635]

The remission of an award does not deprive it of legal effect. It continues to operate so as to make the tribunal *"functus officio"*, unable to alter the award, on those matters which were not remitted.[636]

8–164   **Setting aside the award.** The Arbitration Act 1996 empowers the court to set aside an award, in whole or in part, upon hearing an application to challenge the tribunal's substantive jurisdiction.[637] Where the ground for challenge is a serious irregularity[638] or the application is in the nature of an appeal against the award on a point of law,[639] the court will only set aside the award (in whole or in part) if it is satisfied that it would be inappropriate to remit it to the tribunal for reconsideration.[640] Thus, where a partial award was made and subsequent events or a change of circumstances had rendered the award unduly advantageous to one party, it was not appropriate to remit that award to the tribunal for further

[629] *Pentonville Shipping Ltd v Transfield Shipping Inc (the Johnny K)* [2006] EWHC 134.
[630] Serious irregularity is defined in s.68(2) of the Arbitration Act 1996. See paras 8–072 *et seq.*
[631] *RC Pillar & Sons Ltd v Edwards* (January 11, 2001) H.H. Judge Thornton Q.C. See also *Miranos v Voc Steel* [2005] EWHC 1812 at [36] and [37].
[632] *Skanska Construction v. Anglo-Amsterdam Corp Ltd* [2002] 84 Con L.R 100. *Vrinera Marin v Eastern Rich Operator (the Vakis T)* [2004] 2 Lloyd's Rep. 465.
[633] *Covington Marine Corp v Xiamen Shipbuilding Industry Co Ltd* [2005] EWHC 2912, [67]; *Montedipe SpA and Another v JTP-RO Jugotanker (The "Jordan Nicolov")* [1990] 2 Lloyd's Rep. 11.
[634] *Glencore Grain Ltd v Flacker Shipping (the "Happy Day")* [2001] 1 Lloyd's Rep. 754 and *Islamic Republic of Iran Shipping Lines v Zannis Compania Naviera SA (The "Tzelepi")* [1991] 2 Lloyd's Rep. 265. See also *Equitorial Traders Ltd v Louis Dreyfus Trading Ltd* [2002] 2 Lloyd's Rep. 638 where the award could not be saved. *Covington Marine Corp v Xiamen Shipping Industry Co Ltd* [2005] EWHC 292 at [67].
[635] *David Taylor & Son Ltd v Barnet Trading Co* [1953] 1 W.L.R. 562. In this case the umpire apparently ignored evidence of illegality of the underlying contract.
[636] *Carter v Harold Simpson Associates* [2004] 2 Lloyd's Rep. 512, PC.
[637] Arbitration Act 1996, s.67(3)(c). For illegality see para.8–031.
[638] Arbitration Act 1996, s.68(3).
[639] Arbitration Act 1996, s.69(7).
[640] Arbitration Act, 1996, ss.68(3) and 69(7).

consideration. Rather, the tribunal should take the new matters into account when making its final award.[641]

Award of no effect. In the case of a serious irregularity under s.68, the court is expressly empowered by the Arbitration Act 1996 to declare the award to be of no effect, in whole or in part.[642] If the tribunal still retains jurisdiction in relation to other matters,[643] it may make a further award within its jurisdiction.[644] It also appears that in the case of lack of substantive jurisdiction under s.67, the court may declare an award to be of no effect, even though such facility does not appear in the list of orders which the court may make under s.67(3). However, the Court of Appeal has decided that the distinction between an order setting aside an award and one declaring it to be of no effect is one without a difference.[645] In such circumstances, the court may permit the tribunal to make a further award in circumstances where it would otherwise have been *functus officio*.[646]

8-165

Grounds for remission, setting aside, etc. The Arbitration Act 1996 does not specify the circumstances in which the court should remit an award to the tribunal, but it does indicate when that power may be available. Although the courts had previously sought to limit the categories of cases in which the power to remit could be exercised,[647] it is now established that the power is a general one.[648] Provided that the conditions for the application or an appeal are fulfilled, the court has power to remit, although in exercising its discretion the court will take account of the relevant circumstances of each particular case. For a discussion on the circumstances in which an award may be remitted to the tribunal see para. 8-163.

8-166

Fresh evidence. If fresh evidence comes to light subsequent to the making of a final award, the tribunal may be unable to take account of it because the tribunal's duties will have been completed.[649] Although there is power to make an additional award, that power is limited to a claim "which was presented to the tribunal but was not dealt with in the award".[650] Given the limits imposed on court intervention by the Arbitration Act 1996,[651] the court apparently lacks power in the

8-167

---

[641] *BMBF v Harland and Wolff Shipbuilding* [2001] 2 All E.R. (Comm) 385, CA.

[642] Section 68(3)(c) of the Arbitration Act 1996.

[643] Where the award is a partial award, for example, the tribunal would still retain jurisdiction in relation to the remaining issues.

[644] *Petroships v Petec Trading (the "Petro Ranger")* [2001] 2 Lloyd's Rep. 348 at 351.

[645] *Hussmann (Europe) Ltd v Pharaon* [2003] EWCA Civ 266; [2003] 1 All E.R. (Comm) 879.

[646] *Hussmann (Europe) Ltd v Pharaon* [2003] EWCA Civ 266; [2003] 1 All E.R. (Comm) 879.

[647] Four categories of cases were identified in *Montgomery Jones & Co v Liebenthal & Co* (1898) 78 L.T. 406, but not all of them still apply.

[648] See *King v Thomas McKenna Ltd* [1991] 1 All E.R. 653 at 660, CA.

[649] See para.6-166 above.

[650] Section 57(3)(b) of the Arbitration Act 1996.

[651] As a result of the repeal of Pt 1 of the Arbitration Act 1950 and the terms of ss.67, 68 or 69 of the Arbitration Act 1996, the court does not seem to retain its right to remit where fresh evidence emerges and the inherent jurisdiction retained by s.81(1) of the Act does not seem to apply here.

absence of serious irregularity[652] to overcome the difficulty by remitting the award to the tribunal for reconsideration in the light of the fresh evidence.[653]

8–168 Further requirements. Even when serious irregularity can be established, the party seeking to challenge the award[654] must at least show that (i) he did not have the evidence at the time of the arbitration (ii) he could not have got it at the time of the arbitration by the exercise of due diligence (iii) had he had it, it would be likely to have had a substantial effect upon the result of the arbitration and (iv) where appropriate, that he had no opportunity to ask for the tribunal to delay issuing the award while he considered whether it was possible to get evidence of the type which he now seeks to introduce.[655]

8–169 Accidental error. Unless the tribunal admits an irregularity,[656] the court no longer has a general power to order remission where the tribunal has made an accidental error in an award[657] which cannot be corrected by the tribunal. When the error consists of a failure to deal with a material issue which has caused or will cause substantial injustice to the applicant,[658] the court may remit the matter to the tribunal for consideration.

8–170 Role of tribunal. The tribunal itself usually has power to correct a clerical error or an accidental slip or omission, or to remove an ambiguity in an award,[659] so the circumstances in which the court will be called upon to order remission for accidental error will be exceptional. This may occur, however, where the tribunal does not comment on the existence or otherwise of the alleged error and the court is satisfied that there is a serious irregularity causing substantial injustice.[660] In this situation however, the applicant may have lost the right to object to the award as if he did not exhaust available recourse to the tribunal.[660a]

---

[652] See para.8–103 above.

[653] *Burnard v Wainwright* (1850) 19 L.J. Q.B. 423; *Re Keighley, Maxsted & Co and Bryan Durant & Co* [1893] 1 Q.B. 405; *Sprague v Allen & Sons* (1899) 15 T.L.R. 150. These decisions were based on the previous law which has been repealed but they probably reflect the position under the current law.

[654] The applicant would have to bring the application under s.68 of the Arbitration Act 1996 and show that there was some irregularity of the kind described in s.68(2)(g) or (i).

[655] In the context of s.68, see *DDT Trucks of North America Ltd v DDT Holdings Ltd* [2007] EWHC 1542, [22], [23]. *The "Stainless Patriot"* [1979] 1 Lloyd's Rep. 589. See also *EM Dower & Co v Corrie, MacColl & Son Ltd* (1925) 22 Lloyd's Rep. 256; *The Ben Line Steamers Ltd v Compagnie Optorg of Saigon* (1936) 42 Com. Cas. 113; *The "Eleftheria Niki"* [1980] 2 Lloyd's Rep. 252.

[656] Section 68(2)(i) of the Arbitration Act 1996 defines such an admission as a serious irregularity, which gives the court power to remit, among others. See s.68(3) of the Act.

[657] *Mutual Shipping Corp v Bayshore Shipping Co Ltd (The "Montan")* [1985] 1 Lloyd's Rep. 189 [1985] 1 W.L.R. 625. The error was admitted in this case.

[658] This additional requirement is necessary to comply with the terms of s.68(2) of the Arbitration Act 1996.

[659] Section 57 of the Arbitration Act 1996 which replaces s.17 of the Arbitration Act 1950. See further paras 6–167 and 6–173.

[660] Section 68 of the Arbitration Act 1996: see para.8–072.

[660a] See paras 8–064, 8–109 and 8–122.

Admitted error. Where the tribunal admits an error in the award (or that something was wrong with the conduct of the proceedings) there will be an irregularity, and if the court considers that the applicant has or will suffer substantial injustice, it may remit the award to the tribunal for correction or vary the award itself.[661] 8–171

Who may apply? The tribunal is no longer entitled to apply to the court to have an award remitted to it in order to correct an error in an award,[662] although it can do so itself under s.57 of the 1996 Act. The application for remission based on serious irregularity is only available to a party to the arbitral proceedings.[663] 8–172

Combined application. An application to set aside the award may be made in conjunction with an application to remove the tribunal and appoint a replacement.[664] An application to set aside is often made in the alternative to an application to remit the award to the tribunal because, unless there is a challenge to the substantive jurisdiction of the tribunal, the court has a discretion which remedy to apply in the event of a successful application.[665] 8–173

Procedural orders. Remission is available only in respect of an award: it cannot be granted in respect of a pre-award ruling.[666] There is no inherent jurisdiction in the court to remit in order to correct procedural errors in the course of the reference or otherwise.[667] 8–174

The tribunal's jurisdiction on remission. When a final award is made the tribunal completes its duties and its jurisdiction over the matters referred comes to an end.[668] The effect of the award being remitted is to confer further jurisdiction on the tribunal, but only so that it may reconsider the matters remitted. If the tribunal purports to decide matters which have not been remitted it will be acting without jurisdiction and the award will once again be capable of challenge, this time on s.67 as well as s.68 grounds.[669] 8–175

---

[661] Section 68(2)(i) of the Arbitration Act 1996.
[662] The observations made about an arbitrator's right to apply to the court in *Mutual Shipping Corp v Bayshore Shipping Co Ltd (The "Montan")* [1985] 1 Lloyd's Rep. 189; [1985] 1 W.L.R. 625 are no longer good law.
[663] This is apparent from the opening words in s.68(1) of the Arbitration Act 1996.
[664] Sections 24(1) and 27 of the Arbitration Act 1996. This was done in *Kalmneft v Glencore International* [2002] 1 All E.R. 76 although the applications in that case were dismissed.
[665] Section 68(3) of the Arbitration Act 1996, replacing the Arbitration Act 1950, s.25(2). See para.8–153.
[666] *Three Valleys Water Committee v Binnie & Partners* [1990] 52 B.L.R. 42.
[667] The court's powers are generally limited by the Arbitration Act 1996, although a limited jurisdiction is preserved by s.81(1) of the Act.
[668] See para.6–166.
[669] *Fidelitas Shipping Co Ltd v v/o Exportchleb* [1965] 1 Lloyd's Rep. 223 at 231. See also *Glencore International AG v Beogradska Plovidba (The "Avala")* [1996] 2 Lloyd's Rep. 311.

8–176   Effect of court order. The Arbitration Act 1996 provides that the following provisions have effect where the court makes an order under s.67, 68 or 69 with respect to an award[670]:

- where the award is varied, the variation has effect as part of the tribunal's award[671];

- where the award is remitted to the tribunal, in whole or in part, for reconsideration, the tribunal shall make a fresh award in respect of the matters remitted within three months of the date of the order for remission or such longer or shorter period as the court may direct[672]; and

- where the award is set aside or declared to be of no effect, in whole or in part, the court may also order that any provision that an award is a condition precedent to the bringing of legal proceedings in respect of a matter to which the arbitration agreement applies, is of no effect as regards the subject matter of the award or, as the case may be, the relevant part of the award.[673]

The last provision is intended to deal with the situation created where the arbitration agreement contains a *Scott v Avery* clause.[674]

8–177   Limitation Acts. The Arbitration Act 1996 provides that the Limitation Acts[675] apply to arbitral proceedings as they apply to legal proceedings.[676] This provision corresponds to the Limitation Act 1980 which provides that the 1980 Act and any other limitation enactment shall apply to arbitrations as they apply to actions in the High Court.[677]

In computing the limitation period for commencing proceedings (including arbitral proceedings) in respect of a dispute where the court has ordered an award to be set aside or declared to be of no effect, the court may exclude the period between the commencement of the arbitration and the date of its order.[678] Further, in determining for the purposes of the Limitation Acts when a cause of action accrued, the Arbitration Act 1996 states that any provision that an award is a condition precedent to the bringing of legal proceedings in respect of a matter to which an arbitration agreement applies shall be disregarded.[679]

---

[670] Arbitration Act 1996, s.71(1).
[671] Arbitration Act 1996, s.71(2).
[672] Arbitration Act 1996, s.71(3).
[673] Arbitration Act 1996, s.71(4).
[674] For *Scott v Avery* clauses, see para.2–022.
[675] The Limitation Acts mean in England and Wales, the Limitation Act 1980, the Foreign Limitation Periods Act 1984 "and any other enactment (whenever passed) relating to the limitation of actions", s.13(4)(a) of the Arbitration Act 1996. See para.7–080.
[676] Section 13(1) of the Arbitration Act 1996. See *Henry Boot v Alstom* [2005] 1 W.L.R. 3850 at 3876.
[677] Section 34(1) of the Limitation Act 1980.
[678] Arbitration Act 1996, s.13(2). See paras 5–021 *et seq.* and 7–080.
[679] Arbitration Act 1996, s.13(3). For *Scott v Avery* clauses generally, see paras 2–022 and 7–052.

9. PROCEDURE FOR ARBITRATION APPLICATIONS

Introduction. The court in which an arbitration claim can and should be   8–178
commenced is specified in the High Court and County Court (Allocation of
Arbitration Proceedings) Order 1996.[680] The effect of that Order may be summarised as follows:

- An arbitration claim to stay court proceedings under s.9 of the Arbitration
  Act, 1996 must be commenced in the court in which the proceedings are
  pending[681];

- A claim to enforce an arbitration award under ss.66 or 101(2) of the Act may
  be commenced in the High Court or in any county court[682];

- Subject to the above two cases, all arbitration claims must be commenced and
  taken in the High Court or the Central London County Court.[683]

The lists in which an arbitration claim form may be issued in the High Court
or the Central London County Court are specified later in this chapter.[684]

Criteria for transfer between court. The criteria for the transfer of   8–179
arbitration applications from one court to another are:

- the financial substance of the dispute referred to arbitration, including the
  value of any claim or counterclaim;

- the nature of the dispute referred to arbitration (for example, whether it
  arises out of a commercial or business transaction or relates to engineering,
  building or other construction work);

- whether the proceedings are otherwise important, and in particular whether
  they raise questions of importance to persons who are not parties;

- the balance of convenience points to having the proceedings taken in the
  Central London County Court Mercantile List; and

- where the financial substance of the dispute exceeds £200,000 the proceedings shall be taken in the High Court unless the proceedings do not raise
  questions of general importance to persons who are not parties.[685]

Contents of this part. This part of the chapter will comment principally on   8–180
arbitration applications made under the Arbitration Act 1996. It will begin with

[680] SI 1996/3215 (L.16), a copy of which is included in Appendix 1.
[681] Article 3 of the above-mentioned Order. See also PD 62.3, para.2.1.
[682] Article 4 of the above-mentioned Order.
[683] Articles 2 and 5 of the above-mentioned Order. See PD 62.3, para2.
[684] See para.8–188.
[685] These criteria appear in art.5(4) of the above-named statutory instrument.

the relevant rules of court and continue by commenting on the procedure for most arbitration applications.[686] Mention will then be made of those applications that have special provisions.[687] It will conclude with the procedure for applications to enforce an award,[688] to set aside an enforcement order[689] and registration of an award.[690]

8–181 **Rules of court.** In order to give effect to the Arbitration Act 1996, amendments were made to the court rules. In particular, the former rule of court was completely redrafted[691] and is now to be found in CPR Pt 62 and the Arbitration Practice Direction. CPR Pt 62 and the Arbitration Practice Direction[691a] apply to arbitration business commenced both in the High Court and in the Central London County Court Mercantile List.[692–694]

8–182 **Application of other rules of court.** Other rules of court apply to arbitration claims, such as those relating to service out of the jurisdiction,[695] depending on the court in which the arbitration claim form is issued or transferred.[696]

8–183 **Form of application.** Subject to the transitional provisions, an arbitration claim form must be made substantially in the form set out in the Arbitration Practice Direction[697] and contain the information specified in that direction.[698] Among other things, it must specify the persons on whom the form is to be served, stating their role in the arbitration and whether they are defendants or state that the application is made without notice.[699] This multi-purpose form will be used for all applications in respect of arbitrations to which the Arbitration Act 1996 applies.[700]

---

[686] See paras 8–181 *et seq.*
[687] See paras 8–210 *et seq.*
[688] See paras 8–219 *et seq.*
[689] See para.8–224.
[690] See para.8–225.
[691] The Rules of the Supreme Court (Amendment) Order 1996 (SI 1996/2892), which came into force on January 31, 1997, and has since been amended, replaced RSC, Ord.73 with CPR Pt 62. See Appendix 1.
[691a] See Appendix 1.
[692–694] See PD 62.3, para.2.3.
[695] CPR Pt 6.24–29—See CPR r.62.5(3) and para.8–191.
[696] CPR Pt 58 and PD 58, supplemented by the Admiralty and Commercial Courts Guide (7th Edition, 2006) apply to claims in the Commercial Court of the Queen's Bench Division of the High Court; CPR Pt 59 and PD 59 and guide apply to claims in the Mercantile Courts; and CPR Pt 60 and PD apply to claims in the Technology and Construction Court.
[697] Practice Direction 62, para.2.2 specifies that an arbitration claim form must be in the form set out at Appendix A to the Practice Direction.
[698] See CPR r.62.4(1) for the information required.
[699] CPR r.62.4(1)(f).
[700] See PD 62, para.2.2.

Content of arbitration claim form. Notes accompany the arbitration   8–184
claim form to assist in its completion.[701] Apart from the formal requirements,[702]
the form must:

- include a concise statement of the remedy claimed and any questions on
  which the decision of the court is sought[703];

- give details of any arbitration award challenged, identifying which part or
  points of the award are challenged and the grounds for the challenge[704];

- show that any statutory requirements have been met[705];

- specify under which section of the Act the claim is made[706];

- identify against which (if any) defendant a costs order is sought[707]; and

- specify the persons on whom the claim form is to be served or state that the
  claim is made without notice and the grounds relied on.[708]

Specify subject of challenge. The grounds of challenge in the claim form   8–185
must be specific enough to permit the court and the other party to know exactly
what is the subject of challenge. Timely permission of the court is needed to add
further grounds of challenge or to rely on evidence not served with the claim
form.[709]

Statement of truth. A statement of truth must be signed by the applicant   8–186
or his solicitor. A witness statement may be filed in support of the arbitration
claim, in which case both documents must be served together.

Details of agreement or permission. Where the application is made   8–187
with the written agreement of all the other parties to the arbitral proceedings or
with the permission of the tribunal, the claim form must also give details of the
agreement or permission and exhibit a copy of the written agreement or any
written permission.[710] The witness statement should be filed and a copy served
with the arbitration claim form.

---

[701] The notes are reproduced with the arbitration claim form in Appendix 1.

[702] Formal requirements include the names of the parties and the court in which the claim is to be filed.

[703] CPR r.62.4(1)(a).

[704] CPR r.62.4(1)(b). If the grounds for the challenge are not set out in the claim form, then leave will be needed to adduce grounds later. Such leave will not lightly be given: *Karl Leibinger v Stryker Trauma GmbH* [2006] EWHC 690.

[705] CPR r.62.4(1)(c)

[706] CPR r.62.4(1)(d)

[707] CPR r.62.4(1)(e)

[708] CPR r.62.4(1)(f).

[709] *Karl Leibinger v Stryker Trauma GmbH* [2006] EWHC 690 at [27]–[31].

[710] CPR r.62.15(5)(c).

8–188   Issue of an arbitration claim form. Except for applications to stay legal proceedings[711] an arbitration claim form may be issued at any of the following courts:

- Admiralty and Commercial Registry at the Royal Courts of Justice in London, in which case it will be entered in the Commercial List;

- Technology and Construction Court Registry at St Dunstan's House, London, where it will be entered in the TCC List;

- District Registry of the High Court where a Mercantile Court has been established, in which case the arbitration application will be entered into the Mercantile List[712];

- District Registry of the High Court with the arbitration claim form marked "Technology and Construction Court" which will be entered in the TCC List;

- Central London County Court, in which case the arbitration claim form will be entered in the Mercantile List.[713]

The judge in charge of the relevant list is empowered to transfer an arbitration application to another court or specialist list.[714]

8–189   Service of application to stay legal proceedings. An application notice seeking a stay of legal proceedings under s.9 of the Arbitration Act 1996 must be served[715] on the party bringing the relevant legal proceedings and on any other party to those proceedings.[716] Where another party to those proceedings has not given an address for service, CPR Pt 62 provides for service at his last known address or at a place where the application is likely to come to his attention.[717] Where there is a dispute about the validity or scope of the arbitration agreement, the court may "decide that question or give directions to enable it to be decided and may order the proceedings to be stayed pending its decision".[718]

8–190   Service within the jurisdiction of other arbitration applications. Any arbitration claim form must be served in accordance with CPR Pt 6,[719] unless an order is obtained for service by an alternative method.[720] For the

---

[711] An application to stay legal proceedings must be made in the court where the legal proceedings have been commenced. See paras 8–189 and 8–190 for service of such an application.
[712] There is a Mercantile Court in Birmingham, Bristol, Liverpool and Manchester.
[713] High Court and County Courts (Allocation of Arbitration Proceedings) Order 1996 (SI 1996/3215) which is to be read with PD 62, para.2.3.
[714] CPR Pts 30, 5 and r.62.3(4). See para.8–179 for the criteria for transfer.
[715] Service is to be effected in accordance with CPR Pts 6 and 2.
[716] CPR r.62.8(1).
[717] CPR r.62.8(2).
[718] CPR r.62.8(3). See para.7–025.
[719] CPR Pts 6 and 2 include service by first class post where there is an address for service within the jurisdiction.
[720] CPR Pts 6 and 8 mention an alternative method.

purpose of service within the jurisdiction an arbitration application is valid for one month unless extended by the court.[721]

Service out of the jurisdiction. Permission of the court is required for 8–191 service out of the jurisdiction of an arbitration claim form[722] on a party to an arbitration[723] and may be given where:

- the claimant seeks to challenge an award or appeal on a question of law arising out of an arbitration award made within the jurisdiction[724]; or

- the claim is made for an order in support of arbitration proceedings under s.44 of the Arbitration Act, 1996; or

- the claimant seeks some other remedy or requires a question to be decided by the court affecting an arbitration (whether started or not), an arbitration agreement or an arbitration award.[725]

It is implicit from CPR Part 62[726] that the court will only entertain a request for permission to serve an arbitration claim form out of the jurisdiction in respect of the relief specified in this paragraph.

Contents of witness statement. The claim form or witness statement in 8–192 support of an application for the grant of permission to serve an arbitration application outside the jurisdiction must:

- state the place or country where the person to be served is or may probably be found,[727] and

- state the grounds on which the application is made[728] in a way that will satisfy the court that the case is a proper one for service out of the jurisdiction.[729]

Application of CPR. CPR Pt 6 rr.24 to 29[730] will apply to the service of an 8–193 arbitration claim form under CPR Pt 62 as they apply to the service of any other

---

[721] CPR r.62.4(2).

[722] CPR r.62.5(1).

[723] CPR r.62.5 applies only to applications by and against parties to an arbitration, not to non-parties—see *Vale da Doce Novegacao v Shanghai Steel* [2000] 2 Lloyd's Rep. 1.

[724] The place where an award is treated as made is determined by s.53 of the Arbitration Act 1996: see para.6–050.

[725] In this last case, it is a requirement that the seat of the arbitration is or will be within the jurisdiction of the court or the conditions in s.2(4) of the Act are satisfied.

[726] CPR r.62.5(1).

[727] CPR r.62.5(2)(b).

[728] CPR r.62.5(2)(a).

[729] Permission will not be given unless the court is so satisfied.

[730] CPR Pt 6.24 to 29 specify the methods and proof for service of a writ out of the jurisdiction of the High Court.

claim form.[731] A certificate of service must be filed within seven days of service on the party concerned.[732]

8–194   Permission can be set aside. Where permission for service out of the jurisdiction is obtained on the basis of a serious non-disclosure, such as on a s.67 application failing to disclose that the issue of the arbitrator's jurisdiction had already been the subject of a decision of a foreign court, the permission will be capable of being set aside.[733]

8–195   The respondents or defendants.[734] The arbitration claim must identify each defendant to an application or appeal and specify his role in the arbitration[735] as well as the relief claimed against him.[736] When the Arbitration Act requires an application to the court to be made on notice to any other party to the arbitration, that notice must be given by making that party a defendant.[737] Where an arbitration claim is made under ss.24, 28 or 56 of the Arbitration Act 1996, each arbitrator must also be made a defendant.[738]

8–196   Notice and service. Where notice must be given to an arbitrator or any other person, it may be given by sending him a copy of the arbitration claim form and any written evidence in support.[739] Service has to be effected in accordance with CPR Pt 6.[740]

8–197   Acknowledgement of service. An acknowledgement of service form[741] should accompany the arbitration claim form when it is served. Further, the arbitration claim form itself includes notes for a defendant on how to respond to the claim. Within 14 days[742] of service of the arbitration claim form, an acknowledgment of service form should be returned to the relevant court office with a copy to the claimant and any other party shown on the claim form.

8–198   Consequences of failing to notify intention to contest application. Failure of a defendant to give timely notice of intention to contest the

---

[731] CPR r.62.5(3).
[732] Practice Direction 62, para.3.2.
[733] *Leibinger v Stryker Trauma GmbH* [2006] EWHC 690, [24]–[26].
[734] Part 62 and the Arbitration Practice Direction are not consistent in terminology. In CPR r.62.4, the term used is "defendant"; in other paragraphs the word "respondent" is used.
[735] CPR r.62.4(1)(f), unless the claim is made without notice under s.44(3) of the Arbitration Act 1996.
[736] CPR r.62.4(1)(e), which relates specifically to a costs order.
[737] CPR r.62.6(3).
[738] CPR r.62.6(1).
[739] CPR r.62.6(2).
[740] For service outside the jurisdiction, see para.8–191.
[741] The acknowledgment of service form (N15) is reproduced in Appendix 1.
[742] Fourteen days is the usual time for a defendant within the jurisdiction. The court will fix a longer time for a defendant served outside the jurisdiction to complete and return the acknowledgment of service form.

arbitration application or to acknowledge service has the following consequences:

- the defendant will not be entitled to contest the application without permission of the court and

- the court will not give that defendant notice of the date on which an arbitration application will be heard

- but the defendant's failure will not affect the applicant's duty to satisfy the court that the order applied for should be made.

Options for an arbitrator who is not made a defendant. Often   8–199
an arbitrator will be joined as a defendant to an arbitration application as much for tactical reasons as anything else and in some extreme cases claims will be made against the arbitrator himself.[743] Where an arbitrator is not made a party to an arbitration application but is sent a copy of the arbitration claim form for his information he has the following options:

- he may take no action and wait until he is notified of the outcome of the application;

- he may make representations in writing to the court[744]; or

- he may apply to be made a defendant.[745]

Court ordering arbitrator to be made defendant. Where an   8–200
arbitrator is ordered by the court to be made a defendant, he must acknowledge service of the arbitration application within 14 days of the making of the order. If the arbitrator chooses to file a witness statement or write to the court, he must as soon as is practicable send a copy of any such document to the claimant.[746] The court has a discretion as to the admissibility and weight to be given to such a document.

Automatic directions. CPR Pt 62 provides that, "unless the Court other-   8–201
wise directs", certain specified directions will apply automatically.[747]
Parties who do not comply with these directions will risk the dates for hearings being vacated and/or adverse costs orders. The directions that apply automatically

---

[743] For a discussion of the rights of the arbitral tribunal when faced with a challenge, see para.7–132. For an example of claims being made against an arbitrator directly, see *A v B* [2006] EWHC 2006.
[744] The representations may be made by filing written evidence or another written communication to the court and sending a copy to the claimant: PD 62, para.4.3. For example, in *Sukuman v Commonwealth Secretariat* [2007] EWHC 188, the chairman of the tribunal made written representations to the court.
[745] Practice Direction 62, para.4.1(1)(a).
[746] Practice Direction 62, para.4.2.
[747] Practice Direction 62, paras 6.1 to 6.7 inclusive.

relate to the filing of evidence, the fixing of a date for the hearing and the preparation and lodging with the court of bundles of documents and skeleton arguments.[748]

8–202 Directions by the court. Apart from the directions that may apply automatically to an arbitration application[749] the court may give such directions as to the conduct of the arbitration application as it thinks best adapted to a just, expeditious and economical determination.[750] To that end, the courts may permit oral evidence and give directions for the examination and cross-examination of witnesses.

8–203 Court power to dismiss application. The court is empowered to dismiss an application that does not comply with the rules or directions or if the court "is satisfied that the applicant is not prosecuting the application with due dispatch". The court may also determine it in the absence of evidence or submission from a respondent if that party fails to comply with the rules or the court's directions.

8–204 Hearing of applications. The court may also decide particular issues without a hearing.[751] The clearest example of this is whether or not to give leave to appeal on a question of law.[751a] The Arbitration Practice Direction gives as an example the question whether the court is satisfied as to the matters set out in s.32(2)(b) or s.45(2)(b) of the Arbitration Act, 1996.[752] The court will also generally decide, without a hearing, whether to extend the time limit under s.70(3) of the Act.[753]

8–205 Public or private hearings and judgments. If the court decides to hear an arbitration claim, it may order that the hearing be in public or in private.[754] CPR r. 62.10 is a starting point, but not a presumption.[755] Unless an application is made to the contrary the hearing, which will start in private, will remain in private. The following two applications will be heard in public, that is in open court, unless the court orders otherwise.[756]

---

[748] See PD 62, paras 6.2 to 6.7.
[749] See para.8–201.
[750] This follows the words "unless the court otherwise orders" in CPR 62.7 and PD 62.7, para.6.1.
[751] In making this decision the court will have regard to the overriding objective of a just, expeditious and economical determination of the issue.
[751a] Section 69(5) of the Arbitration Act 1996. See para.8–149.
[752] Practice Direction 62.8, para.10.1, but the example is narrower than contemplated by PD 62.7, para.9.3.
[753] Practice Direction 62.8, para.10.2.
[754] CPR r.62.10(1).
[755] *Department of Economic Policy and Development of Moscow v Bankers Trust and Another* [2005] Q.B. 207, *per* Mance L.J. at [42].
[756] CPR r.62.10(3) is expressed to be subject to an order of the court.

- The determination of a preliminary point of law under s.45 of the Arbitration Act 1996,[757] but not the preliminary question whether the court is satisfied of the matters set out in s.45(2)(b)[758] and

- An appeal under s.69 of the Arbitration Act 1996 on a question of law arising out of an award,[759] but not an application for permission to appeal.[760]

If a party wants any other application heard in public, it should request the court so to order. If no request is made and the application is heard in private, the decision of the court may then be marked private and not published. However, the Court of Appeal, in the leading case on this issue, has emphasised the difference between a hearing "in private"[761] and the following judgment, which should normally be given in public.[762] The consideration that the parties have elected to arbitrate confidentially cannot dictate the position in respect of arbitration claims under CPR Pt 62. The proceedings are no longer consensual and where possible general policy considerations err in favour of the proceedings and certainly the judgment being made public. The names of the parties can be changed if needs be to protect confidence.[763] Indeed, the judge should bear in mind that judgments, especially those under s.68, should be made public and should where possible draft judgments with that aim in mind, avoiding the unnecessary disclosure of confidential information in relation to the underlying arbitration. The Court of Appeal has even mooted the possibility of a separate confidential appendix to the judgment containing the necessary sensitive information in order that the judgment can be made public.[764] Even where a hearing starts in private the court should be "ready to hear representations from one or other party that the hearing should be continued in public".[765] As a matter of practice, the sheer number of available decisions in arbitration applications suggests that more often than not judgments are usually made public.[766]

Security for costs. In the absence of the any agreement as to security for costs[767] the court may order any applicant (including an applicant who has been   8–206

---

[757] CPR r.62.10(3)(a)(i).

[758] CPR r.62.10(4)(a).

[759] CPR r.62.10(3)(a)(ii).

[760] CPR r.62.10(4)(b). There will usually not be a hearing to determine an application for permission to appeal. See para.8–149.

[761] The phrase "in private" in both CPRs r.39.2 and r.62.10 have been taken to refer to "situation in which a hearing would formerly have been described as being in camera or in secret, not simply in chambers." *Department of Economic Policy and Development of Moscow v Bankers Trust and Another* [2005] Q.B. 207, *per* Mance L.J. at 227.

[762] *Department of Economic Policy and Development ibid*; Court of Appeal.

[763] For example, see *C v D* [2007] EWHC 1541.

[764] *Department of Economic Policy and Development of Moscow v Bankers Trust and Another* [2005] Q.B. 207, *per* Sir Andrew Morritt V.C., at [54].

[765] *Department of Economic Policy and Development of Moscow v Bankers Trust and Another* [2005] Q.B. 207, *per* Mance L.J. at [38].

[766] Interestingly, despite the general pro-public nature of the decision in *Department of Economic Policy and Development of Moscow v Bankers Trust and Another*, the s.68 judgment in that case was not made public, apparently because the judgment did contain sensitive information. No request for publication had been made in advance and so the judge had not drafted his judgment in such a way as to de-emphasise or omit the sensitive information.

[767] Section 67 of the Arbitration Act 1996 is not mandatory and may be varied by agreement.

granted permission to appeal) to provide security for the costs of any arbitration claim made under ss.67, 68 or 69 of the Arbitration Act, 1996.[768] If such an order is made the court will direct that the application or appeal shall be dismissed if the order is not complied with.[769]

8–207   **Grounds for exercising power.** The court's power to order security for costs will not be exercised on the ground that the applicant is an individual ordinarily resident outside the United Kingdom or a corporation or association incorporated or formed under the law of a country outside the United Kingdom or whose central management and control is exercised outside the United Kingdom.[770] This section has now been considered by the Court of Appeal, which decided that even where agreement had been reached on security between the parties the court could revise that sum upon a material change of circumstances. Although of limited application, the Court of Appeal's decision appears to confirm that the court's discretion to order security is, save for the second part of s.70(6), unfettered, and it is suggested is likely to be influenced by the CPR criteria.[771] In other words, the application has to be based on grounds other than the origin of the party against whom security is sought. Where the court has awarded security in respect of the whole of an application it will not make a further order in the absence of a material change of circumstances.[772]

8–208   **Security for the award.** In the absence of any agreement to the contrary,[773] the court may also order that any money payable under the award shall be brought into court or otherwise secured pending the determination of the application or appeal.[774] In either case the court is likely to direct that the application or appeal be dismissed if the order is not complied with.

The court's power to order money payable under the award to be secured is only applicable to applications under ss.67, 68 and 69 of the Act and not to other sections.[775] Further, in most cases, it will only be exercised where the party opposing the appeal demonstrates that the challenge is flimsy or otherwise lacks substance.[776] The court will also distinguish between making an order, the effect of which is to diminish the ability of the losing party to dishonour the award, if

[768] Section 70(6) of the Arbitration Act 1996.
[769] The principles on which the court will exercise its discretion were discussed in the *Azov Shipping Co v Baltic Shipping Co* [1999] 2 Lloyd's Rep. 39, *per* Longmore J. at [41] and following.
[770] This is the relevant provision in s.70(6) of the Arbitration Act 1996 to which the court's power is subjected when ordering security for costs in respect of an arbitration claim.
[771] *Kazakhstan v Istil Group Inc* [2006] 1 W.L.R 596, [31].
[772] In *Kazakhstan v Istil Group Inc* [2006] 1 W.L.R 596, the Court of Appeal ordered further security in the circumstances of that case.
[773] Section 67 of the Arbitration Act 1996 is not mandatory and may be varied by agreement.
[774] Section 70(7) of the Arbitration Act 1996.
[775] For example, s.32 of the Act. This limit to the scope of s.70(7) of the Act was emphasised in *Peterson Farms v C&M Farming Ltd* [2004] 1 Lloyd's Rep. 614 at [23].
[776] *Peterson Farms, ibid.* at [35].

upheld, from an order that requires a third party to put the losing party in funds.[777]

General rules about costs. Costs orders will be approached by the court 8–209
on the usual basis, the familiar issues being the extent and basis on which costs orders should be made against parties to the arbitration application in respect of costs incurred in the application (not any underlying arbitration).[778] Where proceedings have been brought in breach of an agreement to arbitrate, the usual principle is that costs of the relevant English proceedings will be awarded against the party acting in breach of the agreement to arbitrate on an indemnity basis.[779] The usual principle however is a flexible one and may be departed from (i.e. only costs on the standard basis awarded) where for example conduct on the part of the successful party has led the party in breach to believe that the chosen forum can be ignored.[780]

Particular applications to the court. The procedure described in the 8–210
preceding paragraphs[781] applies to all arbitration claims to which Pt 1 of the Arbitration Act 1996 relates except for an application to enforce an award, which is governed by a separate section of CPR Pt 62.[782] There are however special provisions for the following arbitration applications:

- to seek a stay of legal proceedings under s.9 of the Arbitration Act, 1996[783];

- to secure the attendance of a witness before an arbitral tribunal pursuant to s.43 of the Arbitration Act 1996[784];

- to obtain the assistance of the court in support of arbitration proceedings pursuant to s.44 of the Arbitration Act 1996[785];

- to determine a question as to the substantive jurisdiction of the arbitral tribunal under s.32 of the Arbitration Act 1996[786];

- to determine a preliminary point of law under s.45 of the Arbitration Act 1996[787];

---

[777] *Peterson Farms, ibid.*, [19].
[778] See CPR r.44.4(2).
[779] *A v B (Costs)* [2007] EWHC 54 at [10]–[11]; *Kyrgyz Mobil Tel and Others v Fellowes International Holdings and Another* [2005] EWHC 1329, at [42].
[780] *A v B (Costs)* [2007] EWHC 54 at [15].
[781] See paras 8–178 *et seq.*
[782] The procedure for the enforcement of an award is governed by s.III of Pt 62. See paras 8–219 *et seq.*
[783] CPR r.62.8: see paras 7–024 *et seq.*
[784] Practice Direction r.62, para.7: see para.7–202.
[785] Practice Direction 62, para.8.1: see paras 7–180 *et seq.*
[786] Practice Direction 62, para.9.1(1): see paras 7–154 *et seq.*
[787] Practice Direction 62, para.9.1(2): see paras 7–165 *et seq.*

- to seek permission to appeal on a question of law arising out of an arbitration award[788]; and

- to obtain an extension of time to challenge an award under s.67 or 68 of the Arbitration Act 1996 or to appeal on a question of law under s.69 of that Act.[789]

Except for the last,[790] these provisions are mentioned earlier in this chapter and in Ch.7 under the paragraphs dealing with the particular subjects.

8–211   Time limit for challenges and appeals. Unless varied by the court[791] the time for applying to the court to challenge or appeal against an award is limited to 28 days from the date of the award or, if there has been any arbitral process of appeal or review, from the date when the applicant or the appellant was notified of the result of that process.[792] In order to comply with that time limit, the arbitration claim form must have been issued and any witness statement in support should have been filed by its expiry.

8–212   Extending the time limit. An application to extend the 28-day time limit may be made whether or not it has expired. If the time limit has not yet expired, the applicant may apply without notice for an order to extend it.[793] Where however the time limit has expired the applicant must serve the application on the other parties.[794] The applicant must state in his arbitration claim form the grounds upon which he maintains that an order extending time should be made.[795] A defendant who wishes to oppose the making of an order extending time, must file written evidence within seven days after service of the arbitration claim form.[796]

8–213   Exercise of discretion. The court has a discretion whether or not to extend the time and in exercising that discretion the court will give proper weight to the relevant considerations. These have been set out by Colman J. in *Kalmneft v Glencore* as follows:

- the length of the delay;

- whether, in permitting the time limit to expire and the subsequent delay to occur, the party was acting reasonably in all the circumstances;

- whether the respondent to the application or the arbitrator caused or contributed to the delay;

---

[788] Practice Direction 62, para.12.1: see paras 8–119 *et seq.*
[789] CPR r.62.9(1).
[790] See paras 8–212 and 8–213.
[791] CPR r.62.9(1) provides that the court may vary this statutory time limit. See para.8–213.
[792] Section 70(3) of the Arbitration Act 1996: see paras 8–063, 8–108 and 8–123.
[793] CPR r.62.9(2).
[794] CPR r.62.9(3)
[795] CPR r.62.9(3)(a)(ii). It is suggested that this requirement must be observed in respect of applications made both before and after the 28 day period has expired.
[796] CPR r.62.9(3)(b).

- whether the respondent to the application would by reason of the delay suffer irremediable prejudice in addition to the mere loss of time if the application were permitted to proceed;

- whether the arbitration has continued during the period of delay and, if so, what impact on the progress of the arbitration or the costs incurred in respect of the determination of the application by the court might now have;

- the strength of the application; and

- whether in the broadest sense it would be unfair to the applicant for him to be denied the opportunity of having the application determined.[797]

Further, the party may lose the right to object if he failed to make a challenge within the requisite time.[798]

Weight to be given to different considerations. The Court of Appeal has endorsed these factors, identifying the first three as the most important.[799] Nonetheless, the relative weight to be given to these considerations in any particular case will of course vary. If for example a challenge is based on an allegedly important document which only comes to light after the end of the 28-day period through no fault of the prospective challenger then it is very likely that an extension of time will be granted.[800] In *Elektrim v Vivendi Universal SA*[801] an application to challenge an award on the grounds that it had been obtained by fraud under s.68(2)(g) was made on the basis of a memorandum which was provided to the prospective applicants 11 days before the 28 day time limit for challenge was due to expire. The applicant instructed English solicitors the next day but neither an application to extend time nor the substantive s.68 application was made until three and a half weeks after the 28 day time limit had expired. Nonetheless, the court extended time for making the s.68 application retrospectively, finding the applicant and their solicitors had acted diligently in the circumstances.[802]   8–214

Stricter application under section 67? The *Kalmneft* criteria may be applied more strictly in relation to s.67 applications where the jurisdiction of the tribunal is being challenged.[803]   8–215

---

[797] *Kalmneft v Glencore* [2001] 2 All E.R. (Comm) 577.
[798] This "gloss" on the consideration quoted above was made in *Peoples's Insurance Co of China v Vysanthi Shipping Co (The Joanna V)* [2003] 2 Lloyd's Rep. 617 as a result of s.67 of the Act.
[799] *Nagusina Naviera v Allied Maritime Inc* [2002] EWCA Civ 1147; the *Kalmneft* criteria were also applied in *Surefire Systems Ltd v Guardian ECL Ltd* [2005] B.L.R. 534.
[800] *Protech Projects Construction (Pty) Ltd v Al-Kharafi & Sons* [2005] 2 Lloyd's Rep. 779, [26].
[801] [2007] EWHC 11.
[802] [2007] EWHC 11, [50], [56] and [72]. The more prudent course would have been to make an application for extension of the 28 day time limit in the 10 day period between instruction of the English solicitors and expiry of the time limit.
[803] *DDT Trucks of North America Ltd v DDT Holdings Ltd* [2007] EWHC 1542, [35].

8–216 Frustrating the arbitration? The court will be mindful not to grant an application which might be seen as part of a pattern of behaviour designed to frustrate the arbitral process: "All the history which I have previously related militates against the granting of any indulgence to the claimants who have taken every step they possibly could to frustrate the arbitration."[804]

8–217 Overlap with section 73. The issue of an extension of time often overlaps with s.73; if the applicant had the requisite knowledge within the 28-day period or could with reasonable diligence have acquired such knowledge then it cannot have been acting reasonably in the context of an extension of time. The same considerations will apply to both issues and it would be futile to grant an extension of time in circumstances where it is clear that the resulting challenge will be barred under s.73.[805]

8–218 No entitlement to hearing. The parties are not entitled to demand a hearing for an application to extend the 28-day time limit, and there will not be one unless it appears to the court that a hearing is required.[806]

8–219 Application to enforce an award. The following provisions apply to all arbitration enforcement proceedings (other than by an action on the award) regardless of when they are commenced and when the arbitral proceedings took place.[807] An application under s.66 or 101 of the Arbitration Act 1996[808] to enforce an award in the same manner as a judgment or order may be made without notice in an arbitration claim form.[809]

The application for permission to enforce an award must be supported by written evidence (usually in the form of a witness statement) which exhibits the arbitration agreement and the award[810] and states:

- the name and address of the applicant as well as the name and the usual or last known place of residence or business of the person against whom it is sought to enforce the award, and

- that the award has not been complied with or, as the case may be, the extent to which it has not been complied with at the date of the application.[811]

---

[804] *Leibinger v Stryker Trauma GmbH* [2006] EWHC 690, [34]. This case involved an application to amend a claim form, not an application for extension of time for service of a claim form.

[805] *Thyssen Canada Ltd v Mariana Maritime SA* [2005] 1 Lloyd's Rep. 640, at [46]–[56].

[806] Practice Direction 62, para.10.2.

[807] CPR rr.62.17 and 62.18(1).

[808] CPR r.62.18(1) also applies to an application for permission under s.26 of the Arbitration Act 1950 or s.3(1)(a) of the Arbitration Act 1975.

[809] CPR r.62.18(1). The relevant form (N8) is reproduced in Appendix 1.

[810] CPR r.62.18(6)(a). For the purposes of the exhibit, a copy will suffice for an application under s.66 of the Arbitration Act 1996. A certified copy is required by s.102 of the Act for a s.101 application. A certified translation will also be required if the arbitration agreement or the award is in a foreign language.

[811] CPR r.62.18(6)(b) and (c).

Where the applicant applies to enforce an agreed award,[812] the application must state that the award is an agreed award and any order made by the court is required to contain such a statement.[813]

Service of application for enforcement. On receipt of the arbitration 8–220 claim form for enforcement, the court may direct that the form should be served on specified parties to the arbitration.[814] Service of the form out of the jurisdiction may be done with permission of the court irrespective of where the award is, or is treated as, made.[815]

Directions in respect of enforcement. Where the court directs that an 8–221 arbitration claim form seeking permission to enforce an award is to be served on another party to the arbitration, the following will apply as they do to other arbitration claims:

- service of the arbitration claim form should be acknowledged by completing the appropriate form of acknowledgement of service[816];

- failure of a respondent to give notice of intention to contest the enforcement application or to acknowledge service will have adverse consequences[817];

- the automatic directions specified in the Arbitration Practice Direction will apply unless the court otherwise directs[818]; and

- the application will be heard in private unless the court orders that it be heard in public.[819]

Statement of interest. Where an applicant seeks to enforce an award of 8–222 interest, and the whole or any part of the interest claimed relates to a period after the date of the award, he must file a statement giving the following particulars[820]:

- whether simple or compound interest was awarded;

- the date from which interest was awarded;

- whether rests were provided for, specifying them;

---

[812] For an agreed award see s.51(2) of the Arbitration Act 1966 and paras 6–023 *et seq.*
[813] CPR r.62.18(5).
[814] CPR r.62.18(2).
[815] CPR r.62.18(4).
[816] CPR r.62.18(3). See para.8–197. The appropriate form of acknowledgement of service (N.15) is reproduced in Appendix 1.
[817] See para.8–198.
[818] Practice Direction 62, para.6.1. See para.8–201.
[819] Part 62 (s.III) does not say so in terms, but CPR r.62.10(3) (s.I) is expressed generally, and the practice supports this interpretation.
[820] CPR r.62.19(1). This rule applies whether the whole or only part of the interest claimed relates to a period after the date of the award.

- the rate of interest awarded; and

- a calculation showing the total amount claimed up to the date of the certificate and any sum which will become due on a daily basis.

A statement containing these particulars must be filed with the court "whenever the amount of interest has to be quantified for the purpose of obtaining a judgment or order under s.66 of the Arbitration Act (enforcement of the award) or for the purpose of enforcing such a judgment or order."[821]

8–223 Service of order. An order giving permission to enforce an award must be drawn up by or on behalf of the applicant and served on the respondent. Service may be effected by delivering a copy to the respondent personally or by sending a copy to him at "his usual or last known place of residence or business"[822] or in such other manner as the court may direct.[823] In the case of a body corporate, the place of residence or business means its registered or principal address.[824] Permission is not required to serve the order outside the jurisdiction.[825]

The copy order served on the respondent must state that it will not be enforced until the period for applying to set the order aside has expired,[826] or any application made by the respondent has been finally disposed of.[827]

8–224 Application to set aside order. The order must contain a statement of the right to apply to set the order aside and the restrictions on enforcement under r.62.18(9)(b).[828] A respondent to the proceedings may apply to set aside an order for enforcement after he receives notice of it.[829] If the order does not contain these required statements it will be formally defective, although this may not be enough of itself to have the order set aside.[830] The application to set aside must be made within 14 days after service of the order within the jurisdiction or such other period as is fixed by the court if the order is served outside the jurisdiction. Where enforcement is sought against a State, the relevant procedures of the State Immunity Act 1978 also need to be adhered to, which in practice means that the 14 day period needs to be extended. In particular, under s.12(1) of the State Immunity Act process on States must be served through diplomatic channels and pursuant to sub-s.(2) any time for entering an appearance only runs from two

---

[821] CPR r.62.19(2).
[822] CPR r.62.18(7).
[823] Practice Direction 62, para.3.1.
[824] CPR r.62.18(11).
[825] CPR r.62.18 (8), which provides that CPR Pt 6.24 to 27 will apply in relation to such an order as they apply in relation to an arbitration claim form.
[826] The period will be 14 days after service within the jurisdiction or such time as the court may fix if service is made outside the jurisdiction.
[827] CPR r.62.18(9)(b).
[828] CPR r.62.18(10).
[829] CPR r.62.18(9)(a).
[830] *IPCO (Nigeria) Ltd v Nigerian National Petroleum Corp* [2005] EWHC 726; [2005] 2 Lloyd's Rep. 326, at [20]. An appropriate sanction might be an order in costs in respect of any premature enforcement proceedings.

months after the date on which the process is received. This time period applies to the applicable period for setting aside an award under CPR 62.18(9) and if the order for enforcement is made in a shorter period it will be premature and may be set-aside.[831]

The grounds for opposing enforcement of an arbitral award are discussed earlier in this chapter.[832] Provided that the application is made within the time specified in the order, the award cannot be enforced until after the application to set aside has been "finally disposed of".[833]

Registration of certain foreign awards. Depending on the award, it 8–225
may be possible to register an award in the High Court under one of the following Acts:

- The Arbitration (International Investment Disputes) Act 1966[834];

- The Multilateral Investment Guarantee Agency Act 1988[835]; or

- The Foreign Judgments (Reciprocal Enforcement) Act 1933, Pt 1.[836]

Registration under one of those Acts has the same effect as if permission to enforce had been obtained because the award is then enforceable in the same manner as a judgment or order of the High Court to the same effect. The rules of the court[837] apply to registration of those awards with some modifications. The modifications vary according to the Act under which the registration is made.[838]

---

[831] *Norsk Hydro ASA v State Property Fund of Ukraine* [2002] EWHC 2120; paras 21–26.
[832] See paras 8–028 et seq. for the grounds for opposing enforcements of a New York Convention award. As for challenges and appeals against an award generally, see paras 8–051 *et seq.*
[833] CPR r.62.18(9)(b). The application may not be finally disposed of until the outcome of any appeal.
[834] See para.8–048. See also CPR r.62.21.
[835] See para.8–050.
[836] See para.8–050. See also CPR r.62.20(1)(a).
[837] CPR rr.62.20(1) and 62.21(2) provide for the application of certain provisions of CPR Pt 74 to registration of these awards.
[838] The modification for each of the three Acts are specified in CPR r.62.20(2). See paras 8–048 and 8–050.

APPENDIX 1

[1] The Arbitration Act 1996 is reproduced in this Appendix with amendments made to the Act before June 30, 2007.

Appendix 1

Arbitration Act 1996[1]

(1996 c. 23)

Arrangement of Sections

Part I

Arbitration Pursuant to an Arbitration Agreement

Introductory

The arbitration agreement

Stay of legal proceedings

Commencement of arbitral proceedings

---

[1] The Arbitration Act 1996 is reproduced in this Appendix with amendments made to the Act before August 31, 2002.

The arbitral tribunal

Jurisdiction of the arbitral tribunal

The arbitral proceedings

Powers of court in relation to arbitral proceedings

The award

Costs of the arbitration

Powers of the court in relation to award

Miscellaneous

Supplementary

PART II

OTHER PROVISIONS RELATING TO
ARBITRATION

Domestic arbitration agreements

Consumer arbitration agreements

Small claims arbitration in the county court

Appointment of judges as arbitrators

Statutory arbitrations

552 *Appendix 1*

PART III

RECOGNITION AND ENFORCEMENT OF CERTAIN FOREIGN AWARDS

Enforcement of Geneva Convention awards

Recognition and enforcement of New York Convention awards

PART IV

GENERAL PROVISIONS

SCHEDULES:

An Act to restate and improve the law relating to arbitration pursuant to an arbitration agreement; to make other provision relating to arbitration and arbitration awards; and for connected purposes

[June 17, 1996]

PART I

ARBITRATION PURSUANT TO AN ARBITRATION AGREEMENT

Introductory

1. General principles

The provisions of this Part are founded on the following principles, and shall be construed accordingly—

(a) the object of arbitration is to obtain the fair resolution of disputes by an impartial tribunal without unnecessary delay or expense;

(b) the parties should be free to agree how their disputes are resolved, subject only to such safeguards as are necessary in the public interest;

(c) in matters governed by this Part the court should not intervene except as provided by this Part.

2. Scope of application of provisions

(1) The provisions of this Part apply where the seat of the arbitration is in England and Wales or Northern Ireland.

(2) The following sections apply even if the seat of the arbitration is outside England and Wales or Northern Ireland or no seat has been designated or determined—

(a) sections 9 to 11 (stay of legal proceedings, &c.), and

(b) section 66 (enforcement of arbitral awards).

(3) The powers conferred by the following sections apply even if the seat of the arbitration is outside England and Wales or Northern Ireland or no seat has been designated or determined—

(a) section 43 (securing the attendance of witnesses), and

(b) section 44 (court powers exercisable in support of arbitral proceedings);

but the court may refuse to exercise any such power if, in the opinion of the court, the fact that the seat of the arbitration is outside England and Wales or Northern Ireland, or that when designated or determined the seat is likely to be outside England and Wales or Northern Ireland, makes it inappropriate to do so.

(4) The court may exercise a power conferred by any provision of this Part not mentioned in subsection (2) or (3) for the purpose of supporting the arbitral process where—

(a) no seat of the arbitration has been designated or determined, and

(b) by reason of a connection with England and Wales or Northern Ireland the court is satisfied that it is appropriate to do so.

(5) Section 7 (separability of arbitration agreement) and section 8 (death of a party) apply where the law applicable to the arbitration agreement is the law of England and Wales or

Northern Ireland even if the seat of the arbitration is outside England and Wales or Northern Ireland or has not been designated or determined.

A1–003   **3. The seat of the arbitration**

In this Part "the seat of the arbitration" means the juridical seat of the arbitration designated—

(a) by the parties to the arbitration agreement, or

(b) by any arbitral or other institution or person vested by the parties with powers in that regard, or

(c) by the arbitral tribunal if so authorised by the parties,

or determined, in the absence of any such designation, having regard to the parties' agreement and all the relevant circumstances.

A1–004   **4. Mandatory and non-mandatory provisions**

(1) The mandatory provisions of this Part are listed in Schedule 1 and have effect notwithstanding any agreement to the contrary.
(2) The other provisions of this Part (the "non-mandatory provisions") allow the parties to make their own arrangements by agreement but provide rules which apply in the absence of such agreement.
(3) The parties may make such arrangements by agreeing to the application of institutional rules or providing any other means by which a matter may be decided.
(4) It is immaterial whether or not the law applicable to the parties' agreement is the law of England and Wales or, as the case may be, Northern Ireland.
(5) The choice of a law other than the law of England and Wales or Northern Ireland as the applicable law in respect of a matter provided for by a non-mandatory provision of this Part is equivalent to an agreement making provision about that matter.

For this purpose an applicable law determined in accordance with the parties' agreement, or which is objectively determined in the absence of any express or implied choice, shall be treated as chosen by the parties.

A1–005   **5. Agreements to be in writing**

(1) The provisions of this Part apply only where the arbitration agreement is in writing, and any other agreement between the parties as to any matter is effective for the purposes of this Part only if in writing.

The expressions "agreement", "agree" and "agreed" shall be construed accordingly.
(2) There is an agreement in writing—

(a) if the agreement is made in writing (whether or not it is signed by the parties),

(b) if the agreement is made by exchange of communications in writing, or

(c) if the agreement is evidenced in writing.

(3) Where parties agree otherwise than in writing by reference to terms which are in writing, they make an agreement in writing.
(4) An agreement is evidenced in writing if an agreement made otherwise than in writing is recorded by one of the parties, or by a third party, with the authority of the parties to the agreement.

(5) An exchange of written submissions in arbitral or legal proceedings in which the existence of an agreement otherwise than in writing is alleged by one party against another party and not denied by the other party in his response constitutes as between those parties an agreement in writing to the effect alleged.

(6) References in this Part to anything being written or in writing include its being recorded by any means.

The arbitration agreement

6. Definition of arbitration agreement   A1–006

(1) In this Part an "arbitration agreement" means an agreement to submit to arbitration present or future disputes (whether they are contractual or not).

(2) The reference in an agreement to a written form of arbitration clause or to a document containing an arbitration clause constitutes an arbitration agreement if the reference is such as to make that clause part of the agreement.

7. Separability of arbitration agreement   A1–007

Unless otherwise agreed by the parties, an arbitration agreement which forms or was intended to form part of another agreement (whether or not in writing) shall not be regarded as invalid, non-existent or ineffective because that other agreement is invalid, or did not come into existence or has become ineffective, and it shall for that purpose be treated as a distinct agreement.

8. Whether agreement discharged by death of a party   A1–008

(1) Unless otherwise agreed by the parties, an arbitration agreement is not discharged by the death of a party and may be enforced by or against the personal representatives of that party.

(2) Subsection (1) does not affect the operation of any enactment or rule of law by virtue of which a substantive right or obligation is extinguished by death.

Stay of legal proceedings

9. Stay of legal proceedings   A1–009

(1) A party to an arbitration agreement against whom legal proceedings are brought (whether by way of claim or counterclaim) in respect of a matter which under the agreement is to be referred to arbitration may (upon notice to the other parties to the proceedings) apply to the court in which the proceedings have been brought to stay the proceedings so far as they concern that matter.

(2) An application may be made notwithstanding that the matter is to be referred to arbitration only after the exhaustion of other dispute resolution procedures.

(3) An application may not be made by a person before taking the appropriate procedural step (if any) to acknowledge the legal proceedings against him or after he has taken any step in those proceedings to answer the substantive claim.

(4) On an application under this section the court shall grant a stay unless satisfied that the arbitration agreement is null and void, inoperative, or incapable of being performed.

(5) If the court refuses to stay the legal proceedings, any provision that an award is a condition precedent to the bringing of legal proceedings in respect of any matter is of no effect in relation to those proceedings.

A1–010 **10. Reference of interpleader issue to arbitration**

(1) Where in legal proceedings relief by way of interpleader is granted and any issue between the claimants is one in respect of which there is an arbitration agreement between them, the court granting the relief shall direct that the issue be determined in accordance with the agreement unless the circumstances are such that proceedings brought by a claimant in respect of the matter would not be stayed.

(2) Where subsection (1) applies but the court does not direct that the issue be determined in accordance with the arbitration agreement, any provision that an award is a condition precedent to the bringing of legal proceedings in respect of any matter shall not affect the determination of that issue by the court.

A1–011 **11. Retention of security where Admiralty proceedings stayed**

(1) Where Admiralty proceedings are stayed on the ground that the dispute in question should be submitted to arbitration, the court granting the stay may, if in those proceedings property has been arrested or bail or other security has been given to prevent or obtain release from arrest—

(a) order that the property arrested be retained as security for the satisfaction of any award given in the arbitration in respect of that dispute, or

(b) order that the stay of those proceedings be conditional on the provision of equivalent security for the satisfaction of any such award.

(2) Subject to any provision made by rules of court and to any necessary modification, the same law and practice shall apply in relation to property retained in pursuance of an order as would apply if it were held for the purposes of proceedings in the court making the order.

Commencement of arbitral proceedings

A1–012 **12. Power of court to extend time for beginning arbitral proceedings, &c**

(1) Where an arbitration agreement to refer future disputes to arbitration provides that a claim shall be barred, or the claimant's right extinguished, unless the claimant takes within a time fixed by the agreement some step—

(a) to begin arbitral proceedings, or

(b) to begin other dispute resolution procedures which must be exhausted before arbitral proceedings can be begun,

the court may by order extend the time for taking that step.

(2) Any party to the arbitration agreement may apply for such an order (upon notice to the other parties), but only after a claim has arisen and after exhausting any available arbitral process for obtaining an extension of time.

(3) The court shall make an order only if satisfied—

(a) that the circumstances are such as were outside the reasonable contemplation of the parties when they agreed the provision in question, and that it would be just to extend the time, or

(b) that the conduct of one party makes it unjust to hold the other party to the strict terms of the provision in question.

(4) The court may extend the time for such period and on such terms as it thinks fit, and may do so whether or not the time previously fixed (by agreement or by a previous order) has expired.

(5) An order under this section does not affect the operation of the Limitation Acts (see section 13).

(6) The leave of the court is required for any appeal from a decision of the court under this section.

13. Application of Limitation Acts

A1–013

(1) The Limitation Acts apply to arbitral proceedings as they apply to legal proceedings.

(2) The court may order that in computing the time prescribed by the Limitation Acts for the commencement of proceedings (including arbitral proceedings) in respect of a dispute which was the subject matter—

(a) of an award which the court orders to be set aside or declares to be of no effect, or

(b) of the affected part of an award which the court orders to be set aside in part, or declares to be in part of no effect,

the period between the commencement of the arbitration and the date of the order referred to in paragraph (a) or (b) shall be excluded.

(3) In determining for the purposes of the Limitation Acts when a cause of action accrued, any provision that an award is a condition precedent to the bringing of legal proceedings in respect of a matter to which an arbitration agreement applies shall be disregarded.

(4) In this Part "the Limitation Acts" means—

(a) in England and Wales, the Limitation Act 1980, the Foreign Limitation Periods Act 1984 and any other enactment (whenever passed) relating to the limitation of actions;

(b) in Northern Ireland, the Limitation (Northern Ireland) Order 1989, the Foreign Limitation Periods (Northern Ireland) Order 1985 and any other enactment (whenever passed) relating to the limitation of actions.

14. Commencement of arbitral proceedings

A1–014

(1) The parties are free to agree when arbitral proceedings are to be regarded as commenced for the purposes of this Part and for the purposes of the Limitation Acts.

(2) If there is no such agreement the following provisions apply.

(3) Where the arbitrator is named or designated in the arbitration agreement, arbitral proceedings are commenced in respect of a matter when one party serves on the other party or parties a notice in writing requiring him or them to submit that matter to the person so named or designated.

(4) Where the arbitrator or arbitrators are to be appointed by the parties, arbitral proceedings are commenced in respect of a matter when one party serves on the other party or

parties notice in writing requiring him or them to appoint an arbitrator or to agree to the appointment of an arbitrator in respect of that matter.

(5) Where the arbitrator or arbitrators are to be appointed by a person other than a party to the proceedings, arbitral proceedings are commenced in respect of a matter when one party gives notice in writing to that person requesting him to make the appointment in respect of that matter.

The arbitral tribunal

A1–015   **15. The arbitral tribunal**

(1) The parties are free to agree on the number of arbitrators to form the tribunal and whether there is to be a chairman or umpire.

(2) Unless otherwise agreed by the parties, an agreement that the number of arbitrators shall be two or any other even number shall be understood as requiring the appointment of an additional arbitrator as chairman of the tribunal.

(3) If there is no agreement as to the number of arbitrators, the tribunal shall consist of a sole arbitrator.

A1–016   **16. Procedure for appointment of arbitrators**

(1) The parties are free to agree on the procedure for appointing the arbitrator or arbitrators, including the procedure for appointing any chairman or umpire.

(2) If or to the extent that there is no such agreement, the following provisions apply.

(3) If the tribunal is to consist of a sole arbitrator, the parties shall jointly appoint the arbitrator not later than 28 days after service of a request in writing by either party to do so.

(4) If the tribunal is to consist of two arbitrators, each party shall appoint one arbitrator not later than 14 days after service of a request in writing by either party to do so.

(5) If the tribunal is to consist of three arbitrators—

(a) each party shall appoint one arbitrator not later than 14 days after service of a request in writing by either party to do so, and

(b) the two so appointed shall forthwith appoint a third arbitrator as the chairman of the tribunal.

(6) If the tribunal is to consist of two arbitrators and an umpire—

(a) each party shall appoint one arbitrator not later than 14 days after service of a request in writing by either party to do so, and

(b) the two so appointed may appoint an umpire at any time after they themselves are appointed and shall do so before any substantive hearing or forthwith if they cannot agree on a matter relating to the arbitration.

(7) In any other case (in particular, if there are more than two parties) section 18 applies as in the case of a failure of the agreed appointment procedure.

A1–017   **17. Power in case of default to appoint sole arbitrator**

(1) Unless the parties otherwise agree, where each of two parties to an arbitration agreement is to appoint an arbitrator and one party ("the party in default") refuses to do so, or

fails to do so within the time specified, the other party, having duly appointed his arbitrator, may give notice in writing to the party in default that he proposes to appoint his arbitrator to act as sole arbitrator.

(2) If the party in default does not within 7 clear days of that notice being given—

(a) make the required appointment, and

(b) notify the other party that he has done so,

the other party may appoint his arbitrator as sole arbitrator whose award shall be binding on both parties as if he had been so appointed by agreement.

(3) Where a sole arbitrator has been appointed under subsection (2), the party in default may (upon notice to the appointing party) apply to the court which may set aside the appointment.

(4) The leave of the court is required for any appeal from a decision of the court under this section.

18. Failure of appointment procedure   A1–018

(1) The parties are free to agree what is to happen in the event of a failure of the procedure for the appointment of the arbitral tribunal.

There is no failure if an appointment is duly made under section 17 (power in case of default to appoint sole arbitrator), unless that appointment is set aside.

(2) If or to the extent that there is no such agreement any party to the arbitration agreement may (upon notice to the other parties) apply to the court to exercise its powers under this section.

(3) Those powers are—

(a) to give directions as to the making of any necessary appointments;

(b) to direct that the tribunal shall be constituted by such appointments (or any one or more of them) as have been made;

(c) to revoke any appointments already made;

(d) to make any necessary appointments itself.

(4) An appointment made by the court under this section has effect as if made with the agreement of the parties.

(5) The leave of the court is required for any appeal from a decision of the court under this section.

19. Court to have regard to agreed qualifications   A1–019

In deciding whether to exercise, and in considering how to exercise, any of its powers under section 16 (procedure for appointment of arbitrators) or section 18 (failure of appointment procedure), the court shall have due regard to any agreement of the parties as to the qualifications required of the arbitrators.

20. Chairman   A1–020

(1) Where the parties have agreed that there is to be a chairman, they are free to agree what the functions of the chairman are to be in relation to the making of decisions, orders and awards.

(2) If or to the extent that there is no such agreement, the following provisions apply.

(3) Decisions, orders and awards shall be made by all or a majority of the arbitrators (including the chairman).

(4) The view of the chairman shall prevail in relation to a decision, order or award in respect of which there is neither unanimity nor a majority under subsection (3).

A1–021   21. Umpire

(1) Where the parties have agreed that there is to be an umpire, they are free to agree what the functions of the umpire are to be, and in particular—

   (a) whether he is to attend the proceedings, and

   (b) when he is to replace the other arbitrators as the tribunal with power to make decisions, order and awards.

(2) If or to the extent that there is no such agreement, the following provisions apply.

(3) The umpire shall attend the proceedings and be supplied with the same documents and other materials as are supplied to the other arbitrators.

(4) Decisions, orders and awards shall be made by the other arbitrators unless and until they cannot agree on a matter relating to the arbitration.

In that event they shall forthwith give notice in writing to the parties and the umpire, whereupon the umpire shall replace them as the tribunal with power to make decisions, orders and awards as if he were sole arbitrator.

(5) If the arbitrators cannot agree but fail to give notice of that fact, or if any of them fails to join in the giving of notice, any party to the arbitral proceedings may (upon notice to the other parties and to the tribunal) apply to the court which may order that the umpire shall replace the other arbitrators as the tribunal with power to make decisions, orders and awards as if he were sole arbitrator.

(6) The leave of the court is required for any appeal from a decision of the court under this section.

A1–022   22. Decision-making where no chairman or umpire

(1) Where the parties agree that there shall be two or more arbitrators with no chairman or umpire, the parties are free to agree how the tribunal is to make decisions, orders and awards.

(2) If there is no such agreement, decisions, orders and awards shall be made by all or a majority of the arbitrators.

A1–023   23. Revocation of arbitrator's authority

(1) The parties are free to agree in what circumstances the authority of an arbitrator may be revoked.

(2) If or to the extent that there is no such agreement the following provisions apply.

(3) The authority of an arbitrator may not be revoked except—

   (a) by the parties acting jointly, or

   (b) by an arbitral or other institution or person vested by the parties with powers in that regard.

(4) Revocation of the authority of an arbitrator by the parties acting jointly must be agreed in writing unless the parties also agree (whether or not in writing) to terminate the arbitration agreement.

(5) Nothing in this section affects the power of the court—

(a) to revoke an appointment under section 18 (powers exercisable in case of failure of appointment procedure), or

(b) to remove an arbitrator on the grounds specified in section 24.

24. Power of court to remove arbitrator

A1–024

(1) A party to arbitral proceedings may (upon notice to the other parties, to the arbitrator concerned and to any other arbitrator) apply to the court to remove an arbitrator on any of the following grounds—

(a) that circumstances exist that give rise to justifiable doubts as to his impartiality;

(b) that he does not possess the qualifications required by the arbitration agreement;

(c) that he is physically or mentally incapable of conducting the proceedings or there are justifiable doubts as to his capacity to do so;

(d) that he has refused or failed:

(i) properly to conduct the proceedings, or

(ii) to use all reasonable despatch in conducting the proceedings or making an award,

and that substantial injustice has been or will be caused to the applicant.

(2) If there is an arbitral or other institution or person vested by the parties with power to remove an arbitrator, the court shall not exercise its power of removal unless satisfied that the applicant has first exhausted any available recourse to that institution or person.

(3) The arbitral tribunal may continue the arbitral proceedings and make an award while an application to the court under this section is pending.

(4) Where the court removes an arbitrator, it may make such order as it thinks fit with respect to his entitlement (if any) to fees or expenses, or the repayment of any fees or expenses already paid.

(5) The arbitrator concerned is entitled to appear and be heard by the court before it makes any order under this section.

(6) The leave of the court is required for any appeal from a decision of the court under this section.

25. Resignation of arbitrator

A1–025

(1) The parties are free to agree with an arbitrator as to the consequences of his resignation as regards—

(a) his entitlement (if any) to fees or expenses,

(b) any liability thereby incurred by him.

(2) If or to the extent that there is no such agreement the following provisions apply.

(3) An arbitrator who resigns his appointment may (upon notice to the parties) apply to the court—

(a) to grant him relief from any liability thereby incurred by him, and

(b) to make such order as it thinks fit with respect to his entitlement (if any) to fees or expenses or the repayment of any fees or expenses already paid.

(4) If the court is satisfied that in all the circumstances it was reasonable for the arbitrator to resign, it may grant such relief as is mentioned in subsection (3)(a) on such terms as it thinks fit.

(5) The leave of the court is required for any appeal from a decision of the court under this section.

A1–026   **26. Death of arbitrator or person appointing him**

(1) The authority of an arbitrator is personal and ceases on his death.

(2) Unless otherwise agreed by the parties, the death of the person by whom an arbitrator was appointed does not revoke the arbitrator's authority.

A1–027   **27. Filling of vacancy, &c**

(1) Where an arbitrator ceases to hold office, the parties are free to agree—

(a) whether and if so how the vacancy is to be filled,

(b) whether and if so to what extent the previous proceedings should stand, and

(c) what effect (if any) his ceasing to hold office has on any appointment made by him (alone or jointly).

(2) If or to the extent that there is no such agreement, the following provisions apply.

(3) The provisions of sections 16 (procedure for appointment of arbitrators) and 18 (failure of appointment procedure) apply in relation to the filling of the vacancy as in relation to an original appointment.

(4) The tribunal (when reconstituted) shall determine whether and if so to what extent the previous proceedings should stand.

This does not affect any right of a party to challenge those proceedings on any ground which had arisen before the arbitrator ceased to hold office.

(5) His ceasing to hold office does not affect any appointment by him (alone or jointly) of another arbitrator, in particular any appointment of a chairman or umpire.

A1–028   **28. Joint and several liability of parties to arbitrators for fees and expenses**

(1) The parties are jointly and severally liable to pay to the arbitrators such reasonable fees and expenses (if any) as are appropriate in the circumstances.

(2) Any party may apply to the court (upon notice to the other parties and to the arbitrators) which may order that the amount of the arbitrators' fees and expenses shall be considered and adjusted by such means and upon such terms as it may direct.

(3) If the application is made after any amount has been paid to the arbitrators by way of fees or expenses, the court may order the repayment of such amount (if any) as is shown to be excessive, but shall not do so unless it is shown that it is reasonable in the circumstances to order repayment.

(4) The above provisions have effect subject to any order of the court under section 24(4) or 25(3)(b) (order as to entitlement to fees or expenses in case of removal or resignation of arbitrator).

(5) Nothing in this section affects any liability of a party to any other party to pay all or any of the costs of the arbitration (see sections 59 to 65) or any contractual right of an arbitrator to payment of his fees and expenses.

(6) In this section references to arbitrators include an arbitrator who has ceased to act and an umpire who has not replaced the other arbitrators.

29. Immunity of arbitrator

(1) An arbitrator is not liable for anything done or omitted in the discharge or purported discharge of his functions as arbitrator unless the act or omission is shown to have been in bad faith.
(2) Subsection (1) applies to an employee or agent of an arbitrator as it applies to the arbitrator himself.
(3) This section does not affect any liability incurred by an arbitrator by reason of his resigning (but see section 25).

Jurisdiction of the arbitral tribunal

30. Competence of tribunal to rule on its own jurisdiction

(1) Unless otherwise agreed by the parties, the arbitral tribunal may rule on its own substantive jurisdiction, that is, as to—

(a) whether there is a valid arbitration agreement,

(b) whether the tribunal is properly constituted, and

(c) what matters have been submitted to arbitration in accordance with the arbitration agreement.

(2) Any such ruling may be challenged by any available arbitral process of appeal or review or in accordance with the provisions of this Part.

31. Objection to substantive jurisdiction of tribunal

(1) An objection that the arbitral tribunal lacks substantive jurisdiction at the outset of the proceedings must be raised by a party not later than the time he takes the first step in the proceedings to contest the merits of any matter in relation to which he challenges the tribunal's jurisdiction.
A party is not precluded from raising such an objection by the fact that he has appointed or participated in the appointment of an arbitrator.
(2) Any objection during the course of the arbitral proceedings that the arbitral tribunal is exceeding its substantive jurisdiction must be made as soon as possible after the matter alleged to be beyond its jurisdiction is raised.
(3) The arbitral tribunal may admit an objection later than the time specified in subsection (1) or (2) if it considers the delay justified.
(4) Where an objection is duly taken to the tribunal's substantive jurisdiction and the tribunal has power to rule on its own jurisdiction, it may—

(a) rule on the matter in an award as to jurisdiction, or

(b) deal with the objection in its award on the merits.

If the parties agree which of these courses the tribunal should take, the tribunal shall proceed accordingly.

(5) The tribunal may in any case, and shall if the parties so agree, stay proceedings whilst an application is made to the court under section 32 (determination of preliminary point of jurisdiction).

A1–032   **32. Determination of preliminary point of jurisdiction**

(1) The court may, on the application of a party to arbitral proceedings (upon notice to the other parties), determine any question as to the substantive jurisdiction of the tribunal. A party may lose the right to object (see section 73).

(2) An application under this section shall not be considered unless—

   (a) it is made with the agreement in writing of all the other parties to the proceedings, or

   (b) it is made with the permission of the tribunal and the court is satisfied—

      (i) that the determination of the question is likely to produce substantial savings in costs,

      (ii) that the application was made without delay, and

      (iii) that there is good reason why the matter should be decided by the court.

(3) An application under this section, unless made with the agreement of all the other parties to the proceedings, shall state the grounds on which it is said that the matter should be decided by the court.

(4) Unless otherwise agreed by the parties, the arbitral tribunal may continue the arbitral proceedings and make an award while an application to the court under this section is pending.

(5) Unless the court gives leave, no appeal lies from a decision of the court whether the conditions specified in subsection (2) are met.

(6) The decision of the court on the question of jurisdiction shall be treated as a judgment of the court for the purposes of an appeal.

But no appeal lies without the leave of the court which shall not be given unless the court considers that the question involves a point of law which is one of general importance or is one which for some other special reason should be considered by the Court of Appeal.

The arbitral proceedings

A1–033   **33. General duty of the tribunal**

(1) The tribunal shall—

   (a) act fairly and impartially as between the parties, giving each party a reasonable opportunity of putting his case and dealing with that of his opponent, and

   (b) adopt procedures suitable to the circumstances of the particular case, avoiding unnecessary delay or expense, so as to provide a fair means for the resolution of the matters falling to be determined.

(2) The tribunal shall comply with that general duty in conducting the arbitral proceedings, in its decisions on matters of procedure and evidence and in the exercise of all other powers conferred on it.

34. Procedural and evidential matters

(1) It shall be for the tribunal to decide all procedural and evidential matters, subject to the right of the parties to agree any matter.

(2) Procedural and evidential matters include—

   (a) when and where any part of the proceedings is to be held;

   (b) the language or languages to be used in the proceedings and whether translations of any relevant documents are to be supplied;

   (c) whether any and if so what form of written statements of claim and defence are to be used, when these should be supplied and the extent to which such statements can be later amended;

   (d) whether any and if so which documents or classes of documents should be disclosed between and produced by the parties and at what stage;

   (e) whether any and if so what questions should be put to and answered by the respective parties and when and in what form this should be done;

   (f) whether to apply strict rules of evidence (or any other rules) as to the admissibility, relevance or weight of any material (oral, written or other) sought to be tendered on any matters of fact or opinion, and the time, manner and form in which such material should be exchanged and presented;

   (g) whether and to what extent the tribunal should itself take the initiative in ascertaining the facts and the law;

   (h) whether and to what extent there should be oral or written evidence or submissions.

(3) The tribunal may fix the time within which any directions given by it are to be complied with, and may if it thinks fit extend the time so fixed (whether or not it has expired).

35. Consolidation of proceedings and concurrent hearings

(1) The parties are free to agree—

   (a) that the arbitral proceedings shall be consolidated with other arbitral proceedings, or

   (b) that concurrent hearings shall be held,

on such terms as may be agreed.

(2) Unless the parties agree to confer such power on the tribunal, the tribunal has no power to order consolidation of proceedings or concurrent hearings.

36. Legal or other representation

Unless otherwise agreed by the parties, a party to arbitral proceedings may be represented in the proceedings by a lawyer or other person chosen by him.

37. Power to appoint experts, legal advisers or assessors

(1) Unless otherwise agreed by the parties—

   (a) the tribunal may—

(i) appoint experts or legal advisers to report to it and the parties, or

(ii) appoint assessors to assist it on technical matters, and may allow any such expert, legal adviser or assessor to attend the proceedings; and

(b) the parties shall be given a reasonable opportunity to comment on any information, opinion or advice offered by any such person.

(2) The fees and expenses of an expert, legal adviser or assessor appointed by the tribunal for which the arbitrators are liable are expenses of the arbitrators for the purposes of this Part.

A1–038 **38. General powers exercisable by the tribunal**

(1) The parties are free to agree on the powers exercisable by the arbitral tribunal for the purposes of and in relation to the proceedings.

(2) Unless otherwise agreed by the parties the tribunal has the following powers.

(3) The tribunal may order a claimant to provide security for the costs of the arbitration.

This power shall not be exercised on the ground that the claimant is—

(a) an individual ordinarily resident outside the United Kingdom, or

(b) a corporation or association incorporated or formed under the law of a country outside the United Kingdom, or whose central management and control is exercised outside the United Kingdom.

(4) The tribunal may give directions in relation to any property which is the subject of the proceedings or as to which any question arises in the proceedings, and which is owned by or is in the possession of a party to the proceedings—

(a) for the inspection, photographing, preservation, custody or detention of the property by the tribunal, an expert or a party, or

(b) ordering that samples be taken from, or any observation be made of or experiment conducted upon, the property.

(5) The tribunal may direct that a party or witness shall be examined on oath or affirmation, and may for that purpose administer any necessary oath or take any necessary affirmation.

(6) The tribunal may give directions to a party for the preservation for the purposes of the proceedings of any evidence in his custody or control.

A1–039 **39. Power to make provisional awards**

(1) The parties are free to agree that the tribunal shall have power to order on a provisional basis any relief which it would have power to grant in a final award.

(2) This includes, for instance, making—

(a) a provisional order for the payment of money or the disposition of property as between the parties, or

(b) an order to make an interim payment on account of the costs of the arbitration.

(3) Any such order shall be subject to the tribunal's final adjudication; and the tribunal's final award, on the merits or as to costs, shall take account of any such order.

(4) Unless the parties agree to confer such power on the tribunal, the tribunal has no such power.

This does not affect its powers under section 47 (awards on different issues, &c.).

40. General duty of parties

(1) The parties shall do all things necessary for the proper and expeditious conduct of the arbitral proceedings.

(2) This includes—

    (a) complying without delay with any determination of the tribunal as to procedural or evidential matters, or with any order or directions of the tribunal, and

    (b) where appropriate, taking without delay any necessary steps to obtain a decision of the court on a preliminary question of jurisdiction or law (see sections 32 and 45).

41. Powers of tribunal in case of party's default

(1) The parties are free to agree on the powers of the tribunal in case of a party's failure to do something necessary for the proper and expeditious conduct of the arbitration.

(2) Unless otherwise agreed by the parties, the following provisions apply.

(3) If the tribunal is satisfied that there has been inordinate and inexcusable delay on the part of the claimant in pursuing his claim and that the delay—

    (a) gives rise, or is likely to give rise, to a substantial risk that it is not possible to have a fair resolution of the issues in that claim, or

    (b) has caused, or is likely to cause, serious prejudice to the respondent,

the tribunal may make an award dismissing the claim.

(4) If without showing sufficient cause a party—

    (a) fails to attend or be represented at an oral hearing of which due notice was given, or

    (b) where matters are to be dealt with in writing, fails after due notice to submit written evidence or make written submissions,

the tribunal may continue the proceedings in the absence of that party or, as the case may be, without any written evidence or submissions on his behalf, and may make an award on the basis of the evidence before it.

(5) If without showing sufficient cause a party fails to comply with any order or directions of the tribunal, the tribunal may make a peremptory order to the same effect, prescribing such time for compliance with it as the tribunal considers appropriate.

(6) If a claimant fails to comply with a peremptory order of the tribunal to provide security for costs, the tribunal may make an award dismissing his claim.

(7) If a party fails to comply with any other kind of peremptory order, then, without prejudice to section 42 (enforcement by court of tribunal's peremptory orders), the tribunal may do any of the following—

    (a) direct that the party in default shall not be entitled to rely upon any allegation or material which was the subject matter of the order;

    (b) draw such adverse inferences from the act of non-compliance as the circumstances justify;

(c) proceed to an award on the basis of such materials as have been properly provided to it;

(d) make such order as it thinks fit as to the payment of costs of the arbitration incurred in consequence of the non-compliance.

Powers of court in relation to arbitral proceedings

A1–042   **42. Enforcement of peremptory orders of tribunal**

(1) Unless otherwise agreed by the parties, the court may make an order requiring a party to comply with a peremptory order made by the tribunal.
(2) An application for an order under this section may be made—

(a) by the tribunal (upon notice to the parties),

(b) by a party to the arbitral proceedings with the permission of the tribunal (and upon notice to the other parties), or

(c) where the parties have agreed that the powers of the court under this section shall be available.

(3) The court shall not act unless it is satisfied that the applicant has exhausted any available arbitral process in respect of failure to comply with the tribunal's order.
(4) No order shall be made under this section unless the court is satisfied that the person to whom the tribunal's order was directed has failed to comply with it within the time prescribed in the order or, if no time was prescribed, within a reasonable time.
(5) The leave of the court is required for any appeal from a decision of the court under this section.

A1–043   **43. Securing the attendance of witnesses**

(1) A party to arbitral proceedings may use the same court procedures as are available in relation to legal proceedings to secure the attendance before the tribunal of a witness in order to give oral testimony or to produce documents or other material evidence.
(2) This may only be done with the permission of the tribunal or the agreement of the other parties.
(3) The court procedures may only be used if—

(a) the witness is in the United Kingdom, and

(b) the arbitral proceedings are being conducted in England and Wales or, as the case may be, Northern Ireland.

(4) A person shall not be compelled by virtue of this section to produce any document or other material evidence which he could not be compelled to produce in legal proceedings.

A1–044   **44. Court powers exercisable in support of arbitral proceedings**

(1) Unless otherwise agreed by the parties, the court has for the purposes of and in relation to arbitral proceedings the same power of making orders about the matters listed below as it has for the purposes of and in relation to legal proceedings.

(2) Those matters are—

(a) the taking of the evidence of witnesses;

(b) the preservation of evidence;

(c) making orders relating to property which is the subject of the proceedings or as to which any question arises in the proceedings—

(i) for the inspection, photographing, preservation, custody or detention of the property, or

(ii) ordering that samples be taken from, or any observation be made of or experiment conducted upon, the property;

and for that purpose authorising any person to enter any premises in the possession or control of a party to the arbitration;

(d) the sale of any goods the subject of the proceedings;

(e) the granting of an interim injunction or the appointment of a receiver.

(3) If the case is one of urgency, the court may, on the application of a party or proposed party to the arbitral proceedings, make such orders as it thinks necessary for the purpose of preserving evidence or assets.

(4) If the case is not one of urgency, the court shall act only on the application of a party to the arbitral proceedings (upon notice to the other parties and to the tribunal) made with the permission of the tribunal or the agreement in writing of the other parties.

(5) In any case the court shall act only if or to the extent that the arbitral tribunal, and any arbitral or other institution or person vested by the parties with power in that regard, has no power or is unable for the time being to act effectively.

(6) If the court so orders, an order made by it under this section shall cease to have effect in whole or in part on the order of the tribunal or of any such arbitral or other institution or person having power to act in relation to the subject-matter of the order.

(7) The leave of the court is required for any appeal from a decision of the court under this section.

45. Determination of preliminary point of law

A1–045

(1) Unless otherwise agreed by the parties, the court may on the application of a party to arbitral proceedings (upon notice to the other parties) determine any question of law arising in the course of the proceedings which the court is satisfied substantially affects the rights of one or more of the parties.

An agreement to dispense with reasons for the tribunal's award shall be considered an agreement to exclude the court's jurisdiction under this section.

(2) An application under this section shall not be considered unless—

(a) it is made with the agreement of all the other parties to the proceedings, or

(b) it is made with the permission of the tribunal and the court is satisfied—

(i) that the determination of the question is likely to produce substantial savings in costs, and

(ii) that the application was made without delay.

(3) The application shall identify the question of law to be determined and, unless made with the agreement of all the other parties to the proceedings, shall state the grounds on which it is said that the question should be decided by the court.

(4) Unless otherwise agreed by the parties, the arbitral tribunal may continue the arbitral proceedings and make an award while an application to the court under this section is pending.

(5) Unless the court gives leave, no appeal lies from a decision of the court whether the conditions specified in subsection (2) are met.

(6) The decision of the court on the question of law shall be treated as a judgment of the court for the purposes of an appeal.

But no appeal lies without the leave of the court which shall not be given unless the court considers that the question is one of general importance, or is one which for some other special reason should be considered by the Court of Appeal.

The award

A1–046   **46. Rules applicable to substance of dispute**

(1) The arbitral tribunal shall decide the dispute—

    (a) in accordance with the law chosen by the parties as applicable to the substance of the dispute, or

    (b) if the parties so agree, in accordance with such other considerations as are agreed by them or determined by the tribunal.

(2) For this purpose the choice of the laws of a country shall be understood to refer to the substantive laws of that country and not its conflict of laws rules.

(3) If or to the extent that there is no such choice or agreement, the tribunal shall apply the law determined by the conflict of laws rules which it considers applicable.

A1–047   **47. Awards on different issues, &c**

(1) Unless otherwise agreed by the parties, the tribunal may make more than one award at different times on different aspects of the matters to be determined.

(2) The tribunal may, in particular, make an award relating—

    (a) to an issue affecting the whole claim, or

    (b) to a part only of the claims or cross-claims submitted to it for decision.

(3) If the tribunal does so, it shall specify in its award the issue, or the claim or part of a claim, which is the subject matter of the award.

A1–048   **48. Remedies**

(1) The parties are free to agree on the powers exercisable by the arbitral tribunal as regards remedies.

(2) Unless otherwise agreed by the parties, the tribunal has the following powers.

(3) The tribunal may make a declaration as to any matter to be determined in the proceedings.

(4) The tribunal may order the payment of a sum of money, in any currency.

(5) The tribunal has the same powers as the court—

(a) to order a party to do or refrain from doing anything;

(b) to order specific performance of a contract (other than a contract relating to land);

(c) to order the rectification, setting aside or cancellation of a deed or other document.

49. Interest

(1) The parties are free to agree on the powers of the tribunal as regards the award of interest.
(2) Unless otherwise agreed by the parties the following provisions apply.
(3) The tribunal may award simple or compound interest from such dates, at such rates and with such rests as it considers meets the justice of the case—

(a) on the whole or part of any amount awarded by the tribunal, in respect of any period up to the date of the award;

(b) on the whole or part of any amount claimed in the arbitration and outstanding at the commencement of the arbitral proceedings but paid before the award was made, in respect of any period up to the date of payment.

(4) The tribunal may award simple or compound interest from the date of the award (or any later date) until payment, at such rates and with such rests as it considers meets the justice of the case, on the outstanding amount of any award (including any award of interest under subsection (3) and any award as to costs).
(5) References in this section to an amount awarded by the tribunal include an amount payable in consequence of a declaratory award by the tribunal.
(6) The above provisions do not affect any other power of the tribunal to award interest.

50. Extension of time for making award

(1) Where the time for making an award is limited by or in pursuance of the arbitration agreement, then, unless otherwise agreed by the parties, the court may in accordance with the following provisions by order extend that time.
(2) An application for an order under this section may be made—

(a) by the tribunal (upon notice to the parties), or

(b) by any party to the proceedings (upon notice to the tribunal and the other parties),

but only after exhausting any available arbitral process for obtaining an extension of time.
(3) The court shall only make an order if satisfied that a substantial injustice would otherwise be done.
(4) The court may extend the time for such period and on such terms as it thinks fit, and may do so whether or not the time previously fixed (by or under the agreement or by a previous order) has expired.
(5) The leave of the court is required for any appeal from a decision of the court under this section.

A1–051   51. **Settlement**

(1) If during arbitral proceedings the parties settle the dispute, the following provisions apply unless otherwise agreed by the parties.

(2) The tribunal shall terminate the substantive proceedings and, if so requested by the parties and not objected to by the tribunal, shall record the settlement in the form of an agreed award.

(3) An agreed award shall state that it is an award of the tribunal and shall have the same status and effect as any other award on the merits of the case.

(4) The following provisions of this Part relating to awards (sections 52 to 58) apply to an agreed award.

(5) Unless the parties have also settled the matter of the payment of the costs of the arbitration, the provisions of this Part relating to costs (sections 59 to 65) continue to apply.

A1–052   52. **Form of award**

(1) The parties are free to agree on the form of an award.

(2) If or to the extent that there is no such agreement, the following provisions apply.

(3) The award shall be in writing signed by all the arbitrators or all those assenting to the award.

(4) The award shall contain the reasons for the award unless it is an agreed award or the parties have agreed to dispense with reasons.

(5) The award shall state the seat of the arbitration and the date when the award is made.

A1–053   53. **Place where award treated as made**

Unless otherwise agreed by the parties, where the seat of the arbitration is in England and Wales or Northern Ireland, any award in the proceedings shall be treated as made there, regardless of where it was signed, despatched or delivered to any of the parties.

A1–054   54. **Date of award**

(1) Unless otherwise agreed by the parties, the tribunal may decide what is to be taken to be the date on which the award was made.

(2) In the absence of any such decision, the date of the award shall be taken to be the date on which it is signed by the arbitrator or, where more than one arbitrator signs the award, by the last of them.

A1–055   55. **Notification of award**

(1) The parties are free to agree on the requirements as to notification of the award to the parties.

(2) If there is no such agreement, the award shall be notified to the parties by service on them of copies of the award, which shall be done without delay after the award is made.

(3) Nothing in this section affects section 56 (power to withhold award in case of non-payment).

A1–056   56. **Power to withhold award in case of non-payment**

(1) The tribunal may refuse to deliver an award to the parties except upon full payment of the fees and expenses of the arbitrators.

(2) If the tribunal refuses on that ground to deliver an award, a party to the arbitral proceedings may (upon notice to the other parties and the tribunal) apply to the court, which may order that—

(a) the tribunal shall deliver the award on the payment into court by the applicant of the fees and expenses demanded, or such lesser amount as the court may specify,

(b) the amount of the fees and expenses properly payable shall be determined by such means and upon such terms as the court may direct, and

(c) out of the money paid into court there shall be paid out such fees and expenses as may be found to be properly payable and the balance of the money (if any) shall be paid out to the applicant.

(3) For this purpose the amount of fees and expenses properly payable is the amount the applicant is liable to pay under section 28 or any agreement relating to the payment of the arbitrators.

(4) No application to the court may be made where there is any available arbitral process for appeal or review of the amount of the fees or expenses demanded.

(5) References in this section to arbitrators include an arbitrator who has ceased to act and an umpire who has not replaced the other arbitrators.

(6) The above provisions of this section also apply in relation to any arbitral or other institution or person vested by the parties with powers in relation to the delivery of the tribunal's award.

As they so apply, the references to the fees and expenses of the arbitrators shall be construed as including the fees and expenses of that institution or person.

(7) The leave of the court is required for any appeal from a decision of the court under this section.

(8) Nothing in this section shall be construed as excluding an application under section 28 where payment has been made to the arbitrators in order to obtain the award.

57. Correction of award or additional award   A1–057

(1) The parties are free to agree on the powers of the tribunal to correct an award or make an additional award.

(2) If or to the extent there is no such agreement, the following provisions apply.

(3) The tribunal may on its own initiative or on the application of a party—

(a) correct an award so as to remove any clerical mistake or error arising from an accidental slip or omission or clarify or remove any ambiguity in the award, or

(b) make an additional award in respect of any claim (including a claim for interest or costs) which was presented to the tribunal but was not dealt with in the award.

These powers shall not be exercised without first affording the other parties a reasonable opportunity to make representations to the tribunal.

(4) Any application for the exercise of those powers must be made within 28 days of the date of the award or such longer period as the parties may agree.

(5) Any correction of an award shall be made within 28 days of the date the application was received by the tribunal or, where the correction is made by the tribunal on its own initiative, within 28 days of the date of the award or, in either case, such longer period as the parties may agree.

(6) Any additional award shall be made within 56 days of the date of the original award or such longer period as the parties may agree.

(7) Any correction of an award shall form part of the award.

A1–058 58. Effect of award

(1) Unless otherwise agreed by the parties, an award made by the tribunal pursuant to an arbitration agreement is final and binding both on the parties and on any persons claiming through or under them.

(2) This does not affect the right of a person to challenge the award by any available arbitral process of appeal or review or in accordance with the provisions of this Part.

Costs of the arbitration

A1–059 59. Costs of the arbitration

(1) References in this Part to the costs of the arbitration are to—

  (a) the arbitrators' fees and expenses,

  (b) the fees and expenses of any arbitral institution concerned, and

  (c) the legal or other costs of the parties.

(2) Any such reference includes the costs of or incidental to any proceedings to determine the amount of the recoverable costs of the arbitration (see section 63).

A1–060 60. Agreement to pay costs in any event

An agreement which has the effect that a party is to pay the whole or part of the costs of the arbitration in any event is only valid if made after the dispute in question has arisen.

A1–061 61. Award of costs

(1) The tribunal may make an award allocating the costs of the arbitration as between the parties, subject to any agreement of the parties.

(2) Unless the parties otherwise agree, the tribunal shall award costs on the general principle that costs should follow the event except where it appears to the tribunal that in the circumstances this is not appropriate in relation to the whole or part of the costs.

A1–062 62. Effect of agreement or award about costs

Unless the parties otherwise agree, any obligation under an agreement between them as to how the costs of the arbitration are to be borne, or under an award allocating the costs of the arbitration, extends only to such costs as are recoverable.

A1–063 63. The recoverable costs of the arbitration

(1) The parties are free to agree what costs of the arbitration are recoverable.

(2) If or to the extent there is no such agreement, the following provisions apply.

(3) The tribunal may determine by award the recoverable costs of the arbitration on such basis as it thinks fit.

If it does so, it shall specify—

  (a) the basis on which it has acted, and

  (b) the items of recoverable costs and the amount referable to each.

(4) If the tribunal does not determine the recoverable costs of the arbitration, any party to the arbitral proceedings may apply to the court (upon notice to the other parties) which may—

    (a) determine the recoverable costs of the arbitration on such basis as it thinks fit, or

    (b) order that they shall be determined by such means and upon such terms as it may specify.

(5) Unless the tribunal or the court determines otherwise—

    (a) the recoverable costs of the arbitration shall be determined on the basis that there shall be allowed a reasonable amount in respect of all costs reasonably incurred, and

    (b) any doubt as to whether costs were reasonably incurred or were reasonable in amount shall be resolved in favour of the paying party.

(6) The above provisions have effect subject to section 64 (recoverable fees and expenses of arbitrators).
(7) Nothing in this section affects any right of the arbitrators, any expert, legal adviser or assessor appointed by the tribunal, or any arbitral institution, to payment of their fees and expenses.

64. Recoverable fees and expenses of arbitrators

A1–064

(1) Unless otherwise agreed by the parties, the recoverable costs of the arbitration shall include in respect of the fees and expenses of the arbitrators only such reasonable fees and expenses as are appropriate in the circumstances.
(2) If there is any question as to what reasonable fees and expenses are appropriate in the circumstances, and the matter is not already before the court on an application under section 63(4), the court may on the application of any party (upon notice to the other parties)—

    (a) determine the matter, or

    (b) order that it be determined by such means and upon such terms as the court may specify.

(3) Subsection (1) has effect subject to any order of the court under section 24(4) or 25(3)(b) (order as to entitlement to fees or expenses in case of removal or resignation of arbitrator).
(4) Nothing in this section affects any right of the arbitrator to payment of his fees and expenses.

65. Power to limit recoverable costs

A1–065

(1) Unless otherwise agreed by the parties, the tribunal may direct that the recoverable costs of the arbitration, or of any part of the arbitral proceedings, shall be limited to a specified amount.
(2) Any direction may be made or varied at any stage, but this must be done sufficiently in advance of the incurring of costs to which it relates, or the taking of any steps in the proceedings which may be affected by it, for the limit to be taken into account.

Appendix 1

Powers of the court in relation to award

A1–066   **66. Enforcement of the award**

(1) An award made by the tribunal pursuant to an arbitration agreement may, by leave of the court, be enforced in the same manner as a judgment or order of the court to the same effect.

(2) Where leave is so given, judgment may be entered in terms of the award.

(3) Leave to enforce an award shall not be given where, or to the extent that, the person against whom it is sought to be enforced shows that the tribunal lacked substantive jurisdiction to make the award.
The right to raise such an objection may have been lost (see section 73).

(4) Nothing in this section affects the recognition or enforcement of an award under any other enactment or rule of law, in particular under Part II of the Arbitration Act 1950 (enforcement of awards under Geneva Convention) or the provisions of Part III of this Act relating to the recognition and enforcement of awards under the New York Convention or by an action on the award.

A1–067   **67. Challenging the award: substantive jurisdiction**

(1) A party to arbitral proceedings may (upon notice to the other parties and to the tribunal) apply to the court—

(a)   challenging any award of the arbitral tribunal as to its substantive jurisdiction; or

(b)   for an order declaring an award made by the tribunal on the merits to be of no effect, in whole or in part, because the tribunal did not have substantive jurisdiction.

A party may lose the right to object (see section 73) and the right to apply is subject to the restrictions in section 70(2) and (3).

(2) The arbitral tribunal may continue the arbitral proceedings and make a further award while an application to the court under this section is pending in relation to an award as to jurisdiction.

(3) On an application under this section challenging an award of the arbitral tribunal as to its substantive jurisdiction, the court may by order—

(a)   confirm the award,

(b)   vary the award, or

(c)   set aside the award in whole or in part.

(4) The leave of the court is required for any appeal from a decision of the court under this section.

A1–068   **68. Challenging the award: serious irregularity**

(1) A party to arbitral proceedings may (upon notice to the other parties and to the tribunal) apply to the court challenging an award in the proceedings on the ground of serious irregularity affecting the tribunal, the proceedings or the award.
A party may lose the right to object (see section 73) and the right to apply is subject to the restrictions in section 70(2) and (3).

(2) Serious irregularity means an irregularity of one or more of the following kinds which the court considers has caused or will cause substantial injustice to the applicant—

(a) failure by the tribunal to comply with section 33 (general duty of tribunal);

(b) the tribunal exceeding its powers (otherwise than by exceeding its substantive jurisdiction: see section 67);

(c) failure by the tribunal to conduct the proceedings in accordance with the procedure agreed by the parties;

(d) failure by the tribunal to deal with all the issues that were put to it;

(e) any arbitral or other institution or person vested by the parties with powers in relation to the proceedings or the award exceeding its powers;

(f) uncertainty or ambiguity as to the effect of the award;

(g) the award being obtained by fraud or the award or the way in which it was procured being contrary to public policy;

(h) failure to comply with the requirements as to the form of the award; or

(i) any irregularity in the conduct of the proceedings or in the award which is admitted by the tribunal or by any arbitral or other institution or person vested by the parties with powers in relation to the proceedings or the award.

(3) If there is shown to be serious irregularity affecting the tribunal, the proceedings or the award, the court may—

(a) remit the award to the tribunal, in whole or in part, for reconsideration,

(b) set the award aside in whole or in part, or

(c) declare the award to be of no effect, in whole or in part.

The court shall not exercise its power to set aside or to declare an award to be of no effect, in whole or in part, unless it is satisfied that it would be inappropriate to remit the matters in question to the tribunal for reconsideration.

(4) The leave of the court is required for any appeal from a decision of the court under this section.

69. Appeal on point of law

A1–069

(1) Unless otherwise agreed by the parties, a party to arbitral proceedings may (upon notice to the other parties and to the tribunal) appeal to the court on a question of law arising out of an award made in the proceedings.

An agreement to dispense with reasons for the tribunal's award shall be considered an agreement to exclude the court's jurisdiction under this section.

(2) An appeal shall not be brought under this section except—

(a) with the agreement of all the other parties to the proceedings, or

(b) with the leave of the court.

The right to appeal is also subject to the restrictions in section 70(2) and (3).

(3) Leave to appeal shall be given only if the court is satisfied—

(a) that the determination of the question will substantially affect the rights of one or more of the parties,

(b) that the question is one which the tribunal was asked to determine,

(c) that, on the basis of the findings of fact in the award

    (i) the decision of the tribunal on the question is obviously wrong, or

    (ii) the question is one of general public importance and the decision of the tribunal is at least open to serious doubt, and

(d) that, despite the agreement of the parties to resolve the matter by arbitration, it is just and proper in all the circumstances for the court to determine the question.

(4) An application for leave to appeal under this section shall identify the question of law to be determined and state the grounds on which it is alleged that leave to appeal should be granted.

(5) The court shall determine an application for leave to appeal under this section without a hearing unless it appears to the court that a hearing is required.

(6) The leave of the court is required for any appeal from a decision of the court under this section to grant or refuse leave to appeal.

(7) On an appeal under this section the court may by order—

(a) confirm the award,

(b) vary the award,

(c) remit the award to the tribunal, in whole or in part, for reconsideration in the light of the court's determination, or

(d) set aside the award in whole or in part.

The court shall not exercise its power to set aside an award, in whole or in part, unless it is satisfied that it would be inappropriate to remit the matters in question to the tribunal for reconsideration.

(8) The decision of the court on an appeal under this section shall be treated as a judgment of the court for the purposes of a further appeal.

But no such appeal lies without the leave of the court which shall not be given unless the court considers that the question is one of general importance or is one which for some other special reason should be considered by the Court of Appeal.

A1–070   **70. Challenge or appeal: supplementary provisions**

(1) The following provisions apply to an application or appeal under section 67, 68 or 69.

(2) An application or appeal may not be brought if the applicant or appellant has not first exhausted—

(a) any available arbitral process of appeal or review, and

(b) any available recourse under section 57 (correction of award or additional award).

(3) Any application or appeal must be brought within 28 days of the date of the award or, if there has been any arbitral process of appeal or review, of the date when the applicant or appellant was notified of the result of that process.

(4) If on an application or appeal it appears to the court that the award—

(a) does not contain the tribunal's reasons, or

(b) does not set out the tribunal's reasons in sufficient detail to enable the court properly to consider the application or appeal, the court may order the tribunal to state the reasons for its award in sufficient detail for that purpose.

(5) Where the court makes an order under subsection (4), it may make such further order as it thinks fit with respect to any additional costs of the arbitration resulting from its order.

(6) The court may order the applicant or appellant to provide security for the costs of the application or appeal, and may direct that the application or appeal be dismissed if the order is not complied with.

The power to order security for costs shall not be exercised on the ground that the applicant or appellant is—

(a) an individual ordinarily resident outside the United Kingdom, or

(b) a corporation or association incorporated or formed under the law of a country outside the United Kingdom, or whose central management and control is exercised outside the United Kingdom.

(7) The court may order that any money payable under the award shall be brought into court or otherwise secured pending the determination of the application or appeal, and may direct that the application or appeal be dismissed if the order is not complied with.

(8) The court may grant leave to appeal subject to conditions to the same or similar effect as an order under subsection (6) or (7).

This does not affect the general discretion of the court to grant leave subject to conditions.

71. Challenge or appeal: effect of order of court

A1–071

(1) The following provisions have effect where the court makes an order under section 67, 68 or 69 with respect to an award.

(2) Where the award is varied, the variation has effect as part of the tribunal's award.

(3) Where the award is remitted to the tribunal, in whole or in part, for reconsideration, the tribunal shall make a fresh award in respect of the matters remitted within three months of the date of the order for remission or such longer or shorter period as the court may direct.

(4) Where the award is set aside or declared to be of no effect, in whole or in part, the court may also order that any provision that an award is a condition precedent to the bringing of legal proceedings in respect of a matter to which the arbitration agreement applies, is of no effect as regards the subject matter of the award or, as the case may be, the relevant part of the award.

Miscellaneous

72. Saving for rights of person who takes no part in proceedings

A1–072

(1) A person alleged to be a party to arbitral proceedings but who takes no part in the proceedings may question—

(a) whether there is a valid arbitration agreement,

(b) whether the tribunal is properly constituted, or

(c) what matters have been submitted to arbitration in accordance with the arbitration agreement,

by proceedings in the court for a declaration or injunction or other appropriate relief.
(2) He also has the same right as a party to the arbitral proceedings to challenge an award—

(a) by an application under section 67 on the ground of lack of substantive jurisdiction in relation to him, or

(b) by an application under section 68 on the ground of serious irregularity (within the meaning of that section) affecting him;

and section 70(2) (duty to exhaust arbitral procedures) does not apply in his case.

A1–073   **73. Loss of right to object**

(1) If a party to arbitral proceedings takes part, or continues to take part, in the proceedings without making, either forthwith or within such time as is allowed by the arbitration agreement or the tribunal or by any provision of this Part, any objection—

(a) that the tribunal lacks substantive jurisdiction,

(b) that the proceedings have been improperly conducted,

(c) that there has been a failure to comply with the arbitration agreement or with any provision of this Part, or

(d) that there has been any other irregularity affecting the tribunal or the proceedings,

he may not raise that objection later, before the tribunal or the court, unless he shows that, at the time he took part or continued to take part in the proceedings, he did not know and could not with reasonable diligence have discovered the grounds for the objection.
(2) Where the arbitral tribunal rules that it has substantive jurisdiction and a party to arbitral proceedings who could have questioned that ruling—

(a) by any available arbitral process of appeal or review, or

(b) by challenging the award,

does not do so, or does not do so within the time allowed by the arbitration agreement or any provision of this Part, he may not object later to the tribunal's substantive jurisdiction on any ground which was the subject of that ruling.

A1–074   **74. Immunity of arbitral institutions, &c**

(1) An arbitral or other institution or person designated or requested by the parties to appoint or nominate an arbitrator is not liable for anything done or omitted in the discharge or purported discharge of that function unless the act or omission is shown to have been in bad faith.
(2) An arbitral or other institution or person by whom an arbitrator is appointed or nominated is not liable, by reason of having appointed or nominated him, for anything done or omitted by the arbitrator (or his employees or agents) in the discharge or purported discharge of his functions as arbitrator.
(3) The above provisions apply to an employee or agent of an arbitral or other institution or person as they apply to the institution or person himself.

75. Charge to secure payment of solicitors' costs   A1–075

   The powers of the court to make declarations and orders under section 73 of the
Solicitors Act 1974 or Article 71H of the Solicitors (Northern Ireland) Order 1976 (power
to charge property recovered in the proceedings with the payment of solicitors' costs) may
be exercised in relation to arbitral proceedings as if those proceedings were proceedings in
the court.

Supplementary

76. Service of notices, &c   A1–076

(1) The parties are free to agree on the manner of service of any notice or other document
required or authorised to be given or served in pursuance of the arbitration agreement or
for the purposes of the arbitral proceedings.
(2) If or to the extent that there is no such agreement the following provisions apply.
(3) A notice or other document may be served on a person by any effective means.
(4) If a notice or other document is addressed, pre-paid and delivered by post—

   (a) to the addressee's last known principal residence or, if he is or has been carrying on
        a trade, profession or business, his last known principal business address, or

   (b) where the addressee is a body corporate, to the body's registered or principal
        office,

it shall be treated as effectively served.
(5) This section does not apply to the service of documents for the purposes of legal
proceedings, for which provision is made by rules of court.
(6) References in this Part to a notice or other document include any form of communication in writing and references to giving or serving a notice or other document shall be
construed accordingly.

77. Powers of court in relation to service of documents   A1–077

(1) This section applies where service of a document on a person in the manner agreed by
the parties, or in accordance with provisions of section 76 having effect in default of
agreement, is not reasonably practicable.
(2) Unless otherwise agreed by the parties, the court may make such order as it thinks
fit—

   (a) for service in such manner as the court may direct, or

   (b) dispensing with service of the document.

(3) Any party to the arbitration agreement may apply for an order, but only after exhausting
any available arbitral process for resolving the matter.
(4) The leave of the court is required for any appeal from a decision of the court under this
section.

78. Reckoning periods of time   A1–078

(1) The parties are free to agree on the method of reckoning periods of time for the
purposes of any provision agreed by them or any provision of this Part having effect in
default of such agreement.

(2) If or to the extent there is no such agreement, periods of time shall be reckoned in accordance with the following provisions.

(3) Where the act is required to be done within a specified period after or from a specified date, the period begins immediately after that date.

(4) Where the act is required to be done a specified number of clear days after a specified date, at least that number of days must intervene between the day on which the act is done and that date.

(5) Where the period is a period of seven days or less which would include a Saturday, Sunday or a public holiday in the place where anything which has to be done within the period falls to be done, that day shall be excluded.

In relation to England and Wales or Northern Ireland, a "public holiday" means Christmas Day, Good Friday or a day which under the Banking and Financial Dealings Act 1971 is a bank holiday.

A1–079   **79. Power of court to extend time limits relating to arbitral proceedings**

(1) Unless the parties otherwise agree, the court may by order extend any time limit agreed by them in relation to any matter relating to the arbitral proceedings or specified in any provision of this Part having effect in default of such agreement.

This section does not apply to a time limit to which section 12 applies (power of court to extend time for beginning arbitral proceedings, &c.).

(2) An application for an order may be made—

    (a) by any party to the arbitral proceedings (upon notice to the other parties and to the tribunal), or

    (b) by the arbitral tribunal (upon notice to the parties).

(3) The court shall not exercise its power to extend a time limit unless it is satisfied—

    (a) that any available recourse to the tribunal, or to any arbitral or other institution or person vested by the parties with power in that regard, has first been exhausted, and

    (b) that a substantial injustice would otherwise be done.

(4) The court's power under this section may be exercised whether or not the time has already expired.

(5) An order under this section may be made on such terms as the court thinks fit.

(6) The leave of the court is required for any appeal from a decision of the court under this section.

A1–080   **80. Notice and other requirements in connection with legal proceedings**

(1) References in this Part to an application, appeal or other step in relation to legal proceedings being taken "upon notice" to the other parties to the arbitral proceedings, or to the tribunal, are to such notice of the originating process as is required by rules of court and do not impose any separate requirement.

(2) Rules of court shall be made—

    (a) requiring such notice to be given as indicated by any provision of this Part, and

    (b) as to the manner, form and content of any such notice.

(3) Subject to any provision made by rules of court, a requirement to give notice to the tribunal of legal proceedings shall be construed—

(a) if there is more than one arbitrator, as a requirement to give notice to each of them, and

(b) if the tribunal is not fully constituted, as a requirement to give notice to any arbitrator who has been appointed.

(4) References in this Part to making an application or appeal to the court within a specified period are to the issue within that period of the appropriate originating process in accordance with rules of court.

(5) Where any provision of this Part requires an application or appeal to be made to the court within a specified time, the rules of court relating to the reckoning of periods, the extending or abridging of periods, and the consequences of not taking a step within the period prescribed by the rules, apply in relation to that requirement.

(6) Provision may be made by rules of court amending the provisions of this Part—

(a) with respect to the time within which any application or appeal to the court must be made,

(b) so as to keep any provision made by this Part in relation to arbitral proceedings in step with the corresponding provision of rules of court applying in relation to proceedings in the court, or

(c) so as to keep any provision made by this Part in relation to legal proceedings in step with the corresponding provision of rules of court applying generally in relation to proceedings in the court.

(7) Nothing in this section affects the generality of the power to make rules of court.

81. Saving for certain matters governed by common law   A1–081

(1) Nothing in this Part shall be construed as excluding the operation of any rule of law consistent with the provisions of this Part, in particular, any rule of law as to—

(a) matters which are not capable of settlement by arbitration;

(b) the effect of an oral arbitration agreement; or

(c) the refusal of recognition or enforcement of an arbitral award on grounds of public policy.

(2) Nothing in this Act shall be construed as reviving any jurisdiction of the court to set aside or remit an award on the ground of errors of fact or law on the face of the award.

82. Minor definitions   A1–082

(1) In this Part—
"arbitrator", unless the context otherwise requires, includes an umpire;
"available arbitral process", in relation to any matter, includes any process of appeal to or review by an arbitral or other institution or person vested by the parties with powers in relation to that matter;
"claimant", unless the context otherwise requires, includes a counter claimant, and related expressions shall be construed accordingly;
"dispute" includes any difference;
"enactment" includes an enactment contained in Northern Ireland legislation;
"legal proceedings" means civil proceedings in the High Court or a county court;

"peremptory order" means an order made under section 41(5) or made in exercise of any corresponding power conferred by the parties;

"premises" includes land, buildings, moveable structures, vehicles, vessels, aircraft and hovercraft;

"question of law" means—

(a) for a court in England and Wales, a question of the law of England and Wales, and

(b) for a court in Northern Ireland, a question of the law of Northern Ireland;

"substantive jurisdiction", in relation to an arbitral tribunal, refers to the matters specified in section 30(1)(a) to (c), and references to the tribunal exceeding its substantive jurisdiction shall be construed accordingly.

(2) References in this Part to a party to an arbitration agreement include any person claiming under or through a party to the agreement.

A1–083   **83. Index of defined expressions: Part I**

In this Part the expressions listed below are defined or otherwise explained by the provisions indicated—

agreement, agree and agreed	section 5(1)
agreement in writing	section 5(2) to (5)
arbitration agreement	sections 6 and 5(1)
arbitrator	section 82(1)
available arbitral process	section 82(1)
claimant	section 82(1)
commencement (in relation to arbitral proceedings)	section 14
costs of the arbitration	section 59
the court	section 105
dispute	section 82(1)
enactment	section 82(1)
legal proceedings	section 82(1)
Limitation Acts	section 13(4)
notice (or other document)	section 76(6)
party—	
–in relation to an arbitration agreement	section 82(2)
–where section 106(2) or (3) applies	section 106(4)
peremptory order	section 82(1) (and see section 41(5))
premises	section 82(1)
question of law	section 82(1)
recoverable costs	sections 63 and 64
seat of the arbitration	section 3
serve and service (of notice or other document)	section 76(6)

substantive jurisdiction (in relation to an arbitral tribunal)	section 82(1) (and see 30(1)(a) to (c))
upon notice (to the parties or the tribunal)	section 80
written and in writing	section 5(6)

84. Transitional provisions

A1–084

(1) The provisions of this Part do not apply to arbitral proceedings commenced before the date on which this Part comes into force.

(2) They apply to arbitral proceedings commenced on or after that date under an arbitration agreement whenever made.

(3) The above provisions have effect subject to any transitional provision made by an order under section 109(2) (power to include transitional provisions in commencement order).

PART II

OTHER PROVISIONS RELATING TO ARBITRATION

Domestic arbitration agreements

85. Modification of Part I in relation to domestic arbitration agreement

A1–085

(1) In the case of a domestic arbitration agreement the provisions of Part I are modified in accordance with the following sections.

(2) For this purpose a "domestic arbitration agreement" means an arbitration agreement to which none of the parties is—

(a) an individual who is a national of, or habitually resident in, a state other than the United Kingdom, or

(b) a body corporate which is incorporated in, or whose central control and management is exercised in, a state other than the United Kingdom,

and under which the seat of the arbitration (if the seat has been designated or determined) is in the United Kingdom.

(3) In subsection (2) "arbitration agreement" and "seat of the arbitration" have the same meaning as in Part I (see sections 3, 5(1) and 6).

86. Staying of legal proceedings

A1–086

(1) In section 9 (stay of legal proceedings), subsection (4) (stay unless the arbitration agreement is null and void, inoperative, or incapable of being performed) does not apply to a domestic arbitration agreement.

(2) On an application under that section in relation to a domestic arbitration agreement the court shall grant a stay unless satisfied—

(a) that the arbitration agreement is null and void, inoperative, or incapable of being performed, or

(b) that there are other sufficient grounds for not requiring the parties to abide by the arbitration agreement.

(3) The court may treat as a sufficient ground under subsection (2)(b) the fact that the applicant is or was at any material time not ready and willing to do all things necessary for the proper conduct of the arbitration or of any other dispute resolution procedures required to be exhausted before resorting to arbitration.

(4) For the purposes of this section the question whether an arbitration agreement is a domestic arbitration agreement shall be determined by reference to the facts at the time the legal proceedings are commenced.

A1–087   **87. Effectiveness of agreement to exclude court's jurisdiction**

(1) In the case of a domestic arbitration agreement any agreement to exclude the jurisdiction of the court under—

(a) section 45 (determination of preliminary point of law), or

(b) section 69 (challenging the award: appeal on point of law),

is not effective unless entered into after the commencement of the arbitral proceedings in which the question arises or the award is made.

(2) For this purpose the commencement of the arbitral proceedings has the same meaning as in Part I (see section 14).

(3) For the purposes of this section the question whether an arbitration agreement is a domestic arbitration agreement shall be determined by reference to the facts at the time the agreement is entered into.

A1–088   **88. Power to repeal or amend sections 85 to 87**

(1) The Secretary of State may by order repeal or amend the provisions of sections 85 to 87.

(2) An order under this section may contain such supplementary, incidental and transitional provisions as appear to the Secretary of State to be appropriate.

(3) An order under this section shall be made by statutory instrument and no such order shall be made unless a draft of it has been laid before and approved by a resolution of each House of Parliament.

Consumer arbitration agreements

A1–089   **89. Application of unfair terms regulations to consumer arbitration agreements**

(1) The following sections extend the application of the Unfair Terms in Consumer Contracts Regulations 1994 in relation to a term which constitutes an arbitration agreement.

For this purpose "arbitration agreement" means an agreement to submit to arbitration present or future disputes or differences (whether or not contractual).

(2) In those sections "the Regulations" means those regulations and includes any regulations amending or replacing those regulations.

(3) Those sections apply whatever the law applicable to the arbitration agreement.

90. Regulations apply where consumer is a legal person　　　　　**A1–090**

The Regulations apply where the consumer is a legal person as they apply where the consumer is a natural person.

91. Arbitration agreement unfair where modest amount sought　　　　　**A1–091**

(1) A term which constitutes an arbitration agreement is unfair for the purposes of the Regulations so far as it relates to a claim for a pecuniary remedy which docs not exceed the amount specified by order for the purposes of this section.
(2) Orders under this section may make different provision for different cases and for different purposes.
(3) The power to make orders under this section is exercisable—

(a) for England and Wales, by the Secretary of State with the concurrence of the Lord Chancellor,

(b) for Scotland, by the Secretary of State [. . .]¹, and

(c) for Northern Ireland, by the Department of Economic Development for Northern Ireland with the concurrence of the Lord Chancellor.

(4) Any such order for Northern Ireland shall be a statutory rule for the purposes of the Statutory Rules (Northern Ireland) Order 1979 and shall be subject to negative resolution; within the meaning of section 41(6) of the Interpretation Act (Northern Ireland) 1954.
(5) Any such order for Northern Ireland shall be a statutory rule for the purposes of the Statutory Rules (Northern Ireland) Order 1979 and shall be subject to negative resolution, within the meaning of section 41(6) of the Interpretation Act (Northern Ireland) 1954.
Note: ¹*Words in square brackets repealed by the Transfer of Functions (Lord Advocate and Secretary of State Order) 1999 (S.I. 1999 No. 678), ag003, art.16.*

Small claims arbitration in the county court

92. Exclusion of Part I in relation to small claims arbitration in the County Court　　　　　**A1–092**

Nothing in Part I of this Act applies to arbitration under section 64 of the County Courts Act 1984.

Appointment of judges as arbitrators

93. Appointment of judges as arbitrators　　　　　**A1–093**

(1) A judge of the Commercial Court or an official referee may, if in all the circumstances he thinks fit, accept appointment as a sole arbitrator or as umpire by or by virtue of an arbitration agreement.
(2) A judge of the Commercial Court shall not do so unless the Lord Chief Justice has informed him that, having regard to the state of business in the High Court and the Crown Court, he can be made available.
(3) An official referee shall not do so unless the Lord Chief Justice has informed him that, having regard to the state of official referees' business, he can be made available.

(4) The fees payable for the services of a judge of the Commercial Court or official referee as arbitrator or umpire shall be taken in the High Court.

(5) In this section—

"arbitration agreement" has the same meaning as in Part I; and

"official referee" means a person nominated under section 68(1)(a) of the Supreme Court Act 1981 to deal with official referees' business.

(6) The provisions of Part I of this Act apply to arbitration before a person appointed under this section with the modifications specified in Schedule 2.

Statutory arbitrations

A1–094   **94. Application of Part I to statutory arbitrations**

(1) The provisions of Part I apply to every arbitration under an enactment (a "statutory arbitration"), whether the enactment was passed or made before or after the commencement of this Act, subject to the adaptations and exclusions specified in sections 95 to 98.

(2) The provisions of Part I do not apply to a statutory arbitration if or to the extent that their application—

(a) is inconsistent with the provisions of the enactment concerned, with any rules or procedure authorised or recognised by it, or

(b) is excluded by any other enactment.

(3) In this section and the following provisions of this Part "enactment"—

(a) in England and Wales, includes an enactment contained in subordinate legislation within the meaning of the Interpretation Act 1978;

(b) in Northern Ireland, means a statutory provision within the meaning of section 1(f) of the Interpretation Act (Northern Ireland) 1954.

A1–095   **95. General adaptation of provisions in relation to statutory arbitrations**

(1) The provisions of Part I apply to a statutory arbitration—

(a) as if the arbitration were pursuant to an arbitration agreement and as if the enactment were that agreement, and

(b) as if the persons by and against whom a claim subject to arbitration in pursuance of the enactment may be or has been made were parties to that agreement.

(2) Every statutory arbitration shall be taken to have its seat in England and Wales or, as the case may be, in Northern Ireland.

A1–096   **96. Specific adaptations of provisions in relation to statutory arbitrations**

(1) The following provisions of Part I apply to a statutory arbitration with the following adaptations.

(2) In section 30(1) (competence of tribunal to rule on its own jurisdiction), the reference in paragraph (a) to whether there is a valid arbitration agreement shall be construed as a reference to whether the enactment applies to the dispute or difference in question.

(3) Section 35 (consolidation of proceedings and concurrent hearings) applies only so as to authorise the consolidation of proceedings, or concurrent hearings in proceedings, under the same enactment.

(4) Section 46 (rules applicable to substance of dispute) applies with the omission of subsection (1)(b) (determination in accordance with considerations agreed by parties).

97. Provisions excluded from applying to statutory arbitrations

A1–097

The following provisions of Part I do not apply in relation to a statutory arbitration—

(a) section 8 (whether agreement discharged by death of a party);

(b) section 12 (power of court to extend agreed time limits);

(c) sections 9(5), 10(2) and 71(4) (restrictions on effect of provision that award condition precedent to right to bring legal proceedings).

98. Power to make further provision by regulations

A1–098

(1) The Secretary of State may make provision by regulations for adapting or excluding any provision of Part I in relation to statutory arbitrations in general or statutory arbitrations of any particular description.

(2) The power is exercisable whether the enactment concerned is passed or made before or after the commencement of this Act.

(3) Regulations under this section shall be made by statutory instrument which shall be subject to annulment in pursuance of a resolution of either House of Parliament.

PART III

RECOGNITION AND ENFORCEMENT OF CERTAIN FOREIGN AWARDS

Enforcement of Geneva Convention awards

99. Continuation of Part II of the Arbitration Act 1950

A1–099

Part II of the Arbitration Act 1950 (enforcement of certain foreign awards) continues to apply in relation to foreign awards within the meaning of that Part which are not also New York Convention awards.

Recognition and enforcement of New York Convention awards

100. New York Convention awards

A1–100

(1) In this Part a "New York Convention award" means an award made, in pursuance of an arbitration agreement, in the territory of a state (other than the United Kingdom) which is a party to the New York Convention.

(2) For the purposes of subsection (1) and of the provisions of this Part relating to such awards—

(a) "arbitration agreement" means an arbitration agreement in writing, and

(b) an award shall be treated as made at the seat of the arbitration, regardless of where it was signed, despatched or delivered to any of the parties.

In this subsection "agreement in writing" and "seat of the arbitration" have the same meaning as in Part I.

(3) If Her Majesty by Order in Council declares that a state specified in the Order is a party to the New York Convention, or is a party in respect of any territory so specified, the Order shall, while in force, be conclusive evidence of that fact.

(4) In this section "the New York Convention" means the Convention on the Recognition and Enforcement of Foreign Arbitral Awards adopted by the United Nations Conference on International Commercial Arbitration on 10th June 1958.

A1–101   **101. Recognition and enforcement of awards**

(1) A New York Convention award shall be recognised as binding on the persons as between whom it was made, and may accordingly be relied on by those persons by way of defence, set-off or otherwise in any legal proceedings in England and Wales or Northern Ireland.

(2) A New York Convention award may, by leave of the court, be enforced in the same manner as a judgment or order of the court to the same effect.

As to the meaning of "the court" see section 105.

(3) Where leave is so given, judgment may be entered in terms of the award.

A1–102   **102. Evidence to be produced by party seeking recognition or enforcement**

(1) A party seeking the recognition or enforcement of a New York Convention award must produce—

(a) the duly authenticated original award or a duly certified copy of it, and

(b) the original arbitration agreement or a duly certified copy of it.

(2) If the award or agreement is in a foreign language, the party must also produce a translation of it certified by an official or sworn translator or by a diplomatic or consular agent.

A1–103   **103. Refusal of recognition or enforcement**

(1) Recognition or enforcement of a New York Convention award shall not be refused except in the following cases.

(2) Recognition or enforcement of the award may be refused if the person against whom it is invoked proves—

(a) that a party to the arbitration agreement was (under the law applicable to him) under some incapacity;

(b) that the arbitration agreement was not valid under the law to which the parties subjected it or, failing any indication thereon, under the law of the country where the award was made;

(c) that he was not given proper notice of the appointment of the arbitrator or of the arbitration proceedings or was otherwise unable to present his case;

(d) that the award deals with a difference not contemplated by or not falling within the terms of the submission to arbitration or contains decisions on matters beyond the scope of the submission to arbitration (but see subsection (4));

(e) that the composition of the arbitral tribunal or the arbitral procedure was not in accordance with the agreement of the parties or, failing such agreement, with the law of the country in which the arbitration took place;

(f) that the award has not yet become binding on the parties, or has been set aside or suspended by a competent authority of the country in which, or under the law of which, it was made.

(3) Recognition or enforcement of the award may also be refused if the award is in respect of a matter which is not capable of settlement by arbitration, or if it would be contrary to public policy to recognise or enforce the award.

(4) An award which contains decisions on matters not submitted to arbitration may be recognised or enforced to the extent that it contains decisions on matters submitted to arbitration which can be separated from those on matters not so submitted.

(5) Where an application for the setting aside or suspension of the award has been made to such a competent authority as is mentioned in subsection (2)(f), the court before which the award is sought to be relied upon may, if it considers it proper, adjourn the decision on the recognition or enforcement of the award.

It may also on the application of the party claiming recognition or enforcement of the award order the other party to give suitable security.

104. Saving for other bases of recognition or enforcement

A1–104

Nothing in the preceding provisions of this Part affects any right to rely upon or enforce a New York Convention award at common law or under section 66.

PART IV

GENERAL PROVISIONS

105. Meaning of "the court": jurisdiction of High Court and county court

A1–105

(1) In this Act "the court" means the High Court or a county court, subject to the following provisions.

(2) The Lord Chancellor may by order make provision—

(a) allocating proceedings under this Act to the High Court or to county courts; or

(b) specifying proceedings under this Act which may be commenced or taken only in the High Court or in a county court.

(3) The Lord Chancellor may by order make provision requiring proceedings of any specified description under this Act in relation to which a county court has jurisdiction to be commenced or taken in one or more specified county courts.

Any jurisdiction so exercisable by a specified county court is exercisable throughout England and Wales or, as the case may be, Northern Ireland.

(4) An order under this section—

(a) may differentiate between categories of proceedings by reference to such criteria as the Lord Chancellor sees fit to specify, and

(b) may make such incidental or transitional provision as the Lord Chancellor considers necessary or expedient.

(5) An order under this section for England and Wales shall be made by statutory instrument which shall be subject to annulment in pursuance of a resolution of either House of Parliament.

(6) An order under this section for Northern Ireland shall be a statutory rule for the purposes of the Statutory Rules (Northern Ireland) Order 1979 which shall be subject to annulment in pursuance of a resolution of either House of Parliament in like manner as a statutory instrument and section 5 of the Statutory Instruments Act 1946 shall apply accordingly.

A1–106 106. Crown application

(1) Part I of this Act applies to any arbitration agreement to which Her Majesty, either in right of the Crown or of the Duchy of Lancaster or otherwise, or the Duke of Cornwall, is a party.

(2) Where Her Majesty is party to an arbitration agreement otherwise than in right of the Crown, Her Majesty shall be represented for the purposes of any arbitral proceedings—

(a) where the agreement was entered into by Her Majesty in right of the Duchy of Lancaster, by the Chancellor of the Duchy or such person as he may appoint, and

(b) in any other case, by such person as Her Majesty may appoint in writing under the Royal Sign Manual.

(3) Where the Duke of Cornwall is party to an arbitration agreement, he shall be represented for the purposes of any arbitral proceedings by such person as he may appoint.

(4) References in Part I to a party or the parties to the arbitration agreement or to arbitral proceedings shall be construed, where subsection (2) or (3) applies, as references to the person representing Her Majesty or the Duke of Cornwall.

A1–107 107. Consequential amendments and repeals

(1) The enactments specified in Schedule 3 are amended in accordance with that Schedule, the amendments being consequential on the provisions of this Act.

(2) The enactments specified in Schedule 4 are repealed to the extent specified.

A1–108 108. Extent

(1) The provisions of this Act extend to England and Wales and, except as mentioned below, to Northern Ireland.

(2) The following provisions of Part II do not extend to Northern Ireland—

section 92 (exclusion of Part I in relation to small claims arbitration in the county court), and

section 93 and Schedule 2 (appointment of judges as arbitrators).

(3) Sections 89,90 and 91 (consumer arbitration agreements) extend to Scotland and the provisions of Schedules 3 and 4 (consequential amendments and repeals) extend to Scotland so far as they relate to enactments which so extend, subject as follows.

(4) The repeal of the Arbitration Act 1975 extends only to England and Wales and Northern Ireland.

109. Commencement   A1–109

(1) The provisions of this Act come into force on such day as the Secretary of State may appoint by order made by statutory instrument, and different days may be appointed for different purposes.
(2) An order under subsection (1) may contain such transitional provisions as appear to the Secretary of State to be appropriate.

110. Short title   A1–110

This Act may be cited as the Arbitration Act 1996.

SCHEDULES

SCHEDULE 1

Section 4(1)

MANDATORY PROVISIONS OF PART I   A1–111

sections 9 to 11 (stay of legal proceedings);
section 12 (power of court to extend agreed time limits);
section 13 (application of Limitation Acts);
section 24 (power of court to remove arbitrator);
section 26(1) (effect of death of arbitrator);
section 28 (liability of parties for fees and expenses of arbitrators);
section 29 (immunity of arbitrator);
section 31 (objection to substantive jurisdiction of tribunal);
section 32 (determination of preliminary point of jurisdiction);
section 33 (general duty of tribunal);
section 37(2) (items to be treated as expenses of arbitrators);
section 40 (general duty of parties);
section 43 (securing the attendance of witnesses);
section 56 (power to withhold award in case of non-payment);
section 60 (effectiveness of agreement for payment of costs in any event);
section 66 (enforcement of award);
sections 67 and 68 (challenging the award: substantive jurisdiction and serious irregularity),
    and sections 70 and 71 (supplementary provisions; effect of order of court) so far as
    relating to those sections;
section 72 (saving for rights of person who takes no part in proceedings);
section 73 (loss of right to object);
section 74 (immunity of arbitral institutions, &c.);
section 75 (charge to secure payment of solicitors' costs).

SCHEDULE 2

Section 93(6)

A1–112   MODIFICATIONS OF PART I IN RELATION TO JUDGE-ARBITRATORS

Introductory

1. In this Schedule "judge-arbitrator" means a judge of the Commercial Court or official referee appointed as arbitrator or umpire under section 93.

General

2. (1) Subject to the following provisions of this Schedule, references in Part I to the court shall be construed in relation to a judge-arbitrator, or in relation to the appointment of a judge-arbitrator, as references to the Court of Appeal.

(2) The references in sections 32(6), 45(6) and 69(8) to the Court of Appeal shall in such a case be construed as references to the House of Lords.

Arbitrator's fees

3. (1) The power of the court in section 28(2) to order consideration and adjustment of the liability of a party for the fees of an arbitrator may be exercised by a judge-arbitrator.

(2) Any such exercise of the power is subject to the powers of the Court of Appeal under sections 24(4) and 25(3)(b) (directions as to entitlement to fees or expenses in case of removal or resignation).

Exercise of court powers in support of arbitration

4. (1) Where the arbitral tribunal consists of or includes a judge-arbitrator the powers of the court under sections 42 to 44 (enforcement of peremptory orders, summoning witnesses, and other court powers) are exercisable by the High Court and also by the judge-arbitrator himself.

(2) Anything done by a judge-arbitrator in the exercise of those powers shall be regarded as done by him in his capacity as judge of the High Court and have effect as if done by that court.

Nothing in this sub-paragraph prejudices any power vested in him as arbitrator or umpire.

Extension of time for making award

5. (1) The power conferred by section 50 (extension of time for making award) is exercisable by the judge-arbitrator himself.

(2) Any appeal from a decision of a judge-arbitrator under that section lies to the Court of Appeal with the leave of that court.

Withholding award in case of non-payment

6. (1) The provisions of paragraph 7 apply in place of the provisions of section 56 (power to withhold award in the case of non-payment) in relation to the withholding of an award for non-payment of the fees and expenses of a judge-arbitrator.

(2) This does not affect the application of section 56 in relation to the delivery of such an award by an arbitral or other institution or person vested by the parties with powers in relation to the delivery of the award.

7. (1) A judge-arbitrator may refuse to deliver an award except upon payment of the fees and expenses mentioned in section 56(1).

(2) The judge-arbitrator may, on an application by a party to the arbitral proceedings, order that if he pays into the High Court the fees and expenses demanded, or such lesser amount as the judge-arbitrator may specify—

(a) the award shall be delivered,

(b) the amount of the fees and expenses properly payable shall be determined by such means and upon such terms as he may direct, and

(c) out of the money paid into court there shall be paid out such fees and expenses as may be found to be properly payable and the balance of the money (if any) shall be paid out to the applicant.

(3) For this purpose the amount of fees and expenses properly payable is the amount the applicant is liable to pay under section 28 or any agreement relating to the payment of the arbitrator.

(4) No application to the judge-arbitrator under this paragraph may be made where there is any available arbitral process for appeal or review of the amount of the fees or expenses demanded.

(5) Any appeal from a decision of a judge-arbitrator under this paragraph lies to the Court of Appeal with the leave of that court.

(6) Where a party to arbitral proceedings appeals under sub-paragraph (5), an arbitrator is entitled to appear and be heard.

Correction of award or additional award

8. Subsections (4) to (6) of section 57 (correction of award or additional award: time limit for application or exercise of power) do not apply to a judge-arbitrator.

Costs

9. Where the arbitral tribunal consists of or includes a judge-arbitrator the powers of the court under section 63(4) (determination of recoverable costs) shall be exercised by the High Court.

10. (1) The power of the court under section 64 to determine an arbitrator's reasonable fees and expenses may be exercised by a judge-arbitrator.

(2) Any such exercise of the power is subject to the powers of the Court of Appeal under sections 24(4) and 25(3)(b) (directions as to entitlement to fees or expenses in case of removal or resignation).

Enforcement of award

11. The leave of the court required by section 66 (enforcement of award) may in the case of an award of a judge-arbitrator be given by the judge-arbitrator himself.

Solicitors' costs

12. The powers of the court to make declarations and orders under the provisions applied by section 75 (power to charge property recovered in arbitral proceedings with the payment of solicitors' costs) may be exercised by the judge arbitrator.

Powers of court in relation to service of documents

13. (1) The power of the court under section 77(2) (powers of court in relation to service of documents) is exercisable by the judge-arbitrator.

(2) Any appeal from a decision of a judge-arbitrator under that section lies to the Court of Appeal with the leave of that court.

Powers of court to extend time limits relating to arbitral proceedings

14. (1) The power conferred by section 79 (power of court to extend time limits relating to arbitral proceedings) is exercisable by the judge-arbitrator himself.

(2) Any appeal from a decision of a judge-arbitrator under that section lies to the Court of Appeal with the leave of that court.

SCHEDULE 3

Section 107(1)

A1–113   CONSEQUENTIAL AMENDMENTS

Merchant Shipping Act 1894 (c.60)

1. In section 496 of the Merchant Shipping Act 1894 (provisions as to deposits by owners of goods), after subsection (4) insert—

"(5) In subsection (3) the expression "legal proceedings" includes arbitral proceedings and as respects England and Wales and Northern Ireland the provisions of section 14 of the Arbitration Act 1996 apply to determine when such proceedings are commenced.".

Stannaries Court (Abolition) Act 1896 (c.45)

2. In section 4(1) of the Stannaries Court (Abolition) Act 1896 (references of certain disputes to arbitration), for the words from "tried before" to "any such reference" substitute "referred to arbitration before himself or before an arbitrator agreed on by the parties or an officer of the court".

Tithe Act 1936 (c.43)

3. In section 39(1) of the Tithe Act 1936 (proceedings of Tithe Redemption Commission)—

(a) for "the Arbitration Acts 1889 to 1934" substitute "Part I of the Arbitration Act 1996";

(b) for paragraph (e) substitute—"(e) the making of an application to the court to determine a preliminary point of law and the bringing of an appeal to the court on a point of law;";

(c) for "the said Acts" substitute "Part I of the Arbitration Act 1996".

Commonwealth Telegraphs Act 1949 (c.39)

5. In section 8(2) of the Commonwealth Telegraphs Act 1949 (proceedings of referees under the Act) for "the Arbitration Acts 1889 to 1934, or the Arbitration Act Northern Ireland) 1937," substitute "Part I of the Arbitration Act 1996".

Lands Tribunal Act 1949 (c.42)

6. In section 3 of the Lands Tribunal Act 1949 (proceedings before the Lands Tribunal)—

(a) in subsection (6)(c) (procedural rules: power to apply Arbitration Acts), and

(b) in subsection (8) (exclusion of Arbitration Acts except as applied by rules),

for "the Arbitration Acts 1889 to 1934" substitute "Part I of the Arbitration Act 1996".

Wireless Telegraphy Act 1949 (c.54)

7. In the Wireless Telegraphy Act 1949, Schedule 2 (procedure of appeals tribunal), in paragraph 3(1)—

(a) for the words "the Arbitration Acts 1889 to 1934" substitute "Part I of the Arbitration Act 1996";

(b) after the word "Wales" insert "or Northern Ireland"; and

(c) for "the said Acts" substitute "Part I of that Act".

Patents Act 1949 (c.87)

8. In section 67 of the Patents Act 1949 (proceedings as to infringement of pre-1978 patents referred to comptroller), for "The Arbitration Acts 1889 to 1934" substitute "Part I of the Arbitration Act 1996".

National Health Service (Amendment) Act 1949 (c.93)

9. In section 7(8) of the National Health Service (Amendment) Act 1949 (arbitration in relation to hardship arising from the National Health Service Act 1946 or the Act), for "the Arbitration Acts 1889 to 1934" substitute "Part I of the Arbitration Act 1996" and for "the said Acts" substitute "Part I of that Act".

Arbitration Act 1950 (c.27)

10. In section 36(1) of the Arbitration Act 1950 (effect of foreign awards enforceable under Part II of that Act) for "section 26 of this Act" substitute "section 66 of the Arbitration Act 1996".

Interpretation Act (Northern Ireland) 1954 (c.33 (N.I.))

11. In section 46(2) of the Interpretation Act (Northern Ireland) 1954 (miscellaneous definitions), for the definition of "arbitrator" substitute—
" "arbitrator" has the same meaning as in Part I of the Arbitration Act 1996;".

Agricultural Marketing Act 1958 (c.47)

12. In section 12(1) of the Agricultural Marketing Act 1958 (application of provisions of Arbitration Act 1950)—

(a) for the words from the beginning to "shall apply" substitute "Sections 45 and 69 of the Arbitration Act 1996 (which relate to the determination by the court of questions of law) and section 66 of that Act (enforcement of awards) apply"; and

(b) for "an arbitration" substitute "arbitral proceedings".

Carriage by Air Act 1961 (c.27)

13. (1) The Carriage by Air Act 1961 is amended as follows.
(2) In section 5(3) (time for bringing proceedings)—

(a) for "an arbitration" in the first place where it occurs substitute "arbitral proceedings"; and

(b) for the words from "and subsections (3) and (4)" to the end substitute "and the provisions of section 14 of the Arbitration Act 1996 apply to determine when such proceedings are commenced.".

(3) In section 11(c) (application of section 5 to Scotland)—

(a) for "subsections (3) and (4)" substitute "the provisions of section 14 of the Arbitration Act 1996"; and

(b) for "an arbitration" substitute "arbitral proceedings".

Factories Act 1961 (c.34)

14. In the Factories Act 1961, for section 171 (application of Arbitration Act 1950), substitute—
"171 Application of the Arbitration Act 1996
Part I of the Arbitration Act 1996 does not apply to proceedings under this act except in so far as it may be applied by regulations made under this Act."

Clergy Pensions Measure 1961 (No.3)

15. In the Clergy Pensions Measure 1961, section 38(4) (determination of questions), for the words "The Arbitration Act 1950" substitute "Part I of the Arbitration Act 1996".

Transport Act 1962 (c.46)

16. (1) The Transport Act 1962 is amended as follows.
(2) In section 74(6)(f) (proceedings before referees in pension disputes), for the words "the Arbitration Act 1950" substitute "Part I of the Arbitration Act 1996".
(3) In section 81(7) (proceedings before referees in compensation disputes), for the words "the Arbitration Act 1950" substitute "Part I of the Arbitration Act 1996".
(4) In Schedule 7, Part IV (pensions), in paragraph 17(5) for the words "the Arbitration Act 1950" substitute "Part I of the Arbitration Act 1996".

Corn Rents Act 1963 (c.14)

17. In the Corn Rents Act 1963, section 1(5) (schemes for apportioning corn rents, &c.), for the words "the Arbitration Act 1950" substitute "Part I of the Arbitration Act 1996".

Lands Tribunal and Compensation Act (Northern Ireland) 1964 (c.29 (N.I))

19. In section 9 of the Lands Tribunal and Compensation Act (Northern Ireland) 1964 (proceedings of Lands Tribunal), in subsection (3) (where Tribunal acts as arbitrator) for "the Arbitration Act (Northern Ireland) 1937" substitute "Part I of the Arbitration Act 1996".

Industrial and Provident Societies Act 1965 (c.12)

20. (1) Section 60 of the Industrial and Provident Societies Act 1965 is amended as follows.

(2) In subsection (8) (procedure for hearing disputes between society and member, &c.)—

(a)   in paragraph (a) for "the Arbitration Act 1950" substitute "Part I of the Arbitration Act 1996"; and

(b)   in paragraph (b) omit "by virtue of section 12 of the said Act of 1950".

(3) For subsection (9) substitute—
"(9) The court or registrar to whom any dispute is referred under subsections (2) to (7) may at the request of either party state a case on any question of law arising in the dispute for the opinion of the High Court or, as the case may be, the Court of Session.".

Carriage of Goods by Road Act 1965 (c.37)

21. In section 7(2) of the Carriage of Goods by Road Act 1965 (arbitrations: time at which deemed to commence), for paragraphs (a) and (b) substitute—
"(a) as respects England and Wales and Northern Ireland, the provisions of section 14(3) to (5) of the Arbitration Act 1996 (which determine the time at which an arbitration is commenced) apply;".

Factories Act (Northern Ireland) 1965 (c.20 (N.I))

22. In section 171 of the Factories Act (Northern Ireland) 1965 (application of Arbitration Act), for "The Arbitration Act (Northern Ireland) 1937" substitute "Part I of the Arbitration Act 1996".

Commonwealth Secretariat Act 1966 (c.10)

23. In section 1(3) of the Commonwealth Secretariat Act 1966 (contracts with Commonwealth Secretariat to be deemed to contain provision for arbitration), for "the Arbitration Act 1950 and the Arbitration Act (Northern Ireland) 1937" substitute "Part I of the Arbitration Act 1996".

Arbitration (International Investment Disputes) Act 1966 (c.41)

24. In the Arbitration (International Investment Disputes) Act 1966, for section 3 (application of Arbitration Act 1950 and other enactments) substitute—

"3 Application of provisions of Arbitration Act 1996

(1) The Lord Chancellor may by order direct that any of the provisions contained in sections 36 and 38 to 44 of the Arbitration Act 1996 (provisions concerning the conduct of arbitral provisions, &c.) shall apply to such proceedings pursuant to the Convention as are specified in the order with or without any modifications or exceptions specified in the order.

(2) Subject to subsection (1), the Arbitration Act 1996 shall not apply to proceedings pursuant to the Convention, but this subsection shall not be taken as affecting section 9 of that Act (stay of legal proceedings in respect of matter subject to arbitration).

(3) An order made under this section—

(a) may be varied or revoked by a subsequent order so made, and

(b) shall be contained in a statutory instrument.".

Poultry Improvement Act (Northern Ireland) 1968 (c.12 (N.I))

25. In paragraph 10(4) of the Schedule to the Poultry Improvement Act (Northern Ireland) 1968 (reference of disputes), for "The Arbitration Act (Northern Ireland) 1937" substitute "Part I of the Arbitration Act 1996".

Industrial and Provident Societies Act (Northern Ireland) 1969 (c.24 (N.I))

26. (1) Section 69 of the Industrial and Provident Societies Act (Northern Ireland) 1969 (decision of disputes) is amended as follows.

(2) In subsection (7) (decision of disputes)—

(a) in the opening words, omit the words from "and without prejudice" to "1937";

(b) at the beginning of paragraph (a) insert "without prejudice to any powers exercisable by virtue of Part I of the Arbitration Act 1996,"; and

(c) in paragraph (b) omit "the registrar or" and "registrar or" and for the words from "as might have been granted by the High Court" to the end substitute "as might be granted by the registrar".

(3) For subsection (8) substitute—

"(8) The court or registrar to whom any dispute is referred under subsections (2) to (6) may at the request of either party state a case on any question of law arising in the dispute for the opinion of the High Court."

Health and Personal Social Services (Northern Ireland) Order 1972 (N.I 14)

27. In Article 105(6) of the Health and Personal Social Services (Northern Ireland) Order 1972 (arbitrations under the Order), for "the Arbitration Act (Northern Ireland) 1937" substitute "Part I of the Arbitration Act 1996".

Consumer Credit Act 1974 (c.39)

28. (1) Section 146 of the Consumer Credit Act 1974 is amended as follows.

(2) In subsection (2) (solicitor engaged in contentious business), for "section 86(1) of the Solicitors Act 1957" substitute "section 87(1) of the Solicitors Act 1974".

(3) In subsection (4) (solicitor in Northern Ireland engaged in contentious business), for the words from "business done" to "Administration of Estates (Northern Ireland) Order 1979" substitute "contentious business (as defined in Article 3(2) of the Solicitors (Northern Ireland) Order 1976."

Friendly Societies Act 1974 (c.46)

29. (1) The Friendly Societies Act 1974 is amended as follows.

(2) For section 78(1) (statement of case) substitute—

"(1) Any arbitrator, arbiter or umpire to whom a dispute falling within section 76 above is referred under the rules of a registered society or branch may at the request of either party state a case on any question of law arising in the dispute for the opinion of the High Court or, as the case may be, the Court of Session.".

(3) In section 83(3) (procedure on objections to amalgamations &c. of friendly societies), for "the Arbitration Act 1950 or, in Northern Ireland, the Arbitration Act (Northern Ireland) 1937" substitute "Part I of the Arbitration Act 1996".

Industry Act 1975 (c.68)

30. In Schedule 3 to the Industry Act (arbitration of disputes relating to vesting and compensation orders), in paragraph 14 (application of certain provisions of Arbitration Acts)—

(a) for "the Arbitration Act 1950 or, in Northern Ireland, the Arbitration Act (Northern Ireland) 1937" substitute "Part I of the Arbitration Act 1996", and

(b) for "that Act" substitute "that Part".

Industrial Relations (Northern Ireland) Order 1976 (N.I.16)

31. In Article 59(9) of the Industrial Relations (Northern Ireland) Order 1976 (proceedings of industrial tribunal), for "The Arbitration Act (Northern Ireland) 1937" substitute "Part I of the Arbitration Act 1996".

Aircraft and Shipbuilding Industries Act 1977 (c.3)

32. In Schedule 7 to the Aircraft and Shipbuilding Industries Act 1977 (procedure of Arbitration Tribunal), in paragraph 2—

(a) for "the Arbitration Act 1950 or, in Northern Ireland, the Arbitration Act (Northern Ireland) 1937" substitute "Part I of the Arbitration Act 1996", and

(b) for "that Act" substitute "that Part".

Patents Act 1977 (c.37)

33. In section 130 of the Patents Act 1977 (interpretation), in subsection (8) (exclusion of the Arbitration Act) for "The Arbitration Act 1950" substitute "Part I of the Arbitration Act 1996".

Judicature (Northern Ireland) Act 1978 (c.23)

34. (1) The Judicature (Northern Ireland) Act 1978 is amended as follows.
(2) In section 35(2) (restrictions on appeals to the Court of Appeal), after paragraph (f) insert—
"(fa) except as provided by Part I of the Arbitration Act 1996, from any decision of the High Court under that Part;".
(3) In section 55(2) (rules of court) after paragraph (c) insert—
"(cc) providing for any prescribed part of the jurisdiction of the High Court in relation to the trial of any action involving matters of account to be exercised in the prescribed manner by a person agreed by the parties and for the remuneration of any such person;".

Health and Safety at Work (Northern Ireland) Order 1978 (N.I.9)

35. In Schedule 4 to the Health and Safety at Work (Northern Ireland) Order 1978 (licensing provisions), in paragraph 3, for "The Arbitration Act (Northern Ireland) 1937" substitute "Part I of the Arbitration Act 1996".

County Courts (Northern Ireland) Order 1980 (N.I.3)

36. (1) The County Courts (Northern Ireland) Order 1980 is amended as follows.
(2) In Article 30 (civil jurisdiction exercisable by district judge)—

(a) for paragraph (2) substitute—

"(2) Any order, decision or determination made by a district judge under this Article (other than one made in dealing with a claim by way of arbitration under paragraph (3)) shall be embodied in a decree which for all purposes (including the right of appeal under Part VI) shall have the like effect as a decree pronounced by a county court judge.";

(b) for paragraphs (4) and (5) substitute—

"(4) Where in any action to which paragraph (1) applies the claim is dealt with by way of arbitration under paragraph (3)—

(a) any award made by the district judge in dealing with the claim shall be embodied in a decree which for all purposes (except the right of appeal under Part VI) shall have the like effect as a decree pronounced by a county court judge;

(b) the district judge may, and shall if so required by the High Court, state for the determination of the High Court any question of law arising out of an award so made;

(c) except as provided by sub-paragraph (b), any award so made shall be final; and

(d) except as otherwise provided by county court rules, no costs shall be awarded in connection with the action.

(5) Subject to paragraph (4), county court rules may—

(a) apply any of the provisions of Part I of the Arbitration Act 1996 to arbitrations under paragraph (3) with such modifications as may be prescribed;

(b) prescribe the rules of evidence to be followed on any arbitration under paragraph (3) and, in particular, make provision with respect to the manner of taking and questioning evidence.

(5A) Except as provided by virtue of paragraph (5)(a), Part I of the Arbitration Act 1996 shall not apply to an arbitration under paragraph (3)."

(3) After Article 61 insert—

"Appeals from decisions under Part I of Arbitration Act 1996

61A. (1) Article 61 does not apply to a decision of a county court judge made in the exercise of the jurisdiction conferred by Part I of the Arbitration Act 1996.

(2) Any party dissatisfied with a decision of the county court made in the exercise of the jurisdiction conferred by any of the following provisions of Part I of the Arbitration Act 1996, namely—

(a) section 32 (question as to substantive jurisdiction of arbitral tribunal);

(b) section 45 (question of law arising in course of arbitral proceedings);

(c) section 67 (challenging award of arbitral tribunal: substantive jurisdiction);

(d) section 68 (challenging award of arbitral tribunal: serious irregularity);

(e) section 69 (appeal on point of law),

may, subject to the provisions of that Part, appeal from that decision to the Court of Appeal.

(3) Any party dissatisfied with any decision of a county court made in the exercise of the jurisdiction conferred by any other provision of Part I of the Arbitration Act 1996

may, subject to the provisions of that Part, appeal from that decision to the High Court.

(4) The decision of the Court of Appeal on an appeal under paragraph (2) shall be final.".

Supreme Court Act 1981 (c.54)

37. (1) The Supreme Court Act 1981 is amended as follows.

(2) In section 18(1) (restrictions on appeals to the Court of Appeal), for paragraph (g) substitute—

"(g) except as provided by Part I of the Arbitration Act 1996, from any decision of the High Court under that Part;".

(3) In section 151 (interpretation, &c.), in the definition of "arbitration agreement", for "the Arbitration Act 1950 by virtue of section 32 of that Act;" substitute "Part I of the Arbitration Act 1996;"

Merchant Shipping (Liner Conferences) Act 1982 (c.37)

38. In section 7(5) of the Merchant Shipping (Liner Conferences) Act 1982 (stay of legal proceedings), for the words from "section 4(1)" to the end substitute "section 9 of the Arbitration Act 1996 (which also provides for the staying of legal proceedings)".

Agricultural Marketing (Northern Ireland) Order 1982 (N.I.12)

39. In Article 14 of the Agricultural Marketing (Northern Ireland) Order 1982 (application of provisions of the Arbitration Act (Northern Ireland) 1937—

(a) for the words from the beginning to "shall apply" substitute "Section 45 and 69 of the Arbitration Act 1996 (which relate to the determination by the court of questions of law) and section 66 of that Act (enforcement of awards)" apply; and

(b) for "an arbitration" substitute "arbitral proceedings".

Mental Health Act 1983 (c.20)

40. In section 78 of the Mental Health Act 1983 (procedure of Mental Health Review Tribunals), in subsection (9) for "The Arbitration Act 1950" substitute "Part I of the Arbitration Act 1996".

Housing Act 1985 (c.68)

42. In section 47(3) of the Housing Act 1985 (agreement as to determination of matters relating to service charges) for "section 32 of the Arbitration Act 1950" substitute "Part I of the Arbitration Act 1996".

Credit Unions (Northern Ireland) Order 1985 (N.I.12)

44. (1) Article 72 of the Credit Unions (Northern Ireland) Order 1985 (decision of disputes) is amended as follows.

(2) In paragraph (7)—

(a) in the opening words, omit the words from "and without prejudice" to "1937";

(b) at the beginning of sub-paragraph (a) insert "without prejudice to any powers exercisable by virtue of Part I of the Arbitration Act 1996,"; and

(c) in sub-paragraph (b) omit "the registrar or" and "registrar or" and for the words from "as might have been granted by the High Court" to the end substitute "as might be granted by the registrar".

(3) For paragraph (8) substitute—

"(8) The court or registrar to whom any dispute is referred under paragraphs (2) to (6) may at the request of either party state a case on any question of law arising in the dispute for the opinion of the High Court.".

Agricultural Holdings Act 1986 (c.5)

45. In section 84(1) of the Agricultural Holdings Act 1986 (provisions relating to arbitration), for "the Arbitration Act 1950" substitute "Part I of the Arbitration Act 1996".

Insolvency Act 1986 (c.45)

46. In the Insolvency Act 1986, after section 349 insert—

"349A Arbitration agreements to which bankrupt is party

(1) This section applies where a bankrupt had become party to a contract containing an arbitration agreement before the commencement of his bankruptcy.

(2) If the trustee in bankruptcy adopts the contract, the arbitration agreement is enforceable by or against the trustee in relation to matters arising from or connected with the contract.

(3) If the trustee in bankruptcy does not adopt the contract and a matter to which the arbitration agreement applies requires to be determined in connection with or for the purposes of the bankruptcy proceedings–

(a) the trustee with the consent of the creditors' committee or

(b) any other party to the agreement,

may apply to the court which may, if it thinks fit in all the circumstances of the case, order that the matter be referred to arbitration in accordance with the arbitration agreement.

(4) In this section–

"arbitration agreement" has the same meaning as in Part I of the Arbitration Act 1996; and "the court" means the court which has jurisdiction in the bankruptcy proceedings".

Building Societies Act 1986 (c.53)

47. In Part II of Schedule 14 to the Building Societies Act 1986 (settlement of disputes: arbitration), in paragraph 5(6) for "the Arbitration Act 1950 and the Arbitration Act 1979 or, in Northern Ireland, the Arbitration Act (Northern Ireland) 1937" substitute "Part I of the Arbitration Act 1996".

Mental Health (Northern Ireland) Order 1986 (N.I.4)

48. In Article 83 of the Mental Health (Northern Ireland) Order 1986 (procedure of Mental Health Review Tribunal), in paragraph (8) for "The Arbitration Act (Northern Ireland) 1937" substitute "Part I of the Arbitration Act 1996".

Multilateral Investment Guarantee Agency Act 1988 (c.8)

49. For section 6 of the Multilateral Investment Guarantee Agency Act 1988 (application of Arbitration Act) substitute—
"6 Application of Arbitration Act
(1) The Lord Chancellor may by order made by statutory instrument direct that any of the provisions of sections 36 and 38 to 44 of the Arbitration Act 1996 (provisions in relation to the conduct of the arbitral proceedings, &c.) apply, with such modifications or exceptions as are specified in the order, to such arbitration proceedings pursuant to Annex II to the Convention as are specified in the order.
(2) Except as provided by an Order under subsection (1) above, no provision of Part I of the Arbitration Act 1996 other than section 9 (stay of legal proceedings) applies to any such proceedings."

Copyright, Designs and Patents Act 1988 (c.48)

50. In section 150 of the Copyright, Designs and Patents Act 1988 (Lord Chancellor's power to make rules for Copyright Tribunal), for subsection (2) substitute—
"(2) The rules may apply in relation to the Tribunal, as respects proceedings in England and Wales or Northern Ireland, any of the provisions of Part I of the Arbitration Act 1996."

Fair Employment (Northern Ireland) Act 1989 (c.32)

51. In the Fair Employment (Northern Ireland) Act 1989, section 5(7) procedure of Fair Employment Tribunal), for "The Arbitration Act (Northern Ireland) 1937" substitute "Part I of the Arbitration Act 1996".

Limitation (Northern Ireland) Order 1989 (N.I.11)

52. In Article 2(2) of the Limitation (Northern Ireland) Order 1989 (interpretation), in the definition of "arbitration agreement", for "the Arbitration Act (Northern Ireland) 1937" substitute "Part I of the Arbitration Act 1996".

Insolvency (Northern Ireland) Order 1989 (N.I.19)

53. In the Insolvency (Northern Ireland) Order 1989, after Article 320 insert—

"Arbitration agreements to which bankrupt is party.

320A. (1) This Article applies where a bankrupt had become party to a contract containing an arbitration agreement before the commencement of his bankruptcy.

(2) If the trustee in bankruptcy adopts the contract, the arbitration agreement is enforceable by or against the trustee in relation to matters arising from or connected with the contract.

(3) If the trustee in bankruptcy does not adopt the contract and a matter to which the arbitration agreement applies requires to be determined in connection with or for the purposes of the bankruptcy proceedings—

(a) the trustee with the consent of the creditors' committee, or

(b) any other party to the agreement,

may apply to the court which may, if it thinks fit in all the circumstances of the case, order that the matter be referred to arbitration in accordance with the arbitration agreement.

(4) In this Article—

'arbitration agreement' has the same meaning as in Part I of the Arbitration Act 1996; and

'the court' means the court which has jurisdiction in the bankruptcy proceedings.".

Social Security Administration (Northern Ireland)
Act 1992 (c.8)

55. In section 57 of the Social Security Administration (Northern Ireland) Act 1992 (procedure for inquiries, &c.), in subsection (6) for "the Arbitration Act (Northern Ireland) 1937" substitute "Part I of the Arbitration Act 1996".

Trade Union and Labour Relations (Consolidation)
Act 1992 (c.52)

56. In sections 212(5) and 263(6) of the Trade Union and Labour Relations (Consolidation) Act 1992 (application of Arbitration Act) for "the Arbitration Act 1950" substitute "Part I of the Arbitration Act 1996".

Industrial Relations (Northern Ireland) Order 1992 (N.I.5)

57. In Articles 84(9) and 92(5) of the Industrial Relations (Northern Ireland) Order 1992 (application of Arbitration Act) for "The Arbitration Act (Northern Ireland) 1937" substitute "Part I of the Arbitration Act 1996".

Registered Homes (Northern Ireland) Order 1992 (N.I.20)

58. In Article 33(3) of the Registered Homes (Northern Ireland) Order 1992 (procedure of Registered Homes Tribunal) for "The Arbitration Act (Northern Ireland) 1937" substitute "Part I of the Arbitration Act 1996".

Roads (Northern Ireland) Order 1993 (N.I.15)

60. (1) The Roads (Northern Ireland) Order 1993 is amended as follows.
    (2) In Article 131 (application of Arbitration Act) for "the Arbitration Act (Northern Ireland) 1937" substitute "Part I of the Arbitration Act 1996".
    (3) In Schedule 4 (disputes), in paragraph 3(2) for "the Arbitration Act (Northern Ireland) 1937" substitute "Part I of the Arbitration Act 1996".

Merchant Shipping Act 1995 (c.21)

61. In Part II of Schedule 6 to the Merchant Shipping Act 1995 (provisions having effect in connection with Convention Relating to the Carriage of Passengers and Their Luggage by Sea), for paragraph 7 substitute—

"7. Article 16 shall apply to arbitral proceedings as it applies to an action; and, as respects England and Wales and Northern Ireland, the provisions of section 14 of the Arbitration Act 1996 apply to determine for the purposes of that Article when an arbitration is commenced".

Industrial Tribunals Act 1996 (c.17)

62. In section 6(2) of the Industrial Tribunals Act 1996 (procedure of industrial tribunals), for "The Arbitration Act 1950" substitute "Part I of the Arbitration Act 1996".

SCHEDULE 4

Schedule 107(2)

Chapter
Extent of repeal

1892 c. 43.
In section 21(b), the words "under the Arbitration Act 1889"

1922 c. 51.
In section 21(3), the words "under the Arbitration Act 1889".

1937 c. 8 (N.I.).
The whole Act.

1949 c. 54.
In Schedule 2, paragraph 3(3).

1949 c. 97.
In section 18(4), the words from "Without prejudice" to "England or Wales".

1950 c. 27.
Part I.
Section 42(3).

1958 c. 47.
Section 53(8).

1962 c. 46.
In Schedule 11, Part II, paragraph 7.

1964 c. 14.
In section 10(4) the words from "or in section 9" to "three arbitrators)".
Section 39(3)(b)(i).

1964 c. 29 (N.I.).
In section 9(3) the words from "so, however, that" to the end.

1965 c. 12.
In section 60(8)(b), the words from "by virtue of section 12 of the said Act of 1950".

1965 c. 37.
Section 7(2)(b).

1965 c. 13
(N.I.).
In section 27(2), the words from "under and in accordance with" to the end.

1969 c. 24
(N.I.).
In section 69(7)—
(a) in the opening words, the words from "and without prejudice" to "1937";
(b) in paragraph (b), the words "the registrar or" and "registrar or".

1970 c. 31.
Section 4.
Schedule 3.

1973 c. 41.
Section 33(2)(d).

1973 N.I.1.
In Article 15(4), the words from "under and in accordance" to the end.
Article 40(4).

In Schedule 7, in paragraph 9(2), the words from "under and in accordance" to the end.

1974 c. 47.
In section 87(1), in the definition of "contentious business", the words "appointed under the Arbitration Act 1950".

1975 c. 3.
The whole Act.

1975 c. 74.
In Part II of Schedule 2
(a) in model clause 40(2), the words "in accordance with the Arbitration Act 1950";
(b) in model clause 40(2B), the words "in accordance with the Arbitration Act (Northern Ireland) 1937".
In Part II of Schedule 3, in model clause 38(2), the words "in accordance with the Arbitration Act 1950".

1976 N.I.12.
In Article 3(2), in the entry "contentious business", the words "appointed under the Arbitration Act (Northern Ireland) 1937".
Article 71H(3).

1977 c. 37.
In section 52(4) the words "section 21 of the Arbitration Act 1950 or, as the case may be, section 22 of the Arbitration Act (Northern Ireland) 1937 (statement of cases by arbitrators); but". Section 131(e).

1977 c. 38.
Section 17(2).

1978 c. 23.
In section 35(2), paragraph (g) (v).
In Schedule 5, the amendment to the Arbitration Act 1950.

1979 c. 42.
The whole Act.

1980 c. 58.
Section 34.

1980 N.I.3.
Article 31(3).

1981 c. 54.
Section 148.

1982 c. 27.
Section 25(3)(c) and (5). In section 26—
(a) in subsection (1), the words "to arbitration or";
(b) in subsection (1)(a)(i), the words "arbitration or";
(c) in subsection (2), the words "arbitration or".

1982 c. 53.
Section 15(6).
In Schedule 1, Part IV.

1984 c. 5.
Section 4(8).

1984 c. 12
Schedule 2, paragraph 13(8).

1984 c. 16.
Section 5.

1984 c. 28.
In Schedule 2, paragraph 70.

1985 c. 61.
Section 58.
In Schedule 9, paragraph 15.

1985 c. 68.
In Schedule 18, in paragraph 6(2) the words from "and the Arbitration Act 1950" to the end.

1985 N.I.12.
In Article 72(7)—
(a) in the opening words, the words from "and without prejudice" to "1937";
(b) in sub-paragraph (b), the words "the registrar or" and "registrar or".

1986 c. 45.
In Schedule 14, the entry relating to the Arbitration Act 1950.

1988 c. 8.
Section 8(3).

1988 c. 21
The whole Act.

1989 N.I.11.
Article 72.
In Schedule 3, paragraph 1.

1989 N.I.19.
In Part II of Schedule 9, paragraph 66.

1990 c. 41.
Sections 99 and 101 to 103.

1991 N.I.7.
In Articles 8(8) and 11(10), the words from "and the provisions" to the end.

1992 c. 40.
In Schedule 16, paragraph
30(1).

1995 c. 8.
Section 28(4).

1995 c. 21.
Section 96(10).
Section 264(9).

1995 c. 42.
Section 3.

1996 S.I. 1921.
Section 31.

1998 c. 14.
Section 54.

1998 S.I. 649.
Section 42(2)(c) and (3).

STATUTORY INSTRUMENTS MADE UNDER THE ARBITRATION ACT 1996

1996 No. 3146 (C.96)

ARBITRATION

The Arbitration Act 1996 (Commencement No.1) Order 1996

A1–115

Made   *16th December 1996*

The Secretary of State, in exercise of the powers conferred on him by section 109 of the Arbitration Act 1996(a), hereby makes the following Order:
1. This Order may be cited as the Arbitration Act 1996 (Commencement No.1) Order 1996.
2. The provisions of the Arbitration Act 1996 ("the Act") listed in Schedule 1 to this Order shall come into force on the day after this Order is made.

3. The rest of the Act, except sections 85 to 87, shall come into force on 31st January, 1997.

4. The transitional provisions in Schedule 2 to this Order shall have effect.

John M Taylor,
Parliamentary Under-Secretary of State
for Corporate and Consumer Affairs,
16th December, 1996   Department of Trade and Industry

SCHEDULE 1

Article 2.

Section 91 so far as it relates to the power to make orders under the section.

Section 105.

Section 107(1) and paragraph 36 of Schedule 3, so far as relating to the provision that may be made by county court rules.

Section 107(2) and the reference in Schedule 4 to the County Courts (Northern Ireland) Order 1980[(a)] so far as relating to the above matter.

Sections 108 to 110.

SCHEDULE 2

Article 4.

1. In this Schedule:

   (a) "the appointed day" means the date specified in Article 3 of this Order;

   (b) "arbitration application" means any application relating to arbitration made by or in legal proceedings, whether or not arbitral proceedings have commenced;

   (c) "the old law" means the enactments specified in section 107 as they stood before their amendment or repeal by the Act.

2. The old law shall continue to apply to:

   (a) arbitral proceedings commenced before the appointed day;

   (b) arbitration applications commenced or made before the appointed day;

   (c) arbitration applications commenced or made on or after the appointed day relating to arbitral proceedings commenced before the appointed day,

and the provisions of the Act which would otherwise be applicable shall not apply.

3. The provisions of this Act brought into force by this Order shall apply to any other arbitration application.

4. In the application of paragraph (b) of subsection (1) of section 46 (provision for dispute to be decided in accordance with provisions other than law) to an arbitration agreement made before the appointed day, the agreement shall have effect in accordance with the rules of law (including any conflict of laws rules) as they stood immediately before the appointed day.

Note: *Sections 85 to 87, which make special provision in relation to domestic arbitration agreements, are not yet in force.*

1996 3215 No. (L.16)

COUNTY COURTS
SUPREME COURT OF ENGLAND AND WALES

The High Court and County Courts (Allocation of Arbitration Proceedings) Order 1996

A1–116

As amended by SI 1999/1010 and SI 2002/439

Made	*19th December, 1996*
Laid before Parliament	*20th December, 1996*
Coming into force	*31st January, 1997*

The Lord Chancellor, in exercise of the powers conferred on him by section 105 of the Arbitration Act 1996(a), hereby makes the following Order:

1. (1) This Order may be cited as the High Court and County Courts (Allocation of Arbitration Proceedings) Order 1996 and shall come into force on 31st January, 1997.

(2) In this Order, "the Act" means the Arbitration Act 1996.

2. Subject to articles 3 to 5, proceedings under the Act shall be commenced and taken in the High Court.

3. Proceedings under section 9 of the Act (stay of legal proceedings) shall be commenced in the court in which the legal proceedings are pending.

4. Proceedings under sections 66 and 101(2) (enforcement of awards) of the Act may be commenced in any county court.

5. (1) Proceedings under the Act may be commenced and taken in the Central London County Court Mercantile List.

(2) Where, in exercise of the powers conferred by sections 41 and 42 of the County Courts Act 1984(b) the High Court or the judge in charge of the Central London County Court Mercantile List orders the transfer of proceedings under the Act which were commenced in the Central London County Court Mercantile List to the High Court, those proceedings shall be taken in the High Court.

(3) Where, in exercise of its powers under section 40(2) of the County Courts Act 1984(c) the High Court orders the transfer of proceedings under the Act which were commenced in the High Court to the Central London County Court Mercantile List, those proceedings shall be taken in the Central London County Court Mercantile List.

(4) In exercising the powers referred to in paragraphs (2) and (3) regard shall be had to the following criteria:

(a) the financial substance of the dispute referred to arbitration, including the value of any claim or counterclaim;

(b) the nature of the dispute referred to arbitration (for example, whether it arises out of a commercial or business transaction or relates to engineering, building or other construction work);

(c) whether the proceedings are otherwise important and, in particular, whether they raise questions of importance to persons who are not parties; and

(d) the balance of convenience points to having the proceedings taken in the Central London County Court Mercantile List,

and, where the financial substance of the dispute exceeds £200,000, the proceedings shall be taken in the High Court unless the proceedings do not raise questions of general importance to persons who are not parties.

(5) The value of any claim or counterclaim shall be calculated in accordance with rule 16.3(6) of the Civil Procedure Rules 1998 [fn1].

(6) In this article: "the Central London County Court Mercantile List" means the Mercantile Court established at the Central London County Court pursuant to Part 59 of the Civil Procedure Rules 1998.

"value" shall be construed in accordance with articles 9 and 10 of the High Court and County Courts Jurisdiction Order 1991(b).

6. Nothing in this Order shall prevent the judge in charge of the commercial list (within the meaning of section 62(3) of the Supreme Court Act 1981 (c)) from transferring proceedings under the Act to another list, court or Division of the High Court to which he has power to transfer proceedings and, where such an order is made, the proceedings may be taken in that list, court or Division as the case may be.

Mackay of Clashfern, C.

Dated December 19, 1996

1996 No. 3211

<small>ARBITRATION</small>

A1–117

The Unfair Arbitration Agreements (Specified Amount) Order 1996

Made	*19th December, 1996*
Laid before Parliament	*20th December, 1996*
Coming into force	*31st January, 1997*

The Secretary of State, in exercise of the powers conferred on him by section 91(3)(a) and (b) of the Arbitration Act 1996(a), with the concurrence (as respects England and Wales) of the Lord Chancellor and (as respects Scotland) of the Lord Advocate, hereby makes the following Order:

1. This Order may be cited as the Unfair Arbitration Agreements (Specified Amount) Order 1996, and shall come into force on 31st January, 1997.

2. The amount of £3,000 is hereby specified for the purposes of section 91 of the Arbitration Act 1996 (arbitration agreement unfair where modest amount sought).

John M. Taylor,
Parliamentary Under-Secretary of State
for Corporate and Consumer Affairs,
Department of Trade and Industry

16th December, 1996

I concur,

Mackay of Clashfern, C.

17th December, 1996

I concur,

Mackay of Drumadoon,
Lord Advocate's Department

19th December, 1996

The High Court and County Courts (Allocation of Arbitration Proceedings) (Amendment) Order 1999

A1–117A

Made	*25th March 1999*
Laid before Parliament	*30th March 1999*
Coming into force	*26th April 1999*

The Lord Chancellor, in exercise of the powers conferred on him by section 105(3) of the Arbitration Act 1996, makes the following Order.

1. This Order may be cited as the High Court and County Courts (Allocation of Arbitration Proceedings) (Amendment) Order 1999 and shall come into force on 26th April 1999.

2. For paragraph (5) of article 5 of the High Court and County Courts (Allocation of Arbitration Proceedings) Order 1996, substitute:—

" (5) The value of any claim or counterclaim shall be calculated in accordance with rule 16.3(6) of the Civil Procedure Rules 1998.".

Irvine of Lairg, C.

Dated 25th March 1999

Arbitration Act 1950

(14 GEO. 6 C. 27)

PART II

ENFORCEMENT OF CERTAIN FOREIGN AWARDS

35. Awards to which Part II applies   A1–118

(1) This Part of this Act applies to any award made after the twenty-eighth day of July, nineteen hundred and twenty-four—

(a) in pursuance of an agreement for arbitration to which the protocol set out in the First Schedule to this Act applies; and

(b) between persons of whom one is subject to the jurisdiction of some one of such Powers as His Majesty, being satisfied that reciprocal provisions have been made, may by Order in Council declare to be parties to the convention set out in the Second Schedule to this Act, and of whom the other is subject to the jurisdiction of some other of the Powers aforesaid; and

(c) in one of such territories as His Majesty, being satisfied that reciprocal provisions have been made, may by Order in Council declare to be territories to which the said convention applies;

and an award to which this Part of this Act applies is in this Part of this Act referred to as "a foreign award".

(2) His Majesty may by a subsequent Order in Council vary or revoke any Order previously made under this section.

(3) Any Order in Council under section one of the Arbitration (Foreign Awards) Act 1930 which is in force at the commencement of this Act shall have effect as if it had been made under this section.

A1–119   36. Effect of foreign awards

(1) A foreign award shall, subject to the provisions of this Part of this Act, be enforceable in England either by action or in the same manner as the award of an arbitrator is enforceable by virtue of [section twenty-six of this Act].

(2) Any foreign award which would be enforceable under this Part of this Act shall be treated as binding for all purposes on the persons as between whom it was made, and may accordingly be relied on by any of those persons by way of defence, set off or otherwise in any legal proceedings in England, and any references in this Part of this Act to enforcing a foreign award shall be construed as including references to relying on an award.

Note: *For the words in square brackets in sub-s.(1) there are substituted the words "Section 66 of the Arbitration Act 1996" by Arbitration Act 1996, s.107(1), Sched. 3, para. 10 as from a day to be appointed.*

A1–120

37. Conditions for enforcement of foreign awards

(1) In order that a foreign award may be enforceable under this Part of this Act it must have—

(a) been made in pursuance of an agreement for arbitration which was valid under the law by which it is governed;

(b) been made by the tribunal provided for in the agreement or constituted in manner agreed upon by the parties;

(c) been made in conformity with the law governing the arbitration procedure;

(d) become final in the country in which it was made;

(e) been in respect of a matter which may lawfully be referred to arbitration under the law of England;

and the enforcement thereof must not be contrary to the public policy or the law of England.

(2) Subject to the provisions of this subsection, a foreign award shall not be enforceable under this Part of this Act if the court dealing with the case is satisfied that—

(a) the award has been annulled in the country in which it was made; or

(b) the party against whom it is sought to enforce the award was not given notice of the arbitration proceedings in sufficient time to enable him to present his case, or was under some legal incapacity and was not properly represented; or

(c) the award does not deal with all the questions referred or contains decisions on matters beyond the scope of the agreement for arbitration:

Provided that, if the award does not deal with all the questions referred, the court may, if it thinks fit, either postpone the enforcement of the award or order its enforcement subject to the giving of such security by the person seeking to enforce it as the court may think fit.

(3) If a party seeking to resist the enforcement of a foreign award proves that there is any ground other than the non-existence of the conditions specified in paragraphs (a), (b) and (c) of subsection (1) of this section, or the existence of the conditions specified in paragraphs (b) and (c) of subsection (2) of this section, entitling him to contest the validity of the award, the court may, if it thinks fit, either refuse to enforce the award or adjourn the hearing until after the expiration of such period as appears to the court to be reasonably sufficient to enable that party to take the necessary steps to have the award annulled by the competent tribunal.

38. Evidence

A1–121

(1) The party seeking to enforce a foreign award must produce—

(a) the original award or a copy thereof duly authenticated in manner required by the law of the country in which it was made; and

(b) evidence proving that the award has become final; and

(c) such evidence as may be necessary to prove that the award is a foreign award and that the conditions mentioned in paragraphs (a), (b) and (c) of subsection (1) of the last foregoing section are satisfied.

(2) In any case where any document required to be produced under subsection (1) of this section is in a foreign language, it shall be the duty of the party seeking to enforce the award to produce a translation certified as correct by a diplomatic or consular agent of the country to which that party belongs, or certified as correct in such other manner as may be sufficient according to the law of England.

(3) Subject to the provisions of this section, rules of court may be made under section [84 of the Supreme Court Act 1981] with respect to the evidence which must be furnished by a party seeking to enforce an award under this Part of this Act.

Note: *The words in square brackets in sub-s.(3) were substituted by the Supreme Court Act 1981, s.152(1), Sch. 5.*

A1–122　39. **Meaning of "final award"**

For the purposes of this Part of this Act, an award shall not be deemed final if any proceedings for the purpose of contesting the validity of the award are pending in the country in which it was made.

A1–123　40. **Saving for other rights, etc.**

Nothing in this Part of this Act shall—

(a) prejudice any rights which any person would have had of enforcing in England any award or of availing himself in England of any award if neither this Part of this Act nor Part I of the Arbitration (Foreign Awards) Act 1930 had been enacted; or

(b) apply to any award made on an arbitration agreement governed by the law of England.

Note: *Arbitration (Foreign Awards) Act 1930, Pt. 1. 20 & 21 Geo 5 C15. That Act was repealed by s.44(3) post.*

A1–124　41. (*Applies to Scotland only.*)

A1–125　42. **Application of Part II to Northern Ireland**

(1) The following provisions of this section shall have effect for the purpose of the application of this Part of this Act to Northern Ireland.

(2) For the references to England there shall be substituted references to Northern Ireland.

(3) For subsection (1) of section thirty-six there shall be substituted the following subsection:

"(1) A foreign award shall, subject to the provisions of this Part of this Act, be enforceable either by action or in the same manner as the award of an arbitrator under the provisions of the Common Law Procedure Amendment Act (Ireland) 1856 was enforceable at the date of the passing of the Arbitration (Foreign Awards) Act 1930".

(4) ...

Notes: *Sub-s.(3) is repealed by the Arbitration Act 1996, s.107(2), Sch. 4 as from a day to be appointed.*
Sub-s.(4) was repealed by the Judicature (Northern Ireland) Act 1978, s.122(2), Sched. 7, Pt. I.
Arbitration (Foreign Awards) Act 1930 was repealed by s.44(3) post.

43. (*Repealed by the SL(R) Act 1978.*)

Civil Procedure Rules Part 62, Arbitration Claims

Contents of this Part

Scope of this Part and interpretation

62.1   (1) This Part contains rules about arbitration claims.   **A1–127**
       (2) In this Part—

(a) 'the 1950 Act' means the Arbitration Act 1950[1];

(b) 'the 1975 Act' means the Arbitration Act 1975[2];

(c) 'the 1979 Act' means the Arbitration Act 1979[3];

(d) 'the 1996 Act' means the Arbitration Act 1996[4];

(e) references to—

    (i) the 1996 Act; or
    (ii) any particular section of that Act

include references to that Act or to the particular section of that Act as applied with modifications by the ACAS Arbitration Scheme (England and Wales) Order 2001[5]; and

(f) 'arbitration claim form' means a claim form in the form set out in the practice direction.

(3) Part 58 (Commercial Court) applies to arbitration claims in the Commercial Court, Part 59 (Mercantile Court) applies to arbitration claims in the Mercantile Court and Part 60 (Technology and Construction Court claims) applies to arbitration claims in the Technology and Construction Court, except where this Part provides otherwise.

I Claims Under the 1996 Act

Interpretation

A1–128   62.2 (1) In this Section of this Part 'arbitration claim' means—

(a) any application to the court under the 1996 Act;

(b) a claim to determine—

    (i) whether there is a valid arbitration agreement;
    (ii) whether an arbitration tribunal is properly constituted; or

what matters have been submitted to arbitration in accordance with an arbitration agreement;

(c) a claim to declare that an award by an arbitral tribunal is not binding on a party; and

(d) any other application affecting—

    (i) arbitration proceedings (whether started or not); or

---

[1] 1950 c. 27.
[2] 1975 c. 3; repealed by the Arbitration Act 1996 (c. 23), section 107(2) and Schedule 4 but continues to apply to claims commenced before 31st January 1997 by virtue of the Arbitration Act 1996 (Commencement No. 1) Order 1996 (S.I. 1996/3146), article 4 and Schedule 2.
[3] 1979 c. 42; repealed by the Arbitration Act 1996 (c. 23), section 107(2) and Schedule 4 but continues to apply to claims commenced before 31st January 1997 by virtue of the Arbitration Act 1996 (Commencement No. 1) Order 1996 (S.I. 1996/3146), article 4 and Schedule 2.
[4] 1996 c. 23.
[5] S.I. 2001/1185.

(ii) an arbitration agreement.

(2) This Section of this Part does not apply to an arbitration claim to which Sections II or III of this Part apply.

Starting the claim

62.3 (1) Except where paragraph (2) applies an arbitration claim must be started by the issue of an arbitration claim form in accordance with the Part 8 procedure.   **A1–129**

(2) An application under section 9 of the 1996 Act to stay legal proceedings must be made by application notice to the court dealing with those proceedings.

(3) The courts in which an arbitration claim may be started are set out in the practice direction.

(4) Rule 30.5(3) applies with the modification that a judge of the Technology and Construction Court may transfer the claim to any other court or specialist list.

Arbitration claim form

62.4 (1) An arbitration claim form must—   **A1–130**

    (a) include a concise statement of—

      (i) the remedy claimed; and
      (ii) any questions on which the claimant seeks the decision of the court;

    (b) give details of any arbitration award challenged by the claimant, identifying which part or parts of the award are challenged and specifying the grounds for the challenge;

    (c) show that any statutory requirements have been met;

    (d) specify under which section of the 1996 Act the claim is made;

    (e) identify against which (if any) defendants a costs order is sought; and

    (f) specify either—

      (i) the persons on whom the arbitration claim form is to be served, stating their role in the arbitration and whether they are defendants; or
      (ii) that the claim is made without notice under section 44(3) of the 1996 Act and the grounds relied on.

(2) Unless the court orders otherwise an arbitration claim form must be served on the defendant within 1 month from the date of issue and rules 7.5 and 7.6 are modified accordingly.

(3) Where the claimant applies for an order under section 12 of the 1996 Act (extension of time for beginning arbitral proceedings or other dispute resolution procedures), he may include in his arbitration claim form an alternative application for a declaration that such an order is not needed.

Service out of the jurisdiction

62.5 (1) The court may give permission to serve an arbitration claim form out of the jurisdiction if—   **A1–131**

(a) the claimant seeks to—

(i) challenge; or
(ii) appeal on a question of law arising out of,
an arbitration award made within the jurisdiction;

(The place where an award is treated as made is determined by section 53 of the 1996 Act.)

(b) the claim is for an order under section 44 of the 1996 Act; or

(c) the claimant—

(i) seeks some other remedy or requires a question to be decided by the court affecting an arbitration (whether started or not), an arbitration agreement or an arbitration award; and
(ii) the seat of the arbitration is or will be within the jurisdiction or the conditions in section 2(4) of the 1996 Act are satisfied.

(2) An application for permission under paragraph (1) must be supported by written evidence—

(a) stating the grounds on which the application is made; and

(b) showing in what place or country the person to be served is, or probably may be found.

(3) Rules 6.24 to 6.29 apply to the service of an arbitration claim form under paragraph (1).

(4) An order giving permission to serve an arbitration claim form out of the jurisdiction must specify the period within which the defendant may file an acknowledgment of service.

Notice

A1–132 62.6 (1) Where an arbitration claim is made under section 24, 28 or 56 of the 1996 Act, each arbitrator must be a defendant.

(2) Where notice must be given to an arbitrator or any other person it may be given by sending him a copy of—

(a) the arbitration claim form; and

(b) any written evidence in support.

(3) Where the 1996 Act requires an application to the court to be made on notice to any other party to the arbitration, that notice must be given by making that party a defendant.

Case management

A1–133 62.7 (1) Part 26 and any other rule that requires a party to file an allocation questionnaire does not apply.

(2) Arbitration claims are allocated to the multi-track.

(3) Part 29 does not apply.

(4) The automatic directions set out in the practice direction apply unless the court orders otherwise.

Stay of legal proceedings

62.8   (1) An application notice seeking a stay of legal proceedings under section 9 of the **A1–134**
1996 Act[6] must be served on all parties to those proceedings who have given an
address for service.

      (2) A copy of an application notice under paragraph (1) must be served on any other
party to the legal proceedings (whether or not he is within the jurisdiction) who
has not given an address for service, at—

         (a) his last known address; or

         (b) a place where it is likely to come to his attention.

      (3) Where a question arises as to whether—

         (a) an arbitration agreement has been concluded; or

         (b) the dispute which is the subject-matter of the proceedings falls within the
terms of such an agreement,

the court may decide that question or give directions to enable it to be decided
and may order the proceedings to be stayed pending its decision.

Variation of time

62.9   (1) The court may vary the period of 28 days fixed by section 70(3) of the 1996 Act   **A1–135**
for—

         (a) challenging the award under section 67 or 68 of the Act; and

         (b) appealing against an award under section 69 of the Act.

      (2) An application for an order under paragraph (1) may be made without notice
being served on any other party before the period of 28 days expires.

      (3) After the period of 28 days has expired—

         (a) an application for an order extending time under paragraph (1) must—

            (i) be made in the arbitration claim form; and

            (ii) state the grounds on which the application is made;

         (b) any defendant may file written evidence opposing the extension of time
within 7 days after service of the arbitration claim form; and

         (c) if the court extends the period of 28 days, each defendant's time for
acknowledging service and serving evidence shall start to run as if the
arbitration claim form had been served on the date when the court's order
is served on that defendant.

Hearings

62.10 (1) The court may order that an arbitration claim be heard either in public or in   **A1–136**
private.

      (2) Rule 39.2 does not apply.

      (3) Subject to any order made under paragraph (1)—

[6] 1996 c. 23.

(a) the determination of—

    (i) a preliminary point of law under section 45 of the 1996 Act; or

    (ii) an appeal under section 69 of the 1996 Act on a question of law arising out of an award,

will be heard in public; and

(b) all other arbitration claims will be heard in private.

(4) Paragraph (3)(a) does not apply to—

(a) the preliminary question of whether the court is satisfied of the matters set out in section 45(2)(b); or

(b) an application for permission to appeal under section 69(2)(b).

II OTHER ARBITRATION CLAIMS

Scope of this Section

A1–137   62.11 (1) This Section of this Part contains rules about arbitration claims to which the old law applies.

    (2) In this Section

(a) 'the old law' means the enactments specified in Schedules 3 and 4 of the 1996 Act as they were in force before their amendment or repeal by that Act; and

(b) 'arbitration claim' means any application to the court under the old law and includes an appeal (or application for permission to appeal) to the High Court under section 1(2) of the 1979 Act.[7]

    (3) This Section does not apply to—

(a) a claim to which Section III of this Part applies; or

(b) a claim on the award.

Applications to Judge

A1–138   62.12   A claim—

(a) seeking permission to appeal under section 1(2) of the 1979 Act;

(b) under section 1(5) of that Act (including any claim seeking permission); or

(c) under section 5 of that Act,

    must be made in the High Court and will be heard by a judge of the Commercial Court unless any such judge directs otherwise.

---

[7] 1979 c. 42; repealed by the Arbitration Act 1996 (c. 23), section 107(2) and Schedule 4 but continues to apply to claims commenced before 31st January 1997 by virtue of the Arbitration Act 1996 (Commencement No. 1) Order 1996 (S.I. 1996/3146), article 4 and Schedule 2.

Starting the claim

62.13 (1) Except where paragraph (2) applies an arbitration claim must be started by the   **A1–139**
          issue of an arbitration claim form in accordance with the Part 8 procedure.

     (2) Where an arbitration claim is to be made in existing proceedings—

        (a) it must be made by way of application notice; and

        (b) any reference in this Section of this Part to an arbitration claim form
            includes a reference to an application notice.

     (3) The arbitration claim form in an arbitration claim under section 1(5) of the 1979
         Act (including any claim seeking permission) must be served on—

        (a) the arbitrator or umpire; and

        (b) any other party to the reference.

Claims in District Registries

62.14   If—   **A1–140**

        (a) a claim is to be made under section 12(4) of the 1950 Act[8] for an order for
            the issue of a witness summons to compel the attendance of the witness
            before an arbitrator or umpire; and

        (b) the attendance of the witness is required within the district of a District
            Registry,

        the claim may be started in that Registry.

Time limits and other special provisions about arbitration claims

62.15 (1) An arbitration claim to   **A1–141**

        (a) remit an award under section 22 of the 1950 Act[9];

        (b) set aside an award under section 23(2) of that Act[10] or otherwise; or

        (c) direct an arbitrator or umpire to state the reasons for an award under section
            1(5) of the 1979 Act,

        must be made, and the arbitration claim form served, within 21 days after the
        award has been made and published to the parties.

     (2) An arbitration claim to determine any question of law arising in the course of a
         reference under section 2(1) of the Arbitration Act 1979 must be made, and the
         arbitration claim form served, within 14 days after—

---

[8] 1950 c. 27; section 12(4) was repealed by the Arbitration Act 1996 (c. 23), section 107(2) and
Schedule 4 but continues to apply to claims commenced before 31st January 1997 by virtue of the
Arbitration Act 1996 (Commencement No. 1) Order 1996 (S.I. 1996/3146), article 4 and
Schedule 2.
[9] 1950 c. 27; section 22 was repealed by the Arbitration Act 1996 (c. 23), section 107(2) and Schedule
4 but continues to apply to claims commenced before 31st January 1997 by virtue of the Arbitration
Act 1996 (Commencement No. 1) Order 1996 (S.I. 1996/3146), article 4 and Schedule 2.
[10] 1950 c. 27; section 23(2) was repealed by the Arbitration Act 1996 (c. 23), section 107(2) and
Schedule 4 but continues to apply to claims commenced before 31st January 1997 by virtue of the
Arbitration Act 1996 (Commencement No. 1) Order 1996 (S.I. 1996/3146), article 4 and
Schedule 2.

(a) the arbitrator or umpire gave his consent in writing to the claim being made; or

(b) the other parties so consented.

(3) An appeal under section 1(2) of the 1979 Act must be filed, and the arbitration claim form served, within 21 days after the award has been made and published to the parties.

(4) Where reasons material to an appeal under section 1(2) of the 1979 Act are given on a date subsequent to the publication of the award, the period of 21 days referred to in paragraph (3) will run from the date on which reasons are given.

(5) In every arbitration claim to which this rule applies—

(a) the arbitration claim form must state the grounds of the claim or appeal;

(b) where the claim or appeal is based on written evidence, a copy of that evidence must be served with the arbitration claim form; and

(c) where the claim or appeal is made with the consent of the arbitrator, the umpire or the other parties, a copy of every written consent must be served with the arbitration claim form.

(6) In an appeal under section 1(2) of the 1979 Act—

(a) a statement of the grounds for the appeal specifying the relevant parts of the award and reasons; and

(b) where permission is required, any written evidence in support of the contention that the question of law concerns—

(i) a term of a contract; or

(ii) an event,

which is not a 'one-off' term or event,

must be filed and served with the arbitration claim form.

(7) Any written evidence in reply to written evidence under paragraph (6)(b) must be filed and served on the claimant not less than 2 days before the hearing.

(8) A party to a claim seeking permission to appeal under section 1(2) of the 1979 Act who wishes to contend that the award should be upheld for reasons not expressed or fully expressed in the award and reasons must file and serve on the claimant, a notice specifying the grounds of his contention not less than 2 days before the hearing.

Service out of the jurisdiction

A1–142   62.16 (1) Subject to paragraph (2)—

(a) any arbitration claim form in an arbitration claim under the 1950 Act or the 1979 Act; or

(b) any order made in such a claim,

may be served out of the jurisdiction with the permission of the court if the arbitration to which the claim relates—

      (i) is governed by the law of England and Wales; or

      (ii) has been, is being, or will be, held within the jurisdiction.

(2) An arbitration claim form seeking permission to enforce an award may be served out of the jurisdiction with the permission of the court whether or not the arbitration is governed by the law of England and Wales.

(3) An application for permission to serve an arbitration claim form out of the jurisdiction must be supported by written evidence—

    (a) stating the grounds on which the application is made; and

    (b) showing in what place or country the person to be served is, or probably may be found.

Rules 6.24 to 6.29 apply to the service of an arbitration claim form under paragraph (1).

(4) omitted.

(5) An order giving permission to serve an arbitration claim form out of the jurisdiction must specify the period within which the defendant may file an acknowledgment of service.

III ENFORCEMENT

Scope of this Section

62.17   This Section of this Part applies to all arbitration enforcement proceedings other than by a claim on the award.   **A1–143**

Enforcement of awards

62.18 (1) An application for permission under—   **A1–144**

    (a) section 66 of the 1996 Act[11];

    (b) section 101 of the 1996 Act;

    (c) section 26 of the 1950 Act[12]; or

    (d) section 3(1)(a) of the 1975 Act,[13]

to enforce an award in the same manner as a judgment or order may be made without notice in an arbitration claim form.

(2) The court may specify parties to the arbitration on whom the arbitration claim form must be served.

---

[11] 1996 c. 23.

[12] 1950 c. 27; section 26 was repealed by the Arbitration Act 1996 (c. 23), section 107(2) and Schedule 4 but continues to apply to claims commenced before 31st January 1997 by virtue of the Arbitration Act 1996 (Commencement No. 1) Order 1996 (S.I. 1996/3146), article 4 and Schedule 2.

[13] 1975 c. 3; repealed by the Arbitration Act 1996 (c. 23), section 107(2) and Schedule 4 but continues to apply to claims commenced before 31st January 1997 by virtue of the Arbitration Act 1996 (Commencement No. 1) Order 1996 (S.I. 1996/3146), article 4 and Schedule 2.

(3) The parties on whom the arbitration claim form is served must acknowledge service and the enforcement proceedings will continue as if they were an arbitration claim under Section I of this Part.

(4) With the permission of the court the arbitration claim form may be served out of the jurisdiction irrespective of where the award is, or is treated as, made.

(5) Where the applicant applies to enforce an agreed award within the meaning of section 51(2) of the 1996 Act—

    (a) the arbitration claim form must state that the award is an agreed award; and

    (b) any order made by the court must also contain such a statement.

(6) An application for permission must be supported by written evidence—

    (a) exhibiting—

        (i) where the application is made under section 66 of the 1996 Act or under section 26 of the 1950 Act, the arbitration agreement and the original award (or copies);

        (ii) where the application is under section 101 of the 1996 Act, the documents required to be produced by section 102 of that Act; or

        (iii) where the application is under section 3(1)(a) of the 1975 Act, the documents required to be produced by section 4 of that Act;

    (b) stating the name and the usual or last known place of residence or business of the claimant and of the person against whom it is sought to enforce the award; and

    (c) stating either—

        (i) that the award has not been complied with; or

        (ii) the extent to which it has not been complied with at the date of the application.

(7) An order giving permission must—

    (a) be drawn up by the claimant; and

    (b) be served on the defendant by—

        (i) delivering a copy to him personally; or

        (ii) sending a copy to him at his usual or last known place of residence or business.

(8) An order giving permission may be served out of the jurisdiction—

    (a) without permission; and

    (b) in accordance with rules 6.24 to 6.29 as if the order were an arbitration claim form.

(9) Within 14 days after service of the order or, if the order is to be served out of the jurisdiction, within such other period as the court may set—

    (a) the defendant may apply to set aside the order; and

    (b) the award must not be enforced until after—

(i) the end of that period; or

(ii) any application made by the defendant within that period has been finally disposed of.

(10) The order must contain a statement of—

(a) the right to make an application to set the order aside; and

(b) the restrictions on enforcement under rule 62.18(9)(b).

(11) Where a body corporate is a party any reference in this rule to place of residence or business shall have effect as if the reference were to the registered or principal address of the body corporate.

Interest on awards

62.19 (1) Where an applicant seeks to enforce an award of interest the whole or any part of which relates to a period after the date of the award, he must file a statement giving the following particulars—   **A1–145**

(a) whether simple or compound interest was awarded;

(b) the date from which interest was awarded;

(c) where rests were provided for, specifying them;

(d) the rate of interest awarded; and

(e) a calculation showing—

(i) the total amount claimed up to the date of the statement; and

(ii) any sum which will become due on a daily basis.

(2) A statement under paragraph (1) must be filed whenever the amount of interest has to be quantified for the purpose of—

(a) obtaining a judgment or order under section 66 of the 1996 Act (enforcement of the award); or

(b) enforcing such a judgment or order.

Registration in High Court of foreign awards

62.20 (1) Where—   **A1–146**

(a) an award is made in proceedings on an arbitration in any part of a United Kingdom Overseas Territory (within the meaning of rule 6.18(f)) or other territory to which Part I of the Foreign Judgments (Reciprocal Enforcement) Act 1933[14] ('the 1933 Act') extends;

(b) Part II of the Administration of Justice Act 1920[15] extended to that part immediately before Part I of the 1933 Act was extended to that part; and

---

[14] 1933 c. 13 (23 & 24 Geo. 5).
[15] 1920 c. 81 (10 & 11 Geo. 5); section 10 of Part II was substituted by the Civil Jurisdiction and Judgments Act 1982 (c. 27), section 35(2) and section 14 of Part II was amended by the Civil Jurisdiction and Judgments Act 1982 (c. 27), section 35(3).

(c) an award has, under the law in force in the place where it was made, become enforceable in the same manner as a judgment given by a court in that place,

Rules 74.1 to 74.7 and 74.9, apply in relation to the award as they apply in relation to a judgment given by the court subject to the modifications in paragraph (2).

(2) The modifications referred to in paragraph (1) are as follows—

(a) for references to the state of origin are substituted references to the place where the award was made; and

(b) the written evidence required by rule 74.4 must state (in addition to the matters required by that rule) that to the best of the information or belief of the maker of the statement the award has, under the law in force in the place where it was made, become enforceable in the same manner as a judgment given by a court in that place.

Registration of awards under the Arbitration (International Investment Disputes) Act 1966

A1–147   62.21 (1) In this rule—

(a) 'the 1966 Act' means the Arbitration (International Investment Disputes) Act 1966[16];

(b) 'award' means an award under the Convention;

(c) 'the Convention' means the Convention on the settlement of investment disputes between States and nationals of other States which was opened for signature in Washington on 18th March 1965[17];

(d) 'judgment creditor' means the person seeking recognition or enforcement of an award; and

(e) 'judgment debtor' means the other party to the award.

(2) Subject to the provisions of this rule, the following provisions of Part 74 apply with such modifications as may be necessary in relation to an award as they apply in relation to a judgment to which Part II of the Foreign Judgments (Reciprocal Enforcement) Act 1933 applies—

(a) rule 74.1;

(b) rule 74.3;

(c) rule 74.4(1), 2(a) to (d) and (4);

(d) rule 74.6 (except paragraph 3(c) to (e)); and (e), rule 74.9(2).

(3) An application to have an award registered in the High Court under section 1 of the 1966 Act[18] must be made in accordance with the Part 8 procedure.

---

[16] 1966 c. 41.

[17] The text of the Convention is set out in the Schedule to the Arbitration (International Investment Disputes) Act 1966 (c. 41).

[18] 1966 c. 41; section 1 was amended by the Administration of Justice Act 1977 (c. 38), sections 4 and 32(4) and Schedule 5, Part I and by the Supreme Court Act 1981 (c. 54), section 152(1) and Schedule 5.

(4) The written evidence required by rule 74.4 in support of an application for registration must—

(a) exhibit the award certified under the Convention instead of the judgment (or a copy of it); and

(b) in addition to stating the matters referred to in rule 74.4(2)(a) to (d), state whether—

(i) at the date of the application the enforcement of the award has been stayed (provisionally or otherwise) under the Convention; and

(ii) any, and if so what, application has been made under the Convention, which, if granted, might result in a stay of the enforcement of the award.

(5) Where, on granting permission to register an award or an application made by the judgment debtor after an award has been registered, the court considers –

(a) that the enforcement of the award has been stayed (whether provisionally or otherwise) under the Convention; or

(b) that an application has been made under the Convention which, if granted, might result in a stay of the enforcement of the award,

the court may stay the enforcement of the award for such time as it considers appropriate.

Practice Direction—Arbitration

This Practice Direction supplements Part 62

CONTENTS OF THIS PART

SECTION I

SECTION II

SECTION III

SECTION I

A1–149   1.1 This Section of this Practice Direction applies to arbitration claims to which Section I of Part 62 applies.

1.2 In this Section 'the 1996 Act' means the Arbitration Act 1996.

1.3 Where a rule provides for a document to be sent, it may be sent—

(1) by first class post;

(2) through a document exchange; or

(3) by fax, electronic mail or other means of electronic communication.

62.3—Starting the claim

A1–150   2.1 An arbitration claim under the 1996 Act (other than under section 9) must be started in accordance with the High Court and County Courts (Allocation of Arbitration Proceedings) Order 1996 by the issue of an arbitration claim form.

2.2 An arbitration claim form must be substantially in the form set out in Appendix A to this practice direction.

2.3 Subject to paragraph 2.1, an arbitration claim form—

(1) may be issued at the courts set out in column 1 of the table below and will be entered in the list set out against that court in column 2;

(2) relating to a landlord and tenant or partnership dispute must be issued in the Chancery Division of the High Court.

Court	List
Admiralty and Commercial Registry at the Royal Courts of Justice, London	Commercial list
Technology and Construction Court Registry, St. Dunstan's House, London	TCC list
District Registry of the High Court (where mercantile court established)	Mercantile list
District Registry of the High Court (where arbitration claim form marked 'Technology and Construction Court' in top right hand corner)	TCC list

2.3A An arbitration claim form must, in the case of an appeal, or application for permission to appeal, from a judge-arbitrator, be issued in the Civil Division of the Court of

Appeal. The judge hearing the application may adjourn the matter for oral argument before two judges of that court.

62.4—Arbitration claim form

Service

3.1 The court may exercise its powers under rule 6.8 to permit service of an arbitration claim form at the address of a party's solicitor or representative acting for him in the arbitration. **A1–151**

3.2 Where the arbitration claim form is served by the claimant he must file a certificate of service within 7 days of service of the arbitration claim form.

(Rule 6.10 specifies what a certificate of service must show).

Acknowledgment of service or making representations by arbitrator or ACAS

4.1 Where—

    (1) an arbitrator; or

    (2) ACAS (in a claim under the 1996 Act as applied with modifications by the ACAS Arbitration Scheme (England and Wales) Order 2001)

is sent a copy of an arbitration claim form (including an arbitration claim form sent under rule 62.6(2)), that arbitrator or ACAS (as the case may be) may—

    (a) apply to be made a defendant; or

    (b) make representations to the court under paragraph 4.3.

4.2 An application under paragraph 4.1(2)(a) to be made a defendant—

    (1) must be served on the claimant; but

    (2) need not be served on any other party.

4.3 An arbitrator or ACAS may make representations by filing written evidence or in writing to the court.

Supply of documents from court records

5.1 An arbitration claim form may only be inspected with the permission of the court. **A1–152**

62.7—Case management

6.1 The following directions apply unless the court orders otherwise. **A1–153**

6.2 A defendant who wishes to rely on evidence before the court must file and serve his written evidence—

    (1) within 21 days after the date by which he was required to acknowledge service; or,

    (2) where a defendant is not required to file an acknowledgement of service, within 21 days after service of the arbitration claim form.

6.3 A claimant who wishes to rely on evidence in reply to written evidence filed under paragraph 6.2 must file and serve his written evidence within 7 days after service of the defendant's evidence.

6.4 Agreed indexed and paginated bundles of all the evidence and other documents to be used at the hearing must be prepared by the claimant.

6.5 Not later than 5 days before the hearing date estimates for the length of the hearing must be filed together with a complete set of the documents to be used.

6.6 Not later than 2 days before the hearing date the claimant must file and serve—

    (1) a chronology of the relevant events cross-referenced to the bundle of documents;

    (2) (where necessary) a list of the persons involved; and

    (3) a skeleton argument which lists succinctly—

        (a) the issues which arise for decision;

        (b) the grounds of relief (or opposing relief) to be relied upon;

        (c) the submissions of fact to be made with the references to the evidence; and

        (d) the submissions of law with references to the relevant authorities.

6.7 Not later than the day before the hearing date the defendant must file and serve a skeleton argument which lists succinctly—

    (1) the issues which arise for decision;

    (2) the grounds of relief (or opposing relief) to be relied upon;

    (3) the submissions of fact to be made with the references to the evidence; and

    (4) the submissions of law with references to the relevant authorities.

Securing the attendance of witnesses

A1–154 7.1 A party to arbitral proceedings being conducted in England or Wales who wishes to rely on section 43 of the 1996 Act to secure the attendance of a witness must apply for a witness summons in accordance with Part 34.

7.2 If the attendance of the witness is required within the district of a district registry, the application may be made at that registry.

7.3 A witness summons will not be issued until the applicant files written evidence showing that the application is made with—

    (1) the permission of the tribunal; or

    (2) the agreement of the other parties.

Interim remedies

A1–155 8.1 An application for an interim remedy under section 44 of the 1996 Act must be made in an arbitration claim form.

Applications under sections 32 and 45 of the 1996 Act

9.1 This paragraph applies to arbitration claims for the determination of—   A1–156

    (1) a question as to the substantive jurisdiction of the arbitral tribunal under section 32 of the 1996 Act; and

    (2) a preliminary point of law under section 45 of the 1996 Act.

9.2 Where an arbitration claim is made without the agreement in writing of all the other parties to the arbitral proceedings but with the permission of the arbitral tribunal, the written evidence or witness statements filed by the parties must set out any evidence relied on by the parties in support of their contention that the court should, or should not, consider the claim.

9.3 As soon as practicable after the written evidence is filed, the court will decide whether or not it should consider the claim and, unless the court otherwise directs, will so decide without a hearing.

Decisions without a hearing

10.1 Having regard to the overriding objective the court may decide particular issues   A1–157
without a hearing. For example, as set out in paragraph 9.3, the question whether the court is satisfied as to the matters set out in section 32(2)(b) or section 45(2)(b) of the 1996 Act.

10.2 The court will generally decide whether to extend the time limit under section 70(3) of the 1996 Act without a hearing. Where the court makes an order extending the time limit, the defendant must file his written evidence within 21 days from service of the order.

62.9—Variation of time

11.1 An application for an order under rule 62.9(1)—   A1–158

    (1) before the period of 28 days has expired, must be made in a Part 23 application notice; and

    (2) after the period of 28 days has expired, must be set out in a separately identified part in the arbitration claim form.

Applications for permission to appeal

12.1 Where a party seeks permission to appeal to the court on a question of law arising out   A1–159
of an arbitration award, the arbitration claim form must—

    (1) identify the question of law; and

    (2) state the grounds

on which the party alleges that permission should be given.

12.2 The written evidence in support of the application must set out any evidence relied on by the party for the purpose of satisfying the court—

(1) of the matters referred to in section 69(3) of the 1996 Act; and

(2) that permission should be given.

12.3 The written evidence filed by the respondent to the application must—

(1) state the grounds on which the respondent opposes the grant of permission;

(2) set out any evidence relied on by him relating to the matters mentioned in section 69(3) of the 1996 Act; and

(3) specify whether the respondent wishes to contend that the award should be upheld for reasons not expressed (or not fully expressed) in the award and, if so, state those reasons.

12.4 The court will normally determine applications for permission to appeal without an oral hearing.

12.5 Where the court refuses an application for permission to appeal without an oral hearing, it must provide brief reasons.

12.6 Where the court considers that an oral hearing is required, it may give such further directions as are necessary.

SECTION II

A1–160 13.1 This Section of this Practice Direction applies to arbitration claims to which Section II of Part 62 applies.

62.13—Starting the claim

A1–161 14.1 An arbitration claim must be started in the Commercial Court and, where required to be heard by a judge, be heard by a judge of that court unless he otherwise directs.

SECTION III

A1–162 15.1 This Section of this Practice Direction applies to enforcement proceedings to which Section III of Part 62 applies.

62.21—Registration of awards under the Arbitration (International Investment Disputes) Act 1966

A1–163 16.1 Awards ordered to be registered under the 1966 Act and particulars will be entered in the Register kept for that purpose at the Admiralty and Commercial Registry.

NB: The court forms attached to this Practice Direction are to be found in Section E of Appendix 6 below.

COURT FORMS

	Claim Form (arbitration)	In the	
		for court use only	
		Claim No.	
		Issue date	

In an arbitration claim between

Claimant

SEAL

Defendant(s)

In the matter of an [intended] arbitration between

Claimant

Respondent(s)   *Set out the names and addresses of persons to be served with the claim form stating their role in the arbitration and whether they are defendants.*

Defendant's name and address

☐ This claim will be heard on:

at   am/pm

☐ This claim is made without notice.

The court office at

When corresponding with the court, please address forms or letters to the Court Manager and quote the case number.

N8 Claim form (arbitration)

	Claim No.	

Remedy claimed and grounds on which claim is made

	Claim No.	

The claimant seeks an order for costs against

Statement of Truth
*(I believe)(The Claimant believes) that the facts stated in these particulars of claim are true.
* I am duly authorised by the claimant to sign this statement

Full name _____

Name of claimant's solicitor's firm _____

signed _____ position or office held _____
     *(Claimant)(Claimant's solicitor)   (if signing on behalf of firm or company)
*delete as appropriate

Claimant's or claimant's solicitor's address to
which documents should be sent if different from
overleaf. If you are prepared to accept service by
DX, fax or e-mail, please add details.

Arbitration Claim - notes for the claimant

Please read these guidance notes before you begin completing the claim form

The arbitration claim form may be used to start proceedings and make an application in existing proceedings. Where an application is being made in existing proceedings, an acknowledgment of service form is not required and the references to an acknowledgment of service form in the Notes for the Defendant should be deleted.

With the exception of:

- applications under section 9 of the Arbitration Act 1996; and
- certain proceedings which may be started only in the High Court or only in a county court - see High Court and County Courts (Allocation of Arbitration Proceedings) Order 1996, arbitration proceedings may be started in the courts set out in the table opposite.

Court	List
Admiralty and Commercial Registry at the Royal Courts of Justice, London	Commercial
Technology and Construction Court Registry, St Dunstan's House, London	TCC
District Registry of the High Court *(where Mercantile court established)*	Mercantile
District Registry of the High Court *(where the Claim form marked 'Technology and Construction Court' in top right hand corner)*	TCC
Central London County Court	Mercantile

Heading

You must fill in the heading of the claim form with:

- the name of the court (High Court or county court); and
- if issued in a District Registry, the name of the District Registry

Claimant and defendant details

You must provide your full name and address and the full names and addresses of the defendants to be served. If a defendant is to be served outside England and Wales, the court's permission may need to be sought *(see Rule 62.5)*.

Remedy claimed and grounds on which claim is made

You must:

- include a concise statement of
  - the remedy claimed; and
  - any questions on which you seek the decision of the court;
- give details of any arbitration award which you challenge, identifying which part or parts of the award are challenged and the grounds for the challenge;
- show that any statutory requirements have been met;

- specify under which section of the Act the claim is made;

Respondents

- if on notice, give the names and addresses of the persons on whom the arbitration claim form is to be served, stating their role in the arbitration and whether they are defendants; or
- state that the claim is made without notice under section 44(3) of the 1966 Act, and the grounds relied on.

Acknowledgment of service form

An acknowledgment of service form N15 must accompany the arbitration claim form. You should complete the heading on this form. Where the claim form is to be served out of the jurisdiction, you must amend the Notes for the Defendant to give the time within which the defendant must acknowledge service and file evidence. The claim form is valid for one month beginning with the date of its issue or, where required to be served out of the jurisdiction, for such period as the court may fix.

Address for documents

You must provide an address for service within England and Wales to which documents should be sent. That address must be either the business address of your solicitor, or your residential or business address.

Statement of Truth

The statement of truth must be signed by you or by your solicitor. Where the statement of truth is not signed by the solicitor and the claimant is a registered company or corporation, the statement of truth must be signed by either a director, the treasurer, secretary, chief executive, manager or other officer of the company and (in the case of a corporation) the mayor, chairman, president or town clerk.

You may rely on the matters set out in the claim form as evidence only if the claim form is verified by a statement of truth. You may also file an affidavit or witness statement in support of the arbitration claim, which must be served with the claim form.

N8A Arbitration claim - notes for claimant (03.02)

Arbitration Claim - notes for the defendant

Please read these guidance notes carefully before you respond to the arbitration claim form

Court staff can help you with procedures but they cannot give legal advice. If you need legal advice, you should contact a solicitor or a Citizens Advice Bureau immediately.

Responding to the claim

If you are:

- named as a defendant in the claim form; and
- served with a copy of it,

you should respond by completing and returning to the court office the acknowledgment of service form which was enclosed with the claim form, within *(14 days) (   ) of the date it was served on you. At the same time you must serve a copy on the claimant and any other party shown on the claim form.

If the claim form was:

- sent by post, the *(14 days) (   ) starts 2 days from the date of the postmark on the envelope;
- delivered or left at your address, the *(14 days) (   ) starts on the day it was given to you;
- handed to you personally, the *(14 days) (   ) starts on the day it was given to you.

The acknowledgment of service

If you:

- fail to complete and file the acknowledgment of service within the time specified; or
- if you indicate that you do not intend to contest the claim,

If you later change your mind, you will not be entitled to contest the claim without the court's permission.

Evidence

If you wish to rely on evidence before the court, you must file and serve your written evidence within *(21 days) (   ) of the date the claim form was served on you.

Statement of truth

The acknowledgment of service must be signed by you or by your solicitor. Where the acknowledgment of service is not signed by your solicitor and you are a registered company or corporation, it must be signed by either a director, the treasurer, secretary, chief executive, manager or other officer of the company and (in the case of a corporation) the mayor. Chairman, president or town clerk.

Notes for arbitrators

If you are:

- an arbitrator; or
- ACAS (in a claim under the 1996 Act as applied with modification by the ACAS (England and Wales) Order 2001),

who has been named as a defendant in the claim form, the above notes apply to you as they do to any other defendant.

If you were, or are:

- an arbitrator in the arbitration which led to this claim; and
- if you are not named as a defendant;

this claim form is sent to you for information

You may either:

- make a request (with notice only to the claimant) to be made a defendant
- may make representations to the court *(see paragraph 4.3 of practice direction to Part 62)*

Claimant should alter where appropriate if the claim form is to be served out of the jurisdiction (see CPR Part6)

N8B Arbitration claim - notes for defendant (03.02)

Acknowledgment of Service
(arbitration claim)

You should read the 'notes for defendant' attached
to the claim form which will tell you how to complete
this form, and when and where to send it.

In the	
Claim No.	
Claimant (including ref)	
Defendant	

Tick and complete sections A - D as appropriate.
In all cases you must complete sections E and F

Section A

☐ I **do not** intend to contest this claim

Section B

☐ I intend to contest this claim

Give brief details of any different remedy you are seeking.

Section C

☐ I intend to dispute the court's jurisdiction
(Please note, any application must be filed within 14 days of the date on which you file this acknowledgment of service)

The court office at

When corresponding with the court, please address forms or letters to the Court Manager and quote the claim number.
N15 Acknowledgment of Service (arbitration) (03.02)

Claim No.	

Section D

☐   I intend to rely on written evidence

My written evidence:

☐   is filed with this form

☐   will be filed and served within 21 days after the date by which I am required to file this acknowledgment of service.

Section E

Full name of defendant filing
this acknowledgment   _____

Section F

Signed
(To be signed by
you or by your
solicitor)

*(I believe)(The defendant believes) that the facts stated in this form are true. *I am duly authorised by the defendant to sign this statement

delete as appropriate

**Position or
office held**
(if signing on
behalf of firm
or company)

Date

**Give an
address in
England or Wales
to which notices
about this case
can be sent to
you**

Postcode

Tel. no.

	if applicable
Ref. no.	
fax no.	
DX no.	
e-mail	

Appendix 2

Departmental Advisory Committee on Arbitration Law Report on The Arbitration Bill and Supplementary Report on The Arbitration Act 1996

Report on The Arbitration Bill

Chairman
The Rt Hon Lord Justice Saville

February 1996

Contents

MEMBERS OF THE COMMITTEE

The Rt Hon. Lord Justice Saville (Chairman)
Professor J. M. Hunter (Deputy Chairman)
Miss C. R. Allen (Secretary)
Mr P. Bovey
Mr A. W. S. Bunch
Mr S. C. Boyd Q.C.
Dr K. G. Chrystie
Lord Dervaird
Mr J. B. Garrett
Professor R. M. Goode C.B.E., Q.C., F.B.A.
Mr B. Harris
Mrs J. Howe
Mrs P. Kirby-Johnson
Mr R. A. MacCrindle Q.C.

Mr A. I. Marriott
Mr K. S. Rokison Q.C.
Mr D. Sarre
Mr J. H. M. Sims
Professor D. R. Thomas
Professor J. Uff Q.C.
Mr V. V. Veeder Q.C.

The DAC has been greatly assisted by the invaluable work done by Mr T. T. Landau of counsel.

CHAPTER 1

INTRODUCTION

A2–000 1. In its Report of June 1989, the Departmental Advisory Committee on Arbitration Law (the DAC), under the chairmanship of Lord Justice Mustill (now Lord Mustill) recommended against England, Wales and Northern Ireland adopting the UNCITRAL Model Law on International Commercial Arbitration. Instead, the DAC recommended that there should be a new and improved Arbitration Act for England, Wales and Northern Ireland, with the following features (Paragraph 108):

"(1) It should comprise a statement in statutory form of the more important principles of the English law of arbitration, statutory and (to the extent practicable) common law.

(2) It should be limited to those principles whose existence and effect are uncontroversial.

(3) It should be set out in a logical order, and expressed in language which is sufficiently clear and free from technicalities to be readily comprehensible to the layman.

(4) It should in general apply to domestic and international arbitrations alike, although there may have to be exceptions to take account of treaty obligations.

(5) It should not be limited to the subject-matter of the Model Law.

(6) It should embody such of our proposals for legislation as have by then been enacted: see paragraph 100 [of the 1989 Report].

(7) Consideration should be given to ensuring that any such new statute should, so far as possible, have the same structure and language as the Model Law, so as to enhance its accessibility to those who are familiar with the Model Law."

2.   In an Interim Report in April 1995, the DAC stated as follows:

> "The original interpretation of [paragraph 108 of the 1989 Report] led to the draft
> Bill which was circulated in February 1994. Although undoubtedly a highly skilful
> piece of work, it now appears that this draft Bill did not carry into effect what most
> users in fact wanted. In the light of the responses, the view of the DAC is that a new
> Bill should still be grounded on the objectives set out in [paragraph 108 of the 1989
> Report], but that, reinterpreted, what is called for is much more along the lines of
> a restatement of the law, in clear and 'user-friendly' language, following, as far as
> possible, the structure and spirit of the Model Law, rather than simply a classic
> exercise in consolidation."

3.   The DAC's proposals in the Interim Report led to a new draft Bill which was
circulated for public consultation in July 1995. This draft was very much the product
of a fresh start. Indeed, it will be noted that whereas the February 1994 draft had the
following long-title:

> "To consolidate, with amendments, the Arbitration Act 1950, the Arbitration Act
> 1975, the Arbitration Act 1979 and related enactments"

this was altered for the July 1995 draft, and now begins:

> "An Act to restate and improve the law relating to arbitration pursuant to an
> arbitration agreement . . . "

4.   The DAC remained of the view, for the reasons given in the Mustill Report, that the
solution was not the wholesale adoption of the Model Law. However, at every stage in
preparing a new draft Bill, very close regard was paid to the Model Law, and it will
be seen that both the structure and the content of the July draft Bill, and the final
draft, owe much to this model.

5.   The task of the Committee has been made far easier by the extraordinary quantity and
quality of responses we received both to the draft Bill published in February 1994 and
to the draft Bill which was published in July 1995. A large number of people put
substantial time and effort into responding to both drafts and putting forward
suggestions, and we are very grateful to all of them. Indeed, both these consultation
exercises have proved invaluable: the former showed that a new approach was
required, while the latter showed that our April 1995 proposals seemed to be on the
right track. Both sets of responses also contained carefully considered suggestions,
many of which have been incorporated in the Bill. It should be emphasized that those
suggestions which have not been adopted were only put on one side after lengthy
consideration.

6.   Among those who responded were a large number of institutions who offer arbitration
services (such as the ICC) or who provide rules and administration for arbitrations
concerning their members (such as the commodity associations). Both domestically
and internationally institutions such as these play a very significant role in the field of
arbitration. It seemed to us that the Bill should specifically recognize this, and that it
should safeguard their spheres of operation. Consequently, there are many references
to such institutions in the Bill, and, indeed, Clause 74 gives them what we believe to
be a necessary degree of immunity from suit.

7. Given the extremely favourable response, the July 1995 draft was taken forward, with certain modifications, to form the basis of the final draft, which is explained in this Report.

8. As well as containing a guide to the provisions of the final draft, this Report also contains supplementary recommendations (in Chapter 6) on certain matters that have come to light since publication of the final draft, and since its second reading in the House of Lords.

Chapter 2

Part I of The Bill

A2–001 9. The title to this Part is *Arbitration Pursuant to an Arbitration Agreement*. It is in this Part that we have attempted to restate within a logical structure the basic principles of our law of arbitration, as it relates to arbitration under an agreement to adopt this form of dispute resolution. The Bill does not purport to provide an exhaustive code on the subject of arbitration. It would simply not be practicable to attempt to codify the huge body of case law that has built up over the centuries, and there would be a risk of fossilising the common law (which has the great advantage of being able to adapt to changing circumstances) had we attempted to do so. Rather, we have sought to include what we consider to be the more important common law principles, whilst preserving all others, in so far as they are consistent with the provisions of the Bill (see Clause 81).

10. A small number of key areas, however, have not been included, precisely because they are unsettled, and because they are better left to the common law to evolve. One such example concerns privacy and confidentiality in arbitrations, which deserves special mention here.

11. Privacy and confidentiality have long been assumed as general principles in English commercial arbitration, subject to important exceptions. It is only recently that the English courts have been required to examine both the legal basis for such principles and the breadth of certain of these exceptions, without seriously questioning the existence of the general principles themselves (see *e.g. The Eastern Saga* [1988] 2 Lloyd's Rep. 373, 379 (Leggatt L.J.); *Dolling-Baker v. Merrett* [1990] 1 W.L.R. 1205, 1213 (Parker L.J.); *Hassneh v. Mew* [1993] 2 Lloyd's Rep. 243 (Colman J.); *Hyundai Engineering v. Active* (unreported, 9 March 1994, Phillips J.); *Ins Company v. Lloyd's Syndicate* [1995] 2 Lloyd's Rep. 272 (Colman J.); *London & Leeds Estates Limited v. Parisbas Limited (No. 2)* (1995) E.G. 134 (Mance J.)).

12. In practice, there is also no doubt whatever that users of commercial arbitration in England place much importance on privacy and confidentiality as essential features of English arbitration (*e.g.* see survey of users amongst the "Fortune 500" U.S. corporations conducted for the LCIA by the London Business School in 1992). Indeed, as Sir Patrick Neill Q.C. stated in his 1995 "Bernstein" Lecture, it would be difficult to

conceive of any greater threat to the success of English arbitration than the removal of the general principles of confidentiality and privacy.

13. Last year's decision of the High Court of Australia in *Esso/BHP v. Plowman* (see [1995] 11 *Arbitration International* 234) reinforced many people's interest in seeking to codify the relevant English legal principles in the draft Arbitration Bill. The implied term as the contractual basis for such principles was not in doubt under English law, and the English Courts were upholding these principles in strong and unequivocal terms. However, the Australian decision was to the effect that, as a matter of Australian law, this contractual approach was unsustainable as regards confidentiality. This has troubled users of commercial arbitration far outside Australia. The first response has been for arbitral institutions to amend their arbitration rules to provide expressly for confidentiality and privacy. The new WIPO Rules have sought to achieve this and we understand that both the ICC and the LCIA are currently amending their respective rules to similar effect.

14. In England, the second response was to consider placing these general principles on a firm statutory basis in the Arbitration Bill. This task was initially undertaken by the DAC mid-1995, and perhaps surprisingly, it soon proved controversial and difficult.

15. Whilst none could reasonably dispute the desirability of placing these general principles beyond all doubt on a firm statutory basis, applicable to all English arbitrations within the scope of the Bill (irrespective of the substantive law applicable to the arbitration agreement), grave difficulties arose over the myriad exceptions to these principles—which are necessarily required for such a statutory provision. There is of course no statutory guidance to confidentiality in the UNCITRAL Model Law whatever; and indeed, in a different context, Lord Mustill has recently warned against an attempt to give in the abstract an accurate exposition of confidentiality at large (see *In re D (Adoption Reports: Confidentiality)* [1995] 3 W.L.R. 483, 496D: "To give an accurate exposition of confidentiality at large would require a much more wide-ranging survey of the law and practice than has been necessary for a decision on the narrow issue raised by the appeal, and cannot in my opinion safely be attempted in the abstract").

16. For English arbitration, the exceptions to confidentiality are manifestly legion and unsettled in part; and equally, there are important exceptions to privacy (*e.g.* in *The Lena Goldfields Case* (1930), the arbitration tribunal in London opened the hearing to the press (but not the public) in order to defend the proceedings against malicious charges made by one of the parties, the USSR). As to the former, the award may become public in legal proceedings under the Arbitration Acts 1950–1979 or abroad under the 1958 New York Convention; the conduct of the arbitration may also become public if subjected to judicial scrutiny within or without England; and most importantly, several non-parties have legitimate interests in being informed as to the content of a pending arbitration, even short of an award: *e.g.* parent company, insurer, P+I Club, guarantor, partner, beneficiary, licensor and licensee, debenture-holder, creditors' committee etc., and of course even the arbitral institution itself (such as the ICC Court members approving the draft award). Whilst non-parties to the arbitration agreement and proceedings, none of these are officious strangers to the arbitration. Further, any provisions as to privacy and confidentiality would have to deal with the duty of a company to make disclosure of, *e.g.*, arbitration proceedings and actual or potential awards which have an effect on the company's financial position. The further

Australian decision in *Commonwealth of Australia v. Cockatoo Dockyard Pty Ltd* (1995) 36 N.S.W.L.R. 662 suggests that the public interest may also demand transparency as an exception to confidentiality: "Can it be seriously suggested that [the parties'] private agreement can, endorsed by a procedural direction of an arbitrator, exclude from the public domain matters of legitimate concern . . . ", *per* Kirby J. This decision raises fresh complications, particularly for statutory corporations. We are of the view that it would be extremely harmful to English arbitration if any statutory statement of general principles in this area impeded the commercial good-sense of current practices in English arbitration.

17.   Given these exceptions and qualifications, the formulation of any statutory principles would be likely to create new impediments to the practice of English arbitration and, in particular, to add to English litigation on the issue. Far from solving a difficulty, the DAC was firmly of the view that it would create new ones. Indeed, even if acceptable statutory guidelines could be formulated, there would remain the difficulty of fixing and enforcing sanctions for non-compliance. The position is not wholly satisfactory. However, none doubt at English law the existence of the general principles of confidentiality and privacy (though there is not unanimity as to their desirability). Where desirable, institutional rules can stipulate for these general principles, even where the arbitration agreement is not governed by English law. As to English law itself, whilst the breadth and existence of certain exceptions remains disputed, these can be resolved by the English courts on a pragmatic case-by-case basis. In due course, if the whole matter were ever to become judicially resolved, it would remain possible to add a statutory provision by way of amendment to the Bill. For these reasons, the DAC is of the view that no attempt should be made to codify English law on the privacy and confidentiality of English arbitration in the Bill. We would, however, draw attention to our supplementary recommendations on this topic in Chapter 6 below.

Clause 1   General Principles

A2–002   18.   The DAC was persuaded by the significant number of submissions which called for an introductory clause setting out basic principles. This Clause sets out three general principles. The first of these reflects what we believe to be the object of arbitration. We have not sought to define arbitration, since this poses difficulties that we discussed in our April 1995 Interim Report, and in the end we were not persuaded that an attempted definition would serve any useful purpose. We do, however, see value in setting out the object of arbitration. Fairness, impartiality and the avoidance of unnecessary delay or expense are all aspects of justice *i.e.* all requirements of a dispute resolution system based on obtaining a binding decision from a third party on the matters at issue. To our minds it is useful to stipulate that all the provisions of the Bill must be read with this object of arbitration in mind.

19.   The second principle is that of party autonomy. This reflects the basis of the Model Law and indeed much of our own present law. An arbitration under an arbitration agreement is a consensual process. The parties have agreed to resolve their disputes by their own chosen means. Unless the public interest otherwise dictates, this has two main consequences. Firstly, the parties should be held to their agreement and secondly, it should in the first instance be for the parties to decide how their arbitration should be conducted. In some cases, of course, the public interest will make inroads on complete party autonomy, in much the same way as there are limitations on freedom of contract. Some matters are simply not susceptible of this

form of dispute resolution (*e.g.* certain cases concerning status or many family matters) while other considerations (such as consumer protection) may require the imposition of different rights and obligations. Again, as appears from the mandatory provisions of the Bill, there are some rules that cannot be overridden by parties who have agreed to use arbitration. In general the mandatory provisions are there in order to support and assist the arbitral process and the stated object of arbitration.

20. So far as the third principle is concerned this reflects article 5 of the Model Law. This article provides as follows:

> "In matters governed by this Law, no court shall intervene except where so provided in this Law."

21. As was pointed out in the Mustill Report (pp. 50–52) there would be difficulties in importing this article as it stands. However, there is no doubt that our law has been subject to international criticism that the courts intervene more than they should in the arbitral process, thereby tending to frustrate the choice the parties have made to use arbitration rather than litigation as the means for resolving their disputes.

22. Nowadays the courts are much less inclined to intervene in the arbitral process than used to be the case. The limitation on the right of appeal to the courts from awards brought into effect by the Arbitration Act 1979, and changing attitudes generally, have meant that the courts nowadays generally only intervene in order to support rather than displace the arbitral process. We are very much in favour of this modern approach and it seems to us that it should be enshrined as a principle in the Bill.

Clause 2   Scope of Application of Provisions

23. International arbitrations can give rise to complex problems in the conflict of laws. A **A2–003** possible solution to some of these problems would have been to provide that all arbitrations conducted in England and Wales or in Northern Ireland should be subject to the provisions of the Bill, regardless of the parties' express or implied choice of some other system of law. We have not adopted this solution, which appears to us contrary to the basic principle that the parties should be free to agree how their disputes should be resolved. There appear to us to be no reasons of public policy to prevent the parties conducting an arbitration here under an agreement governed by foreign law or in accordance with a foreign procedural law. Clause 4(5) also follows the same basic principle. Of course, cases may well arise where considerations of our own concepts of public policy would lead to the refusal of the court here to enforce an arbitration award. This, however, is covered by Clause 66(3).

24. The rules of the conflict of laws as they apply to arbitration are complex, and to some extent still in a state of development by the courts. It therefore seems to us inappropriate to attempt to codify the relevant principles, beyond the simple statements set out in clause 2(1). Thus, as Clause 2(2) provides, matters referable to the arbitration agreement are governed by the law of England and Wales or of Northern Ireland, as the case may be, where that is the law applicable to the arbitration agreement, and matters of procedure are governed by that law where the seat of the arbitration is in England and Wales or in Northern Ireland: "seat" is defined in Clause 3. Beyond that we have not attempted to state the relevant rules of the conflict of laws, nor to embark on the issues of characterisation by which they are invoked.

25. Subsection (3) concerns the powers of the court to support the arbitration by staying proceedings brought in breach of an agreement to arbitrate, by compelling the attendance of witnesses, by granting those forms of interim relief which are set out in Clause 44, and by enforcing the award at common law by summary procedure. Such powers should obviously be available regardless of whether the seat of the arbitration is in England and Wales or in Northern Ireland, and regardless of what law is applicable to the arbitration agreement or the arbitral proceedings. Since we have used the expression "whatever the law applicable . . . ", it follows that Clause 2(3) is in no way restricted by Clause 2(1). It will be noted that in extending the power of the court to grant interim relief in support of arbitrations to arbitrations having a foreign seat we have given effect to our recommendation that section 25 of the Civil Jurisdiction and Judgments Act 1982 should be extended to arbitration proceedings. It should be appreciated that Rules of Court will have to be amended to give proper effect to the extension of the court's jurisdiction in Clause 2(3) (*i.e.* so as to allow service out of the jurisdiction in cases where it is necessary). Subsection (4) enables the court to refuse to exercise its power in such cases, where the fact that the arbitration has a foreign seat makes it inappropriate to exercise that power.

Clause 3   The Seat of the Arbitration

A2–004   26. The definition of "seat of the arbitration" is required by Clause 2, and as part of the definition of "domestic arbitration" in Clause 85. The concept of the "seat" as the juridical seat of the arbitration is known to English law but may be unfamiliar to some users of arbitration. Usually it will be the place where the arbitration is actually conducted: but this is not necessarily so, particularly if different parts of the proceedings are held in different countries.

27. In accordance with the principle of party autonomy, Clause 3 provides that the seat may be designated by the parties themselves or in some other manner authorised by them. Failing that it must be determined objectively having regard to the parties' agreement and all other relevant circumstances. English law does not at present recognise the concept of an arbitration which has no seat, and we do not recommend that it should do so. The powers of the court where the seat is in England and Wales or in Northern Ireland are limited to those necessary to carry into effect the principles enshrined in Clause 1. Where the seat is elsewhere, the court's powers are further limited by Clause 2(4). The process of consultation identified no need for an arbitration which was "delocalised" to a greater extent than this.

Clause 4   Mandatory and Non-mandatory Provisions

A2–005   28. This provision is designed to make clear that the Bill has certain provisions that cannot be overridden by the parties; and for ease of reference these are listed in Schedule 1 to the Bill. The Clause also makes clear that the other provisions of this Part can be changed or substituted by the parties, and exist as "fall-back" rules that will apply if the parties do not make any such change or substitution, or do not provide for the particular matter in question. In this way, in the absence of any other contrary agreement, gaps in an arbitration agreement will be filled.

29. Subsection (5). Although we believe that the choice of a foreign law would anyway have the effect set out in this provision, it seemed for the sake of clarity to be useful to state this expressly, so as to remind all concerned that a choice of a foreign law does amount to an agreement of the parties to which due regard should be paid.

30. It should be made clear that the phrase "mandatory" is not used in either of the two senses that it is used, for example, in Articles 3 and 7 of the Rome Convention (see Goode, *Commercial Law* (2nd ed.) at 1118): the mandatory provisions of Part 1 of the Bill are only mandatory in so far as the provisions of Part 1 apply (*i.e.* by virtue of Clause 2). The mandatory provisions would have no application if Part 1 does not apply.

Clause 5 Agreements to be in Writing

(a) Arbitration Agreements

31. Article 7 of the Model Law requires the arbitration agreement to be in writing. We have not followed the precise wording of this article, for the reasons given in the Mustill Report (p. 52), though we have incorporated much of that article in the Bill. **A2–006**

32. The requirement for the arbitration agreement to be in writing is the position at present under section 32 of the Arbitration Act 1950 and section 7 of the Arbitration Act 1975. If an arbitration agreement is not in writing then it is not completely ineffective, since the common law recognises such agreements and is saved by Clause 81(2)(a).

33. We remain of the view expressed in the Consultative Paper issued with the draft Clauses published in July 1995, that there should be a requirement for writing. An arbitration agreement has the important effect of contracting out of the right to go to the court, *i.e.* it deprives the parties of that basic right. To our minds an agreement of such importance should be in some written form. Furthermore the need for such form should help to reduce disputes as to whether or not an arbitration agreement was made and as to its terms.

34. We have, however, provided a very wide meaning to the words "in writing". Indeed this meaning is wider than that found in the Model Law, but in our view, is consonant with Article II.2 of the English text of the New York Convention. The non-exhaustive definition in the English text ("shall include") may differ in this respect from the French and Spanish texts, but the English text is equally authentic under Article XVI of the New York Convention itself, and also accords with the Russian authentic text ("ключает"); see also the 1989 Report of the Swiss Institute of Comparative Law on Jurisdictional Problems in International Commercial Arbitration (by Adam Samuel), at pages 81 to 85. It seems to us that English law as it stands more than justifies this wide meaning; see, for example, *Zambia Steel v. James Clark* [1986] 2 Lloyd's Rep. 225. In view of rapidly evolving methods of recording we have made clear that "writing" includes recording by any means.

(b) Other Agreements

35. These we have also made subject to a "writing" requirement. Had we not done so, we could envisage disputes over whether, for example, something the parties had agreed to during the conduct of the arbitration amounted to a variation of the arbitration **A2–007**

agreement and required writing, or could be characterised as something else. By introducing some formality with respect to all agreements, the possibility of subsequent disputes (*e.g.* at the enforcement stage) is greatly diminished. Indeed it seemed to us that with the extremely broad definition we have given to writing, the advantages of requiring some record of what was agreed with regard to any aspect of an arbitration outweighed the disadvantages of requiring a specific form for an effective agreement.

(c) Further Points

A2–008 36. Subsection 5(3). This is designed to cover, amongst other things, extremely common situations such as salvage operations, where parties make an oral agreement which incorporates by reference the terms of a written form of agreement (*e.g.* Lloyd's Open Form), which contains an arbitration clause. Whilst greatly extending the definition of "writing", the DAC is of the view that given the frequency and importance of such activity, it was essential that it be provided for in the Bill. The reference could be to a written agreement containing an arbitration clause, or to a set of written arbitration rules, or to an individual written arbitration agreement. This provision would also cover agreement by conduct. For example, party A may agree to buy from party B a quantity of goods on certain terms and conditions (which include an arbitration clause) which are set out in writing and sent to party B, with a request that he sign and return the order form. If, which is by no means uncommon, party B fails to sign the order form, or send any document in response to the order, but manufactures and delivers the goods in accordance with the contract to party A, who pays for them in accordance with the contract, this could constitute an agreement "otherwise than in writing by reference to terms which are in writing . . . ", and could therefore include an effective arbitration agreement. The provision therefore seeks to meet the criticisms that have been made of article 7(2) of the Model Law in this regard (see, *e.g.* the Sixth Goff Lecture, delivered by Neil Kaplan Q.C. in Hong Kong in November 1995, (1996) 12 *Arb. Int.* 35). A written agreement made by reference to separate written terms would, of course, be caught by Clause 5(2).

37. Subsection 5(4). There has been some concern that a writing requirement with respect to every agreement might unduly constrain the parties' freedom and flexibility with respect to, for example, minor matters of procedure during a hearing. This subsection seeks to avoid this. An agreement will be evidenced in writing if recorded by, amongst others, a third party with the authority of the parties to the agreement. Given that this third party could of course be the tribunal, the parties are free during a hearing to make whatever arrangements or changes to the agreed procedure they wish, as long as these are recorded by the tribunal. The DAC is of the view that this presents no serious hindrance to the parties' flexibility, and has the merit of reducing the risk of disputes later on as to what exactly was agreed. Clearly, this subsection also has a wider effect, allowing for the recording of an oral agreement at any stage.

38. Subsection 5(5). This provision is based on article 7(2) of the Model Law, but with certain important changes. The DAC has been careful to emphasize that for there to be an effective arbitration agreement for the purposes of this Part, it is not enough for one party to allege in a written submission that there is an arbitration agreement, in circumstances where the other party simply fails to respond at all. If this were enough,

an unfair obligation would be placed on any party (including a stranger to the proceedings in question) to take the active step of serving a written submission in order to deny this allegation. Therefore, in order to satisfy this subsection, there must be a failure to deny an allegation by a party who has submitted a response submission.

39. It has been suggested that the term "written submissions" is too narrow, and that this should be replaced by "documents". The DAC does not agree with this, given that this would include the most informal of letters. It may well be unjust, for example, for one party to be able to point to one sentence in one letter in a long exchange with another party, in which there is an allegation that there exists an arbitration clause, and where this has not been denied.

40. Reference should also be made to subsection 23(4). Whilst any agreement as to an arbitration must be in writing, the DAC is of the view that it is impracticable to impose a writing requirement on an agreement to terminate an arbitration. Parties may well simply walk away from proceedings, or allow the proceedings to lapse, and it could be extremely unfair if one party were allowed to rely upon an absence of writing at some future stage. Where a claimant allows an arbitration to lapse, Clause 41(3) may be utilised.

The Arbitration Agreement

Clause 6   Definition of Arbitration Agreement

41. The first subsection reflects article 7(1) of the Model Law and provides a more informative definition than that in section 32 of the 1950 Act. We have used the word "disputes" but this is defined in Clause 82 as including "differences" since there is some authority for the proposition that the latter term is wider than the former; see *Sykes v. Fine Fare Ltd* [1967] 1 Lloyd's Rep. 53.   A2–009

42. The second subsection reflects article 7(2) of the Model Law. In English law there is at present some conflicting authority on the question as to what is required for the effective incorporation of an arbitration clause by reference. Some of those responding to the July 1995 draft Clauses made critical comments of the views of Sir John Megaw in *Aughton v. M F Kent Services* [1991] 57 B.L.R. 1 (a construction contract case) and suggested that we should take the opportunity of making clear that the law was as stated in the charterparty cases and as summarised by Ralph Gibson L.J. in *Aughton*. (Similar disquiet has been expressed about decisions following *Aughton*, such as *Ben Barrett v. Henry Boot Management Ltd* [1995] Constr. Ind. Law Letter 1026). It seemed to us, however, that although we are of the view that the approach of Ralph Gibson L.J. should prevail in all cases, this was really a matter for the court to decide. The wording we have used certainly leaves room for the adoption of the charterparty rules in all cases, since it refers to references to a document containing an arbitration clause as well as a reference to the arbitration clause itself. Thus the wording is not confined to cases where there is specific reference to the arbitration clause, which Sir John Megaw (but not Ralph Gibson L.J.) considered was a requirement for effective incorporation by reference.

Clause 7   Separability of Arbitration Agreement

43. This Clause sets out the principle of separability which is already part of English law (see *Harbour Assurance v. Kansa* [1993] Q.B. 701), which is also to be found in article   A2–010

16(1) of the Model Law, and which is regarded internationally as highly desirable. However, it seems to us that the doctrine of separability is quite distinct from the question of the degree to which the tribunal is entitled to rule on its own jurisdiction, so that, unlike the Model Law, we have dealt with the latter elsewhere in the Bill (Clause 30).

44.   In the draft Clauses published in July 1995 we inserted a provision to make clear that the doctrine of separability did not affect the question whether an assignment of rights under the substantive agreement carried with it the right or obligation to submit to arbitration in accordance with the arbitration agreement. This is now omitted as being unnecessary, since we have re-drafted subsection (1) in order to follow the relevant part of article 16 of the Model Law more closely, and to make clear that the doctrine of separability is confined to the effect of invalidity etc of the main contract on the arbitration agreement, rather than being, as it was in the July 1995 draft, a free-standing principle. Similarly, in being so restricted, this Clause is not intended to have any impact on the incorporation of an arbitration clause from one document or contract into another (which is addressed in Clause 6(2)).

45.   A number of those responding to our drafts expressed the wish for the Bill to lay down rules relating to assignment, *e.g.* that the assignment of rights under the substantive agreement should be subject to any right or obligation to submit to arbitration in accordance with the arbitration agreement unless either of these agreements provided otherwise. Indeed we included such a provision in the illustrative draft published in April 1995. However, on further consideration, we concluded that it would not be appropriate to seek to lay down any such rules.

46.   There were two principal reasons for reaching this view.

  i.   In the first place, under English law the assignability of a contractual right is governed by the proper law of that right, while the effectiveness of the assignment is governed by the proper law of the assignment. However, where the law governing the substantive agreement (or the arbitration agreement) is not English law, different rules may well apply and there is an added problem in that those rules (under the foreign law in question) may be categorised as either substantive or procedural in nature. The Bill would therefore have to address such problems whilst simultaneously not interfering with substantive rights and obligations. We were not persuaded that it would be either practicable or of any real use to attempt to devise general rules which would deal satisfactorily with this matter.

  ii. In the second place, English law distinguishes between legal and equitable assignments, so that any rules we devised would have to take this into account. In our view, an attempt to devise rules relating to assignments where no foreign law elements are involved is more the subject of reform of the law of assignment generally than of a Bill relating exclusively to arbitration.

47.   Finally, it should be noted that the substantive agreement of which the arbitration agreement forms part need not itself be in writing for the Bill to apply, provided of course that the arbitration agreement itself is in writing. This should be clarified as we suggest in our supplementary recommendations in Chapter 6 below.

Clause 8   Whether Agreement discharged by Death of a Party

A2–011   48.   This Clause sets out the present statutory position. The common law was that an arbitration agreement was discharged by the death of a party. That rule was altered by the Arbitration Act 1934 as re-enacted by section 2 of the Arbitration Act 1950. We have avoided using the technical expression "right of action" which is to be found in section 2(3) of the 1950 Act and which could perhaps give rise to problems for the reasons given in the consultative paper published with the draft Clauses in July 1995. In line with party autonomy, we have provided that the parties can agree that death shall have the effect of discharging the arbitration agreement.

49. This Clause deals only with the arbitration agreement. The effect of the death of a party on the appointment of an arbitrator (also to be found in section 2 of the 1950 Act) is now dealt with in that part of the Bill concerned with the arbitral tribunal (see Clause 26(2)).

Stay of Legal Proceedings

Clause 9   Stay of Legal Proceedings

50. We have proposed a number of changes to the present statutory position (section 4(1) A2–012
of the 1950 Act and section 1 of the 1975 Act), having in mind article 8 of the Model Law, our treaty obligations, and other considerations.

51. We have made it clear that a stay can be sought of a counterclaim as well as a claim. The existing legislation could be said not to cover counterclaims, since it required the party seeking a stay first to enter an "appearance" which a defendant to counterclaim could not do. Indeed, "appearance" is no longer the appropriate expression in the High Court in any event, and never was the appropriate expression in the county court. We have also made clear that an application can be made to stay part of legal proceedings, where other parts are not subject to an agreement to arbitrate.

52. Further, the Clause provides that an application is only to be made by a party against whom legal proceedings are brought (as opposed to any other party).

53. We have provided that an application may be made for a stay even where the matter cannot be referred to arbitration immediately, because the parties have agreed first to use other dispute resolution procedures. This reflects *dicta* of Lord Mustill *Channel Tunnel v. Balfour Beatty* [1993] A.C. 334.

54. In this Clause we have made a stay mandatory unless the court is satisfied that the arbitration agreement is null and void, inoperative, or incapable of being performed. This is the language of the Model Law and of course of the New York Convention on the Recognition and Enforcement of Foreign Arbitral Awards, presently to be found in the Arbitration Act 1975.

55. The Arbitration Act 1975 contained a further ground for refusing a stay, namely where the Court was satisfied that "there was not in fact any dispute between the parties with regard to the matter agreed to be referred". These words do not appear in the New York Convention and in our view are confusing and unnecessary, for the reasons given in *Hayter v. Nelson* [1990] 2 Lloyd's Rep. 265.

56. In Part II of the Bill these provisions are altered in cases of "domestic arbitration agreements" as there defined.

57. We have included a provision (subsection (5)) that where the court refuses to stay the legal proceedings, any term making an award a condition precedent to the bringing of

legal proceedings (known as a *Scott v. Avery* clause) will cease to have effect. This avoids a situation where the arbitration clause is unworkable, yet no legal proceedings can be successfully brought. Whilst one respondent suggested that this may go too far, it appears to be a matter of basic justice that a situation in which a party can neither arbitrate nor litigate must be avoided.

Clause 10   Reference of Interpleader Issue to Arbitration

A2–013   58.   This Clause is based on section 5 of the 1950 Act. We have however taken the opportunity of making a stay mandatory so as to comply with the New York Convention, as well as trying to express the provision in simpler, clearer terms. The Clause is required because "interpleader" arises where one party claiming no right himself in the subject matter, is facing conflicting claims from other parties and does not know to which of them he should account. English law allows such a party to bring those in contention before the court which may order the latter to fight out the question between themselves. If they have agreed to arbitrate the matter then Clause 9 would not itself operate, since the party seeking interpleader relief would not be making a claim which he had agreed to arbitrate.

59.   We have not defined "interpleader", although some suggested that we should, given that this is a legal term of art, which goes far beyond arbitration contexts.

Clause 11   Retention of Security where Admiralty Proceedings Stayed

A2–014   60.   This Clause is not intended to do more than re-enact the present statutory position as found in section 26 of the Civil Jurisdiction and Judgments Act 1982.

61.   Clauses 9 to 11 are, of course, mandatory.

Commencement of Arbitral Proceedings

Clause 12   Power of Court to Extend Time for Beginning Arbitral Proceedings, etc.

A2–015   62.   We have proposed a number of changes to the existing law.

63.   The major change concerns the test that the court must apply before extending the time.

64.   The power of the court to extend a contractual time limit which would otherwise bar the claim first appeared in our law in section 16(6) of the Arbitration Act 1934, which was re-enacted in section 27 of the Arbitration Act 1950.

65.   From paragraph 33 of the Report of the MacKinnon Committee presented to Parliament in March 1927 it can be seen that the reason for suggesting that the court should have power to extend the time was that the vast majority of submissions to arbitration are contained in printed forms of contract, which cannot be carefully examined in the transaction of business and alteration of which it would be difficult for most people to secure. The Committee concluded that it might be sound policy to create a power to modify unconscionable provisions as regards common forms of submission in printed forms. It is also clear from paragraph 34 of the Report that the Committee had in mind cases where the time limit was very short, *i.e.* measured in

days. The Committee suggested that the test should be whether the time limit created an "unreasonable hardship".

66. As can be seen from the Notes on Clauses to the 1934 Act, it was later felt that since the justification for giving the power was presumably either ignorance of the existence of the provision in the contract, or the acceptance of the provision through undue pressure by the other party, which could be the case whether or not the contract was in a common form, the power should not be limited to such forms.

67. Section 27 of the 1950 Act, with its test of undue hardship, seems to many to have been interpreted by the courts in a way hardly envisaged by those who suggested the power in the first place. Indeed that interpretation seems to have changed over the years: see the discussion in Mustill and Boyd, *Commercial Arbitration* (2nd ed.), pp. 201–215. Some responses indicated dissatisfaction with the way the Courts were using Clause 27 to interfere with the bargain that the parties had made. The present legal position would seem to owe much to a time, now some 20 years ago, when the courts were flirting with the idea that they enjoyed some general power of supervisory jurisdiction over arbitrations.

68. The justification for time limits is that they enable commercial concerns (and indeed others) to draw a line beneath transactions at a much earlier stage than ordinary limitation provisions would allow. It should be mentioned, however, that other responses suggested that the position presently reached by the courts should be maintained.

69. The present Committee re-examined section 27 in the light of the underlying philosophy of the Bill, namely that of party autonomy. This underlying philosophy seems to have been generally welcomed in this country and abroad and of course it fits with the general international understanding of arbitration. Party autonomy means, among other things, that any power given to the court to override the bargain that the parties have made must be fully justified. The idea that the court has some general supervisory jurisdiction over arbitrations has been abandoned.

70. It seemed to us in today's climate that there were three cases where the power could be justified in the context of agreed time limits to bring a claim. These are, firstly, where the circumstances are such as were outside the reasonable contemplation of the parties when they agreed the provision in question and that it would be fair to extend the time, secondly, where the conduct of one party made it unjust to hold the other to the time limit, and thirdly, where the respective bargaining position of the parties was such that it would again be unfair to hold one of them to the time limit.

71. The third of these cases seems to us to reflect the thinking of the MacKinnon Committee, while the other two have developed through the courts' interpretation of section 27. However this third category is really an aspect of what nowadays would be called "consumer protection". This part of the Bill is not concerned with consumer protection, for which provision is made elsewhere and in respect of which there is a growing body of European law.

72. In these circumstances it seemed to us to be appropriate to set out in this part of the Bill the first and second of the cases we have described. Apart from anything else, this will give the courts the opportunity to reconsider how to proceed in the light of the philosophy underlying the Bill as a whole, namely that of party autonomy. As the

MacKinnon Committee itself intimated, great care must be taken before interfering with the bargain that the parties have made.

73.   It was suggested to the DAC that the principal matter to be taken into account by the court should be the length of the contractual period in question. The DAC is of the view that this is only one of several relevant matters, another factor being, for example, the contemplation of the parties. For this reason, the DAC concluded that a simple test of "substantial injustice", without more, would not suffice.

74.   There are some other changes.

   i.   Firstly, Clause 12(1)(b) contains a reference to other dispute resolution procedures. We understand that there is an increasing use of provisions which call for mediation and other alternative dispute resolution procedures to precede recourse to arbitration, so that we thought it proper to add this to the other step covered by the Clause, namely to begin arbitral proceedings. We do not intend to widen the scope of the Clause beyond this, so that unless the step in question is one of the two kinds described, the Clause will not operate. Thus this represents only a small but we think logical extension to the present law.

   ii. Secondly, it is made a pre-condition that the party concerned first exhausts any available arbitral process for obtaining an extension of time. In the view of the Committee it would be a rare case indeed where the court extended the time in circumstances where there was such a process which had not resulted in an extension, for it would in the ordinary case be difficult if not impossible to persuade the court that it would be just to extend the time or unjust not to do so, where by an arbitral process to which *ex hypothesi* the applying party had agreed, the opposite conclusion had been reached.

   iii. Thirdly, we have made any appeal from a decision of the court under this Clause subject to the leave of that court. It seems to us that there should be this limitation, and that in the absence of some important question of principle, leave should not generally be granted. We take the same view in respect of the other cases in the Bill where we propose that an appeal requires the leave of the court.

   iv. Fourthly, whereas the existing statutory provision refers to terms of an agreement that provide that claims shall be "barred", this has been extended to read "barred, or the claimant's right extinguished".

75.   For obvious reasons, this Clause is mandatory.

Clauses 13 and 14   Application of Limitation Acts and Commencement of Arbitral Proceedings

A2–016   76.   The first of these provisions is designed to restate the present law. The reference to the Foreign Limitation Periods Act 1984 avoids (subject to the provisions of that Act) the imposition of an English limitation period where an applicable foreign law imposes a different period. The second provision reflects to a degree article 21 of the Model Law, but sets out the various cases, including one not presently covered by the law. It will be noted that we have used the word "matter" rather than the word "disputes". This is to reflect the fact that a dispute is not the same as a claim; *cf.* Mustill and Boyd, *op.cit.* at p. 29 and *Commission for the New Towns v. Crudens* (1995) C.I.L.L. 1035. The neutral word "matter" will cover both, so that an arbitration clause which refers to claims will be covered as well as one which refers to disputes.

77. Clause 13 is a mandatory provision.

The Arbitral Tribunal

Clause 15   The Arbitral Tribunal

78. Article 10(1) of the Model Law provides that the parties are free to determine the   A2–017
number of arbitrators. We have included a like provision.

79. Article 10(2) of the Model Law stipulates that failing such determination, the number
of arbitrators shall be three. This we have not adopted, preferring the existing English
rule that in the absence of agreement the default number shall be one. The employment of three arbitrators is likely to be three times the cost of employing one, and it
seems right that this extra burden should be available if the parties so choose, but not
imposed on them. The provision for a sole arbitrator also accords both with common
practice in this country, and the balance of responses the DAC received. The Model
Law default does not, of course, cater for the situation where there are more than two
parties to the arbitration.

Clause 16   Procedure for the Appointment of Arbitrators

80. Again we have had the Model Law (article 11) very much in mind in drafting these   A2–018
provisions, though we have attempted to cater for more cases and also for the fact that
under our law, there can be either an umpire or a chairman. We should note that this
has caused some confusion abroad, particularly in the United States, where what we
would describe as a "chairman" is called an "umpire". In Clauses 20 and 21 we set
out the differences between these two which (in the absence of agreement between the
parties) is the present position under English law.

81. The time limits we have imposed for appointments we consider to be fair and
reasonable. They can be extended by the Court under Clause 79, but the power of the
court in this regard is limited as set out in that Clause. In the ordinary case we would
not expect the court to allow a departure from the Clause 16 time limits.

82. It might be noted that periods of 28 days, rather than 30 days (as in the Model Law)
have been used throughout the Bill, in order to reduce the likelihood of a deadline
expiring on a weekend.

Clause 17   Power in Case of Default to Appoint Sole Arbitrator

83. This Clause is intended to replace the present rules concerning the appointment of   A2–019
a sole arbitrator where the other party is in default (section 7(b) of the 1950 Act). It
only applies to a two party case. We have stipulated that the party in default must not
only appoint his arbitrator within the specified period but also inform the other party
that he has done so. This in our view is a significant improvement on the present law,
where the defaulting party was under no obligation to say that he had made an
appointment. This was calculated to cause unnecessary delay, confusion and
expense.

84. Some of those responding objected to this Clause. The DAC, however, remains of the
view that this provision is an example of the Court supporting the arbitral process,

and reducing the opportunities available for a recalcitrant party. The DAC is advised that section 7(b) of the 1950 Act is used a great deal, and that its very existence constitutes a deterrent to those contemplating dilatory tactics. The alternative would be to simply provide for recourse to court. This would be overly burdensome in most cases, and is available, in any event, under the provisions of the Bill.

85.   It has been suggested that the Bill should set out grounds upon which the court should exercise its discretion in Clause 17(3). The DAC is of the view, however, that this is best left for the courts to develop, given the specific circumstances of each case, and in the light of the overall philosophy of the Bill.

86.   One respondent queried the use of the word "refuses" in Clause 17(1). The advantage of this is that if a party does actually refuse to appoint an arbitrator, rather than simply failing to do so, the non-defaulting party need not wait for the expiration of the relevant time period within which the defaulting party may make such an appointment, but could use the mechanism in Clause 17 straight away.

Clause 18   Failure of Appointment Procedure

A2–020   87.   Again we have had the Model Law in mind when drafting this provision, The starting point is any agreement the parties may have made to deal with a failure of the appointment procedure. In the absence of any such agreement, the court is given the power to make appointments. This is a classic case of the court supporting and helping to carry through the arbitration process.

88.   It will be noted that we have given the court power to revoke any appointments already made. This is to cover the case where unless the court took this step it might be suggested thereafter that the parties had not been fairly treated, since one had his own choice arbitrator while the other had an arbitrator imposed on him by the court in circumstances that were no fault of his own. This situation in fact arose in France in the *Dutco* case, where an award was invalidated for this reason.

89.   The Model Law stipulates that there shall be no appeal from a decision of the court. We have not gone as far as this, since there may well be questions of important general principle which would benefit from authoritative appellate guidance.

Clause 19   Court to have regard to Agreed Qualifications

A2–021   90.   This comes from article 11(5) of the Model Law, which itself seeks to preserve as much of the parties' agreement as possible.

Clauses 20 and 21   Chairman and Umpire

A2–022   91.   The parties are, of course, free to make what arrangements they like about the functions and powers of Chairmen or Umpires. We have set out what we believe to be the position under English law in the absence of any such agreement. As we understand the current position, in the absence of an agreement between the parties, an umpire can neither take part nor attend an arbitration until the arbitrators have disagreed.

92.   A cause of delay and expense often exists under our umpire system where the umpire does not attend the proceedings and it is only at an advanced stage (when the arbitrators disagree) that he takes over, for much that has gone on may have to be repeated before him. Equally, the time and expense of an umpire may be wasted if he

attends but the arbitrators are able to agree on everything. We have decided that it would be preferable to stipulate that (in the absence of agreement between the parties) the umpire should attend the proceedings (as opposed to taking part in the proceedings) and be supplied with the same documents and materials as the other arbitrators. We hope, however, that common sense will prevail and that the parties will make specific agreement over this question, tailored to the circumstances of the particular case.

93. Subsection 21(4) caused some concern amongst a few respondents, but this subsection simply reflects what is understood to be the current position.

94. We should record that we considered whether the peculiarly English concept of an umpire should be swept away in favour of the more generally used chaired tribunal. As we have pointed out above, in the United States what we would describe as a chairman is called an umpire. In the end we decided not to recommend this, and to continue to provide default provisions for those who wanted to continue to use this form of arbitral tribunal.

Clause 22   Decision-making where no Chairman or Umpire

95. We decided to include this situation for the sake of completeness, though the default   **A2–023**
provision can only work if there is unanimity or a majority. If there is neither, then it would appear that the arbitration agreement cannot operate, unless the parties can agree, or have agreed, what is to happen.

Clause 23   Revocation of Arbitrator's Authority

96. Statutory provisions making it impossible unilaterally to revoke the authority of an   **A2–024**
arbitrator have existed since 1833. The present Clause is designed to reflect the current position, save that we have imposed a writing requirement and thought it helpful to make express reference to arbitral institutions etc. These of course only have such powers as the parties have agreed they shall have, so that strictly this provision is not necessary, but we consider that an express reference makes for clarity.

97. Some of those responding suggested that the parties' right to agree to revoke an arbitral appointment should be limited (*e.g.* that court approval should be required in every case). The DAC has not adopted these suggestions since any tribunal is properly regarded as the parties' tribunal and to do so would derogate from the principle of party autonomy.

98. It will be seen that various terms are used in the Bill with respect to the termination of an arbitral appointment, such as "removal" and "revocation of authority". Different terms have been adopted simply as a matter of correct English usage. The difference in terms is not intended to be of any legal significance.

99. Subsection 23(4). Whilst any agreement as to an arbitration must be in writing, as defined earlier, the DAC is of the view that it is impracticable to impose a writing requirement on an agreement to terminate an arbitration. Parties may well simply walk away from proceedings, or allow the proceedings to lapse, and it could be extremely unfair if one party were allowed to rely upon an absence of writing at some future stage. Where a Claimant allows an arbitration to lapse, Clause 41(3) may be utilised.

Clause 24   Power of Court to Remove Arbitrator

A2–025   100. We have set out the cases where the court can remove an arbitrator.

101. The Model Law (article 12) specifies justifiable doubts as to the independence (as well as impartiality) of an arbitrator as grounds for his removal. We have considered this carefully, but despite efforts to do so, no-one has persuaded us that, in consensual arbitrations, this is either required or desirable. It seems to us that lack of independence, unless it gives rise to justifiable doubts about the impartiality of the arbitrator, is of no significance. The latter is, of course, the first of our grounds for removal. If lack of independence were to be included, then this could only be justified if it covered cases where the lack of independence did not give rise to justifiable doubts about impartiality, for otherwise there would be no point including lack of independence as a separate ground.

102. We can see no good reason for including "non-partiality" lack of independence as a ground for removal and good reasons for not doing so. We do not follow what is meant to be covered by a lack of independence which does not lead to the appearance of partiality. Furthermore, the inclusion of independence would give rise to endless arguments, as it has, for example, in Sweden and the United States, where almost any connection (however remote) has been put forward to challenge the "independence" of an arbitrator. For example, it is often the case that one member of a barristers' Chambers appears as counsel before an arbitrator who comes from the same Chambers. Is that to be regarded, without more, as a lack of independence justifying the removal of the arbitrator? We are quite certain that this would not be the case in English law. Indeed the Chairman has so decided in a case in Chambers in the Commercial Court. We would also draw attention to the article "Barristers' Independence and Disclosure" by Kendall in (1992) 8 *Arb. Int.* 287. We would further note in passing that even the oath taken by those appointed to the International Court of Justice; and indeed to our own High Court, refers only to impartiality.

103. Further, there may well be situations in which parties desire their arbitrators to have familiarity with a specific field, rather than being entirely independent.

104. We should emphasise that we intend to lose nothing of significance by omitting reference to independence. Lack of this quality may well give rise to justifiable doubts about impartiality, which is covered, but if it does not, then we cannot at present see anything of significance that we have omitted by not using this term.

105. We have included, as grounds for removal, the refusal or failure of an arbitrator properly to conduct the proceedings, as well as failing to use all reasonable despatch in conducting the proceedings or making an award, where the result has caused or will cause substantial injustice to the applicant. We trust that the courts will not allow the first of these matters to be abused by those intent on disrupting the arbitral process. To this end we have included a provision allowing the tribunal to continue while an application is made. There is also Clause 73 which effectively requires a party to "put up or shut up" if a challenge is to be made.

106. We have every confidence that the courts will carry through the intent of this part of the Bill, which is that it should only be available where the conduct of the arbitrator is such as to go so beyond anything that could reasonably be defended that substantial injustice has resulted or will result. The provision is not intended to allow the court to substitute its own view as to how the arbitral proceedings should be conducted.

Thus the choice by an arbitrator of a particular procedure, unless it breaches the duty laid on arbitrators by Clause 33, should on no view justify the removal of an arbitrator, even if the court would not itself have adopted that procedure. In short, this ground only exists to cover what we hope will be the very rare case where an arbitrator so conducts the proceedings that it can fairly be said that instead of carrying through the object of arbitration as stated in the Bill, he is in effect frustrating that object. Only if the court confines itself in this way can this power of removal be justified as a measure supporting rather than subverting the arbitral process.

107. We have also made the exhaustion of any arbitral process for challenging an arbitrator a pre-condition to the right to apply to the court. Again it will be a very rare case indeed where the court will remove an arbitrator notwithstanding that that process has reached a different conclusion.

108. If an arbitrator is removed by the court, we have given the court power to make orders in respect of his remuneration. We would expect this power to be exercised where the behaviour of the arbitrator is inexcusable to the extent that this should be marked by depriving him of all or some of his fees and expenses. This subsection is also the subject of a supplementary recommendation in Chapter 6 below.

109. As a matter of justice, we have stipulated that an arbitrator is entitled to be heard on any application for his removal.

110. This is a mandatory provision. It seems to us that an agreement to contract out of the cases we specify would really be tantamount to an agreement to a dispute resolution procedure that is contrary to the basic principles set out in Clause 1.

Clause 25   Resignation of Arbitrator

111. In theory it could be said that an arbitrator cannot unilaterally resign if this conflicts with the express or implied terms of his engagement. However, as a matter of practical politics an arbitrator who refuses to go on cannot be made to do so, though of course he may incur a liability for breach of his agreement to act.

A2–026

112. In this Clause we have given an arbitrator who resigns the right to go to the court to seek relief from any liability incurred through resigning and to make orders relating to his remuneration and expenses, unless the consequences of resignation have been agreed with the parties (*e.g.* by virtue of having adopted institutional rules).

113. We have chosen the words of subsection (1) with care so that the agreement referred to is confined to an agreement as to the consequences of resignation. A simple agreement not to resign (or only to resign in certain circumstances) with no agreement as to what will happen if this promise is broken is not within the subsection. This has to be so since otherwise (by virtue of subsection (2)), subsections (3) and (4) would never or hardly ever operate, for the arbitrator will not be under any liability or at risk as to his fees or expenses unless he is in breach by resigning.

114. In the July draft we suggested a provision which would have entitled the court to grant relief in all circumstances including those where the arbitrator had made an agreement as to the consequences of his resignation. However, as the result of a response that we received we have concluded that where the parties have agreed with an arbitrator on the consequences it would be wrong to give the court a power to adjust the position.

115. The reason we propose this is that circumstances may well arise in which it would be just to grant such relief to a resigning arbitrator. For example, the arbitrator may (reasonably) not be prepared to adopt a procedure agreed by the parties (*i.e.* under Clause 34) during the course of an arbitration, taking the view that his duty under Clause 33 conflicts with their suggestions (the relationship between the duty of arbitrators in Clause 33 and the freedom of the parties in Clause 34, is discussed in more detail below). Again, an arbitration may drag on for far longer than could reasonably have been expected when the appointment was accepted, resulting in an unfair burden on the arbitrator. In circumstances where the court was persuaded that it was reasonable for the arbitrator to resign, it seems only right that the court should be able to grant appropriate relief.

Clause 26   Death of Arbitrator or Person Appointing Him

A2–027   116. This Clause complements Clause 8 and is included for the same reason. Clause 26(1) is mandatory—it is difficult to see how parties could agree otherwise.

Clause 27   Filling of Vacancy, etc.

A2–028   117. This Clause reflects article 15 of the Model Law, but also deals with certain other important ancillary matters. It should be noted that we do not propose to re-enact the power given to the court under section 25 of the Arbitration Act 1950 to fill a vacancy created by its removal of an arbitrator. It seems to us that (in the absence of agreement between the parties) it is preferable for the original appointment procedure to be used, for otherwise (as in the *Dutco* case mentioned above) it might be argued that the parties were not being treated equally.

118. We have given the tribunal the right (when reconstituted) to determine to what extent the previous proceedings should stand, though we have also made clear that this does not affect any right a party may have to challenge what has happened.

119. Further, we have provided in Clause 27(5) that the fact of an arbitrator ceasing to hold office will not affect any appointment made by him (whether alone or jointly) of another arbitrator, unless the parties have otherwise agreed pursuant to Clause 27(1)(c).

Clause 28   Joint and Several Liability of Parties to Arbitrators for Fees and Expenses

A2–029   120. Arbitration proceedings necessarily involve the incurring of expenditure. The arbitrators have to be paid, and the parties incur expense in presenting their cases to the tribunal. The issue of costs involves at least three quite discrete elements:

    i. As a matter of general contract law, arbitrators, experts, institutions and any other payees whatsoever are entitled to be paid what has been agreed with them by any of the parties. Therefore, for example, if a party appoints an arbitrator for an agreed fee, as a matter of general contract law (rather than anything in this Bill), that arbitrator is entitled to that fee.

    ii. It is generally accepted that all parties are jointly and severally liable for the fees of an arbitrator. This is an issue as to the entitlement of arbitrators, and as such is quite distinct from the third element.

    iii. As in court litigation, when one party is successful, that party should normally recover at least a proportion of his costs. This issue, being where the burden of costs should lie, is an issue as between the parties.

121. The Bill contains provisions as to costs and fees in two separate parts: the joint and several liability owed by the parties to the arbitrators (the second element) is addressed in this clause, whilst the third element (*i.e.* the responsibility for costs as between the parties) is addressed in Clauses 59–65. The first element, being a matter of general contract law, is not specifically addressed by either set of provisions, but is preserved in both. It is extremely important to distinguish between these provisions.

122. Clause 28 is concerned with the rights of the arbitrators in respect of fees and expenses. As subsection (5) makes clear, and as explained above, this provision is not concerned with which of the parties should (as between themselves) bear these costs as the result of the arbitration, which is dealt with later in the Bill, nor with any contractual right an arbitrator may have in respect of fees and expenses.

123. As we understand the present law, the parties are jointly and severally liable to the arbitrator for his fees and expenses. The present position seems to be that if these are agreed by one party, the other party becomes liable, even if he played no part in making that agreement; and circumstances may arise in which that party is unable to obtain a reduction of the amount by taxation. It seems to us that whilst arbitrators should be protected by this joint and several liability of the parties, a potentially unfair result must be avoided: a party who never agreed to the appointment by another party of an exceptionally expensive arbitrator should not be held jointly and severally liable for that arbitrator's exceptional fees. To this end, we have stipulated, in Clause 28(1), that a party's joint and several liability to an arbitrator only extends to "reasonable fees". Of course, if a party has agreed an exceptional fee with an arbitrator, that party may still be pursued by that arbitrator, under general contract law, which is preserved in Clause 28(5).

124. We have proposed a mechanism to allow a party to go to the court if any question arises as to the reasonableness of the arbitrator's charges. The court is empowered to adjust fees and expenses even after they have been paid, since circumstances may well arise in which a question about the level of fees and expenses only arises after payment has been made. For example, a large advance payment may be made at a time when it is considered that the arbitration will take a long time, but this does not turn out to be the case. However, the court must be satisfied that it is reasonable in the circumstances to order repayment. Thus an applicant who delays in making an application is likely to receive short shrift from the court, nor is the court likely to order repayment where the arbitrator has in good faith acted in such a way that it would be unjust to order repayment. It seems to us that it is necessary to set out expressly in the Bill that the power of the court extends to dealing with fees and expenses already paid, since otherwise there could be an argument that this power is confined to fees and expenses yet to be paid.

125. These provisions are extended by subsection (6) to include an arbitrator who has ceased to act and an umpire who has not replaced the other arbitrators. An arbitrator may cease to act through the operation of Clauses 23 to 26, or if an umpire takes over following a disagreement.

126. The liability in Clause 28(1) is to "the parties". It seems to us to follow that a person who has not participated at all, and in respect of whom it is determined that the arbitral tribunal has no jurisdiction, would not be a "party" for the purposes of this clause (*cf.* Clause 72). More difficult questions may well arise in respect of persons

who have participated, for there the doctrine of *Kompetenz-Kompetenz* (Clauses 30 and 31) may have to be weighed against the proposition that a party can hardly be under any liability in respect of the fees and expenses of the tribunal which he has successfully established should not have been acting at all on the merits of the dispute.

127. It is to be noted that arbitrators' fees and expenses include, by virtue of Clause 37(2), the fees and expenses of tribunal appointed experts, etc.

128. It seems that the present joint and several liability of the parties to an arbitrator for his fees may rest on some implied contract said to exist between them. Be this as it may, such an implied contract (in so far as it related to fees and expenses) would not survive by virtue of Clause 81 of this Bill, because this only saves rules of law which are consistent with Part I. Any implied contract imposing a liability for more than reasonable fees and expenses would clearly be inconsistent with Clause 28(1). Furthermore, since Clause 28(1) gives a statutory right there remains no good reason for any implied contractual right. As stated above, any specific contract would, however, of course be preserved by Clause 28(5).

129. Contrary to some suggestions made to us, it seems to us that rights of contribution between the parties in relation to their statutory liability under Clause 28(1) can best be left to the ordinary rules which relate to joint and several liability generally.

130. Clause 28 is made mandatory, since otherwise the parties could by agreement between themselves deprive the arbitrators of what seems to us to be a very necessary protection.

Clause 29 Immunity of Arbitrators

A2–030 131. Although the general view seems to be that arbitrators have some immunity under the present law, this is not entirely free from doubt. We were firmly of the view that arbitrators should have a degree of immunity, and most (though not all) the responses we received expressed the same view.

132. The reasons for providing immunity are the same as those that apply to judges in our courts. Arbitration and litigation share this in common, that both provide a means of dispute resolution which depends upon a binding decision by an impartial third party. It is generally considered that an immunity is necessary to enable that third party properly to perform an impartial decision making function. Furthermore, we feel strongly that unless a degree of immunity is afforded, the finality of the arbitral process could well be undermined. The prospect of a losing party attempting to re-arbitrate the issues on the basis that a competent arbitrator would have decided them in favour of that party is one that we would view with dismay. The Bill provides in our view adequate safeguards to deal with cases where the arbitral process has gone wrong.

133. This is a mandatory provision. Given the need and reason for immunity, it seems to us to follow that as a matter of public policy, this should be so.

134. The immunity does not, of course, extend to cases where it is shown that the arbitrator has acted in bad faith. Our law is well acquainted with this expression and although we considered other terms, we concluded that *there* were unlikely to be any

difficulties in practice in using this test: see, for example, *Melton Medes Ltd v. Securities and Investment Board* [1995] 3 All E.R.

135. Subsection 29(3). There was a concern that if a provision such as this was not included, Clause 25, when read together with Clause 29, could be said to preclude a claim against an arbitrator for resigning in breach of contract and similarly a defence (based on resignation) to a claim by an arbitrator for his fees, unless "*bad faith*" is proved.

136. Since the publication of the final draft of the Bill, we have concluded that the court should be given power to remove or modify the immunity as it sees fit when it removes an arbitrator. We consider this further in Chapter 6 below.

Jurisdiction of the Arbitral Tribunal

Clause 30   Competence of Tribunal to Rule on its own Jurisdiction

137. This Clause states what is called the doctrine of "*Kompetenz-Kompetenz*". This is an internationally recognized doctrine, which is also recognized by our own law (*e.g. Christopher Brown v. Genossenschaft Osterreichlischer Waldbesitzer* [1954] 1 Q.B. 8), though this has not always been the case.   A2–031

138. The great advantage of this doctrine is that it avoids delays and difficulties when a question is raised as to the jurisdiction of the tribunal. Clearly the tribunal cannot be the final arbiter of a question of jurisdiction, for this would provide a classic case of pulling oneself up by one's own bootstraps, but to deprive a tribunal of a power (subject to court review) to rule on jurisdiction would mean that a recalcitrant party could delay valid arbitration proceedings indefinitely by making spurious challenges to its jurisdiction.

139. The Clause and the following Clause are based on article 16 of the Model Law, but unlike that model we have not made this provision mandatory so that the parties, if they wish, can agree that the tribunal shall not have this power. We have also spelt out what we mean by "substantive jurisdiction".

Clause 31   Objection to Substantive Jurisdiction of Tribunal

140. In this Clause we set out how a challenge to the jurisdiction can be made, and the circumstances in which it must be made (following article 16 of the Model Law). This reflects much of the Model Law but we have, for example, refrained from using expressions like "submission of the statement of defence" since this might give the impression, which we are anxious to dispel, that every arbitration requires some formal pleading or the like.   A2–032

141. The Clause, in effect, sets out three ways in which the matter may proceed.

   i. The first is that the tribunal may make an award on the question of jurisdiction. If it does so then that award may be challenged by a party under Clause 67.

   ii. The second way is for the tribunal to deal with the question of jurisdiction in its award on the merits. Again on the jurisdiction aspect the award may be challenged under Clause 67.

We have provided these two methods because, depending on the circumstances, the one or the other may be the better course to take, bearing in mind the duty (in Clause 33) to adopt procedures suitable to the circumstances of the particular case, avoiding unnecessary delay or expense.

iii. The third way of proceeding is for an application to be made to the court before any award (pursuant to Clause 32). Again this third course is designed to achieve the same objective (albeit in limited circumstances). For example, cases arise where a party starts an arbitration but the other party, without taking part, raises an objection to the jurisdiction of the tribunal. In such circumstances, it might very well be cheaper and quicker for the party wishing to arbitrate to go directly to the court to seek a favourable ruling on jurisdiction rather than seeking an award from the tribunal. Such an approach would be very much the exception, and, to this end, Clause 32 is narrowly drawn. In this connection it must be remembered that a party who chooses not to take any part in an arbitration cannot in justice be required to take any positive steps to challenge the jurisdiction, for to do otherwise would be to assume against that party (before the point has been decided) that the tribunal has jurisdiction. We return to this topic when considering Clause 72.

142. Article 16(3) of the Model Law provides that the arbitral tribunal may rule on a plea as to jurisdiction either as a preliminary question or in an award on the merits. The DAC is of the view that it is unnecessary to introduce a new concept of a "preliminary ruling", which is somehow different from an award. Clause 31(4) therefore only refers to awards. This has the advantage that awards on jurisdiction will have the benefit of those provisions on awards generally (*e.g.* costs, lien, reasons, additional awards, etc.), and, if appropriate, may be enforced in the same way as any other award.

143. A challenge to jurisdiction may well involve questions of fact as well as questions of law. Since the arbitral tribunal cannot rule finally on its own jurisdiction, it follows that both its findings of fact and its holdings of law may be challenged. The regime for challenging such awards is set out in Clause 67.

144. Clause 31(1) replaces the requirement set out in article 16(2) of the Model Law (that a challenge to the overall jurisdiction of the tribunal must be raised no later than the submission of a statement of defence) with a requirement that such an objection be raised no later than the time a party takes the first step in the proceedings to contest the merits of any matter in relation to which he challenges the tribunal's jurisdiction. This allows for alternative procedures where there is no "statement of defence" as such.

145. Clause 31 is a mandatory provision. Under Clause 30, of course, the parties can agree that the tribunal shall not have power to rule on its own jurisdiction, but while this means (as subsection (4) points out) that the tribunal cannot then make an award on jurisdiction, the compulsory nature of Clause 31 means that the objection must be raised as there stipulated. It seems to us that this is highly desirable by way of support for the object of arbitration as set out in Clause 1.

146. It has been suggested to the DAC that there should be a mechanism whereby an objecting party, or even a non-objecting party, could require the tribunal forthwith to make an award as to jurisdiction, rather than merely incorporating a ruling in an award on the merits. The DAC disagrees with this. Unless the parties agree otherwise, the choice as to which course to take will be left with the tribunal, who will decide

what is to be done consistent with their duty under Clause 33 (see below). Indeed, in some cases it may be simply impracticable to rule on jurisdiction, before determining merits. If, however, the parties agree which course is to be taken, and if, of course, their agreement is effective (*i.e.* it does not require the tribunal to breach its mandatory duty under Clause 33) then the provision under discussion requires the tribunal to take the course chosen by the parties.

Clause 32 Determination of Preliminary Point of Jurisdiction

147. In this Clause we have set out the procedure for the third of the possible ways of dealing with a challenge to the jurisdiction. As stated above, this Clause provides for exceptional cases only: it is not intended to detract from the basic rule as set out in Clause 30. Hence the restrictions in Clause 32(2), and the procedure in Clause 32(3). It will be noted that we have required either the agreement of the parties, or that the court is satisfied that this is, in effect, the proper course to take. It is anticipated that the courts will take care to prevent this exceptional provision from becoming the normal route for challenging jurisdiction. Since this Clause concerns a power exercisable by the court in relation to the jurisdiction of the tribunal, it is in our view important enough to be made mandatory.   A2–033

148. Under this Clause the tribunal may continue the arbitral proceedings and make an award whilst the application to the Court is pending. Thus a recalcitrant party will not be able to mount spurious challenges as a means of delaying the arbitral process. Under subsection (5) of the preceding Clause the tribunal can, of course (and must if the parties agree) stay the arbitral proceedings whilst an application is made. Which course the tribunal takes (where it has power to choose) will of course depend once again on what it sees its Clause 33 duty to be.

149. The right of appeal from court rulings is limited in the way set out in the Clause.

The Arbitral Proceedings

Clause 33 General Duty of the Tribunal

150. This is one of the central proposals in our Bill (grounded on article 18 of the Model Law). It is a mandatory provision, since, as is explained below, we fail to see how a proceeding which departed from the stipulated duties could properly be described as an arbitration. We endeavour to set out, in the simplest, clearest terms we have been able to devise, how the tribunal should approach and deal with its task, which is to do full justice to the parties. In the following Clauses we set out in detail the powers available to the tribunal for this purpose.   A2–034

151. It has been suggested that the generality of Clause 33 may be problematic: that it may be an invitation to recalcitrant parties to launch challenges, or that vagueness will give rise to arguments. The advantage of arbitration is that it offers a dispute resolution system which can be tailored to the particular dispute to an extent which litigation finds it difficult to do. Thus depending on the nature of the dispute, there will be numerous ways in which the arbitration can be conducted. It is quite impossible to list all the possible variants and to set out what may or may not be done. Indeed any attempt to do so would defeat one of the main purposes of the Bill, which is to encourage arbitral tribunals not slavishly to follow court or other set procedures. It follows that the only limits can be those set out in the present clause. It is to be hoped

that the Courts will take a dim view of those who try to attack awards because of suggested breaches of this clause which have no real substance. At the same time, it can hardly be suggested that awards should not be open to attack when the tribunal has not acted in accordance with the principles stated.

152. It has further been suggested that this part of the Bill will cause the demise of the amateur arbitrator. If by this is meant the demise of people who purport to act as arbitrators but who are either unable or unwilling (or both) to conduct the proceedings in accordance with what most would regard as self-evident rules of justice, then we indeed hope that this will be one of the results. But since these rules of justice are generally accepted in our democratic society, and are not merely theoretical considerations that concern lawyers alone, we can see no reason why the Bill should discourage anyone who is ready willing and able to apply them. Indeed we consider that the Bill will encourage and support all such people.

153. Sometimes the parties to an arbitration employ lawyers who seek, in effect, to bully a non-legal arbitrator into taking a course of action which is against his better instincts, by seeking to blind him with legal "science" to get their way. Again, in some circles it is thought that somehow the procedures in an arbitration should be modelled on court procedures, and that to adopt other methods would be "misconduct" (an expression that the Bill does not use) on the part of the arbitrator. This part of the Bill is designed to prevent such bullying and to explode the theory that an arbitration has always to follow court procedures. If an arbitrator is satisfied that the way he wants to proceed fulfils his duty under this Clause and that the powers he wants to exercise are available to him under the following Clauses, then he should have the courage of his own convictions and proceed accordingly, unless the parties are agreed that he should adopt some other course.

The Relationship Between Clauses 1(b), 33 and 34(1)

A2–035   154. It has been suggested to us there could be a conflict between:

  i. the mandatory duty cast on arbitrators by Clause 33 and

  ii. the principle of party autonomy in Clause 1(b) and the proviso in Clause 34(1).

As we explain below, the DAC does not consider that there is any inconsistency between these two principles.

155. Under the principle of party autonomy, the parties are free to agree upon anything to do with the arbitration, subject only to such safeguards as are necessary in the public interest (Clause 1(b)). The mandatory provisions set out those matters which have effect notwithstanding any agreement to the contrary: see Clause 4. It seems to us that the public interest dictates that Clause 33 must be mandatory, *i.e.* that the parties cannot effectively agree to dispense with the duty laid on arbitrators under Clause 33. In other words, they cannot effectively agree that the arbitrators can act unfairly, or that the arbitrators can be partial, or that the arbitrators can decide that the parties (or one of them) should not have a reasonable opportunity of putting his case or answering that of his opponent, or indeed that the arbitrators can adopt procedures that are unsuitable for the particular circumstances of the case or are unnecessarily slow or expensive, so that the means for resolving the matters to be determined is unfair. It is, of course, extremely unlikely in the nature of things that the parties would wish deliberately to make such bizarre agreements, but were this to happen, then it

seems to us that such agreements should be ineffective for the purposes of this Bill, *i.e.* not binding on the parties or the tribunal.

156. However, a situation could well arise in practice in cases where the parties are agreed on a method of proceeding which they consider complies with the first of the general principles set out in Clause 1 (and which therefore the tribunal could adopt consistently with its duty under Clause 33) but the tribunal takes a different view, or where they are agreed in their opposition to a method of proceeding which the tribunal considers should be adopted in order to perform its Clause 33 duty.

157. In our view it is neither desirable nor practicable to stipulate that the tribunal can override the agreement of the parties. It is not desirable, because the type of arbitration we are discussing is a consensual process which depends on the agreement of the parties who are surely entitled (if they can agree) to have the final say on how they wish their dispute to be resolved. It is not practicable, since there is no way in which the parties can be forced to adopt a method of proceeding if they are agreed that this is not the way they wish to proceed. The latter is the case even if it could be established that their agreement was ineffective since it undermined or prevented performance of the duty made mandatory by Clause 33.

158. A party would be unable to enforce an ineffective agreement against the other parties, nor would such an agreement bind the tribunal, but the problem under discussion only exists while the parties are *in fact* at one, whether or not their agreement is legally effective.

159. In circumstances such as these, the tribunal (assuming it has failed to persuade the parties to take a different course) has the choice of adopting the course preferred by the parties or of resigning. Indeed, resignation would be the only course if the parties were in agreement in rejecting the method preferred by the tribunal, and no other way of proceeding was agreed by them or considered suitable by the tribunal.

160. We have stipulated elsewhere in the Bill that the immunity we propose for arbitrators does not extend to any liability they may be under for resigning (Clause 29) though under Clause 25 they may seek relief in respect of such liability from the court. The reason for the limitation on immunity is that cases may arise where the resignation of the arbitrator is wholly indefensible and has caused great delay and loss. In our view Clause 25 would suffice to protect arbitrators who resigned because they reasonably believed that the agreement of the parties prevented them from properly performing their Clause 33 duty. Furthermore, arbitrators could always stipulate for a right to resign in such circumstances as a term of their appointment.

161. If, on the other hand, the tribunal adopted a method of proceeding agreed by the parties, it seems to us that none of the parties could afterwards validly complain that the tribunal had failed in its Clause 33 duty, since the tribunal would only have done what the parties had asked it to do. Again, the fact that as between the parties such an agreement may have been ineffective as undermining or preventing performance of the Clause 33 duties seems to us to be wholly irrelevant. It could of course be said that the tribunal had breached its Clause 33 duty, but this would have no practical consequences since the parties themselves would have brought about this state of affairs, and would therefore be unable to seek any relief in respect of it.

162. Some people have expressed concern that there is a danger that lawyers will agree between themselves a method of proceeding which the tribunal consider to be unnecessarily long or expensive. However, if a tribunal considered, for example, that lawyers were trying either deliberately to "churn" the case for their own private advantage or were simply but misguidedly seeking to adopt unnecessary procedures, etc., the obvious solution would be to ask them to confirm that their respective clients had been made aware of the views of the tribunal but were nevertheless in agreement that the course proposed by their lawyers should be adopted. At the end of the day, however, the fact remains that the only sanction the arbitrators have is to resign.

163. In summary, therefore, we consider that the duty of the arbitrators under Clause 33 and the right of the parties to agree how the arbitration should be conducted do fit together. Under Clause 33 the tribunal have the specified duties. Under Clause 34 therefore, the tribunal must decide all procedural and evidential matters, subject to the right of the parties to agree any matter. If the parties reach an agreement on how to proceed which clashes with the duty of the tribunal or which the tribunal reasonably considers does so, then the arbitrators can either resign and have the protection of Clause 25, or can adopt what the parties want and will not afterwards be liable to the parties for doing so.

Further Points

A2–036   164. In this Clause we have provided that the tribunal shall give each party a "reasonable opportunity" of putting his case and dealing with that of his opponent. Article 18 of the Model Law uses the expression "full opportunity".

165. We prefer the word "reasonable" because it removes any suggestion that a party is entitled to take as long as he likes, however objectively unreasonable this may be. We are sure that this was not intended by those who framed the Model Law, for it would entail that a party is entitled to an unreasonable time, which justice can hardly require. Indeed the contrary is the case, for an unreasonable time would *ex hypothesi* mean unnecessary delay and expense, things which produce injustice and which accordingly would offend the first principle of Clause 1, as well as Clauses 33 and 40.

Clause 34   Procedural and Evidential Matters

A2–037   166. We trust that the matters we have listed in this Clause (which are partly drawn from articles 19, 20, 22, 23 an 24 of the Model Law) are largely self-evident. We have produced a non-exhaustive checklist because we think it will be helpful both to arbitrating parties and to their arbitrators. We cannot emphasise too strongly that one of the strengths of the arbitral process is that it is able much more easily than any court system to adapt its procedures to suit the particular case. Hence we have spelt this out as a duty under the preceding Clause. The list of powers helps the tribunal (and indeed the parties) to choose how best to proceed, untrammelled by technical or formalistic rules.

167. Some of those responding suggested that we should include a special code to deal with the arbitration of small claims. We have not adopted this suggestion for the very reason we have just stated. Any such code would have to have detailed rules, arbitrary monetary or other limits and other complicated provisions. In our view, proper adherence to the duties in Clause 33 will achieve the same result. A small claim will simply not need all the expensive procedural and other paraphernalia which might be required for the resolution of some huge and complicated international dispute.

168. Furthermore, we consider that associations and institutions concerned with specific areas of trade, etc. can play a very significant part in formulating rules and procedures for arbitrating disputes concerning their members. Such bodies have the detailed knowledge and experience required to enable them properly to address this task, in relation both to small claims and otherwise. We feel strongly that it would be wrong for a Bill of the present kind to seek to lay down a rigid structure for any kind of case; and that different methods must be developed to suit different circumstances, by arbitral tribunals as well as those who have the necessary practical knowledge of those circumstances. Finally, of course, the Bill in no way impinges upon small claims procedures developed for use through the court system.

169. Subsection (a). Whilst article 20(1) of the Model law states that, in the absence of the agreement of the parties, "the place of arbitration shall be determined by the arbitral tribunal having regard to the circumstances of the case, including the convenience of the parties", subsection 34(2)(a) does not state that the tribunal should have the convenience of the parties in mind, given that this is a consideration that is really subsumed under the general duty of the Tribunal in Clause 33, and, further, because the DAC was of the view that like considerations apply to other parts of Clause 34, such as subsection (b), even though the Model Law does not appear to reflect this. Unlike the Model Law, subsection (a) also refers to "when", as well as "where".

170. Subsection (f) makes it clear that arbitrators are not necessarily bound by the technical rules of evidence. In his 1993 Freshfields Lecture ((1994) *Arbitration International* Vol. 10, p. 1), Lord Steyn questioned why the technical rules of evidence should apply to arbitration, even if (as he doubted) there was authority for this. This provision clarifies the position. It is to be noted that Clause 34(2)(f) helps to put an end to any arguments that it is a question of law whether there is material to support a finding of fact.

171. Subsection (g). Some anxiety was expressed at the power to act inquisitorially, to be found in subsection (g), on grounds that arbitrators are unused to such powers and might, albeit in good faith, abuse them.

172. We do not share this view. Once again it seems to us that provided the tribunal in exercising its powers follows its simple duty as set out in Clause 33 (and subsection (2) of this Clause tells the tribunal that this is what they must do) then in suitable cases an inquisitorial approach to all or some of the matters involved may well be the best way of proceeding. Clause 33, however, remains a control, such that, for example, if an arbitrator takes the initiative in procuring evidence, he must give all parties a reasonable opportunity of commenting on it.

173. A number of arbitrators who responded to our July 1995 draft suggested that the tribunal should be entitled to have the last word *i.e.* should be given the power to override the agreement of the parties to follow a different course. The interrelationship of the tribunal's duties and party autonomy has already been discussed above. As is clear from that discussion, we disagree with this view for the following reasons:

    i. To give the tribunal such a power would be contrary to article 19 of the Model Law. It would also be contrary to the present position under English law.

    ii. To allow the tribunal to override the agreement of the parties would to our minds constitute an indefensible inroad into the principle of party autonomy, upon which the Bill is based.

iii. It is difficult to see how such a power could be backed by any effective sanction. If the parties agree not to adopt the course ordered by the tribunal, there is nothing the tribunal can do except resign.

iv. It seems to us that the problem is more apparent than real. In most cases the parties rely on the tribunal to decide how to conduct the case and do not sit down and agree between themselves how it is to be done. In order to reflect what actually happens in practice we have accordingly reversed the way many of the other Clauses begin and stated that it is for the tribunal to decide all procedural and evidential matters, subject to the right of the parties to agree any matter. In our view, however, since arbitration is the parties' own chosen method of dispute resolution, we cannot see why they should be deprived of the right to decide what form the arbitration should take.

174. As we have made clear above, it is of course open to those who frame rules for arbitration which the parties incorporate into their agreement, to stipulate that the tribunal is to have the last word, and likewise arbitrators can stipulate this as a term of their agreement to act, though once again there would be no means, apart from persuasion or the threat of resignation, of enforcing such a stipulation if the parties later jointly took a different view.

175. It has been suggested that there could be a conflict between the proviso in Clause 34(1) and Clause 40. This is said to arise, for example, where the parties have agreed a procedural or evidential matter which they are entitled to do under Clause 34(1), but the tribunal are intent on taking a different course. Does the parties' agreement override their duty under Clause 40?

The DAC considers that no such conflict exists:

i. The parties are free to agree on all procedural and evidential matters, pursuant to Clause 34(1).

ii. However, any such agreement will only be effective, if it is consistent with Clause 33, being a mandatory provision.

iii. Any such agreement made pursuant to Clause 34(1), and consistent with Clause 33, will define the scope of Clause 40—*i.e.* the parties will have agreed on how the arbitration is to be conducted, or, in the words of Clause 40, what is to constitute the "proper and expeditious conduct of the arbitral proceedings". The determinations of the tribunal should follow that agreement (which would not be the case if such an agreement was inconsistent with Clause 33) and *ex hypothesi* the parties should be obliged to comply.

iv. If there are matters on which the parties have not agreed, then the tribunal will fill the gap under Clause 34(1) and Clause 40(1) will again operate without conflict.

176. It has also been suggested that the Bill should include a provision that the arbitrator should encourage the parties to use other forms of ADR when this was considered appropriate. This suggestion has not been adopted, since the Bill is concerned with arbitration where the parties have chosen this rather than any other form of dispute resolution.

Clause 35   Consolidation of Proceedings and Concurrent Hearings

177. This Clause makes clear that the parties may agree to consolidate their arbitration   A2–038
with other arbitral proceedings or to hold concurrent hearings.

178. During the consultation exercises, the DAC received submissions calling for a provision that would empower either a tribunal or the court (or indeed both) to order consolidation or concurrent hearings. These were considered extremely carefully by the committee.

179. The problem arises in cases where a number of parties are involved. For example, in a construction project a main contractor may make a number of sub-contracts each of which contains an arbitration clause. A dispute arises in which a claim is made against one sub-contractor who seeks to blame another. In court, of course, there is power to order consolidation or concurrent hearings, as well as procedures for allowing additional parties to be joined. In arbitrations, however, this power does not exist. The reason it does not exist is that this form of dispute resolution depends on the agreement of the contracting parties that their disputes will be arbitrated by a private tribunal, not litigated in the public courts. It follows that unless the parties otherwise agree, only their own disputes arising out of their own agreement can be referred to that agreed tribunal.

180. In our view it would amount to a negation of the principle of party autonomy to give the tribunal or the court power to order consolidation or concurrent hearings. Indeed it would to our minds go far towards frustrating the agreement of the parties to have their own tribunal for their own disputes. Further difficulties could well arise, such as the disclosure of documents from one arbitration to another. Accordingly we would be opposed to giving the tribunal or the court this power. However, if the parties agree to invest the tribunal with such a power, then we would have no objection.

181. Having said this, the DAC appreciates the common sense behind the suggestion. We are persuaded, however, that the problem is best solved by obtaining the agreement of the parties. Thus those who are in charge of drafting standard forms of contract, or who offer terms for arbitration services which the parties can incorporate into their agreements, (especially those institutions and associations which are concerned with situations in which there are likely to be numerous contracts and sub-contracts) could include suitable clauses permitting the tribunal to consolidate or order concurrent hearings in appropriate cases. For example, the London Maritime Arbitrators Association Rules have within them a provision along these lines. In order to encourage this, we have made clear in this Clause that with the agreement of the parties, there is nothing wrong with adopting such procedures.

182. It will be noted that whereas Clause 39 uses the expression "[t]he parties are free to agree that the tribunal shall have power to order . . . ", Clause 35 simple states that "[t]he parties are free to agree . . . " This difference is easily explained. In both cases the parties are free to endow the tribunal with the power in question. This is implicit in Clause 35(1) by virtue of Clause 35(2). Under Clause 35(1), the parties may agree between themselves to consolidate two arbitrations, or to have concurrent hearings, before a tribunal has been appointed. This could, of course, have a bearing on how the tribunal is to be appointed in such a situation. Indeed the parties may agree on institutional rules that provide for this. However, an equivalent arrangement is difficult to imagine in the context of Clause 39. Overall, the difference in wording is

not intended to impede the parties' freedom to agree what they like, when they like, in either case.

Clause 36   Legal or Other Representation

A2–039   183. It seems to us that this reflects a basic right, though of course the parties are free to dispense with it if they wish.

184. In the draft produced in July we used the phrase "a lawyer or other person of his choice". We have changed this, because we felt that it might give the impression that a party could stubbornly insist on a particular lawyer or other person, in circumstances where that individual could not attend for a long time, thus giving a recalcitrant party a good means of delaying the arbitral process. This should not happen. "A lawyer or other person chosen by him" does not give this impression: if a party's first choice is not available, his second choice will still be "a lawyer or other person chosen by him". The right to be represented exists but must not be abused. Furthermore the right must be read with the first principle of Clause 1, as well as Clauses 33 and 40. If this is done then we trust that attempts to abuse the right will fail.

185. It has been suggested to the DAC that there should be some provision requiring a party to give advance notice to all other parties if he intends to be represented at a hearing. Whilst in some ways an attractive proposal, this would be difficult to stipulate as a statutory provision, given that it may be impossible in some circumstances, or simply unnecessary in others. Further, different sanctions may be appropriate depending on the particular case. It is clearly desirable that, as a general rule, such notice be given. If it is not, one sanction may be for the tribunal to adjourn a hearing at the defaulting party's cost. In the end, however, this must be a matter for the tribunal's discretion in each particular case.

186. It has been suggested that this Clause provides an opportunity of extending by statute the privilege enjoyed by legal advisers to non-legal advisers or representatives. We have not adopted this suggestion. It seems to us that it would be necessary to define with great precision which non-legal advisers or representatives are to be included (*e.g.* what relationship they must have to the arbitration and its conduct), and the precise classes of privilege which should be extended to them. Further, any such provision would necessarily have an impact on the position beyond arbitration. In short, it seems to us that this question cannot be confined to arbitrations and raises matters of general principle far beyond those of our remit.

Clause 37   Power to Appoint Experts, Legal Advisers or Assessors

A2–040   187. This to our minds would be a useful power in certain cases. We trust that the provisions we suggest are self-evident. Of course, the power can only be exercised if in the circumstances of the particular case its exercise falls within the scope of the duty of the tribunal set out in Clause 33.

188. Subsection (2) is made mandatory, to avoid the risk of the parties agreeing otherwise and thus disabling the tribunal from recovering from the parties expenses properly incurred.

Clause 38   General Powers Exercisable by the Tribunal

A2–041   189. These provisions represent a significant re-drawing of the relationship between arbitration and the court. Wherever a power could properly be exercised by a tribunal rather than the court, provision has been made for this, thereby reducing the need to incur the expense and inconvenience of making applications to court during arbitral proceedings.

190. The first of the powers in this Clause is one which enables the tribunal to order security for costs. The power presently given to the court to order security for costs in arbitrations is removed in its entirety.

191. This is a major change from the present position where only the court can order security for costs. The theory which lay behind the present law is that it is the duty of an arbitral tribunal to decide the substantive merits of the dispute referred to it and that it would not be performing this duty if it stayed or struck out the proceedings pending the provision of security: see for example, *Re Unione Stearinerie Lanza and Weiner* [1917] 2 K.B. 558.

192. We do not subscribe to this theory, which Parliament has already abandoned in the context of striking out a claim for want of prosecution. In our view, when the parties agree to arbitrate, they are agreeing that their dispute will be resolved by this means. To our minds (in the absence of express stipulations to the contrary) this does not mean that the dispute is necessarily to be decided on its substantive merits. It is in truth an agreement that it will be resolved by the application of the agreed arbitral process. If one party then fails to comply with that process, then it seems to us that it is entirely within what the parties have agreed that the tribunal can resolve the dispute on this ground.

193. Apart from this, the proposition that the court should involve itself in such matters as deciding whether a claimant in an arbitration should provide security for costs has received universal condemnation in the context of international arbitrations. It is no exaggeration to say that the recent decision of the House of Lords in *S.A. Coppee Lavalin NV v. Ken-Ren Chemicals and Fertilisers* [1994] 2 W.L.R. 631 was greeted with dismay by those in the international arbitration community who have at heart the desire to promote our country as a world centre for arbitration. We share those concerns.

194. It has been suggested to the DAC that the court should retain a power to order security for costs that may be incurred up to the appointment of the tribunal. We have not been persuaded, however, that this is really necessary.

195. It has been pointed out that in some cases an application for security before an arbitral tribunal might involve disclosing to that tribunal the fact that an offer of settlement had been or was about to be made. Under the court system, such disclosure can be made to a court other than that which will try the merits of the case.

196. We are not disturbed by this. It seems to us that a tribunal, properly performing its duty under Clause 33, could and should not be influenced by such matters, if the case proceeds to a hearing on the merits, nor do we accept that the disclosure of such information could somehow disqualify the tribunal from acting.

197. Clause 38(3) has been the subject of significant criticism since the Bill was introduced. In the light of this, we have concluded that it must be redrawn. Chapter 6, to which reference should be made, contains a full discussion of the problems with this provision as currently drafted, and our recommendations for its amendment.

198. Whilst the sanction in court for a failure to provide security for costs is normally a stay of the action, this is inappropriate in arbitration: if an arbitrator stayed proceedings, the arbitration would come to a halt without there necessarily being an award which could be challenged (*e.g.* if a party seeks to continue the proceedings). We have therefore included a specific sanction with respect to a failure to provide security for costs, which is to be found in Clause 41(6). This provision also follows the practice of the English Commercial Court, which changed from the old practice of ordering a stay of proceedings if security was not provided. The disadvantage of the latter course was that it left the proceedings dormant but alive, so that years later they could be revived by the provision of security.

199. Clause 38 provides the tribunal with other powers in relation to the arbitration proceedings. We trust that these are self-explanatory.

Clause 39   Power to Make Provisional Awards

A2–042 200. In the July 1995 draft Clauses, this power did not require the agreement of the parties. As the result of responses, we have concluded on further consideration that this is necessary.

201. In *The Kostas Melas* [1981] 1 Lloyd's Rep. 18 at 26, Goff J., as he then was, made clear that it was no part of an arbitrator's function to make temporary or provisional financial arrangements between the parties. Furthermore, as can be demonstrated by the abundance of court cases dealing with this subject (in the context of applications for summary judgment, interim payments, *Mareva* injunctions and the like) enormous care has to be taken to avoid turning what can be a useful judicial tool into an instrument of injustice. We should add that we received responses from a number of practising arbitrators to the effect that they would be unhappy with such powers, and saw no need for them. We should note in passing that the July 1995 draft would arguably (and inadvertently) have allowed arbitrators to order *ex parte Mareva* or even *Anton Piller* relief. These draconian powers are best left to be applied by the courts, and the provisions of the Bill with respect to such powers have been adjusted accordingly.

202. There is a sharp distinction to be drawn between making provisional or temporary arrangements, which are subject to reversal when the underlying merits are finally decided by the tribunal; and dealing severally with different issues or questions at different times and in different awards, which we cover in Clause 47. It is for this reason that in this provision we draw attention to that Clause.

203. These considerations have led us firmly to conclude that it would only be desirable to give arbitral tribunals power to make such provisional orders where the parties have so agreed. Such agreements, of course, will have to be drafted with some care for the reasons we have stated. Subject to the safeguards of the parties' agreement and the arbitrators' duties (Clause 33), we envisage that this enlargement of the traditional jurisdiction of arbitrators could serve a very useful purpose, for example in trades and industries where cash flow is of particular importance.

Clause 40   General Duty of the Parties

A2–043 204. This is a mandatory provision, since it would seem that an ability to contract out of it would be a negation of the arbitral process.

205. We were asked what the sanction would be for non-compliance. The answer lies in other Clauses of the Bill. These not only give the tribunal powers in relation to recalcitrant parties (*e.g.* Clause 41), but stipulate time limits for taking certain steps (*e.g.* applications to the court, etc.) and (in Clause 73) making clear that undue delay will result in the loss of rights.

Clause 41   Powers of Tribunal in Case of Party's Default

206. The first part of this Clause sets out the present law (section 13A of the 1950 Act, which was inserted by section 102 of the Courts and Legal Services Act 1990) giving the arbitral tribunal power to strike out for want of prosecution.   **A2–044**

207. The second part makes clear that in the circumstances stipulated, a tribunal may proceed *ex parte*, though we have forborne from using this expression (or indeed any other legal Latin words or phrases) in the Bill. The Clause has its roots in article 25 of the Model Law.

208. It is a basic rule of justice that a court or tribunal should give all parties an opportunity to put their case and answer that of their opponents. That is why this appears in Clause 33 of the Bill. Equally, however, and for reasons already mentioned, that opportunity should, again for reasons of justice, be limited to a reasonable one. If for no good reason such an opportunity is not taken by a party then to our minds it is only fair to the other party that the tribunal should be able to proceed as we have set out in this Clause.

209. The last part of this Clause sets out a system of peremptory orders. It will be noted that a peremptory order must be "to the same effect" as the preceding order which was disobeyed (subsection (5)). It could be quite unfair for an arbitrator to be able to make any type of peremptory order, on any matter, regardless of its connection with the default in question.

210. For the reasons mentioned earlier, subsection (6) provides that where a party fails to comply with a peremptory order to provide security for costs, the tribunal may make an award dismissing the claim, thereby following the practice of the English Commercial Court, and avoiding the danger that the proceedings are halted indefinitely, without there being anything to challenge before the court.

211. So far as failure to comply with other peremptory orders is concerned, we have provided a range of remedies. They do not include a power simply to make an award against the defaulting party. The reason for this is that (unlike a failure to comply with a peremptory order to provide security) it seems to us that this is too draconian a remedy, and that the alternatives we have provided very much better fit the justice of the matter.

Powers of Court in Relation to Arbitral Proceedings

Clause 42   Enforcement of Peremptory Orders of Tribunal

212. Although in Clause 41 we have provided the tribunal with powers in relation to peremptory orders, it seemed to us that the court should have power to order compliance with such orders, though (unless both parties have agreed) these can only be invoked with the permission of the tribunal. In our view there may well be   **A2–045**

circumstances where in the interests of justice, the fact that the court has sanctions which in the nature of things cannot be given to arbitrators (*e.g.* committal to prison for contempt) will assist the proper functioning of the arbitral process. This Clause is a good example of the support the court can give to that process. Subsection (3) requires that any other available recourse within the arbitral process be first exhausted.

Clause 43   Securing the Attendance of Witnesses

A2–046   213. This Clause (which corresponds to article 27 of the Model Law, and is derived from section 12(4) and (5) of the 1950 Act) is also designed to provide court support for the arbitral process. It will be noted, in particular, that the agreement of the parties or the permission of the tribunal is required. The reason for this is to make sure that this procedure is not used to override any procedural method adopted by the tribunal, or agreed by the parties, for the arbitration. Thus, for example, if the tribunal has decided that there shall be no oral evidence, then (unless all parties agree otherwise) this procedure cannot be used to get round that decision.

Clause 44   Court Powers Exercisable in Support of Arbitral Proceedings

A2–047   214. This provision corresponds in part to article 9 of the Model Law. As part of the redefinition of the relationship between arbitration and the court, which was mentioned above, the powers we have given the court are intended to be used when the tribunal cannot act or act effectively, as subsection (5) makes clear. It is under this Clause that the court has power to order *Mareva* or *Anton Piller* relief (*i.e.* urgent protective measures to preserve assets or evidence) so as to help the arbitral process to operate effectively. Equally, there may be instances where a party seeks an order that will have an effect on a third party, which only the court could grant. For the same reason the court is given the other powers listed.

215. In order to prevent any suggestion that the court might be used to interfere with or usurp the arbitral process, or indeed any attempt to do so, we have stipulated that except in cases of urgency with regard to the preservation of assets or evidence, the court can only act with the agreement of the parties or the permission of the tribunal. We have excepted cases of urgency, since these often arise before the tribunal has been properly constituted or when in the nature of things it cannot act quickly or effectively enough.

216. Furthermore, under subsection (6) the court, after making an order, can in effect hand over to the tribunal the task of deciding whether or not that order should cease to have effect. This is a novel provision, but follows from the philosophy behind these provisions: if a given power could possibly be exercised by a tribunal, then it should be, and parties should not be allowed to make unilateral applications to the court. If, however, a given power could be exercised by the tribunal, but not as effectively, in circumstances where, for example, speed is necessary, then the court should be able to step in.

Clause 45   Determination of Preliminary Point of Law

A2–048   217. This Clause preserves what used to be the old Consultative Case procedure, though its availability is limited as we have set out, in order not to interfere with the arbitral process. The Clause is based on section 2 of the 1979 Act, with certain important changes.

218. It seems to us that with the limitations we have provided, this procedure can have its uses. For example, an important point of law may arise which is of great general interest and potentially the subject of a large number of arbitrations. This not infrequently happens when some major event occurs, as, for example, the closure of the Suez Canal or the United States embargo on the export of soya beans. It may well be considered by those concerned that in such special circumstances it would be cheaper and better for all to obtain a definitive answer from the court at an early stage.

219. However, under subsection (1), unless the parties agree, the court must now be satisfied that determination of the given question of law will substantially affect the rights of one or more of the parties. This last point is a departure from the 1979 Act, section 1 of which makes this precondition in relation to an appeal in respect of questions of law arising out of the award, but section 2 of which does not impose it in relation to the determination of a preliminary point of law.

220. Further, unless the parties agree, the court will now have to be satisfied of the matters set out in subsection (2) before considering an application, so that the procedure can only be used (even with the permission of the tribunal) in cases where its adoption will produce a substantial saving in costs to the parties or one of them. The condition in section 2(2) of the 1979 Act, which requires that the question of law be one in respect of which leave to appeal would be likely to be given under section 1(3)(b) of that Act, is not repeated.

221. It has been suggested to the DAC that the right to refer to the court under this Clause be removed from all non-domestic arbitrations, unless the parties otherwise agree. For the reasons given above as to the value of this provision, and for the reasons given below with respect to preserving the right of appeal in Clause 69, we were not persuaded by this.

The Award

Clause 46   Rules Applicable to Substance of Dispute

222. This Clause reflects much, though not all, of article 28 of the Model Law. We have not, for example, directed the tribunal to "take into account the usages of the trade applicable to the transaction". If the applicable law allows this to be done, then the provision is not necessary; while if it does not, then it could be said that such a direction overrides that law, which to our minds would be incorrect.

A2–049

223. Subsection (1)(b) recognizes that the parties may agree that their dispute is not to be decided in accordance with a recognised system of law but under what in this country are often called "equity clauses", or arbitration "ex aequo et bono", or "amiable composition", *i.e.* general considerations of justice and fairness, etc. It will be noted that we have avoided using this description in the Bill, just as we have avoided using the Latin and French expressions found in the Model Law. There appears to be no good reason to prevent parties from agreeing to equity clauses. However, it is to be noted that in agreeing that a dispute shall be resolved in this way, the parties are in effect excluding any right to appeal to the court (there being no "question of law" to appeal).

224. Subsection (2) does, in effect, adopt the rule found in article 28 of the Model Law, thereby avoiding the problems of *renvoi*.

225. Subsection (3) caters for the situation where there is no choice or agreement. This again is the language of the Model Law. In such circumstances the tribunal must decide what conflicts of law rules are applicable, and use those rules in order to determine the applicable law. It cannot simply make up rules for this purpose. It has been suggested to the DAC that more guidance be given as to the choice of a proper law, but it appears to us that flexibility is desirable, that it is not our remit to lay down principles in this highly complex area, and that to do so would necessitate a departure from the Model Law wording.

Clause 47   Awards on Different Issues, etc.

A2–050   226. We regard this as a very important provision. Some disputes are very complex, raising a large number of complicated issues which, if they are all addressed and dealt with at one hearing, would necessarily take a very long time and be very expensive. Disputes concerning large scale construction contracts are a good example, though there are many other cases.

227. In recent years both the Commercial Court and the Official Referees Court in England (which deal with large cases) have adopted a different approach. The judge plays much more of a managerial role, suggesting and indeed directing ways in which time and money can be saved. One of the ways is to select issues for early determination, not necessarily on the basis that they will be *legally* determinative of the entire litigation, but where they may well be *commercially* determinative, in the sense that a decision is likely to help the parties to resolve their other differences themselves without the need to spend time and money on using lawyers to fight them out. This has a further advantage. Cases fought to the bitter end often result in a permanent loss of goodwill between the warring factions, thus impeding or preventing future profitable relationships between them. The result is often in truth a loss to all the parties, whether or not they were the "winners" in the litigation.

228. In court therefore, the old idea that a party is entitled to a full trial of everything at once has now largely disappeared: see, for example, the decision of the House of Lords in *Ashmore v. Corporation of Lloyd's* [1992] 2 Lloyd's Rep. 1. Furthermore, this method of approach is reflected in the views expressed by Lord Woolf in his current consideration of how to improve our system of civil justice. The same reasoning, of course, applies to arbitrations.

229. As we have said earlier, arbitration enjoys an advantage over litigation, since the arbitral tribunal is appointed to deal with the particular dispute that has arisen, and is thus in a better position to tailor the procedure to suit the particular circumstances of that dispute. Furthermore, an arbitral tribunal is often able, for the same reason, to move much quicker than the court.

230. For these reasons, we have tried to make clear in this Clause that the tribunal is empowered to proceed in this way. This is an aspect of the duty cast upon the tribunal to adopt procedures suitable to the circumstances of the particular case, which is set out in Clause 33(1)(a). We would encourage arbitrators to adopt this approach in any case where it appears that time and money will be saved by doing so, and where such an approach would not be at the expense of any of the other requirements of justice.

231. In this connection we would draw attention to the decision of Goff J. (now Lord Goff) in *The Kostas Melas, op. cit.* As we observed when considering Clause 39, the function of arbitrators is not to make temporary financial adjustments between the parties pending the resolution of the dispute, unless this is what they have agreed the arbitrators can do. As this case shows, there is a clear distinction between such arrangements and the right to make a permanent binding decision after considering the arguments, even though the later resolution of other issues (if this becomes necessary) may overall produce a different result.

232. We should emphasize that in this Clause we are not intending to give arbitral tribunals greater or different powers from those they presently have, but to emphasise how their powers should, in suitable cases, be exercised.

233. It might also be noted that we have been careful to avoid use of the term "interim award", which has become a confusing term, and in its most common use, arguably a misnomer.

Clause 48   Remedies

234. We trust that the matters addressed in this Clause are self-evident. We have excluded specific performance of land contracts, so as not to change the law in this regard, but clarified the power of arbitrators to award injunctive relief. Given that the parties are free to agree on the remedies that a tribunal may order, there is nothing to restrict such remedies to those available at Court.   **A2–051**

Clause 49   Interest

235. The responses we received demonstrated to us that there was a general desire to give arbitral tribunals a general power to award compound interest.   **A2–052**

236. There is no doubt that the absence of such a power adds to the delays (and thus the expense) of arbitrations and causes injustice, for it is often in a party's interest to delay the proceedings and the honouring of an award, since the interest eventually payable is less than can be made by holding on to funds which should be paid over to the other party, who of course is losing out by a like amount.

237. Some of those responding were fearful that arbitrators would abuse this power, and may, for example, award compound interest on a punitive rather than compensatory basis. We do not share those fears. To our minds any competent arbitrator seeking to fulfil the duties laid on him by the Bill will have no more difficulty in making decisions about compound interest than he will in deciding in any other context what fairness and justice require. Anyone who has such difficulties demonstrates, in our view, that he is really not fit to act as an arbitrator. In such a case, the award and the arbitrator will be susceptible of challenge.

238. Clause 84 and 111 allow for transitional measures. In the context of this Clause, we understand that these may prove necessary in relation to the enforcement of awards through the county courts, who we are told are not presently equipped to calculate compound interest payable from the date of the award.

Clause 50   Extension of Time for Making Award

A2–053   239. This Clause re-enacts the existing law, though with two qualifications:

    i. arbitral procedures for obtaining an extension must be exhausted before recourse to the court; and

    ii. the court must be satisfied that substantial injustice would be done if the time were not extended.

It seems to us that these qualifications are needed so as to ensure that the court's power is supportive rather than disruptive of the arbitral process. For the same reason, it seems to us that it would be a rare case indeed where the court extended the time notwithstanding that this had not been done through an available arbitral process.

Clause 51   Settlement

A2–054   240. This Clause reflects article 30 of the Model Law. It enables an agreed settlement of the dispute to be given the status of an arbitral award, which could then be enforced as such.

241. Concern has been expressed that this provision (taken from article 30 of the Model Law) might be used by the parties either to obtain an award in respect of matters which are simply not arbitrable (*e.g.* matters which under our law cannot be settled by agreement between the parties), or to mislead third parties (*e.g.* the tax authorities). It was suggested that any agreed award should have to state on its face that it is such.

242. Dealing first with deception, in our view there is no material difference between Clause 51 and our present law: *cf.* p. 59 of the Mustill Report. As that Report observes, article 30 and our present law recognise the right of the tribunal to refuse to make an award on agreed terms if it contains an objectionable feature, *e.g.* is structured to mislead third parties. Clause 51 preserves that right. Thus unless the tribunal is itself prepared to be a party to an attempted deception, we consider the risk that misleading awards will be made to be very small. If the tribunal is prepared to conspire with the parties, then nothing we could put in Clause 51 is likely to deter it. Furthermore, the whole of Clause 51 is based upon the assumption that there is a dispute between the parties which has been referred to arbitration and then settled. Nothing in the Clause would assist parties to mislead others where there was no genuine dispute or genuine reference or genuine settlement. The Clause would simply not apply to such a situation.

243. So far as arbitrability is concerned, this is a question that goes beyond agreed awards. We discuss this question when considering Clause 66 (see also the supplementary recommendations in Chapter 6 below).

244. We are not persuaded that we should require that any agreed award should state that it is such. Both under this Clause and Clause 52 the parties are free to agree on the form the award should take. In our view this is not only the position under the Model Law but also the position under our present law. A requirement that an agreed award should state that it is such would have to be made a mandatory provision to be effective. We are not aware of any problems arising under our present law and are reluctant to impose this formal requirement. Moreover, it would of course be open to the tribunal to record the agreement in the award if they thought it was appropriate

to do so. However, at the enforcement stage we agree that the Court should be informed if the award is an agreed award, if this is not apparent from the award itself. We return to this point when considering Clause 66 below (see also Chapter 6).

Clause 52   Form of Award

245. This Clause follows closely article 31 of the Model Law. There are, however, two matters worthy of particular note.   **A2–055**

246. In the first place, as in the Model Law, we have required the tribunal to give reasons, unless the award is an agreed award or the parties have agreed that reasons need not be given.

247. To our minds, it is a basic rule of justice that those charged with making a binding decision affecting the rights and obligations of others should (unless those others agree) explain the reasons for making that decision. This was also the view of the majority of those who commented on this.

248. It was suggested that having to give reasons would be likely to add to the cost of arbitrations and encourage applications for leave to appeal to the court.

249. We do not agree. The need for reasons is that which we have explained above and has nothing to do with the question whether or not a court should hear an appeal from an award. Further, we have introduced stricter conditions for the bringing of appeals in any event. As to cost, it is always open to the parties to agree to dispense with reasons if they wish to do so, though in the case of domestic arbitrations this can only be done after the dispute has arisen: see Clauses 69(1) and 87.

250. The second noteworthy point is that we have used the word "seat" instead of the Model Law phrase "place of arbitration". We consider that the Model Law uses this phrase to mean the seat (there being no obvious legal reason to stipulate the geographical place where the award was made), and since we have used this word earlier in the Bill (see Clauses 2 and 3) it would in our view only cause confusion not to use it here. Of course the seat is only of importance in international arbitrations or where the question arises as to the enforcement of an award abroad. Therefore, in a purely domestic arbitration, if an arbitrator were to fail to state the "seat", or to state this incorrectly, it is extremely unlikely that the award could be challenged under Clause 68(2)(h), given that such a failure would be unlikely to result in "substantial injustice".

251. Subsection (3) provides that the award shall be in writing and signed by all the arbitrators or, alternatively, by all those assenting to the award. An earlier draft of this subsection had only stipulated that all arbitrators assenting to an award sign it. It was pointed out to the DAC, however, that (for whatever reason) some dissenting arbitrators may not wish to be identified as such, and that the provision should therefore be amended to provide for this.

252. It has been suggested to the DAC that there should be a provision allowing for somebody to sign on behalf of an arbitrator. This could invoke complicated principles of agency, and, overall, is better left to be resolved in each particular case.

Clause 53   Place Where Award is Treated as Made

A2–056   253. This Clause is designed to avoid disputes over where an award is made and (in cases where Part I of the Bill applies to the arbitration in question) it reverses the decision (although not the result) of the House of Lords in *Hiscox v. Outhwaite* [1992] 1 A.C. 562.

Clause 54   Date of Award

A2–057   254. We trust this provision is self-explanatory.

Clause 55   Notification of Award

A2–058   255. This provision we also trust is self-explanatory. The obligation on the tribunal to notify the parties by service on them of copies of the award is important, given that certain time limits in the Bill for, *e.g.* challenging the award, run from the date of the award (which, under Clause 54, in the absence of any other agreement, is the date upon which it is signed). Time periods, of course, can be extended: see Clause 79. We have required the award to be notified to the "parties" so as to prevent one party from obtaining the award and sitting on it without informing the other party until the expiry of time limits for appeal etc, which we are aware has happened in practice.

256. Clause 55(3) provides that nothing in this section affects the power to withhold an award in the case of non-payment. However, it should be noted that the duty to notify all parties would of course revive once the tribunal's "lien" has been satisfied.

Clause 56   Power to Withhold Award in Case of Non-payment

A2–059   257. These provisions enable a party to seek the assistance of the court if he considers that the arbitrators are asking too much for the release of their award, though it is important to note from subsection (4) that there is no recourse if there is already arbitral machinery for an appeal or review of the fees or expenses demanded.

258. Subsection (8) makes clear that this Clause does not affect the right to challenge fees and expenses under Clause 28, *i.e.* that paying them to get the award does not lose this right. The reason for this provision is that it may be important for a party to obtain the award quickly, rather than going to the court for an order about fees and expenses before getting the award.

259. Unlike section 19 of the 1950 Act, this provision gives the court a discretion to specify that a lesser amount than that claimed by the arbitrators be paid into court, in order to have the award released. If this were not so, an arbitrator could demand an extortionate amount, in effect preventing a party from taking advantage of the mechanism provided for here.

260. For obvious reasons, this provision is mandatory.

Clause 57   Correction of Award or Additional Award

A2–060   261. This Clause reflects article 33 of the Model Law. In our view this is a useful provision, since it enables the arbitral process to correct itself, rather than requiring applications to the court. In order to avoid delay, we have stipulated time limits for seeking corrections, etc.

Clause 58   Effect of Award

262. This provision in effect simply restates the existing law.   A2–061

263. It has been suggested that what is described as the other side of subsection (1) should be spelt out in the Bill, *i.e.* that whatever the parties may or may not agree, the award is of no substantive or evidential effect against any one who is neither a party nor claiming through or under a party.

264. Such a provision would, of course, have to be mandatory. It would have to confine itself to cases exclusively concerned with the laws of this country, for otherwise it could impinge on other applicable laws which have a different rule. Even where the situation was wholly domestic, it would also have to deal with all those cases (*e.g.* insurers) who are not parties to the arbitration but whose rights and obligations may well be affected by awards (agreed or otherwise) in one way or another. In our view it would be very difficult to construct an acceptable provision and we are not persuaded that it is needed.

Costs of the Arbitration

Clause 59   Costs of the Arbitration

Clause 60   Agreement to Pay Costs in Any Event

Clause 61   Award of Costs

Clause 62   Effect of Agreement or Award about Costs

Clause 63   The Recoverable Costs of the Arbitration

Clause 64   Recoverable Fees and Expenses of Arbitrators

Clause 65   Power to Limit Recoverable Costs

265. In these Clauses we have attempted to provide a code dealing with how the costs or   A2–062
an arbitration should be attributed between the parties. The question of the right of the arbitrators to fees and expenses is dealt with earlier in that part of the Bill concerned with the arbitral tribunal: see Clause 28.

266. Clause 59 defines costs.

267. Clause 60 is a mandatory provision preventing effective agreements to pay the whole or part of the costs in any event unless made after the dispute has arisen. The Clause is based on section 18(3) of the Arbitration Act 1950. The Committee are of the view that public policy continues to dictate that such a provision should remain.

268. Clause 62 empowers the arbitrators to make an award in relation to costs. Subsection (2) sets out the general principle to be applied, which is the same principle that is applicable in court.

269. It has been suggested that arbitral tribunals should not be fettered in this way, but to our minds it is helpful to state the principle, especially for those who may not be

lawyers and who otherwise might not know how to proceed. Furthermore, it seems to us that there is no reason why the general principle should not apply to arbitrations: it certainly does under the present law. The parties are, of course, free to agree on other principles, subject to Clause 60.

270. Clauses 63 and 64 are we hope more or less self-explanatory. Clearly there has to be a special regime for the fees and expenses of the arbitrators, for otherwise they would be left with the power to decide for themselves whether or not they had over-charged!

271. Clause 64(4) preserves any contractual right an arbitrator may have to payment of his fees and expenses. If a party has agreed these, then it would in our view be wrong to allow the court to adjust the amount, *i.e.* to rewrite that agreement.

272. Clause 65 contains a new proposal. It gives the tribunal power to limit in advance the amount of recoverable costs. We consider that such a power, properly used, could prove to be extremely valuable as an aid to reducing unnecessary expenditure. It also represents a facet of the duty of the tribunal as set out in Clause 33. The Clause enables the tribunal to put a ceiling on the costs, so that while a party can continue to spend as much as it likes on an arbitration it will not be able to recover more than the ceiling limit from the other party. This will have the added virtue of discouraging those who wish to use their financial muscle to intimidate their opponents into giving up through fear that by going on they might be subject to a costs order which they could not sustain.

Powers of the Court in Relation to Award

Clause 66   Enforcement of the Award

A2–063   273. This reflects article 35 of the Model Law. Enforcement through the court provides the classic case of using the court to support the arbitral process. Subsection (3)(a) is intended to state the present law: see Mustill & Boyd, *Commercial Arbitration* (2nd (ed.) at p. 546. Subsection (3)(b) is intended to cover cases where public policy would not recognise the validity of an award, for example awards purporting to decide matters which our law does not accept can be resolved by this means. For obvious reasons, this provision is mandatory.

274. Reference should be made to Chapter 6, where certain supplementary recommendations are made with respect to this Clause.

Clause 67   Challenging the Award: Substantive Jurisdiction

A2–064   275. Jurisdiction has already been considered in the context of that part of the Bill dealing with the jurisdiction of the arbitral tribunal: see Clauses 30 to 32.

276. Clause 31 allows the tribunal (where it has power to rule on its own jurisdiction) to make a "jurisdiction" award, either on its own, or as part of its award on the merits. Clause 67 provides the mechanism for challenging the jurisdiction rulings in such awards, and is a mandatory provision. It also provides a mechanism for challenges to the jurisdiction by someone who has taken no part in the arbitral proceedings. We deal with such persons below, when considering Clause 72.

277. To avoid the possibility of challenges to the jurisdiction causing unnecessary delay, the rights given by this Clause are subject to qualifications, which explains the reference in subsection (1) to three other sections. In addition, subsection (2) means that a challenge to jurisdiction does not stop the tribunal from proceeding with other aspects of the arbitration while the application is pending.

Clause 68   Challenging the Award: Serious Irregularity

278. We have drawn a distinction in the Bill between challenges in respect of substantive   A2–065
jurisdiction (*i.e.* those matters listed in Clause 30) and challenges in respect of what we have called "serious irregularity". We appreciate that cases may arise it which it might be difficult to decide into which category a particular set of circumstances should be placed, but since the time limits etc for both Clause 67 and Clause 68 are the same, this should cause no procedural difficulties. We are firmly of the view, however, that it is useful to have two categories.

279. The reason for this is that where jurisdiction is concerned, there can be no question of applying a test of "substantial injustice" or the like. An award of a tribunal purporting to decide the rights or obligations of a person who has not given that tribunal jurisdiction so to act simply cannot stand, though of course, if the party concerned has taken part in the arbitration, there is nothing wrong in requiring him to act without delay in challenging the award.

280. Irregularities stand on a different footing. Here we consider that it is appropriate, indeed essential, that these have to pass the test of causing "substantial injustice" before the court can act. The court does not have a general supervisory jurisdiction over arbitrations. We have listed the specific cases where a challenge can be made under this Clause. The test of "substantial injustice" is intended to be a applied by way of support for the arbitral process, not by way of interference with that process. Thus it is only in those cases where it can be said that what has happened is so far removed from what could reasonably be expected of the arbitral process that we would expect the court to take action. The test is not what would have happened had the matter been litigated. To apply such a test would be to ignore the fact that the parties have agreed to arbitrate, not litigate. Having chosen arbitration, the parties cannot validly complain of substantial injustice unless what has happened simply cannot on any view be defended as an acceptable consequence of that choice. In short, Clause 68 is really designed as a long stop, only available in extreme cases where the tribunal has gone so wrong in its conduct of the arbitration that justice calls out for it to be corrected.

281. By way of example, there have been cases under our present law where the court has remitted awards to an arbitral tribunal because the lawyers acting for one party failed (or decided not to) put a particular point to the tribunal: see, for example *Indian Oil Corporation v. Coastal (Bermuda) Ltd* [1990] 2 Lloyd's Rep. 407; *King v. Thomas McKenna* [1991] 2 Q.B. 480; *Breakbulk Marine v. Dateline* 19 March 1992, unreported (jurisdiction recognised but not exercised).

282. The responses we received were critical of such decisions, on the grounds that they really did amount to an interference in the arbitral process agreed by the parties. We agree. The Clause we propose is designed not to permit such interference, by setting out a closed list of irregularities (which it will not be open to the court to extend), and instead reflecting the internationally accepted view that the court should be able to

correct serious failure to comply with the "due process" of arbitral proceedings: *cf.*
article 34 of the Model Law.

283. This Clause is, of course, mandatory.

Clause 69   Appeal on Point of Law

A2–066   284. We received a number of responses calling for the abolition of any right of appeal on
the substantive issues in the arbitration. These were based on the proposition that by
agreeing to arbitrate their dispute, the parties were agreeing to abide by the decision
of their chosen tribunal, not by the decision of the court, so that whether or not a
court would reach the same conclusion was simply irrelevant. To substitute the
decision of the court on the substantive issues would be wholly to subvert the
agreement the parties had made.

285. This proposition is accepted in many countries. We have considered it carefully, but
we are not persuaded that we should recommend that the right of appeal should be
abolished. It seems to us, that with the safeguards we propose, a limited right of
appeal is consistent with the fact that the parties have chosen to arbitrate rather than
litigate. For example, many arbitration agreements contain an express choice of the
law to govern the rights and obligations arising out of the bargain made subject to that
agreement. It can be said with force that in such circumstances, the parties have
agreed that that law will be properly applied by the arbitral tribunal, with the
consequence that if the tribunal fail to do this, it is not reaching the result contemplated by the arbitration agreement.

286. In these circumstances what we propose is a right to apply to the court to decide a
point of law arising out of an award. This right is limited, however, in several
ways.

i. The point of law must substantially affect the rights of one or more of the parties.
This limitation exists, of course, in our present law.

ii. The point of law must be one that was raised before the tribunal. The responses
showed that in some cases applications for leave to appeal have been made and
granted on the basis that an examination of the reasons for the award shows an
error on a point of law that was not raised or debated in the arbitration. This
method of proceeding has echoes of the old and long discarded common law rules
relating to error of law on the face of the award, and is in our view a retrograde
step. In our view the right to appeal should be limited us we suggest.

iii. There have been attempts, both before and after the enactment of the Arbitration
Act 1979, to dress up questions of fact as questions of law and by that means to
seek an appeal on the tribunal's decision on the facts. Generally these attempts
have been resisted by the courts, but to make the position clear, we propose to state
expressly that consideration by the court of the suggested question of law is made
on the basis of the findings of fact in the award.

iv. We have attempted to express in this Clause the limits put on the right to appeal
by the House of Lords in *Pioneer Shipping Ltd v. BTP Tioxide Ltd (The Nema)*
[1982] A.C. 724.

287. With respect to the last point, we think it is very important to do this. Many of those
abroad who do not have ready access to our case law were unaware that the Arbitration

Act 1979 had been construed by the House of Lords in a way that very much limited the right of appeal, and which was not evident from the words of the Act themselves.

288. The test we propose is whether, in the ordinary case, the court is satisfied that the decision of the tribunal is obviously wrong. The right of appeal is only available for such cases, for the reasons discussed above. Where the matter is one of general public importance, the test is less onerous, but the decision must still be open to serious doubt.

289. We propose a further test, namely whether, despite the agreement of the parties to resolve the matter by arbitration, it is just and proper in all the circumstances for the court to determine the question.

290. We have been asked why we suggest this addition. The reason is that we think it desirable that this factor should be specifically addressed by the court when it is considering an application. It seems to us to be the basis on which the House of Lords acted as it did in *The Nema, op. cit.*. The court should be satisfied that justice dictates that there should be an appeal; and in considering what justice requires, the fact that the parties have agreed to arbitrate rather than litigate is an important and powerful factor.

291. It will be noted that we have included a provision that the court should determine an application without a hearing unless it appears to the court that a hearing is required. This again reflects what was said in *The Nema, op. cit.* about the tendency for applications for leave being turned into long and expensive court hearings. In our view, the tests for leave (*i.e.* obviously wrong or open to serious doubt) are such that in most cases the court will be able to decide whether to allow or reject the application on written material alone.

292. Finally, a question has been raised as to whether an agreement in advance of the proceedings (*i.e.* contained in an arbitration clause mor in the underlying contract) would satisfy Clause 69(2)(a). The Clause is intended to encompass such agreements, and in our view it plainly does so since the word agreement is not qualified. However, such an agreement will not automatically allow an appeal unless it complies with the other conditions set out in Clause 69 and 70.

Clause 70   Challenge or Appeal: Supplementary Provisions

Clause 71   Challenge or Appeal: Effect of Order of the Court

293. These provisions contain time-limits and other matters in relation to challenges to the award and applications and appeals. Some of these provisions are mandatory.   A2–067

294. The time limit in Clause 70(3) runs from the date of the award, or, where applicable, the date when a party was notified of the result of any arbitral process of appeal or review. It has been suggested that difficulties might arise if an award is held back by the arbitrators, pending payment by the parties (*i.e.* under Clause 56). It is possible that the time limit in Clause 70(3) will have expired by the time an award is released. However, the DAC is of the view that the date of the award is the only incontrovertible date from which the time period should run. Any other starting point would result in great uncertainty (*e.g.* as to the exact point at which an award is "released" or

"delivered"). Further, any difficulties arising from specific circumstances can be easily remedied by way of an extension of time under Clause 79.

Miscellaneous

Clause 72   Saving for Rights of Person who Takes no Part in Proceedings

A2–068   295. To our minds this is a vital provision. A person who disputes that an arbitral tribunal has jurisdiction cannot be required to take part in the arbitration proceedings or to take positive steps to defend his position, for any such requirement would beg the question whether or not his objection has any substance and thus be likely to lead to gross injustice. Such a person must be entitled, if he wishes, simply to ignore the arbitral process, though of course (if his objection is not well-founded) he runs the risk of an enforceable award being made against him. Those who do decide to take part in the arbitral proceedings in order to challenge the jurisdiction are, of course, in a different category, for then, having made that choice, such people can fairly and properly be required to abide by the time limits etc. that we have proposed.

296. This is a mandatory provision.

Clause 73   Loss of Right to Object

A2–069   297. Recalcitrant parties or those who have had an award made against them often seek to delay proceedings or to avoid honouring the award by raising points on jurisdiction, etc. which they have been saving up for this purpose or which they could and should have discovered and raised at an earlier stage. Article 4 of the Model Law contains some provisions designed to combat this sort of behaviour (which does the efficiency of arbitration as a form of dispute resolution no good) and we have attempted to address the same point in this Clause. In particular, unlike the Model Law, we have required a party to arbitration proceedings who has taken part or continued to take part without raising the objection in due time, to show that at that stage he neither knew nor could with reasonable diligence have discovered the grounds for his objection (the latter being an important modification to the Model Law, without which one would have to demonstrate actual knowledge, which may be virtually impossible to do). It seems to us that this is preferable to requiring the innocent party to prove the opposite, which for obvious reasons it might be difficult or impossible to do.

298. For the reasons explained when considering Clause 72, the provision under discussion cannot, of course, be applied to a party who has chosen to play no part at all in the arbitral proceedings.

Clause 74   Immunity of Arbitral Institutions, etc.

A2–070   299. In this mandatory provision we have provided institutions and individuals who appoint arbitrators with a degree of immunity.

300. The reason for this proposal is that without such an immunity, there is in our view a real risk that attempts will be made to hold institutions or individuals responsible for the consequences of their exercise of the power they may be given to appoint or nominate arbitrators, or for what their appointed or nominate arbitrators then do or fail to do. This would provide a means of reopening matters that were referred to

arbitration, something that might be encouraged if arbitrators were given immunity (as we have also proposed in Clause 29) but nothing was said about such institutions or individuals.

301. There is an additional point of great importance. Many organisations that provide arbitration services, including Trade Associations as well as bodies whose sole function it is to provide arbitration services, do not in the nature of things have deep pockets. Indeed much of the work is done by volunteers simply in order to promote and help this form of dispute resolution. Such organisations could find it difficult if not impossible to finance the cost of defending legal proceedings or even the cost of insurance against such cost. In our view the benefits which these organisations (and indeed individuals) have on arbitration generally fully justify giving them a measure of protection so that their good work can continue.

Clause 75   Charge to Secure Payment of Solicitors' Costs

302. This is a technical provision designed to maintain the present position.   A2–071

Supplementary

Clause 76   Service of Notices, etc.

303. The subject matter of this Clause was touched on in the MacKinnon Report which   A2–072
led to the Arbitration Act 1934, but at that time no action was taken.

304. In this Clause we have attempted to do three things.

   i. We have stipulated that the parties can agree on how service of notices and other documents can be done.

   ii. We have made clear that in the absence of agreement, service by *any* effective means will suffice.

   iii. We have provided in subsection (4) an option which can best be described as a "fail-safe" method, which a party may employ if he wishes, for example if he is not sure that other methods will be effective. We should emphasise that this fail-safe method is not a compulsory or preferred method for service, but merely a means which, if employed, will be treated as effective.

305. These provisions do not apply in respect of service in court proceedings, for the obvious reason that such service must comply with the rules of the court concerned.

Clause 77   Powers of Court in Relation to Service of Documents

306. In this Clause we have given the court powers to support the arbitral process so that   A2–073
it is not delayed or frustrated through difficulties over service. In the nature of human affairs, it is sadly the case that potential respondents to arbitration proceedings quite often go to considerable lengths to avoid service and thus to achieve this state of affairs, by making normal methods difficult or even impossible to use effectively. This Clause should, in appropriate cases, help to deal with such cases.

Clause 78   Reckoning Periods of Time

307. In our view it would be of great assistance to set out a code to deal with the reckoning   A2–074
of time, thus avoiding the need to refer to other sources. Hence this provision.

Clause 79   Power of Court to Extend Time Limits Relating to Arbitral Proceedings

A2–075   308. Here we propose that the court should have a general right to extend time limits, except time limits for starting an arbitration, which is dealt with specifically in Clause 12. We propose that the wording of the Clause be clarified as set out in Chapter 6 below.

309. This power is limited in the ways set out in this Clause. In particular, no extension will be granted unless a substantial injustice would otherwise be done and any arbitral process for obtaining an extension must first be exhausted. As we have said in other contexts, it would be a rare case indeed where we would expect the court to grant an extension where such has not been obtained through that process. With these limitations we take the view that this provision can properly be described as supporting the arbitral process.

Clause 80   Notice and other Requirements in Connection with Legal Proceedings

A2–076   310. Legal proceedings must of course be subject to the rules of the court concerned. We have made clear, therefore, that where the Bill provides for notice of legal proceedings to be given to others, this is a reference to such rules as the court concerned may make; and is not a separate requirement over and above those rules.

Clause 81   Saving for Certain Matters governed by Common Law

A2–077   311. As we have stated earlier, and as was stated in the Mustill Report, it would be neither practicable nor desirable to attempt to codify the whole of our arbitration law. Hence subsections (1) and (2) of this Clause.

312. It was suggested to us that a provision preserving the common law would enable arguments to be raised and accepted which were contrary to the spirit and intent of the Bill. We do not think that this will happen, in view of the opening words of the Clause and indeed the statements of principle in Clause 1. Equally, it seems to us to be necessary to make clear that the common law (so far as it is consistent with the Bill) will continue to make its great contribution to our arbitration law, a contribution that has done much to create and preserve the world wide popularity of arbitration in our country.

313. Subsection (3) is technically necessary to make clear that the repeal of the existing statutes does not have the effect of reviving the common law rules relating to errors on the face of the award.

Clause 82   Minor Definitions

Clause 83   Index of Defined Expressions: Part I

A2–078   314. The first of these Clauses provides the definition of words and phrases which are often repeated in the body of the Bill, so that repetition of the meaning is avoided, as well as providing a ready means of discovering the meaning of certain important words and phrases. The second of these Clauses is also designed to help the reader by identifying the place where other important words and phrases are defined or explained.

Clause 84   Transitional Provisions

315. This Clause sets out the general proposition, namely that the Bill will apply to arbitral   A2–079
proceedings commenced after the legislation comes into force, whenever the arbitration agreement is made. There are respectable precedents for this, since the Arbitration Acts 1889, and 1934 contained a like provision. The 1950 Act, of course, was not a precedent, since this was a consolidating measure. We consider this to be a useful provision, since some arbitration agreements have a very long life indeed (for example, rent review arbitration agreements under leases) and it would be most unsatisfactory if the existing law and the proposed legislation were to run in parallel (if that is the right expression) indefinitely into the future.

316. Reference should also be made to Clause 111.

CHAPTER 3

PART II OF THE BILL

OTHER PROVISIONS RELATING TO ARBITRATION

Domestic Arbitration Agreements

Clause 85   Modification of Part I in Relation to Domestic Arbitration Agreements

Clause 86   Staying of Legal Proceedings

Clause 87   Effectiveness of Agreement to Exclude Court's Jurisdiction

Clause 88   Power to Repeal or Amend ss.85 to 87

317. Under our present law, a distinction is drawn between domestic and other arbitrations   A2–080
for two main purposes.

318. In the first place, the rules for obtaining a stay of legal proceedings differ. The reason for this is that under international Conventions, a stay in favour of an arbitration is mandatory except in certain specified circumstances. The current Convention is the New York Convention and the rules under that Convention we have now set out in Clause 9. With an exception that we have already discussed above, Clause 9 simply re-enacts the Arbitration Act 1975 so far as it concerns this matter.

319. Section 1 of the Arbitration Act 1975 does not apply to domestic arbitrations as there defined. These continue to be governed by section 4(1) of the Arbitration Act 1950, which makes the grant of a stay discretionary.

320. It is our view that consideration should be given to abolishing this distinction and applying the New York Convention rules to all cases. It seems to us that these rules fit much more happily with the concept of party autonomy than our domestic rules, which were framed at a time when attitudes to arbitration were very different and the courts were anxious to avoid what they described as usurpation of their process.

321. For example, there are cases justifying the refusal of a stay in cases where the court considers that the party seeking to arbitrate has no defence to the claim and is merely seeking to delay the day of judgment. This has been explained on the basis that since there is no defence to the claim, there is no dispute that can be arbitrated. The difficulty with this argument is that it logically follows that only disputable matters can be arbitrated, or, in other words, that the arbitrators have no jurisdiction to deal with cases where there is no real defence. This in turn means that a claimant cannot refer a claim to arbitration where there is no real defence, since *ex hypothesi* the arbitrators would have no jurisdiction. In short, this argument leads to consequences that in our view have only to be stated to be rejected. As to delaying tactics, it has been our intention throughout the Bill to provide the means whereby an agreement to arbitrate can produce (in suitable cases) a very quick answer indeed. Indeed, if in truth there is no defence to a claim, then it should not take more than a very short time for an arbitral tribunal to deal with the matter and produce an award.

322. For these reasons, which are those discussed in *Nelson v. Hayter* [1990] 2 Lloyd's Rep. 265, we consider that this ground for preserving the distinction between domestic and other arbitrations so far as stays are concerned is highly unconvincing.

323. The domestic rules have also been used to refuse stays where the disputes are likely to involve other parties, who could not be brought into the arbitration, since the agreement to arbitrate only binds those who were party to it. Here the justification for refusing to stay legal proceedings is that it would be much better for all the concerned parties to be brought into one proceeding, so that the whole matter can be sorted out between them all.

324. This reasoning of course is in one sense supported by common sense and justice, for in certain cases it would be better and fairer for all the disputes between all the parties involved to be dealt with by one tribunal, thereby avoiding delay and the possibility of inconsistent findings by different tribunals. However, as we observed in the context of considering whether there should be a power (without the agreement of the parties) to order consolidation or concurrent hearings in arbitrations (Clause 35), to refuse a stay because other parties are involved involves tearing up the arbitration agreement that the applicant for a stay has made. In other words, with the benefit of hindsight, the court adjusts the rights and obligations of contracting parties.

325. We fully accept that for reasons of consumer protection, this on occasion can and should be done, but we are not persuaded that it should be a general rule in the context of stays of domestic arbitrations, for it sits uneasily with the principle of party autonomy and amounts to interference with rather than support for the arbitral process.

326. We should also note that the distinction drawn between domestic and other arbitrations produces odd results. An arbitration agreement between two English people is a domestic arbitration agreement, while an agreement between an English person and someone of a different nationality is not, even if that person has spent all his time in

England. Furthermore, we are aware that it could be said that the distinction discriminates against European Community nationals who are not English, and is thus contrary to European law.

327. Notwithstanding the foregoing, we do not propose in this Bill to abolish the distinction. Some defend it and we have not had an opportunity to make all the soundings we would like on this subject. What we have done is to put the domestic arbitration rules in a separate part of the Bill, and provided in Clause 88 for a power of repeal through the mechanism of a positive joint resolution of each House of Parliament.

328. What we have felt able to do is to redraft the domestic rules on stays and to make two changes. Firstly we have removed the discretion and instead set out words which are wide enough to encompass the circumstances which the cases have developed as grounds for refusing a stay. Secondly and more importantly, we have reversed the existing burden of proof (and incidentally got rid of a double or perhaps treble negative in the previous legislation). It seemed to us that it was for the party seeking to litigate something which he had previously agreed to arbitrate to persuade the court that he should be allowed to go back on his agreement.

329. The second purpose served by making a distinction between domestic and other arbitrations is to prevent the parties in a domestic case from effectively agreeing to exclude the jurisdiction of the court to deal with preliminary points of law or with an appeal from an award on a point of law, until after the commencement of the arbitral proceedings. This necessarily means that until the arbitration starts such parties cannot make an effective agreement to dispense with reasons, for that is treated as an agreement to exclude the jurisdiction of the court—see, now, Clause 69(1).

330. Again we are not persuaded of the value or the validity of this, but we have preserved the existing law for the same reason as we have preserved the present position on stays. Our own view is that this distinction should disappear.

331. It should be noted that we have not preserved the "special categories" dealt with in section 4 of the Arbitration Act 1979. These were intended as a temporary measure, and the weight of the responses received persuaded us that they should now go.

Consumer Arbitration Agreements

Clauses 89 to 93

332. In these Clauses we have consolidated the provisions of the Consumer Arbitration Agreements Act 1988. We have suggested this in order to bring within the Bill all the current major enactments on arbitration, so as to provide as complete a code as possible. **A2–081**

333. We did not regard it as part of our remit to redraft this legislation, so we have not sought responses on it. However, we are aware that problems have arisen in construing this Act. For example, it has been suggested that what now appears as Clause 89 makes it far from clear whether a building contract made by a consumer falls outside the Act if the consumer has sought a number of quotes for the work.

334. We are also aware of a more fundamental problem. This country has recently implemented Council Directive 93/13 through the Unfair Terms in Consumer

Contracts Regulations 1994 (S.I. 1994/3159). These Regulations came into force on 1st July 1995. Thus at the moment a situation exists where there are two parallel regimes for protecting consumer interests in the context of arbitration agreements.

335. To our minds this is an unsatisfactory state of affairs, likely to cause confusion and difficulties. Although we have not attempted to trespass into the field of consumer protection, it does seem to us that it would be unfortunate if the opportunity were not taken to clarify the position. On the face of it, the solution would seem to be to maintain the suggested repeal of the 1988 Act and to omit Clauses 89 to 92 of the Bill. If this were to be done, then we would welcome at least a cross-reference in the Bill to the Regulations, so that anyone reading the Bill will be made aware of them. As we understand it, the Regulations would not affect our international obligations regarding arbitrations (for example, the New York Convention) though doubtless those charged with the question of consumer protection will consider this aspect of the matter.

336. We would, however, emphasise that the arbitration community is extremely anxious that the Bill should not be delayed. The fact is that this country has been very slow to modernise its arbitration law and this has done us no good in our endeavour to retain our pre-eminence in the field of international arbitration, a service which brings this country very substantial amounts indeed by way of invisible earnings.

337. It is for these reasons that we have included in Clause 88 a power to amend or repeal Clauses 89 to 93. If the situation cannot be clarified or settled without delaying the progress of the Bill, then this mechanism could allow the Bill to go forward with the Consumer Arbitration Agreements Act in it, and the matter dealt with later.

Small Claims Arbitration in the County Court

Clause 94   Exclusion of Part 1 in Relation to Small Claims in the County Court

A2–082   338. There is an entirely separate regime for the arbitration of small claims in the county court. The Bill is not intended to affect this.

339. As we observed earlier in the Report, we considered the suggestion that we should incorporate in the Bill another system for the arbitration of small claims, but for the reasons given, we have not adopted this suggestion and do not recommend it.

Appointment of Judges as Arbitrators

Clause 95   Appointment of Judges as Arbitrators

A2–083   340. In this Clause we have set out the existing provisions for the appointment of Commercial Judges and Official Referees as arbitrators.

341. We firmly of the view that provision should be made for any judge to be appointed as an arbitrator, rather than limiting the power to the two kinds of judge presently included. It was not, however, possible to obtain agreement to this proposal from the concerned departments in time to put it in the Bill.

342. We appreciate that in view of the court commitments of judges generally, it is not possible to allow judges to act as arbitrators whenever they are asked and are willing to do so. Hence the present requirement now set out in subsections (2) and (3). We would suggest that the same or a similar provision is used for all other judges.

343. We are told that the problem is particularly acute in the field of patents and the like, where the parties are anxious to arbitrate but where the only acceptable arbitrators are judges.

Statutory Arbitrations

Clauses 96 to 101

344. These provisions adapt Part 1 to statutory arbitrations. This exercise is not within our remit and we have played no part in it.   A2–084

Chapter 4

Part III of The Bill

Clauses 102 to 107

345. The purpose of Part III is to re-enact the substance of the provisions relating to the recognition and enforcement of foreign arbitral awards contained in Part II of the Arbitration Act 1950 and the Arbitration Act 1975, which gave effect to the U.K.'s treaty obligations under the Geneva and New York Conventions respectively.   A2–085

346. The Geneva Convention only remains in force as between state parties to that Convention which have *not* subsequently become parties to the New York Convention. So far as the U.K. is concerned, it is believed that only a few states (*e.g.* Malta) remain in that category. Accordingly, in the interest of brevity, Clause 102 states simply that Part II of the Arbitration Act 1950 continues to apply to Geneva Convention awards which are not also New York Convention awards rather than restating or reframing the non-user friendly language of Part II of that Act.

347. The New York Convention on the Recognition and Enforcement of Foreign Arbitral Awards adopted by the U.N. Conference on International Arbitration on 10 June 1958 is not only the cornerstone of international dispute resolution; it is an essential ingredient more generally of world trade. If it did not exist, or even if it were not to have been widely adopted by the world's trading nations, contracting parties from different legal cultures might be reduced to resolving their disputes in the courts of a country which would be alien to either one or both of them (because of doubts as to the enforceability across national boundaries of arbitration awards made in a neutral country). Clauses 102 to 107 of the Bill restate the current implementing legislation (contained in the 1975 Act) in concise and simple language.

348. As we have indicated earlier in Chapter 2, we take the view that the definition of "in writing" is consonant with Article II.2 of the New York Convention. For clarity

therefore, we consider that the Bill can be improved by including an express cross-reference to this definition in Clause 103(2). This would have the added advantage of ensuring that the enforcement of foreign awards under Clause 66 and enforcement under the New York Convention are in this respect in line with each other.

349. One intriguing question was highlighted by the decision of the House of Lords in *Hiscox v. Outhwaite* [1992] 1 A.C. 562. This concerns the case of an arbitration with its "seat" in country A and an award that states expressly that it was "made" in country B. Country A might be a New York Convention country, and B not—or vice versa. (Article I.1 of the Convention provides that it shall apply to " . . . *awards made in the territory of a State other than the State in which recognition and enforcement of such awards are sought* . . . " (emphasis added)).

350. Distinguished authors (writing before the decision in *Hiscox*) are split on the question. Dr A.J. van den Berg in the first edition of his authoritative book on the Convention (at pp. 294/295) states: "*The award must be deemed to be made in the country which is indicated in the award as [the] place where the award was made.*" (emphasis added).

351. But the late Dr F.A. Mann Q.C. (in [1985] *Arb. Int.* 107/108) wrote, after recalling that little learning then existed on the question of where an award is made,

> "It is submitted that an award is 'made' at the place at which the arbitration is held, i.e. the arbitral seat . . . admittedly the view suggested here attributes a somewhat strained meaning to the word 'made'. But for the reasons given the natural meaning of the word leads to such strange consequences that a less literal interpretation would seem to be justified".

352. In *Hiscox* the question arose as to whether, where the "seat" of the arbitration was in England and for all practical purposes it was a domestic "English" arbitration, the award became a "foreign" award for the purposes of the Convention merely because it stated expressly on its face that it was signed in Paris? According to the House of Lords, applying a literal interpretation of Article I.1 of the Convention, the answer was "Yes".

353. So far as arbitrations held in England, Wales or Northern Ireland are concerned, the "strange consequences" of this result have been removed by Clause 53 of the Bill (see above).

354. The DAC is of the view that this question should be resolved by incorporating into Part III of the proposed new legislation an equivalent provision to that contained in Clause 53—to the effect that an award shall be treated as made at the seat of the arbitration, regardless of where it was signed, despatched or delivered to any of the parties. It seems to us that this is consonant with the U.K.'s treaty obligations under the New York Convention.

CHAPTER 5

PART IV OF THE BILL

355. We have drawn attention to Clause 111 under Clause 84. The other Clauses in this   A2–086
Part we trust are self-evident, and were not within the remit of the DAC, although we
do welcome the inclusion of Northern Ireland.

CHAPTER 6

SUPPLEMENTARY RECOMMENDATIONS

356. The foregoing discussion is based on the text of the Bill as it was introduced in   A2–087
December 1995. Since that date we have had the advantage of considering the
speeches made in the House of Lords on the Second Reading and some comments
and suggestions from others, as well as looking once again at the text of the Bill in the
course of preparing this Report. In consequence, we make the following recommendations.

Clause 2   Scope of Application
357. A number of foreign readers have expressed the view that Clause 2(2)(a) does not   A2–088
sufficiently make clear that the applicable law referred to is the law applicable to the
arbitration agreement, rather than the law applicable to the substantive agreement
(which would have far reaching and wholly unintended consequences). For the sake
of clarity, we would suggest an amendment along the following lines:

> " . . . where the applicable law to that agreement is the law of England and Wales
> or Northern Ireland; and . . . "

Clause 7   Separability of Arbitration Agreement
358. In view of the definition of "agreement" in Clause 5, we suggest that the words   A2–089
"(whether or not in writing)" be inserted after the words "another agreement" in
Clause 7, since otherwise it could be said that this Clause is only effective in relation
to such other agreements as are in writing. This is not the intention.

Clause 14(5)   Commencement of Arbitral Proceedings
359. It has been suggested that the words "gives notice" should be replaced by "serves",   A2–090
in conformity with Clauses 14(3) and 14(4). This is a matter for Parliamentary
Counsel to consider.

Clause 16(6)(b) and Clause 21(4)
360. The word "any" follows a negative and so could be read as meaning "all". This is not   A2–091
the intention. We therefore suggest that the words "one or more matters" follow the
word "any" in these provisions.

Clause 24(4)   Power of Court to Remove Arbitrator

A2–092   361.   We have explained in Chapter 1 above the reasoning behind Clause 29(3). Upon
further reflection, it appears to us that Clause 24(4) needs to be altered for the same
reason. As currently drafted, if an arbitrator resigns and is sued for his fees, he is not
protected from such a breach of contract action by the immunity in Clause 29. Rather,
he can apply to the court for protection under Clause 25(3), and the court may see fit
to grant this, if appropriate. However, if an arbitrator does not resign, but is removed
by the court under Clause 24, it would appear that he will have the benefit of the
immunity in Clause 29, come what may. In such circumstances, the parties could not
sue him for breach of contract, unless they could demonstrate "bad faith". This is
anomalous. The DAC therefore recommends that Clause 24(4) be amended to provide
that as well as making such order as it thinks fit with respect to an arbitrator's
entitlement to fees, where the court removes an arbitrator, it also be given a discretion
to make such order as it thinks fit with respect to an arbitrator's immunity under
Clause 29. Such wide words would enable the court, for example, to remove the
immunity but impose a ceiling on the amount of any liability.

362.   Arbitrators may also be removed by agreement of the parties. However, the DAC does
not consider that a similar provision be made with respect to this, given that it would
be contrary to the whole basis of Clause 29 for parties to be able to agree on the
removal of an arbitrator's immunity.

Clause 25(2)   Resignation of Arbitrator

A2–093   363.   There is a rogue "in writing" in this subsection, which should be deleted by virtue
of Clause 5(1).

Clause 38(3)   Security for Costs

A2–094   364.   In the draft Clauses published in July 1995, the power to order security for costs was
expressed in very general terms. This elicited a number of responses which expressed
concern that there were no principles or guidelines for the exercise of this power. It
is certainly the case that the power to order security for costs, unless exercised with
great care, can all too easily work injustice rather than justice.

365.   The rules and principles applied by the courts with respect to security for costs have
been carefully worked out over many years, and are contained in a large amount of
case law that has developed alongside Order 23 of the Rules of the Supreme Court.
Given the concerns referred to above, the DAC considered whether to set out these
rules and principles in the Bill. In the end we decided that this would be simply
impracticable: a codification of all the relevant case law would be extremely difficult,
would result in very lengthy and complicated provisions, and may well have an
unintended impact on how this area is approached by the courts.

366.   Clause 38(3) of the current draft of the Bill reflects what we initially concluded was
the only solution to this difficulty: it provides that arbitrators are to have power to
order a party to provide security for costs "wherever the court would have power . . ."
and that this power is to be exercised: "on the same principles as the court". In the
light of many comments received since the Bill was introduced (including a significant
number of criticisms of this subsection from foreign arbitration specialists and
institutions), we have had to reconsider this area, and, after much careful thought, we
have concluded that Clause 38(3) requires amendment for the following reasons:

i. As drafted, this subsection is very far from being "user-friendly". Without referring to the Rules of the Supreme Court, and the case law referred to in the relevant part of the White Book, it would be impossible for any domestic or foreign user to determine what the nature and scope of the power conferred here is. Lay arbitrators may have difficulty locating or even, perhaps, understanding the relevant law (any error of law, of course, being a potential ground for appeal). In the case of a foreign arbitration that has its seat in this country for the sole reason that this is a neutral forum, it would be extremely undesirable for parties to have to instruct English lawyers in order to make sense of this provision. This alone could constitute a powerful disincentive to selecting this country as an arbitral seat. Indeed, throughout the Bill, we have been very careful to avoid any such express cross-references to other legal sources.

ii. One of the grounds on which an order for security for costs may be made in court is that the plaintiff is ordinarily resident out of the jurisdiction: see Order 23, Rule 1(1)(a) of the Rules of the Supreme Court. On further consideration of the matter, we have concluded that it would be very damaging to this country's position as the leading centre for international arbitrations to make this ground available to arbitral tribunals. It would reasonably appear to those abroad who are minded to arbitrate their claims here that foreigners were being singled out for special and undeserved treatment. (Of course if the parties agree to invest their tribunal with power to order security for costs on this ground, they are free to do so).

iii. On reflection, the concerns expressed above as to the potential scope of the power conferred by Clause 38(3) and the possibilities of injustice may be overstated. The other provisions of the Bill confer very far-reaching powers on arbitrators, and it has been made clear throughout that this is tempered, for example, by the mandatory duty in Clause 33. The same would be true of the power to order security for costs: in exercising the power, the tribunal would have to comply with Clause 33, and any serious irregularity could form the basis of a challenge. In agreeing to arbitration, parties in effect agree that their disputes could be decided differently from a court, although in accordance with principles of justice. The fact that arbitrators may decide an issue as to security for costs differently from a judge appears to be no more than an aspect of this. It is true that if this power is improperly exercised, a claim could, for example, be stifled without justification. It is equally true, however, that the Bill contains mechanisms for parties to challenge any such injustice or improper conduct, and sufficient warnings to arbitrators as to their mandatory duties.

367. We remain of the view that the power to order security for costs is an important one, and should be given to arbitrators, and also that some basic restrictions should be set out in this Clause, in the light of the points made above. To this end, we recommend that Clause 38(3) be deleted, and replaced with a new provision along the following lines:

"(3) The tribunal may order a claimant to provide security for the costs of the arbitration.

Such power shall not be exercised on the grounds only that such party is—

(a) an individual ordinarily resident in a state other than the United Kingdom,

(b) a body corporate which was incorporated in or has its central management and control exercised in a state other than the United Kingdom."

368. Such a provision would allow arbitrators a flexibility in exercising this power, within the confines of their strict duty in Clause 33. The risk of an order on the sole ground that a party is from abroad, would be removed. Similarly, there would be no need for an arbitrator, whether domestic or foreign, to discern the English or Northern Irish law in this area, or, indeed, to instruct local lawyers in this respect. An arbitrator may well exercise this power differently from a court (as with many other powers conferred by the Bill), but any misuse could be corrected under the other provisions of the Bill.

369. It is of course the case that orders for security are not to be made automatically, but only when the justice of the case so requires. We appreciate that cases are likely to arise when deciding what is just may be very difficult. For example, a claimant may contend that he might be prevented from continuing if he has to put up security, whilst at the same time a respondent is contending that unless security is provided, he is likely to be ruined. However, to our minds, this is merely an example of the balancing of factors in order to achieve the most just result possible which is part of the essential function of arbitrators.

370. The power to award security for costs under the proposed provision could be exercised against counter-claimants as well as claimants. This we have covered in the definition Clause (see Clause 82(1)).

Clause 66   Enforcement of Award

A2–095   371. In the present Bill, we have provided that leave by a court to enforce an award may not be given if the award was so defective in form or substance that it is incapable of enforcement, if its enforcement would be contrary to public policy or if the tribunal lacked substantive jurisdiction.

372. These are what are described as "passive" defences to the enforcement of an award. The "positive" steps that may be taken are those we have set out in Clauses 67 to 69, together with the rights preserved in Clause 72 for someone who has taken no part in the arbitral proceedings.

373. In our view the way we have drafted Clause 66 sufficed to cover all the cases where enforcement should be refused. However, since the Bill was published it has been suggested to us that it would be advisable to spell out in more detail two particular cases, namely those where the arbitral tribunal has purported to decide matters which are simply not capable of resolution by arbitration, whatever the parties might have agreed (*e.g.* custody of a child) and those where the tribunal has made an award which (if enforced) would improperly affect the rights and obligations of those who were not parties to the arbitration agreement.

374. On the present wording, even if it could be said that either or both these cases fell outside the three categories where leave to enforce shall not be given, it does not follow that the Clause somehow sanctions enforcement in those cases. The reason for this is that the Clause does not require the court to order enforcement, but only gives it a discretion to do so. That discretion is only fettered in a negative way, *i.e.* by setting out certain cases where enforcement shall not be ordered. To our minds there is

nothing to prevent a court from refusing to enforce an award in other appropriate cases. Unlike, for example, Clause 68, there is no closed list of cases where leave to enforce an award may be refused. However, on reflection we consider that it would be preferable to set out the two cases as further instances where the discretion of the court is negatively fettered, and we would suggest that a further category is added to subsection (3) along the following lines:

> "it purports to decide matters which are not capable of resolution by arbitration or grants relief which (if enforced as a judgment or order of the court) would improperly affect the rights of persons other than the parties to the arbitration agreement."

375. Such a provision would best appear before the catch all case of public policy. It will be noted that this wording takes advantage of the definition of parties to an arbitration agreement to be found in Clause 82(2). Furthermore, to put the matter beyond any doubt, we would suggest that it is made clear that subsection (3) is not a closed list, by inserting suitable words.

376. It is vital to include some such word as "improperly" since there is no doubt that there are many cases where third party rights and obligations are perfectly properly affected, such as guarantors or insurers who have agreed to pay the amount of an award to which they are not a party. Furthermore, it must always be borne in mind that the parties' rights and obligations may well be governed by a law other than our own, under which, for example, matters are arbitrable which would not be the case under our own law. In such cases it would not automatically follow that the court would refuse to enforce the award, unless of course public policy dictated that course.

377. Apart from the enforcement procedure set out in this clause, under our law it is possible to bring an action on an award, in much the same way as an action is brought on an agreement. This method is expressly saved in Clause 81(2)(b). There is also an oblique reference to this in Clause 66(5) in the reference to "rule of law". On reflection, it seems to us that it would make for greater clarity to add the words "or by an action on the award" at the end of this subsection.

378. There is one further point. It seems to us that there is much to be said for a suggestion that the court must be informed on an application for enforcement if the award is an agreed award (see Clause 51) if this is not apparent from the award itself, and that any enforcement order or judgment of the court should also state that it is made in respect of an agreed award, thus putting everyone concerned on notice of that fact and avoiding the risk that third parties might be misled into believing that the award was one made at arm's length. We suggest that these requirements be added to Clause 66.

Clause 69   Appeal on Point of Law

379. It has been pointed out that Clause 69(8) sets out the two pre-conditions to an appeal to the Court of Appeal as alternatives, whereas they should be cumulative (as with the similar pre-conditions in section 1(7) of the 1979 Act). We recommend that the Clause be amended accordingly.

A2–096

Clause 70 Challenge or Appeal: Supplementary Provisions

A2–097 380. We note that the power to order security or bring the money payable under the award into court only extends at present to applications under Clauses 67 or 68. This should be extended so that the court can impose these requirements as a condition of granting leave to appeal under Clause 69. This is a tool of great value, since it helps to avoid the risk that while the appeal is pending, the ability of the losing party to honour the award may (by design or otherwise) be diminished.

Clause 74 Immunity of Arbitral Institutions, etc.

A2–098 381. On reflection we consider that the wording of Clause 74(2) should be tightened so as to make clear that the institution or person concerned is not liable without more for anything done or omitted to be done by the arbitrator. Thus we suggest that the words "by reason only of" should be substituted for the word "for" in this subsection.

Clause 79 Powers of Court to Extend Time Limits Relating to Arbitral Proceedings

A2–099 382. It has been pointed out to us that Clause 79(1) as presently drafted could be said to be inapplicable to, for example, Clause 70(3) where the time stipulated is not one having effect in default of agreement between the parties. We agree with this comment and suggest that Clause 79(1) be amended along the following lines:

> " . . . the court may by order extend any time limit agreed by them in relation to any matter relating to the arbitral proceedings or applicable by virtue of any provision of this Part".

Clause 81 Saving for Certain Matters Governed by Common Law

A2–100 383. We suggest that two additions should be made to the specific cases mentioned in subsection (2).

384. The first of these relates to confidentiality. For reasons we have explained, we have not included specific provisions dealing with this matter. However, it seems to us that it would be valuable to highlight the fact that our law does deal with it. Thus we suggest a further category which could perhaps be in the following words:

> "confidentiality and privacy in relation to arbitrations".

385. The second addition we propose relates to arbitrability, which we have discussed in the context of Clause 66. Again there is a lot of important law on this topic. We suggest a further category which could perhaps be in the following words:

> "whether a matter is capable of resolution by arbitration".

386. The title to this Clause is "Saving for certain matters governed by common law". We would prefer the expression "other rules of law" to the words "common law" as this would include legislation and be clearer to non-lawyers and those from abroad.

Clause 82 Minor Definitions

A2–101 387. The definition of "question of law" started life as part of the Clause dealing with appeals to the court; now Clause 69. The objective was to make clear that there was no question of an appeal in respect of a matter of foreign law. Our law treats questions of foreign law as questions of fact. Furthermore, we can see no good reason for allowing an appeal on foreign law, since *ex hypothesi* the court cannot give a definitive or authoritative ruling on such matters. The courts have refused to grant leave to appeal on questions of foreign law, but attempts are still made and it would be desirable to put the matter beyond doubt.

388. The definition was moved to this Clause. It had, of course, to accommodate the fact that the Bill is expressed to apply to Northern Ireland as well as England and Wales. However the present definition, while it does this, also seems to indicate that where the seat of the arbitration is in neither of these places, the meaning of "question of law" is not confined to questions of (respectively) English law or the law of Northern Ireland. We would suggest that the definition be amended, so that "question of law" means a question of law of England and Wales where the application for leave to appeal is made to a court in England and Wales, and a question of the law of Northern Ireland, where an application for leave to appeal is made to a Court in Northern Ireland.

Clause 85   Domestic Arbitration Agreements

389. It has been pointed out to us that the way "domestic arbitration agreements" is defined (which is taken from the existing legislation) means that agreements made by sovereign states which incorporate an arbitration clause fall into this category. We are sure that this was not the intention, so that if the distinction between domestic and non-domestic arbitrations is to remain, the opportunity should be taken to correct this anomaly.   A2–102

Clause 95   Appointment of Judges as Arbitrators

390. For the reasons set out in our discussion of this Clause in Chapter 1, we recommend that this provision be extended to judges generally.   A2–103

Clauses 96–100   Statutory Arbitrations

391. Although the application of Part 1 to statutory arbitrations is not part of our remit, we note that during the Second Reading Lord Lester suggested that it might be a requirement of European law in cases of compulsory arbitration that the arbitrators should be independent as well as impartial. We can offer no view on this point, but if it is felt appropriate to include any such requirement in the context of statutory arbitrations, great care should be taken to make clear that this requirement has no application to private or other consensual arbitrations, so as to avoid any risk of this concept being imported into other cases. This, for the reasons already given, would in our view be most damaging. We understand that Lord Lester shares our view that a requirement of independence for private or other consensual arbitrations is neither necessary nor desirable.   A2–104

Clause 103   New York Convention Awards

392. For the reasons set out in our discussion in Chapter 3, this Clause should be amended so as to cross-refer to the definition of writing to be found in Part I of the Bill, and should also incorporate the recommendation that an award should be treated as made at the seat of the arbitration, regardless of where it was signed, despatched or delivered to any of the parties.   A2–105

Clause 107   Saving for Other Bases of Recognition or Enforcement

A2–106   393. It has been pointed out that, as drafted, this Clause may not save enforcement under Part II of the 1950 Act. This is a matter for Parliamentary Counsel to consider.

CHAPTER 7

CONCLUSIONS

A2–107   394. The Arbitration Bill and this Report are the result of a long and wide-ranging process of consultation with interested parties, probably the most comprehensive for any Bill of this kind. Our recommendations are based on the many responses that we have received as well as our own researches and discussions. In a number of cases, of course, we have had to make decisions on matters where more than one point of view has been expressed. What we should emphasize, however, is that all were agreed that it is high time we had new legislation, to the extent that many people have stated to us that for this reason they were not disposed to delay progress by stubbornly insisting on their point of view on particular points; and have demonstrated that this is the case by being ready and willing to reach compromise solutions. We are convinced (as all are) that further delay will do grave and probably irretrievable damage to the cause of arbitration in this country, thus damaging our valuable international reputation as well as the promotion here of this form of dispute resolution.

395. We have attempted to produce a draft which can be read, understood and applied by everyone, not just lawyers learned in this branch of our law. Thus our aim has been to make the text "user-friendly" and the rules it contains clear and readily comprehensible, so that arbitration is available to all who wish to use it. This has not been an easy task, since in the nature of things this form of dispute resolution raises highly complex and sophisticated matters. We have attempted it, however, in the hope that our efforts will not only encourage and promote arbitration, but also help to achieve what we believe to be the true object of this form of dispute resolution, namely (in the words of Clause 1 of the Bill itself) to obtain the fair resolution of disputes by an impartial tribunal without unnecessary delay or expense.

SUPPLEMENTARY REPORT ON THE ARBITRATION ACT 1996

Chairman
The Rt Hon Lord Justice Saville

January 1997

Supplement
to
The DAC Report on the Arbitration Bill, of February 1996

CONTENTS

CHAPTER 1

INTRODUCTION

1. In our Report of February 1996 we discussed the provisions of the Arbitration Bill as introduced in the House of Lords in December 1995. In Chapter 6 of that Report we   A2–108

set out some recommendations for changes to some of the provisions of the Bill, having considered the speeches made in the House of Lords on the Second Reading and some comments and suggestions from others; and having also carried out our own re-examination of the Bill. This Report discusses the changes that were made to the Bill during its passage through Parliament and thus the differences between that Bill and the Arbitration Act 1996, which received the Royal Assent on 17 June 1996. All these changes were recommended by the Committee, though some differ from or are in addition to the suggestions originally made in Chapter 6. Not all the changes suggested in Chapter 6 were adopted, but again this met with the approval of the Committee, after yet further reflection and consideration of comments and suggestions made to us.

2. Certain decisions were also taken by the DAC after the Act received Royal Assent, with respect to the commencement of its provisions. These are also discussed with respect to the particular sections affected, and in the context of the transitional provisions.

3. This Supplementary Report is to be read in conjunction with our Report of February 1996. The numbering of sections corresponds to the Act in its final form. As several sections were added to the Bill during its passage through Parliament, some of the references are slightly different from those in Chapter 6 of our February 1996 Report.

4. The new Order 73 of the Rules of the Supreme Court, together with the new Allocation Order (which stipulates the Courts to which arbitration applications may be made) have been included in Appendix A to this Report, together with a short commentary. The new Order 73 has been completely recast in order to reflect the changes brought about by the Act and to simplify the procedure for Court applications concerning arbitration. Although drafted in consultation with some members of the DAC, the new rules were not within the latter's remit, and are therefore included here simply for ease of reference.

5. By the Arbitration Act (Commencement No. 1) Order 1996 (S.I. 1996 No. 3146 (C. 96)), the Act (with the qualifications set out in that Order) comes into force on 31st January 1997. This Order also contains transitional provisions. The Order is reproduced in Appendix B, together with a short commentary.

CHAPTER 2

PART I OF THE ACT

Section 2   Scope of Application

A2–109   6.   Clause 2 of the Bill as introduced in the House of Lords in December 1995, read as follows:

> "2.–(1) The provisions of this Part apply where the law of England and Wales or Northern Ireland is applicable, or the powers of the court are exercisable, in accordance with the rules of the conflict of laws.

(2) They apply, in particular—

    (a) to matters relating to or governed by the arbitration agreement, where the applicable law is the law of England and Wales or Northern Ireland; and

    (b) to matters governed by the law applicable to the arbitral proceedings, where the seat of the arbitration is in England and Wales or Northern Ireland.

(3) The following provisions apply whatever the law applicable to the arbitration agreement or the arbitral proceedings—

    (a) sections 9 to 11 (stay of legal proceedings);

    (b) section 43 (securing the attendance of witnesses) and section 44 (court powers exercisable in support of arbitral proceedings); and

    (c) section 66 (enforcement of arbitral awards).

(4) The court may refuse to exercise any power conferred by this Part if, in the opinion of the court, the fact that the seat of the arbitration is outside England and Wales or Northern Ireland, or that when designated or determined the seat is likely to be outside England and Wales or Northern Ireland, makes it inappropriate to exercise that power."

7.   This provision was explained at paragraphs 23 to 25 of our Report of February 1996. The intention was to set out a clear statement identifying the scope of application of the Act, without attempting to codify any rules of the conflict of laws. The basic elements of this clause, as originally drafted, may be summarised as follows:

    i. Clause 2(1) simply provided that the Act applies wherever English law is found to be applicable to an arbitration, or where the powers of the English court are exercisable in relation to an arbitration. Whether or not English law is applicable, and whether or not the powers of the English court are exercisable, are both matters to be determined by reference to appropriate rules of the conflict of laws, which are to be found elsewhere.

    ii. Clause 2(2), as originally drafted, further refined this basic principle by recognising that different elements in an arbitration may well be governed by different laws. The law governing the merits of the dispute (*e.g.* a choice of law clause in a contract) may not necessarily govern the arbitration clause itself, as the latter constitutes a separate agreement. Similarly, the law governing the procedure of the arbitration may well be a different law from that governing the merits of the dispute. Consequently, if the arbitration agreement was governed by English law, those provisions in the Act which concern arbitration agreements would apply (Clause 2(2)(a)). Similarly, if the seat of the arbitration was in England and Wales or Northern Ireland, those parts of the Act which concern the arbitral procedure (as distinct from matters of substance) would apply (Clause 2(2)(b)).

This further refinement was necessary in order to avoid the danger that all the provisions of Part I of the Act would be imported if English law is found to govern one particular aspect of an arbitration. For example, an arbitration may have a French seat, with French law governing the procedure, but English law governing the arbitration agreement. In such a situation, only those provisions of the Act which concern arbitration agreements should apply. It would be quite wrong to apply provisions of the Act which concern arbitral procedure, as this would be governed by French law. Indeed, if this were not the case, a choice of English law to govern an arbitration agreement would entitle a party to invoke the jurisdiction of the English court wherever the seat of the arbitration might be, thereby endowing the English court with an unacceptable extra-territorial jurisdiction.

   iii. The remaining parts of the original Clause 2 made specific provision for the New York Convention (Clause 2(3)(a) and (b)—stays of legal proceedings and the enforcement of awards) and enacted section 25 of the Civil Jurisdiction and Judgments Act 1982 (Clause 2(3)(b)—powers in support of foreign arbitrations).

8.   In Chapter 6 of our February 1996 Report, at paragraph 357, we recommended that the original Clause 2(2)(a) be slightly amended in order to make clear that the applicable law referred to there was the law applicable to the arbitration agreement, rather than the law applicable to the substantive agreement.

9.   Following the introduction of the Bill into Parliament, we had the benefit of further detailed discussions with a number of leading arbitration experts from abroad, and took the opportunity of reconsidering this provision. It is fair to say that whilst there was unanimous support for the inclusion of such a provision identifying the scope of the Act, there was considerable disquiet as to the clause as drafted. It was felt that the provision was sound in principle, but unworkable in practice, for the following reasons:

   i. The clause was complicated and extremely difficult to understand. To this end, it appeared to defeat its own object.

   ii. In order to apply Clause 2(2), it was necessary to be able to identify all those provisions of the Act which concerned the arbitration agreement, as distinct from all those that concerned the arbitral procedure. As explained above, if for example English law governed the arbitration agreement, but not the arbitral procedure, by virtue of Clause 2(2) only those provisions in the Act which concerned the arbitration agreement (as opposed to the arbitral procedure) would apply. The provisions of the Act had therefore to be individually characterised and separated in this way.

However, the original clause made no attempt to characterise each provision of the Act, precisely because this had proved an extremely difficult and complex exercise. Many provisions concern both arbitration agreements and arbitral procedure, and there appeared to be a divergence of view with respect to many others.

   iii. There was a feeling amongst certain foreign experts that the original clause gave the wrong impression, in that it appeared to endow the English court with inappropriate extra-territorial powers, when this was clearly not intended.

10.   In the light of these difficulties, the DAC decided to recommend recasting the whole provision in a different form that would be far easier to understand and that would be entirely workable in practice. The policy behind the section, however, was not materially altered. The final section 2 provides a clear and simple scheme, which was welcomed by all those who had originally expressed concerns.

11.   Section 2(1) states the basic rule: Part I of the Act applies to arbitrations which have their seat in England and Wales or Northern Ireland. The concept of a "seat" was referred to in our February 1996 Report, and is defined in section 3 of the Act. The seat of an arbitration refers to its legal place, as opposed to its geographical location.

It is, of course, perfectly possible to conduct an arbitration with an English seat at any convenient location, whether in England or abroad.

12. If the seat of an arbitration is in England and Wales or Northern Ireland, the arbitration will be governed by this Act. If, however, a foreign law has been chosen to govern any particular aspect of the arbitration, such as the arbitral procedure or the arbitration agreement, or is otherwise applicable to any such aspect, this is catered for by section 4(5). Therefore, reference may be made to this Act in the first instance, and then back to another law with respect to a specific issue. Whilst a process of characterisation may still have to be done, the combination of section 2 and section 4(5) avoids the dangers that:

— a choice of English law with respect to one part of an arbitration will import other parts of the Act that concern other aspects of the arbitration;

— a choice of England as the seat of the arbitration will necessarily entail the imposition of every provision of the Act.

13. Sections 2(2) to (5) set out a series of deviations from the basic rule in section 2(1).

14. Section 2(2) caters for the New York Convention. Under the terms of this Convention, the English courts are obliged to recognise and enforce foreign arbitration agreements and foreign arbitral awards. Sections 9 to 11 (stays of legal proceedings, etc.) and section 66 (enforcement) could not, therefore, be restricted to arbitrations with a seat in England and Wales or Northern Ireland. These particular sections therefore apply even if the seat of an arbitration is abroad. Equally, these sections will apply if no seat has been designated or determined.

15. Section 2(3) extends the power of the court to grant interim relief in support of arbitrations with a foreign seat, thereby giving effect to section 25 of the Civil Jurisdiction and Judgments Act 1982, as was intended by the original Clause 2(3)(b). The power of the court to exercise these powers is restricted in the last part of this section to appropriate cases. There may well be situations in which it would be quite wrong for an English court to make an interim order in support of a foreign arbitration, where this would result in a possible conflict with another jurisdiction.

16. Section 2(4) deals with those cases where a seat has still to be designated or determined, but where recourse to the court is necessary in the meantime. For example, an arbitration agreement may provide that the tribunal, once constituted, will designate the seat of the arbitration. The agreement may also provide that any arbitration must be commenced within a specified time period. If that time period is exceeded, could a party make an application to the English Court pursuant to section 12 of the Act for an Order extending time for the commencement of proceedings (*e.g.* in order that a seat may be designated)? See, *e.g. International Tank & Pipe S.A.K. v. Kuwait Aviation Fuelling Co. K.S.C.* [1975] Q.B. 224 (CA). Clearly this would not be possible under section 2(1), as long as the arbitration was without an English or Northern Irish seat. It was our view, however, that the English court should be able to exercise supportive powers if there is a sufficient connection with England and Wales or Northern Ireland such that this is appropriate (*i.e.* the requirement in section 2(4)(b)), and if there will be no clash with a foreign jurisdiction. For example, there will be cases where it is extremely likely that once a seat is designated, that seat will be England and Wales or Northern Ireland.

17.   Section 2(4) therefore gives the English court powers where that court is satisfied, as a matter of English law, that the arbitration in question does not have a seat elsewhere. As long as there is no seat elsewhere, there could be no possible conflict with any other jurisdiction.

18.   Both sections 2(3) and 2(4) are based on a very clear policy: the English court should have effective powers to support an actual or anticipated arbitration that does not fall within section 2(1). However, such powers should not be used where any other foreign court is already, or is likely to be, seized of the matter, or where the exercise of such powers would produce a clash with any other more appropriate forum.

19.   Section 2(5) provides that section 7 (separability) and section 8 (death of a party) apply whenever the law applicable to an arbitration agreement is English law, even if the seat of the arbitration is abroad. Without this provision, reference would have to be made to the old English common law with respect to separability and the effect of death in every arbitration where the arbitration agreement is governed by English law, but the seat is not in England and Wales or Northern Ireland, such as to be within section 2(1). This would be an absurd result.

Section 7   Separability of Arbitration Agreement

A2–110   20.   As we said in Chapter 6, we suggested that the words "(whether or not in writing)" be inserted after the words "another agreement" in view of the definition of "agreement" in what is now section 5, in order to preclude any argument that section 7 only applies where the other agreement is in writing. This amendment was duly made.

Section 14(5)   Commencement of Arbitral Proceedings

A2–111   21.   Parliamentary Counsel considered that it was not necessary to make the amendment suggested in paragraph 359 of Chapter 6 and we accepted his advice.

Section 16(6)(b) and Section 21(4)

A2–112   22.   The Bill used the word "any" after a negative which could thus be read as meaning "all". This was not intended. We suggested a form of wording in paragraph 360 of Chapter 6 but were persuaded that a neater solution was to replace "any" with "a" and this was done.

Section 24(4)   Power of Court to Remove Arbitrator

A2–113   23.   In paragraph 361 of Chapter 6, we drew attention to the fact that the immunity of an arbitrator, under what is now section 29, did not extend to protect an arbitrator from the consequences of resigning, though some protection is available under what is now section 25(3). This we contrasted with what is now section 24, since an arbitrator removed by the court still enjoyed the section 29 immunity. We thought that this was anomalous and that the court should be given a discretionary power to make such order as it thought fit with regard to the immunity of an arbitrator it removed.

24.   This suggestion was not adopted. After further consideration we concluded that the anomaly was more apparent than real and that the suggestion would undermine the reasons for providing arbitrators with the immunity expressed in section 29. As will be seen from paragraph 362 of Chapter 6, we were against adopting the same suggestion when the parties agreed to remove an arbitrator under what is now section 23. What it seemed to us would be likely to happen if our original suggestion were adopted is that the parties, instead of privately agreeing to remove an arbitrator, would

instead apply to the court in the hope that the immunity would be wholly or partially removed. This seemed to us to be undesirable.

25. It should be remembered, of course, that while an arbitrator retains his immunity if removed by the court, what is now section 24(4) does give the court the power to make orders about his fees and expenses, including those already paid.

Section 25(2) Resignation of Arbitrator
26. At paragraph 363 of Chapter 6 we noted that the words "in writing" appeared,   **A2–114** though by virtue of section 5(1) this was unnecessary. These words were duly removed by amendment.

Section 32, Section 45 and Section 69
27. The Bill used the words "unless the court certifies". These were changed by   **A2–115** amendment to "which shall not be given unless the court considers". This amendment was made to make clear that where an appeal is desired from a decision of the court, leave must be obtained from that court itself, and will always be required. Leave may not be obtained from the Court of Appeal. As originally drafted, the incorrect impression was given that leave of the court may not be necessary where that court certified the issue as being one of general importance or one which for some other special reason should be considered by the Court of Appeal.

Section 38(3) Security for Costs
28. The power for arbitrators to order security for costs was included in the Bill for the   **A2–116** reasons set out at paragraphs 189 to 199 of our February 1996 Report. In the Bill as introduced, we included a provision that the arbitral tribunal should apply the same principles as the court in exercising this power. This was an attempt to meet the concerns of those who considered that since under the existing law arbitrators had no power to order security (unless the parties had expressly agreed to confer such a power), there was a need to set out some principles to guide arbitrators. However, as we explained a paragraphs 364 to 370 of Chapter 6, we concluded in the end that this was not a good idea and that it would be better to amend this part of the Bill, by deleting the references to court principles and by making clear that the fact that a claimant or counter-claimant came from abroad was not a ground for ordering security. Our suggestions were adopted. We proposed a specific amendment, but Parliamentary Counsel improved upon it, in particular by not using the word "only" since this might enable it to be argued that the fact that the claimant or counter-claimant came from abroad could be taken into account so long as there were other supporting factors as well. This, of course, was not our intention.

29. It should also be noted that the Bill as introduced used the word "party" in relation to orders for security for costs. This did not matter so long as there was a reference to court principles, but once this was deleted, it was necessary to change this to "claimant", since it was not our intention to give arbitral tribunals the power to order respondents to provide security. Section 82 defines claimant as including counter-claimant.

Section 46(1)(b) "Equity Clauses"
30. Whilst the provisions of Part I of the Act apply to arbitrations commenced after the   **A2–117** Act comes into force, regardless of when the arbitration agreement was made (by virtue of section 84), strong representations were made to the DAC that section

46(1)(b) should be commenced differently—in such a way as to preserve the existing law on the validity of "equity clauses" with respect to arbitration agreements that already exist and were made before the Act comes into force. Many existing contracts contain standard clauses which read as if they are "equity clauses", but which have been interpreted differently by the courts. This is the case, for example, with so-called "honourable engagement" clauses in reinsurance treaties. It was thought that if section 46(1)(b) were to apply to existing arbitration agreements, this would entail a retrospective substantive change in the meaning and effect of existing contracts, different from that which the contracting parties would have contemplated at the time of contracting. The DAC agreed with this view, and recommended that section 46(1)(b) should not apply to arbitration agreements that were made before the Act comes into force. Existing case law on the interpretation and effect of "equity clauses" will therefore continue to apply to such agreements. Transitional provisions have been put in place accordingly (see Appendix B).

Section 57   Correction of Award or Additional Award

A2–118   31.   A minor drafting change was made to section 57(3)(b).

Section 66   Enforcement of Award

A2–119   32.   In paragraphs 371 to 378 of Chapter 6 we made various suggestions for changes to the provision as it then appeared in the Bill. We were concerned that we had not covered enough of the cases where leave to enforce an award could be refused. We also suggested that it should be made clear that the list was not a closed list. However, on further reflection we concluded that it would be preferable, instead of having a list which would have to expressed as not closed, to have no list at all; instead relying on the fact (as noted at paragraphs 373 and 374) that the opening words of the provision do not require the court to order enforcement, but only give it a discretion to do so. Thus what was subsection (3) of the Bill was deleted by amendment. However, it will be noted that in what is now section 81 it is made clear (by an amendment to the Bill as introduced) that any rule of law relating in particular to matters which are not capable of settlement by arbitration or to the refusal of recognition or enforcement of an arbitral award on the grounds of public policy continues to operate.

33.   The suggestion that there should be an express reference to an action on the award was adopted and this reference is now to be found in section 66(4) of the Act. This in turn meant that the reference to an action on an award in what is now section 81 was unnecessary and this latter reference was accordingly removed by amendment.

34.   In paragraph 378 of Chapter 6 we suggested that where the application was to enforce an agreed award, the court should be notified of that fact, which should also be recorded in any order for enforcement. Upon reflection, however, it seemed to us that such requirements would be better placed in the relevant Rules of Court, and this, we are informed, will be done.

Section 68   Challenging the Award: Serious Irregularity

A2–120   35.   In the Bill, one of the grounds for challenging an award was expressed as "uncertainty or ambiguity of the award". It was pointed out to us that this wording might encourage attempts to challenge an award under this provision on the grounds that the reasoning of the decision was uncertain or ambiguous. This was certainly not our intention. What we wanted to cover were cases where the result of the award was uncertain or ambiguous. Where the quality of the award was in question, there would only be recourse under the limited right to appeal under section 69. To make matters clear, this part of the section was amended and now reads "uncertainty or ambiguity as to the effect of the award".

Section 70   Challenge or Appeal: Supplementary Provisions

36.   In paragraph 380 of Chapter 6 we suggested that the power to order security or that the amount of the award be brought into court should be extended so as to apply to applications and appeals under what is now section 69, as well as what are now sections 67 and 68. This suggestion was adopted and the appropriate amendments made to section 70.   A2–121

37.   Subsection 70(6) (security for costs) was further amended in order to bring this provision into line with the amended section 38(3), which has been referred to above.

Section 74   Immunity of Arbitral Tribunals, etc.

38.   In paragraph 381 of Chapter 6 we suggested tightening the wording of subsection 2. This suggestion was adopted by inserting into this subsection after the word "liable" the words "by reason of having appointed or nominated him". Without this amendment it could have been suggested that an immunity existed even where, for example, an institution conspired with an arbitrator to act partially.   A2–122

Section 76   Service of Notices, etc.

39.   Some minor textual amendments were made to the Bill as introduced, in order to tie this provision with others concerning the giving of notices.   A2–123

Section 77   Powers of Court in Relation to Service of Documents

40.   What was subsection (5) of Clause 77 in the Bill as introduced was deleted on amendment as being unnecessary. The point was already covered by section 76(6).   A2–124

Section 79   Power of Court to Extend Time Limits Relating to Arbitral Proceedings

41.   In paragraph 382 of Chapter 6 we noted that this provision did not cover cases where the time stipulated was not one having effect in default of agreement between the parties, *e.g.* what is now section 70(3). We suggested an amendment to what is now section 79(1). This suggestion was not adopted, but the point was covered by adding the words "the extending or abridging of periods" to what is now section 80(5).   A2–125

Section 80

42.   The word "appeal" was added by amendment to this provision, so it would cover appeals as well as applications.   A2–126

43.   A minor change was also made to subsection (5) (insertion of the words "the extending or abridging of periods") in order to tie this provision in with relevant Rules of Court.

Section 81   Saving for Certain Matters Governed by Common Law

44.   In paragraphs 383 to 386 of Chapter 6 we made a number of suggestions. First we suggested a reference to privacy and confidentiality. This suggestion was not adopted,   A2–127

since we finally concluded (especially as the law on this topic is in a stage of development) that it would be better to have no express reference at all, and to rely instead as necessary on the general opening words of this section. The second suggestion (namely an express reference to whether a matter is capable of resolution by arbitration) was adopted and the words "matters which are not capable of settlement by arbitration" added by amendment. We also suggested changing the words "common law" in the title, but were persuaded that this was not really necessary.

Sections 82 to 83   Minor Definitions

A2–128   45.   In paragraphs 387 and 388 of Chapter 6 we raised a point of drafting on the definition of "question of law". This was dealt with by deleting the words "where the seat of the arbitration is" and inserting in their place the words "for a court".

46.   Further minor amendments were made to sections 82 and 83 in the light of the new section 105 that was added (meaning of "court").

CHAPTER 3

PART II OF THE ACT

Sections 85–87   Domestic Arbitration Agreements

A2–129   47.   In paragraphs 317 to 331 of our February 1996 Report, we set out the reasons why the rules governing domestic arbitration agreements had been grouped together in sections 85 to 87 of Part II of the Act, and our provisional view as to whether or not the distinction in English law between international and domestic arbitration should be maintained. In July 1996, the Department of Trade and Industry published a consultation document on the commencement of the Act in which, amongst other matters, views were sought on this issue. The majority of respondents were in favour of the abolition of this distinction, and the application of the international regime throughout (*i.e.* a mandatory stay of legal proceedings in all cases, and the ability to exclude the right to appeal on a point of law at any stage in all cases).

48.   At about the same time as this consultation document was published, the Court of Appeal upheld the decision of Waller J. in *Phillip Alexander Securities and Futures Limited v. Bamberger and others* (unreported: 8 May 1996 [Commercial Court]; 12 July 1996 [Court of Appeal]), in which it was held (in the context of the Consumer Arbitration Agreements Act 1988) that the distinction between international and domestic arbitration is incompatible with European Community law because it amounts to a restriction on the freedom to provide services contrary to Article 59 of the Treaty of Rome and/or unlawful discrimination contrary to Article 6.

49.   In the light of the responses to the consultation document, the decision of the Court of Appeal, and the factors we had originally set out in our February 1996 Report, the DAC has since decided that, as matters currently stand, there is no option but to

abolish this distinction. Indeed, on one view, in the light of the *Phillip Alexander* case, the distinction has already been removed from current English law. However, it is to be noted that (at the time of going to press) an application for leave to appeal the *Phillip Alexander* is pending before the House of Lords, and there remains the possibility that the question will be referred to the European Court.

50.   In these circumstances, sections 85 to 87 have not been brought into force by the Commencement Order.

Section 85

51.   In paragraph 389 of Chapter 6 we noted an anomaly in the definition of "domestic   **A2–130** arbitration agreement" and suggested that the opportunity should be taken to correct it. However, in view of the position with respect to the future of the distinction between domestic and non-domestic arbitration agreements, this suggestion was not adopted.

52.   Various other minor textual amendments were also made to this section, which now are of no consequence.

Section 88

53.   A minor textual amendment was made to this section, in order to reflect the   **A2–131** amendments made to the consumer provisions of the Act (the new sections 89 to 91).

Sections 89 to 91   Consumer Arbitration Agreements

54.   Clauses 89 to 93 of the Bill as introduced into Parliament reproduced the Consumer   **A2–132** Arbitration Agreements Act 1988. These provisions were removed by amendment, and replaced by what is now sections 89 to 91, which refer to the Unfair Terms in Consumer Contracts Regulations 1994 (implementing E.C. Council Directive 93/13 EEC). The consumer provisions of the Act were beyond the remit of the DAC, and are therefore not commented upon here. For an explanation of these amendments, reference should be made to Hansard at H.L. Vol. 571 No. 72 Cols 152–5 (2 April 1996).

Section 93   Appointment of Judges as Arbitrators

55.   Our suggestion in paragraph 390 of Chapter 6 was not adopted.   **A2–133**

Sections 94–98   Statutory Arbitrations

56.   The issue that we noted at paragraph 391 of Chapter 6 concerning the requirement   **A2–134** of "independence" in statutory (compulsory) arbitration was debated in the House of Lords (see Hansard H.L. Vol. 569 No. 51 Col. CWH 26–28 (28 February 1996)), but did not result in an amendment to the Bill.

57.   The words "or difference" were inserted in section 96(2) by way of tidying up.

CHAPTER 4

PART III OF THE ACT

Section 100(2)   New York Convention Awards

A2–135   58.   In paragraph 392 of Chapter 6, we recommended that this provision be amended so as to cross-refer to the definition of writing to be found in Part I of the Act, and also to incorporate our recommendation that an award be treated as made at the seat of the arbitration, regardless of where it was signed, despatched or delivered to any of the parties. This recommendation was adopted.

Section 101

A2–136   59.   A minor textual amendment was made to section 101(2), in order to refer to the new section 105, that was added.

Section 102   Evidence to be Produced

A2–137   60.   The wording of this provision was amended in order to bring it back into line with the wording of the New York Convention itself.

Section 104   Saving for Other Bases of Recognition or Enforcement

A2–138   61.   The concern recorded at paragraph 393 of Chapter 6 did not lead to any amendment.

CHAPTER 5

PART IV OF THE ACT

Section 105   Meaning of "the Court": Jurisdiction of High Court and County Court

A2–139   62.   This is a new section. It was added in order to confer order-making powers on the Lord Chancellor to allocate matters as between different courts, thereby providing for more flexibility than was provided for by existing rules. Reference should be made to the Allocation Order set out at Appendix B.

APPENDIX A

THE NEW RSC ORDER 73 & ALLOCATION ORDER

Introduction by His Hon. Judge Diamond Q.C.
Scope of the Order

63. The Order had to govern not only applications to the Court under the Arbitration Act 1996, but also applications under the Arbitration Acts 1950 to 1979, which continue to apply to arbitrations commenced before 31st January 1997, the date when, by virtue of the Arbitration Act 1996 (Commencement No. 1) Order 1996, the 1996 Act came into force. So as to cater for both classes of arbitration application, the new Order has been divided into three parts and a table has been inserted at the beginning of the Order to indicate to the user which part is appropriate, a matter which depends on the date when the relevant arbitration proceedings were commenced and the date of the application to the Court (see Chapter 7 of this Report). Part I is concerned with applications to the Court relating to arbitrations to which Part I of the 1996 Act applies. Part II of the Order preserves the procedure of the former Order 73 for arbitrations governed by the earlier statutes. Part III is concerned with all applications to enforce arbitration awards (save by action on the award), whether under the 1950, 1975 or 1996 Acts or under certain other enactments.   A2–140

The General Scheme of Part I

64. Part I of the new Order completes and puts flesh on the general scheme set out in the 1996 Act governing applications to the Court. For example the Act provides that in some instances notice of an application is to be given "to the other parties" and in others "to the other parties and to the tribunal". The Order provides how that notice is to be given. In the case of parties (rule 10(1)) this is to be done by making them respondents to the application and by effecting formal service of the proceedings upon them. In the case of arbitrators, notice of applications under sections 24, 28 and 56 of the Act must be given in a similar manner (rule 10(2)) but notice of all other applications to arbitrators may be given by sending the papers to them at their last known address "for information" (rule 10(3)). Similarly, the Order sets out the rights of parties and arbitrators who have been given notice of an application, to appear and be heard in the proceedings or, in the case of arbitrators who are given notice "for information", to make informal representations to the court or to appear at their option.   A2–141

Particular Features of Part I

65. While it was necessary for the Order to give some guidance as to whether arbitration applications should be heard in open court or in Chambers, it was considered that this was a matter which depended essentially on the particular circumstances of each   A2–142

application. One consideration is the privacy of the arbitration process; another is whether the application raises points of principle which may be relevant in other cases. rules 15(2) and 15(3) set out a *prima facie* presumption that all arbitration applications shall be heard in Chambers save for the determination of a preliminary point of law under section 45 of the Act and an appeal on a question of law under section 69 which should both be heard in open court. The court may however order that any arbitration application be heard in open court or in Chambers depending on the particular circumstances.

66. Part I of the Order contains provisions designed to minimise the cost and delay involved in serving proceedings out of the jurisdiction. Where the respondent to the arbitration application is or was represented in the arbitration proceedings by a solicitor or other agent, the court may give leave (on an *ex parte* application) for the proceedings to be served on that solicitor or agent (rule 7(2)). While service out of the jurisdiction may still be necessary for the first application arising out of an arbitration or arbitration agreement, subsequent applications by either party can be served at the address for service within the jurisdiction given in the first application (rule 7(4)).

67. When deciding in which court to bring an arbitration application, the user needs to refer both to the High Court and County Courts (Allocation of Arbitration Proceedings) Order 1996 and also to rule 5 of the new Order 73. Rule 5 also contains provisions designed to ensure that, wherever the application is issued, the Commercial Court is able to preserve some consistency of approach both to the application and to the interpretation of Order 73. All arbitration applications brought in the Royal Courts of Justice are, for this reason, to be issued out of the Admiralty and Commercial Registry (rule 5(3)) so that the Commercial Court can act as a "filter" and the judge in charge of the Commercial Court may transfer them elsewhere if he thinks fit (rule 5(5)). In the case of applications brought in a Mercantile List or in the Central London County Court Business List, the control of the Commercial Court is preserved by provisions (rules 5(5) and 5(6)) that the application will be reviewed by the judge in charge of the list who, in consultation with the judge in charge of the Commercial Court, may transfer the application to the Commercial Court or to another court or List.

68. Rule 4(1) introduces a new form of originating process for applications governed by the 1996 Act, called simply an "arbitration application". This supersedes the two different forms of originating summons and the form of notice of motion used under the old procedure (which, however, is retained in Part II of the Order for applications governed by the old law).

General

A2–143 69. Though necessarily detailed, the new Order 73 is designed to be "user friendly". Users should be assisted by the table, to which reference has previously been made, indicating whether Part I or Part II of the Order is appropriate for a particular application. Similarly, rule 4 attempts to assist users by setting out in table form the most important statutory requirements that need to be satisfied and referred to in any arbitration application made under the 1996 Act.

APPENDIX B

TRANSITIONAL PROVISIONS

70. As we said in paragraph 315 of our February 1996 Report, we decided to use the precedent of previous arbitration statutes so that the new Act applies to arbitrations commenced after it came into force, whenever the arbitration agreement was made. The transitional provisions reflect this, but of course also have to deal with arbitration agreements and arbitrations which are to remain governed by the pre-existing law.

A2–144

71. Section 84(1) of the Act is a limiting provision, in that it stipulates that the Act does not apply to arbitrations commenced before the date on which Part I comes into force, and this is of course reflected in paragraph 2(a) of Schedule 2 to the Commencement No. 1 Order.

72. Section 84(2) is an enlarging provision, since it applies the Act to arbitrations commenced after Part I comes into force, even if the agreement is made at an earlier time.

73. The remaining transitional provisions in paragraph 2 of Schedule 2 to the Commencement No. 1 Order, deal with arbitration applications to the court. Paragraph 2(b) is designed to ensure that the pre-existing law applies to all applications to court made before Part I comes into force, and that this will remain the case even if an arbitration is commenced after Part I comes into force. Paragraph 2(c) is designed to ensure that applications relating to arbitral proceedings commenced before Part I comes into force are themselves governed by the pre-existing law so as to avoid one law applying to the arbitration proceedings and another to arbitration applications to the court.

74. Paragraph 4 of Schedule 2 deals with the question of "equity clauses" in arbitration agreements, which we deal with in paragraph 30 of this Report.

Appendix 3

Statutory Arbitration

A3–001   **Introduction.** An agreement is one of the features which distinguishes arbitration from litigation.[1] That statement must be qualified because arbitration can be imposed upon parties by statute.[2] The Acts of Parliament are not, however, consistent in their approach. Some make arbitration of particular disputes compulsory (i.e. not only is no agreement required but the parties have no choice); others make arbitration optional at the instance of one or both parties.

A3–002   **Definition.** Statutory arbitration is a creature of statute: it arises where the reference to arbitration derives from an enactment of Parliament other than the Arbitration Act 1996.[3] The source of the arbitration is not an agreement of the parties (the arbitration clause or agreement) but a s.of a particular Act of Parliament.[4] The main Pt of this book is devoted to contractual arbitration; this appendix comments on statutory arbitration.

A3–003   **The seat.** Irrespective of any agreement a statutory arbitration will be taken to have its seat in England and Wales.[5] The procedure for a statutory arbitration will thus derive from the statute giving rise to that particular arbitration or from the Arbitration Act 1996.[6]

A3–004   **Application of the Arbitration Act.** The provisions of Pt 1 of the Arbitration Act 1996 apply to every statutory arbitration "whether the enactment[7] was passed or made before or after the commencement of this Act, subject to the adaptations and exclusions

---

[1] This is a summary of para.1–002.

[2] Since the Human Rights Act 1998 came into force, it is doubtful whether a party to a statutory arbitration who has not voluntarily or freely agreed to it will effectively waive his right to a public hearing. See paras 1–038 and 1–039.

[3] Arbitration Act 1996, ss.94 to 98 inclusive. An arbitral tribunal appointed pursuant to other Acts of Parliament should be distinguished from a tribunal appointed under the Tribunal and Inquiries Act 1992. The latter conducts an inquiry on behalf of a Minister, who appoints the Chairman. Its procedure is regulated by rules made by the Lord Chancellor.

[4] For example, s.12 of the Agricultural Holdings Act 1986.

[5] Section 95(2) of the Arbitration Act 1996. The provision is mandatory.

[6] The procedure may be "ad hoc" but it derives from statute. In this context an arbitration scheme established pursuant to statute should be distinguished from a voluntary scheme. Both may operate in a particular industry (e.g. disputes concerning the supply of electricity—see paras A3–029 *et seq.*).

[7] "Enactment" includes an enactment contained in subordinate legislation—see s.94(3) of the Arbitration Act 1996. This includes rules made under an Act, e.g. County Court rules made under s.64(1) of the County Courts Act 1984.

specified in ss.95 to 98"[8] and subject to exclusion by or inconsistency with the enactment concerned.[9] Usually any exclusion will be expressed in the Act of Parliament giving rise to the statutory arbitration,[10] but even in the event of an inconsistency that Act will prevail over the provisions of Pt 1 of the Arbitration Act 1996.[11]

Where the provisions of Pt 1 of the Arbitration Act 1996 are not excluded they will apply to a statutory arbitration:

"as if the arbitration were pursuant to an arbitration agreement and as if the enactment were that agreement, and
as if the persons by and against whom a claim subject to arbitration in pursuance of the enactment may be or has been made were parties to that agreement."[12]

Thus, for the purposes of the Arbitration Act 1996 an arbitration pursuant to another statute is treated as if it were a contractual arbitration, subject to the adaptions and exclusions mentioned in the following paragraphs.[13]

The adaptions. In the case of a statutory arbitration Pt 1 of the Arbitration Act 1996   **A3–005** is adapted in three respects. First, an arbitral tribunal appointed pursuant to such an arbitration may decide "whether the enactment applies to the dispute in difference or question"; which means that the tribunal may determine its own jurisdiction.[14] Second, any consolidation of proceedings or concurrent hearings in proceedings of a statutory arbitration can only occur under the same enactment.[15] This provision limits the tribunal's jurisdiction to the particular statute even where the dispute also arises under another statute. Third, the tribunal must decide a dispute referred to statutory arbitration in accordance with the law chosen by the parties as applicable to the substance of the dispute.[16] Accordingly, a statutory arbitration must be decided in accordance with the law; it cannot be decided according to other considerations.[17]

The provisions excluded by the Arbitration Act. Three provisions of Pt 1   **A3–006** of the Arbitration Act 1996 are expressly excluded in respect of a statutory arbitration. First, the death of a party may discharge a statutory arbitration.[18] Personal representatives of a claimant cannot therefore pursue a claim in that arbitration, unless the particular Act authorises them to do so. Second, the court has no power under s.12 of the Arbitration

---

[8] Section 94(1) of the Arbitration Act 1996 which replaced s.31 of the Arbitration Act 1950. The adaptations and exclusions from Pt 1 of the Arbitration Act 1996 are mentioned in the following paras A3–005 to A3–006.

[9] See para.A3–007.

[10] See, for example, s.92 of the County Courts Act 1984 and paras A3–010 *et seq.*

[11] For example, the provision for stating a special case contained in the Industry Act 1975—see para.A3–028.

[12] Section 95(1) of the Arbitration Act 1996.

[13] Paragraphs A3–005 to A3–006.

[14] Section 30(1) of the Arbitration Act 1996 is adapted accordingly: see s.96(2) of that Act.

[15] Section 35 of the Arbitration Act 1996 is adapted accordingly: see s.96(3) of that Act.

[16] Section 46(1)(b) of the Arbitration Act 1996 cannot apply to a statutory arbitration—see s.96(4) of that Act.

[17] The other consideration referred to in s.46(1)(b) of the Act (e.g. equitable principles) are discussed in paras 4–141 *et seq.*

[18] Section 8 of the Arbitration Act 1996 is excluded by s.97(a), which replaced s.31(2) of the Arbitration Act 1950 as amended by s.8(2)(d) of the Arbitration Act 1975.

Act[19] to extend the time for bringing a statutory arbitration[20] although other time limits may be extended.[21] Third, a provision that an award is a condition precedent to the bringing of legal proceedings may not cease to have effect, in contrast with the consequences of certain court orders about contractual arbitrations subject to the same condition precedent.[22]

There were more exclusions under the former arbitration legislation[23] but the three mentioned above are all that are mentioned in the Arbitration Act 1996 although there is power to make further provision by regulation for "adapting or excluding any provision of Pt 1 in relation to statutory arbitrations in general or statutory arbitrations of any particular descriptions".[24]

A3–007 **Provisions that may be excluded by another enactment.** Another enactment may, in respect of a particular statutory arbitration, exclude all or some of Pt 1 of the Arbitration Act 1996, either expressly or because the Arbitration Act is "inconsistent with the provisions of the enactment concerned or with any rules or procedure authorised or recognised by it".[25] The scope of such an exclusion was considered in *Tustian v Johnston*[26] where the judge decided that the Agricultural Holdings Act 1986, excluded the whole of the previous arbitration legislation so that the Court had no discretion but to stay an action. As will be apparent however from the rest of this Appendix Pt 1 of the Arbitration Act 1996, as amended by ss.96 and 97, does apply to many statutory arbitrations.[27]

A3–008 **The scope and procedure of statutory arbitration.** The Acts of Parliament which refer disputes to arbitration extend across a huge range of subjects, including agriculture, financial services, friendly societies, industry, road traffic maintenance and utilities. The procedure for the conduct of statutory arbitrations is not specified in the Act giving rise to the statutory arbitration. Instead it is to be found in rules made pursuant to the Act concerned[28] or derived from Pt 1 of the Arbitration Act 1996. In some cases, however, parties are encouraged to resort to an arbitration agreement and contractual rules even though there is a clear statutory reference.[29]

A3–009 **The layout of this Appendix.** This appendix will proceed to identify and comment upon some statutory arbitrations by reference to various Acts of Parliament.[30] It

---

[19] Power may however be conferred on the Court by the Act giving rise to the particular statutory arbitration.

[20] Section 97(b) of the Act.

[21] Section 79 of the Arbitration Act 1996 is not excluded by s.97 of the Act.

[22] Sections 9(5), 10(2) and 71(4) of the Arbitraton Act 1996 are excluded for statutory arbitration by s.97(c) of that Act.

[23] Section 31(2) of the Arbitration Act 1950, which has been repealed by the Arbitration Act 1996, contained a longer list of exclusions.

[24] Section 98(1) of the Arbitration Act 1996.

[25] Section 94(2) of the Arbitration Act 1996, which replaced s.31(1) of the Arbitration Act 1950.

[26] [1993] 2 All E.R. 673.

[27] In the 20th edition of Russell on Arbitration it is said that there is a "widespread tendency to exclude the Arbitration Acts in modern statutes", p.14. That statement is not borne out by recent public Acts. Indeed, it seems that this is the exception rather than the rule.

[28] For example, the rules made under the Financial Services Act 1996.

[29] Utilities are increasingly adopting voluntary arbitration schemes for settlement of their disputes (see paras A3–026 *et seq.*).

[30] The Appendix does not attempt to list all references to statutory arbitration but it will proceed to identify some of the principal examples.

will then identify those institutions to whom the various statutes refer and offer some comments on their role.[31-32]

1. AGRICULTURE

Agriculture provides a good source of statutory arbitrations. Two important examples will be mentioned in the following paragraphs but there are others.[33]   **A3–010**

The Agricultural Holdings Act 1986 contains provisions which require certain disputes to be referred to arbitration[34] and the court retains jurisdiction to decide whether a transaction falls within the ambit of those provisions.[35] That Act also provides that other disputes must be referred if either party requests it.[36] The result is that arbitration is compulsory (at least if one party requests it) for the resolution of almost all disputes that may arise between landlord and tenant in respect of agricultural land.[37]   **A3–011**

The Agricultural Holdings Act provides that the arbitrator shall be a person appointed by agreement between the parties or, in default of agreement, by the President of the Royal Institution of Chartered Surveyors ("RICS"). The procedure is well described in *Muir Watt & Moss on Agricultural Holdings*.[38]   **A3–012**

The Agricultural Tenancies Act 1995 also contains provisions for statutory arbitration. Any dispute[39] between the landlord and tenant under a farm business tenancy must be determined by arbitration[40] under that Act unless the dispute concerned is referred to a third party for determination pursuant to an agreed provision in the tenancy agreement.[41] The arbitration will be conducted by a sole arbitrator appointed by the President of the RICS.[42]   **A3–013**

The provisions of Pt 1 of the Arbitration Act 1996,[43] with the adaptions and exclusions already mentioned, apply to an arbitration under the Agricultural Tenancies Act 1995.[44]   **A3–014**

2. FINANCIAL SERVICES

Arbitration schemes which had existed under the previous regulatory regime were replaced by the Financial Services and Markets Act 2000 into a single ombudsman   **A3–015**

[31-32] Paragraphs A3–038 *et seq.*

[33] For example, the Dairy Produce Quota Regulations 1989 (now 1993) which were made under the European Communities Act 1972 and were considered in *Holdcraft v Staffordshire County Council* [1994] 28 E.D. 131.

[34] For example, ss.2 and 12 of the Agricultural Holdings Act 1986.

[35] *Goldsack v Shore* [1950] 1 All E.R. 276, a decision based on the previous Agricultural Holdings Act.

[36] Section 6 of the 1986 Act is an example.

[37] See *Grammer v Lane* [1999] New Property Cases 149 for a case where the arbitrator was faced with an unresolved dispute as to the existence of a tenancy.

[38] See Ch.14 (14th edn), published by Sweet & Maxwell. See also Ch.21 of Scammell & Densham's *Law on Agricultural Holdings* (8th edn), published by Butterworths. Schedule 11 of the Agricultural Holdings Act 1986 has been repealed.

[39] There are three exceptions, see s.28(5) of the Agricultural Tenancies Act 1995.

[40] Section 28(1) of the Agricultural Tenancies Act 1995.

[41] Section 29 of the Agricultural Tenancies Act 1995.

[42] Section 30 of the Agricultural Tenancies Act 1995.

[43] See s.84(1) of the Agricultural Holdings Act 1986, as amended by the Arbitration Act 1996, Sch.3, para.45 which was construed in *Tustian v Johnston* [1993] 2 All E.R. 673.

[44] As a result of amendments made in 2006 to the Agricultural Holdings Act 1986, the provisions of Pt 1 of the Act also appear to apply to the 1986 Act.

scheme.[45] Arbitration schemes established by the Finance and Leasing Association and the Consumer Credit Trade Association continue to exist.[46]

3. FRIENDLY SOCIETIES

A3–016   The Friendly Societies Act 1992 provides for the determination by arbitration of certain disputes with a registered Friendly Society[47] or branch in the manner directed by the rules of that society or branch.[48] That provision is not intended to inhibit a Society from establishing internal procedures for the resolution of complaints or providing for their settlement by adjudication, but a registered Friendly Society cannot thereby prevent a member from referring a dispute to arbitration.[49] Pt 1 of the Arbitration Act 1996 applies to such an arbitration, subject to the adaptions and exclusions mentioned.

As an alternative to arbitration, the parties may agree that their dispute shall be determined by a county court.[50] If the matter is determined by arbitration, an application to enforce an award may be made to the county court.[51]

4. INDUSTRIAL RELATIONS

A3–017   The Trade Union and Labour Relations (Consolidation) Act 1992 provides for referring a trade dispute[52] to arbitration. Consent of all parties to the dispute is needed and any available procedure for settlement of the dispute should usually[53] be exhausted. Where however all parties do consent to a request for arbitration the Advisory, Conciliation and Arbitration Service ("ACAS") is empowered to refer "all or any of the matters to which the dispute relates for settlement to the arbitration of" the Central Arbitration Committee[54] or to one or more arbitrators.[55] In either event, Pt 1 of the Arbitration Act 1996 will not apply.[56]

---

[45] Part XVI and Sch.17.

[46] These are referred to in s.5 of the Banking Code established with effect from July 1, 1997 by the British Bankers' Association, the Building Societies Association and the Association for Payment Clearing Services.

[47] A dispute between a member and a Society which is not a registered Friendly Society may be decided in the manner directed by the rules of that Society which need not include arbitration: see s.76 of the Friendly Societies Act 1974.

[48] Section 80(1) of the Friendly Societies Act 1992. The disputes include those between a member or former member and a registered Friendly Society or branch.

[49] Section 81(1) of the Friendly Societies Act 1992.

[50] Section 80(5) of the Friendly Societies Act 1992.

[51] Section 80(2) of the Friendly Societies Act 1992.

[52] A trade dispute is defined in s.218 of the Trade Union and Labour Relations (Consolidation) Act 1992. This practice of referring industrial disputes in essential services to arbitration is a practice which has also been adopted in other common law jurisdictions. See for example in Belize, the Settlement of Disputes in Essential Services Act (Cap. 298), available at *www.belizelaw.org*.

[53] ACAS has power to refer the matter to arbitration if all parties consent even though an available procedure has not been exhausted; s.212(3) of the Trade Union and Labour Relations (Consolidation) Act 1992.

[54] Section 212(1)(b) of the Trade Union and Labour Relations (Consolidation) Act 1992.

[55] Section 212(1)(a) of the Trade Union and Labour Relations (Consolidation) Act 1992.

[56] Section 212(5) and 263(6) of the Trade Union and Labour Relations (Consolidation) Act 1992.

Where the matter is referred to the Central Arbitration Committee, the Act provides for the Committee to determine its own procedure and for publication of its awards.[57] It sits as a committee of three. Where ACAS refers a trade dispute to an arbitral tribunal, that tribunal may decide upon its own procedure, but any award may only be published if ACAS so decides and all parties consent.[58] The overwhelming majority of ACAS arbitrations are heard by a single arbitrator.

A3–018

Employment disputes are decided not by arbitration but by an employment tribunal,[59] although industrial tribunals do make use of the conciliation services of ACAS.

A3–019

5. INDUSTRY

The Industry Act 1975[60] makes provision for arbitration in respect of vesting and compensation orders that may be made under s.20 of that Act in relation to the transfer of control of important manufacturing undertakings to non-residents. A certain formality attaches to the appointment of an arbitral tribunal appointed under that schedule,[61] and there is a requirement for the statement of a special case,[62] but no rules of procedure have yet been made in respect of this statutory arbitration.[63]

A3–020

Only a limited number of provisions of Pt 1 of the Arbitration Act 1996 apply to an arbitration under the Industry Act.[64]

A3–021

6. ROAD TRAFFIC AND CONSTRUCTION/MAINTENANCE

The Road Traffic Act 1991 and the New Roads and Street Works Act 1991 contain various provisions for arbitration of disputes. For example any matter which, under Pt III of the second Act is to be settled by arbitration, must be referred to a single arbitrator appointed by agreement between the parties concerned or, in default of agreement, by the President of the Institution of Civil Engineers.[65] An application to stay court proceedings was dismissed in *Road Management Services (AB) Plc v London Power Networks*[66] because the dispute did not fall within the scope of the statutory provision.[67]

A3–022

The provisions of Pt 1 of the Arbitration Act 1996, subject to the adaptions and exclusions mentioned, apply to an arbitration conducted under these two Acts.

A3–023

---

[57] Section 263(5) and 264 of the Trade Union and Labour Relations (Consolidation) Act 1992.
[58] Section 212(4)(b) of the Trade Union and Labour Relations (Consolidation) Act 1992.
[59] Employment Tribunals Act 1996.
[60] Schedule 3 to the Industry Act 1975.
[61] See Sch.3, paras 3 and 4.
[62] See para.15.
[63] See para.17 of that Schedule.
[64] The four matters are specified in para.14 of Sch.3 as amended by the Arbitration Act 1996, s.107(1) Sch.3, para.30.
[65] Section 99 of the New Road and Street Works Act 1991.
[66] [2003] B.L.R. 303.
[67] The relevant provision was s.96(3) of the New Roads and Street Works Act, 1991.

7. UTILITIES

(a) Coal

A3–024   Regulations[68] made under the Coal Industry Act 1994 and the Coal Mining Subsidence Act 1991 have established two schemes for the coal industry which provide for arbitration of certain disputes concerning subsidence affecting land.[69] One scheme relates to householders and the other is a general arbitration scheme.

A3–025   Details of the schemes, including the procedure to be followed, are set out in the schedules to the Regulations.

A3–026   The British Coal Corporation have arranged for the Chartered Institute of Arbitrators to operate the schemes with special cost provisions designed for householders.

(b) Electricity

A3–027   The Electricity Act 1989 contains several provisions for referring disputes to arbitration,[70] and Pt 1 of the Arbitration Act 1996, subject to the adaptions and exclusions mentioned, apply to such arbitrations.

A3–028   The Director General of Electricity Supply has power either to decide disputes himself or to refer them to an arbitrator. In the case of some disputes the Director determines the practice and procedure.[71] Other disputes are referred directly to an arbitrator, appointed in default of agreement, by the President of the Chartered Institute of Arbitrators in some cases, or by the Lord Chancellor in other cases.

A3–029   Since the establishment of the Electricity Arbitration Association, the use made of arbitration is very wide, ranging from National Power Plc to individual electricity consumers. The rules of arbitration, which are adopted by agreement, provide a flexible procedure that encourages the arbitrator to play an active role in the conduct of the proceedings.[72]

(c) Gas

A3–030   The Gas Act 1986 contains several provisions for arbitration.[73] Some disputes are required to be referred to a single arbitrator to be appointed by the parties or in default by the Gas and Electricity Markets Authority.[74]

Other disputes[75] may either be decided by the Authority or, if it thinks fit, be referred to an arbitrator appointed by it. In the latter event, the Authority may indicate the practice

---

[68] The Coal Mining Subsidence (Arbitration Schemes) Regulations 1994 (SI 2566).
[69] The regulations were the results of a review following the Waddilove Report in 1984 and the subsequent report of a Select Committee on Energy in 1990.
[70] For example, ss.23 and 44A.
[71] Those disputes are referred to in s.23 as arising out of ss.16 to 22 of the Electricity Act 1989.
[72] For example, r.5.3 of the Rules of Arbitration of the Electricity Arbitration Association.
[73] The Gas Act 1986 has been amended by the Competition and Service (Utilities) Act 1992, the Gas (Exempt Supplies) Act 1993, the Gas Act 1995 and the Utilities Act 2000.
[74] For example, a dispute over the opening up of a street or bridge by a public gas transporter: see s.9 and Sch.4 to the Gas Act 1986. The Gas and Electricity Markets Authority took over the functions of the Director General of Gas Supply (which was abolished by the Utilities Act 2000).
[75] Those between a gas supplier and tariff customer, for example, see s.27A of the Gas Act 1986.

and procedure to be followed in connection with the determination of the dispute.[76] In any event, Pt 1 of the Arbitration Act 1996, subject to the adaptions and exclusions mentioned, applies to these statutory arbitrations.

(d) Water

The Water Resources Act 1991,[77] the Water Industry Act 1994[78] and the Land Drainage Act 1991[79] and the Water Act 2003[80–81] all contain provisions for arbitration.   A3–031

Different wording is used throughout the Acts with regards to how disputes should be settled. There seems to be no good reason for those differences, although disputes about withholding of consent tend to be referred to arbitration. Other disputes may be determined by the minister.   A3–032

Part 1 of the Arbitration Act 1996, subject to the adaptions and exclusions mentioned, apply to all arbitrations arising under these Acts.   A3–033

(e) Telecommunications

The Communications Act 2003 provides that disputes about discrimination in fixing charges, billing disputes and complaints about deposits may be decided by the Director General of Telecommunications or be referred to an arbitrator appointed by him.   A3–034

Part 1 of the Arbitration Act 1996, subject to the adaptions and exclusions mentioned, apply to arbitrations arising under the Telecommunications Act 1984. The Chartered Institute of Arbitrators administers BT's arbitration scheme.   A3–035

8. INSTITUTIONS INVOLVED IN STATUTORY ARBITRATION

The statutory arbitrations identified above refer to a number of institutions. Some, like the Chartered Institute of Arbitrators, are involved in the arbitral process; others simply act as an appointing authority. Their role is not limited to statutory arbitration, but some observations on them follow.   A3–036

Advisory Conciliation and Arbitration Service. ACAS receives about 1,200 cases per year for conciliation (i.e. assisting parties to reach agreement). Of these, between 150 and 200 will then be referred to arbitration. These figures have been the same for about a decade.   A3–037

The ACAS annual report details how their work is divided up, but most of it involves pay disputes or disputes regarding terms and conditions of employment. There are certain principles by which ACAS arbitrations are conducted and these are stated in a short leaflet available from the ACAS head office.

---

[76] See s.27A(4) of the Gas Act 1986.
[77] Sections 108(6) and 110(4) of the Water Resources Act 1991.
[78] For example, ss.42(6), 44, 99(6), and 101 of the Water Industry Act, 1991.
[79] Section 23(5) of the Land Drainage Act, 1991.
[80–81] Section 569 of the Water Act 2003.

A3–038 **The Chartered Institute of Arbitrators.** The President appoints arbitrators, but this institution also provides rules for arbitration, conducts arbitration schemes and trains arbitrators.

The Chartered Institute has both standard arbitration rules and short form rules. In neither its rules nor its appointments does the Chartered Institute make a distinction between statutory arbitrations and contractual arbitrations.

Many requests to appoint an arbitrator come from utility-related disputes. For example, both the Telecom and the coal industries have schemes with the Chartered Institute under which the latter appoints arbitrators. Provision for arbitration is made in standard consumer contracts, and it is from here, rather than from any statute, that the authority of the Chartered Institute arises.

A3–039 **The Lord Chancellor's Department.** The Lord Chancellor is empowered to act as an appointing authority under various Acts, but he is rarely called upon to exercise that power.

A3–040 **The Institution of Civil Engineers.** The President of the ICE acts only as an appointing authority. The ICE maintains and publishes a list of arbitrators from which he makes his choice depending on the type of dispute. The ICE also provides its own arbitration procedure.

Only two or three cases each year are referred to the President under an Act of Parliament. The vast majority of cases arise from use of standard ICE contracts and the sub-contracts that go with them. These contain a dispute resolution clause which provides for all disputes to be resolved by an arbitral tribunal appointed by agreement between the parties, or in default of agreement, by the President of the ICE.

A3–041 **The Royal Institution of Chartered Surveyors.** The President of the RICS acts only as an appointing authority. Only a small number of disputes referred to the President of the RICS arise under statute. Most cases arise from commercial leases. There were 617 cases in 1996. Those disputes arose mainly under the Agricultural Holdings Act 1986, and involved rent reviews.

The RICS has two application forms for statutory arbitration; one for rent review disputes and another for other kinds of disputes.

A3–042 **Director General of Electricity Supply.** The office of Director General of Electricity Supply was established by the Electricity Act 1989. Before the Competition and Services (Utilities) Act 1992 came into force, the Director occasionally used his powers to appoint an arbitrator where there was a dispute about someone being required to give security to the Electricity Board. Since 1992 the scope for statutory appointments has increased, but disputes concerning electricity supply are invariably referred to the Electricity Arbitration Association.

A3–043 **The Gas and Electricity Markets Authority.** The Gas and Electricity Markets Authority was established by the Utilities Act 2000[82] and took over the functions

---

[82] Section 1.(3) of the Utilities Act 2000.

of the office of the Director General of Gas Supply which was abolished.[82a] As originally enacted, the Gas Act 1986 had few arbitration provisions, but the Competition and Service (Utilities) Act 1992 introduced a number of provisions for the determination of disputes between domestic customers and public gas transporters and gas suppliers. The Gas Consumers' Council also has the power to investigate some matters.[82b]

The most important provision deals with disputes involving domestic customers. The Secretary of State may, by regulations, make provision for billing disputes to be referred to the Authority, which regulations may give the Authority the power either to determine disputes itself or to appoint an arbitrator. Formal references to the Authority for arbitration are very rare. The Authority has recently entered into a Memorandum of Understanding with the Ombudsmen Service Ltd in relation to the Energy Supply Ombudsman Service, an alternative dispute resolution mechanism set up to resolve disputes arising from customers of the member companies of the Energy Supply Ombudsman Service.

9. CONCLUSION

Most statutes do not exclude the relevant provisions of the Arbitration Act 1996 but either make rules consistent with that Act or, more often, leave the arbitral tribunal or appointing authority to determine the procedure. There is little purpose in seeking an explanation for the inconsistencies in the various statutes. A few observations are however appropriate.   **A3–044**

The preferred appointing authority for disputes about whether consent to certain proposed works was unreasonably withheld by a public body, seems to be the President of the Institution of Civil Engineers. On the other hand the Chartered Institute of Arbitrators seems to be the favourite for consumer disputes.   **A3–045**

The arbitration procedures also vary; some may be dictated by the director responsible, as in the Gas Act; others follow the domestic practice of the appointing authority (e.g. the Chartered Institute of Arbitrators).   **A3–046**

Despite the replacement of the so called small claims arbitration[83] by the small claims track procedure[84] statutory arbitration continues under a variety of schemes. This appendix does not contain all references to statutory arbitration; there are a number of others.[85]   **A3–047**

[82a] The Office of Director General of Gas Supply was established by the Gas Act1986.

[82b] See, for example, s.32 of the Gas Act 1986.

[83] CCR Ord.19 was revoked in 2002.

[84] CPR Pt 27.

[85] A limited number of disputes are referred to arbitration under the Building Societies Act 1986, Sch.14 para.4 and under the Further and Higher Education Act 1992, Sch.5 para.4.

APPENDIX 4

COMPARISON BETWEEN THE ARBITRATION ACT 1996 AND THE UNCITRAL MODEL LAW ON INTERNATIONAL COMMERCIAL ARBITRATION ("MODEL LAW")

INTRODUCTION

A4–001   The Model Law was adopted by the United Nations Commission on International Trade Law ("UNCITRAL") on June 21, 1985.[1] It was the result of a comprehensive study into the various arbitration laws throughout the world and was intended to provide a model that would lead to greater uniformity. It was preceded by the Convention on the Recognition and Enforcement of Foreign Arbitral Awards (1958), better known as the New York Convention, which has been adopted by more than 140 States. Though not adopted so widely, the influence of the Model Law has been considerable. A number of countries have adopted the Model Law; others have amended their laws to take account of its provisions.[2]

A4–002   In the United Kingdom reports on the Model Law were published by two influential committees, the Department of Advisory Committee on Arbitration law ("the DAC")[3] and the Scottish Advisory Committee on Arbitration law ("the Scottish Committee").[4] In short the DAC advised that the Model Law should not be adopted as, or part of, the arbitration law of England and Wales, but the Scottish Committee advised that the Model Law should be adopted by Scotland. One justification for the first report, which is somewhat ironic, given the stated intention of the Model Law, was the differences between English and Scottish arbitration laws.[5]

A4–003   The DAC went on to advise, however, that there should be a new and improved Arbitration Act for England, Wales and Northern Ireland. In February 1994 a Consultation

---

[1] The Model Law is contained in United Nations document A/40/17, Annex 1. It should be distinguished from the UNCITRAL Rules of Arbitration, which consist of a standard set of procedural rules for the conduct of an arbitration, (e.g. like those of the ICC or the LCIA) rather than a Model Law for arbitration.

[2] By 2007, legislation based on the Model Law had been enacted in 50 countries and six States of the USA. Some of those countries did not adopt the Model Law but amended their laws to take account of its provisions.

[3] A new Arbitration Act ? The response of the Departmental Advisory Committee to the UNCITRAL Model Law on International Commercial Arbitration: HMSO 1989. Subsequent reports have been published by the DAC—see para.1–044.

[4] Departmental Advisory Committee on Arbitration Law and Scottish Advisory Committee on Arbitration Law. The UNCITRAL Model Law on International Commercial Arbitration: A Consultation Document: October 1987.

[5] 1990 Arbitration Int. 3.

paper on Draft Clauses and Schedules of an Arbitration Bill was published. The Consultation Paper contained the draft of an Arbitration Bill, on which comments were invited.[6] As a result of that consultation the DAC reconsidered the matter, the Bill was completely redrafted and a new report was issued.[7] In the explanatory memorandum it was said that the Bill, which has since been enacted[8]

" . . . reflects as far as possible the format and provisions of UNCITRAL Model Law on International Commerce Arbitration".[9]

Revisions to Arts 1, 2 A, 7, 17 and 35 of the Model Law were adopted in 2006 (and, as yet, may not be reflected in the arbitration laws of countries which previously adopted the Model Law).

A4–004

In view of its significance to the development of arbitration law in the United Kingdom and abroad, the provisions of the Model Law (as revised) have been reproduced in this appendix with comments on each article. The purpose of these comments is to indicate the similarities and the differences of the Model Law to English arbitration law. The 2006 revisions are noted in the footnotes. It should be noted that references to a Model Law jurisdiction could now refer to the Model Law either pre or post-amendment, although at present almost all so-called Model Law jurisdictions have based their law on the pre-amendment version.

THE UNCITRAL MODEL LAW ON INTERNATIONAL COMMERCIAL ARBITRATION (WITH COMMENTARY)

(Grateful acknowledgement is made to the United Nations Commission on International Trade Law for granting permission to reproduce this text from www.uncitral.org.)

CHAPTER I. GENERAL PROVISIONS

Article 1. Scope of Application*

(1) This Law applies to international commercial** arbitration, subject to any agreement in force between this State and any other State or States.

(2) The provisions of this Law, except Arts 8, 9, 17H, 17I, 17J[10], 35 and 36, apply only if the place of arbitration is in the territory of this State.

---

[6] Department of Trade and Industry. A Consultation Paper and Draft Clauses and Schedules of an Arbitration Bill February 1994: The quotation is taken from Pt III p.1.

[7] The DAC report: see abbreviations for the full title of this report.

[8] Arbitration Act 1996

[9] Explanatory memorandum to the Arbitration Bill ordered to be printed on December 18, 1995. In the DAC report on the Arbitration Bill dated February 1996 it was said that "very close regard was paid to the Model Law" and that the final draft owes "much to this model" (para.4).

[10] Articles 17H, 17I and 17J were added in 2006.

(3) An arbitration is international if:

    (a) the parties to an arbitration agreement have, at the time of the conclusion of that agreement, their places of business in different States; or

    (b) one of the following places is situated outside the State in which the parties have their place of business;

        (i) the place of arbitration if determined in, or pursuant to, the arbitration agreement;

        (ii) any place where a substantial part of the obligations of the commercial relationship is to be performed or the place with which the subject-matter of the dispute is most closely connected; or

    (c) the parties have expressly agreed that the subject-matter of the arbitration agreement relates to more than one country.

(4) For the purposes of para.(3) of this article:

    (a) if a party has more than one place of business, the place of business is that which has the closest relationship to the arbitration agreement;

    (b) if a party does not have a place of business, reference is to be made to his habitual residence.

(5) This Law shall not affect any other law of this State by virtue of which certain disputes may not be submitted to arbitration or may be submitted to arbitration only according to provisions other than those of this Law.

* Article headings are for reference purposes only and are not to be used for purposes of interpretation.

** The term "commercial" should be given a wide interpretation so as to cover matters arising from all relationships of a commercial nature, whether contractual or not. Relationships of a commercial nature include, but are not limited to, the following transactions: any trade transaction for the supply or exchange of goods or services; distribution agreement; commercial representation or agency; factoring; leasing; construction of works; consulting; engineering; licensing; investment; financing; banking; insurance; exploitation agreement of concession; joint venture and other forms of industrial or business co-operation; carriage of goods or passengers by air, sea, rail or road.

Commentary

A4–005   **International**—Part 1 of the Arbitration Act 1996 applies to all arbitrations where the seat of arbitration is in England and Wales or Northern Ireland (s.2(1)). For the purposes of English law it does not matter if the dispute is between two English parties over real property in England or if it is one where the parties and/or the subject matter is foreign. As a result of the decision not to bring into force ss.85 to 87 of the Arbitration Act 1996, (see para.2–004) there is no longer a distinction between domestic and non-domestic arbitrations.

Commercial—Arbitration is not limited to commercial disputes under English law. A4–006

Other agreements between States—The intention of this provision of the A4–007
Model Law is to give overriding effect to Conventions such as the New York Convention
and Washington Convention, which have been incorporated into English law: see paras
8–011 *et seq.*

Place of Arbitration—The strict territorial application of the Model Law differs A4–008
from English law which is more susceptible to the intention of the parties.

Arbitrability—According to the DAC report of 1989, the primary purpose of this A4–009
provision is to deal with "constitutional problems, which are of little, if any, importance in
England", but see paras 1–027 *et seq.*

Article 2. Definitions and rules of interpretation
For the purposes of this Law:

(a) "arbitration" means any arbitration whether or not administered by a permanent
arbitral institution;

(b) "arbitral tribunal" means a sole arbitrator or a panel of arbitrators;

(c) "court" means a body or organ of the judicial system of a State;

(d) where a provision of this Law, except Art.28, leaves the parties free to determine a
certain issue, such freedom includes the right of the parties to authorise a third
party, including an institution, to make that determination;

(e) where a provision of this Law refers to the fact that the parties have agreed or that
they may agree or in any other way refers to an agreement of the parties, such
agreement includes any arbitration rules referred to in that agreement;

(f) where a provision of this Law, other than in Arts 25(a) and 32(2)(a), refers to a claim,
it also applies to a counter-claim, and where it refers to a defence, it also applies to
a defence to such counter-claim.

Commentary
Arbitration is not defined in the Arbitration Act 1996, (see para.1–002) but it is apparent A4–010
from the Act that the arbitral tribunal may not only include a sole arbitrator and a panel of
arbitrators but also an umpire. The court, unless its context otherwise requires, is said to
mean the High Court or a county court (see s.82). Appointing authorities (para.(d) above)
and arbitration rules (para.(e)) which may include a provision on the lines of para.(f) are
also well known to English law. (see para.3–045).

Article 2A. International origin and general principles
(1) In the interpretation of this Law, regard is to be had to its international origin and
to the need to promote uniformity in its application and the observance of good
faith.

(2) Questions concerning matters governed by this Law which are not expressly settled
      in it are to be settled in conformity with the general principles on which this Law
      is based.[11]

Commentary

For obvious reasons, no such provision is reflected in the Arbitration Act 1996.

Article 3. Receipt of written communications

(1) Unless otherwise agreed by the parties:

(a) any written communication is deemed to have been received if it is delivered to
      the addressee personally or if it is delivered at his place of business, habitual
      residence or mailing address; if none of these can be found after making a
      reasonable inquiry, a written communication is deemed to have been received if
      it is sent to the addressee's last-known place of business, habitual residence or
      mailing address by registered letter or any other means which provides a record
      of the attempt to deliver it;

(b) the communication is deemed to have been received on the day it is so deliv-
      ered.

(2) The provisions of this article do not apply to communications in court proceed-
      ings.

Commentary

A4–011   The Arbitration Act 1996 contains a similar provision (s.76). (See paras 5–033 and
5–034.)

Article 4. Waiver of right to object

A party who knows that any provision of this Law from which the parties may derogate
or any requirement under the arbitration agreement has not been complied with and yet
proceeds with the arbitration without stating his objection to such non-compliance without
undue delay or, if a time-limit is provided therefor, within such a period of time, shall be
deemed to have waived his right to object.

Commentary

A4–012   The Arbitration Act 1996 contains a similar provision (se.73). (See paras 7–105, 8–032
and 8–051.)

Article 5. Extent of Court Intervention

In matters governed by this Law, no court shall intervene except where so provided in
this Law.

Commentary

A4–013   Of all articles, this most clearly illustrates the tensions between international arbitration
and the national courts. Article 5 tries to limit court intervention to specific instances.

A4–014   The Arbitration Act 1996 states as a general principle that in matters governed by Pt 1
of the Act "the court should not intervene except as provided by this Part" (s.1(c)) and it

---

[11] Article 2A was added in 2006.

specifies those occasions when intervention may occur. The parties may contract out of some but not all of these occasions. (See s.4 and the list of mandatory provisions in Sch.1 and Chs 7 and 8.)

Article 6. Court or other authority for certain functions of arbitration assistance and supervision

The functions referred to in Arts 11(3), 11(4), 13(3), 14, 16(3) and 34(2) shall be performed by [Each State enacting this model law specifies the court, courts or, where referred to therein other authority competent to perform these functions.]

Commentary

The High Court or a county court may exercise the functions of assistance and supervision identified in these articles. (Arbitration Act 1996, s.82(1)), (see Chs 7 and 8.)

A4–015

CHAPTER II. ARBITRATION AGREEMENT

OPTION I

Article 7. Definition and form of arbitration agreement

(1) "Arbitration agreement" is an agreement by the parties to submit to arbitration all or certain disputes which have arisen or which may arise between them in respect of a defined legal relationship, whether contractual or not. An arbitration agreement may be in the form of an arbitration clause in a contract or in the form of a separate agreement.

(2) The arbitration agreement shall be in writing.

(3) An arbitration agreement is in writing if its content is recorded in any form, whether or not the arbitration agreement or contract has been concluded orally, by conduct, or by other means.

(4) The requirement that an arbitration agreement be in writing is met by an electronic communication if the information contained therein is accessible so as to be useable for subsequent reference; "electronic communication" means any communication that the parties make by means of data messages; "data message" means information generated, sent, received or stored by electronic, magnetic, optical or similar means, including, but not limited to, electronic data interchange (EDI), electronic mail, telegram, telex or telecopy.

(5) Furthermore, an arbitration agreement is in writing if it is contained in an exchange of statements of claim and defence in which the existence of an agreement is alleged by one party and not denied by the other.

(6) The reference in a contract to any document containing an arbitration clause constitutes an arbitration agreement in writing, provided that the reference is such as to make that clause part of the contract.

Option II

Article 7. Definition of arbitration agreement

"Arbitration agreement" is an agreement by the parties to submit to arbitration all or certain disputes which have arisen or which may arise between them in respect of a defined legal relationship, whether contractual or not.[12]

Commentary

A4–016   A somewhat broader definition of "arbitration agreement" appears in the Arbitration Act 1996, s.6 as that section contains no express restriction to a "defined legal relationship" which appears in both options for Article 7.

A4–017   Both the Article 7, Option 1 of the Model Law and the Arbitration Act 1996, s.6, require that an arbitration agreement be "written" or in writing. Article 7, Option 1 and the Arbitration Act 1996, s.5 recognise that the requirement of writing is to be broadly interpreted (the Model Law recognises that an arbitration agreement is in writing if "its content is recorded in any form" and the Arbitration Act 1996, s.5 notes only that it must be "evidenced in writing"). Article 7, Option 2 of the Model Law is, on its face, considerably broader, not requiring an arbitration agreement to be in writing. Oral arbitration agreements are recognised by English law, but they fall outside the scope of the Arbitration Act 1996—see paragraphs 2–045).

Article 8. Arbitration agreement and substantive claim before court

(1) A court before which an action is brought in a matter which is the subject of an arbitration agreement shall, if a party so requests not later than when submitting his first statement on the substance of the dispute, refer the parties to arbitration unless it finds that the agreement is null and void, inoperative or incapable of being performed.

(2) Where an action referred to in para.(1) of this article has been brought, arbitral proceedings may nevertheless be commenced or continued, and an award may be made, while the issue is pending before the court.

Commentary

A4–018   As a result of the decision not to bring into force ss.85 to 87 inclusive of the Arbitration Act 1996, an English court has no discretion but to stay the action brought in breach of a valid arbitration agreement, whether it be domestic or non-domestic (s.9). Thus, although

---

[12] The two options in Article 7 were added in 2006. Before the 2006 amendments, Article 7 read as follows: "Article 7. Definition and form of arbitration agreement

    (1) 'Arbitration agreement' is an agreement by the parties to submit to arbitration all or certain disputes which have arisen or which may arise between them in respect of a defined legal relationship, whether contractual or not. An arbitration agreement may be in the form of an arbitration clause in a contract or in the form of a separate agreement.

    (2) The arbitration agreement shall be in writing. An agreement is in writing if it is contained in a document signed by the parties or in an exchange of letters, telex, telegrams or other means of telecommunication which provide a record of the agreement, or in an exchange of statements of claim and defence in which the existence of an agreement is alleged by one party and not denied by another. The reference in a contract to a document containing an arbitration clause constitutes an arbitration agreement provided that the contract is in writing and the reference is such as to make that clause part of the contract."

there are some minor differences of definition, Art.8(1) of the Model Law reflects the English law position in respect of all arbitrations, (see paras 7–005 *et seq.*).

Article 8(2) of the Model Law is consistent with the Arbitration Act 1996, s.32(4) which unless otherwise agreed by the parties, authorises the arbitral tribunal to continue the arbitration proceedings and to make an award while an application to the court is pending in order to determine a question as to its substantive jurisdiction (see s.24(3) and para.7–031). **A4–019**

Article 9. Arbitration agreement and interim measures by court

It is not incompatible with an arbitration agreement for a party to request, before or during arbitral proceedings, from a court an interim measure of protection and for a court to grant such measure.

Commentary

This provision is also consistent with English law. Subject to certain restrictions, a party to an arbitration agreement can apply at any time to the court for a wide range of interim measures to preserve assets (e.g. a *Mareva* injunction) and to secure evidence. The Arbitration Act 1996, s.44 gives the court express power (unless otherwise agreed by the parties) to make orders, about the matters listed in s.44(2), but "only if and to the extent that" the arbitral tribunal or any institution agreed by the parties "has no power or is unable for the time being to act effectively" (s.44(5)). The court no longer has power to order disclosure or security for costs. (See paras 7–129 *et seq.*). **A4–020**

CHAPTER III. COMPOSITION OF ARBITRAL TRIBUNAL

Article 10. Number of arbitrators

(1) The parties are free to determine the number of arbitrators.

(2) Failing such determination, the number of arbitrators shall be three.

Commentary

The first paragraph of this article is consistent with English law but the second paragraph is not, for unless a contrary intention is expressed in the arbitration agreement (or in arbitration rules incorporated into that agreement) there will be a sole arbitrator (Arbitration Act 1996, s.15), (see paras 4–006 and 4–062). **A4–021**

As an aside, it is worth repeating here the observation made in the DAC report (1989), namely that the Model Law does not recognise the system of two arbitrators and an umpire, (contrast Arbitration Act 1996, s.15(2) and see para.4–009). **A4–022**

Article 11. Appointment of Arbitrators

(1) No person shall be precluded by reason of his nationality from acting as an arbitrator, unless otherwise agreed by the parties.

(2) The parties are free to agree on a procedure of appointing the arbitrator or arbitrators, subject to the provisions of paragraphs (4) and (5) of this article.

(3) Failing such agreement

(a) in an arbitration with 3 arbitrators, each party shall appoint one arbitrator, and the 2 arbitrators thus appointed shall appoint the third arbitrator; if a party fails to appoint the arbitrator within 30 days of receipt of a request to do so from the other party, or if the 2 arbitrators fail to agree on the third arbitrator within 30 days of their appointment, the appointment shall be made, upon request of a party, by the court or other authority specified in Art.6;

(b) in an arbitration with a sole arbitrator, if the parties are unable to agree on the arbitrator, he shall be appointed, upon request of a party, by the court or other authority specified in Art.6.

(4) Where, under an appointment procedure agreed upon by the parties,

(a) a party fails to act as required under such procedure, or

(b) the parties, or 2 arbitrators, are unable to reach an agreement expected of them under such procedure, or

(c) a third party, including an institution, fails to perform any function entrusted to it under such procedure,

any party may request the court or other authority specified in article 6 to take the necessary measure, unless the agreement on the appointment procedure provides other means for securing the appointment.

(5) A decision on a matter entrusted by para.(3) or (4) of this article to the court or other authority specified in Art.6 shall be subject to no appeal. The court or other authority, in appointing an arbitrator, shall have due regard to any qualifications required of the arbitrator by the agreement of the parties and to such considerations as are likely to secure the appointment of an independent and impartial arbitrator and, in the case of a sole or third arbitrator, shall take into account as well the advisability of appointing an arbitrator of a nationality other than those of the parties.

Commentary

A4–023   Although there is no express provision to this effect, English law does not impose any nationality restriction on arbitrators. There is no limitation on the parties' freedom to agree upon a procedure for the appointment of an arbitral tribunal (Arbitration Act 1996, s.16(1)), although if such an agreement breaks down (or if there is no agreement) the court will appoint one or more arbitrators upon the application of the parties (s.18). The court will also take account of any qualification requirement (e.g. a Q.C. or "individual with commercial expertise") required of an arbitrator (s.19), (see para.4–024).

A4–024   Where the arbitration agreement provides for the appointment of two arbitrators, one by each party, there is no equivalent in the Model Law to the provision contained in s.17 of the Arbitration Act 1996, whereby failure to appoint a second arbitrator may result in a party-appointed arbitrator becoming sole arbitrator contrary to the express terms of the arbitration agreement (see para.4–064).

Article 12. Grounds for Challenge

(1) When a person is approached in connection with his possible appointment as an arbitrator, he shall disclose any circumstances likely to give rise to justifiable doubts as to his impartiality or independence. An arbitrator, from the time of his appointment and throughout the arbitral proceedings, shall without delay disclose any such circumstances to the parties unless they have already been informed of them by him.

(2) An arbitrator may be challenged only if circumstances exist that give rise to justifiable doubts as to his impartiality or independence, or if he does not possess

qualifications agreed to by the parties. A party may challenge an arbitrator appointed by him, or in whose appointment he has participated, only for reasons of which he becomes aware after the appointment has been made.

Commentary

There is no provision for disclosure under English law (as opposed to arbitration rules) A4–025 equivalent to the first paragraph of this article. A party to arbitration proceedings may however, apply to the court to remove an arbitrator because "circumstances exist that give rise to justifiable doubts as to his impartiality" or because "he does not possess the qualifications required by the arbitration agreement" and for other grounds (Arbitration Act 1996, s.24, see paras 4–029 *et seq.*, 5–052 and 7–074 *et seq.*).

Article 13. Challenge procedure

(1) The parties are free to agree on a procedure for challenging an arbitrator, subject to the provisions of para.(3) of this article.

(2) Failing such agreement, a party who intends to challenge an arbitrator shall, within 15 days after becoming aware of the constitution of the arbitral tribunal or after becoming aware of any circumstances referred to in Art.12(2), send a written statement of the reasons for the challenge to the arbitral tribunal. Unless the challenged arbitrator withdraws from his office or the other party agrees to the challenge, the arbitral tribunal shall decide on the challenge.

(3) If a challenge under any procedure agreed upon by the parties or under the procedure of para.(2) of this article is not successful, the challenging party may request, within 30 days after having received notice of the decision rejecting the challenge, the court or other authority specified in Art.6 to decide on the challenge, which decision shall be subject to no appeal; while such a request is pending, the arbitral tribunal, including the challenged arbitrator, may continue the arbitral proceedings and make an award.

Commentary

Although not expressed in the same terms, there is a challenge procedure in the A4–026 Arbitration Act 1996 (s.24) which also recognises that the parties may agree on recourse to a third party or institution (e.g. to the London Court of International Arbitration—see Art.3 of the LCIA Rules of Arbitration). There is no time limit for applying to the court, although a party may in due course lose his right to challenge (s.73, see para.4–209).

Article 14. Failure or impossibility to act

(1) If an arbitrator becomes *de jure* or *de facto* unable to perform his functions or for other reasons fails to act without undue delay, his mandate terminates if he withdraws from his office or if the parties agree on the termination. Otherwise, if a controversy remains concerning any of these grounds, any party may request the court or other authority specified in Art.6 to decide on the termination of the mandate, which decision shall be subject to no appeal.

(2) If, under this article or Art.13(2), an arbitrator withdraws from his office or a party agrees to the termination of the mandate of an arbitrator, this does not imply acceptance of the validity of any ground referred to in this Article or Art.12(2).

Commentary

There is no provision in English law for the automatic termination of an arbitrator's A4–027 mandate if he fails to act. On the contrary, unless the parties agree otherwise, the authority of an arbitral tribunal once appointed is irrevocable except as provided by the Arbitration Act 1996, s.23. There is however a provision which empowers the court to remove an arbitrator in the circumstances described in Art.14(1) above, (i.e. s.24(1)) for refusal to act and for among other things undue delay) (see Ch.7).

Article 15. Appointment of substitute arbitrator

Where the mandate of an arbitrator terminates under Arts 13 or 14 or because of his withdrawal from office for any other reason or because of the revocation of his mandate by agreement of the parties or in any other case of termination of his mandate, a substitute arbitrator shall be appointed according to the rules that were applicable to the appointment of the arbitrator being replaced.

Commentary

A4–028   In the absence of an applicable arbitration rule or agreement by the parties the court is empowered to appoint a substitute arbitrator or umpire (the Arbitration Act 1996, s.18(3)(d), see para.7–094).

CHAPTER IV. JURISDICTION OF ARBITRAL TRIBUNAL

Article 16. Competence of arbitral tribunal to rule on its jurisdiction

(1) The arbitral tribunal may rule on its own jurisdiction, including any objections with respect to the existence or validity of the arbitration agreement. For that purpose, an arbitration clause which forms part of a contract shall be treated as an agreement independent of the other terms of the contract. A decision by the arbitral tribunal that the contract is null and void shall not entail ipso jure the invalidity of the arbitration clause.

(2) A plea that the arbitral tribunal does not have jurisdiction shall be raised not later than the submission of the statement of defence. A party is not precluded from raising such a plea by the fact that he has appointed, or participated in the appointment of, an arbitrator. A plea that the arbitral tribunal is exceeding the scope of its authority shall be raised as soon as the matter alleged to be beyond the scope of its authority is raised during the arbitral proceedings. The arbitral tribunal may, in either case, admit a later plea if it considers the delay justified.

(3) The arbitral tribunal may rule on a plea referred to in para.(2) of this article either as a preliminary question or in an award on the merits. If the arbitral tribunal rules as a preliminary question that it has jurisdiction, any party may request, within 30 days after having received notice of that ruling, the court specified in article 6 to decide the matter, which decision shall be subject to no appeal; while such a request is pending, the arbitral tribunal may continue the arbitral proceedings and make an award.

Commentary

A4–029   Unless otherwise agreed by the parties, the Arbitration Act 1996 provides for:

(a) the separability of the arbitration agreement from other terms of the contract (s.7);

(b) the arbitral tribunal ruling on its own substantive jurisdiction (s.30(1); and

(c) challenge of that ruling by "any available arbitral process of appeal or review or in accordance with the provisions" of Pt 1 of the Act (s.30(2).

The Arbitration Act 1996 (ss.31 and 32) contain similar but not identical provisions to those in Arts 16(2) and (3) above (see paras 2–049 *et seq.* and 7–097 *et seq.*).

CHAPTER IVA INTERIM MEASURES AND PRELIMINARY ORDERS

Section 1. Interim measures

Article 17. Power of arbitral tribunal to order interim measures

(1) Unless otherwise agreed by the parties, the arbitral tribunal may, at the request of a party, grant interim measures.

(2) An interim measure is any temporary measure, whether in the form of an award or in another form, by which, at any time prior to the issuance of the award by which the dispute is finally decided, the arbitral tribunal orders a party to:

(a) Maintain or restore the status quo pending determination of the dispute;

(b) Take action that would prevent, or refrain from taking acting that is likely to cause, current or imminent harm or prejudice to the arbitral process itself;

(c) Provide a means of preserving assets out of which a subsequent award may be satisfied; or

(d) Preserve evidence that may be relevant and material to the resolution of the dispute.[13]

Article 17A. Conditions for granting interim measures

(1) The party requesting an interim measure under Art.17, para.2(a), (b) and (c) shall satisfy the arbitral tribunal that:

(a) Harm not adequately reparable by an award of damages is likely to result if the measure is not ordered, and such harm substantially outweighs the harm that is likely to result to the party against whom the measure is directed if the measure is granted; and

(b) There is a reasonable possibility that the requesting party will succeed on the merits of the claim. The determination on this possibility shall not affect the discretion of the arbitral tribunal in making any subsequent determination.

(2) With regard to a request for an interim measure under Art.17, para.2(d), the requirements in para.1(a) and (b) of this article shall apply only to the extent the arbitral tribunal considers appropriate.

---

[13] The interim measures provisions were expanded considerably as a result of the 2006 amendments, with the amendment of Article 17 and the addition of Articles 17A to 17J. Article 17 previously read as follows: "Article 17. Power of arbitral tribunal to order interim measures.
  Unless otherwise agreed by the parties, the arbitral tribunal may, at the request of a party, order any party to take such interim measures of protection as the arbitral tribunal may consider necessary in respect of the subject-matter of the dispute. The arbitral tribunal may require any party to provide appropriate security in connection with such measure."

Section 2. Preliminary orders

Article 17B. Applications for preliminary orders and conditions for granting preliminary orders

(1) Unless otherwise agreed by the parties, a party may, without notice to any other party, make a request for an interim measure together with an application for a preliminary order directing a party not to frustrate the purpose of the interim measure requested.

(2) The arbitral tribunal may grant a preliminary order provided it considers that prior disclosure of the request for the interim measure to the party against whom it is directed risks frustrating the purpose of the measure.

(3) The conditions defined under Art.17A apply to any preliminary order, provided that the harm to be assessed under Art.17A, para.1(a), is the harm likely to result from the order being granted or not.

Article 17C. Specific regime for preliminary orders

(1) Immediately after the arbitral tribunal has made a determination in respect of an application for a preliminary order, the arbitral tribunal shall give notice to all parties of the request for the interim measure, the application for the preliminary order, the preliminary order, if any, and all other communications, including by indicating the content of any oral communication, between any party and the arbitral tribunal in relation thereto.

(2) At the same time, the arbitral tribunal shall give an opportunity to any party against whom a preliminary order is directed to present its case at the earliest practicable time.

(3) The arbitral tribunal shall decide promptly on any objection to the preliminary order.

(4) A preliminary order shall expire after twenty days from the date on which it was issued by the arbitral tribunal. However, the arbitral tribunal may issue an interim measure adopting or modifying the preliminary order, after the party against whom the preliminary order is directed has been given notice and an opportunity to present its case.

(5) A preliminary order shall be binding on the parties but shall not be subject to enforcement by a court. Such a preliminary order does not constitute an award.

Section 3. Provisions applicable to interim measures and preliminary orders

Article 17D. Modification, suspension, termination

The arbitral tribunal may modify, suspend or terminate an interim measure or a preliminary order it has granted, upon application of any party or, in exceptional circumstances and upon prior notice to the parties, on the arbitral tribunal's own initiative.

Article 17E. Provision of security

(1) The arbitral tribunal may require the party requesting an interim measure to provide appropriate security in connection with the measure.

(2) The arbitral tribunal shall require the party applying for a preliminary order to provide security in connection with the order unless the arbitral tribunal considers it inappropriate or unnecessary to do so.

Article 17F. Disclosure

(1) The arbitral tribunal may require any party promptly to disclose any material change in the circumstances on the basis of which the measure was requested or granted.

(2) The party applying for a preliminary order shall disclose to the arbitral tribunal all circumstances that are likely to be relevant to the arbitral tribunal's determination whether to grant or maintain the order, and such obligation shall continue until the party against whom the order has been requested has had an opportunity to present its case. Thereafter, para.1 of this article shall apply.

Article 17G. Costs and damages

The party requesting an interim measure or applying for a preliminary order shall be liable for any costs and damages caused by the measure or the order to any party if the arbitral tribunal later determines that, in the circumstances, the measure or the order should not have been granted. The arbitral tribunal may award such costs and damages at any point during the proceedings.

Section 4. Recognition and enforcement of interim measures

Article 17H. Recognition and enforcement

(1) An interim measure issued by an arbitral tribunal shall be recognized as binding and, unless otherwise provided by the arbitral tribunal, enforced upon application to the competent court, irrespective of the country in which it was issued, subject to the provisions of Art.17I.

(2) The party who is seeking or has obtained recognition or enforcement of an interim measure shall promptly inform the court of any termination, suspension or modification of that interim measure.

(3) The court of the State where recognition or enforcement is sought may, if it considers it proper, order the requesting party to provide appropriate security if the arbitral tribunal has not already made a determination with respect to security or where such a decision is necessary to protect the rights of third parties.

Article 17I. Grounds for refusing recognition or enforcement*

(1) Recognition or enforcement of an interim measure may be refused only:

(a) At the request of the party against whom it is invoked if the court is satisfied that:

(i) Such refusal is warranted on the grounds set forth in Art.36, para.1(a)(i), (ii), (iii) or (iv); or

---

* The conditions set forth in Art.17I are intended to limit the number of circumstances in which the court may refuse to enforce an interim measure. It would not be contrary to the level of harmonization sought to be achieved by these model provisions if a State were to adopt fewer circumstances in which enforcement may be refused.

(ii) The arbitral tribunal's decision with respect to the provision of security in connection with the interim measure issued by the arbitral tribunal has not been complied with; or

(iii) The interim measure has been terminated or suspended by the arbitral tribunal or, where so empowered, by the court of the State in which the arbitration takes place or under the law of which that interim measure was granted; or

(b) If the court finds that:

(i) The interim measure is incompatible with the powers conferred upon the court unless the court decides to reformulate the interim measure to the extent necessary to adapt it to its own powers and procedures for the purposes of enforcing that interim measure and without modifying its substance; or

(ii) Any of the grounds set forth in Art.36, para.1(b)(i) or (ii), apply to the recognition and enforcement of the interim measure.

(2) Any determination made by the court on any ground in para.1 of this article shall be effective only for the purposes of the application to recognise and enforce the interim measure. The court where recognition or enforcement is sought shall not, in making that determination, undertake a review of the substance of the interim measure.

Section 5. Court-ordered interim measures

Article 17J. Court-ordered interim measures

A court shall have the same power of issuing an interim measure in relation to arbitration proceedings, irrespective of whether their place is in the territory of this State, as it has in relation to proceedings in courts. The court shall exercise such power in accordance with its own procedures in consideration of the specific features of international arbitration.

Commentary

A4–030   The recent amendment to Art.17 is a major re-statement and extension of the circumstances in which arbitral tribunals have the power to issue interim measures in support of arbitration An innovative provision in the form of 17H and I has also been introduced to provide for enforcement internationally of orders granting interim measures issued by tribunals. This has previously been a difficult area, as often orders granting interim measures have not been capable of enforcement outside the place of the seat of arbitration. The powers of the arbitral tribunal to grant interim measures apply unless otherwise agreed by the parties.

Similarly, under the Arbitration Act 1996, interim measures can be granted by the arbitral tribunal or the court. Unless otherwise agreed by the parties, an arbitral tribunal has powers conferred by s.38 which include the power to order the claimant to provide security for costs (a power previously reserved to the court, (see para.5–098)) and the power to direct the preservation of property. The powers under Art.17A however are broader.

Under s.44 of the Arbitration Act, the court has various powers exercisable in support of arbitration proceedings including to order the preservation of evidence and, most notably, the granting of interim injunctive relief (see para.7–181 to 7–202). In non-urgent cases, the court may only act upon the application by one party made with the consent of the arbitral tribunal or the agreement of the other parties. The court's s.44 powers are available unless otherwise agreed by the parties (whereas the powers conferred by Art.17J are absolute).

CHAPTER V. CONDUCT OF ARBITRAL PROCEEDINGS

Article 18. Equal treatment of parties
The parties should be treated with equality and each party shall be given a full opportunity of presenting his case.

Commentary
Although not expressed in quite the same terms, the Arbitration Act 1996 imposes a general duty on the arbitral tribunal to act "fairly and impartially as between the parties" (s.33).   A4–031

That duty requires the tribunal to give each party a reasonable (as opposed to a full) opportunity to put his case and to deal with that of his opponent and to "adopt procedures suitable to the circumstances of the particular case, avoiding unnecessary delay or expense, so as to provide a fair means for the resolution of the matters falling to be determined". (Section 33(1)(b)). This modification to the Model Law provision is intended to complement the English concept of natural justice and to recognise the fact that in an informal arbitration there is often no oral hearing and the parties are not legally represented (see DAC report (1989) p.55 and para.5–050).   A4–032

Article 19. Determination of rules of procedure
(1) Subject to the provisions of this Law, the parties are free to agree on the procedure to be followed by the arbitral tribunal in conducting the proceedings.

(2) Failing such agreement, the arbitral tribunal may, subject to the provision of this Law, conduct the arbitration in such manner as it considers appropriate. The power conferred upon the arbitral tribunal includes the power to determine the admissibility, relevance, materiality and weight of any evidence.

Commentary
Parties are free to agree on a procedure for an English arbitration. In the absence of agreement the Arbitration Act 1996 provides that "it shall be for the tribunal to decide all procedural and evidentiary matters" (s.34(1)). Those matters give the arbitral tribunal a wide discretion on how to conduct the proceedings, and are expressed to include power to determine "the admissibility, relevance or weight" of evidence (s.34(2)). Unless the parties agree otherwise the tribunal is free to decide whether to apply strict rules of evidence or "any other rules". (s.34(2) see para.5–155).   A4–033

Article 20. Place of arbitration
(1) The parties are free to agree on the place of arbitration. Failing such agreement, the place of arbitration shall be determined by the arbitral tribunal having regard to the circumstances of the case, including the convenience of the parties.

(2) Notwithstanding the provisions of para.(1) of this article, the arbitral tribunal may, unless otherwise agreed by the parties, meet at any place it considers appropriate for consultation among its members, for hearing witnesses, experts or the parties, or for inspection of goods, other property or documents.

Commentary

A4–034   In an English arbitration the parties are free to agree "when and where any part of the proceedings is to be held" (Arbitration Act 1996 (s.34)). Failing such agreement, the Act provides that "it shall be for the tribunal to decide" the matter (s.34(2)(a)).

A4–035   There is no provision in the Arbitration Acts 1996 similar to Art.20(2) of the Model Law. On the contrary, s.34 indicates that if a place of arbitration has been agreed by the parties (e.g. in the arbitration clause) the arbitral tribunal cannot without their consent sit elsewhere. (see para.5–092).

Article 21. Commencement of arbitral proceedings

Unless otherwise agreed by the parties, the arbitral proceedings in respect of a particular dispute commence on the date which a request for that dispute to be referred to arbitration is received by the respondent.

Commentary

A4–036   Parties are free to agree "when arbitration proceedings are to be regarded as commenced for the purposes of "the Limitation Acts and Part 1" of the Arbitration Act 1996, s.14(1). If there is no agreement on the commencement date of proceedings in respect of a particular dispute the provisions of s.14 of the Arbitration Act 1996 will be applied to determine the matter (ss.14(2) *et seq.*: see paras 5–005 *et seq.*).

A4–037   English law places emphasis on service of the notice requesting arbitration rather than on receipt by the respondent (see s.14(3) and (4) of the Arbitration Act 1996). Section 79 of the Act empowers the court to extend contractual, but not statutory, time limits for commencing arbitration proceedings (see paras 7–033 *et seq.*).

Article 22. Language

(1) The parties are free to agree on the language or languages to be used in the arbitral proceedings. Failing such agreement, the arbitral tribunal shall determine the language or languages to be used in the proceedings. This agreement or determination, unless otherwise specified therein, shall apply to any written statement by a party, any hearing and any award, decision or other communication by the arbitral tribunal.

(2) The arbitral tribunal may order that any documentary evidence shall be accompanied by a translation into the language or languages agreed upon by the parties or determined by the arbitral tribunal.

Commentary

A4–038   The Arbitration Act 1996 also expresses the freedom of the parties to agree on the "language or languages to be used in the proceedings" (s.34(2)(b)). Failing any agreement, the arbitral tribunal is required to decide any language issue, which may extend to written submissions, directions or an award, as well as "whether translations of any relevant documents are to be supplied" (s.34(2)(b): see paras 5–180 *et seq.*).

Article 23. Statements of claim and defence

(1) Within the period of time agreed by the parties or determined by the arbitral tribunal, the claimant shall state the facts supporting his claim, the points at issue and the relief or remedy sought, and the respondent shall state his defence in respect of these particulars, unless the parties have otherwise agreed as to the required elements of such statements. The parties may submit with their statements

all documents they consider to be relevant or may add a reference to the documents or other evidence they will submit.

(2) Unless otherwise agreed by the parties, either party may amend or supplement his claim or defence during the course of the arbitral proceedings, unless the arbitral tribunal considers it inappropriate to allow such amendment having regards to the delay in making it.

Commentary

The Arbitration Act 1996 gives the arbitral tribunal a wide discretion to decide (subject to the right of the parties to agree any particular matter) whether and if so what form of written statements of claim and defence can be used, when these should be supplied and the extent to which such statements can be later amended (s.34(2)(c)) as well as whether any and if so which documents or classes of documents should be disclosed between and produced by the parties and at what stage (s.34(2)(d)).

A4–039

Formal arbitrations conducted in England tend to proceed on the lines indicated in Art.23(1) of the Model law with points of claim followed by a statement of the defence and counterclaim, if any, and other written pleading. Disclosure of documents usually takes place after close of pleadings. There is, however, considerable flexibility in practice, and arbitral institutions publish their own particular rules. Informal arbitrations often follow a simplified procedure (see paras 5–110 *et seq.*).

A4–040

Provided that the amendments fall within the scope of the reference, the Arbitration Act 1996 gives the arbitral tribunal a discretion to allow a party to amend or supplement the claim or defence during the course of the proceedings (see s.34(2)(c) and para.5–148).

Article 24. Hearings and written proceedings

(1) Subject to any contrary agreement by the parties, the arbitral tribunal shall decide whether to hold oral hearings for the presentation of evidence or for oral argument, or whether the proceedings shall be conducted on the basis of documents and other materials. However, unless the parties have agreed that no hearings shall be held, the arbitral tribunal shall hold such hearings at an appropriate stage of the proceedings, if so requested by a party.

(2) The parties shall be given sufficient advance notice of any hearing and of any meeting of the arbitral tribunal for the purposes of inspection of goods, other property or documents.

(3) All statements, documents or other information supplied to the arbitral tribunal by one party shall be communicated to the other party. Also any expert report or evidentiary document on which the arbitral tribunal may rely in making its decision shall be communicated to the parties.

Commentary

Within the general duty contained in s.33 and subject to the right of the parties to agree otherwise (e.g. to a "documents only" arbitration) the Arbitration Act 1996 gives the tribunal a discretion whether and to what extent there should be "oral or written evidence or submissions" or both (s.34(2)(h)). The Arbitration Act does not require that there shall be a hearing even if one party requests it, although in most cases such a request would be granted (see para.5–210).

A4–041

Under English law an arbitral tribunal is required to give each party a reasonable opportunity of putting his case and dealing with that of his opponent (s.33(1)(a) Arbitration

A4–042

Act 1996) and to conduct the arbitral proceedings so as to comply with that general duty. (Section 33(2).) Thus, although with one exception Arts 24(2) and (3) of the Model law are not expressed in the Arbitration Act, they are implicit from s.33. The exception is contained in s.37(1)(b) of the Act, which requires that the parties are given a reasonable opportunity to comment on any information, opinion or advice offered by an expert appointed by the tribunal, (see paras 5–173 *et seq.*).

Article 25. Default of a party
Unless otherwise agreed by the parties, if, without showing sufficient cause

    (a) the claimant fails to communicate his statement of claim in accordance with Art.23(1), the arbitral tribunal shall terminate the proceedings;

    (b) the respondent fails to communicate his statement of defence in accordance with Art.23(1), the arbitral tribunal shall continue the proceedings without treating such failure in itself as an admission of the claimant's allegations;

    (b) any party fails to appear at a hearing or to produce documentary evidence, the arbitral tribunal may continue the proceedings and make the award on the evidence before it.

Commentary
A4–043   An arbitral tribunal has no power under English law to terminate the proceedings if a claimant fails to communicate his statement of claim within an agreed period, although the parties may agree to confer power on the tribunal in case of a party's failure to do something necessary for the proper and expeditious conduct of the arbitration (s.41(1) Arbitration Act 1996). In the absence of agreement the tribunal does, however, have power to dismiss certain claims for want of prosecution,—(s.41(3) and see para.5–240).

A4–044   The provision in Art.25(b) and (c) of the Model Law broadly represents English law, when after due notice the tribunal may proceed *ex parte* in default of a pleading or evidence or the appearance of a party at the hearing, but without treating such failure in itself as an admission. (Arbitration Act 1996, s.41(4): see paras 5–216 and 5–217).

Article 26. Expert appointed by arbitral tribunal
    (1) Unless otherwise agreed by the parties, the arbitral tribunal

        (a) may appoint one or more experts to report to it on specific issues to be determined by the arbitral tribunal;

        (b) may require a party to give the expert any relevant information or to produce, or to provide access to, any relevant documents, goods or other property for his inspection.

    (2) Unless otherwise agreed by the parties, if a party so requests or if the arbitral tribunal considers it necessary, the expert shall, after delivery of his written or oral report, participate in a hearing where the parties have the opportunity to put questions to him and to present expert witnesses in order to testify on the points at issue.

Commentary
A4–045   The Arbitration Act 1996 contains a similar provision in s.37(1). The English provision extends expressly to legal advisers and assessors, and perhaps as a consequence the tribunal

has a wider discretion under English law than is apparent from Art.26(2) whether to allow the expert to be questioned by the parties at the hearing.

Despite the statutory power to appoint an expert, the English practice is to let each party (as opposed to the tribunal) adduce expert evidence if required and to allow examination of the expert witness after exchange of reports and possibly a "without prejudice" meeting with the other party's expert. (See paras 5–172 *et seq.*)   **A4–046**

Article 27. Court assistance in taking evidence

The arbitral tribunal or a party with the approval of the arbitral tribunal may request from a competent court of this State assistance in taking evidence. The court may execute the request within its competence and according to its rules on taking evidence.

Commentary

The Arbitration Act 1996 contains provisions that will secure the attendance of witnesses before the tribunal as well as make available the powers of the court to take evidence. A party to an arbitration may with the permission of the tribunal or with the agreement of the other parties to the arbitration issue a *subpoena* out of the court directing a witness to attend before the arbitral tribunal to give oral evidence or to bring documents to a hearing (s.43), see para.5–171 and paras 7–125 and 7–126. A party may also apply to the court for "the taking of the evidence of witnesses" (s.44(2)) which may include the issue of a commission or request for the examination of a witness out of the jurisdiction. (See para.7–134.)   **A4–047**

CHAPTER VI. MAKING AWARD AND TERMINATION OF PROCEEDINGS

Article 28. Rules applicable to substance of dispute

(1) The arbitral tribunal shall decide the dispute in accordance with such rules of law as are chosen by the parties as applicable to the substance of the dispute. Any designation of the law or legal system of a given State shall be construed, unless otherwise expressed, as directly referring to the substantive law of that State and not to its conflict of laws rules.

(2) Failing any designation by the parties, the arbitral tribunal shall apply the law determined by the conflict of laws rules which it considers applicable.

(3) The arbitral tribunal shall decide *ex aequo et bono* or as amiable compositeur only if the parties have expressly authorised it to do so.

(4) In all cases, the arbitral tribunal shall decide in accordance with the terms of the contract and shall take into account the usages of the trade applicable to the transaction.

Commentary

The Arbitration Act 1996, s.46 contains provisions similar to those in Art.28. The terms of Art.28(3) are expressed somewhat more broadly in s.46(1)(b) of the Arbitration Act and there is no express equivalent to Art.28(4), but such differences as exist between English law and the Model law on the rules applicable to the substance of the dispute are more significant in practice than in the words used (see paras 4–164 *et seq.*).   **A4–048**

Article 29. Decision making by panel of arbitrators

In arbitral proceedings with more than one arbitrator, any decision of the arbitral tribunal shall be made, unless otherwise agreed by the parties, by a majority of all its members.

However, questions of procedure may be decided by a presiding arbitrator, if so authorised by the parties or all members of the arbitral tribunal.

Commentary

A4–049   In this matter English law does not make the same distinction between decisions and procedural questions. Although all members of an arbitral tribunal are required to participate in the decision making, if they cannot agree upon a "decision, order or award", it shall be decided by a majority of them, failing which "the view of the chairman shall prevail" in the absence of another method of decision making agreed by the parties (Arbitration Act 1996, s.20) see para.6–059.

Article 30. Settlement

(1) If, during arbitral proceedings, the parties settle the dispute, the arbitral tribunal shall terminate the proceedings and, if requested by the parties and not objected by the arbitral tribunal, record the settlement in the form of an arbitral award on agreed terms.

(2) An award on agreed terms shall be made in accordance with the provisions of Art.31 and shall state that it is an award. Such an award has the same status and effect as any other award on the merits of the case.

Commentary

A4–050   The Arbitration Act 1996, s.51 contains similar provisions for an "agreed award" in the event that the arbitral proceedings are settled and the parties do not agree some other provisions. Section 51(5) also provides for how costs should be dealt with in the absence of agreement, (see paras 6–023 *et seq.*).

Article 31. Form and contents of award

(1) The award shall be made in writing and shall be signed by the arbitrator or arbitrators. In arbitral proceedings with more than one arbitrator, the signatures of the majority of all members of the arbitral tribunal shall suffice, provided that the reason for any omitted signature is stated.

(2) The award shall state the reasons upon which it is based, unless the parties have agreed that no reasons are to be given or the award is an award on agreed terms under Art.30.

(3) The award shall state its date and the place of arbitration as determined in accordance with Art.20(1). The award shall be deemed to have been made at that place.

(4) After the award is made, a copy signed by the arbitrators in accordance with para.(1) of this article shall be delivered to each party.

Commentary

A4–051   The Arbitration Act 1996, s.52 expresses the freedom of the parties to agree on the form of the award. In the absence of agreement, the section requires that the award:

(a) shall be in writing signed by all the arbitrators or all those assenting to the award (s.52(3));

(b) shall contain the reasons for the award unless it is an "agreed award" or the parties have agreed to dispense with reasons (s.52(4)); and

(c) shall state the seat of the arbitration and the date when the award is made (s.52(5)).

The deeming provision in Art.31(3) is reflected in s.53 of the Arbitration Act 1996 where the seat of the arbitration is in England or Wales, unless otherwise agreed by the parties. Section 54 of the Act also provides how the date of an award is determined in the absence of an agreement by the parties or a decision by the arbitral tribunal, (see paras 6–045 *et seq.*).

A parol award can be given (e.g. in an emergency) although it is invariably confirmed in writing, if only for the purpose of enforcement. Further, the power given to the tribunal to correct a clerical mistake or error in the award implies that it will be reduced to writing, (s.57(3): see paras 6–049 and 6–194).

Article 32. Termination of proceedings

(1) The arbitral proceedings are terminated by the final award or by an order of the arbitral tribunal in accordance with para.(2) of this article.

(2) The arbitral tribunal shall issue an order for the termination of the arbitral proceedings when:

(a) the claimant withdraws his claim, unless the respondent objects thereto and the arbitral tribunal recognises a legitimate interest on his part in obtaining a final settlement of the dispute;

(b) the parties agree on the termination of the proceedings;

(c) the arbitral tribunal finds that the continuation of the proceedings has for any other reason become unnecessary or impossible.

(3) The mandate of the arbitral tribunal terminates with the termination of the arbitral proceedings, subject to the provisions of Arts 33 and 34(4).

Commentary

Subject to any power to correct the award or make an additional award (s.57) under English law, an arbitral tribunal ceases to hold office once the final award is published to the parties, (see paras 6–193 *et seq.*). There is no express provision in the Arbitration Act 1996 for the arbitration proceedings to terminate in that event. Indeed, the court may remit an award, including a final award for the reconsideration of the tribunal (s.68(3) and 69(7) or direct the tribunal to give sufficient reasons for the award (s.70(4), see para.8–060). **A4–052**

The parties and the arbitral tribunal can always agree on the termination of arbitration proceedings, but otherwise the tribunal has no power under English law to terminate an arbitration even if the proceedings become unnecessary or impossible. A tribunal is however empowered to make an award dismissing a claim if it appears that certain conditions are satisfied (e.g. those specified in s.41(3): see paras 5–240 *et seq.*). **A4–053**

Article 33. Correction and interpretation

(1) Within 30 days of receipt of the award, unless another period of time has been agreed upon by the parties:

(a) a party, with notice to the other party, may request the arbitral tribunal to correct in the award any errors in computation, any clerical or typographical errors or any errors of similar nature;

(b) if so agreed by the parties, a party, with notice to the other party, may request the arbitral tribunal to give an interpretation of a specific point or part of the award

If the arbitral tribunal considers the request to be justified, it shall make the correction or give the interpretation within 30 days of receipt of the request. The interpretation shall form part of the award.

(2) The arbitral tribunal may correct any error of the type referred to in para.(1)(a) of this article on its own initiative within 30 days of receipt of the award.

(3) Unless otherwise agreed by the parties, with notice to the other party, may request, within 30 days of receipt of the award, the arbitral tribunal to make an additional award as to claims presented in the arbitral proceedings but omitted from the award. If the arbitral tribunal considers the request to be justified, it shall make the additional award within 60 days.

(4) The arbitral tribunal may extend, if necessary, the period of time within which it shall make a correction, interpretation or an additional award under paras (1) or (3) of this article.

(5) The provisions of article 31 shall apply to a correction or interpretation of the award or to an additional award.

Commentary

A4–054   The Arbitration Act 1996, s.57 empowers an arbitral tribunal, in the absence of a contrary agreement by the parties , to correct an award so as to remove "any clerical mistake or error" arising from accidental slip or omission or to clarify or remove any ambiguity in the award. This power may be exercised on the initiative of the tribunal or in response to a request from one of the parties. There is a time limit of 28 days.

A4–055   Section 57 also empowers the tribunal to make an additional award. Parties can also resort to the court for an order to remit certain matters referred for the reconsideration of an arbitral tribunal, which the court is empowered to do in certain cases (s.68(3)(a) and 69(7)(d): see paras 6–193 *et seq.*).

CHAPTER VII. RECOURSE AGAINST AWARD

Article 34. Application for setting aside as exclusive recourse against arbitral award

(1) Recourse to a court against an arbitral award may be made only by an application for setting aside in accordance with paras (2) and (3) of this article.

(2) An arbitral award may be set aside by the court specified in Art.6 only if:

(a) the party making the application furnishes proof that:

(i) a party to the arbitration agreement referred to in Art.7 was under some incapacity; or the said agreement is not valid under the law to which the parties have subjected it or, failing any indication thereon, under the law of this State; or

(ii) the party making the application was not given proper notice of the appointment of an arbitrator or of the arbitral proceedings or was otherwise unable to present his case; or

(iii) the award deals with a dispute not contemplated by or not failing within the terms of the submission to arbitration, or contains decisions on matters beyond the scope of the submission to arbitration, provided that, if the decisions on matters submitted to arbitration can be separated from those not so submitted, only that part of the award which contains decisions on matters not submitted to arbitration may be set aside; or

(iv) the composition of the arbitral tribunal or the arbitral procedure was not in accordance with the agreement of the parties, unless such agreement was in conflict with a provision of this Law from which the parties cannot derogate, or, failing such agreement, was not in accordance with this Law; or

(b) the court finds that:

(i) the subject-matter of the dispute is not capable of settlement by arbitration under the law of this State; or

(ii) the award is in conflict with the public policy of this State.

(3) An application for setting aside may not be made after 3 months have elapsed from the date on which the party making that application had received the award or, if a request has been made under Art.33, from the date on which that request had been disposed of by the arbitral tribunal.

(4) The court, when asked to set aside an award, may, where appropriate and so requested by a party, suspend the setting aside proceedings for a period of time determined by it in order to give the arbitral tribunal an opportunity to resume the arbitral proceedings or to take such other action as in the arbitral tribunal's opinion will eliminate the grounds for setting aside.

Commentary

There are several means of recourse against an award under English law. First, there is the kind of recourse mentioned in Art.34(1) and (2) above where the Court can set aside an award on an application of one of the parties where there has been a "serious irregularity affecting the tribunal the proceedings or the award" (s.68). The words quoted from those sections are wide enough to embrace the grounds specified in Art.34(2), which derive from the New York Convention. There is a time limit of 28 days for such an application, (s.70(3): see paras 8–035 *et seq.*).   **A4–056**

Second, quite apart from its power to set aside an award, the court can in appropriate cases remit "the award to the tribunal, in whole or in part, for reconsideration . . . " (ss.68(3)(a) and 69(7)(c) but not under s.67). There is an important distinction between the court's wide powers of remission under English law and the court's limited power to suspend setting aside proceedings under Art.34(4) of the Model Law while the tribunal consider a correction under Art.33, (see paras 8–075 *et seq.*).   **A4–057**

Third, and there is no equivalent in the Model Law, a party may, as an alternative to seeking recourse under s.67 or 68 of the Act, apply to the court for leave to appeal against an award on a question of law provided that there is no valid exclusion agreement (s.69). If leave is obtained the court may review the award, although leave will only be given in limited circumstances: (s.69, see paras 8–054 *et seq.*).   **A4–058**

CHAPTER VIII. RECOGNITION AND ENFORCEMENT OF AWARDS

Article 35. Recognition and enforcement

(1) An arbitral award, irrespective of the country in which it was made, shall be recognised as binding and, upon application in writing to the competent court, shall be enforced subject to the provisions of this article and of Art.36.

(2) The party relying on an award or applying for its enforcement shall supply the original award or a copy thereof. If the award is not made in an official language of this State, the court may request the party to supply a translation thereof into such language.***[14]

*** The conditions set forth in this paragraph are intended to set maximum standards. It would, thus, not be contrary to the harmonisation to be achieved by the model law if a State retained even less onerous conditions.

Commentary

A4–059   This article and the following Art.36 closely follow Arts III, IV and V of the New York Convention to which the United Kingdom acceded. The Arbitration Act, 1996, which implements the New York Convention provides for the recognition and enforcement of New York Convention awards (s.101) and specifies the evidence required (s.102). A New York Convention award is defined in the Act as "an award made, in pursuance of an arbitration agreement, in the territory of a State (other than the United Kingdom), which is a party to the New York Convention" (s.100(1) and see para.6–035).

A4–060   In view of the number of foreign States which have been recognised by the United Kingdom as a party to the New York Convention, the provision for enforcement under the 1996 Act of awards made abroad is very wide, but it is not unlimited (contrast Art.35 above). Enforcement may also be achieved by suing on the award. There is however a summary procedure which is available for the enforcement of New York Convention awards and other awards, including domestic awards (s.66) that can be invoked by originating summons, although the grounds for opposition vary according to the nature of the award (see the comment on the next article and Ch.8).

Article 36. Grounds for refusing recognition or enforcement

(1) Recognition or enforcement of an arbitral award, irrespective of the country in which it was made, may be refused only:

(a) at the request of the party against whom it is invoked, if that party furnishes to the competent court where recognition or enforcement is sought proof that:

(i) a party to the arbitration agreement referred to in Art.7 was under some incapacity; or the said agreement is not valid under the law to which the parties have subjected it or, failing any indication thereon, under the law of the country where the award was made; or

---

[14] Article 35(2) was amended in 2006 to make the requirements for a party wishing to rely on, or enforce, an award less stringent. Article 35(2) previously read as follows:

"The party relying on an award or applying for its enforcement shall supply the duly authenticated original award or a duly certified copy thereof., and the original arbitration agreement referred to in article 7 or a duly certified copy thereof. If the award or agreement is not made in an official language of this State, the court may request the party shallto supply a duly certified translation thereof into such language."

(ii) the party against whom the award is invoked was not given proper notice of the appointment of an arbitrator or of the arbitral proceedings or was otherwise unable to present his case; or

(iii) the award deals with a dispute not contemplated by or not falling within the terms of the submission to arbitration, or it contains decisions on matters beyond the scope of the submission to arbitration, provided that, if the decisions on matters submitted to arbitration can be separated from those not so submitted, that part of the award which contains decisions on matters submitted to arbitration may be recognised and enforced; or

(iv) the composition of the arbitral tribunal or the arbitral procedure was not in accordance with the agreement of the parties or, failing such agreement, was not in accordance with the law of the country where the arbitration took place; or

(v) the award has not yet become binding on the parties or has been set aside or suspended by a court of the country in which, under the law of which, that award was made; or

(b) if the court finds that:

(i) the subject-matter of the dispute is not capable of settlement by arbitration under the law of this State; or

(ii) the recognition or enforcement of the award would be contrary to the public policy of this State.

(2) If an application for setting aside or suspension of an award has been made to a court referred to in para.(1)(a)(v) of this Article, the court where recognition or enforcement is sought may, if it considers it proper, adjourn its decision and may also, on the application of the party claiming recognition or enforcement of the award, order the other party to provide appropriate security.

Commentary

As mentioned in the previous para.0–61, this article follows closely (but not exactly) Article V of the New York Convention. Enforcement of a New York Convention award (as defined) may only be refused by an English court if the person against whom it is invoked proves at least one of the grounds listed in s.103 of the Arbitration Act 1996 which are almost identical to the grounds specified in Art.36(1)(a) above. The defences of public policy and non-arbitrability are treated in s.103(3) of the Arbitration Act 1996 and correspond broadly, but not exactly, for New York Convention awards to Art.36(1)(b) above. Under English law other grounds of opposition are available to the enforcement of an award made abroad, which is not a New York Convention award, as they are to an award made in England (see paras 8–028 *et seq.*).   **A4–061**

A provision for adjournment of enforcement proceedings similar to that specified in Art.36 (2) above (i.e. in the event of recourse against the award in the State where it was made) is contained in s.103(5) of the Arbitration Act 1996, but is limited to New York Convention awards (see para.8–020).   **A4–062**

Appendix 5

List of Appointing Authorities

A5–001 This Appendix 5 contains a list of the major institutions acting as appointing authorities in arbitrations. It does not purport to be exhaustive and for ease of reference is divided between the major international institutions and domestic/specialist bodies.

International
The Arbitration Institute of the Stockholm Chamber of Commerce (SCC Institute)
P.O. Box 16050
SE-103 21 Stockholm
Sweden

Tel: 00 46 8 555 100 50
Fax: 00 46 8 566 316 50

E-mail: arbitration@chamber.se
Website: *http://www.sccinstitute.com/uk/Home/*

The China International Economic and Trade Arbitration Commission (CIETAC)
6/F Liang Ma Qiao Road
Chaoyang District,
Beijing 100016
P.R. China

Tel: 00 86 10 64646688
Fax: 00 86 10 64643500/64643520

Email: info@cietac.org
Web Site: *www.cietac.org*

The Hong Kong International Arbitration Centre (HKIAC)
38th Floor Two Exchange Square
8 Connaught Place
Hong Kong S.A.R.
China

Telephone: 00 852 2525 2381
Fax: 00 852 2524 2171

Email: adr@hkiac.org
Web Site: *http://www.hkiac.org/HKIAC/HKIAC_English/main.html*

The International Centre for Dispute Resolution (ICDR) of the American Arbitration Association
ICDR International Case Management Center
1633 Broadway, 10th Floor
New York 10019–6708
United States

Tel: 001 212 484 4115
Fax: 001 212–246 7274

Web Site: *http://www.adr.org/about_icdr*
Email: VentroneT@adr.org

The International Court of Arbitration of the International Chamber of Commerce
38, Cours Albert 1er
75008 Paris
France

Tel: 00 331 49 53 29 05
Fax: 00 331 49 53 29 33

Web Site: *www.iccwbo.org*

International Centre for Settlement of Investment Disputes (ICSID)
1818 H Street NW
Washington DC 20433
USA

Tel: 001 202 458 1534
Fax: 001 202 522 2615

Web Site: *http://www.worldbank.org/icsid/index.html*

London Court of International Arbitration (LCIA)
70 Fleet Street
London EC4Y 1EU

Tel: 020 79367007
Fax: 020 79367008
E-mail: casework@lcia.org/lcia@lcia.org

Web Site: *www.lcia-arbitration.com*

The Singapore International Arbitration Centre (SIAC)
City Hall
3 St Andrew's Road
Singapore 178958

Tel: 00 65 6334 1277
Fax: 00 65 6334 2942

Web Site: *http://www.siac.org.sg*

National/Specialist
The Academy of Experts
3 Gray's Inn Square
London WC1R 5AH

Tel: 020 7430 0666
Fax: 020 7637 1893
DX 283 London Chancery Lane

E-mail: admin@academy-experts.org
Web Site: *www.academy-experts.org*

The Centre for Dispute Resolution (CEDR)
International Dispute Resolution Centre
70 Fleet Street
London EC4Y 1EU

Tel: 020 7536 6000
Fax: 020 7536 6001

Web Site: *www.cedr.co.uk*

The Chartered Institute of Arbitrators
24 City Road
Angelgate
London EC1Z 2PT

Tel: 020 7520 3800
Fax: 020 7520 3828

Web Site: *www.arbitrators.org*

The Chartered Institute of Management Accountants
26 Chapter Street
London SW1P 4NP

Tel: 020 7663 5441
Fax: 020 7663 5442

Web Site: *www.cimaglobal.com*

The Chartered Institute of Patent Attorneys
3rd Floor
95 Chancery LaneLondon WC2A 1DT

Tel: 020 7405 9450
Fax: 020 7430 0471

E-mail: mail@cipa.org.uk
Web Site: *www.cipa.org.uk/*

The City Disputes Panel
24 Angelgate
City Road
London EC1V 2PT

Tel: 020 7520 3800
Fax: 020 7520 3829

E-mail: info@citydisputespanel.org
Web Site: *www.citydisputespanel.org*

Coffee Trade Federation
Blackfriars Foundry
156 Blackfriars RoadLondon SE1 8EN

Tel: 020 7328 5222
Fax: 020 7328 5444

E-mail: secretariat@coffeetradefederation.org.uk
Web Site: *www.coffeetradefederation.org.uk*

The Electricity Arbitration Association
5 Meadow Road
Great Gransden
Sandy
Beds

Tel: 01767 677043
Fax: 01767 677043

Federation of Cocoa Commerce Ltd
Cannon Bridge House
1 Cousin Lane
London EC4R 3XX

Tel: 020 7379 2884
Fax: 020 7379 2389

E-mail: fcc@liffe.com
Web Site: *www.cocoafederation.com*

Federation of Oil Seeds and Fats Association Ltd (Fosfa)
20 St Dunstans Hill
London EC3R 8NQ

Tel: 020 7283 5511
Fax: 020 7623 1310

E-mail: contact@fosfa.org
Web Site: *www.fosfa.org*

The Grain and Feed Trade Association (Gafta)
Gafta House
6 Chapel Place
Rivington Street
London EC2A 3SH

Tel: 020 7814 9666
Fax: 020 7814 8383

E-mail: arbitration@gafta.com
Web Site: *www.gafta.com*

The General Council of the Bar of England and Wales
3 Bedford Row
London WC1R 4DB

Tel: 020 7242 0082
Fax: 020 7831 9217

Web Site: *http://www.barcouncil.org.uk/*

The Institute of Actuaries
Staple Inn Hall
High Holborn
London WC1V 7QJ

Tel: 020 7632 2100
Fax: 020 7632 2111

E-mail: institute@actuaries.org.uk
Web Site: *www.actuaries.org.uk*

The Institute of Chartered Accountants in England and Wales
PO Box 433
Chartered Accountants Hall
Moorgate Place
London EC2P 2BJ

Tel: 020 7920 8100
Fax: 020 7920 0547

Web Site: *http://www.icaew.co.uk/*

Institute of Civil Engineers
1–7 Great George Street
London SW1 3AA

Tel: 020 7222 7722
Fax: 020 7222 7500

E-mail: contractsanddisputes@ice.org.uk
Web Site: *www.ice.org.uk*

The Institution of Chemical Engineers
Davis Building
165–189 Railway Terrace
Rugby
CV21 3HQ

Tel: 01788 578214
Fax: 01788 560833

E-mail: www.icheme.org
Web Site: *www.icheme.org*

Institution of Mechanical Engineers
1 Birdcage Walk
London SW1H 9JJ

Tel: 020 7222 7899
Fax: 020 7222 4557

E-mail: s_rogers@imeche.org
Web Site: *www.imeche.org/industries/consult*

The Energy Institute
61 New Cavendish Street
London W1G 7AR

Tel: 020 7467 7100
Fax: 020 7255 1472

E-mail: info@energyinst.org.uk
Web Site: *www.energyinst.org.uk*

Institution of Structural Engineers
11 Upper Belgrave Street
London SW1X 8BH

Tel: 020 7235 4535
Fax: 020 7235 4294

Web Site: *www.istructe.org*

The Law Society of England and Wales
113 Chancery Lane
London WC2A 1PL

Tel: 020 7242 1222
Fax: 020 7831 0344

Web Site: *www.lawsociety.org.uk*

London Common Law and
Commercial Bar Association
3 Verulam Buildings
Grays Inn
London WC1R 5NT

Tel: 020 7831 8441
Fax: 020 78318479

Web Site: *www.lclcba.com*

London Maritime Arbitrators Association
124 Aldersgate Street
London EC1A 4JQ

Tel: 020 74907334
Fax: 020 74904383

E-mail: lmaa@btinternet.com
Web Site: *www.lmaa.org.uk*

London Metal Exchange Ltd
56 Leadenhall Street
London EC3A 2DX

Tel: 020 7264 5555
Fax: 020 7680 0505

Web Site: *www.lme.com*

The Refined Sugar Association/The Sugar Association of London
Forum House
Lime Street
London EC3M 7AQ

Tel: 020 7626 1745
Fax: 020 7283 3831

E-mail: durhamn@sugar-assoc.co.uk
Web Site: *www.sugarassociation.co.uk*

Royal Institute of British Architects
66 Portland Place
London W1B 1AD

Tel: 020 7580 5533
Fax: 020 7255 1541

E-mail: info@inst.riba.org
Web Site: *www.riba.org*

The Royal Institution of Chartered
Surveyors
Surveyor Court
Westwood Way
Coventry
CV4 8JE

Tel: 020 7222 7000
Fax: 020 7334 3802

Web Site: *www.rics.org*

INDEX